D0884112

Chernick-Mellins

Basic Mechanisms of Pediatric Respiratory Disease

SECOND EDITION

Gabriel G. Haddad, MD
Professor
Department of Pediatrics

Chief
Section of Respiratory Medicine
Yale University School of Medicine
Yale-New Haven Children's Hospital
New Haven, Connecticut

Steven H. Abman, MD
Professor
Department of Pediatrics
University of Colorado School of Medicine

Director
Pediatric Heart Lung Center
The Children's Hospital
Denver, Colorado

Victor Chernick, MD, FRCPC
Professor
Department of Pediatrics
University of Manitoba
Children's Hospital Winnipeg
Winnipeg, Manitoba

2002
BC Decker Inc
Hamilton • London

BC Decker Inc.
20 Hughson Street South
P.O. Box 620, LCD 1
Hamilton, Ontario L8N 3K7
Tel: 905-522-7017; 1-800-568-7281
Fax: 905-522-7839; 1-888-311-4987
E-mail: info@bcdecker.com
Website: www.bcdecker.com

02 03 04 05 / FP / 9 8 7 6 5 4 3 2 1

ISBN 1-55009-159-X
Printed in Canada

Sales and Distribution

United States
BC Decker Inc.
P.O. Box 785
Lewiston, NY 14092-0785
Tel: 905-522-7017; 1-800-568-7281
Fax: 905-522-7839; 1-888-311-4987
E-mail: info@bcdecker.com
Website: www.bcdecker.com

Canada
BC Decker Inc.
20 Hughson Street South
P.O. Box 620, LCD 1
Hamilton, ON L8N 3K7
Tel: 905-522-7017; 1-800-568-7281
Fax: 905-522-7839; 1-888-311-4987
E-mail: info@bcdecker.com
Website: www.bcdecker.com

Foreign Rights
John Scott & Co.
International Publishers' Agency
P.O. Box 878
Kimberton, PA 19442
Tel: 610-827-1640
Fax: 610-827-1671
E-mail: jsco@voicenet.com

UK, Europe, Scandinavia, Middle East
Elsevier Science
Customer Service Department
Foots Cray High Street
Sidcup, Kent
DA14 5HP, UK
Tel: 44 (0) 208 308 5760
Fax: 44 (0) 181 308 5702
E-mail: cservice@harcourt.com

Australia, New Zealand
Elsevier Science Australia
Customer Service Department
STM Division
Locked Bag 16
St. Peters, New South Wales, 2044
Australia
Tel: 61 02 9517-8999
Fax: 61 02 9517-8930
E-mail: stmp@harcourt.com.au
Website: www.harcourt.com.au

Japan
Igaku-Shoin Ltd.
Foreign Publications Department
3-24-17 Hongo, Bunkyo-ku
Tokyo 113-8719, Japan
Tel: 81 3 3817 5680
Fax: 81 3 3815 6776
E-mail: fd@igaku-shoin.co.jp

Singapore, Malaysia, Thailand, Philippines, Indonesia, Vietnam, Pacific Rim, Korea
Elsevier Science Asia
583 Orchard Road
#09/01, Forum
Singapore 238884
Tel: 65-737-3593
Fax: 65-753-2145

Contributors

Steven H. Abman, MD
Department of Pediatrics
University of Colorado School of Medicine
Pediatric Heart Lung Center
The Children's Hospital
Denver, Colorado

Julian Allen, MD
Department of Pediatrics
University of Pennsylvania School of Medicine
Children's Hospital of Philadelphia
Philadelphia, Pennsylvania
Development of the Thoracic Cage

Michael Apkon, MD, PhD
Department of Pediatrics
Yale University School of Medicine
New Haven, Connecticut
Regulation of Cerebral Vascular Function by Oxygen

Alia Bazzy-Asaad, MD
Department of Pediatrics
Yale University School of Medicine
Yale-New Haven Children's Hospital
New Haven, Connecticut
Respiratory Muscle Function: Implications for Ventilatory Failure

Jeffrey P. Bailey, BS
Department of Anesthesiology
Mayo Clinic
Rochester, Minnesota
Structural and Functional Development of Respiratory Muscle

H. Scott Baldwin, MD
Department of Pediatrics
University of Pennsylvania School of Medicine
Children's Hospital of Philadelphia
Philadelphia, Pennsylvania
Mechanisms of Lung Vascular Development

Zuhair K. Ballas, MD
Department of Veterans Affairs
University of Iowa College of Medicine
Iowa City, Iowa
Immunology and Cellular Defense Mechanisms in the Lung

Merton Bernfield, MD
Departments of Pediatrics and Cell Biology
Harvard Medical School
Department of Medicine
Children's Hospital
Boston, Massachusetts
Responses of the Developing Lung to Injury

C.E. Blanco, MD, PhD
Department of Pediatrics
University of Maastricht
University Hospital Maastricht
Maastricht, The Netherlands
Fetal Respiratory Control and Changes at Birth

Clifford W. Bogue, MD
Department of Pediatrics
Yale University
Yale-New Haven Children's Hospital
New Haven, Connecticut
Genetic and Molecular Basis of Airway and Lung Development

Dara Brodsky, MD
Department of Newborn Medicine
Harvard Medical School
Children's Hospital
Brigham and Women's Hospital
Beth Israel Deaconess Medical Center
Boston, Massachusetts
Responses of the Developing Lung to Injury

David P. Carlton, MD
Department of Pediatrics
University of Wisconsin
Madison, Wisconsin
Pulmonary Edema and Injury to the Developing Lung

Todd Carpenter, MD
Department of Pediatrics
University of Colorado Health Sciences Center
The Children's Hospital
Denver, Colorado
Effects of Hypoxia on the Developing Pulmonary Circulation

Robert L. Chatburn, RRT, FAARC
Department of Pediatrics
Case Western Reserve University
Department of Respiratory Care
University Hospitals of Cleveland
Cleveland, Ohio
Respiratory Function in Infants

Victor Chernick, MD, FRCPC
Department of Pediatrics
University of Manitoba
Children's Hospital
Winnipeg, Manitoba
Physiology of Cough
Laryngeal Function and Respiratory System Neural Reflexes

Helen Christou, MD
Department of Newborn Medicine
Harvard University
Children's Hospital
Brigham and Women's Hospital
Boston, Massachusetts
Responses of the Developing Lung to Injury

Dan Michael Cooper, MD
Department of Pediatrics
University of California Irvine College of Medicine
Irvine, California
Interacting Mechanisms of Physical Activity and Growth in Children

Jonathan M. Davis, MD
Department of Pediatrics
SUNY Stony Brook School of Medicine
Winthrop University Hospital
Mineola, New York
The Role of Oxidant Injury in the Pathogenesis of Bronchopulmonary Dysplasia

Daphne E. deMello, MD
Departments of Pathology and Pediatrics
Saint Louis University Health Sciences Center
Cardinal Glennon Children's Hospital
St. Louis, Missouri
Prenatal and Postnatal Development of the Pulmonary Circulation

Juliann M. Di Fiore, BSEE
Department of Pediatrics
Rainbow Babies and Children's Hospital
Case Western Reserve University
Cleveland, Ohio
Respiratory Function in Infants

Marie E. Egan, MD
Department of Pediatrics, and Cellular and Molecular Physiology
Yale University School of Medicine
Yale-New Haven Hospital
New Haven, Connecticut
Ion Flux and Homeostasis in the Lung

Oliver Eickelberg, MD
Department of Pathology
Yale University School of Medicine
New Haven, Connecticut
Fibroproliterative Response: Molecular Mediators and Pathophysiologic Relevance

Sandra J. England, PhD
Department of Pediatrics
University of Medicine and Dentistry of New Jersey
Robert Wood Johnson Medical School
New Brunswick, New Jersey
Laryngeal Function and Respiratory System Neural Reflexes

John Fahey, MD
Department of Pediatrics
Yale University
Yale-New Haven Hospital
New Haven, Connecticut
Oxygen Transport

Jay P. Farber, PhD
Department of Physiology
University of Oklahoma Health Sciences Center
Oklahoma City, Oklahoma
Postnatal Development of Respiratory Control

Terence R. Flotte, MD
Department of Pediatrics
University of Florida Genetics Institute
Powell Gene Therapy Center
Gainesville, Florida
Approach to Pulmonary Diseases with a Genetic Basis

J. Julio Pérez Fontán, MD
Department of Pediatrics
Washington University School of Medicine
St. Louis Children's Hospital
St. Louis, Missouri
Pulmonary Gas Exchange

James E. Gern, MD
Department of Pediatrics
University of Wisconsin Medical School
Madison, Wisconsin
Virus-Induced Inflammation in Airways

David Gozal, MD
Department of Pediatrics
University of Louisville
Kosair Children's Hospital Research Institute
Louisville, Kentucky
Sleep and Respiratory Control

Karen W. Gripp, MD
Department of Pediatrics
Thomas Jefferson University Jefferson College of Medicine
Philadelphia, Pennsylvania
Alfred I. duPont Hospital for Children
Wilmington, Delaware
Development of the Thoracic Cage

Gabriel G. Haddad, MD
Department of Pediatrics
Yale University School of Medicine
Yale-New Haven Children's Hospital
New Haven, Connecticut
Cellular and Molecular Mechanisms in Hypoxic Injury or Adaptation
Laryngeal Function and Respiratory System Neural Reflexes

M.A. Hanson, MA, DPhil, Cert Ed, FRCOG
Center for Fetal Origins of Adult Disease
University of Southampton
Southampton, United Kingdom
Fetal Respiratory Control and Changes at Birth

Ronald M. Harper, PhD
Department of Neurobiology
University of California at Los Angeles School of Medicine
Los Angeles, California
Sleep and Respiratory Control

Peter M. Henson, DVM, PhD
Department of Pathology
University of Colorado Health Sciences Center
Denver, Colorado
Pulmonary Macrophages: Origins, Functions, and Clearance

Marc B. Hershenson, MD
Department of Pediatrics
University of Chicago
Chicago, Illinois
Airway Smooth Muscle

Brian A. Hyatt, PhD
Department of Pediatrics
Children's Hospital Medical Center
Cincinnati, Ohio
Tissue Interactions in Lung Organogenesis

Alan H. Jobe, MD, PhD
Department of Pediatrics
University of Cincinnati School of Medicine
Children's Hospital Medical Center
Cincinnati, Ohio
Developmental Biology of Surfactant

Michael Kashgarian, MD
Department of Pathology
Yale University School of Medicine
Diagnostic Electron Microscopy and Renal Pathology
New Haven, Connecticut
Ciliary Abnormalities

Young-Jee Kim, MD
Department of Pediatrics
University of Chicago
Chicago, Illinois
Airway Smooth Muscle

Stella Kourembanas, MD
Department of Pediatrics
Harvard Medical School
Division of Newborn Medicine
Children' Hospital
Brigham and Women's Hospital
Boston, Massachusetts
Responses of the Developing Lung to Injury

Margaret W. Leigh, MD
Department of Pediatrics
University of North Carolina
University of North Carolina Hospitals
Chapel Hill, North Carolina
Airway Secretions

George Lister, MD
Department of Pediatrics
Yale University
Yale-New Haven Hospital
New Haven, Connecticut
Oxygen Transport

Carlos B. Mantilla, MD
Department of Anesthesiology
Mayo Clinic
Rochester, Minnesota
Structural and Functional Development of Respiratory Muscle

Richard J. Martin, MB, BS, FRACP
Departments of Pediatrics, Reproductive Biology, Physiology, and Biophysics
Case Western Reserve University
Rainbow Babies and Children's Hospital
Cleveland, Ohio
Respiratory Function in Infants

Jacopo P. Mortola, MD
Department of Physiology
McGill University
Montreal, Quebec
Comparative Aspects of Neonatal Respiratory Mechanics

Susan Niermeyer, MD
Department of Pediatrics
University of Colorado Health Sciences Center
The Children's Hospital
Denver, Colorado
Cardiopulmonary Physiology at Altitude

Lawrence M. Nogee, MD
Department of Pediatrics
Johns Hopkins University School of Medicine
Baltimore, Maryland
Genetics of Lung Disease: Surfactant Protein B Deficiency

Hugh O'Brodovich, MD
Department of Pediatrics
University of Toronto
Department of Respiratory Medicine
Hospital for Sick Children
Toronto, Ontario
Disorders of Ion Transport

Lawrence E. Ostrowski, PhD
Department of Medicine
The University of North Carolina at Chapel Hill School of Medicine
Cystic Fibrosis/Pulmonary Research and Treatment Center
Chapel Hill, North Carolina
Ciliogenesis of Airway Epithelium

Richard Parad, MD, MPH
Department of Pediatrics
Harvard Medical School
Department of Newborn Medicine
Brigham and Women's Hospital
Boston, Massachusetts
The Role of Oxidant Injury in the Pathogenesis of Bronchopulmonary Dysplasia

Lynne M. Reid, MD
Department of Pathology
Harvard Medical School
Children's Hospital
Boston, Massachusetts
Prenatal amd Postnatal Development of the Pulmonary Circulation

David W.H. Riches, PhD
Department of Immunology
University of Colorado Health Sciences Center
Denver, Colorado
Pulmonary Macrophages: Origins, Functions, and Clearance

Steven M. Scharf, MD, PhD
Department of Medicine
Albert Einstein College of Medicine
Long Island Jewish Medical Center
New Hyde Park, New York
Heart-Lung Interactions

Susan Schachtner, MD
Department of Pediatrics
University of Pennsylvania School of Medicine
Children's Hospital of Philadelphia
Philadelphia, Pennsylvania
Mechanisms of Lung Vascular Development

John M. Shannon, PhD
Department of Pediatrics
Children's Hospital Medical Center
Cincinnati, Ohio
Tissue Interactions in Lung Organogenesis

Anthony S. Sica, PhD
Department of Medicine
Albert Einstein College of Medicine
Long Island Jewish Medical Center
New Hyde Park, New York
Heart-Lung Interactions

Gary C. Sieck, PhD
Departments of Physiology and Biophysics/Anesthesiology
Mayo Medical School
Mayo Graduate School
Rochester, Minnesota
Structural and Functional Development of Respiratory Muscle

Julian Solway, MD
Departments of Medicine and Pediatrics
University of Chicago
Chicago, Illinois
Airway Smooth Muscle

Kurt R. Stenmark, MD
Department of Pediatrics
University of Colorado Health Sciences Center
The Children's Hospital
Denver, Colorado
Effects of Hypoxia on the Developing Pulmonary Circulation

Erik R. Swenson, MD
Department of Medicine
University of Washington
VA Puget Sound Health Care System
Seattle, Washington
Tissue and Cellular Carbon Dioxide Transport and Acid-Base Balance

Darren Taichman, MD, PhD
Department of Medicine
University of Pennsylvania School of Medicine
Philadelphia, Pennsylvania
Mechanisms of Lung Vascular Development

Rene Vandenboom, PhD
Anesthesia Research
Mayo Clinic
Rochester, Minnesota
Structural and Functional Development of Respiratory Muscle

Alfin G. Vicencio, MD
Department of Pediatrics
Yale University School of Medicine
New Haven, Connecticut
Fibroproliferative Response: Molecular Mediators and Pathophysiologic Relevance

Timothy E. Weaver, PhD
Division of Pulmonary Biology
University of Cincinnati College of Medicine
Children's Hospital Medical Center
Cincinnati, Ohio
Developmental Biology of Surfactant

Contents

III. DEVELOPMENTAL PHYSIOLOGY OF THE RESPIRATORY SYSTEM

Mechanics

PREFACE TO THE SECOND EDITION

The second edition of *Basic Mechanisms of Pediatric Respiratory Disease* has been able to build upon the major achievements of the first edition by maintaining its unique approach to childhood respiratory illness. This approach emphasizes the importance of the integration of molecular, cellular, and physiologic strategies in the development of a new understanding of pediatric respiratory disorders. Unlike other textbooks in this field, which provide encyclopedic discussions of specific illnesses and their treatment, the goal of this book is to provide state-of-the-art information about fundamental systems underlying the pathogenesis and pathophysiology of lung disease in children. This textbook fills a rather unique niche in several respects, both through its multidisciplinary approach and through its integration of basic and clinical science. In addition, this volume brings together many diverse clinical disciplines related to lung disease, including the fields of pediatric respiratory medicine, neonatology, critical care medicine, and allergy and immunology. Finally, this text seeks to integrate a number of diverse basic science approaches: molecular biology, cell biology, genetics, developmental biology, and cell physiology.

Exciting new developments in the field of pediatric respiratory disease provide the rationale for the second edition. As a discipline, respiratory medicine in general has come a long way since the early days of tuberculosis at the turn of the century. In pediatrics, respiratory and critical care medicine and perinatal medicine have been especially enhanced by a variety of discoveries over the past several decades that have led to major advances in those fields. For example, early work on surfactant led to critical insights into the pathophysiology of respiratory distress syndrome in premature neonates, which then led to the now routine clinical practice of surfactant replacement therapy. More recently, exciting work has led to new insights into surfactant biology, including understanding the critical role of surfactant proteins in lung defense mechanisms. Additionally, the field of cystic fibrosis has exploded with new information about its genetic basis, about the role of modifier genes, and about how various mutations lead to the pathophysiology and complex manifestations of lung disease. Insights into basic mechanisms of vascular development have also led to a greater understanding of pulmonary hypertension as well as novel findings on its genetic basis. In fact, it is important to note that numerous research areas have made important advances in the recent past, including basic studies of hypoxia and the regulation of tissue injury, the adaptation and mechanisms of cell death, the pathophysiology and genetics of asthma, and cell signaling in airway smooth muscle.

Overall, this past decade has seen more biomedical discoveries and breakthroughs than perhaps any other decade in human history, including the discoveries mentioned above. It is for this reason that the editors of this edition decided to again galvanize an outstanding group of experts and leaders from diverse backgrounds to address the various facets of pediatric respiratory medicine at the molecular, cellular, and integrative levels. Hence, one of the main aims of this new edition is to reflect some of these exciting new discoveries.

This text is divided into four sections: "Genetic and Developmental Biology of the Respiratory System", "Developmental Anatomy of the Respiratory System", "Developmental Physiology of the Respiratory System", and "Inflammation and Pulmonary Defense Mechanisms." As a result of extensive new developments in pediatric respiratory medicine, the second edition of this volume has expanded upon the first, growing by 13 chapters. These new chapters either further develop previous discussions or add new subjects (such as developmental genetics, organogenesis, molecular mechanisms underlying the response to injury, ionic homeostasis and transport across lung epithelia, cell and molecular aspects of tissue hypoxia, ciliogenesis, the neurobiology of sleep, and the physiology of cough). This volume has indeed developed into an exciting endeavor, which parades the molecular and integrative basis of respiratory diseases as currently understood at the beginning of this new century.

We are indebted to the contributing authors of this new edition without whom this endeavor would never have been possible. As well, we would like to thank Mr. Brian Decker for his advice and encouragement, and Ms. Heather Kidd at BC Decker whose diligence, ideas, and gentle hounding have been invaluable.

Gabriel G. Haddad, MD
Steven H. Abman, MD
Victor Chernick, MD, FRCPC
November 2001

Preface to the First Edition

The exciting advances in modern cellular and molecular biology offer promise of providing new and dramatic solutions to problems confronted at the bedside. Cell growth, differentiation, and maturation have always been a central focus of pediatrics; thus it is not surprising that these advances at the basic level serve to enhance our understanding of pediatric pulmonary diseases and disorders. These advances have come from diverse disciplines in the basic sciences as well as in pediatrics and adult medicine. Because the number of journals containing material relevant to the lung is now so extensive, it seemed timely to summarize the new scientific advances in one book. To be relevant at the bedside, our challenge is to relate changes in cellular physiology to organ pathophysiology, and this also is a major aim of this book. We believe the book should be useful for anyone interested in pulmonary disease, particularly those with a special interest in the developing lung.

Many diseases share common pathophysiologic mechanisms at the cellular level. The orientation of this book is toward the disease mechanism rather than the clinical manifestations. Wherever possible, the authors have pointed to the clinical relevance of the new insights at the cellular level.

We are indebted to the contributors of various chapters for their excellent scholarship. Any kudos for this book that may accrue are entirely due to their expertise and scholarly writing. We are also indebted to Mary Mansor at BC Decker Inc whose wise advise, continual encouragement, and occasional gentle nudging made this project become a reality.

Victor Chernick, MD
Robert B. Mellins, MD

Foreword

In the decade since the first edition, three developments have made a revision an exciting undertaking: pediatric pulmonary medicine has been recognized as a separate clinical discipline; advances in molecular medicine have raised the possibility of using modern science to understand the organizing principles of the lung and respiration in ways that have not been possible before; and advances in genomics have offered the promise of developing ways to prevent such lung diseases as asthma and cystic fibrosis, thus shifting the focus from disease treatment to health promotion. Subspecialties such as pediatric respiratory medicine have evolved in ways that are not dissimilar to biological systems. As they develop, they differentiate into more specialized functions—in the modern era, these are defined in cellular and molecular terms—and, as they mature, broader concepts of disease mechanisms emerge that allow us to relate structure to function in the developing respiratory system. Thus, the second edition is focused on molecular, cellular, and integrated aspects of the biology of the developing respiratory system. At the same time, it reaches out to a wide variety of related disciplines that have enriched our understanding of the respiratory system at rest as well as during exercise, during sleep, during exposure to hypoxia and high altitude, and under conditions of critical illness. In the process, our understanding of lung-related ion and fluid transport, allergy, immunology and inflammation as well as lung injury and repair have deepened.

When basic science was at the level of organ physiology, moving to clinical relevance was straightforward and direct. As basic science has moved to the cellular and molecular levels, clinical relevance has depended on the integration of concepts that reveal underlying mechanisms of disease. The authors have wisely chosen to strike out in some new directions rather than simply to update the previous edition. The result is a text that will be useful to scientists, medical students, residents, and postdoctoral fellows interested in the developmental biology of the respiratory system as well as to practitioners who wish to understand the basis for their clinical decisions.

Robert B. Mellins, MD
Professor of Pediatrics
Columbia University

To my late father George and mother Ida, who always encouraged me,
and to my wife, Karen, and my children, Chris, Diana, and Justin, whose love and support
was so essential throughout the years—GGH

To my wife, Carolyn, and my children, Ryan, Lauren, Mark, and Megan,
whose love has nourished me, and to my colleagues Frank Accurso and John Kinsella,
whose friendships have sustained my professional life—SHA

To all of my students,
some of whom have now become my teachers—VC

To Vic Chernick and Bob Mellins,
our mentors and teachers—GGH & SHA

SECTION I
GENETIC AND DEVELOPMENTAL BIOLOGY OF THE RESPIRATORY SYSTEM

CHAPTER 1

APPROACH TO PULMONARY DISEASES WITH A GENETIC BASIS

TERENCE R. FLOTTE, MD

As the human genome project nears its completion, there is a unique opportunity to identify the genetic basis of disease predisposition in a wide range of clinical settings, including common pulmonary illnesses. At present the genetic basis of two fairly common pulmonary disorders, cystic fibrosis (CF) and α_1-antitrypsin (AAT) deficiency are known, along with a few other rare genetic disorders that either affect the lungs primarily or as a result of multiorgan dysfunction. In the current chapter we focus on the two common single-gene disorders, CF and AAT deficiency. It is likely that similar protein transfer and gene transfer methods could eventually be useful in more common and complex pulmonary disorders, like asthma and chronic obstructive pulmonary disease (COPD).

Cystic Fibrosis

Cystic fibrosis is a common autosomal recessive disorder with an incidence of 1 in 3,300 live births. It is due to defects in the CF transmembrane conductance regulator (*CFTR*) gene, which is located on chromosome 7.[1] The CFTR protein shares structural homology with the adenosine triphosphate (ATP)-binding cassette superfamily of transmembrane transporters.[2] Its deduced structure includes two transmembrane domains, each consisting of six transmembrane α helixes, two nucleotide binding folds (NBF), and a regulatory domain rich in phosphorylation sites. *CFTR* can function as a cyclic adenosine monophosphate (cAMP)-activated chloride channel.[3,4] It requires phosphorylation by protein kinase A (PKA) for activation, and channel opening is enhanced by binding of ATP to the first NBF.[5,6]

The role of *CFTR* in maintaining normal airway function is not entirely clear. *CFTR* is found in the apical membrane of ciliated cells on the airway surface in both distal and proximal airways and in serous cells of the bronchial submucosal glands.[7,8] *CFTR* may function in the secretion of chloride at the apical surface, which could, in turn, control the volume and composition of the airway surface fluid (ASF). *CFTR* also acts as a regulator of other chloride channels, such as the outwardly rectifying chloride channel,[9,10] and of the epithelium sodium channel.[11]

There is evidence that *CFTR* defects can lead to excessive NFκB activation.[12] This is associated with an exaggerated release of proinflammatory cytokines by airway epithelial cells in response to exposure to *Pseudomonas aeruginosa* or lipopolysaccharide. Specifically, cells from CF patients secrete excessive amounts of interleukin (IL)-8 and tumor necrosis factor-α (TNF-α) and decreased amounts of IL-10, an anti-inflammatory cytokine.[13] Similar findings have been reported recently in a *Pseudomonas*-infected *CFTR* knockout mouse model.[14] In that model, *CFTR* knockout mice have a fourfold greater mortality than normal mice by 10 days after inoculation of *Pseudomonas* embedded in agarbeads (Figure 1–1). Although these findings remain controversial, they could explain the excessive neutrophil-mediated airway inflammation that is the hallmark of CF lung disease.

Other competing theories of CF pathogenesis have also been proposed. These include a hypothesis that abnormal ion channel function in the airway epithelium leads to an increase in the concentration of sodium and chloride in the ASF, which, in turn, renders some important antimicrobial activity ineffective.[15] The isolation of a salt-sensitive defensin peptide, human β defensin (HβD-1), raised the possibility that dysfunction of this molecule represented a primary link between the ion channel defect and the increased susceptibility to *Pseudomonas* infection that has been observed.[16] Further studies have indicated, however, that the difference in ASF composition between individuals with CF and unaffected individuals is not sufficient to cause a significant difference in HβD-1 activity, which only decreases at NaCl concentrations greater than 300 mM. Finally, there have been a series of studies that have indicated a difference between

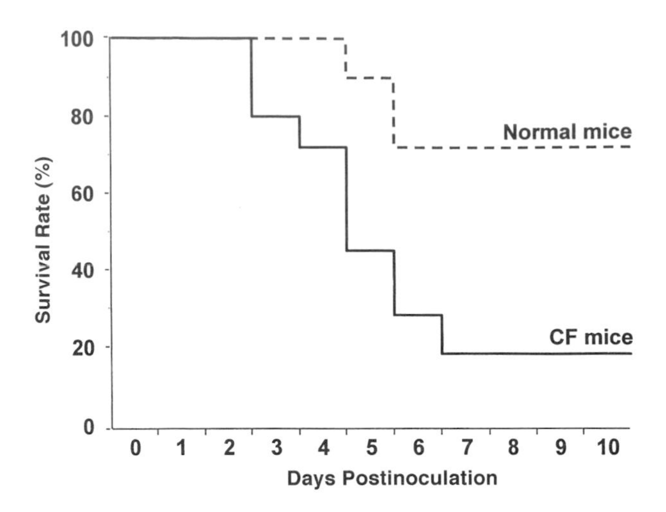

FIGURE 1–1. Mortality of cystic fibrosis mice and wild-type littermates after intratracheal inoculation with sterile agarbeads or beads laden with *Pseudomonas aeruginosa* strain M57–15. (Adapted from Heeckeren AR et al.[14])

CF and normal epithelial cells with regard to their ability to bind and/or internalize *Pseudomonas aeruginosa* and *Staphylococcus aureus*.

While several theories remain with regard to the initiation of airway infection and inflammation in CF, the major consequences of this event have been studied in detail. The cardinal feature of CF lung disease is ongoing inflammation of the small airways, apparently triggered by the presence of the offending bacterial pathogens. Despite the chronic nature of this response, the cells and mediators involved include many of those typically associated with acute inflammation. Polymorphonuclear (PMN) neutrophilic leukocytes are present in very high numbers along with elevated levels of proinflammatory cytokines such as IL-8, (TNF-α, and IL-1β). With the infiltration of PMNs into the airway, high levels of PMN-derived products are released including neutrophil elastase (NE) and human neutrophil peptides (HNPs, part of the α defensin group), both of which amplify the signal from inflammatory mediators and participate directly in the destruction of cells and extracellular matrix molecules. Furthermore, the death and subsequent breakdown of PMNs lead to the release of free macromolecules, such as deoxyribonucleic acid (DNA) and polymerized actin (F-actin), which can increase the viscosity of airway secretions and further impair airway clearance.

There are two major consequences of the massive inflammatory response described above that are relevant for gene therapy. First, there is a self-sustaining nature to the inflammatory response and the lung damage that is associated with it. Since the role of *CFTR* defects in precipitating this process is not well understood, it is not entirely clear how efficient *CFTR* expression will need to be to reverse this process. Second, gene transfer vectors themselves are exposed to a number of inflammatory effector cells and their products that are present in very elevated amounts in the CF airways. Factors such as free DNA, NE, cathepsins, and other proteases all are present in high concentrations in the airway lumen and might present a significant barrier to vector particles and hence to gene transfer.[17] For example, a recent study by our group has indicated that the efficiency of recombinant adeno-associated virus (rAAV)-mediated gene transfer was inhibited by CF bronchoalveolar lavage (BAL) fluid.[18] Furthermore, the efficiency of gene transfer was inversely proportional to the concentration of neutrophil-derived α defensins in the BAL fluid (Figure 1–2).

Gene Transfer Vectors

Based on the microanatomy and architecture of the lung, it is clear that therapeutic gene transfer for CF lung disease must be accomplished in vivo. That is, the vectors will require the ability to transduce the cells in situ, rather than undergoing gene transfer ex vivo prior to reimplantation, as can be done with hematopoietic progenitors or lymphocytes. There are, in fact, only a handful of vector systems that have been explored to date that are capable of such in vivo gene transfer. These include recombinant adenoviruses (Ad), rAAV, lentiviruses (including human immunodeficiency virus 1[HIV-1] and equine infectious anemia virus [EIAV]), cationic liposomes, and molecular

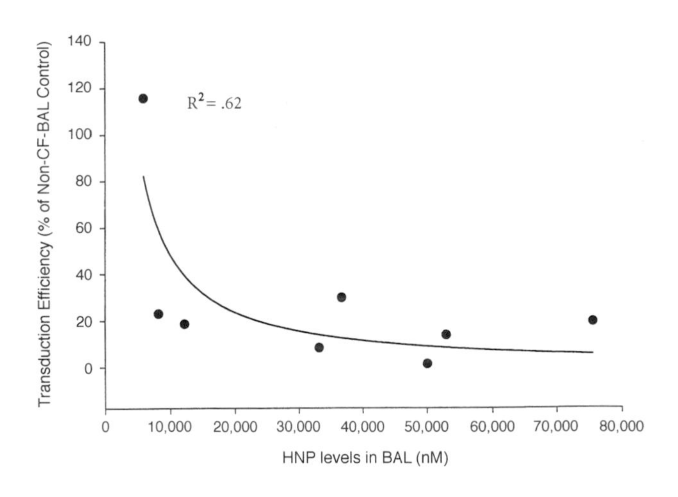

FIGURE 1–2. Inverse correlation between transduction efficiency and neutrophil defensin levels. The efficiency of gene transfer of recombinant adeno-associated virus (rAAV) was assessed in vitro by infection of cystic fibrosis (CF) bronchial epithelial cells with an rAAV-green fluorescent protein reporter virus in the presence of CF broncho-alveolar lavage (BAL) fluid. The efficiency was scored by fluorescence microscopy at 48 hours postinfection and normalized to a non-CF-BAL control. The efficiency was then correlated with the amount of neutrophil-derived α defensin. HNP = human neutrophil peptide. (Adapted from Virella-Lowell I et al.[18])

conjugates. Each of these offers potential advantages and disadvantages, particularly in the setting of ongoing inflammation in the CF lung. Our group has focused on the development of rAAV vectors.

Recombinant adeno-associated virus

Adeno-associated virus is a nonpathogenic human parvovirus that has a natural mechanism for long-term persistence in human cells. Wild-type AAV is unique in that it undergoes stable integration of its DNA into a specific region of human chromosome 19, the AAVS1 site,[19–22] a process that our group has recently described in vivo in rhesus macaques.[23] This site-specificity appears to be mediated by specific interactions between the nonstructural protein Rep and the sequence-specific binding elements within the AAVS1 site.[24] Adeno-associated virus vectors have been developed by deleting the two AAV genes *REP* and *CAP* from the viral genome, and substituting transgenes such as *CFTR*.[25,26] Since the *REP* gene is deleted, these vectors generally do not integrate in a site-specific manner, yet they do persist long-term in mammalian cells through a complicated process that involves both episomal persistence and random-site integration.[27–29]

The packaging capacity of rAAV is rather limited, only 5 kb, including the AAV inverted terminal repeats (ITRs) that are required in cis for replication and packaging of vector genomes. This leaves only 4.7 kb for the coding sequence, promoter, and polyadenylation signal. In the case of *CFTR*, the coding sequence consists of 4.44 kb of DNA. Therefore, the use of small promoters and/or truncated versions of *CFTR* has been investigated by several groups. Vectors of rAAV expressing full-length *CFTR* have been developed using either the AAV-p5 promoter,[30] the herpes simplex virus–thymidine kinase (HSV-Tk) promoter, or the cryptic promoter sequences present within the ITR.[31,32] Vectors of AAV-*CFTR* have been shown to be active for stable complementation of the *CFTR* defect in vitro[9,31,33] and for in vivo gene transfer in the lungs of rabbits[9,34] and rhesus macaques.[28,35] In each of these settings, rAAV-*CFTR* transduction has been stable and has not been associated with acute inflammatory responses or other toxicities.

Based on these data, several phase I trials of rAAV-*CFTR* in CF patients were initiated by our group. A total of 50 patients have been treated to date. The first of these trials, involving a combined nasal and bronchial administration, is still ongoing.[36] The results of a second phase I trial of delivery of rAAV-*CFTR* to the maxillary sinuses of individuals with CF have recently been reported.[37–39] These results indicate that gene transfer occurred in a dose-dependent fashion, with a maximal efficiency of one vector genome copy per cell. Gene transfer was stable for up to 70 days after a single instillation. Furthermore, the vector-treated sinuses showed a dose-related increase in cAMP-activated chloride conductance as judged by transepithelial potential difference measurement in vivo. Perhaps even more promising was a trend toward decreased levels of IL-8 in sinus lavage fluid after rAAV-*CFTR* therapy. Additional studies of administration to the sinuses, nose, and lung are ongoing. A preliminary analysis of the BAL fluid from several of the CF patients involved in the bronchial gene transfer trial has shown inhibition of rAAV, and there is some indication that this effect correlates with the degree of inflammation present in the airways. While these sorts of barriers may be overcome simply by increasing the vector dosage, it is also possible that transient anti-inflammatory therapy may be helpful. Concern has also been raised about the availability of receptors for AAV on the apical surface of bronchial epithelial cells.[40–42] However, data from both our own laboratory[28,34,43,44] and that of Dusty Miller,[45] indicate that pulmonary gene transfer with rAAV is feasible and that it is persistent once it occurs. Ultimately, treating the lungs with this vector may be done optimally at a young age, prior to the onset of severe airway inflammation.

Anti-inflammatory Gene Therapy

Several attempts have been made to interrupt the inflammatory process in CF lung disease by use of oral anti-inflammatory corticosteroids[46,47] or nonsteroidal anti-inflammatory drugs such as ibuprofen.[48] In general these studies have supported the concept that reduction of inflammation can improve outcome variables associated with CF lung disease. Attempts are being made to localize anti-inflammatory therapy using various inhalants, such as inhaled corticosteroids or aerosolized AAT.[49] Several early studies have yielded promising results.

Gene therapy could be used as a means for sustained local delivery of biologically active anti-inflammatory molecules. Gene therapy based on rAAV might pose the advantage of being more sustained, thus necessitating far less effort on the part of patients who often are already using a number of other chronic medications, such as pancreatic enzyme replacement, bronchodilators, inhaled antibiotics, and mucolytics. The feasibility of such an approach has been investigated recently in our laboratory in the context of single intratracheal injections of rAAV vectors expressing human AAT (hAAT) from either the cytomegalovirus (CMV) immediate early promoter (C-AT) or the CMV enhancer/chicken β actin hybrid promoter (Cβ-AT).[50] A single dose of 2×10^9 IU of rAAV-Cβ-AT administered intratracheally was sufficient to mediate expression of >1,000 μg/mL of hAAT in the *serum* of some treated animals. Local levels in the lung are presumably significantly higher. Also of note, the levels of AAT expression were dose-related and were sustained for over 16 weeks with no evidence of decline.

These data are encouraging, because they confirm the feasibility of using rAAV vectors in the lung for locally high stable levels of anti-inflammatory molecules. The dose-dependence of expression would potentially provide some level of control in and of itself. For an agent such as AAT, which is not known to have dose-related side effects from overexpression, this level of control may be sufficient.

However, our group has also begun investigating the use of the tetracycline-controlled system, which will be particularly useful for molecules such as IL-10 that are likely to be immunosuppressive when present at high levels, or when significant systemic levels are produced, as in the example above. Preliminary data from our laboratory indicates that a tetracycline-responsive element-driven IL-10 vector transfected in murine myoblast cultures along with a rAAV-*reverse* tetracycline transactivator (rtTA;TetOn) vector demonstrated approximately 100-fold induction over a range of doxycycline concentrations from 0 to 1,000 μg/mL. The induction was also rapidly reversible in culture, returning to baseline within 24 hours. For the current application, we plan to use the original tetracycline transactivator (TetOff) system to avoid the potential confounding antibiotic effect of doxycyline in the *Pseudomonas*-infected mouse model.

α_1-Antitrypsin Deficiency

α_1-Antitrypsin is a 52-kD serum protein that is normally produced in the hepatocytes within the liver and circulates at serum levels sufficient to be detected by serum protein electrophoresis (> 20 μol/L). Mutations in AAT are designated by their protease inhibitor (Pi) type, as determined by isoelectric focusing (IEF) gel electrophoresis.[51] Clinical deficiency of AAT is most commonly due to homozygosity for the PiZ allele (Glu342Lys). Compound heterozygotes for PiZ and PiS (Glu264Val)[52] are also at risk for lung disease if the level of activity is less than 11 μM.[52,53] Null mutants (with total absence of AAT expression) are also prone to emphysema, although these mutations are less common.[54] The PiZ protein is defective for transport out of the Golgi complex. The accumulation of mutant AAT protein in hepatocytes results in clinical liver disease in approximately 10 to 15% of individuals with the PiZZ genotype. Approximately 63% of AAT-deficient patients will have obstructive pulmonary disease listed as a diagnosis at the time of death, although the phenotype of this disease is strongly influenced by environmental factors, particularly exposure to cigarette smoke.

Emphysema develops when the network elastin fibers in the lung parenchyma, which normally support the structure of the alveoli and tether open the small airways, are destroyed, resulting in overdistention of distal air spaces, destruction of alveolar architecture, air-trapping, and impaired gas exchange. It is now known that the destruction of elastin in the lung results from the disturbance of a physiologic balance between antiproteases and proteases, such as NE, within the lung.[55] Processes that increase the activity of protease or decrease available antiprotease (eg, inherited deficiency of AAT) will increase the likelihood of the development of emphysema. The pulmonary disease in AAT deficiency is similar to cigarette smoking-related emphysema except for the following: (1) the histologic pattern in AAT deficiency is that of panacinar emphysema, as opposed to centriacinar in smoking-related emphysema; (2) the regional distribution is skewed to the lower lung fields in AAT deficiency; and (3) the age of onset is much earlier in AAT-deficient patients.[51] Individuals with an AAT deficiency who smoke may develop emphysema in their twenties or thirties, whereas those who are not exposed to smoke may have their presentation delayed by 10 to 15 years. The effect of cigarette smoke in this disorder is primarily due to a reduction in the association rate constant of AAT with NE,[55] although smoke exposure also causes a modest increase in phagocytes within the lung.[56] Deficiency of AAT is implicated in 2.7% of all deaths due to obstructive pulmonary disease among persons in the 35 to 44-year-old age group.

Animal Models

Human AAT is one of a family of serine proteinase inhibitors (serpins) that serve diverse functions in mammalian species, most often involving the regulation of protease cascades such as those involved in inflammation, coagulation, and fibrinolysis.[57] A review of the murine homologues, the α1AP genes, is relevant since mice provide useful reagents for studies of immunology and transgenic models of disease. There are two strains of mice, tight-skin and pallid, that develop emphysema and seem to have an inherited deficiency of serum antiprotease activity.[58] Of these, the *pallid* strain more closely reflects the human version of AAT deficiency, in that emphysema develops gradually over the first 12 months of life and is clearly not related to an increased neutrophil burden.[58,59] The actual mutation accounting for pallid has been identified recently as a syntaxin-like protein involved in vesicle docking.[60] Presumably, the systemic AAT deficiency is caused by this defect in the last step in the AAT secretory pathway.

The first isolation and characterization of a murine *α1AP* gene was by Krauter et al.[61] They described a genomic clone from Balb/c mice that mapped to chromosome 12 and corresponded with a copy DNA (cDNA) expressed in murine liver. This clone was found to show about 60 to 70% homology with monkey and human *α1AT* genes and about 30% homology with other mammalian serpins. Subsequently Borriello and Krauter[62] have shown that the C57Bl/6 mice possess a family of five related homologues. However, only two of the five possess the active site P1-methionine, which is felt to be crucial for substrate specificity and regulation of AAT by oxidation.

These two genes have been designated *DOM1* and *DOM2*. Inactivation of these two loci would therefore be hypothesized to result in a functional knockout of AAT activity, and thus potentially provide a model for AAT-deficient lung disease. Our group recently has succeeded in sequencing three genomic BAC clones covering exons 2 through 5 of the two active murine genes *DOM1* and *DOM2*. The first targeting vectors for homologous recombination-mediated knockout in embryonic stem cells have been prepared, and electroporation of these vectors into ES cells will commence shortly.

The more relevant model for AAT-deficient liver disease is the transgenic overexpression of the PiZ mutant AAT-protein. Geller et al[63] published a description of such a model. Their PiZ transgenic model developed chronic hepatitis, which eventually progressed to hepatocarcinoma, in a manner reminiscent of human AAT-deficient liver disease.

Approaches to Therapy

Protein replacement therapy is available for prevention of the progression of lung disease due to AAT deficiency; it consists of weekly repeated intravenous infusions of hAAT. Since 1996, thousands of doses of recombinant hAAT have been administered, with only rare side effects that were generally limited to immunoglobulin A (IgA)-deficient patients. Furthermore, hAAT is present in high levels in a wide range of plasma-containing blood products that have been administered to normal and AAT-deficient individuals without incident. Immunologic responses specific to hAAT have not been reported. Of particular note, protein replacement therapy generally does not result in the development of serum antibodies, even in patients who possess the null/null genotype. Aerosolized protein replacement also has been evaluated and found to be safe, although perhaps less effective.

The prevention of lung disease in AAT deficiency is a relatively straightforward concept, since the presence of serum levels of 11 μM or 800 μg/mL is a clear indicator of a restored antiprotease defense. The pathophysiology of AAT-deficient liver disease is much more complex, however. As stated above, AAT-deficient liver disease relates to toxicity for the mutant AAT molecule within the hepatocyte. In the most common mutation, the PiZ mutant, AAT protein undergoes polymerization within the endoplasmic reticulum. The mutant protein is then targeted for ubiquitination and protease-mediated degradation. Prevention of degradation of PiZ AAT in cell cultures allows for the secretion of the mutant protein, which retains functional antiprotease activity. However, inefficient degradation of PiZ AAT may actually predispose patients to liver disease. Again, this may be due to toxic effects from AAT degradation products. In any case, the clinical presentation of AAT-deficient liver disease is quite distinct from that of the lung disease. While the lung disease presents in early adulthood, the liver disease frequently presents in infancy or early childhood and causes progressive cirrhosis, often leading to liver failure. Adults can also have chronic liver disease due to the effects of PiZ AAT, and their risk of hepatocellular carcinoma is significantly increased.

Several gene therapy approaches for AAT replacement have been evaluated in vivo including recombinant Ad and cationic liposome vector delivery to the bronchial epithelium,[64,65] the peritoneal surface,[66] the liver,[67,68] and the skin.[69] Retroviral vectors,[70] naked DNA injection[71] and gene-particle bombardment (gene gun) delivery[72] techniques also have been evaluated. The results of these studies have been encouraging in that secretion of AAT into the serum from a variety of ectopic sites has been demonstrated. This includes the direct demonstration that myofibers of skeletal muscle are capable of secretion of biologically active AAT into the serum.[72] A recent study by Guo and collaborators[73] evaluated the relative strength of a wide range of promoters with particular attention to their ability to achieve therapeutic levels of AAT in mice. In that study, the human elongation factor 1α promoter had the highest stable levels of expression, 2 mg/mL, well above the threshold value for prevention of emphysema, which is 0.8 mg/mL or 11 μM. While the first-generation Ad system itself is still limited by immunologic rejection of transduced cells, this work clearly shows the feasibility of gene augmentation as a therapy for AAT deficiency.

The remaining obstacle to the use of gene transfer for therapy of AAT deficiency is the availability of a vector system that can provide efficient and *sustained* expression. Two recent publications have indicated that transduction of skeletal muscle, either with helper-dependent high-capacity Ad vectors[74] or with rAAV vectors[75] is capable of achieving therapeutic levels in mice in a stable manner.

Since AAT-deficient liver disease is due to a deleterious effect of the mutant protein, rather than to a lack of activity of the wild-type protein, it is not likely that gene augmentation with a single PiM allele into a PiZZ hepatocyte will prevent the development of pathology. It is possible that the liver disease due to PiZ will demonstrate a dominant negative phenotype. In fact, there is evidence that chronic liver failure is more common in adults who are heterozygous for PiZ.[76] In that case, gene therapy for AAT-deficient liver disease would require downregulation of PiZ allele. The feasibility of knocking out an overexpressed gene in somatic cells with an rAAV vector has been demonstrated recently. Lewin, et al[77] showed that the use of hairpin and hammerhead ribozymes in an rAAV vector were capable of efficiently decreasing expression from a mutant allele in a rodent model of autosomal dominant retinitis pigmentosa. The correction they observed was sustained for ≥ 8 months and was sufficient to restore vision to these animals that otherwise are prone to progressive blindness.

Conclusions

The genetic component of more common diseases affecting the respiratory tract, such as asthma and COPD, will likely be better defined in the coming years. Experience with the more common single-gene defects affecting the lung, CF and AAT-deficiency, suggests that the identification of a genetic cause, although not leading to an immediate cure for the disease, is an important step. Discovery of the genetic basis for a given disease opens up new opportunities for research into disease pathogenesis and for the production of animal models in which to test new therapies. The promise of gene therapy remains a long-term goal. In the future, newer vectors based on rAAV may provide safe and long-lasting therapeutic effects.

Acknowledgment

Supported in part by grants from the NHLBI (HL59412, HL51811), NIDDK (DK51809), NCRR (RR00082), the Cystic Fibrosis Foundation, and the Alpha One Foundation.

References

1. Riordan JR, Rommens JM, Kerem B, et al. Identification of the cystic fibrosis gene: cloning and characterization of complementary DNA [published erratum appears in Science 1989;245:1437]. Science 1989;245:1066–73.
2. Welsh MJ, Smith AE. Molecular mechanisms of CFTR chloride channel dysfunction in cystic fibrosis. Cell 1993;73:1251–4.
3. Anderson MP, Rich DP, Gregory RJ, et al. Generation of cAMP-activated chloride currents by expression of CFTR. Science 1991;251:679–82.
4. Rich DP, Anderson MP, Gregory RJ, et al. Expression of cystic fibrosis transmembrane conductance regulator corrects defective chloride channel regulation in cystic fibrosis airway epithelial cells [see comments]. Nature 1990;347:358–63.
5. Berger HA, Anderson MP, Gregory RJ, et al. Identification and regulation of the cystic fibrosis transmembrane conductance regulator-generated chloride channel. J Clin Invest 1991;88:1422–31.
6. Schultz BD, Venglarik CJ, Bridges RJ, Frizzell RA. Regulation of CFTR Cl- channel gating by ADP and ATP analogues. J Gen Physiol 1995;105:329–61.
7. Engelhardt JF, Yankaskas JR, Ernst SA, et al. Submucosal glands are the predominant site of CFTR expression in the human bronchus. Nat Genet 1992;2:240–8.
8. Sehgal A, Presente A, Engelhardt JF. Developmental expression patterns of CFTR in ferret tracheal surface airway and submucosal gland epithelia. Am J Respir Cell Mol Biol 1996;15:122–31.
9. Egan M, Flotte T, Afione S, et al. Defective regulation of outwardly rectifying Cl-channels by protein kinase A corrected by insertion of CFTR [see comments]. Nature 1992;358:581–4.
10. Schwiebert EM, Egan ME, Hwang TH, et al. CFTR regulates outwardly rectifying chloride channels through an autocrine mechanism involving ATP. Cell 1995; 81:1063–73.
11. Stutts MJ, Rossier BC, Boucher RC. Cystic fibrosis transmembrane conductance regulator inverts protein kinase A-mediated regulation of epithelial sodium channel single channel kinetics. J Biol Chem 1997;272: 14037–40.
12. DiMango E, Ratner AJ, Bryan R, et al. Activation of NF-kappaB by adherent *Pseudomonas aeruginosa* in normal and cystic fibrosis respiratory epithelial cells. J Clin Invest 1998;101:2598–605.
13. Dosanjh AK, Elashoff D, Robbins RC. The bronchoalveolar lavage fluid of cystic fibrosis lung transplant recipients demonstrates increased interleukin-8 and elastase and decreased IL-10 [in process citation]. J Interferon Cytokine Res 1998;18:851–4.
14. Heeckeren AR, Walenga MW, Konstan T, et al. Excessive inflammatory response of cystic fibrosis mice to bronchopulmonary infection with *Pseudomonas aeruginosa.* J Clin Invest 1997;100:2810–5.
15. Smith JJ, Travis SM, Greenberg EP, Welsh MJ. Cystic fibrosis airway epithelia fail to kill bacteria because of abnormal airway surface fluid [published erratum appears in Cell 1996;87:following 355]. Cell 1996;85:229–36.
16. Goldman MJ, Anderson GM, Stolzenberg ED, et al. Human beta-defensin-1 is a salt-sensitive antibiotic in lung that is inactivated in cystic fibrosis. Cell 1997;88:553–60.
17. Stern M, Caplen NJ, Browning JE, et al. The effect of mucolytic agents on gene transfer across a CF sputum barrier in vitro. Gene Ther 1998;5:91–8.
18. Virella-Lowell I, Poirier A, Chesnut KA, et al. Inhibition of recombinant adeno-associated virus (rAAV) transduction by bronchial secretions from cystic fibrosis patients. Gene Ther 2000;7:1783–9.
19. Kotin RM, Siniscalco M, Samulski RJ, et al. Site-specific integration by adeno-associated virus. Proc Natl Acad Sci U S A 1990;87:2211–5.
20. Kotin RM, Menninger JC, Ward DC, Berns KI. Mapping and direct visualization of a region-specific viral DNA integration site on chromosome 19q13-qter. Genomics 1991;10:831–4.
21. Kotin RM, Linden RM, Berns KI. Characterization of a preferred site on human chromosome 19q for integration of adeno-associated virus DNA by non-homologous recombination. EMBO J 1992;11:5071–8.
22. Samulski RJ, Zhu X, Xiao X, et al. Targeted integration of adeno-associated virus (AAV) into human chromosome 19 [published erratum appears in EMBO J 1992; 11:1228]. EMBO J 1991;10:3941–50.
23. Hernandez YJ, Wang J, Kearns WG, et al. Latent adeno-associated virus infection elicits humoral but not cell-mediated immune responses in a nonhuman primate model [in process citation]. J Virol 1999;73:8549–58.
24. Weitzman MD, Kyostio SR, Kotin RM, Owens RA. Adeno-associated virus (AAV) Rep proteins mediate complex formation between AAV DNA and its integra-

tion site in human DNA. Proc Natl Acad Sci U S A 1994;91:5808–12.
25. Tratschin JD, West MH, Sandbank T, Carter BJ. A human parvovirus, adeno-associated virus, as a eucaryotic vector: transient expression and encapsidation of the procaryotic gene for chloramphenicol acetyltransferase. Mol Cell Biol 1984;4:2072–81.
26. Hermonat PL, Muzyczka N. Use of adeno-associated virus as a mammalian DNA cloning vector: transduction of neomycin resistance into mammalian tissue culture cells. Proc Natl Acad Sci U S A 1984;81:6466–70.
27. Flotte TR, Afione SA, Zeitlin PL. Adeno-associated virus vector gene expression occurs in nondividing cells in the absence of vector DNA integration. Am J Respir Cell Mol Biol 1994;11:517–21.
28. Afione SA, Conrad CK, Kearns WG, et al. In vivo model of adeno-associated virus vector persistence and rescue. J Virol 1996;70:3235–41.
29. Kearns WG, Afione SA, Fulmer SB, et al. Recombinant adeno-associated virus (AAV-CFTR) vectors do not integrate in a site-specific fashion in an immortalized epithelial cell line. Gene Ther 1996;3:748–55.
30. Flotte TR, Solow R, Owens RA, et al. Gene expression from adeno-associated virus vectors in airway epithelial cells. Am J Respir Cell Mol Biol 1992;7:349–56.
31. Flotte TR, Afione SA, Solow R, et al. Expression of the cystic fibrosis transmembrane conductance regulator from a novel adeno-associated virus promoter. J Biol Chem 1993;268:3781–90.
32. Baudard M, Flotte TR, Aran JM, et al. Expression of the human multidrug resistance and glucocerebrosidase cDNAs from adeno-associated vectors: efficient promoter activity of AAV sequences and in vivo delivery via liposomes. Hum Gene Ther 1996;7:1309–22.
33. Schwiebert EM, Flotte T, Cutting GR, Guggino WB. Both CFTR and outwardly rectifying chloride channels contribute to cAMP-stimulated whole cell chloride currents. Am J Physiol 1994;266:C1464–77.
34. Flotte TR, Afione SA, Conrad C, et al. Stable in vivo expression of the cystic fibrosis transmembrane conductance regulator with an adeno-associated virus vector. Proc Natl Acad Sci U S A 1993;90:10613–7.
35. Conrad CK, Allen SS, Afione SA, et al. Safety of single-dose administration of an adeno-associated virus (AAV)-CFTR vector in the primate lung. Gene Ther 1996; 3:658–68.
36. Flotte T, Carter B, Conrad C, et al. A phase I study of an adeno-associated virus-CFTR gene vector in adult CF patients with mild lung disease. Hum Gene Ther 1996; 7:1145 59.
37. Wagner JA, Reynolds T, Moran ML, et al. Efficient and persistent gene transfer of AAV-CFTR in maxillary sinus [letter]. Lancet 1998;351:1702–3.
38. Wagner JA, Moran ML, Messner AH, et al. A phase I/II study of tgAAV-CF for the treatment of chronic sinusitis in patients with cystic fibrosis. Hum Gene Ther 1998;9: 889–909.
39. Wagner JA, Moran ML, Daifuku R, et al. Safety and biological efficacy of an adeno-associated virus vector-cystic fibrosis transmembrane conductance regulator (AAV-CFTR) in the cystic fibrosis maxillary sinus. Laryngoscope 1999;109:266–74.
40. Teramoto S, Bartlett JS, McCarty D, et al. Factors influencing adeno-associated virus-mediated gene transfer to human cystic fibrosis airway epithelial cells: comparison with adenovirus vectors. J Virol 1998;72:8904–12.
41. Duan D, Yue Y, Yan Z, et al. Polarity influences the efficiency of recombinant adenoassociated virus infection in differentiated airway epithelia [in process citation]. Hum Gene Ther 1998;9:2761–76.
42. Bals RXW, Sang N, Weiner DJ, et al.Transduction of well-differentiated airway epithelium by recombinant adeno-associated virus is limited by vector entry. J Virol 1999; 73:6085–88.
43. Flotte TR, Barraza-Ortiz X, Solow R, et al. An improved system for packaging recombinant adeno-associated virus vectors capable of in vivo transduction. Gene Ther 1995; 2:29–37.
44. Flotte TR, Beck SE, Chesnut K, et al. A fluorescence video-endoscopy technique for detection of gene transfer and expression. Gene Ther 1998;5:166–73.
45. Halbert CL, Standaert TA, Wilson CB, Miller AD. Successful readministration of adeno-associated virus vectors to the mouse lung requires transient immunosuppression during the initial exposure. J Virol 1998; 72: 9795–805.
46. Eigen H, Rosenstein BJ, FitzSimmons S, Schidlow DV. A multicenter study of alternate-day prednisone therapy in patients with cystic fibrosis. Cystic Fibrosis Foundation Prednisone Trial Group. J Pediatr 1995;126:515–23.
47. Rosenstein BJ, Eigen H. Risks of alternate-day prednisone in patients with cystic fibrosis. Pediatrics 1991;87:245–6.
48. Konstan MW, Byard PJ, Hoppel CL, Davis PB. Effect of high-dose ibuprofen in patients with cystic fibrosis [see comments]. N Engl J Med 1995;332:848–54.
49. Konstan MW. Therapies aimed at airway inflammation in cystic fibrosis. Clin Chest Med 1998;19:505–13, vi.
50. Virella-Lowell I, Zusman B, Conlon T, et al. A CMV/beta actin hybrid promoter enhances rAAV vector expression in the lung. Submitted 2001.
51. Crystal RG. The alpha 1-antitrypsin gene and its deficiency states. Trends Genet 1989;5:411–7.
52. Ogushi F, Hubbard RC, Fells GA, et al. Evaluation of the S-type of alpha-1-antitrypsin as an in vivo and in vitro inhibitor of neutrophil elastase. Am Rev Respir Dis 1988;137:364–70.
53. Brantly ML, Wittes JT, Vogelmeier CF, et al. Use of a highly purified alpha 1-antitrypsin standard to establish ranges for the common normal and deficient alpha 1-antitrypsin phenotypes. Chest 1991;100:703–8.
54. Cox DW, Levison H. Emphysema of early onset associated with a complete deficiency of alpha-1-antitrypsin (null homozygotes). Am Rev Respir Dis 1988;137:371–5.
55. Ogushi F, Hubbard RC, Vogelmeier C, et al. Risk factors for emphysema. Cigarette smoking is associated with a reduction in the association rate constant of lung alpha 1-antitrypsin for neutrophil elastase. J Clin Invest 1991; 87:1060–5.
56. Casolaro MA, Fells G, Wewers M, et al. Augmentation of lung antineutrophil elastase capacity with recombinant

human alpha-1-antitrypsin. J Appl Physiol 1987; 63:2015–23.

57. Patterson SD. Mammalian alpha 1-antitrypsins: comparative biochemistry and genetics of the major plasma serpin. Comp Biochem Physiol Biochem Mol Biol 1991; 100:439–54.
58. Martorana PA, Brand T, Gardi C, et al. The pallid mouse. A model of genetic alpha 1-antitrypsin deficiency. Lab Invest 1993;68:233–41.
59. de Santi MM, Martorana PA, Cavarra E, Lungarella G. Pallid mice with genetic emphysema. Neutrophil elastase burden and elastin loss occur without alteration in the bronchoalveolar lavage cell population. Lab Invest 1995;73:40–7.
60. Huang L, Kuo YM, Gitschier J. The pallid gene encodes a novel, syntaxin 13-interacting protein involved in platelet storage pool deficiency. Nat Genet 1999;23:329–32.
61. Krauter KS, Citron BA, Hsu MT, et al. Isolation and characterization of the alpha 1-antitrypsin gene of mice. DNA 1986;5:29–36.
62. Borriello F, Krauter KS. Multiple murine alpha 1-protease inhibitor genes show unusual evolutionary divergence. Proc Natl Acad Sci U S A 1991;88:9417–21.
63. Geller SA, Nichols WS, Kim S, et al. Hepatocarcinogenesis is the sequel to hepatitis in Z # 2 alpha 1-antitrypsin transgenic mice: histopathological and DNA ploidy studies. Hepatology 1994:19:389–97.
64. Canonico AE, Conary JT, Meyrick BO, Brigham KL. Aerosol and intravenous transfection of human alpha 1-antitrypsin gene to lungs of rabbits. Am J Respir Cell Mol Biol 1994;10:24–9.
65. Rosenfeld MA, Siegfried W, Yoshimura K, et al. Adenovirus-mediated transfer of a recombinant alpha 1-antitrypsin gene to the lung epithelium in vivo [see comments]. Science 1991;252:431–4.
66. Setoguchi Y, Jaffe HA, Chu CS, Crystal RG. Intraperitoneal in vivo gene therapy to deliver alpha 1-antitrypsin to the systemic circulation. Am J Respir Cell Mol Biol 1994; 10:369–77.
67. Alino SF, Crespo J, Bobadilla M, et al. Expression of human alpha 1-antitrypsin in mouse after in vivo gene transfer to hepatocytes by small liposomes. Biochem Biophys Res Commun 1994;204:1023–30.
68. Barr D, Tubb J, Ferguson J, et al. Strain related variations in adenovirally mediated transgene expression from mouse hepatocytes in vivo: comparisons between immunocompetent and immunodeficient inbred strains. Gene Ther 1995;2:151–5.
69. Setoguchi Y, Jaffe HA, Danel C, Crystal RG. Ex vivo and in vivo gene transfer to the skin using replication-deficient recombinant adenovirus vectors. J Invest Dermatol 1994;102:415–21.
70. Kay MA, Li Q, Liu TJ, et al. Hepatic gene therapy: persistent expression of human alpha 1-antitrypsin in mice after direct gene delivery in vivo. Hum Gene Ther 1992; 3:641–7.
71. Levy MY, Barron LG, Meyer KB, Szoka FC Jr. Characterization of plasmid DNA transfer into mouse skeletal muscle: evaluation of uptake mechanism, expression and secretion of gene products into blood. Gene Ther 1996;3:201–11.
72. Qui P, Zeigelhoffer P, Sun J, Yang NS. Gene gun delivery of mRNA in situ results in efficient gene transgene expression and genetic immunization. Gene Ther 1996; 3:262–8.
73. Guo ZS, Wang LH, Eisensmith RC, Woo SL. Evaluation of promoter strength for hepatic gene expression in vivo following adenovirus-mediated gene transfer. Gene Ther 1996;3:802–10.
74. Schiedner G, Morral N, Parks RJ, et al. Genomic DNA transfer with a high-capacity adenovirus vector results in improved in vivo gene expression and decreased toxicity [published erratum appears in Nat Genet 1998; 18:298]. Nat Genet 1998;18:180–3.
75. Song S, Morgan M, Ellis T, et al. Sustained secretion of human alpha-1-antitrypsin from murine muscle transduced with adeno-associated virus vectors. Proc Natl Acad Sci U S A 1998;95:14384–8.
76. Graziadei IW, Joseph JJ, Wiesner RH, et al. Increased risk of chronic liver failure in adults with heterozygous alpha1-antitrypsin deficiency. Hepatology 1998;28:1058–63.
77. Lewin AS, Drenser KA, Hauswirth WW, et al. Ribozyme rescue of photoreceptor cells in a transgenic rat model of autosomal dominant retinitis pigmentosa [published erratum appears in Nat Med 1998;4:1081]. Nat Med 1998;4:967–71.

CHAPTER 2

Genetic and Molecular Basis of Airway and Lung Development

Clifford W. Bogue, MD

The mammalian respiratory system is a complex organ comprising two parts—the trachea and the lungs—which both develop from the foregut. The respiratory system has arisen relatively late in vertebrate evolution, and its primary function is gas exchange, a function critical to survival of the organism. In humans, the lungs originate as the laryngotracheal groove in the endodermal epithelium lining the floor of the primitive embryonic anterior pharynx at 5 weeks of gestation. The laryngotracheal groove deepens and finally constricts, thereby dividing the foregut tube into a ventral trachea and a dorsal esophagus. At the same time, the tracheal rudiment outgrowth elongates caudally and bifurcates to form two bronchial lung buds. These two primary buds then begin a reproducible bilaterally asymmetric pattern of stereotypic branching, followed by dichotomous branching into the surrounding splanchnic mesenchyme. This developmental process results in a bilobed left and trilobed right lung. Branching of these secondary bronchi occurs over and over for a total of twenty-three generations in the human. This process is completed in the latter part of gestation; alveolization begins at around 20 weeks of gestation and is completed postnatally.

Lung development in the mouse closely parallels human lung development, and it is therefore used as a model in this chapter. Histologically, mouse lung development has been divided into four chronologic stages: (1) the pseudoglandular stage (embryonic days 9.5 to 16.5 [E9.5 to 16.5]), when the bronchial and respiratory tree develops and an undifferentiated primordial system forms; (2) the canalicular stage (E16.5 to 17.5), when terminal air sacs develop and vascularization begins; (3) the terminal sac stage (E17.5 to postnatal day five [P5]), during which the number of terminal sacs and blood vessels increases and type I and II cells differentiate; and (4) the alveolar stage (P5 to 30), characterized by terminal sacs developing into mature alveolar ducts and alveoli.

Obviously, this commonly used classification of the stages of lung development begins with initial lung budding and trachea formation. However, it has become increasingly clear over the past several years that the biologic processes and genetic pathways that influence lung development begin well before the lung buds actually form as ventral outpouchings of the foregut. In general, the development of endodermal organs can be divided into four fundamental stages: (1) gastrulation and formation of the three principal germ layers, including endoderm; (2) gut tube morphogenesis; (3) budding of organ domains from the gut tube; and (4) differentiation of organ-specific cell types within the growing organ buds. It is through these four distinct developmental events that the endoderm forms from totipotent cells of the epiblast.[1] Once the endoderm is formed, it is transformed from a single sheet of cells into a primitive tube that becomes the gut from which the organ buds grow, branch, and eventually form differentiated functioning parenchymal organs. Based on this general developmental scheme for the formation of all organs from the endoderm, the development of the mammalian lung can therefore be categorized as follows: (1) endoderm formation; (2) foregut formation and patterning; (3) lung bud and trachea formation; and (4) morphogenesis and differentiation (Figure 2–1). This chapter highlights many of the important molecular events and genetic factors involved in these different stages of lung development.

Endoderm Formation

At E6.0, just prior to onset of gastrulation, the embryonic portion of the developing embryo is composed of two epithelial layers—the epiblast, which forms the entire embryo, and the visceral endoderm (or hypoblast), which is replaced by definitive gut endoderm during gastrulation and eventually contributes only to the extraembryonic yolk sac.[2] Gastrulation begins at E6.5 with the formation of the primitive streak on the posterior side of the embryo; epiblast cells undergo an epithelial-mesenchymal transformation to generate mesoderm (for an excellent review, see Tam and Behringer[3]) (Figure 2–2). With the formation of the primitive streak on the posterior side of the embryo, the anterioposterior (A-P) axis of the embryo becomes obvious morphologically. Over the ensuing 24 hours, the streak elongates and moves along the rim of the egg cylinder toward its distal tip. It is here, at the anterior end of the primitive streak, that a specialized structure, known as the "node," forms. The node generates axial mesendoderm, which includes the mesoderm that contributes to the prechordal plate and notochord as well as

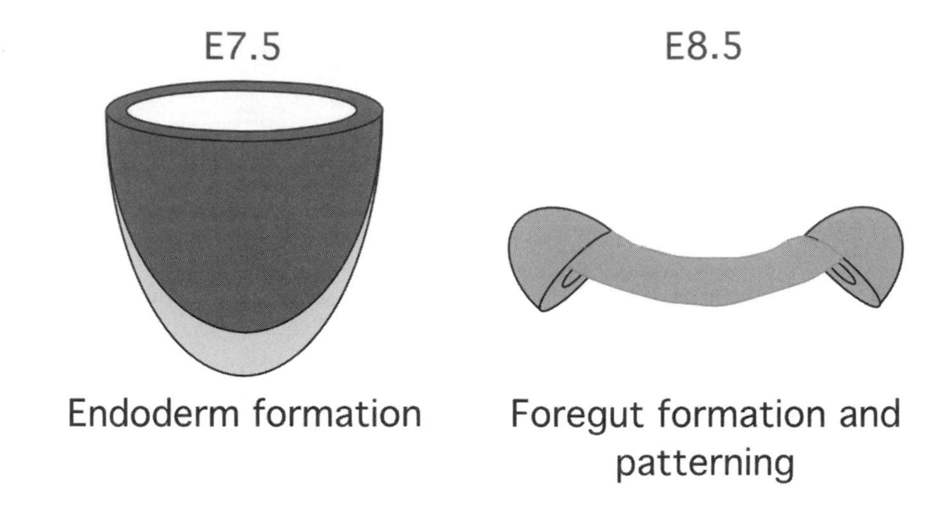

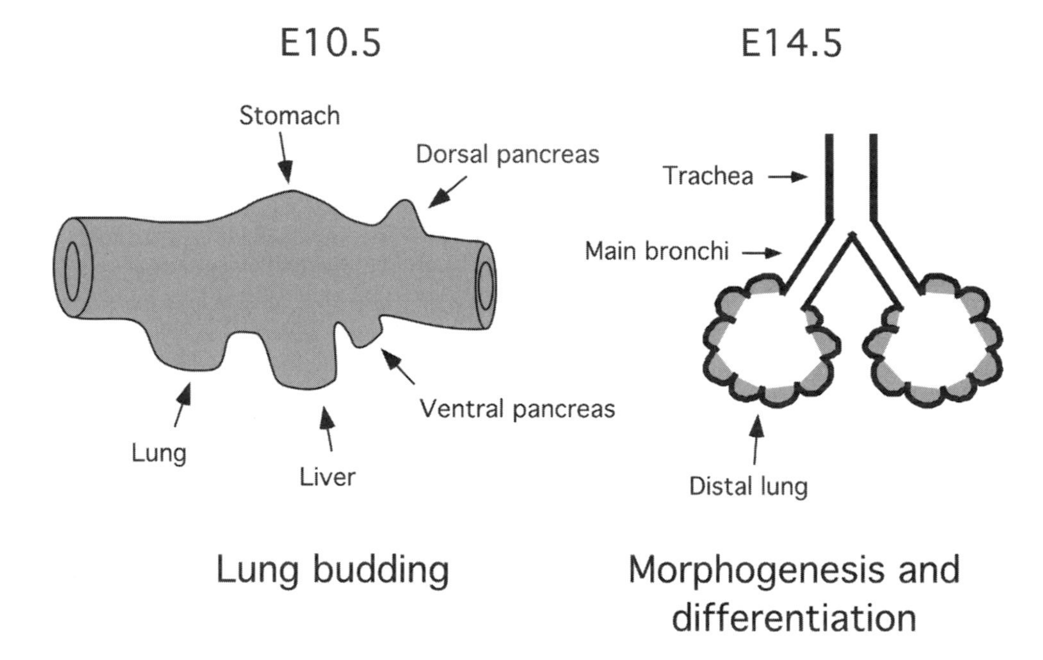

FIGURE 2–1. Stages of lung development. The panels illustrate the four stages of lung development and morphogenesis, corresponding to ages E7.5 to 14 in the mouse. *Top left*, At E7.5, the endoderm is only one cell-layer thick and forms a cup-like structure overlying the mesoderm and ectoderm. The embryonic endoderm is shown here as light, and the visceral endoderm as dark. *Top right*, By E8.5, morphogenetic cell movements transform this cup-like sheet of cells into a three-dimensional tube-like structure that is patterned along the anteroposterior and dorsoventral axes. *Bottom left*, At E10.5, the lungs, along with other gut-derived organs, have begun to bud into the surrounding mesenchyme. The relative positions of the various organs are shown. *Bottom right*, By E14.5, the initial lung buds have been transformed into a highly branched lung. The foregut has undergone septation to form the trachea and esophagus, the two main bronchi are present, as are distal lung buds. Significant differentiation of lung-specific cell types has begun. (Adapted from Wells JM and Melton DA.[1] ©1999 by Annual Reviews, www.AnnualReviews.org.)

the definitive gut endoderm. The posterior end of the primitive streak gives rise to extraembryonic mesoderm, and the lateral plate and paraxial mesoderm arise from the intervening regions of the streak. The definitive endoderm moves anteriorly, replacing the anterior visceral endoderm, and eventually gives rise to the endoderm of the fore- and midgut. The foregut begins as a ventral folding of endoderm tissue at the anterior end of the embryo. As the foregut begins to close off, several tissue buds begin to form; they later become important parenchymal organs, such as the thyroid, thymus, lung, liver, and pancreas. Therefore, proper formation of the

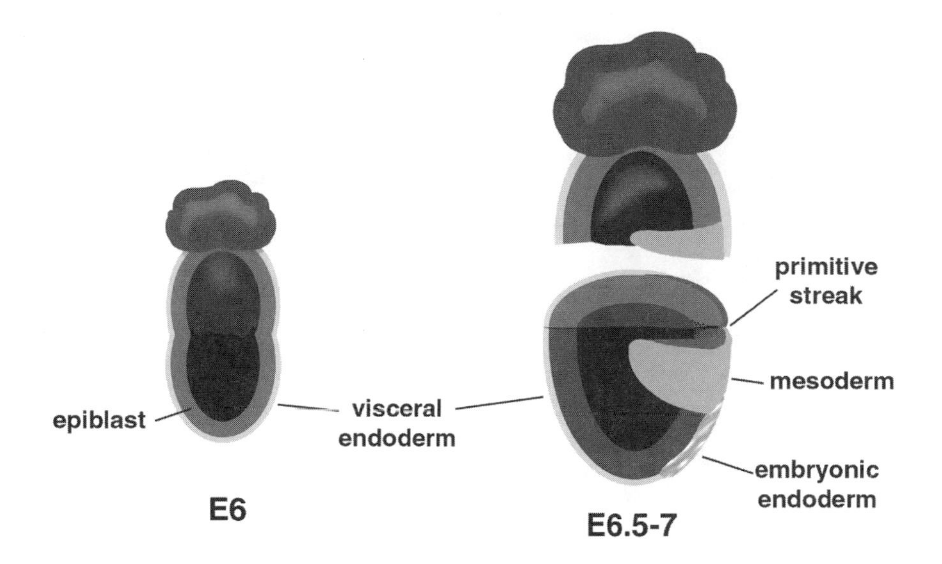

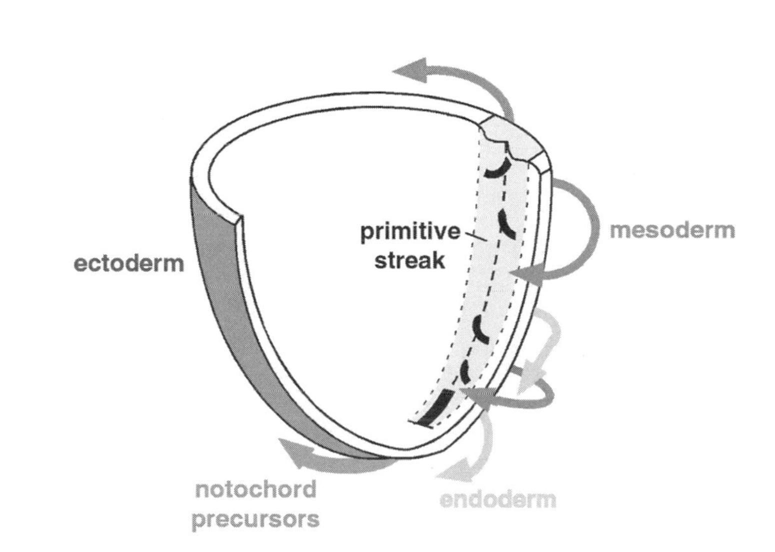

FIGURE 2–2. Gastrulation and endoderm formation. *Top panel*, Relative positions of the embryonic ectoderm (*dark gray*), mesoderm (*light gray*), and endoderm (*hatched*) during gastrulation of the mouse embryo in a partially cut away view. All embryonic tissues derive from the *light gray* region of the E6 embryo, which is called the primitive ectoderm or epiblast at this stage. The layer of cells surrounding the E6 epiblast, the visceral endoderm, does not contribute to the embryonic gut but does contribute to extraembryonic structures such as the yolk sac. Gastrulation begins at E6 when cells migrate out of the epiblast through the primitive streak (PS) at a site that marks the future posterior of the embryo. Within 24 hours (early to mid-PS), the embryo has a well-formed PS, and mesoderm (*light gray*) has begun to ingress between the endoderm and ectoderm in a medial and lateral direction. Embryonic endoderm (*hatched*), which is first detected over the anterior PS, migrates along the midline in an anterior direction. Migration of endoderm and mesoderm continues throughout gastrulation (E7 to 7.5) and is shown in more detail in the *bottom panel*. The arrows show the relative paths of migration of cells during mouse gastrulation. Notochord, endoderm, and mesoderm all derive from the epiblast/PS. Endoderm migrate from the anterior part of the PS and follow an anterior path of migration similar to that of the notochord precursor cells, in contrast to the lateral migration of mesoderm. (Reproduced with permission from Wells JM and Melton DA.[1] ©1999 by Annual Reviews, www.AnnualReviews.org.)

foregut is a critical step in lung development. Interestingly, relatively little is known about endoderm development compared with the knowledge that has accumulated regarding the mechanisms involved in mesoderm and ectoderm formation.

Although mesoderm and endoderm cells both arise from the epiblast and migrate through the primitive streak,[4] it is unclear when or how these cells decide between the two germ cell fates. It also is unclear how the early A-P patterns of gene expression are established.

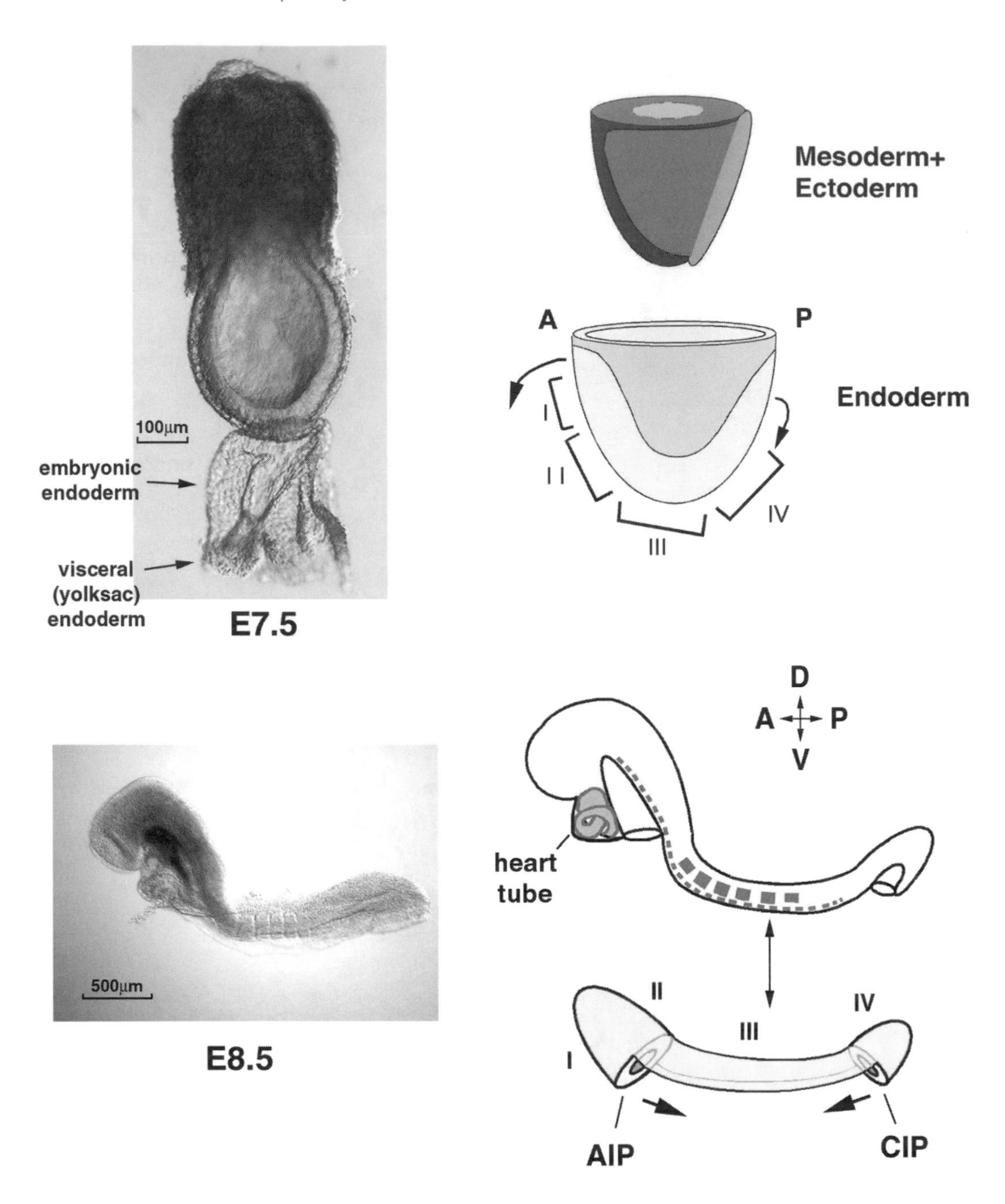

FIGURE 2–3. Formation of the gut tube. *Top left panel,* An E7.5 embryo with the endoderm layer peeled off the underlying mesoderm and ectoderm but still attached at the node. *Bottom left panel,* An E8.5 embryo with a well-formed foregut. The *right panels* show the endoderm separated from the mesoderm and ectoderm. The endoderm of the E7.5 embryo (*light gray and hatched areas, top right*) was fate mapped to the forming E8.5 gut tube (*lower right*). The *right panels* also show the endoderm separated from the mesoderm and ectoderm. The original fate map, of which this is a schematic, was generated by injection of single endoderm cells with a tracer (horseradish peroxidase [HRP]), followed by 24 to 48 hours in culture (see Lawson et al[7]). Roman numerals I to IV represent regions of E7.5 endoderm that fate map to regions I to IV of the E8.5 gut. The anterior-most endoderm (region I) of the E7.5 embryo (*upper right*) contributes to the ventral foregut adjacent to the developing heart and gives rise to organs such as the liver and ventral pancreas (*lower right*). Regions II and III (*upper right*) give rise to dorsal foregut and midgut (*lower right*) that are adjacent to the notochord (*dotted line*) and somites (*dark boxes*). These regions ultimately contribute to stomach, pancreas, duodenum, and part of the intestine. Region IV (*upper right*) forms the hindgut, which contributes to the large intestine and colon (*lower right*). The foregut tube forms as region I folds over region II (*arrow*) and migrates in a posterior direction, whereas the hindgut tube forms when region IV folds over and migrates in an anterior direction (*arrow*). The posterior migration of the anterior intestinal portal (AIP) and the anterior migration of the caudal intestinal portal (CIP), in combination with embryonic turning, close the midgut and form a primitive gut tube by E9. (Reproduced with permission from Wells JM and Melton DA.[1] ©1999 by Annual Reviews, www.AnnualReviews.org.)

Regional expression of genes suggests that endoderm cells have an A-P identity by the end of gastrulation, and recent evidence points to the fact that a series of reciprocal inductions between germ layers results in A-P specification of the endoderm. Although it is not known how all regions of the endoderm become specified, endoderm does interact with many different structures, including the notochord plate, presumptive head ectoderm, the node, lateral mesoderm, and the primitive streak. In vitro experiments using germ layer explants show that the germ layers that are adjacent to the endoderm provide soluble temporally specific signals that induce organ-specific gene expression in the endoderm. One of these signals appears to be the secreted fibroblast growth factor (FGF)4.[5] Interestingly, these signals are instructive rather than permissive; anterior endoderm can be re-specified when placed more posteriorly. This suggests that the A-P nature of the endoderm is not irreversibly determined by E7.5, and it can be altered by changing the spatial source of the adjacent signal.

Evidence from chimeric mouse studies has shown that the formation of definitive endoderm is dependent also on the effector molecule *Smad2*.[6] The smad proteins act downstream of transforming growth factor (TGF)-β receptors and, with other smad proteins, form heteromeric complexes, which are then transported to the nucleus and gain the ability to function as transcriptional regulators via their interactions with other deoxyribonucleic acid (DNA)-binding proteins such as FAST-1 or *Mix* family members. These studies demonstrated that *Smad2* signals promote the recruitment of epiblast cells to form the gut endoderm. In addition, these chimeric studies also suggested that a small number of precursor cells actually give rise to the definitive endoderm. Thus, it is likely that highly localized TGF-β signals cause epiblast derivatives to form the outermost population of endodermal cells.

Foregut Formation and Patterning

At the end of gastrulation (E7.5), the endoderm is a two-dimensional sheet of cells that extends from the anterior headfold to the primitive streak posteriorly. As was noted above, although the endoderm at this point appears morphologically homogeneous, there are differences along the A-P axis. Over the next 24 hours, the gut is transformed into a three-dimensional tube by a series of morphogenetic movements. The foregut begins as a ventral folding of endodermal tissue at the anterior end of the embryo and, as the foregut begins to close off, several tissue buds begin to form, which later become important parenchymal organs. Fate mapping studies performed in the mouse,[7] in which single endoderm cells of the late gastrulation embryo were injected with an intracellular tracer, reveal that specific regions of the E7.5 endoderm give rise to analogous organ domains and regions of the E8.5 gut tube (Figure 2–3). In particular, the anterior-most endoderm (region I) of the E7.5 embryo contributes to the yolk sac and to the ventral foregut adjacent to the developing heart. Subsequently this ventral foregut region gives rise to the liver, ventral pancreas, lungs, and stomach. Region II maps to the dorsal foregut endoderm, contributing to esophagus, stomach, dorsal pancreas, and duodenum. In turn, region III maps to midgut/trunk endoderm, which forms the small intestine, and region IV gives rise to posterior trunk endoderm/hindgut, which forms the large intestine. The opening to the foregut, which is termed the anterior intestinal portal, is pushed caudally, while the opening to the hindgut, the caudal intestinal portal (CIP), is pushed rostrally. These movements, in combination with the turning of the embryo, close up the midgut and form the primitive gut tube by E9 in the mouse. During this time, the endodermal cells change from a flat squamous epithelium to a thick, columnar epithelium. Then discrete regions of the gut tube begin to express different sets of genes, which appear to give rise to specific organs.

Several important developmental events occur between E7.5 and E8.5 to form and pattern the foregut. As mentioned previously, at E7.5 the gut endoderm is not yet irreversibly specified.[5] At this stage, large regions of the foregut endoderm have the potential to adopt a specific organ fate if given the correct developmental cues. This is termed "competence." For instance, regions of the foregut that are not normally destined to become liver are, in fact, capable of expressing hepatic genes in the pre- and early somite embryo. The development of competence is one of the earliest developmental steps in foregut organ formation. Gualdi et al,[8] using a tissue explant assay, demonstrated that in the 7–8 somite stage mouse, inductive events between the ventral foregut endoderm and cardiac mesoderm are necessary for initiating hepatic gene expression. However, these studies also showed that regions of dorsal endoderm, when freed from contact with other dorsal tissues and cultured in the absence of cardiac mesoderm, often initiated liver-specific gene (albumin) expression. This suggests that a large region of the developing endoderm (but not the whole gut endoderm) is competent to initiate the hepatic gene program, and that a combination of both positive (cardiac mesoderm) and negative (dorsal mesoderm and ectoderm) signals restricts the expression of liver-specific genes to the ventral foregut endoderm.

Two genes that have been proposed to act as hepatic competency factors are *HNF3ß* and *GATA-4*.[9–12] The HNF3 proteins were first discovered as factors abundantly expressed in liver[2] and that functioned as transcription factors that regulated the expression of a host of genes in gut-derived endodermal cells.[11] There are three HNF3 isoforms encoded by different genes (designated α, β, and γ) and they have a high degree of sequence similarity in their DNA binding domain, known as the HNF3/forkhead, or winged helix, domain.[13] At the time of gastrulation (E6.5), *HNF3ß* is expressed in the node at the anterior end of the primitive streak and is seen shortly thereafter in the definitive endoderm as well as the notochord and the neural floor plate.[14–17] *HNF3ß* is capable of inducing the expression of Sonic hedgehog (*Shh*) during development,[18,19] and *Shh* expression appears, in turn, to maintain the expression of *HNF3ß*.[20,21] A crucial role for *HNF3ß* in foregut development has been established through gene-targeting experiments. Inactivation of both copies of *HNF3ß* leads to severe defects in foregut morphogenesis as well as abnormalities in notochord formation.[22,23] Recently, Dufort et al demonstrated an intrinsic requirement for *HNFß* in foregut/midgut endoderm development in chimeric mice.[24] In the lung, *HNF3ß* expression is confined to the pulmonary epithelium during development and, in adult lung, is seen in fully differentiated bronchiolar-alveolar epithelium.[15,25] In vitro studies have revealed that several pulmonary epithelium-specific genes are regulated by *HNF3ß*, including *Nkx2.1*,[26] human surfactant protein B (SP-B),[27,28] and Clara cell secretory protein (CCSP or CC10).[29–31] It is not known what role, if any, *HNF3ß* may play in determining pulmonary competence of the foregut or in later aspects of lung development. However, it clearly is necessary for foregut morphogenesis. *GATA-4* is another gene integral to foregut development. *GATA-4* is expressed in the precardiac splanchnic mesoderm and adjacent foregut endoderm during the time of foregut invagination and heart tube formation; homozygous inactivation of the gene results in severe defects of foregut and heart morphogenesis and absence of ventral endoderm.[32,33]

The term "specification" refers to a stage of development in which a group of cells, if isolated and cultured in a neutral environment, will develop more or less according to their normal fate.[34] In the mouse it appears that the gut endoderm is specified by approximately E8.5. Although the endoderm needs and receives ongoing developmental "instructions" as organ development proceeds, the basic regional pattern of the endoderm appears to be established by this early stage of development. And as with earlier stages of development, specification of endodermal cells to particular developmental fates involves signals from adjacent structures. However, at this stage, these signals are permissive rather than instructive. For instance, in liver development, explant studies indicate that signals from the cardiac mesoderm are permissive, because when cardiac mesoderm is combined with endodermal regions other than the anterior ventral endoderm (liver region), hepatic gene expression is not induced.[35,36] A significant effort has been, and continues to be, made in identifying transcription factors that play a role in gut morphogenesis and organ specification. For example, the homeobox gene *Pdx1* has been shown to be necessary for pancreas development in both mice and humans,[37,38] and mice with a null mutation in *Hex* do not form livers.[39,40] Each of these genes appears to function as a specification factor in foregut organ development, as they are expressed in discrete domains of the gut prior to organ budding, and organ formation is not initiated in their absence. To date, no such specification factor expressed in the foregut endoderm that is necessary for lung development has been identified.

Another group of genes likely to play a role in foregut patterning and in determination of the site of lung budding is the *Hox* genes. The *Hox* genes are a murine subfamily of homeobox genes containing over 30 members that are located in four clusters, each on a separate chromosome (chromosomes 2, 6, 11, and 15). Characteristic of this subfamily is a homeodomain with a high degree of homology to that of *Antennapedia (Antp)*, a *Drosophila* homeobox gene that controls leg versus antenna development.[41] In the developing mouse, the temporal and spatial pattern of expression of each *Hox* gene is determined by its position on the chromosome relative to the other genes in the *Hox* cluster—the 5′ genes are expressed later and more posteriorly, while the 3′ genes are expressed earlier and more anteriorly.[42] Pattern formation appears to be governed, in large part, by a network of these transcription factors, as is evidenced by the fact that they have both self- and cross-regulatory properties.[43]

A number of *Hox* genes are known to be expressed in the developing lung, with the *Hoxa* and *Hoxb* clusters being particularly well represented in surveys of pulmonary *Hox* gene expression.[44–50] Data examining the expression of *Hoxb-2, b-3, b-4*, and *b-5* in the foregut at the time of lung budding (E9.5) have shown that *Hoxb-2* was expressed most proximally and *b-3, b-4*, and *b-5* were expressed progressively more distally in the foregut mesenchyme.[45] This pattern of expression is collinear with a gene's position on the chromosome and is consistent with the general pattern of *Hox* gene expression in the developing central nervous system, where genes on the 3′ end of the cluster have spatial expression domains that are more anterior than are the domains of genes that are closer to 5′ in the cluster. Interestingly, lung buds form in the region of the foregut that corresponds to the anterior boundary of *Hoxb-5* expression, which may suggest that *Hoxb-5* helps determine the site of lung budding, similar to the role that it plays in determining the position of the limb buds along the A-P axis.[51] Despite the fact that a large number of *Hox* genes are expressed in the developing lung, most mice with null mutations in individual *Hox* genes do not appear to have significant lung budding and branching defects. One exception is *Hoxa-5*. *Hoxa-5* is expressed in the mesenchyme of the trachea, bronchi, and distal lung, and mice with a null mutation in *Hoxa-5* die of respiratory failure, apparently due to laryngotracheal abnormalities that lead to tracheal occlusion, as well as marked decrease in SP production, and decreased lung branching.[52] In addition to the effect on SPs, which are produced by pulmonary epithelial cells, the expression of three developmentally important genes expressed in the pulmonary epithelium—*Nkx2.1*, *HNF3ß*, and *N-myc*—also was altered. This suggests that the lack of *Hoxa-5* expression leads to a disruption in normal epithelial-mesenchymal interactions in the lung.

Lung Bud and Trachea Formation

In the mouse, the trachea and lungs develop from the foregut at E9.5, a stage when the foregut is a single tube of epithelial endoderm surrounded by splanchnic mesoderm. Lung and trachea development are first recognized at this stage as a ventral epithelial outpouching of the foregut comprising two parts—the future trachea and two primordial lung buds. Interestingly, these two parts of the mammalian respiratory system are formed and develop in completely different ways. Namely, the trachea develops by the division of the foregut into two tubes—the esophagus (dorsal) and the trachea (ventral)—by a longitudinal septum. In contrast the lung, which includes the two main bronchi, subsequent distal bronchial branches, and alveoli, is formed primarily by branching morphogenesis of the two primary lung buds that develop from the ventral foregut. Many factors have been determined to play a role in branching morphogenesis of the lung, as are discussed in the next section. Yet the identification of factors proven to be necessary for lung budding is limited to members of the Gli and FGF gene families.

The vertebrate Gli gene family currently consists of three members, *Gli*, *Gli2*, and *Gli3*, that encode DNA-binding proteins with five zinc fingers and are homologous to *Drosophila Ci*.[53] The Gli family of genes has been implicated as a transducer of *Shh* signaling. During development of the foregut and lung, all three *Gli* genes are expressed in both the splanchnic and lung mesenchyme, with higher levels generally seen in the distal rather than the proximal mesoderm.[53,54] The role of all three *Gli* genes in foregut and lung development has been examined by targeted deletion. Mice with a deletion of the *Gli3* gene have the mildest lung phenotype, consisting of localized size reductions and changes in the shape of the lobes.[54] A more dramatic phenotype is seen in embryos with mutations in *Gli2* and in embryos with compound mutations in both *Gli2* and *Gli3*.[55] At E11.5, *Gli2–/–* animals develop only one lobe on the right, instead of the usual four, while the left lung appears to branch normally. As development proceeds, both right and left lungs are hypoplastic and characterized by thick mesenchymal layers and small air sacs. 5-Bromo-2′-deoxyuridine incorporation studies suggest that the lung hypoplasia is due to a decrease in cell proliferation at later stages of lung development. Additionally, both the trachea and esophagus are hypoplastic, indicating a more generalized effect on the foregut. The phenotype of *Gli2–/–;Gli3+/–* lungs is even more severe, consisting of animals with esophageal atresia, tracheoesophageal fistulas, and a single-lobed lung in the midline. Two other foregut derived organs, the pancreas and liver, appear to bud normally from the foregut endoderm at E9.5. The most severe phenotype was seen in *Gli2–/–;Gli3–/–* animals, which completely lack esophagus, trachea, and lungs. Other foregut derivatives such as stomach, liver, pancreas, and thymus are reduced in size, but are present, and the expression of *HNF3ß* appears to be decreased. This suggests that Gli3 is important for foregut formation when one of the other Gli proteins is missing. To date, the *Gli2–/–;Gli3–/–* mice are the only mouse mutants that completely lack trachea and lungs. However, their specific role in the early lung development remains unclear. The *Gli* genes are expressed broadly in the mesoderm rather than being concentrated at the sites of lung budding, and there is no evidence that they influence the expression levels of other factors in the mesoderm that are known to be mediators of epithelial-mesenchymal interactions, such as members of the *FGF* or bone morphogenetic protein (*BMP*) families. Identification of the direct targets of the *Gli* genes is likely to yield important information on lung budding.

The FGF family of genes includes at least 18 members that encode growth factors that regulate a number of different biologic processes during development, including cellular proliferation, migration, and differentiation. Fibroblast growth factors exert their effects by binding to their receptors (FGFRs), which are tyrosine kinase receptors. During embryogenesis, interactions between FGFs and FGFRs have important roles in mediating epithelial-mesenchymal interactions.[56,57] Several members of the FGF family, and their receptors, are expressed in the developing lung and are necessary for normal lung development. At least three FGFs appear to have important roles in lung development and branching morphogenesis. A number of recent studies indicate that FGF-10 is the most critical FGF for branching morphogenesis of the lung. Early in lung development, *Fgf-10* expression is present in the mesenchyme of the primary lung buds at E9.75.[58] As development proceeds, the expression of *Fgf-10* is dynamic, with highest levels seen in the mesoderm where the endoderm is forming a bud or where bud outgrowth is continuing.[58,59] In fact, the expression domain of *Fgf-10* in the developing mesoderm appears to prefigure the site of endodermal budding, consistent with observations that FGF-10 can induce budding from endodermal lung buds cultured in the absence of mesenchyme[58] and is a potent chemotactic factor that is able to direct the outgrowth of lung buds in whole lung organ culture.[60] Gene ablation studies have unequivocally proven a role for FGF-10 in lung development. In *Fgf-10–/–* mice, septation of the foregut into the trachea and esophagus occurred, but formation of lung buds did not occur.[61,62] The FGF receptor FGFR2-IIIb, which binds both FGF-7 and FGF-10 with high affinity, is highly expressed in the lung endoderm at early stages of lung development.[63,64] It is notable that the critical determinant of the branching pattern of the *Drosophila* trachea is the *branchless* (*bnl*) gene, a member of the FGF gene family.[65] *Bnl* expression is seen in groups of cells surrounding the tracheal sacs just prior to the time when primary branches form. The receptor for *bnl* is *breathless* (*btl*), a member of the FGF receptor family. Secreted *bnl* binds to the *btl* receptor on adjacent tracheal cells, resulting in a signaling cascade that guides the migration of the tracheal cells during the primary budding process.[66–69] Expression of *bnl* in *Drosophila* trachea development is dynamic, with expression levels dropping significantly as the primary branch moves toward a cluster of cells expressing *bnl*, and the primary branch stops growing. Thus, it is likely that *Fgf-10* is the mammalian homologue of *bnl*, and that there are highly conserved mechanisms of branching morphogenesis between flies and mammals.

The genetic factors and pathways required for mouse trachea formation remain relatively obscure. As stated above, it generally is accepted that the formation of the trachea and lungs are coordinated but separate events—the lungs forming by bud formation and branching morphogenesis, and the trachea by septation of the common foregut tube into the ventral trachea and dorsal esophagus. Incomplete septation of the esophagus and trachea is a somewhat common congenital malformation in children, and recent studies in gene-targeted mice have identified some of the genes involved. The gene *Nkx2.1*, also known as *TTF-1* and *T/ebp-1*, is a divergent homeobox gene expressed in the lung. *Nkx2.1* is expressed in the endoderm of the ventral foregut at E9.5, as the foregut is undergoing septation into the ventral trachea and dorsal esophagus,[70] as well as in the thyroid and discrete regions of the brain.[71] Mice with a null mutation in *Nkx2.1* have no septation of the foregut into trachea and esophagus, similar to the anatomic findings of humans with tracheoesophageal fistula. In addition, the lungs form the two main bronchi but fail to undergo subsequent branching morphogenesis. The result is highly dilated sacs lined with columnar epithelium and no distal epithelium, instead of well-formed lungs. Recently, two siblings with hypothyroidism and respiratory failure were determined to have an interstitial chromosomal deletion resulting in deletion of *Nkx2.1*.[72]

Shh is a vertebrate homologue of Drosophila hedgehog (*hh*), a segment polarity gene that encodes a secreted signaling protein regulating *Dpp* and *Wingless* (*Wg*) in target cells.[73–76] In vertebrates, Shh exists as a proprotein that is cleaved into two functional moieties—a 19-kD NH_2-terminal petide that is modified by the addition of cholesterol and serves as a cell membrane anchor, and a 26- to 28-kD COOH-terminal peptide that freely diffuses between cells and is able to exert distant effects in a concentration-dependent manner.[77] *Shh* mediates its effects on adjacent cells by binding to the transmembrane receptor *patched* (*ptc*), which, in turn, results in increased levels of the *Gli* genes, mammalian homologues of *Ci*. In the lung, *Shh* is expressed in the epithelium throughout development and into adulthood. At E9.5, *Shh* is prominently expressed in the tracheal diverticulum, an endodermal outpouching from the ventral foregut,[78] and, as lung development proceeds, expression is particularly high in the epithelium of the distal tips of the lung buds.[79–81] Mice homozygous for a deletion of *Shh* have abnormalities of septation and development of the esophagus and trachea as well as abnormalities in branching morphogenesis of the lung.[78,82] Several interesting observations have been made in the analysis of the *Shh* null mutants. First, the abnormal division of the foregut into the anteriorly placed trachea and posteriorly placed esophagus indicates that this developmental process is likely to be dependent on epithelial-mesenchymal interactions that require *Shh* signaling. Second, although the lungs are quite abnormal (simple sacs lined with respiratory epithelia and covered by a sparse loose mesenchyme), they are present. Therefore, although *Shh* is clearly necessary for normal branching of the lung to occur, it is not necessary for the initiation of lung budding from the foregut. Interestingly, the lungs of *Shh*-null mutants showed evidence of development of both proximal and distal respiratory epithelium, indicating that *Shh* is not necessary for normal proximal-distal epithelial development to occur.

Morphogenesis and Differentiation

Branching Morphogenesis

Once the lung bud has formed, it undergoes a series of highly stereotypic patterning events termed branching morphogenesis. Branching morphogenesis is fundamental to the growth and differentiation of many vertebrate organs, including the lung, thyroid, pancreas, kidney, and mammary gland. In this process the lung primordium, which is a simple bud of undifferentiated epithelial cells surrounded by mesenchyme, is transformed into a highly ramified tree-like organ through the combination of bud outgrowth, tube elongation, and subdivision of terminal buds (a process excellently reviewed by Hogan[83]). In the lung, like other vertebrate organs, this process requires dynamic and reciprocal interactions between two cell populations, the mesenchyme and the epithelium. Over the last several years, valuable insight into the molecular and cellular basis of branching morphogenesis of the embryonic lung has been gained, which suggests that *Fgf-10*, *Bmp4*, *Shh*, and TGF-β play important roles in the process.

It is now clear that *Fgf-10*, in addition to being involved in initial lung bud formation from the foregut, also plays a key role in the reiterative budding and branching that occurs during lung morphogenesis. *Fgf-10* has a highly dynamic temporal and spatial pattern of expression in the lung mesenchyme as development proceeds. Expression of *Fgf-10* is highest in the mesoderm at discrete sites in the distal mesoderm where a prospective bud will form.[58] Expression is not seen in the proximal mesoderm, a tissue that does not promote lung budding. As a lung bud develops, the expression level of *Fgf-10* near the tip of the bud decreases and, subsequently, increased transcript levels are seen laterally at the site of the next lung bud. In vitro experiments in both whole lungs in culture and in single isolated lung buds show that FGF-10 promotes lung budding and acts as both a mitogen and chemoattractant for lung epithelium to promote outgrowth of the lung epithelium toward a source of FGF-10.[60,84] Transgenic mice, in which a dominant-negative form of the *Fgfr2-IIIb* receptor messenger ribonucleic acid (mRNA) was expressed in the lung epithelium under the control of the SP-C promoter or a soluble dominant-negative form of the receptor was ubiquitously expressed, developed normal tracheae and main-stem bronchi but did not develop secondary or terminal lung buds,[63,85] consistent with the idea that *Fgf-10* plays a crucial role in lung budding. Other genetic studies support a role of *Fgf* signaling in lung budding: *Fgf-10–/–* mice do not develop lung buds (see above), and an identical phenotype has been reported in mice with mutations of the receptor for *Fgf-10*, FGFR2.[86,87]

Interestingly, during lung branching morphogenesis, there are regions of mesoderm lateral to the developing lung bud that continue to express low levels of *Fgf-10*, suggesting there may be some factor or factors produced by the mesoderm that locally inhibit or downregulate *Fgf-10* expression, thereby controlling the sites of lateral branching. *Bmp4* is a member of a large family of evolutionally conserved signaling molecules that belong to the TGF-β superfamily. The BMP family members are known to be involved in a number of embryonic patterning events[2] and mediate their effects through transmembrane serine-threonine kinase receptors that form heterodimers/tetramers of two different subunits.[88] *Bmp4* has been placed into a subfamily with *Bmp2* and *Dpp* based on a comparison of the sequence of the carboxy-terminal mature region of the protein.[2] Transcripts for *Bmp5*, *Bmp7*, and *Bmp4* have been detected in the developing lung. *Bmp5* is expressed ubiquitously in the mesenchyme,[89] while *Bmp7* is expressed ubiquitously in the endoderm.[90] *Bmp4* expression is dynamic, and there appear to be two distinct sites of expression during lung development. Prior to lung budding, *Bmp4* is expressed in the ventral mesenchyme surrounding the foregut and expression in the ventral mesenchyme persists during the early stages of lung development (until approximately E11.5). Starting at E10.0, expression can be detected in the lung endoderm and, by E11.5, the endodermal expression is limited to the distal lung bud. Expression in the distal endoderm is maintained at least through E17.5.[91] Examination of *Bmp4* expression in mice with a *LacZ* reporter gene linked to *Bmp4* (*Bmp4*^{lacZ})[92] showed that high expression of *Bmp4*^{lacZ} was always associated with periods of bud extension, rather than lateral bud initiation; this suggests that *Bmp4* is not required for bud outgrowth.[84] In vitro studies with lung explants reveal that *Bmp4* expression is regulated by *Fgf-10* signaling; FGF-10 induces the expression of *Bmp4* in the epithelium, and this induction is not dependent on the presence of mesenchyme.[84,93] It is not clear whether this induction is direct or indirect.

Genetic studies using *Bmp4 –/–* mice are not informative for lung development, because the mice die by approximately E10.0.[92,94] To study the function of *Bmp4* in lung development, Bellusci et al overexpressed *Bmp4* in transgenic mice under the control of the SP-C promoter, which targets gene expression to the distal respiratory epithelium.[90] They found that the lungs of SP-C-*Bmp4* transgenic mice were abnormal, showing the formation of cystic terminal sacs and decreased epithelial proliferation. Inhibition of *Bmp4* signaling in transgenic mice expressing either the *Bmp* antagonist noggin or a dominant-negative *Bmp* receptor in the distal lung epithelium resulted in a marked reduction in distal epithelial cell types and an increase in proximal cell types in the distal part of the lung.[91] In lungs in culture, treatment with exogenous *Bmp4* inhibits the outgrowth and alters the morphology of lung endoderm exposed to an FGF-soaked bead.[84] This, coupled with the mouse transgenic and in vivo expression data, suggests that two functions of *Bmp4* in vivo are to locally inhibit lung budding and to promote the differentiation of proximal epithelial cell types.

As mentioned above, Shh is a secreted molecule that is predominately expressed in the distal lung epithelium, forms a complex with patched (*ptc*) and smoothened (Smo), and activates signaling in the mesenchyme.[79,95] Studies in transgenic and knockout mice and organs in culture indicate that one function of *Shh* is to promote the proliferation of pulmonary mesenchyme. In *Shh–/–* mice, the lungs exhibited enhanced cell death and decreased cell proliferation in the mesenchyme.[78] Mice in which *Shh* was overexpressed in the distal lung epithelium showed an overabundance of lung mesenchyme associated with upregulation of *ptc* expression.[79] *Shh* also appears to inhibit *Fgf-10* expression both in cultured lungs and in transgenic animals overexpressing *Shh*,[79,93] and, in the absence of *Shh*, the expression domain of *Fgf-10* is no longer highest at sites of bud formation but is diffuse.[82] Thus, in addition to being a trophic factor for the pulmonary mesenchyme, *Shh* appears to downregulate *Fgf-10* expression and may function to extinguish *Fgf-10* expression as the lung bud grows distally.

TGF-β1, -2, and -3 are peptides that are members of the TGF-β superfamily, which includes the BMPs. The different TGF-β family members and their cognate

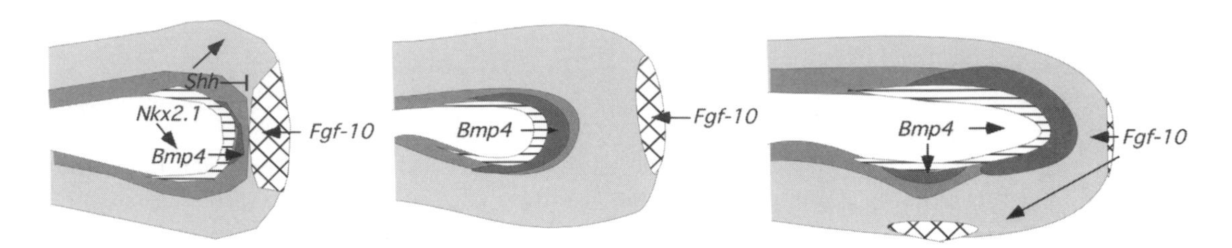

FIGURE 2–4. Model for lung bud outgrowth and new bud formation. *Left panel,* Lung bud shortly after bud initiation. *Fgf-10 (cross hatching)* is highly expressed in the distal bud mesenchyme, promoting both the proliferation and chemotaxis of the underlying epithelium toward the *Fgf-10* expressing cells. *Shh (medium gray)* is expressed in the endoderm throughout branching morphogenesis and is thought to signal the adjacent mesenchyme to proliferate. *Shh* also may downregulate *Fgf-10* expression at the bud tip. *Nkx2.1 (horizontal hatching)* is expressed in the endoderm throughout lung branching and appears to be necessary for *Bmp4* expression. At the initiation of lung bud formation, low levels of *Bmp4 (dark gray)* are expressed in the distal endoderm. *Middle panel,* As bud growth continues, endodermal expression of *Bmp4* increases, while expression of *Fgf-10* in the distal mesoderm diminishes. The mechanisms controlling these changes in expression are not known. Increased expression of *Bmp4* probably serves to limit adjacent bud formation to a specific distance from the existing bud. *Right panel,* Formation of an adjacent lateral bud begins as the domain of *Fgf-10* expression shifts laterally, controlled by unknown mechanisms. Bud formation begins only in areas where *Bmp4* expression is below a certain threshold. (Modified from Hogan BL[83] and Weaver M et al.[84])

receptors are differentially expressed in the developing lung, and evidence from in vitro studies suggests that activation of TGF-β signaling in the lung influences several aspects of lung development and pulmonary cell differentiation. In general, it appears that exogenous TGF-β ligands exert negative regulatory influences on lung development. The addition of exogenous TGF-β1 and TGF-β2 to embryonic mouse lungs in culture, as well as the lung epithelial cell specific overexpression of TGF-β1 in transgenic mice using a SPC-TGF-β1 chimeric transgene, results in varying degrees of pulmonary hypoplasia.[96,97] Conversely, abrogation of TGF-β signaling in mouse lungs in culture by inhibiting TGF-β receptors results in enhanced lung branching.[98–100] Recent evidence using antisense oligonucleotides on rat lungs in culture reveals a role for TGF-β2, and not TGF-β1 or TGF-β3, in early lung branching.[101] A null mutation in TGF-β2 results in mice who die apparently from respiratory failure and who have primitive-appearing lungs with decreased alveolization.[102] It also appears that TGF-β1 interferes with chemoattraction mediated by *Fgf-10,* since treatment of lung explants with TGF-β1 decreases the levels of *Fgf-10* mRNA,[93] and endogenous expression of TGF-β1 is present in regions of the subepithelial mesenchyme that do not express *Fgf-10.* It is clear that the effects of TGF-β signaling in development are complex. The varying effects on lung development (inhibitory and stimulatory) are likely to be highly dependent on the precise amount and timing of TGF-β expression. Interestingly, excessive TGF-β signaling has been linked to several pathologic states in the lung, including chronic fibrosis[103,104] and bronchopulmonary dysplasia.[105]

A model for the roles of *Bmp4, Fgf-10,* and *Shh* in lung development has been proposed in which (as in limb bud and feather bud development) the three interact to direct lung bud formation and branching[84,91] (Figure 2–4). Once a lung bud has been initiated, localized expression of *Fgf-10* in the mesenchyme promotes both the proliferation and chemotaxis of the underlying epithelium toward the *Fgf-10*-expressing cells. As the bud extends, the distal epithelium detects high levels of *Fgf-10* that, in turn, induce the expression of *Bmp4* in the most distal epithelium of the extending bud. The enhanced expression of *Bmp4* at the bud tip inhibits lateral budding, resulting in the continued outgrowth of a single bud rather than a cluster of buds. Thus, only in areas at specific discrete distances from the lung bud, where there are relatively high levels of *Fgf-10* and low levels of *Bmp4,* can a new bud form. *Shh* expression, which is highest in the epithelium of the lung bud, signals the adjacent mesenchyme to proliferate as the lung bud grows. In addition once *Shh* reaches a specific threshold, it may act to downregulate *Fgf-10* expression at the bud tip. Gradually, the level of *Fgf-10* expression at the bud tip decreases and shifts laterally. In the case of a lateral bud, the shift in the *Fgf-10* expression domain is asymmetric, while, in a dichotomous branch, the shift is symmetric to both sides of the bud. In both cases, bud formation occurs only in areas of high *Fgf-10* and low *Bmp4* expression. The factors controlling the complex domains of *Fgf-10* expression are unknown. Hogan has suggested two models that are not mutually exclusive.[83] In one model the sites of lung budding are genetically predetermined, or "hardwired," as in *Drosophila* tracheal development, and are related to the dorsoventral, proximodistal and mediolateral axes of the foregut and primary lung buds. The second model is termed "generative" and is a dynamic process in which multiple factors expressed in both the endoderm and mesoderm interact to determine where lung budding and branching will occur; it involves both stimulatory and inhibitory genetic interactions.

ALVEOLIZATION

Alveolar formation can be considered, in very general terms, to consist of two steps. First, existing walls of distal air spaces become thinner through the flattening of epithelial cells and the reduction in epithelial cell number by apoptosis, generating saccules. At the same time, the capillary network becomes more complex. Next, secondary crests develop and extend to make new alveolar septa, effectively increasing the gas-exchange area, while simultaneously decreasing mean alveolar size. Secondary septal formation involves coordinated outgrowth of epithelial cells, a capillary network, and alveolar myofibroblasts at alveolar septal tips. The signals directing this process remain largely unknown. It appears that there is a critical period in development in which septation occurs. For example, treatment of rats with dexamethasone during the period in which they would normally undergo lung septation prevents septation from occurring, and spontaneous development of septa when dexamethasone is withdrawn does not occur.[106–109] It has become clear that elastic fibers are critical elements of the supporting framework of the lung and are essential for the process of alveolar septation. Therefore, it is not surprising that the elastin gene has become an important candidate in the study of alveolization. Several lines of investigation suggest a link between factors that alter the level of elastin expression and failure of alveolization. For instance, it is clear that retinoids are important in the maintenance of normal lung homeostasis and are required for normal alveolization. In several model systems, retinoic acid (RA) has been shown to enhance alveolization. First, daily treatment of normal rats with RA from age 4 though 13 days results in a 50% increase in the number of alveoli formed without a concomitant increase in the total lung volume.[110] Second, RA treatment of *tight skin* mice results in a reversal of the lung septation defect that is present.[111] *Tight skin* mice have a tandem duplication in *fibrillin-1*, a gene whose expression in elastic organs (ie, lung and skin) peaks just prior to and during the period of peak elastin expression. It is presumed that one or more genes involved in elastic microfibril assembly are affected by RA. Retinoic acid also partially rescues alveolar septation in mice treated with dexamethasone,[111] while RA treatment of adult rats made emphysematous by the intratracheal administration of elastase induces septation and abrogates many of the features seen in both human and experimental emphysema.[112] Most recently it was shown that mice with a null mutation in the RA receptor γ, which perturbs the signaling of RA and its downstream targets, have decreased levels of tropoelastin mRNA in lung fibroblasts and decreased lung elastic tissue and numbers of alveoli.[113]

Exactly how treatment with RA stimulates alveolization remains unknown. Retinoic acid has long been known to be a morphogen, important in many aspects of vertebrate development. In the lung, RA has been shown to affect lung morphogenesis and differentiation of the respiratory epithelium.[44,114–117] During development, RA appears to mediate most of its effects by binding to retinoid receptors, which, in turn, bind to RA reponse elements present in the regulatory regions of target genes. Retinoic acid has been shown to regulate the expression of a number of developmentally important genes, including growth signaling molecules,[118] lung epithelial genes,[114,119] and homeobox genes.[120,121] Thus, the identification of genes responsive to RA will yield important insight into the factors directing lung development in general, and alveolization in particular. The results of studies using RA in rodents with alveolization defects are particularly exciting because RA is the first treatment shown to induce alveolus formation. This is clinically relevant because there are at least three pathologic states of lung alveolization in which there may be too few alveoli for adequate gas exchange. Two of these, diffuse interstitial fibrosis and pulmonary emphysema, are characterized by alveolar destruction. The third, bronchopulmonary dysplasia, is characterized primarily by a failure of lung septation due to a perturbation of normal lung development by premature birth, or possibly due to dexamethasone administration. In addition, there may be a component of alveolar destruction.

Several other factors have been shown to affect the process of sacculation/alveolization. As mentioned previously, TGF-β signaling is likely to be involved in alveolization and pulmonary cell differentiation as well as branching morphogenesis. Mice in which TGF-β1 is overexpressed in lung epithelial cells have lungs that are arrested in the late pseudoglandular stage and show inhibited development of distal cell types.[97] Mice with a null mutation of TGF-β2, along with other defects, have lungs with marked developmental abnormalities. They die of respiratory failure at birth and have lungs that appear arrested at the pseudoglandular stage of development with marked alveolar hypoplasia.[102] Two additional families of peptide growth factors that have been shown to be important in alveolization are the members of the FGF and platelet-derived growth factor (PDGF) families. The role of FGFs in lung branching has been discussed above. A role for this family of molecules in the late stage of lung development has been shown in mice doubly homozygous for *Fgfr3* and *Fgfr4*. These mice, which display novel phenotypes not present in either single mutant, have pronounced dwarfism and a complete failure of alveogenesis due to lack of septation.[122] In addition, they appear to have abnormally prolonged elastin synthesis. Failure of alveolization also has been seen in PDGF-A-deficient mice.[123,124] The *Pdgf-A–/–* mice exhibited reduced deposition of elastin fibers in the lung parenchyma and developed a pathologic condition similar to emphysema due to a failure of alveolus formation. The lung phenotype of the *Pdgf-A–/–* mice was quite similar to that of the *Fgfr3–/–;Fgfr4–/–* double mutants. However, in the case of the *Pdgf-A–/–* mice, depletion of myofibroblasts from alveolar walls resulted in an absence of elastic fibers. It is likely that many more genes necessary for alveolization will be discovered in the years to come.

References

1. Wells JM, Melton DA. Vertebrate endoderm development. Annu Rev Cell Dev Biol 1999;15:393–410.
2. Hogan BL. Bone morphogenetic proteins: multifunctional regulators of vertebrate development. Genes Dev 1996;10:1580–94.
3. Tam PPL, Behringer RR. Mouse gastrulation: the formation of a mammalian body plan. Mech Dev 1997; 68:3–25.
4. Lawson KA, Meneses JJ, Pedersen RA. Clonal analysis of epiblast fate during germ layer formation in the mouse embryo. Development 1991;113:891–911.
5. Wells JM, Melton DA. Early mouse endoderm is patterned by soluble factors from adjacent germ layers. Development 2000;127:1563–72.
6. Tremblay KD, Hoodless PA, Bikoff EK, Robertson EJ. Formation of the definitive endoderm in mouse is a Smad2-dependent process. Development 2000; 127:3079–90.
7. Lawson KA, Meneses JJ, Pedersen RA. Cell fate and cell lineage in the endoderm of the presomite mouse embryo, studied with an intracellular tracer. Dev Biol 1986;115:325–39.
8. Gualdi R, Bossard P, Zheng M, et al. Hepatic specification of the gut endoderm in vitro: cell signaling and transcriptional control. Genes Dev 1996;10:1670–82.
9. Bossard P, Zaret KS. GATA transcription factors as potentiators of gut endoderm differentiation. Development 1998;125:4909–17.
10. Shim EY, Woodcock C, Zaret KS. Nucleosome positioning by the winged helix transcription factor HNF3. Genes Dev 1998;12:5–10.
11. Zaret K. Developmental competence of the gut endoderm: genetic potentiation by GATA and HNF3/fork head proteins. Dev Biol 1999;209(1):1–10.
12. Zaret KS. Liver specification and early morphogenesis. Mech Dev 2000;92(1):83–8.
13. Weigel D, Jackle H. The fork head domain: a novel DNA binding motif of eukaryotic transcription factors? Cell 1990;63:455–6.
14. Ang SL, Wierda A, Wong D, et al. The formation and maintenance of the definitive endoderm lineage in the mouse: involvement of HNF3/forkhead proteins. Development 1993;119:1301–15.
15. Monaghan AP, Kaestner KH, Grau E, Schutz G. Postimplantation expression patterns indicate a role for the mouse forkhead/HNF-3 α, β and γ genes in determination of the definitive endoderm, chordamesoderm and neuroectoderm. Development 1993;119:567–78.
16. Ruiz i Altaba A, Prezioso VR, Darnell JE, Jessell TM. Sequential expression of HNF-3 β and HNF-3 α by embryonic organizing centers: the dorsal lip/node, notochord and floor plate. Mech Dev 1993;44(2–3):91–108.
17. Sasaki H, Hogan BL. Differential expression of multiple fork head related genes during gastrulation and axial pattern formation in the mouse embryo. Development 1993;118:47–59.
18. Epstein DJ, McMahon AP, Joyner AL. Regionalization of Sonic hedgehog transcription along the anteroposterior axis of the mouse central nervous system is regulated by Hnf3-dependent and -independent mechanisms. Development 1999;126:281–92.
19. McMahon AP. Mouse development. Winged-helix in axial patterning. Curr Biol 1994;4:903–6.
20. Echelard Y, Epstein DJ, St-Jacques B, et al. Sonic hedgehog, a member of a family of putative signaling molecules, is implicated in the regulation of CNS polarity. Cell 1993;75:1417–30.
21. Sasaki H, Hogan BL. HNF-3 β as a regulator of floor plate development. Cell 1994;76:103–15.
22. Ang SL, Rossant J. HNF-3 β is essential for node and notochord formation in mouse development. Cell 1994;78:561–74.
23. Weinstein DC, Ruiz i Altaba A, Chen WS, et al. The winged-helix transcription factor HNF-3 β is required for notochord development in the mouse embryo. Cell 1994;78:575–88.
24. Dufort D, Schwartz L, Harpal K, Rossant J. The transcription factor HNF3β is required in visceral endoderm for normal primitive streak morphogenesis. Development 1998;125:3015–25.
25. Zhou L, Lim L, Costa RH, Whitsett JA. Thyroid transcription factor-1, hepatocyte nuclear factor-3β, surfactant protein B, C, and Clara cell secretory protein in developing mouse lung. J Histochem Cytochem 1996; 44:1183–93.
26. Ikeda K, Shaw-White JR, Wert SE, Whitsett JA. Hepatocyte nuclear factor 3 activates transcription of thyroid transcription factor 1 in respiratory epithelial cells. Mol Cell Biol 1996;16:3626–36.
27. Clevidence DE, Overdier DG, Peterson RS, et al. Members of the HNF-3/forkhead family of transcription factors exhibit distinct cellular expression patterns in lung and regulate the surfactant protein B promoter. Dev Biol 1994;166(1):195–209.
28. Bohinski RJ, Di Lauro R, Whitsett JA. The lung-specific surfactant protein B gene promoter is a target for thyroid transcription factor 1 and hepatocyte nuclear factor 3, indicating common factors for organ-specific gene expression along the foregut axis. Mol Cell Biol 1994;14:5671–81.
29. Bingle CD, Hackett BP, Moxley M, et al. Role of hepatocyte nuclear factor-3 α and hepatocyte nuclear factor-3 β in Clara cell secretory protein gene expression in the bronchiolar epithelium. Biochem J 1995;308(Pt 1):197–202.
30. Sawaya PL, Stripp BR, Whitsett JA, Luse DS. The lung-specific CC10 gene is regulated by transcription factors from the AP-1, octamer, and hepatocyte nuclear factor 3 families. Mol Cell Biol 1993;13:3860–71.
31. Sawaya PL, Luse DS. Two members of the HNF-3 family have opposite effects on a lung transcriptional element; HNF-3 α stimulates and HNF-3 β inhibits activity of

region I from the Clara cell secretory protein (CCSP) promoter. J Biol Chem 1994;269:22211–6.
32. Kuo CT, Morrisey EE, Anandappa R, et al. GATA4 transcription factor is required for ventral morphogenesis and heart tube formation. Genes Dev 1997;11:1048–60.
33. Molkentin JD, Lin Q, Duncan SA, Olson EN. Requirement of the transcription factor GATA4 for heart tube formation and ventral morphogenesis. Genes Dev 1997;11:1061–72.
34. Wolpert L. Principles of development. London: Current Biology Ltd, 1998.
35. LeDouarin NM. Etude experimentale de l'oraganogenese du tube digestif et du foie l'embryon de poulet. Bull Biol Fr Bel 1964;XCVIII:543–676.
36. LeDouarin NM. Induction de l'endoderm pre-hepatique par le mesoderme de l'aire cardiaque chez l'embryon de poulet. J Embryol Exp Morphol 1964;12:651–64.
37. Jonsson J, Carlsson L, Edlund T, Edlund H. Insulin-promoter-factor 1 is required for pancreas development in mice. Nature 1994;371:606–9.
38. Stoffers DA, Zinkin NT, Stanojevic V, et al. Pancreatic agenesis attributable to a single nucleotide deletion in the human IPF1 gene coding sequence. Nat Genet 1997;15:106–10.
39. Keng VW, Yagi H, Ikawa M, et al. Homeobox gene hex is essential for onset of mouse embryonic liver development and differentiation of the monocyte lineage. Biochem Biophys Res Commun 2000;276:1155–61.
40. Martinez Barbera JP, Clements M, Thomas P, et al. The homeobox gene Hex is required in definitive endodermal tissues for normal forebrain, liver and thyroid formation. Development 2000;127:2433–45.
41. Graham A, Papalopulu N, Krumlauf R. The murine and Drosophila homeobox gene complexes have common features of organization and expression. Cell 1989; 57:367–78.
42. McGinnis W, Krumlauf R. Homeobox genes and axial patterning. Cell 1992;68:283–302.
43. Affolter M, Schier A, Gehring WJ. Homeodomain proteins and the regulation of gene expression. Curr Opin Cell Biol 1990;2:485–95.
44. Bogue CW, Gross I, Vasavada H, et al. Identification of Hox genes in newborn lung and effects of gestational age and retinoic acid on their expression. Am J Physiol 1994;266(4 Pt 1):L448–54.
45. Bogue CW, Lou LJ, Vasavada H, et al. Expression of *Hoxb* genes in the developing mouse foregut and lung. Am J Respir Cell Mol Biol 1996;15:163–71.
46. Cardoso WV. Transcription factors and pattern formation in the developing lung. Am J Physiol 1995;269(4 Pt 1):L429–42.
47. Gaunt SJ, Krumlauf R, Duboule D. Mouse homeo-genes within a subfamily, Hox-1.4, -2.6 and -5.1, display similar anteroposterior domains of expression in the embryo, but show stage- and tissue-dependent differences in their regulation. Development 1989;107:131–41.
48. Graham A, Papalopulu N, Lorimer J, et al. Characterization of a murine homeo box gene, *Hox-2.6*, related to the *Drosophila Deformed* gene. Genes Dev 1988; 2:1424–38.
49. Krumlauf R, Holland PWH, McVey JH, Hogan BLM. Developmental and spatial patterns of expression of the mouse homeobox gene, Hox 2.1. Development 1987;99:603–17.
50. Mollard R, Dziadek M. Homeobox genes from clusters A and B demonstrate characteristics of temporal colinearity and differential restrictions in spatial expression domains in the branching mouse lung. Int J Dev Biol 1997;41:655–66.
51. Rancourt DE, Tsuzuki T, Capecchi MR. Genetic interaction between hoxb-5 and hoxb-6 is revealed by nonallelic noncomplementation. Genes Dev 1995;9:108–22.
52. Aubin J, Lemieux M, Tremblay M, et al. Early postnatal lethality in Hoxa-5 mutant mice is attributable to respiratory tract defects. Dev Biol 1997;192:432–45.
53. Hui CC, Slusarski D, Platt KA, et al. Expression of three mouse homologs of the *Drosophila* segment polarity gene cubitus interruptus, Gli, Gli-2, and Gli-3, in ectoderm- and mesoderm-derived tissues suggests multiple roles during postimplantation development. Dev Biol 1994;162:402–13.
54. Grindley JC, Bellusci S, Perkins D, Hogan BL. Evidence for the involvement of the Gli gene family in embryonic mouse lung development. Dev Biol 1997;188:337–48.
55. Motoyama J, Liu J, Mo R, et al. Essential function of Gli2 and Gli3 in the formation of lung, trachea and oesophagus. Nat Genet 1998;20:54–7.
56. Martin GR. The roles of FGFs in the early development of vertebrate limbs. Genes Dev 1998;12:1571–86.
57. Goldfarb M. Functions of fibroblast growth factors in vertebrate development. Cytokine Growth Factor Rev 1996;7:311–25.
58. Bellusci S, Grindley J, Emoto H, et al. Fibroblast growth factor 10 (FGF10) and branching morphogenesis in the embryonic mouse lung. Development 1997;124:4867–78.
59. Hogan BL, Grindley J, Bellusci S, et al. Branching morphogenesis of the lung: new models for a classical problem. Cold Spring Harb Symp Quant Biol 1997;62:249–56.
60. Park WY, Miranda B, Lebeche D, et al. FGF-10 is a chemotactic factor for distal epithelial buds during lung development. Dev Biol 1998;201:125–34.
61. Min H, Danilenko DM, Scully SA, et al. Fgf-10 is required for both limb and lung development and exhibits striking functional similarity to *Drosophila* branchless. Genes Dev 1998;12:3156–61.
62. Sekine K, Ohuchi H, Fujiwara M, et al. Fgf10 is essential for limb and lung formation. Nat Genet 1999;21:138–41.
63. Peters K, Werner S, Liao X, et al. Targeted expression of a dominant negative FGF receptor blocks branching morphogenesis and epithelial differentiation of the mouse lung. EMBO J 1994;13:3296–301.
64. Cardoso WV, Itoh A, Nogawa H, et al. FGF-1 and FGF-7 induce distinct patterns of growth and differentiation in embryonic lung epithelium. Dev Dyn 1997;208:398–405.
65. Sutherland D, Samakovlis C, Krasnow MA. Branchless encodes a *Drosophila* FGF homolog that controls tracheal cell migration and the pattern of branching. Cell 1996;87:1091–101.
66. Glazer L, Shilo BZ. The *Drosophila* FGF-R homolog is expressed in the embryonic tracheal system and appears

to be required for directed tracheal cell extension. Genes Dev 1991;5:697–705.
67. Shilo BZ, Gabay L, Glazer L, et al. Branching morphogenesis in the *Drosophila* tracheal system. Cold Spring Harb Symp Quant Biol 1997;62:241–7.
68. Klambt C, Glazer L, Shilo BZ. Breathless, a *Drosophila* FGF receptor homolog, is essential for migration of tracheal and specific midline glial cells. Genes Dev 1992;6:1668–78.
69. Lee T, Hacohen N, Krasnow M, Montell DJ. Regulated Breathless receptor tyrosine kinase activity required to pattern cell migration and branching in the *Drosophila* tracheal system. Genes Dev 1996;10:2912–21.
70. Minoo P, Su G, Drum H, et al. Defects in tracheoesophageal and lung morphogenesis in Nkx2.1(-/-) mouse embryos. Dev Biol 1999;209(1):60–71.
71. Lazzaro D, Price M, De Felice M, Di Lauro R. The transcription factor TTF-1 is expressed at the onset of thyroid and lung morphogenesis and in restricted regions of the foetal brain. Development 1991;113:1093–104.
72. Iwatani N, Mabe H, Devriendt K, et al. Deletion of NKX2.1 gene encoding thyroid transcription factor-1 in two siblings with hypothyroidism and respiratory failure. J Pediatr 2000;137:272–6.
73. Capdevila J, Pariente F, Sampedro J, et al. Subcellular localization of the segment polarity protein patched suggests an interaction with the wingless reception complex in *Drosophila* embryos. Development 1994;120:987–98.
74. Heberlein U, Wolff T, Rubin GM. The TGF β homolog dpp and the segment polarity gene hedgehog are required for propagation of a morphogenetic wave in the *Drosophila* retina. Cell 1993;75:913–26.
75. Ingham PW. Localized hedgehog activity controls spatial limits of wingless transcription in the *Drosophila* embryo. Nature 1993;366:560–2.
76. Basler K, Struhl G. Compartment boundaries and the control of Drosophila limb pattern by hedgehog protein. Nature 1994;368:208–14.
77. Tabin CJ, McMahon AP. Recent advances in Hedgehog signaling. Trends Cell Biol 1997;7:442–6.
78. Litingtung Y, Lei L, Westphal H, Chiang C. Sonic hedgehog is essential to foregut development. Nat Genet 1998;20:58–61.
79. Bellusci S, Furuta Y, Rush MG, et al. Involvement of Sonic hedgehog (Shh) in mouse embryonic lung growth and morphogenesis. Development 1997;124:53–63.
80. Bitgood MJ, McMahon AP. Hedgehog and Bmp genes are coexpressed at many diverse sites of cell-cell interaction in the mouse embryo. Dev Biol 1995;172(1):126–38.
81. Urase K, Mukasa T, Igarashi H, et al. Spatial expression of Sonic hedgehog in the lung epithelium during branching morphogenesis. Biochem Biophys Res Commun 1996;225:161–6.
82. Pepicelli CV, Lewis PM, McMahon AP. Sonic hedgehog regulates branching morphogenesis in the mammalian lung. Curr Biol 1998;8:1083–6.
83. Hogan BL. Morphogenesis. Cell 1999;96:225–33.
84. Weaver M, Dunn NR, Hogan BL. Bmp4 and Fgf10 play opposing roles during lung bud morphogenesis. Development 2000;127:2695–704.
85. Celli G, LaRochelle WJ, Mackem S, et al. Soluble dominant-negative receptor uncovers essential roles for fibroblast growth factors in multi-organ induction and patterning. EMBO J 1998;17:1642–55.
86. De Moerlooze L, Spencer-Dene B, Revest J, et al. An important role for the IIIb isoform of fibroblast growth factor receptor 2 (FGFR2) in mesenchymal-epithelial signaling during mouse organogenesis. Development 2000;127:483–92.
87. Arman E, Haffner-Krausz R, Gorivodsky M, Lonai P. Fgfr2 is required for limb outgrowth and lung-branching morphogenesis. Proc Natl Acad Sci U S A 1999;96:11895–9.
88. Massague J, Weis-Garcia F. Serine/threonine kinase receptors: mediators of transforming growth factor β family signals. Cancer Surv 1996;27:41–64.
89. King JA, Marker PC, Seung KJ, Kingsley DM. BMP5 and the molecular, skeletal, and soft-tissue alterations in short ear mice. Dev Biol 1994;166(1):112–22.
90. Bellusci S, Henderson R, Winnier G, et al. Evidence from normal expression and targeted misexpression that bone morphogenetic protein (Bmp-4) plays a role in mouse embryonic lung morphogenesis. Development 1996;122:1693–702.
91. Weaver M, Yingling JM, Dunn NR, et al. Bmp signaling regulates proximal-distal differentiation of endoderm in mouse lung development. Development 1999;126:4005–15.
92. Lawson KA, Dunn NR, Roelen BA, et al. Bmp4 is required for the generation of primordial germ cells in the mouse embryo. Genes Dev 1999;13:424–36.
93. Lebeche D, Malpel S, Cardoso WV. Fibroblast growth factor interactions in the developing lung. Mech Dev 1999;86(1–2):125–36.
94. Winnier G, Blessing M, Labosky PA, Hogan BL. Bone morphogenetic protein-4 is required for mesoderm formation and patterning in the mouse. Genes Dev 1995;9:2105–16.
95. Stone DM, Hynes M, Armanini M, et al. The tumour-suppressor gene patched encodes a candidate receptor for Sonic hedgehog. Nature 1996;384:129–34.
96. Serra R, Pelton RW, Moses HL. TGF β 1 inhibits branching morphogenesis and N-myc expression in lung bud organ cultures. Development 1994;120:2153–61.
97. Zhou L, Dey CR, Wert SE, Whitsett JA. Arrested lung morphogenesis in transgenic mice bearing an SP-C-TGF-β 1 chimeric gene. Dev Biol 1996;175:227–38.
98. Zhao J, Sime PJ, Bringas P Jr, et al. Epithelium-specific adenoviral transfer of a dominant-negative mutant TGF-β type II receptor stimulates embryonic lung branching morphogenesis in culture and potentiates EGF and PDGF-AA. Mech Dev 1998;72(1–2):89–100.
99. Zhao J, Lee M, Smith S, Warburton D. Abrogation of Smad3 and Smad2 or of Smad4 gene expression positively regulates murine embryonic lung branching morphogenesis in culture. Dev Biol 1998;194:182–95.
100. Zhao J, Bu D, Lee M, et al. Abrogation of transforming growth factor-β type II receptor stimulates embryonic mouse lung branching morphogenesis in culture. Dev Biol 1996;180(1):242–57.

101. Liu J, Tseu I, Wang J, et al. Transforming growth factor β2, but not β1 and β3, is critical for early rat lung branching. Dev Dyn 2000;217:343–60.
102. Kaartinen V, Voncken JW, Shuler C, et al. Abnormal lung development and cleft palate in mice lacking TGF-β 3 indicates defects of epithelial-mesenchymal interaction. Nat Genet 1995;11:415–21.
103. Border WA, Noble NA. Transforming growth factor β in tissue fibrosis. N Engl J Med 1994;331:1286–92.
104. Sime PJ, Xing Z, Graham FL, et al. Adenovector-mediated gene transfer of active transforming growth factor-β1 induces prolonged severe fibrosis in rat lung. J Clin Invest 1997;100:768–76.
105. Kotecha S, Wangoo A, Silverman M, Shaw RJ. Increase in the concentration of transforming growth factor β-1 in bronchoalveolar lavage fluid before development of chronic lung disease of prematurity. J Pediatr 1996;128:464–9.
106. Blanco LN, Frank L. The formation of alveoli in rat lung during the third and fourth postnatal weeks: effect of hyperoxia, dexamethasone, and deferoxamine. Pediatr Res 1993;34:334–40.
107. Massaro GD, Massaro D. Formation of alveoli in rats: postnatal effect of prenatal dexamethasone [published errata appear in Am J Physiol 1992;263(3 Pt 1) and 1993;264(2 Pt 1): section L following Table of Contents]. Am J Physiol 1992;263(1 Pt 1):L37–41.
108. Blanco LN, Massaro GD, Massaro D. Alveolar dimensions and number: developmental and hormonal regulation. Am J Physiol 1989;257(4 Pt 1):L240–7.
109. Massaro D, Teich N, Maxwell S, et al. Postnatal development of alveoli. Regulation and evidence for a critical period in rats. J Clin Invest 1985;76:1297–305.
110. Massaro GD, Massaro D. Postnatal treatment with retinoic acid increases the number of pulmonary alveoli in rats. Am J Physiol 1996;270(2 Pt 1):L305–10.
111. Massaro GD, Massaro D. Retinoic acid treatment partially rescues failed septation in rats and in mice. Am J Physiol Lung Cell Mol Physiol 2000;278:L955–60.
112. Massaro GD, Massaro D. Retinoic acid treatment abrogates elastase-induced pulmonary emphysema in rats [published erratum appears in Nat Med 1997;3:805]. Nat Med 1997;3:675–7.
113. McGowan S, Jackson SK, Jenkins-Moore M, et al. Mice bearing deletions of retinoic acid receptors demonstrate reduced lung elastin and alveolar numbers. Am J Respir Cell Mol Biol 2000;23:162–7.
114. Bogue CW, Jacobs HC, Dynia DW, et al. Retinoic acid increases surfactant protein mRNA in fetal rat lung in culture. Am J Physiol 1996;271(5 Pt 1):L862–8.
115. Cardoso WV, Williams MC, Mitsialis SA, et al. Retinoic acid induces changes in the pattern of airway branching and alters epithelial cell differentiation in the developing lung in vitro. Am J Respir Cell Mol Biol 1995;12:464–76.
116. Cardoso WV, Mitsialis SA, Brody JS, Williams MC. Retinoic acid alters the expression of pattern-related genes in the developing rat lung. Dev Dyn 1996;207(1):47–59.
117. Malpel S, Mendelsohn C, Cardoso WV. Regulation of retinoic acid signaling during lung morphogenesis. Development 2000;127:3057–67.
118. Han GR, Dohi DF, Lee HY, et al. All-trans-retinoic acid increases transforming growth factor-β2 and insulin-like growth factor binding protein-3 expression through a retinoic acid receptor-α-dependent signaling pathway. J Biol Chem 1997;272:13711–6.
119. Naltner A, Ghaffari M, Whitsett JA, Yan C. Retinoic acid stimulation of the human surfactant protein B promoter is thyroid transcription factor 1 site-dependent. J Biol Chem 2000;275:56–62.
120. Bogue CW, Gross I, Vasavada H, et al. Identification of *Hox* genes in newborn lung and the effects of gestational age and retinoic acid on their expression. Am J Physiol 1994;266:L448–54.
121. Packer AI, Mailutha KG, Ambrozewicz LA, Wolgemuth DJ. Regulation of the Hoxa4 and Hoxa5 genes in the embryonic mouse lung by retinoic acid and TGFβ1: implications for lung development and patterning. Dev Dyn 2000;217:62–74.
122. Weinstein M, Xu X, Ohyama K, Deng CX. FGFR-3 and FGFR-4 function cooperatively to direct alveogenesis in the murine lung. Development 1998;125:3615–23.
123. Lindahl P, Karlsson L, Hellstrom M, et al. Alveogenesis failure in PDGF-A-deficient mice is coupled to lack of distal spreading of alveolar smooth muscle cell progenitors during lung development. Development 1997;124:3943–53.
124. Bostrom H, Willetts K, Pekny M, et al. PDGF-A signaling is a critical event in lung alveolar myofibroblast development and alveogenesis. Cell 1996;85:863–73.

CHAPTER 3

Genetics of Lung Disease: Surfactant Protein B Deficiency

Lawrence M. Nogee, MD

Pulmonary surfactant is the mixture of lipids and proteins needed to reduce alveolar surface tension at the air–liquid interface and prevent end-expiratory collapse. A deficiency of surfactant owing to immaturity is the principal cause of respiratory distress syndrome (RDS) in prematurely born infants.[1] The risk of RDS is related to gestational age, with more immature infants being at highest risk.[2,3] However, a potential genetic contribution to the development of RDS has been recognized through familial cases.[4] The recognition that mutations in the gene encoding one of the surfactant proteins (SPs), surfactant protein B (SP-B), cause lethal neonatal respiratory disease in full-term infants supports the hypothesis that respiratory failure in some newborn infants has a genetic basis. The disease also provides a model for how genetic factors could influence the development of lung disease. Although a rare condition, hereditary SP-B deficiency also has provided insights into normal surfactant function and homeostasis. Finally, because SP-B is expressed primarily in lung epithelial cells, and the respiratory disease caused by the lack of SP-B is rapidly lethal without an effective therapy, SP-B deficiency is a potentially important model for gene therapy in the lung. This chapter reviews the clinical, laboratory, and research aspects of hereditary SP-B deficiency, with emphasis on this disease as a model for the contribution of how genetic factors can cause or contribute to lung disease.

Pulmonary Surfactant Proteins

Pulmonary surfactant contains approximately 90% lipid and 10% protein by weight. Whereas the phospholipid components of surfactant are critical for its ability to lower surface tension, the surface tension–lowering properties of surfactant phospholipids are enhanced by two extremely hydrophobic proteins, SP-B and SP-C.[5,6] Surfactant proteins B and C are important components of mammalian-derived surfactant preparations used to treat premature infants with RDS.[5] Both SP-B and SP-C are derived from proteolytic processing of much larger precursor proteins encoded by single genes on chromosomes 2 and 8, respectively.[7,8] Both are highly expressed in alveolar type II cells, although SP-B is also expressed in bronchiolar epithelial cells in the lung and in some epithelial cells outside the lung.[9–11] The expression of both proteins is developmentally regulated and increases with advancing gestation.[12] The mature forms of SP-B and SP-C are routed to lamellar bodies, the storage organelles for surfactant in the alveolar type II cell, and secreted along with surfactant phospholipids.[13]

Pulmonary surfactant also contains two larger glycoproteins, SP-A and SP-D. Both SP-A and SP-D have an N-terminal collagenous domain and a C-terminal lectin-like domain and are part of the collectin family.[14] Surfactant protein A inhibits surfactant release from type II cells and stimulates reuptake by alveolar type II cells of surfactant phospholipids in vitro.[15,16] However, the roles of SP-A and SP-D in the lung are more likely related to local host cell defense rather than surfactant function or metabolism.[17] Genetically engineered SP-A-deficient mice do not develop neonatal respiratory disease or have disturbances of surfactant metabolism.[18–20] Such animals do appear to have an increased susceptibility to infection with a variety of organisms that are relevant to human neonates, including group B streptococcus and respiratory syncytial virus.[21,22] Similarly, SP-D is also thought to be important in local immunity. Surfactant protein D-deficient mice develop lung disease as they age, with both emphysema and fibrosis suggesting a role in regulating chronic inflammation and lipoproteinosis suggesting a possible role in surfactant homeostasis.[23–26] Surfactant proteins A and D are encoded in a multigene complex on human chromosome 10, containing two genes and a pseudogene for SP-A, and a single gene for SP-D.[27] Human diseases definitively linked to mutations in the SP-A and SP-D loci have not been reported.

Hereditary SP-B Deficiency

Hereditary SP-B deficiency was first recognized as a cause of neonatal lung disease in 1993, with the report of three siblings who developed respiratory failure at birth.[28] All three were born at term and had progressive lung disease despite maximal medical therapy. A lung biopsy done on the proband revealed striking findings of alveolar proteinosis: an accumulation of granular, eosinophilic material that filled distal air spaces with foamy macrophages trapped within the proteinaceous debris. Alveolar proteinosis in older individuals is usually a disease of more insidious onset, and the accumulated material is rich in

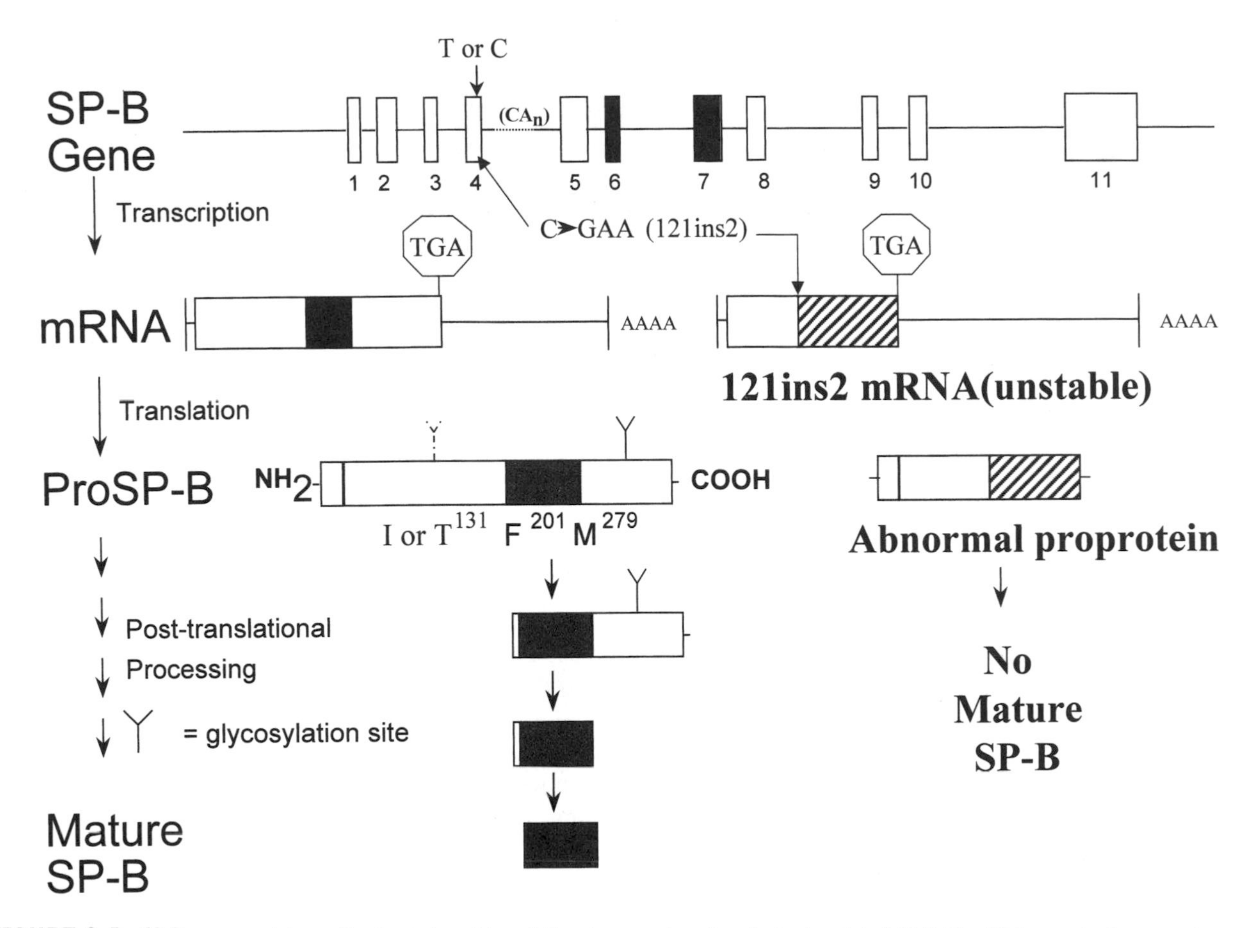

FIGURE 3–1. SP-B gene, protein synthesis, and post-translational processing of surfactant protein (SP)-B. The SP-B gene is shown at the top, with the 11 exons represented by boxes and the introns represented by lines. The locations of the 121ins2 mutation and a coding polymorphism resulting in either isoleucine (I) or threonine (T) in exon 4 and variable nucleotide repeat sequences (CA_n) in intron IV are indicated. Mature SP-B is encoded in exons 6 and 7 of the gene and corresponds to amino acids 201 (phenylalanine, F) to 279 (methionine, M) of the proprotein (*shaded*). Normal transcription and processing of SP-B are outlined on the left. The consequences of the frameshift introduced by the 121ins2 mutation are shown on the right, with the hatched portion of transcript representing the altered reading frame, the amino acid sequence of which would be unrelated to normal proprotein SP-B, and the location of the premature termination codon indicated by the octagon.

surfactant phospholipids and proteins, with lung lavage material from adults with alveolar proteinosis often having been used as the starting material for the purification of the SPs.[29–31] Thus, this finding indicated a disorder of surfactant metabolism in these infants. This histopathology had been observed previously in full-term neonates presenting with apparent RDS and intractable respiratory failure, including familial cases suggestive of an autosomal-recessive inheritance pattern.[32–35] Collectively, these observations supported the hypothesis that an inherited abnormality of one of the SPs could be the basis for disease in these children. To test this hypothesis, the expression of SP-A, SP-B, and SP-C proprotein (proSP-C) were examined in the lung tissue by western blotting and immunohistochemical staining. Whereas SP-A and proSP-C were present in amounts comparable to that observed in control tissues, a complete absence of SP-B was observed in the lung tissue of the affected infants.[28] Moreover, SP-B messenger ribonucleic acid (mRNA), which should have been present in amounts similar to those observed in adult lung tissue, was completely undetectable, indicating that the absence of SP-B was attributable to an inability to produce SP-B at a pretranslational level, supporting a genetic mechanism.

The inability to produce SP-B was proven to be the cause of lung disease in this family when a mutation that accounted for the lack of SP-B was found on both SP-B alleles of all three affected infants.[36] The SP-B gene contains 11 exons, the last of which is untranslated. The gene is transcribed into a 2-kb mRNA that directs the synthesis of a 381 amino acid precursor protein (proSP-B). The hydrophobic mature SP-B peptide found in the air spaces corresponds to codons 201 (encoding phenylalanine) to 279 (encoding methionine) of the mRNA and is encoded in exons 6 and 7 of the gene (Figure 3–1).[37] The mutation identified involved the substitution of three bases (GAA) for one (C) in codon 121 of the SP-B mRNA, corresponding to exon 4 of the SP-B gene. The net insertion of two bases altered the reading frame, resulting in the introduction of a premature codon for

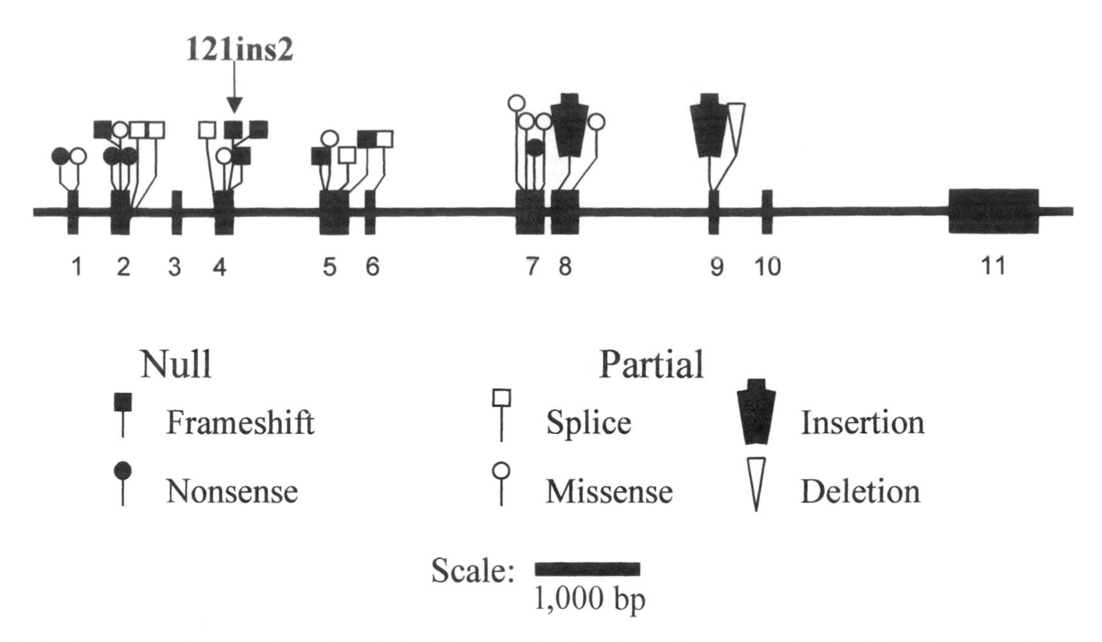

FIGURE 3–2. Locations and nature of mutations in the SP-B gene. The locations of known mutations in the SP-B gene are indicated by different symbols corresponding to the nature of the mutation. Exons are represented by boxes and introns by lines.

the termination of translation in exon 6, thus completely precluding production of mature SP-B. The resulting transcript is also unstable because of the frameshift accounting for the lack of SP-B mRNA.[38] The affected infants were homozygous for this mutation (termed 121ins2 for the net insertion of two bases into codon 121), and both parents were found to be carriers as suggested by the autosomal-recessive inheritance pattern. As there was no history of consanguinity in the family, the finding of the same mutation on both alleles was unexpected and suggested that this mutation might not be unique to this family. The same mutation was then found on seven of eight SP-B alleles from unrelated infants with the same phenotype, which confirmed that this mutation was a frequent, although not exclusive, cause of disease.[36]

Over two dozen different mutations have subsequently been identified throughout the SP-B gene, including those introducing nonsense codons and frameshifts that completely preclude SP-B production and missense mutations or in-frame deletions or insertions that allow for the production of proSP-B containing altered amino acid sequences (Figure 3–2).[39–44] These latter mutations prevented the normal processing of the proSP-B containing mutations to mature SP-B, resulting in the lack of mature SP-B in lung tissue and tracheal secretions of affected infants.[45] SP-B proprotein is organized into three tandem domains, of which the repeating periodicity of cysteines and hydrophobic residues suggests structural homology to the saposins, lysosomal proteins that bind lipids and activate lysosomal hydrolases.[46] The role(s) of the amino- and carboxy-terminal flanking domains of proSP-B are uncertain but may be important in the transport of SP-B through the cell or have a more direct biologic function.[47–49] The amino-terminal domain is removed first in a step that is not thought to be cell specific. The subsequent removal of the carboxy-terminal domain occurs distal to the trans-golgi during transport from multivesicular to lamellar bodies and is type II cell specific.[50,51] The middle domain corresponds to mature SP-B, which is stored in lamellar bodies and secreted into the air spaces. Mutations in the region of the gene encoding mature SP-B could theoretically result in the production of a mature SP-B protein with abnormal surface properties. However, a synthetic peptide containing one such mutation (R236C) was able to augment surface tension lowering normally in an in vitro system,[52] suggesting that the disease in infants with this mutation also resulted from impaired processing of proSP-B containing the mutation.

Epidemiology and Molecular Genetics

The incidence of SP-B deficiency is unknown. The number of reported cases is relatively small (approximately 50),[28,36,39–44,53–57] and population-based studies to determine the incidence of disease have not been performed. The finding of a common mutation allows for an estimate of disease incidence by population screening for the frequency of this mutation. The 121ins2 mutation has accounted for approximately two thirds of the mutant alleles identified, and in the only study performed to date, a carrier frequency between 1:1,000 and 1:3,000 individuals was observed for this mutation.[58] This implies that between 1 in 667 and 1 in 2,000 individuals in the population carries an SP-B gene mutation. Since there is a 25% chance of having an affected child if both parents have a mutation for an autosomal-recessive disorder, this implies a disease incidence of between 1 in 1.8 million (667 × 667 × 4) and 1 in 16 million. Although SP-B deficiency is likely a very rare disease, this is probably an underestimate. The number of infants diagnosed with the SP-B deficiency in the United States since its recognition is greater than this estimate suggests, and it is likely that some affected infants died without the diagnosis having been made.[59] Most studies to date also have focused on children with either the 121ins2 mutation and/or very severe lung disease, and children with mutations resulting in milder disease also have been unrecognized.

One explanation for the finding of a common mutation is that there is a common ancestral origin for the 121ins2 mutation ("founder effect"), which has been found mainly in individuals of Northern European descent.[60] In support of this hypothesis, analyses of genetic markers within and near the SP-B gene demonstrated a similar genetic background for chromosomes containing the 121ins2 mutation.[61] However, two other SP-B gene mutations (122delC, 122delT) have been identified within five nucleotides of the site of the common mutation, suggesting that this region of the SP-B gene may also represent a "hot spot" for mutation.[43,55] Mutations in close physical proximity to one another also have been identified in exons 2 and 9. Other mutations have been found in unrelated individuals from different ethnic groups, including individuals of Asian (1043ins3), Middle Eastern (122delT), and French-Canadian (c.479G>T) descent. The frequency of these mutations and hence the likely disease incidence in these populations have not been determined.

Clinical Aspects of Hereditary SP-B Deficiency

The usual clinical presentation of an infant with SP-B deficiency is that of a full-term infant who develops symptoms and signs of respiratory distress consistent with surfactant deficiency within the first several hours of life. The most typical radiographic findings are those consistent with surfactant deficiency, including hypoexpanded lungs, diffuse granularity, and air bronchograms, although this has not been examined systematically.[62] Initial diagnoses of affected infants have included transient tachypnea of the newborn, pneumonia, persistent pulmonary hypertension, and meconium aspiration.[59] The respiratory disease may be severe, often requiring support with extracorporeal membrane oxygenation when available. However, the initial severity of respiratory disease is variable, with some affected infants not needing mechanical ventilation for several weeks. The factors responsible for modifying the course of the illness in these infants are unclear. The infants' genotypes do not explain all of the clinical variability observed as some infants homozygous for null mutations have had initially mild disease, whereas infants with mutations associated with some SP-B production have had severe disease beginning at birth. Regardless of the initial presentation, the lung disease in affected infants worsens with time, with an escalating need for respiratory support and progressive alveolar and interstitial infiltrates radiographically. Air leak is common, as is secondary pulmonary hypertension. An initial beneficial response to exogenous surfactant therapy may be observed, although this response generally is not sustained with subsequent doses. Some affected infants appear to benefit from glucocorticoids, perhaps because they have mutations that allow for some SP-B production, but these infants generally still have progressive lung disease and worsen when steroid therapy is withdrawn.[39] Hereditary SP-B deficiency is a rapidly fatal disease, with >80% of affected infants dying within 3 months, even with aggressive supportive measures.[59,60]

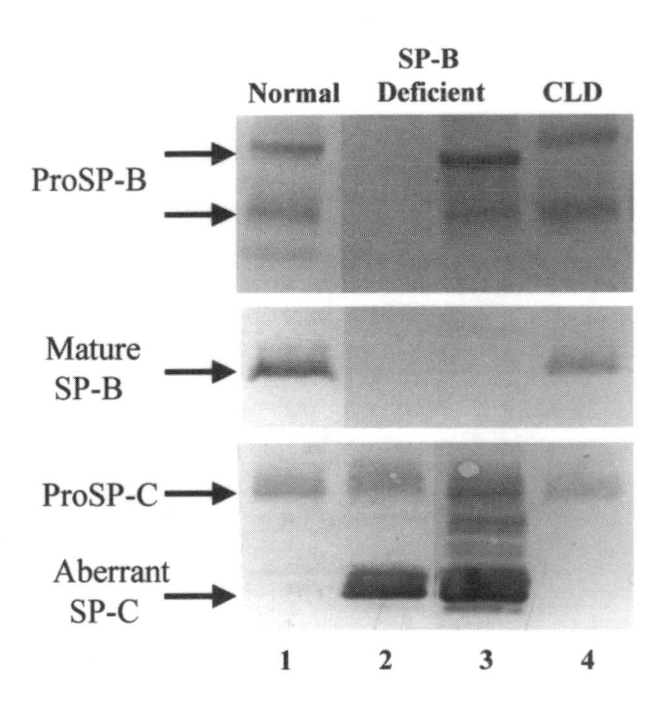

FIGURE 3–3. Protein blotting for proSP-B and mature SP-B and SP-C in lung tissue. Western blotting using antisera to proSP-B (top), mature SP-B (*middle*), and proSP-C (*bottom*) in lung tissue from two control (*lanes 1 and 4*) and two affected (*lanes 2 and 3*) infants is shown. Surfactant protein B was not detected in the lungs of the affected infants, which also contained large amounts of proteins immunoreactive with anti-proSP-C antiserum that were not observed in control tissues. SP-B proprotein was not detected in the lung tissue from one of the affected infants (*lane 2*), who was homozygous for the 121ins2 mutation. SP-B protein migrating at a lower molecular weight than that detected in controls was detected in the lung tissue of the other affected infant (*lane 3*), who had a mutation affecting RNA splicing, resulting in a shortened proprotein. CLD = chronic lung disease.

Secondary Changes in Other Surfactant Components

Along with the absence of SP-B, secondary changes have been observed in the composition and/or metabolism of other surfactant components in the lung fluid and tissue of infants with hereditary SP-B deficiency. These include a relative paucity of surfactant phospholipids and, in particular, phosphatidylglycerol,[63,64] and an accumulation of incompletely or aberrantly processed proSP-C peptides, which are generally abundant in both the lung tissue and lung lavage fluid of affected infants (Figure 3–3). This aberrant processing of proSP-C may also result in a relative deficiency of mature SP-C in affected infants, although the block in SP-C processing does not appear to be complete.[65] The mechanisms underlying these secondary changes are unknown. On ultrastructural analysis, the lungs of affected infants also lack normally formed lamellar bodies, the intracellular storage organelles of surfactant (Figure 3–4), and tubular myelin, a lattice-like extracellular form of surfactant, the formation of which requires SP-B.[66,67] The final processing steps for both SP-B and SP-C take place in lamellar bodies; thus, a hypothesis to account for these observations is that the lack of this organelle results in incompletely processed proSP-C and inadequate packaging of surfactant components for secretion.

As in the initial infants reported with the disorder, findings of alveolar proteinosis are often striking in the lung histopathology of infants with hereditary SP-B deficiency. The proteinosis material likely contains a relative paucity of surfactant phospholipids, along with abundant SP-A and secreted, aberrantly processed proSP-C peptides. Although the exact composition of these aberrantly processed SP-C peptides has not been determined, they likely contain both hydrophobic and hydrophilic epitopes. Thus, they are not likely to be very surface active and are present in large enough amounts that they may interfere with normal surfactant function. The exact mechanisms leading to the appearance of alveolar proteinosis are not well understood. The findings of alveolar proteinosis are highly variable in SP-B-deficient infants, and not all affected infants have had this pathology, although the material may be more evi-

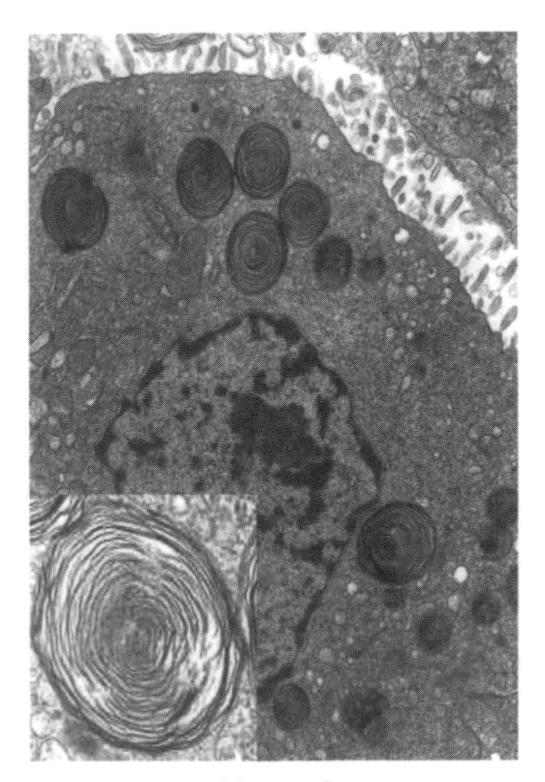

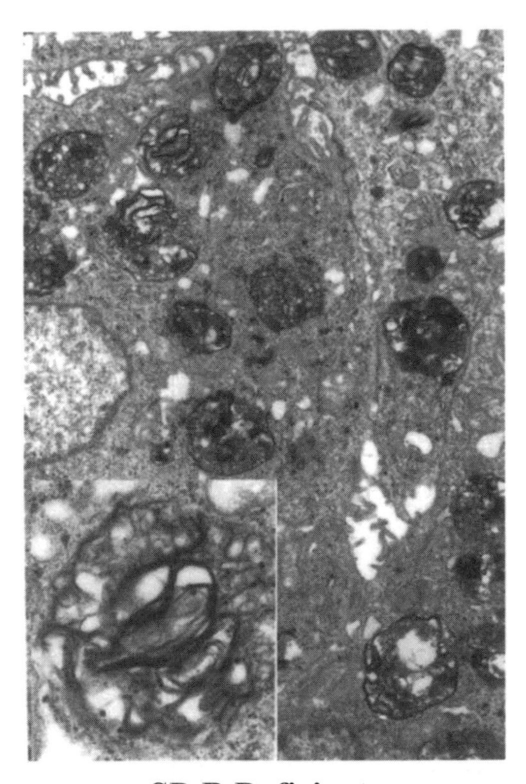

FIGURE 3–4. Ultrastructure of SP-B-deficient lung tissue. An electron micrograph of an alveolar type II cell from normal lung tissue demonstrating well-organized lamellar bodies is shown on the left (shown at a higher magnification on the inset). In contrast, abnormal-appearing lamellar bodies with loosely packed, disorganized membranes are seen in an elctron micrograph from an SP-B-deficient infant homozygous for the 121ins2 mutation on the right (original magnification × 5,000). (Photographs courtesy of Drs. Ernest Cutz, The Hospital for Sick Children, Toronto, ON, and Susan Wert, Children's Hospital Medical Center, Cincinnati, OH.)

dent after immunostaining with antisera directed against SP-A or proSP-C. Additionally, not all neonates with a finding of alveolar proteinosis have hereditary SP-B deficiency as a mechanism for their lung disease (Figure 3–5).[68,69] Mechanisms other than SP-B deficiency result in similar histopathology, including deficiencies of granulocyte-macrophage colony-stimulating factor or its receptor.[70] Hence, the term congenital alveolar proteinosis should *not* be used synonymously with hereditary SP-B deficiency. Other histopathologic findings in SP-B deficiency are nonspecific and include alveolar type II cell hyperplasia, interstitial fibrosis, and nonspecific alveolar damage.

Variants of SP-B Deficiency and Role of SP-B Gene Variants in Other Lung Diseases

Mutations that allow the production of some SP-B and are associated with longer survival than those that do not allow for any SP-B production have been recognized ("partial deficiency"). These have included missense mutations that interfered with the normal processing of proSP-B to mature SP-B or mutations that affected mRNA splicing but allowed for some normal transcript to be produced.[39,44] One such mutation resulted in the

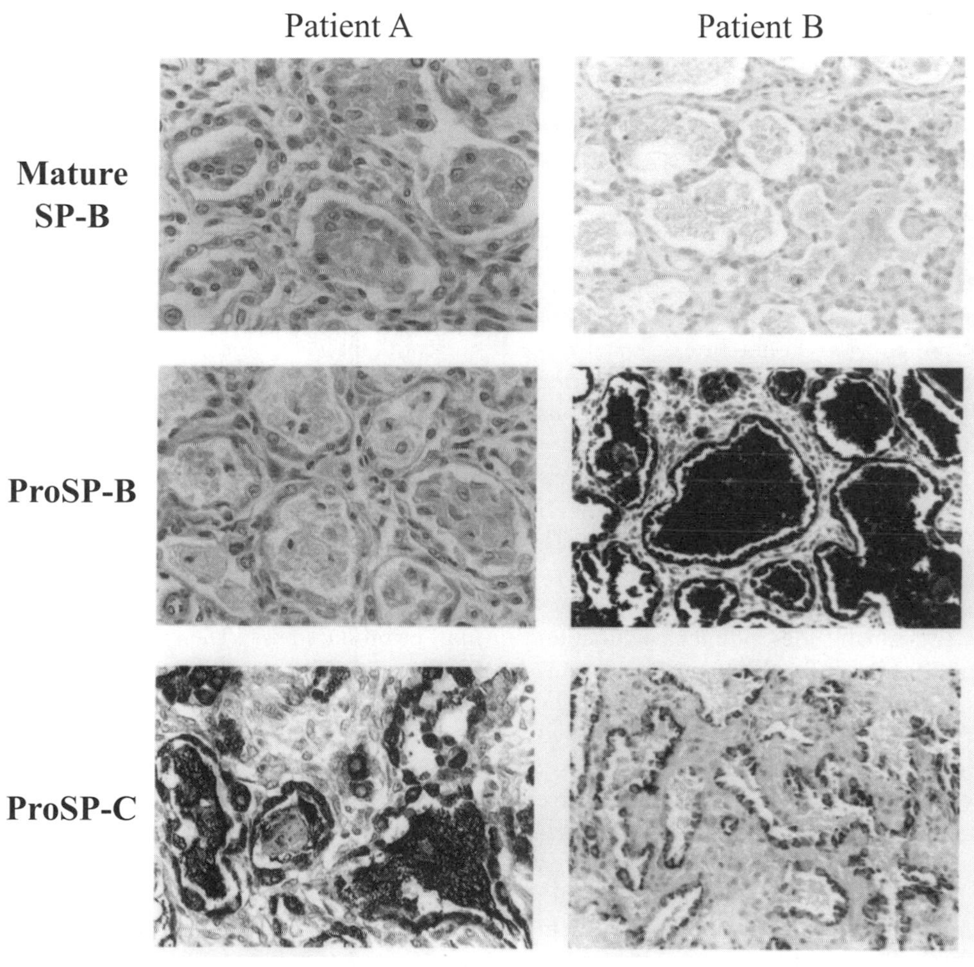

FIGURE 3–5. Immunohistochemical staining of lung tissue from two neonates with findings of alveolar proteinosis. Immunostaining of lung tissue from two full-term infants with respiratory failure for mature SP-B demonstrated no detectable staining in either child (*top*). After antigen retrieval to enhance the sensitivity of staining, immunoreactive material was observed in patient B but not patient A (*not shown*). This was similar to the staining pattern for proSP-B (*middle*), with absent staining observed in patient A, but intense staining for proSP-B was observed in both the extracellular proteinaceous material and the alveolar epithelium in patient B. Intense immunostaining with antiserum directed against proSP-C was also observed in extracelluar proteinaceous material in patient A, whereas proSP-C staining was confined to the alveolar epithelium in patient B (*bottom*). Patient A was found to be homozygous for the 121ins2 mutation. Patient B did not have a SP-B gene mutation identified, and the underlying cause of disease in this child remains undetermined (staining performed as described in reference 41, original magnification × 250 [approximately]). (Photographs courtesy of Dr. Susan Wert, Children's Hospital Medical Center, Cincinnati, OH.)

production of an abnormal transcript that encoded a stable, abnormal proprotein containing the majority of the amino- and carboxy-terminal domains of proSP-B but lacked the domain corresponding to mature SP-B. Whether this resultant abnormal proprotein retained some functions that allowed for the less severe course observed in the children with this mutation, one of whom is ambulatory at 8 years of age, remains unknown. Transient deficiency of SP-B also has been observed in a child with severe, but eventually reversible, lung disease in the neonatal period who had an SP-B mutation on only one allele and an apparently normal second allele.[40] Collectively, these observations suggest that there is a critical level of SP-B needed for normal lung function, although the precise level of SP-B needed for normal lung function is unknown.

This hypothesis is supported by experiments with mice genetically engineered to be unable to produce SP-B. Animals homozygous for the null SP-B allele do not have detectable SP-B mRNA or protein in their lungs, do not inflate their lungs at birth, and die within minutes from respiratory insufficiency.[71] These animals also have secondary abnormalities in their lungs similar to those observed in human infants with hereditary SP-B deficiency, including aberrant processing of proSP-C and abnormal lamellar body formation.[71,72] Mice heterozygous for a null SP-B allele have half the normal levels of SP-B mRNA and protein, and do not have neonatal respiratory disease, although they may develop abnormal compliance as they age.[73] However, these heterozygous SP-B-deficient mice were more susceptible to pulmonary oxygen toxicity than their wild-type littermates.[74,75] Levels of SP-B protein also have been observed to be low in bronchoalveolar lavage (BAL) from adult patients with acute RDS, but it is unclear whether this primarily contributes to their pulmonary dysfunction or is a secondary effect.[76,77] In a small series, pulmonary function tests in human adult carriers for the 121ins2 mutations did not differ from controls.[78] Population studies will be necessary to determine whether there are risks associated with carrying one abnormal SP-B allele.

Frequently occurring variants in the SP-B gene have been identified that could potentially affect SP-B expression. A single-nucleotide polymorphism (SNP) has been identified in the last codon in exon 4, encoding either threonine or isoleucine.[9,37,41,55,79] The polymorphism encoding threonine allows a recognition site for N-linked glycosylation, which could potentially have functional significance for the proprotein structure or affect its routing through the cell. The polymorphism encoding threonine was associated with an increased risk of acute RDS in adults in a recent study.[80] Further studies are needed in larger populations, but this observation supports the notion that functionally significant alterations in the SP-B gene resulting in small differences in SP-B function or metabolism could be important in the pathogenesis of lung disease in older children and adults. Exon 8 also contains a cryptic splice site, the use of which would result in an SP-B proprotein with four amino acids deleted from the carboxy-terminal domain.[36] This splice variant has been detected in human lung tissue and may be increased relative to the normal transcript in diseased tissue.[81] Whether this increase is a cause or consequence of disease, whether this splice variant is translated, and, if so, whether the resulting proprotein is processed normally are unknown.

A variable nucleotide tandem repeat sequence is located within intron IV of the SP-B gene, and alleles containing different numbers of repeats have been characterized. Variants from the predominant allele were found more frequently in a cohort of infants with RDS as compared to a control group in one study.[82] However, the interpretation of these results is complicated by the finding that the infants with RDS had a significantly lower mean gestational age than the controls, a known risk factor for RDS. The populations from which these cohorts were drawn also were ethnically heterogeneous. No functional differences in SP-B expression have been demonstrated with respect to the different intron IV variants. Thus, the significance of these polymorphic variants remains unknown, but they may provide useful markers for linkage to SP-B alleles with functional importance. Single-nucleotide polymorphisms have also been identified in other noncoding regions of the SP-B gene, the functional significance of which likewise remains unknown.[55,69]

The potential significance of both naturally occurring SP-B gene coding variants and mutations, as well as in vitro constructs designed to alter or eliminate regions of the proSP-B molecule to determine their potential functional significance, can be assessed using animal models. A transgenic mouse expressing an SP-B variant of interest must be produced first. Then these mice can be bred with heterozygous SP-B-deficient mice, and then the offspring of these animals that have both the transgene expressing the variant of interest and that are heterozygous for a null SP-B allele can be interbred. The effects of the SP-B gene variant then are assessed by examining the lung disease (or lack thereof) in the subset of mice expressing only the transgene in the deficient background. For example, mice expressing only an SP-B construct encoding a truncated proSP-B that lacked the carboxy-terminal domain were able to produce mature SP-B and survived.[49] Interestingly, nonsense mutations have not been identified yet in the region of the gene encoding the carboxy-terminal domain of proSP-B. Although the number of known SP-B mutations is small, it is possible that such mutations may not result in lung disease.

Given its importance in surfactant function, other mechanisms that impair SP-B production or accelerate its catabolism are likely to be associated with disease. To date, the term hereditary SP-B deficiency has been applied to children with a primary inability to produce SP-B owing to mutations in the SP-B gene. Given the complex and cell-specific processing of SP-B, it is likely that mutations in genes needed for proper processing of proSP-B to mature SP-B could result in disease. Familial examples of children with reduced amounts of SP-B as detectable by immunostaining, or with reduced or undetectable amounts of SP-B in the BAL fluid, but without mutations to account for the lack of SP-B have been reported.[69,83] The mechanisms for disease in these children are unknown. The observation of abnormal lamellar bodies in one of these kindreds is consistent with the possibility of an abnormality in surfactant packaging and/or secretion.[84,85] Recently, a mutation in the gene encoding SP-C was identified in a child who had reduced immunostaining for SP-B (and SP-C) in her lung tissue, although SP-B was readily detected by Western blotting.[65] These observations support the notion that there may be important intracellular interactions between SP-B and SP-C and that mutations in other genes may affect SP-B metabolism. These observations underscore the importance of a systematic approach to the diagnosis and collection of samples in children with severe neonatal lung disease of unclear etiology, including the need for ultrastructural examination.

Evaluation of Infants with Suspected SP-B Deficiency

The diagnosis of SP-B deficiency should be considered in full-term infants with respiratory distress that is not explained by history and does not improve after the first week of life or in infants who have died from lung disease of unclear etiology. A family history of neonatal lung disease also should prompt suspicion for the diagnosis. The differential diagnosis includes RDS, infection, persistent pulmonary hypertension, unrecognized cardiac malformations, and developmental anomalies of the lung such as alveolar capillary dysplasia.

Routine laboratory findings in SP-B-deficient infants are nonspecific. Tracheal aspirate samples for lecithin-to-sphingomyelin ratios have been reported as low and within the normal range but have not been evaluated systematically as such testing is not done routinely on full-term infants.[35,86] Specific tests are needed to establish the diagnosis but are not widely available. The presence or absence of SP-B in tracheal aspirate or BAL fluid can be analyzed by either enzyme-linked immunosorbent or Western blotting assays. Currently, such assays are available only on a research basis, and the sensitivity and specificity of such testing are unknown. The potential for both false-positive and false-negative results exists. Either immaturity or injury to alveolar type II cells could globally lower surfactant production, leading to false-negative results. Exogenous surfactant preparations used to treat infants with RDS contain variable amounts of SP-B and, if the infant has received such preparations, could be a source of false-positive results as most polyclonal antisera do not distinguish between human and bovine or porcine SP-B. Finally, the disease may be caused by mutations that allow for some SP-B production, and the SP-B levels that distinguish such infants from unaffected infants are unknown.

As a common mutation has been identified that is responsible for disease, genetic testing may be of help in establishing the diagnosis. The 121ins2 introduces a new recognition site for the restriction endonuclease *Sfu* I, thus facilitating its analysis by amplification of the region containing the mutation by polymerase chain reaction and restriction analysis (Figure 3–6).[36] Such testing is noninvasive and can be performed rapidly, and a finding of this mutation on both alleles is diagnostic for the disorder. Assays for this mutation are available in clinical diagnostic laboratories and on a research basis. However, as many mutations have been identified, the majority of which are "private" in that they have been found in only one unrelated kindred, the sensitivity of genetic testing is limited. Moreover, a finding of the 121ins2 mutation on only one allele does not distinguish between affected infants who are compound heterozygotes for two different SP-B mutations and those who may only be carriers for SP-B deficiency and either transiently deficient or have lung disease for other reasons.

Immunohistochemical staining of biopsy or autopsy lung tissue may be used to establish the diagnosis. However, this either requires a lung biopsy in a critically ill, unstable child or is limited to a postmortem approach. Such studies can be performed on archived lung specimens, allowing for retrospective diagnosis of children who may have died many years ago. Care must be taken in the interpretation of immunohistochemical staining. An absence of staining for mature SP-B is consistent with the diagnosis but not definitive as this pattern has been observed in children in whom mutations in the SP-B gene were not identified or in whom other mechanisms for their lung disease were subsequently identified (see Figure 3–5). Additionally, the staining pattern for proSP-B and mature SP-B is variable in affected infants and dependent on the nature of the mutation(s) responsible for disease. Null mutations that preclude SP-B production are associated with absent staining for both proSP-B and mature SP-B, but variable staining for both proSP-B and mature SP-B may be observed in association with mutations that allow for some SP-B production and hence a source of false-positive results.[41] The sensitivity and specificity of staining for SP-B have not been determined. In contrast to staining for SP-B, the finding of extracellular staining for proSP-C has correlated well with the finding of mutations in the SP-B gene.

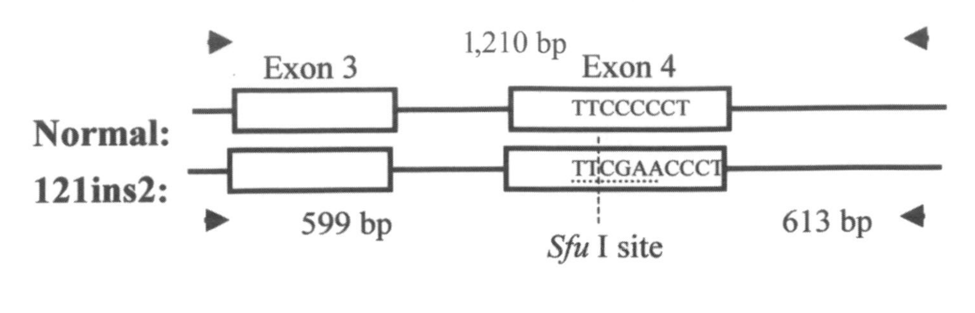

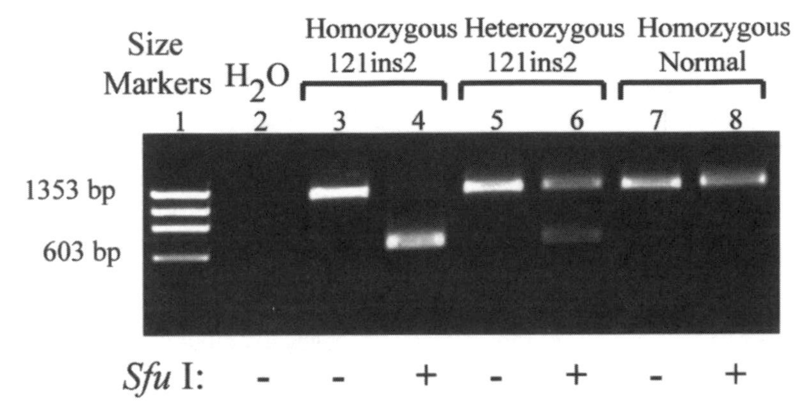

FIGURE 3–6. Restriction analysis for the 121ins2 mutation. The location of the 121ins2 mutation in exon 4 and primers used to amplify the DNA sequence spanning the site of the mutation are shown on the top. Agarose gel electrophoresis analysis of the polymerase chain reaction (PCR) products from three patients before and after digestion with a restriction endonuclease that cuts at a site created by the 121ins2 mutation are shown below. The appearance of bands at 613 and 599 bp (not resolved under these conditions) indicates the presence of the mutation. Lane 1 contains size markers; lane 2 contains the product from a PCR reaction without DNA added (negative control). The 1,212-bp PCR products from a patient with only the 121ins2 mutation (*lane 3*) were completely digested to 613/599 bp by *Sfu* I (*lane 4*). In contrast, the 1,210-bp PCR products from a patient who does not have the 121ins2 mutation on either allele (*lane 7*) were unaffected by *Sfu* I digestion (*lane 8*). Lanes 5 and 6 contain PCR products from a patient who has the 121ins mutation on one allele, as indicated by bands at both 1,210 bp and 613/599 bp following *Sfu* I digestion.

Finally, it is likely that SP-B deficiency is only one of a number of genetic defects that may result in abnormal surfactant production and present with the nonspecific phenotype of RDS. There are likely many other important enzymes and factors needed for the proper production, intracellular routing and packaging, secretion, and metabolism of other surfactant components, and mutations in the genes for these proteins are likely candidates to result in lung disease. An analogy may be drawn from inborn errors of intermediary metabolism, in which infants may present with a nonspecific appearance of a sepsis-like illness and metabolic disturbances. Similarly, inborn errors of lung cell metabolism may present with a nonspecific picture of neonatal respiratory distress and radiographically diffuse lung disease. Elucidation of these inborn errors should enhance our understanding of normal surfactant metabolism and may provide clues to the pathogenesis of lung diseases outside the neonatal period.

Treatment

Currently, there is no effective treatment for hereditary SP-B deficiency aside from lung transplantation. The response to exogenous surfactant replacement therapy is usually transient, and sustained replacement therapy (> 80 doses) did not alter the course in an antenatally diagnosed infant treated from birth.[86] Several factors could account for the failure of replacement therapy to improve the disease. Purified preparations of SP-B are not available for replacement therapy, and exogenous replacement surfactants contain variable amounts of SP-B and other surfactant components. The amount of SP-B provided may have been insufficient, or there may have been toxicity from overtreatment with surfactant lipids and SP-C. Exogenous SP-B also may be recognized as a foreign protein and induce an immunologic response in children with mutations that do not allow for any SP-B production. Finally, it seems likely from the secondary disturbances in SP-C processing and lamellar body biogenesis that endogenously synthesized proSP-B or mature SP-B have critical intracellular roles in the packaging and processing of surfactant. Exogenously administered mature SP-B may not be able to serve these functions either because they require proSP-B epitopes or because exogenous SP-B does not reach the necessary cellular compartments.

Because of the relative tissue specificity of SP-B expression and the lethal nature of the lung disease caused by its absence, SP-B deficiency is a candidate for gene therapy. Viral vectors capable of directing SP-B expression have been generated and tested in in vitro and animal systems.[87–89] However, considerable barriers need to be overcome before gene therapy may be considered for human infants. A high level of SP-B expression, both within individual cells and throughout the lung, will likely be needed to prevent disease. Such expression also must be sustained for long periods of time, and continued replacement treatment will be needed. The potential toxicity of the viral vectors is an additional concern. Since the most common mutation resulting in SP-B deficiency is a null mutation, SP-B and proSP-B may be recognized as foreign antigens and elicit an immune response. Anti-SP-B antibodies have had adverse effects in experimental animals, and the development of such antibodies could thus limit replacement strategies for this disease.[90–92] Such an anti-SP-B antibody was detected in the serum of a child homozygous for the 121ins2 mutation who underwent lung transplantation.[63] However, the child's lung function improved despite the presence of the antibody, and the significance of this observation remains unclear.

Currently, the only therapy available for SP-B deficiency is lung transplantation. Infants who are SP-B deficient have been successfully transplanted, with correction of the underlying biochemical abnormalities and encouraging short-term outcomes.[63] However, the ultimate prognosis for these children remains unknown, with the need for long-term immunosuppressive therapy and the risks of infection and rejection. In addition to economic considerations, lung transplantation is available only at a limited number of medical centers, and the availability of donor lungs is limited. As SP-B deficiency is a fatal disorder, compassionate care is an option once a diagnosis is established. The parents of affected children should receive formal genetic counseling. Identification of the mutation(s) responsible for disease in an affected child may allow for prenatal diagnosis in subsequent pregnancies.[93]

Summary

The identification of hereditary SP-B deficiency has provided an explanation for fatal lung disease in some full-term infants that was not previously understood. More importantly, by demonstrating the essential role for SP-B, it illustrates a mechanism by which genetic variability can either directly cause or contribute to neonatal lung disease and likely has implications for lung disease beyond the neonatal period. Finally, as with other inborn errors of metabolism, understanding the pathogenesis of lung disease resulting from the lack of SP-B will provide insights into normal surfactant and lung cell function and metabolism. For example, it is clear that SP-B plays an important role in lamellar body biogenesis and is important in the metabolism of other surfactant components, such as the post-translational processing of proSP-C to mature SP-C.

Many questions remained unanswered with respect to SP-B deficiency. The pathophysiology of the disease, in particular the roles of misprocessing of SP-C and secondary effects on metabolism of other surfactant components, needs to be better understood. The intracellular role of SP-B and whether mature SP-B epitopes or domains of the proprotein are critical for function needs to be determined. Other genes and environmental factors that may have roles in modifying the course of the disease need to be identified. Finally, the incidence of the disease and contribution of SP-B gene defects to other lung diseases, including whether haploinsufficiency for SP-B is a risk factor for development of lung disease in the neonatal period and later in life, remain to be determined.

Acknowledgments

The author wishes to thank Dr. Susan Wert for providing photographs of immunostained lung tissue from patient samples and an electron micrograph of normal lung tissue, and Dr. Ernest Cutz for providing electron micrographs of lung tissue from an SP-B deficient infant.

Supported by grants from the National Institutes of Health (HL-54703) and the Eudowood Foundation.

References

1. Farrell PM, Avery ME. Hyaline membrane disease. Am Rev Respir Dis 1975;111:657–88.
2. Miller HC, Futrakul P. Birth weight, gestational age, and sex as determining factors in the incidence of respiratory distress syndrome of prematurely born infants. J Pediatr 1968;72:628–35.
3. Usher RH, Allen AC, McLean FH. Risk of respiratory distress syndrome related to gestational age, route of delivery, and maternal diabetes. Am J Obstet Gynecol 1971; 111:826–32.
4. Nagourney BA, Kramer MS, Klebanoff MA, Usher RH. Recurrent respiratory distress syndrome in successive preterm pregnancies. J Pediatr 1996;129:591–6.
5. Whitsett JA, Ohning BL, Ross G, et al. Hydrophobic surfactant-associated protein in whole lung surfactant and its importance for biophysical activity in lung surfactant extracts used for replacement therapy. Pediatr Res 1986;20:460–7.
6. Johansson J, Curstedt T, Robertson B. The proteins of the surfactant system. Eur Respir J 1994;7:372–91.
7. Weaver TE. Synthesis, processing and secretion of surfactant proteins B and C. Biochim Biophys Acta 1998; 1408:173–9.
8. Nogee LM. Genetics of the hydrophobic surfactant proteins. Biochim Biophys Acta 1998;1408:323–33.
9. Glasser SW, Korfhagen TR, Weaver T, et al. cDNA and deduced amino acid sequence of human pulmonary surfactant-associated proteolipid SPL(Phe). Proc Natl Acad Sci U S A 1987;84:4007–11.

10. Glasser SW, Korfhagen TR, Weaver TE, et al. cDNA, deduced polypeptide structure and chromosomal assignment of human pulmonary surfactant proteolipid, SPL(pVal). J Biol Chem 1988;263:9–12.
11. Paananen R, Glumoff V, Sormunen R, et al. Expression and localization of lung surfactant protein B in eustachian tube epithelium. Am J Physiol 2001;280:L214–20.
12. Whitsett JA, Weaver TE, Clark JC, et al. Glucocorticoid enhances surfactant proteolipid Phe and pVal synthesis and RNA in fetal lung. J Biol Chem 1987;262:15618–23.
13. Voorhout WF, Weaver TE, Haagsman HP, et al. Biosynthetic routing of pulmonary surfactant proteins in alveolar type II cells. Microsc Res Tech 1993;26:366–73.
14. Crouch EC. Collectins and pulmonary host defense. Am J Respir Cell Mol Biol 1998;19:177–201.
15. Rice WR, Ross GF, Singleton FM, et al. Surfactant-associated protein inhibits phospholipid secretion from type II cells. J Appl Physiol 1987;63:692–8.
16. Wright JR, Wager RE, Hawgood S, et al. Surfactant apoprotein Mr = 26,000–36,000 enhances uptake of liposomes by type II cells. J Biol Chem 1987;262:2888–94.
17. Crouch E, Hartshorn K, Ofek I. Collectins and pulmonary innate immunity. Immunol Rev 2000;173:52–65.
18. Korfhagen TR, Bruno MD, Ross GF, et al. Altered surfactant function and structure in SP-A gene targeted mice. Proc Natl Acad Sci U S A 1996;93:9594–9.
19. Ikegami M, Korfhagen TR, Bruno MD, et al. Surfactant metabolism in surfactant protein A-deficient mice. Am J Physiol 1997;272:L479–85.
20. Korfhagen TR, LeVine AM, Whitsett JA. Surfactant protein A (SP-A) gene targeted mice. Biochim Biophys Acta 1998;1408:296–302.
21. LeVine AM, Bruno MD, Huelsman KM, et al. Surfactant protein A-deficient mice are susceptible to group B streptococcal infection. J Immunol 1997;158:4336–40.
22. LeVine AM, Gwozdz J, Stark J, et al. Surfactant protein-A enhances respiratory syncytial virus clearance in vivo. J Clin Invest 1999;103:1015–21.
23. Korfhagen TR, Sheftelyevich V, Burhans MS, et al. Surfactant protein-D regulates surfactant phospholipid homeostasis in vivo. J Biol Chem 1998;273:28438–43.
24. Botas C, Poulain F, Akiyama J, et al. Altered surfactant homeostasis and alveolar type II cell morphology in mice lacking surfactant protein D. Proc Natl Acad Sci U S A 1998;95:11869–74.
25. Wert SE, Yoshida M, LeVine AM, et al. Increased metalloproteinase activity, oxidant production, and emphysema in surfactant protein D gene-inactivated mice. Proc Natl Acad Sci U S A 2000;97:5972–7.
26. Crouch E, Wright J. Surfactant proteins a and d and pulmonary host defense. Annu Rev Physiol 2001;63:521–54.
27. Floros J, Hoover RR. Genetics of the hydrophilic surfactant proteins A and D. Biochim Biophys Acta 1998;1408:312–22.
28. Nogee LM, de Mello DE, Dehner LP, Colten HR. Brief report: deficiency of pulmonary surfactant protein B in congenital alveolar proteinosis. N Engl J Med 1993; 328:406–10.
29. Chauhan MS, Jayaswal R, Rajan RS, et al. Pulmonary alveolar proteinosis (with review of literature). J Assoc Physicians India 1988;36:445–6.
30. Voss T, Schafer KP, Nielsen PF, et al. Primary structure differences of human surfactant-associated proteins isolated from normal and proteinosis lung. Biochim Biophys Acta 1992;1138:261–7.
31. Beers MF, Bates SR, Fisher AB. Differential extraction for the rapid purification of bovine surfactant protein B. Am J Physiol 1992;262:L773–8.
32. Coleman M, Dehner LP, Sibley RK, et al. Pulmonary alveolar proteinosis: an uncommon cause of chronic neonatal respiratory distress. Am Rev Respir Dis 1980;121:583–6.
33. Knight DP, Knight JA. Pulmonary alveolar proteinosis in the newborn. Arch Pathol Lab Med 1985;109:529–31.
34. Schumacher RE, Marrogi AJ, Heidelberger KP. Pulmonary alveolar proteinosis in a newborn. Pediatr Pulmonol 1989;7:178–82.
35. Moulton SL, Krous HF, Merritt TA, et al. Congenital pulmonary alveolar proteinosis: failure of treatment with extracorporeal life support. J Pediatr 1992;120: 297–302.
36. Nogee LM, Garnier G, Dietz HC, et al. A mutation in the surfactant protein B gene responsible for fatal neonatal respiratory disease in multiple kindreds. J Clin Invest 1994;93:1860–3.
37. Pilot-Matias TJ, Kister SE, Fox JL, et al. Structure and organization of the gene encoding human pulmonary surfactant proteolipid SP-B. DNA 1989;8:75–86.
38. Beers MF, Hamvas A, Moxley MA, et al. Pulmonary surfactant metabolism in infants lacking surfactant protein B. Am J Respir Cell Mol Biol 2000;22:380–91.
39. Ballard PL, Nogee LM, Beers MF, et al. Partial deficiency of surfactant protein B in an infant with chronic lung disease. Pediatrics 1995;96:1046–52.
40. Klein JM, Thompson MW, Snyder JM, et al. Transient surfactant protein B deficiency in a term infant with severe respiratory failure. J Pediatr 1998;132:244–8.
41. Nogee LM, Wert SE, Proffit SA, et al. Allelic heterogeneity in hereditary surfactant protein B (SP-B) deficiency. Am J Respir Crit Care Med 2000;161:973–81.
42. Tredano M, van Elburg RM, Kaspers AG, et al. Compound SFTPB 1549C—>GAA (121ins2) and 457delC heterozygosity in severe congenital lung disease and surfactant protein B (SP-B) deficiency. Hum Mutat 1999;14:502–9.
43. Somaschini M, Wert S, Mangili G, et al. Hereditary surfactant protein B deficiency resulting from a novel mutation. Intensive Care Med 2000;26:97–100.
44. Dunbar AE 3rd, Wert SE, Ikegami M, et al. Prolonged survival in hereditary surfactant protein B (SP-B) deficiency associated with a novel splicing mutation. Pediatr Res 2000;48:275–82.
45. Vorbroker DK, Profitt SA, Nogee LM, Whitsett JA. Aberrant processing of surfactant protein C in hereditary SP-B deficiency. Am J Physiol 1995;268:L647–56.
46. Hawgood S, Derrick M, Poulain F. Structure and properties of surfactant protein B. Biochim Biophys Acta 1998; 1408:150–60.
47. Lin S, Phillips KS, Wilder MR, Weaver TE. Structural requirements for intracellular transport of pulmonary surfactant protein B (SP-B). Biochim Biophys Acta 1996; 1312:177–85.

48. Lin S, Akinbi HT, Breslin JS, Weaver TE. Structural requirements for targeting of surfactant protein B (SP-B) to secretory granules in vitro and in vivo. J Biol Chem 1996;271:19689–95.
49. Akinbi HT, Breslin JS, Ikegami M, et al. Rescue of SP-B knockout mice with a truncated SP-B proprotein. Function of the C-terminal propeptide. J Biol Chem 1997; 272:9640–7.
50. Hawgood S, Latham D, Borchelt J, et al. Cell-specific posttranslational processing of the surfactant-associated protein SP-B. Am J Physiol 1993;264:L290–9.
51. Weaver TE, Lin S, Bogucki B, Dey C. Processing of surfactant protein B proprotein by a cathepsin D-like protease. Am J Physiol 1992;263:L95–103.
52. Mbagwu N, Bruni R, Hernandez-Juviel JM, et al. Sensitivity of synthetic surfactants to albumin inhibition in preterm rabbits. Mol Genet Metab 1999;66:40–8.
53. Ball R, Chetcuti PA, Beverley D. Fatal familial surfactant protein B deficiency [letter]. Arch Dis Child Fetal Neonatal Ed 1995;73:F53.
54. de la Fuente AA, Voorhout WF, deMello DE. Congenital alveolar proteinosis in the Netherlands: a report of five cases with immunohistochemical and genetic studies on surfactant apoproteins. Pediatr Pathol Lab Med 1997;17: 221–31.
55. Lin Z, deMello DE, Wallot M, Floros J. An SP-B gene mutation responsible for SP-B deficiency in fatal congenital alveolar proteinosis: evidence for a mutation hotspot in exon 4. Mol Genet Metab 1998;64:25–35.
56. Williams GD, Christodoulou J, Stack J, et al. Surfactant protein B deficiency: clinical, histological and molecular evaluation. J Paediatr Child Health 1999;35:214–20.
57. Andersen C, Ramsay JA, Nogee LM, et al. Recurrent familial neonatal deaths: hereditary surfactant protein B deficiency. Am J Perinatol 2000;17:219–24.
58. Cole FS, Hamvas A, Rubinstein P, et al. Population-based estimates of surfactant protein B deficiency. Pediatrics 2000;105:538–41.
59. Nogee LM, Wert SE, Hamvas A, et al. Phenotypic variability in hereditary surfactant protein B (SP-B) deficiency. Am J Respir Crit Care Med 2000;161:A523.
60. Hamvas A, Nogee LM, deMello DE, Cole FS. Pathophysiology and treatment of surfactant protein-B deficiency. Biol Neonate 1995;67:18–31.
61. Nogee LM, Irrizary K, Hamvas A, et al. Evidence for a common ancestral origin for the most frequent mutation responsible for surfactant protein B (SP-B) deficiency. Pediatr Res 2000;47:370A.
62. Herman TE, Nogee LM, McAlister WH, Dehner LP. Surfactant protein B deficiency: radiographic manifestations. Pediatr Radiol 1993;23:373–5.
63. Hamvas A, Nogee LM, Mallory GB Jr, et al. Lung transplantation for treatment of infants with surfactant protein B deficiency. J Pediatr 1997;130:231–9.
64. Beers MF, Hamvas A, Moxley MA, et al. Pulmonary surfactant metabolism in infants lacking surfactant protein B. Am J Respir Mol Cell Biol 2000;22:380–91.
65. Nogee LM, Dunbar AE, Wert SE, et al. A mutation in the surfactant protein C gene associated with familial interstitial lung disease. N Engl J Med 2001;344:573–9.
66. Williams MC, Hawgood S, Hamilton RL. Changes in lipid structure produced by surfactant proteins SP-A, SP-B, and SP-C. Am J Respir Cell Mol Biol 1991;5:41–50.
67. deMello DE, Heyman S, Phelps DS, et al. Ultrastructure of lung in surfactant protein B deficiency. Am J Respir Cell Mol Biol 1994;11:230–9.
68. deMello DE, Nogee LM, Heyman S, et al. Molecular and phenotypic variability in the congenital alveolar proteinosis syndrome associated with inherited surfactant protein B deficiency. J Pediatr 1994;125:43–50.
69. Lin Z, deMello DE, Batanian JR, et al. Aberrant SP-B mRNA in lung tissue of patients with congenital alveolar proteinosis (CAP). Clin Genet 2000;57:359–69.
70. Dirksen U, Nishinakamura R, Groneck P, et al. Human pulmonary alveolar proteinosis associated with a defect in GM- CSF/IL-3/IL-5 receptor common beta chain expression. J Clin Invest 1997;100:2211–7.
71. Clark JC, Wert SE, Bachurski CJ, et al. Targeted disruption of the surfactant protein B gene disrupts surfactant homeostasis, causing respiratory failure in newborn mice. Proc Natl Acad Sci U S A 1995;92:7794–8.
72. Stahlman MT, Gray MP, Falconieri MW, et al. Lamellar body formation in normal and surfactant protein B-deficient fetal mice. Lab Invest 2000;80:395–403.
73. Clark JC, Weaver TE, Iwamoto HS, et al. Decreased lung compliance and air trapping in heterozygous SP-B-deficient mice. Am J Respir Cell Mol Biol 1997;16:46–52.
74. Tokieda K, Iwamoto HS, Bachurski C, et al. Surfactant protein-B-deficient mice are susceptible to hyperoxic lung injury. Am J Respir Cell Mol Biol 1999;21:463–72.
75. Tokieda K, Ikegami M, Wert SE, et al. Surfactant protein B corrects oxygen-induced pulmonary dysfunction in heterozygous surfactant protein B-deficient mice. Pediatr Res 1999;46:708–14.
76. Gregory TJ, Longmore WJ, Moxley MA, et al. Surfactant chemical composition and biophysical activity in acute respiratory distress syndrome. J Clin Invest 1991;88: 1976–81.
77. Greene KE, Wright JR, Steinberg KP, et al. Serial changes in surfactant-associated proteins in lung and serum before and after onset of ARDS. Am J Respir Crit Care Med 1999;160:1843–50.
78. Yusen RD, Cohen AH, Hamvas A. Normal lung function in subjects heterozygous for surfactant protein-B deficiency. Am J Respir Crit Care Med 1999;159:411–4.
79. Jacobs KA, Phelps DS, Steinbrink R, et al. Isolation of a cDNA clone encoding a high molecular weight precursor to a 6–kDa pulmonary surfactant-associated protein [published erratum appears in J Biol Chem 1988;263: 1093]. J Biol Chem 1987;262:9808–11.
80. Lin Z, Pearson C, Chinchilli V, et al. Polymorphisms of human SP-A, SP-B, and SP-D genes: association of SP-B Thr131Ile with ARDS. Clin Genet 2000;58:181–91.
81. Lin Z, Wang G, Demello DE, Floros J. An alternatively spliced surfactant protein B mRNA in normal human lung: disease implication. Biochem J 1999;343(Pt 1):145–9.
82. Floros J, Veletza SV, Kotikalapudi P, et al. Dinucleotide repeats in the human surfactant protein-B gene and respiratory-distress syndrome. Biochem J 1995;305:583–90.

83. Tryka AF, Wert SE, Mazursky JE, et al. Absence of lamellar bodies with accumulation of dense bodies characterize a novel form of congenital surfactant deficiency. Pediatr Dev Pathol 2000;3:335–45.
84. Cutz E, Wert SE, Nogee LM, Moore AM. Deficiency of lamellar bodies in alveolar type II cells associated with fatal respiratory disease in a full-term infant. Am J Respir Crit Care Med 2000;161:608–14.
85. Tryka AF, Wert SE, Mazursky JE, et al. Absence of lamellar bodies with accumulation of dense bodies characterizes a novel form of congenital surfactant defect. Pediatr Dev Pathol 2000;3:335–45.
86. Hamvas A, Cole FS, deMello DE, et al. Surfactant protein B deficiency: antenatal diagnosis and prospective treatment with surfactant replacement. J Pediatr 1994; 125:356–61.
87. Yei S, Bachurski CJ, Weaver TE, et al. Adenoviral-mediated gene transfer of human surfactant protein B to respiratory epithelial cells. Am J Respir Cell Mol Biol 1994; 11:329–36.
88. Korst RJ, Bewig B, Crystal RG. In vitro and in vivo transfer and expression of human surfactant SP-A- and SP-B-associated protein cDNAs mediated by replication-deficient, recombinant adenoviral vectors. Hum Gene Ther 1995;6:277–87.
89. Strayer MS, Guttentag SH, Ballard PL. Targeting type II and Clara cells for adenovirus-mediated gene transfer using the surfactant protein B promoter. Am J Respir Cell Mol Biol 1998;18:1–11.
90. Kobayashi T, Nitta K, Takahashi R, et al. Activity of pulmonary surfactant after blocking the associated proteins SP-A and SP-B. J Appl Physiol 1991;71:530–6.
91. Robertson B, Kobayashi T, Ganzuka M, et al. Experimental neonatal respiratory failure induced by a monoclonal antibody to the hydrophobic surfactant-associated protein SP-B. Pediatr Res 1991;30:239–43.
92. Grossmann G, Suzuki Y, Robertson B, et al. Pathophysiology of neonatal lung injury induced by monoclonal antibody to surfactant protein B. J Appl Physiol 1997; 82:2003–10.
93. Stuhrmann M, Bohnhorst B, Peters U, et al. Prenatal diagnosis of congenital alveolar proteinosis (surfactant protein B deficiency). Prenat Diagn 1998;18:953–5.

CHAPTER 4

Developmental Biology of Surfactant

Alan H. Jobe, MD, PhD, Timothy E. Weaver, PhD

What is Surfactant?

A review of the developmental biology of surfactant must start with a definition of surfactant, which is complicated by the multiple components and functions of surfactant. Is pulmonary surfactant defined by its biophysical properties, its lipid and protein components, its innate host defense properties, or its function in the lung? Of course, all these functions and characteristics of surfactant need to be integrated into a balanced view of the role of surfactant in the lung. This review emphasizes the integrated nature of surfactant function based on lessons learned from animals that lack surfactant proteins. The goal is to emphasize aspects of surfactant biology with relevance to lung diseases in infants and children.

Surfactant Metabolism: An Overview

The Mature Lung

Most of the information about the metabolism of surfactant has resulted from evaluations of the major surfactant component dipalmitoylphosphatidylcholine (DPPC) (Figure 4–1). After being synthesized in the endoplasmic reticulum, DPPC is transferred to lamellar bodies along with the other lipids of surfactant and the surfactant proteins (SP) B and C by multivesicular bodies (Figure 4–2).[1,2] The lamellar bodies are the storage and secretory granules for surfactant that contain stacked arrays of lipid and protein in a high Ca^{+2} environment. Lamellar bodies fuse with the plasma membrane during secretion. The regulators of the homeostatic regulation of secretion are not known, but surfactant secretion can be stimulated by stretch of the type II cell, by β-agonists, and by purinergic agonists such as adenosine triphosphate (ATP).[3] Once secreted to the hypophase, the lamellar bodies unravel to form tubular myelin and vesicular structures. These three-dimensional arrays of lipid and protein adsorb to an air-water interface and spread rapidly on the surface to decrease the equilibrium surface tension of 72 mN/m to a value of about 25 mN/m. A small percentage of surface area compression results in very low surface tensions that stabilize the alveoli and prevent collapse.[4]

The hypophase is a very thin fluid layer covering the distal epithelium of the lung that contains about 0.5 to 1 mL fluid per kg body weight and a surfactant concentration of about 5 to 10 mg/mL, based on an alveolar pool size of about 4 mg/kg of surfactant in the adult human alveolus.[5] The hypophase is thickest in the corners of the alveoli where type II cells tend to localize and is very thin over the surface of type I cells. The surface film is primarily DPPC in a monolayer or multilayers of lipids. The high local concentration of surfactant together with multiple layers at the surface assures rapid adsorption on film expansion and rapid replacement of surfactant in the normal lung. To achieve the very low and stable surface tensions of natural surfactant, the surface film must be primarily DPPC. This implies that DPPC is selectively adsorbed to the surface or that the other lipid and protein components are lost or squeezed out with film formation and with changes in the surface area of the film.[6] Of the DPPC present in the hypophase, about 50% is in lamellar bodies and loose lipid arrays and 50% is in small vesicles.[7] The small vesicles are unilamellar liposomes that have a lipid composition equivalent to lamellar bodies but lack SP-A, SP-B, and SP-C. The small vesicles are not very surface active and are thought to be the catabolic forms of

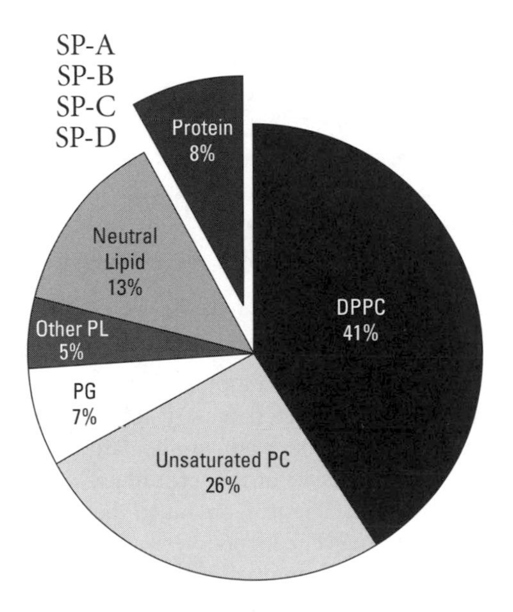

FIGURE 4–1. Composition of surfactant. DPPC = dipalmitoylphosphatidylcholine; PC = phosphatidylcholine; PG = phosphatidylglycerol; PL = phospholipids.

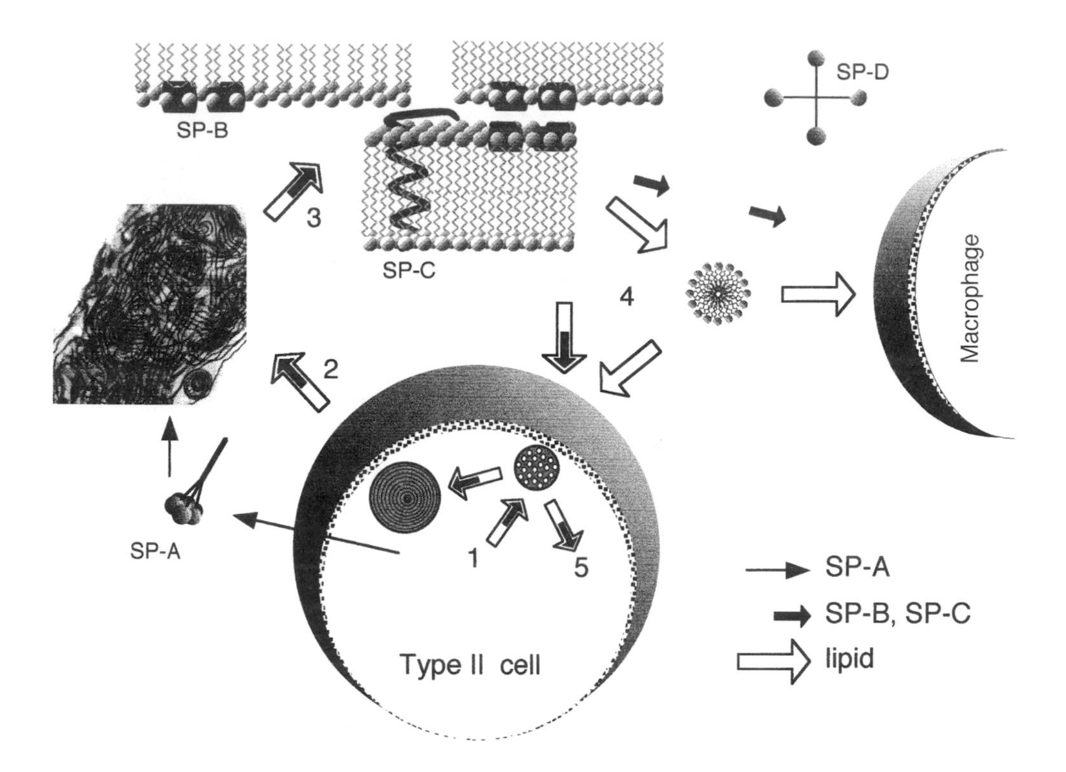

FIGURE 4–2. Diagram of surfactant metabolism. Surfactant lipids, SP-B and SP-C are synthesized in the endoplasmic reticulum and processed in multivesicular bodies before storage in lamellar bodies (*arrow 1*). Secretion (*arrow 2*) to the hypophase followed by tubular myelin formation results from the association of constitutively secreted SP-A with the other surfactant components. The tubular myelin and other lipoprotein forms adsorb to form the lipoprotein surface film (*arrow 3*). Lipid components are lost from the film as liposomes, and are recycled or catabolized (*arrows 4 and 5*). The catabolic pathways from the surface film taken by the surfactant proteins (SPs) are not known.

the lipids. Surfactant lipids are cleared from alveoli by macrophages and are taken up by type II cells. Macrophage catabolism accounts for about 20% of the catabolic activity of DPPC in the rabbit; the rest of the DPPC is cleared by type II cells.[8] About 50% of the DPPC taken up by type II cells is recycled intact back into lamellar bodies for resecretion, and the rest is catabolized via lysosomal degradative pathways.[9] The turnover time for DPPC in small mammals is about 5 hours, indicating that the lipid components of surfactant are participating in complex and dynamic metabolic pathways, which assures a continued supply of new surfactant to maintain lung function.[10]

Metabolic Pathways in the Developing Lung

The fetal lung accumulates large amounts of DPPC during the last third of gestation. After term birth, the amount of alveolar surfactant is 10-fold higher than in the adult lung, and there are similar large increases of DPPC in the lung tissue of the term fetus.[11] At term, the composition of surfactant is similar to that of surfactant from the adult lung. The kinetics from synthesis to secretion of DPPC in the preterm and term lung is slower than in the adult lung.[12] Once secreted, the turnover time is longer, and as much as 90% of the DPPC is recycled back into type II cells for resecretion, in part because there are few macrophages in the fetal lung. Another difference between the preterm and adult lung is that catabolism is very slow. For example, the half-life of DPPC in the newborn lamb is 6 days in contrast to half-life values of 9 to 12 hours for the adult lung. Therefore, fetal and term newborn lungs have slower metabolic rates, and term lungs have much larger pool sizes and decreased catabolism, which assure large amounts of surfactant for the initiation of breathing. The lungs of preterm infants with respiratory distress syndrome (RDS) contain alveolar pools of 2 to 10 mg/kg DPPC, which are similar in size to those of the adult lung.[11] However, this surfactant has decreased biophysical function and is more sensitive to inactivation by inhibitors such as plasma, presumably because it contains lower amounts of the surfactant proteins.[13] Measurements of the metabolic characteristics of surfactant using stable isotopes in infants with RDS are similar to measurements with radiolabeled precursors in term animals.[14] Therefore, the results of the many measurements in animal models are useful for understanding surfactant metabolism in the human, where few measurements are available.

Surfactant Metabolism with Lung Injury

Surfactant metabolism during lung injury in children and adults has not been extensively evaluated. The composition and function of the surfactant can change with

TABLE 4–1. Alterations in Surfactant during Acute Lung Injury

Decreased alveolar pool size
Dilution with edema fluid (lowers concentration)
Composition changes
Decreased phosphatidylglycerol and increased PI
Decreased dipalmitoylphosphatidylcholine
Decreased SP-A and SP-B
Increased SP-D
Changes in function
Decreased amounts of biophysically active forms
Decreased function of biophysically active forms
Inhibition by proteins and products of inflammation
Oxidation of surfactant components

PI = phosphatidylinositol; SP = surfactant protein.

lung injury (Table 4–1). Ventilated preterm baboons developing chronic lung disease have distal saccules lined with atypical type II cells, although the lung tissue contains very high pool sizes of DPPC, SP-A, and SP-D.[15,16] Despite high intracellular pools, the alveolar surfactant pools of DPPC and SP-A remain low for several weeks. These preterm animals have an uncharacterized abnormality of secretion as well as abnormal function of the surfactant that is in the alveoli. Chronic lung injury in the preterm results in multiple disturbances in the surfactant system.

In adult animal models the alveolar pool size decreases with acute injury to type I and type II cells and then increases as the type II cells repopulate the gaps in the epithelium. Acute injury results in decreased amounts of the large aggregate surface active forms of surfactant and increased amounts of the vesicular or catabolic forms of surfactant that have poor biophysical function. The large aggregate forms from the injured lung also have decreased biophysical function, and mechanical ventilation can further degrade their function. The net effect is a decrease in the amount of biophysically active surfactant. The function of the alveolar surfactant will be further compromised by dilution of the hypophase with edema fluid and by surfactant inhibitors from plasma and inflammatory products of the injury.

Surfactant Components and Developmental Profiles

Lipids

Phosphatidylcholines

The composition of surfactant is quite constant across mammalian species, with small differences that probably are of no physiologic significance except in hibernating mammals.[17] Phosphatidylcholine (PC) species constitute about 70% of the lipid in surfactant. About 60% of the PC species is DPPC (see Figure 4–1.) The majority of the other PCs contain palmitate (C-16) in the 1 position and the C-18 monounsaturated oleate or diunsaturated linoleate in the 2 position. Phosphatidylcholines with fatty acids of higher orders of unsaturation and longer chain lengths are minor species in surfactant. The only lipid component in surfactant that can lower surface tensions to very low values is DPPC, but it is a solid at 37°C and cannot adsorb or spread on a surface.[4] The unsaturated PCs, other lipids, and the surfactant proteins facilitate the adsorption of DPPC. Phosphatidylcholine is synthesized by all cells with predominantly 1-palmitoyl, 2-unsaturated fatty acid species in the endoplasmic reticulum. In the mature lung a deacylation-reacylation reaction in type II cells converts the unsaturated PC to DPPC before the lipids and lipophilic proteins SP-B and SP-C are assembled into lamellar bodies.[2] The amount of DPPC in the fetal lung increases concurrently with the appearance of lamellar bodies after about 22 weeks in the human lung.[18] The percent saturation of the PC in surfactant can be decreased by lung injury by two mechanisms:[19] injury can (1) allow unsaturated species of PC to contaminate the surfactant (eg, PC from plasma and red blood cell membranes) and (2) impair the ability of the type II cell to synthesize and secrete normal surfactant. Surfactant function will be poor if the percentage of saturated PC is low.

Acidic phospholipids

All mammalian surfactant contains 5 to 15% phosphatidylglycerol and/or phosphatidylinositol (PI), which are both acidic phospholipids that can enhance adsorption and film formation of saturated PC.[17] These acidic phospholipids change with development and lung injury. As the developing mammalian lung begins to synthesize and store surfactant, PI is the primary acidic phospholipid.[20] Phosphatidylinositol is replaced by phosphatidylglycerol when lung maturation is sufficient to permit delivery without RDS. Analyses of amniotic fluid for the presence of phosphatidylglycerol are used to predict lung maturation clinically. With recovery from RDS, the amount of PI in surfactant decreases, and phosphatidylglycerol appears.[21] If RDS progresses to chronic lung disease, the appearance of phosphatidylglycerol can be delayed for weeks. The surfactant in children and adults with acute lung injury loses phosphatidylglycerol, and PI again predominates; recovery is accompanied by a normalization of these acidic phospholipids.[22] These alterations are presumed to reflect injury to type II cells and perhaps a recapitulation of the fetal maturation sequence as type II cells recover and repopulate the pulmonary epithelium.

The other major class of lipids in surfactant are neutral lipids, primarily cholesterol ester. Cholesterol can increase the adsorption rate of saturated PC, but surfactant with a high cholesterol content can not achieve the low surface tensions of natural surfactant. There are trace amounts of free fatty acids and other lipids that probably contribute little to function.

The Hydrophobic Proteins

Surfactant protein B

The SP-B isolated from lung lavage is a 79 amino acid homodimer of about 18 kD that comprises 1 to 2% of surfactant by weight. The messenger ribonucleic acid (mRNA) for SP-B first appears in the maturing alveolar type II cells concurrently with lamellar bodies. Subsequently, SP-B mRNA is localized exclusively to type II cells and Clara cells, although complete processing of the 42-kD proprotein to the mature peptide occurs only in type II cells. Surfactant containing SP-B and lipids can restore the pressure-volume curves of surfactant deficient lungs to normal and effectively treat surfactant deficiency in animal models of RDS.[23] Surfactant protein B is essential for tubular myelin formation, and SP-B promotes surface adsorption of DPPC in lipid mixtures.[24] Presumably its biophysical function derives from its ability to "solubilize" into lipids, resulting in vesicle fusion and rearrangement of the lipid structures. Surfactant protein B is thought to position itself below the surface film in contact with the headgroups of the phospholipids. In vivo, SP-B is clearly important for the function of surfactant; however, surfactants that contain only lipids and SP-C also can restore pressure-volume curves of surfactant-deficient lungs and treat surfactant deficiency in animal models.[23,25]

The essential function of SP-B is its absolute requirement for packaging of surfactant phospholipids in lamellar bodies of type II cells. In transgenic mice or term infants that lack SP-B, normal appearing lamellar bodies are absent from type II cells.[26,27] Although DPPC synthesis is preserved with SP-B deficiency, SP-C can not be processed to its active peptide, and no secretion of normal surfactant occurs.[28] Both mice and humans that lack SP-B die soon after birth of a severe RDS-like syndrome. Surfactant treatment is not effective, presumably because there are no pathways for reprocessing the surfactant. The diagnosis can be made by demonstrating the SP-C precursor and no SP-B in airway samples or amniotic fluid. Therefore, the absolute requirement for SP-B results from its intracellular functions to permit surfactant component processing, storage, and secretion to occur.[2]

Deficiency of SP-B most frequently occurs because of a 121ins2 frame shift mutation, although multiple compound mutations have been described. The gene frequency of this frame shift maturation is 1 per 1,000 to 3,000 individuals.[29] Deficiency of SP-B from all mutations accounts for about 30% of infants that die of severe RDS at birth, because of possible genetic causes for the respiratory failure.[26] Some mutations result in low expression that may increase with glucocorticoid treatment. Infants with low expression may have chronic progressive lung disease indistinguishable from bronchopulmonary dysplasia.[30] Acute lung injury (adult respiratory distress syndrome [ARDS]) can depress SP-B levels in airway samples from adults.[31] Inflammation resulting in tumor necrosis factor α (TNF–α) release in the lungs will depress SP-B levels,[32] but it is not clear if the decreased levels of SP-B contribute directly to the respiratory failure.

Surfactant protein C

The SP-C in lung lavage is a 35 amino acid monomer of 4.2 kD that is 1 to 2% of the surfactant by weight.[33] Most of the SP-C is a dipalmitoylated peptide with palmitic acid residues on Cys-5 and Cys-6. The mRNA and proprotein for SP-C are present from early lung morphogenesis at the distal tips of the developing airways.[34] Subsequently SP-C expression occurs only in type II cells. Despite the localization and specificity of expression of the SP-C from early gestation, the proprotein is not processed to the mature peptide and secreted until day 28 of the 31-day term gestation in the rabbit.[35] As with SP-B, SP-C is processed in multivesicular bodies to the mature peptide that is stored in lamellar bodies and secreted together with mature SP-B and DPPC.[2] The mature peptide is one of the most hydrophobic proteins known, and it forms an amphipathic helix of the correct length to span a phospholipid bilayer.[33] The palmitates may interdigitate with an adjacent phospholipid monolayer or bilayer, resulting in membrane stacking. Surfactant protein C promotes film adsorption, and mixtures of SP-C and lipids can function effectively as a pulmonary surfactant.

Although highly conserved across species, SP-C deficiency in mice does not recapitulate SP-B deficiency.[36] Mice that lack SP-C process SP-B normally and survive without apparent lung disease. The surfactant from SP-C-deficient mice has normal surface properties, and surfactant metabolism is normal. However, in humans SP-C deficiency may result in a progressive deterioration of lung function in the early years of life. The spectrum of lung disease resulting from SP-C deficiency remains to be explored.

The effects of lung injury on SP-C levels have not been well studied. Until recently, there was no practical way to measure the amounts of active SP-C.[35] Messenger RNA of SP-C is decreased in experimental models by TNF-α and viral injuries.[37,38] Presumably, in vivo SP-B and SP-C interact to provide the biophysical properties to surfactant. A lung injury resulting in increased TNF-α expression that decreases both proteins likely will degrade surfactant function. These proteins also make surfactant less sensitive to inhibitors by plasma proteins.

The Collectins

Surfactant protein A

Surfactant protein A is primarily expressed in the lung and is assembled from 26-kD monomers; these are glycosylated and assembled to form a functional protein of about 650 kD comprising 6 tetramers to yield a bouquet-like structure.[39] This complex protein has a proline-rich collagen domain that allows tetramer formation and a C terminal carbohydrate recognition domain. This combination of collagen and carbohydrate domains also is present in mannose-binding protein and SP-D—the family of proteins called collectins. Expression of SP-A is detectable in nonmucus tracheal glands, bronchial glands, and a few cells in the developing airways in the second trimester human fetus.[40] By late gestation, and subsequently in the mature lung, SP-A is expressed predominantly in type II cells and Clara cells with some expression in tracheal glands. The protein appears in fetal lung fluid in parallel with the phospholipids during late gestation, but its metabolic pathways are distinct from the phospholipids. De novo synthesized SP-A is secreted constitutively and separately from the DPPC, SP-B, and SP-C that are packaged in lamellar bodies in both the late fetal and adult lung.[41,42] Once in the air space, SP-A associates with the surfactant lipids to form tubular myelin and to alter the structure of the loose lipid arrays. In vitro SP-A binds phospholipids and causes aggregation of lipid vesicles. Surfactant protein A is about 5% of surfactant by weight. It is cleared from the air spaces with a biologic half life similar to DPPC by macrophages and type II cells, and some of the SP-A appears to be recycled via lamellar bodies for resecretion.[43]

The important biologic activities of SP-A have become apparent from evaluations of mice that lack SP-A. These mice have normal lung function despite the lack of tubular myelin.[44] The biophysical properties of the surfactant are comparable to surfactant from mice that have SP-A, except at high dilution. Although SP-A-deficient mice have increased amounts of small aggregate surfactant (the biophysically inactive form) and the SP-A-deficient surfactant is more sensitive to inhibition by plasma, SP-A-deficient mice are not more susceptible to injury than are normal mice.[45,46] Mice that are SP-A deficient have normal amounts of the other surfactant components, and metabolism of those components is normal.[47] There are extensive in vitro results demonstrating that SP-A interacts with the type II cell to decrease surfactant secretion and increase surfactant uptake,[48,49] but these activities are not evident in SP-A-deficient mice.

Surfactant protein A functions primarily as an innate host defense molecule in the alveolus and airways.[50,51] Innate or nonimmune defenses against pathogen invasion include a multitude of factors such as lysozyme, the defensins, SP-A, and SP-D. The ability of SP-A to bind carbohydrates and to interact with immune cells in the lungs contributes to host defense. It binds endotoxin avidly, and it also binds a wide range of gram-positive and gram-negative organisms, and fungi (such as *Aspergillus fumigatus*), and other organisms such as mycobacteria and *Pneumocystis carinii.* Macrophages have receptors for SP-A, and SP-A promotes phagocytosis and killing of microorganisms by alveolar macrophages. Surfactant protein A also acts as an opsonin for the phagocytosis of viruses, such as herpes simplex, influenza A, and respiratory syncytial virus (RSV).

The interactions between SP-A and macrophages to promote pathogen clearance and killing have been established in the SP-A-deficient mouse. Mice that lack SP-A have less effective clearance and killing both of bacteria and of viruses, and the infections are more likely to become systemic (Figure 4–3).[52,53] The defect in host defenses can be corrected by treating SP-A-deficient mice with SP-A. Another component to the host defense role of SP-A is modulation of the inflammatory response to infection.[52,54] Production of NO by macrophages is increased by SP-A to promote pathogen killing. Surfactant protein A also downregulates the general inflammatory response of the lung that generates TNF-α and other proinflammatory cytokines, which decreases granulocyte recruitment and activation. Thus, SP-A promotes clearance of pathogens by resident macrophages while, at the same time, modulating a more generalized inflammatory response.

Two closely related genes express SP-A in man, but no genetically based deficiency state has been identified.[10] However, an acquired decrease in SP-A is probably common in patients with severe lung injury. Infants born with very low SP-A-to-DPPC ratios are at increased risk of dying or developing bronchopulmonary dysplasia (BPD).[55] Even if a low amount of SP-A is an indicator of severe lung immaturity, it is not clear whether it predicts functional abnormalities. Infants and ventilated preterm baboons with chronic lung disease have decreased amounts of SP-A relative to DPPC in airway samples.[16] Levels of SP-A are depressed in ARDS and in infants with RSV pneumonia.[16] Secondary bacterial pneumonias may occur in part because of the low levels of SP-A. There may be a therapeutic role for SP-A, because treatment of SP-A-deficient mice with SP-A restores the ability to clear and kill organisms.[53] Treatments with SP-A also might modulate the inflammatory response of the lung to minimize injury.

Surfactant protein D

Surfactant protein D has similarities in structure and function to SP-A, but distinct differences also are apparent.[56] The 43-kD monomer of SP-D assembles into a tetramer by the collagen domain, with subsequent aggregation of tetramers into a 560-kD protein that also exists in higher aggregate forms. The carbohydrate recognition domain binds endotoxin, gram-negative organisms, and a variety of other lung pathogens with a specificity that overlaps, but is distinct from, SP-A. Surfactant protein D binds PI in vitro, but the majority of SP-D is not associated

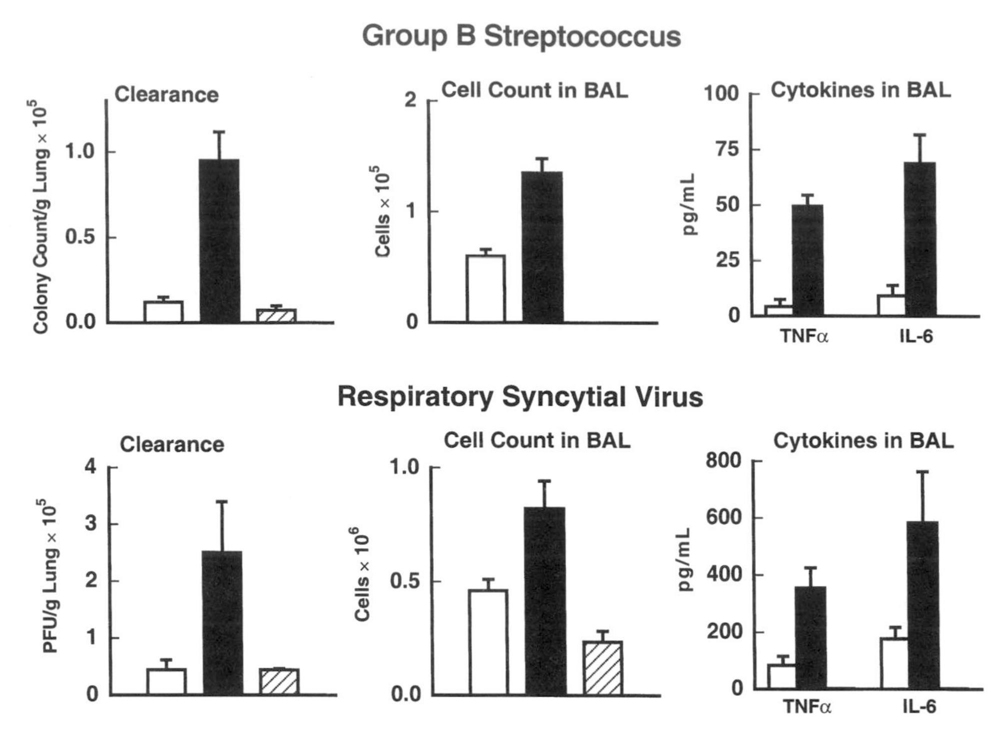

FIGURE 4–3. Effect of SP-A on infections caused by group B streptococcus and respiratory syncytial virus (RSV). Wild-type mice (□), mice that were SP-A deficient because of deletion of the SP-A gene (■), and SP-A-deficient mice given SP-A by tracheal injection (▨) were challenged with intratracheal injections of group B streptococci or RSV. Relative to the wild-type or SP-A-treated mice, the SP-A deficient mice had decreased clearances of both agents. Cell counts were higher in bronchoalveolar lavage (BAL) from SP-A-deficient mice, as were levels of the proinflammatory cytokines tumor necrosis factor (TNF-α) and interleukin (IL)-6. PFU = plaque forming unit. (Adapted from LeVine AM et al.[52,53])

with the surfactant lipids. The protein is present in alveolar lavage fluid at 10 to 33% of the level of SP-A. In contrast to SP-A, SP-D expression is widely distributed in epithelial surfaces in the body.[57] In the lung SP-D is expressed in type II cells, Clara cells, and other airway cells and glands. Expression of SP-D in the lung increases from late gestation, and achieves adult levels after term; glucocorticoids increase SP-D expression.

Surfactant protein D has all the characteristics of an innate host defense protein. It binds bacteria and fungi, and aggregates viruses, promoting opsonization and phagocytosis by macrophages.[58] It binds to macrophages by receptors yet to be characterized. This protein also may modulate the proinflammatory responses of leukocytes in the lung. There is not much information about how SP-D levels change with lung injury. In contrast to SP-A, SP-D increases with acute lung injury and following the intratracheal instillation of endotoxin. Mice that express interleukin (IL)-4 in Clara cells have an alveolar proteinosis phenotype and a 90-fold increase in SP-D.[59]

Mice that lack SP-D have increased tissue and alveolar pools of surfactant lipids without proportionate increases in the other surfactant proteins.[60,61] These mice develop emphysema after several months of age. Surfactant metabolism in SP-D deficiency is altered, although surfactant function is normal.[62] Mice that are SP-D deficient have a greater inflammatory response when given RSV.[63] The mechanisms by which SP-D deficiency alters surfactant metabolism and causes emphysema remain to be characterized. No SP-D deficiency has been identified in man, and its contribution to the pathogenesis of acute lung injury or secondary infections has not been defined.

Surfactant and Lung Development

Glucocorticoids

Glucocorticoids are generally considered the primary regulators of both normal lung maturation and induced lung maturation.[64] Glucocorticoids, acting through glucocorticoid receptors, modulate gene transcription and upregulate surfactant proteins. However, a number of clinical and experimental observations challenge a preeminent role of glucocorticoids in lung maturation. Human fetal lung explants at 15 to 20 weeks' gestation rapidly develop seemingly mature type II cells, surfactant proteins, and alveolar-like structures when grown in explant culture without hormones.[65,66] Therefore, the human fetal lung can differentiate at early gestational ages without cortisol. Infants born without hypothalamic and pituitary function also have mature lungs. Transgenic mice that are glucocorticoid-receptor deficient have lungs that are not structurally mature at term, but surfactant lipids and protein mRNAs are normal.[67,68] Newborn mice that are corticotropin-releasing hormone deficient

(CRH–/–) are normal if born to CRH+/– dams or to dams given corticosterone in their drinking water.[69] In contrast, CRH–/– mice born to CRH–/– dams die of respiratory failure at birth. These latter mice have lungs with essentially normal surfactant but poorly developed distal saccules. These results with transgenic mice models indicate that glucocorticoids are not necessary for normal development of the surfactant system. Very low levels of maternal-to-fetal transfer of corticosterone in CRH–/– fetal mice are sufficient to sustain normal anatomic development of the lung.[69]

The effectiveness of glucocorticoids to induce early lung maturation also is less compelling than is generally appreciated. Antenatal glucocorticoid treatments of women at risk of preterm delivery decrease the incidence of RDS by about 50% (Figure 4–4).[70] The converse is that glucocorticoids seem to have no benefit in about 50% of patients. Retrospective nonrandomized studies suggest that repetitive courses of antenatal glucocorticoids given at 7 to 10-day intervals do not consistently cause a further decrease in the risk of RDS.[71,72] The mechanism that has been proposed for the early lung maturation associated with stressed pregnancies has been elevation of fetal cortisol.[73,74] However, RDS is not decreased in infants born with fetal growth restriction, preeclampsia, or preterm prolonged rupture of membranes.[75–77] These clinical situations should cause sufficient fetal stress to increase fetal cortisol. Nevertheless, it is clear that early lung maturation is a real finding. Although the human fetal lung does not mature sufficiently to support normal lung function in the infant until about 36 weeks' gestation,[78] about 30% of preterm infants with birth weights less than 1 kg have minimal or no RDS.[79,80] The inducers of this early lung maturation are not known, and endogenous glucocorticoids may or may not participate in this early maturation in the human.

In animal models, antenatal glucocorticoids can augment surfactant pools and alter lung structure.[64] Maternal treatment of monkeys with glucocorticoids for 3 to 13 days at midgestation causes fetal lung maturation by thinning of the mesenchyme and by increase of lung gas volume after preterm delivery.[81,82] However, the process of alveolarization is disrupted, such that the lungs are simplified with fewer and larger alveoli if delivery occurs at term. Similar findings have been reported in postnatal newborn rats treated with glucocorticoids during the period of initiation of alveolarization.[83] Although mRNA for the SP-A, SP-B, and SP-C increases within 24 hours of glucocorticoid exposure of the sheep fetus, the mRNA levels return to baseline within several days.[84] The alveolar pool sizes of the surfactant phospholipids or the surfactant proteins do not increase consistently until about 7 days after glucocorticoid treatments. Repetitive glucocorticoid treatments at weekly intervals are required for substantial increases in surfactant pool

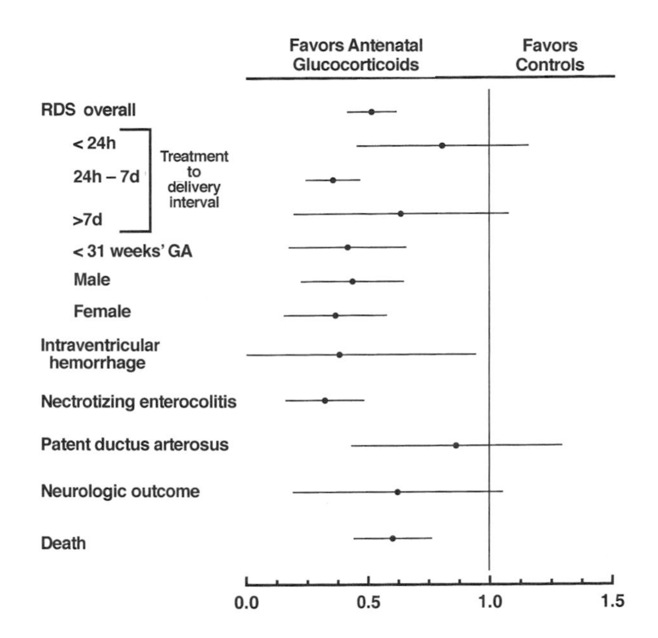

FIGURE 4–4. Meta-analysis of outcomes of antenatal glucocorticoid treatments for women at risk of preterm labor. Values are given as odds ratios (*solid dots*) and 95% confidence limits (*lines*). RDS = respiratory distress syndrome; GA = gestational age. (Adapted from Crowley P.[70])

sizes in the fetal sheep.[85] Fetal exposure to glucocorticoids seems to be more important for lung structural maturation than for the rapid stimulation of the surfactant system.

A single course of antenatal glucocorticoids is recommended for women in preterm labor who are at risk of preterm delivery before 34 weeks' gestational age.[86] There are no major contraindications to the treatments, and the benefits in terms of decreased RDS, decreased death, and decreased intraventricular hemorrhage are substantial.[70] The most effective treatment schedule appears to be betamethasone given as a 1-to-1 mixture of the acetate and phosphate salts at a dose of 12 mg by intramuscular injection, with the dose repeated 24 hours later if preterm delivery has not occurred. Dexamethasone may be less effective and result in more adverse outcomes.[87]

Repetitive courses of glucocorticoids

A meta-analysis of the clinical trials of antenatal glucocorticoid treatments evaluated the effect of treatment to delivery interval.[70] An interval from treatment to delivery of 24 hours was not beneficial (note: all deliveries that occurred at less than 24 hours were combined). In fetal sheep, 15 hours is sufficient to improve lung function, and 8 hours is sufficient to increase the blood pressure of the preterm newborn.[88] Therefore, maternal glucocorticoids should be given unless delivery is imminent. However, the clinical data suggest that the

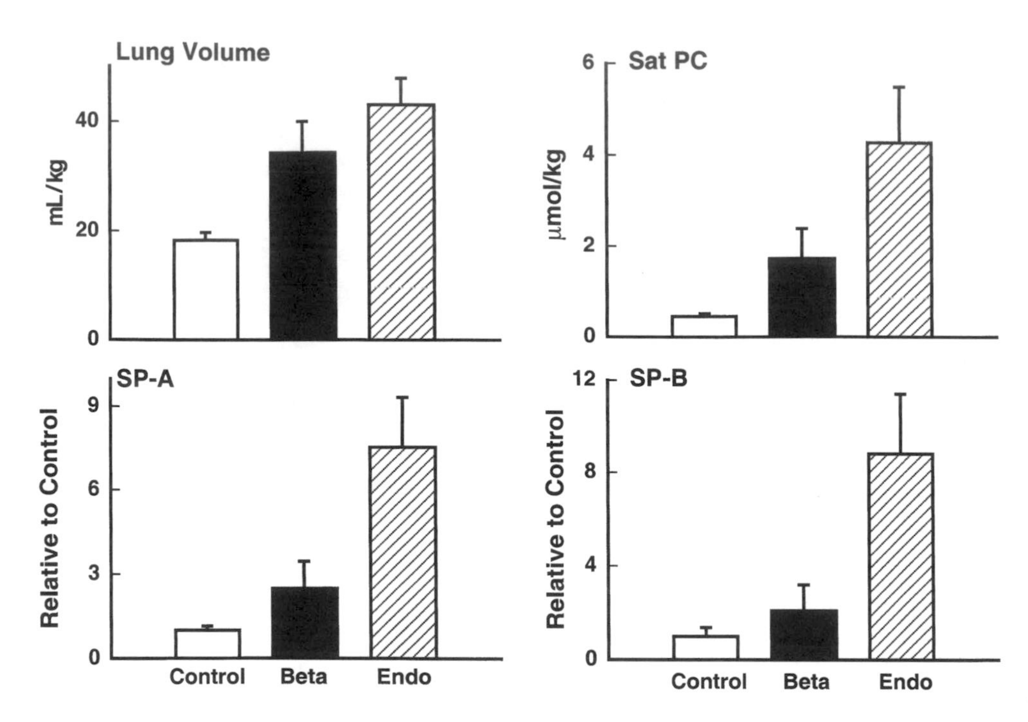

FIGURE 4–5. A comparison of lung maturational effects of maternal betamethasone or intra-amniotic endotoxin in preterm sheep. Seven days after maternal betamethasone or intra-amniotic endotoxin, lung gas volumes increased. The endotoxin stimulus increased the amount of saturated phosphatidylcholine (Sat PC), surfactant protein A (SP-A), and SP-B in alveolar washes more than did betamethasone. Endotoxin did not increase fetal cortisol levels. (Adapted from Jobe AH et al.[105])

beneficial glucocorticoid effect may be lost after 7 to 10 days if delivery does not occur.[70] Consequently, repetitive courses of antenatal glucocorticoids are being given to try to improve neonatal outcomes. In fetal mice, rats, and sheep, repetitive doses of maternal glucocorticoids increased indicators of surfactant maturation more than did single doses. However, multiple doses decreased fetal weights more than did single courses, and also increased the adrenal suppression.[89–91] There are no randomized controlled trials of repetitive courses of antenatal glucocorticoids in humans, although several trials are in progress. Retrospective analyses suggest both risk and benefit of repetitive treatment strategies. Of concern, decreased fetal weights and head circumferences, and increased death were reported without improved respiratory outcomes after repetitive courses of antenatal glucocorticoids.[71]

Thyrotropin Releasing Hormone and Other Agents

Glucocorticoids can interact synergistically with other factors such as β-agonists, thyroid hormones, and prolactin to promote early lung maturation in fetal lambs.[87,92] Liggins et al[93] found virtually no effect of cortisol or thyrotropin releasing hormone (TRH) infusions on lung gas volumes or surfactant lipids in lambs delivered prematurely, but the simultaneous infusion of cortisol and TRH was effective. Although the initial clinical trials to evaluate the benefit of adding TRH to glucocorticoid treatments of women at risk for preterm delivery were positive,[94] subsequent multicenter trials have shown no benefit and perhaps some risk.[95,96]

Inflammatory Modulation of Lung Maturation

A perplexing clinical scenario that frequently occurs is the very preterm infant without significant RDS that then progresses to BPD over several weeks. The BPD develops without initial exposure to much supplemental oxygen or mechanical ventilation.[79] Preterm infants with postnatal pneumonia or sepsis are at increased risk of BPD,[97] and infants destined to develop BPD have elevated levels of proinflammatory cytokines and inflammatory cells in airway samples relative to comparably ventilated infants that do not progress to BPD.[98] Infants born before about 30 weeks' gestation are at high risk of exposure in utero to chronic amnionitis and commensal organisms such as *Ureaplasma urealyticum*.[99] The presence of inflammatory indicators such as TNF-α, IL-1b, IL-6, and transforming growth factor α in amniotic fluid prior to preterm delivery is a risk factor for the subsequent development of BPD.[100,101] Therefore, antenatal or postnatal inflammatory stimuli are associated with lung injury in the preterm. The contraintuitive association is that very preterm infants exposed to histologic chorioamnionitis have a lower incidence of RDS but a higher incidence of BPD than infants not exposed to chorioamnionitis before birth.[102]

The intriguing possibility to explain BPD in infants without RDS is that proinflammatory stimuli can simultaneously promote both early lung maturation as well as lung injury.[103] Bry et al[104] reported that the proinflammatory cytokine IL-1α can increase lung compliance and SP-A and SP-B mRNA levels when given by intra-amniotic injection to preterm rabbits. Intra-amniotic endotoxin–induced chorioamnionitis improved lung function in lambs. The endotoxin response increased surfactant components after preterm birth without an increase in fetal plasma cortisol (Figure 4–5).[105] The endotoxin-mediated improvement in lung function after preterm delivery was more striking than the early maturation induced with maternal glucocorticoids. These experiments suggest that potent promotors of lung maturation other than glucocorticoids remain to be identified.

Treatment with Surfactant

In the postnatal mature lung, acute lung injuries such as ARDS and RSV pneumonia decrease surfactant proteins.[22] Cystic fibrosis does not cause large changes in surfactant.[106] There have been no pharmacologic therapies other than surfactant treatment developed to increase surfactant pools. High-dose glucocorticoids increase surfactant lipid and SP-A pools in the adult rat lung,[107] but effects of glucocorticoids on surfactant in the adult human lung have not been evaluated.

Surfactant treatment of infants with RDS has been strikingly successful and has changed the respiratory care of these infants.[108] Surfactant treatments of term infants with lung injury resulting from meconium aspiration and pneumonia has improved oxygenation and outcomes in several small trials.[109,110] Surfactant treatments also can decrease the need for extracorporeal membrane oxygenation for infants with severe respiratory failure.[111] These successes suggest that surfactant should be beneficial for older infants and children with acute lung injury associated with edema, inflammation, and decreased compliance. Several small trials have demonstrated some benefit, but the results have not been compelling to date.[112] Similarly, surfactant treatments for adults with ARDS have shown no benefit in one large trial,[113] striking improvements in oxygenation in a small trial,[114] and indications of decreased death in another small trial.[115] Treatment of acute respiratory failure in the mature lung differs from treatment of the preterm lung in a number of ways.[116] The preterm lung generally is not injured and has a primary surfactant deficiency, which surfactant treatment can minimize. In contrast in the mature lung severe injury causes respiratory failure, and surfactant tends to be less effective in animal models after injury has occurred. There are also uncertainties about how best to treat the mature lung, and strategies have ranged from aerosolization of surfactant, to lavage with dilute surfactant suspensions and directed bronchial instillation. The efficacy of surfactant treatments for children with ARDS remains to be demonstrated.

Acknowledgment

This work was supported in part by grants HL61646 and HD-12714.

References

1. Hawgood S, Derrick M, Poulain F. Structure and properties of surfactant protein B. Biochim Biophys Acta 1998; 1408:150–60.
2. Weaver TE. Synthesis, processing and secretion of surfactant proteins B and C. Biochim Biophys Acta 1998;1408: 173–9.
3. Mason RJ, Voelker DR. Regulatory mechanisms of surfactant secretion. Biochim Biophys Acta 1998;1408:226–40.
4. Goerke J. Pulmonary surfactant: functions and molecular composition. Biochim Biophys Acta 1998;1408:79–89.
5. Rebello CM, Jobe AH, Eisele JW, Ikegami M. Alveolar and tissue surfactant pool sizes in humans. Am J Respir Crit Care Med 1996;154:625–8.
6. Schurch S, Green FHY, Bachofen H. Formation and structure of surface films: captive bubble surfactometry. Biochim Biophys Acta 1998;1408:180–202.
7. Savov J, Silbajoris R, Young SL. Mechanical ventilation of rat lung: effect on surfactant forms. Am J Physiol 1999; 277:L320–6.
8. Rider ED, Ikegami M, Jobe AH. Localization of alveolar surfactant clearance in rabbit lung cells. Am J Physiol 1992;263:L201–9.
9. Jacobs HC, Ikegami M, Jobe AH, et al. Reutilization of surfactant phosphatidylcholine in adult rabbits. Biochim Biophys Acta 1985;837:77–84.
10. Jobe AH, Rider ED. Catabolism and recycling of surfactant. In: Robertson B, van Golde LMG, Batenburg JJ, eds. Pulmonary surfactant: from molecular biology to clinical practice. Amsterdam: Elsevier Publishing, 1992:313–37.
11. Jobe A, Ikegami M. Surfactant for the treatment of respiratory distress syndrome. Am Rev Respir Dis 1987; 136:1256–75.
12. Ikegami M, Jobe AH. Surfactant metabolism. In: Creasy RK, Warshaw JB, eds. Seminars in perinatology. Philadelphia: WB Saunders; 1993:223–40.
13. Ueda T, Ikegami M, Jobe AH. Developmental changes of sheep surfactant: in vivo function and in vitro subtype conversion. J Appl Physiol 1994;76:2701–6.
14. Bunt JE, Zimmerman LJ, Wattimena D, et al. Endogenous surfactant turnover in preterm infants measured with stable isotope. Am J Respir Crit Care Med 1998; 157:810–4.
15. Seidner SR, Jobe AH, Coalson JJ, Ikegami M. Abnormal surfactant metabolism and function in preterm ventilated baboons. Am J Respir Crit Care Med 1998;158:1982–9.
16. Awasthi S, Coalson JJ, Crouch E, et al. Surfactant proteins A and D in premature baboons with chronic lung injury. Evidence for an inhibition of secretion. Am J Respir Crit Care Med 1999;160:942–9.

17. Veldhuizen R, Nag K, Orgeig S, Possmayer F. The role of lipids in pulmonary surfactant. Biochim Biophys Acta 1998;1408:90–108.
18. Clements JA. Kinetics of surface active material in fetal lung. In: Hodson WA, ed. Development of the lung. New York: Marcel Dekker, Inc., 1977.
19. Jobe AH. Surfactant-edema interactions. In: Weir EK, et al, eds. The pathogenesis and treatment of pulmonary edema. Armonk (NY): Futura Publishing Company, Inc., 1998.
20. Hallman M, Kulovich M, Kirkpatrick E, et al. Phosphatidylinositol and phosphatidylglycerol in amniotic fluid: indices of lung maturity. Am J Obstet Gynecol 1976; 125:613–7.
21. Obladen M. Alterations in surfactant composition. In: Merritt TA, Northway WH, Boynton BR, eds. Contemporary issues in fetal and neonatal medicine. Boston: Blackwell Scientific Publications, 1988.
22. Lewis JF, Jobe AH. Surfactant and the adult respiratory distress syndrome. Am Rev Respir Dis 1993;147:218–33.
23. Rider ED, Ikegami M, Whitsett JA, et al. Treatment responses to surfactants containing natural surfactant proteins in preterm rabbits. Am Rev Respir Dis 1993; 147:669–76.
24. Suzuki Y, Fujita Y, Kogishi K. Reconstitution of tubular myelin from synthetic lipids and proteins associated with pig pulmonary surfactant. Am Rev Respir Dis 1989;140:75–81.
25. Davis AJ, Jobe AH, Häfner D, Ikegami M. Lung function in premature lambs and rabbits treated with a recombinant SP-C surfactant. Am J Respir Crit Care Med 1998; 157:553–9.
26. Nogee LM. Genetics of the hydrophobic surfactant proteins. Biochim Biophys Acta 1998;1408:323–33.
27. Clark JC, Wert SE, Bachurski CJ, et al. Targeted disruption of the surfactant protein B gene disrupts surfactant homeostasis, causing respiratory failure in newborn mice. Proc Natl Acad Sci U S A 1995;92:7794–8.
28. Beers MF, Hamvas A, Moxley MA, et al. Pulmonary surfactant metabolism in infants lacking surfactant protein B. Am J Respir Cell Mol Biol 2000;22:380–91.
29. Cole FS, Hamvas A, Rubinstein P, et al. Population-based estimates of surfactant protein B deficiency. Pediatrics 2000;105:538–41.
30. Nogee LM, Wert SE, Profitt SA, et al. Allelic heterogeneity in hereditary SP-B deficiency. Am J Respir Crit Care Med 2000;161:973–81.
31. Gregory TJ, Longmore WJ, Moxley MA, et al. Surfactant chemical composition and biophysical activity in acute respiratory distress syndrome. J Clin Invest 1991; 188:1976–81.
32. Pryhuber GS, Bachurski C, Hirsch R, et al. Tumor necrosis factor-alpha decreases surfactant protein B mRNA in murine lung. Am J Physiol 1996;270:L714–21.
33. Johansson J. Structure and properties of surfactant protein C. Biochim Biophys Acta 1998;1408:161–72.
34. Wert SE, Glasser SW, Korfhagen TR, Whitsett JA. Transcriptional elements from the human SP-C gene direct expression in the primordial respiratory epithelium of transgenic mice. Dev Biol 1993;156:426–43.
35. Ross GF, Ikegami M, Steinhilber W, Jobe AH. Surfactant protein C (SP-C) levels in fetal and ventilated preterm rabbit lungs. Am J Physiol 1999;277:L1104–8.
36. Glasser SW, Burhans MS, Korfhagen TR, et al. Generation of an SP-C deficient mouse by targeted gene inactivation. Am J Respir Crit Care Med 2000;161:A43.
37. Zsengeller Z, Wert SE, Bachurski CJ, et al. Recombinant adenoviral vector disrupts surfactant homeostasis in mouse lung. Hum Gene Ther 1997;8:1331–44.
38. Bachurski CJ, Pryhuber GS, Glasser SW, et al. Tumor necrosis factor-alpha inhibits surfactant protein C gene transcription. J Biol Chem 1995;270:19402–7.
39. McCormack FX. Structure, processing and properties of surfactant protein A. Biochim Biophys Acta 1998; 1408:109–31.
40. Mendelson CR, Gao E, Li J, et al. Regulation of expression of surfactant protein-A. Biochim Biophys Acta 1998; 1408:132–49.
41. Ikegami M, Lewis JF, Tabor B, et al. Surfactant protein-A metabolism in preterm ventilated lambs. Am J Physiol 1992;262:L765–72.
42. Ikegami M, Ueda T, Purtell J, et al. Surfactant protein A labeling kinetics in newborn and adult rabbits. Am J Respir Cell Mol Biol 1994;10:413–8.
43. Ueda T, Ikegami M, Jobe AH. Clearance of surfactant protein A from rabbit lungs. Am J Respir Cell Mol Biol 1995;12:89–94.
44. Korfhagen TR, Bruno MD, Ross GF, et al. Altered surfactant function and structure in SP-A gene targeted mice. Proc Natl Acad Sci U S A 1996;93:9594–9.
45. Ikegami M, Korfhagen TR, Whitsett JA, et al. Characteristics of surfactant from SP-A deficient mice. Am J Physiol 1998;275:L247–58.
46. Ikegami M, Jobe AH, Whitsett J, Korfhagen T. Tolerance of SP-A deficient mice to hyperoxia or exercise. J Appl Physiol. [In press 2000]
47. Ikegami M, Korfhagen TR, Bruno MD, et al. Surfactant metabolism in surfactant protein A–deficient mice. Am J Physiol 1997;272:L479–85.
48. Dobbs LG, Wright JR, Hawgood S, et al. Pulmonary surfactant and its components inhibit secretion of phosphatidylcholine from cultured rat alveolar Type II cells. Proc Natl Acad Sci U S A 1987;84:1010–4.
49. Rice WR, Ross GF, Singleton FM, et al. Surfactant-associated protein inhibits phospholipid secretion from Type II cells. J Appl Physiol 1987;63:692–8.
50. Wright JR. Immunomodulatory functions of surfactant. Physiol Rev 1997;77:931–62.
51. Haagsman HP. Interactions of surfactant protein A with pathogens. Biochim Biophys Acta 1998;1408:264–77.
52. LeVine AM, Kurak KE, Wright JR, et al. Surfactant protein-A (SP-A) binds group B streptococcus enhancing phagocytosis and clearance from lungs of surfactant protein-A deficient mice. Am J Respir Mol Cell Biol 1999;20:279–86.
53. LeVine AM, Gwozdz J, Stark J, et al. Surfactant protein-A enhances respiratory syncytial virus clearance in vivo. J Clin Invest 1999;103:1015–21.
54. Harrod KS, Trapnell BC, Otake K, et al. SP-A enhances viral clearance and inhibits inflammation after pulmonary adenoviral infection. Am J Physiol 1999;277:L580–8.

55. Hallman M, Merritt TA, Akino T, Bry K. Surfactant protein-A, phosphatidylcholine, and surfactant inhibitors in epithelial lining fluid—correlation with surface activity, severity of respiratory distress syndrome, and outcome in small premature infants. Am Rev Respir Dis 1991; 144:1376–84.
56. Crouch EC. Collectins and pulmonary host defense. Am J Respir Cell Mol Biol 1998;19:177–201.
57. Hull W, Stahlman M, Gray MP, et al. Immunolocalization of SP-D in human secretory tissues. Am J Respir Crit Care Med 2000;161:A42.
58. Crouch EC. Structure, biologic properties, and expression of surfactant protein D (SP-D). Biochim Biophys Acta 1998;1408:278–89.
59. Ikegami M, Chroneos Z, Whitsett JA, Jobe AH. Interleukin-4 increases surfactant and regulates metabolism in vivo. Am J Physiol 2000;278:L75–80.
60. Korfhagen TR, Sheftelyevich V, Burhans MS, et al. Surfactant protein-D regulates surfactant phospholipid homeostasis in vivo. J Biol Chem 1998;43:28438–43.
61. Botas C, Poulain F, Akiyama J, et al. Altered surfactant homeostasis and alveolar type II cell morphology in mice lacking surfactant protein D. Proc Natl Acad Sci U S A 1998;95:11869–74.
62. Wert SE, Yoshida M, LeVine AM, et al. Increased metalloproteinase activity, oxidant production, and emphysema in surfactant protein D gene-inactivated mice. Proc Natl Acad Sci U S A 2000;97:5972–7.
63. LeVine AM, Gwozdz J, Fisher J, et al. Surfactant protein D modulates lung inflammation with respiratory syncytial virus infection in vivo. Am J Respir Crit Care Med 2000; 161:A515.
64. Ballard PL. Hormones and lung maturation. Monographs on endocrinology. New York: Springer-Verlag, 1986.
65. Liley HG, White RT, Benson BJ, Ballard PL. Glucocorticoids both stimulate and inhibit production of pulmonary surfactant protein A in fetal human lung. Proc Natl Acad Sci U S A 1988;85:9096–100.
66. Gonzales LW, Ballard PL, Ertsey R, Williams MC. Glucocorticoids and thyroid hormones stimulate biochemical and morphological differentiation of human fetal lung in organ culture. J Clin Endocrinol Metab 1986;62:678–91.
67. Reichardt HM, Kaestner KH, Tuckermann J, et al. DNA binding of the glucocorticoid receptor is not essential for survival. Cell 1998;93:531–41.
68. Cole TJ, Blendy JA, Monaghan AP, et al. Targeted disruption of the glucocorticoid receptor gene blocks adrenergic chromaffin cell development and severely retards lung maturation. Gene Dev 1995;9:1608–21.
69. Muglia LJ, Bae DS, Brown TT, et al. Proliferation and differentiation defects during lung development in corticotropin-releasing hormone-deficient mice. Am J Respir Cell Mol Biol 1999;20:181–8.
70. Crowley P. Antenatal corticosteroid therapy: a meta-analysis of the randomized trials—1972–1994. Am J Obstet Gynecol 1995;173:322–35.
71. French NP, Hagan R, Evans SF, et al. Repeated antenatal corticosteroids: size at birth and subsequent development. Am J Obstet Gynecol 1999;180:114–21.
72. Banks BA, Cnaan A, Morgan MA, et al. Multiple courses of antenatal corticosteroids and outcome of premature neonates. Am J Obstet Gynecol 1999;181:709–17.
73. Watterberg KL, Scott SM, Naeye RL. Chorioamnionitis, cortisol, and acute lung disease in very low birth weight infants. Pediatrics 1997;99:E6.
74. Gagnon R, Langridge J, Inchley K, et al. Changes in surfactant-associated protein mRNA profile in growth-restricted fetal sheep. Am J Physiol 1999;276:L459–65.
75. Tyson JE, Kennedy K, Broyles S, Rosenfeld CR. The small for gestational age infant: accelerated or delayed pulmonary maturation? Increased or decreased survival? Pediatrics 1995;95:534–8.
76. Friedman SA, Schiff E, Kao L, Sibai BM. Neonatal outcome after preterm delivery for preeclampsia. Am J Obstet Gynecol 1995;172:1785–92.
77. Hallak M, Bottoms SF. Accelerated pulmonary maturation from preterm premature rupture of membranes: a myth. Am J Obstet Gynecol 1993;169:1045–9.
78. Chasen ST, Madden A, Chervenak FA. Cesarean delivery of twins and neonatal respiratory disorders. Am J Obstet Gynecol 1999;181:1052–6.
79. Bancalari E, Gonzalez A. Clinical course and lung function abnormalities during development of neonatal chronic lung disease. In: Bland RD, Coalson JJ, eds. Chronic lung disease in early infancy. New York: Marcel Dekker, Inc., 2000:41–64.
80. Stevenson DK, Wright LL, Lemons JA, et al. Very low birth weight outcomes of the National Institute of Child Health and Human Development Neonatal Research Network, January 1993 through December 1994. Am J Obstet Gynecol 1998;179:1632–9.
81. Bunton TE, Plopper CG. Triamcinolone-induced structural alterations in the development of the lung of the fetal rhesus macaque. Am J Obstet Gynecol 1984;148: 203–15.
82. Johnson JWC, Mitzner W, Beck JC, et al. Long-term effects of betamethasone on fetal development. Am J Obstet Gynecol 1981;141:1053–61.
83. Massaro GD, Massaro D. Formation of pulmonary alveoli and gas-exchange surface area: quantitation and regulation. Annu Rev Physiol 1996;58:73–92.
84. Tan RC, Ikegami M, Jobe AH, et al. Developmental and glucocorticoid regulation of surfactant protein mRNAs in preterm lambs. Am J Physiol 1999;277:L1142–8.
85. Ballard PL, Ning Y, Polk D, et al. Glucocorticoid regulation of surfactant components in immature lambs. Am J Physiol 1997;273:L1048–57.
86. National Institutes of Health. Consensus development panel on the effect of corticosteroids for fetal maturation on perinatal outcomes. Effect of corticosteroids for fetal maturation on perinatal outcomes. JAMA 1995; 273:413–8.
87. Ballard PL, Ballard RA. Scientific basis and therapeutic regimens for use of antenatal glucocorticoids. Am J Obstet Gynecol 1995;173:254–62.
88. Ikegami M, Polk D, Jobe A. Minimum interval from fetal betamethasone treatment to postnatal lung responses in preterm lambs. Am J Obstet Gynecol 1996;174: 1408–13.

89. Stewart JD, Sienko AE, Gonzalez CL, et al. Placebo-controlled comparison between a single dose and a multidose of betamethasone in accelerating lung maturation of mice offspring. Am J Obstet Gynecol 1998; 179:1241–7.
90. Pratt L, Magness RR, Phernetton T, et al. Repeated use of betamethasone in rabbits: effects of treatment variation on adrenal suppression, pulmonary maturation, and pregnancy outcome. Am J Obstet Gynecol 1999; 180:995–1005.
91. Jobe AH, Newnham J, Willet K, et al. Fetal versus maternal and gestational age effects of repetitive antenatal glucocorticoids. Pediatrics 1998;102:1116–25.
92. Schellenberg JC, Liggins GC, Manzai M, et al. Synergistic hormonal effects on lung maturation in fetal sheep. J Appl Physiol 1988;65:94–100.
93. Liggins GC, Schellenberg JC, Manzai M, et al. Synergism of cortisol and thyrotropin-releasing hormone in lung maturation in fetal sheep. J Appl Physiol 1988;65:1880–4.
94. Moya FR, Gross I. Combined hormonal therapy for the prevention of respiratory distress syndrome and its consequences. Semin Perinatol 1993;17:267–74.
95. Ballard RA, Ballard PL, Cnaan A, et al. Antenatal thyrotropin-releasing hormone to prevent lung disease in preterm infants. North American Thyrotropin-Releasing Hormone Study Group. N Engl J Med 1998;338:493–8.
96. ACTOBAT. Australian collaborative trial of antenatal thyrotropin-releasing hormone (ACTOBAT) for prevention of neonatal respiratory disease. Lancet 1995; 345:877–82.
97. Palta M, Sadek M, Barnet JH, et al. Evaluation of criteria for chronic lung disease in surviving very low birth weight infants. J Pediatr 1998;132:57–63.
98. Groneck P, Speer CP. Inflammatory mediators and bronchopulmonary dysplasia. Arch Dis Child 1995;73:F1–3.
99. Romero R, Mazor K, Wu Y, et al. Infection in the pathogenesis of preterm labor. Semin Perinatol 1988;12:262–79.
100. Hitti J, Krohn MA, Patton DL, et al. Amniotic fluid tumor necrosis factor-alpha and the risk of respiratory distress syndrome among preterm infants. Am J Obstet Gynecol 1997;177:50–6.
101. Yoon BH, Romero R, Jun JK, et al. Amniotic fluid cytokines (interleukin-6, tumor necrosis factor-alpha, interleukin-1 beta, and interleukin-8) and the risk for the development of bronchopulmonary dysplasia. Am J Obstet Gynecol 1997;177:825–30.
102. Watterberg KL, Demers LM, Scott SM, Murphy S. Chorioamnionitis and early lung inflammation in infants in whom bronchopulmonary dysplasia develops. Pediatrics 1996;97:210–5.
103. Jobe AH. The new BPD: an arrest of lung development. Pediatr Res 1999;46:641–3.
104. Bry K, Lappalainen U, Hallman M. Intraamniotic interleukin-1 accelerates surfactant protein synthesis in fetal rabbits and improves lung stability after premature birth. J Clin Invest 1997;99:2992–9.
105. Jobe AH, Newnham JP, Willet KE, et al. Effects of antenatal endotoxin and glucocorticoids on the lungs of preterm lambs. Am J Obstet Gynecol 2000;182:401–8.
106. Hull J, South M, Phelan P, Grimwood K. Surfactant composition in infants and young children with cystic fibrosis. Am J Respir Crit Care Med 1997;156:161–5.
107. Young SL, Ho YS, Silbajoris RA. Surfactant apoprotein in adult rat lung compartments is increased by dexamethasone. Am J Physiol 1991;260:L161–7.
108. Jobe AH. Pulmonary surfactant therapy. N Engl J Med 1993;328:861–8.
109. Auten RL, Notter RH, Kendig JW, et al. Surfactant treatment of full-term newborns with respiratory failure. Pediatrics 1991;87:101–7.
110. Findlay RD, Taeusch WH, Walther FJ. Surfactant replacement therapy for meconium aspiration syndrome. Pediatrics 1996;97:48–52.
111. Lotze A, Mitchell BR, Bulas DI, et al. Multicenter study of surfactant (beractant) use in the treatment of term infants with severe respiratory failure. Survanta in Term Infants Study Group. J Pediatr 1998;132:40–7.
112. Tibby SM, Hatherill M, Wright SM, et al. Exogenous surfactant supplementation in infants with respiratory syncytial virus bronchiolitis. Am J Respir Crit Care Med 2000;162(4 Pt 1):1251–6.
113. Anzueto A, Baughman R, Guntupalli R, et al. Aerosolized surfactant in adults with sepsis-induced ARDS. N Engl J Med 1996;334:1417–21.
114. Walmrath D, Gunter A, Ghofrani HA, et al. Bronchoscopic surfactant administration in patients with severe ARDS and sepsis. Am J Respir Crit Care Med 1996; 154:57–62.
115. Gregory TJ, Steinberg KP, Spragg R, et al. Bovine surfactant therapy for patients with acute respiratory distress syndrome. Am J Respir Crit Care Med 1997;155:1309–15.
116. Jobe AH, Ikegami M. Surfactant and acute lung injury. Proc Assoc Am Physicians 1998;110:489–95.

SECTION II
STRUCTURE-FUNCTION RELATIONS OF THE RESPIRATORY SYSTEM DURING DEVELOPMENT

CHAPTER 5

MECHANISMS OF LUNG VASCULAR DEVELOPMENT

SUSAN SCHACHTNER, MD, DARREN TAICHMAN, MD, PHD,
H. SCOTT BALDWIN, MD

Over the last several years significant advances have been made in uncovering critical mechanisms of vascular development in the embryo. However, study of the pulmonary vasculature has been surprisingly limited. The establishment of a dual blood supply (pulmonary and bronchial), considerable vascular development after birth, and an apparent dependence on airway formation as well as blood flow, all make pulmonary vascular ontogeny an extremely challenging field of investigation. The purpose of this chapter is to briefly review what is known about molecular regulation of vascular ontogeny, with a specific focus on regulation of pulmonary vascular growth.

Vessel Formation: Angiogenesis and Vasculogenesis

The establishment of the cardiovascular system represents an early critical event essential for normal embryonic development.[1-3] Two different processes are thought to be involved in embryonic and extraembryonic blood vessel formation: *angiogenesis*, the budding and branching of vessels from pre-existing vessels, and *vasculogenesis*, the de novo differentiation of endothelial cells from mesoderm and organization of endothelial progenitors into a primitive vascular plexus (Figure 5–1). This plexus then expands through sprouting angiogenesis, intussusceptive growth, and intercalation of new endothelial cells. Finally, this vascular plexus is remodeled by pruning, fusion, and regression of pre-existing vessels into a vascular tree composed of arteries, capillaries, and veins.[4] Formation of the yolk sac circulation, differentiation of the endocardium of the heart, and development of larger vascular networks occur by vasculogenesis, while other organs, such as the brain and kidney, appear to be vascularized primarily by angiogenesis. While angiogenesis can occur in both the embryo and the adult (eg, wound healing, tumor neovascularization), it was initially believed that vasculogenesis was restricted to embryonic development. However, recent identification of endothelial progenitor cells isolated from circulating blood and bone marrow[5,6] has raised speculation that vasculogenesis also might occur in postnatal neovascularization.[7]

Pulmonary Vascular Development

Lung development traditionally has been divided into four or five distinct, but overlapping, stages based primarily on epithelial processes, as shown in Figure 5–2[8] and

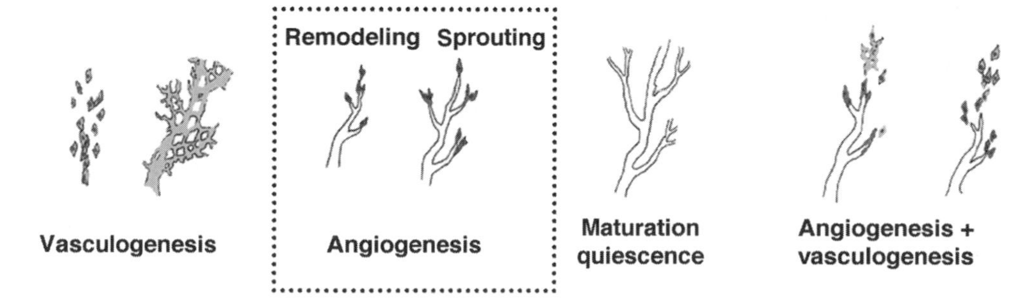

FIGURE 5–1. Mechanisms of vascular development. Vessels form by vasculogenesis, angiogenesis, or a combination of the two mechanisms. The primitive structure can be remodeled to form the mature structure.

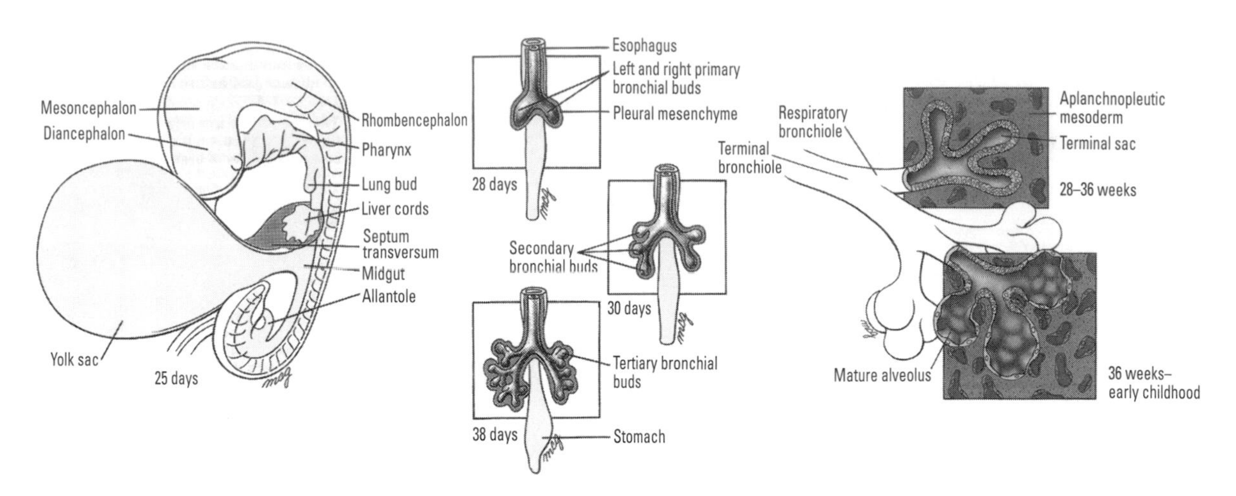

FIGURE 5–2. Summary of in utero pulmonary development. The formation of the lung from the foregut endoderm extending into and being surrounded by the splanchnopleuric mesoderm is shown. (Adapted from Larsen WJ.[8])

Table 5–1. The embryonic stage, or lung bud stage, (embryonic days [E] 9.5 to 14.2 in the mouse) occurs as the foregut endoderm pushes out into, and becomes surrounded by, the splanchnic mesoderm. The pseudoglandular stage (E14.2 to 16.6) has been characterized by rapid and extensive epithelial branching. The primary phase of vessel formation has been described as occurring during the canalicular stage (E16 to 17.5), as vascular structures extend more peripherally following the airway branches that have already formed. Two maturation stages, the saccular (or newborn) stage and the alveolar stage (neonatal or postconception (pc) days 5 to 30) also have been described. In the latter stage thick-walled saccules that are capable of respiratory function eventually become thin and form the delicate septa of mature alveoli.[9,10]

While branching morphogenesis and epithelial development have been the subject of intense investigation,[11,12] the number of studies on mechanisms regulating pulmonary vascular ontogeny have been surprisingly limited. Current information is primarily descriptive in nature. The lung may be unique in its process of vascularization, with angiogenesis and vasculogenesis occurring simultaneously.[13] Early pulmonary development represents the paradigm of de novo regulation of endothelial differentiation from mesodermal cells by the subjacent endoderm,

TABLE 5–1. Stages of Human and Mouse Pulmonary Development

Stage	Mouse	Human
Embryonic	E9–14.2	3–7 wk
Pseudoglandular	E14.2–16.6	5–17 wk
Canalicular	E16–17.5	16–26 wk
Saccular	E17.5–5d pc	24–38 wk
Alveolor	5–30 pc	36 wk–1 or 2 yr

E = embryonic day; pc = post conception.
Reprinted with permission from Schachtner SK, Wang Y, Baldwin HS. Qualitative and quantitative analysis of embryonic pulmonary vessel formation. Am J Respir Cell Mol Biol 2000;22:157–65.

that is, vasculogenesis.[14] Simultaneous differentiation of a primary ventral pulmonary vascular plexus in the mesoderm surrounding the protruding endoderm was initially described by Chang and has been confirmed subsequently by recent studies using contemporary markers of endothelial differentiation.[15–18] deMello and colleagues used a combination of light, transmission and scanning electron microscopy, barium-gelatin angiograms, and Mercox vascular casts to elegantly define vessels formed by central sprouting angiogenesis that subsequently communicate with peripheral vessels developed by vasculogenesis in the lung.[19] Smith et al have used a novel technique of micromagnetic resonance imaging to define the formation of the pulmonary arterial tree in the mouse embryo.[20] While significant controversy still exists about the exact mechanism by which pulmonary arterial and venous connections are made to the developing embryonic circulation, the importance of initial endothelial differentiation and subsequent angiogenic remodeling has clearly been established.[1]

Vascular Cytokines and Receptors

Vascular development is marked by the carefully timed expression of numerous growth factors and endothelial specific receptors.[2,3,21–24] Members of the vascular endothelial, platelet derived, basic, and transforming growth factor families are produced by various cell types and influence endothelial cell proliferation, migration, and function. Several groups of receptors on endothelial cells mediate signals from these growth factors and other molecules. The importance of the carefully controlled expression of each of these factors is emphasized by the embryonic lethality seen in recombinant animals lacking gene function (Figure 5–3). Such knockout animals have identified distinct roles and periods of action for these factors in modulating vascular development. For example, the loss of

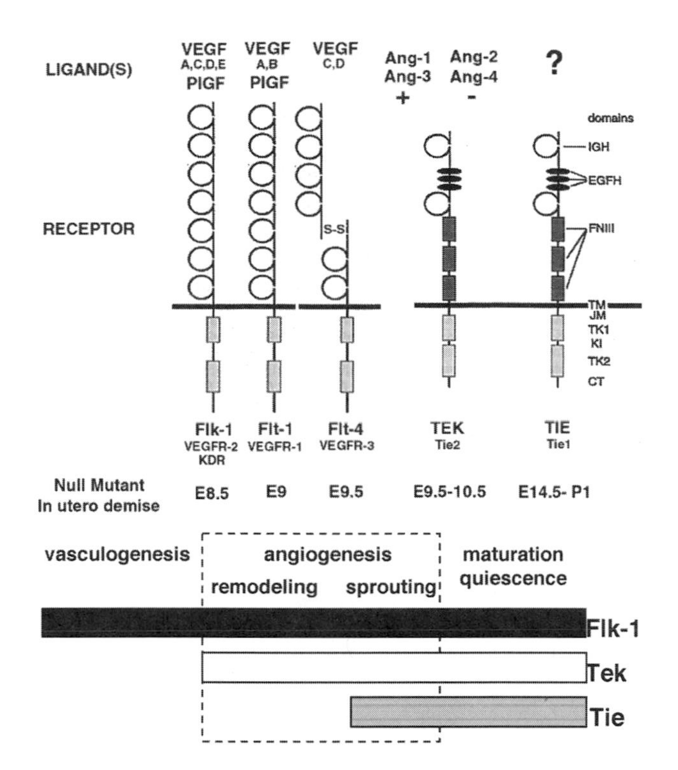

FIGURE 5–3. Schematic of structure for several vascular cytokine receptors, their ligands, stage of embryonic demise in null mutants, and role in vessel development. VEGFR = vascular endothelial growth factor receptor; PlGF = placental growth factor; E = embryonic day; Ang = angiopoietin.

vascular endothelial growth factor (*VEGF*) signaling (through deletion of the growth factor itself or its endothelial receptors) results in failure of initial vessel formation. By contrast, other genes, such as those mediating signaling through the angiopoietins, appear to act later in the remodeling of vascular networks and the maintenance of vessel integrity. However, because the pulmonary vasculature develops relatively late in gestation, the early embryonic lethality of many gene knockouts has prevented a true delineation of their role in pulmonary vascular ontogeny. As is detailed below, a mechanistic role for many genes can only be inferred currently from the available data.

Vascular endothelial growth factor

Signaling involving VEGF appears to play a pivotal role in vascular development; this is emphasized by the unique finding of embryonic lethality in animals missing even a single *VEGF* allele.[25–29] Embryonic death secondary to loss of gene function in other recombinant animal models has required homozygous null mutations. In addition to its role in cardiovascular development in general, recently the roles of *VEGF* and *Flk1* (a receptor tyrosine kinase [RTK]) in pulmonary development have begun to be defined.[17,18,30] In addition to refining the descriptive observations outlined previously, these studies have documented a continuous increase in both *VEGF* and *Flk1* expression within the developing lung that begins at the onset of lung bud formation and continues through the neonatal period. In addition, relatively high levels of both *VEGF* and *Flk1* are maintained in the adult period. This surprising observation calls into question the concept that *VEGF-Flk1* interactions are important only during early embryonic development.

Coordinated development of the lung's airways and vasculature is essential for matched ventilation and perfusion in the mature organ. Inductive signaling between epithelial and mesenchymal cells is likely vital to such coordinated development, and may involve both cell-cell and cell-matrix interactions. Central to these interactions is the production of *VEGF* by alveolar epithelial cells; this induces differentiation of endothelial precursors in the parenchyma of the embryonic lung. *VEGF* messenger ribonucleic acid (mRNA) and protein have been identified in the developing lungs of many mammalian embryos, including humans, and are found most prominently at the distal tips of the developing epithelial buds and in the surrounding extracellular matrix (ECM).[30–36] Simultaneously, *VEGF* receptor 2 (*VEGF2*) *Flk1* expression is seen on the emerging endothelial cells within the mesenchyme surrounding these developing airways.[17,30,35,37] These findings are consistent with a critical role for *VEGF*-signaling between epithelial and mesenchymal cells in linking the development of airway and vascular structures. Indeed, in vitro cultures of pulmonary embryonic mesenchyme demonstrate a dependence on signals from epithelial cells for growth and development. In the absence of contact with pulmonary epithelial cells, mesenchyme-derived cultures fail to produce *Flk*-positive cells, and ultimately undergo necrosis.[17] The importance of the epithelium in initiating vascular morphogenesis through production of *VEGF* is well established, but *VEGF* production by nonepithelial mesenchymal cells recently has challenged the dogma of exclusive epithelial production of this critical cytokine.[17]

At least six highly related *VEGF*-type ligands have been identified (*VEGFs* A to E and placental growth factor [PlGF]), with distinct tissue distributions and affinities for the known *VEGF* receptors. Embryonic expression of *VEGF-D* is relatively restricted to the murine lung, where activity is upregulated just prior to birth and persists into adulthood,[38] suggesting a distinct (although not yet elucidated) role in pulmonary vascular development and function. Alternative splicing and post-translational modifications can alter the secretion of *VEGF*, as well as its receptor affinity, mitogenic activity, and solubility.[39] For example, the presence of heparin-binding regions influences attachment to the ECM and, thereby, a *VEGF* isoform's ability to diffuse. Such differences might limit the activity of highly ECM-bound isoforms while allowing other more diffusible isoforms to have more widespread effects.

Lung-specific differences in *VEGF* isoform expression have been studied in the developing rabbit.[39] Adult organs differ in the relative proportions of *VEGF* mRNA splice variants expressed. Within the lung itself, changes in the relative expression of these isoforms occur with continued embryonic and postnatal growth. With advancing fetal age, the expression of a highly diffusible form (*VEGF 165*) declines, while that of a highly matrix-bound (and less diffusible) isoform (*VEGF 189*) increases. Further, this poorly soluble *VEGF 189* remains more abundant in the adult lung than in any other organ, suggesting a unique role in the development and maintenance of the pulmonary vasculature. One such role might be to influence the anatomic relationship of alveolar and vascular structures as lung maturation proceeds. By switching to the production of a less soluble *VEGF* isoform, maturing epithelial cells might alter the location of developing capillaries from the center of alveolar septa in the fetus to a position more directly adjacent the epithelial basement membrane seen with continued septation/maturation in the postnatal period.

The best known regulator of VEGF expression is oxygen. Numerous cell culture systems have demonstrated increased *VEGF* mRNA expression in response to hypoxia and, conversely, a decrease on exposure to increased levels of O_2.[40] Midtrimester human embryonic lung, which normally develops in a low-oxygen environment, also expresses increased levels of *VEGF* mRNA and protein when cultured in vitro under low-oxygen (2%) conditions as compared with incubation in 20% O_2.[31] *VEGF* message and protein levels also are responsive to O_2 levels in vivo, as seen in the lungs of newborn rabbits exposed to hyperoxia.[39] In addition to differences at the cellular level, changes in environmental oxygen tensions occurring at birth likely signal vascular growth (or quiescence) in the lung's postnatal development.

Perturbing *VEGF* signaling emphasizes the importance of its delicate regulation in normal pulmonary development. The overexpression of *VEGF* under control of a surfactant (surfactant protein C) promoter in a transgenic mouse results in marked disruption of both vascular and acinar structures.[37] *VEGF* transgene expression by respiratory alveolar cells is associated with increased vasculogenic activity in the surrounding mesenchyme. Further, vascular formations demonstrate increased expression of RTKs (*Flk1* and *Tie1*) and abnormally dilated lumens. In addition to its effects on vascular structures, the increased expression of *VEGF* also appears to affect the airways themselves where aberrantly dilated respiratory tubules and altered differentiation of type I and II alveolar cells are seen. Whether these represent primary effects of *VEGF* expression itself or secondary changes resulting from the altered vascular development is unknown.

Receptor signaling

VEGF signaling is initiated upon binding one of its structurally related endothelial RTKs (see Figure 5–3). These vascular endothelial growth factor receptors (VEGFRs) each contain extracellular immunoglobulin (Ig)-like domains that appear to dictate ligand binding and functional specificity. Activation of VEGFR involves homotypic receptor dimerization (although evidence to suggest heterotypic interaction also has been reported), which results in activation of TK activity. Multiple downstream effector proteins participate in regulating the transmission of *VEGF*-induced intracellular signaling (eg, P13-kinase [P13K], SHP-2, and members of the Ras/MAP kinase cascade) by each of the VEGFRs.[3]

Within the developing lung the expression of ***VEGFR2/Flk1*** has been studied specifically. As noted above, expression of this RTK in the fetal rat lung is seen in association with the message for its *VEGF* ligand.[17] *Flk1*-positive cells are seen from the earliest point studied (E13, which corresponds to E14.5 to 15 in the mouse), becoming more abundant with further embryonic as well as postnatal lung development. Intermittent surges are observed immediately prior to birth and again in the early postnatal periods, and levels drop off in the adult. In contrast to the declining levels reported in the rat, a steady rise in *Flk1* mRNA is reported in the mouse from midgestation (E13) until full postnatal maturation, with persistence in the adult animal.[30] Finally, transgenic mice expressing the reporter gene *LacZ*, under control of the *Flk1* promoter, have been used to study the kinetics of vascular development in the lung.[18,28] Assessment of β-galactosidase activity as a marker of gene expression demonstrates a continuous increase in *Flk1* message as well as its persistence in the adult animal, (Figures 5–4 and 5–5 and Table 5–2). Whether these differences in the reported kinetics in *Flk1* message between species represent distinctions in this RTK's function or discrepancies in the assays employed has yet to be determined.

The ***Tie1*** and ***Tie2*** RTKs are another class of highly related endothelial cell-specific molecules vital to vascular morphogenesis. Each consists of a highly conserved cytoplasmic region composed of TK domains and similar (although less conserved) extracellular domains of two Ig-like loops separated by three tandem epidermal growth factor (*EGF*)-like repeats.[41] Four *Tie* receptor ligands, the angiopoietins (Ang), have been shown to bind to *Tie2*. The most completely characterized members, Ang 1 and 2, appear to have opposing actions in promoting and inhibiting vessel quiescence, respectively.

Relatively abundant *Tie1* message is found in the fetal and adult lungs of mice and humans.[42] Given the highly vascularized nature of the lung, it is perhaps not surprising that a relatively large amount of *Tie1* signal is found in the lung compared with that in other organs. However, the mature pulmonary vasculature appears to have an absolute requirement for *Tie1* expression. Compelling evidence for the importance of *Tie1* comes from chimeric animals composed of wild-type and recombinant cells

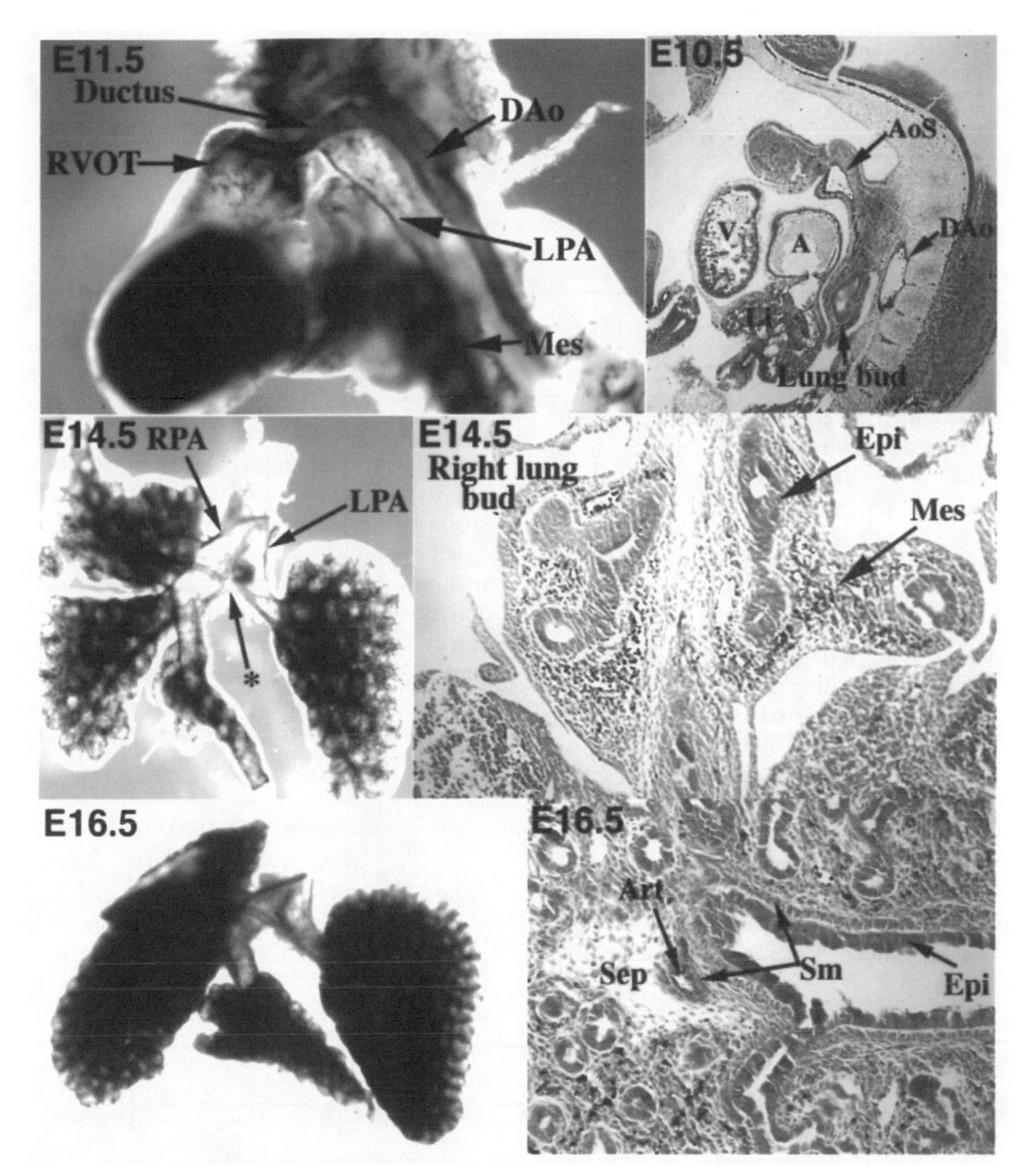

FIGURE 5–4. *Flk-LacZ* expression in pulmonary vascular development at several embryonic stages in the mouse (E10.5 to 16.5). The expression pattern identifies vessel formation from the earliest stages through later stages of pulmonary vascular ontogeny. *LacZ* under Flk expression identifies the pulmonary arterial outflow from the heart, the pulmonary arteries, capillaries, and veins including the pulmonary venous confluence (*). Dao = dorsal aorta; RVOT = right ventricular outflow tract; LPA = left pulmonary artery; Mes = pulmonary mesenchyme; AoS = aortic sac; V = cardiac ventricle; A = cardiac atrium; Li = liver; RPA = right pulmonary artery; Epi = pulmonary epithelium; Art = pulmonary arteriole; Sep = septum; Sm = smooth muscle (X = gal stain).

lacking a functional *Tie* allele (expressing a reporter gene in its place).[27,43] While *Tie1*-deficient cells are incorporated normally into embryonic pulmonary vessels, they fail to survive within the vasculature of the adult organ. The kinetics of *Tie1* mRNA expression during development also differs between organs. In the lung, *Tie1* expression appears to be enhanced in the perinatal period (in comparison to other RTKs), suggesting a unique role in the newborn (Taichman and Baldwin, unpublished observation). Of note, the ligands for *Tie2*, Ang 1 and 2, are both found throughout prenatal development in the murine lung.[44]

A third class of RTKs, the *Eph* family of receptors, has more recently been implicated in vascular development.[3,45,46] Unlike the *VEGF* and *Tie* RTKs, the Eph receptors and their ligands, the ephrins, are expressed in a wide range of cell types, having been characterized originally by their activity in axon patterning of the nervous system. Animals lacking function of certain members of the Eph family, as well as those of their ligands, are unable to

TABLE 5–2. Protein Content and Quantitative Analysis of Vascular Development in Murine Lungs

Age	Protein/Lung (μg) ±SEM	β-gal/lung (ng) ±SEM	β-gal(pg)/ protein (μg)
E12.5	35 ± 2	12 ± 1	343
E13.5	240 ± 18	108 ± 3	450
E15.5	1,713 ± 75	777 ± 17	454
E18	2,351 ± 130	1,196 ± 61	509
2 wk	6,456 ± 476	3,215 ± 219	498

E = embryonic day; β-gal = β-galactosidase.
Reprinted with permission from Schachtner SK, Wang Y, Baldwin HS. Quantitative and qualitative analysis of embryonic pulmonary vessel formation. Am J Respir Cell Mol Biol 2000;22:157–65.

properly remodel their developing vascular beds, similar to the phenotype demonstrated by *Tie2*-knockout animals.[27,47] Distinct from other classes of RTK ligands, the ephrin ligands must be cell bound to activate their Eph receptors. Thus, this signal transduction system would appear to function in the regulation of local cell-cell interactions (such as coordinating the development of arterial and venous endothelial channels). Such cross-talk in the development of arterial and venous connections is emphasized by the finding that the absence of an ephrin ligand normally localized to arterial endothelial cells (ephrin B2) results not only in abnormal arterial structures, but in defective neighboring venous channels as well.[47] Although expression of an ephrin B2 has been demonstrated in the developing lung,[48] specific involvement of this signaling pathway in pulmonary vascular development has not been explored.

Cell differentiation in numerous tissues and organs involves signaling through a family of transmembrane proteins termed "*Notch*".[49–52] Members of this highly conserved family of Notch molecules act to control cell fate specification in many developmental pathways, and disruption of Notch member function perturbs development in diverse species from insects to mammals. Recently, abnormal vascular remodeling resulting in embryonic death has been demonstrated in animals lacking each of several *Notch* genes (eg, either alone or in combination) as well as that of a Notch ligand, *Jagged1*.[53–55] As in other knockout models causing death from deficient cardiovascular development, fetal demise in *Notch*-deficient animals occurs too early to allow for an assessment of gene function in the development of the pulmonary vasculature. It is intriguing, however, that Notch ligands and *Jagged1* are expressed within the developing and postnatal murine lung and, indeed, on its vasculature.[56] Further, mutations in human *Jagged1* result in Alagille syndrome, which, in addition to hepatic dysfunction, is associated in many patients with cardiovascular abnormalities including abnormalities of the pulmonary vasculature.[57,58] The development of inducible systems to control gene function later in embryonic (and postnatal) development will allow for clarification of the role of Notch signaling in pulmonary morphogenesis, and specifically that of its vasculature.

Adhesion Molecules, Cell-Cell, and Cell-Matrix Interactions

Formation and stabilization of endothelial cells into large- and medium-sized vessels complete with elastic laminae, smooth muscle media, and pericytes, or into

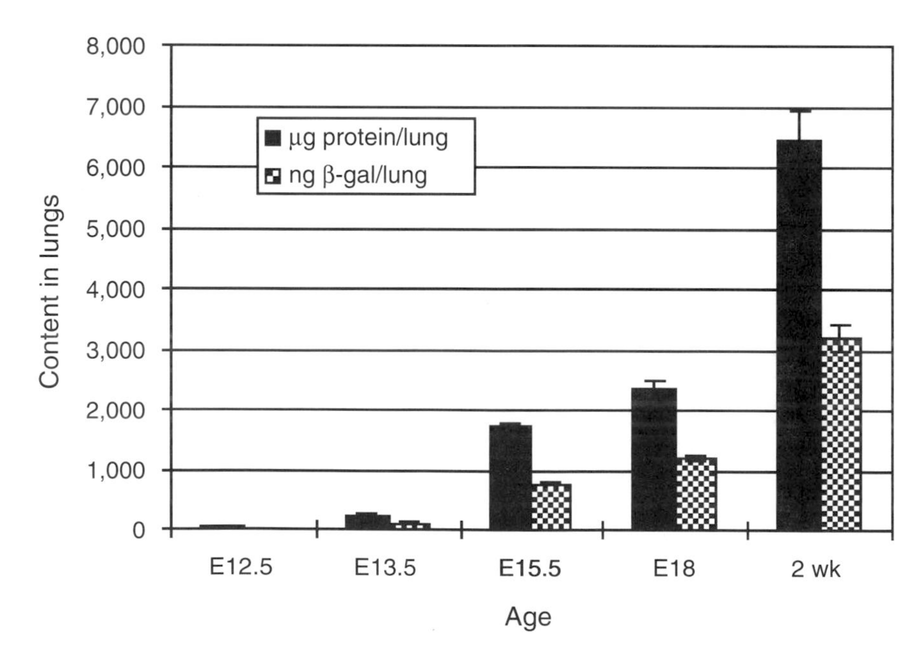

FIGURE 5–5. Graphic illustrating protein content and quantitative analysis of vascular development in murine lungs, as outlined in Table 5–2. E = embryonic day; β-gal = β-galactosidase. (Reproduced with permission from Schachtner SK et al.[18])

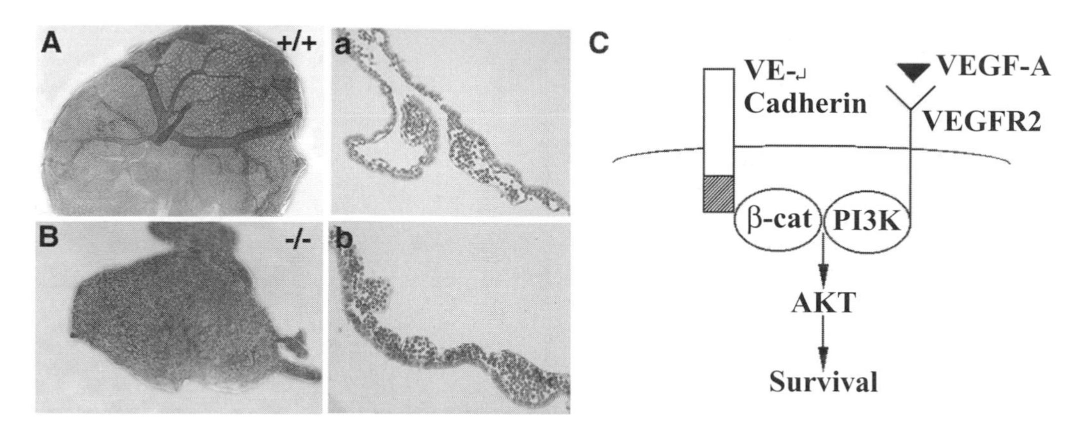

FIGURE 5–6. Yolk sacs from E9.25 wild-type embryos (*A*) and embryos homozygous for a truncation mutation of the VE-cadherin cytoplasmic domain (*B*) stained with antibody to platelet endothelial cell adhesion molecule 1. Significant endothelial differentiation has occurred but the primitive vascular plexus was unable to remodel to form an arborized vasculature in the mutated embryos (ve = vitello-embryonic vessels). *C*, The proposed model of the role of vascular endothelial cadherin (VE-cadherin) in *VEGF*-A mediated survival of endothelial cells via formation of a multi-component junctional complex between VE-cadherin, β-catenin (β-cat), P13-kinase (P13K) and VEGFR2. VE-cadherin promotes *VEGF*-A-mediated activation of Akt and endothelial survival. *VEGF* = vascular endothelial growth factors; VEGFR2 = *VEGF* receptor 2; Akt = serine/threonine protein kinase (protein kinase B). (Reproduced with permission from Carmeliet P et al.[61])

microvascular networks, requires cell-cell communication as well as coordinated cellular interaction with the ECM. In the lung, particularly intricate cellular interactions must take place with the apposition of endothelial and epithelial cells at the level of the alveoli. These interactions are mediated through cellular adhesion molecules (CAMs), integrins, matrix proteins, and proteases, among others.

Adhesion molecules are known to function in vascular cell-cell and cell-matrix interactions and include members of the Ig superfamily such as platelet endothelial CAM 1 (PECAM-1), intercellular adhesion molecule 1 (ICAM-1), and vascular CAM 1 (VCAM-1); as well as members of the selectin family, E-selectin and P-selectin; and cadherins. Many of these molecules are expressed in arteries, arterioles, and veins of the normal human adult lung, where they have an ongoing role in vascular maintenance[59] (Table 5–3).

Vascular endothelial cadherin, **VE-cadherin**, a member of the cadherin family of CAMs, is a calcium-dependent homotypic adhesive protein expressed at interendothelial junctions.[60] The cadherin cytoplasmic domain associate with molecules called catenins as well as with endothelial growth factor receptors, and these associations are necessary for VE-cadherin function.[61] Vascular endothelial cadherin is expressed in endothelial cells of all vessels including arteries, veins, and the microvasculature. In contrast to other endothelial cell markers, it is not found in blood cells or hematopoietic precursors.[62] Evidence for the role of VE-cadherin in vascular development comes initially from cell culture work and targeted disruption studies in embryoid bodies. In vitro studies have found inhibition of fibrin- or collagen-induced capillary tube formation by a VE-cadherin antibody. Although cells grown as a monolayer do not lose intercellular contact in the presence of this antibody, addition of antibody to preformed capillaries results in disruption of the capillary network.[63] These data support a role for VE-cadherin in vessel formation and stabilization. Loss-of-function embryoid bodies (VE-cadherin-/-) have impaired formation of vascular structures; however, they maintain expression of other endothelial cell markers.[64] These findings suggest a role for VE-cadherin in vascular assembly but not in endothelial cell differentiation. In addition, *VEGF* expression results in tyrosine phosphorylation of VE-cadherin, indicating that VE-cadherin is a downstream mediator of *VEGF* action.[65] Interestingly, in vitro data suggest there may be complementary roles for VE-cadherin and PECAM-1 (discussed below) during the process of vasculogenesis.[66,67] However, this has not been confirmed by in vivo studies.

The role of VE-cadherin in vascular assembly has been confirmed in vivo; VE-cadherin transcripts are first identified at E7.5, and mice lacking a functional VE-cadherin gene, either from deletion or mutation, die by E9.5.[61,62] Blood islands of the yolk sac show clusters of angioblasts that fail to form a capillary plexus, despite intercellular junction formation by endothelial cells (Figure 5–6). There is incomplete organization of endothelial cells into

TABLE 5–3. Expression of Adhesion Molecules in Vessel Types

	Vessel Type		
Adhesion Molecule	Arteries	Veins	Venules/Arterioles
ICAM-1	+	+	++
VCAM-1	++	++	+++
E-selectin	+	++	++
P-selectin	++	+++	+++

ICAM-1 = intercellular adhesion molecule 1; VCAM-1 = vascular cell adhesion molecule 1.

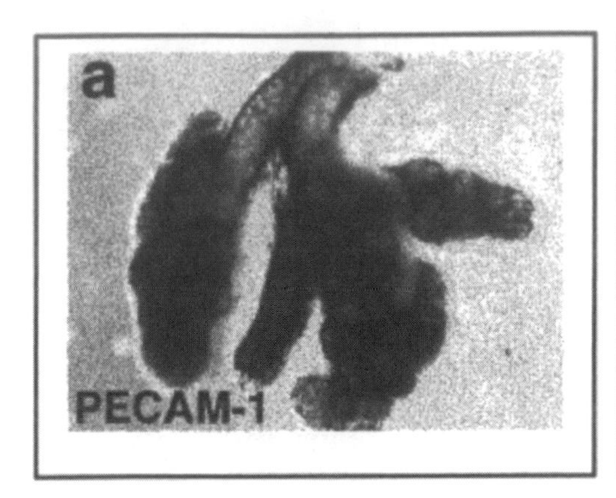

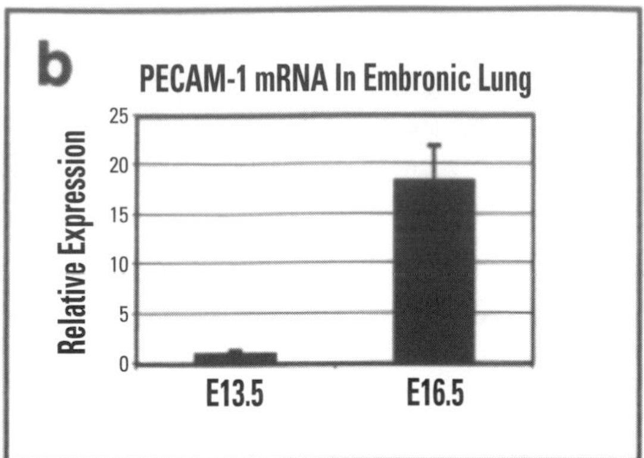

FIGURE 5–7. *A*, Whole-mount alkaline phosphatase detected immunostaining for platelet endothelial cell adhesion molecule 1 (PECAM-1) antibody in murine lung at E13.5 and *B*, mRNA expression of PECAM-1 at E13.5 and E16.5 showing an increase consistent with vascular development (Alkaline phosphatase stain, original magnification × 10).

large vessels and impaired angiogenesis.[61,62] Increased endothelial cell apoptosis results from an ineffective response to the survival signals induced by *VEGF-A*. This effect is mediated by a loss of VE-cadherin interaction with β-catenin, PI3K, and the *VEGF* receptor *Flk1* (*VEGFR2*). However, a normal cell survival response occurs indicating the cell survival signal occurs via an alternate pathway. Differentiation of endothelial cells appears to be normal; however, subsequent expansion, remodeling, and prevention of regression of the primitive network are impaired.[61] Hematopoiesis is not altered in these mice, and expression of other markers of endothelial cell differentiation such as *Flk*, *Flt*, *Tie2*, *Tie1*, and PECAM in null embryos is not affected.[62] These data support a role for VE-cadherin in the assembly of endothelial cells during both vasculogenesis and angiogenesis; VE-cadherin does not appear to be necessary for endothelial cell differentiation.

As mentioned previously, it is felt that the vasculature of the lung forms through a combination of vasculogenesis and angiogenesis. While not yet evaluated, it is likely that VE-cadherin is involved in vascular assembly in the lung during the processes of vasculogenesis and angiogenesis. Due to recent studies, an additional role for VE-cadherin in vascular maintenance and prevention of apoptosis in the pulmonary vasculature is suspected. Significant expression of VE-cadherin mRNA is found in highly vascularized organs, and VE-cadherin promoter studies have shown particularly high levels of marker gene expression in the lung and heart of adult mice.[68] In situ studies of day 13.5 embryos reveal expression in the mesenchyme and forming vasculature of the lung. An interaction of VE-cadherin with the *VEGF* receptor *Flk1*, which is also found in lung mesenchyme and on all endothelial cells of the lung during development, is suggested by these and the aforementioned studies. Blocking VE-cadherin function results in increased lung vessel permeability and interstitial edema.[69] In addition, another member of this family, VE-cadherin-2, is highly expressed in lung.[70] Further work into the role of VE-cadherin during lung development and in the adult lung should provide more information on the role of VE-cadherin in angiogenesis, vasculogenesis, and mature vessel maintenance.

During development **PECAM-1** (or CD31), a member of the Ig superfamily, is expressed in all endothelial cells after initial differentiation in embryonic and extraembryonic tissues.[71] This early expression occurs shortly after the expression of *Flk1*, and PECAM-1 is therefore considered one of the earliest markers of endothelial cell differentiation. It has multiple isoforms produced by alternative splicing, is localized to areas of endothelial cell contact, and is known to interact with integrins.[72,73] Changes in integrin-PECAM-1 engagement, in particular with β_1 integrin subunit, can modulate tyrosine phosphorylation on endothelial cells and affect cell migration.[74]

In developmental studies in the lung, PECAM-1 is seen as early as E9.5 to 10 in the mouse while a marker of mature endothelial cells, factor VIII, is initially found at E11.5.[16] Large and small (noncapillary) vessels express both factor VIII and PECAM at this early stage in lung formation. However, endothelial cells of capillaries express only PECAM early in development; PECAM-1 is therefore an excellent marker of lung endothelial development (Figure 5–7). Thus maturation of endothelial cells in the developing lung occurs first in the larger vessels and later in the capillary beds, consistent with the sequence of vessel development in the lung. Platelet endothelial CAM 1 continues to be expressed in the adult lung and appears to have a particularly specific role as shown by PECAM-antibody-targeted transduction studies in animals.[75–77] In these studies anti-PECAM antibody was conjugated to polyethylenimine (PEI), a cationic polymer and target plasmid, or to streptavidin and a target enzyme, and then delivered systemically into rodents. In both studies, the conjugated target was found

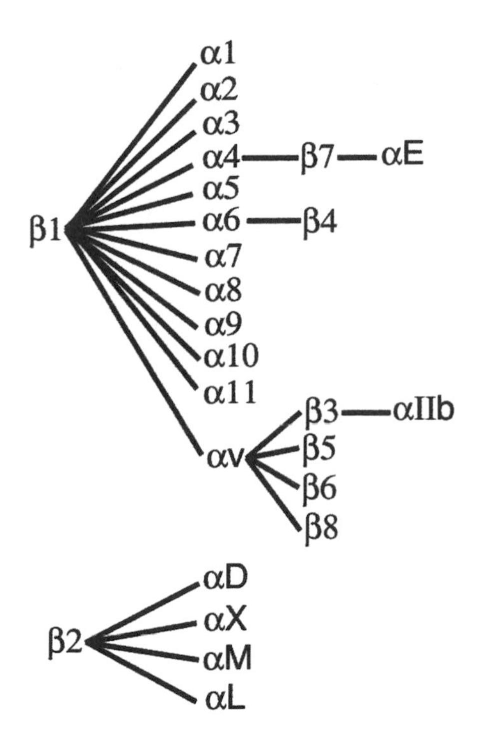

FIGURE 5–8. Schematic representation of known integrin pairing. The ligand specificity is determined by the heterodimeric α-β pairing of subunits.

predominantly in the lung, despite the systemic administration. The in vitro function assays, expression studies, and PECAM-antibody-targeted experiments indicate PECAM-1 likely has a significant role in endothelial cell function during development, contributing to intercellular communication and migration. In addition, in the mature lung, PECAM-1 appears to contribute to endothelial maintenance and vessel stabilization. However, null mutations in PECAM-1 are not embryonic lethal and show only subtle defects in white cell diapedesis and platelet function.[78]

In addition to their role in endothelial cell development, cell adhesion molecules have a role in the coordination of other cell types in vascular development., Vascular cell adhesion molecule 1, **VCAM-1** another member of the Ig superfamily, is important in developing vascular smooth muscle; VCAM-1 and its integrin ligand α_4 (see "Integrins" below) are expressed in smooth muscle cells of developing human aorta at 10 weeks' gestation. This expression decreases by 24 weeks and disappears in adulthood.[79] In vitro, blockade of VCAM and α_4 with antibodies prevents the expression of smooth muscle markers of differentiation in cultured fetal smooth muscle cells.[79] In the developing lung α_4 and VCAM are found in mesenchyme and around blood vessels in a pattern similar to α-smooth muscle actin, but they are not found around bronchi, implicating a role specifically in vascular smooth muscle development;[16,80] α_4 continues to be expressed in α-smooth muscle actin positive cells into the perinatal period. Targeted disruption of VCAM-1 or α_4 results in embryonic death around E10 or 11.[81,82] Evaluation of these embryos reveals a failure in placentation, loss of interaction between the epicardium and subjacent myocardium, and abnormal or absent coronary development. A role for VCAM-α_4 interactions in pulmonary smooth muscle development can be suspected; however, the lethality at this developmental stage prevents assessment of the role of VCAM or α_4 in pulmonary vascular development in these animals. Further work using conditional knockout technology may allow for the determination of function of VCAM and α_4 during pulmonary vascular ontogeny.

Integrins

Integrins are well-characterized heterodimeric transmembrane proteins that function as cell-ECM adhesive proteins and cell signaling receptors (Figure 5–8).[83–85] As with other transmembrane receptors, the cytoplasmic tail transmits signals from integrin occupancy, resulting in changes of pH, calcium levels, and tyrosine phosphorylation. This "outside-in" signaling can affect cellular differentiation, activation, gene expression, and proliferation. In addition, integrin activation can result in "inside-out" signaling, whereby ligand engagement creates an extracellular effector response such as cell anchorage or assembly of a fibronectin matrix. Different combinations of α and β subunits determine ligand-binding specificity. For example, depending on the coordinate α subunit, β_1 can bind fibronectin or laminin, and β_3 can bind fibronectin, tenascin, vitronectin, or osteopontin.

β_1 integrin pairing with α_3 has been shown to be necessary for lung development. $\alpha_3\beta_1$-deficient mice survive to birth in the homozygous state; however, these animals die during the perinatal period due to abnormal branching in both the kidney and the lung.[86] In addition to its effect on epithelial development, β_1 likely has a role in pulmonary vascular formation. $\alpha_5\beta_1$, a receptor for fibronectin, appears to have a definitive role in the final stages of tube formation during vascular development. In chick embryo experiments a function blocking monoclonal antibody against β_1 has no effect on the initial stages of vasculogenesis (ie, angioblast differentiation and vascular chord formation). However, a later stage of vessel lumen formation is disrupted by this antibody.[87] β_1 integrin also interacts with vascular cytokines. β_1 mediates endothelial cell attachment to collagen in vitro, and this attachment and cell migration can be altered by basic fibroblast growth factor (bFGF).[88] Likewise, bFGF-induced differentiation of cultured capillary endothelial cells can be inhibited by treatment with an anti-β_1 integrin IgG.[89] In addition, evaluation of teratomas created in mice found β_1 influences the vascular development response to *VEGF*; β_1-null embryonic stem cells form small teratomas with small irregular vessels that are not responsive to *VEGF*, while β_1-expressing cells form large teratomas with prominent vessels.[90] Although β_1 clearly has a function in branching morphogenesis in the lung, the role of β_1 and its interaction with *bFGF* and *VEGF* during pulmonary vascular development has yet to be evaluated. β_1-null mutations result in pregastrulation embryonic demise, precluding study of pulmonary vascular events.[91]

α integrin subunits have been studied in lung development. Collagen and laminin receptor α subunits have been evaluated, with α_1 found on endothelial cells and smooth muscle cells surrounding airways and large blood vessels.[92] In addition, the lung mesenchyme expresses high levels of α_2 and α_6, while the epithelium expresses α_6 and α_3, with α_2 present at branching tips.

The αv subunit paired with β_3 or β_5 clearly has a role in postnatal angiogenesis, but the requirement for these specific integrins in development has been questioned. Mice with all αv integrins deleted show a surprising amount of development of the vasculature, progressing to E9.5 before 80% of the embryos die. These mice die before any significant lung development has occurred. The 20% that progress further in development are found to have intracerebral and intestinal hemorrhages, and they die at birth.[93] Although the lungs appear grossly normal, it is difficult to assess whether normal function of the alveolar-capillary interface is present. Lung development is not complete in mice until about 30 days, and so the question of whether any of the αv integrins plays a role in developing a functional or mature lung remains unanswered. A recent study evaluating the expression pattern of $\alpha v\beta_3$ in adult rats revealed that $\alpha v\beta_3$ protein and mRNA were present in the endothelium of alveolar and extra-alveolar microvessels, vascular smooth muscle, and in large bronchial epithelium.[94] Little expression was found in other systemic organs, indicating that $\alpha v\beta_3$ may have a lung-specific role in maintaining the vasculature, perhaps interacting with *VEGF*. The lack of vascular abnormalities found during the early stages of development in the αv-knockout mice contrasts with results of experiments performed in chicks in which antibody to $\alpha v\beta_3$ integrin resulted in a defect of vasculogenesis and blocked chicks in *bFGF*- or tumor necrosis factor α (TNF-α)-stimulated angiogenesis, while blocking of $\alpha v\beta_5$ prevented angiogenesis stimulated by *VEGF*, transforming growth factor (TGF-α), or phorbol ester.[95,96] This difference in results may be due to species variability in requirement of integrins for pulmonary vascular development. Conversely, absence of αv in the null mutant animals may be "compensated for" by the very early upregulation of other CAMs that does not occur when these integrins are inactivated later.

Other integrins also are expressed in the vasculature. Resting endothelium expresses $\alpha_6\beta_1$, $\alpha_5\beta_1$, $\alpha_2\beta_1$, and $\alpha_v\beta_3$,[97] as well as the individual subunits α_2 and α_3.[98] Smooth muscle cells express β_1, αv, α_1, and α_3 sub-units.[98,99] In the lung, $\alpha_5\beta_3$, a receptor for laminin, has been found in early bronchial epithelial cells.[100] $\alpha_5\beta_1$, a fibronectin receptor, is found in bronchial epithelial cells and co-localizes with α-smooth muscle actin in smooth muscle cells at all stages of lung development.[101,102] However, α_5 knockout mice are embryonic lethal by E10 to 11, showing defects in both the embryonic and extraembryonic vasculature, precluding evaluation of α_5 function in lung vessel development in these mice.[103]

α_6 expression is seen in a similar time-course as is PECAM in the lung; however, it shows a wider expression pattern, being found on mesenchymal cells (both PECAM positive and negative) as well as in bronchial epithelial cells. Later in development α_6 is not found on endothelial cells of major vessels, but its vascular expression is restricted to smaller vessels and capillaries.[16] While it is clear that integrins have a role in many cell processes and work coordinately with matrix, cytokines, and other cell types to affect shape, attachment, and other cellular responses, new in vitro and pulmonary-specific gene targeting strategies are required specifically to elucidate the purpose of integrins in pulmonary vascular ontogeny.

Extracellular Matrix

Fibronectin, an adhesive glycoprotein found in ECMs, is highly expressed in developing lung.[104] Cellular actions such as migration, adhesion, and differentiation are affected by its interaction with integrin receptors such as $\alpha_5\beta_1$, $\alpha_4\beta_1$, and $\alpha_3\beta_1$. During the embryonic stage of lung development, fibronectin is expressed and deposited at the epithelial-mesenchymal interface of developing airways and in the mesenchyme.[101,104] Its expression increases with ongoing branching morphogenesis and is highest during the pseudoglandular stage of lung development. At this stage it is again found at the epithelial-mesenchymal interface and also surrounds spindle-shaped cells that are likely to be differentiating smooth muscle cells.[101] By E16 fibronectin is seen around developing vessels.[101] In addition to effects on epithelial-matrix interactions, fibronectin promotes vascular cell migration and can affect the ability of endothelial cells to form vessel-like cords in vitro.[105] During lung maturation fibronectin expression is gradually replaced by laminin in the matrix, a transition seen when immature vessels mature and the basement membrane is established.[101,106,107] A severe phenotype of mesodermal defects is seen in fibronectin-knockout mice consisting of arrested axis elongation, absent somites, disorganized notochord, and defective vasculogenesis in the yolk sac, with death occurring prior to lung development.[108,109] The severity of cardiovascular defects appears to be related to the particular strain of mice used, indicating that additional modifying factors determine the ultimate phenotype.[110] Interestingly, in bronchopulmonary dysplasia, a lung disease in premature newborns that partially results from arrested epithelial and vascular development, expression of fibronectin message is increased in vascular and smooth muscle cells.[111] This increase in expression may represent a lack of transition to the more mature laminin expression pattern.

Laminin, another ECM glycoprotein, is found to selectively bind myofibroblasts of developing fetal mouse lungs. A subpopulation of mesenchymal cells isolated from E16 lungs bind specifically to the alpha chain of laminin 2. These cells are also found to express α-smooth muscle actin, vimentin, and desmin, indicating they are of smooth muscle lineage.[112] As the preceding studies indicate, differentiation of both epithelial and mesenchymal components during lung development is correlated with matrix production. Further studies to evaluate the roles fibronectin, laminin, and other matrix molecules play in development of individual lung components and in epithelial-mesenchymal interactions are clearly indicated.

Vascular Smooth Muscle Development

Coordination of endothelial and smooth muscle cell differentiation during formation of muscularized vessels is not unique to the lung. However, muscularization of the pulmonary vasculature is necessary for vascular stabilization, and precise control is required for normal physiologic and hemodynamic responses. Extension of the musculature onto smaller normally nonmuscularized or partially muscularized vessels results in pulmonary hypertension. Precise control of the location and extent of muscularization is therefore critical during development. There is evidence for multiple pathways of vascular smooth muscle differentiation in the lung. Four different smooth muscle cell phenotypes have been identified in the mature bovine pulmonary artery.[113] During development each cell population progresses along a different developmental pathway, suggesting the existence of multiple cell lineages. During human prenatal development, pulmonary vascular smooth muscle cells have been reported to arise from three different sources: by extension from pre-existing bronchial smooth muscle cells, by differentiation from mesenchyme surrounding the endothelial tubes, and by transdifferentiation from endothelial cells.[114] Investigation into molecular regulation of these processes has begun recently.

A gradient of smooth muscle differentiation from proximal-to-distal structures is seen in the lung during development. With the onset of pulmonary budding, messages for α-smooth muscle actin, smooth muscle myosin, and metavinculin (indicative of a contractile phenotype) are expressed sequentially.[115] By E12.5 smooth muscle actin, generally the earliest marker of smooth muscle differentiation, is seen surrounding developing large vessels in the lung as well as around clusters of endothelial cells that are beginning to organize, form lumens, and produce a laminin-containing basement membrane. Smooth muscle is absent around those clusters of endothelial cells that have not yet begun to organize (Figure 5–9).[16] As branching continues and mesenchymal cells around developing airways and vessels differentiate into smooth muscle, initial expression of α-actin is followed by intermediate filament expression of vimentin, then desmin, and smooth muscle myosin (the latter a more specific marker of smooth muscle), indicating a more differentiated phenotype. This maturation gradient is seen earlier around branching airways as compared with developing vessels.[116] Myofibroblasts and pericytes, which express smooth muscle characteristics in the mature animal, are not identified before birth.[115]

Other factors known to influence smooth muscle replication and development are beginning to be evaluated in developing lung. **Angiotensin converting enzyme** (ACE) has been implicated in the process of medial hypertrophy in pulmonary hypertension. Analysis of ACE expression in fetal and young rats shows early (E15) endothelial expression in the hilar pulmonary arteries, with expression extending more distally as development progresses. By term, endothelial cells of all muscularized arteries and alveolar capillaries express ACE,[117] and overall ACE activity increases rapidly in the early postnatal period (2 to 4 weeks), reaching adult levels. Angiotensin I receptor expression is found in the periphery of the lung first, on day 17 in nonepithelial mesenchymal cells. This pattern of expression likely indicates cell signaling and interaction between maturing endothelial cells and the developing smooth muscle cells in the surrounding mesenchyme. In addition it confirms that factors involved in normal prenatal development may become re-activated during pathologic processes later in life.

Prostacyclin and Nitric Oxide

Prostacyclin, a postnatal pulmonary vascular dilator, is produced by cyclooxygenase (COX) conversion of arachidonic acid to prostaglandin, which then is converted to prostacyclin by action of prostaglandin-I synthase (PGIS). Prostacyclin is known to have a significant regulatory function on pulmonary vascular tone in the perinatal and postnatal periods. Expression of COX-1 and COX-2 mRNA rises progressively from fetal to postnatal periods in lamb. Protein analysis reveals COX-1 expression in endothelial cells pre- and postnatally, and in airway smooth muscle in the postnatal period.[118] **Nitric oxide**, another potent pulmonary vasodilator synthesized by nitric oxide synthase (*NOS*), is present during the early stages of fetal bovine lung development and in the rat by E16, implicating a potential role in formation of the vasculature.[119,120] As development proceeds synthesis of both PGIS and *NOS* increase, especially near term when the vasculature must respond to rapid changes in blood flow and alveolar gas composition.[121] In persistent pulmonary hypertension of the newborn, *NOS* expression has been found to be decreased in both humans and rats.[122,123]

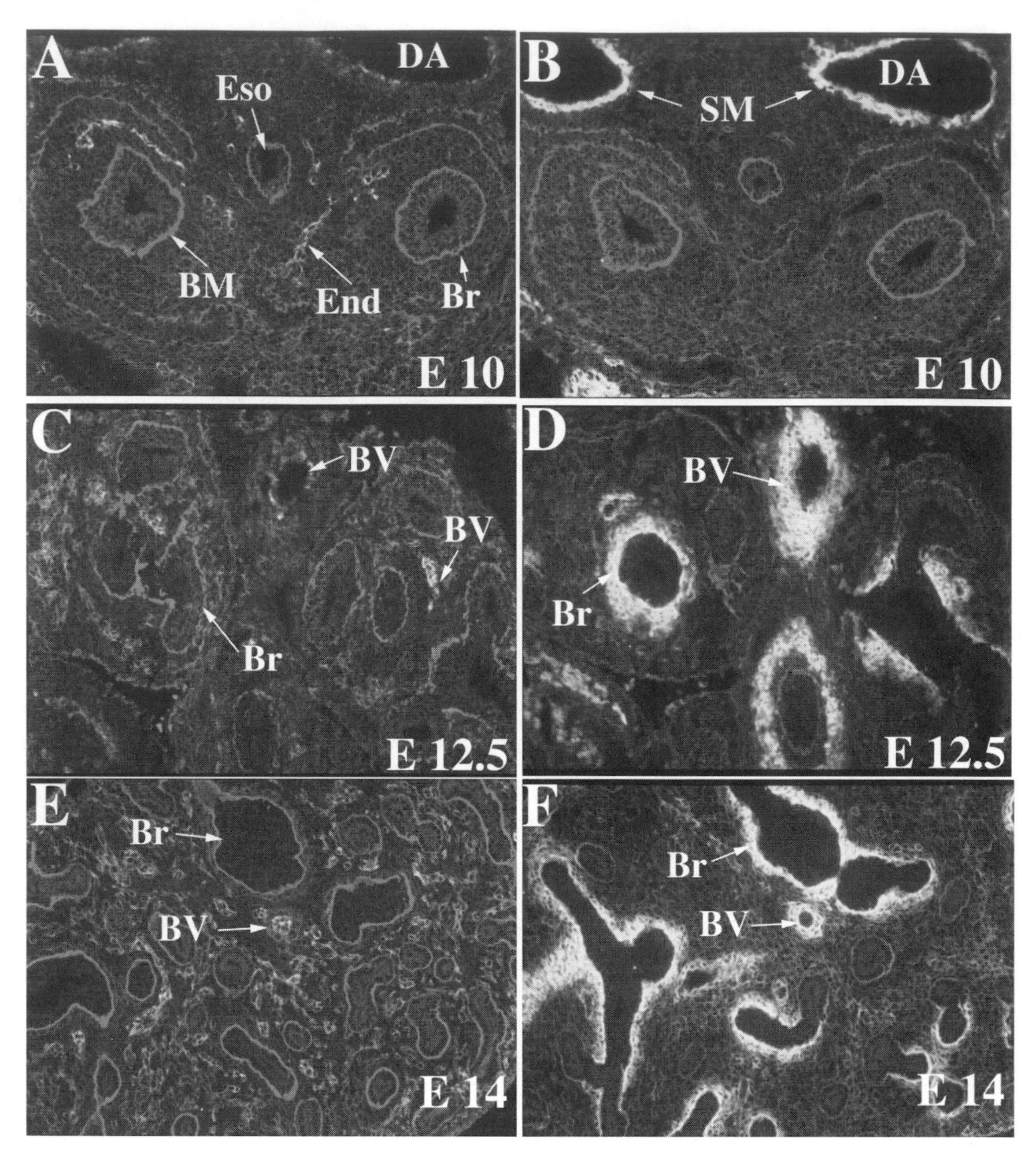

FIGURE 5–9. Vascular and smooth muscle staining in murine embryos from E10 to 14. Fluorescein isothiocynate (*light gray*) staining is used for anti-PECAM-1 (platelet endothelial cell adhesion molecule 1) antibody (*A, C, E*) or anti-α-smooth muscle actin (*B, D, E*) and all panels are stained for antilaminin. Eso = esophagus; DA = dorsal aorta; End = endothelium; BM = basement membrane; Br = bronchial epithelium; SM = smooth muscle; BV = blood vessel. (Reproduced with permission from Buck CA et al.[16])

Analysis of both the prostacyclin and nitric oxide synthetic pathways, expression patterns, and determination of function are needed during earlier stages of pulmonary vascular development.

Proteases

Matrix metalloproteinases (**MMP**) have been implicated in angiogenic processes. Existing endothelial cells secrete proteolytic enzymes including MMPs and plasminogen activators that degrade ECM, activate cytokines, and permit endothelial cells to divide and migrate into the tissue to be vascularized. The angiogenic cytokine *VEGF* has been shown to influence smooth muscle cell migration, and this effect can be blocked by MMP inhibition.[124] Only one recent study has focused on MMPs in developing lung.[125] In this study of several stages during the second half of gestation, Fukuda et al found membrane type 1 MMP (MT1-MMP), MMP-1, and MMP-9 expressed in the epithelium of fetal rabbits, while MMP-2 and TIMP-2 were present in both the epithelium and mesenchyme. Further analysis of proteases and MMP activity in lung during vascular development is needed.

Thrombin is a protease that affects mesenchymal cell proliferation and endothelial cell production of growth factors and adhesion molecules. Messages for prothrombin and tissue factor, both proteases involved in converting prothrombin to thrombin, are detected on embryonic epithelial cells by E12. Thrombin receptor mRNA is detected in embryos from E9.5 to 16, initially widely in the mesenchyme during organogenesis, but by E16.5 its expression is restricted to certain neurons, endocardial and endothelial cells, and the lung and liver.[126] Studies indicate a potential role for thrombin and its receptors in epithelial-mesenchymal interactions in the developing lung.

Transcription Factors

Transcription factors are proteins that control the temporal and tissue-specific expression of many genes. Several of these regulatory components are expressed in the lung during development; their roles in development are incompletely understood. ***GATA-5***, a member of the zinc finger transcription factor family known to regulate cell lineage differentiation, is expressed diffusely in the pulmonary mesenchyme from E12.5.[127] The pattern of *GATA-5* expression overlaps with the pattern of *SM22α*; however, it is more diffuse. As development progresses SM22α is expressed in both bronchial and pulmonary artery smooth muscle cells. Another member, ***GATA-6***, is expressed in bronchial cells at E12.5, but its expression becomes restricted at later stages (E18) to arterial smooth muscle cells.[127] Chimeric studies in mice reveal that *GATA-6* may have a crucial role in lung development in that it is required for in vivo and in vitro branching morphogenesis.[128]

Hox genes (homeobox-containing) are sequence-specific deoxyribonucleic acid (DNA) transcription factors involved in regulation of embryonic and fetal morphogenesis, including lung development. Many members of the *Hoxb* gene family show restricted expression to the mesenchyme early in lung development, and patterns of *Hoxb* genes differentiate proximal and distal lung mesenchyme.[129] *Hoxb-5* is expressed in mesenchyme early during development of the lungs, but it is present in epithelium only during late stages of embryonic lung formation.[130] The location and specific patterns of *Hoxb* family member expression likely indicate a role in epithelial-mesenchymal communication and may control the response of mesenchyme from different parts of the lung to epithelial signals, and vice versa. The *Hox* genes also are likely involved in specific programs of mesenchymal differentiation, including endothelial cell differentiation and migration. *Hoxd-3* has been shown in vitro to regulate endothelial cell phenotype; stimulation of endothelial cells with bFGF resulted in upregulation of *Hoxd-3*, and direct upregulation of *Hoxd-3* resulted in transition of endothelial cells into the invasive angiogenic phenotype.[131] Regulation of endothelial cell differentiation and remodeling in the processes of vasculogenesis and angiogenesis in lung development are possibly under the control of *Hox* genes, and the direct effect of these transcription factors remains to be determined.

The transcription factors ***ets-1*** and ***ets-2*** are expressed during murine organogenesis in the lung and in developing vascular structures such as the heart, arteries, and capillaries.[132] *Ets-1* influences MMP expression in vitro and is required for invasion and spreading of endothelial cells on vitronectin.[133] In chicken and human embryos, there is evidence that *ets-1* may regulate transcription of matrix-degrading proteases necessary for angiogenesis.[134] In addition, *VEGF* receptors *flk* and *flt*, and VE-cadherin have ets binding sites.[135,136] *Ets-1* is induced by *VEGF*, *aFGF*, *bFGF*, and *EGF* in endothelial cells, and blocking of ets-1 by antisense oligonucleotides inhibits endothelial cell migration and tube formation induced by cytokines.[137,138] These data and the localization of ets-1 and ets-2 in developing murine lung indicate potential interactions of ets, cytokines, and MMPs during endothelial cell/vascular development in the fetal lung.

Remodeling and Negative Regulatory Genes

Two novel regulatory genes recently have been described in the lung. ***Del-1*** is an early endothelial cell marker that is deposited into the ECM and has a role in vascular remodeling.[139] In addition to early expression in endothelial and mesodermal components of the yolk sac, differentiating endothelial cells of the dorsal aorta, and cells migrating into the endocardium, it is expressed at later developmental stages in the microvasculature of the lung, gut, neural tube, and kidney. Consistent with a role in vascular morphogenesis, *del-1* is expressed as endothelial cells differentiate from the mesenchyme, and expression of *del-1* declines after endothelial cells contribute to vascular structures. In the same manner, *del-1* is expressed diffusely throughout the mesenchyme of the lung in a similar pattern and time course to that of other endothelial cell markers such as Flk and PECAM-1; however, in contrast to these markers, which continue to be expressed after vascularization of the lung, *del-1* disappears once vessels are formed, and it is not found after birth in any tissue.

Endothelial monocyte-activating polypeptide II, ***EMAP II***, is an antiangiogenic factor in tumor development that has recently been found expressed in the developing lung.[140] Levels of *EMAP II* are high in the early stages of murine lung development, decrease during vascular formation, and then increase during vascular maturation. This expression pattern suggests that the presence of *EMAP II* is high when endothelial cells are not dividing rapidly, and is thus associated with a stabilization of the lung vasculature.

Potential Regulating Role of Oxygen

Hypoxia is an important regulator of both vasculogenesis and angiogenesis. Many of the genes that regulate vascular development, such as *VEGF*, *Flk1*, *Flt1*, *Tie2*, platelet-derived growth factor β (PDGFβ), *bFGF*, inducible NOS, and endothelin-1, are known to be affected, directly or indirectly by hypoxia.[141] *VEGF-A* is markedly upregulated by hypoxia and has become the most studied model for hypoxia-induced gene expression. Hypoxia is also known to stabilize *VEGF* mRNA. The primary increase of *VEGF* is mediated by the actions of the protein complex hypoxia-inducible factor (HIF).[142] Activity of HIF is initiated by heterodimerization of two basic helix-loop-helix (bHLH)-Per-Arnt/AhR-Sim (PAS) proteins, HIF1α and HIF1β (also known as ARNT), which bind to the HIF-responsive elements in the *VEGF* promoter. Oxygen-dependent HIF1 expression is detected by virtually all cell types in the lung, and arterial smooth muscle cells express HIF1 even under normoxic conditions.[143] The central role of the HIFs in regulating vascular development is demonstrated by marked defects and embryonic death at E10.5 described in both HIF1α- and ARNT-null mutant embryos, closely resembling that seen in *VEGF-A*-deficient embryos.[144–149] Interestingly, a novel bHLH-PAS factor has been identified and designated endothelial PAS protein (EPAS)-1 (also known as HIF2α, HRF, or HLF) that is both endothelial specific and expressed abundantly in the lung. Its expression is enhanced at birth, and it may mediate VEGF expression under normoxic conditions.[150–152] In contrast to mutations in HIF components, embryos carrying a null mutation in EPAS-1 appear to develop a normal vascular system but die of bradycardia and congestive heart failure between El2.5 and E15.5, thus preventing a direct evaluation of the role of EPAS-1 in pulmonary ontogeny.[153]

Studies focusing on the role of hypoxia in regulating pulmonary vascular development are extremely limited. This is particularly surprising, as the embryo develops in a relatively hypoxic environment, with tissue O_2 saturations between 3 and 5%;[141] thus hypoxia likely plays a significant role in pulmonary vascular morphogenesis. Acarregui and colleagues studied midtrimester human lung explants and documented *VEGF* mRNA and protein levels that were significantly increased by hypoxic conditions (2% O_2) compared with normoxia (20% O_2) after only 2 days in culture.[31] Similar results were obtained using midgestation kidney explants from rat embryos.[154]

The role of hyperoxia in producing a syndrome of pulmonary toxicity that includes epithelial cell damage, interstitial edema, pleural fluid accumulation, lung hemorrhages, and inflammation has been well described, particularly in the adult animal.[155,156] While studies have primarily focused on damage to the airway epithelium, it is quite clear that there is simultaneous damage to alveolar endothelial cells, and that impaired function or loss of microvascular endothelial cells may play a major role in pathologic processes.[157] One of the most intriguing aspects of hyperoxic lung injury is the high oxygen tolerance of young animals compared with the intolerance found in adults.[158,159] Again, studies primarily have focused on epithelial damage and evaluation of antioxidant defenses, with identification of a "critical period" for alveolar develop ment in the early neonatal period.[160] However, there is evidence that pulmonary vascular development is impaired as well. Several investigators have documented that prolonged exposure (8 weeks) to hyperoxia can result in decreased parenchymal and vascular growth with increased muscularity.[161] Other investigators have shown that in rat pups there is a pronounced decrease in the branching of distal arterial segments, a decrease in microvascular density, and a decrease in capillary formation, all occurring within 6 days of exposure to hyperoxia.[162] While hyperoxia is not fatal to newborn animals, and the potential for "recovery" exists, brief periods of hyperoxic exposure during this critical period of alveolarization (immediately after birth) frequently result in permanent vascular alterations, including a decreased number of small pulmonary arteries, elevated right ventricular pressure, and emphysema-like changes in the air spaces.[163,164]

The role of hyperoxia in pulmonary vascular development is a potentially important consideration in the occurrence of lung abnormalities in the extremely low-birth-weight infant. Since the lung normally develops in a hypoxic environment, as described above, even ambient oxygen conditions represent a significant hyperoxic challenge. Other than the descriptive studies mentioned above, little is known about the mechanisms of hyperoxia-induced pulmonary vascular changes in the neonate, and there is little information on developmental differences in the vascular response to O_2. Maniscalco and colleagues have shown that *VEGF* declines in both newborn and adult rabbit lungs following hyperoxic injury, correlating with the loss of endothelial cells.[34] They also have documented an increase in *VEGF* production by type II epithelial cells that correlates with endothelial cell proliferation during recovery.[165] This group has gone on to describe similar differences in *VEGF* isoform expression in neonates and adults following hyperoxic injury and recovery, and they have documented an increase of *VEGF* protein in lung lavage fluid during recovery.[39] However, the significance of these observations is yet to be determined.

Summary

The explosion of information on molecular regulation of vascular development has implicated several classes of proteins as being potentially critical to pulmonary vascular ontogeny. However, the relatively late development of the lung in combination with the frequent occurrence of early embryonic lethality in null mutant embryos has prevented the delineation of the roles of many of these proteins in lung morphogenesis. Thus, new models and pulmonary-specific gene-targeting strategies need to be developed to unravel the steps in this important developmental process. The accentuation of pulmonary vascular growth during late gestation and the early newborn period make the pulmonary vasculature a particularly accessible target for both diagnostic and corrective interventional strategies. However, further investigation into the basic mechanisms of pulmonary vascular development is essential to identify the most efficient pathways in which to intervene.

References

1. Baldwin HS. Early embryonic vascular development. Cardiovasc Res 1996;31:E35–45.
2. Risau W. Mechanisms of angiogenesis. Nature 1997; 386:671–4.
3. Tallquist MD, Soriano P, Klinghoffer RA. Growth factor signaling pathways in vascular development. Oncogene 1999;18:7917–32.
4. Carmeliet P, Collen D. Role of vascular endothelial growth factor and vascular endothelial growth factor receptors in vascular development. Curr Top Microbiol Immunol 1999;237:133–58.
5. Shi Q, Rafii S, Wu MH, et al. Evidence for circulating bone marrow-derived endothelial cells. Blood 1998;92:362–7.
6. Takahashi T, Kalka C, Masuda H, et al. Ischemia- and cytokine-induced mobilization of bone marrow-derived endothelial progenitor cells for neovascularization. Nature Medicine 1999;5:434–8.
7. Isner JM, Asahara T. Angiogenesis and vasculogenesis as therapeutic strategies for postnatal neovascularization. J Clin Invest 1999;103:1231–6.
8. Larsen WJ, ed. Human embryology. 2nd Ed. New York: Churchill Livingstone Inc., 1997:138–9.
9. Ten Have-Opbroek AAW. Lung development in the mouse embryo. Exper Lung Res 1991;17:111–30.
10. Thurlebeck WM. Pre- and postnatal organ development. In: Chernick V, Mellins RB, eds. Basic mechanisms of pediatric respiratory disease: cellular and integrative. Philadelphia: B.C. Decker, 1991:23–5.
11. Perl AK, Whitsett JA. Molecular mechanisms controlling lung morphogenesis. Clin Genet 1999;56:14–27.
12. Warburton D, Schwarz M, Tefft D, et al. The molecular basis of lung morphogenesis. Mech Dev 2000;92:55–81.
13. Pardanaud L, Yassine F, Dieterlen-Lievre F. Relationship between vasculogenesis, angiogenesis and haemopoiesis during avian ontogeny. Development 1989; 105:473–85.
14. Pardanaud L, Altmann C, Kitos P, et al. Vasculogenesis in the early quail blastodisc as studied with a monoclonal antibody recognizing endothelial cells. Development 1987;100:339–49.
15. Chang C. On the origin of the pulmonary vein. Anat Rec 1931;50:1–8.
16. Buck CA, Edelman JM, Buck CE, et al. Expression patterns of adhesion receptors in the developing mouse lung: functional implications. Cell Adhes Commun 1996; 4:69–87.
17. Gebb SA, Shannon JM. Tissue interactions mediate early events in pulmonary vasculogenesis. Dev Dyn 2000; 217:159–69.
18. Schachtner SK, Wang Y, Baldwin HS. Qualitative and quantitative analysis of embryonic pulmonary vessel formation. Am J Respir Cell Mol Biol 2000;22:157–65.
19. deMello DE, Sawyer D, Galvin N, Reid LM. Early fetal development of lung vasculature. Am J Respir Cell Mol Biol 1997;16:568–81.
20. Smith BR, Johnson GA, Groman EV, Linney E. Magnetic resonance microscopy of mouse embryos. Proc Natl Acad Sci U S A 1994;91:3530–3.
21. Folkman J, D'Amore PA. Blood vessel formation: what is its molecular basis [comment; review]. Cell 1996; 87:1153–5.
22. Hanahan D. Signaling vascular morphogenesis and maintenance [comment]. Science 1997;277:48–50.
23. Mustonen T, Alitalo K. Endothelial receptor tyrosine kinases involved in angiogenesis. J Cell Biol 1995;129:895–8.
24. Petrova TV, Makinen T, Alitalo K. Signaling via vascular endothelial growth factor receptors. Exp Cell Res 1999; 253:117–30.
25. Ferrara N, Carver-Moore K, Chen H, et al. Heterozygous embryonic lethality induced by targeted inactivation of the VEGF gene. Nature 1996;380:439–42.
26. Fong GH, Rossant J, Gertsenstein M, Breitman ML. Role of the flt1 receptor tyrosine kinase in regulating the assembly of vascular endothelium. Nature 1995;376:66–70.
27. Sato TN, Tozawa Y, Deutsch U, et al. Distinct roles of the receptor tyrosine kinases tie-1 and tie-2 in blood vessel formation. Nature 1995;376:70–4.
28. Shalaby F, Rossant J, Yamaguchi TP, et al. Failure of blood-island formation and vasculogenesis in flk1 deficient mice. Nature 1995;376:62–6.
29. Carmeliet P, Ferreira V, Breier G, et al. Abnormal blood vessel development and lethality in embryos lacking a single VEGF allele. Nature 1996;380:435–9.
30. Bhatt AJ, Amin SB, Chess PR, et al. Expression of vascular endothelial growth factor and Flk-1 in developing and glucocorticoid-treated mouse lung. Pediatr Res 2000; 47:606–13.
31. Acarregui M, Penisten ST, Goss KL, et al. Vascular endothelial growth factor gene expression in human fetal lung in vitro. Am J Respir Cell Mol Biol 1999;20:14–23.
32. Breier G, Albrecht U, Sterrer S, Risau W. Expression of vascular endothelial growth factor during embryonic angiogenesis and endothelial cell differentiation. Development 1992;114:521–32.
33. Kaipainen A, Korhonen J, Pajusola K, et al. The related FLT4, FLT1, and KDR receptor tyrosine kinases show distinct expression patterns in human fetal endothelial cells. J Exp Med 1993;178:2077–88.
34. Maniscalco WM, Watkins RH, D'Angio CT, Ryan RM. Hyperoxic injury decreases alveolar epithelial cell expression of vascular endothelial growth factor (VEGF) in neonatal rabbit lung. Am J Respir Cell Mol Biol 1997;16:557–67.
35. Millauer B, Wizigmann-Voos S, Schnurch H, et al. High

affinity VEGF binding and developmental expression suggest Flk-1 as a major regulator of vasculogenesis and angiogenesis. Cell 1993;72:835–46.
36. Shifren JL, Doldi N, Ferrara N, et al. In the human fetus, vascular endothelial growth factor is expressed in epithelial cells and myocytes, but not vascular endothelium: implications for mode of action. J Clin Endocrinol Metab 1994;79:316–22.
37. Zeng X, Wert SE, Federici R, et al. VEGF enhances pulmonary vasculogenesis and disrupts lung morphogenesis in vivo. Dev Dyn 1998;211:215–27.
38. Farnebo F, Piehl F, Lagercrantz J. Restricted expression pattern of VEGF-D in the adult and fetal mouse: high expression in the embryonic lung. Biochem Biophy Res Commun 1999;257:891–4.
39. Watkins RH, D'Angio CT, Ryan RM, et al. Differential expression of VEGF mRNA splice variants in newborn and adult hyperoxic lung injury. Am J Physiol 1999; 276:L858–67.
40. Minchenko A, Bauer T, Salceda S, Caro J. Hypoxic stimulation of vascular endothelial growth factor expression in vitro and in vivo. Lab Invest 1994;71:374–9.
41. Partanen J, Dumont DJ. Functions of Tie1 and Tie2 receptor tyrosine kinases in vascular development. Curr Top Microbiol Immunol 1999;237:159–72.
42. Korhonen J, Polvi A, Partanen J, Alitalo K. The mouse tie receptor tyrosine kinase gene: expression during embryonic angiogenesis. Oncogene 1994;9:395–403.
43. Partanen J, Puri MC, Schwartz L, et al. Cell autonomous functions of the receptor tyrosine kinase TIE in a late phase of angiogenic capillary growth and endothelial cell survival during murine development. Development 1996;122:3013–21.
44. Colen KL, Crisera CA, Rose MI, et al. Vascular development in the mouse embryonic pancreas and lung. J Pediatr Surg 1999;34:781–5.
45. Holder N, Klein R. Eph receptors and ephrins: effectors of morphogenesis. Development 1999;126:2033–44.
46. Yancopoulos GD, Klagsbrun M, Folkman J. Vasculogenesis, angiogenesis, and growth factors: ephrins enter the fray at the border [comment]. Cell 1998;93:661–4.
47. Wang HU, Chen ZF, Anderson DJ. Molecular distinction and angiogenic interaction between embryonic arteries and veins revealed by ephrin-B2 and its receptor Eph-B4 [comments]. Cell 1998;93:741–53.
48. Cerretti DP, Vanden Bos T, Nelson N, et al. Isolation of LERK-5: a ligand of the eph-related receptor tyrosine kinases. Mol Immunol 1995;32:1197–205.
49. Artavanis-Tsakonas S, Matsuno K, Fortini ME. Notch signaling. Science 1995;268:225–32.
50. Greenwald I, Rubin GM. Making a difference: the role of cell-cell interactions in establishing separate identities for equivalent cells. Cell 1992;68:271–81.
51. Kopan R, Cagan R. Notch on the cutting edge. Trends Genet 1997;13:465–7.
52. Simpson P. Notch signaling in development. Perspect Dev Neurobiol 1997;4:297–304.
53. Krebs LT, Xue Y, Norton CR, et al. Notch signaling is essential for vascular morphogenesis in mice. Genes Dev 2000;14:1343–52.
54. McCright B, Gao X, Shen L, et al. Defects in development of the kidney, heart and eye vasculature in mice homozygous for a hypomorphic Notch2 mutation. Development 2001;128:491–502.
55. Xue Y, Gao X, Lindsell CE, et al. Embryonic lethality and vascular defects in mice lacking the Notch ligand Jagged1. Hum Mol Genet 1999;8:723–30.
56. Loomes KM, Underkoffler LA, Morabito J, et al. The expression of Jagged1 in the developing mammalian heart correlates with cardiovascular disease in Alagille syndrome. Hum Mol Genet 1999;8:2443–9.
57. Li L, Krantz ID, Deng Y, et al. Alagille syndrome is caused by mutations in human Jagged1, which encodes a ligand for Notch1. Nat Genet 1997;16:243–51.
58. Oda T, Elkahloun AG, Pike BL, et al. Mutations in the human Jagged1 gene are responsible for Alagille syndrome. Nat Genet 1997;16:235–42.
59. Feuerhake F, Fuchsl G, Bals R, Welsch U. Expression of inducible cell adhesion molecules in the normal human lung: immunohistochemical study of their distribution in pulmonary blood vessels. Histochem Cell Biol 1998;110:387–94.
60. Gory-Faure S, Prandini MH, Pointu H, et al. Role of vascular endothelial-cadherin in vascular morphogenesis. Development 1999;126:2093–102.
61. Carmeliet P, Lampugnani MG, Moons L, et al. Targeted deficiency or cytosolic truncation of the VE-cadherin gene in mice impairs VEGF-mediated endothelial survival and angiogenesis. Cell 1999;98:147–57.
62. Breier G, Breviario F, Caveda L, et al. Molecular cloning and expression of murine vascular endothelial-cadherin in early stage development of cardiovascular system. Blood 1996;87:630–41.
63. Bach TL, Barsigian C, Chalupowicz DG, et al. VE-cadherin mediates endothelial cell capillary tube formation in fibrin and collagen gels. Exp Cell Res 1998;238:324–34.
64. Vittet D, Buchou T, Schweitzer A, et al. Targeted null-mutation in the vascular endothelial-cadherin gene impairs the organization of vascular-like structures in embryoid bodies. Proc Natl Acad Sci U S A 1997;94:6273–8.
65. Esser S, Lampugnani MG, Corada M, et al. Vascular endothelial growth factor induces VE-cadherin tyrosine phosphorylation in endothelial cells. J Cell Sci 1998;111:1853–65.
66. Yang S, Graham J, Kahn JW, et al. Functional roles for PECAM-1 (CD31) and VE-cadherin (CD144) in tube assembly and lumen formation in three-dimensional collagen gels. Am J Pathol 1999;155:887–95.
67. Matsumura T, Wolff K, Petzelbauer P. Endothelial cell tube formation depends on cadherin 5 and CD31 interactions with filamentous actin. J Immunol 1997;158:3408–16.
68. Gory S, Vernet M, Laurent M, et al. The vascular endothelial-cadherin promoter directs endothelial-specific expression in transgenic mice. Blood 1999; 93:184–92.
69. Corada M, Mariotti M, Thurston G, et al. Vascular endothelial-cadherin is an important determinant of microvascular integrity in vivo. Proc Natl Acad Sci U S A 1999;96:9815–20.
70. Telo' P, Breviario F, Huber P, et al. Identification of a novel cadherin (vascular endothelial cadherin-2) located at

intercellular junctions in endothelial cells. J Biol Chem 1998;273:17565–72.
71. Baldwin HS, Shen H-M, Yan H-C, et al. Platelet endothelial cell adhesion molecule-1 (PECAM-1/CD31): alternatively spliced, functionally distinct isoforms expressed during mammalian cardiovascular development. Development 1994;120:2539–53.
72. Yan HC, Baldwin HS, Sun J, et al. Alternative splicing of a specific cytoplasmic exon alters the binding characteristics of murine platelet/endothelial cell adhesion molecule-1 (PECAM-1). J Biol Chem 1995;270:23672–80.
73. Jackson DE, Ward CM, Wang R, Newman PJ. The protein-tyrosine phosphatase SHP-2 binds platelet/endothelial cell adhesion molecule-1 (PECAM-1) and forms a distinct signaling complex during platelet aggregation. Evidence for a mechanistic link between PECAM-1- and integrin-mediated cellular signaling. J Biol Chem 1997;272:6986–93.
74. Lu TT, Yan LG, Madri JA. Integrin engagement mediates tyrosine dephosphorylation on platelet-endothelial cell adhesion molecule 1. Proc Natl Acad Sci U S A 1996; 93:11808–13.
75. Muzykantov VR, Christofidou-Solomidou M, Balyasnikova I, et al. Streptavidin facilitates internalization and pulmonary targeting of an anti-endothelial cell antibody (platelet-endothelial cell adhesion molecule 1): a strategy for vascular immunotargeting of drugs. Proc Natl Acad Sci U S A 1999;96:2379–84.
76. Christofidou-Solomidou M, Pietra GG, Solomides CC, et al. Immunotargeting of glucose oxidase to endothelium in vivo causes oxidative vascular injury in the lungs. Am J Physiol Lung Cell Mol Physiol 2000;278:L794–805.
77. Li S, Tan Y, Viroonchatapan E, et al. Targeted gene delivery to pulmonary endothelium by anti-PECAM antibody. Am J Physiol Lung Cell Mol Physiol 2000;278:L504–11.
78. Duncan GS, Andrew DP, Takimoto H, et al. Genetic evidence for functional redundancy of platelet/endothelial cell adhesion molecule-1 (PECAM-1): CD31-deficient mice reveal PECAM-1-dependent and PECAM-1-independent functions. J Immunol 1999;162:3022–30.
79. Duplaa C, Couffinhal T, Dufourcq P, et al. The integrin very late antigen-4 is expressed in human smooth muscle cell. Involvement of alpha 4 and vascular cell adhesion molecule-1 during smooth muscle cell differentiation. Circ Res 1997;80:159–69.
80. Sheppard AM, Onken MD, Rosen GD, et al. Expanding roles for alpha 4 integrin and its ligands in development. Cell Adhes Commun 1994;2:27–43.
81. Kwee L, Baldwin HS, Shen HM, et al. Defective development of the embryonic and extraembryonic circulatory systems in vascular cell adhesion molecule (VCAM-1) deficient mice. Development 1995;121:489–503.
82. Yang JT, Rayburn H, Hynes RO. Cell adhesion events mediated by alpha 4 integrins are essential in placental and cardiac development. Development 1995; 121:549–60.
83. Shattil SJ, Ginsberg MH. Integrin signaling in vascular biology. J Clin Invest 1997;100:S91–5.
84. Luscinskas FW, Lawler J. Integrins as dynamic regulators of vascular function. FASEB J 1994;8:929–38.
85. De Arcangelis A, Georges-Labouesse E. Integrin and ECM functions: roles in vertebrate development. Trends Genet 2000;16:389–95.
86. Kreidberg JA, Donovan MJ, Goldstein SL, et al. Alpha 3 beta 1 integrin has a crucial role in kidney and lung organogenesis. Development 1996;122:3537–47.
87. Drake CJ, Davis LA, Little CD. Antibodies to beta 1-integrins cause alterations of aortic vasculogenesis, in vivo. Dev Dyn 1992;193:83–91.
88. Hoying JB, Williams SK. Effects of basic fibroblast growth factor on human microvessel endothelial cell migration on collagen I correlates inversely with adhesion and is cell density dependent. J Cell Physiol 1996;168:294–304.
89. Kanda S, Tomasini-Johansson B, Klint P, et al. Signaling via fibroblast growth factor receptor-1 is dependent on extracellular matrix in capillary endothelial cell differentiation. Exp Cell Res 1999;248:203–13.
90. Bloch W, Forsberg E, Lentini S, et al. Beta 1 integrin is essential for teratoma growth and angiogenesis. J Cell Biol 1997;139:265–78.
91. Stephens LE, Sutherland AE, Klimanskaya IV, et al. Deletion of beta 1 integrins in mice results in inner cell mass failure and peri-implantation lethality. Genes Dev 1995;9:1883–95.
92. Wu JE, Santoro SA. Differential expression of integrin alpha subunits supports distinct roles during lung branching morphogenesis. Dev Dyn 1996;206:169–81.
93. Bader BL, Rayburn H, Crowley D, Hynes RO. Extensive vasculogenesis, angiogenesis, and organogenesis precede lethality in mice lacking all αv integrins. Cell 1998; 95:507–19.
94. Singh B, Fu C, Bhattacharya J. Vascular expression of the alpha(v)beta(3)-integrin in lung and other organs. Am J Physiol Lung Cell Mol Physiol 2000;278:L217–26.
95. Drake CJ, Cheresh DA, Little CD. An antagonist of integrin alpha v beta 3 prevents maturation of blood vessels during embryonic neovascularization. J Cell Sci 1995; 108:2655–61.
96. Friedlander M, Brooks P, Shaffer R, et al. Definition of two angiogenic pathways by distinct αv integrins. Science 1995;270:1500–2.
97. Conforti G, Dominguez-Jimenez C, Zanetti A, et al. Human endothelial cells express integrin receptors on the luminal aspect of their membrane. Blood 1992;80:437–46.
98. Damjanovich L, Albelda SM, Mette SA, Buck CA. Distribution of integrin cell adhesion receptors in normal and malignant lung tissue. Am J Respir Cell Mol Biol 1992;6:197–206.
99. Liaw L, Skinner MP, Raines EW, et al. The adhesive and migratory effects of osteopontin are mediated via distinct cell surface integrins. Role of alpha v beta 3 in smooth muscle cell migration to osteopontin in vitro. J Clin Invest 1995;95:713–24.
100. Elices MJ, Urry LA, Hemler ME. Receptor functions for the integrin VLA-3: fibronectin, collagen, and laminin binding are differentially influenced by Arg-Gly-Asp peptide and by divalent cations. J Cell Biol 1991; 112:169–81.
101. Roman J, McDonald JA. Expression of fibronectin, the integrin α5, and α-smooth muscle actin in heart and

lung development. Am J Respir Cell Mol Biol 1992; 6:472–80.
102. Roman J, Little CW, McDonald JA. Potential role of RGD-binding integrins in mammalian lung branching morphogenesis. Development 1991;112:551–8.
103. Yang JT, Rayburn H, Hynes RO. Embryonic mesodermal defects in alpha 5 integrin-deficient mice. Development 1993;119:1093–105.
104. Roman J. Fibronectin and fibronectin receptors in lung development. Exp Lung Res 1997;23:147–59.
105. Spargo BJ, Testoff MA, Nielsen TB, et al. Spatially controlled adhesion, spreading, and differentiation of endothelial cells on self-assembled molecular monolayers. Proc Natl Acad Sci U S A 1994;91:11070–4.
106. Chen WT, Chen JM, Mueller SC. Coupled expression and colocalization of 140K cell adhesion molecules, fibronectin, and laminin during morphogenesis and cytodifferentiation of chick lung cells. J Cell Biol 1986;103:1073–90.
107. Risau W, Lemmon V. Changes in the vascular extracellular matrix during embryonic vasculogenesis and angiogenesis. Dev Biol 1988;125:441–50.
108. George EL, Georges-Labouesse EN, Patel-King RS, et al. Defects in mesoderm, neural tube and vascular development in mouse embryos lacking fibronectin. Development 1993;119:1079–91.
109. Georges-Labouesse EN, George EL, Rayburn H, Hynes RO. Mesodermal development in mouse embryos mutant for fibronectin. Dev Dyn 1996;207:145–56.
110. George EL, Baldwin HS, Hynes RO. Fibronectins are essential for heart and blood vessel morphogenesis but are dispensable for initial specification of precursor cells. Blood 1997;90:3073–81.
111. Sinkin RA, Roberts M, LoMonaco MB, et al. Fibronectin expression in bronchopulmonary dysplasia. Pediatr Dev Pathol 1998;1:494–502.
112. Flores-Delgado G, Bringas P, Warburton D. Laminin 2 attachment selects myofibroblasts from fetal mouse lung. Am J Physiol 1998;275:L622–30.
113. Frid MG, Moiseeva EP, Stenmark KR. Multiple phenotypically distinct smooth muscle cell populations exist in the adult and developing bovine pulmonary arterial media in vivo. Circ Res 1994;75:669–81.
114. Hall SM, Hislop AA, Pierce CM, Haworth SG. Prenatal origins of human intrapulmonary arteries. Formation and smooth muscle maturation. Am J Respir Cell Mol Biol 2000;23:194–203.
115. Jostarndt-Fogen K, Djonov V, Draeger A. Expression of smooth muscle markers in the developing murine lung: potential contractile properties and lineal descent. Histochem Cell Biol 1998;110:273–84.
116. Mitchell JJ, Reynolds SE, Leslie KO, et al. Smooth muscle cell markers in developing rat lung. Am J Respir Cell Mol Biol 1990;3:515–23.
117. Morrell NW, Grieshaber SS, Danilov SM, et al. Developmental regulation of angiotensin converting enzyme and angiotensin type 1 receptor in the rat pulmonary circulation. Am J Respir Cell Mol Biol 1996;14:526–37.
118. Brannon TS, MacRitchie AN, Jaramillo MA, et al. Ontogeny of cyclooxygenase-1 and cyclooxygenase-2 gene expression in ovine lung. Am J Physiol 1998;274:L66–71.
119. Halbower AC, Tuder RM, Franklin WA, et al. Maturation-related changes in endothelial nitric oxide synthase immunolocalization in developing ovine lung. Am J Physiol 1994;267:L585–91.
120. North AJ, Star RA, Brannon TS, et al. Nitric oxide synthase type I and type III gene expression are developmentally regulated in rat lung. Am J Physiol 1994; 266:L635–41.
121. Shaul PW. Regulation of vasodilator synthesis during lung development. Early Hum Dev 1999;54:271–94.
122. Villanueva ME, Zaher FM, Svinarich DM, Konduri GG. Decreased gene expression of endothelial nitric oxide synthase in newborns with persistent pulmonary hypertension. Pediatr Res 1998;44:338–43.
123. North AJ, Moya FR, Mysore MR, et al. Pulmonary endothelial nitric oxide synthase gene expression is decreased in a rat model of congenital diaphragmatic hernia. Am J Respir Cell Mol Biol 1995;13:676–82.
124. Wang H, Keiser JA. Vascular endothelial growth factor upregulates the expression of matrix metalloproteinases in vascular smooth muscle cells. Circ Res 1998; 83:832–40.
125. Fukuda Y, Ishizaki M, Okada Y, et al. Matrix metalloproteinases and tissue inhibitor of metalloproteinase-2 in fetal rabbit lung. Am J Physiol Lung Cell Mol Physiol 2000;279:L555–61.
126. Soifer SJ, Peters KG, O'Keefe J, Coughlin SR. Disparate temporal expression of the prothrombin and thrombin receptor genes during mouse development. Am J Pathol 1994;144:60–9.
127. Morrisey EE, Ip HS, Tang Z, et al. GATA-5: a transcriptional activator expressed in a novel temporally and spatially restricted pattern during embryonic development. Dev Biol 1997;183:21–36.
128. Keijzer R, van Tuyl M, Meijers C, et al. The transcription factor GATA6 is essential for branching morphogenesis and epithelial cell differentiation during fetal pulmonary development. Development 2001;128:503–11.
129. Bogue CW, Gross I, Vasavada H, et al. Identification of Hox genes in newborn lung and effects of gestational age and retinoic acid on their expression. Am J Physiol 1994;266:L448–54.
130. Chinoy MR, Volpe MV, Cilley RE, et al. Growth factors and dexamethasone regulate Hoxb5 protein in cultured murine fetal lungs. Am J Physiol 1998;274:L610–20.
131. Boudreau N, Andrews C, Srebrow A, et al. Induction of the angiogenic phenotype by Hox D3. J Cell Biol 1997;139:257–64.
132. Maroulakou IG, Papas TS, Green JE. Differential expression of ets-1 and ets-2 proto-oncogenes during murine embryogenesis. Oncogene 1994;9:1551–65.
133. Oda N, Abe M, Sato Y. ETS-1 converts endothelial cells to the angiogenic phenotype by inducing the expression of matrix metalloproteinases and integrin beta3. J Cell Physiol 1999;178:121–32.
134. Wernert N, Raes MB, Lassalle P, et al. c-ets1 proto-oncogene is a transcription factor expressed in endothelial cells during tumor vascularization and other forms

of angiogenesis in humans. Am J Pathol 1992;140: 119–27.
135. Valter MM, Hugel A, Huang HJ, et al. Expression of the Ets-1 transcription factor in human astrocytomas is associated with Fms-like tyrosine kinase-1 (Flt-1)/ vascular endothelial growth factor receptor-1 synthesis and neoangiogenesis. Cancer Res 1999;59:5608–14.
136. Gory S, Dalmon J, Prandini MH, et al. Requirement of a GT box (Sp1 site) and two Ets binding sites for vascular endothelial cadherin gene transcription. J Biol Chem 1998;273:6750–5.
137. Chen Z, Fisher RJ, Riggs CW, et al. Inhibition of vascular endothelial growth factor-induced endothelial cell migration by ETS1 antisense oligonucleotides. Cancer Res 1997;57:2013–9.
138. Iwasaka C, Tanaka K, Abe M, Sato Y. Ets-1 regulates angiogenesis by inducing the expression of urokinase-type plasminogen activator and matrix metalloproteinase-1 and the migration of vascular endothelial cells. J Cell Physiol 1996;169:522–31.
139. Hidai C, Zupancic T, Penta K, et al. Cloning and characterization of developmental endothelial locus-1: an embryonic endothelial cell protein that binds the $\alpha v\beta_3$ integrin receptor. Genes Dev 1998;12:21–33.
140. Schwarz M, Lee M, Zhang F, et al. EMAP II: a modulator of neovascularization in the developing lung. Am J Physiol 1999;276:L365–75.
141. Maltepe E, Simon MC. Oxygen, genes, and development: an analysis of the role of hypoxic gene regulation during murine vascular development. J Mol Med 1998; 76:391–401.
142. Semenza GL. HIF-1: mediator of physiological and pathophysiological responses to hypoxia. J Appl Physiol 2000;88:1474–80.
143. Yu AY, Frid MG, Shimoda LA, et al. Temporal, spatial, and oxygen-regulated expression of hypoxia-inducible factor-1 in the lung. Am J Physiol 1998;275:L818–26.
144. Iyer NV, Kotch LE, Agani F, et al. Cellular and developmental control of O_2 homeostasis by hypoxia-inducible factor 1 alpha. Genes Dev 1998;12:149–62.
145. Ryan HE, Lo J, Johnson RS. HIF-1 alpha is required for solid tumor formation and embryonic vascularization. EMBO J 1998;17:3005–15.
146. Carmeliet P, Dor Y, Herbert JM, et al. Role of HIF-1 alpha in hypoxia-mediated apoptosis, cell proliferation and tumour angiogenesis [published erratum appears in Nature 1998;395:525]. Nature 1998;394:485–90.
147. Kozak KR, Abbott B, Hankinson O. ARNT-deficient mice and placental differentiation. Dev Biol 1997; 191:297–305.
148. Maltepe E, Schmidt JV, Baunoch D, et al. Abnormal angiogenesis and responses to glucose and oxygen deprivation in mice lacking the protein ARNT. Nature 1997;386:403–7.
149. Adelman DM, Gertsenstein M, Nagy A, et al. Placental cell fates are regulated in vivo by HIF-mediated hypoxia responses. Genes Dev 2000;14:3191–203.
150. Ema M, Taya S, Yokotani N, et al. A novel bHLH-PAS factor with close sequence similarity to hypoxia-inducible factor 1 alpha regulates the VEGF expression and is potentially involved in lung and vascular development. Proc Natl Acad Sci U S A 1997;94:4273–8.
151. Flamme I, Frohlich T, von Reutern M, et al. HRF, a putative basic helix-loop-helix-PAS-domain transcription factor is closely related to hypoxia-inducible factor-1 alpha and developmentally expressed in blood vessels. Mech Dev 1997;63:51–60.
152. Tian H, McKnight SL, Russell DW. Endothelial PAS domain protein 1 (EPAS1), a transcription factor selectively expressed in endothelial cells. Genes Dev 1997; 11:72–82.
153. Tian H, Hammer RE, Matsumoto AM, et al. The hypoxia-responsive transcription factor EPAS1 is essential for catecholamine homeostasis and protection against heart failure during embryonic development. Genes Dev 1998;12:3320–4.
154. Tufro-McReddie A, Norwood VF, Aylor KW, et al. Oxygen regulates vascular endothelial growth factor-mediated vasculogenesis and tubulogenesis. Dev Biol 1997; 183:139–49.
155. Crapo JD. Morphologic changes in pulmonary oxygen toxicity. Annu Rev Physiol 1986;48:721–31.
156. Smith LJ. Hyperoxic lung injury: biochemical, cellular, and morphologic characterization in the mouse. J Lab Clin Med 1985;106:269–78.
157. Fracica PJ, Knapp MJ, Piantadosi CA, et al. Responses of baboons to prolonged hyperoxia: physiology and qualitative pathology. J Appl Physiol 1991;71:2352–62.
158. Frank L, Bucher JR, Roberts RJ. Oxygen toxicity in neonatal and adult animals of various species. J Appl Physiol Respir Environ Excr Physiol 1978;45:699–704.
159. Frank L. Developmental aspects of experimental pulmonary oxygen toxicity. Free Radic Biol Med 1991;11:463–94.
160. Massaro D, Teich N, Maxwell S, et al. Postnatal development of alveoli. Regulation and evidence for a critical period in rats. J Clin Invest 1985;76:1297–305.
161. Wilson WL, Mullen M, Ollcy PM, Rabinovitch M. Hyperoxia-induced pulmonary vascular and lung abnormalities in young rats and potential for recovery. Pediatr Res 1985;19:1059–67.
162. Roberts RJ, Weesner KM, Bucher JR. Oxygen-induced alterations in lung vascular development in the newborn rat. Pediatr Res 1983;17:368–75.
163. Shaffer SG, O'Neill D, Bradt SK, Thibeault DW. Chronic vascular pulmonary dysplasia associated with neonatal hyperoxia exposure in the rat. Pediatr Res 1987; 21:14–20.
164. Randell SH, Mercer RR, Young SL. Neonatal hyperoxia alters the pulmonary alveolar and capillary structure of 40-day-old rats. Am J Pathol 1990;136:1259–66.
165. Maniscalco WM, Watkins RH, Finkelstein JN, Campbell MH. Vascular endothelial growth factor mRNA increases in alveolar epithelial cells during recovery from oxygen injury. Am J Respir Cell Mol Biol 1995;13:377–86.

CHAPTER 6

Tissue Interactions in Lung Organogenesis

John M. Shannon, PhD, Brian A. Hyatt, PhD

The metabolic load of cellular respiration in air-breathing mammals and amphibians requires an efficient means for providing systemic oxygen that is met by the lungs, which provide a very large surface area (estimated at 70 to 100 m^2 in the adult human) for gas exchange. The lung is a complex organ that comprises over 40 distinct cell types, each of which plays a role in normal lung functions, such as maintenance of alveolar patency, protection against inhaled particulates and toxins, and innate host immunity. Despite its eventual complexity, the lung has a simple beginning, arising from the floor of the foregut endoderm as the seventh pair of pharyngeal pouches. In humans, the first evidence of lung development is the formation of the laryngotracheal groove, which bifurcates at its posterior end to form the primary bronchi and lung rudiments. Initiation of lung development in rodents is slightly different as the lung rudiments arise as paired endodermal outgrowths into mesenchyme derived from splanchnic mesoderm. In both cases, however, the induced endoderm undergoes a series of dichotomous and lateral branchings to give rise to the pulmonary tree, a process classically referred to as branching morphogenesis. Alveolarization begins toward the end of gestation and continues postnatally. The extensive arborization of the pulmonary epithelium is accompanied by parallel development of a highly ordered pulmonary vasculature. This parallel development of the distal pulmonary epithelium and vasculature in the embryo and fetus generate what will postnatally become the functional gas exchange system.

Concomitant with branching morphogenesis is the specification of the various cell types throughout the lung that will constitute the mature organ. Pattern formation and the spatially correct differentiation of the different cell types within the developing lung require the coordinated expression of multiple genes in the correct place at the proper time. Elucidation of the genes controlling lung development is just beginning, but one tenet has emerged: mesenchyme specifies epithelial morphogenesis and cytodifferentiation by means of a proximate induction.

Tissue Interactions in the Developing Lung

Studies in both mammals[1–3] and birds[4,5] have established that epithelial branching morphogenesis and differentiation in the lung require an interaction between the endodermal epithelium and its subtending mesenchyme. This is but one example of a number of short-range secondary inductions that are commonly referred to as epithelial–mesenchymal interactions, which have been described in the lung, salivary gland,[6] pancreas,[7] mammary gland,[8] kidney,[9] tooth,[10] limb,[11] urogenital tract,[12] and other organs.

In the lung, the first report of a mesenchymal requirement for lung morphogenesis was made over 65 years ago by Rudnick,[5] who observed that embryonic chick lung rudiments would branch when grafted onto chorioallantoic membranes in ovo, but all development ceased when the mesenchyme was removed. The development of in vitro techniques for embryonic lung rudiments allowed these observations to be confirmed and extended in both birds[4] and mammals.[2,13,14] Even the earliest events in lung organogenesis can occur in vitro: primary lung buds will form in cultured guts taken from embryos as early as the 2-somite stage. Extensive branching occurs, however, only if the guts are taken from embryos at the 25-somite stage, when the primary lung downgrowths have just emerged from the floor of the gut tube.[2]

The development of tissue recombination techniques advanced the study of epithelial–mesenchymal interactions. At particular stages of development, embryonic organ rudiments that are treated with proteolytic enzyme incubation followed by mechanical dissection can be separated into purified epithelium and mesenchyme. Then the tissues are recombined and cultured in vitro. Particularly informative studies have compared the response of an epithelium to its own mesenchyme (homotypic recombinant) versus an unrelated mesenchyme (heterotypic recombinant). A number of studies involving the separation, recombination, and culture of embryonic lung rudiments have produced several consistent observations

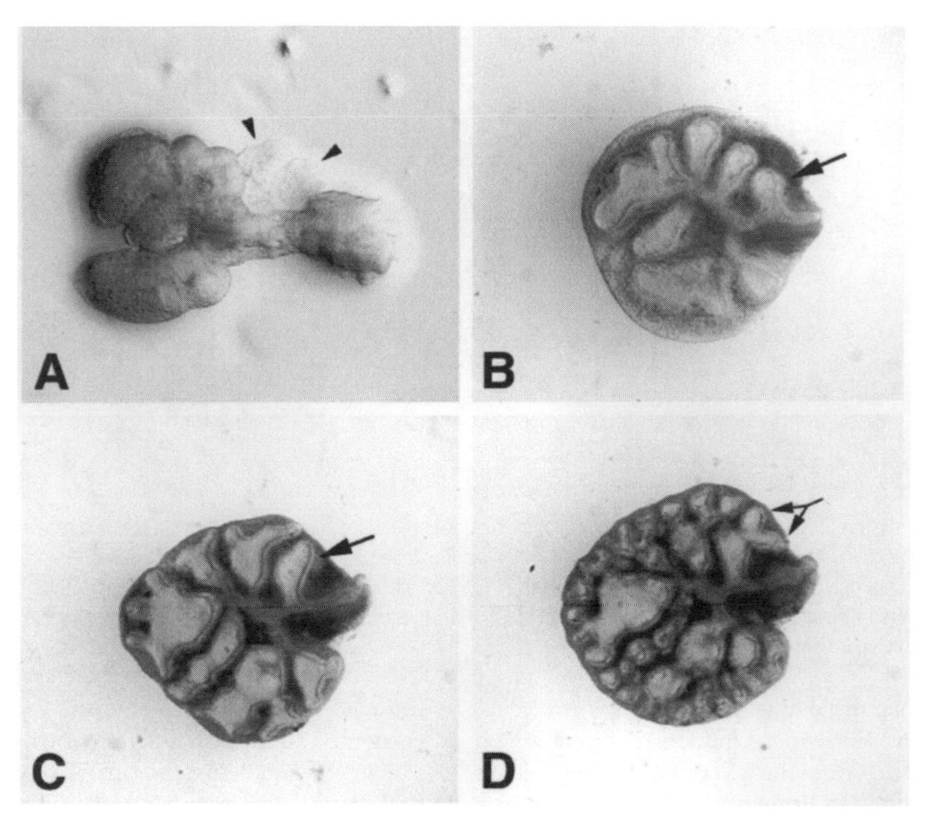

FIGURE 6–1. Lung mesenchyme specifies epithelial morphogenesis. *A*, A lung-trachea complex taken from a gestational day 13 rat embryo in which the mesenchyme has been surgically removed from the trachea and replaced with same-stage distal lung mesenchyme (*arrowheads*). *B*, After 24 hours of culture, the lung mesenchyme has induced a supernumerary bud (*arrow*) from the wall of the tracheal epithelium. *C*, After 48 hours, the induced bud (arrow) has elongated and expanded. *D*, After 72 hours, the induced bud has begun to branch (*double-headed arrow*) in a pattern identical to the untreated lung tissue (original magnification × 18.5).

concerning the role of epithelial–mesenchymal interactions in lung development. First, embryonic lung epithelium cannot survive for an extended period in the absence of mesenchyme. Masters demonstrated that embryonic mouse lung epithelial rudiments undergo necrosis by 72 hours when cultured in the absence of mesenchyme;[14] a minimal amount of mesenchyme is required for epithelial survival in vitro, and the extent of epithelial differentiation is related to the amount of mesenchyme present in the tissue recombinants.

Second, branching morphogenesis of embryonic lung epithelium requires a specific interaction with lung mesenchyme. Embryonic lung epithelium can survive in a heterotypic mesenchyme, although further proliferation and lung-like branching are arrested. Dameron demonstrated that the chick lung epithelial rudiments survive when recombined with mesonephric, somitic, or chorioallantoic mesenchyme but only branch normally in the presence of lung mesenchyme[4]; limited branching can be induced by metanephric mesenchyme. Spooner and Wessells showed that cultured 25-somite (gestational day 9) mouse gut endoderm forms lung buds in response to salivary gland mesenchyme but branches only in the presence of lung mesenchyme.[2] The response of embryonic lung epithelium to salivary gland mesenchyme is variable and depends on the stage at which the epithelium is isolated: epithelial lung rudiments isolated from day 12 mice or day 13 rats show no response when recombined with salivary gland mesenchyme, whereas epithelial rudiments isolated from lungs only 1 day older (when secondary branches have formed) show a limited branching response.[15,16] Similar results were seen in recombinations of day 15 rat salivary gland mesenchyme with day 12 rat lung epithelium.[17] The pattern of branching in these recombinants is specified by the mesenchyme, in this case, like the salivary gland. The cytodifferentiated phenotype of the lung epithelial cells responding to recombination with salivary gland mesenchyme was not determined. Whether salivary gland mesenchyme was permissively supporting lung epithelial cell cytodifferentiation or instructively reprogramming the expression of a new phenotype is unknown.

Another system that demonstrated the instructive capabilities of lung mesenchyme and also served as a model for early events in lung development was originally described by Alescio and Cassini.[18] In these studies, a portion of mesenchyme is surgically removed from the day 11 to 12 mouse trachea and replaced by a heterotypic

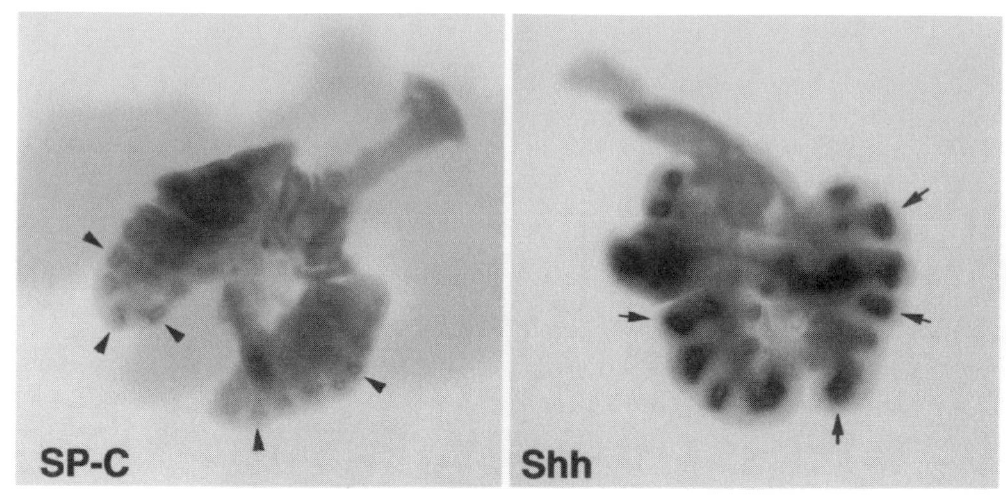

FIGURE 6–2. Expression of SP-C and Sonic hedgehog (Shh) in the developing lung. Lung-trachea complexes were taken from embryonic mice on gestational days 13 (*left*) and 12 (*right*) and hybridized with digoxigenin-labeled antisense RNA probes to either SP-C or Shh. Note that SP-C is expressed (dark staining) only in the most distal lung buds (*arrowheads*), which are the precursors of the alveolar epithelium. In contrast, Shh is expressed (dark staining) throughout the respiratory epithelium but is most intense in the distal lung buds (*arrows*), which serve as signaling centers in the developing lung (original magnification × 5.5).

mesenchyme. When distal lung mesenchyme is grafted as the replacement mesenchyme, it induces the formation of a supernumerary bud from the wall of the tracheal epithelium that continues to branch in a lung-like fashion (Figure 6–1). These data were extended by Wessells, who demonstrated that mesenchyme from several unrelated tissues also can induce the formation of a supernumerary bud when grafted onto denuded tracheal epithelium.[3] Importantly, however, only lung mesenchyme supports branching subsequent to initial bud formation. Furthermore, Wessells showed that tracheal mesenchyme inhibits branching of lung epithelium when grafted onto denuded lung epithelium.[3] Thus, important differences clearly exist between lung and tracheal mesenchyme, even though both have a similar spatial origin within the embryo.

Third, epithelial cell phenotype is dependent on the type of mesenchyme from which it receives inductive signals. A question arising from the tracheal grafting studies concerned the cellular phenotype of the induced tracheal epithelium. We addressed this question by grafting distal embryonic lung mesenchyme onto same-stage tracheal epithelium that was denuded of its own mesenchyme.[19] Identical to prior observations in the mouse, distal embryonic rat lung mesenchyme grafted onto tracheal epithelium induces a supernumerary bud that branches in a lung-like pattern. Histologic and ultrastructural analyses indicate that the tracheal epithelium has been reprogrammed to express a distal lung epithelial phenotype. We also took advantage of the observation that surfactant protein C (SP-C) is an alveolar type II epithelial cell-specific marker in fetal rodents (Figure 6–2),[20,21] and epithelial cells of the rodent trachea have never been shown to express SP-C at any point in development. The branching structures induced in tracheal epithelium by distal lung mesenchyme exhibit cells intensely positive for SP-C messenger ribonucleic acid (mRNA) in the most distal aspects, and the expression of SP-C mRNA is detected as soon as 24 hours after recombination (Figure 6–3). The distal pattern of SP-C mRNA expression is identical to that seen in control cultures of intact lung explants from the same animals, which suggests that the lung mesenchyme induces the tracheal epithelium to follow a spatially correct pattern of development. From these molecular, histochemical, and ultrastructural data, it was concluded that the lung mesenchyme is acting instructively on the tracheal epithelium; that is, the cells have been reprogrammed to express a new phenotype that would not have occurred in the absence of lung mesenchyme. The ability of tracheal epithelium to respond to lung mesenchyme is temporally restricted, however, since day 16 epithelium is not competent to respond to day 13 mesenchyme. Furthermore, lung mesenchyme was unable to induce a response in other gut-derived endodermal derivatives such as esophagus and intestine, indicating that these epithelia are already restricted at this time point.

As will be discussed below, the conservation of the basic mechanisms underlying branching of the respiratory system may extend evolutionarily back to *Drosophila*. The conservation of permissive induction by lung mesenchyme from different species also holds true for epithelial cytodifferentiation: when day 16 mouse lung epithelium is directly recombined with chick lung mesenchyme, the epithelium branches, when cultured for 2 to 5 days, and the resultant epithelial cells contain copious numbers of lamellar bodies, indicating that type II cell differentiation has occurred.[22]

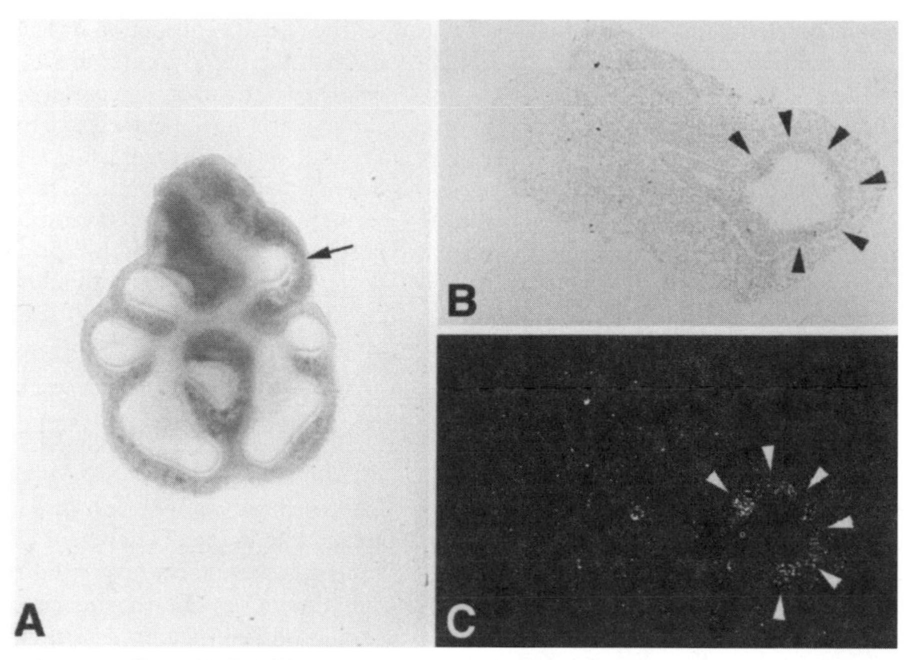

FIGURE 6–3. Lung mesenchyme specifies epithelial differentiated phenotype. *A*, This panel depicts a supernumerary bud (*arrow*) that has been induced by grafting distal lung mesenchyme onto tracheal epithelium that has had a portion of its mesenchyme surgically removed. *B* and *C*, Tissue-section autoradiography of the supernumerary bud shown in panel *A*, which has been hybridized with a radiolabeled antisense RNA probe to SP-C. Surfactant protein-C is a molecular marker specific for the distal epithelium and is not present in the trachea. The induced bud (*circumscribed by arrowheads*) consists of multiple cell layers (*B*). Darkfield optics of the autoradiogram (*C*) demonstrate that SP-C has been induced in the supernumerary bud, indicating that the tracheal epithelium has been reprogrammed to express a distal lung phenotype. Note that the tracheal epithelium is completely negative for SP-C expression.

The effects of lung mesenchyme on stimulating lung epithelial branching appear to be short range and mediated by a diffusible factor(s). This was shown in transfilter tissue recombinations performed using the techniques pioneered by Grobstein in his benchmark studies on the developing kidney and salivary gland.[23] Using this model system, Taderera isolated lung epithelial and mesenchymal rudiments and cultured them in apposition to each other, with a 0.45-mm Millipore filter interposed between them.[13] These filters allow the passage of macromolecules between the two tissues but do not allow direct cell-to-cell contact by virtue of the tortuous pathways traversing these mesh-type filters. The results showed that the epithelium do not branch in the absence of mesenchyme but rather spread over the surface of the plasma clot substratum. In the presence of lung mesenchyme, however, lung-like branching ensues. An important additional observation in these experiments was that chick lung mesenchyme is as effective as mouse lung mesenchyme in supporting branching, again suggesting that the inductive molecules required for branching morphogenesis are evolutionarily conserved.

Reciprocity in epithelial–mesenchymal interactions also occurs in lung development. As noted above, Taderera demonstrated that the ability of lung mesenchyme to support epithelial branching is maintained when a filter is interposed between the two tissues, and direct contact between the epithelium and mesenchyme is not discernible.[13] Additional observations made in these experiments concerned the effects of the epithelium on the mesenchyme: vascular and stromal cells develop only in the mesenchyme when it is cultured transfilter to lung epithelium. In the absence of epithelium, lung mesenchyme fails to express pulmonary connective tissue cell types. Furthermore, spinal cord and salivary epithelia fail to influence lung mesenchymal histogenesis, suggesting that the epithelial contribution to mesenchymal histogenesis is a specific one. If development of the specialized cell types in the nonepithelial compartment of the lung is dependent on the presence of lung epithelium, reciprocity would exist: epithelial proliferation and differentiation are induced by an as-yet-unidentified mesenchymal cell population. Then the induced epithelium would, in turn, produce factors inducing mesenchymal cell proliferation, differentiation, and organization.

In summary, lung epithelium has a highly specific, evolutionarily conserved interaction with lung mesenchyme that is required for normal proliferation and branching to occur. The requisite factors are diffusible and do not require direct cell-to-cell contact. Lung mesenchyme can act either instructively, as in the reprogramming of tracheal epithelium, or permissively, as in supporting salivary gland epithelial cytodifferentiation. Whether heterotypic mesenchymes can permissively support lung epithelial cell differentiation in the absence of cell proliferation and branching is unknown.

Mediators of Tissue Interactions in Lung Development

The list of hormones, growth factors, other signaling molecules, and components of the extracellular matrix that have been shown to affect lung development is extensive. Space limitations preclude a discussion of all of these factors, which have been the subject of several recent reviews.[24–26] Instead, we will limit our discussion to two families of molecules that act as critical mediators of tissue interactions during early lung morphogenesis: the fibroblast growth factor (FGF) family and Sonic hedgehog (Shh). These two examples illustrate the complexity of the molecular mechanisms underlying tissue interactions in lung development.

Fibroblast Growth Factors and Their Receptors

The FGF family comprises at least 21 related ligands. All of the known members of the FGF family share significant protein sequence identity within a core of approximately 120 amino acids that is responsible for one characteristic of this family: the ability to bind heparin.[27] Acidic and basic FGFs (hereafter FGF1 and FGF2, respectively) were the first FGF family members to be identified and, along with FGF9, differ from the other FGFs in that they do not contain a signal peptide for classic protein secretion. Fibroblast growth factors signal through high-affinity fibroblast growth factor receptors (FGFRs), which are one of nine subclasses of tyrosine kinase receptors. Four FGFRs have been identified; all are found in the lung,[28] and all share a common general structure. A secretory signal sequence at the N-terminus is followed by two or three immunoglobulin (Ig)-like disulfide loops that constitute the extracellular domain. A transmembrane domain anchors the receptors to the plasma membrane, thus defining the FGFR as cell surface receptors. The intracellular portion of the FGFR consists of two tyrosine kinase domains, which are divided by a short interkinase domain.

The complexity of the FGFR family is increased significantly by alternate RNA splicing. One functionally important variant occurs in the C-terminal portion of the third Ig-like loop, which affects ligand specificity and affinity. Alternative splicing of 49 amino acids in the C-terminal half of the third Ig-like loop in FGFR2 results in what have been termed the IIIb and IIIc splice variants of this receptor. This single variation has a profound effect on receptor function. The IIIb variant binds FGF1, FGF3, FGF7, and FGF10 with high affinity and FGF2 with lower affinity, whereas the IIIc variant binds FGF1, FGF2, FGF4, FGF6, and FGF9.[29] Use of this single splice variant has important implications for lung development.

The relevant interaction of FGFs with heparin occurs through their low-affinity binding of the related molecule, heparan sulfate. Heparan sulfate is found on cell surfaces and in the extracellular matrix in the form of heparan sulfate proteoglycan (HSPG). Currently, it is believed that HSPGs bind FGFs and induce or stabilize formation of FGF dimers or a ternary complex composed of ligand plus high- and low-affinity receptors. Beyond acting as co-receptors for FGFs on the cell surface, the HSPG that exists in the extracellular matrix can bind FGFs and thus may act as a reservoir for FGFs in the extracellular space.[30]

Fibroblast Growth Factors as Mediators of Tissue Interactions in the Developing Lung

Evidence from many systems has shown that FGFs play a critical role in the development of organs, affecting cells from all three germ layers. Fibroblast growth factor family members cause changes in cell proliferation, morphology, differentiation, and migration during organogenesis. All of these responses effected by FGFs have been demonstrated in the developing lung. Fibroblast growth factors 1,[31] 2,[32,33] 7,[34,35] 9,[36] 10,[37] and 18[38] all have been localized to the developing lung. Information on some of these ligands is sketchy, whereas other ligands have been investigated in much greater detail. Of these FGFs, only FGF10 has been shown to be absolutely essential for lung development. Expression of FGF10 has been demonstrated in the lungs of humans[39] and rodents,[40,41] where it has been localized to mesenchymal cells around distal lung epithelial tips.[37,42] Since the primary receptor for FGF10 (FGFR2IIIb) is found in the lung epithelium, FGF10 has been considered a primary candidate effector molecule of epithelial–mesenchymal interactions. Fibroblast growth factor 10 appears to be the evolutionarily conserved homologue of the *Drosophila* gene *branchless*, which interacts with its receptor *breathless* to guide tracheal epithelial buds to specific sites within the larva, thereby playing a primary role in patterning the *Drosophila* respiratory system.[43] Similarly, FGF10-soaked beads induce dramatic chemotaxis of embryonic lung epithelium,[42,44] supporting its role in determining the spatial coordinates of the early lung. The importance of FGF10 to lung development was most strikingly demonstrated in FGF10 null mice, which show no lung development below the trachea.[45,46] Thus, FGF10 plays a unique role in the induction of lung patterning that cannot be compensated by other FGF ligands.

Fibroblast growth factor 7 (keratinocyte growth factor) has no demonstrated effects on fibroblasts and instead is a potent mitogen and differentiation factor for epithelial cells. Like FGF10, FGF7 is present only in mesenchymal cells of the developing lung, although its distribution is more widespread. Also, like FGF10, FGF7 binds and activates FGFR2IIIb. Fibroblast growth factor

7 has potent effects on both the prenatal and postnatal lung. Targeted overexpression of FGF7 to the developing lung epithelium using the SP-C promoter results in abnormal development resembling pulmonary cystadenomatoid malformation.[47] Similarly, increasing FGF7 levels in the postnatal lung, either by instillation[48] or by conditional, targeted overexpression,[49] leads to epithelial hyperplasia. Fibroblast growth factor 7 also has potent effects in vitro. Lung explants treated with FGF7 show epithelial hyperplasia[50] and dilation.[51] Purified embryonic lung epithelia treated with FGF7 exhibit extensive proliferation and widespread expression of SP-C when given with other competence factors.[52] Furthermore, FGF7 is necessary (but not sufficient by itself) to reprogram embryonic tracheal epithelium to express an alveolar type II cell phenotype.[53] Importantly, however, mice with a targeted deletion of FGF7 exhibit no apparent lung abnormalities,[54] suggesting functional compensation by another FGF ligand(s). The data demonstrating functional differences between FGF7 and FGF10 present a paradox since they both predominantly bind the same receptor (FGFR2IIIb) splice variant in the lung epithelium. Thus, the effects of FGFs on morphogenetic patterning and cellular differentiation may be separable processes in the lung.

Fibroblast growth factor 1, which binds all four FGFRs, is detectable in both the epithelium and mesenchyme of the embyronic lung. A role for FGF1 in lung development has been suggested by the observation that FGF1 elicits growth and budding of day E11 mouse lung epithelium in mesenchyme-free culture.[55] Importantly, mice null for FGF1 exhibit no abnormalities in lung development, suggesting that its loss can be compensated for by other FGFs.[56]

Localization of FGF2 in the developing lung by immunohistochemistry has given variable results, with some investigators finding expression in the epithelium,[32] whereas others do not.[57] The developing human lung epithelium, however, contains FGF2 mRNA.[58] Fibroblast growth factor 2 has been shown to affect lung epithelial cell differentiation, inducing significant increases in expression of SP-A, SP-B, and SP-C mRNAs in midgestation fetal rat lung epithelial cells.[59] These data suggest a potential autocrine role for FGF2, but confirmation of this awaits a more detailed description of FGF2 expression in the developing lung. How these FGF2 effects on the lung epithelium are mediated is unclear since high-affinity receptors for FGF2 are located in the lung mesenchyme; it should be noted, however, that FGF2 has been shown to bind FGFR2IIIb but at a much lower affinity than FGF7 or FGF10.[60] If FGF2 plays a role in lung development, it can be compensated for by other FGFs since mice with a targeted deletion for FGF2 or null for both FGF1 and FGF2 have completely normal lungs.[56,61] Beyond the fact that they have been localized to the developing lung, little is known about how FGF9 and FGF18 affect lung morphogenesis and differentiation.

The most compelling data suggesting a primary role for FGFs in lung development come from studies in which FGF signaling pathways are disrupted by the alteration or elimination of FGF receptors. Using the SP-C promoter to target overexpression of a dominant-negative FGFR2IIIb to the surface of lung epithelial cells, Peters et al demonstrated that lung development does not progress beyond the generation of the trachea and two unbranched bronchi.[62] Celli et al used the metallothionein promoter to express a soluble dominant-negative FGFR2IIIb throughout the entire developing embryo and also observed lung bud initiation but no branching morphogenesis.[29] Targeted deletion of the FGFR2 gene results in embryonic lethality shortly after implantation owing to trophectoderm defects.[63] When these defects were circumvented by using tetraploid fusion chimeras, FGFR2 null mice showed no development of the respiratory tree below the trachea.[64] Using the Cre-loxP recombination system, De Moerlooze et al demonstrated that pulmonary agenesis results when the DNA coding for the IIIb exon is deleted.[65] This suggests a critical role for those FGF ligands that bind FGFR2IIIb in early lung development. Fibroblast growth factor receptor 2 is not the only FGF receptor signaling system used in the developing lung. Although mice null for FGFR3 or FGFR4 have no abnormal lung phenotype, mice null for both FGFR3 and FGFR4 show defective alveolar septation and abnormally elevated elastin content.[28] The role of FGFR1-mediated signaling in lung development is at present unknown since animals null for FGFR1 die early in development.[66]

Sonic Hedgehog, Patched, and Gli's

Sonic hedgehog, the mammalian homologue of the *Drosophila hedgehog* gene, is a secreted protein involved in many early developmental processes.[67,68] During early lung development, Shh is expressed in the epithelium of the entire respiratory tree but not in a uniform pattern: expression is increased markedly in the most distal epithelium, where epithelial–mesenchymal interactions are actively ongoing (see Figure 6–2). Whereas Shh is expressed by the developing lung epithelium, its predominant receptor, patched-1 (Ptc), is expressed in the lung mesenchyme and mirrors the expression pattern of Shh, being higher in the most distal aspects of the embryonic lung. These observations support a role for Shh in epithelium-to-mesenchyme signaling. The binding of Ptc by Shh derepresses the seven-pass transmembrane protein smoothened, which leads to activation of the Gli family of zinc finger transcription factors. The downstream target genes of the gli transactivators have not yet been elucidated.

Mice null for Shh expression exhibit developmental abnormalities in a variety of organs, including the lungs.[69,70] Sonic hedgehog knockout mice have delayed initiation of lung buds from the foregut endoderm, and growth and branching are severely retarded. Left-to-right asymmetry of the lung is completely absent, and separation of the tracheal and esophageal tubes fails to occur. Although a lack of Shh signaling leads to defects in patterning of the respiratory tree, epithelial differentiation apparently is not affected since clara cell secretory protein and SP-C, markers of the proximal and distal epithelium, respectively, are expressed in a spatially correct pattern.

Although these data demonstrate that expression of Shh is required for normal lung development, the amount and spatial distribution of Shh expression also play an important role in morphogenesis. This was shown in experiments in which the human SP-C promoter was used to drive overexpression of Shh in transgenic mice. These animals die at birth from respiratory failure, and examination of their lungs reveals an abnormal amount of mesenchyme and a lack of normal alveolar formation.[71] Whereas the abnormal amount and distribution of Shh in these animals may account for the disruption in lung development, it also is possible that temporal factors also are involved since the SP-C promoter sustained high-level Shh expression at stages of lung development when Shh is normally decreasing.

The three members of the Gli family of transcription factors are expressed in distinct but overlapping areas of the lung mesenchyme.[72] Mice with individual targeted deletions of Gli2 or Gli3 exhibit reduced lung size and changes in segmentation.[72,73] Mice null for both Gli2 and Gli3, however, have a much more severe phenotype, completely lacking both lungs and tracheae.[73] This outcome is much more severe than that seen in Shh knockout mice, in which lung development is initiated. This suggests that Gli family members may be part of a signaling cascade(s) that does not involve Shh yet is crucial for the initial events of lung development.

As noted above, lung morphogenesis and differentiation are influenced by a large number of hormones, growth factors, cytokines, and other signaling molecules. The complexity generated by this array is increased further by the fact that these signaling cascades interact. One such interaction is between one member of the FGF family, FGF10, and Shh. Surfactant protein C promoter-driven overexpression of Shh in the mouse lung leads to decreased expression of FGF10 and increased proliferation of mesenchymal cells,[71] and fetal lung mesenchymal cells treated with recombinant Shh in vitro retard FGF10 expression.[74] Furthermore, FGF10 expression in Shh knockout mice is spread throughout the lung mesenchyme as opposed to its normally discrete localization to the mesenchyme subtending distal lung buds.[70] These observations have led to a model in which Shh produced in the distal lung epithelial cells acts on mesenchymal cells to extinguish FGF10 expression, thereby limiting FGF10-directed bud outgrowth and expansion. Regulation of this "signaling center" is complicated yet further by its interaction with two other factors, bone morphogenetic protein 4[44,75] and transforming growth factor β-1.[74,76]

Classic techniques of embryology have demonstrated that normal lung organogenesis requires tissue interactions that are highly specific in time and space. The application of molecular biology to the study of lung development has initiated the elucidation of the molecular basis for these interactions, of which the FGF family and Shh are but two of many players. The advent of new technologies, such as functional genomics and proteomics, will lead to a great expansion of our understanding of lung growth and differentiation, which, in turn, should produce new strategies for the prevention and treatment of pathologies resulting from aberrant lung development.

References

1. Sampaolo G, Sampaolo L. Observations histologiques sur le poumon de foetus de Cobaye, cultive in vitro. Comput Rend Assoc Anat 1959;45:707–14.
2. Spooner BS, Wessells NK. Mammalian lung development: interactions in primordium formation and bronchial morphogenesis. J Exp Zool 1970;175:445–54.
3. Wessells N. Mammalian lung development: interactions in formation and morphogenesis of tracheal buds. J Exp Zool 1970;175:455–66.
4. Dameron F. Etude de la morphogenese de la bronche de l'embryon de Poulet associee a differents mesenchymes en culture in vitro. Comput Rend Acad Sci 1961;262: 1642–45.
5. Rudnick D. Developmental capacities of the chick lung in chorioallantoic grafts. J Exp Zool 1933;66:125–54.
6. Grobstein C, Cohen J. Collagenase: effect on the morphogenesis of embryonic salivary epithelium in vitro. Science 1965;150:626–8.
7. Rutter WJ, Wessells NK, Grobstein C. Controls of specific synthesis in the developing pancreas. Natl Cancer Inst Monogr 1964;13:51–65.
8. Kratochwil K. Organ specificity in mesenchymal induction demonstrated in the embryonic development of the mammary gland of the mouse. Dev Biol 1969;20:46–71.
9. Lehtonen E. Epithelio-mesenchymal interface during mouse kidney tubule induction in vivo. J Embryol Exp Morphol 1975;34:695–705.
10. Kollar EJ, Baird G. Tissue interaction in developing mouse tooth germs. II. The inductive role of the dental papilla. J Embryol Exp Morphol 1970;24:173–86.
11. Harrison RG. Experiments on the development of the forelimb of *Amblystoma*, a self-differentiating equipotential system. J Exp Zool 1918;25:413–61.
12. Cunha GR. Epithelial-stromal interactions in the development of the urogenital tract. Int Rev Cytol 1976;47: 137–94.
13. Taderera JT. Control of lung differentiation in vitro. Dev Biol 1967;16:489–512.

14. Masters JRW. Epithelial-mesenchymal interaction during lung development: the effect of mesenchymal mass. Dev Biol 1976;51:98–108.
15. Lawson KA. The role of mesenchyme in the morphogenesis and functional differentiation of rat salivary epithelium. J Embryol Exp Morphol 1972;27:497–513.
16. Lawson KA. Mesenchyme specificity in rodent salivary gland development: the response of salivary epithelium to lung mesenchyme in vitro. J Embryol Exp Morphol 1974;32:469–93.
17. Ball WD. Development of the rat salivary glands. III. Mesenchymal specificity in the morphogenesis of the embryonic submaxillary and sublingual glands of the rat. J Exp Zool 1974;188:277–88.
18. Alescio T, Cassini A. Induction in vitro of tracheal buds by pulmonary mesenchyme grafted on tracheal epithelium. J Exp Zool 1962;150:83–94.
19. Shannon JM. Induction of alveolar type II cell differentiation in fetal tracheal epithelium by grafted distal lung mesenchyme. Dev Biol 1994;166:600–14.
20. Kalina M, Mason RJ, Shannon JM. Surfactant protein C is expressed in alveolar type II cells but not in Clara cells of rat lung. Am J Respir Cell Mol Biol 1992;6:595–600.
21. Wert SE, Glasser SW, Korfhagen TR, Whitsett JA. Transcriptional elements from the human SP-C gene direct expression in the primordial respiratory epithelium of transgenic mice. Dev Biol 1993;156:426–43.
22. Hilfer S, Rayner R, Brown J. Mesenchymal control of branching pattern in the fetal mouse lung. Tissue Cell 1985;17:523–38.
23. Grobstein C. Mechanisms of organogenetic tissue interaction. Natl Cancer Inst Monogr 1967;26:279–99.
24. Cardoso WV. Molecular regulation of lung development. Annu Rev Physiol 2001;63:471–94.
25. Warburton D, Schwarz M, Tefft D, et al. The molecular basis of lung morphogenesis. Mech Dev 2000;92:55–81.
26. Shannon JM, Deterding RR. Epithelial-mesenchymal interactions in lung development. In: McDonald JA, ed. Lung growth and development. Vol. 1. New York: Marcel Dekker, 1997:81–118.
27. McKeehan WL, Wang F, Kan M. The heparan sulfate-fibroblast growth factor family: diversity of structure and function. Prog Nucleic Acid Res Mol Biol 1998; 59:135–76.
28. Weinstein M, Xu X, Ohyama K, Deng CX. FGFR-3 and FGFR-4 function cooperatively to direct alveogenesis in the murine lung. Development 1998;125:3615–23.
29. Celli G, LaRochelle WJ, Mackem S, et al. Soluble dominant-negative receptor uncovers essential roles for fibroblast growth factors in multi-organ induction and patterning. EMBO J 1998;17:1642–55.
30. Mason IJ. The ins and outs of fibroblast growth factors. Cell 1994;78:547–52.
31. Fu YM, Spirito P, Yu ZX, et al. Acidic fibroblast growth factor in the developing rat embryo. J Cell Biol 1991; 114:1261–73.
32. Gonzalez A-M, Buscaglia M, Ong M, Baird A. Distribution of basic fibroblast growth factor in the 18-day rat fetus: localization in the basement membranes of diverse tissues. J Cell Biol 1990;110:753–65.
33. Han RNN, Mawdsley C, et al. Platelet-derived growth factors and growth-related genes in rat lung. III. Immunolocalization during fetal development. Pediatr Res 1992; 31:323–9.
34. Finch PW, Cunha GR, Rubin JS, et al. Pattern of keratinocyte growth factor and keratinocyte growth factor receptor expression during mouse fetal development suggests a role in mediating morphogenetic mesenchymal-epithelial interactions. Dev Dyn 1995;203:223–40.
35. Mason IJ, Fuller-Pace F, Smith R, Dickson C. FGF-7 (keratinocyte growth factor) expression during mouse development suggests roles in myogenesis, forebrain regionalisation and epithelial-mesenchymal interactions. Mech Dev 1994;45:15–30.
36. Colvin JS, Feldman B, Nadeau JH, et al. Genomic organization and embryonic expression of the mouse fibroblast growth factor 9 gene. Dev Dyn 1999;216:72–88.
37. Bellusci S, Grindley J, Emoto H, et al. Fibroblast growth factor 10 (FGF10) and branching morphogenesis in the embryonic mouse lung. Development 1997;124:4867–78.
38. Hu MC, Qiu WR, Wang YP, et al. FGF-18, a novel member of the fibroblast growth factor family, stimulates hepatic and intestinal proliferation. Mol Cell Biol 1998;18: 6063–74.
39. Emoto H, Tagashira S, Mattei MG, et al. Structure and expression of human fibroblast growth factor-10. J Biol Chem 1997;272:23191–4.
40. Tagashira S, Harada H, Katsumata T, et al. Cloning of mouse FGF10 and up-regulation of its gene expression during wound healing. Gene 1997;197:399–404.
41. Yamasaki M, Miyake A, Tagashira S, Itoh N. Structure and expression of the rat mRNA encoding a novel member of the fibroblast growth factor family. J Biol Chem 1996;271:15918–21.
42. Park WY, Miranda B, Lebeche D, et al. FGF–10 is a chemotactic factor for distal epithelial buds during lung development. Dev Biol 1998;201:125–34.
43. Sutherland D, Samakovlis C, Krasnow MA. *Branchless* encodes a *Drosophila* FGF homolog that controls tracheal cell migration and the pattern of branching. Cell 1996;87:1091–101.
44. Weaver M, Dunn NR, Hogan BL. Bmp4 and Fgf10 play opposing roles during lung bud morphogenesis. Development 2000;127:2695–704.
45. Min H, Danilenko DM, Scully SA, et al. Fgf-10 is required for both limb and lung development and exhibits striking functional similarity to *Drosophila branchless*. Genes Dev 1998;12:3156–61.
46. Sekine K, Ohuchi H, Fujiwara M, et al. Fgf10 is essential for limb and lung formation. Nat Genet 1999;21:138–41.
47. Simonet WS, DeRose ML, Bucay N, et al. Pulmonary malformation in transgenic mice expressing human keratinocyte growth factor in the lung. Proc Natl Acad Sci U S A 1995;92:12461–5.
48. Ulich TR, Yi ES, Longmuir K, et al. Keratinocyte growth factor is a growth factor for type II pneumocytes in vivo. J Clin Invest 1994;93:1298–306.
49. Tichelaar JW, Lu W, Whitsett JA. Conditional expression of fibroblast growth factor-7 in the developing and mature lung. J Biol Chem 2000;275:11858–64.

50. Shiratori M, Oshika E, Ung LP, et al. Keratinocyte growth factor and embryonic rat lung morphogenesis. Am J Respir Cell Mol Biol 1996;15:328–38.
51. Zhou L, Graeff RW, McCray PB Jr, et al. Keratinocyte growth factor stimulates CFTR-independent fluid secretion in the fetal lung in vitro. Am J Physiol 1996;271:L987–94.
52. Deterding RR, Shannon JM. Proliferation and differentiation of fetal rat pulmonary epithelium in the absence of mesenchyme. J Clin Invest 1995;95:2963–72.
53. Shannon JM, Gebb SA, Nielsen LD. Induction of alveolar type II cell differentiation in embryonic tracheal epithelium in mesenchyme-free culture. Development 1999; 126:1675–88.
54. Guo L, Yu QC, Fuchs E. Targeting expression of keratinocyte growth factor to keratinocytes elicits striking changes in epithelial differentiation in transgenic mice. EMBO J 1993;12:973–86.
55. Nogawa H, Ito T. Branching morphogenesis of embryonic mouse lung epithelium in mesenchyme-free culture. Development 1995;121:1015–22.
56. Miller DL, Ortega S, Bashayan O, et al. Compensation by fibroblast growth factor 1 (FGF1) does not account for the mild phenotypic defects observed in FGF2 null mice [published erratum appears in Mol Cell Biol 2000; 20:3752]. Mol Cell Biol 2000;20:2260–8.
57. Han RNN, Liu J, Tanswell AK, Post M. Expression of basic fibroblast growth factor and receptor: immunolocalization studies in developing rat fetal lung. Pediatr Res 1992;31:435–40.
58. Gonzalez AM, Hill DJ, Logan A, et al. Distribution of fibroblast growth factor (FGF)-2 and FGF receptor-1 messenger RNA expression and protein presence in the mid-trimester human fetus. Pediatr Res 1996;39:375–85.
59. Matsui R, Brody JS, Yu Q. FGF-2 induces surfactant protein gene expression in foetal rat lung epithelial cells through a MAPK-independent pathway. Cell Signal 1999;11:221–8.
60. Wang F, Kan M, Xu J, et al. Ligand-specific structural domains in the fibroblast growth factor receptor. J Biol Chem 1995;270:10222–30.
61. Ortega S, Ittmann M, Tsang SH, et al. Neuronal defects and delayed wound healing in mice lacking fibroblast growth factor 2. Proc Natl Acad Sci U S A 1998;95:5672–7.
62. Peters K, Werner S, Liao X, et al. Targeted expression of a dominant negative FGF receptor blocks branching morphogenesis and epithelial differentiation of the mouse lung. EMBO J 1994;13:3296–301.
63. Arman E, Haffner-Krausz R, Chen Y, et al. Targeted disruption of fibroblast growth factor (FGF) receptor 2 suggests a role for FGF signaling in pregastrulation mammalian development. Proc Natl Acad Sci U S A 1998;95:5082–7.
64. Arman E, Haffner-Krausz R, Gorivodsky M, Lonai P. Fgfr2 is required for limb outgrowth and lung-branching morphogenesis. Proc Natl Acad Sci U S A 1999;96:11895–9.
65. De Moerlooze L, Spencer-Dene B, Revest J, et al. An important role for the IIIb isoform of fibroblast growth factor receptor 2 (FGFR2) in mesenchymal-epithelial signaling during mouse organogenesis. Development 2000;127: 483–92.
66. Ciruna BG, Schwartz L, Harpal K, et al. Chimeric analysis of fibroblast growth factor receptor-1 (Fgfr1) function: a role for FGFR1 in morphogenetic movement through the primitive streak. Development 1997;124:2829–41.
67. Hammerschmidt M, Brook A, McMahon AP. The world according to hedgehog. Trends Genet 1997;13:14–21.
68. McMahon AP. More surprises in the hedgehog signaling pathway. Cell 2000;100:185–8.
69. Litingtung Y, Lei L, Westphal H, Chiang C. Sonic hedgehog is essential to foregut development. Nat Genet 1998; 20:58–61.
70. Pepicelli CV, Lewis PM, McMahon AP. Sonic hedgehog regulates branching morphogenesis in the mammalian lung. Curr Biol 1998;8:1083–6.
71. Bellusci S, Furuta Y, Rush MG, et al. Involvement of Sonic hedgehog (Shh) in mouse enbryonic lung growth and morphogenesis. Development 1997;124:53–63.
72. Grindley JC, Bellusci S, Perkins D, Hogan BLM. Evidence for the involvement of the Gli gene family in embryonic mouse lung development. Dev Biol 1997;188:337–48.
73. Motoyama J, Liu J, Mo R, et al. Essential function of Gli2 and Gli3 in the formation of lung, trachea and oesophagus. Nat Genet 1998;20:54–7.
74. Lebeche D, Malpel S, Cardoso WV. Fibroblast growth factor interactions in the developing lung. Mech Dev 1999; 86:125–36.
75. Bellusci S, Henderson R, Winnier G, et al. Evidence from normal expression and targeted misexpression that bone morphogenetic protein-4 (Bmp-4) plays a role in mouse embryonic lung morphogenesis. Development 1996; 122:1693–702.
76. Zhou L, Dey CR, Wert SE, Whitsett JA. Arrested lung morphogenesis in transgenic mice bearing an SP-C—TGF-β1 chimeric gene. Dev Biol 1996;175:227–38.

CHAPTER 7

Prenatal and Postnatal Development of the Pulmonary Circulation

Daphne E. deMello, MD, Lynne M. Reid, MD

With the vast and sparkling explosion of information about genes, transcription factors, growth factors, and receptors, there is a growing need to relate this new information to the whole organ and its pathophysiology. Knockout models such as the cystic fibrosis transmembrane regulator (CFTR) model, which fails to recapitulate the pathology of the human disease, are pointed examples of how much is yet to be learned about gene function in relation to organ development and physiology.

Anatomy

General Lung Development

The development of the pulmonary circulation is part of a well-integrated program of lung development; and yet, on occasion, it has surprising autonomy. The following three laws of lung development are a summary of the latest stages of intrauterine development and provide a simple framework within which the vessels, the particular interest of this chapter, can be related to the air spaces, both airways, and alveoli:

1. *Airways.* Branching of the airways, bronchi, and bronchioli is complete by the 16th week of intrauterine life.[1]
2. *Alveoli.* At birth, the alveolar spaces are sometimes well developed and are sometimes just primitive saccules, as described by Boyden.[2] A wide variation in the number of alveoli has been reported. Early reports, at birth, were of the order of $\times 10^6$ for both lungs.[3,4] In a later report for only the left lung, the range in the first 4 months of life is from 68×10^6 to 128×10^6.[5]
3. *Vascular—arteries and veins.* The development of the circulation is linked to both of the above Laws. The pre-acinar branches of the pulmonary artery develop as the airways divide: the intra-acinar or respiratory surface vessels appear as alveoli multiply. Muscularization lags behind the appearance of the vessels so that in the infant and child, larger arteries are nonmuscular as compared with those in the adult.

Development includes (a) growth in the size or mass of tissue and (b) differentiation, which represents maturation of function. The steady increase in volume or weight and increase in the number and size of alveolar units that occurs with age can be considered a "magic lantern growth." The other, more intriguing type of growth represents a change in template, indicating a shift in program that produces a new stage of maturation or a different balance between the lungs' constituent units or tissues. Such shifts represent "windows," often quite short, when the growing lung is susceptible to signal for maturation or injury.

Pulmonary Vascular Systems

The lung has a double arterial supply and double venous drainage, which do not correspond precisely. The pulmonary artery supplies the intra-acinar structures: it branches with the airways but does not break into a capillary bed until it reaches the respiratory bronchiolus. The bronchial artery, the nutrient artery to the lung, supplies the capillary bed within the bronchial wall and also the structures of the perihilar region. The arterial supply to the pleura, except at the hilar region, is from the pulmonary artery. All intrapulmonary structures drain to the pulmonary vein, whereas the hilar structures drain to the so-called true bronchial veins and then to the azygos system.

From the right ventricle to the left atrium, a vascular loop can be identified that passes through artery, capillary, and vein but in the lung also has special pre- and postcapillary segments. The precapillary segment lies between the resistance artery and the capillary and includes arteries in which a muscular coat is present around only part of the circumference, before disappearing, from vessels still bigger than capillaries (Figure 7–1). By light microscopy, these are identified as either partially or nonmuscular arteries. A similar structural pattern can be identified in the postcapillary or venous stretch. We prefer to call all vessels upstream from the capillary arteries—thus avoiding the word "arteriole" since this is used with various connotations—and all vessels downstream veins.

The heterogeneity of vascular structure and even greater heterogeneity of metabolism and reactivity are achieved by just three cell types: the endothelial cell of the intima, the fibroblast of the adventitia, and for the media, a contractile cell—the smooth muscle cell or one of its precursor cells, the intermediate cell or pericyte.

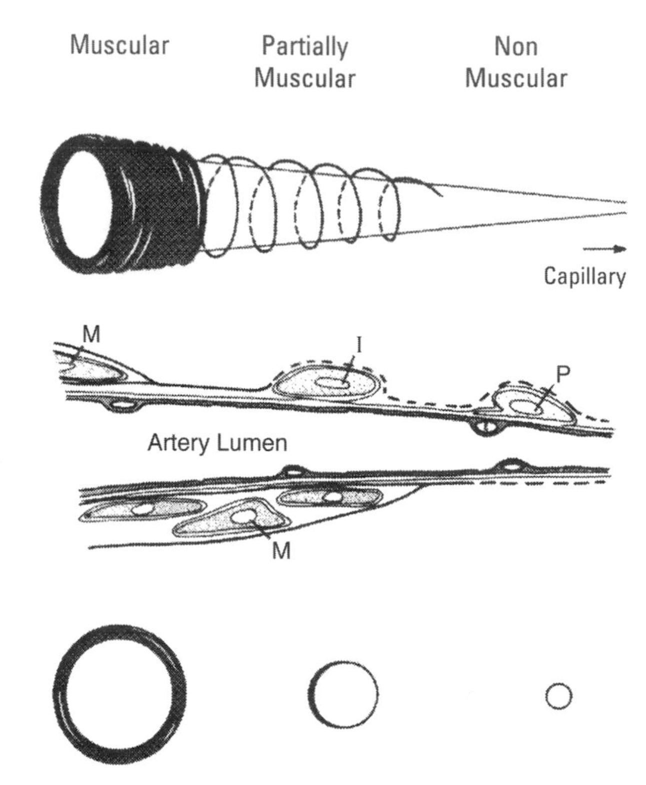

FIGURE 7–1. Along any arterial pathway > by light microscopy a completely muscular coat becomes incomplete, appearing as a spiral before disappearing to give a nonmuscular structure, still in arteries larger than the capillary (*top*). The bottom view shows these appearances in cross-section. The central diagram adds the features that are apparent by electron microscopy (Em). In the nonmuscular part of the artery, contractile cells are sometimes still present, although their processes are extremely thin. Proceeding distally, at first such cells are typical of a smooth muscle cell (M) and then of an intermediate cell (I), and in the immediately precapillary region pericytes (P) are found. The intermediate cell and pericyte are precursor smooth muscle cells. (Part of this diagram is from the Scientific Basis of Medicine Annual Review Series, 1968.)

Increasingly, mediators, cytokines, growth factors, or hormones (the difference between these terms is becoming blurred) that determine and modulate these differences are being identified.

Nerves are present in the walls of arteries and veins.

Species Variation

Broadly, the features of the human lung are found in the lung of most other species. Species differences in the structure and rate of lung growth do occur and need to be analyzed precisely in interpreting experimental results. For example, in the sheep, a major burst of lung development in the immediately prenatal period means relatively less change than in the human between birth and adulthood. Features that develop only during childhood in the human lung are prenatal in the sheep. It is likely that this prenatal growth burst is typical of animals that within hours of birth can run and keep up with the adult flock. In other mammals, such as the rat, mouse, piglet, and human, that are not immediately mobile, lung development takes relatively longer.

Prenatal Development

Normal-Embryonic and Early and Late Fetal

Landmarks of the prenatal period

During intrauterine development, the following features are established in the normal lung:

1. By the 6th week, connections between the double arterial supply and double venous drainage of the lung are made with the left and right heart chambers.
2. By the 16th week, branching of the bronchial tree is completed. The bronchial tree at term is the adult in miniature.
3. The "primitive" bronchial arteries disappear by the 6th week, and between the 9th and 12th weeks, definitive bronchial arteries develop.[6]
4. Pre-acinar and resistance arteries are present by the 28th week; but muscularization increases to term.[7]
5. An intra-acinar alveolar region is established by the 28th week; additional saccules and even mature alveoli appear to term.[8]
6. By the 28th week, a blood-gas barrier of thickness similar to that in the adult has developed.[9,10]

The epithelial outpouchings from the trachea that represent future air spaces of the lung are invested with mesoderm. Mesenchymal–epithelial interaction is necessary for normal lung development.[11] In the bursa cloacalis of the chick, Schoenwolf and colleagues concluded that for epithelial buds to develop, association with an arterial branch is necessary.[12] Their observations support the hypothesis that blood vessels induce formation of epithelial buds. Such detail has not been established for the human lung. In pulmonary artery atresia, however, when pulmonary blood flow is provided by collateral systemic vessels, the distribution is that of a pulmonary artery.[13] Perhaps this points to a generally maintained pattern of distal distribution and behavior.

The differentiation of the alveolar epithelium is a critical stage in the formation of the blood-gas barrier. The fusion of epithelial and endothelial basement membranes over part of the capillary circumference is an important stage of lung development that occurs usually between the 20th and 30th week. This is probably the single most important feature that determines viability of the fetus.

The acinus is the unit of lung supplied by a terminal bronchiolus. It includes several generations of respiratory bronchioli and alveolar ducts as well as the distal alveoli. Three to five such acini make up a lobule. The pulmonary arteries run with the airways but give off many more branches than an airway. Two main types of arterial branch can be distinguished.[14] "Conventional" describes the *long* pulmonary artery branch that runs with an airway, dividing as the airway divides, and finally is distributed to the capillary bed beyond the level of the terminal bronchiolus. "Supernumerary" describes those additional branches that arise from the pulmonary artery between the conventional branches, run a *short* course, and supply the capillary bed of alveoli immediately around the pulmonary artery.

Recently, in cattle, a distinct V-shaped musculoelastic cushion that forms a baffle projecting over the supernumerary artery lumen has been described.[15] This valve is responsive to vasoconstrictive agents, suggesting that it may be responsible for regulation of blood flow into the supernumerary artery. It is noteworthy that these two types of pulmonary artery have different pharmacologic profiles; for example, response to a vasoconstrictor such as 5-hydroxytryptamine (5-HT) was 30 times more potent in supernumerary arteries than in conventional arteries, and endogenous NO selectively attenuates the vasoconstrictor response to 5-HT in the supernumerary but not in the conventional artery.[16]

In the prelobular region, the ratio of conventional to supernumerary is of the order of 1 to 2. Along the pre- and intra-acinar stretch of the intralobular artery, the supernumeraries are even more numerous, giving a ratio of 1 to 3.[7,14,17]

The venous pattern resembles the arterial in that there are many more venous tributaries than airway branches, and similarly, two types of veins can be identified. "Conventional" veins, for example, arise from the points of division of an airway, pass to the periphery of the given unit, and combine to form increasingly large venous tributaries. Tributaries to the pulmonary veins also arise from the pleura and connective tissue septa.[18] Within the lung, the anatomic distribution of the arteries and veins is characteristic. The bronchoarterial bundle includes the airway with the bronchial artery capillary bed: the pulmonary artery is immediately adjacent and shares the single adventitial sheath. The veins always run at the periphery of any unit, whether it is the acinus, lobule, or segment. At the hilum, the veins join to form superior and inferior pulmonary veins that drain to the left atrium; they have a different distribution within the mediastinum from the pulmonary artery.

Primitive and definitive bronchial arteries

In the embryo, primitive bronchial arteries supplying the central airways arise in the neck from the dorsal aorta near the coeliac axis.[19] The central extrapulmonary part disappears at about the 6th week of gestation. Between the 9th and 12th weeks, definitive bronchial arteries arise from the aorta, grow along the superior surface of the airways, and induce communication with the capillary bed in the airway walls. Sometimes, the primitive bronchial arteries persist, as when such an artery supplies a sequestrated lung segment. In this case, the artery is found to have migrated with the coeliac axis to an origin below the diaphragm, which it traverses before entering the lung through the inferior pulmonary ligament. Venous drainage of a sequestration has been reported in various sites including the portal vein, azygos system, inferior vena cava, and subclavian vein.[20–23]

Vascular development within pulmonary mesenchyme

A detailed analysis of the origin of the cells and vessels of the pulmonary circulation has not yet been made. Certain emerging principles of angiogenesis allow speculation on processes that probably contribute to normal lung growth and explain certain unusual conditions of disturbed growth.

The origin of the vascular system is mesodermal, but angioblasts interact with other mesenchymal cells and also show unique patterns of behavior.[24] Development of a mature vascular system is ordered by central events that determine for a given vessel direction of blood flow, its region of distribution or drainage, and its central connections. Local or peripheral events determine the fine structure of the vessels as they supply the ultimate functioning unit of a given organ. Experimentally, information on control of vascular development has been obtained in the fetus by surgical excision or division of tissue and by transplanting tissue. Study of chimeric organisms has added considerably to our understanding of angiogenesis, as it has to other events in development.[25]

It is established that branching occurs at the end of a pathway and that lengthening and widening of a given segment involve cell multiplication. Generally, it is accepted that new blood vessels arise by branching from postcapillary or venous structures.[26] Differences between the endothelial cells at various sites have been reported. Rowan and Maxwell described alkaline phosphatase in the endothelium of the new sprouts but not in adjacent cells.[27] Characteristic features are reported for the cells at the tips of the bud distal to the level of sprouting. A lumen develops within an island of angioblasts and ultimately communicates with other hollow channels to produce vessels. The appearance of such an isolated lumen often occurs just distal or adjacent to a branching point and implies a region of organizer activity. This indicates a fusion of cells and cell lysis, ultimately with reformation of cell membrane to give a hollow tube. A particularly intriguing behavior is that there is widespread and rapid migration of individual angioblasts for a considerable distance from their region of origin. Even relatively large arteries include chimeric cells, indicating fusion by migrating cells with cells already in situ.

The transcription factor TAL1/SCL is a marker of angioblasts.[28] In the presence of extracellular matrix, endothelial cell precursors form protrusions that result in

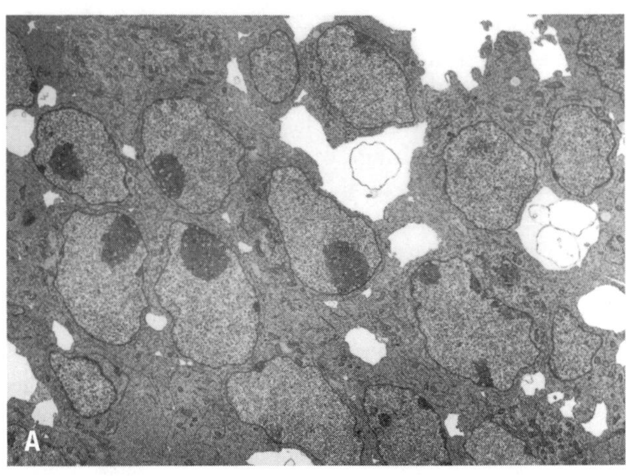

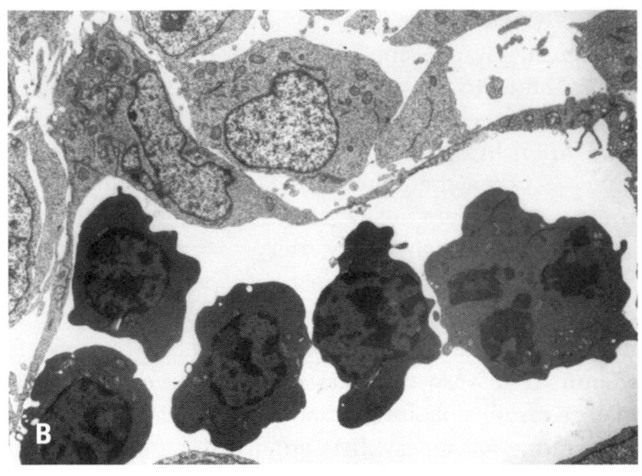

FIGURE 7–2. Transmission electron micrographs of fetal mouse thorax. *A*, At 9 days, intercellular spaces are seen between densely packed mesenchymal cells around the developing lung bud. Membrane-bound vesicles and membranous fragments within the spaces suggest that the spaces result from discharge of intracytoplasmic vesicles (original magnification ×707). *B*, At 10 days, hematopoietic precursors are seen within the "lakes," and the lining cells appear thin, like endothelial cells (original magnification ×1,458). (Reproduced with permission from deMello DE et al.[34])

the formation of vascular cords and then vessels. This process requires integrin-mediated adhesions.[29,30] Vascular endothelial growth factor (VEGF) plays a role as a mitogen and as a vascular morphogen in vasculogenesis.[31] Whereas vascular smooth muscle cells arise through progenitors within the mesoderm, they also are derived from endothelial cells.[32]

Overexpression of VEGF in the lung results in the formation of oversized vessels. It is not clear whether this is the result of fusion of multiple small vessels, interstitial growth, or dilation.[33] Overexpression of VEGF in the lung also disrupts airway morphogenesis.

Presumably, excessive amounts of VEGF alter the balance in the mesoderm, resulting in the recruitment of an abnormally large number of mesodermal cells to endothelial lineage. A resulting deficiency of nonvascular mesoderm could explain the abnormalities in airway branching.

Angiogenesis, vasculogenesis, fusion: mouse and human

Noden has described in the yolk sac of the chicken embryo, two processes of blood vessel formation: angiogenesis, the branching of new vessels from pre-existing ones, and vasculogenesis, the development of blood lakes that undergo transformation into vessels.[24]

We speculated previously that both conventional and supernumerary branches from the main pulmonary artery result from angiogenesis and that the more distal vessels, those of the future alveolar region, arise by vasculogenesis (ie, from a lumen that appears locally within the mesenchyme). This speculation has been proved by recent studies of early lung vascular development in the mouse and human.[34,35]

Since little was known about the development of the vasculature within an organ, we undertook a study in the mouse lung to determine what processes contribute to blood vessel assembly in early lung development.[34] Using a combination of techniques—light and transmission electron microscopy of tissue and scanning electron microscopy of Mercox vascular casts—we delineated lung vascular development in mouse embryos and fetuses aged 9 to 20 days. Vascular casts provided a means of determining "function," (ie, the presence of a vascular lumen) and continuity between the various vascular segments. This study showed that in mouse between 9 and 10 days, primitive angioblast precursors within the mesenchyme surrounding the lung bud form vascular lakes that have hematopoietic cells in their lumen (Figure 7–2). At 12 days, there are four generations of central arterial branches but no luminal connection between these and the lakes in the peripheral lung mesenchyme, where already a dense collection of lakes containing hematopoietic cells is present. By 14 days, five to seven generations of central artery branches, supernumerary and conventional, are present. There is now a connection between the central vessels and the peripheral system so that casts of the peripheral vessels are obtained by central injection. Between 15 days and term, there is increasing complexity of the peripheral vascular casts, reflecting an increase in the connections between the central and peripheral systems (Figures 7–3 and 7–4). This study demonstrated that two processes, angiogenesis and vasculogenesis, are involved in mouse lung vascular development. It showed that these processes occur separately but concurrently and that a third process, fusion, between these two systems is necessary for the circulation to be established.

To determine whether the same three processes are involved in human lung vascular development, we studied human embryos from the Carnegie Collection of Human Embryos housed in the Carnegie Institute of

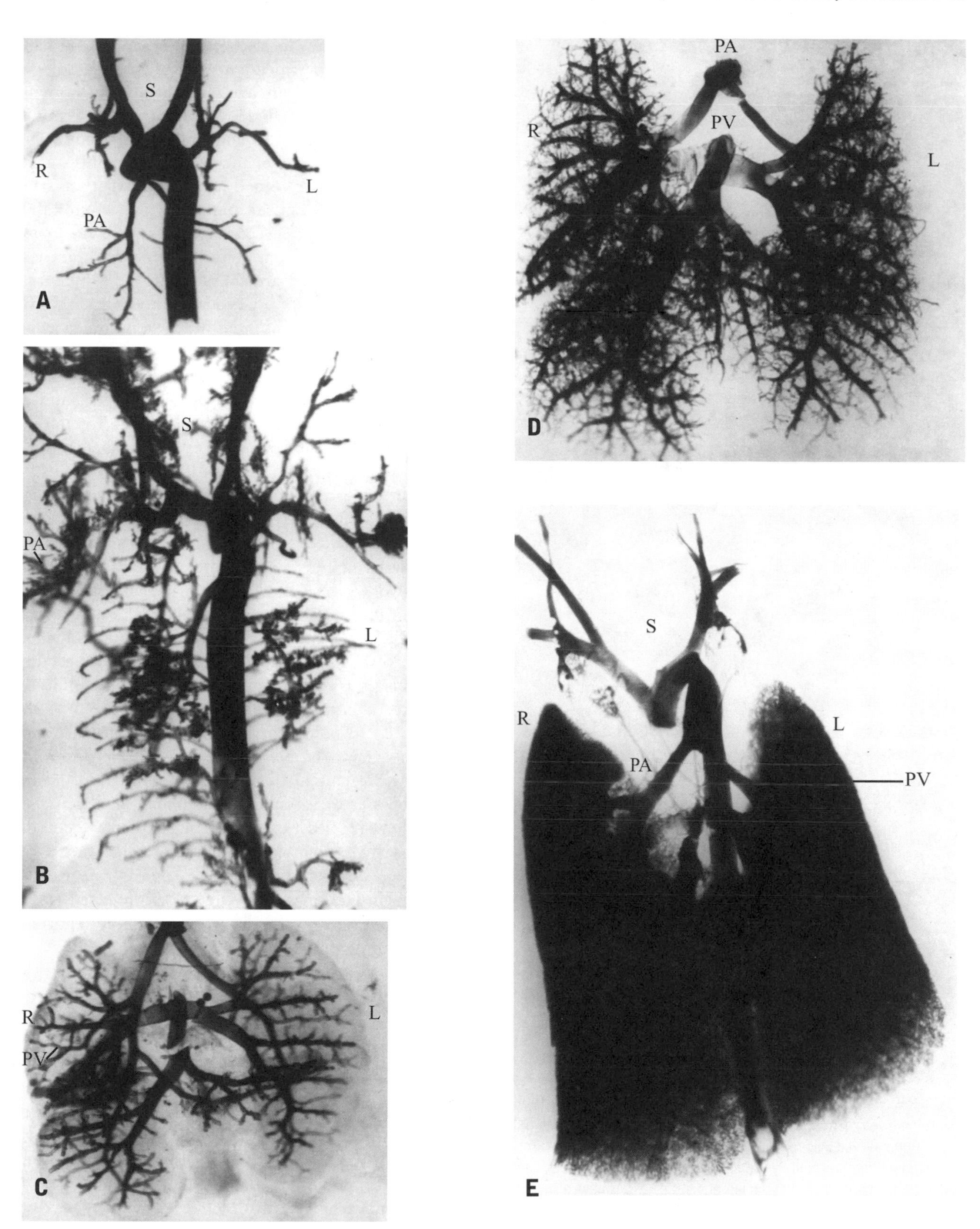

FIGURE 7–3. Photomicrographs of Mercox casts of mouse pulmonary vasculature. *A*, At 12 days, there is no vascular connection to the peripheral lung, and only four generations of arterial central branches are present. *B*, At 13 days, the first peripheral vessels are seen. *C*, At 14 days, peripheral vessels of both the arterial (upper) and venous (lower) systems are seen. *D*, At 15 days, the density of small peripheral vessels is increased. *E*, At 16 days, the cast is dense and complex. S = systemic; R = right; L = left; PA = pulmonary artery; PV= pulmonary vein. (Reproduced with permission from deMello DE et al.[34])

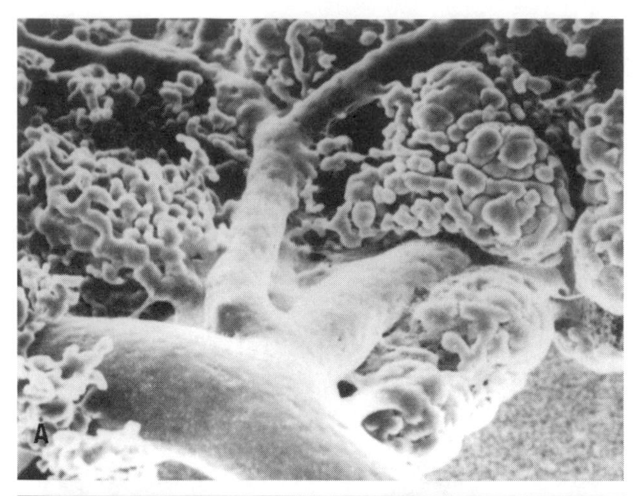

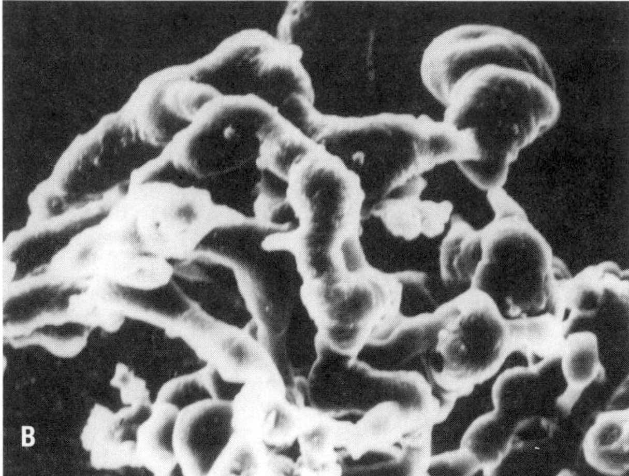

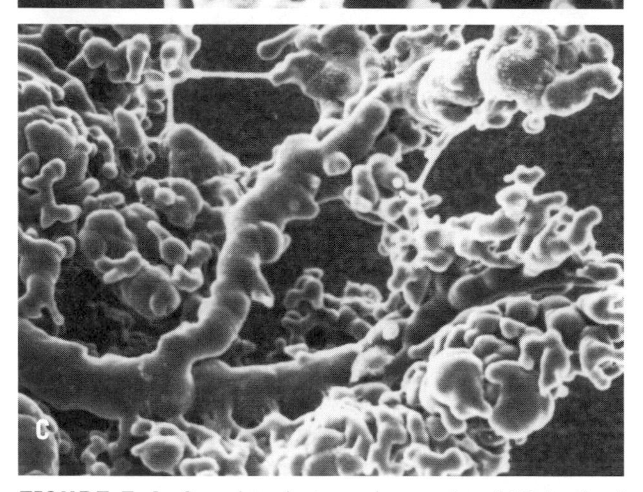

FIGURE 7–4. Scanning electron micrographs of 15-day fetal mouse lung vascular casts. Extensive connections between the central and peripheral systems are reflected by a complex peripheral network. The blind-ending precapillary branches approach the future capillary bed at right angles. Note that the larger central vessels have a smooth profile, whereas the smaller peripheral vessels are irregular, perhaps reflecting their derivation by angiogenesis or vasculogenesis, respectively (original magnification ×320). (Reproduced with permission from deMello DE et al.[34])

Washington, DC, now located in the Museum of Human Development in the Armed Forces Institute of Pathology in Washington, DC. Complete serial sections of human embryos from stages 10 to 23 were studied to determine the sites of origin, pathways, and ending of a given structure (ie, pulmonary arteries and veins).[35] From this study, we determined that the blood lakes are the first to form and are present in the primitive mesenchyme around the lung bud in the neck between stages 14 and 18 (32 to 44 days). At stage 20 (50.5 days), five to six airway branches have formed and lakes are abundant in the subpleural mesenchyme. The pulmonary artery, however, accompanies the bronchi only as far as the third or fourth generation. No continuity between the peripheral and central systems is present at this time. The first connection to the hilum was between peripheral lakes and a thin-walled hilar vein. It was seen at stage 22 (54 days), indicating that venous drainage is established before pulmonary artery supply. At stage 23 (56.5 days), pulmonary artery branches accompany the airways but lag behind the airway by two to three generations. The artery is thick walled and ends blindly in a solid cord of cells. Between 12 and 16 weeks, there is an extensive capillary network in the subpleural mesenchyme surrounding the most distal airway buds. The vascular network is separated widely from the airway buds by mesenchyme. By 22 to 23 weeks, the capillary network approaches the airway epithelium and bulges into the air space, indicating that blood barriers have formed (Figures 7–5 to 7–7). At this time, the pulmonary artery accompanies even the most distal airway branch just beneath the pleura. From this study, we concluded that in the human also, the three processes of vascular development, angiogenesis, vasculogenesis, and fusion, occur. Further, we determined that the venous circulation is established first.

There are several examples of a condition in which the microcirculation appears to be disconnected from the central vessels. Several cases have now been reported as absence of pulmonary artery capillaries.[36–38]

Loss or gain of function experiments: genes, factors, and receptors

The processes involved in vascular assembly, namely angiogenesis, vasculogenesis, and fusion, are effected by genes and their products such as growth factors, hormones (endocrine, exocrine, and paracrine), mediators, and the appropriate receptors. The role of genes and their products can be deduced from experiments in which overexpression, or deprivation, is produced and related to the resulting disorder of growth. By way of illustration, a few of these players in the complex drama of vascular assembly are discussed, notably VEGF, transforming growth factor beta (*TGF-ß*) and the *tie* receptor.

Vascular endothelial growth factor is an important chemoattractant and mitogen for endothelial cells.[39–41]

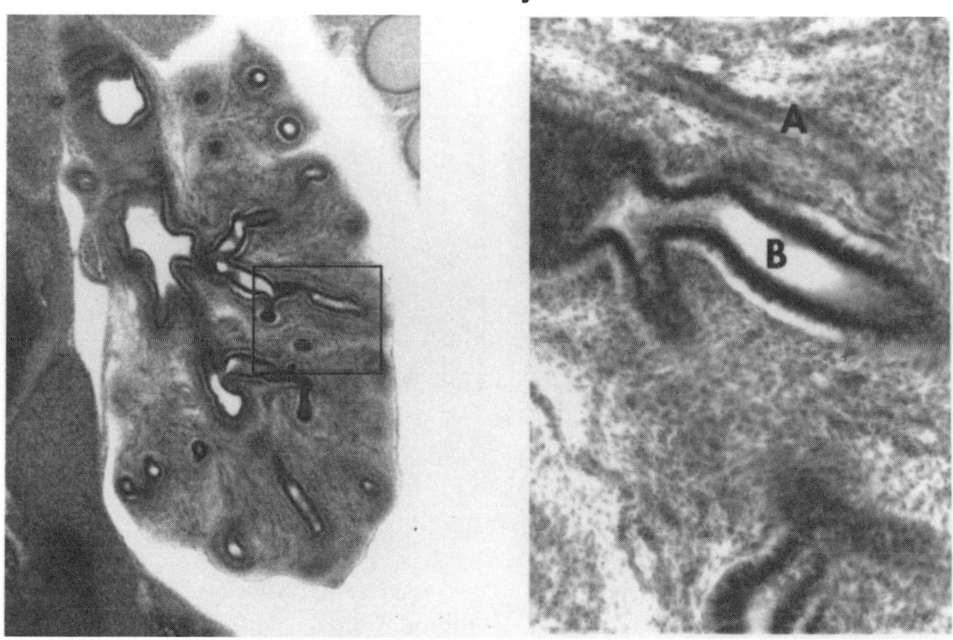

FIGURE 7–5. Low (*left,* hematoxylin and eosin stain, original magnification × 40) and high (*right,* hematoxylin and eosin stain, original magnification × 100) magnification views of a sagittally sectioned human embryo. The segmental pulmonary arteries (A) accompany the airways (B) but end as blind solid cords proximal to the distal end of the airway. An extensive vascular network exists in the intervening mesenchyme between airways. (Reproduced with permission from deMello DE. Structural elements of human fetal and neonatal lung vascular development. In: Weir EK, Archer SL, Reeves JT, eds. The fetal and neonatal pulmonary circulations. Armonk, NY: Futura, 1999:37–64.)

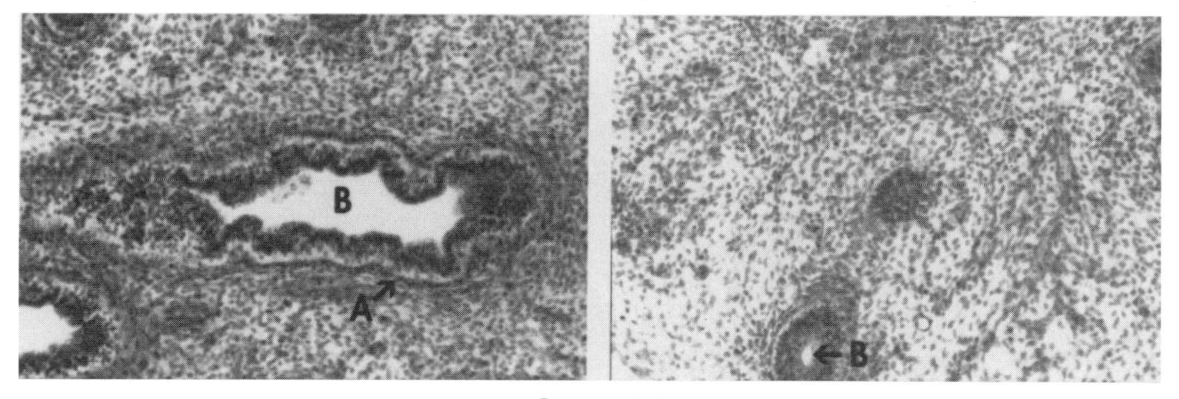

FIGURE 7–6. Photomicrographs of human embryonic lung. The pulmonary artery (A) accompanies the airway (B) to its distal tip. The arborizing network within the mesenchyme surrounding the most peripheral airway branches is separated from the airway by intervening mesenchyme (hematoxylin and eosin stain, original magnification × 100). (Reproduced with permission from deMello DE. Structural elements of human fetal and neonatal lung vascular development. In: Weir EK, Archer SL, Reeves JT, eds. The fetal and neonatal pulmonary circulations. Armonk, NY: Futura, 1999:37–64.)

In the human, VEGF is expressed in epithelial cells and myocytes but not in vascular endothelial cells. It is the VEGF receptor tyrosine kinases, *flt*-1 (VEGF-R1) and *flk*-1/KDR (VEGF-R2), which are expressed in endothelium.[42,43] In prematurely born infants, the level of VEGF measured in lung lavage fluid tripled between days 1 and 3 of life, and higher levels were present in the more immature infants.[44] The importance of VEGF is reflected by the fact that in mouse embryonic development, even the loss of one allele (heterozygosity) results in embry-

17 Weeks

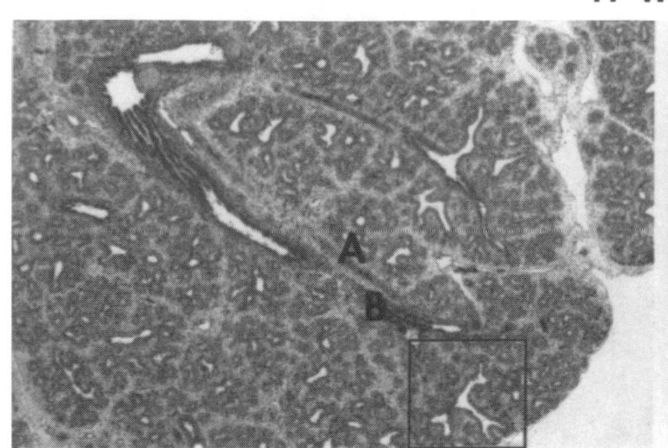

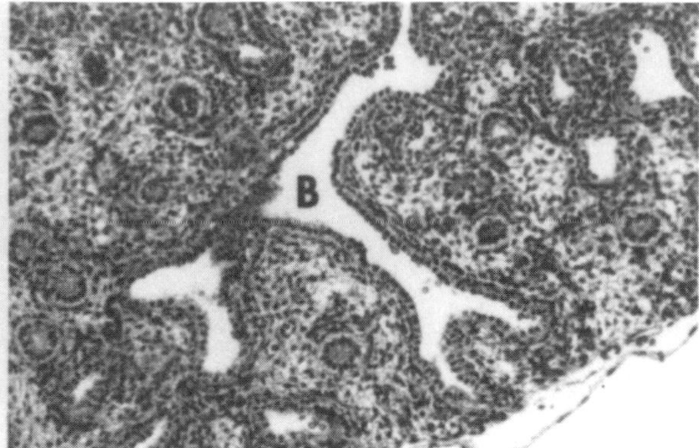

FIGURE 7–7. By 17 weeks, the pulmonary artery (A) accompanies the airway and has reached the distal end. The mesenchyme between airways is significantly reduced (hematoxylin and eosin stain, original magnification × 200). (Reproduced with permission from deMello DE. Structural elements of human fetal and neonatal lung vascular development. In: Weir EK, Archer SL, Reeves JT, eds. The fetal and neonatal pulmonary circulations. Armonk, NY: Futura, 1999:37–64.)

onic death at days 11 to 12 with "defects in vessel formation."[45,46] A dose-dependent effect of VEGF on the developing vasculature was further demonstrated in avian embryo studies, in which VEGF dose, increased by either microinjection of the agent or by VEGF-expressing retroviruses, produced an overgrowth of vessels.[31,47] In mouse embryos in which the VEGF receptor flt-1 is knocked out, defective angiogenesis is reported, with embryonic death between 8.5 and 9.5 days.[48] A similar knockout of the receptor flk-1 also produces embryonic death between days 8.5 and 9.5.[49] The almost complete lack of vascular structures in these animals points to a failure of angiogenesis and vasculogenesis.[49]

Transforming Growth Factor/Beta. Transforming growth factor beta is activated by interactions between endothelial cells and undifferentiated mesenchymal cells, smooth muscle cells, or pericytes.[50,51] Activated TGF-β inhibits endothelial and smooth muscle cell multiplication and migration and induces differentiation of mesenchymal cells into smooth muscle cells and pericytes.[52–56] Transforming growth factor beta null mice have defective hematopoieses and vasculogenesis.[57] In the human, mutations in genes encoding for the TGF binding protein endoglin and activin receptor-like kinase 1 have been identified in patients with hereditary hemorrhagic telangiectasia.[58,59] These receptors are expressed in endothelial cells, which suggests that disruption in TGF-β signaling leads to the abnormal vessels of telangiectasia.

Tie Receptor: These receptor tyrosine kinases are specific for vascular endothelium. In the lung, the family of genes responsible for these kinases plays an important role in the regulation of both processes, vasculogenesis and angiogenesis. In the mouse, expression of the *tie-1* gene is apparent early in gestation (embryonic age 8.5) in angioblasts and continues throughout gestation.[60] In the adult, expression is limited to capillaries within lung alveolar septa. Knockout of the tie-1 receptor causes death of the mice from respiratory distress shortly after birth. It is reported that there are "ultrastructural abnormalities" in the endothelium.[60]

Vascular structure and size

In genetic and molecular studies, there is a need for more precise analysis of cellular and tissue abnormality. Four main features need to be assessed to establish the normality of vascular structure and its appropriateness to age: (a) the number of pre-acinar branches, (b) the number of intra-acinar branches and vascular density in relation to alveolar growth, (c) the structure of the vessel at a given level in branching, and (d) the size of the artery usually assessed as the external diameter between the external elastic lamina. The two latter features need to be related to the level of the artery in the pattern of branching (Figure 7–8). This is conveniently judged by landmarking a vessel by reference to its accompanying airway.[61]

Examples of Abnormal Development

Hypoplasia, dysplasia, and hyperplasia

When the lung is hypoplastic or underdeveloped, its circulation usually demonstrates growth failure. If the lung is small, but this is part of a general systemic failure to grow, then relating lung to body weight may be appropriate. It is when lung weight to body weight is reduced that we apply the term "lung hypoplasia." The lung can be the solitary organ affected. In hypoplasia, lung volume or lung weight may be reduced, and yet the full complement of structures is present. More typically, there is a differential effect on airways, alveoli, and vascular structures that needs to be assessed to identify the nature of the underdevelopment.[62–65] Small lungs sometimes have blood vessels the size of which is appropriate to the volume,[66] but often these are selectively hypoplastic

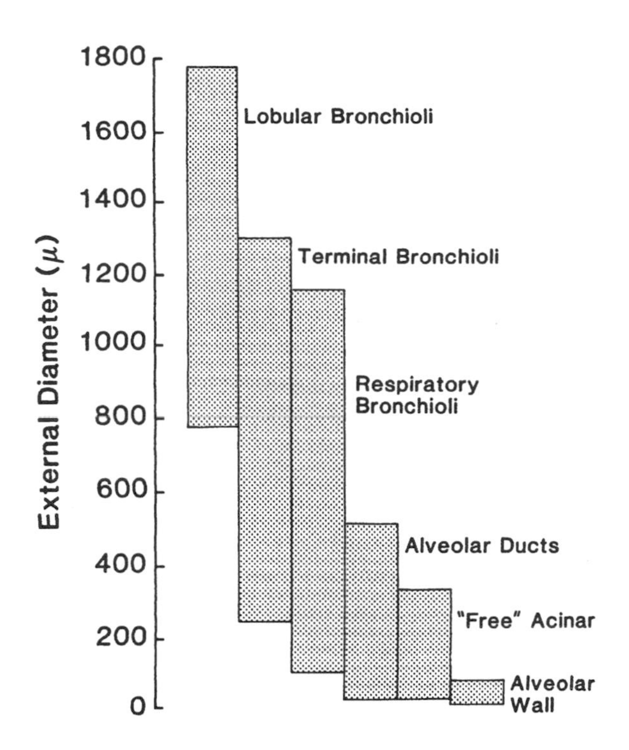

FIGURE 7–8. Arterial diameter—range of diameter of arteries accompanying peripheral airways and within the acinus. The arteries had been distended with a barium gelatin suspension before fixation. "Free" acinar refers to alveolar wall arteries with a connective tissue adventitia apparent by light microscopy.

even when related to volume. A severe degree of precocious muscularization in utero is found in many cases of lung hypoplasia.[67–69] A striking example of this was reported by Goldstein and Reid[70]—small lungs, reduced airway, and alveolar number in an infant with absent phrenic nerves and amyotrophy of the diaphragm. Even in relation to lung volume, the diameter of the pulmonary arteries was greatly reduced with excessive muscularization as judged both by medial thickness and the abnormally distal level at which muscle was found.

Hyperplasia can be applied for a lung excessive in volume or weight. The solitary lung in so-called agenesis of lung can have the volume of two lungs—hyperplasia—and yet detailed examination of this case showed that airway number is reduced—hypoplasia—but alveolar number and total lung volume were equivalent to two lungs.[71] In a maldeveloped lung, it is necessary to assess more than one feature to characterize the lobe. The above lung and its acini are "polyalveolar."[71] We have not seen or heard of a condition in which there is an excessive number of airways in an otherwise normal lung. Relative excess seems to occur only with alveoli or sometimes with blood vessels, as in hypoplastic left heart syndrome.[72,73] Possibly, a cystadenomatoid malformation in which cystic airways open to alveoli and to proximal airways could be considered an example of excessive airway development. These sometimes disappear after birth. This line of thought allows us to include a range of anomalies and dysplasias suggesting that excessive stimulation of airway growth does occur.[74] By implication, the terms hypoplasia and hyperplasia, in this context, are used when the structure is a reasonable approximation to the normal. The term "dysplasia" is used when the alveolar region, in particular, does not show the normal organization and fine structure associated with normal function.[75] The dysplasia of the newborn lung at term can include alveolar wall thickening without a normal blood-gas barrier.

Alveolar capillary dysplasia

Absence of capillaries in the alveolar region[36–38] is reported to be associated sometimes with what has been considered a misalignment of veins. Prominent dilated veins are present, but because pulmonary veins normally arise in the airway and run in the connective tissue septa, this appearance suggests that the veins may be receiving more than the usual blood flow through the bronchial system. The precise path of the pulmonary artery blood flow in these patients is not clear. Some of the reported cases have relatively mild clinical symptoms in the first few days of life, suggesting that some form of pulmonary artery blood flow occurs and that this drains through the bronchial system to the bronchial veins. In this condition, cardiac catheterization has shown that central venous connections are normal, but details of the post-acinar–intrapulmonary venous channels have not been established.[76]

Prematurity and its impact on catch-up growth

Before birth, growth and differentiation seem to predominate at different times. One patient who illustrates the seemingly inverse relationship between these two functions is illustrated in Figure 7–9.[77] Although, at birth, this premature infant was very small, she did not have hyaline membrane disease (respiratory distress of the newborn). At the time she was discharged from the hospital, the patient was the smallest newborn to leave. Over the next months, she had some feeding problems but was clinically satisfactory until 4 to 6 weeks before her death at 9 months from respiratory failure. During her life, her lungs failed to achieve even the structural features of a normal newborn (Figures 7–10 and 7–11). It seems that the lungs had differentiated sufficiently to prevent hyaline membrane disease but at the expense of growth.

The adaptation by the pulmonary artery branches to the obliterative lesions in the axial arteries illustrates the way a collateral circulation opens up between branches proximal and distal to the block; supernumerary and conventional branches participate (see Figures 7–9 and 7–11). Such arcades are seen in cases of congenital heart disease, severe panacinar emphysema (as in α1-antiprotease deficiency), and pulmonary fibrosis.

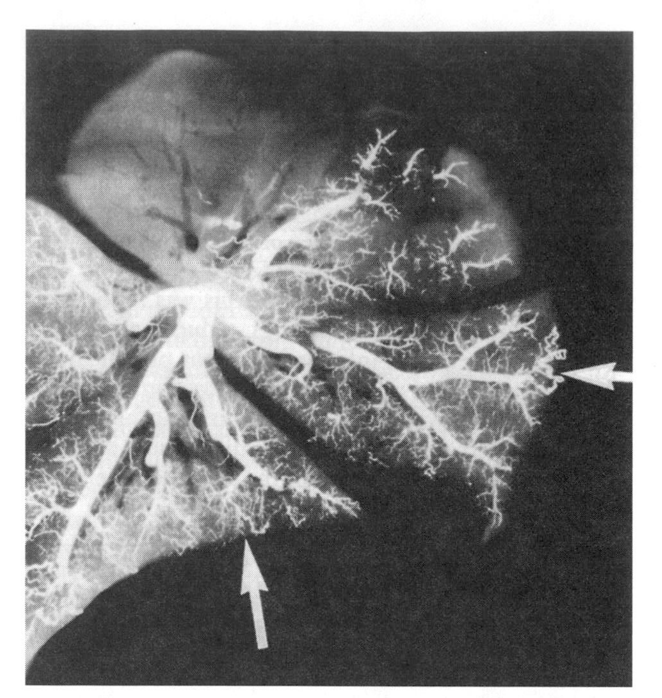

FIGURE 7–9. Arteriogram of a 1-cm slice of lung of a premature infant dying at 9 months of age from pulmonary hypertension with hypoplasia of the pulmonary vascular bed. The arteriogram shows tortuous dilated vessels and interpulmonary artery arcades (*at arrows*). (Reproduced with permission from Rendas A, Brown ER, Avery ME, Reid L. Prematurity, hypoplasia of the pulmonary vascular bed and hypertension: fatal outcome in 10 month old infant. Am Rev Respir Dis 1980;121:873–80.)

Metabolic defects: kidney-lung axis and chondro-osseous disorders

On the basis of some recent studies, we feel justified in considering renal dysplasia and osteogenesis imperfecta as two examples of defective fetal metabolism that interferes with lung growth and, in particular, with vascular development. Lung hypoplasia is sometimes seen with oligohydramnios but also is associated with polyhydramnios, and with both conditions, lung may be normal. Early in development, the kidney produces proline in excess of its own needs and exports the amino acid to other organs. Clemmons has shown experimentally that administration of nephrotoxins during development of the meso- or metanephros is associated with reduced uptake of proline by the lung and lung dysplasia.[78] In renal agenesis, the central and axial arteries appear abnormal, being widely dilated so that the overall impression is of excessive vascular volume.[79] In a recent study, we reported a similar arteriogram in a patient with osteogenesis imperfecta.[65] Impaired lung development had been reported in this condition, but arterial injections were not performed.[80] In this study, we reported patterns of hypoplasia associated with osseochondrous disorders.[65] For example, in three cases of thanatophoric dwarfism, the lung showed greatly reduced volumes (assessed as lung to body weight ratio) and a significant reduction in airway branching and excessive muscularization of peripheral arteries (Figure 7–12).

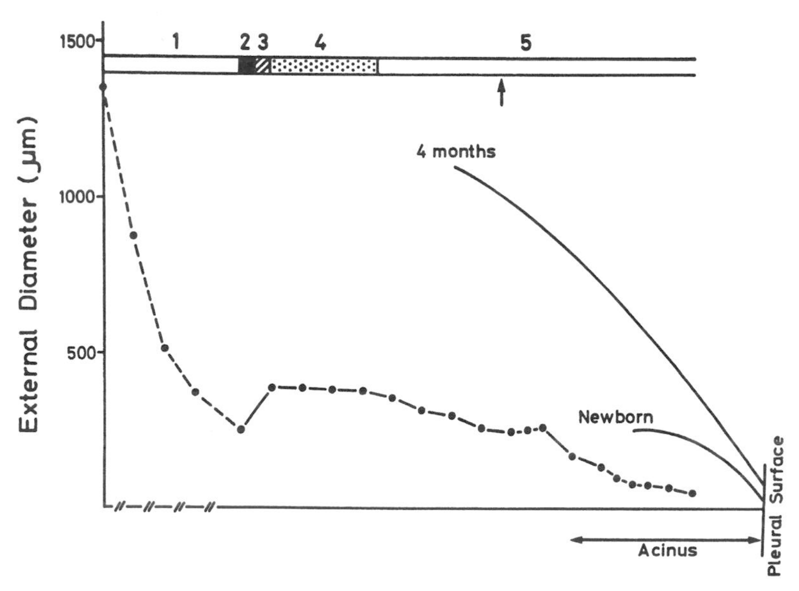

FIGURE 7–10. Diagrammatic representation of the serial reconstruction of the posterior basal arterial pathway from hilum to pleural surface, relating external diameter of artery (μm) (*vertical axis*) to the distance from the hilum (*horizontal axis*). Also shown for comparison is the arterial diameter for a normal newborn and a 4-month-old infant. Present case: proximal, 19.7 mm of pathway traced by dissection and microscopy; distal, 2.3 mm traced in step sections 50 μm apart. The bar at the top of the diagram indicates the state of the artery at various levels: (1) patent and filled with injection medium; (2) lumen occluded; (3) dilated but without injection medium; (4) normal diameter, thin walled, patent, and not filled with injection medium; (5) filled with injection medium; the wall is thickened but there is no intimal change. The arrow indicates the position of the anastomosis or arcade with an adjacent pulmonary artery. (Reproduced with permission from Rendas A, Brown ER, Avery ME, Reid L. Prematurity, hypoplasia of the pulmonary vascular bed and hypertension: fatal outcome in 10 month old infant. Am Rev Respir Dis 1980;121:873–80.)

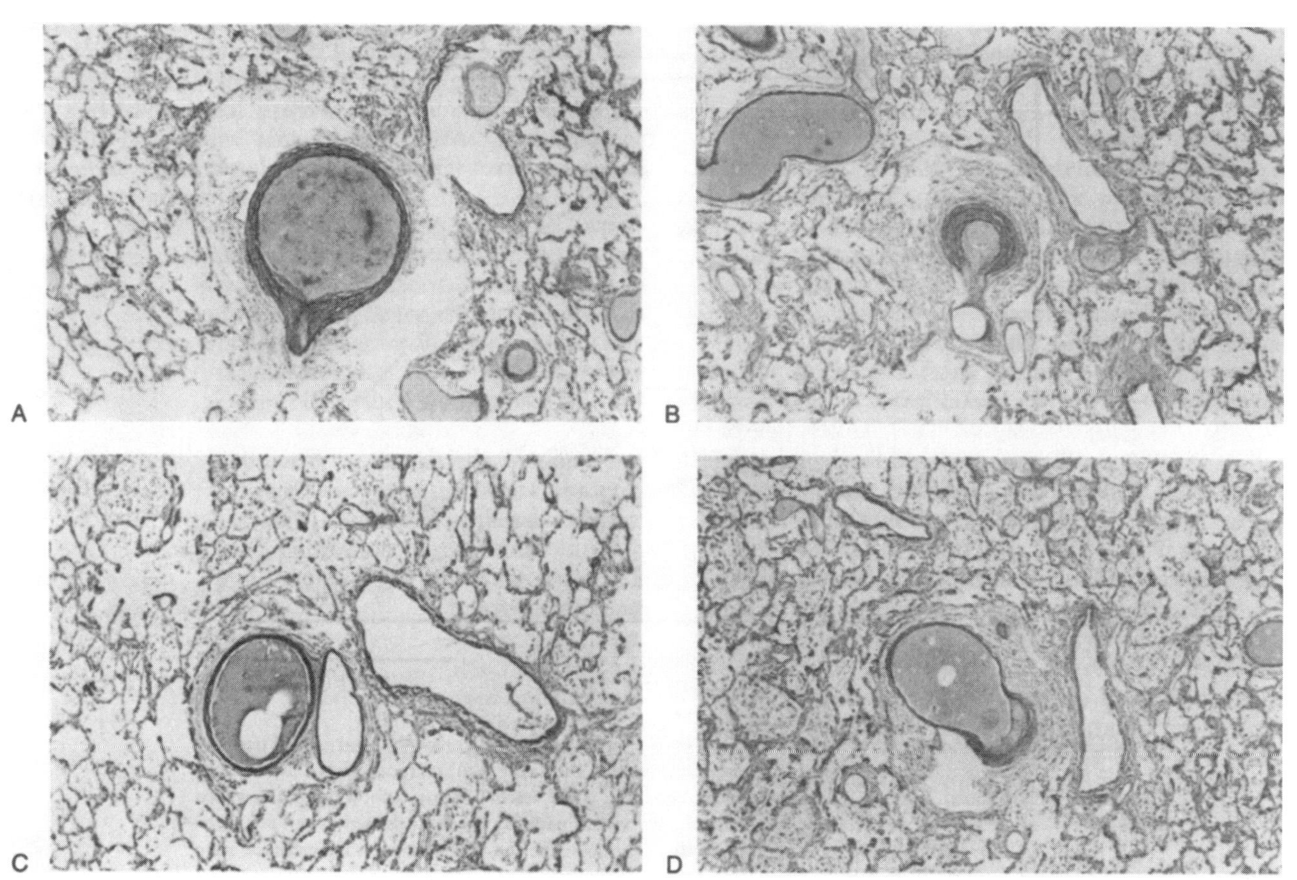

FIGURE 7–11. Photomicrographs of successive levels from the hilum to the periphery of the posterior basal axial artery (*A*) proximal level, patent and filled with injection medium; (*B*) narrowed artery with intimal occlusion; (*C*) side branches of the axial artery from beyond the blockage, dilated and filled with injection medium, although at this level the axial artery (*at right*) is not; (*D*) the level where the axial artery again fills with injection medium. As related to the bar at the top of FIGURE 7–10, *A*, corresponds to region 1, *B* to region 2, *C* to side branches at region 3, and *D* to 5. (Reproduced with permission from Rendas A, Brown ER, Avery NE, Reid L. Prematurity, hypoplasia of the pulmonary vascular bed and hypertension: Fatal outcome in 10 month old infant. Am Rev Respir Dis 1980;121:873–80.)

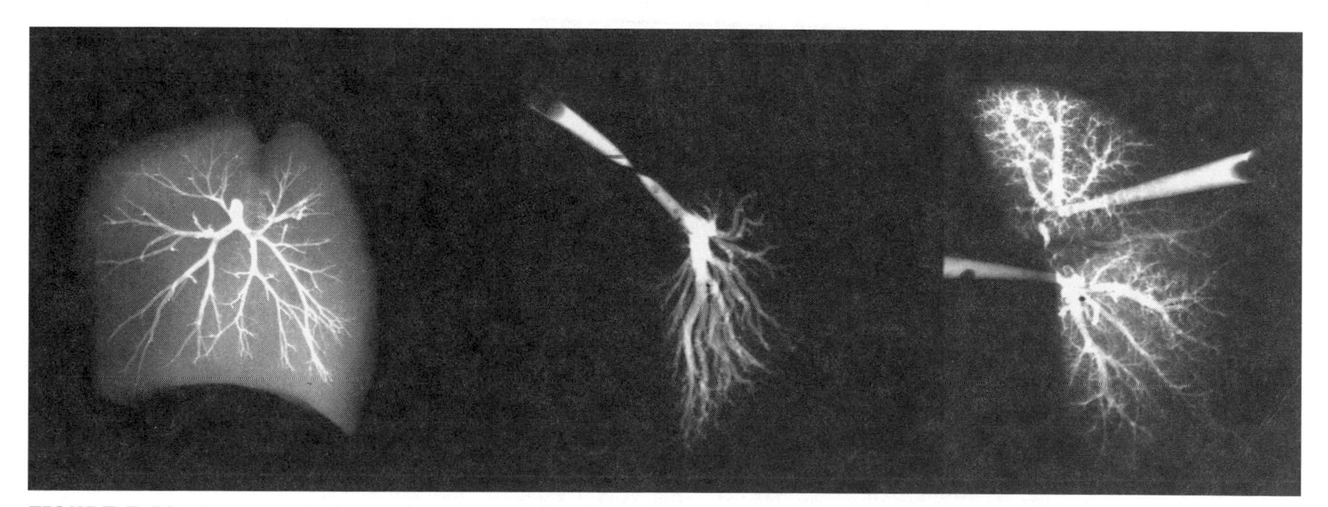

FIGURE 7–12. Postmortem barium angiograms of newborn human lungs show a range of abnormal growth patterns for pre- and intra-acinar pulmonary arteries reflecting deranged angiogenesis. *Left*, arterial hypoplasia is reflected by the reduced branching and small caliber of the pulmonary arteries in an infant whose mother used cocaine throughout her pregnancy; *center*, in osteogenesis imperfecta there is tortuosity and crowding of the arteries in addition to reduced branching; *right*, in camptomelic dwarfism, although lung volume is small, arterial size and branching are not severely affected. (Reproduced with permission from deMello DE. Structural elements of human fetal and neonatal lung vascular development. In: Weir EK, Archer SL, Reeves JT, eds. The fetal and neonatal pulmonary circulations. Armonk, NY: Futura, 1999:37–64.)

Inherited defects: Down syndrome and α1-antiprotease deficiency

Examples of genetic or inherited defects that affect lung growth are seen in Down syndrome and α1-antiprotease deficiency. In Down syndrome, the basis for interference in lung development is not clear, but abnormal adhesiveness of the cells has been reported as a likely basis for the endocardial cushion defects.[81] In the lung, the pattern varies.[81] The lungs are sometimes small. What is more intriguing is that the airway number can be normal or reduced; whereas alveolar number can be reduced, appropriate, or even increased for age.[82] Airway and alveolar patterns do not necessarily correlate. The polyalveolar condition of some of the lobes in Down syndrome was striking. In one child, the number was in the adult range. There is an often quoted clinical observation that for a given cardiac lesion, a patient with Down syndrome is likely to present earlier and with worse symptoms than a child without Down syndrome. Structural vascular analysis usually reveals that hypertensive arterial changes are appropriate for the given cardiac lesion and degree of hypertension. It may be that the clinical condition reflects the inappropriateness of other aspects of lung development.

Alpha 1-antiprotease deficiency is associated with liver, but not lung, manifestations in the newborn. Lung function is affected significantly later, but it is by no means clear whether interference with lung growth contributes to this or whether a loss of lung structure occurs after normal growth.

Congenital cardiac lesions

Some congenital heart lesions do not interfere with hemodynamic pulmonary function before birth; others do. In the latter, adaptive structural changes during prenatal development are a striking feature of the pulmonary circulation. For example, in pulmonary atresia, the small size of the pulmonary arteries but with normal distribution of muscle is in contrast to the increased vascular density and increased muscularization of the microcirculation in hypoplastic left heart syndrome (Figure 7–13).[83]

Environmental factors including drugs like cocaine

Maternal nutrition and environmental factors such as exposure to drugs and toxins can interfere with fetal growth. A number of studies have investigated the effect of these factors on lung growth but none with special reference to the blood vessels. Hypoxia has been considered a cause of pulmonary hypertension in the newborn. However, the effect, both clinically and experimentally, is that hypoxia of the mother, as at altitude, produces a small-for-dates baby, but no selective interference with lung blood vessels has been identified.[84]

COCAINE. The effect of maternal cocaine ingestion on growth of the pulmonary vasculature is not clear. There are no reports of neonatal lung vascular disease, although we have one example of a newborn with severe hypoplasia of the pulmonary vascular tree demonstrated by a postmortem angiogram (see Figure 7–12). No maternal risk factors were identified other than cocaine

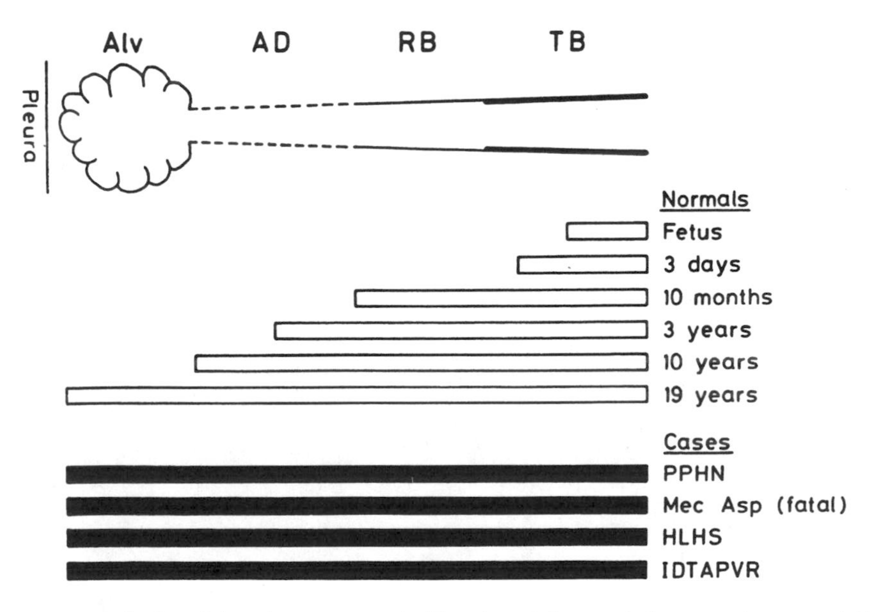

FIGURE 7–13. Precocious muscularization of the pulmonary artery bed in selected disease. A diagrammatic representation of the acinus, the respiratory unit supplied by the terminal bronchiolus that includes several generations of respiratory bronchioli, alveolar ducts, and alveoli. The length of the bars indicates the size that has the highest percentage of partially muscular arteries; ie, it is a level beyond which most arteries are nonmuscular. PPHN-persistent pulmonary hypertension of the newborn, Mec Asp (fatal) = fatal cases of meconium aspiration; HLHS = hypoplastic left heart syndrome; IDTAPVR = infradiaphragmatic total anomalous pulmonary venous return.

ingestion throughout pregnancy. If etiologically related, the mechanism of action of this interference with pulmonary vascular growth is unknown. Clinical and animal studies suggest that fetal growth including brain development and function, fetal renal arterial flow and urine output, and necrosis and inflammation of the gastrointestinal tract are all affected by maternal cocaine use.[85–90] Quite possibly, the mode of maternal use and the dose and duration of use during pregnancy influence the variety and severity of effect in the fetus.

Perinatal Adaptation

Normal

In the perinatal period, the main features of development are concerned with maturation, adaptation to air breathing, and a major increase in pulmonary blood flow.[91] As lung liquid is replaced with air, there is a volume increase in lung and a change in the nature and physical behavior of the alveolar lining, the tissue-gas interface.

The main circulatory change is the drop in pulmonary artery pressure with an increase in flow to the lung, reflected in a major drop in pulmonary vascular resistance. Dilation and lengthening of arteries presumably affect the pre-acinar vessels in particular since in the newborn this includes the resistance segment and upstream channels. Some muscularization, either partial or to give a complete circumferential layer, is found in the region of the respiratory bronchiolus, but a completely muscular coat is unusual at the level of the alveolar duct or in the alveolar wall. A special feature is the change in the resistance arteries as though they have been treated by a tenderizer: the external diameter increases and the thickness of the medial coat reduces.[92,93] Although, at birth, there is likely to be variation in structure from one normal infant to another, typically the intra-acinar arterial and venous bed are virtually nonmuscular in the normal newborn.

Abnormal

Persistent pulmonary hypertension

Persistent pulmonary hypertension (PPHN) is an important problem in the newborn.[94] It may be idiopathic, that is, unexplained or secondary to an identified cause as with certain congenital heart lesions. In six infants who died within the first 6 days of life, we were able to prepare the arteries by distention before fixation so that a quantitative analysis could be made.[95] Structural abnormality of the pulmonary microarteries was identified that could explain the failure to respond to treatment. The small peripheral arteries within the alveolar wall showed severe muscularization often associated with a reduced external diameter, a well-developed internal and external lamina, and a thick collagenous adventitia. The upstream arteries were more thickly walled than normal, so centrally the arterial lumen also was reduced in diameter, and the adventitia was dense and well developed. In some cases, thinning of the muscular arteries at the pre-acinar level had occurred.

Meconium aspiration syndrome

In cases in which meconium aspiration was associated with PPHN, we expected that the pulmonary hypertension resulted from failure of the perinatal adaptation rather than from a structural abnormality. However, in this group we found in 10 of 11 cases the same structural abnormality as that described above.[96] This indicated that the passage of meconium was not the cause of the hypertension but rather a marker of the seriousness of the vascular changes. This fits with the earlier clinical study of Fox and his colleagues who found that they could not predict which infants with aspiration of meconium would be chronically sick.[91] Regardless of the severity of meconium aspiration, only those infants who developed pulmonary hypertension were clinically ill; all of the deaths occurred in this group of patients, of whom about half died. In all of these cases of PPHN, the pulmonary veins were normal, and no congenital cardiac lesion was identified.

The remodeling of PPHN seems to occur in the well-developed lung. We do not know the cytokines and mediators that are responsible for this excessive muscularization. Two suggestions that hypoxemia in utero and injestion of indomethacin or a similar drug by the mother would produce it have failed in an experimental model to cause the hemodynamic or structural changes.[84,97,98] In a recent series of experiments, we investigated the effect on perinatal structural adaptation of delivery into a hypoxic environment.[92] The newborn rabbit was delivered into either hypoxia or air, and the structural changes followed for up to 48 hours for the hypoxic animals and up to 72 hours for the controls. Before the vessels were examined, the lungs were treated with potassium cyanide to eliminate tone.

Additional features of adaptation were identified. Within the first hour or so, a drop in medial coat thickness was seen in all animals, suggesting that fluid had left the intracellular compartment of the muscle layer.

Over the next hours, there was a return to the thickness level at birth, suggesting that hypertrophy from synthetic activity was responsible. In both groups of animals, fluid was seen in the perivascular and alveolar spaces only in the first hours after birth. In the normal, animals it was possible to compare the pulmonary circulation in spontaneously delivered animals with those that by cesarean section had been delivered into air.[92] The drop in wall thickness and increase in external diameter of the resistance arteries were apparent in both groups between 48 and 72 hours. Considering that the -

spontaneously delivered animals could be anything up to 12 hours older than the cesarean derived, this suggested that the important component for this adaptation was between 48 and 72 hours of air breathing.

Postnatal Development

Normal

Pre-acinar and pre-lobular arteries

The branching pattern of the arteries and airways in this region of the lung is complete by the 16th week of intrauterine life.[7] Postnatal growth is characterized by an increase in arterial diameter, which reflects cell multiplication. At a given position, the diameter of an artery shows a linear relationship to the length of its distal course. Thus, regardless of age, the diameter of arteries 1 cm from their peripheral end is similar. During fetal life, in the pre-acinar region the proximal part of the axial pathway increases in diameter faster than the peripheral portion; after birth, both increase at a similar rate. Both conventional and supernumerary arteries increase at the same rate. Size increases rapidly during the first 18 months of life, and then the rate of growth becomes slower.[17] The structure of the pre-acinar arterial tree is established in fetal life and does not change postnatally.[7] At the hilum, the pulmonary artery is elastic.[99] It has a well-defined internal and external elastic lamina limiting the media that consists of layers of smooth muscle cells with several additional central elastic laminae. Passing distally, the central elastic laminae become progressively fragmented to give the typical appearance of a muscular artery, a compact layer of muscle cells between an internal and external lamina. Brenner defined an elastic artery as having eight or more central laminae and a transitional artery as having four to seven.[99] Serial sections of an axial pathway of the inferior basal segment revealed that 43% of the length is elastic, 10% transitional, and 47% muscular. The first six generations of the artery were elastic, the next three transitional, and beyond muscular. In the adult, structure and size are related: arteries in the range of 150 to 2,000 microns are muscular, and those larger than 2,000 microns are either transitional or elastic.[18]

Post-acinar and post-lobular veins

The venous pathways develop when the arteries develop so that all post-acinar veins are present in fetal life. At a given level, conventional and supernumerary veins appear together, and their numbers maintain the same ratio to each other during childhood and in adulthood.[18]

Intra-acinar arteries and veins

Postnatally, the main burst of growth is within the acinus.[8] As alveoli multiply and new alveolar ducts are formed, the intra-acinar vessels increase in number and density. Although few new conventional vessels appear, supernumerary arteries increase considerably, their number exceeding the conventional arteries of this region. The increase in the density of small arteries is reflected in specimen arteriograms: at birth, these show no background haze, but by 10 months, a dense haze caused by filled small vessels is apparent and obscures main vessels. In the first few years of life, alveolar multiplication is so rapid that even as the chest wall grows, alveolar size does not increase. The prominent intra-acinar arteries increase in size, and new alveolar wall vessels grow to supply the increasing gas exchange surface.

Genetic programming for vascular development and response to changes in hemodynamic conditions both seem responsible for intra-acinar vessel growth. As the vessels increase in density and size, wall structure is remodeled upstream and downstream from the capillary bed. A muscle or medial coat develops within smaller and more distal vessels, thus accompanying respiratory bronchioli, alveolar ducts, and, finally, alveolar walls. Therefore, in late childhood and adulthood many intra-acinar arteries have muscle in their wall.[5,100] Although, between individuals, variability is wide, in the fetus and newborn muscular arteries are rare within the acinus or accompanying alveolar ducts. There is also considerable overlap in the size range of the three structural artery types. By about 10 years of age, the largest nonmuscular arteries are about 230 microns in diameter, whereas the smallest muscular arteries are about 180 microns; for the adult, these figures are 90 and 50 microns, respectively.

Local conditions, both hemodynamic and ventilatory, as well as inflammation, can markedly modify the normal structure of intra-acinar vessels, for example, congenital heart disease with left to right shunts, bronchiolitis obliterans, cystic fibrosis (CF), and scoliosis. The density and size of intra-acinar arteries are modified as well as the size distribution of arterial structural types.[13,101–103]

New veins, conventional and supernumerary, develop in the intra-acinar region along with the arteries. Supernumerary veins are more numerous in this region. Within the alveolar wall, nonmuscular and partially muscular arteries and veins cannot be distinguished reliably by light microscopy. An advantage of injecting one of the systems with an identifiable medium permits their recognition.

Nerve supply to the pulmonary circulation

Nerve trunks run in the adventitia of the lung's vessels and are found mainly with large arteries and veins. In the large arteries, nerve fibers are distributed through the outer third of the muscle coat of the elastic or muscular vessels. Nerve fibers are not typically found with alveolar wall vessels.

Both noradrenergic and cholinergic nerves are identified,[104] and usually contain other putative transmitters, which have been the subject of a recent investigation. Allen and colleagues investigated a series of peptides-vasoactive intestinal peptide predominant in parasympathetic nerves: substance P, the neurokinins and calcitonin gene-related peptide all present in sensory nerves, and the neuropeptide tyrosine found in sympathetic nerves.[105] Synaptophysin is a membrane protein associated with small secretory vesicles thought to contain the classic neurotransmitters in nerve terminals.

Neuropeptide tyrosine and tyrosine hydralase immunoreactivity are the most common substances identified. Other subpopulations are uncommon, but of these, fibers containing vasoactive intestinal peptide are the most abundant. Such fibers, albeit sparse, are most commonly associated with the small muscular arteries immediately proximal to the respiratory unit.

Nerves are present in vein walls; their distribution is different from that in the arteries. In veins, a dense network is present throughout the adventitia, and furthermore, nerve fibers penetrate the muscle coat and extend to the subendothelium. Neuropeptide tyrosine, tyrosine hydralase, and somatostatin are present in the veins, but the other peptides are rare. More synaptophysin immunoreactive fibers are present in veins than in arteries. The atrial natriuretic peptide is found in myocardial cells around the hilar veins but nowhere else in the lung.

The bronchial arteries show nerves at the border between the media and adventitia; they are predominantly immunoreactive to neuropeptide tyrosine and tyrosine hydralase.

Changes with age are confined to the arteries of the respiratory unit. In children aged 1 to 4 months, about one-third of the arteries accompanying alveolar ducts are without innervation, but by 2.5 years, almost all are innervated, and in the adult they are invariably so. Of the arteries with alveolar ducts, immunoreactivity to protein gene product 9.5 and neuropeptide tyrosine is common; rare fibers contain vasoactive intestinal peptide. In individuals under 1.5 years, the veins within the alveolar region do not seem to have nerve fibers, although in those older than 2.5 years, a small proportion does.

In rats, afferent lung innervation, abolished by transplantation, is spontaneously re-established and functioning in the ipsilateral vagus nerve 8 months after pulmonary isografting.[106] In the guinea pig, arterial innervation is more developed than that of veins. In the arterial tree, nitrergic axons are restricted to large (> 700 microns) extrapulmonary arteries, whereas noradrenergic and substance P-containing axons are present from the pulmonary trunk to the smallest intrapulmonary vessels and cholinergic axons are present in arteries up to 50 microns in diameter.[107]

Examples of Abnormal Development

Bronchopulmonary dysplasia

The term "bronchopulmonary dysplasia" (BPD) was used originally to describe a complication of the idiopathic respiratory distress syndrome of the newborn, also known as hyaline membrane disease—the changes in the lung of infants born prematurely, who develop hyaline membrane disease and are treated by ventilator and high oxygen.[108] Bronchopulmonary dysplasia now describes lung changes in any infant so treated in the perinatal period who develops radiographic shadows. The diagnosis is made now after only 3 weeks of treatment. Bronchopulmonary dysplasia represents a palimpsest, whereon the multiple events that have affected the lung can be detected.[109] The infant is born prematurely so that the latter part of intrauterine lung growth and maturation has not occurred, and then, at birth, there is the injury characteristic of hyaline membrane disease of the newborn in which high-protein edema develops in the intra-alveolar space with damage to the epithelium of small airways and the lining of the alveolar space. Ventilation and high oxygen are administered as treatment, and each produces injury. The lung adapts to these new levels of high oxygen, and then if weaning is too sudden, there may be additional injury from relative hypoxia.[110–112] Adaptation, resolution, healing, and scar formation take further toll on the lung structure. The changes are of a focal nature so that lung units, whether lobe, segment, lobule, or acinus, are not uniformly affected (Figure 7–14).

All components of the lung are affected, although probably each to a different degree. In larger airways, epithelial changes include ciliary loss, hyperplasia, and squamous metaplasia, whereas in the smaller airways, there is growth of exuberant granulation tissue that sometimes occludes the lumen and leads to retention of mucus and ultimately bronchiolitis obliterans. Bronchial smooth muscle is frequently hypertrophic.

Scars of collapsed lung represent a significant loss of alveolar number, a scar representing the original lung of considerably greater volume than the final scar. Alveoli supplied by conducting airways that undergo luminal occlusion are protected from exposure to high ventilatory pressures. Collateral ventilation can help such blocked alveoli aerate; consequently, such areas are likely to undergo late compensatory growth when the airway resumes, but alveolar multiplication will not occur normally. Whatever the reason, in BPD, foci of alveolar condensation alternate with emphysema that reflects overdistention of alveoli and their failure to multiply. These changes in air spaces probably determine the eventual pattern of the pulmonary vasculature as well (Figure 7–15).

The arterial branching pattern is normal,[4] reflecting normal early intrauterine development, but there is

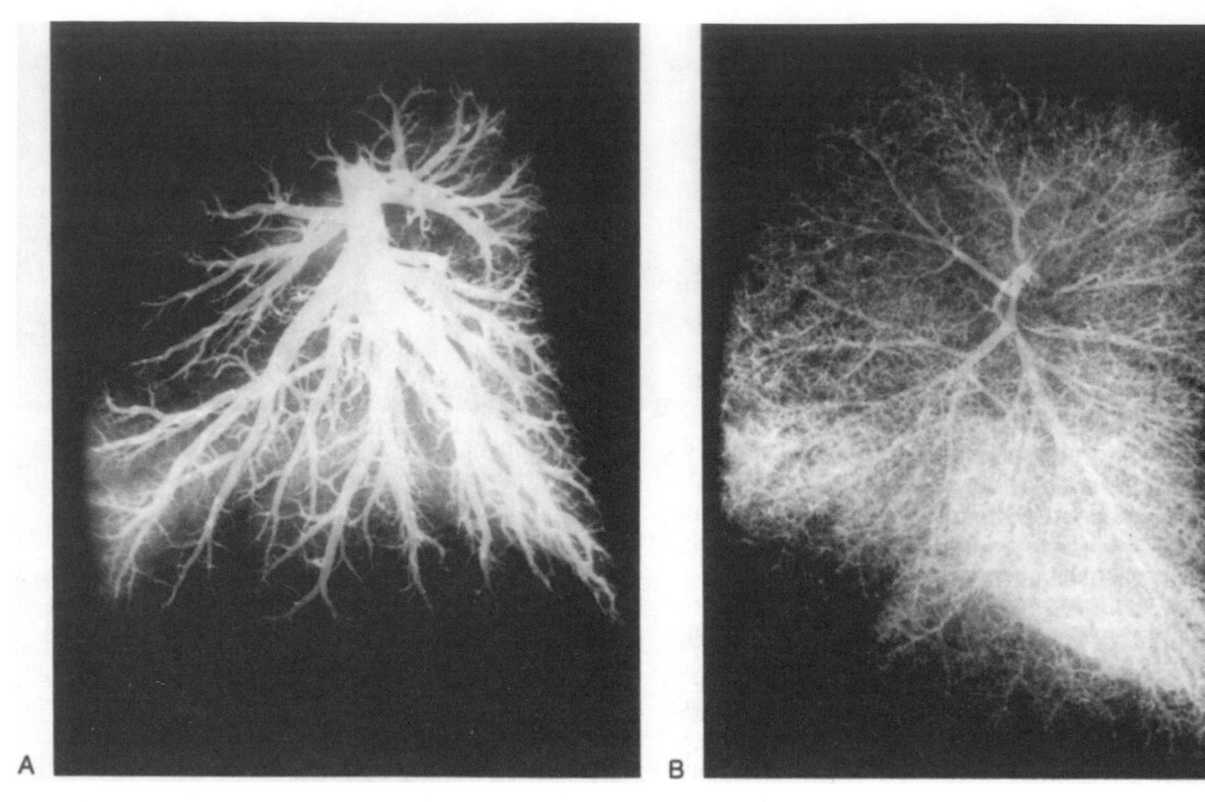

FIGURE 7–14. Postmortem arteriograms showing marked variations in central arterial size and peripheral vascular density in two cases of BPD. The postconception age of *A* is 32.5 weeks and that of *B* 38.0 weeks. Note the large central artery size and relative lack of peripheral vascular density in *A* compared with *B*. The pattern of *A* is common in infants who die in the newborn period. The pattern of *B* is uncommon. Whether this pattern is peculiar to BPD is not known. (Reprinted with permission from Tomashefski J et al.[112])

considerable variation in vessel size, perhaps reflecting the state of the alveolar region supplied by a given artery. The scarred regions are supplied by the smallest vessels; those undergoing alveolar multiplication receive the largest vessels. Vascular congestion is sometimes apparent in the dilated capillary loops within the thickened alveolar wall. This picture has led some to the belief that there is focal formation of double capillary loops,[61] but it is equally likely that this picture is the result of congestion and relaxation in scarred areas unable to expand with respiration.

Congenital diaphragmatic hernia

Interference with intrauterine lung growth has a profound effect on postnatal adaptation and growth. A good example is congenital diaphragmatic hernia. In this condition, a defect in the early stages of development of the diaphragm allows herniation into the thorax of the gut and other abdominal organs. The reduction of available thoracic space restricts lung growth, inhibiting airway and blood vessel branching; this affects both sides but is usually worse on the ipsilateral side.[66,70,113] Thus, the arteries are small (but often appropriate to lung volume) and also reduced in density. Surgical correction of the hernia postnatally allows the lung to expand considerably, even to fill the thorax (Figure 7–16). Pulmonary artery size is then clearly inappropriate to the distended lung volume. This artery size is probably a good postnatal and postoperative indicator of the degree of hypoplasia present at birth. Lung growth does occur after correction, but to what extent is not clear (Figure 7–17). Reduced alveolar number and alveolar overdistention, a type of hypoplastic emphysema, are apparent months after correction. Good function has been shown to be maintained into the teens, although reduced perfusion to the ipsilateral lung persists.[114]

The structure of the arterial tree also is not normal, typically with the muscle coat being thicker and extending further into smaller arteries than is normal. The abnormal structure is reflected in the abnormal postnatal pulmonary vascular adaptation and the PPHN that is frequent postoperatively.[70] The distortion of central airways and arteries persists even after repair, and when the lung expands postoperatively, abnormal configuration of the airways may lead to their kinking and to foci of collapse and emphysema.[66] In this condition, emphysema is a hypoplastic form resulting from great overdistention of a hypoplastic lobe[113] or from air trapping, usually in the ipsilateral lower lobe.[115] This, in turn, further

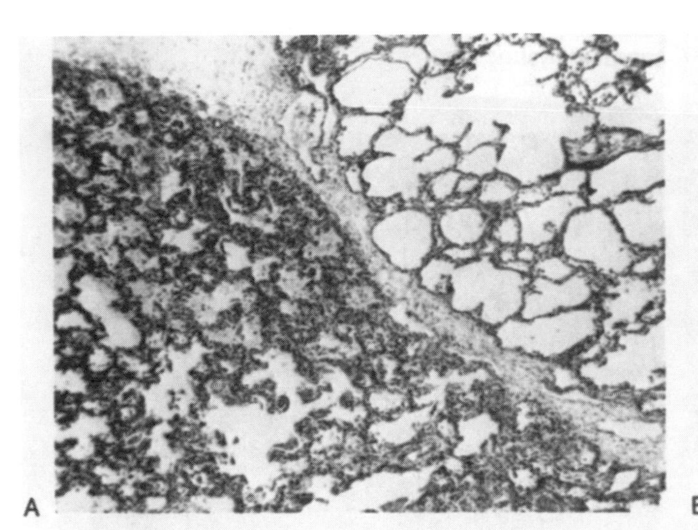

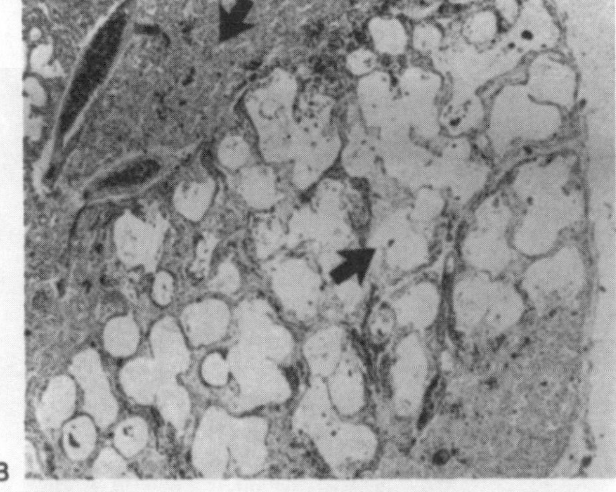

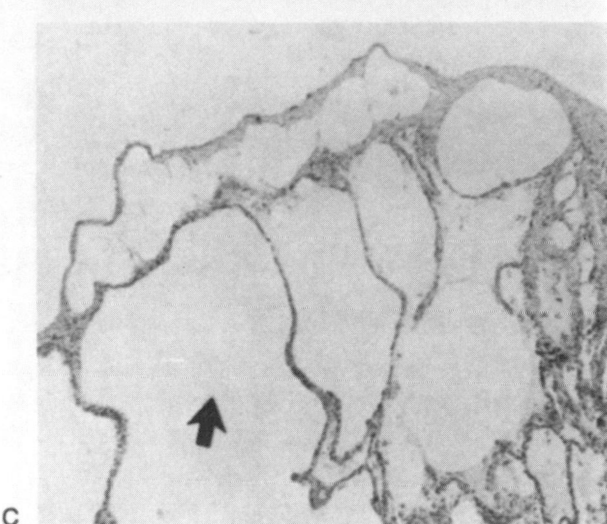

FIGURE 7–15. Photomicrographs from the lung of patients with bronchopulmonary dysplasia. *A*, Photomicrograph of a section of lung showing to the left small alveoli containing hyaline membranes and to the right larger and better aerated alveoli. Focally irregular changes are apparent. The two areas of lung are separated by a connective tissue septum. *B*, Late BPD. Aerated lung (*lower arrow*) with alveolar wall fibrosis alternates with collapsed alveolar spaces (*upper arrow*). Radiologically, this appears as streaky densities or finely bubbly lung. This is from an infant born at 7 months of gestational age who died 2 months later after having hyaline membrane disease (HMD), erythroblastosis fetalis, and BPD. *C*, Late BPD. Pleural interstitial emphysema and large, fibrous tissue-lined air spaces (*arrow*) lacking alveolar subdivision. Such changes often are most pronounced in the lower lobes and are one reason for the overdistention and cystic appearance seen radiologically. This is from an infant weighing 1,000 g at birth who died 7 months later after HMD and BPD. (Reprinted with permission from Tomashefski J et al.[112])

compromises pulmonary circulation and may require eventual resection of the emphysematous lobe. If such regions appear hyperlucent, inspiration expiration films can exclude air trapping. Ventilation perfusion scans provide additional information.

Scoliosis

Scoliosis is another example of modified lung growth from restriction of space, but since the restriction usually develops after birth, the effect is on postnatal lung growth.[116,117] In contrast to congenital diaphragmatic hernia, branching of the bronchial tree and pre-acinar arteries should be complete; it is multiplication of postnatal alveoli and small vessels that is impaired.[118] The effect on alveolar growth and size varies with the shape of the thorax as the lung grows and remodels to fit the distorted thoracic cage. In addition, pressure atrophy is a secondary effect. Thus, alveoli of the lung stretched over the convexity of the spine are often atrophic, whereas those within the spinal concavity are enlarged. Artery size and density are reduced. From the straight radiograph, distribution of lung function cannot be predicted since the most obvious lung in the radiogram can represent one of the smaller lobes and thus be receiving less blood flow.

The severity of functional impairment depends on the time of onset of scoliosis and the rapidity with which it develops. Initially, despite the distortion of lung shape, function is good because there is no obstruction of airways. Should airway obstruction occur, perhaps secondary to infection or blockage by secretions, the problems of chronic airways obstruction are superimposed on those resulting from mechanical distortion. In this setting, cor pulmonale is likely to develop quickly. Reduction of arterial size and number parallels alveolar impairment, and arterial wall smooth muscle may be increased, extending into more peripheral vessels than normal.[118]

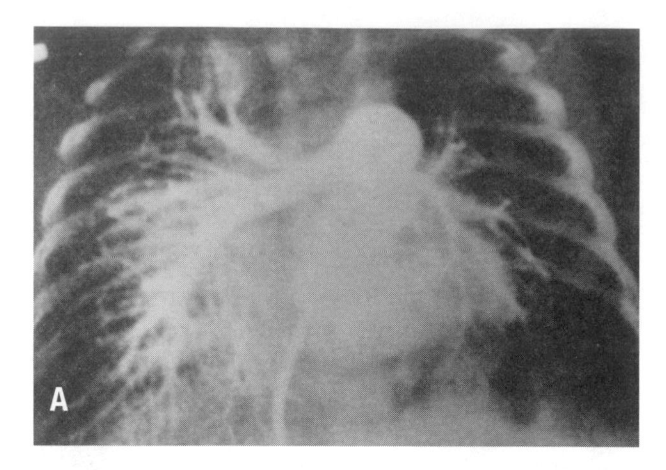

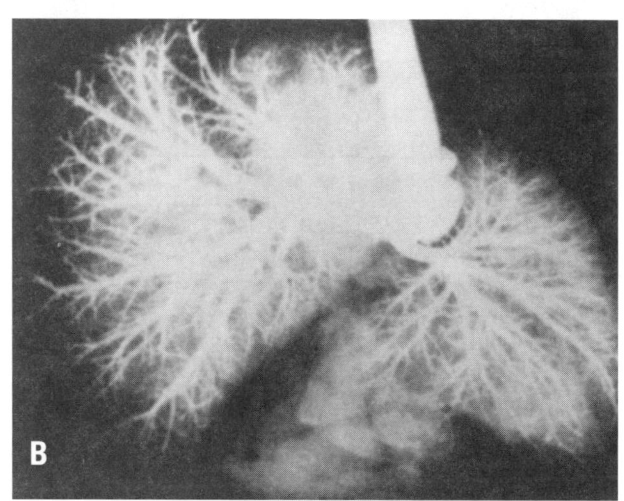

FIGURE 7–16. Congenital diaphragmatic hernia repair. *A*, Pulmonary angiogram at 1 month. The right pulmonary artery is normal in size and the peripheral lung is well filled. The left pulmonary artery is small and the peripheral filling is poor. *B*, Postmortem arteriogram of both lungs. The left lung is small and the arteries are reduced in size and number compared with the right lung, which has normal-sized arteries for age.[113]

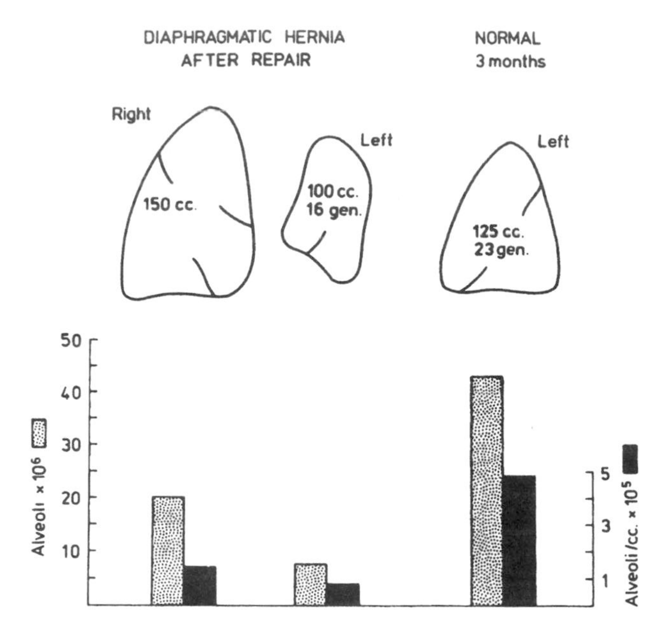

FIGURE 7–17. Diagram illustrating the quantitative findings in the airways and alveoli in diaphragmatic hernia. The number of airway generations (gen) is reduced; the total alveolar number is reduced, as is alveolar density. The alveoli are too large, ie, emphysematous. (Reproduced with permission from Hislop A and Reid L.[113])

The alveoli are commonly abnormally large, and the presence of excessive muscularization of the small arteries, as judged by both size and position within the branching pattern, suggests that the additional muscularization that occurs during childhood and adolescence to achieve adult levels in these cases occurs rather earlier than normal. It is difficult to decide how much the changes seen at autopsy reflect hypoxia and hypoxemia in the last months to years and how much they represent a precocious muscularization as evidence of early maturation.

Cystic fibrosis

Recently, the gene that causes CF in about 70% of patients has been identified.[119] It is present in chromosome 7 and shows a specific deletion of the codon for one amino acid, phenylalanine. It produces what has been named the transmembrane regulatory protein of cystic fibrosis —CFTR protein, which is thought to influence ion conduction in epithelial cells. The lungs are structurally normal in contrast to other sites such as pancreas, duodenum, and vas deferens, in which abnormalities are manifested in utero or in the early postnatal period. Unfortunately, this mutation seems to account for only about 70% of the mutations responsible for clinical cystic fibrosis. Genotype-phenotype studies have demonstrated that the degree of correlation between CFTR genotype and CFTR phenotype varies between its clinical patterns; it is highest for pancreatic status and lowest for pulmonary disease. This suggests an influence of environmental and secondary genetic factors, CF modifiers, for example, a CF modifier for meconium ileus on human chromosome 19q13.2. Beyond classic CF, there are monosymptomatic diseases such as obstructive azoospermia, idiopathic pancreatitis, and disseminated bronchiectasis, which are associated with CFTR mutations uncharacteristic for CF.[120] Normal sweat chloride tests should not exclude the diagnosis of CF if lung disease is consistent with CF. Genotyping in such patients has revealed compound heterozygotic CF mutations delta F508/3849 + 10kb C – > T.[121]

In the CF lung, postnatal structural abnormalities result from the repeated injury of infection[122,123]; there is as yet no known explanation for this increased susceptibility to infection. The mucus in CF is no more viscid than that in chronic bronchitis if the secretions are of equal purulence.[124–127] Mucus hypersecretion develops, and mucus plugging of airways occurs. The repeated episodes of infection predominantly affect the small airways, throughout the lung,[127] with no predilection for apex or base, suggesting that the increased susceptibility to infection is humoral and that stasis and gravity are not the primary cause. It also is striking that infection does not usually lead to obliteration of the pleural space; pneumothorax is a common late complication.

The involvement of small airways has a profound effect on subsequent growth of the intra-acinar structures. The severity of growth impairment largely depends on the timing of the infection during the postnatal growth phase. Acute and chronic bronchiolitis and bronchitis eventually lead to obliterative lesions. Although collapse does occur, collateral ventilation is often effective in maintaining aeration distal to obstruction. Where it is ineffective, collapse does occur, even of a whole lobe. The wall of the dilated airway upstream from the obliterated point is often without muscle; it represents an endobronchial abscess that has extended through the wall.

The blood vessels in CF reflect changes in the airways and alveoli (Figure 7–18).[128] Interference with alveolar ventilation and alveolar multiplication lead to reduced flow; hypoxemia causes structural remodeling and perhaps vasoconstriction. A combination of small arterial size, reduced number, and increased wall thickness

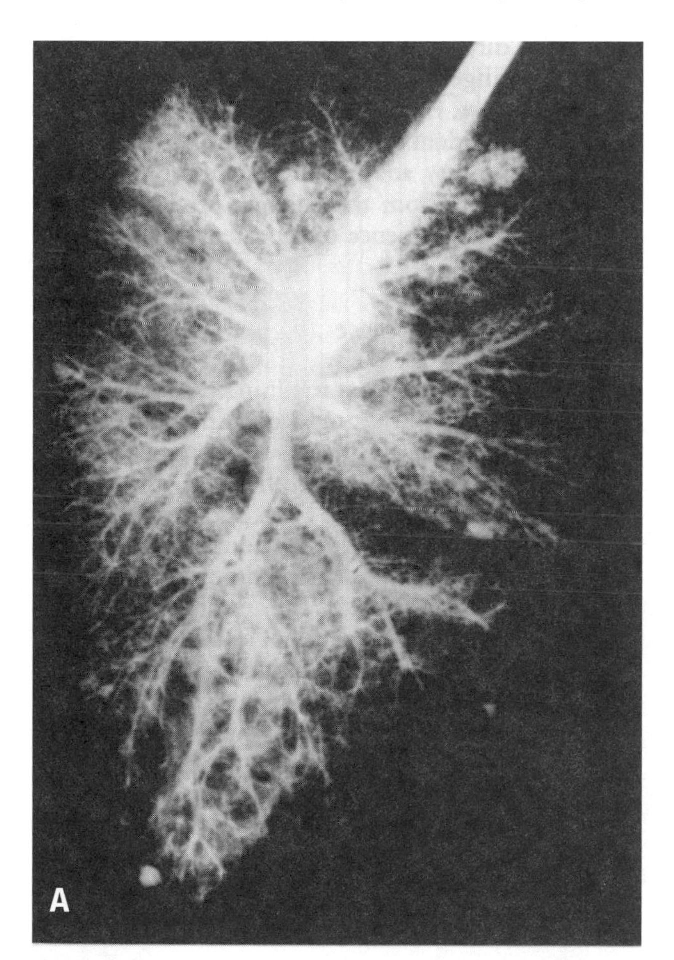

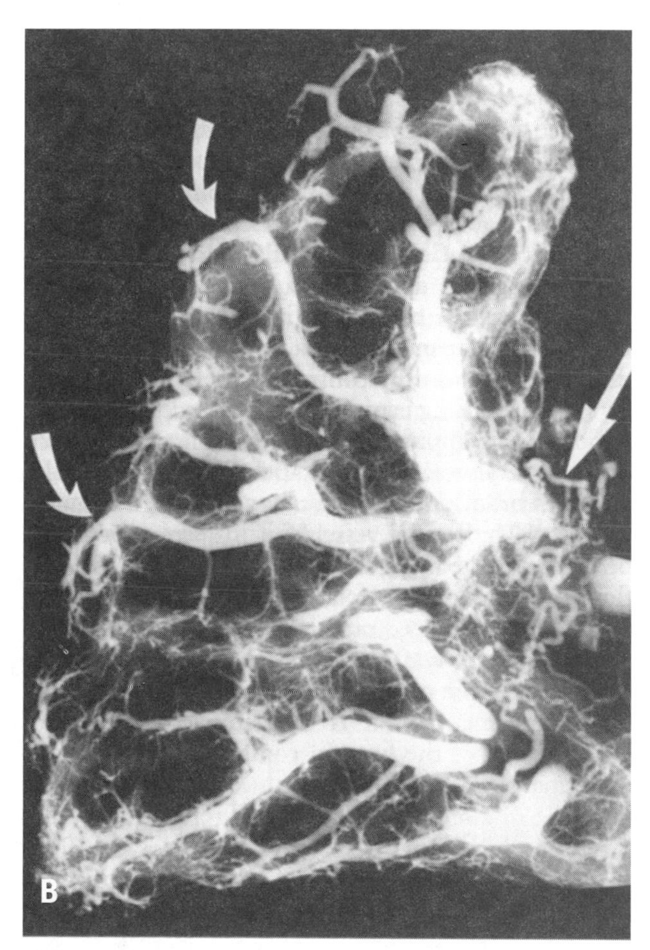

FIGURE 7–18. Arteriograms from two fatal cases of cystic fibrosis. *A*, Postmortem pulmonary arteriogram of the left lung of a boy aged 6 years, 2 months. Cystic fibrosis was first diagnosed when he was 6 months of age. During the next 2.5 years, he had acute respiratory infections, which were treated carefully, but by the age of 4 years, he had chronic cough productive of the purulum sputum and began to complain of breathlessness on exertion. During the next year, his condition worsened, and he became deeply cyanosed, with gross clubbing of the fingers. Signs of heart failure were apparent only for 2 weeks before death. The left upper lobe volume was relatively reduced compared with the left lower. The proximal arteries are narrow in all areas but particularly centrally. The peripheral filling was abnormal: in the posterior basal region the vessels were "stretched" around cystic bronchiectatic cavities. Muscle extended into arteries smaller than normal. At each diameter range, the wall thickness showed a wide range always greater than normal. This increase was striking even in the larger arteries. *B*, Postmortem arteriogram of a bronchiectatic upper lobe. The large pulmonary artery branches (*curved arrows*) extend to the pleural surface with markedly decreased peripheral filling. The narrower bronchial arteries (*straight arrows*) form a plexus in the hilum and run with the airways and pulmonary arteries to the periphery in the bronchoarterial bundle. (Reprinted with permission from Tomashefski JF et al.[127])

produces a hypoplastic or restricted pulmonary artery bed; ultimately, hypertrophy of the right ventricle develops but usually only a year or two before death. In fatal cases of CF, the degree of right ventricle hypertrophy correlates with the degree of arterial and venous muscularity. The degree of response of the pulmonary hypertension varies widely,[129,130] particularly when bronchiectasis is present.

Polycythemia is seen rarely in patients with CF, even when they have been hypoxic for some time. This does not seem to be nutritional because of failure to absorb iron. Development of collateral circulation between large bronchial and pulmonary arteries sometimes develops (see Figure 7–18). The dilated bronchial arteries within the walls of bronchiectatic cavities often cause hemoptysis in these patients. Selective bronchial artery embolization and surgical resection of the most severely affected lobe are used to treat this complication.

Bronchiolitis obliterans

As the name bronchiolitis obliterans implies, the inflammatory process predominantly affects the small airways.[131] Sometimes, both lungs are diffusely affected; sometimes, it is localized. In the acute stages, epithelial necrosis and inflammation destroy ciliary activity. Although the inflammatory process may resolve, more often it becomes subacute or chronic, and the ensuing organization leads to an obliteration of the lumen. When the airway block is complete, the peripheral lung supplied by that airway undergoes collapse. Frequently, collateral ventilation provides aeration of the alveolar regions supplied by the obliterated airways. Airway obliteration also may lead to the formation of endobronchial abscesses. Collateral ventilation favors inspiration with air-trapping and a consequent reduction in blood flow. The minute blood flow in the lung is influenced by total ventilation and therefore occurs mainly during inspiration. Alveolar blood flow is greatest during expiration and is reduced by overinflation or air-trapping. Alveolar multiplication is affected, and normal alveolar multiplication does not occur. In bronchiolitis obliterans, blood vessels are reduced in number and size. The central vessels fail to increase in volume because of the reduced ventilation and thus reduce blood flow. Alveolar blood vessels do not achieve normal density, concomitant with the failure in alveolar multiplication.

The MacLeod syndrome represents a striking example of this sort of pathologic process.[132] As originally described, it is characterized by unilateral hyperlucency of the lung in combination with a small or normal-sized lung. The hyperlucency may be confined to a lobe or a segment of lobe and represents localized accentuation of

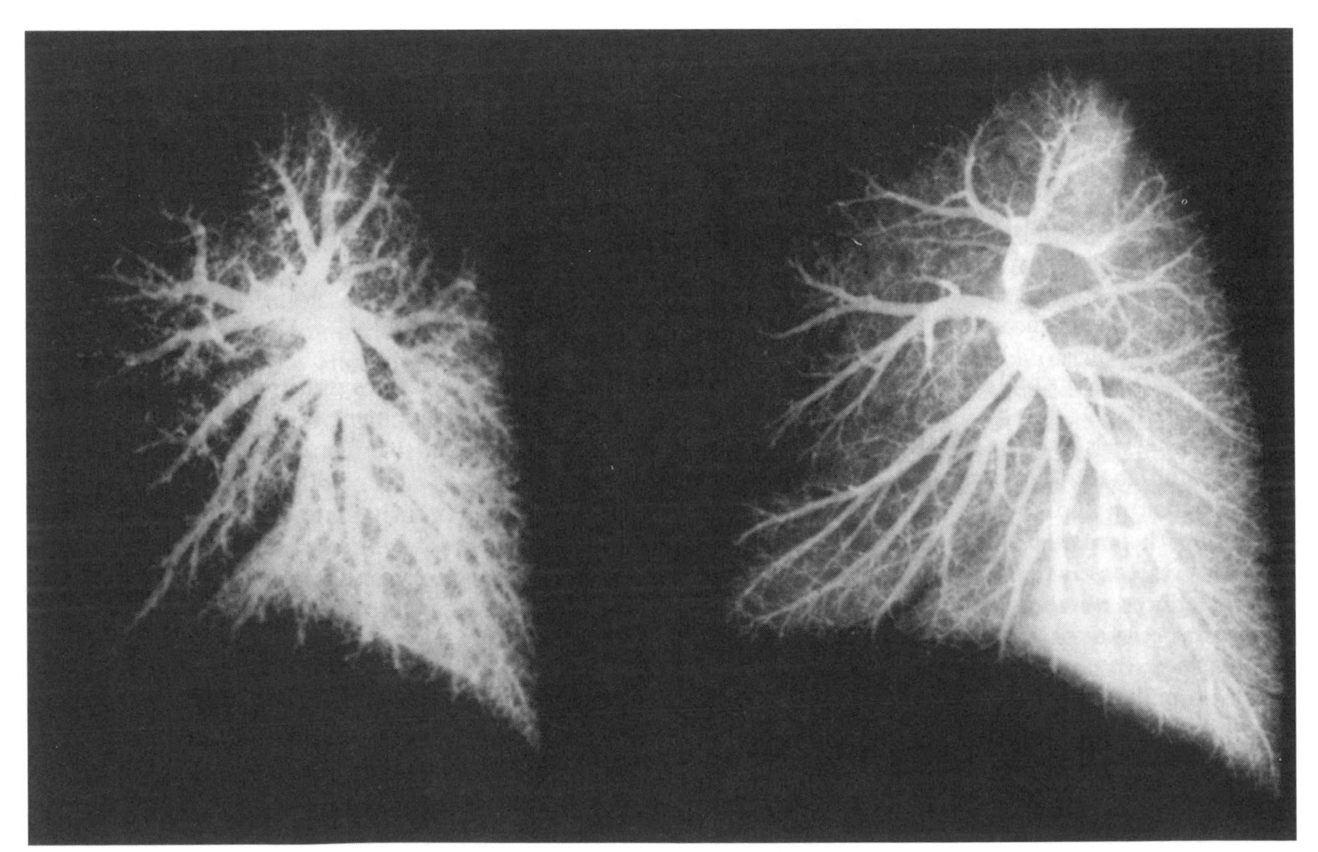

FIGURE 7–19. Arteriogram (*right*) of a patient with ventricular septal defect and acute and chronic pulmonary congestion, showing reduction of luminal size of the main and axial arteries. The control is at *left*.

a more widespread process. Careful examination of bronchograms of what appears to be the "normal" lung often shows localized foci of bronchiolectasis. Although arteriograms reveal the main pulmonary arteries to be reduced in diameter, direct inspection shows them to be within the normal range, indicating that the angiogram reflects reduced blood flow. Bronchiolitis obliterans usually results from a single incident of infection that goes through the various stages: injury, adaptation, resolution, repair, and scarring. It differs from the changes produced by CF, which are the consequence of repeated episodes of infection.

Congenital heart disease

In many congenital heart lesions, the pulmonary circulation is functionally and structurally normal at birth. If hemodynamic abnormality occurs prenatally, pulmonary vascular structural remodeling develops in utero. This process continues postnatally until the defect is repaired. In other cases, the vascular bed is structurally normal at birth, and disturbance of growth is postnatal. Thus, the pulmonary arterial tree is susceptible to extensive prenatal and postnatal structural alterations (Figure 7–19). Pulmonary vascular occlusive disease in older patients is a common complication of congenital heart lesions. The severity of these structural changes have been graded by Heath and Edwards on a scale of 1 to 6.[133] In children, pulmonary vascular structure reflects both a remodeling process and interference with prenatal and postnatal pulmonary arterial growth (Figure 7–20). To appropriately evaluate these alterations, which include precocious muscularization of small intra-acinar arteries, increased medial thickness of normally muscular arteries, and reduced size and density of small vessels, we have graded additional features that reflect the correlation between the structural vascular abnormalities and clinical and hemodynamic findings.[103,134]

If the pulmonary microcirculation is normal at birth, the perinatal adaptation of a drop in resistance can occur normally. This is seen, for example, in most cases of ventricular septal defect, in which at birth an increase in pulmonary flow does not prevent the drop in pressure. Pressure and resistance then increase steadily as a response to flow increase, and structural remodeling occurs. In a relatively uncommon form of the ventricular septal defect, the structure of the microcirculation indicates that perinatal adaptation did not occur normally.[101] In a group of children who died within the first year of life, it was apparent that the medial thickness of the resistance arteries was well above anything that is seen in patients with ventricular septal defect who had survived some years. In those children in whom pulmonary hypertension developed later, although the microcirculation showed an increase in medial thickness, it was not at the fetal level.

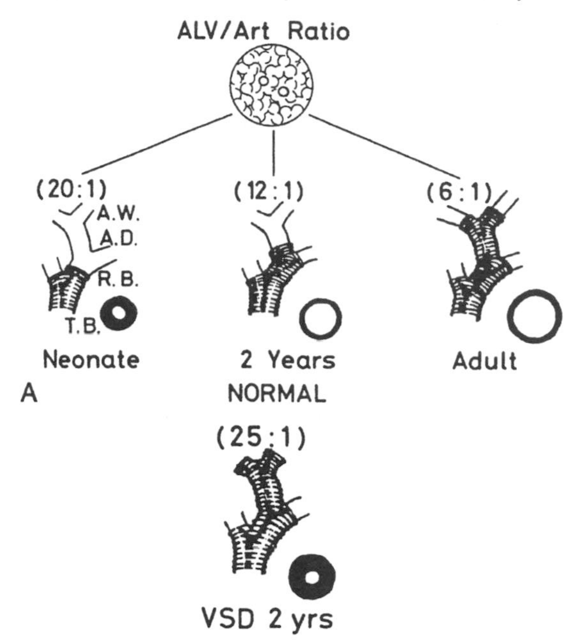

FIGURE 7–20. Biopsy analysis of structural changes in ventricular septal defect (VSD). The number of alveoli (ALV) and the number of arteries (Art) per unit area are given as a ratio. *A*, AW = alveolar wall; AD = alveolar duct; RB = respiratory bronchiolus; TB = terminal bronchiolus. The progressive extension to the periphery is illustrated at three ages. The size and wall thickness of the artery with terminal bronchiolus is shown in cross-section. *B*, Findings in a case of VSD, in a patient aged 2 years. The number of arteries is decreased, the arterial muscle is abnormally far to the periphery, and the artery is smaller, with an abnormally thick wall. (Reproduced with permission from Rabinovitch M et al.[102])

Acknowledgment

Supported in part by a grant from the NIH #HL55600 (DEdM).

References

1. Bucher UG, Reid L. Development of the intra segmental bronchial tree: the pattern of branching and development of cartilage at various stages of intrauterine life. Thorax 1961;16:207–18.
2. Boyden EA. The mode of origin of pulmonary acini and respiratory bronchioles in the fetal lung. Am J Anat 1974;141:317–28.
3. Dunnill MS. Post-natal growth of the lung. Thorax 1962; 17:329–33.
4. Davies GM, Reid L. Growth of the alveoli and pulmonary arteries in childhood. Thorax 1970;25:669–81.
5. Hislop AA, Wigglesworth JS, Desai R. Alveolar development in the human fetus and infant. Early Hum Dev 1986;13:1–11.

6. Boyden EA. The developing bronchial arteries in a fetus of the 12th week. Am J Anat 1970;129:357–68.
7. Hislop A, Reid L. Intrapulmonary arterial development during fetal life—branching pattern and structure. J Anat 1972;113:35–48.
8. Hislop A, Reid L. Development of the acinus in the human lung. Thorax 1974;29:90–4.
9. Hislop A, Reid L. Lung development in relation to gas exchange capacity. Bull Physiopathol Respir 1973; 9:1317–43.
10. DiMaio M, Gil J, Ciurea D, et al. Structural maturation of the human fetal lung: a morphometric study of the development of air blood barriers. Pediatr Res 1989; 26:88–93.
11. Hislop A, Reid L. Growth and development of the respiratory system—anatomical development. In: Davis JA, Dobbing J, eds. Scientific foundations of pediatrics. London: William Heinemann, 1974:214–54.
12. Schoenwolf GC, Bell LA, Watterson RL. Vasculogenesis of the bursa cloacalis (fabricius) of the chick embryo. J Morphol 1981;167:35–42.
13. Rabinovitch M, Herrera-deLeon V, Castaneda AR, Reid L. Growth and development of the pulmonary vascular bed in patients with tetralogy of Fallot with or without pulmonary atresia. Circulation 1981;64:1234–49.
14. Elliott FM, Reid L. Some new facts about the pulmonary artery and its branching pattern. Clin Radiol 1965; 16:193–8.
15. Shaw AM, Bunton DC, Fisher A, et al. V-shaped cushion at the origin of bovine pulmonary supernumerary arteries: structure and putative function. J Appl Physiol 1999; 87:2348–56.
16. Bunton DC, MacDonald A, Brown T, et al. 5-Hydroxytryptamine and U46619-mediated vasoconstriction in bovine pulmonary conventional and supernumerary arteries: effect of endogenous nitric oxide. Clin Sci 2000;98:81–9.
17. Hislop A, Reid L. Pulmonary arterial development during childhood: branching pattern and structure. Thorax 1973;28(a):129–35.
18. Hislop A, Reid L. Fetal and childhood development of the intrapulmonary veins in man—branching pattern and structure. Thorax 1973;28(b):313–9.
19. Boyden EA. The time lag in the development of bronchial arteries. Anat Rec 1970;166:611–4.
20. Kamata S, Sawai T, Nose K, et al. Extralobar pulmonary sequestration with venous drainage to the portal vein: a case report. Pediatr Radiol 2000;30:492–4.
21. Shaffrey JK, Brinker DA, Horton KM, et al. Atypical extralobar sequestration: CT-pathological correlation. Clin Imaging 1999;23:223–6.
22. Serrano A, Santonja C, Calderon JA, et al. Intralobar pulmonary sequestration as the cause of neonatal respiratory distress. Arch Bronconeumol 1996;32:310–2.
23. Gamillscheg A, Beitzke A, Smolle-Juttner FM, et al. Extralobar sequestration with unusual arterial supply and venous drainage. Pediatr Cardiol 1996;17:57–9.
24. Noden DM. Embryonic origins and assembling of blood vessels. Am Rev Respir Dis 1989;140:1097–03.
25. LeDouarin NM. A biological labelling technique and its use in experimental embryology. Dev Biol 1973;30:217–22.
26. Folkman J, Weisz PB, Joullie MM, et al. Control of angiogenesis with synthetic heparin substitutes. Science 1989;243:1490–3.
27. Rowan RA, Maxwell DS. An ultrastructural study of vascular proliferation and vascular alkaline phosphatase activity in the developing cerebral cortex of the rat. Am J Anat 1981;160:257–65.
28. Drake CJ, Brandt SJ, Trusk TC, et al. TAL1/SCL is expressed in endothelial progenitor cells/angioblasts and defines a dorsal to ventral gradient of vasculogenesis. Dev Biol 1997;191:1–14.
29. Drake CJ, Davis LA, Little CD. Antibodies to Beta 1 integrins cause alterations of aortic vasculogenesis in vivo. Dev Dyn 1992;193:83–91.
30. Drake CJ, Cheresh DA, Little CD. An antagonist of integrin α vβ3 prevents maturation of blood vessels during embryonic neovascularization. J Cell Sci 1995;108: 2655–61.
31. Drake CJ, Little CD. Exogenous vascular endothelial growth factor induces malformed and hyperfused vessels during embryonic neovascularization. Proc Natl Acad Sci U S A 1995;92:7657–61.
32. deRuiter MC, Poelmann RE, Van Munsteren JC, et al. Embryonic endothelial cells transdifferentiate into mesenchymal cells expressing smooth muscle actins in vivo and in vitro. Circ Res 1997;80:444–51.
33. Zeng X, Wert SE, Federici R, et al. VEGF enhances pulmonary vasculogenesis and disrupts lung morphogenesis in vivo. Dev Dyn 1998;221:215–27.
34. deMello DE, Sawyer D, Galvin N, Reid L. Early fetal development of lung vasculature. Am J Respir Cell Mol Biol 1997;16:568–81.
35. deMello DE, Reid LM. Embryonic and early fetal development of human lung vasculature and its functional implications. Pediatr Dev Pathol 2000;3:439–49.
36. Janney CG, Askin FB, Kuhn C. Congenital alveolar capillary dysplasia—an unusual cause of respiratory distress in the newborn. Am J Clin Pathol 1981;76:722–7.
37. Cater G, Thibeault DW, Beatty EC, et al. Misalignment of lung vessels and alveolar capillary dysplasia: a cause of persistent pulmonary hypertension. J Pediatr 1989; 114:293–300.
38. Wagenvoort CA. Misalignment of lung vessels: a syndrome causing persistent neonatal pulmonary hypertension. Hum Pathol 1986;17:727–30.
39. Shifren JL, Doldi N, Ferrara N, et al. In the human fetus, vascular endothelial growth factor is expressed in epithelial cells and myocytes, but not vascular endothelium: implications for mode of action. J Clin Endocrinol Metab 1994;79:316–22.
40. Beck L Jr, D'Amore PA. Vascular development: cellular and molecular regulation. FASEB J 1997;11:365–73.
41. Stenmark KR, Mecham RP. Cellular and molecular mechanisms of pulmonary vascular remodeling. Annu Rev Physiol 1997;59:89–144.
42. Breier G, Clauss M, Risau W. Coordinate expression of vascular endothelial growth factor receptor-1 (flt-1) and its

ligand suggests a paracrine regulation of murine vascular development. Dev Dyn 1995;204:228–39.

43. Kaipainen A, Korhonen J, Pajusola K, et al. The related flt4, flt1, and kdr receptor tyrosine kinases show distinct expression patterns in human fetal endothelial cells. J Exp Med 1993;178:2077–88.
44. D'Angio CT, Maniscalco WM, Ryan RM, et al. Vascular endothelial growth factor in pulmonary lavage fluid from premature infants: effects of age and postnatal dexamethasone. Biol Neonate 1999;76:266–73.
45. Carmeliet P, Ferreira V, Breier G, et al. Abnormal blood vessel development and lethality in embryos lacking a single VEGF allele. Nature 1996;380:435–9.
46. Ferrara N, Carver-Moore K, Chen H, et al. Heterozygous embryonic lethality induced by targeted inactivation of the VEGF gene. Nature 1996;380:439–42.
47. Flamme I, von Reutern M, Drexler HCA, et al. Overexpression of vascular endothelial growth factor in the avian embryo induces hypervascularization and increased vascular permeability without alterations of embryonic pattern formation. Dev Biol 1995;171:399–414.
48. Fong GH, Rossant J, Gertsenstein M, et al. Role of the flt-1 receptor tyrosine kinase in regulating the assembly of vascular endothelium. Nature 1995;376:66–70.
49. Shalaby F, Rossant J, Yamaguchi TP, et al. Failure of blood-island formation and vasculogenesis in Flk-1 deficient mice. Nature 1995;376:62–6.
50. Rohovsky SA, Hirschi KK, D'Amore PA. Growth factor effects on a model of vessel formation. Surg Forum 1996;47:390–1.
51. Antonelli-Orlidge A, Saunders KB, Smith SR, et al. An activated form of transforming growth factor β is produced by cocultures of endothelial cells and pericytes. Proc Natl Acad Sci U S A 1989;86:4544–8.
52. Orlidge A, D'Amore PA. Inhibition of capillary endothelial cell growth by pericytes and smooth muscle cells. J Cell Biol 1987;105:1455–62.
53. Sato Y, Rifkin DB. Inhibition of endothelial cell movement by pericytes and smooth muscle cell: activation of a latent transforming growth factor-β 1-like molecule by plasmin during co-culture. J Cell Biol 1989;109: 309–15.
54. D'Amore PA, Smith SR. Growth factor effects on cells of the vascular wall: a survey. Growth Factors 1993;8:61–75.
55. Heimark RL, Twardzik DR, Schwartz SM. Inhibition of endothelial regeneration by type-β transforming growth factor from platelets. Science 1986;233:1078–80.
56. Battegay EJ, Raines EW, Seifert RA, et al. TGF-β induces bimodal proliferation of connective tissue cells via complex control of an autocrine PDGF loop. Cell 1991; 63:515–24.
57. Dickson MC, Martin JS, Cousins FM, et al. Defective hematopoiesis and vasculogenesis in transforming growth factor-β1 knock-out mice. Development 1995;121:1845–54.
58. McAllister KA, Grogg KM, Johnson DW, et al. Endoglin, a TGF-β binding protein of endothelial cells, is the gene for hereditary hemorrhagic telangiectasia type I. Nat Enet 1994;8:345–51.
59. Johnson DW, Berg JN, Baldwin MA, et al. Mutations in the activin receptor-like kinase 1 gene in hereditary hemorrhagic telangiectasia type 2. Nat Genet 1996;13:189–95.
60. Korhonen J Polvi A, Partanen J, et al. The mouse tie receptor tyrosine kinase gene: expression during embryonic angiogenesis. Oncogene 1994;9:395–403.
61. Davies P, deMello D, Reid L. Methods in experimental pathology of pulmonary vasculature. In: Gil J, Kleinerman J, eds. Models of lung disease: microscopy and structural methods. New York: Marcel Dekker, 1990: 843–904.
62. Areechon W, Reid L. Hypoplasia of lung with congenital diaphragmatic hernia. BMJ 1963;i:230–3.
63. Reid L, Simmon G. The role of alveolar hypoplasia in some types of emphysema. Br J Dis Chest 1964;58:158–68.
64. deMello DE, Davies P, Reid LM. Lung growth and development. In: Simmons D, ed. Current pulmonology. Chicago: Yearbook Medical, 1989:10:159–208.
65. deMello D, Reid L. Patterns of disturbed lung growth in newborns with skeletal dysplasia. Mod Pathol 1990; 3(1):2P.
66. Kitagawa N, Hislop A, Boyden EA, Reid L. Lung hypoplasia in congenital diaphragmatic hernia. A quantitative study of airway, artery and alveolar development. Br J Surg 1971;58:342–6.
67. Goldstein JD, Rabinovitch N, Van Praagh R, Reid L. Unusual vascular anomalies causing persistent pulmonary hypertension in a newborn. Am J Cardiol 1979;43:962–8.
68. Geggel RL, Reid L. The structural basis of PPHN. In: Phillips JB III, ed. Clinics in perinatology. Vol. 11, No. 3. Symposium on neonatal pulmonary hypertension. Philadelphia: WB Saunders, 1984:525–49.
69. Geggel R, Murphy J, Langleben D, et al. Congenital diaphragmatic hernia: arterial structural changes and persistent pulmonary hypertension after surgical repair. J Pediatr 1985;107:457–64.
70. Goldstein JD, Reid L. Pulmonary hypoplasia resulting from phrenic nerve agenesis and diaphragmatic amyoplasia. J Pediatr 1980;97:282–7.
71. Ryland D, Reid L. Pulmonary aplasia—a quantitative analysis of the development of the single lung. Thorax 1971;26:602–9.
72. Hislop A, Reid L. New pathologic findings in emphysema of childhood: 1. Polyalveolar lobe with emphysema. Thorax 1970;25:682–90.
73. Haworth SG, Reid L. Quantitative structural study of pulmonary circulation in the newborn with aortic atresia, stenosis or coarctation. Thorax 1977;32:121–8.
74. Stocker T, Stocker JT, Pladwell SE, et al. Congenital cystic adenomatoid malformation of the lung: classification and morphologic spectrum. Hum Pathol 1977;8:155.
75. Hislop A, Sanderson M, Reid L. Unilateral congenital dysplasia of lung associated with vascular anomalies. Thorax 1973;28:435–41.
76. Hintz SR, Vincent JA, Pitlick PT, et al. Alveolar capillary dysplasia: diagnostic potential for cardiac catheterization. J Perinatol 1999;19:441–6.
77. Rendas A, Brown ER, Avery ME, Reid L. Prematurity, hypoplasia of the pulmonary vascular bed and hyper-

tension: fatal outcome in 10 month old infant. Am Rev Respir Dis 1980;121:873–80.
78. Clemmons JJW. Embryonic renal injury: a possible factor in fetal malnutrition [abstract]. Pediatr Res 1977;11:404.
79. Hislop A, Hay E, Reid L. The lungs in congenital bilateral renal agenesis and dysplasia. Arch Dis Child 1979;54:32–8.
80. Shapiro JR, Reid L, Burn VE, et al. Pulmonary hypoplasia and osteogenesis imperfecta type II with defective synthesis of alpha (1) procollagen. Bone 1989;10:165–79.
81. Kurnit DM, Aldridge JF, Matsuoka R, et al. Increased adhesiveness of trisomy 21 cells and arterial ventricular canal malformations in Down's syndrome: a stochastic model. Am J Med Genet 1985;20:385–99.
82. Schloo BL, Vawter GF, Reid L. Down syndrome: patterns of disturbed lung growth. Hum Pathol 1991;22:919–23.
83. Haworth SG, Reid LM. Quantitative structural study of pulmonary circulation in the newborn with pulmonary atresia. Thorax 1977;32:129–33.
84. Geggel RL, Aronovitz MJ, Reid LM. Effects of chronic in utero hypoxemia in rat neonatal pulmonary arterial structure. J Pediatr 1986;108:756–9.
85. Mirochnick M, Frank DA, Cabral H, et al. Relation between meconium concentration of the cocaine metabolite benzoylecgonine and fetal growth. J Pediatr 1995;126:636–8.
86. Olsen GD. Potential mechanisms of cocaine-induced developmental neurotoxicity: a minireview. Neurotoxicology 1995;16:159–67.
87. Hepper PG. Human fetal behaviour and maternal cocaine use: a longitudinal study. Neurotoxicology 1995;16:139–43.
88. Mitra SC, Ganesh V, Apuzziom JJ. Effect of maternal cocaine abuse on renal arterial flow and urine output of the fetus. Am J Obstet Gynecol 1994;171:1556–9.
89. Mitra SC, Seshan SV, Salcedo JR, Gil J. Maternal cocaine abuse and fetal renal arteries: a morphometric study. Pediatr Nephrol 2000;14:315–8.
90. Kilic N, Buyukunal C, Dervisoglu S, et al. Maternal cocaine abuse resulting in necrotizing enterocolitis. An experimental study in a rat model. II: Results of perfusion studies. Pediatr Surg Int 2000;16:176–8.
91. Fox WW, Gewitz MH, Dinwiddie R, et al. Pulmonary hypertension in the perinatal aspiration syndromes. Pediatrics 1977;59:205–11.
92. deMello DE, Hu LM, Gashi-Luci L, et al. The effect of hypoxia on post-natal vascular structure in newborn rabbits. FASEB J 1988;2:1181.
93. Haworth SG, Hislop AA. Adaptation of the pulmonary circulation to extra-uterine life in the the pig and its relevance to the human infant. Cardiovasc Res 1981;15:108–19.
94. Haworth SG, Reid L. Persistent fetal circulation: newly recognized structural features. J Pediatr 1976;88:614–20.
95. Murphy JD, Rabinovitch M, Goldstein JD, et al. The structural basis of persistent pulmonary hypertension in the newborn. J Pediatr 1981;98:962–7.
96. Murphy JD, Vawter GF, Reid LM. Pulmonary vascular disease in fatal meconium aspiration. J Pediatr 1984;104:758–62.
97. deMello D, Murphy J, Aronovitz M, et al. Effects of indomethacin in utero on the pulmonary vasculature of the newborn guinea pig. Pediatr Res 1987;22:693–7.
98. Murphy J, Aronovitz M, Reid L. Effects of chronic in utero hypoxia on the pulmonary vasculature of the newborn guinea pig. Pediatr Res 1986;20:292–5.
99. Brenner O. Pathology of the vessels of the pulmonary circulation, part I. Arch Intern Med 1935;56:211–37.
100. Hislop A, Reid L. Formation of the pulmonary vasculature. In: Hodson WA, ed. Development of the lung. Vol. 6. In: L'enfant C, exec. ed. Lung biology in health and disease. New York: Marcel Dekker, 1977:37–86.
101. Haworth SG, Sauer U, Buhlmeyer K, et al. The development of the pulmonary circulation in ventricular septal defect: a quantitative structural study. Am J Cardiol 1977;40:781–8.
102. Rabinovitch M, Haworth SG, Castaneda A, et al. Lung biopsy in congenital heart disease: a morphometric approach to pulmonary vascular disease. Circulation 1978;58:1107–22.
103. Rabinovitch M. Pulmonary vascular disease. In: Glenn WWL, Baue AE, Geha AS, et al, eds. Thoracic and cardiovascular surgery. 4th Ed. Norwalk, CT: Appleton-Century-Crofts, 1983:655–67.
104. Bevan RD. Trophic effects of peripheral allergic nerves on vascular structure. Hypertension 1984;6(Suppl 3):19–26.
105. Allen KM, Wharton J, Pollak JM, Haworth S. A study of nerves containing peptides in the pulmonary vasculature of healthy infants and children and of those with pulmonary hypertension. Br Heart J 1989;62:353–60.
106. Kawaguchi AT, Shirai M, Yamano M, et al. Afferent reinnervation after lung transplantation in the rat. J Heart Lung Transplant 1998;17:341–8.
107. Haberberger R, Schemann M, Sann H, Kummer W. Innervation pattern of guinea pig pulmonary vasculature depends on vascular diameter. J Appl Physiol 1997;82:426–34.
108. Northway WH Jr, Rosan RC, Porter DY. Pulmonary disease following respiratory therapy of hyaline membrane disease, bronchopulmonary dysplasia. N Engl J Med 1967;17:357–68.
109. Reid LM. The lung: its growth and remodeling in health and disease. Edward BD Neuhauser lecture. AJR Am J Roentgenol 1977;129:777–88.
110. Meyrick B, Reid L. Normal post-natal development of the media of the rat hilar pulmonary artery and its remodeling by chronic hypoxia. Lab Invest 1982;46:505–14.
111. Tomashefski JF, Oppermann HC, Vawter GF, Reid L. Bronchopulmonary dysplasia: a morphometric study with emphasis on the pulmonary vasculature. Pediatr Pathol 1984;2:469–87.
112. Tomashefski J, Vawter G, Reid L. Pathologic observations on infants who do not survive the respiratory distress syndrome. In: Nelson GH, ed. Pulmonary development transition from intrauterine to extrauterine life. Vol. 27. In: L'enfant C, ex. ed, Lung biology in health and disease. New York: Marcel Dekker, 1985;27:387–429.
113. Hislop A, Reid L. Persistent hypoplasia of the lung after repair of congenital diaphragmatic hernia. Thorax 1976;31:450–5.

114. Wohl MEB, Griscom NT, Strieder DJ, et al. The lung following repair of congenital diaphragmatic hernia. J Pediatr 1977;90:405–14.
115. Berdon WE, Baker DH, Amoury R. The role of pulmonary hypoplasia in the prognosis of newborn infants with diaphragmatic hernia and eventration. AJR Am J Roentgenol 1968;103:413–21.
116. Reid L. Autopsy studies of the lungs in kyphoscoliosis. In: Zorab PA, ed. A symposium on scoliosis. Action for the crippled child monograph. London: Garden City Press, 1966:71–8.
117. Reid L. Pathological changes in the lungs in scoliosis. In: Zorab PA, ed. Scoliosis. Springfield, IL: Charles C. Thomas, 1969:67–86.
118. Davies G, Reid L. Effect of scoliosis on growth of alveoli and pulmonary arteries and on right ventricle. Arch Dis Child 1971;46:623–32.
119. Kerem BS, Rommens JM, Buchanan JA, et al. Identification of the cystic fibrosis gene: genetic analysis. Science 1989;245:1073–80.
120. Zielenski J. Genotype and phenotype in cystic fibrosis. Respiration 2000;67:117–33.
121. Stewart B, Zabner J, Shuber AP, et al. Normal sweat chloride values do not exclude the diagnosis of cystic fibrosis. Am J Respir Crit Care Med 1995;151:899–903.
122. Reid L, DeHaller R. Lung changes in cystic fibrosis. In: Hubble D, ed. Cystic fibrosis. London: Chest and Heart Association, 1964:21.
123. Reid L. Cardiopulmonary pathology. In: Sturgess JM, ed. Perspectives in cystic fibrosis. Proceedings of the 8th International Cystic Fibrosis Congress. Toronto: Canadian Cystic Fibrosis Foundation, 1980:198–214.
124. Lopez-Vidriero MT, Reid L. Pathophysiology of mucus secretion in cystic fibrosis. Mod Prob Paediatr 1977; 19:120–8.
125. Bhaskar KR, Reid L. Application of density gradient methods to study the composition of sol and gel phases of CF sputa and the isolation and characterization of epithelial glycoprotein from the two phases. In: Sturgess JM, ed. Perspectives in cystic fibrosis. Proceedings of the 8th International Cystic Fibrosis Congress. Toronto: Canadian Cystic Fibrosis Foundation, 1980:113–21.
126. Reid L. Bronchial mucus and its glycoproteins in cystic fibrosis. In: Warwick WJ, ed. One thousand years of cystic fibrosis—collective papers. NHLBI University of Minnesota Department of Pediatrics in cooperation with the International Cystic Fibrosis Association, Minneapolis, MN. 1981:179–84.
127. Tomashefski JF, Vawter GF, Reid L. Pulmonary pathology. In: Hodson NE, Norman AP, Batten JC, eds. Cystic fibrosis. London: Bailliere Tindall, 1983:31–51.
128. Ryland D, Reid L. The pulmonary circulation in cystic fibrosis. Thorax 1975;30:285–92.
129. Geggel R, Dozor A, Fyler D, Reid L. The effect of vasodilators at rest and during exercise in young adults with cystic fibrosis and chronic cor pulmonale. Am Rev Respir Dis 1985;131:531–6.
130. Reid L. Chronic obstructive pulmonary diseases. In: Fishman AP, ed. Pulmonary diseases and disorders. Vol. 2. New York, NY: McGraw-Hill, 1988:1247–72.
131. Reid LM. The pathology of obstructive and inflammatory airway diseases. Eur J Respir Dis 1986;69:26–37.
132. MacLeod WM. Abnormal transradiancy of one lung. Thorax 1954;9:147–53.
133. Heath D, Edwards JE. The pathology of hypertensive pulmonary vascular disease: a description of six grades of structural changes in the pulmonary arteries with special reference to congenital cardiac septal defects. Circulation 1958;18:533–47.
134. Haworth SG, Reid L. A morphometric study of regional variation in lung structure in infants with pulmonary hypertension and congenital cardiac defect: a justification of lung biopsy. Br Heart J 1978;40:825–37.

CHAPTER 8

Responses of the Developing Lung to Injury

Dara Brodsky, MD, Helen Christou, MD, Merton Bernfield, MD, Stella Kourembanas, MD

The response of the developing lung to injury encompasses a multitude of cellular and molecular interactions. These interactions determine whether a specific injury will lead to regeneration and repair or will proceed to growth arrest, irreversible tissue destruction, and/or fibrosis. The preterm newborn lung is at a critical stage of development and is susceptible to injury from mechanical ventilation, oxidant toxicity, intrauterine infection, and chronic inflammation. Lung injury in premature infants can lead to an arrest of alveolar septation, altered pulmonary vascularization, and abnormal lung development. This arrest of lung development is the hallmark of bronchopulmonary dysplasia (BPD), the most common complication in infants born at less than 27 weeks gestation. This chapter focuses on specific cellular responses following lung injury, including those of epithelial, mesenchymal, vascular, neuroendocrine, and migratory cells, as well as the responses of the extracellular matrix. In addition, the effector molecules that mediate intercellular and intracellular communication in the normal developing lung and in response to lung injury will be discussed (Figure 8–1). A broader understanding of the mechanisms leading to injury of the developing lung will enhance our ability to provide preventive and therapeutic strategies for pediatric pulmonary diseases.

Normal Lung Development

Fetal lung development has traditionally been staged according to the lung's histologic appearance (Table 8–1). In humans, the embryonic stage (0 to 7 weeks gestation) encompasses early differentiation of the primitive foregut into the primordial lung bud. This is followed by the pseudoglandular stage (8–16 weeks gestation), during which airway branching morphogenesis occurs into the surrounding mesenchyme. In parallel, formation of cartilage, muscle, blood vessels, and lymphatics begins. The canalicular period of lung development (17–24 weeks gestation) is characterized by thinning of the epithelium, widening of distal airway lumens, and formation of the terminal bronchioles. The final stage of fetal lung development, the terminal sac period (25 weeks gestation to birth), involves the further differentiation of gas exchange units as the terminal bronchioles differentiate into terminal clusters of saccules. True alveoli form in late gestation (> 36 weeks) during the alveolar stage and continue to grow postnatally. Since fetal rodent and primate lung development follows the same stages as the human lung and continues perinatally, animals studies provide significant insights into the mechanisms of lung development and responses to injury. In the next section, we focus on the cell-specific changes that occur during these phases of normal lung development and in response to perinatal injury.

Cellular Responses

Epithelial Cells

Three types of epithelial cells (type I pneumocytes, type II pneumocytes, and Clara cells) play a critical role in lung development, normal pulmonary function, and the lung's response to injury. Type I pneumocytes, the principal cells lining the alveoli, are squamous epithelial cells that are derived from type II cells during fetal lung development.[1] Type I pneumocytes are first observed during the canalicular stage of lung development, and gradually increase in number until the alveolar stage, when they comprise 96%

TABLE 8–1. Normal Lung Development

Stage	Time Period	Events
Embryonic stage	0–7 weeks gestation	Early differentiation of primitive foregut into lung bud
Pseudoglandular stage	8–16 weeks gestation	Airway branching morphogenesis
Canalicular stage	17–24 weeks gestation	Epithelial thinning Widening of distal airway lumens Formation of terminal bronchioles
Terminal sac stage	25 weeks gestation to birth	Differentiation of gas exchange units—saccule formation
Alveolar stage	> 36 weeks gestation to 2 years of age	Formation of alveoli

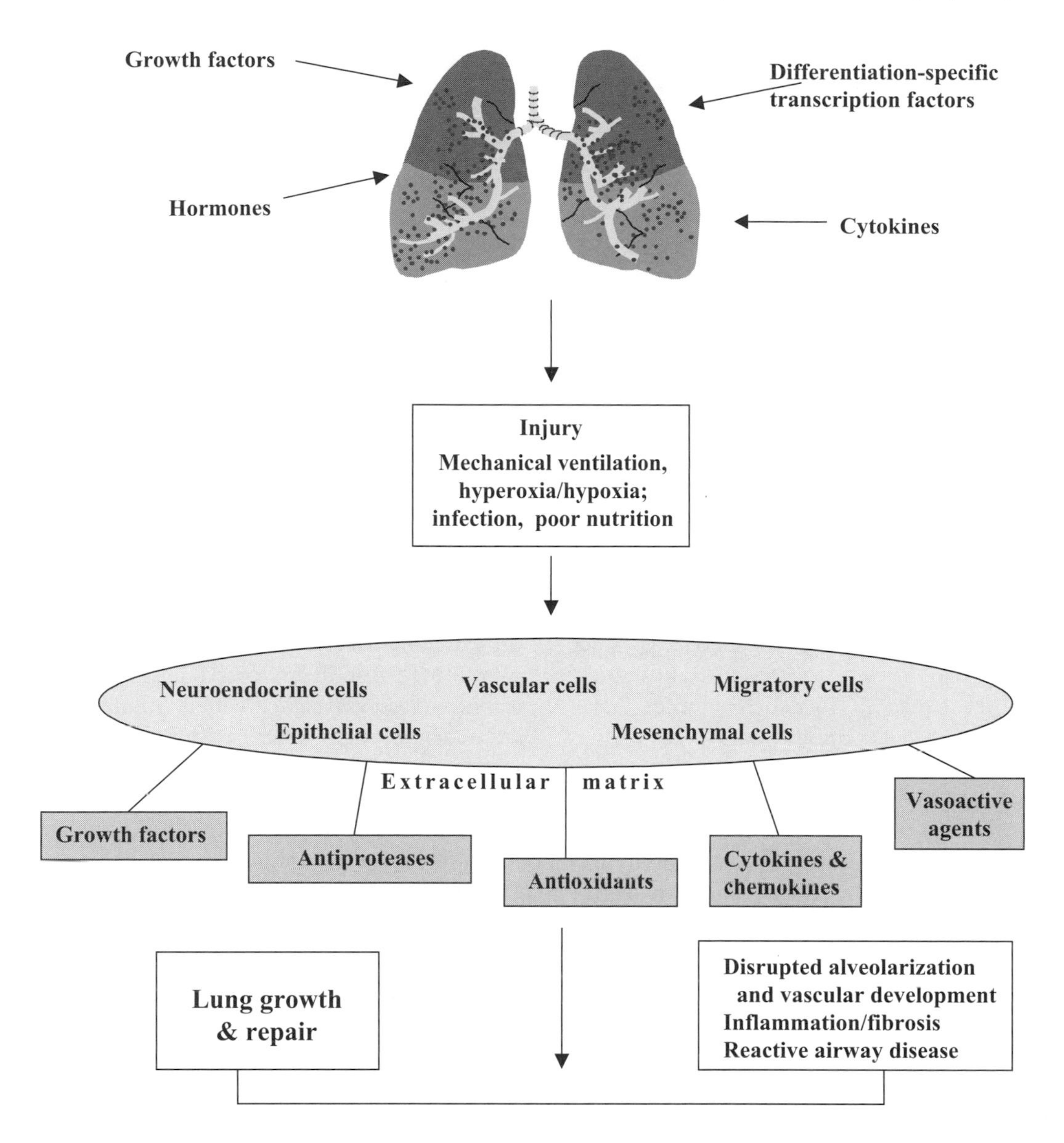

FIGURE 8–1. The developing lung and lung injury. Injurious agents, cellular responses, and effector molecules modulate the balance of growth, repair, and injury in the developing lung. These interactions determine whether a specific injury will lead to regeneration and repair or will proceed to disrupted lung development, irreversible tissue destruction, and/or fibrosis.

of the alveolar surface area. Type I cells provide the short diffusion pathway essential for gas exchange, and participate in the regulation of transepithelial fluid transport in the lung. Injury to type I cells leads to loss of epithelial barrier function and promotes pulmonary edema. During the recovery phase, these injured cells are replaced by differentiated type II pneumocytes.[2]

Morphologically identifiable type II pneumocytes first appear in fetal lungs during the pseudoglandular stage of lung development.[3,4] At this stage, they are cuboidal in shape and exclusively line the prospective pulmonary acinus. Their shape and ultrastructural characteristics transform with advancing gestational age. These intracellular changes, including decreased glycogen concentration and increased lamellar bodies,[5] are accelerated by hormones such as corticosteroids and thyroid hormones.[6] Eventually, type II cells are spherical and comprise only 4% of the alveolar surface area. Type II pneumocytes have diverse functions, including synthesis and secretion of surfactant, xenobiotic metabolism, transepithelial movement of water, and regeneration of the alveolar epithelium following lung injury.[2]

Alveolar type II cell proliferation occurs in response to lung injury[7] and is thought to play a critical role in alveolar epithelial repair.[8,9] Similar to lung development, successful restoration of normal architecture after lung injury is a result of complex and incompletely understood cell-cell and cell-matrix interactions that are mediated by secreted growth factors, adhesion molecules, and chemotactic factors.[10] Reactive hyperplasia of progenitor type II cells as well as adherence of type II cells to the provisional matrix proteins are central to the renewal of the type I cell population after lung injury.[11]

Whereas type I and type II pneumocytes are located within the alveoli, the nonciliated bronchiolar epithelial cells, Clara cells, are located at the critical junction between conducting airways and alveoli. Their phenotype as well as their susceptibility to injury varies according to proximal or distal airway localization.[12] Studies in rat and mouse lungs[13] suggest that Clara cells are immature at birth and that their maturation may be delayed by prenatal factors such as maternal malnutrition.[12] Clara cells are progenitors of ciliated cells in the small airways and secrete components of the extracellular layer that lines small airways.[12]

Clara cells secrete multiple proteins including surfactant proteins (SPs), Clara cell secretory protein (CCSP; also known as CC10 and CC16), leukocyte protease inhibitor, β-galactosidase-binding lectin and trypsin-like protease (30-kD Clara cell tryptase). CC10 inhibits phospholipase A_2,[14] binds surfactant phospholipids,[15] and has been reported to provide protection against pulmonary oxidant stress. CC10-deficient mice have demonstrated increased susceptibility to hyperoxic lung injury and an exaggerated inflammatory response.[16] Leukocyte protease inhibitor inhibits leukocyte proteases such as elastase and may play an important role in maintaining the protease-antiprotease balance in the lung.[17] The function of the other proteins secreted by Clara cells is not clearly determined.

Clara cells are particularly vulnerable to injury following exposure to environmental toxins. This is due to increased levels of metabolically active enzymes, including cytochrome P450 monooxygenases and flavin-containing monooxygenases that are present within these cells.[17] Neonatal mice[18] and rabbits are particularly susceptible to Clara cell injury via bioactivated lung toxicants. Indeed, injury to the differentiating Clara cells in the newborn rabbit greatly affects repair of the bronchiolar epithelium by inhibiting epithelial differentiation and organization later in life.[19]

Mesenchymal Cells

Mesenchymal cell hyperplasia and collagen deposition in the lung is a well-recognized pattern of response to injury. Mesenchymal cells, including fibroblasts, peribronchial and vascular smooth muscle cells, and myofibroblasts, are present in the developing lung. Their differentiation, migration and ability to replicate or undergo apoptosis are important determinants of the fate of the fibroproliferative response to injury.[20]

Myofibroblasts are ultrastructurally and metabolically distinctive connective tissue cells that are localized in alveolar septa. The process by which myofibroblasts are derived from activated fibroblasts is mediated by platelet-derived growth factor (PDGF), transforming growth factor β (TGF-β)[21–22] and other cytokines.[23] The expression of alpha smooth muscle actin and the presence of contractile elements distinguishes myofibroblasts from fibroblasts. Platelet-derived growth factor A appears to have a critical role in alveolar myofibroblast ontogeny in mice. Postnatally surviving PDGF-A-null mice demonstrate absence of alveolar myofibroblasts and deficiency in elastic fiber deposits.[24] This leads to failure of alveolar septation and emphysema, suggesting a morphogenetic function of myofibroblasts in the mouse. Although myofibroblasts are present in normal terminal airways in the developing human lung,[22] their role in development is not clearly defined.

It is widely recognized that myofibroblasts are key participants in tissue remodeling following acute lung injury.[22,25–28] Following diffuse alveolar injury from hyperoxia,[28] bleomycin,[27] or paraquat,[29] these cells increase in number, migrate to the intra-alveolar space, acquire desmin contractile filaments, and form bundles encircling terminal air spaces. They produce collagen and contribute to extracellular matrix deposition in the lung parenchyma in association with pulmonary fibrosis.[30] In a rat model of lung injury,[25] PDGF-B was shown to at least partially mediate these cellular effects. In addition, PDGF receptor-α was upregulated in the lung prior to mesenchymal cell hyperplasia.[25] In studies of human lungs with diffuse alveolar injury, the proliferation and migration of myofibroblasts at sites of injury is also associated with the presence of TGF-β,[22,26] which inhibits myofibroblast apoptosis and, thus, may contribute to the progression of pulmonary fibrosis.[30]

Vascular Cells

Blood vessel formation in the lung occurs via angiogenesis and vasculogenesis during all stages of fetal development[31] as well as postnatally during alveolarization.[32] Endothelial cell (EC) proliferation and differentiation is controlled primarily by vascular endothelial growth factor (VEGF). This endothelial cell mitogen is produced by adjacent pulmonary epithelial and mesenchymal cells, and acts in a paracrine manner. Disruption of the VEGF gene in embryonic stem cells leads to abnormal angiogenesis and blood-island formation, resulting in death of mouse embryos between days 11 and 12.[33] Vascular endothelial cells also play a critical role in the transition of the fetal circulation at birth. Indeed, endothelial cell nitric oxide synthase activity dramatically increases in late gestation and early postnatal life, leading to decreased pulmonary vascular resistance at birth.[34,35]

Endothelial cell injury with loss of barrier function is seen in different models of lung injury including lipopolysaccharide,[36] hyperoxia,[37] monocrotaline,[38] and oleic acid.[39] Elaboration of adhesion molecules by the injured endothelium leads to recruitment of inflammatory cells and the cascade of cellular and molecular interactions that amplify the inflammatory response in the lung. Loss of barrier function also sets off a series of events that lead to pulmonary vascular remodeling and pulmonary hypertension. Thus, ECs play a critical role in the response of the lung to injury.

Vascular smooth muscle cell (VSMC) differentiation and maturation in the lung follows nonvascular smooth muscle development.[40] Mature VSMCs produce and respond to a number of effector molecules involved in the maintenance of lung homeostasis and the response to injury. Vascular endothelial growth factor,[41] prostacyclin,[42] nitric oxide,[43] and carbon monoxide[44] are examples of important SMC-derived mediators with autocrine and paracrine effects in the pulmonary vasculature. In addition, VSMCs participate in pulmonary inflammation by producing proinflammatory arachidonic acid metabolites in response to cytokines such as interleukin (IL)-1β and tumor necrosis factor α (TNF-α).[45]

The reciprocal interaction between ECs and VSMCs is of critical importance to pulmonary homeostasis and the response to lung injury. Nitric oxide derived from ECs is a key regulator of pulmonary vascular tone, particularly in the perinatal adaptation to extrauterine life.[46] During hypoxic lung injury, increased production of the EC-derived SMC mitogens endothelin-1 (ET-1) and PDGF-B leads to increased proliferation and migration of pulmonary VSMCs observed in pulmonary hypertension.[47,48] Furthermore, increased VEGF production from hypoxic VSMCs may stimulate EC proliferation in a paracrine manner. In contrast, SMC-derived carbon monoxide (CO) is a negative regulator of VSMC growth under hypoxia.[49] Carbon monoxide inhibits the expression of cell cycle–specific transcription factors resulting in decreased VSMC proliferation. Moreover, CO prevents the hypoxic induction of ET-1 and PDGF-B by ECs, indirectly inhibiting VSMC growth. Thus, the balance of vasoactive mediators and growth factors produced by vascular cells determines the contractile and proliferative state of the pulmonary vasculature.

Pericytes are precursors of VSMCs that are found in the precapillary pulmonary vessels during development.[50] Proliferation and migration of pericytes, mediated by growth factors,[51,52] leads to pulmonary vessel formation during development. Platelet-derived growth factor B is a critical growth factor involved in this pathway since PDGF-B-deficient mice have loss of pericytes and formation of microaneurysms.[53] Exaggerated pericyte proliferation and migration, mediated by growth factors and endotoxins,[54] underlies the structural remodeling of pulmonary vessels observed in pulmonary hypertension. Increased numbers of intra-acinar pericytes are also found in hypoplastic human lungs, which is consistent with the increased muscularization of intra-acinar arteries and persistent fetal circulation observed in hypoplastic lungs.[50]

Neuroendocrine Cells

Pulmonary neuroendocrine cells (PNECs) are predominantly found at branching points of airways and regulate both lung morphogenesis and inflammatory responses in the developing lung. Single PNECs first appear in humans at 8 weeks' gestation, which is prior to type I and II cell differentiation. By 20 weeks' gestation, PNECs form innervated cell clusters known as neuroepithelial bodies. Pulmonary neuroendocrine cells have long dendritic processes that extend into the basement membrane and dense core vesicles that contain calcitonin-gene related peptide, serotonin, and the bombesin-like peptide (BLP) known as gastrin releasing peptide. Peak BLP messenger ribonucleic acid (mRNA) levels are found in midgestation and coincide with the appearance of neuroepithelial bodies.[55] Increased density of PNECs[56] and BLP receptors is found at airway branching points, suggesting a role for these cells and their products in airway branching morphogenesis. Indeed, BLP has been shown to promote branching morphogenesis and stimulate type II cell differentiation in organ cultures.[57,58]

Postnatally, BLP receptors are found mostly in mesenchymal cells at cleft regions of branching airways and pulmonary blood vessels as well as in macrophages and airway epithelial cells.[59] This close proximity of expression suggests a paracrine mechanism of action. Bombesin-like peptides are potent bronchoconstrictors as well as growth factors for pulmonary fibroblasts and epithelial cells.[60] In addition, BLPs stimulate migration of airway epithelial cells, an important process of healing and restoration of function after airway injury.[60] By inducing cellular proliferation, BLP indirectly stimulates the production of fibronectin and laminin, which are important in branching morphogenesis and in tissue repair.

Postnatally, PNECs are believed to function as oxygen chemosensors since they degranulate and proliferate in response to airway hypoxia.[61] In addition, hyperoxia initially leads to the induction of BLP and its receptors in hamster lungs.[62] Hyperplasia of PNEC is observed in fetal lungs following maternal nicotine exposure, premature lungs with bronchopulmonary dysplasia (BPD), adult lungs with bronchiectasis, lungs of adult smokers, and lung tumors.[63] Studies in a baboon model of BPD showed increased urine BLP levels in animals that later developed BPD.[59] Treatment of these animals with monoclonal antibodies against BLP prevented the development of BPD, suggesting that BLP might play a critical role during abnormal lung development.[59]

Migratory Cells

Migratory cells such as neutrophils, macrophages, and monocytes, provide an important inflammatory response following lung injury. The critical role of neutrophils in the host defense response is well known. However, in the course of defending the host against microbial invasion, neutrophils release a potent arsenal of mediators consisting of proteases and oxidants that can damage host tissues. Neutrophil-mediated lung injury may occur as a result of (1) inability to regulate neutrophil influx, (2) abnormal neutrophil activation within the lung, (3) inhibition of neutrophil apoptosis, and (4) ineffective neutrophil removal by macrophages. At sites of inflammation, azurophilic granules containing the serine proteinases, elastase and cathepsin G, as well as the non-enzymatic defensins are released, leading to the degradation of elastin, collagen, proteoglycan, and basement membrane. In vitro studies have shown that these mediators cause lung injury by altering the integrity of the lung epithelium, decreasing the ciliary beat, increasing mucus secretion, and stimulating epithelial cells to produce chemokines, attracting more neutrophils to the site of inflammation.[64] In a model of lipopolysaccharide-induced pulmonary vascular injury in rats, the inhibition of neutrophil activation significantly decreased injury to the lung.[65]

Macrophages represent the majority of phagocytes in the lower respiratory tract and are morphologically and functionally heterogenous within the alveoli, interstitium, vasculature, and airway of the lung.[66] In response to environmental stimuli, lung macrophages clear most of the particles and organisms in the distal airways and alveolar spaces. In addition, macrophages play a critical role in pulmonary inflammation by releasing oxygen radicals and proteolytic enzymes, and by recruiting neutrophils to the site.[66] By extruding growth-promoting and inhibiting factors, macrophages can influence lung repair as well as induce injury to the lung.

Monocytes are activated and recruited in the lung during acute inflammatory injury. In rodents and rabbits monocytes, in the form of pulmonary intravascular macrophages, localize circulating pathogens to the lungs and concentrate the inflammatory response to the lung during systemic disease.[67] The role of monocytes in lung injury is mediated by adhesion molecules, cytokines, and chemokines and involves complex interactions among vascular and inflammatory cells as well as effector molecules.[67–69]

Extracellular Matrix

The extracellular matrix (ECM) has an important role in the regulation of lung development by providing a structural framework and assisting in repair following lung injury. The functional role of the ECM differs by location. In the conducting airways, the ECM acts as a stabilizer, preventing airway collapse during expiration. In the respiratory and transitional zones, the ECM is more dynamic, accommodating to changes in alveolar volume during inspiration and expiration. In the pulmonary alveoli, it provides structural support for the alveolar-capillary network.

The basal lamina (BL), a principal component of the ECM, provides structural support to the lung and allows for gas exchange to occur between type I epithelium and capillary endothelium. Experiments by Vracko have shown that an intact basal lamina is essential for organized regeneration of lung tissue.[70] Lung injury induced by oleic acid in dogs led to epithelial, endothelial, and interstitial cell injury without disruption of BL integrity. Three days after injury, organized regeneration of epithelial and endothelial cells occurred, guided by the intact acellular BL.[70] In contrast to regenerating skeletal muscle and kidney, the regenerating cells of the lung did not form a new layer of BL, but instead grew directly on pre-existing BL.[70] Moreover, the cells that grew along the BL, were always the same cell type that had been supported by the BL before the injury, probably due to cell-specific markers that identify the BL as belonging to a specific cell type. By 3 weeks, the structure and function of the lung were almost completely re-established.[70]

Abnormal repair of the lung may occur if the initial lesion damages the BL. Without the BL acting as a scaffold to establish epithelial continuity, interalveolar gaps can form, creating enlarged air spaces and an emphysematous appearance.[70] Furthermore, the disruption of the alveolar interface leads to exudation of plasma proteins into the alveolar spaces, followed by intra-alveolar fibrin deposition. Thus, if the BL is destroyed, orderly regeneration of the lung does not occur, resulting in formation of scar tissue and loss of function. If the BL is damaged in the developing lung, abnormal differentiation of alveolar epithelial cells and an abnormal ratio of type II to type I cells occurs, further exacerbating the response to injury.

In addition to the BL, the ECM is composed of proteins such as laminin, fibronectin, and tenascin that are important during lung development as well as during lung injury. Laminin is a glycoprotein that affects growth, differentiation, cellular migration, and adhesion. It is present in the lung throughout development, and treatment of embryonic lung cultures with antilaminin antibodies markedly inhibits tube formation and terminal branching.[71] This suggests that laminin is an important regulator of branching morphogenesis.[72]

Fibronectin is secreted by fibroblasts and converted to insoluble matrices in the extracellular space. In utero maximal expression of lung fibronectin is observed at the pseudoglandular stage when maximal cell proliferation occurs. Fibronectin abundance in the lung decreases with advancing gestation, although low levels persist in normal neonatal and adult lungs. This component of the ECM influences lung morphogenesis by its effects on cell adhesion, cell shape, and cytoskeletal organization.[73] During lung injury, fibronectin abundance greatly increases and may contribute to the fibroproliferative response associated with lung injury.[73,74]

Tenascin, produced by lung fibroblasts and endothelial cells during fetal lung development, is another important component of the ECM. Tenascin plays a role in matrix organization and cell-cell interactions during lung development.[75] Cadherins,[76] syndecans,[77] epimorphin,[78] and the *wnt*[79] family of proteins also mediate cell-cell and cell-matrix interactions during lung development. Accumulating evidence suggests involvement of these ECM proteins in the pulmonary responses to injury, and these responses appear to be developmentally regulated.[72]

During development, the ECM regulates cellular growth, differentiation, and function. Extracellular matrix molecules can modulate the cellular responses to growth factors and vasoactive agents by determining cell shape.[80] Several ECM components such as proteoglycans, collagen, laminin, and fibronectin also have been shown to alter the function of differentiated epithelial cells in the lung by modifying surfactant production.[81,82] The mechanisms by which contact of type II cells with ECM components enhances transcription of SP-A, SP-B, and SP-C mRNA in culture remain unclear.[83]

Effector Molecules

Growth Factors

Peptide growth factor signaling is necessary for lung morphogenesis, maintenance of pulmonary cell growth, and response to lung injury (Table 8–2). A number of in vitro and in vivo studies have extensively characterized this multifunctional group, which includes TGF-β, keratinocyte growth factor (KGF), hepatocyte growth factor (HGF), epidermal growth factor (EGF), PDGF, basic fibroblast growth factor (bFGF), and insulin-like growth factors (IGFs). The role of growth factors mediating intercellular communications in the developing lung and during lung injury has been well studied. In general, peptide growth factor signaling through tyrosine kinase intracellular signaling domains (ie, EGF, FGF, HGF, IGF, and PDGF) stimulate lung morphogenesis, whereas the receptors with serine/threonine kinase intracellular domains such as TGF-β are inhibitory.[84] Although the same growth factors may regulate both development and repair, there are specific temporal, spatial, and quantitative differences that determine the appropriate role of these mediators.

Transforming growth factor β

Transforming growth factor β is a 25-kD homodimer produced and secreted by most cells and has many autocrine and paracrine effects in the lung: TGF-β can stimulate mesenchymal cell growth, inhibit epithelial cell proliferation, and alter ECM production. In addition, TGF-β can induce the production of other mitogens, adding even more diversity to its function.

The TGF-β family plays a critical role in lung development. Signaling from TGF-β1 and TGF-β2 has been shown to suppress lung morphogenesis. Exogenous TGF-β1 and TGF-β2 administration have suppressed airway branching morphogenesis and led to decreased thyroid transcription factor 1 and SP-C expression.[85] Blockage of TGF-β type II receptor function with antisense oligonucleotides or blocking antibodies has stimulated lung development two- to threefold in embryonic murine lungs undergoing branching morphogenesis in ex vivo cultures.[86] Furthermore, transgenic mice overexpressing TGF-β1 in the lung were perinatally lethal and were found to have arrested lung morphogenesis in the pseudoglandular stage at embryonic day 18.5. Nontransgenic littermates had progressed to the more mature saccular stage of lung development by embryonic day 18.5.[87]

In contrast to the negative regulators TGF-β1 and TGF-β2, TGF-β3 is believed to promote lung development since TGF-β3-null mutant mice exhibit abnormal lung morphogenesis and do not survive the newborn period.[88] Shi et al[88] found that the lungs of these mutant mice on embryonic day 18.5 had not formed normal saccular structures and had a thick mesenchyme between the terminal air spaces. In addition, fewer pulmonary cells expressed SP-C, further suggesting impaired lung development.[88] In vitro studies suggest that TGF-β3 might mediate the glucocorticoid regulation of fetal lung development. Fetal lung fibroblasts exposed to cortisol have demonstrated increased TGF-β3 mRNA expression in a time- and dose-dependent manner.[89] Maternal administration of dexamethasone also increased TGF-β3 expression in fetal lung fibroblasts.[89] However, as shown in TGF-β3-null mutant animals, glucocorticoid signaling in the lung can use alternative pathways and exert its effect in promoting lung maturation without the presence of TGF-β3.[88]

Alveolar macrophages are recruited to the lungs after different types of injury and produce TGF-β. In addition, epithelial cells and probably fibroblasts release TGF-β.[90] A number of in vitro studies suggest that TGF-β alters ECM protein components, leading to an increase in fibronectin and collagen. Transforming growth factor β decreases plasmin production by increasing plasminogen activator inhibitor 1,[91] and suppresses fibroblast-derived proteases, leading to excessive accumulation of fibronectin. In addition, TGF-β leads to enhanced collagen synthesis and decreased collagen degradation by decreasing fibroblast collagenase and increasing the collagenase inhibitor, TIMP-1 (tissue inhibitor of metalloproteinase-1).[92]

Excessive production of TGF-β can lead to fibrotic lung disease, a prominent feature of chronic lung disease. During the development of fibrosis, mesenchymal cells and ECM replace normal lung tissue. Santana et al[93] used a bleomycin-induced model of pulmonary fibrosis in rats and showed enhanced mRNA and protein levels of all three TGF-β isoforms during the "inflammatory phase" (days 1 and 3) in the injured areas.[93] There was a further

TABLE 8–2. Growth Factors: Function and Role in Lung Injury

Growth Factors	Sites of Production	Biologic Function In Lung Development	Role in Lung Injury
TGF-ß	Alveolar macrophages Epithelial cells Fibroblasts (probable)	Stimulates mesenchymal growth Inhibits epithelial cell proliferation Alters ECM production Induces other mitogens TGF-ß1 and TGF-ß2: suppress lung morphogenesis TGF-ß3: promotes lung development	Alters ECM components: increases fibronectin and collagen, decreases plasmin Incites fibrosis
HGF	Mesenchymal cells	Mediates epithelial-mesenchymal interactions Potent mitogen for type II epithelial cells	Induces epithelial proliferation
KGF	Fibroblasts	Mediates epithelial-mesenchymal interactions Potent mitogen for type II epithelial cells Possible role in lung airway branching	Induces epithelial proliferation Promotes alveolar cell migration Upregulates surfactant proteins
EGF	Mesenchymal cells	Induces branching morphogenesis Accelerates lung maturation	Involved in fibroproliferative response
PDGF	Vascular endothelial cells Alveolar macrophages Fibroblasts Airway epithelial cells Airway smooth muscle cells	Potent mesenchymal cell mitogen Chemotaxin Role in alveolar myofibroblast development	Modulates fibroproliferative response Leads to emphysematous lung formation
FGF	Airway epithelial cells Mesenchymal cells	Mitogen for epithelial and epidermal cells Stimulates fibroblast and endothelial cell growth Induces surfactant protein expression Induces branching morphogenesis	Important in fibroproliferative response
IGF	IGF-I: Mesenchymal cells, alveolar macrophages IGF-II: Epithelial cells, endothelial cells	IGF-I: Potent mitogen of fibroblasts Stimulates collagen synthesis Significant role in pulmonary growth	Role in fibroproliferative response Maintenance of epithelial cells following lung injury

TGF = transforming growth factor; HGF = hepatocyte growth factor; KGF = keratinocyte growth factor; EGF = epidermal growth factor; PDGF = platelet-derived growth factor; FGF = fibroblast growth factor; IGF = insulin-like growth factor; ECM = extracellular matrix.

increase in TGF-β expression in the areas of developing fibrosis during the later "reparative phase" (days 7 and 14).[93] This corresponded with an increase in collagen production 7 days after injury, which peaked at 14 days.[94] Interestingly, mice strains with greater pulmonary TGF-β expression were found to be at greater risk of developing severe fibrosis.[95] Indeed, TGF-β levels are increased in tracheal aspirates of infants with chronic lung disease compared to infants with resolved respiratory distress syndrome and control groups.[96] This provides indirect evidence that TGF-β may contribute to the fibrotic component of chronic lung disease in premature infants.

Hepatocyte and keratinocyte growth factors

Hepatocyte growth factor and keratinocyte growth factor (KGF) are two extremely potent mitogens for alveolar type II epithelial cells.[97] Mesenchymal cells produce HGF, which is thought to act as a mediator of epithelial-mesenchymal interactions.[97] Keratinocyte growth factor is a member of the FGF family (also designated FGF7) that, unlike other FGF members, only binds to the epithelial cell-specific KGF receptor. As a paracrine mediator of epithelial cell proliferation and differentiation, KGF is important in epithelial cell repair.

In situ hybridization has shown that HGF and the HGF receptor are expressed respectively in mesenchymal and epithelial cells in the developing fetal lung.[98] In utero HGF may regulate interactions between these two cell types. In vitro cultures show that HGF reorganizes fetal lung epithelial cells on a basement membrane extract into structures similar to alveoli.[99] Exogenous HGF in the presence of FGF or KGF also induces epithelial branching in the developing lung.[98] In addition to endogenous pulmonary HGF, the high levels of HGF in fetal amniotic fluid probably also have a direct effect on fetal lung development. In support of this hypothesis, amniotic fluid from pregnant women between 14 and 31 weeks of gestation induced fetal alveolar type II cell migration in vitro and this effect was proportional to HGF levels and was neutralized by anti-HGF antibodies.[100]

Similar to HGF, KGF is a regulator of mesenchymal-epithelial interactions in the developing lung. Expression of KGF is detected in mesenchymal embryonic rat lung, whereas the KGF receptor is expressed in the epithelium.[101] Medium conditioned from 13-day lung mesenchymal cells stimulated DNA synthesis of embryonic lung epithelial cells, and this effect was reduced by a neutralizing KGF antibody.[101] Blocking of endogenous HGF with antibodies in fetal lung cultures did not inhibit the KGF-induced lung branching, suggesting that KGF may play a more important role in lung branching than HGF.[102]

Transgenic mice overexpressing human KGF in the lung did not survive to term.[103] These animals had disrupted lung development during the pseudoglandular stage.[103] By embryonic day 15.5, lungs appeared cystic and were composed of numerous dilated saccules lined with epithelial cells containing glycogen.[103] Furthermore, the normal distribution of SP-C in distal tubules was altered, and there was decreased SP-C observed in the columnar epithelial cells. Although the mesenchyme was preserved, the architectural relationship of the epithelium to the mesenchyme was altered.[103] Following lung injury, HGF and KGF levels increase in an attempt to induce alveolar epithelial cell proliferation.[97] Keratinocyte growth factor also promotes cell migration and spreading of type II alveolar cells, enabling the regenerating epithelium to cover the alveolar surface.[97] In addition, upregulation of surfactant proteins in cultured cells by KGF and the possible role of KGF in enhancing alveolar clearance may provide further reparative pathways following lung injury.[97,104]

Numerous studies have demonstrated that administration of exogenous KGF can prevent or attenuate various types of lung injury. Intratracheal instillation of recombinant human KGF (rhKGF) in rats 48 or 72 hours prior to bleomycin-induced lung injury led to minimal lung injury compared with the moderate to severe injury observed in control animals.[105] Similar protective effects of KGF were observed in rats treated with intratracheal rhKGF prior to hyperoxic exposure.[106] In addition to a dramatic decrease in mortality, rhKGF-treated animals had fewer pulmonary hemorrhages and did not have intra-alveolar exudates.[106] Intratracheal instillation of rhHGF promoted alveolar type II cell proliferation and provided protection against hyperoxia.[107] Whether direct delivery of KGF (and/or HGF) to the human premature lung will prove efficacious in preserving or restoring the alveolar epithelium during exposure to hyperoxia and other injurious agents remains to be elucidated.

Epidermal growth factor

Epidermal growth factor is a low-molecular weight polypeptide with structural and functional similarity to other members of the EGF family, such as TGF-α, amphiregulin, heparin-binding EGF, and betacellulin. These factors bind to the EGF receptor (EGFR), a tyrosine kinase receptor, and activate type I protein kinase A, thereby inducing a mitogenic response via the mitogen-activated protein kinase (MAPK) pathway.[108] Whereas EGF, TGF-α, and EGFR are localized to epithelial and smooth muscle cells of bronchioles as well as epithelial cells of saccules in fetal rat lungs,[109] fetal human lungs express these compounds in mesenchymal cells.[110] Receptors for EGF also are found in differentiated type II cells in human fetal lung explants.[111]

Epidermal growth factor enhances branching morphogenesis and accelerates lung maturation in fetal lung cultures.[112] This paracrine effect requires the presence of mesenchyme[113] and interaction with TGF-β,[114] and may be modulated by the induction of matrix-degrading metalloproteinases.[115] Exogenously administered EGF has increased choline incorporation into phosphatidylcholine (PC) and disaturated PC in fetal rat lungs in a dose-dependent fashion,[116] and it has accelerated type II cell maturation in fetal rhesus monkeys.[117] The observation that premature lambs[118] and rhesus monkeys[119] were rescued from the development of respiratory distress syndrome (RDS) following in utero infusion of EGF provides further evidence that EGF is critical for lung development.

The role of EGFR in embryonic development was studied in EGFR-null mutant mice.[120–122] Although the genetic background of the mice influenced the mutant phenotype, in one strain[120] the mice survived up to 8 days after birth but had impaired epithelial development in several organs including the lungs. The histologic appearance of their lungs resembled that of neonatal RDS with diffuse atelectasis and decreased surfactant production.[123] Alveolar septa were thicker and more cellular compared to control animals. Expression of EGFR was significantly decreased in human fetuses with pulmonary hypoplasia,[124] emphasizing the role of EGF in human lung development. Treatment with either EGF alone or in combination with TGF-α restored lung growth and branching in two animal models of lung hypoplasia,[124,125] suggesting a potential of EGF to induce pulmonary growth.

The role of EGF in lung injury has been studied in several injury models. Following naphthalene-induced Clara cell injury in the mouse, there is increased expression of EGF, EGFR, and TGF-α in clusters of squamous epithelial cells of the distal bronchioles.[126] Hyperoxia in vitro and in vivo has increased EGF bioactivity in rat type II cells and rat lungs.[127] Expression of EGFR also was upregulated in rat lungs following bleomycin-induced injury[128] as well as in fibrotic mouse lungs that were exposed to silica dust.[129] The important role of EGF during lung injury is also suggested by the lack of EGF staining in human bronchiolar epithelium beyond 24 weeks of gestation unless there had been lung injury, such as chronic lung disease of prematurity.[130] Furthermore, EGF immunostaining was observed in alveolar macrophages in infants with BPD.[131] Thus, EGF and EGFR probably play a role in the fibroproliferative response following acute lung injury.

Platelet-derived growth factor

Platelet-derived growth factor, a 30-kD dimeric peptide composed of A and/or B chains, is produced by vascular endothelial cells, alveolar macrophages, fibroblasts, and airway epithelial cells and smooth muscle cells. Platelet-derived growth factor is a potent mesenchymal cell mitogen, which serves as an important chemotaxin.[132] The two PDGF receptors (α and β) belong to the protein tyrosine kinase receptor family with variable cellular expression that influences the PDGF binding affinity as well as the response to PDGF.

There is increasing evidence to suggest that PDGF plays a crucial role in fetal lung growth and morphogenesis. Both PDGF-AA and PDGF-BB are present in developing airway epithelial cells of fetal rat lung as early as day 12 of gestation and, in mesenchymal cells, 2 days later (day 22=term).[133] The corresponding PDGF receptors are detected similarly by immunohistochemistry in both cells as early as 13 days' gestation.[134] Both PDGF-AA and PDGF-BB protein levels are elevated in airway epithelial and mesenchymal cells during the embryonic and pseudoglandular stage of lung development; they decrease with advancing gestation.[133] As shown by studies in PDGF-A-null mice, PDGF-A is required for development of alveolar myofibroblasts. Mice that survive postnatally develop lung emphysema following failure of alveolar septation.[24] This inhibition of alveolar development is attributed to decreased elastin deposition and inadequate formation of alveolar myofibroblasts.[24]

In addition to its role in lung embryogenesis, PDGF signaling contributes to the development of pulmonary fibrosis, emphysema, and probably pulmonary vascular cell hypertrophy following lung injury. It modulates the fibroproliferative response following acute lung injury, whereby interstitial mesenchymal cells migrate into the alveolar space, proliferate, and deposit connective tissue.[135] Alveolar macrophages isolated from patients with acute lung injury or idiopathic pulmonary fibrosis, and rat lung fibroblasts following asbestos-induced fibrosis, have increased PDGF levels.[136,137] Three related PDGF peptides detected in bronchoalveolar lavage of patients with acute lung injury are believed to play an important role in signaling mesenchymal cell migration and replication.[135] Neonatal transgenic mice overexpressing PDGF-B have enlarged saccules and thickened primary septa as early as 1 week of age, corresponding to aspects of both emphysema and fibrotic lung disease.[138] Furthermore, PDGF might contribute to the pulmonary vascular cell hypertrophy observed after exposure to hyperoxia, since increased expression of PDGF (especially PDGF-B) and its receptors precede hyperplasia of VSMCs.[139]

Fibroblast growth factor

The family of fibroblast growth factors (FGFs) consists of 16- to 17-kD peptides composed of basic and hydrophobic domains. These polypeptides typically are released following leakage of damaged cells, and function as potent mitogens for a wide variety of mesodermal and neuroectodermal derived cells. Acidic FGF (FGF-1) and basic FGF (FGF-2) are expressed ubiquitously and stimulate fibroblast and EC growth. Throughout development, FGF is immunolocalized to airway epithelial cells, BMs, and mesenchymal cells associated with buds and SMCs of large airways and vessels.[140–143] The initial FGF signaling pattern appears to be established during the early embryonic period with modifications at each stage of branching by genetic feedback controls.[144]

Signaling from FGF is an important regulator of the embryonic lung, controlling its epidermal cell proliferation, differentiation, and branching morphogenesis. Fibroblast growth factors 1, 2, and 7 (KGF) were the most potent mitogens to stimulate in vitro lung epithelial cell proliferation when compared with IGF-1, EGF, and HGF.[145] Fibroblast growth factor 2 was found to be the most effective inducer of lung epithelial cell-specific SP-A, SP-B, and SP-C expression.[145]

The clinical involvement of FGF in branching morphogenesis is supported by multiple in vivo and in vitro observations. Mice deficient in FGF-10 were perinatal lethal due to the complete absence of lungs.[146] Although these knockout mice had normal trachea, the mainstem bronchi and subsequent pulmonary branching was completely disrupted.[146] This is similar to the phenotype of the Drosophila mutant branchless, an FGF homologue, suggesting that the function of these genes has been conserved during evolution. In addition, extensive budding is observed in endodermal and mesenchymal cultured lung tissue following addition of FGF-10.[147] Furthermore, newborn mice expressing a dominant-negative FGF receptor 2 (ligands include FGF-1, FGF-7 [KGF], and FGF-10) in lung bud epithelium had abnormally developed lungs consisting of two undifferentiated epithelial tubes that extended from the bifurcation of the trachea to the diaphragm, resulting in perinatal death.[148] Regulation of FGF is also critical during postnatal lung development, since knockout mice for FGF receptors 3 and 4 were unable to undergo alveogenesis despite normal lung development at birth.[149]

Due to the ability of FGF to stimulate fibroblast growth, this family has been associated with the fibroproliferative process following lung injury. In a model of lung fibrosis using paraquat and hyperoxia, rat lungs had increased FGF-1 and FGF receptor expression in alveolar epithelial cells and macrophages as compared with control lungs.[150] Similarly, the development of asbestos-induced fibrosis in rat lungs correlated with increased FGF levels that persisted for 6 months.[151]

Insulin-like growth factors

Insulin-like growth factor I and IGF-II are small peptides (about 7.5 kD), with structural homology to proinsulin, that bind to type I IGF receptor (IGF-IR). These growth factors stimulate cellular proliferation, induce cellular differentiation, and influence fetal growth.[152] Type II IGF receptor (IGF-IIR) does not transduce mitogenic signals but appears to regulate the levels of its ligand available to the growth-promoting IGF-IR.[153] Specific binding proteins, such as IGF binding proteins (IGFBP)-1 through-6, both positively and negatively modulate the biologic effects of the IGFs.

All components of the IGF system are expressed in the developing rat or mouse lung and appear to be developmentally regulated.[154–156] Abundance of IGF-I mRNA is relatively constant in fetal and adult lungs, whereas IGF-II mRNA levels decrease in late gestation.[154] Whereas fetal rat lung IGF-I mRNA is present in mesenchymal cells such as fibroblasts,[157] IGF II mRNA localizes predominantly to epithelia. Type I IGF-R is widely expressed in all cells, and IGF-IIR is confined to mesenchyme. This pattern of distribution of receptors and ligands suggests both a paracrine and an autocrine role of IGFs in cellular proliferation during lung growth and development. The IGFBPs also have a complex pattern of regulated expression in fetal rat lungs, and this may serve to modulate IGF action at specific target sites.[153]

In the human, in situ hybridization studies have demonstrated IGF mRNA (predominantly IGF-II mRNA) in the lung throughout gestation. There is decreasing expression of both IGFs after 20 weeks of gestation. Whereas IGF mRNA is mostly localized in undifferentiated mesenchyme of the lung buds with weak epithelial localization, IGF II is expressed consistently in endothelium throughout gestation.[158] Postnatally, alveolar macrophages express IGF I, and type II pneumocytes express IGF-II.[159]

Involvement of the IGF family in the lung's response to injury has been studied in numerous models of lung injury. Exposure of neonatal rats to hyperoxia has led to increased IGF-I and IGF-II mRNA levels in the lungs, with a spatial pattern similar to that seen during fetal lung development.[159] In vitro exposure of type II cells to hyperoxia has led to increased IGF-II expression with arrested cell growth, associated with increased levels of IGFBP-2 and IGF IIR.[160] In vivo, hyperoxia of moderate severity (60% oxygen for 2 weeks) led to formation of parenchymal thickening in newborn rat lungs, correlating with increased type II cell proliferation and increased immunoreactive IGF-I and IGF-IR levels.[161] Hypoxia also led to increased expression of IGF-I and IGF-IR mRNA in newborn rat lungs.[162] The relative contribution of each component of the IGF family to the lung's response to oxidant injury is difficult to discern. Most studies suggest that if the oxidant stress induces IGFBP-2 and IGF-IIR, arrested cell growth occurs. In contrast, if the oxidant injury increases IGF-I and IGF-IR, proliferation of type II cells along with fibroblast proliferation and migration ensues.[163]

Proteases and Antiproteases

Serine proteases such as elastase and cathepsin G are hydrolases that use serine's hydroxyl group to cleave internal peptide bonds. They are present in all mammalian tissues, including the lung and airway. Elastase and cathepsin G are located in cytosolic granules within leukocytes and some monocytes, and are secreted in response to inflammatory stimuli. These proteins degrade many components of the extracellular matrix,[164] have direct cytotoxic effects on endothelial cells,[164,165] and lead to increased airway epithelial cell permeability.[166,167] Instillation of elastase into dog lungs in vivo leads to the degradation of elastic fibers as well as other alveolar septal elements, resulting in anatomic changes consistent with emphysema.[168]

The activity of these enzymes is limited by numerous endogenous serine protease inhibitors (serpins) including α-antitrypsin (also known as α-proteinase inhibitor), human elastase inhibitor, secretory leukocyte proteinase inhibitor (SLPI), and elastase-specific inhibitor (elafin). It is postulated that the smaller compounds SLPI and elafin provide the first line of defense against elastase activity by inhibiting enzyme that is already attached to elastin fibers.[169] A product of epithelial cells, SLPI is localized to the cytosol of neutrophils in the upper airway during inflammation.[170] Studies have shown that α-antitrypsin, localized to peripheral blood monocytes, epithelial cells, and tissue macrophages, can be regulated by elastase.[171]

A number of studies have shown that administration of elastase inhibitors can prevent various types of lung injury. ONO-5046, a specific inhibitor of neutrophil elastase, attenuated the lipopolysaccharide-induced acute lung injury in guinea pigs[172] and in rats,[173] the acute pulmonary injury induced by TNF-α in isolated perfused rat lungs,[174] and the phorbol myristate acetate-induced injury in isolated dog lung.[175] Similarly, the neutrophil elastase inhibitor L-680,833 and recombinant monocyte/neutrophil elastase inhibitor almost completely prevented the hemorrhage observed after instilling airway secretions from cystic fibrosis patients into lungs of healthy rats.[176,177] Furthermore, intratracheal instillation of recombinant secretory leukocyte proteinase inhibitor significantly diminished the development of lipopolysaccharide-induced pulmonary emphysema in hamsters.[178] Finally, α_1-antitrypsin protected neonatal rats from the pulmonary parenchymal and vascular effects resulting from hyperoxic exposure.[179]

An imbalance between serine proteases with their endogenous inhibitors can lead to lung injury. Patients with homozygous or heterozygous deficiency of α_1-antitrypsin have a high risk of developing emphysema due to unopposed elastase in the lung.[180] Similarly, the association of smoking with the development of emphysema is attributed to the accumulation of leukocytes and macrophages leading to an excess protease load[181] as well as the direct inactivation of α_1-proteinase inhibitors by the oxidizing activity of tobacco smoke.[168] Indeed, transgenic mice lacking macrophage elastase did not develop emphysema in response to long-term exposure to cigarette smoke.[182] The massive neutrophilic influx to the lungs of patients with cystic fibrosis and the associated

TABLE 8–3. Transcription Factors: Role in Lung Development

Transcription Factor	Biologic Role	Interactions
TTF-1	Cellular proliferation during branching morphogenesis	HNF binding site
	Peripheral lung cell lineage determination	GATA-6
	Alters SP expression	Binding sites on SPs A, B, C, D and CC-10
Gli 2 and *Gli 3*	Epithelial and mesenchymal proliferation during fetal lung growth	*Shh*
Shh	Mesenchymal cell proliferation	*Gli 2* and *Gli 3*
Hox	Airway branching and patterning during lung development	Retinoic acid
Retinoic acid	Branching morphogenesis	*Hox b-5*
	Alveolar septation	
NFκB and *NF-IL-6*	Induction of proinflammatory mediator IL-8	TNF-α
	NFκB also role in hyperoxic and asbestos-induced lung injury	

TTF = thyroid transcription factor; *Shh* = Sonic hedgehog; NFκB = nuclear factor κB; NF-IL-6 = nuclear factor interleukin-6; HNF = hepatocyte nuclear factor; IL = interleukin; SP = surfactant protein; TNF = tumor necrosis factor.

excess neutrophil elastase levels leads to enhanced mucus secretion, injured airway tissues, and decreased opsonization and elimination of bacterial pathogens.[183]

The persistent inflammation that contributes to the development of BPD in premature infants is also associated with a protease-antiprotease imbalance. Although bronchoalveolar lavage elastase-to-α_1-proteinase inhibitor ratios did not differ in newborns with RDS, there was a significant increase in this ratio between 1 to 4 weeks of life in patients who developed BPD.[96,184,185] Dexamethasone treatment in ventilated premature infants with BPD was associated with a significant decrease in bronchoalveolar lavage elastase activity and suggests one mechanism by which corticosteroid treatment decreases lung inflammation. Perhaps early therapy with recombinant protease inhibitors to premature infants will help to decrease the incidence of BPD.

Endogenous vascular elastase

The protease-antiprotease balance in the lung extends to the pulmonary vascular bed. Endogenous vascular elastase (EVE) is a developmentally regulated 20-kD elastolytic enzyme produced by VSMCs.[186] It is expressed at sites of vascular remodeling in the embryo, and its activity is modulated by the 9-kD serine proteinase inhibitor elafin, which is also expressed in embryonic and postnatal vessel walls. Postnatal activation of EVE in response to lung injury contributes to the pathogenesis of the pulmonary vascular remodeling accompanying pulmonary hypertension. Degradation of elastin and extracellular proteoglycans by EVE leads to release of EM-bound growth factors that induce SMC proliferation and migration. Inhibitors of EVE have been used in animal models of pulmonary hypertension to reverse this process.[187,188]

Transcription Factors

Transcription factors are important regulators of lung morphogenesis (Table 8–3). Orderly cellular proliferation during branching morphogenesis is positively regulated by the thyroid transcription factor 1 (TTF-1) family, which is also involved in peripheral lung cell lineage determination.[189] Since TTF-1 binding sites are found at the 5′ promoter regions of several peripheral lung-specific genes including SPs (A, B, C and D) and Clara cell protein 10 (CC-10), TTF-1 probably plays an important role in SP expression.[85] The close proximity of TTF-1 binding sites with the hepatocyte nuclear factor (HNF) binding sites enables cooperation between TTF-1 and HNF in determining the future of pulmonary epithelial cell lineage.[85] Thyroid transcription factor 1 may also interact with GATA-6, a member of the zinc finger family of transcription factors that is coexpressed with TTF-1 in respiratory epithelium.[190]

The two zinc finger transcription factors *Gli 2* and *Gli 3* play an important role in fetal lung growth.[191] Studies in mutant mice demonstrate that abnormalities in *Gli* gene expression are accompanied by decreased epithelial and mesenchymal cell proliferation, resulting in abnormal airway branching.[191] *Gli* genes also mediate *Sonic hedgehog (Shh)* signaling. Overexpression of *Shh* in the developing lung leads to increased mesenchymal and epithelial cell proliferation with an increase in the ratio of interstitial mesenchyme to epithelial tubules.[192] This results in absence of normal alveoli and death in the newborn period, suggesting that *Shh* regulates lung mesenchymal cell proliferation in vivo.[193] Conversely, mice lacking *Shh* expression have fewer mesenchymal cells, leading to tracheoesophageal atresia and other tracheal and lung abnormalities.[194]

The *Hox* genes also encode important transcription factors that are required for airway branching and patterning during lung development.[195] The poor survival in mice lacking *Hoxa-3* results from pulmonary maldevelopment, as evidenced by small trachea and disorganized bronchial epithelium.[196] Mice lacking *Hoxa-5* also die perinatally, partly due to respiratory failure from abnormal tracheal development as well as abnormal distal airways.[197] Indeed, *Hoxb-5* also plays a critical role in normal lung development by influencing branching embryogenesis in the embryonic lung.[198]

The transcription factor *Trachealess (trh)*, the Drosophila homologue of hypoxia inducible factor 1α (HIF-1α), regulates tubulogenesis in the respiratory organs of Drosophila.[199] In contrast, a possible role for the homologous HIF-1α in the development of human lungs has not been fully characterized. In mammalian lungs HIF-1α is induced in response to profound hypoxia, regulating numerous hypoxia-inducible genes.[200] Mice that are HIF-1α null are embryonic lethal due to extensive cardiovascular malformations and neural tube defects.[201,202] Mice heterozygous for HIF-1α are partially protected from hypoxia-induced pulmonary hypertension,[203] suggesting that HIF-1α participates in the development of abnormal pulmonary vascular tone and structure following hypoxic exposure. Further studies are necessary to elucidate the role of HIF-1α in human lung development.

Several developmentally regulated signaling pathways that are important in lung development are reactivated during acute lung injury. Retinoic acid enhances cell proliferation and branching activity in the developing lung, probably by increasing EGFR expression.[204] Massaro and Massaro showed that postnatal treatment with retinoic acid increased the number of pulmonary alveoli in rats by promoting alveolar septation.[205] Treatment with retinoic acid reversed elastase-induced pulmonary emphysema in adult rats (long after septation had ceased), supporting the principle that developmental mechanisms can be exploited during tissue repair.[206]

Another category of transcription factors with important roles in lung responses to injury are the transcription factors related to redox state and inflammation such as nuclear factor κB (NFκB), nuclear factor interleukin-6 (NF-IL-6), activated protein 1 (AP-1), and early growth response 1 (EGR-1). The redox sensitive transcription factors NFκB and NF-IL-6 are implicated in the TNF-α induction of the proinflammatory mediator IL-8 in pulmonary epithelial cells.[207] Nuclear factor κB is also involved in the lung's response to hyperoxic[208] and asbestos-induced injury.[209] The CCAAT enhancer binding family of proteins (C/EBP),[210] as well as the serum amyloid A activating factor 1 and NFκB, is induced in response to inflammatory stimuli in rabbit lungs.[210] Studies in humans have not systematically assessed the role of transcription factors in the response of the developing lung to injury.

Hormones

Hormonal influences, similar to transcription factors, play an important role during lung development. Glucocorticoids, thyroid hormones, and prolactin have been associated with lung differentiation.[6] The well-known effect of prenatal betamethasone treatment to accelerate the maturation of the surfactant system of the fetal lung has provided tremendous benefit to premature infants.[211] However, prenatal treatment with dexamethasone is less likely to accelerate lung maturation if it is administered to sheep less than 125 days' gestation.[212] Postnatal administration of dexamethasone also can inhibit lung growth, since rats who received dexamethasone after birth had decreased alveoli.[213] In addition, postnatal dexamethasone inhibits septation of saccules in the rat,[214] accelerates alveolar wall thinning, and alters wall composition by delaying conversion of type II cells to type I cells.[215] Inhibition of inflammatory pathways by systemic glucocorticoids has led to their clinical use for prevention and treatment of chronic lung disease of prematurity.[216,217] However, there are ongoing concerns about the arrest of lung development as well as long-term neurologic effects of postnatal systemic glucocorticoids.

Thyroid hormones further enhance the stimulatory effect of glucocorticoids on surfactant synthesis.[6] However, clinical trials of antenatal thyroid-releasing hormone treatment concomitant with glucocorticoid administration showed conflicting results,[218,219] and, thus, thyroid hormones are not currently used clinically to enhance fetal lung maturation. Thyroid hormones also are known to play a role in the postnatal architectural maturation of the lung by increasing gas exchange surface area. This effect is due to receptor-mediated cell replication of epithelial cells in response to thyroid hormones.[220]

The role of sex hormones in lung development has been suggested because of the delayed lung maturation in male fetuses compared with female fetuses. In the rabbit, female lung explants have increased baseline incorporation of glycerol to diphosphatidylcholine compared with male explants. In addition, male explants are less responsive to exogenous EGF.[221] Klein and Nielson demonstrated that male hormones or androgens, induce a delay in EGFR binding activity associated with decreased EGFR density.[222] In addition, the male hormone dihydrotestosterone was reported to inhibit fetal lung fibroblast-pneumocyte factor.[223] In rats, there is sexual dimorphism in the lung's gas exchange surface area that presents at the onset of sexual maturity. This is attributed to estrogen's stimulatory effect on alveolar septation, which leads to a greater number of smaller alveoli in female rats compared with male rats.[224] Thus, whereas male hormones attenuate lung growth, female hormones may enhance pulmonary growth.

Nonimmune Defenses

Surfactant proteins

The four surfactant proteins (SPs), A, B, C, and D, are transcriptionally regulated in the developing lung, and their functions have recently been characterized. Surfactant protein A and SP-D are members of the collectin family of host defense molecules that are expressed and secreted primarily by type II and nonciliated bronchiolar epithelial cells.

Surfactant protein A dramatically increases during late gestation in the human lung, and its expression is induced by glucocorticoids. Messenger RNA of SP-D is first detected in the second trimester and rises steadily during late fetal and postnatal lung development. In addition to their role in surfactant phospholipid homeostasis, these proteins play critical roles in the innate immune system of the lung, which is critical for immediate antibody-independent host defense.[225] Surfactant protein A-null mutant mice show ineffective lung clearance after intratracheal administration of group B streptococci,[226] *Pseudomonas aeruginosa*,[227] and adenovirus.[228] Although these mice had increased pulmonary inflammation, there was decreased phagocytosis and attenuated superoxide radical generation by alveolar macrophages.[226] Surfactant protein D–null mutant mice manifest altered surfactant lipid homeostasis with progressive accumulation of surfactant lipid, SP-A, and SP-B in the alveolar space.[229] Both SP-A and SP-D are believed to participate in the response of the lung to injury by binding and opsonizing pathogens, thus enhancing their phagocytosis and clearance,[230] and by modulating the inflammatory responses in the lung.[227] Acute hyperoxia[231] or intratracheal instillation of lipopolysaccharide in rats[232] is associated with differential alterations in SP-A and SP-D by type II and Clara cells. As shown in studies in the premature baboon model of chronic lung disease, the total collectin pool in lavage fluid is significantly reduced. Since these collectins may bind and opsonize pathogens, reduced levels may present additional risk to those premature infants who require prolonged ventilatory support.[233]

Surfactant protein B and SP-C are hydrophobic proteins that accelerate surface film formation by surfactant phospholipids. Their mRNAs are detected as early as 13 weeks of gestation in the human, prior to the appearance of SP-A and surfactant lipids.[234] Their expression in the fetal lung is induced by glucocorticoids.[234] Surfactant protein B is a 79-amino acid protein produced by type II and Clara cells. Its critical role in postnatal lung function and surfactant homeostasis is demonstrated in studies of homozygous SP-B-deficient mice that die from respiratory failure at birth.[235] More importantly, hereditary deficiency of SP-B in humans is recognized as a rare cause of respiratory failure in full-term newborns.[236–238] Heterozygous SP-B-deficient mice are highly susceptible to oxygen-induced lung injury, suggesting a protective role for SP-B during exposure to hyperoxia.[239,240] Surfactant protein C is expressed exclusively in alveolar type II cells in the mouse and is secreted in lamellar bodies. Its main function appears to be modulation of the biophysical properties of surfactant phospholipid.

Endogenous antioxidants

Numerous endogenous antioxidants, such as copper-zinc or manganese superoxide dismutase (SOD), catalase, ceruloplasmin, and glutathione peroxidase, serve as important defenses against oxidant-induced lung injury. They are produced by pulmonary epithelial cells and are secreted in the airway epithelial lining fluid with mucus and surfactants. Inhaled oxidants can then be inactivated by interacting with the epithelial lining fluid.[241] In addition, heme oxygenase and its enzymatic product bilirubin are induced during oxidative stress and provide an important antioxidant defense system in the lung.[242,243]

Oxidants are generated in the setting of hyperoxia, infection, or interaction of biologic messengers such as nitric oxide (NO) with oxygen. Reactive oxygen species such as superoxide, hydrogen peroxide, and hydroxyl radicals induce direct injury of the pulmonary cells by intracellular generation of toxic oxidants that cause oxidation and/or nitrosylation of cellular components and alter cellular protein expression. This injury is further exacerbated by stimulation of the inflammatory response.[244]

The oxidant-antioxidant balance determines the magnitude of injury to the lung. Recent evidence suggests that an oxidant-antioxidant imbalance exists in premature infants. They have lower erythrocyte copper-zinc SOD, red blood cell catalase, and glutathione peroxidase activities compared to full-term infants.[245–249] Similarly, the premature infant's inability to induce pulmonary SOD activity following hyperoxic exposure has corresponded with the severity of RDS.[250] A preliminary study demonstrated that ventilated neonates with severe RDS who received bovine SOD had less radiographic evidence and fewer clinical signs of BPD, although no difference in length of oxygen therapy was detected.[251] In a follow-up study, intratracheal administration of one dose of recombinant human SOD to preterm infants was associated with significantly lower concentrations of the acute lung injury markers, tracheal aspirate fluid neutrophil chemotactic activity, and albumin.[252] In addition to suppressed antioxidant activity, premature infants have an excessive production of oxidants due to the prolonged hyperoxic exposure in the setting of surfactant deficiency. This relative excess of oxidants can further exacerbate the chronic lung injury.

Cytokines and Chemokines

Chemotactic cytokines (chemokines) are produced in the lung predominantly by stimulated macrophages but also from a variety of other cell types including neutrophils, fibroblasts, and epithelial cells.[253,254] They play a major role in the recruitment of inflammatory cells during acute lung injury.[255] Several animal models of lung injury[253,255–257] have demonstrated increased levels of macrophage inflammatory proteins (MIPs), monocyte chemoattractant protein 1 (MCP-1), TNF-α, and interleukins in the lung. In vitro and in vivo studies have demonstrated a critical role for early response cytokines (TNF-α, and IL 1) in the initiation and maintenance of the inflammatory responses in the lung.[258] Anti-inflammatory cytokines such as IL-10 also have been identified. Differences in intensity, timing, and distribution of chemokine abundance in the newborn lung compared with the adult lung have been reported and may explain differences in susceptibility to lung injury[256,259] (see Chapter 36 for more details).

Biologic Messengers

Nitric oxide is a potent vasodilator and VSMC antiproliferative agent. All three isoforms of NO synthase (endothelial, neuronal, and inducible) are expressed in the developing lung, and the lung epithelium constitutes an important source of NO throughout lung development.[260] The role of the endothelium-derived NO in the normal cardiopulmonary transition at birth is well recognized,[261] whereas nonvascular functions of NO during lung development have not been studied.[34]

Increased endothelial NO synthase (NOS) activity in the late-gestation fetus is responsible for the dramatic increase in pulmonary blood flow at birth, whereas attenuated expression of endothelial NOS contributes to the pathogenesis of neonatal pulmonary hypertension.[262] Hence, clinical use of inhaled NO to treat pulmonary hypertension in the neonate has been successful.[263,264] The activity of NOS is altered in several models of lung injury.[260,262,265] Although the vasodilating and antiproliferative effects of NO may be beneficial in the setting of acute lung injury, the ability of NO to react with oxygen radicals affects oxidant metabolism, which, depending on the local oxidant-antioxidant balance, may be injurious.[34]

Carbon monoxide is produced in the lung by the action of heme oxygenase (HO), the rate-limiting enzyme of heme degradation. The inducible isoform, HO-1 is developmentally regulated,[266] and accumulating evidence supports its role as a protective stress protein.[267] A protective role for HO-1 has been shown in several models of lung injury, including hyperoxia, endotoxin-induced lung injury, and hypoxia-induced pulmonary hypertension.[268–271] The anti-inflammatory effect of HO-1 is attributed to CO,[272] which also has vasodilator[273] and anti-proliferative properties in VSMCs.[44,274] Although CO may have a protective role in lung injury, the interaction of CO with NO may lead to increased reactive oxygen species with potential deleterious effects.[275]

Conclusion

The lung response to acute injury encompasses a multitude of cellular and molecular interactions. Following lung injury, there is an enhancement of effector molecules, recruitment of cells, and initiation of a fibroproliferative response, cumulatively leading to tissue regeneration and repair. The developmental stage at the time of injury plays a critical role in the effectiveness of these processes. For example, some pathways may be absent, incompletely developed, or immature and thereby lead to an inadequate or exaggerated response. In addition, injury to the developing lung may interfere with normal lung development. Ultimately, the development-dependent cellular responses determine whether a specific injury will lead to regeneration and repair or will proceed to growth arrest, irreversible tissue destruction, and/or fibrosis.

Understanding the complex genetic, cellular, and molecular mechanisms that govern normal lung development is crucial to our ability to enhance lung repair and promote normal lung development in the setting of lung injury. Potential approaches include enhancement of inadequate defenses, modulation of exaggerated responses, and use of morphogenetic and growth-promoting factors. Moreover, an understanding of factors interfering with normal lung development will lead to novel strategies to prevent lung injury.

References

1. Danto SI, Zabski SM,Crandall ED. Late appearance of a type I alveolar epithelial cell marker during fetal rat lung development. Histochem 1994;102:297–304.
2. Castranova V, Rabovsky J, Tucker JH, Miles PR. The alveolar type II epithelial cells: a multifunctional pneumocyte. Toxicol Appl Pharmacol 1988;93:472–83.
3. Ten Have-Opbroek AA, Plopper CG. Morphogenetic and functional activity of type II cells in early fetal rhesus monkey lungs: a comparison between primates and rodents. Anat Rec 1992;234:93–104.
4. Ten Have-Opbroek AA, Dubbeldam JA, Otto-Verberne CJ. Ultrastructural features of type II alveolar epithelial cells in early embryonic mouse lung. Anat Rec 1988; 221:846–53.
5. Post M, Smith BT. Histochemical and immunocytochemical identification of alveolar type II epithelial cells isolated from fetal rat lung. Am Rev Respir Dis 1988; 137:525–30.
6. Boshier DP, Holloway H, Liggins GC, Marshall RJ. Morphometric analysis of the effects of thyrotropin releasing hormone and cortisol on the lungs of fetal sheep. J Dev Physiol 1989;12:49–54.
7. Finkelstein JN. Physiologic and toxicologic responses of alveolar type II cells. Toxicology 1990;60:41–52.
8. Daly HE, Baecher-Allan CM, Paxhia AT, et al. Cell-specific gene expression reveals changes in epithelial cell populations after bleomycin treatment. Lab Invest 1998; 78:393–400.
9. Piedboeuf B, Frenette J, Petrov P, et al. In vivo expression of intercellular adhesion molecule I in type II pneumocytes during hyperoxia. Am J Respir Cell Mol Biol 1996; 15:71–7.
10. Lesur O, Arsalane K, Lane D. Lung alveolar epithelial cell migration in vitro: modulators and regulation processes. Am J Physiol 1996;270:L311–9.
11. Kim HJ, Ingbar DH, Henke CA. Integrin mediation of type II cell adherence to provisional matrix. Am J Physiol 1996;271:L277–86.
12. Massaro GD. The Clara cells: secretory and developmental studies in the rat. Eur J Respir Dis 1987;71:52–8.
13. Fanucchi MV, Murphy ME, Buckpitt A, et al. Pulmonary cytochrome P450 monooxygenase and Clara cell differentiation in mice. Am J Respir Cell Mol Biol 1997; 17:302–14.
14. Andersson O, Nordlund-Moller L, Barnes HJ, Lund J. Heterologous expression of human uteroglobin/

polychlorinated biphenyl-binding protein: determination of ligand binding parameters and mechanism of phospholipase A2 inhibition in vitro. J Biol Chem 1994; 269:19081–7.
15. Singh G, Katyal SL. Clara cells and Clara cell 10kD protein (CC10). Am J Respir Cell Mol Biol 1997;17:141–3.
16. Johnston CJ, Mango GW, Finkelstein JN, Stripp BR. Altered pulmonary response to hyperoxia in Clara cell secretory protein deficient mice. Am J Respir Cell Mol Biol 1998; 17:147–55.
17. Massaro GD, Singh G, Mason R, et al. Conference report: biology of the Clara cell. Am J Physiol 1994;265:L101–6.
18. Stevens TP, McBride JT, Peake JL, et al. Naphthalene cytotoxicity of differentiating Clara cells in neonatal mice. Toxicol Appl Pharmacol 1997;144:96–104.
19. Smiley-Jewell SM, Nishio SJ, Weir AR, Plopper CG. Neonatal Clara cell toxicity by 4-ipomeanol alters bronchiolar organization in adult rabbits. Am J Physiol 1998;274:L485–98.
20. Bitterman PB, Polunovsky VA, Inghar DH. Repair after acute lung injury. Chest 1994;105:118–21S.
21. Montesano R, Orci L. Transforming growth factor beta stimulates collagen-matrix contraction by fibroblasts: implications for wound healing. Proc Natl Acad Sci U S A 1988;85:4894–7.
22. Toti P, Buonocore G, Tanganelli P, et al. Bronchopulmonary dysplasia of the premature baby: an immunohistochemical study. Pediatr Pulmonol 1997;24:22–8.
23. Sime PJ, Marr RA, Gauldie D, et al. Transfer of tumor necrosis factor-alpha to rat lung induces severe pulmonary inflammation and patchy interstitial fibrogenesis with induction of transforming growth factor-beta 1 and myofibroblasts. Am J Pathol 1998;153:825–32.
24. Bostrom H, Willetts K, Pekny M, et al. PDGF-A signaling is a critical event in lung alveolar myofibroblast development and alveogenesis. Cell 1996;85:863–73.
25. Bonner JC, Lindroos PM, Rice AB, et al. Induction of PDGF receptor-alpha in rat myofibroblasts during pulmonary fibrogenesis in vivo. Am J Physiol 1998;274:L72–80.
26. Pache JC, Christakos PG, Gannon DE, et al. Myofibroblasts in diffuse alveolar damage of the lung. Mod Pathol 1998;11:1064–70.
27. Zhang K, Flanders KC, Phan SH. Cellular localization of transforming growth factor-beta expression in bleomycin-induced pulmonary fibrosis. Am J Pathol 1995;147:352–61.
28. Thet LA, Parra SC, Shelburne JD. Sequential changes in lung morphology during the repair of acute oxygen-induced lung injury in adult rats. Exp Lung Res 1986;11:209–28.
29. Fukuda Y, Ferrans VJ, Schoenberger CI, et al. Patterns of pulmonary structural remodeling after experimental paraquat toxicity: the morphogenesis of intraalveolar fibrosis. Am J Pathol 1985;118:452–75.
30. Zhang HY, Phan SH. Inhibition of myfibroblast apoptosis by transforming growth factor β1. Am J Respir Cell Mol Biol 1999;21:658–65.
31. Schachtner SK, Wang Y, Scott Baldwin H. Qualitative and quantitative analysis of embryonic pulmonary vessel formation. Am J Respir Cell Mol Biol 2000;22:157–65.
32. Maniscalco WM, Watkins RH, D'Angio CT, Ryan RM. Hyperoxic injury decreases alveolar epithelial cell expression of vascular endothelial growth factor (VEGF) in neonatal rabbit lung. Am J Respir Cell Mol Biol 1997;16:557–67.
33. Ferrara N, Carver-Moore K, Chen H, et al. Heterozygous embryonic lethality induced by targeted inactivation of the VEGF gene. Nature 1996;380:439–42.
34. Kawai N, Bloch DB, Filippov G, et al. Constitutive endothelial nitric oxide synthase gene expression is regulated during lung development. Am J Physiol 1995;268 (4 Pt 1): L589–95.
35. Parker TA, le Cras TD, Kinsella JP, Abman SH. Developmental changes in endothelial nitric oxide synthase expression and activity in ovine fetal lung. Am J Physiol Lung Cell Mol Physiol 2000;278:L202–8.
36. Fujita M, Kuwano K, Kunitake R, et al. Endothelial cell apoptosis in lipopolysaccharide-induced lung injury in mice. Int Arch Allergy Immunol 1998;117:202–8.
37. Piedboeuf B, Gamache M, Frenette J, et al. Increased endothelial cell expression of platelet-endothelial cell adhesion molecule-1 during hyperoxic lung injury. Am J Respir Cell Mol Biol 1998;19:543–53.
38. Lappin PB, Ross KL, King LE, et al. The response of pulmonary vascular endothelial cells to monocrotaline pyrrole: cell proliferation and DNA synthesis in vitro and in vivo. Toxicol Appl Pharmacol 1998;150:37–48.
39. Beilman G. Pathogenesis of oleic acid-induced lung injury in the rat: distribution of oleic acid during injury and early endothelial cell changes. Lipids 1995;30:817–23.
40. Woodcock-Mitchell J, White S, Stirewalt W, et al. Myosin isoform expression in developing and remodeling rat lung. Am J Respir Cell Mol Biol 1993;8:617–25.
41. Klekamp JG, Jarzecha K, Hoover RL, et al. Vascular endothelial growth factor is expressed in ovine pulmonary vascular smooth muscle cells in vitro and regulated by hypoxia and dexamethasone. Pediatr Res 1997;42:744–9.
42. Wen FQ, Watanabe K, Yoshida M. Lipopolysaccharide and cytokines enhance bradykinin-stimulated production of PGI2 by cultured human pulmonary artery smooth muscle cells. Cell Biol Int 1997;21:321–7.
43. Degnim AC, Nakayama DK. Nitric oxide and the pulmonary artery smooth muscle cell. Semin Pediatr Surg 1996;5:160–4.
44. Morita T, Mitsialis SA, Koike H, et al. Carbon monoxide controls the proliferation of hypoxic vascular smooth muscle cells. J Biol Chem 1997;272:32804–9.
45. Wen FQ, Watanabe K, Yoshida M. Eicosanoid profile in cultured human pulmonary artery smooth muscle cells treated with IL-1 beta and TNF alpha. Prostaglandins Leukot Essent Fatty Acids 1998;59:71–5.
46. Abman SH, Chatfield BA, Hall SL, McMurty IF. Role of endothelium-derived relaxing factor during transition of pulmonary circulation at birth. Am J Physiol 1990; 259:H1921–7.
47. Kourembanas S, Marsden PA, McQuillan LP, Faller DV. Hypoxia induces endothelin gene expression and secretion in cultured human endothelium. J Clin Invest 1991;88:1054–7.
48. Kourembanas S, Hannan RL, Faller DV. Oxygen tension regulates the expression of the platelet-derived growth

factor-B chain gene in human endothelial cells. J Clin Invest 1990;86:670–4.
49. Morita T, Mitsialis SA, Koike H, et al. Carbon monoxide controls the proliferation of hypoxic vascular smooth muscle cells. J Biol Chem 1997;272:32804–9.
50. Barghorn A, Koslowski M, Kromminga R, et al. Alpha-smooth muscle actin distribution in the pulmonary vasculature comparing hypoplastic and normal fetal lungs. Pediatr Pathol Lab Med 1998;18:5–22.
51. Khouri J, Langleben D. Platelet-activating factor stimulates lung pericyte growth in vitro. Am J Physiol 1996; 270:L298–304.
52. Hellstrom M, Kal NM, Lindahl P, et al. Role of PDGF-B and PDGFR-beta in recruitment of vascular smooth muscle cells and pericytes during embryonic blood vessel formation in the mouse. Development 1999; 126:3047–55.
53. Lindahl P, Johansson BR, Leveen P, Betsholtz C. Pericyte loss and microaneurysm formation in PDGF-B-deficient mice. Science 1997;277:242–5.
54. Khoury J, Langleben D. Effects of endotoxin on lung pericytes in vitro. Microvasc Res 1998;56:71–84.
55. Spindel ER, Sunday ME, Hofler H, et al. Transient elevation of messenger RNA encoding gastrin-releasing peptide, a putative pulmonary growth factor in human fetal lung. J Clin Invest 1987;80:1172–9.
56. King KA, Torday JS, Sunday ME. Bombesin and [Leu8] phyllolitorin promote fetal mouse lung branching morphogenesis via a receptor-mediated mechanism. Proc Natl Acad Sci U S A 1995;9:4357–61.
57. Aguayo SM, Schuyler WE, Murtagh JJ Jr, Roman J. Regulation of lung branching morphogenesis by bombesin-like peptides and neutral endopeptidase. Am J Respir Cell Mol Biol 1994;10:635–42.
58. Emanuel RL, Torday JS, Mu Q, et al. Bombesin-like peptides and receptors in normal fetal baboon lung: roles in lung growth and maturation. Am J Physiol 1999;277: L1003–17.
59. Sunday ME, Yoder BA, Cuttitta F, et al. Bombesin-like peptide mediates lung injury in a baboon model of bronchopulmonary dysplasia. J Clin Invest 1998;102:584–94.
60. Spurzem JR, Rennard SI, Romberger DJ. Bombesin-like peptides and airway repair: a recapitulation of lung development? Am J Respir Cell Mol Biol 1997;16:209–11.
61. Johnson DE, Georgieff MK. Pulmonary neuroendocrine cells; their secretory products and their potential roles in health and chronic lung disease in infancy. Am Rev Respir Dis 1989;140:1807–12.
62. Sunday ME, Willett CG. Induction and spontaneous regression of intense pulmonary neuroendocrine cell differentiation in a model of preneoplastic lung injury. Cancer Res 1992;52:2677–86s.
63. Johnson DE, Anderson WR, Burke BA. Pulmonary neuroendocrine cells in pediatric lung disease: alterations in airway structure in infants with bronchopulmonary dysplasia. Anat Rec 1993;236:115–9.
64. Hiemstra PS, van Wetering S, Stolk J. Neutrophil serine proteases and defensins in chronic obstructive pulmonary disease: effects on pulmonary epithelium. Eur Respir J 1998;12:1200–8.
65. Murakami K, Okajima K, Uchiba M. The prevention of lipopolysaccharide-induced pulmonary vascular injury by pretreatment with cepharanthine in rats. Am J Respir Crit Care Med 2000;161:57–63.
66. Sibille Y, Reynolds HY. Macrophages and polymorphonuclear neutrophils in lung defenses and injury. Am Rev Respir Dis 1990;141:471–501.
67. Warner AE. Pulmonary intravascular macrophages. Role in acute lung injury. Clin Chest Med 1996;17:125–35.
68. Shanley TP, Schmal H, Friedl HP, et al. Role of macrophage inflammatory protein-1 alpha (MIP-1 alpha) in acute lung injury in rats. J Immunol 1995;154:4793–802.
69. Warren JS, Jones ML, Flory CM. Analysis of monocyte chemoattractant protein 1-mediated lung injury using rat lung organ cultures. Am J Pathol 1993;143:894–906.
70. Vracko R. Significance of basal lamina for regeneration of injured lung. Virchows Arch A Pathol Anat 1972; 355:264–74.
71. Schuger L, O'Shea S, Rheinheimer J, Varani J. Laminin in lung development: effects of anti-laminin antibody in murine lung morphogenesis. Dev Biol 1990;137:26–32.
72. McGowan SE. Extracellular matrix and the regulation of lung development and repair. FASEB J 1992;6:2895–904.
73. Limper AH, Roman J. Fibronectin: a versatile matrix protein with roles in thoracic development, repair and infection. Chest 1992;101:1663–73.
74. Sinkin RA, Sanders RS, Horowitz S, et al. Cell-specific expression of fibronectin in adult and developing rat lung. Pediatr Res 1995;37:189–95.
75. Zhao Y, Young SL. Tenascin in rat lung development: in situ localization and cellular sources. Am J Physiol 1995; 269:L482–91.
76. Hirai Y, Nose A, Kobayashi S, Takeichi M. Expression and role of E- and P-cadherin adhesion molecules in embryonic histogenesis. Development 1989;105:263–70.
77. Romaris M, Bassols A, David G. Effect of transforming growth factor-beta 1 and basic fibroblast growth factor on the expression of cell surface proteoglycans in human lung fibroblasts: enhanced glycanation and fibronectin-binding of CD44 proteoglycan and downregulation of glypican. Biochem J 1995;310:73–81.
78. Koshida S, Hirai Y. Identification of cellular recognition sequence of epimorphin and critical role of cell/epimorphin interaction in lung branching morphogenesis. Biochem Biophys Res Commun 1997;234:522–5.
79. Levay-Young BK, Navre M. Growth and developmental regulation of wnt-2 (irp) gene in mesenchymal cells of fetal lung. Am J Physiol 1992;262:L672–83.
80. Huang S, Ingber DE. The structural and mechanical complexity of cell-growth control. Nat Cell Biol 1999; 1:E131–8.
81. Albeda SM. Endothelial and epithelial cell adhesion molecules. Am J Respir Cell Mol Biol 1991;4:195–203.
82. Hilfer SR, Rayner RM, Brown JW. Mesenchymal control of branching pattern in the fetal mouse lung. Tissue Cell 1985;7:523–38.
83. Shannon JM, Emrie A, Fisher JH, et al. Effect of a reconstituted basement membrane on expression of surfactant apoproteins in cultured adult rat alveolar type II cells. Am J Respir Cell Mol Biol 1990;2:183–92.

84. Warburton D, Wuenschell C, Flores-Delgado G, Anderson K. Commitment and differentiation of lung cell lineages. Biochem Cell Biol 1998;76:971–5.
85. Warburton D, Olver RE. Coordination of genetic, epigenetic and environmental factors in lung development, injury, and repair. Chest 1997;111:119–22S.
86. Zhao J, Tefft JD, Lee M, et al. Abrogation of betaglycan attenuates TGF-beta-mediated inhibition of embryonic murine lung branching morphogenesis in culture. Mech Dev 1998;75:67–79.
87. Zhou L, Dey CR, Wert SE, Whitsett JA. Arrested lung morphogenesis in transgenic mice bearing an SP-C-TGF-beta 1 chimeric gene. Dev Biol 1996;175:227–38.
88. Shi W, Heisterkemp N, Groffen J, et al. TGF-beta3-null mutation does not abrogate fetal lung maturation in vivo by glucocorticoids. Am J Physiol 1999;277:L1205–13.
89. Wang J, Kuliszewski M, Yee W, et al. Cloning and expression of glucocorticoid-induced genes in fetal rat lung fibroblasts: transforming growth factor-beta 3. J Biol Chem 1995;270:2722–8.
90. Assoian RK, Fleurdelys BE, Stevenson HC, et al. Expression and secretion of type beta transforming growth factor by activated human macrophages. Proc Natl Acad Sci U S A 1987;84:6020–4.
91. Laiho M, Saksela O, Keski-Oja J. Transforming growth factor beta induction of type-1 plasminogen activator-inhibitor: pericellular deposition and sensitivity to exogenous urokinase. J Biol Chem 1987;262:17467–74.
92. Edwards DR, Murphy G, Reynolds JJ, et al. Transforming growth factor beta modulates the expression of collagenase and metalloproteinase inhibitor. EMBO J 1987; 6:1899–904.
93. Santana A, Saxena B, Noble NA, et al. Increased expression of transforming growth factor beta isoforms (beta 1, beta 2, beta 3) in bleomycin-induced pulmonary fibrosis. Am J Respir Cell Mol Biol 1995;13:34–44.
94. Khalil N, Bereznay O, Sporn M, Greenberg AH. Macrophage production of transforming growth factor beta and fibroblast collagen synthesis in chronic pulmonary inflammation. J Exp Med 1989;170:727–37.
95. Finkelstein JN, Horowitz S, Sinkin RA, Ryan RM. Cellular and molecular responses to lung injury in relation to induction of tissue repair and fibrosis. Clin Perinatol 1992;19:603–20.
96. Kotecha S, Chan B, Azam N, et al. Increase in interleukin-8 and soluble intercellular adhesion molecule-1 in bronchoalveolar lavage fluid from premature infants who develop chronic lung disease. Arch Dis Child Fetal Neonatal Ed 1995;72:F90–6.
97. Adamson IYR, Bakowska J. Relationship of keratinocyte growth factor and hepatocyte growth factor levels in rat lung lavage fluid to epithelial cell regeneration after bleomycin. Am J Pathol 1999;155:949–54.
98. Ohmichi H, Koshimizu U, Matsumoto K, Nakamura T. Hepatocyte growth factor (HGF) acts as a mesenchyme-derived morphogenic factor during fetal lung development. Development 1998;125:1315–24.
99. Sato N, Takahashi H. Hepatocyte growth factor promotes growth and lumen formation of fetal lung epithelial cells in primary culture. Respirology 1997;2:185–91.
100. Itakura A, Kurauchi O, Morikawa S, et al. Human amniotic fluid mitogenic activity for fetal alveolar type II cells by way of hepatocyte growth factor. Obstet Gynecol 1997;89:729–33.
101. Post M, Souza P, Liu J, et al. Keratinocyte growth factor and its receptor are involved in regulating early lung branching. Development 1996;122:3107–15.
102. Shiratori M, Oshika E, Ung LP, et al. Keratinocyte growth factor and embryonic rat lung morphogenesis. Am J Respir Cell Mol Biol 1996;15:328–38.
103. Simonet WS, DeRose ML, Bucay N, et al. Pulmonary malformation in transgenic mice expressing human keratinocyte growth factor in the lung. Proc Natl Acad Sci U S A 1995;92:12461–5.
104. Sugahara K, Rubin JS, Mason RJ, et al. Keratinocyte growth factor increases in mRNAs for SP-A and SP-B in adult rat alveolar type II cells in culture. Am J Physiol 1995;169:L344–50.
105. Deterding RR, Havill A, Yano T, et al. Prevention of bleomycin-induced lung injury in rats by keratinocyte growth factor. Proc Assoc Am Physicians 1997; 109:254–68.
106. Panos RJ, Bak PM, Simonet WS, et al. Intratracheal instillation of keratinocyte growth factor decreases hyperoxia-induced mortality in rats. J Clin Invest 1995;96:2026–33.
107. Panos RJ, Patel R, Bak PM. Intratracheal administration of hepatocyte growth factor/scatter factor stimulates rat alveolar type II cell proliferation in vivo. Am J Respir Cell Mol Biol 1996;15:574–81.
108. Ciardello F, Tortora G. Interactions between the epidermal growth factor receptor and type I protein kinase A: biological significance and therapeutic implications. Clin Cancer Res 1998;4:821–8.
109. Strandjord TP, Clark JG, Madtes DK. Expression of TGF-alpha, EGF, and EGF receptor in fetal rat lung. Am J Physiol 1994;267:L384–9.
110. Ruocco S, Lallemand A, Tournier JM, Gaillard D. Expression and localization of epidermal growth factor, transforming growth factor-alpha and localization of their common receptor in fetal human lung development. Pediatr Res 1996;39:448–55.
111. Klein JM, Fritz BL, McCarthy TA, et al. Localization of epidermal growth factor receptor in alveolar epithelium during human fetal lung development in vitro. Exp Lung Res 1995;21:917–39.
112. Nielsen HC, Martin A, Volpe MV, et al. Growth factor control of growth and epithelial differentiation in embryonic lung. Biochem Mol Med 1997;60:38–48.
113. Nogawa H, Ito T. Branching morphogenesis of embryonic mouse lung epithelium in mesenchyme-free culture. Development 1995;121:1015–22.
114. Chinoy MR, Zgleszewski SE, Cilley RE, et al. Influence of epidermal growth factor and transforming growth factor beta-1 on patterns of fetal mouse lung branching morphogenesis in organ culture. Pediatr Pulmonol 1991;25:244–56.
115. Ganser GL, Stricklin GP, Matrisian LM. EGF and TGF alpha influence in vitro lung development by the induction of matrix-degrading metalloproteinases. Int J Dev Biol 1991;35:453–61.

116. Gross I, Dynia DW, Rooney SA, et al. Influence of epidermal growth factor on fetal rat lung development in vitro. Pediatr Res 1986;20:473–7.
117. Edwards LA, Read LC, Nishio SJ, et al. Comparison of the distinct effects of epidermal growth factor and betamethasone on the morphogenesis of the gas exchange region and differentiation of alveolar type II cells in lung of fetal rhesus monkeys. J Pharmacol Exp Ther 1995;274:1025–32.
118. Sundell HW, Gray ME, Serenius FS, et al. Effects of epidermal growth factor on lung maturation in fetal lambs. Am J Pathol 1980;100:707–25.
119. Goetzman BW, Read LC, Plopper CG, et al. Prenatal exposure to epidermal growth factor attenuates respiratory distress syndrome in rhesus infants. Pediatr Res 1994; 35:30–6.
120. Miettinen PJ, Berger JE, Meneses J, et al. Epithelial immaturity and multiorgan failure in mice lacking epidermal growth factor receptor. Nature 1995;376:337–41.
121. Threadgill DW, Dlugosz AA, Hansen LA, et al. Targeted disruption of mouse EGF receptor: effect of genetic background on mutant phenotype. Science 1995; 269:230–4.
122. Sibilia M, Wagner EF. Strain-dependent epithelial defects in mice lacking the EGF receptor. Science 1995;269:234–8.
123. Miettinen PJ, Warburton D, Bu D, et al. Impaired lung branching morphogenesis in the absence of functional EGF receptor. Dev Biol 1997;186:224–36.
124. Yoshimura S, Masuzaki H, Miura K, et al. Effect of epidermal growth factor on lung growth in experimental lung pulmonary hypoplasia. Early Hum Dev 2000; 57:61–9.
125. Zgleszewski SE, Cilley RE, Krummel TM, Chinoy MR. Effects of dexamethasone, growth factors, and tracheal ligation on the development of nitrofen-exposed hypoplastic murine fetal lungs in organ culture. J Pediatr Surg 1999;34:1187–95.
126. Van Winkle LS, Isaac JM, Plopper CG. Distribution of epidermal growth factor receptor and ligands during bronchiolar epithelial repair from napthalene-induced Clara cell injury in the mouse. Am J Pathol 1997; 151:443–59.
127. Nici L, Medina M, Frackleton AR. The epidermal growth factor receptor network in type 2 pneumocytes exposed to hyperoxia in vitro. Am J Physiol 1996;270:L242–50.
128. Madtes DK, Bushby HK, Strandjord TP, Clark JG. Expression of transforming growth factor-alpha and epidermal growth factor receptor is increased following bleomycin-induced lung injury in rats. Am J Respir Cell Mol Biol 1994;11:540–51.
129. Kumar RK, Velan GM, O'Grady R. Epidermal growth factor-like activity in bronchoalveolar lavage fluid in experimental silicosis. Growth Factors 1994;10:163–70.
130. Stahlman MT, Orth DN, Gray ME. Immunocytochemical localization of epidermal growth factor in the developing human respiratory system in acute and chronic lung disease in the neonate. Lab Invest 1989;60:539–47.
131. Strandjord TP, Clark JG, Guralnick DE, Madtes DK. Immunolocalization of transforming growth factor-alpha, epidermal growth factor (EGF), and EGF-receptor in normal and injured developing human lung. Pediatr Res 1995;38:851–6.
132. Ross R. Platelet-derived growth factor. Lancet 1989; i:1179–82.
133. Han RN, Mawdsley C, Souza P, et al. Platelet-derived growth factors and growth-related genes in rat lung. III. Immunolocalization during fetal development. Pediatr Res 1992;31:323–9.
134. Han RN, Liu J, Tanswell AK, Post M. Ontogeny of platelet-derived growth factor receptor in fetal rat lung. Microsc Res Tech 1993;26:381–8.
135. Snyder LS, Hertz MI, Peterson MS, et al. Acute lung injury: pathogenesis of intraalveolar fibrosis. J Clin Invest 1991;20:113–21.
136. Martinet Y, Rom WM, Grotendorst GR, et al. Exaggerated spontaneous release of platelet-derived growth factor by alveolar macrophage from patients with idiopathic pulmonary fibrosis. N Engl J Med 1987;317:202–9.
137. Lasky JA, Tonthat B, Liu JY, et al. Upregulation of the PDGF-alpha receptor precedes asbestos-induced lung fibrosis in rats. Am J Respir Crit Care Med 1998; 157:1652–7.
138. Hoyle GW, Li J, Finkelstein JB, et al. Emphysematous lesions, inflammation, and fibrosis in the lungs of transgenic mice overexpressing platelet-derived growth factor. Am J Pathol 1999;153:1763–75.
139. Powell PP, Klagsbrun M, Abraham JA, Jones RC. Eosinophils expressing heparin-binding EGF like growth factor mRNA localize around lung microvessels in pulmonary hypertension. Am J Pathol 1993;143:784–93.
140. Powell PP, Wang CC, Horinouchi H, et al. Differential expression of fibroblast growth factor receptors 1 and 4 and ligand genes in late fetal and early postnatal rat lung. Am J Respir Cell Mol Biol 1998;19:563–72.
141. Sannes PL. Differences in basement membrane-associated microdomains of type I and type II pneumocytes in the rat and rabbit lung. J Histochem Cytochem 1984; 32:827–33.
142. Gonzalez AM, Hill DJ, Logan A, et al. Distribution of fibroblast growth factor (FGF-2) and FGF receptor-1 messenger RNA expression and protein presence in the mid-trimester human fetus. Pediatr Res 1996; 39:375–85.
143. Han RN, Liu J, Tanswell AK, Post M. Expression of basic fibroblast growth factor and receptor: immunolocalization studies in developing rat fetal lung. Pediatr Res 1992;31:435–40.
144. Metzger RJ, Krasnow MA. Genetic control of branching morphogenesis. Science 1999;284:221–8.
145. Matsui R, Brody JS, Yu Q. FGF-2 induces surfactant protein gene expression in foetal rat lung epithelial cells through a MAPK-independent pathway. Cell Signal 1999;11:221–8.
146. Min H, Danilenko DM, Scully SA, et al. FGF-10 is required for both limb and lung development and exhibits striking function similarity to Drosophila branchless. Genes Dev 1998;12:3156–61.
147. Bellusci S, Grindley J, Emoto J, et al. Fibroblast growth factor-10 (FGF-10) and branching morphogenesis in the embryonic mouse lung. Development 1997;124:4867–78.

148. Peters K, Werner S, Liao X, et al. Targeted expression of a dominant negative FGF receptor blocks branching morphogenesis and epithelial differentiation of the mouse lung. EMBO J 1994;12:3296–301.
149. Weinstein M, Xu X, Ohyama K, Deng CX. FGFR-3 and FGFR-4 function cooperatively to direct alveogenesis in the murine lung. Development 1998;125:3615–23.
150. Barrios R, Pardo A, Ramos C, et al. Upregulation of acidic fibroblast growth factor during development of experimental lung fibrosis. Am J Physiol 1997;273:L451–8.
151. Lemaire I, Beaudoin H, Dubois C. Cytokine regulation of lung fibroblast proliferation. Pulmonary and systemic changes in asbestos-induced pulmonary fibrosis. Am Rev Respir Dis 1986;134:653–8.
152. Stiles AD, D'Ercole AJ. The insulin-like growth factors and the lung. Am J Respir Cell Mol Biol 1990;3:93–100.
153. Retsch-Bogart GZ, Moats-Staats BM, Howard K, et al. Cellular localization of messenger RNAs for insulin-like growth factors (IGFs), their receptors and binding proteins during fetal rat lung development. Am J Respir Cell Mol Biol 1996;14:61–9.
154. Moats-Staats BM, Price WA, Xu L, et al. Regulation of the insulin-growth factor system during normal rat lung development. Am J Respir Cell Mol Biol 1997;12:56–64.
155. Wallen LD, Myint W, Nygard K, et al. Cellular distribution of insulin-like growth factor binding protein mRNAs and peptides during rat lung development. J Endocrinol 1997;155:313–27.
156. Melnick M, Chen H, Rich KA, Jaskoll T. Developmental expression of insulin-like growth factor II receptor (IGF-IIR) in congenic mouse embryonic lungs: correlation between IGF-IIR mRNA and protein levels and heterochronic lung development. Mol Reprod Dev 1996;44:159–70.
157. Stiles AD, Moats-Staats BM. Production and action of insulin-like growth factor I/somatomedin C in primary cultures of fetal lung fibroblasts. Am J Respir Cell Mol Biol 1989;1:21–6.
158. Lallemand AV, Ruocoo SM, Joly PM, Gaillard DA. In vivo localization of the insulin-like growth factors I and II (IGF I and IGF II) gene expression during human lung development. Int J Dev Biol 1995;39:529–37.
159. Veness-Meehan KA, Moats-Staats BM, Price WA, Stiles AD. Re-emergence of a fetal pattern of insulin-like growth factor expression during hyperoxic rat lung injury. Am J Respir Cell Mol Biol 1997;16:538–48.
160. Cazals V, Mouhieddine B, Maitre B, et al. Insulin-like growth factors, their binding proteins, and transforming growth factor-beta 1 in oxidant-arrested lung alveolar epithelial cells. J Biol Chem 1994;269:14111–7.
161. Han RN, Buch S, Tseu I, et al. Changes in structure, mechanics, and insulin-like growth factor-related gene expression in the lungs of newborn rats exposed to air or 60% oxygen. Pediatr Res 1996;39:921–9.
162. Moromisato DY, Moromisato MY, Zanconato S, Roberts CTJ. Effect of hypoxia on lung, heart, and liver insulin-like growth factor-I gene and receptor expression in the newborn rat. Crit Care Med 1996;24:919–24.
163. Melloni B, Lesur O, Bouhadiba T, et al. Effect of exposure to silica on human alveolar macrophages in supporting growth activity in type II epithelial cells. Thorax 1996;51:781–6.
164. Bless NM, Smith D, Charlton J, et al. Protective effects of an aptamer inhibitor of neutrophil elastase in lung inflammatory lung. Curr Biol 1997;7:877–80.
165. Peterson MW. Neutrophil cathepsin G increases transendothelial albumin flux. J Lab Clin Med 1989; 113:297–308.
166. Peterson MW, Walter ME, Nygaard SD. Effect of neutrophil mediators on epithelial permeability. Am J Respir Cell Mol Biol 1995;13:719–27.
167. Rochat T, Casale J, Hunninghake GW, Peterson MW. Neutrophil cathepsin G increases permeability of cultured type II pneumocytes. Am J Physiol 1988; 255:C6603–11.
168. Janoff A, White R, Carp H, et al. Lung injury induced by leukocyte proteases. Am J Pathol 1979;97:111–36.
169. Knight KR, Burdon JG, Cook L, et al. The proteinase-antiproteinase theory of emphysema: a speculative analysis of recent advances into the pathogenesis of emphysema. Respirology 1997;2:91–5.
170. Sallenave JM, Si-Ta har M, Cox G, et al. Secretory leukocyte proteinase inhibitor is a major leukocyte elastase inhibitor in human neutrophils. J Leukoc Biol 1997; 61:695–702.
171. Perlmutter DH, Travis J, Punsal PI. Elastase regulates the synthesis of its inhibitor, alpha-1-proteinase inhibitor, and exaggerates the defect in homozygous PiZZ alpha 1 PI deficiency. J Clin Invest 1988;81:1775–80.
172. Sakamaki F, Ishizaka A, Urano T, et al. Effect of a specific neutrophil elastase inhibitor, ONO-5046, on endotoxin-induced acute lung injury. Am J Respir Crit Care Med 1996;153:391–7.
173. Uchiba M, Okajima K, Murakami K, et al. Endotoxin-induced pulmonary vascular injury is mainly mediated by activated neutrophils in rats. Thromb Res 1995; 78:117–25.
174. Miyazaki Y, Inoue T, Kyi M, et al. Effects of a neutrophil elastase inhibitor (ONO-5046) on acute pulmonary injury induced by tumor necrosis factor alpha and activated neutrophils in isolated perfused rabbit lungs. Am J Respir Crit Care Med 1998;157:89–94.
175. Wang HG, Shibamoto T, Miyahara T, et al. Effect of ONO-5046, a specific neutrophil elastase inhibitor, on the phorbol myristate acetate-induced injury in isolated dog lung. Exp Lung Res 1999;25:55–67.
176. Rees DD, Brain JD. Effects of cystic fibrosis airway secretions on rat lung: role of neutrophil elastase. Am J Physiol 1995;269:L195–202.
177. Rees DD, Rogers RA, Cooley J, et al. Recombinant human monocyte/neutrophil elastase inhibitor protects rat lungs against injury from cystic fibrosis airway secretions. Am J Respir Cell Mol Biol 1999;20:69–78.
178. Rudolphus A, Stolk J, Dijkman JH, Kramps JA. Inhibition of lipopolysaccharide-induced pulmonary emphysema by intratracheally instilled recombinant secretory leukocyte proteinase inhibitor. Am Rev Respir Dis 1993; 147:442–7.
179. Koppel R, Han RN, Cox D, et al. Alpha-1-antitrypsin protects neonatal rats from pulmonary vascular and

parenchymal effects of oxygen toxicity. Pediatr Res 1994;36:763–70.
180. Weitz JI, Silverman EK, Thong B, Campbell EJ. Plasma levels of elastase-specific fibrinopeptides correlate with proteinase inhibitor phenotype: evidence for increased elastase activity in subjects with homozygous and heterozygous deficiency of alpha-1-proteinase inhibitor. J Clin Invest 1992;89:766–73.
181. Virca GD, Schnebli HP. The elastase/alpha 1-proteinase inhibitor balance in the lung. Schweiz Med Wochenschr 1984;114:895–8.
182. Hautamaki RD, Kobayashi DK, Senior RM, Shapiro SD. Requirement for macrophage elastase for cigarette smoke-induced emphysema in mice. Science 1997; 277:2002–4.
183. Allen ED. Opportunities for the use of aerosolized alpha-1-antitrypsin for the treatment of cystic fibrosis. Chest 1996;110:256–60S.
184. Ogden BE, Murphy SA, Saunders GC, et al. Neonatal lung neutrophils and elastase/proteinase inhibitor imbalance. Am Rev Respir Dis 1984;130:817–21.
185. Watterberg KL, Carmichael DF, Gerdes JS, et al. Secretory leukocyte protease inhibitor and lung inflammation in developing bronchopulmonary dysplasia. J Pediatr 1994;125:264–9.
186. Rabinovitch M. EVE and beyond, retro and prospective insights. Am J Physiol 1999;277:L5–12.
187. Maruyama K, Ye C, Woo H, et al. Chronic hypoxic pulmonary hypertension in rats and increased elastolytic activity. Am J Physiol 1991;261:H1716–26.
188. Ye C, Rabinovitch M. Inhibition of elastolysis by SC-37698 reduces development and progression of monocrotaline pulmonary hypertension. Am J Physiol 1991; 261:H1255–67.
189. Bingle CD. Thyroid transcription factor-1. Int J Biochem Cell Biol 1997;29:1471–3.
190. Shaw-White JR, Bruno MD, Whitsett JA. GATA-6 activates transcription of thyroid transcription factor-1. J Biol Chem 1999;274:2658–64.
191. Motoyama J, Liu J, Mo R, et al. Essential function of Gli2 and Gli3 in the formation of lung, trachea and oesophagus. Nat Genet 1998;20:54–7.
192. Grindley JC, Bellusci S, Perkins D, Hogan BL. Evidence for the involvement of the *Gli* gene family in embryonic mouse lung development. Dev Biol 1997;188:337–48.
193. Bellusci S, Furuta Y, Rush MG, et al. Involvement of Sonic hedgehog (Shh) in mouse embryonic lung growth and morphogenesis. Development 1997;124:53–63.
194. Litingtung Y, Lei L, Westphal H, Chiang C. *Sonic hedgehog* is essential to foregut development. Nat Genet 1998; 20:58–61.
195. Krumlauf R. *Hox* genes in vertebrate development. Cell 1994;78:191–201.
196. Kappen C. *Hox* genes in the lung. Am J Respir Cell Mol Biol 1996;15:156–62.
197. Aubin J, Lemieux M, Tremblay M, et al. Early postnatal lethality in Hoxa-5 mutant mice is attributable to respiratory tract defects. Dev Biol 1997;192:432–45.
198. Volpe MV, Martin A, Vosatka RJ, et al. Hoxb-5 expression in the developing mouse lung suggests a role in branching morphogenesis and epithelial cell fate. Histochem Cell Biol 1997;108:495–504.
199. Isaac DD, Andrew DJ. Tubulogenesis in Drosophila: a requirement for the trachealess gene product. Genes Dev 1996;10:103–7.
200. Yu Ay, Frid MG, Shimoda LA, et al. Temporal, spatial and oxygen-regulated expression of hypoxia-inducible factor-1 in the lung. Am J Physiol 1998;275:L818–26.
201. Iyer NV, Kotch LE, Agani F, et al. Cellular and developmental control of O_2 homeostasis by hypoxia-inducible factor 1α. Genes Dev 1998;12:149–62.
202. Ryan HE, Lo J, Johnson RS. HIF-1α is required for solid tumor formation and embryonic vascularization. EMBO J 1998;17:3005–15.
203. Yu AY, Shimoda LA, Iyer NV, et al. Impaired physiological responses to chronic hypoxia in mice partially deficient for hypoxia-inducible factor 1α. J Clin Invest 1999; 103:691–6.
204. Schuger L, Varani J, Mitra RJ, Gilbride K. Retinoic acid stimulates mouse lung development by a mechanism involving epithelial-mesenchymal interaction and regulation of epidermal growth factor receptors. Dev Biol 1993;159:462–73.
205. Massaro GD, Massaro D. Postnatal treatment with retinoic acid increases the number of pulmonary alveoli in rats. Am J Physiol 1996;270:L305–10.
206. Massaro GD, Massaro D. Retinoic acid treatment abrogates elastase-induced pulmonary emphysema in rats. Nat Med 1997;3:675–7.
207. Simeonova PP, Leonard S, Flood L, et al. Redox-dependent regulation of interleukin-8 by tumor necrosis factor-α in lung epithelial cells. Lab Invest 1999;79:1027–37.
208. Cazals V, Nabeyrat E, Corroyer S, et al. Role for NF-kappa B in mediating the effects of hyperoxia on IGF-binding protein 2 promoter activity in lung alveolar epithelial cells. Biochim Biophys Acta 1999;1448:349–62.
209. Luster MI, Simeonova PP. Asbestos induces inflammatory cytokines in the lung through redox sensitive transcription factors. Toxicol Lett 1998;102:271–5.
210. Ray A, Ray BK. Persistent expression of serum amyloid A during experimentally induced chronic inflammatory condition in rabbit involves differential activation of SAF, NF-kappa B and C/EBP transcription factors. J Immunol 1999;163:2143–50.
211. Ballard RA, Ballard PL, Granberg JP, Sniderman S. Prenatal administration of betamethasone for prevention of respiratory distress syndrome. J Pediatr 1979; 94:97–101.
212. Schellenberg JC, Liggins GC. New approaches to hormonal acceleration of fetal lung maturation. J Perinat Med 1987;15:447–52.
213. Massaro GD, Massaro D. Formation of alveoli in rats: postnatal effect of prenatal dexamethasone. Am J Physiol 1992;263:L37–41.
214. Massaro D, Teich N, Maxwell S, et al. Postnatal development of alveoli: regulation and evidence for a critical period. J Clin Invest 1985;76:1297–305.
215. Massaro D, Massaro GD. Dexamethasone accelerates postnatal alveolar wall thinning and alters wall composition. Am J Physiol 1986;251:R218–24.

216. Harkavy KL, Scanlong JW, Chowdhry PK, Grylack LJ. Dexamethasone therapy for chronic lung disease in ventilator- and oxygen-dependent infants: a controlled trial. J Pediatr 1989;115:979–83.
217. O'Shea TM, Kothadia JM, Klinepeter KL, et al. Follow-up of preterm infants treated with dexamethasone for chronic lung disease. Am J Dis Child 1993;147:658–61.
218. Anonymous. Australian collaborative trial of antenatal thyrotropin-releasing hormone (ACTOBAT) for prevention of neonatal respiratory disease. Lancet 1995; 345:877–82.
219. Ballard RA, Ballard PL, Creasy RK, et al. Respiratory disease in very-low-birthweight infants after prenatal thyrotropin-releasing hormone and glucocorticoid. Lancet 1992;339:510–5.
220. Massaro D, Teich N, Massaro GD. Postnatal development of pulmonary alveoli: modulation in rats by thyroid hormones. Am J Physiol 1986;250:R51–5.
221. Klein JM, Nielsen HC. Sex-specific differences in rabbit fetal lung maturation in response to epidermal growth factor. Biochim Biophys Acta 1992;1133:121–6.
222. Klein JM, Nielsen HC. Androgen regulation of epidermal growth factor receptor binding activity during fetal rabbit lung development. J Clin Invest 1993;91:425–31.
223. Floros J, Nielsen HC, Torday JS. Dihydrotestosterone blocks fetal lung fibroblast-pneumocyte factor at a pretranslational level. J Biol Chem 1987;262:13592–8.
224. Massaro GD, Mortola JP, Massaro D. Estrogen modulates the dimensions of the lung's gas exchange surface area and alveoli in female rats. Am J Physiol 1996;270:L110–4.
225. Crouch EC. Collectins and pulmonary host defense. Am J Respir Cell Mol Biol 1998;19:177–201.
226. LeVine AM, Kurak KE, Wright JR, et al. Surfactant protein-A binds group B streptococcus enhancing phagocytosis and clearance from lungs of surfactant protein-A-deficient mice. Am J Respir Cell Mol Biol 1999;20:279–86.
227. LeVine A, Kurak KE, Bruno MD, et al. Surfactant protein-A-deficient mice are susceptible to *Pseudomonas aeruginosa* infection. Am J Respir Cell Mol Biol 1998; 19:700–8.
228. Harrod KS, Trapnell BC, Otake K, et al. SP-A enhances viral clearance and inhibits inflammation after pulmonary adenoviral infection. Am J Physiol 1999; 277:L580–8.
229. Botas C, Poulain F, Akiyama J, et al. Altered surfactant homeostasis and alveolar type II cell morphology in mice lacking surfactant protein D. Proc Natl Acad Sci U S A 1998;95:11869–74.
230. Restrepo CI, Dong Q, Savov J, et al. Surfactant protein D stimulates phagocytosis of *Pseudomonas aeruginosa* by alveolar macrophages. Am J Respir Cell Mol 1999; 21:576–85.
231. Horowitz S, Watkins RH, Auten RLJ, et al. Differential accumulation of surfactant protein A, B, and C mRNAs in two epithelial cell types of hyperoxic lung. Am J Respir Cell Mol Biol 1991;5:511–5.
232. McIntosh JC, Swyers AH, Fisher JH, Wright JR. Surfactant proteins A and D increase in response to intratracheal lipopolysaccharide. Am J Respir Cell Mol Biol 1996; 15:509–19.
233. Awasthi S, Coalson JJ, Crouch E, et al. Surfactant proteins A and D in premature baboons with chronic lung injury. Evidence for an inhibition of secretion. Am J Respir Crit Care Med 1999;160:942–9.
234. Liley HG, White RT, Warr RG, et al. Regulation of messenger RNAs for the hydrophobic surfactant proteins in human lung. J Clin Invest 1989;83:1191–7.
235. Tokieda K, Whitsett JA, Clark JC, et al. Pulmonary dysfunction in neonatal SP-B-deficient mice. Am J Phsyiol 1997;273:L875–82.
236. deMello DE, Nogee LM, Heyman S, et al. Molecular and phenotypic variability in the congenital alveolar proteinosis syndrome associated with inherited surfactant protein B deficiency. J Pediatr 1994;125:43–50.
237. Nogee LM, Garnier G, Dietz HC, et al. A mutation in the surfactant protein B gene responsible for fatal neonatal respiratory disease in multiple kindreds. J Clin Invest 1994;93:1860–3.
238. Nogee LM, deMello DE, Dehner LP, Colten HR. Brief report: deficiency of pulmonary surfactant protein B in congenital alveolar proteinosis. N Engl J Med 1993; 328:406–10.
239. Tokieda K, Iwamoto HS, Bachurski C, et al. Surfactant protein-B-deficient mice are susceptible to hyperoxic lung injury. Am J Respir Cell Mol Biol 1999;21:463–72.
240. Tokieda K, Ikegami M, Wert SE, et al. Surfactant protein B corrects oxygen-induced pulmonary dysfunction in heterozygous surfactant protein B-deficient mice. Pediatr Res 1999;46:708–14.
241. Putman E, van Golde LM, Haagsman HP. Toxic oxidant species and their impact on the pulmonary surfactant system. Lung 1997;175:75–103.
242. Yang L, Quan S, Abraham NG. Retrovirus-mediated HO gene transfer into endothelial cells protects against oxidant-induced injury. Am J Physiol 1999;277:L127–33.
243, Dennery PA, Spitz DR, Yang G, et al. Oxygen toxicity and iron accumulation in the lungs of mice lacking heme oxygenase-2. J Clin Invest 1998;101:1001–11.
244. Brigham KL. Oxidant stress and adult respiratory distress syndrome. Eur Respir J Suppl 1990;11:482–4S.
245. Dobashi K, Asayama K, Hayashibe H, et al. Immunohistochemical study of copper-zinc and manganese superoxide dismutases in the lungs of human fetuses and newborn infants: developmental profile and alterations in hyaline membrane disease and bronchopulmonary dysplasia. Virchows Arch A Pathol Anat Histopathol 1993;423:177–84.
246. Phylactos AC, Leaf AA, Costeloe K, Crawford MA. Erythrocyte cupric/zinc superoxide dismutase exhibits reduced activity in preterm and low-birthweight infants at birth. Acta Paediatr 1995;84:1421–5.
247. Huertas JR, Palomino N, Ochoa JJ, et al. Lipid peroxidation and antioxidants in erythrocyte membranes of full-term and preterm newborns. Biofactors 1998; 8:133–7.
248. Saugstad OD. Mechanisms of tissue injury by oxygen radicals: implications for neonatal disease. Acta Pediatr 1996;85:1–4.
249. Jain A, Mehta T, Auld PA, et al. Glutathione metabolism in newborns: evidence for glutathione deficiency in

plasma, bronchoalveolar lavage fluid, and lymphocytes in prematures. Pediatr Pulmonol 1995;29:160–6.

250. Frank L, Autor AP, Roberts RJ. Oxygen therapy and hyaline membrane disease: the effect of hyperoxia on pulmonary superoxide dismutase activity and the mediating role of plasma or serum. J Pediatr 1977; 90:105–10.
251. Rosenfeld W, Evans H, Concepcion L, et al. Prevention of bronchopulmonary dysplasia by administration of bovine superoxide dismutase in preterm infants with respiratory distress syndrome. J Pediatr 1984;105:781–5.
252. Rosenfeld WN, Davis JM, Parton L, et al. Safety and pharmacokinetics of recombinant human superoxide dismutase administered intratracheally to premature neonates with respiratory distress syndrome. Pediatrics 1996;97:811–7.
253. Smith RE. Chemotactic cytokines mediate leukocyte recruitment in fibrotic lung disease. Biol Signals 1996; 5:223–31.
254. Driscoll KE. Macrophage inflammatory proteins: biology and role in pulmonary inflammation. Exp Lung Res 1994;20:473–90.
255. Johnston CJ, Finkelstein JN, Gelein R, Overdorster G. Pulmonary cytokine and chemokine mRNA levels after inhalation of lipopolysaccharide in C57BL/6 mice. Toxicological Sci 1998;46:300–7.
256. D'Angio CT, Johnston CJ, Wright TW, et al. Chemokine mRNA alterations in newborn and adult mouse lung during acute hyperoxia. Exp Lung Res 1998;24:685–702.
257. Brieland JK, Jones ML, Clarke SJ, et al. Effect of acute inflammatory lung injury on the expression of monocyte chemoattractant protein-1 (MCP-1) in rat pulmonary alveolar macrophages. Am J Respir Cell Mol Biol 1992;7:134–9.
258. Czermak BJ, Sarma V, Bless NM, et al. In vitro and in vivo dependency of chemokine generation on C5a and TNF-alpha. J Immunol 1999;162:2321–5.
259. D'Angio CT, LoMonaco MB, Chaudhry SA, et al. Discordant pulmonary proinflammatory cytokine expression during acute hyperoxia in the newborn rabbit. Exp Lung Res 1999;25(5):443–65.
260. Sherman TS, Chen Z, Yuhanna IS, et al. Nitric oxide synthase isoform expression in the developing lung epithelium. Am J Physiol 1999;276:L383–90.
261. Shaul PW, Pace MC, Chen Z, Brannon TS. Developmental changes in prostacyclin synthesis are conserved in cultured pulmonary endothelium and vascular smooth muscle. Am J Respir Cell Mol Biol 1999;20:113–21.
262. Shaul PW. Regulation of vasodilator synthesis during lung development. Early Hum Dev 1999;54:271–94.
263. Roberts JD Jr, Fineman JR, Morin FC III, et al. Inhaled nitric oxide and persistent pulmonary hypertension of the newborn. N Engl J Med 1997;336:605–10.
264. Group NINOS. Inhaled nitric oxide in full-term and nearly full-term infants with hypoxic respiratory failure. N Engl J Med 1997;336:597–604.
265. Steudel W, Watanabe M, Dikranian K, et al. Expression of nitric oxide synthase isoforms (NOS II and NOS III) in adult rat lung in hyperoxic pulmonary hypertension. Cell Tissue Res 1999;295:317–29.
266. Bergeron M, Ferriero DM, Sharp FR. Developmental expression of heme oxygenase-1 (HSP32) in rat brain: an immunocytochemical study. Dev Brain Res 1998; 105:181–94.
267. Wong HR,Wispe JR. The stress response and the lung. Am J Physiol 1997;273:L1–9.
268. Jia YX, Sekizawa K, Okinaga S, et al. Role of heme oxygenase in pulmonary response to antigen challenge in sensitized rats in vivo. Int Arch Allergy Immunol 1999;120:141–5.
269. Otterbein LE, Kolls JK, Mantell LL, et al. Exogenous administration of heme oxygenase-1 by gene transfer provides protection against hyperoxia-induced lung injury. J Clin Invest 1999;103:1047–54.
270. Otterbein LE, Sylvester SL, Choi AM. Hemoglobin provides protection against lethal endotoxemia in rats: the role of heme oxygenase-1. Am J Respir Cell Mol Biol 1995;13:595–601.
271. Christou H, Morita T, Hsieh C-M, et al. Prevention of hypoxia-induced pulmonary hypertension by enhancement of endogenous heme oxygenase-1 in the rat. Circ Res. 2000;86:1224–9.
272. Otterbein LE, Mantell LL,Choi AM. Carbon monoxide provides protection against hyperoxic lung injury. Am J Physiol 1999;276:L688–94.
273. Lefer AM, Ma X-L, Lefer DJ. Vasodilator and anti-neutrophil activities of carbon monoxide compared with nitric oxide. Circulation 1993;88:A3036.
274. Morita T, Kourembanas S. Endothelial cell expression of vasoconstrictors and growth factors is regulated by smooth muscle cell–derived carbon monoxide. J Clin Invest 1995;96:2676–82.
275. Thom SR, Ohnishi ST, Fisher D, et al. Pulmonary vascular stress from carbon monoxide. Toxicol Appl Pharmacol 1999;154:12–9.

CHAPTER 9

Development of the Thoracic Cage

Julian Allen, MD, Karen W. Gripp, MD

The chest wall, including the rib cage and respiratory muscles, comprises the "pump" component of the respiratory system. The pump component is responsible for the ventilatory (as opposed to gas exchange) function of the system.[1] Ventilatory success depends not on pump function alone but on a balance between pump function and the magnitude of the load upon which the pump is acting[2] (Figure 9–1). Respiratory loads are primarily elastic and resistive and can arise from the lung or the chest wall itself. The thoracic cage can thus occupy both sides of the balance shown in Figure 9–1, and disorders of the thoracic cage can affect both components as well. This chapter describes how chest wall function changes with development, some of the basic mechanisms by which congenital abnormalities of the chest wall are produced, and the evaluation of chest wall dysfunction.

Growth and Development of the Chest Wall

The Rib Cage

Structural changes

Ossification of the chest wall begins in utero and continues until approximately the 25th year. Vertebral and rib ossification start by the end of the embryonic period (7th week of gestation).[3] Sternal ossification begins during the 5th month of fetal life. Ossification is complete by age 25 years,[4] although progressive calcification of the costal cartilages can continue into old age.[5]

Major configurational changes occur in the chest wall with growth; these changes have important functional implications for respiratory pump efficiency and function. In infancy, the orientation of the ribs is horizontal; the ribs start to slope downward with assumption of the upright position, and by the age of 10 years this downward slope has reached the adult configuration (Figure 9–2).[6]

Functional changes

The chest wall stiffens with growth. While specific lung compliance (Cl) changes little with growth, compliance of the chest wall (Cw) progressively decreases. In infancy Cw can be 2 to 6 times greater than Cl, and even higher in premature infants.[7–11] In childhood and adulthood Cw decreases to approximately equal Cl, and can be half Cl in the elderly.[11–13] These changes in Cw are caused by increasing muscle mass and ossification.[14–16]

Since passive relaxation (resting) lung volume (Vr) is determined by the balance of the outward recoil of the chest wall and the inward recoil of the lung, a chest wall that is highly compliant relative to the lung results in a lowered Vr (Figure 9–3).[17] Low Vr can predispose the infant to atelectasis and low oxygen reserves. Full-term infants actively maintain end-expiratory lung volume (EEV) above Vr by prolonging the expiratory time constant (t) relative to the time available for expiration (Figure 9–4).[18] Expiratory flow is therefore "interrupted" at a lung volume above the relaxed level. This active prolongation of the expiratory time constant occurs through (1) postinspiratory activity of the diaphragm (Figure 9–5)[19] and (2) expiratory "braking" by the upper airway muscles.[20,21] As the chest wall stiffens, active maintenance of end-expiratory volume becomes unnecessary and is no longer present by 1 to 2 years of age.[22]

There are few studies on developmental changes in chest wall resistance. The chest wall accounts for approximately 30 to 35% of total respiratory system resistance in adults[23] and may be proportionately less in infants (20 to 25%).[24] In adult humans the chest wall contributes significantly to the viscoelastic properties of the respiratory system;[25,26] this contribution probably increases after 5 years of age.[27]

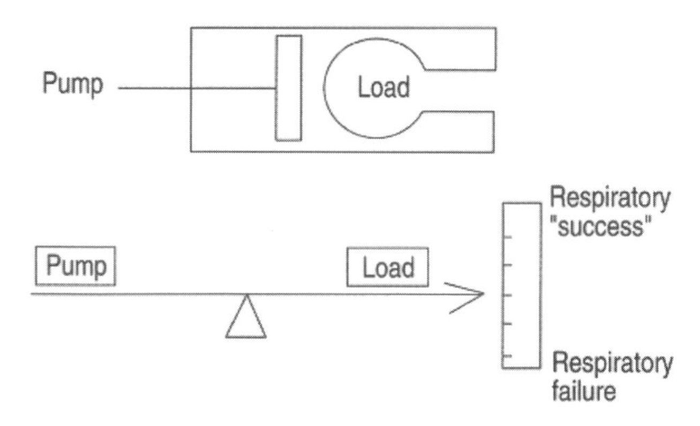

FIGURE 9–1. The ability of the respiratory pump to exceed the mechanical load of the respiratory system determines whether respiratory "success" or failure ensues. (Reproduced with permission from Allen J. Respiratory function in children with neuromuscular disease. Monaldi Arch Chest Dis 1996;51:230–5.)

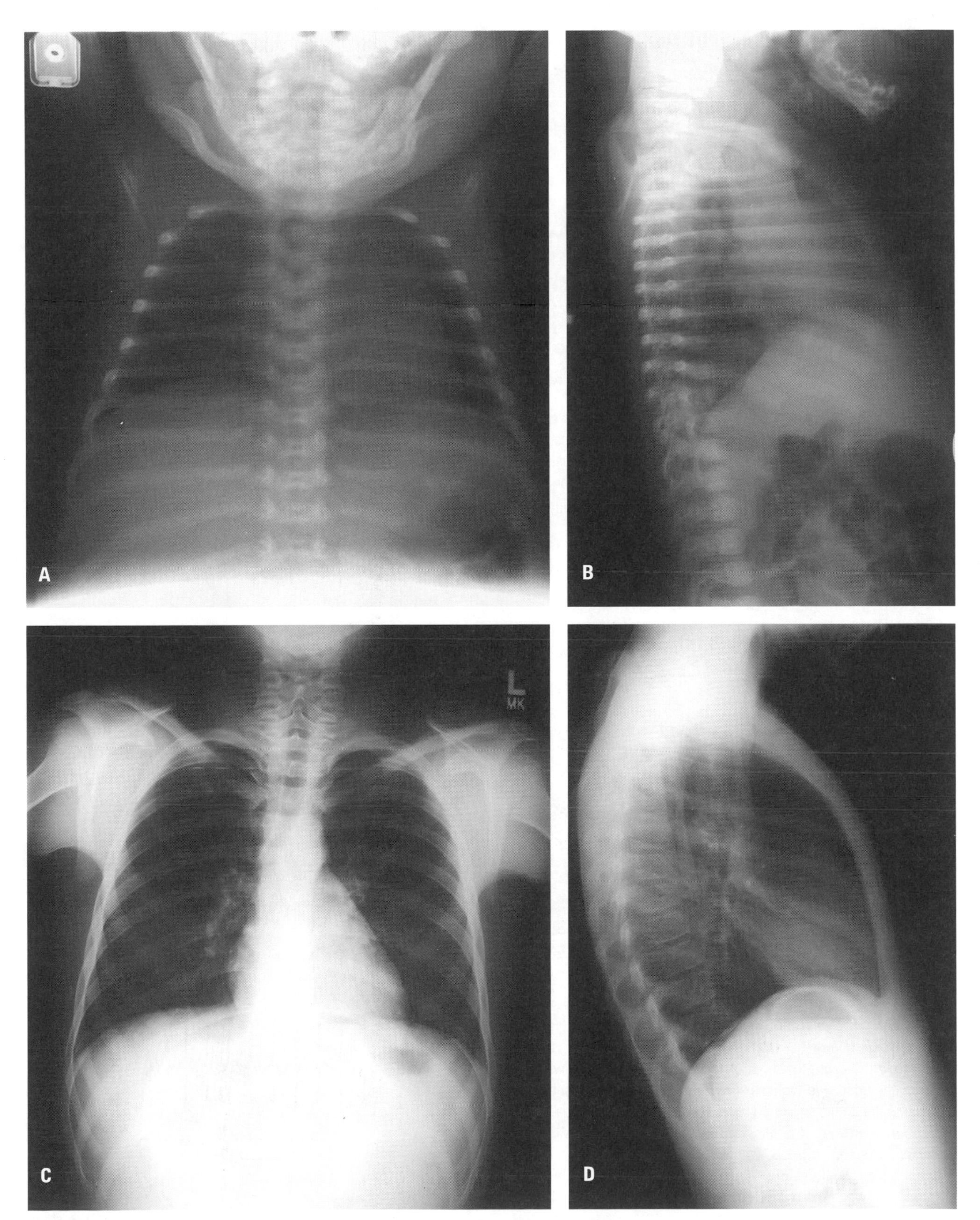

FIGURE 9–2. Changes in rib cage morphometry with growth. *A*, Posteroanterior and *B*, lateral chest radiographs of a 4-month-old infant. *C*, Posteroanterior and *D*, lateral chest radiographs of a 14-year-old male. In the infant the slope of the ribs is nearly horizontal, while in the 14 year old there is a downward declination of the ribs. (Reproduced with permission from Allen JL, Wohl MEB. Neuromuscular and chest wall disorders. In: Taussig LM, Landau LI, editors. Pediatric respiratory medicine. New York: Mosby 1999.)

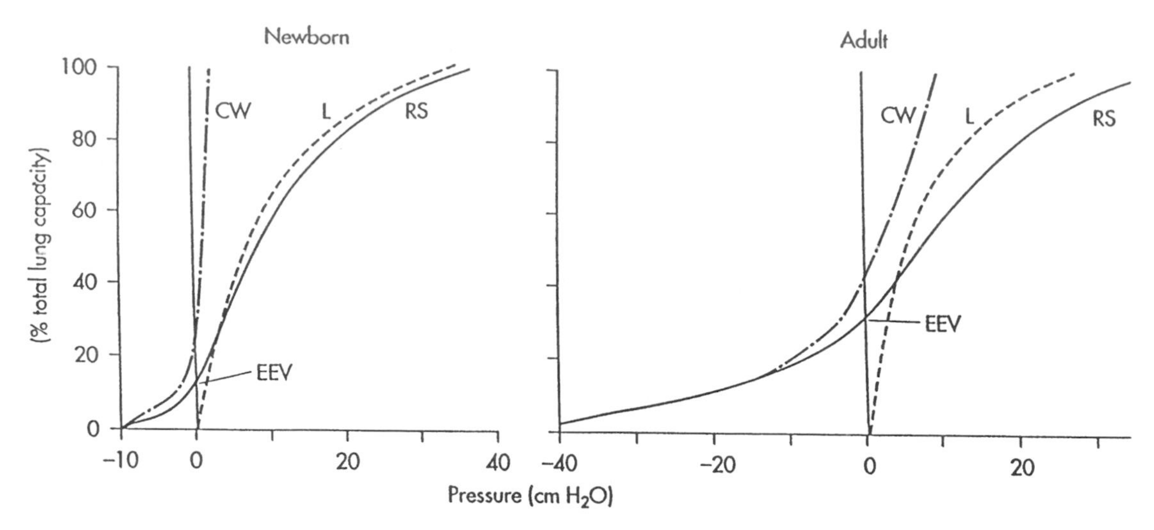

FIGURE 9–3. Respiratory system pressure-volume (PV) curves in the newborn and adult human. The slope of each curve at a given lung volume represents the compliance at that volume. The *solid curve* in each diagram is the PV curve of the respiratory system (RS) and represents the sum of the pressures resulting from the chest wall PV curve (*left dashed line*; CW) and the lung PV curve (*right dashed line*; L) at a given lung volume. Passive end-expiratory lung volume (EEV) is represented by the point at which the solid curve crosses the zero pressure axis. It is relatively lower in the newborn than in the adult because of the relatively high compliance of the newborn chest wall curve. (Reproduced with permission from Agostoni E and Mead J.[17])

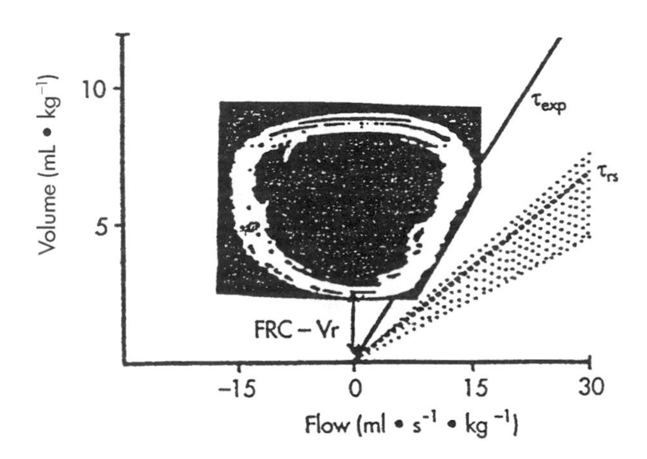

FIGURE 9–4. Elevation of end expiratory lung volume (EEV) by active prolongation of the respiratory system time constant (τ). The *solid line* is the expiratory limb of the tidal flow volume curve. The slope of the solid line (volume/flow) has the units of seconds and represents the active expiratory time constant (τ_{exp}). The slope of the *dotted line* represents the passive time constant of the system (τ_{rs}) following an end-inspiratory occlusion, which activates the Hering-Breuer reflex and therefore relaxes the respiratory muscles. The difference between the two slopes ($\tau_{exp} > \tau_{rs}$) is caused by the slowing of expiration by active respiratory muscle braking. These lines intersect at the passive relaxation volume (Vr). The volume difference between Vr and the active flow volume curve EEV reflects active maintenance of functional residual capacity (FRC). (Reproduced with permission from Mortola JP and Saetta M.[18])

The Respiratory Muscles

The diaphragm has three major inspiratory actions.[28,29] First, by acting as a piston, the diaphragm decreases intrapleural pressure, causing inward airflow through the mouth and nose. Second, by increasing intra-abdominal pressure, the diaphragm expands the lower rib cage. This lower rib cage expansion occurs because a substantial portion of intra-abdominal contents resides within the rib

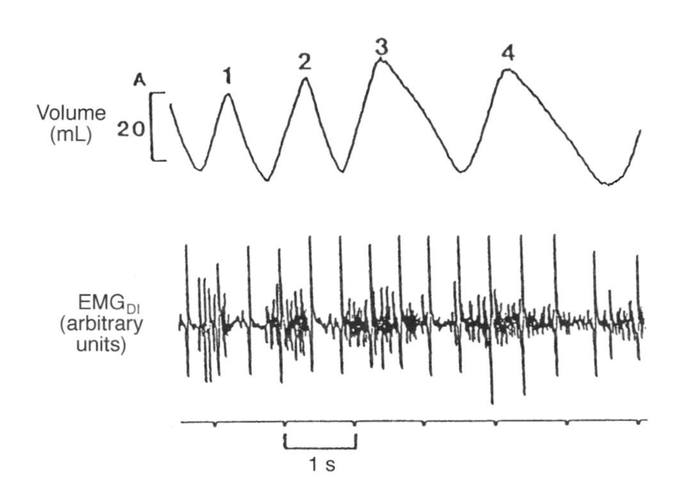

FIGURE 9–5. Postinspiratory activity of the diaphragm. The sharp spikes are cardiac artifact. Diaphragmatic electromyogram (EMG_{DI}) of breaths 3 and 4 shows electrical activity after inspiration ends, which slows expiratory airflow. (Reproduced with permission from Kosch PC and Stark AR.[19])

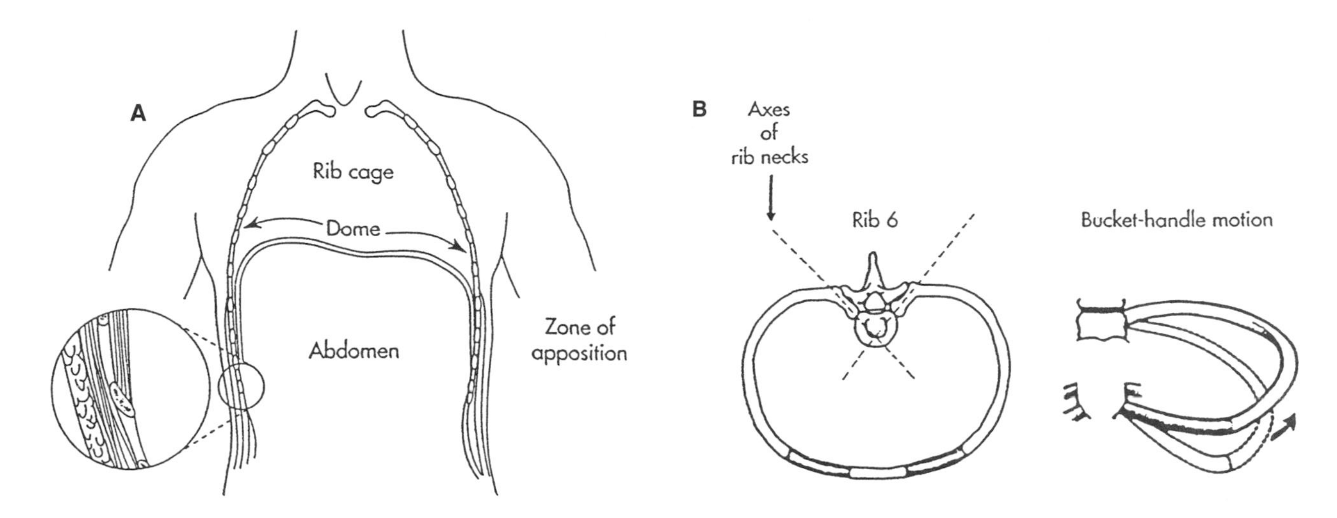

FIGURE 9–6. Functional anatomy of the rib cage. *A*, Zone of apposition. (Reproduced with permission from DeTroyer A and Estenne M.[28]) *B*, Bucket-handle effect. (Reproduced with permission from De Troyer A and Loring SH.[29])

cage (Figure 9–6*A*). Third, the diaphragm acts to elevate the lower ribs through its area of apposition to the inner rib cage wall. This elevation of the lower ribs also expands lower thoracic cross-sectional area by causing the downward-sloping ribs to assume a more horizontal position, the "bucket-handle" effect (Figure 9–6*B*).

The differences between the adult and infant chest wall outlined above can affect the diaphragm's inspiratory action. Since less of the rib cage's contents are intra-abdominal, and the area of apposition is less in the infant than in the older child and adult (Figure 9–7),[30,31] there is a diminished bucket-handle effect. In addition, the highly compliant chest wall of the infant results in a less efficient respiratory pump. By decreasing pleural pressure, the respiratory muscles, inwardly distort the chest wall. This can result in diaphragmatic pressure-volume work exceeding pulmonary work by up to sevenfold.[32]

While the mechanical inefficiencies of the infant chest wall may interfere with the diaphragm's ability to generate pressure, these inefficiencies may be overcome by the law of Laplace. This law states that the smaller radius of curvature of the infant's diaphragm relative to the adult should improve its pressure generating ability at a given level of tension. In fact, maximal inspiratory occlusion

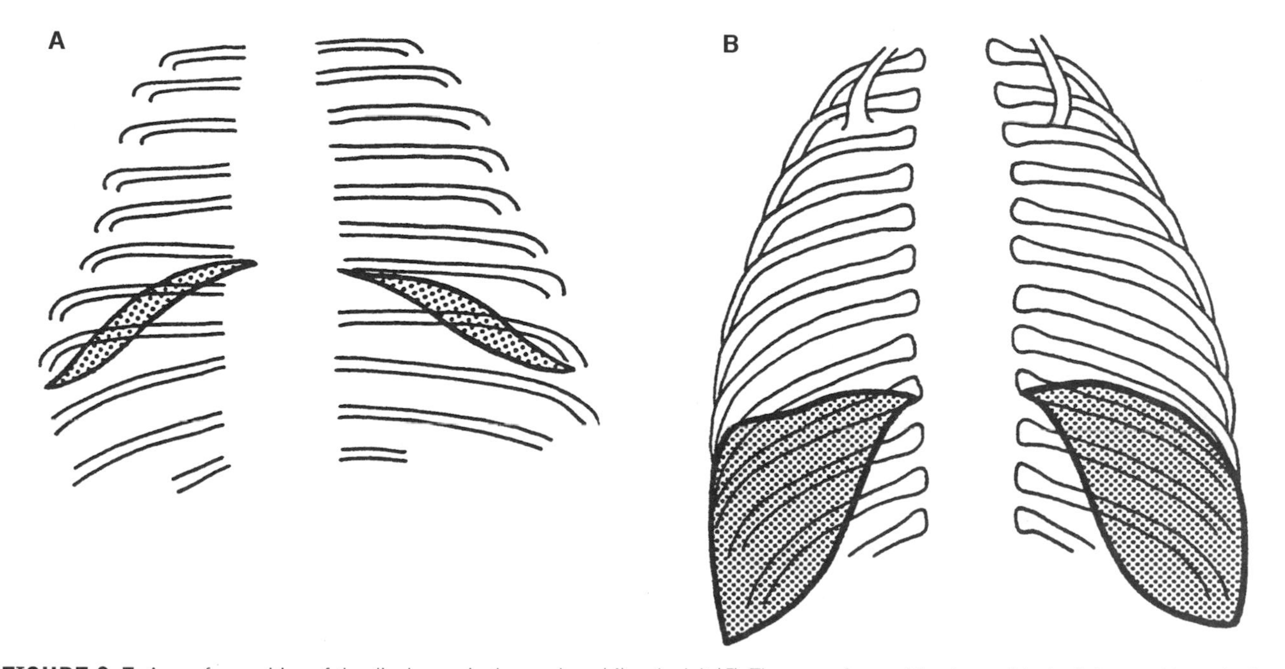

FIGURE 9–7. Area of apposition of the diaphragm in the newborn (*A*) and adult (*B*). The area of apposition is small in the infant and large in the adult. (Adapted from Devlieger H.[30])

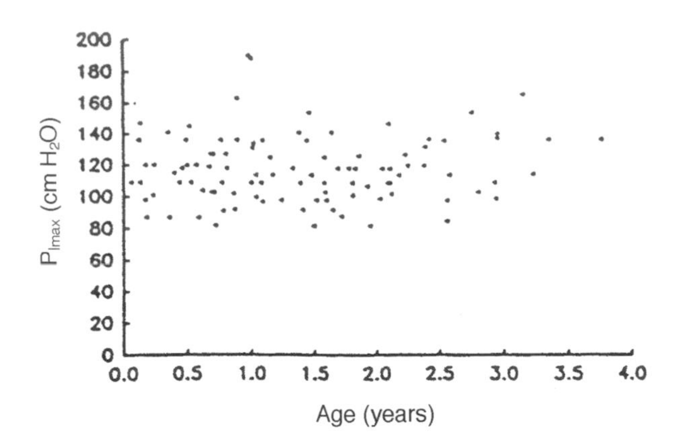

FIGURE 9–8. Maximal inspiratory pressures P_{Imax} in infants measured by occluding the airway at the beginning of inspiratory effort during crying. (Reproduced with permission from Shardonofsky FR et al.[33])

pressures (see "Assessment of Respiratory Muscle Strength," below) measured in infants at the mouth during crying are not much lower than those during voluntary efforts in older children and adults (Figure 9–8),[33,34] suggesting that the mechanical disadvantages of the infant diaphragm are offset by its smaller radius of curvature. Recent studies do indicate, however, that maximal inspiratory pressure in premature infants increases between 32 and 40 weeks postconceptional age.[35]

While expiration is primarily driven by the passive elastic recoil of the respiratory system at lung volumes above functional residual capacity (FRC), neonates, like adults, can recruit abdominal muscles to promote active expiration under conditions of hypercapnea and hypercarbia.[36,37] Such recruitment is less effective in rapid eye movement (REM) sleep than in non-REM sleep. Maximal expiratory occlusion pressures increase with age (see "Assessment of Respiratory Muscle Strength," below).[34] This may be due to increasing intercostal and abdominal muscle strength with age, and an increased chest wall contribution to respiratory system inward recoil pressure at the high lung volumes at which maximal expiratory pressure measurements occur.

The mechanical disadvantage imposed by a highly compliant chest wall has been thought to predispose the premature and newborn infants to respiratory muscle fatigue and consequent pump failure.[38–40] However the contractile properties and fatigue resistance of respiratory muscles undergo complex changes with development that challenge the notion that the newborn is highly prone to fatigue.[41–44] This is discussed further in Chapter 10.

Developmental Disorders of the Chest Wall

Congenital abnormalities of the thorax occur in numerous syndromes.[45,46] These abnormalities may be structural, resulting from a primary malformation of the structure, or secondary, due to disruption or mechanical deformation of an originally well-formed organ (Table 9–1). Structural malformations may be further due to dysplasia, for example, disorganized cell or tissue structure. Disorders with structural abnormalities of the chest wall include the Jarcho-Levin syndrome (severely malformed vertebrae and ribs), the cerebrocostomandibular syndrome (gaps in the posterior aspects of the ribs), and the Fryns syndrome (diaphragmatic hernias in combination with multiple other anomalies). The causative gene mutations for these disorders have not yet been identified. The pattern of malformation seen in Jarcho-Levin syndrome is suggestive of abnormal segmentation in early embryologic development. Fryns syndrome is inherited as an autosomal recessive trait, and the multiple affected organ systems are suggestive of underlying mutations in a gene widely expressed during early development.

Skeletal dysplasias may lead to severe pulmonary complications, due either to pulmonary hypoplasia or to respiratory pump failure. The underlying defect in skeletal dysplasia may affect either the extracellular matrix or the intracellular metabolism of cells forming skeletal structures. There are three major genetic mechanisms leading to skeletal dysplasias: (1) abnormal gene product dominant negative action (eg, in osteogenesis imperfecta and Marfan syndrome), (2) gain-of-function mutations (eg, in achondroplasia), and (3) loss-of-function mutations. In some loss-of-function disorders (eg, achondrogenesis type IB[46]), both alleles typically affecting an enzyme or transporter protein have to lose their function to produce the phenotype. In these disorders the loss of function is inherited as a recessive trait.[46] In other disorders, loss of function affecting only one of the two alleles is enough to produce the phenotype; this mechanism is called haploinsufficiency and is inherited as a dominant trait. Disorders caused by haploinsufficiency typically are due to deletions of or mutations in genes encoding transcription factors, for example, *CBFA1* in cleidocranial dysplasia. Transcription factors are proteins regulating the expression of other genes downstream in a pathway. Diseases exemplifying these three basic genetic mechanisms are described in detail below.

Osteogenesis imperfecta, an example of a disorder caused by abnormal gene product dominant negative action, is characterized by a decreased integrity and strength of bones and connective tissue, and is caused by mutations in genes coding for structural proteins forming the extracellular matrix.[47,48] The extracellular matrix of bone, ligaments, and skin consists largely of type I collagen. The mature type I collagen molecule is assembled from two α1(I) and one α2(I) procollagen molecules, encoded by the *COL1A1* gene on chromosome 17 and the *COL1A2* gene on chromosome 7, respectively. These procollagen molecules contain long stretches of three amino acid repetitions, consisting of one glycine and two variable

TABLE 9–1. Malformation Syndromes Affecting the Thorax*

Category	Disorder	Major Findings	Thoracic Involvement	Respiratory Complications	Inheritance Pattern	Gene	Mutation
Dominant negative action	Osteogenesis imperfecta	Multiple fractures, joint laxity, blue sclera, dentinogenesis imperfecta	Rib fractures	Pulmonary hypoplasia in severe forms; unstable thorax after multiple rib fracture	Autosomal dominant	*COL1A1* or *COL1A2* (procollagen molecules)	Multiple
Dominant negative action	Marfan syndrome	Arachnodactyly, joint laxity, aortic dilatation	Scoliosis, kyphosis, and pectus excavatum or carinatum	Rarely respiratory distress due to abnormal thorax	Autosomal dominant	*FBN1*	Multiple
Dominant negative action	Beals' syndrome	Camptodactyly, arachnodactyly, crumpled ears	Kyphoscoliosis	Rare	Autosomal dominant	*FBN2*	Multiple
Gain of function	Achondroplasia	Rhizomelic dwarfism, macrocephaly	Small rib cage, kyphosis	May occur in infancy; upper airway obstruction possible	Autosomal dominant	*FGFR3*	Gly380Arg
Gain of function	Thanatophoric dysplasia	Short limbs, lethal dwarfism	Narrow thorax due to shortened ribs; flat vertebral bodies	Lethal shortly after birth, often due to respiratory insufficiency	Sporadic cases due to new mutation	*FGFR3*	Arg248Cys, Lys650Glu, others
Haploinsufficiency	Campomelic dysplasia	Bowing of long bones, male-to-female sex reversal, micrognathia	Small thoracic cage with slender ribs or decreased number of ribs; kyphoscoliosis	Respiratory insufficiency may cause death in early infancy; failure to thrive in survivors	Autosomal dominant	*SOX9* (transcription factor)	Multiple
Haploinsufficiency	Cleidocranial dysplasia	Wide anterior fontanel with delayed closure; excess teeth; mild short stature	Partially or completely absent clavicle; narrow chest	Rare	Autosomal dominant	*CBFA1* (transcription factor)	Multiple
Loss of function	Ellis-van Creveld syndrome (chondroectodermal dysplasia)	Short distal extremities, polydactyly, nail hypoplasia, cardiac defects	Small thoracic cage with short ribs	Respiratory distress may occur due to the small thorax or the cardiac defect	Autosomal recessive	*EVC*	Multiple
Loss of function	Hypophosphatasia (neonatal form)	Undermineralized, hypoplastic, and fragile bones; rachitic rosary; hypercalcemia	Short ribs and small thoracic cage	Death due to respiratory insufficiency in neonatal period common	Autosomal recessive	*ALPL*	Multiple
Loss of function	Jarcho-Levin syndrome (spondylothoracic dysplasia; spondylocostal dysostosis)	Short neck, long digits with camptodactyly	Short thorax with multiple vertebral defects and abnormal ribs	Respiratory distress due to small thoracic volume causes death in infancy	Autosomal recessive; most cases of Puerto Rican ancestry	*DLL3*	Multiple
Unknown	Jeune's syndrome (asphyxiating thoracic dystrophy)	Short limbs, polydactyly, cystic renal lesions or chronic nephritis	Small, bell-shaped rib cage, hypoplastic lungs	Usually fatal neonatal asphyxia	Autosomal recessive	Unknown	Unknown
Unknown	Cerebrocostomandibular syndrome	Severe micrognathia; prenatal growth deficiency	Small, bell-shaped thorax, gaps between posterior ossified and anterior cartilagineous ribs	Respiratory insufficiency may cause neonatal death	Possibly autosomal recessive or autosomal dominant	Unknown	Unknown

*Category refers to the presumed genetic mechanism by which the mutations cause the phenotype (see text). Mutations in the listed genes have been identified in the respective disorders. In some disorders there is a strict correlation between the genotype (ie, a specific mutation or a mutation in a specific gene), while in others heterogeneity is suspected or has been proven (eg, not all patients with Jarcho-Levin syndrome have mutations in *DLL3*).

FBN = fibrillin; *FGFR* = fibroblast growth factor receptor; Gly = glycine; Arg = arginine; Cys = cysteine; Lys = lysine; Glu = glutamic acid; *ALPL* = alternative phosphatase; DLL = delta-like.

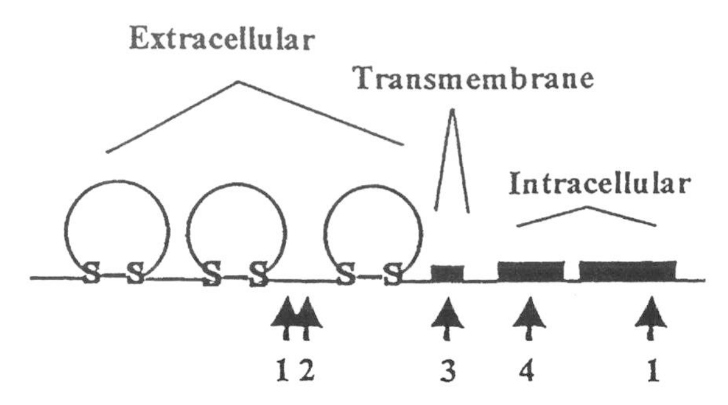

FIGURE 9–9. The fibroblast growth factor receptor 3 (*FGFR3*) protein with the extracellular ligand binding and the transmembrane and intracellular split tyrosine kinase domains. The locations of mutations causing autosomal dominant skeletal disorders are indicated: 1 = thanatophoric dysplasia; 2 = coronal synostosis; 3 = achondroplasia; 4 = hypochondroplasia.

other amino acids, the glycine (Gly)-X-Y motif. These long stretches of Gly-X-Y motif repetition give rise to a helical structure allowing the three procollagen chains to form the triple helical structure of the mature collagen protein. An interruption of this Gly-X-Y repetition, in particular a substitution of the glycine residue (the smallest amino acid) by another amino acid, results in bulges or kinks of the triple helical structure and secondary overmodification by glycosylation and hydroxylation, ultimately causing excretion and/or incorporation of abnormal collagen into the extracellular matrix. Paradoxically, subtle mutations lead to qualitative abnormalities of the procollagen molecule, leading to severe clinical findings, because the abnormal protein is processed and incorporated into mature collagen[49]—hence the term "dominant negative action." In contrast, mutations causing major changes, such as premature protein termination, may result in a milder phenotype due to the lack of incorporation of the abnormal protein into the matrix.[50]

A second example of a connective tissue disorder caused by abnormal gene product dominant negative action affecting the rib cage is Marfan syndrome, a disorder often presenting with severe scoliosis and pectus deformations. Marfan syndrome is due to mutations in the *FBN1* gene coding for fibrillin.[51] Fibrillin is the major constitutive element of extracellular microfibrils. Similar to the mechanism in collagen molecules, the incorporation of an abnormal fibrillin protein disrupts the macromolecular structure of the extracellular microfibrils. A third example of a disease caused by dominant negative action is the lethal achondrogenesis type II, a disorder of type II collagen caused by a mutation in the *COL2A1* gene.[52]

Achondroplasia is an example of a disease caused by a gain-of-function mutation. Achondroplasia, with a frequency of ~1/10,000 people,[53] is the most common of the skeletal dysplasias. In this disorder respiratory compromise can be caused by short flared ribs forming a shallow thorax. Chest wall circumference is small.[54] In addition, patients often have severe midfacial hypoplasia causing obstructive apnea, or central apnea due to brain-stem compression secondary to a small foramen magnum and mild hydrocephalus. Achondroplasia is due to a disturbance in an intracellular tyrosine kinase signaling pathway, leading to decreased endochondral growth rates resulting in short limb dwarfism. The gene mutated in achondroplasia encodes the fibroblast growth factor receptor 3 and is called *FGFR3*.[55] Its protein product is one of four transmembrane receptors for the 19 currently identified fibroblast growth factors. Ligand binding leads to dimerization of receptor molecules, initiating tyrosine kinase activity of the intracellular domains (Figure 9–9), thus triggering an intracellular signaling cascade that ultimately regulates cell proliferation and differentiation. Nearly all patients with achondroplasia are heterozygous for a missense mutation resulting in a glycine-to-arginine amino acid substitution at position 380 in the transmembrane domain.[56,57] This mutation is thought to cause ligand-independent activation of the signaling pathway by dimerization of the mutant receptors, thus leading to a gain of function by constitutive activation. The normal function of the receptor is negative regulation of endochondral growth, as is indicated by the skeletal overgrowth seen in mice lacking both functional copies of the gene.[58] Increased activation of this pathway through constitutive activation of the *FGFR3* results in shortened growth plates causing short limb dwarfism. The rare patients with homozygous achondroplasia, having inherited the *FGFR3* mutation from both parents, show a much more severe phenotype and die in early infancy, often from respiratory complications. A second lethal skeletal dysplasia, thanatophoric dysplasia, is also caused by mutations in *FGFR3*. While several different mutations have been reported, the most common are missense mutations affecting amino acid 248 in the extracellular domain and amino acid 650 in the intracellular tyrosine kinase domain.[59] Two other skeletal disorders not typically leading to respiratory problems are also caused by *FGFR3* mutations: hypochondroplasia, a mild form of short-limbed dwarfism,[60] and Muenke craniosynostosis.[61,62] These disorders are due to missense mutations located in the intracellular and extracellular domains, respectively (see Figure 9–9). While all *FGFR3* mutations are presumed to exert their effect by a gain-of-function mechanism, it is not completely understood how they cause the distinctive phenotypes.

Achondrogenesis type IB is an example of a chest wall disorder caused by a loss-of-function mutation. This disorder causes a clinical syndrome of extreme short stature, poor ossification of the skull and vertebral bodies, severe micromelia of the limbs, extremely short ribs, and stellate long bones (Figure 9–10).[63] The mutation resides in the diastrophic dysplasia sulfate transporter (*DTDST*) gene,[64]

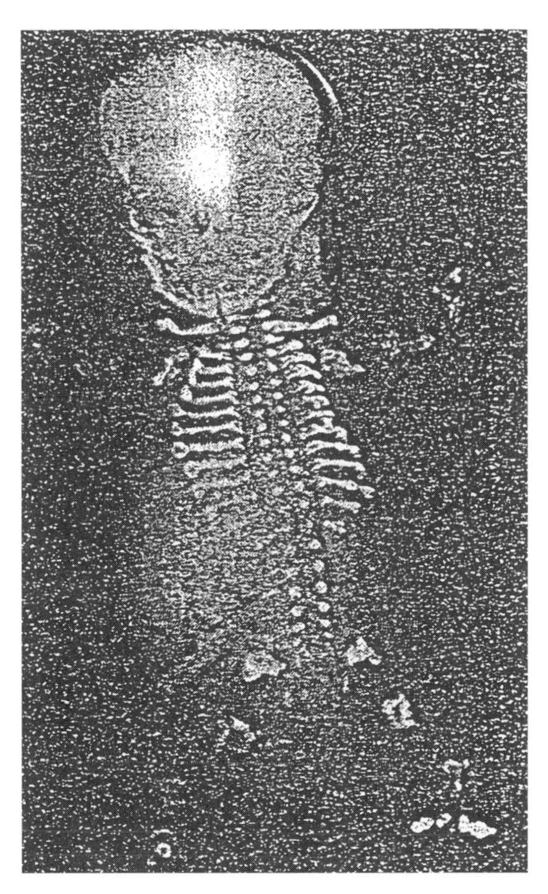

FIGURE 9–10. Small chest wall in an infant with achondrogenesis type IB. (Reproduced with permission from Lyons Jones K.[45])

leading to decreased or absent sulfate transport[65] and abnormalities in cartilage proteoglycans sulfation.

Cleidocranial dysplasia is due to haploinsufficiency for the transcription factor *CBFA1* (also called *RUNX2*), a transcriptional activator of bone formation. The characteristic findings of cleidocranial dysplasia are wide late-closing fontanelles, hypoplastic or absent clavicles, and supernumerary teeth. More subtle abnormalities include moderate short stature, a narrow thorax with short ribs, hypoplastic pubic bones, and brachydactyly. Respiratory distress may occur, but it is relatively rare.

Other clinical malformation syndromes affecting the thorax and their genetic bases (where known) are listed in Table 9–1.

Methods for Assessing Chest Wall Function

Physical Examination

Paradoxic motion of the rib cage (RC) and abdomen (AB) is readily identified. The phase of respiration should be noted in addition to the presence of paradox. Inward RC motion and outward AB motion during inspiration denotes intercostal muscle or rib cage dysfunction. This pattern is commonly noted in infants with severe airflow obstruction and in some normal premature infants, especially during REM sleep. It is also seen in patients with neuromuscular disease with intercostal muscle weakness but intact diaphragmatic function, for example, quadriplegia. Inward AB and outward RC motion during inspiration denotes diaphragmatic dysfunction. It often is noted in adults with severe airflow obstruction and impending diaphragmatic fatigue. It also is seen in patients with phrenic nerve paralysis.

An observed pattern of "respiratory alternans" during inspiratory resistive loaded breathing, in which the contributions of the diaphragm and intercostal accessory muscles alternate in time, has been suggested as a respiratory muscle strategy that can postpone the onset of fatigue.[66] This produces an alternating pattern of RC and AB motion, each compartment's displacement alternating in magnitude. Asynchronous RC-AB motion may also merely reflect the magnitude of the load itself, rather than respiratory muscle fatigue per se.[67–69]

Palpation of the abdominal muscles (eg, rectus abdominis) may reveal active contraction during expiration. This is seen in patients with severe obstructive lung disease, in whom passive recoil of the respiratory system may provide insufficient pressure to overcome expiratory airflow obstruction.

Chest Wall Motion

The measurement of chest wall motion by respiratory inductive plethysmography can provide information about both chest wall function and underlying lung function.[70,71] The magnitude of the RC and AB compartments' contribution to tidal volume, and timing relationships between the two compartments can be quantitated. Newborn infants breathe predominantly with their abdominal compartments, as opposed to adults who are primarily rib cage breathers. Hershenson et al[72] estimated the rib cage's contribution to tidal breathing during quiet sleep in the newborn at 35% of tidal volume (range, 20 to 50%), increasing gradually over the first year to the normal adult value of 65%.

Timing relationships between RC and AB can be measured by plotting RC against AB motion (with time as an implicit variable) in a Lissajous, or Konno-Mead figure[73] and calculating the "phase angle" as an index of thoracoabdominal asynchrony (TAA) (Figure 9–11). This phase angle can range from 0° (synchronous RC-AB motion) to 180° (paradoxic RC-AB motion). Normal chest wall motion is synchronous in full-term infants (mean phase angle 8°) (Figure 9–12) and children (mean phase angle 1.5°) during quiet sleep.[68,74,75] Chest wall motion becomes more asynchronous as chest wall stiffness decreases and/or pleural pressure swings increase, because the chest wall is less able to withstand the decrease in pleural pressure during inspiration. Under these conditions, outward motion

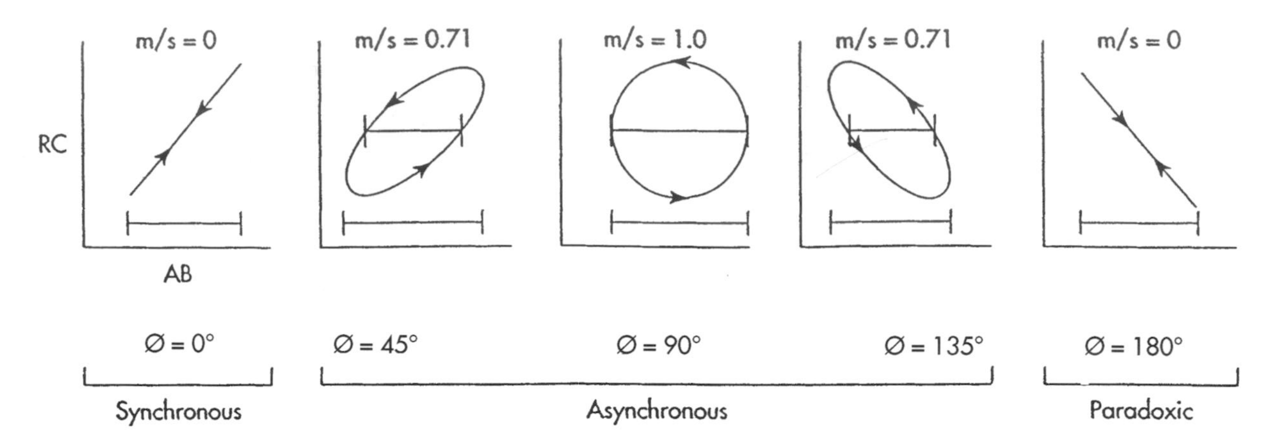

FIGURE 9–11. Lissajous figures of rib cage (RC) versus abdominal wall (AB) motion. Increasing phase angle (Ø) is an index of increasing thoracoabdominal asynchrony. For phase angles 0° < Ø < 90°, sin Ø = m/s, where m is the width of the figure at mid-RC excursion and s is the width of the figure at the extremes of AB excursion; for 90° < Ø < 180°, Ø = 180 - μ, where sin μ = m/s. (Reproduced with permission from Allen JL et al.[68])

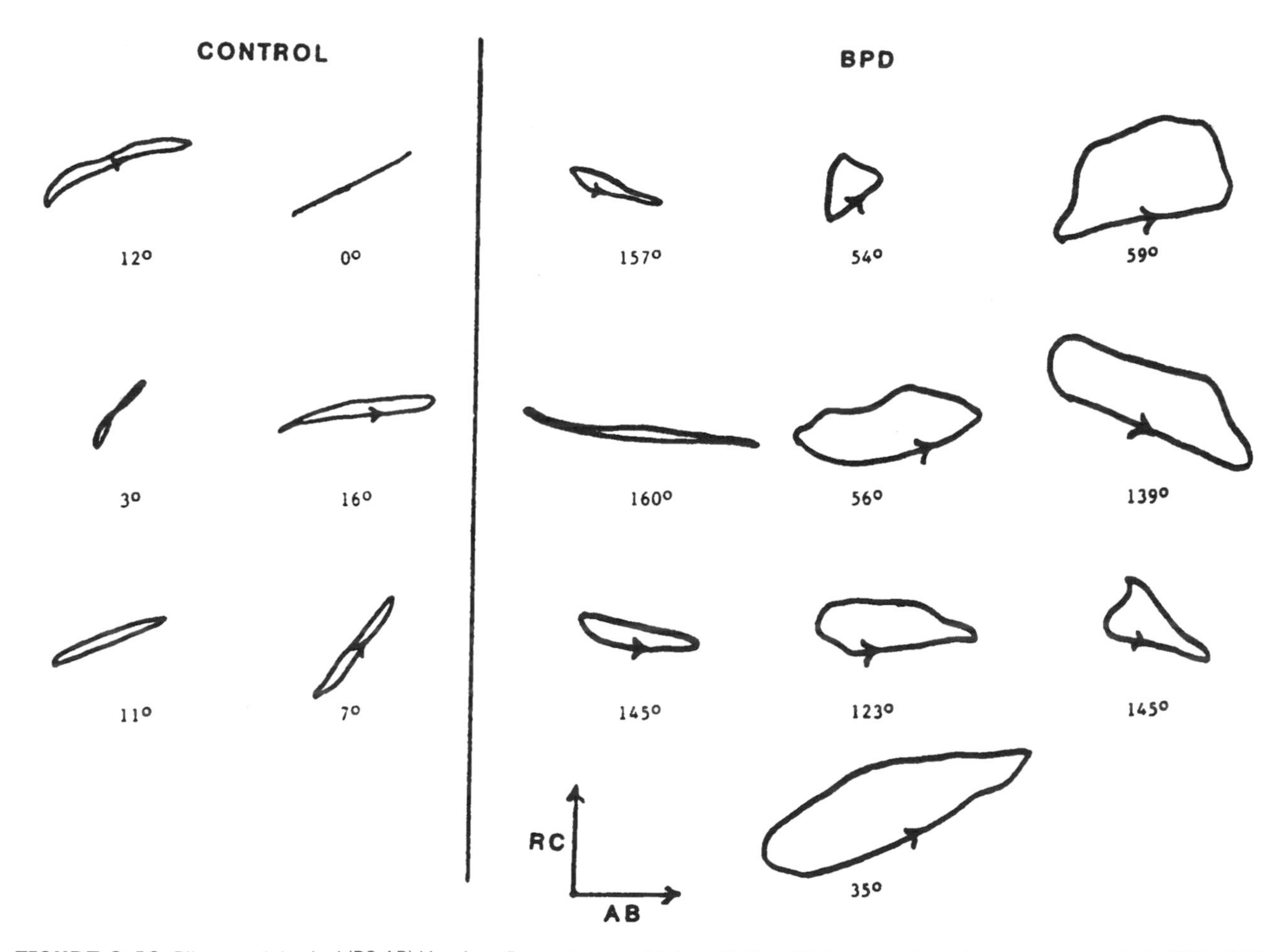

FIGURE 9–12. Rib cage-abdominal (RC-AB) Lissajous figures in normal infants (*left*) and infants with bronchopulmonary dysplasia (BPD; *right*). The calculated phase angles are shown. (Reproduced with permission from Allen JL et al.[68])

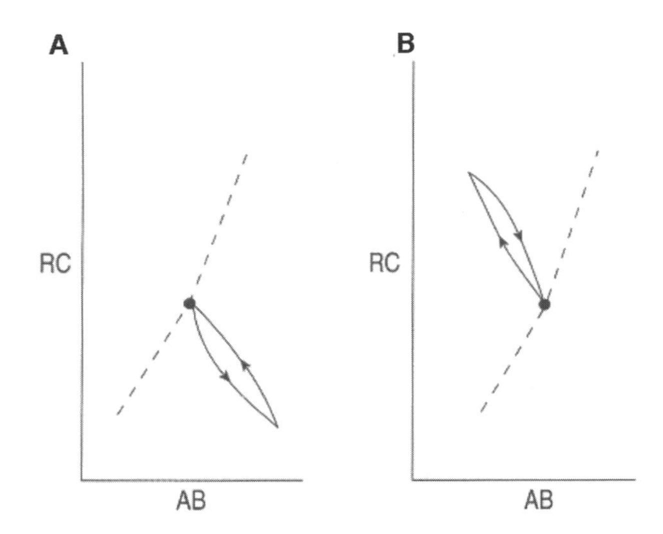

FIGURE 9–13. Konno-Mead figures in patients with neuromuscular disease during breathing at rest. The *dashed line* represents the relaxation curve of the chest wall, along which normal breathing usually occurs. The *closed circle* represents end-expiration. RC = rib cage; AB = abdomen. *A*, Intercostal weakness. *B*, Diaphragmatic paralysis. (Reproduced with permission from Allen J.[2])

of the rib cage can lag behind that of the abdomen or become paradoxic. An example of this may be found in premature infants, who frequently breathe asynchronously or paradoxically during quiet sleep (mean phase angle 58°; range, 0° to 157°).[69] Another example is infants with bronchopulmonary dysplasia, who can have markedly asynchronous breathing (see Figure 9–12), the degree of which can be related to the magnitude of abnormality in lung resistance and compliance.[68] Asynchrony improves significantly after use of bronchodilators in infants with lower airway obstruction[74] and after use of racemic epinephrine in children with upper airway obstruction.[76] Thus, quantitation of asynchrony can be used as a noninvasive indirect index of airway obstruction.

Short runs of inspiratory resistive-loaded breathing can increase TAA in preterm, but not full-term, infants.[69] The fact that full-term infants with chronic lung disease (an intrinsic resistive load) display TAA, while normal full-term infants subjected to acute extrinsic resistive loads of similar magnitude do not display the same degree of TAA, suggests that factors other than the magnitude of the load can influence the development of TAA. Such factors may include differences in central respiratory drive, respiratory muscle neuromuscular transmission, and the development of respiratory muscle fatigue.

Chest wall motion also can be affected by primary chest wall disease. Paradoxic breathing is seen in patients with neuromuscular disease, and, as described above, the pattern of RC-AB paradox can give important clues to the underlying disorder. Patients with primary intercostal muscle weakness display inward RC motion during inspiration (Figure 9–13*A*),[77] while patients with primary diaphragmatic paralysis display inward abdominal motion during inspiration (Figure 9–13*B*).[78,79]

In summary, while measures of TAA may give useful information about the mechanical resistive and elastic loads of the respiratory system, they also are influenced by central drive and affected by respiratory muscle weakness and fatigue. It may be better to think of measures of TAA as an integrated functional measure that reflects the ability of the respiratory pump to handle its mechanical load (see Figure 9–1). As such, TAA may reflect the likelihood of susceptibility to respiratory muscle fatigue (see below); this requires further study.

Assessment of Respiratory Muscle Strength

Normal adults can develop maximal inspiratory and expiratory pressures against an occluded airway in excess of 100 and 200 cm H_2O, respectively. As discussed earlier, after full-term birth, maximal inspiratory pressures (PI_{max}) remain constant throughout development, while maximal expiratory pressures (PE_{max}) increase.[33,34,80,81] Occlusion pressures during crying have been measured in premature infants[35] and in term infants from the age of 3 months onward.[33] From infancy onward, PI_{max} (mean ± standard deviation (SD) = 118 ± 21 cm H_2O) is relatively constant with age and is similar to that of adults; PE_{max} increases with age (mean ± SD = 125 ± 35 cm H_2O from 3 months to 3 years;[33] 138 ± 36 cm H_2O from ages 8 to 17 years;[81] nearly 200 cm H_2O in adults). After puberty, there are gender differences as well: occlusion pressures are greater in boys than in girls.[34,80,81]

Assessment of Respiratory Muscle Fatigue

The ability to assess respiratory pump function is particularly desirable in the settings of impending respiratory failure and weaning from mechanical ventilation. Maximal inspiratory force is sometimes used as an index of ability to wean from mechanical ventilation; such measurements, while reproducible, may not be reliable indicators of true respiratory muscle strength,[82] and may therefore not be reliable predictors of successful weaning. Transdiaphragmatic pressure (PDI) is an index of diaphragmatic strength rather than global respiratory muscle strength. It is more difficult to measure, however, requiring the placement of a gastric and esophageal pressure sensor. Both of these measures have the disadvantage that they measure strength, not fatigue.

Pump fatigue is ultimately defined as a falling minute ventilation and PDI in the face of continued respiratory load. Sophisticated research tests can diagnose respiratory pump fatigue and distinguish between the various sites of failure (eg, central, neuromuscular transmission, and respiratory muscle). Central fatigue is defined as decreasing neural output measured at the phrenic nerve during respiratory loading. It also has been inferred from decreasing ventilation resulting from a fall in respiratory frequency. Neuromuscular transmission failure is inferred from a fall in integrated respiratory muscle electromyographic (EMG) activity, which *precedes* a fall in PDI and occurs despite stable or increasing phrenic nerve output. Respiratory muscle contractile failure is defined as falling PDI despite increasing phrenic nerve and integrated EMG activity. The assessment of the site of respiratory pump failure is technically difficult in the clinical setting, especially in infants. Two indirect indices have been proposed as clinically useful indicators of *impending* respiratory failure. These are measurement of the tension-time index (TTI) and frequency pattern assessment of diaphragmatic EMG activity.

Tension-time index

The development of fatigue is closely linked to the force and duration of muscle contraction.[83] The TTI has been developed to predict whether respiratory muscle fatigue will occur. This index is the dimensionless product of (1) the ratio of mean inspiratory transdiaphragmatic pressure (PDI) to maximal transdiaphragmatic pressure (PDI_{max}) and (2) the ratio of the inspiratory time (TI) to the respiratory cycle time (TTOT). Thus,

$$TTI = PDI/PDI_{max} \cdot TI/TTOT.$$

For example, diseases such as asthma, cystic fibrosis, and adult respiratory distress syndrome can increase the TTI by increasing PDI to overcome abnormal airway resistance or lung compliance. Neuromuscular diseases, on the other hand, can increase the TTI by decreasing PDI_{max}. Upper airway obstruction (eg, croup or epiglottitis) increases TTI by increasing TI.

In adults, when the TTI is less than 0.1, it is unlikely that diaphragmatic fatigue will occur. When the TTI exceeds 0.2, it is highly likely that fatigue will occur. From 0.1 to 0.2 is a critical zone (Figure 9–14).[84] Studies have not been done in infants to determine whether the above values of the TTI are applicable in this age group.

The measurement of the TTI requires the ability to assess PDI and PDI_{max}, which can be technically difficult, since PDI measurements require placement of both esophageal and gastric pressure transducers. Gaultier et al[85] described an approach to measuring the TTI that has the advantages of being non-invasive and of measuring the TTI of all the inspiratory muscles, not just the diaphragm. The mean pressure generated during inspiration is estimated by measuring mouth pressure 100 ms after an occlusion at the beginning of inspiration (P100), and extrapolating this pressure to end inspiration and calculating the mean inspiratory pressure for the breath, PI (see Figure 9–15 for details). While P100 is usually thought of as a measure of respiratory drive,[86] it also is related to respiratory mechanical load.[85,87–91] The ratio of PI to maximal

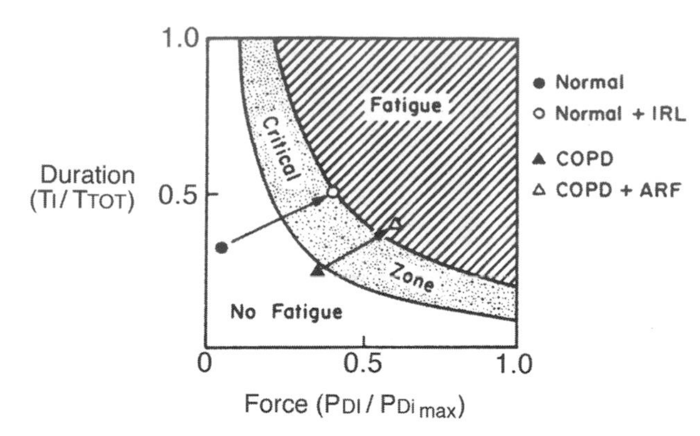

FIGURE 9–14. Graphic representation of the tension-time index, (TTI). Isobars of the dimensionless product of tension × time are shown. For TTI in the *lower left* of the figure, fatigue will not occur; for TTI in the *upper right*, fatigue will occur. IRL = inspiratory resistive load; COPD = chronic obstructive pulmonary disease; ARF = acute respiratory failure. TI = inspiratory time; TTOT = respiratory cycle time; PDI = mean inspiratory transdiaphragmatic pressure; PDI_{max} = maximal transdiaphragmatic pressure. (Reproduced with permission from Rochester DF and Arora NS.[84])

inspiratory pressure measured at the mouth (MIP) is then used to calculate a non-invasive TTI:[85,90]

$$TTI = PI/MIP \cdot TI/TTOT.$$

In adults there is an excellent correlation between invasive and non-invasive measurements of the TTI.[90] Children with obstructive lung disease[88] and cystic fibrosis[91] have an elevated TTI relative to normal controls. In cystic fibrosis,

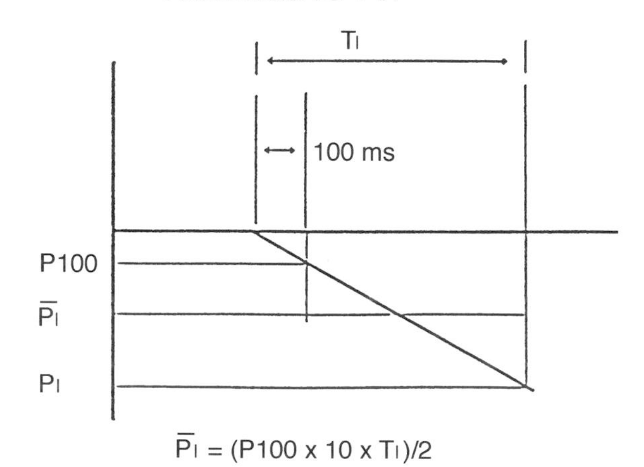

FIGURE 9–15. Noninvasive measurement of the tension-time index (TTI) requires estimation of the average pressure generated during the breath by the inspiratory muscles. If a linear rise in mouth pressure over the breath is assumed, inspiratory pressure at the end of the breath is the mouth occlusion pressure at 100 ms (P100) × 10 × inspiratory time (TI); this is divided by 2 to give the average inspiratory pressure ($\bar{P}I$).

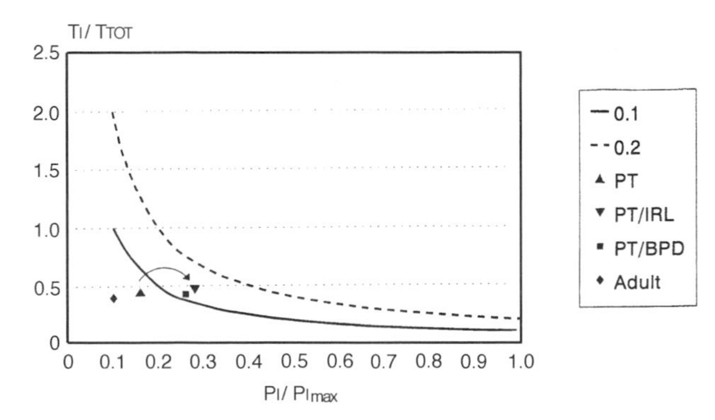

FIGURE 9–16. Noninvasive measurement of the tension-time index (TTI) in normal preterm (PT) infants before and after inspiratory resistive loading (IRL), and in preterm infants with bronchopulmonary dysplasia (BPD). The *dashed* and *solid lines* are TTI isobars. Both IRL and BPD move the TTI in the direction of respiratory muscle fatigue. TI = inspiratory time; TTOT = respiratory cycle time; PI = mean inspiratory pressure; PI_{max} = maximal inspiratory pressure. (Adapted from Greenspan JS et al;[89] assuming PI_{max} as reported by Dimitriou et al[35] for preterm infants.)

the TTI is inversely related to body mass index.[91] Measurements of the TTI are also feasible in infants, since P100 can be measured, as can MIP from inspiratory occlusions during crying (Figure 9–16).

Diaphragmatic electromyography

Spectral frequency analysis of the surface diaphragmatic EMG during fatiguing loads has been shown to indicate diaphragmatic muscle fatigue in adults.[92] Muller et al[93,94] performed similar analyses in infants, showing that diaphragmatic fatigue produces a decrease in the high-frequency power and an increase in the low-frequency power of the EMG. During weaning from mechanical ventilation, the EMG power spectrum remained normal in infants who were able to be weaned successfully, while in infants in whom mechanical ventilation had to be reinstituted, a decrease in the high-to-low-power spectrum ratio was seen that preceded CO_2 retention and clinical deterioration. The clinical usefulness of diaphragmatic EMG measurements is uncertain; shifts in the diaphragmatic EMG power spectrum may occur during loaded breathing in the absence of fatigue,[95] and may also be seen with muscle lengthening.[96] Furthermore, ventilatory failure induced by resistive-loaded breathing can occur in the absence of EMG power spectrum changes.[97]

In conclusion, since most children with chronic respiratory failure have respiratory pump dysfunction, better means of assessing the respiratory pump are needed. Such tests will be especially useful in designing regimens for weaning from chronic ventilator assistance and in designing strategies to improve respiratory muscle strength and endurance.

References

1. Roussos C, Macklem PT. The respiratory muscles [review]. N Engl J Med 1982;307:786–97.
2. Allen J. Respiratory function in children with neuromuscular disease. Monaldi Arch Chest Dis 1996;51:230–5.
3. Moore KL. The developing human. Clinically oriented embryology. 1st ed. Philadelphia: WB Saunders Co., 1973:284–7.
4. Warwick R, Williams PL. Gray's anatomy. 35th ed. Philadelphia: WB Saunders Co., 1973:254.
5. Scott W, Scott P, Treretola S. Radiology of the thoracic skeleton. Philadelphia: B.C. Decker, Inc., 1991:5.
6. Openshaw P, Edwards S, Helms P. Changes in rib cage geometry during childhood. Thorax 1984;39:624–7.
7. Davis GM, Coates AL, Papageorgiou A, Bureau MA. Direct measurement of static chest wall compliance in animal and human neonates. J Appl Physiol 1998;65:1093–8.
8. Reynolds RN, Etsten BE. Mechanics of respiration in apneic anesthetized infants. Anesthesiology 1966;27:13–9.
9. Richard CC, Bachman L. Lung and chest wall compliance in apneic paralyzed infants. J Clin Invest 1961;40:273–8.
10. Gerhardt T, Bancalari E. Chest wall compliance in full term and premature infants. Acta Paediatr Scand 1980; 69:359–64.
11. Papastamelos C, Panitch H, England S, Allen J. Developmental changes in chest wall compliance in infancy and early childhood. J Appl Physiol 1995;78:179–84.
12. Sharp JT, Druz WS, Balagot RC, et al. Total respiratory compliance in infants and children. J Appl Physiol 1970; 29:775–9.
13. Mittman C, Edelman NH, Norris AH, Shock NW. Relationship between chest wall and pulmonary compliance and age. J Appl Physiol 1965;20:1211–6.
14. Leiter JC, Mortola JP, Tenney SM. A comparative analysis of contractile characteristics of the diaphragm and of respiratory system mechanics. Respir Physiol 1980; 64:267–76.
15. Davidson MB. The relationship between diaphragm and body weight in the rat. Growth 1968;32:221–3.
16. Kikuchi Y, Stamenovich D, Loring SH. Dynamic behavior of excised dog rib cage: dependence on muscle. J Appl Physiol 1991;70:1059–67.
17. Agostoni E, Mead J. Statics of the respiratory system. In: Fenn WO, Rahn H, eds. Handbook of physiology. Vol. 1. Washington (DC): American Physiological Society, 1964:401.
18. Mortola JP, Saetta M. Measurements of respiratory mechanics in the newborn: a simple approach. Pediatr Pulmonol 1987;3:123–30.
19. Kosch PC, Stark AR. Dynamic maintenance of end-expiratory lung volume in full-term infants. J Appl Physiol Respir Environ Exerc Physiol 1984;57:1126–33.
20. England SJ. Laryngeal function. In: Chernick V, Mellins RB. Basic mechanisms of pediatric respiratory disease: cellular and integrative. Philadelphia: B.C. Decker, Inc., 1991:72–9.
21. Kosch PC, Hutchison AA, Wozniak JA, et al. Posterior cricoarytenoid and diaphragm activities during tidal breathing in neonates. J Appl Physiol 1988;64:1968–78.

22. Colin AA, Wohl MEB, Mead J, et al. Transition from dynamically maintained to relaxed end-expiratory volume in human infants. J Appl Physiol 1989;67:2107–11.
23. Ferris BG Jr, Mead J, Opie LH. Partitioning of respiratory flow resistance in man. J Appl Physiol 1964;19:653–8.
24. Wohl MEB, Stigol LC, Mead J. Resistance of the total respiratory system in healthy infants and infants with bronchiolitis. Pediatrics 1969;43:495–509.
25. Similowski T, Levy P, Corbeil C, et al. Viscoelastic behavior of lung and chest wall in dogs determined by flow interruption. J Appl Physiol 1989;67:2219–29.
26. D'Angelo E, Robatto FM, Calderini E, et al. Pulmonary and chest wall mechanics in anesthetized paralyzed humans. J Appl Physiol 1991;70:2602–10.
27. Lanteri CJ, Sly PD. Changes in respiratory mechanics with age. J Appl Physiol 1993;74:369–78.
28. DeTroyer A, Estenne M. Functional anatomy of the respiratory muscles [review]. Clin Chest Med 1988;9:175–93.
29. DeTroyer A, Loring SH. Action of the respiratory muscles. In: Macklem PT, Mead J, eds. Handbook of physiology. The respiratory system. Mechanics of breathing. Vol. III. Bethesda (MD): American Physiological Society, 1986:453.
30. Devlieger H. The chest wall in the preterm infant. Leuven (Belgium): KU Leuven, 1987.
31. Devlieger H, Daniels H, Marchal G, et al. The diaphragm of the newborn infant: anatomical and ultrasonographic studies. J Dev Physiol 1991;16:321–9.
32. Heldt GP, McIlroy MB. Distortion of chest wall and work of diaphragm in preterm infants. J Appl Physiol 1987; 62:164–9.
33. Shardonofsky FR, Perez-Chada D, Carmuega E, Milic-Emili J. Airway pressures during crying in healthy infants. Pediatr Pulmonol 1989;6:14–8.
34. Gaultier C, Zinman R. Maximal static pressures in healthy children. Respir Physiol 1983;51:45–61.
35. Dimitriou G, Greenough A, Dyke H, Rafferty GF. Maximal airway pressures during crying in healthy preterm and term neonates. Early Hum Dev 2000;57:149–56.
36. Watchko JF, Brozanski BS, O'Day TL, et al. Contractile properties of the rat external abdominal oblique and diaphragm muscles during development. J Appl Physiol 1992;72:1432–6.
37. Praud J-P, Egreteau L, Benlabed M, et al. Abdominal muscle activity during CO_2 rebreathing in sleeping neonates. J Appl Physiol 1991;70:1344–50.
38. Keens TG, Bryan AC, Levison H, Ianuzzo CD. Developmental pattern of muscle fiber types in human ventilatory muscles. J Appl Physiol Respir Environ Exerc Physiol 1978;44:909–13.
39. Le Souef PN, England SJ, Stogryn HAF, Bryan AC. Comparison of diaphragmatic fatigue in newborn and older rabbits. J Appl Physiol 1988;65:1040–4.
40. Muller N, Volgyesi G, Eng P, et al. The consequences of diaphragmatic muscle fatigue in the newborn infant. J Pediatr 1979;95:793–7.
41. Watchko JF, Mayock DE, Standaert TA, Woodrum DE. The ventilatory pump: neonatal and developmental issues [review]. Adv Pediatr 1991;38:109–34.
42. Sieck GC, Fournier M. Developmental aspects of diaphragm muscle cells: structural and functional organization [review]. In: Haddad GG, Farber JP, eds. Developmental neurobiology of breathing. New York: Dekker, 1991: 375–428.
43. Watchko JF, Sieck GC. Respiratory muscle fatigue resistance relates to myosin phenotype and SDH activity during development. J Appl Physiol 1993;75:1341–7.
44. Watchko JF, Daood MJ, Sieck GC. Myosin heavy chain transitions during development. Functional implications for the respiratory musculature. Comp Biochem Physiol B Biochem Mol Biol 1998;119:459–70.
45. Lyons Jones K. Smith's recognizable patterns of human malformation. Philadelphia: WB Saunders, 1988.
46. Dreyer SD, Zhou G, Lee B. The long and short of it: developmental aspects of the skeletal dysplasias. Clin Genet 1998;54:464–73.
47. Byers PH, Steiner RD. Osteogenesis imperfecta. Annu Rev Med 1992;43:269–82.
48. Tosi LL. Osteogenesis imperfecta. Curr Opin Pediatr 1997;9:94–9.
49. Stacey A, Bateman J, Choi T, et al. Perinatal lethal osteogenesis imperfecta in transgenic mice bearing an engineered mutant pro-alpha 1(I) collagen gene. Nature 1988; 332:131–6.
50. Bonadio J, Saunders TL, Tsai E, et al. Transgenic mouse model of the mild dominant form of osteogenesis imperfecta. Proc Natl Acad Sci U S A 1990;87:7135–49.
51. Hayward C, Brock DJ. Fibrillin-1 mutations in Marfan syndrome and other type-I fibrillinopathies. Hum Mutat 1997;10:415–23.
52. Vissing H, M DA, Lee B, et al. Glycine to serine substitution in the triple helical domain of pro-alpha 1 (II) collagen results in a lethal perinatal form of short-limbed dwarfism. J Biol Chem 1989;264:18265–7.
53. Orioli IM, Castilla EE, Barbosa-Neto JG. The birth prevalence rates for the skeletal dysplasias. J Med Genet 1986;23:328–32.
54. Hunter AGW, Reid CS, Pauli RM, Scott CI. Standard curves of chest circumference in achondroplasia and the relationship of chest circumference to respiratory problems. Am J Med Genet 1996;62:91–7.
55. Horton WA. Fibroblast growth factor receptor 3 and the human chondrodysplasias. Curr Opin Pediatr 1997; 9:437–42.
56. Shiang R, Thompson LM, Zhu YZ, et al. Mutations in the transmembrane domain of FGFR3 cause the most common genetic form of dwarfism, achondroplasia. Cell 1994;78:335–42.
57. Francomano CA. The genetic basis of dwarfism. N Engl J Med 1995;332:58–9.
58. Colvin JS, Bohne BA, Harding GW, et al. Skeletal overgrowth and deafness in mice lacking fibroblast growth factor receptor 3. Nat Genet 1996;12:390–7.
59. Tavormina PL, Shiang R, Thompson LM, et al. Thanatophoric dysplasia (types I and II) caused by distinct mutations in fibroblast growth factor receptor 3. Nat Genet 1995;9:321–8.
60. Bellus GA, McIntosh I, Smith EA, et al. A recurrent mutation in the tyrosine kinase domain of fibroblast growth factor receptor 3 causes hypochondroplasia. Nat Genet 1995;10:357–9.

61. Bellus GA, Gaudenz K, Zackai EH, et al. Identical mutations in three different fibroblast growth factor receptor genes in autosomal dominant craniosynostosis syndromes. Nat Genet 1996;14:174–6.
62. Muenke M, Gripp KW, McDonald-McGinn DM, et al. A unique point mutation in the fibroblast growth factor receptor 3 gene (FGFR3) defines a new craniosynostosis syndrome. Am J Hum Genet 1997;60:555–64.
63. Lyons Jones K. Smith's recognizable patterns of human malformation. Philadelphia: Saunders; 1988:278–9.
64. Superti-Furga A, Hastbacka J, Wilcox WR, et al. Achondrogenesis type IB is caused by mutations in the diastrophic dysplasia sulfate transporter gene. Nat Genet 1996;12:100–2.
65. Rossi A, Bonaventure J, Delezoide AL, et al. Undersulfation of proteoglycans synthesized by chondrocytes from a patient with achondrogenesis type IB homozygous for an L483P substitution in the diastrophic dysplasia sulfate transporter. J Biol Chem 1996;271:18456–64.
66. Roussos C, Fixley M, Gross D, Macklem PT. Fatigue of inspiratory muscles and their synergic behaviour. J Appl Physiol Respir Environ Exerc Physiol 1979; 46:897–904.
67. Tobin MJ, Perez W, Guenther SM, et al. Does rib cage-abdominal paradox signify respiratory muscle fatigue? J Appl Physiol 1987;63:851–60.
68. Allen JL, Greenspan JS, Deoras KS, et al. Interaction between chest wall motion and lung mechanics in normal infants and infants with bronchopulmonary dysplasia. Pediatr Pulmonol 1991;11:37–43.
69. Deoras KS, Greenspan JS, Wolfson MR, et al. Effects of inspiratory resistive loading on chest wall motion and ventilation: differences between preterm and full term infants. Pediatr Res 1992;32:589–94.
70. Adams JA. Respiratory inductive plethysmography. In: Stocks J, Sly PD, Tepper RS, Morgan WJ. Infant respiratory function testing. New York: Wiley-Liss, 1996:139–64.
71. Allen JL, Sivan Y. Measurements of chest wall function. In: Stocks J, Sly PD, Tepper RS, Morgan WJ. Infant respiratory function testing. New York: Wiley-Liss, 1996:329–54.
72. Hershenson MB, Colin AA, Wohl MEB, Stark AR. Changes in the contribution of the rib cage to tidal breathing during infancy. Am Rev Respir Dis 1990;41:922–5.
73. Konno K, Mead J. Measurement of the separate volume changes of rib cage and abdomen during breathing. J Appl Physiol 1967;2:407–22.
74. Allen JL, Wolfson MR, McDowell K, Shaffer TH. Thoracoabdominal asynchrony in infants with airflow obstruction. Am Rev Respir Dis 1990;41:337–42.
75. Colin AA, Hunter JM, Stark AR,Wohl MEB. Normal infants and children have minimal thoracoabdominal asynchrony assessed by respiratory inductive plethysmography [abstract]. Am Rev Respir Dis 1993;147:A966.
76. Sivan Y, Deakers TW, Newth CJL. Thoraco-abdominal asynchrony in acute upper airway obstruction in small children. Am Rev Respir Dis 1990;142:540–4.
77. Mortola JP, Sant'Ambrogio G. Motion of the rib cage and the abdomen in tetraplegic patients. Clin Sci Mol Med 1978;54:25–32.
78. DeTroyer A, Kelly S. Chest wall mechanics in dogs with acute diaphragm paralysis. J Appl Physiol Respir Environ Exerc Physiol 1982;53:373–9.
79. Higgenbottam T, Allen D, Loh L, Clark TJH. Abdominal wall movement in normals and patients with hemidiaphragmatic and bilateral diaphragmatic palsy. Thorax 1977;32:589–95.
80. Cook CD, Mead J, Orzalesi MM. Static volume pressure characteristics of the respiratory system during maximal efforts. J Appl Physiol 1964;19:1016–22.
81. Wagener JS, Hibbert ME, Landau LI. Maximal respiratory pressures in children. Am Rev Respir Dis 1984; 129:873–5.
82. Multz AS, Aldrich TK, Prezant DJ, et al. Maximal inspiratory pressure is not a reliable test of inspiratory muscle strength in mechanically ventilated patients. Am Rev Respir Dis 1990;142:529–32.
83. Bellemare F, Grassino A. Effect of pressure and timing of contraction on human diaphragm failure. J Appl Physiol 1982;53:1190–95.
84. Rochester DF, Arora NS. Respiratory muscle failure [review]. Med Clin North Am 1983;67:573–97.
85. Gaultier C, Boule M, Girard F. Inspiratory force reserve of the respiratory muscles in children with chronic obstructive pulmonary disease. Am Rev Respir Dis 1985; 131:811–5.
86. Whitelaw WA, Derenne J-P, Milic-Emili J. Occlusion pressure as a measure of respiratory center output in conscious man. Respir Physiol 1975;23:181–99.
87. Bureau MA, Lupien L, Begin R. Neural drive and ventilatory strategy of breathing in normal children, and in patients with cystic fibrosis and asthma. Pediatrics 1981; 68:187–94.
88. Gaultier C, Perret L, Boule M, et al. Occlusion pressure and breathing pattern in children with chronic obstructive pulmonary disease. Bull Eur Physiopathol Respir 1982; 18:851–62.
89. Greenspan JS, Wolfson MR, Locke RG, et al. Increased respiratory drive and limited adaptation to loaded breathing in bronchopulmonary dysplasia. Pediatr Res 1992; 32:356–9.
90. Ramonatxo M, Boulard P, Prefaut C. Validation of a noninvasive tension-time index of inspiratory muscles. J Appl Physiol 1995;78:646–53.
91. Hayot M, Guillaumont S, Ramonatxo M, et al. Determinants of the tension-time index of inspiratory muscles in children with cystic fibrosis. Pediatr Pulmonol 1997;23:336–43.
92. Gross D, Grassino A, Macklem PT. Electromyogram pattern of diaphragm fatigue. J Appl Physiol 1979;46:1–7.
93. Muller N, Gulston G, Dade C, et al. Diaphragmatic muscle fatigue in the newborn. J Appl Physiol Respir Environ Exerc Physiol 1979;46:688–95.
94. Muller N, Volgyesi G, Bryan MH, Bryan AC. The consequence of diaphragmatic muscle fatigue in the newborn infant. J Pediatr 1979;95:793–7.
95. Sieck GC, Mazar A, Belman JM. Changes in diaphragmatic EMG spectra during hypercapneic loads. Respir Physiol 1985;61:137–52.

96. Bazzy AR, Korten JB, Haddad GG. Increase in electromyogram low frequency power in non-fatigued contracting skeletal muscle. J Appl Physiol 1986;61:1012–7.
97. Watchko JF, Standaert TA, Mayock DE, Woodrum DE. Diaphragmatic electromyogram power spectral analysis during ventilatory failure in infants. In: Gennser G, Marsal K, Svennigsen N, Lindstrom K, eds. Fetal and neonatal physiologic measurements. III. Proceedings of the Third International Conference on Fetal and Neonatal Physiological Measurements. Malmö, Sweden. Flenhags, Tryckeri, 1989:445–9.

CHAPTER 10

Structural and Functional Development of Respiratory Muscle

Gary C. Sieck, PhD, Rene Vandenboom, PhD, Carlos B. Mantilla, MD, Jeffrey P. Bailey, BS

The diaphragm muscle (DIAm) is the major inspiratory muscle in mammals. Thus, although other skeletal muscles are involved in respiration, this chapter focuses primarily on the pre- and early postnatal development of the DIAm. The DIAm appears rather late in evolution, whereas other ventilatory strategies dominate in lower vertebrates. The DIAm is rhythmically active prenatally (fetal respiratory movements) and must function to sustain ventilation from birth. Pre- and postnatal DIAm pathologies may lead to ventilatory failure and premature death. Given its vital importance, it is not surprising that the development and growth of the DIAm has attracted considerable interest. Yet, apart from general descriptive morphometric and histologic information, we know little about the mechanisms underlying DIAm development. Much information about myogenesis is available from in vitro model systems, but the applicability of these regulatory processes to in vivo DIAm development remains to be established. In this regard, it is particularly important to consider DIAm development in the context of maturation of other systems, for example, the central nervous system, the lung, and the thoracic and abdominal walls. Such integrative information is lacking.

There are a number of potential internal and external factors that can influence myogenesis. It is beyond the scope of this chapter to comprehensively assess all of these factors. However, there is abundant evidence that neural innervation and mechanical activation affect muscle plasticity and remodeling, even in the adult. Therefore, this chapter focuses on the role of innervation and mechanical activation on DIAm development. There is remarkable coincidence among the key developmental benchmarks of changes in DIAm innervation, mechanical activation, and contractile protein expression that reflect the establishment of different DIAm fiber phenotypes (Figure 10–1). Although seemingly circumstantial, the coincidence of these developmental benchmarks may provide insights into possible triggering and/or modulatory influences on DIAm development.

In this chapter we focus on the developmental benchmarks appearing in the rat DIAm (see Figure 10–1). The

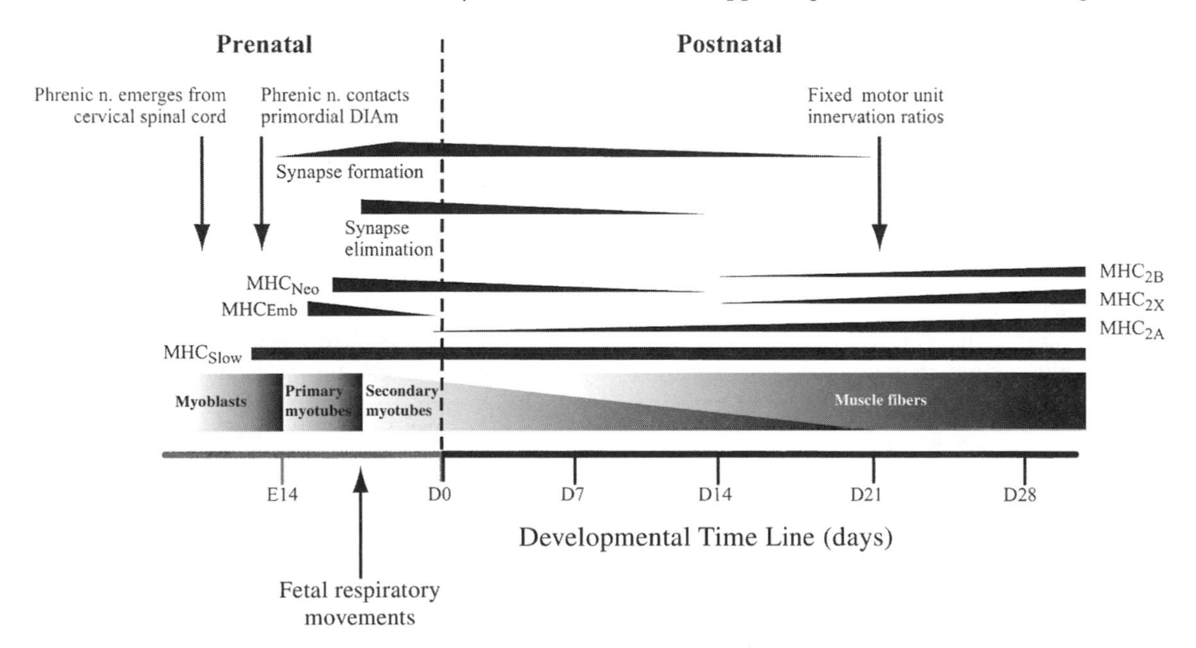

FIGURE 10–1. Schematic demonstrating the time lines of the major developmental landmarks for innervation, myosin heavy chain (MHC) isoform expression, muscle fiber formation, and fetal respiratory movements in the rat diaphragm muscle (DIAm).

rat serves as an animal model; it is assumed that comparable changes occur in humans. The rat is selected because of the abundant literature in this area on rodents. The gestational and postnatal benchmarks in mice generally are comparable to those in rats, and the use of this species affords the advantages of genetic manipulation. Unfortunately, at present there is little information specific to the DIAm in mice. In the rat, the DIAm developmental benchmarks span a period from embryonic day 12 (E12), when the phrenic nerve emerges from the spinal cord, to postnatal day 28 (D28), when the adult complement of DIAm fiber types is present. Between E12 and E17, DIAm fibers are innervated by phrenic motoneurons. This initial innervation of DIAm fibers is polyneuronal, as multiple phrenic motoneurons contact individual muscle fibers, and persists until the second postnatal week.[1] The initial fusion of myoblasts to form primary myotubules also takes place at the onset of innervation (E14 to E17). Subsequent to primary myotubule formation, contractile proteins are expressed including myosin heavy chain (MHC). The transitions in expression of MHC isoforms serve as a surrogate for the expression of a complement of contractile proteins that define the adult contractile phenotype. Important in this process is the formation of functional sarcomeres, which allow mechanical action. Shortly thereafter, fetal respiratory movements of the DIAm occur; these may further promote myogenesis. During this period and into the third postnatal week, secondary myotubules are formed by the fusion of myoblasts, and additional muscle fibers are added. Only then, is there establishment of the final innervation ratio of motor units (ie, the number of muscle fibers innervated by a single phrenic motoneuron). Myoblast proliferation may be particularly important in secondary myotubule formation, and this proliferative capacity remains important in the adult, as satellite cell activation participates in the injury and repair process.

Polyneuronal innervation of rat DIAm fibers is withdrawn through elimination of synapses before or at D14. Concurrently, expression of adult fast MHC isoforms (MHC_{2X} and MHC_{2B}) emerge, and their expression increases until D28 when the adult pattern of MHC isoform expression is fully established. Subsequently, muscle fiber type is established, but changes in the relative contribution of each fiber type can change due to disproportionate growth, for example, fibers expressing MHC_{2X} and MHC_{2B} grow disproportionately compared to fibers expressing MHC_{Slow} and MHC_{2A}.[2–4] Based on the temporal associations between innervation and the major developmental events in myogenesis, it would seem reasonable that the nervous system can either directly (eg, activity or nerve traffic) or indirectly (eg, secretion of neurotrophic factors) influence DIAm development. However, the precise mechanisms by which activation history and/or neurotrophic factors influence DIAm development remain largely unknown.

During the perinatal period, individual DIAm fibers undergo dramatic alterations in phenotype. Transformations in expression of key proteins such as MHC from embryonic to neonatal to adult isoforms occur and define at least one aspect of muscle fiber differentiation. Postnatal development of DIAm fibers is marked by remarkable plasticity in terms of MHC expression and contractile properties.[4] The following sections will discuss each of these aspects of DIAm development in greater detail.

Gross Embryologic Development of the Diaphragm Muscle

It is commonly thought that the DIAm is derived from three embryonic structures: the septum transversum, the pleuroperitoneal membranes, and esophageal mesenchyme.[5,6] The septum transversum forms a transverse partition that separates the coelomic cavity into thoracic (superior) and abdominal (inferior) portions. The superior portion contains the developing heart and the primitive pericardial cavity; the inferior portion contains the future peritoneal cavity. The peritoneum and pericardial cavities communicate through two large dorsolateral openings, the pleural canals. The left pleural canal is larger than the right and closes at a later stage in development, which may account for differences in the incidence of congenital DIAm hernias, which are more common on the left side. The differential growth of the embryonic axis causes a progressive caudal displacement of the septum transversum. The anterior edge of the septum transversum eventually becomes attached at the midthoracic level and the dorsal edge at the lowest thoracic level. Myoblasts differentiate within the septum transversum and eventually form part of the future DIAm. The phrenic nerves exit the cervical spinal cord and classically are thought to follow the migrating septum transversum.[6,7] More recently, it has been suggested that the initial targets of the phrenic nerves are the pleuroperitoneal membranes.[1,8] These transverse membranes grow ventrally to fuse with the posterior margin of the septum transversum. As the pleuropericardial folds develop from the lateral wall of the thoracic cavity, the phrenic nerve migrates toward the central tendon of the diaphragm and its more medial location between the pericardial and pleural cavities. The underlying mechanisms guiding phrenic nerve outgrowth continue to be poorly understood; the migration of the phrenic nerves and associated primordial DIAm might be interdependent.

The bulk of the DIAm develops within the pleuroperitoneal fold, although the right and left crural portions of the DIAm derive from the esophageal mesenchyme. Fibers of the crural DIAm originate from the upper lumbar vertebral column and insert into the dorsomedial portion of the central tendon. Because of the different origin of the crural portions of the DIAm and the fact that they may arise from the esophageal mesenchyme, some authors attribute the innervation of the crural portion of the DIAm to lumbar spinal nerves.[6,7] However, there is now consensus that the entire DIAm is innervated by cervical spinal cord segments.[9–12] Indeed, there is a somatotopic pattern of innervation in both costal and crural portions of the DIAm, with the more ventral aspects being innervated by phrenic motoneurons located in more rostral cervical spinal cord segments, compared with the dorsal aspects of both DIAm regions. This somatotopic innervation pattern may reflect either the embryonic migration of the phrenic nerves or the migration of myoblasts/myotubules in the DIAm. Certainly, despite the long-standing interest in development of the DIAm, there is still considerably more to learn about the embryologic development of this important and unique muscle.

Innervation of the Diaphragm Muscle

In the rat, phrenic motoneuron axons and the axons of the brachial plexus emerge from the cervical spinal cord at E11.[1] Migration of phrenic motoneuron axons to the pleuroperitoneal membrane (primordial DIAm) is complete by E13 to E14. Thereafter, phrenic motoneuron axons branch, and primary myotubules form in association with nerve terminals. Functional synapses do not form until E17, at which time fetal respiratory movements begin indicating intact inspiratory drive. The formation of functional synapses involves specialization of both pre- and postsynaptic elements (Figure 10–2). A number of regulatory processes are involved in guiding axonal growth, targeting to the pleuroperitoneal fold and directing specific patterns of branching. There is abundant in vitro literature to indicate a close interaction between the extracellular matrix and axonal outgrowth and branching. On the postsynaptic side, cholinergic receptors aggregate, a process that may involve agrin secretion by the nerve terminal, its incorporation into the basal lamina, and activation of MuSK receptors at the postsynaptic membrane, leading to rapsyn-mediated cholinergic receptor clustering.[13] It has been demonstrated clearly that the morphology of neuromuscular junction varies with DIAm fiber type in the adult rat (see Figure 10–2).[14] However, the evolution of these differences in neuromuscular junction structure during the perinatal period has not been explored fully. It appears that neuromuscular junctions in the neonatal DIAm are far less elaborate than those on adult fibers.

During early postnatal development, it has been demonstrated that the rat DIAm is far more susceptible to neuromuscular transmission failure during repetitive activation compared with that of the adult.[15–18] At least part of this increased susceptibility to neuromuscular transmission failure may reflect failure of action potential propagation at axonal branch points.[16,18–20] Due to polyneuronal innervation, there is more extensive branching of phrenic motoneurons during the pre- and early postnatal period. There also appears to be differences in presynaptic neurotransmitter release and/or cholinergic receptor activation, which could affect neuromuscular transmission failure. Differences in endplate potential amplitude suggest either reduced neurotransmitter release and/or disproportionately smaller endplate regions (ie, fewer cholinergic receptors) in the early postnatal DIAm.[15–17]

Recent evidence in the rat indicates that adult phrenic motoneurons express various neurotrophic factors including NT3, NT4/5, and brain-derived neurotrophic factor (BDNF).[21,22] It has been demonstrated that these neurotrophic factors are produced by spinal cord neurons during embryonic development; however, whether phrenic motoneurons specifically express these neurotrophic factors remains unknown. Receptors for NT3 (TrkC), NT4/5, and BDNF (TrkB) are present in adult skeletal muscle, including the rat DIAm.[21] The presence of these neurotrophic factor receptors in developing muscle has not been adequately explored. It is possible that secretion of neurotrophic factors by phrenic motoneurons may partially influence DIAm myogenesis. It should be noted that homozygous NT3- and BDNF-null mutant mice do not survive after birth.[23,24] Clearly, there are abnormalities in the central nervous systems of these knockout mice. Unfortunately, there is no specific information available concerning development of the phrenic nerve; nor have structural abnormalities in the DIAm been explored.

Myogenesis

The formation of skeletal muscle fibers involves two basic and readily discernible stages: commitment and terminal differentiation (Figure 10–3). Commitment (also known as determination) refers to the transformation of mesodermal progenitor cells to myoblasts. Neural-derived proteins (eg, Sonic hedgehog and wnt 1, 3, and 4) act to promote myoblast commitment within the myotome.[25] The process for myoblast commitment for hypaxial muscles (eg, limb muscles, chest and abdominal wall muscles, and DIAm) is distinct from that for epaxial muscles (eg, back and neck muscles).[26] In both cases, the commitment process is marked by the expression of *Pax-3*. However, hypaxial muscles do not depend on axial neural structures for the commitment of myoblasts, suggesting that myogenic determination can be initiated in the absence of neuraxial structures and, in fact, may be repressed in vivo until migration occurs. The explanted lateral half of avian somites express MyoD, which can be inhibited in vitro by bone morphogenic protein 4 or fibroblast growth factor 5.[27]

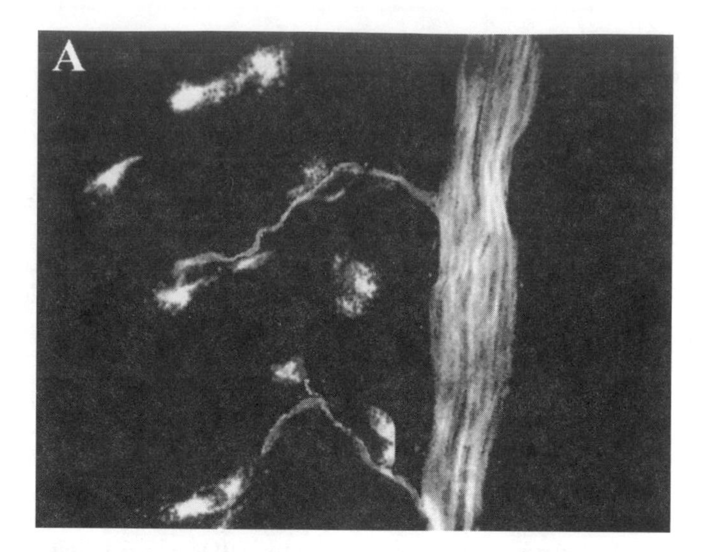

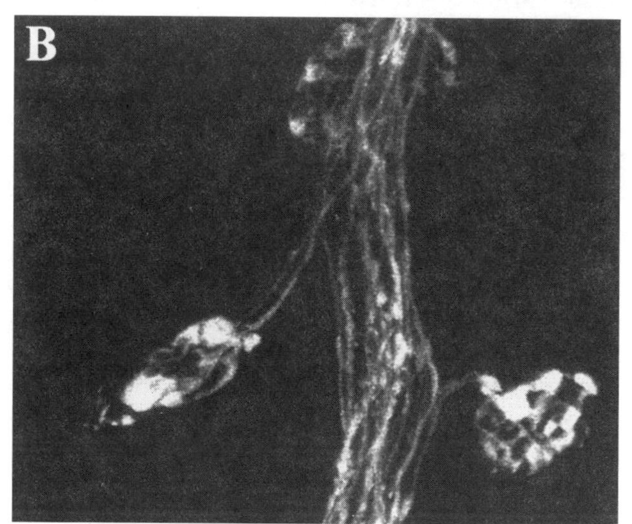

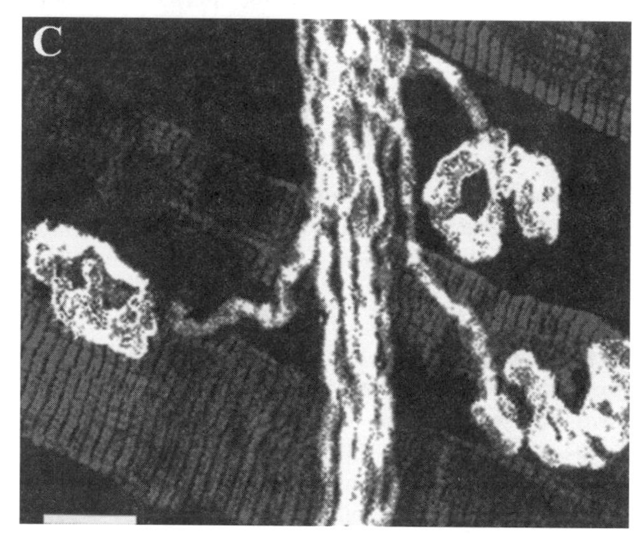

FIGURE 10–2. Microscopic images of phrenic motor axons and neuromuscular junctions at E17 (*A*), D0 (*B*), and adult (*C*) diaphragm muscle (DIAm). In the adult, immunoreactivity for slow myosin heavy chain (MHC_{Slow}) and MHC_{2A} (N2.261 antibody) is also displayed. Bar represents 25 μm. Motor endplates were labeled using rhodamine-conjugated α-bungarotoxin and phrenic motor axons were labeled with rabbit immunoglobulin G (IgG) anti-PGP9.5 and Cy5-conjugated antirabbit IgG. Images were collected using a laser-scanning confocal microscope. Note that in the E17 DIAm (*A*), many clusters of cholinergic receptors are not yet innervated. Also, the pattern of polyneuronal innervation is not clearly established at this early stage of synapse formation. At D0 (*B*), polyneuronal innervation of endplate regions is clearly evident. Note also that at this age, the neuromuscular junctions are not as elaborate as those in the adult (*C*).

These factors have been implicated in the maintenance of the proliferative myoblast phenotype and inhibition of differentiation. Myoblasts for hypaxial muscles migrate out of the lateral dermomyotome and express Myf-5 and c-met (a tyrosine kinase receptor for hepatocyte growth factor/scatter factor). Myoblast differentiation does not occur in vivo until myoblasts migrate to the thoracic or abdominal walls or to the limbs. Note that this is a simplified view of this complex process, and other factors may be involved. For hypaxial muscles, including the DIAm, expression of Myf-5 and subsequent myoblast commitment begins at ~E10 and continues through E12.[28]

Terminal differentiation refers to the subsequent, nonreversible transformation of committed mononucleated myoblasts to multinucleated myotubules containing contractile proteins (see Figure 10–3). Terminal differentiation begins when a population of proliferating myoblasts irreversibly exits the cell cycle. In other words, the proliferative phase of myoblast cell formation must cease for terminal differentiation to occur. However, a pool of myoblasts capable of proliferation persists into adulthood as satellite cells. Proliferating myoblasts are susceptible to apoptosis (ie, programmed cell death) until they exit the cell cycle. It has been suggested that this mechanism may exist to control the total number of myoblasts committed to a muscle cell phenotype.[29]

Differentiation of skeletal muscle fibers requires that mononucleated myoblasts fuse to produce myotubules

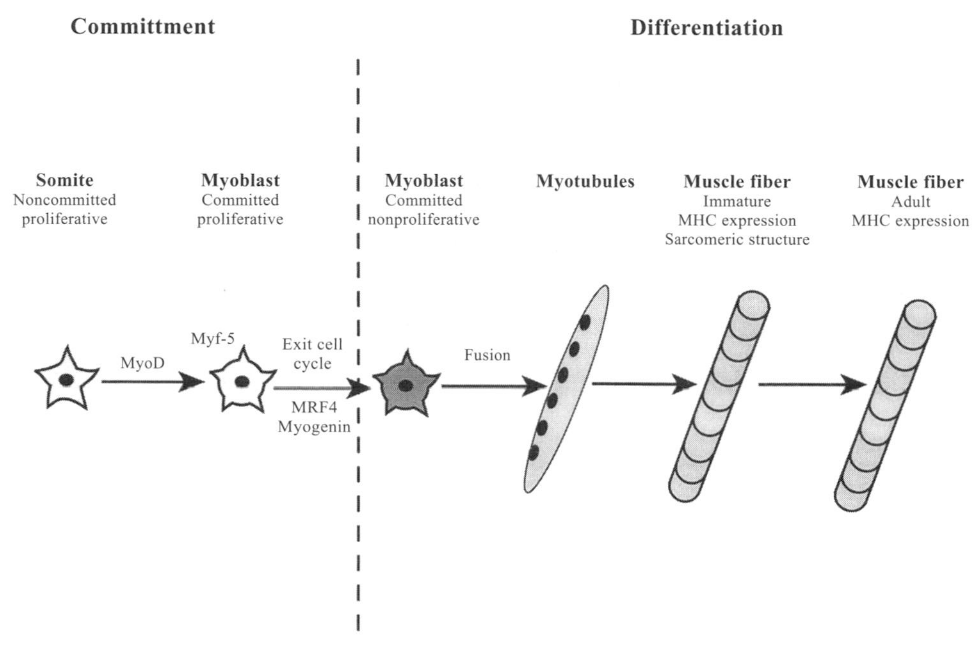

FIGURE 10–3. Schematic demonstrating the stages involved in the formation of skeletal muscle fibers during myogenesis. In the first stage, somite expression of MyoD and Myf-5 marks the beginning of the process of commitment to proliferative myoblasts. With the expression of MRF4 and myogenin, myoblasts exit the cell cycle to begin the stage of differentiation. These nonproliferative myoblasts then fuse to form myotubules. With the formation of distinct sarcomeres, muscle fibers are formed, and the differentiation process continues until adult fiber types are formed.

(see Figure 10–3).[30–32] Myoblast proliferation must cease before this phase of terminal differentiation can occur (ie, these events appear to be mutually exclusive). Myotubule formation in the rat DIAm occurs in two phases: the formation of primary myotubules (E14 to E17) followed by the formation of secondary myotubules (E17 to D21; Figure 10–4).[2,33] The fusion of myoblasts to form primary myotubules coincides temporally and spatially with the arrival and branching of the phrenic nerve. It has been suggested that formation of primary myotubules is independent of innervation.[34] However, this suggestion is based on the use of neuromuscular blocking agents, which does not exclude a potential neurotrophic influence. The formation of secondary myotubules is dependent on intact and functional innervation;[30,31,33–36] this is a distinguishing characteristic of secondary myotubules. However, it is unclear whether the dependence of secondary myotubules on innervation reflects the influence of activation (eg, fetal respiratory movements) or neurotrophic factors. It has been suggested that primary myotubules differentiate into fibers expressing the slow MHC isoform. In contrast, secondary myotubes can differentiate into fibers expressing either fast or slow MHC isoforms.[31,35,36] At present, we are unaware of any specific markers distinguishing primary from secondary myotubules, which complicates the interpretation of cell lineage studies.

An important step in the formation of myotubules is the fusion of myoblasts. The regulation of myoblast fusion depends on the expression of several proteins, including those in the extracellular matrix (eg, fibronectins and laminins), basal lamina (eg, muscle cell adhesion molecule [M-CAM]), neural cell adhesion molecule (N-CAM; M-cadherin), cell membrane (eg, β_1-integrin), and cytoskeleton (eg, actin and desmin) (Figure 10–5).[37] Abundant literature has focused on the in vitro properties of culture systems; however, little is known about the complex interactions that may exist in vivo.

Effect of Mechanical Activity

Mechanical effects on developing muscle may be either active (due to neural activation and muscle contraction) or passive strain imposed by the growing skeleton. Fetal respiratory movements begin with the formation of functional neuromuscular junctions and inspiratory neural drive. As mentioned above, neuromuscular blockade has no apparent effect on primary myotubule formation but does inhibit secondary myotubule formation.[30,31,33–36] It is possible that the effects of neuromuscular blockade result from the removal of the mechanical effects of neural activation rather that innervation per se. The influence of passive mechanical strain on muscle has been demonstrated clearly. Vandenburgh and co-workers[38,39] reported that in vitro passive stretching resulted in both hyperplasia and hypertrophy of myotubules. Thus, both proliferation and differentiation of myoblasts were affected by passive stretch. Further, in the presence of medium containing no growth factors, passive stretch prevented the atrophy of myotubules that normally occurs. Stretch-induced growth of muscle may be mediated by an

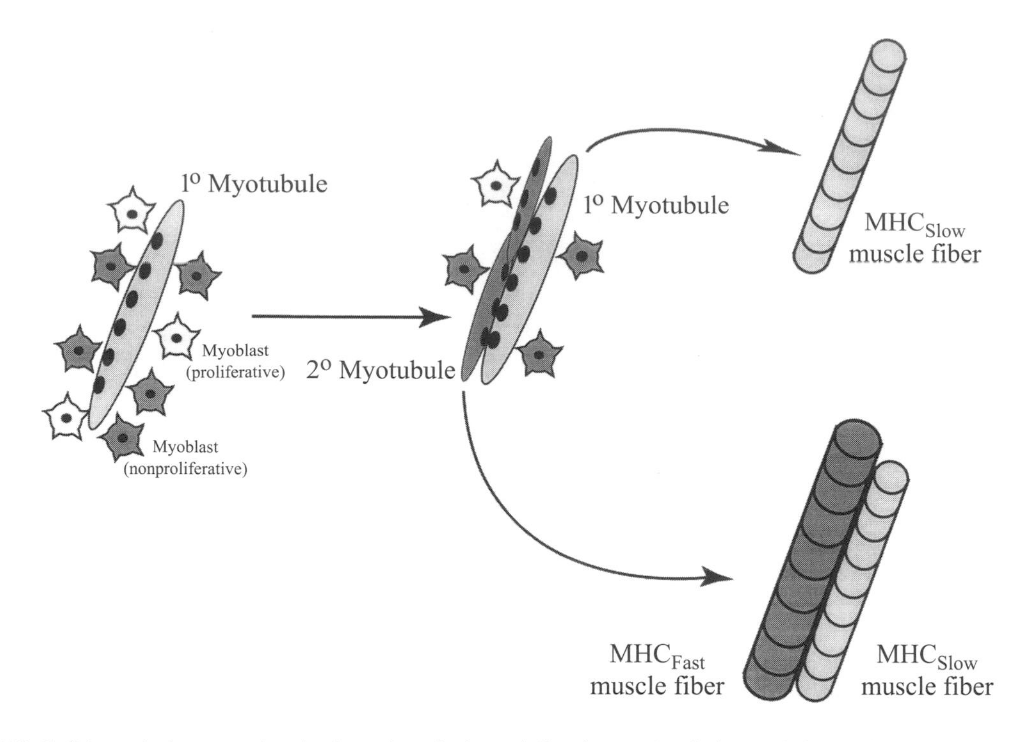

FIGURE 10–4. Schematic demonstrating the formation of primary (1°) and secondary (2°) myotubules, and the lineage-specific expression of myosin heavy chain (MHC) isoforms. Primary myotubules are formed from the fusion of nonproliferative myoblasts in the first phase of myotubule formation. Primary myotubules differentiate to become muscle fibers expressing the MHC_{Slow} isoform. Subsequently, secondary myotubules are formed by fusion of nonproliferative myoblasts surrounding primary myotubules. Secondary myotubules differentiate to become muscle fibers expressing either slow or fast MHC isoforms. A pool of quiescent nondifferentiated myoblasts capable of proliferation persist into adulthood (satellite cells—not shown).

increase in $PDGF_{2\alpha}$.[39] These data suggest that fetal respiratory movements may influence DIAm development by promoting secondary myotubule formation.

Regulation of Myogenesis by Basic Helix-Loop-Helix Proteins

Striated muscle is among the most ancient of all cell types. One wonders how expression of muscle-specific genes was first initiated and then maintained in the primitive host. It is unknown whether mesoderm has an intrinsic tendency to express the myogenic program or if myogenesis needs to be induced by positive signals; it also may be possible that myogenesis proceeds unless repressed by inhibitory signals.[25] Although none of these potential mechanisms can, at present, be ruled out, it has been demonstrated that myogenesis can be induced in a variety of nonmuscle cells by the forced expression of members of the basic helix-loop-helix (bHLH) superfamily of proteins.[40,41] These so-called muscle regulatory factors (MRFs) include MyoD,[42] myogenin,[43] Myf-5,[44] and MRF4 (also known as herculin) (Figure 10–6).[45] In human muscle, MRF4 has been independently isolated as Myf-6.[46]

The identification of the superfamily of bHLH proteins has provided a molecular mechanism for the regulation of myogenesis. Expression of MRFs may provide the signaling network required for both the initiation and continuation of the myogenic program in cells fated to a muscle lineage. The MRFs also may be involved in fine tuning myogenesis by determining the precise expression of MHC species in adult muscle.[47] The similar function of the different MRF proteins, that is, the induction of the myogenic program in nonmuscle cells, may be due to a highly conserved basic deoxyribonucleic acid (DNA) binding domain for sequence-specific DNA binding. In addition, the HLH region may be important for forming heterodimers with E proteins.[48] Outside these regions there appears to be little sequence similarity between different MRFs.

The initiation of skeletal muscle phenotype in various nonmuscle cell types by the overexpression of MRFs indicates that at some point in the evolutionary process, control of muscle-specific gene expression came to be mediated by muscle-specific transcription factors, acting through *cis*-acting regulatory elements on the DNA strand. Signals emanating from the neural tube or notochord may commit mesodermal cells to a muscle cell lineage and thus initiate myogenesis by releasing suppression of specific MRFs.[27] A candidate mediator of this positive regulation is Sonic hedgehog.[49] The initial upregulation of MRFs may initiate a complex cascade of signals that continues through differentiation and helps

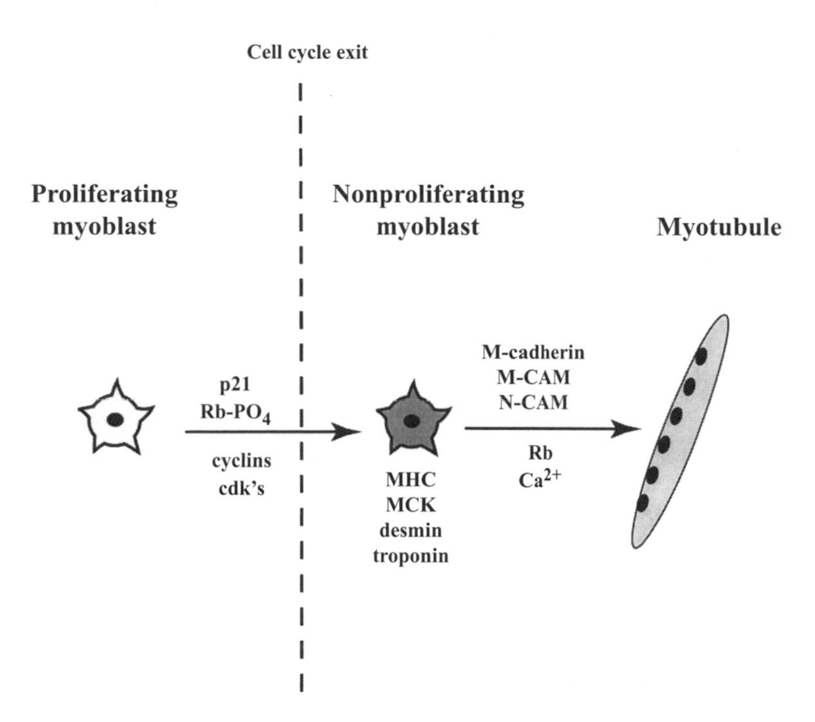

FIGURE 10–5. Schematic demonstrating the multiple factors involved in the regulation of myoblast fusion. The exit of proliferating myoblasts from the cell cycle is marked by the expression of p21 and phosphorylation of the retinoblastoma protein (Rb). Key cyclins and cyclin dependent kinases (cdk's) can modulate the exit of myoblasts from the cell cycle and, thus, keep the myoblast in the proliferative phase. After exiting the cell cycle, myoblasts begin to express muscle specific markers, such as myosin heavy chain (MHC), M-creatine kinase (MCK), desmin, and troponin. Expression of the cell adhesion molecules (CAMs) M-cadherin, muscle CAM (M-CAM), and neural CAM (N-CAM), along with the presence of the inactive dephosphorylated form of Rb and elevation of cytosolic Ca^{2+} participate in the fusion of myoblasts into myotubules.

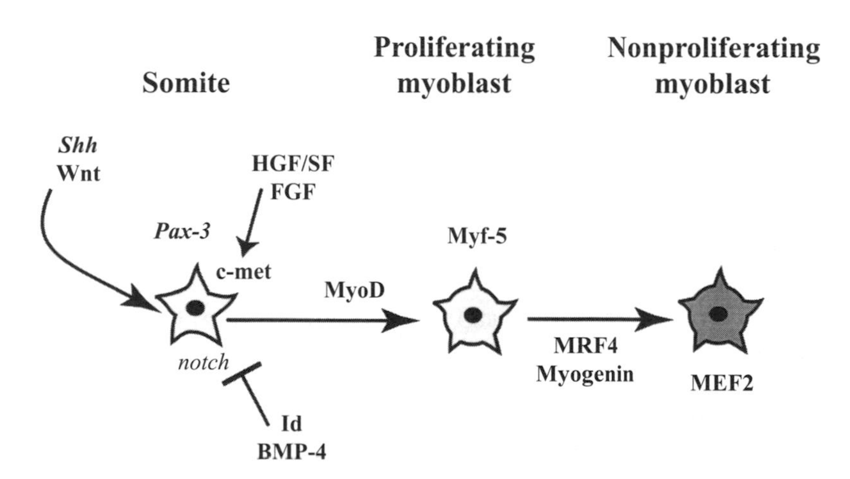

FIGURE 10–6. Schematic demonstrating the role of myogenic regulatory factors (MRFs) and other regulatory factors in myogenesis. Formation of somites is controlled by the expression of Sonic hedgehog (Shh), wingless family proteins (Wnt), and *Pax-3*. Commitment of somitic muscle cell precursors to become myoblasts is controlled by MyoD and Myf-5, as well as c-met and its ligand hepatocyte growth factor/scatter factor (HGF/SF). For hypaxial muscle, the somitic muscle cell precursors must migrate before myoblasts are formed. Factors that inhibit precursor cell migration (bone morphogenic protein 4 [BMP-4]) will thus block myoblast formation. Myoblast formation also is inhibited by an inhibitor of differentiation (Id), *notch*, and general growth factors. Further differentiation into nonproliferating myoblasts is affected by the expression of myogenin, as well as MRF4. The expression of many muscle-specific genes (ie, MHC) may be controlled through the interaction of the MRFs with myocyte-enhancing factor (MEF2).

sustain myogenesis. Induction of MyoD, occurring first, may initiate a cascade of reactions that result in expression of Myf-5, MRF4, and myogenin. Tissues, such as the DIAm, derived from hypaxial myotome show this order; whereas, in epaxial muscle, Myf-5 is expressed first.[50] The timing of induction of various MRFs also seems to be critical for initiating or continuing specific stages of prenatal muscle development. MyoD and Myf-5 are highly expressed in proliferating myoblasts, suggesting a primary role for the MRFs during this stage of development.[42]

The critical role of different MRFs during development has been elucidated by gene-targeting experiments. For example, in mice, single knockout models for MyoD[51] and MRF4[52] produce offspring with apparently normal skeletal muscles. Myf-5-deficient pups succumb to asphyxiation soon after birth due to rib abnormalities, but they, also, have apparently normal skeletal muscle.[53] In MyoD- and MRF4-deficient pups, Myf-5 and myogenin, respectively, are upregulated. This suggests that, in these animals, normal skeletal muscle development is "rescued" by redundancies in the MRF regulatory network. Myogenin single knockouts produce animals that have only myoblasts where limb muscles should be,[54,55] implying that myogenin alone among the MRFs is indispensable for formation of primary myotubules. Double knockouts of Myf-5 and MyoD produce offspring that lack even myoblasts. Consistent with the idea that expression of some MRFs is autoregulatory, this study suggests that expression of both these MRFs is required for initiating precursor cell commitment to a muscle lineage.[56] Double knockouts of Myf-5 and MRF4 produce offspring that resemble Myf-5 knockouts, suggesting that MRF4 regulates later aspects of myogenesis and may be substituted with myogenin.

Deoxyribonucleic acid enhancer regions have been identified for several of the MRFs. For example, MyoD expression is regulated by upstream and downstream enhancers, regions that may be important for controlling MyoD expression at different points during development.[57,58] Importantly, expression of specific MRFs may be dependent upon upstream induction of other MRF proteins. For example, induction of MyoD depends in part on Myf-5 expression, suggesting that induction of MRFs is, at least in part, autoregulatory in nature.[59] The paired-box protein Pax-3 may also positively regulate MRF expression, as ectopic expression of Pax-3 induces both MyoD and Myf-5 in embryonic tissue.[60] After expression, MRFs function as molecular switches, initiating myogenesis by inducing the expression of a host of muscle-specific genes. The molecular mechanism mediating this function may be the binding of the bHLH motif to *cis*-acting DNA control elements of muscle-specific genes, known as E boxes.[61] The E-box is a CANNTG sequence-containing motif present in the promoter regions of many skeletal muscle specific genes. The E box functions to mediate gene activation in an MRF-dependent manner.[62] In addition to bHLH region binding, binding of nonconserved domains in the NH_2 and/or COOH termini of the MRFs may help activate transcription.[25]

Upstream regulation of bHLH binding to DNA may be regulated by dimerization of MRFs with other bHLH proteins. This mechanism may produce heterodimers with varying characteristics. Thus, MRF binding to DNA E boxes (and, thus, the expression of muscle-specific genes) may be either inhibited or promoted in a heterodimer-specific manner. The myocyte-enhancer factor 2 (MEF2A to D) family of MCM1, *a*gamus *d*eficiens, and *s*erum response factor (MADS)-box proteins may aid positive regulation of the myogenic program by MRFs. Interaction between MRFs and MEF2 proteins may account for how muscle specificity can be established for genes that lack MRF binding domains. Sites of MEF2 are located in the promotor regions of many muscle-specific genes. The muscle-promoting ability of MEF2 transcription factors may be due to MEF2 protein binding to muscle-specific promotor/enhancer regions on DNA, a mechanism that might aid the transcription process. It is important to note, however, that MEF2 protein binding alone is not thought to be sufficient for the induction of myogenesis. Binding sites of MEF2 have been located in the promotor region of myogenin, suggesting that expression of MRFs and MEFs is autoregulatory in nature.

In direct contrast to the positive role of MEF2 protein binding, the mesoderm may be prevented from expressing the myogenic program by the presence of inhibitory signals that suppress MRF expression/activity. Activity of MRFs is suppressed by binding of a class of HLH proteins lacking a basic DNA binding region. These inhibitor of differentiation factors (Id1 to Id4) inhibit MRF activity by forming heterodimers with E2 products (ubiquitously expressed HLH-containing proteins encoded for by E2 genes). These products prevent dimerization with MRFs and subsequent activation of skeletal muscle-specific genes.[63] Because they lack the basic DNA binding domain, heterodimerization of bHLH proteins with Id proteins prevents the strong binding to DNA by either E proteins or MRFs.[64] In mice, the twist protein may inhibit MRFs by sequestration of E proteins, thus preventing the formation of MRF-E protein heterodimers.[65] Another inhibitory factor is Mist1, a protein that binds with MyoD to form an inactive heterodimer, because Mist1 lacks a transactivation domain.[66] Teleologically, negative regulation of the myogenic program may be necessary to prevent the ectopic formation of skeletal muscle. It also may be important to prevent myogenesis in nonmyotomal somite cells.

Myosin Heavy Chain

Myosin is expressed ubiquitously in eukaryotic cells. There are at least 11 distinct myosin classes, coded for by a multigene family located on chromosome 17 (human)

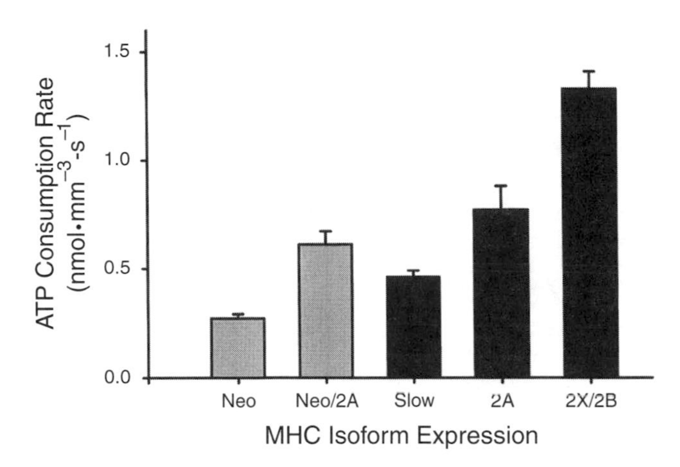

FIGURE 10–7. Comparison of maximal isometric myofibrillar adenosine triphosphate (ATP) consumption rates (nmol ATP consumed/fiber volume) of rat diaphragm muscle (DIAm) fibers expressing different myosin heavy chain (MHC) isoforms. Coexpression of MHC_{Neo} and MHC_{2A} is prevalent in the developing (D0 to D14) DIAm, whereas coexpression of MHC_{2X} and MHC_{2B} is prevalent in the adult DIAm. Myofibrillar ATP consumption rate was measured using a NADH-linked fluorometric procedure in single triton-X permeabilized fibers at 15°C.

and 11 (mouse).[67] Myosin II is the predominant myosin found in mammalian skeletal muscle, where it is both a structural and functional protein. In skeletal muscles such as the DIAm, myosin forms the thick filaments of the sarcomere, comprising approximately 50% of all muscle proteins. Functionally, all myosin types function as molecular motors, converting the chemical energy stored in the terminal phosphate bonds of adenosine triphosphate (ATP) into mechanical energy, thus driving muscle contraction.[68]

Myosin is a hexamer protein (MW = 480 kD) comprising two heavy chains and four light chains. The molecular structure of myosin was first described using crystallized chicken myosin.[69,70] At the COOH terminus, the myosin molecule is rod-shaped, as a result of the dimerization of the two heavy chains (MW = 200 kD) into a 200-nm α-helical tail. Bundled together, this portion of the MHC forms the thick filament backbone. At the NH_3 terminus, the heavy chains separate and branch out to form two distinct heads (S-1). S-1 is asymmetric, being 16.5 nm long and 4.5 to 6.5 nm wide. S-1 is the kinetic domain of myosin, containing actin and nucleotide binding domains. The mechanism whereby S-1 converts chemical energy into mechanical work may involve stereo-specific docking of S-1 with actin that reverses intramolecular conformational changes induced by ATP hydrolysis.[71] The ATPase activity of S-1 varies with MHC isoform (Figure 10–7),[72–75] a specificity that forms the molecular basis for differences in mechanical function between different skeletal muscle fiber types. Although the amino acid sequences of different MHC isoforms generally are conserved, sequence divergence does exist in the COOH terminal as well as in the flexible hinge region of the neck. The lack of amino acid homology in these sequences may underlie this difference in ATPase activity between MHC isoforms.[76] Bound to S-1 are the ~20-kD essential (MLC_{20}) and regulatory myosin light chains (MLC17); MLC binding provides structural support to the MHC.[70] Different isoforms of MLC may modulate the kinetic properties of MHC.[77] The MLC_{17} binds Ca^{2+} and can be phosphorylated, modifications that may further modulate S-1 activity of MHC species.[78–80]

Pre- and early postnatal development (E17 to D28) of the rat DIAm is characterized by dramatic transitions in MHC isoform expression.[81–84] During late embryonic development (E17 to E21), the predominant MHC isoforms expressed in the rat DIAm are MHC_{Slow}, MHC_{Emb}, and MHC_{Neo}.[81–84] As mentioned above, primary myotubules appear to express MHC_{Slow}, perhaps in combination with MHC_{Emb}, although such coexpression is difficult to discern at this stage. Secondary myotubules apparently express MHC_{Emb} with rapid transition to MHC_{Neo}. By birth, the predominant isoform expressed in the rat DIAm is MHC_{Neo} (~70% of total). It should also be noted that MHC_{Emb} expression is undetectable at birth, whereas MHC_{Slow} and MHC_{2A} are expressed overtly. Neo myosin heavy chain continues to be expressed in the rat DIAm until D21, usually in combination with MHC_{Slow} and/or MHC_{2A} isoforms. During this gradual disappearance of MHC_{Neo}, MHC_{Slow} and MHC_{2A} expression increases. Expression of MHC_{2X} and MHC_{2B} does not appear until D14, coincident with the completion of synapse elimination and disappearance of polyneuronal innervation of muscle fibers. It remains unknown whether synapse elimination is linked to muscle fiber lineage and MHC isoform expression. Through secondary myotubule formation, the number of DIAm fibers

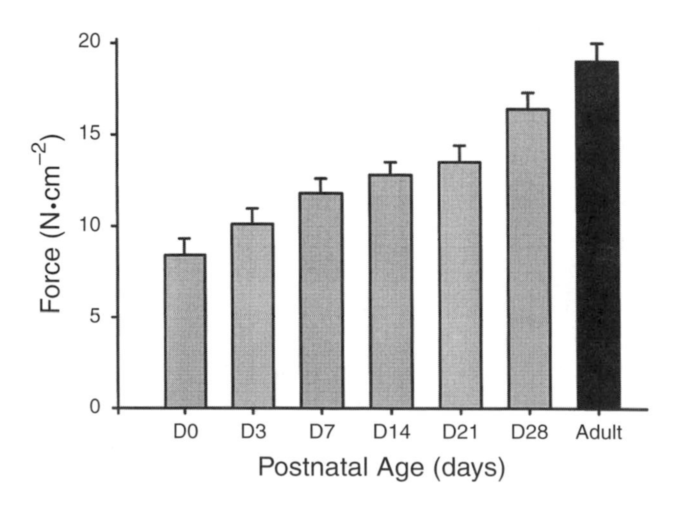

FIGURE 10–8. Maturational changes in maximum specific force of rat diaphragm muscle. Maximum specific force of muscle fiber strips was measured at 27°C.

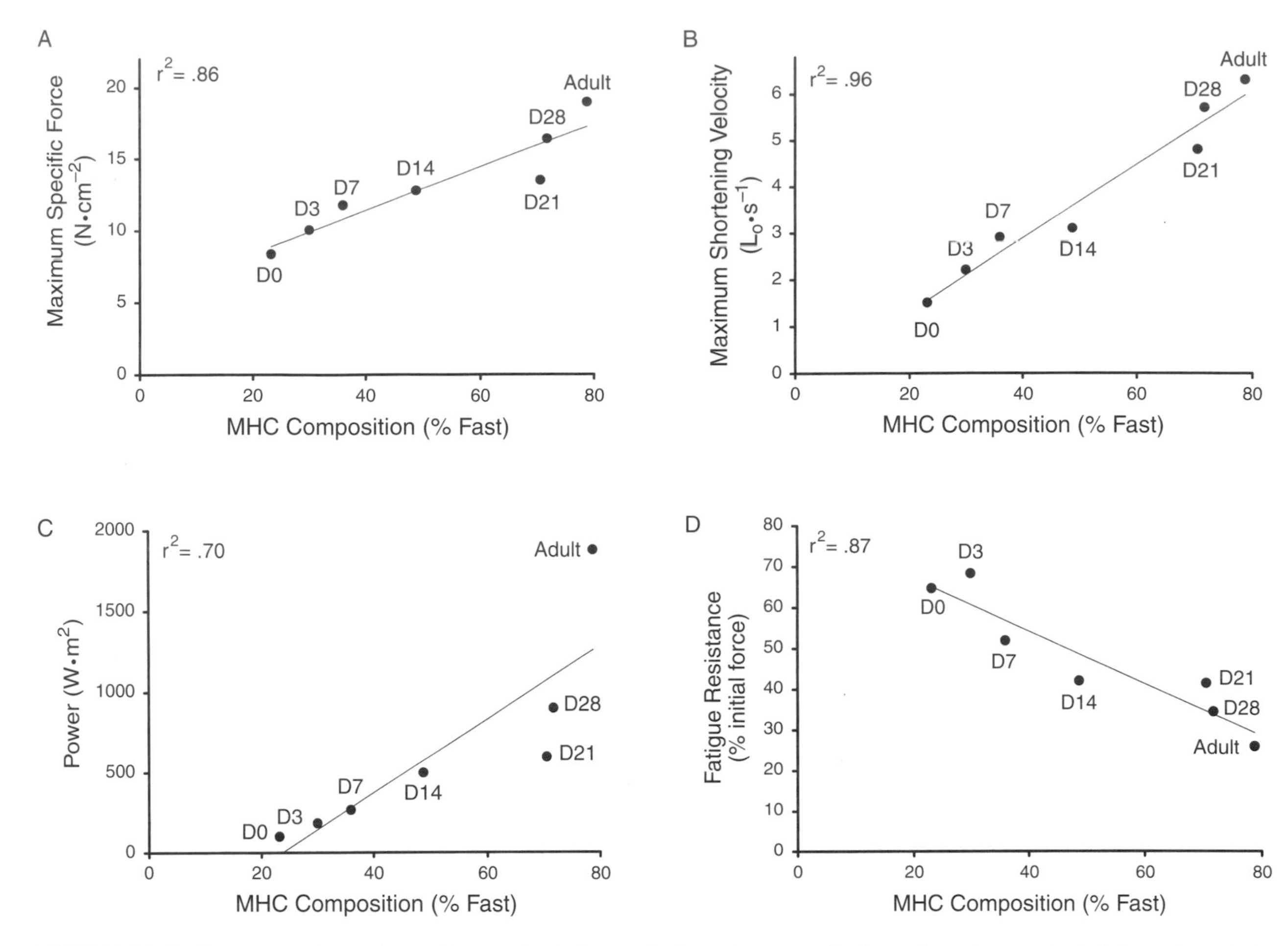

FIGURE 10–9. Linear regression analyses of maturational changes in *A*, maximum specific force, *B*, maximum unloaded shortening velocity, *C*, maximum power output, and *D*, fatigue resistance in relation to changes in the relative expression of fast MHC isoforms. Data were obtained from mixed fiber bundles in the rat diaphragm muscle at 27°C.

increases until D21.[85] Thus, innervation ratio (ie, the number of muscle fibers innervated by a single phrenic motoneuron) is not established until D21. By D28 the adult pattern of MHC expression in the rat DIAm is complete, with MHC_{2X} and MHC_{2B} isoforms accounting for ~45% of total MHC expression, with MHC_{Slow} and MHC_{2A} accounting for ~30% and ~25%, respectively. This dramatic shift in MHC isoform expression in the DIAm across a 4 to 5-week period represents an important stage of muscle fiber differentiation, especially with respect to the development of mature contractile properties.

The time course for developmental transitions in MHC isoform expression in the DIAm, particularly for the expression of MHC_{Neo} and fast MHC isoforms, differs from that described for limb muscles. It is presumed that factors such as activation history (eg, fetal respiratory movements and early breathing requirements), hormonal milieu (eg, thyroid hormones, growth hormone, and insulin-like growth hormone), and innervation (polyneuronal innervation and synapse elimination) play major roles in determining these developmental transitions. For example, MHC expression is known to be sensitive to thyroid hormone levels.[86] To examine the effect of hypothyroidism on the postnatal development of the rat DIAm, pregnant female rats were administered propyl-2-thiouracil beginning at gestational day 10.[87] The effect of hypothyroidism on MHC isoform transitions was then assessed. We found that perinatal hypothyroidism delayed the transition from MHC_{Neo} to adult fast MHC isoforms. Even in rats at D28, MHC_{Neo} was still expressed at the expense of all fast MHC isoforms. Unfortunately, we did not evaluate MHC isoform expression at later stages. The results of this study were confounded by the simultaneous blunting of normal growth, which could affect secondary myotubule formation. In another study in which pregnant female rats were undernourished, and subsequently the growth curves of pups were blunted, we found a reduced number of DIAm fibers (predominantly type II or fast fibers) reflecting an inhibition of secondary myotubule formation.[2] In a third study the effect of unilateral denervation of the phrenic nerve at D7 on MHC isoform transitions in the rat DIAm was examined.[88] Similar to the effects of hypothyroidism, we found that denervation delayed the normal transition from MHC_{Neo}

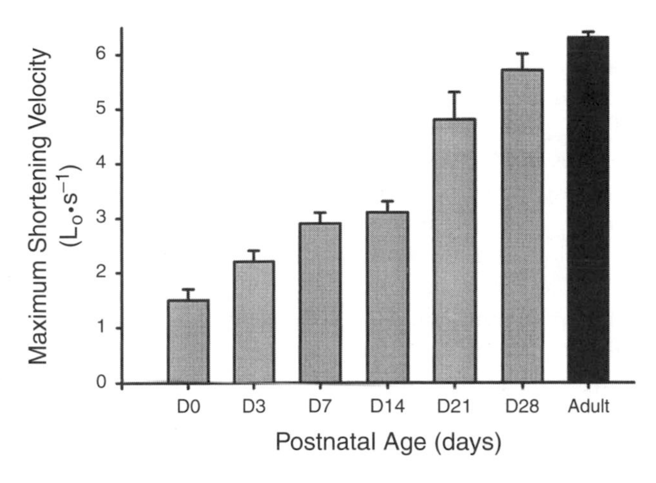

FIGURE 10–10. Maturational changes in maximum unloaded shortening velocity (expressed as $L_o \cdot s^{-1}$) of the rat diaphragm muscle. Maximum unloaded shortening velocity was measured in muscle fiber strips at 27°C.

to adult fast MHC isoforms. However, by D28 the adult pattern of MHC isoform expression was present.

Myosin Heavy Chain Isoform Expression and Muscle Contractile Properties

A number of studies have demonstrated that the contractile properties of skeletal muscle correlates with fiber type composition. A number of histochemical fiber type classification schemes have been proposed, but the most widely used and accepted scheme is based on the pH lability of myofibrillar ATPase staining.[89] Based on this scheme, muscle fibers are classified as type I, IIa, and IIb, and in a modified version, type IIx fibers also can be classified in some species.[90] In the adult, there is a correlation between MHC isoform expression and fiber type classification, based on the pH lability of myofibrillar

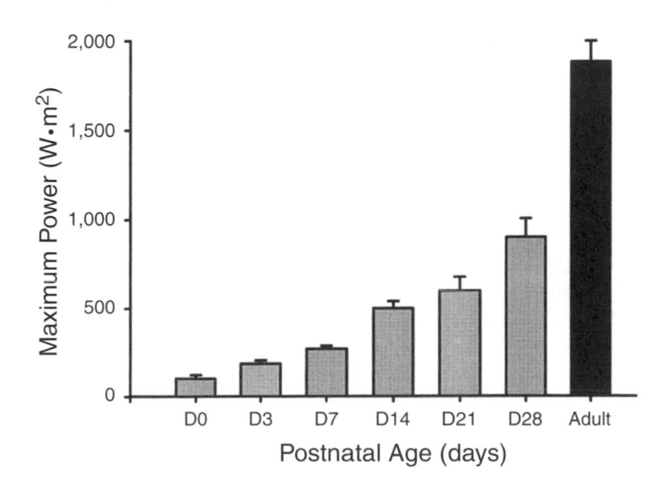

FIGURE 10–11. Maturational changes in maximum power output of the rat diaphragm muscle. Power was determined in muscle fiber strips at 27°C.

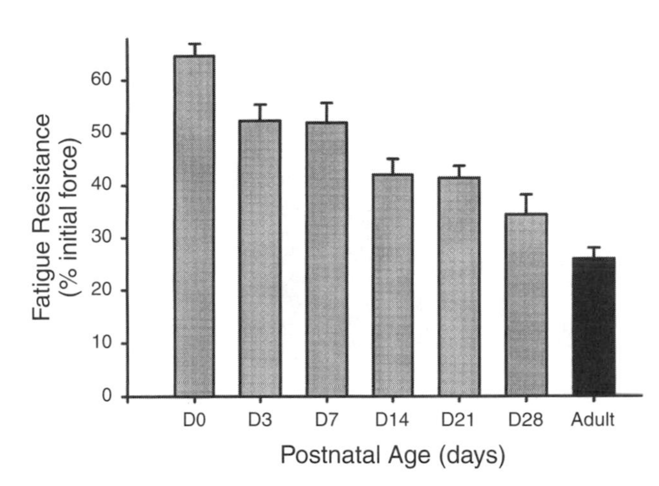

FIGURE 10–12. Maturational changes in fatigue resistance of the rat diaphragm muscle. Fatigue resistance was determined in muscle strips at 27°C using a standard fatigue test (40 Hz in 330 ms trains repeated each second for a 2-min period). Fatigue resistance was calculated as the force generated after 2 min divided by initial force.

ATPase staining.[67] Accordingly, fibers classified as type I express MHC_{Slow}, type IIa fibers express MHC_{2A}, and type IIb fibers express MHC_{2B} and/or MHC_{2X}.[91–93] Several studies, including our own, have demonstrated an association between MHC isoform composition of the rat DIAm and muscle contractile properties.[84] During early postnatal development, the contractile properties of the DIAm change dramatically, and these changes correlate with transitions in MHC isoform composition. Specific force (ie, force generated per muscle cross-sectional area) of the rat DIAm more than doubles from birth to adulthood (Figure 10–8),[2,4,87,88,94–96] and this increase in specific force correlates with an increase in the relative expression of fast MHC isoforms (Figure 10–9*A*). Maximum unloaded shortening velocity (V_o) of the DIAm increases by over fivefold from D0 to D28 (Figure 10–10),[87,88,96] which also correlates with the relative expression of fast MHC isoforms (see Figure 10–9*B*). Accompanying these changes in contractile properties, the maximum power output and work performance of the rat DIAm markedly increase from birth to D28 (Figures 10–9*C* and 10–11).[96] Not surprisingly, fatigue resistance of the neonatal DIAm to repeated activation is much higher compared to the adult, and this correlates with the changing relative amount of fast MHC isoforms expressed as well as the oxidative capacity of DIAm fibers (Figures 10–9*D* and 10–12).[4,95,96]

These changes in contractile properties at the whole-muscle level reflect the relationship between MHC isoform expression and contractile properties of individual muscle fibers. Fibers expressing MHC_{Slow} generate less specific force (Figure 10–13) and have a slower V_o (Figure 10–14) compared with fibers expressing fast MHC isoforms. It has been reported that fibers expressing immature MHC isoforms (MHC_{Neo} and MHC_{Emb}) also

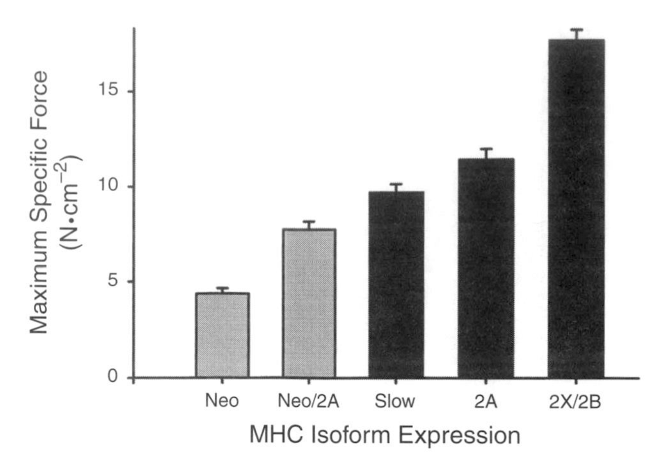

FIGURE 10–13. Comparison of maximum specific force of rat diaphragm muscle fibers expressing different myosin heavy chain (MHC) isoforms. Maximum specific force was measured in single triton-X permeabilized fibers at a sarcomere length of 2.5 μm (15°C).

display lower specific force and slower V_o than do adult fibers expressing fast MHC isoforms.[97] In the adult DIAm, the lower maximum specific force of fibers expressing MHC_{Slow} is at least partially explained by differences in MHC protein content per half-sarcomere (ie, fewer crossbridges in parallel). It is likely that the specific force of the neonatal DIAm is also due, at least in part, to a lower MHC content per half-sarcomere.[98] The slower V_o and greater fatigue resistance of the neonatal DIAm may partly reflect the slower ATP consumption rate of fibers expressing MHC_{Slow} and MHC_{Neo} (see Figure 10–7), which are the predominant isoforms expressed at this age.[95] Although it is clear that during early development the contractile properties of the DIAm undergo profound shifts that correspond to the transitions in MHC isoform expression, the signals driving these changes are not yet known.

Changes in contractile properties induced by pathophysiologic conditions may not always be reflected by changes in MHC isoform composition alone. For example, with perinatal hypothyroidism there is a dramatic reduction in maximum specific force and a slowing of V_o in the rat DIAm that cannot be attributed fully to the moderate changes in MHC isoform composition. Similarly, following unilateral denervation of the DIAm at D7, there is a marked reduction in maximum specific force and a slowing of V_o that are not predicted from the slight changes in MHC isoform composition. As mentioned above, the changes in specific force may reflect the total MHC content per half-sarcomere of DIAm fibers,[98] rather than MHC isoform expression per se. The slowing of V_o is more difficult to explain. Clearly, these results indicate that crossbridges cycling kinetics can be slowed independent of the MHC isoform expressed. It is possible that these pathophysiologic conditions affect actomyosin ATPase activity of the myosin S-1 fragment, or that there is an increased internal resistance to shortening. In support, we observed that following unilateral denervation of the adult rat DIAm, maximum isometric ATP consumption rate was reduced independent of MHC isoform expression.[99]

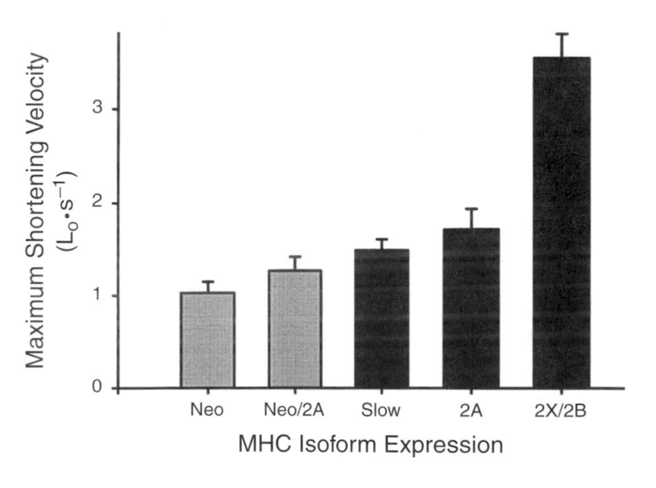

FIGURE 10–14. Comparison of maximum unloaded shortening velocity of rat diaphragm muscle fibers expressing different myosin heavy chain (MHC) isoforms. Maximum unloaded shortening velocity was measured in single triton-X permeabilized fibers using the slack test at 15°C.

Functional Implications of Developmental Stages of the Diaphragm Muscle

The DIAm plays a vital role in sustaining ventilation from the time of birth. Thus, it must be capable of meeting this essential role. Maturation of other structures may impact DIAm performance. For example, the lung is stiffer due to greater alveolar recoil, which is offset by maturation of surfactant expression. The chest and abdominal walls are more compliant, and the DIAm must generate greater relative power to produce the necessary intrathoracic pressures, inspiratory airflow, and tidal volumes. At the same time, maximum power output and work performance are considerably lower for the neonatal DIAm compared with the adult (see Figure 10–11). Thus, a far greater fraction of maximum power output must be recruited to accomplish ventilation, and there is a correspondingly lower reserve capacity. The polyneuronal innervation of DIAm fibers may be particularly important as a neural strategy to accomplish greater fractional recruitment of DIAm fibers (ie, larger motor units). With synapse elimination and the expression of less energy-efficient MHC_{2X} and MHC_{2B} isoforms, DIAm motor behaviors that require greater power output can be accomplished, but at the expense of greater susceptibility to fatigue.[100,101] Typically, these are short-duration, high-pressure, expulsive behaviors that may be less necessary in the neonate than in the adult. However, it would appear that the neonate may be more susceptible to aspiration and asphyxiation than the adult, if they are unable to clear the airway via expulsive behaviors. This may account for the greater hypoxic tolerance of the immature central nervous system. It is important that more research be conducted to explore these important integrative aspects of development, and to place the genetic regulation of myogenesis and changing innervation patterns in this more global context.

References

1. Greer JJ, Allan DW, Martin-Caraballo M, Lemke RP. An overview of phrenic nerve and diaphragm muscle development in the perinatal rat. J Appl Physiol 1999; 86:779–86.
2. Prakash YS, Fournier M, Sieck GC. Effects of prenatal undernutrition on developing rat diaphragm. J Appl Physiol 1993;75:1044–52.
3. Johnson BD, Wilson LE, Zhan WZ, et al. Contractile properties of the developing diaphragm correlate with myosin heavy chain phenotype. J Appl Physiol 1994; 77:481–7.
4. Sieck GC, Fournier M. Developmental aspects of diaphragm muscle cells: structural and functional organization. In: Haddad GG, Farber JP, eds. Developmental neurobiology of breathing. New York: Marcel Dekker, 1991:375–428.
5. Wells LJ. Development of the human diaphragm and pleural sacs. Contrib Embryol 1954;35:107–34.
6. Larsen WJ. Human embryology. Hong Kong: Churchill Livingstone Inc., 1997.
7. Last RJ. Last's anatomy: regional and applied. Edinburgh: Churchill Livingstone Inc., 1994.
8. Allan DW, Greer JJ. Embryogenesis of the phrenic nerve and diaphragm in the fetal rat. J Comp Neurol 1997; 382:459–68.
9. Gordon DC, Richmond FJ. Topography in the phrenic motoneuron nucleus demonstrated by retrograde multiple-labelling techniques. J Comp Neurol 1990; 292:424–43.
10. Hammond CG, Gordon DC, Fisher JT, Richmond FJ. Motor unit territories supplied by primary branches of the phrenic nerve. J Appl Physiol 1989;66:61–71.
11. Fournier M, Sieck GC. Topographical projections of phrenic motoneurons and motor unit territories in the cat diaphragm. In: Sieck GC, Gandevia SC, Cameron WE, eds. Respiratory muscles and their neuromotor control. New York: Alan R. Liss, Inc., 1987:215–26.
12. Laskowski MB, Sanes JR. Topographic mapping of motor pools onto skeletal muscles. J Neurosci 1987;7:252–60.
13. Gautam M, DeChiara TM, Glass DJ, et al. Distinct phenotypes of mutant mice lacking agrin, MuSK, or rapsyn. Brain Res Rev Dev Brain Res 1999;114:171–8.
14. Prakash YS, Miller SM, Huang M, Sieck GC. Morphology of diaphragm neuromuscular junctions on different fibre types. J Neurocytol 1996;25:88–100.
15. Feldman JD, Bazzy AR, Cummins TR, Haddad GG. Developmental changes in neuromuscular transmission in the rat diaphragm. J Appl Physiol 1991;71:280–6.
16. Fournier M, Alula M, Sieck GC. Neuromuscular transmission failure during postnatal development. Neurosci Lett 1991;125:34–6.
17. Bazzy AR, Donnelly DF. Failure to generate action potentials in newborn diaphragms following nerve stimulation. Brain Res 1993;600:349–52.
18. Sieck GC, Prakash YS. Fatigue at the neuromuscular junction. Branch point vs. presynaptic vs. postsynaptic mechanisms. Adv Exp Med Biol 1995;384:83–100.
19. Krnjevic K, Miledi R. Failure of neuromuscular propagation in rats. J Physiol (Lond) 1958;140:440–61.
20. Krnjevic K, Miledi R. Presynaptic failure of neuromuscular propagation in rats. J Physiol (Lond) 1959;149:1–22.
21. Mantilla CB, Yiman Y, Zhan WZ, et al. Alterations in neurotrophin receptor expression in rat diaphragm neuromuscular junction following spinal cord hemisection. Neurosci Abstr 1999;25:511.
22. Johnson RA, Okragly AJ, Haak-Frendscho M, Mitchell GS. Cervical dorsal rhizotomy increases brain-derived neurotrophic factor and neurotrophin-3 expression in the ventral spinal cord. J Neurosci 2000;20:RC 77.
23. Conover JC, Yancopoulos GD. Neurotrophin regulation of the developing nervous system: analyses of knockout mice. Rev Neurosci 1997;8:13–27.
24. Liu X, Jaenisch R. Severe peripheral sensory neuron loss and modest motor neuron reduction in mice with combined deficiency of brain-derived neurotrophic factor, neurotrophin 3 and neurotrophin. Dev Dyn 2000; 218:94–101.
25. Arnold HH, Braun T. Genetics of muscle determination and development. Curr Top Dev Biol 2000;48:129–65.
26. Tajbakhsh S, Cossu G. Establishing myogenic identity during somitogenesis. Curr Opin Gen Dev 1997;7:634–41.
27. Cossu G, Tajbakhsh S, Buckingham M. How is myogenesis initiated in the embryo? Trends Genet 1996;12:218–23.
28. Buckingham ME, Lyons GE, Ott MO, Sassoon DA. Myogenesis in the mouse. Ciba Found Symp 1992; 165:111–24.
29. Walsh K, Perlman H. Cell cycle exit upon myogenic differentiation. Curr Opin Gen Dev 1997;7:597–602.
30. Harris WA. Neural activity and development. Annu Rev Physiol 1981;43:689–710.
31. Ross JJ, Duxson MJ, Harris AJ. Formation of primary and secondary myotubes in rat lumbrical muscles. Development 1987;100:383–94.
32. Wilson SJ, McEwan JC, Sheard PW, Harris AJ. Early stages of myogenesis in a large mammal: formation of successive generations of myotubes in sheep tibialis cranialis muscle. J Muscle Res Cell Motil 1992;13:534–50.
33. Harris AJ. Embryonic growth and innervation of rat skeletal muscles. I. Neural regulation of muscle fibre numbers. Phil Trans R Soc Lond 1981;293(1065):257–77.
34. Wilson SJ, Harris AJ. Formation of myotubes in aneural rat muscles. Dev Biol 1993;156:509–18.
35. McLennan IS. Neural dependence and independence of myotube production in chicken hindlimb muscles. Dev Biol 1983;98:287–94.
36. Ross JJ, Duxson MJ, Harris AJ. Neural determination of muscle fibre numbers in embryonic rat lumbrical muscles. Development 1987;100:395–409.

37. Knudsen KA. Cell adhesion molecules in myogenesis. Curr Opin Cell Biol 1990;2(5):902–6.
38. Vandenburgh H, Hatfludy S, Karlisch P, Shansky J. Skeletal muscle growth is stimulated by intermittent stretch-relaxation in tissue culture. Am J Physiol 1989; 256:C674–82.
39. Vandenburgh HH. Mechanical forces and their second messengers in stimulating cell growth in vitro. Am J Physiol 1992;262:R350–5.
40. Weintraub H, Davis R, Tapscott S, et al. The myoD gene family: nodal point during specification of the muscle cell lineage. Science 1991;251:761–6.
41. Weintraub H, Dwarki VJ, Verma I, et al. Muscle-specific transcriptional activation by MyoD. Genes Dev 1991; 5:1377–86.
42. Davis RL, Weintraub H, Lassar B. Expression of a single transfected cDNA converts fibroblasts to myoblasts. Cell 1987;51:987–1000.
43. Braun T, Bober E, Buschhausen-Denker G, et al. Differential expression of myogenic determination genes in muscle cells: possible autoactivation by the Myf gene products. EMBO J 1989;8:3617–25.
44. Braun T, Buschhausen-Denker G, Bober E, et al. A novel human muscle factor related to but distinct from MyoD1 induces myogenic conversion in 10T1/2 fibroblasts. EMBO J 1989;8:701–9.
45. Rhodes SJ, Konieczny SF. Identification of MRF4: a new member of the muscle regulatory factor gene family. Genes Dev 1989;3:2050–61.
46. Braun T, Winter B, Bober E, et al. Myf-6, a new member of the human gene family of myogenic determination factors: evidence for a gene cluster on chromosome 12. EMBO J 1990;9:821–31.
47. Hughes SM, Koishi K, Rudnicki M, Maggs AM. MyoD protein is differentially accumulated in fast and slow skeletal muscle fibres and required for normal fibre type balance in rodents. Mech Dev 1997;61:151–63.
48. Megeney LA, Rudnicki MA. Determination versus differentiation and the MyoD family of transcription factors. Biochem Cell Biol 1995;73:723–32.
49. Borycki AG, Brunk B, Tajbakhsh S, et al. Sonic hedgehog controls epaxial muscle determination through Myf5 activation. Development 1999;126:4053–63.
50. Sabourin LA, Rudnicki MA. The molecular regulation of myogenesis. Clin Genet 2000;57:16–25.
51. Rudnicki MA, Braun T, Hinuma S, Jaenisch R. Inactivation of MyoD in mice leads to up-regulation of the myogenic HLH gene Myf-5 and results in apparently normal muscle development. Cell 1992;71:383–90.
52. Zhang W, Behringer RR, Olson EN. Inactivation of the myogenic bHLH gene MRF4 results in up-regulation of myogenin and rib anomalies. Genes Dev 1995; 9:1388–99.
53. Braun T, Rudnicki MA, Arnold H-H, Jaenisch R. Targeted inactivation of the muscle regulatory genes Myf-5 results in abnormal rib development and perinatal death. Cell 1992;71:269–82.
54. Hasty P, Bradley A, Morris JH, et al. Muscle deficiency and neonatal death in mice with a targeted mutation in the myogenin gene. Nature 1993;364:501–6.
55. Nabeshima Y, Hanaoka K, Hayasaka M, et al. Myogenin gene disruption results in perinatal lethality because of severe muscle defect. Nature 1993;364:532–5.
56. Rudnicki MA, Schnegelsberg PN, Stead RH, et al. MyoD or Myf-5 is required for the formation of skeletal muscle. Cell 1993;75:1351–9.
57. Tapscott SJ, Lassar AB, Weintraub H. A novel myoblast enhancer element mediates MyoD transcription. Mol Cell Biol 1992;12:4994–5003.
58. Goldhamer DJ, Brunk BP, Faerman A, et al. Embryonic activation of the myoD gene is regulated by a highly conserved distal control element. Development 1995; 121:637–49.
59. Tajbakhsh S, Rocancourt D, Cossu G, Buckingham M. Redefining the genetic hierarchies controlling skeletal myogenesis: Pax-3 and Myf-5 act upstream of MyoD. Cell 1997;89:127–38.
60. Maroto M, Reshef R, Munsterberg AE, et al. Ectopic Pax-3 activates MyoD and Myf-5 expression in embryonic mesoderm and neural tissue. Cell 1997;89:139–48.
61. Olson EN. Signal transduction pathways that regulate skeletal muscle gene expression. Mol Endocrinol 1993; 7:1369–78.
62. Buckingham M. Which myogenic factors make muscle? Curr Biol 1994;4:61–3.
63. Benezra R, Davis RL, Lassar A, et al. Id: a negative regulator of helix-loop-helix DNA binding proteins. Control of terminal myogenic differentiation. Ann N Y Acad Sci 1990;599:1–11.
64. Jen Y, Weintraub H, Benezra R. Overexpression of Id protein inhibits the muscle differentiation program: in vivo association of Id with E2A proteins. Genes Dev 1992; 6:1466–79.
65. Spicer DB, Rhee J, Cheung WL, Lassar AB. Inhibition of myogenic bHLH and MEF2 transcription factors by the bHLH protein Twist. Science 1996;272:1476–80.
66. Lemercier C, To RQ, Carrasco RA, Konieczny SF. The basic helix-loop-helix transcription factor Mist1 functions as a transcriptional repressor of myoD. EMBO J 1998; 17:1412–22.
67. Schiaffino S, Reggiani Cg. Molecular diversity of myofibrillar proteins: gene regulation and functional significance. Physiol Rev 1996;76:371–423.
68. Cooke R. The actomyosin engine. FASEB J 1995;9:636–42.
69. Rayment I, Rypniewski WR, Schmidt-Base K, et al. Three-dimensional structure of myosin subfragment-1: a molecular motor. Science 1993;261:50–8.
70. Rayment I, Holden HM, Whittaker M, et al. Structure of the actin-myosin complex and its implications for muscle contraction. Science 1993;261:58–65.
71. Rayment I, Holden HM, Sellers JR, et al. Three-dimensional structure of myosin subfragment-1: a molecular motor. Science 1995;261:50–8.
72. Barany M. ATPase activity of myosin correlated with speed of muscle shortening. J Gen Physiol 1967; 50:197–216.
73. Stienen GJM, Kiers JG, Bottinelli R, Reggiani C. Myofibrillar ATPase activity in skinned human skeletal muscle fibres: fibre type and temperature dependence. J Physiol (Lond) 1996;493:299–309.

74. Sieck GC, Han YS, Prakash YS, Jones KA. Cross-bridge cycling kinetics, actomyosin ATPase activity and myosin heavy chain isoforms in skeletal and smooth respiratory muscles. Comp Biochem Physiol 1998;119:435–50.
75. Sieck GC, Prakash YS. Cross-bridge kinetics in respiratory muscles [see comments]. Eur Respir J 1997;10:2147–58.
76. Uyeda TQ, Ruppel KM, Spudich JA. Enzymatic activities correlate with chimaeric substitution at the actin-binding domain of myosin. Nature 1994;368:567–9.
77. Reiser PJ, Moss RL, Giulian GG, Greaser ML. Shortening velocity in single fibers from adult rabbit soleus muscles is correlated with myosin heavy chain composition. J Biol Chem 1985;260:9077–80.
78. Perrie WT, Smillie LB, Perry SB. A phosphorylated light-chain component of myosin from skeletal muscle. Biochem J 1973;35:151–64.
79. Diffee GM, Greaser ML, Reinach FC, Moss RL. Effects of a non-divalent cation binding mutant of myosin regulatory light chain on tension generation in skinned skeletal muscle fibers. Biophys J 1995;68:1443–52.
80. Patel JR, Diffee GM, Moss RL. Myosin regulatory light chain modulates the Ca2+ dependence of the kinetics of tension development in skeletal muscle fibers. Biophys J 1996;70:2333–40.
81. LaFramboise WA, Daood MJ, Guthrie RD, et al. Myosin isoforms in neonatal rat extensor digitorum longus, diaphragm, and soleus muscles. Am J Physiol 1990; 259:L116–22.
82. LaFramboise WA, Daood MJ, Guthrie RD, et al. Emergence of the mature myosin phenotype in the rat diaphragm muscle. Dev Biol 1991;144:1–15.
83. Watchko JF, Daood MJ, Vazquez RL, et al. Postnatal expression of myosin isoforms in an expiratory muscle-external abdominal oblique. J Appl Physiol 1992;73:1860–6.
84. Watchko JF, Daood MJ, Sieck GC. Myosin heavy chain transitions during development. Functional implications for the respiratory musculature. Comp Biochem Physiol 1998;119:459–70.
85. Prakash YS, Smithson KG, Sieck GC. Growth-related adaptations of endplates on diaphragm muscle fibers: a 3D study using confocal microscopy. Soc Neurosci Abstr 1994;20:1599.
86. Izumo S, Nadal-Ginard B, Mahdavi V. All members of the MHC multigene family respond to thyroid hormone in a highly tissue-specific manner. Science 1986;231:597–600.
87. Sieck GC, Wilson LE, Johnson BD, Zhan WZ. Hypothyroidism alters diaphragm muscle development. J Appl Physiol 1996;81:1965–72.
88. Sieck GC, Zhan WZ. Denervation alters MHC isoform expression and contractile properties of developing rat diaphragm muscle. J Appl Physiol 2000;89:1106–13.
89. Brooke MH, Kaiser KK. Muscle fiber types: how many and what kind? Arch Neurol 1970;23:369–79.
90. Schiaffino S, Reggiani C. Myosin isoforms in mammalian skeletal muscle. J Appl Physiol 1994;77:493–501.
91. Bar A, Pette D. Three fast myosin heavy chains in adult rat skeletal muscle. FEBS Lett 1988;235:153–5.
92. Schiaffino S, Gorza L, Ausoni S. Muscle fiber types expressing different myosin heavy chain isoforms. Their functional properties and adaptive capacity. In: Pette D, ed. The dynamic state of muscle fibers. Berlin: De Gruyter, 1990:329–41.
93. Sieck GC, Zhan WZ, Prakash YS, et al. SDH and actomyosin ATPase activities of different fiber types in rat diaphragm muscle. J Appl Physiol 1995;79:1629–39.
94. Watchko JF, Brozanski BS, O'Day TL, et al. Contractile properties of the rat external abdominal oblique and diaphragm muscles during development. J Appl Physiol 1992;72:1432–6.
95. Watchko JF, Sieck GC. Respiratory muscle fatigue resistance relates to myosin phenotype and SDH activity during development. J Appl Physiol 1993;75:1341–7.
96. Zhan W-Z, Watchko JF, Prakash YS, Sieck GC. Isotonic contractile and fatigue properties of developing rat diaphragm muscle. J Appl Physiol 1998;84:1260–8.
97. Johnson BD, Austrup ML, Sieck GC. Diaphragm contractile properties in transgenic mice overexpressing CuZn-superoxide dismutase. Am J Respir Crit Care Med 1994;149:A322.
98. Geiger PC, Cody MJ, Macken RL, Sieck GC. Maximum specific force depends on myosin heavy chain content in rat diaphragm muscle fibers. J Appl Physiol 2000;89:695–703.
99. Han YS, Iyanoye A, Geiger PC, et al. Effects of denervation on mechanical and energetic properties of single fibers in rat diaphragm muscle. Biophys J 1999;76:A34.
100. Sieck GC. Neural control of the inspiratory pump. NIPS 1991;6:260–4.
101. Sieck GC, Prakash YS. The diaphragm muscle. In: Miller AD, Bianchi AL, Bishop BP, eds. Neural control of the respiratory muscles. Boca Raton: CRC Press, 1996:7–20.

SECTION III
DEVELOPMENTAL PHYSIOLOGY OF THE RESPIRATORY SYSTEM

CHAPTER 11

Respiratory Function in Infants

Juliann M. Di Fiore, BSEE, Robert L. Chatburn, RRT, FAARC,
Richard J. Martin, MB, BS, FRACP

Infant respiratory function testing can be a useful tool for providing information on the mechanical structure and contractile responses of the respiratory system. For example, measurements of airway resistance, time constant, and the flow-volume curve can be used to identify patients with bronchoconstriction or airway disease.[1–5] Once identified, these same variables then can be used to measure airway responsiveness to clinical interventions.[6–13] Although values of respiratory mechanics are being used currently in both research and clinical settings, these measurements are still limited in their usefulness in a pediatric environment. This is due to many factors that include lack of patient cooperation and lack of standardization of mathematical models and techniques used for calculating respiratory mechanics, despite the increasing availability of reference values.[14–15]

This chapter reviews current issues related to determination of respiratory mechanics in children, including a description of the equipment and mathematical models currently being used in the infant population. Our goal is to improve understanding of the many options and corresponding limitations in this field that have impeded the widespread use of respiratory mechanics in a clinical environment.

Mathematical Models of Respiratory Function

One of the most useful models in pulmonary mechanics is that of a single flow conducting tube (representing the airways) connected to a single elastic compartment (representing the lungs and chest wall), as shown in Figure 11–1*A*. The model can be expanded by adding another elastic component to represent the chest wall (Figure 11–1*B*). A common mathematical model referred to as the **equation of motion** of the respiratory system relating variables pressure, volume, and flow has the form:

$$\text{pressure} = \text{elastance} \times \text{volume} + \text{resistance} \times \text{flow}$$

where *pressure* is the driving pressure (ie, inspiratory pressure – expiratory pressure in a mechanically ventilated infant **or** esophageal pressure in a spontaneously breathing infant), *volume* is tidal volume, and *flow* is inspiratory flow. The parameters *elastance* (often expressed as its reciprocal, compliance) and *resistance* are constants in the equation and are defined in terms of the variables:

$$\text{elastance} = \Delta\ \text{pressure} / \Delta\ \text{volume}$$
$$\text{compliance} = \Delta\ \text{volume} / \Delta\ \text{pressure}$$
$$\text{resistance} = \Delta\ \text{pressure} / \Delta\ \text{flow}$$

The locations at which pressures are measured are used to define the particular system of interest.[16] For example, if the pressure difference between the airway opening and the body surface is measured, an imaginary "respiratory system" can be defined that exists between these two locations and is modeled by its physical behavior relating changes in "transrespiratory pressure" to changes in volume and flow. Thus, respiratory system parameters are calculated from measurements of transrespiratory pressure: pulmonary (lung) parameters are calculated from transpulmonary pressure measurements, and chest wall parameters are calculated from transmural pressure measurements such that:

$$\text{transrespiratory pressure} = \text{airway opening pressure} - \text{body surface pressure}$$

$$\text{transpulmonary pressure} = \text{airway opening pressure} - \text{pleural pressure}$$

$$\text{transmural pressure} = \text{pleural pressure} - \text{body surface pressure}$$

Signals Needed for Measurement of Respiratory Mechanics

The four signals available for measurement of respiratory mechanics are pressure, flow, tidal volume, and lung

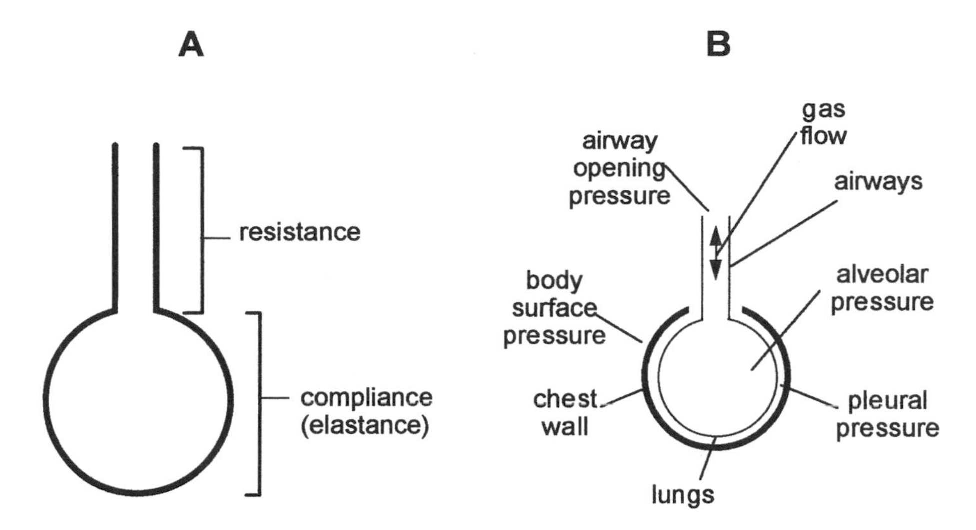

FIGURE 11–1. *A*, A single-compartment model of the respiratory system, in which the airways are represented by a flow-resistive conduit, and the lungs and chest wall are represented by an elastic compartment. *B*, More detail can be achieved by adding another compartment, such that the lungs can be distinguished from the chest wall. The system can be described mathematically by first specifying measurable variables (ie, the equation of motion). The separate components of the model (ie, airway, lungs, and chest wall) are thus imaginary structures, whose physical extents are mathematically defined by the points in space between which the pressures are measured. For example, the airway is defined as anything that exists between the airway opening and the alveoli (which might include an endotracheal tube), the lungs are anything that exists between the alveoli and the pleural space, and the chest wall is anything that exists between the pleural space and the body surface. (Reproduced with permission from Chatburn RL, Di Fiore JM. Assessment of respiratory function in infants and children. In: Pierson DJ, Kacmarek RM, eds. Foundations of respiratory care. Edinburgh: Churchill Livingstone, 1992:642.)

volume. There are many types of equipment and technology available to measure these variables each with advantages and disadvantages. However, regardless of the technology used, it should be confirmed that the equipment is appropriate for use by following basic guidelines that include linearity, frequency response, filtering, and digitization.

Measurement of *linearity* represents the ability of the output of the device to accurately represent the input applied to the system. If the waveforms being measured are too large, the output of the device can become attenuated or even saturated, thus making the output signal inaccurate for useful interpretation of data (Figure 11–2). The output signal can also be distorted when it is measuring changes in amplitude that cover a very small percentage of the total range of the device. This is often the case when trying to make measurements in infants using equipment that initially was designed for measurements in adults.

The *frequency* response of the system can best be described as the highest frequency at which the output can accurately represent the input of the system.[17,18] Since infants have a higher respiratory rate than do adults, they require equipment that can respond at a faster rate. If the device does not have a fast enough frequency response, signals may not only become attenuated but may be delayed in time (also known as phase lag) in respect to other waveforms, resulting in error when calculating lung mechanics.

Waveforms also can be delayed in time by overfiltering. A *filter* is a network that passes signals of certain frequencies while blocking signals of other frequencies. Although signals should be filtered to eliminate unwanted background noise, care must be taken to set thresholds high enough so that higher frequency components that may occur in infants are not removed.

Last, since calculations of respiratory mechanics are performed via computer, the raw waveforms must be stored in a *digital* format. Since the digitization routines are already imbedded in commercially available algorithms, usually little thought is put into this process when a monitor is purchased with sample rates established by the manufacturer. However, due to infants' increased respiratory rate, waveforms acquired in infants must be sampled at a higher rate than those in adults to achieve adequate resolution and to minimize error during calculation of lung mechanics. Although there are no published standards, a minimum sampling rate of 50 Hz[19] is thought to be sufficient in spontaneously breathing infants, and up to 200 Hz for techniques that require very rapid responses such as the interrupter technique (see "Compliance"). Lower sample rates should be used with caution, especially in young infants who tend to have rapid changes in flow, volume, and pressure during early inspiration.

Pressure

During mechanical ventilation the driving force for the respiratory system is the ventilator. In this case respiratory

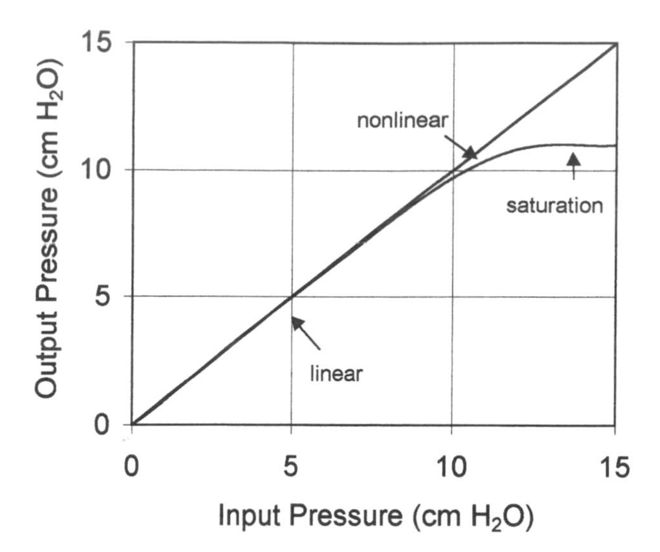

FIGURE 11–2. The linear range of a device is denoted by the area where any increase in input results in a comparable increase in output. As the input increase approaches the capacity of the measuring device, the output will become attenuated or nonlinear with a given increase in input. This attenuation in output will increase to the point where there is no further output response, known as the point of saturation.

mechanics require the measurement of transrespiratory pressure (see above) for the calculation of resistance and compliance using pressure at the airway opening.

During spontaneous breathing, the pressure driving the respiratory system is generated by the ventilatory muscles. Although this pressure cannot be measured in a noninvasive manner, it is possible to estimate the pressure difference between the airway opening and pleural pressure. This pressure drop is known as transpulmonary pressure. Transpulmonary pressure is estimated in spontaneous breathing patients using an esophageal catheter. The catheter is placed in the lower third of the esophagus and is referenced to atmosphere. There are three types of catheters used to measure esophageal pressure: fluid-filled, balloon, and microtip catheters.

Fluid-filled catheter

Fluid-filled catheters were first used in infants in 1982.[20] Pressures are transmitted through a liquid medium, accomplished with a 5F nasogastric tube attached to a pressure transducer. Once placed in the esophagus, the catheter is flushed to achieve adequate pressure transmission. Secretions at the tip of the catheter or adherence to the wall of the esophagus may attenuate or even totally eliminate the pressure signal. This is resolved by additional gentle flushing of the catheter. During this procedure care must be taken to eliminate all bubbles, as they can result in additional attenuation or nonlinear transmission of the pressure waveform.

Balloon catheter

Balloon catheters were first introduced in the 1950s.[21] Although reasonable pressure transmission was achieved, it was highly dependent on catheter placement, balloon size, thickness, and volume. Beardsmore et al[22] created multiple handmade balloon catheters with varying lengths, diameters, and thicknesses to establish the most suitable design to optimize the largest range where pressure transmission was independent of the volume of the balloon. However, balloon catheters now are commercially available with even thinner walls, creating the need for validation of the working range of the catheter if it is not stated by the manufacturer.

Microtip catheter

Microtip catheters, initially designed for cardiovascular measurements of venous flow, have been adopted into use for esophageal pressure measurement. The advantage of the microtip catheter is that a transducer is attached to the tip of the catheter, eliminating the need for flushing or pressure distortion due to improper balloon inflation. However, the catheter is stiff and additional care is required during placement. In addition, adherence to the wall of the esophagus resulting in attenuation of the pressure signal still can occur.

Pressure signal

Regardless of the type of catheter, the pressure signal should be verified for accurate pressure transmission. This can be accomplished by occluding the system and comparing the esophageal pressure waveform with the pressure measured at the airway opening. If the transmission of pleural pressure is reliable, the two pressure waveforms should be similar. In young infants with compliant rib cages, transmission of pleural pressure has been found to be compromised with the occurrence of increased chest wall distortion.[23] However, Coates et al[24] located a finite area above the cardia but below the carina where esophageal pressure transmission was reliable, independent of chest wall distortion.

Flow

There is a wide range of devices available that can measure flow; some are less invasive than others. However, the less invasive devices give qualitative measurements of flow, which limits their usefulness in the measurement of lung mechanics. On the other hand qualitative noninvasive devices can be used over longer periods of time, increasing the chance of detection of an anomalous respiratory pattern.

Pneumotachometer

The pneumotachometer is considered the gold standard for measuring airflow. The basic design consists of a resistive element inserted between two cylinders. As air flows

FIGURE 11–3. *A*, Diagram of a pneumotachometer. *B*, A pneumotachometer built into a nasal mask-used to measure airflow in a spontaneously breathing infant. Rib cage and abdominal bands are for respiratory inductance plethysmography.

through the resistive element, a pressure drop occurs. This pressure drop can be measured by a differential pressure transducer attached to the pneumotachometer via ports on either side of the resistive element and calibrated to record in units of flow. The material used to create the pressure drop across the pneumotachometer can vary from capillary networks to mesh screens (Figure 11–3*A*). Since humidity can affect the accuracy of flow measurement, some pneumotachometer designs have a heater element incorporated to reduce humidity that may build up during expiration. To accurately quantify flow all air must pass through the pneumotachometer. Thus, in a ventilated patient the pneumotachometer can be attached to the endotracheal tube with leaks minimized by using a cuffed tube or by applying gentle pressure to the neck. For a spontaneously breathing patient, the pneumotachometer must be incorporated into a nasal and/or oral mask that is tightly sealed around the patient's nose and/or mouth,[25] as shown in Figure 11–3*B*. In infants a tight mask seal can be accomplished by applying gentle pressure to the face. In addition, clay or lubricant can be used to seal any leaks that may occur. The pneumotachometer is not designed for long-term studies, especially in spontaneously breathing patients where it must be held in place to prevent leaks. Furthermore, facial stimulation may alter the ventilatory pattern in infants.[26]

Thermistor and thermocouple

The thermistor and thermocouple are temperature sensors that detect increases in temperature as warm air from the body crosses the sensor during expiration; inspiration of air from the atmosphere cools the sensor back to room temperature. Thus, the sensor is actually an expiratory-flow sensing device. Even though these devices are applied to the facial area, they are usually well tolerated and can be used unattended for long periods of time. Although thermistor/thermocouple waveforms have been widely used to document hypopnea,[27] the waveforms have been shown to have a poor correlation with the plethysmograph in acquiring quantitative measurements of flow.[28] Therefore, the thermistor or thermocouple is a useful qualitative device for documentation of the presence or absence of airflow, as occurs during apnea,[29] and either can be used in conjunction with sensors measuring chest wall motion to confirm airway obstruction.

End-tidal carbon dioxide

Although, end-tidal CO_2 monitors initially were incorporated into the montage of many sleep laboratories, these monitors have come to be used as detectors of airflow and hypoventilation. The level of exhaled CO_2 has a poor correlation with tidal volume amplitude, therefore, partial pressure of end-tidal CO_2 ($P_{ET_{CO_2}}$) should only be used as a qualitative device to detect the presence or total absence of flow.[30] This is especially true in infants with chronic lung disease, as $P_{ET_{CO_2}}$ may significantly underestimate the corresponding arterial CO_2.

Impedance

Electrical impedance is measured using two electrodes placed on either side of the chest above and below the insertion of the diaphragm. This measurement is based on the principle that air has a much higher level of impedance than tissue. A very small current is passed through the body, and the electrodes detect increases in impedance as the air-to-tissue ratio changes with air entering the lung during an inspiratory effort. Although, the measurement of impedance also has been shown to have minimal capabilities in quantifying actual breath amplitudes when compared to the pneumotachometer,[31,32] it can permit detection of the absence of airflow and, thus, the occurrence of central apnea. However, since air can move back and forth within the chest wall cavity during airway obstruction, impedance cannot distinguish obstructive apnea from normal respiration.

Forced expiration

Maximal expiratory flow at functional residual capacity (FRC) measured by rapid thoracoabdominal compression is an index of small airway function. A forced expiratory maneuver can be simulated in neonates by wrapping an inflatable cuff around the chest and abdomen and pressurizing it at the end of inspiration.[33,34] The cuff is inflated rapidly by hand or by a solenoid valve triggered by a computer. Initially these maneuvers were performed during normal tidal volume. Recently this technique has been modified by delivering one[35] or a few[36,37] large "sigh-like" breaths before the rapid compression to achieve a fuller expiratory flow volume curve. Normal values need to be indexed to FRC or weight, so that comparisons of different-sized infants can be made.

Tidal Volume

As with flow, many devices are available to measure both qualitative and quantitative measurements of volume. Whereas qualitative devices may assist in distinguishing respiratory events such as central versus obstructive apnea, quantitative devices are needed when applying algorithms for calculation of resistance and compliance.

Pneumotachometer

As previously described, the pneumotachometer is calibrated to provide a measure of flow. Once the flow signal is acquired, it can be put through the process of integration via electronic integrator amplifier or software algorithm to achieve volume. This device provides the most accurate measurement of volume when compared with the gold standard of volumetric displacement (ie, with a syringe), however, there are still the limitations of facial stimulation and the need to hold the pneumotachometer in place for spontaneously breathing infants that prohibit its use for extended periods of time.

Plethysmograph

Plethysmography requires the patient to be placed in a well-sealed box with ports attached to a differential pressure transducer. The principle of plethysmography is Boyle's law, which states that in a closed system with constant temperature (which is often not the case[38]), changes in pressure will be proportional to changes in volume. Although plethysmography is used more commonly for measurements of lung volume (see "Thoracic Gas Volume"), Helms et al showed that tidal volume measurements by plethysmography are within 7% of tidal volume measurements obtained with the pneumotachometer.[39] In addition, there have been many studies using plethysmography to measure resistance and compliance.[40–42] However, since it is an enclosed device, it is difficult to use without patient cooperation, which is rare from infants and small children.

Strain gauges

Strain gauges consist of hollow rubberized bands filled with mercury. These bands can be placed around the abdomen and/or chest wall with adhesive and are well tolerated in the infant population. As the bands expand, the mercury column elongates, thus changing the resistance of the band. These changes in resistance are converted to changes in voltage and are recorded on an output device. Studies have tried to calibrate strain gauges with known volumes with limited success.[31,32] However, when used in addition to a flow-sensing device applied to the facial area, two strain gauges applied to the chest wall and abdomen can be used to distinguish central apnea from obstructive apnea.

Respiratory inductance plethysmograph

The respiratory inductance plethysmograph (RIP) consists of two bands placed around the abdomen and rib cage. Each band is made of elastic and contains a flexible wire, shaped in a sinusoidal pattern. These bands stretch as the chest wall expands during respiration to correspond with changes in abdominal or rib cage cross-sectional area. Inductance bands are used along with a flow-sensing device in many sleep laboratories to distinguish obstructive apnea from central apnea (Figure 11–4).

This technology has advanced to the point where RIP can be calibrated so that a flow sensor is no longer needed for apnea detection.[43–45] The technology assumes two degrees of freedom where changes in area of the abdomen summed with changes in area of the rib cage compartment that occur during normal ventilation are proportional to changes in tidal volume. Three methods have been developed to calibrate the RIP signals: the regression method, the Isovolume method, and the Qualitative Diagnostic Calibration (QDC).

The regression method uses the relationship

$$V_T = A \times Vrc + B \times Vab$$

where V_T is tidal volume from a known source such as a pneumotachometer, Vrc is the volume change of the rib cage, and Vab is the volume change of the abdomen. Using multiple measurements of V_T, Vrc, and Vab, the calibration coefficients A and B can be solved.

Eliminating the need for a pneumotachometer, the Isovolume method begins with the relationship that states:

$$V = A \times Vrc + Vab$$

where V is the total volume, Vrc is the volume of the rib cage, and Vab is the volume of the abdomen. The patient then must shift volume from the rib cage to the abdominal compartments simulating an obstructive apnea. Therefore: $V = 0$ and

$$A = -Vab/Vrc$$

Using this maneuver the software adjusts the gain of Vrc by the factor A. This method works fine for patients that can cooperate, but it cannot be applied to infants who cannot perform this maneuver.

The QDC[46] method does not require patient cooperation. During 5 minutes of normal quiet respiration, measurements of Vrc and Vab movement are documented. To estimate a relatively constant V_T, only those breaths that fall within ±1 standard deviation (SD) are used for calculation of the calibration coefficient, where

$$A = -SDVab/SDVrc$$

and SDVab and SDVrc are the standard deviation of all rib cage and abdominal volumes falling within the initial ±1 SD range. As with the Isovolume method, the gain of Vrc is corrected by the calibration coefficient then added to Vab to achieve a sum value. This sum value is not a true quantitative estimate of tidal volume but, rather, a value from which all sequential measurements are referenced. In other words, all values for the sum will be expressed as a percentage of the V_T during the 5-min calibration period.

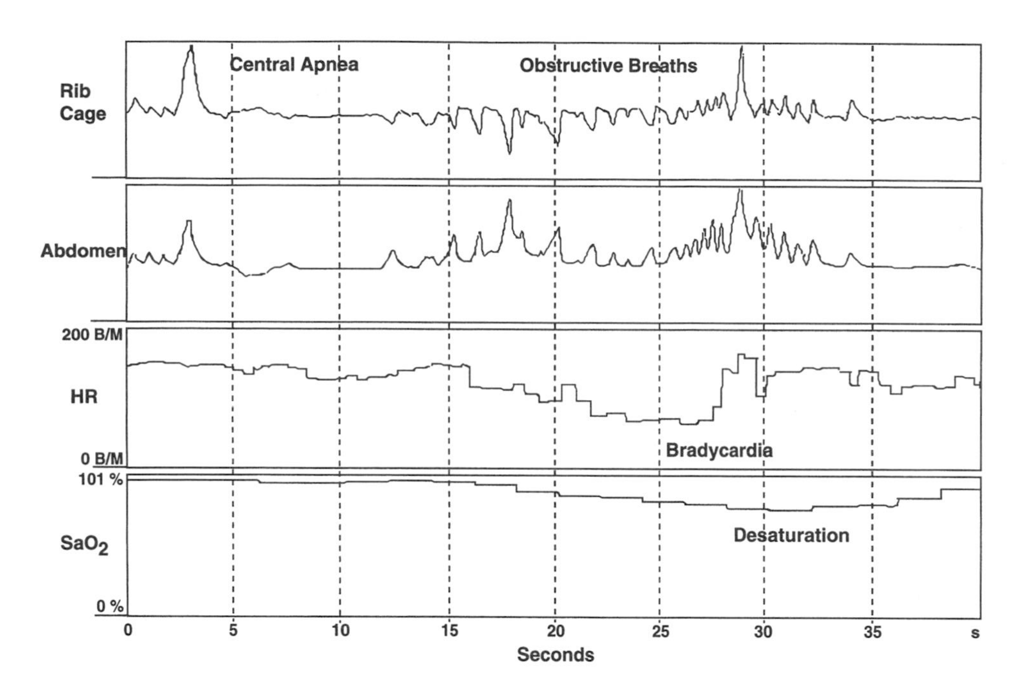

FIGURE 11–4. An example of rib cage and abdominal waveforms acquired with respiratory inductance plethysmography in a premature infant. Normal respiration is shown for the first three breaths followed by a central apnea. During the apnea obstructed respiratory efforts appear, as shown by out-of-phase deflections on the rib cage and abdominal waveforms; this is followed by airway opening and resolution of the event. B/M = beats per minute; HR = heart rate; SaO_2 = oxygen saturation.

Since RIP uses the rib cage and abdominal excursions to measure ventilation, studies have examined the effect of body position, sleep state, and chest wall asynchrony on its accuracy. Zimmerman et al[47] showed that postural changes had a varying effect on RIP volume measurements (when compared with spirometric volume changes) that were dependent on the calibration technique used. Cantineau et al[48] showed an increase in error of volume measurements during sleep versus wakefulness, when compared with volume measurements acquired with a pneumotachograph in adults. Using similar volume measurements made in premature infants, Brooks et al[49] found no change in the relationship between RIP and pneumotachometer volume measurements with alterations in body position, chest wall asynchrony, and respiratory rate. When comparing tidal volume measurements in anesthetized infants from QDC calibrated RIP and pneumotachometer, Brown et al[50] found the QDC method was limited by the need to analyze ≥ 20 breaths.

Given these findings, RIP technology is probably the most promising method for obtaining qualitative measurements of tidal volume in a pediatric setting, since it does not require patient cooperation, there is no need for a pneumotachometer, no equipment is attached to the facial area, and it can be used for extended periods of time with minimal discomfort to the patient. However, there is variability when RIP is compared with measurements of tidal volume from a pneumotachometer on a breath-by-breath basis. Since small variations in tidal volume and flow can create large errors in resistance and compliance, the current trend of extending RIP technology to the field of respiratory mechanics should be explored with caution.

Lung Volume

Levels of end-expiratory lung volume are actively controlled in infants[51–53] due to laryngeal adduction and/or postinspiratory diaphragm activation. Because infant and pediatric lung diseases often are characterized by changes in lung volume, its measurement is of diagnostic value. Although measurements of lung volume are reported as outcome variables (ie, Lee et al showed a delay in the establishment of lung volumes in infants born by cesarean section versus vaginally[54]), lung volume measurements often are used to index volume-dependent parameters such as resistance and compliance. For example, compliance is dependent not only on the elastic properties of the lungs but also on the lung volume and the size of the subject in whom the measurements are made. Thus, the calculation of specific compliance (compliance/FRC), allows the comparison of the elastic properties of different-sized lungs.

Functional residual capacity

By definition, FRC includes only the volume of gas in the lungs at end expiration in communication with open airways. Thus, the use of indicator dilution techniques is appropriate. Both the closed-system helium-dilution technique and the nitrogen washout technique have been used in newborn infants.[55–58] With the helium technique, the patient's airway is connected to a bag with a known volume containing a known concentration of helium. The dilution caused by the addition of the FRC volume to the system causes the helium concentration to drop. If the distribution of ventilation in the lungs is normal, the helium concentration in the bag stabilizes at a lower value within 30 to 60 seconds. The FRC is then estimated using an equation based on a simple mass balance:

$$FRC = \frac{[(Vi)(Hei)] - [(Vf)(Hef)]}{Hef}$$

where Vi and Vf are the initial and final volumes of the bag and Hei and Hef are the initial and final helium concentrations.

The underlying assumption of this technique is that no helium is lost from the system. Thus, any leaks, such as those around masks or uncuffed endotracheal tubes, will cause errors. Schwartz et al[59] have described a mathematical analysis that corrects for changes in He concentration due to endotracheal tube leaks. If the patient's distribution of ventilation is impaired, the equilibration time may be extended to the point at which hypercapnia and hypoxia may occur, requiring the addition of oxygen and absorption of carbon dioxide; this further complicates the procedure.

In the nitrogen washout technique, the infant breathes 100% oxygen in an open system. After washout of nitrogen from the lungs, FRC is calculated using measurements of the volume of exhaled gas collected and the initial nitrogen concentration, and the nitrogen concentration in end-tidal gas. One improvement on this technique involves the continuous measurement and integration of nitrogen concentration in exhaled gas that has passed through a mixing chamber.[58] A further improvement has been described by Richardson et al[60] using a computerized sampling system that requires that the patient take only four breaths of 100% oxygen. With this technique, FRC can be determined in less than 1 minute, allowing repeated measurements in critically ill infants and reducing the risk of the potentially toxic effects of oxygen (eg, retinopathy and absorption atelectasis). Despite the improvements that have been made, both the helium and the nitrogen washout techniques still only approximate FRC, due to the inclusion of the dead space volume of the equipment being used.

Thoracic gas volume

Thoracic gas volume (TGV) measurement via plethysmography includes all the gas in the thorax, regardless of communication with open airways. The procedure involves placing the infant's body inside the plethysmograph (with the head or face exposed to the atmosphere) and measuring the pressure both at the airway opening and inside the plethysmograph.[61,62] When the airway is occluded at end expiration, subsequent inspiratory efforts cause an increase in the volume of the thorax, which causes a decrease in the pressure measured at the airway opening. At the same time, the expansion of the thorax causes a decrease in the internal volume of the plethysmograph and, hence, an increase in pressure. These pressure changes are multiplied by a calibration factor to convert changes to volume, and are then used to calculate TGV. A comprehensive description of plethysmograph designs and lung volume measurements can be found in the European Respiratory Society/American Thoracic Society workshop report series by Coates et al.[63] Unfortunately, TGV technique is cumbersome and is impractical for use in critically ill infants.

Variables of Pulmonary Function Testing

Compliance

In practice the equation of motion is used to derive estimates of compliance and resistance in measurements of pressure, volume, and flow under two experimental conditions. Under static conditions compliance is measured at two moments in time when the respiratory system is held motionless (eg, at end expiration and end inspiration). Such measurements may be made with an inspiratory pause during mechanical ventilation, which yields a so-called plateau pressure, or by training the patient to perform the required breathing maneuvers. However, when dealing with small children and infants, it is often more convenient to calculate dynamic estimates of compliance by analyzing data points obtained during continuous ventilation (either spontaneous or mechanical). For normal lungs at normal frequencies, static and dynamic estimates yield similar values. However, dynamic compliance is generally lower in lungs that have a nonhomogeneous distribution of mechanical properties.

Dynamic compliance

The term dynamic compliance has been a source of some confusion, as it occasionally has been used erroneously to indicate the value calculated from the total pressure change required to deliver a tidal volume. Thus, during mechanical ventilation this value would be calculated as the tidal volume divided by the difference between peak inspiratory pressure (PIP) and positive end-expiratory pressure (PEEP). However, this pressure difference reflects not only the force necessary to overcome elastic recoil, but also the component of pressure required to overcome flow resistance, because Peak pressure occurs during inspiratory flow.

The correct definition of dynamic compliance is the ratio of tidal volume to the pressure difference measured

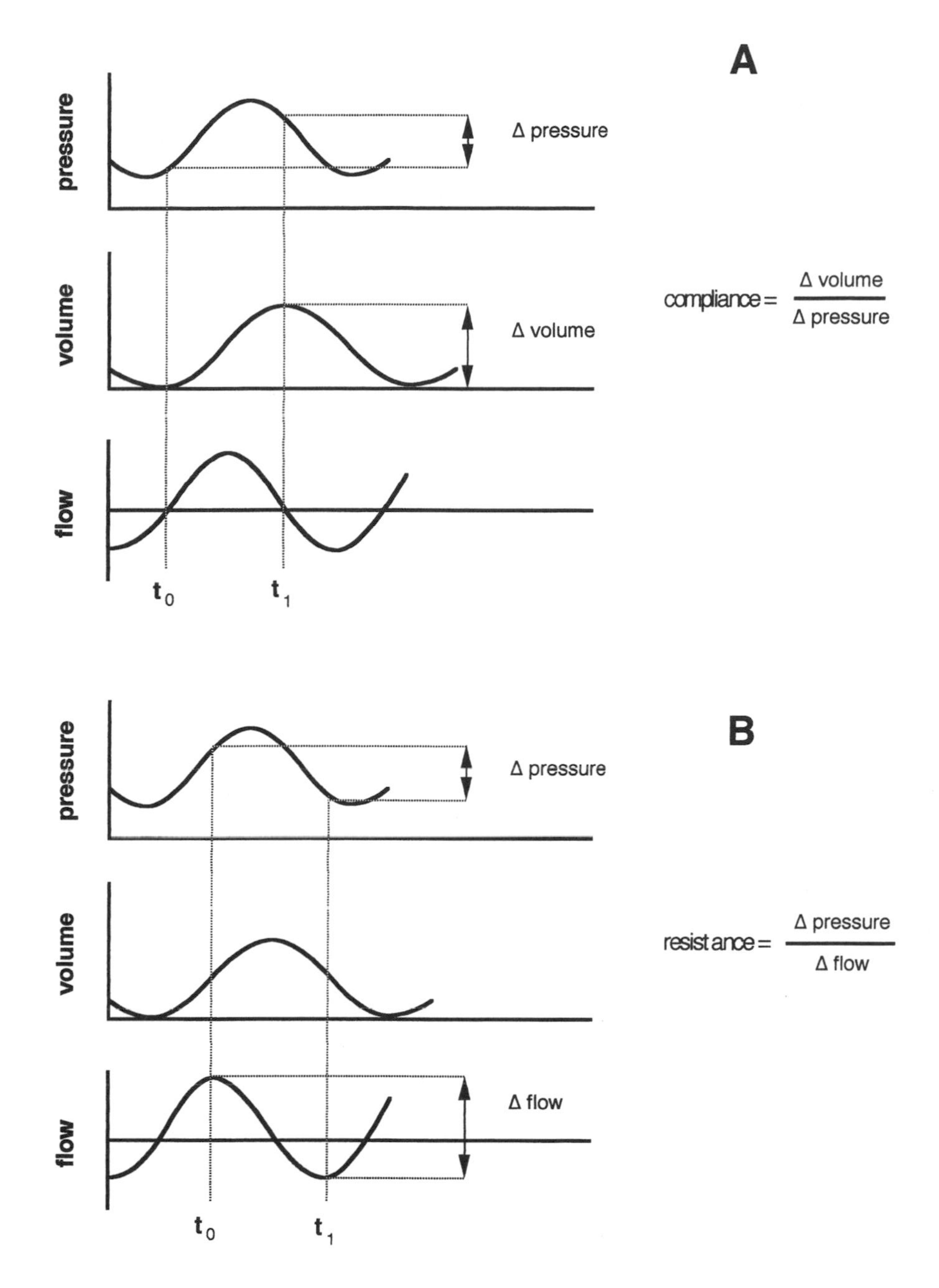

FIGURE 11–5. *A*, Data analysis for the calculation of dynamic compliance based on esophageal pressure changes and volume changes measured between two points in time (t_0 and t_1) when flow at the airway opening is zero. *B*, Data analysis for the calculation of pulmonary resistance based on pressure and flow changes between two points in time (t_0 and t_1) when lung volumes are equal. (Reproduced with permission from Chatburn RL, Di Fiore JM. Assessment of respiratory function in infants and children. In: Pierson DJ, Kacmarek RM, eds. Foundations of respiratory care. Edinburgh: Churchill Livingstone, 1992:652.)

between two points in time when flow at the airway opening (but not necessarily in the lungs) is zero (Figure 11–5*A*). Dynamic compliance is intended to be an *estimate* of static compliance. However, flow can be zero at the airway opening and still exist between lung units that have different time constants, a condition known as pendelluft. In this situation, dynamic compliance is less than static compliance. In addition, measurement of dynamic compliance assumes that the relationship between pressure and volume is constant throughout the breath. This may be true for low tidal volumes, but with overdistension of the lung that may occur during mechanical ventilation, in the presence of airway disease, or even in normal spontaneously breathing preterm infants,[64] compliance can decrease with higher lung volumes (Figure 11–6). Under these conditions measurements of dynamic compliance become invalid.

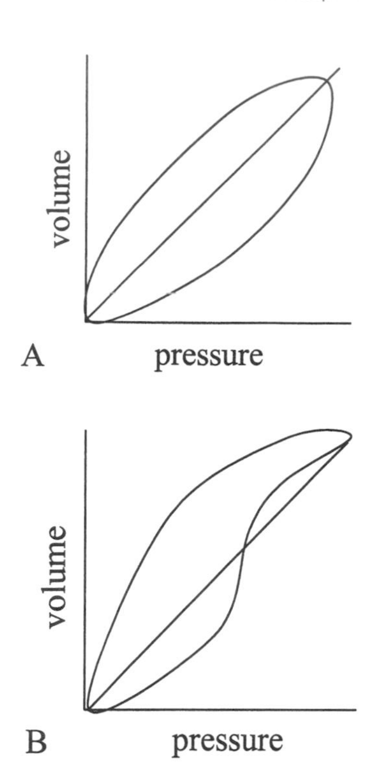

FIGURE 11–6. Pressure-volume curve for *A*, linear and *B*, nonlinear compliance. Nonlinear compliance values can occur with overdistension of the lung during mechanical ventilation.

Static compliance

Static compliance is calculated as the ratio of tidal volume to the pressure difference measured between two points in time when flow throughout the lungs has ceased. During mechanical ventilation, this is achieved by instituting an inspiratory pause or airway occlusion of sufficient duration. Once inspiratory flow has stopped (and flow within the lungs decays to zero), airway pressure drops from the ventilator pressure immediately preceding the occlusion to a steady-state plateau pressure (Pplt), which reflects the true elastic recoil pressure:

$$\text{static compliance} = \text{tidal volume}/(\text{Pplt} - \text{PEEP}).$$

A single occlusion can be used to calculate static compliance when compliance is constant throughout a breath. However, in certain conditions such as pulmonary fibrosis or overdistension of the lung during mechanical ventilation, static compliance becomes volume dependent with compliance decreasing with increasing volume. To estimate the changes in compliance in relation to volume, the occlusion technique can be extrapolated to its logical extreme by the application of the "interrupter" technique (Figure 11–7).[65]

In this method, expiratory flow is interrupted multiple times by a computer-controlled valve. This initial pressure slowly decays to a plateau, reflecting tissue stress relaxation and redistribution of gases between lung units (pendelluft).[66] The plateau pressure is used with the associated volume measurement to calculate respiratory system compliance, with multiple determinations of compliance revealing nonlinearities within a single breath.

Measurements of static compliance can also be used in a spontaneously breathing child. However, the occlusion technique relies on the ability to evoke the Hering-Breuer reflex. This reflex inhibits inspiratory muscle activation with airway occlusion and allows for a passive pressure plateau. Rabbette et al assessed the presence of the Hering-Breuer reflex in infants and found that it could be elicited until the end of the first year of life.[67]

Confounding parameters

In addition to disease state and lung overdistension, values of compliance can be affected by anesthesia. Using the multiple-occlusion technique, Fletcher et al[68] compared compliance in infants and young children during sedation and anesthesia. Compliance was found to be reduced with anesthesia, with the decrease in compliance being due to a reduction in tidal volume.

Time Constant

Another important concept in modeling respiratory system mechanics is that of the "time constant." The variables for the equation of motion, as described earlier, are understood to be functions of time. The mechanical response of the respiratory system to sudden (ie, step) changes in transrespiratory pressure is of particular interest. This happens during inspiration with a pressure-limited, time-cycled mode of mechanical ventilation. It also happens in passive exhalation. If the equation of motion is modified by substituting a constant value for pressure and solving for volume and flow as functions of time (t), we get for inspiration:

$$\text{volume (t)} = \text{compliance x (PIP} - \text{PEEP)}(1 - e^{-t/RC})$$
$$\text{flow (t)} = (\text{PIP} - \text{PEEP})(1 - e^{-t/RC})/\text{resistance}$$

and for expiration:

$$\text{volume (t)} = \text{compliance x (PIP} - \text{PEEP)}(e^{-t/RC})$$
$$\text{flow (t)} = -(\text{PIP} - \text{PEEP})(e^{-t/RC})/\text{resistance}$$
$$\text{time constant} = \text{resistance x compliance}$$

where e = the base of natural logarithms (2.72) and RC is the product of resistance and compliance, known as the time constant. The time constant has units of time (usually seconds) and is defined as the time required for an exponential function to achieve 63% of its steady state value. If the terms $(1 - e^{-t/RC})$ and $(e^{-t/RC})$ are isolated in the above equations and plotted against time in units of RC (ie, time constant units), then the curves shown in Figure 11–8 are achieved. From these curves the time necessary for inspiration and expiration can be predicted based on estimates of respiratory system resistance and compliance.

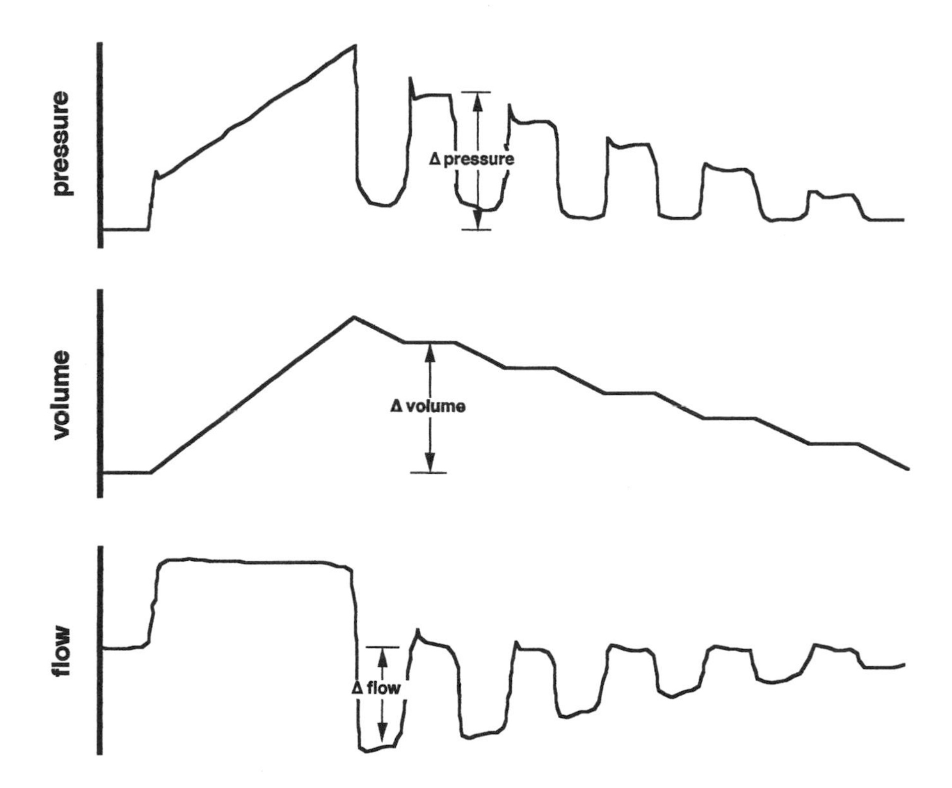

FIGURE 11–7. An example of one breath with multiple occlusions used for the calculation of static compliance and resistance with the interrupter technique. Static compliance is defined as Δ volume/Δ pressure and resistance as Δ pressure/Δ flow for each occlusion. In this example five values of compliance and resistance can be calculated at different volumes throughout the breath to reveal any nonlinear relationship. (Reproduced with permission from Chatburn RL, Di Fiore JM. Assessment of respiratory function in infants and children. In: Pierson DJ, Kacmarek RM, eds. Foundations of respiratory care. Edinburgh: Churchill Livingstone, 1992:651.)

Resistance

Measurement of resistance is a useful tool for establishing baseline parameters regarding the mechanical structure of developing airways. In addition, it can be used in a clinical environment to estimate airway responses to interventions. The precluding factor in using this variable for general clinical application is the lack of standardization of methods being used. There are many algorithms used to calculate resistance that can yield different values for the same breath. This has resulted in a wide range of published values for any given patient population that, compounded with normal intersubject variability, makes it difficult to define threshold values for comparison between normal and diseased states.

The basic definition of resistance states that:

$$R = \Delta P_{res}/\Delta F \text{ (Equation 1)}$$

where R is resistance, ΔP_{res} is the change in pressure, and ΔF is the change in flow. P_{res} is the change in pressure due to the resistive component of the pressure waveforms; it is calculated by subtracting the elastic component of pressure and is represented by:

$$P_{res} = P - 1/C^{\times}(V) \text{ (Equation 2)}$$

where P is pressure, C is compliance, and V is volume. Many mathematical models have been developed that use equations 1 and 2 as a starting point.

Mead-Whittenberger technique

The Mead-Whittenberger technique was first described in 1953.[69] This method subtracts the elastic from the resistive components of the transpulmonary signal. It has been used to calculate resistance at a given volume (usually half the maximal volume) (see Figure 11–5*B*) or at a given flow, as shown by point a in Figure 11–9.

Least-Squares Regression technique

The Least-Squares Regression technique uses the equation of motion that states:

$$P = (1/C)^{\times}V + R^{\times}F$$

or substituting equation 2,

$$P_{res} = P - (1/C)^{\times}V = R^{\times}F$$

where P is pressure, R is resistance, F is flow, C is compliance, V is volume, and P_{res} is the resistive component of pressure. Using known values for pressure, flow, and volume, the regression equation is solved for the coefficients

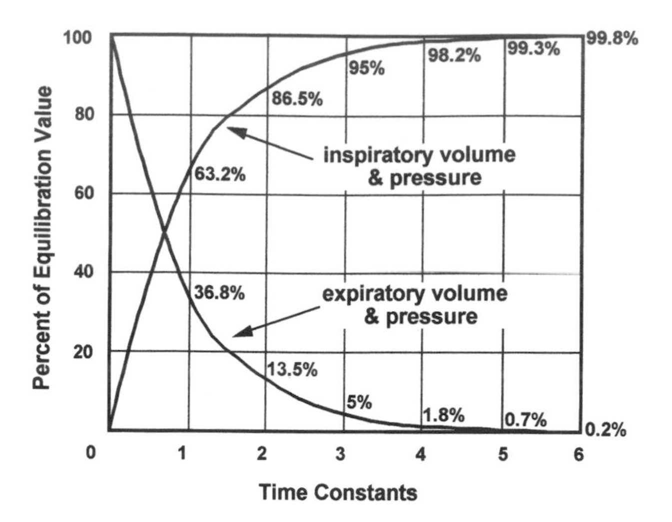

FIGURE 11–8. The exponential rise and fall of lung pressure and volume during inspiration and expiration in terms of time constants. (Reproduced with permission from Chatburn RL. Principles and practice of neonatal mechanical ventilation. Respir Care 1991;36:569–95.)

of resistance (see Figure 11–9) and compliance. Since a regression equation can be applied to any set of data, even when the relationship of the signals is poor, most commercially available systems require the correlation coefficient to be ≥.95 before measurements of resistance and compliance are thought to be reliable.

Multiple Linear Regression technique

The Mead-Whittenberger and Least-Squares techniques make the assumption that the relationship between pressure and flow remains constant throughout a breath. However, as can be seen in Figure 11–10*A*, which represents a typical breath in a premature infant, this often is not the case.[70] At low pressures resistance is independent of flow. However, as pressure increases a point is reached where the flow response to increases in pressure is attenuated (Figure 11–10*B*).

This change in the pressure-flow relationship can occur due to a phenomenon called the Bernoulli effect. This can best be described by visualizing flow through a rigid tube (Figure 11–11). Low pressure gradients cause the gas molecules to move in a straight line, with molecules near the wall moving slower due to the frictional properties of the wall. This is known as the laminar flow range, where the increase in flow is proportional to the increase in pressure. As the pressure in the tube increases the movement of the gas molecules increases to the point where the gas molecules begin to move in a chaotic manner. This is known as turbulent flow, where pressure is proportional to flow^2. In extreme cases this can progress to the point where the rate of flow remains constant, regardless of any increase in pressure. This is known as the point of flow limitation.

The Multiple Linear Regression technique adds a term to the equation of motion, to account for the nonlinear relationship between pressure and flow with increasing levels of pressure. This leads to the equation:

$$P = (1/C) \times V + R \times F + K \times F^2$$

or substituting equation 2,

$$P_{res} = P - (1/C) \times V = R \times F + K \times F^2$$

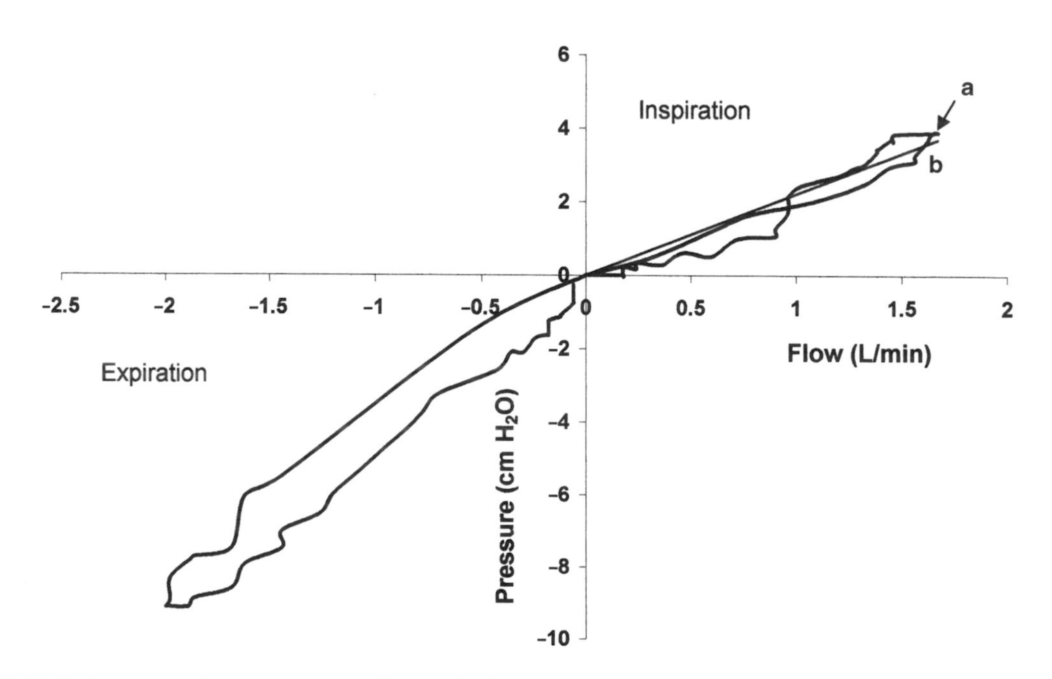

FIGURE 11–9. A representative pressure-versus-flow tracing in a premature infant. Calculation of resistance is made for inspiration using (a) the Mead-Whittenberger technique (R=140 cm H_2O/L/s) or (b) the Linear Regression technique (R=133 cm H_2O/L/s).

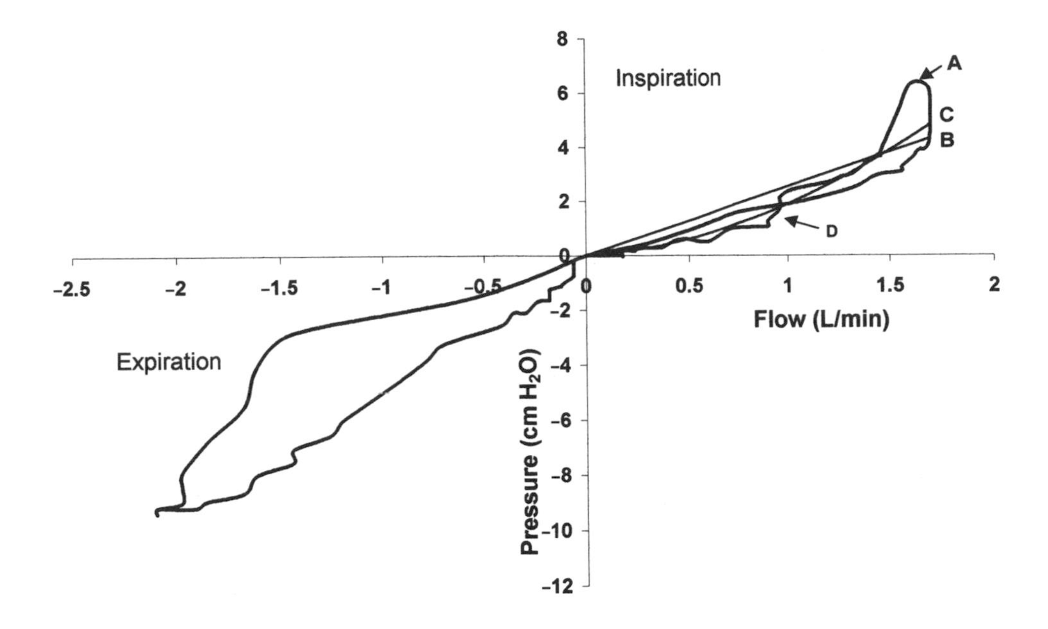

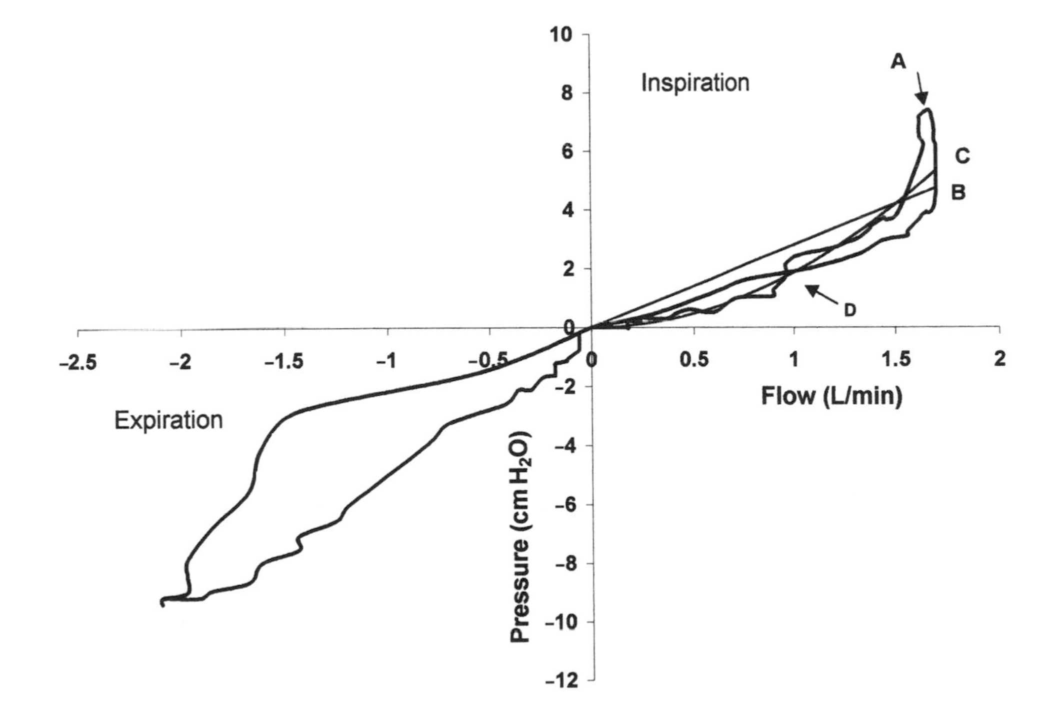

FIGURE 11–10. *A*, As resistance changes within a breath becoming flow dependent, the values of resistance among various techniques begin to diverge (A) Mead-Whittenberger (R=20 cm H_2O/L/s) (B) Linear Regression (R=152 cm H_2O/L/s) (C) Multiple Regression (R=32 cm H_2O/L/s) and (D) the Linear Portion of the Curve (R=106 cm H_2O/L/s). *B*, Once flow limitation occurs, further increases in pressure have little benefit except to increase the nonlinear segment of the pressure-flow curve. This nonlinear segment has differing effects on resistance that are technique dependent. For example, when compared to the resistance value in part *A*, the following changes in resistance would occur: (A) Mead-Whittenberger (30% increase), (B) Linear Regression (10% increase) (C) Multiple Regression (99% decrease), and (D) the Linear Portion of the Curve (no change).

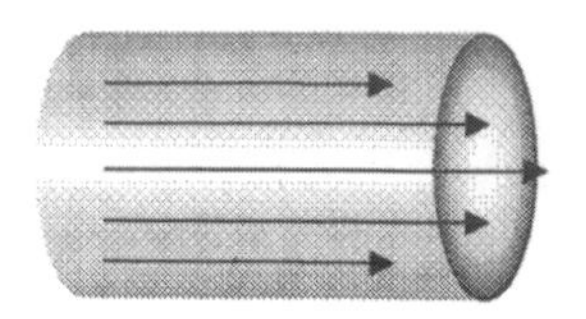

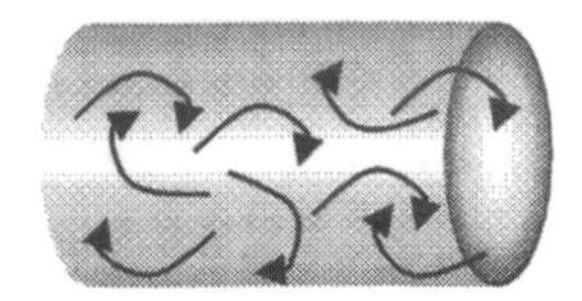

FIGURE 11–11. Laminar flow occurs when gas molecules move in a straight line, with molecules near the wall moving slower due to increased friction of the walls. As the pressure gradient increases, the gas molecules continue to increase in speed until they begin to move in a chaotic manner, known as turbulent flow.

where K is the coefficient corresponding to the turbulent portion of airflow. Application of this regression equation is shown in Figure 11–10.

Linear Portion of the Curve technique

As the Multiple Linear Regression technique tries to use the entire pressure-versus-flow curve and adjust the coefficients for resistance and compliance, the Linear Portion of the Curve technique avoids this area. In this case, using visual inspection, only the area in which resistance is constant and independent of flow is used for calculations (see Figure 11–10).

Summary

When resistance is constant within a breath, all of the techniques yield similar results. However, as seen in Figure 11–10*A*, when resistance is flow dependent, application of the above techniques can lead to different results for the same breath, with the Mead-Whittenberger method yielding the highest value of resistance and the Linear Portion of the Curve technique yielding the lowest. If the breath in Figure 11–10*A* were representative of that of a premature infant on a ventilator, and if the pressure of the ventilator were increased slightly, the pressure-versus-flow curve would appear as that in Figure 11–10*B*, with the further increase in ventilator pressure resulting in a minimal increase in flow.

As shown in Figure 11–10*B*, application of the same four techniques to the new pressure-versus-flow curve results in a variety of outcomes when compared with the initial outcomes in Figure 11–10*A*. However, the mechanical properties of the airways have not changed. From these results it can be seen that it is important to understand the mathematical model being used for calculation of resistance when acquiring data or reviewing the literature.

Confounding parameters

As discussed under "Pressure," the driving pressure for the respiratory system comes from one of two sources, depending on whether the breath is spontaneous or mechanical in origin. Therefore, the type of respiration should be noted when comparing values of respiratory mechanics between studies, as these values may differ.[71]

Studies of mechanically ventilated infants have been reported using a variety of techniques for calculating lung mechanics. Independent of the technique, is the need to account for the resistance of the endotracheal tube before reporting results. LeSouef et al[72] have shown that for a small group of infants recovering from respiratory distress syndrome (RDS), pneumonia, and transient tachypnea of the newborn, total respiratory system resistance averaged 128 cm H_2O/L/s for those with 3.0-mm inside diameter (ID) endotracheal tubes (ETTs) and 73 cm H_2O/L/s for those with 3.5-mm ID ETTs. After extubation, the resistance for these two groups dropped to 75 and 37 cm H_2O/L/s, respectively. Based on these data, the 3.0-mm ETT had an effective resistance of about 53 cm H_2O/L/s, whereas the 3.5-mm ETT had an effective resistance of about 36 cm H_2O/L/s.

Resistance of the ETT is dependent on its diameter and length. Fontan et al[73] measured resistance of 2.5-, 3.0-, and 3.5-mm ID ETTs. Resistance was found to decrease with increasing diameter size, which was expected, but, in addition, it became flow dependent at very low flow rates. Therefore, the mechanical characteristics need to be known for each size of ETT before measurements are made in infants. In addition, care must be taken to minimize leaks around the tube, which may further compound errors in measurement.[74] Kondo et al[75] found that a leak of 38% resulted in an overestimation of respiratory resistance by 51% and an underestimation of elastance by 23%. However, resistance for the expiratory phase of the breath was not affected, and elastance during expiration increased by only 6.1%. Although the ideal situation requires total elimination of any leak in the system, this study shows that when this cannot be achieved, measurements of lung mechanics during the expiratory phase of the breath would yield the most accurate results.

As premature infants generally tolerate procedures better than do term infants, sedation is not usually required. Term infants may not be as cooperative, and usually need to be sedated. Sedation, in doses most commonly given for lung function tests, has been shown to have little effect on respiratory pattern, resting lung volume, and sleep state,[76–79] although chloral hydrate may decrease upper airway muscle tone in patients with upper airway obstruction.

Clinical Applications

Due to the current availability of commercial equipment, the use of pulmonary mechanics is slowly being incorporated into the pediatric arena. To fully apply this field in a clinical setting, a solid set of reference values must be established to distinguish normal from disease states. Unfortunately, the references currently in the literature are few, and many reference values are based on small populations. In addition, attempts to determine normalization of variables are inconsistent and use various parameters of body size such as weight and lung volume. Since the initially high values of airway resistance decrease rapidly during the first year of life,[80] the current recommendation by the American Thoracic Society/ European Respiratory Society is to normalize respiratory mechanics by thoracic gas volume whenever possible.[14]

Measurements of lung mechanics also can vary with the technique used. In general, however, values for dynamic lung compliance for infants and newborns range from 1.1 to 2.0 mL/kg/cm H_2O, with specific dynamic compliance ranges from 0.04 to 0.08 mL/cm H_2O/mL FRC or volume of thoracic gas.[81–90] Values for resistance in normal healthy infants (newborn to 2 years old) range from 30 to 80 cm H_2O/L/s.[37,11] Mean values for FRC using gas dilution techniques have ranged from 20 to 24 mL/kg in infants up to 18 months of age.[34,91–96]

Measurements of lung mechanics have been useful in documenting changes in the respiratory system in response to different treatments. For example, Miller et al[11] have shown a decrease in both total pulmonary and supraglottic resistance in response to nasal continuous positive airway pressure (CPAP) in healthy preterm infants, with 60% of the decrease occurring in the supraglottic airway.

Studies showing the effect of surfactant therapy on respiratory mechanics have demonstrated that such data must be interpreted with caution and a clear understanding of the techniques employed. Kelly et al[96] showed an increase in FRC, oxygenation, and static compliance in response to surfactant therapy with no improvement in dynamic compliance. However, Davis et al[12] did see an increase in dynamic compliance in response to surfactant therapy, but only after ventilator pressures were decreased and/or patients were extubated, suggesting that the regional overdistension of the lung after surfactant therapy may have prevented the anticipated immediate improvement in lung function.

Respiratory mechanics in conjunction with other parameters have been applied to the process of weaning infants from mechanical ventilation. Fox et al[97] found that infants with a combination of low birth weight, low gestational age, and high pulmonary resistance at the time of pre-extubation were more likely to require reintubation. Dreizzin et al measured static compliance in preterm infants with RDS, weaned from mechanical ventilation. Those infants were found to have higher compliance values than acutely ill infants requiring ventilation and oxygen therapy, and other infants who subsequently developed bronchopulmonary dysplasia (BPD). They concluded that low compliance may be predictive of the development of BPD.[98] It also has been shown that preterm infants who have elevated lung resistance are predisposed to development of BPD.[2] Therefore, pulmonary mechanics measurements may identify those infants destined to develop chronic neonatal lung injury. For those infants and children who develop BPD, there is a large body of literature on their impairment in lung function and predisposition to airway reactivity,[1,99–101] which is beyond the scope of this chapter.

One potential area of advancement in measuring respiratory mechanics is the existence of mechanical ventilators that have the capability to measure both static and dynamic mechanics. Identification of clinically useful patterns of pressure-volume curves may help in avoidance of lung overdistention.[13] Other values of respiratory mechanics may assist in maximizing ventilation to the infant while minimizing trauma to the lung. Stenson et al[102] performed a randomized controlled trial of 245 mechanically ventilated neonates comparing duration of ventilation, adverse outcome, and oxygen supplementation, and found no difference between results of routine clinical management and clinical management supplemented with values of compliance. However, the survivors who received routine clinical management had a longer duration of ventilation (median 5 versus 3 days).

Studies performed primarily in animal models have revealed that larger central airways, more distal airways, and lung parenchyma contribute to total lung resistance.[103,104] The contribution of tissue resistance (comprising distal lung units, measured via alveolar capsules) to total lung resistance ranges from 40 to 70% during the first 3 weeks of life in the piglet. Inhalation of nitric oxide has been shown to decrease total lung and tissue resistance with a variable reduction in airway resistance in open-chested piglets.[104] Unfortunately, there currently is no noninvasive way to partition lung resistance into airway and tissue components. There is, however, considerable interest in the role of inhaled NO in decreasing the risk of chronic neonatal lung injury, and whether a reduction in lung resistance contributes to this beneficial effect.

In summary, although it may be technically challenging, measurement of respiratory mechanics is possible in infants and has a potential role in the clinical environment. Progress needs to be made in the following areas: (1) standardization of measurements techniques, (2) consistency of normalization of values, and (3) data acquisition from large normal populations for establishment of baseline values. Simultaneous efforts should be directed toward incorporating newer techniques into clinical trials to unravel pathophysiologic mechanisms underlying pediatric lung disease and its management. These requirements need to be met before respiratory mechanics can be a general clinical application in the pediatric environment.

References

1. Gerhardt T, Hehre D, Feller R, et al. Serial determination of pulmonary function in infants with chronic lung disease. J Pediatr 1987;110:448–56.

2. Goldman SL, Gerhardt T, Sonni R, et al. Early prediction of chronic lung disease by pulmonary function testing. J Pediatr 1983;102:613–7.
3. Motoyama EK, Fort MD, Klesh KW, et al. Early onset of airway reactivity in premature infants with BPD. Am Rev Respir Dis 1987;136:50–7.
4. Baraldi E, Pettenazzo A, Filippone M, et al. Rapid improvement of static compliance after surfactant treatment in preterm infants with respiratory distress syndrome. Pediatr Pulmonol 1993;15:157–62.
5. Tasker RC, Dundas I, Laverty A, et al. Distinct patterns of respiratory difficulty in young children with achondroplasia: a clinical, sleep and lung function study. Arch Dis Child 1998;79:99–108.
6. Kao LC, Warburton D, Platzker ACG, et al. Effect of isoproterenol inhalation on airway resistance in chronic bronchopulmonary dysplasia. Pediatrics 1984;73:509–14.
7. Kao LC, Durand DJ, Nickerson BG. Effects of inhaled metaproterenol and atropine on the pulmonary mechanics of infants with bronchopulmonary dysplasia. Pediatr Pulmonol 1989;6:36–41.
8. Kraemer R, Frey U, Sommer CW, Russi E. Short-term effect of albuterol, delivered via a new auxiliary device. Am Rev Respir Dis 1991;144:347–51.
9. Soto ME, Sly PD, Uren E, et al. Bronchodilator response during acute viral bronchitis in infancy. Pediatr Pulmonol 1985;1:85–90.
10. Prabhu VG, Keszler M, Dhanireddy R. Pulmonary function changes after nebulised and intravenous frusemide in ventilated premature infants. Arch Dis Child 1997; 77:F32–5.
11. Miller MJ, Di Fiore JM, Strohl KP, et al. Effects of nasal CPAP on supraglottic and total pulmonary resistance in preterm infants. J Appl Physiol 1990;68:141–6.
12. Davis JM, Veness-Neehan K, Notter RH, et al. Changes in pulmonary mechanics after the administration of surfactant to infants with respiratory distress syndrome. N Engl J Med 1988;319:476–9.
13. Fisher JB, Manuel MC, Coleman M, et al. Identifying lung overdistension by using volume-pressure loops. Pediatr Pulmonol 1988;5:10–4.
14. American Thoracic Society/European Respiratory Society Joint Committee. Respiratory mechanics in infants: physiologic evaluation in health and disease. Am Rev Respir Dis 1993;147:474–96.
15. Stocks J, Quanjer PHH. Reference values for residual volume, functional residual capacity and total lung capacity. Eur Respir J 1995;8:492–506.
16. Primiano FP Jr, Chatburn RL. The use of models in pulmonary physiology. In: Chatburn RL, Craig KC, eds. Fundamentals of respiratory care research. East Norwalk (CT): Appleton & Lange, 1988:39–57.
17. Vallinis P, Retfalvi S, Davis GM, et al. A simplified method for determining the frequency response of pneumotachographs used in infants. Pediatr Pulmonol 1993; 16:109–15.
18. Turner MJ, Macleod IM, Rothberg AD. Measurement of the frequency response and common-mode gain of neonatal respiratory pressure and flow measurement systems. Part 1: Apparatus. Clin Phys Physiol Meas 1989; 10:219–30.
19. Sly PD, Davis GM. Equipment requirements for infant respiratory testing. In: Stocks J, Sly PD, Tepper RS, et al, eds. Infant respiratory function testing. Wiley-Liss, 1996:45–80.
20. Asher MI, Coates AL, Collinge J-M, et al. Measurement of pleural pressure in neonates. J Appl Physiol 1982; 52:491–4.
21. Milic-Emili J, Mead J, Turner JM, et al. Improved technique for estimating pleural pressure from esophageal balloons. J Appl Physiol 1964;19:207–16.
22. Beardsmore CS, Helms P, Stocks J, et al. Improved esophageal balloon technique for use in infants. J Appl Physiol 1980;49:735–42.
23. LeSouef PN, Lopes JM, England SJ, et al. Influence of chest wall distortion on esophageal pressure. J Appl Physiol 1983;55;353–8.
24. Coates AL, Davis GM, Vallinis P, et al. Liquid-filled esophageal catheter for measuring pleural pressure in preterm neonates. J Appl Physiol 1989;67:889–93.
25. Anderson JV, Martin RJ, Lough MD, et al. An improved nasal mask pneumotachometer for measuring ventilation in neonates. J Appl Physiol 1982;53:1307–9.
26. Dolfin T, Duffty P, Wilkes D, et al. Effects of a face mask and pneumotachograph on breathing in sleeping infants. Am Rev Respir Dis 1983;128:977–9.
27. Moser NJ, Phillips BA, Berry DTR, et al. What is hypopnea anyway? Chest 1994;105:426–8.
28. Berg S, Haight JSJ, Yap V, et al. Comparison of direct and indirect measurements of respiratory airflow: implications for hypopneas. Sleep 1997;1:60–4.
29. Dransfield DG, Fox WW. A noninvasive method for recording central and obstructive apnea with bradycardia in infants. Crit Care Med 1980;8:663–6.
30. Weese-Mayer DE, Corwin MJ, Peucker MR, et al. Comparison of apnea identified by respiratory inductance plethysmography with that detected by end-tidal CO_2 or thermistor. The CHIME Study Group. Am J Respir Crit Care Med 2000; 162:471–80.
31. Baird TM, Neuman MR. Effect of infant position on breath amplitude measured by thoracic impedance and strain gauges. Pediatr Pulmonol 1991;10:52–6.
32. Adams JA, Zabaleta IA, Stroh D, et al. Measurement of breath amplitudes: comparison of three noninvasive respiratory monitors to integrated pneumotachograph. Pediatr Pulmonol 1993;16:254–8.
33. Taussig LM, Landau LI, Godfrey S, et al. Determinants of forced expiratory flows in newborn infants. J Appl Physiol 1982;53:1220–7.
34. Tepper RS, Morgan WJ, Cota A, et al. Physiologic growth and development of the lung during the first year of life. Am Rev Respir Dis 1986;134:513–9.
35. Turner DJ, Stick SM, LeSouef KL, et al. A new technique to generate and assess forced expiration from raised lung volume in infants. Am J Respir Crit Care Med 1995; 151:1441–50.
36. Feher A, Castile R, Kisling J, et al. Flow limitation in normal infants: a new method for forced expiratory

maneuvers from raised lung volumes. J Appl Physiol 1996;80:2019–25.
37. Hayden MJ, Sly PD, Devadason SG, et al. Influence of driving pressure on raised-volume forced expiration in infants. Am J Respir Crit Care Med 1997;156:1876–83.
38. Sly PD, Lanteri CJ, Bates JHT. Effect of the thermodynamics on an infant plethysmograph on the measurement of thoracic gas volume. Pediatr Pulmonol 1990;8:203–8.
39. Helms PJ, Hatch DJ, Cunningham K. Measuring tidal volume in the infant. Prog Respir Res 1981;17:22–34.
40. Kraemer R. Whole body plethysmography in the clinical assessment of infants with bronchopulmonary disease. Respiration 1993;15:1–8.
41. Beardsmore CS, Thompson JR, Williams A, et al. Pulmonary function in infants with cystic fibrosis: the effect of antibiotic treatment. Arch Dis Child 1994;71:133–7.
42. Dundas I, Dezateux CA, Fletcher ME, et al. Comparison of single-breath and plethysmograph measurements of resistance in infancy. Am J Respir Crit Care Med 1995; 151:1451–8.
43. Chadha TS, Watson H, Birch S, et al. Validation of respiratory inductive plethysmography using different calibration procedures. Am Rev Respir Dis 1982;125:644–9.
44. Dolfin T, Duffty P, Wilkes DL, et al. Calibration of respiratory induction plethysmography (respitrace) in infants. Am Rev Respir Dis 1982;126:577–9.
45. Cohn MA, Rao ASV, Broudy M, et al. The respiratory inductive plethysmograph: a new non-invasive monitor of respiration. Bull Eur Physiopathol Respir 1982;18:643–58.
46. Sackner MA, Watson H, Belsito AS, et al. Calibration of respiratory inductive plethysmograph during natural breathing. J Appl Physiol 1989;66:410–20.
47. Zimmerman PV, Connellan SJ, Middleton HC, et al. Postural changes in rib cage and abdominal volume-motion coefficients and their effect on the calibration of a respiratory inductance plethysmograph. Am Rev Respir Dis 1983;127:209–14.
48. Cantineau JP, Escourrou P, Sartene R, et al. Accuracy of respiratory inductive plethysmography during wakefulness and sleep in patients with obstructive sleep apnea. Chest 1992;102:1145–51.
49. Brooks LJ, Di Fiore JM, Martin RJ, et al. Assessment of tidal volume over time in preterm infants using respiratory inductance plethysmography. Pediatr Pulmonol 1997; 23:429–33.
50. Brown K, Aun C, Jackson E, et al. Validation of respiratory inductive plethysmography using the qualitative diagnostic calibration method in anaesthetized infants. Eur Respir J 1998;12:935–43.
51. Kosch PC, Stark AR. Dynamic maintenance of end-expiratory lung volume in full-term infants. J Appl Physiol 1984;57:1126–33.
52. Mortola JP, Milic-Emili J, Noworaj A, et al. Muscle pressure and flow during expiration infants. Am Rev Respir Dis 1984;129:49–53.
53. Stark AR, Cohlan BA, Waggener TB, et al. Regulation of end-expiratory lung volume during sleep in premature infants. J Appl Physiol 1987;62:1117–23.
54. Lee S, Hassan A, Ingram D, et al. Effects of different modes of delivery on lung volumes of newborn infants. Pediatr Pulmonol 1999;27:318–21.
55. Kraus AN, Auld PAM. Measurement of functional residual capacity in distressed neonates by helium rebreathing. J Pediatr 1970;77:228–32.
56. Nelson NM, Prod'hom LS, Cherry RB, et al. Pulmonary function in the newborn infant. I. Methods: ventilation and gaseous metabolism. Pediatrics 1962;30:963–74.
57. Gappa M, Fletcher ME, Dezateux CA, et al. Comparison of nitrogen washout and plethysmographic measurements of lung volume in healthy infants. Am Rev Respir Dis 1993;148:1496–501.
58. Gerhardt T, Hehre D, Bancalari E, et al. A simple method for measuring functional residual capacity by N_2 washout in small animals and newborn infants. Pediatr Res 1985;19:1165–9.
59. Schwartz JG, Fox WW, Schaffer TH. A method for measuring functional residual capacity in neonates with endotracheal tubes. IEEE Trans Biomed Eng 1978;25:304–7.
60. Richardson P, Galway W, Olsen S, et al. Computerized estimates of functional residual capacity in infants. Ann Biomed Eng 1981;9:243–55.
61. Klaus M, Tooley WH, Weaver KL, et al. Lung volume in the newborn infant. Pediatrics 1962;30:111–6.
62. Stocks J, Levy NM, Godfrey S. A new apparatus for the accurate measurement of airway resistance in infancy. J Appl Physiol 1977;43:155–9.
63. Coates AL, Peslin R, Rodenstein D, et al. Measurement of lung volumes by plethysmography. Eur Respir J 1997; 10:1415–27.
64. Neto GS, Gerhardt T, Silberberg, et al. Nonlinear pressure/volume relationship and measurements of lung mechanics in infants. Pediatr Pulmonol 1992;12:146–52.
65. Fletcher ME, Dezateux CA, Stocks J. Respiratory compliance in infants—a preliminary evaluation of the multiple interrupter technique. Pediatr Pulmonol 1992;14:118–25.
66. Bates JHT, Baconnier P, Milic-Emili J. A theoretical analysis of interrupter technique for measuring respiratory mechanics. J Appl Physiol 1988;64:2204–14.
67. Rabbette PS, Fletcher ME, Dezateux CA, et al. Hering-Breuer reflex and respiratory system compliance in the first year of life: a longitudinal study. J Appl Physiol 1994;76:650–6.
68. Fletcher ME, Stack C, Ewart M, et al. Respiratory compliance during sedation, anesthesia and paralysis in infants and young children. J Appl Physiol 1991;70:1977–82.
69. Mead J, Whittenberger JL. Physical properties of human lung measured during spontaneous respiration. J Appl Physiol 1953;5:779–96.
70. Stocks J, Thomson A, Silverman M, et al. Numerical analysis of pressure-flow curves in infancy. Pediatr Pulmonol 1985;1:19–26.
71. Mammel MC, Fisher JB, Bing DR, et al. Effect of spontaneous and mechanical breathing on dynamic lung mechanics in hyaline membrane disease. Pediatr Pulmonol 1990;8:222–5.
72. LeSouef PN, England SJ, Bryan AC. Total resistance of the respiratory system in preterm infants with and without an endotracheal tube. J Pediatr 1984;104:108–11.

73. Fontan JJP, Heldt GP, Gregory GA. Resistance and inertia of endotracheal tubes used in infants during periodic flow. Crit Care Med 1985;13:1052–5.
74. Brick HJ, Chatburn RL. The effect of airway leak on respiratory mechanics calculations. Respir Care 1998;43:876.
75. Kondo T, Matsumoto I, Lanteri CJ, et al. Respiratory mechanics during mechanical ventilation: a model study on the effects of leak around a tracheal tube. Pediatr Pulmonol 1997;24:423–8.
76. Jackson EA, Rabbette PS, Dezateux C, et al. The effect of triclofos sodium sedation on respiratory rate, oxygen saturation and heart rate in infants and young children. Pediatr Pulmonol 1991;10:40–5.
77. Mallol J, Sly PD. Effect of chloral hydrate on arterial oxygen saturation in wheezy infants. Pediatr Pulmonol 1988;5:96–9.
78. Rabbett PS, Dezateux CA, Fletcher ME, et al. Influence of sedation on the Hering-Breuer inflation reflex in healthy infants. Pediatr Pulmonol 1991;11:217–22.
79. Turner DJ, Morgan SEG, Landau LI, et al. Methodological aspects of flow-volume studies in infants. Pediatr Pulmonol 1990;8:289–93.
80. Stocks J, Godfrey S. Specific airway conductance in relation to post-conceptual age during infancy. J Appl Physiol 1977;43:144–5.
81. Olinsky A, Bryan AC, Bryan MH. A simple method for measuring total respiratory system compliance in newborn infants. S Afr Med J 1976;50:128–30.
82. Cook CD, Helliesen PJ, Agathon S. Relation between mechanics of respiration, lung size and body size from birth to young adulthood. J Appl Physiol 1958; 13:349–52.
83. Cook CD, Sutherland JM, Segal S, et al. Studies of respiratory physiology in the newborn infant. II. Measurements of mechanics in respiration. J Clin Invest 1957;37:440–8.
84. Swyer PR, Reiman RC, Wright JJ. Ventilation and ventilatory mechanics in the newborn. J Pediatr 1960;34:525–32.
85. Chu JS, Dawson P, Klaus M, et al. Lung compliance and lung volume measured concurrently in normal full-term and premature infants. Pediatrics 1964;34:525–32.
86. Gerhardt T, Hehre D, Feller R, et al. Pulmonary mechanics in normal infants and young children during the first 5 years of life. Pediatr Pulmonol 1987;3:309–16.
87. Phelan PD, Williams HE. Ventilatory studies in healthy infants. Pediatr Res 1969;3:425–32.
88. Kreiger I. Studies on mechanics of respiration in infancy. Am J Dis Child 1963;105:51–60.
89. Howlett G. Lung mechanics in normal infants with congenital heart disease. Arch Dis Child 1972;47:707–15.
90. Hanrahan JP, Tager IB, Castile RG, et al. Pulmonary function measures in healthy infants. Variability and size correction. Am Rev Respir Dis 1990;141:1127–35.
91. Gaultier CI, Boule M, Allaire Y, et al. Growth of lung volumes during the first three years of life. Bull Eur Physiopathol Respir 1979;15:1103–16.
92 Taussig LM, Harris TR, Lebowitz MD, et al. Lung function in infants and young children. Am Rev Respir Dis 1977;116:233–9.
93. Bar-Yishay E, Shulman DL, Beardsmore CS, et al. Functional residual capacity in healthy preschool children lying supine. Am Rev Respir Dis 1987;135:954–6.
94. Sjoqvist BA, Sanberg K, Hjalmarson O, et al. Calculation of lung volume in newborn infants by means of a computer-assisted nitrogen washout method. Pediatr Res 1984; 18:1160–4.
95. Gerhardt T, Reifenberg L, Hehre D, et al. Functional residual capacity in normal neonates and children up to 5 years of age determined by a N_2 washout method. Pediatr Res 1986;20:668–71.
96. Kelly E, Bryan H, Possmayer F. Compliance of the respiratory system in newborn infants pre- and postsurfactant replacement therapy. Pediatr Pulmonol 1993;15:225–30.
97. Fox WW, Schwartz JG, Shaffer TH. Successful extubation of neonates: clinical and physiological factors. Crit Care Med 1982;9:823–6.
98. Dreizzin E, Migdal M, Praud JP, et al. Passive compliance of total respiratory system in preterm newborn infants with respiratory distress syndrome. J Pediatr 1988;36:264–8.
99. Gross SJ, Iannuzzi DM, Kveselis DA, et al. Effect of preterm birth on pulmonary function at school age: a prospective controlled study. J Pediatr 1998;133:188–92.
100. Jacob SV, Coates AL, Lands LC, et al. Long-term pulmonary sequelae of severe bronchopulmonary dysplasia. J Pediatr 1998;133:193–200.
101. Santuz P, Baraldi E, Zaramella P, et al. Factors limiting exercise performance in long-term survivors of bronchopulmonary dysplasia. Am J Crit Care Med 1995;152:1284–9.
102. Stenson BJ, Glover RM, Wilkie RA, et al. Randomized controlled trial of respiratory system compliance measurements in mechanically ventilated neonates. Arch Dis Child Fetal Neonatal Ed 1998;78:F15–9.
103. Dreshaj IA, Haxhiu MA, Potter CF, et al. Maturational changes in responses of tissue and airway resistance to histamine. J Appl Physiol 1996;81:1785–91.
104. Potter CF, Dreshaj IA, Haxhiu MA, et al. Effect of exogenous and endogenous nitric oxide on the airway and tissue components of lung resistance in the newborn piglet. Pediatr Res 1997;41:886–91.

CHAPTER 12

Comparative Aspects of Neonatal Respiratory Mechanics

Jacopo P. Mortola, MD

Newborns of different species vary greatly in body size and development. Many rodents are born with a body weight of only a few grams and are quite helpless at birth. Very short gestations occur in marsupials, typically born at an extremely early stage of development. Other species, such as many ungulates, have a large body weight and a precocial appearance at birth. Comparisons among species can be used as a tool to analyze the adaptation to the diversity in size and development and to gain further insights into physiologic function. The goal of this chapter is to use the comparative approach to analyze the mechanical properties of the respiratory system of newborn mammals.

How to Compare: The Problems of Normalization

Comparison of data among animals is a common occurrence in biologic research. Similarities and differences are evaluated and interpreted as physiologic aspects of adaptation and specialization, or expression of methodologic and biologic variability ("signals" versus "noise"[1]). Occasionally, direct comparison of the absolute values is physiologically meaningful, such as time-derived parameters like breathing rate or the mechanical time constant in respiratory physiology. In most cases, however, direct comparison is of little interest. For example, it would not be surprising that the lung volume of a rat is smaller than that of a horse, or that the respiratory compliance of an infant is less than that of an adult man. Undoubtedly more meaningful would be a comparison that takes into account the differences in size. Body weight, length, and height are common parameters used for such comparisons. In respiratory mechanics lung volume or lung weight (wet or dry) also are commonly used as normalizing parameters. It is important to realize that each normalization parameter has some usefulness, but none is completely satisfactory. For example, comparison of pulmonary functions based on body weight (W) may be confounded by the inclusion of the weight of the head, limbs, and other organs that have little to do with the functions of the lungs. This limitation becomes even more important when comparing the mechanical properties of the lungs between newborns and adults, since the relative contribution of the lungs and other organs to the total W varies with age. On the other hand, if the comparisons were made with the intention of assessing the role of the lungs in fulfilling the oxygen needs of the whole organisms, then the normalization by W would be not only practical, but also physiologically meaningful. In the present discussion W will be the normalizing parameter adopted for most of the interspecies comparisons.

The allometric analysis is a commonly used approach for interspecies comparison by W.[1–3] The variable of interest (Y) is related to W according to the function $Y = a \cdot W^b$. This exponential function is conveniently expressed by its log-transformed version $\log Y = \log a + b \cdot \log W$, where the original exponent b becomes the slope of the log-function, and a is the antilog of its intercept. When $b = 1$, Y increases in direct proportion to W, and Y/W is an interspecies constant. When b differs from unity, Y is not directly proportional to W; therefore, Y/W is not an interspecies constant.

Metabolic and Ventilatory Needs

Before comparing and discussing the mechanical properties of the neonatal respiratory system it is necessary to address a few preliminary questions. First, in newborn mammals is the respiratory system the only route for gas exchange? Second, what are the metabolic and ventilatory needs of the newborns? In general, the answer to the first question is affirmative, although, in contrast with original beliefs,[4] an important exception occurs in some marsupials. In fact, gas exchange through the skin that is many times more important than that provided by the lungs has been demonstrated in the Julia Creek dunnart, a marsupial born after only 12 days of gestation, and, being ~4 mm long and ~15 mg in W, one of the smallest newborn mammals (Figure 12–1).[5,6] After 2 weeks the gas exchange through the skin of the dunnart pouch young is comparable to that of its lungs, and only after 3 weeks it is reduced to minor importance. At the day of birth the Tammar wallaby joey also has a large fraction of gas exchange through the skin[7] and it is possible that the same phenomenon may occur in other very small marsupials.

Measurements of oxygen consumption ($\dot{V}_{O_2}$) have been performed on many newborn species. The data are scattered, as one perhaps would anticipate given the

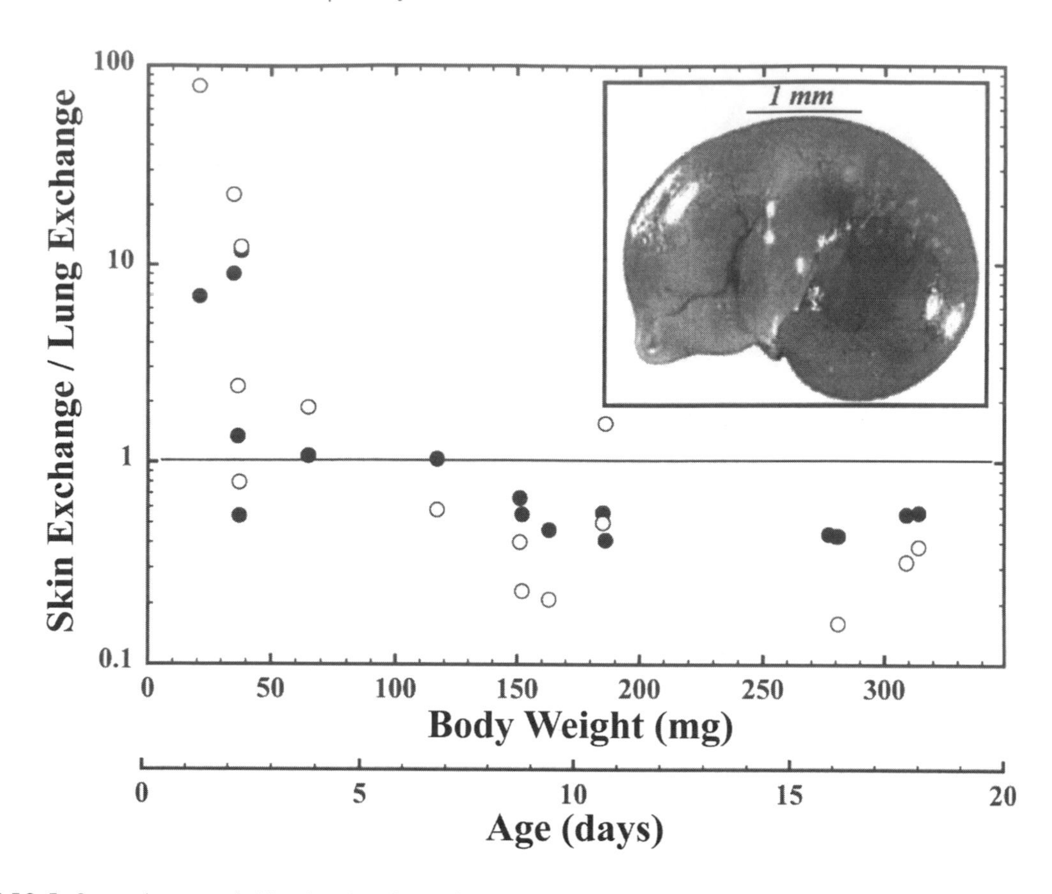

FIGURE 12–1. Oxygen (*open symbols*) and carbon dioxide (*filled symbols*) exchanged through the skin in the pouch young Julia Creek dunnart (*inset*: a 1 day old dunnart: the air sacs of the lungs are visible through the skin). Skin exchange is expressed as ratio of that occurring through the lungs. Total oxygen consumption (skin + lungs) averaged ~15 mL • kg^{-1} • min^{-1} at all ages. In this marsupial during the first postnatal week the skin is the most important contributor to gas exchange. (Data from Mortola JP et al,[5] Frappell PB and Mortola JP.[6])

numerous factors potentially confounding the measurements. For example, many newborn species commonly live at temperatures lower than thermoneutrality*; yet, thermoneutrality is the ambient temperature range most often chosen for the $\dot{V}_{O_2}$ measurements. Also, $\dot{V}_{O_2}$ can change rapidly during the first postnatal days and at different rates among species, such that seemingly small differences in postnatal age can add noise to the results. Despite these and other uncertainties, it seems clear that the allometric relation of $\dot{V}_{O_2}$ for newborn species has an exponent much higher than the classic adult value of 0.75;[8,9] in fact, the exponent is ~0.9—higher than 0.75 but significantly below unity.[10,11] Therefore, $\dot{V}_{O_2}$/W is not an interspecies constant, and, on a W basis, small newborn species exchange larger quantities of O_2 and CO_2 than do larger species.

Given that $\dot{V}_{O_2}$/W is larger in smaller species and that in the large majority of newborn mammals gas exchange occurs through the lungs, we should expect alveolar ventilation ($\dot{V}_A$) to be proportional to gas exchange and, therefore, $\dot{V}_A$/W to be larger in the smaller species. Data on $\dot{V}_A$ are few, but there is reason to believe that $\dot{V}_A$ is proportional to external, or pulmonary, ventilation ($\dot{V}_E$), which is the product of breathing frequency (f) and tidal volume (V_T). Measurements of $\dot{V}_E$ and breathing pattern have been performed on numerous newborn species. The results confirm the expectations that $\dot{V}_E$ is linearly proportional to $\dot{V}_{O_2}$ (Figure 12–2); hence, $\dot{V}_E$/W also is larger in the smaller newborn species. This interspecies difference in $\dot{V}_E$/W is due almost exclusively to differences in f, whereas V_T/W does not change systematically with the species size and averages ~10 mL/kg. Therefore, the breathing pattern of newborn species in the lower, intermediate, and higher spectrums of size can be represented schematically as in Figure 12–3.

*Thermoneutrality is the range in ambient temperature over which a body temperature is maintained with minimal $\dot{V}_{O_2}$ in normoxia.

Scaling Respiratory Mechanics in Newborn Species

Expectations

Given that flow rates and $\dot{V}_E$/W are higher in smaller newborn species, one may expect corresponding differences in the mechanical design of the respiratory system. For example, one may hypothesize that the greater flows require a larger muscle mass or larger lungs. Alternatively, for the same muscle force and pressure, the mechanical

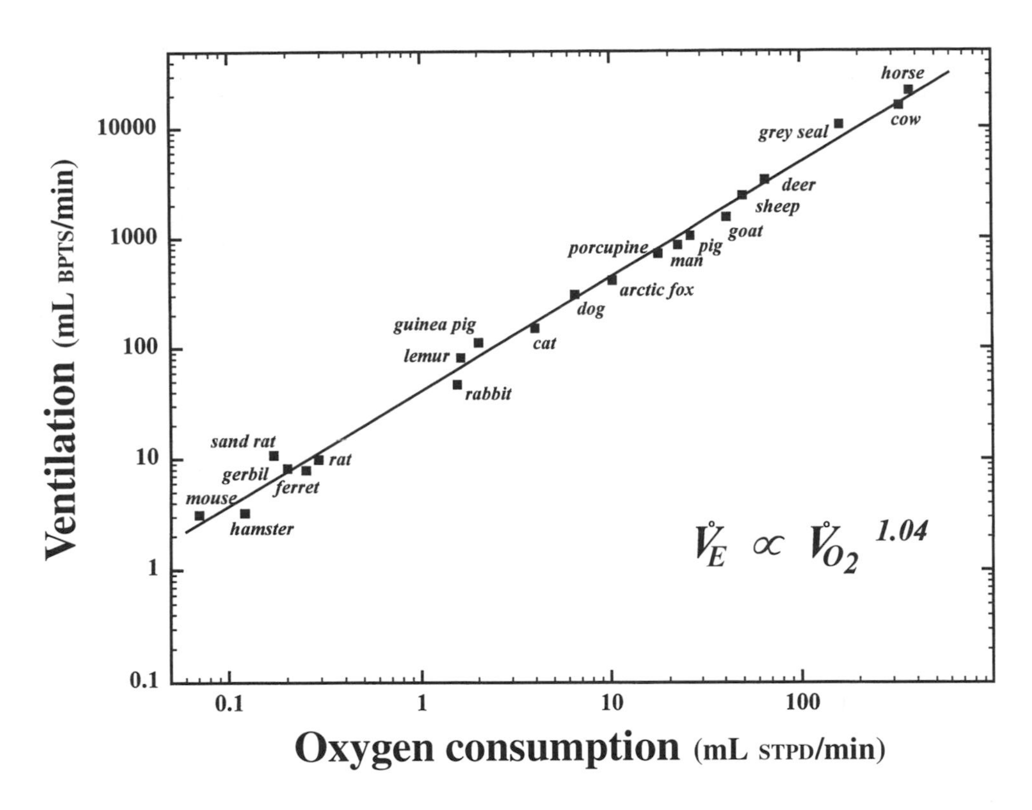

FIGURE 12–2. Average values of oxygen consumption and ventilation in newborn mammalian species. The two variables bear a direct proportionality to each other. BTPS = body temperature, pressure, saturation; STPD = standard temperature, pressure, dry. (Reproduced with permission from Mortola JP,[11] which includes references for the individual species.)

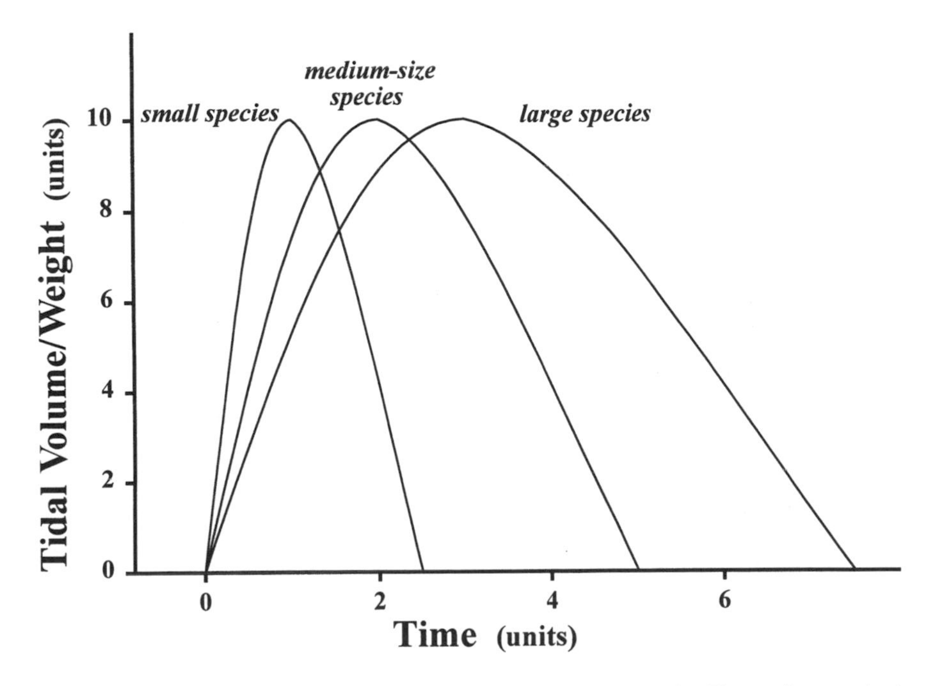

FIGURE 12–3. Schematic spirometric records representative of three groups of newborn species. The smallest species breathe quickly, and the biggest ones breathe more slowly; however tidal volume per unit of body weight is species-independent.

response time of the respiratory system could be faster in smaller newborn species. Because the time constant of the respiratory system (τrs), by analogy with a first-order mechanical system, is the product of its compliance (Crs) and resistance (Rrs), a shorter τrs in smaller newborns should require either a small Crs, or a small Rrs, in any combination. The former could be achieved with lungs that are disproportionately small relative to W, or with tissue characteristics that increase the pulmonary stiffness. Because Rrs is contributed largely by the resistance to flow within the airways, a small Rrs could occur in lungs with disproportionately short airways or with a large cross-sectional area. Some experimental data are available to test which of these expectations is most supported.

Respiratory Muscles

The total mass of the main respiratory muscles—the diaphragm and intercostals—represents a similar fraction of W, ~0.4%, in both small and large species.[10] Because pressure equals force/surface area and the force generated by a muscle is proportional to its cross-sectional area, the interspecies similarity of muscle mass/W is in agreement with experimental observations that the swing in pleural pressure generated during breathing is similar among species. In the respiratory muscles of adults the percentage of fast-twitch fibers and the mitochondria concentration are inversely related to the species W,[12,13] which may explain the faster response time of diaphragmatic contraction in the smaller species.[14] Whether or not these or similar differences in the biochemical characteristics of the respiratory muscles also occur among neonatal species is not known.

Lungs

At birth, the amount of lung tissue is a constant fraction of body mass, that is, ~0.4% for the dry lung mass or ~2% for the fresh wet mass,[10,11] independent of the species size. The extent of the similarity in the lung tissue constituents is not known, because data on the biochemical components of the lungs are available for only a few species. The number of alveoli is usually very low at birth, and the process of alveolar formation seems to match the appearance of elastic fibers.

The elastic characteristics of the lungs often are quantified as the changes in V per unitary changes in transpulmonary pressure (P_L) under conditions of zero flow, or lung compliance ($C_L = \Delta V/\Delta P_L$). Lung compliance, measured by different techniques in many species spanning in W from a few grams to several kilograms, is proportional to the first power of W, with values between 2 and 3 mL • cm H_2O^{-1} • kg^{-1} in most species.[9] Mathematic analysis of the deflation P-V curve has indicated profound similarities among newborn species of very different size, with the possible exception of the guinea pig, an animal born after a long gestation and at an advanced stage of development.[15,16]

The notion that C_L/W is an interspecies constant permits some interesting predictions. Because the pressure required to inflate the lungs is mostly determined by the lung's elastic characteristics, the interspecies similarity in V_T/W mentioned earlier implies that the pleural pressure swing (Ppl) during tidal breathing should be similar, even among species of very different dimensions. The interspecies similarity in Ppl also means that alveolar surface pressure is rather similar among newborns, because the major component of the lung elastic recoil pressure is due to surface tension at the alveolar air-liquid interface. According to the Young-Laplace relationship, surface pressure is proportional to surface tension (γ) and inversely proportional to the radius of the air-liquid interface, which is the alveolar radius in the lungs. Since γ is a constant, one is left with the conclusion that alveolar dimensions must be similar in small and large species; stated differently, large lungs, in comparison to small lungs, should have more alveoli, not necessarily bigger ones. To a large extent this prediction was supported by experimental measurements on lungs of many newborn species.[17]

Respiratory System Compliance and Resistance

Data on Crs and Rrs of newborn mammals have been collected for many years. In comparing results from different publications, one notices a substantial scatter in the data, largely because these measurements are sensitive to the technique and experimental conditions. Nevertheless, after averaging the results of different studies on any given species[10,11] and plotting the data in allometric form, the conclusion can be reached that Crs increases in direct proportion to the species W ($Crs \propto W^{1.02}$, whereas Rrs decreases less than expected by direct proportionality, or $Rrs \propto W^{-0.80}$ (Figure 12–4). This pattern is qualitatively similar to that emerged from analysis of adult species.[1,2,14] Hence, Crs/W is an interspecies constant, whereas Rrs/W is progressively lower the smaller the newborn species. The structural basis for the nonproportional relation between Rrs and W is not known; nor is it known whether it could be attributed to possible differences in airway dimensions occurring systematically with changes in body size. At any rate, the important functional implication is that the product of these two variables, τrs, is not directly proportional to W. In fact, from the allometric relations of Crs ($\propto W^{1.02}$) and Rrs ($\propto W^{-0.80}$), one can calculate that τrs should scale to W with an exponent of 1.02–0.80, or $\propto W^{0.22}$. Stated in other words, the mechanical response of the respiratory system is faster in smaller species. Some direct experimental measurements of τrs are in agreement with this conclusion. For example, in the 3 to 4-kg human infant, τrs can be close to 200 ms, in 500-g to 1-kg newborn dogs and piglets, τrs is ~130 to 150 ms, and in 2 to 4-g newborn mice and hamsters, it is 40 to 50 ms.[10,18]

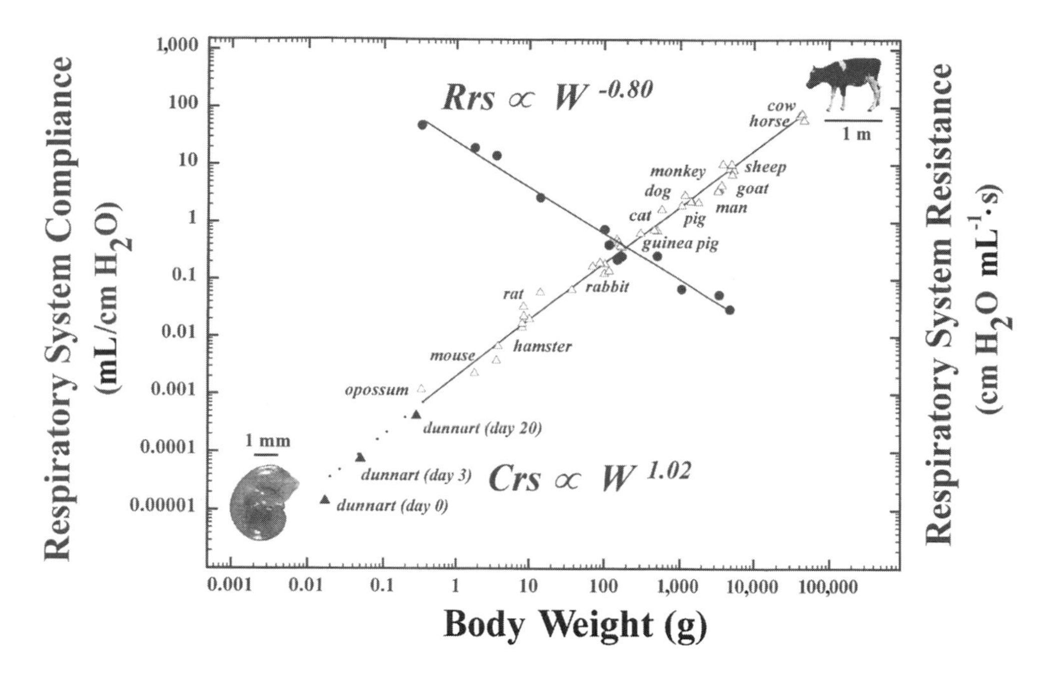

FIGURE 12–4. Allometric relations of the compliance (Crs) and resistance (Rrs) of the respiratory system. Each symbol is the mean value of a particular study. The smallest species represented is the dunnart pouch young (~17 mg); the largest is the calf (~45 kg). Although all data points are represented, the regression lines were calculated after averaging the values pertinent to any particular species. Δ, ▲ = Crs; • = Rrs. (Adapted from Mortola JP,[11] which includes references for the individual species.)

In conclusion, it appears that the interspecies differences in metabolic and ventilatory requirements are not met by differences in muscle or pulmonary mass, nor in lung or respiratory system compliance. Rather, the faster breathing of the smaller newborn species finds a functional correspondence in the lower resistance and shorter time constant of the respiratory system.

"Active" Mechanical Behavior of the Respiratory System

The finding that neonatal τrs varies with species size in accordance with metabolic and ventilatory needs is in agreement with expectations, but it is not necessarily conclusive. In fact, the data of Crs and Rrs just discussed were obtained in "passive" conditions, that is, when no muscle force is applied to the system. If we want to extend the analysis of the mechanical design in relation to the metabolic requirements, we need to ask to what extent in "active" conditions (ie, when the respiratory muscles are operating) the mechanical behavior resembles the passive situation. Further, within the context of the present discussion, if differences between active and passive properties do occur, we then would like to know whether these differences vary systematically with the species size.

Inspiration

During the first phase of the active breathing cycle (ie, inspiration), several factors could modify the effective mechanical properties of the system. Probably the main factor is the propensity of the neonatal chest wall to become deformed when the muscles contract, a distortion that cannot occur during passive inflation. This propensity finds its structural basis in the characteristically high ratio between chest wall and lung compliance of newborn mammals (Figure 12–5). For example, in the adult man this ratio is approximately 1, whereas in infants the compliance of the chest wall can be 4 to 5 times higher than that of the lungs. The propensity for distortion during inspiration implies that more muscle force needs to be generated than is expected simply from the measurements of Crs and Rrs. In fact, energy is lost because of the inward movement of the rib cage during inspiration, which does not contribute to lung inflation; if the extradiaphragmatic muscles are recruited to stabilize the rib cage during inspiration, this compensatory contraction increases the energetic cost of breathing. Either way, whether the chest distortion actually occurs or is compensated for by concurrent contraction of rib cage muscles, a high chest wall compliance implies that, for the same VT, in active conditions some force is required in addition to that expected from the passive measurements.

There are other reasons for the inspiratory active-passive difference. For example, lung compliance during breathing† is usually less than the passive value, due to the

†Lung compliance measured during tidal breathing is often called "dynamic" compliance.

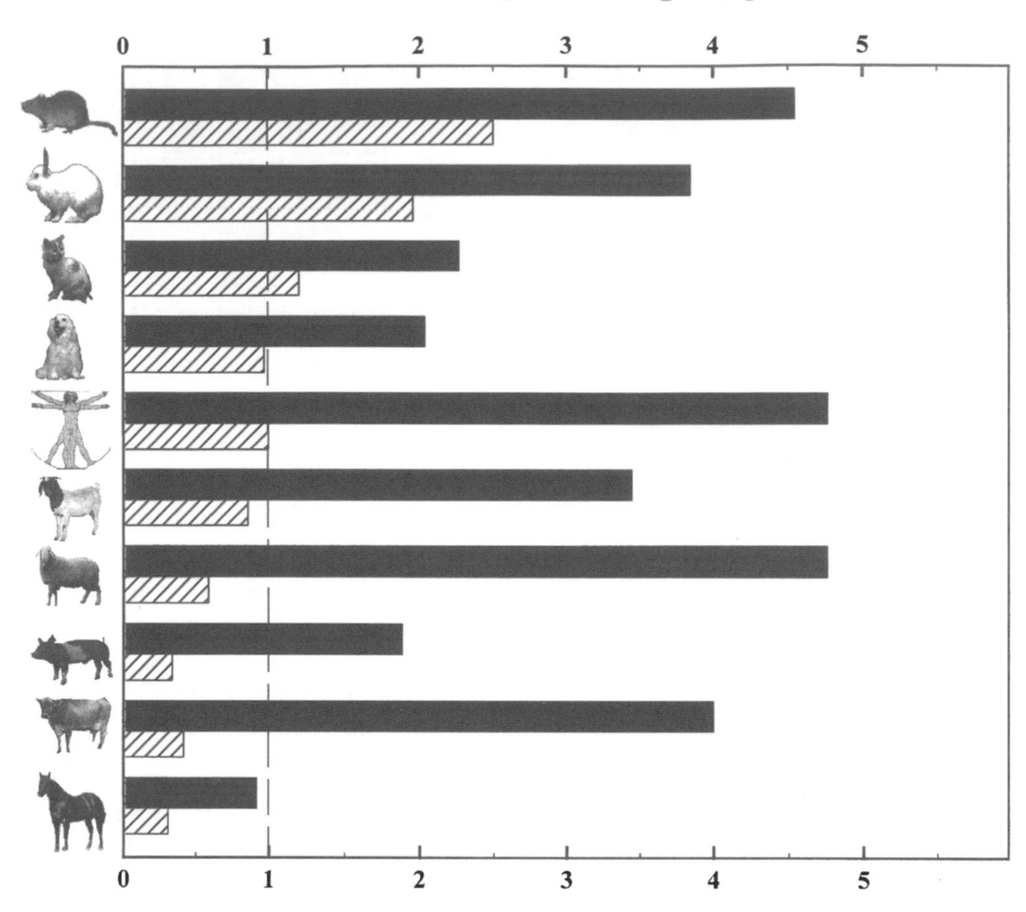

FIGURE 12–5. Ratio between the compliance of the chest wall and that of the lungs in newborn and adult mammals of several species. The values represent averages compiled from various studies. ■ = ratio in newborns; ▨ = ratio in adults. (Adapted from Mortola JP,[11] which includes references for the individual species.)

high viscous characteristics of the neonatal pulmonary tissue and, possibly, due to some peripheral airway closure determined by lung deformation.[9,20,21] How much higher is the muscle pressure required to breathe, compared with the passive measurements, cannot be said with certainty, because estimates are very indirect.[10] In infants during active breathing the effective compliance could be only about half of Crs.[22]

The functional implication of an effective reduction in Crs during breathing is that the response time of the system is shorter than τrs. Furthermore, pulmonary resistance can decrease during breathing to below the value measured in passive conditions. Indeed, when pulmonary tissue viscosity is high and is an important contributor to the total resistance (as is the case in newborn lungs), Rrs does not increase; in fact, it actually decreases with breathing rate.[23] In the newborn opossum, mouse, and hamster,[18] this mechanism has been estimated to further reduce τrs by ~ 30%. In conclusion, in newborns during inspiration active Crs and Rrs are both likely to be less than the corresponding passive values, with the result of shortening of the response time of the system.

Expiration

During the second phase of the breathing cycle (ie, expiration), two mechanisms are the primary factors modifying the mechanical behavior of the respiratory system: the postinspiratory activity of the inspiratory muscles and the laryngeal control of expiratory flow. The latter consists in the narrowing of the vocal folds during expiration, a physiologic phenomenon that can be exaggerated in conditions of respiratory distress into what is known clinically as "grunting." These two mechanisms prolong the time required for deflation, such that the expiratory time constant (τexp) is longer than τrs. In the human infant, for example, at the normal breathing rate, the active prolongation of the expiratory time constant is such that the expiratory time is not sufficient for a complete deflation to the passive resting volume, Vr; hence, the lung volume at end-expiration (or functional residual capacity, FRC) is larger than Vr.[24–26] A similar pattern has been observed in other newborn species.[27] Because the characteristic high chest wall compliance of the newborn favors a low Vr, the dynamic elevation of FRC can be considered a protective mechanism against the risks of small airway closure, which would have major consequences for gas exchange and the cost of breathing. In infants intubated under anesthesia, postinspiratory muscle activity is reduced and the larynx is bypassed. In these conditions blood gases deteriorate unless an end-expiratory pressure is added to the ventilatory circuit for the purpose of increasing FRC.[28,29]

Interspecies Differences in Active Respiratory Mechanics

Besides the human infant, a quantitative assessment of chest distortion has been attempted in only a few species, such as the piglet and the lamb. Hence, the information is too scanty for conclusions about the implications of chest distortion on the ventilatory requirements of the different species.

On the other hand, in several newborn species τexp has been computed from the flow-volume expiratory curve during resting breathing. The general conclusion is that in infants and in other species of medium or large size, τexp exceeds τrs. In contrast, in the smallest species breathing at high rates, τexp is similar or even shorter than τrs.[27] The mechanism for this latter phenomenon is the previously mentioned reduction in dynamic lung compliance below the passive value during conditions of high-frequency breathing; this is also known as frequency-dependence of dynamic C_L. Hence, in the smallest newborns the very short τexp limits the extent of the dynamic elevation of FRC, which would otherwise be large, because these small species breathe quickly and with short expiratory times. Several reasons may explain why in small newborns a high FRC may not be advantageous. Whenever FRC is above Vr, some muscle pressure must be generated at the onset of inspiration to overcome the recoil of the respiratory system before inspiratory flow can be produced. Also, the higher is the FRC, the more pronounced is the input from the airway stretch receptors inhibiting inspiratory activity. Neither mechanism is desirable in the smallest species, which have high metabolic requirements and the necessity of high ventilatory rates. In summary, the dynamic elevation of FRC is an appropriate solution to the condition of a low Vr, which is characteristic of the neonatal respiratory system. However, an important increase in FRC may pose some problems in the smallest species, which have high ventilatory rates. Therefore, the dynamic elevation of FRC is mainly observed in newborns of medium-size and large species, including the human infant, in which the metabolic and ventilatory demands are not as great as those in the smallest species.

Conclusion

The metabolic and ventilatory differences among newborns of different body size are accompanied by some differences in the mechanical design of the respiratory system. Hence, some parameters are interspecies constants, meaning that they change in direct proportion to the species W, whereas others are flexible, varying among species and not in proportion to W. The mass of the lungs and of the respiratory muscles, and lung volumes are interspecies constants. Among the implications of this constancy is that alveolar dimensions and the pressures applied to the respiratory system, including the tidal pleural pressure swing, are interspecies constants. The parameters that vary to accommodate the different metabolic and ventilatory needs imposed by the differences in body size are time-dependent variables. Hence, breathing frequency and timing, flows, and resistances change not in direct proportion to W, but in proportion to $\dot{V}_{O_2}$ and $\dot{V}_E$. The result is that the mechanical time constant varies among species accommodating the ventilatory requirements imposed by the differences in size. Therefore, in newborns the solution to the problems introduced by differences in body size is, from the view point of the mechanics of breathing, similar to that of the adults.[14,30] An important difference from the adults is represented by the numerous mechanisms that collectively modify the mechanical behavior during active conditions. These mechanisms are needed namely to counteract the functional problems introduced by the high chest wall compliance of the neonatal period.

At the lowermost end of the range in body size, in the domain of the small marsupials, the general rules in the design of the neonatal respiratory system may no longer apply. For example, in the newborn opossum, which weighs ~ 300 mg, the lungs are made of air sacs with a disproportionately large volume.[18] In the newborn dunnart, which is one order of magnitude smaller, we cannot even find coordinated respiratory muscle contraction, and, as mentioned earlier, the skin, not the lungs, are the major route for gas exchange.[5,6] Presumably, at this extreme end of the spectrum in body size, where the physiologic distinctions between mammals and lower vertebrates are blurry, a lung design and ventilation according to the allometric rules of the larger species would present unsurmountable engineering problems, and evolution has opted for different priorities and strategies of gas exchange.

References

1. Leith DE. Comparative mammalian respiratory mechanics. Physiologist 1976;19:485–510.
2. Stahl WR. Scaling of respiratory variables in mammals. J Appl Physiol 1967;22:453–60.
3. Schmidt-Nielsen K. Scaling. Why is animal size so important? Cambridge: Cambridge University Press, 1984: 126–42.

4. Baudinette RV, Gannon BJ, Ryall RG, Frappell PB. Changes in metabolic rates and blood respiratory characteristics during pouch development of a marsupial, *Macropus eugenii*. Respir Physiol 1988;72:219–28.
5. Mortola JP, Frappell PB, Woolley PA. Breathing through skin in a newborn mammal. Nature 1999;397:660.
6. Frappell PB, Mortola JP. Respiratory function in a newborn marsupial with skin gas exchange. Respir Physiol 2000; 120:35–45.
7. MacFarlane PM, Frappell PB. Convection requirements is established by total metabolic rate in the newborn tammar wallaby. Respir Physiol 2001;126:221–31.
8. Brody S. Bioenergetics and growth. New York: Reinhold Publishing Co., 1945 [a reprint of this 1945 edition is available from New York: Hafner, 1974].
9. Kleiber M. The fire of life: an introduction to animal energetics. New York: Wiley, 1961:454.
10. Mortola JP. Dynamics of breathing in newborn mammals. Physiol Rev 1987;67:187–243.
11. Mortola JP. Respiratory physiology of newborn mammals. A comparative perspective. Baltimore: Johns Hopkins University Press, 2000.
12. Gauthier GF, Padikula HA. Cytological studies of fiber types in skeletal muscle. A comparative study of the mammalian diaphragm. J Cell Biol 1966;28:333–54.
13. Davies AS, Gunn HM. Histochemical fibre types in the mammalian diaphragm. J Anat 1972;112:41–60.
14. Leiter JC, Mortola JP, Tenney SM. A comparative analysis of contractile characteristics of the diaphragm and of respiratory system mechanics. Respir Physiol 1986; 64:267–76.
15. Gaultier C, Harf A, Lorino AM, Atlan G. Lung mechanics in growing guinea pigs. Respir Physiol 1984;56:217–28.
16. Saetta M, Mortola JP. Exponential analysis of the lung pressure-volume curve in newborn mammals. Pediatr Pulmonol 1985;1:193–7.
17. Bartlett D Jr, Areson JG. Quantitative lung morphology in newborn mammals. Respir Physiol 1977;29:193–200.
18. Frappell PB, Mortola JP. Respiratory mechanics in small newborn mammals. Respir Physiol 1989;76:25–36.
19. Sullivan KJ, Mortola JP. Age related changes in the rate of stress relaxation within the rat respiratory system. Respir Physiol 1987;67:295–309.
20. Sullivan KJ, Mortola JP. Effect of distortion on the mechanical properties of newborn piglet lung. J Appl Physiol 1985;59:434–42.
21. Sullivan KJ, Mortola JP. Dynamic lung compliance in newborn and adult cats. J Appl Physiol 1986;60:743–50.
22. Mortola JP, Saetta M, Fox G, et al. Mechanical aspects of chest wall distortion. J Appl Physiol 1985;59:295–304.
23. Kochi T, Okubo S, Zin WA, Milic-Emili J. Chest wall and respiratory system mechanics in cats: effects of flow and volume. J Appl Physiol 1988;64:2636–46.
24. Mortola JP, Fisher JT, Smith B, et al. Dynamics of breathing in infants. J Appl Physiol 1982;52:1209–15.
25. Mortola JP, Milic-Emili J, Noworaj A, et al. Muscle pressure and flow during expiration in infants. Am Rev Respir Dis 1984;129:49–53.
26. Kosch PC, Stark AR. Dynamic maintenance of end-expiratory lung volume in full-term infants. J Appl Physiol 1984;57:1126–33.
27. Mortola JP, Magnante D, Saetta M. Expiratory pattern of newborn mammals. J Appl Physiol 1985;58:528–33.
28. Gregory GA, Kitterman JA, Phibbs RH, et al. Treatment of the idiopathic respiratory-distress syndrome with continuous positive airway pressure. N Engl J Med 1971; 284:1333–40.
29. Berman LS, Fox WW, Raphaely RC, Downes JD Jr. Optimum levels of CPAP for tracheal extubation of newborn infants. J Pediatr 1976;89:109–12.
30. Bennett FM, Tenney SM. Comparative mechanics of mammalian respiratory system. Respir Physiol 1982; 49:131–40.

CHAPTER 13

PHYSIOLOGY OF COUGH

VICTOR CHERNICK, MD, FRCPC

Cough is a complex defense mechanism designed to protect the lungs against inhalation of foreign objects or noxious substances and to enhance the clearance of mucus from the tracheobronchial tree.[1] Cough probably also enhances mucus clearance in normal individuals by stimulating the mucociliary apparatus.[2] Cough is the most common symptom of respiratory disease; cough prevalence in the general population is estimated to be between 5 and 40%, although it is infrequent in healthy individuals.[3] Nonproductive or irritative cough may be seen in many patients, such as those with asthma and gastroesophageal reflux, in which the mechanism of stimulation is obviously different. The potentially dire consequences of the inability to cough become obvious in clinical situations when the cough reflex is impaired. Atelectasis, lobar collapse, or frequent pneumonia may occur because of retained lung secretions.

Mechanics of Cough

Cough has four distinct phases whether initiated reflexly or voluntarily: inspiration, compression, expiration, and relaxation (Figure 13–1).[4]

INSPIRATION

The initial phase of cough is an inspiratory effort associated with an active abduction of the glottis caused by contraction of the abductor muscle of the arytenoid cartilage. Inspiratory volume varies from less than 50% of tidal volume to 50% of vital capacity. In adults the volume at which glottic closure occurs is 200 to 3,500 mL above functional residual capacity.[5,6] Larger inspiratory volumes allow the generation of greater subglottic pressure, because of greater mechanical efficiency of the expiratory muscles and a greater elastic recoil of the lung. Studies of inspiratory volumes in relation to glottic closure have not been done in children.

COMPRESSION

In compression thoracoabdominal expiratory muscles contract isometrically against the closed glottis causing a rapid rise in intrathoracic and intra-abdominal pressures. Lung volume decreases due to gas compression (Boyle's law). Glottic closure lasts for about 200 ms, and subglottic pressures may reach values as high as 300 cm H_2O.[7]

Cough may be effective in clearing mucus from the tracheobronchial tree even in the absence of glottic closure. For example, cough may be effective in patients with a tracheostomy or following laryngectomy.[8,9] Presumably isotonic contraction of expiratory muscles, although associated with a reduced expiratory flow, compensate with a longer duration of contraction. Voluntary brief forced expiratory movements with an open glottis ("huffing") can be effective in clearing the airway in normal subjects and in patients with cystic fibrosis.[10,11]

EXPIRATION (EXPULSION)

Once the glottis opens there is an explosive expiratory flow that causes passive vocal cord and gas vibration and the characteristic noise.[4] Peak flow dissipates rapidly, plateaus, and then decreases (see Figure 13–1). Pressure in the large airways decreases rapidly, and the high intrapleural pressure causes dynamic compression and

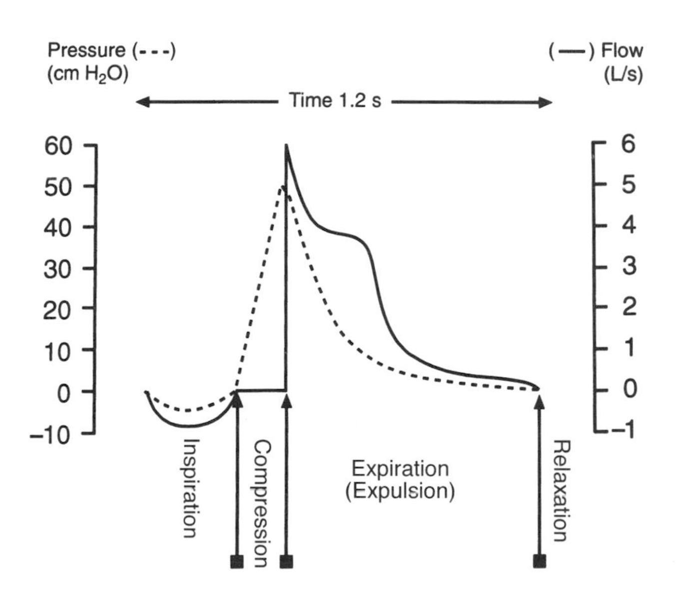

FIGURE 13–1. Diagrammatic representation of a cough. *Dashed line* represents sublottic pressure and *solid line* represents flow. Flow is negative during inspiration, zero during glottic closure, and positive during expiration when there is an initial rapid increase, a plateau, and then a decrease in flow to zero. (Adapted from Yamagihara N et al.[4])

collapse of the central airways. Peak flow at the mouth can exceed 10 L/s. Flow velocities are considerably higher in central airways than in peripheral airways, because they have a lower total cross-sectional area and are dynamically compressed.[12] During cough tracheal cross-sectional area may be decreased up to 80%. Dynamic compression and increased linear velocity of flow are thought to enhance mucus clearance. The expulsive phase of cough may be prolonged with a large expiratory volume, or it may be interrupted in a series of short expiratory efforts, each having compressive and expulsive phases.

Relaxation

In the fourth phase muscles of expiration relax and intrapleural and intra-abdominal pressures fall to resting values. Transmural pressures of the central airways also return to normal.

The Cough Reflex

The involuntary initiation of cough involves (1) cough "receptors," (2) afferent vagal nerves, (3) the cough "center," and (4) efferent neural pathways and the muscles of inspiration and expiration (effectors).

Cough Receptors

Surprisingly, the precise physiology and pathophysiologic mechanisms involving the so-called cough receptors have not been elucidated, and the subject remains controversial. Animal studies have been extrapolated to the human and may or may not be pertinent. Three sensory nerves in the lung are possible cough receptors: (1) rapidly adapting myelinated fibers (A delta) located in the airway epithelium, (2) bronchial C fibers (nonmyelinated), and (3) pulmonary C fibers (nonmyelinated fibers located in alveolar walls). However, whether C fiber activation can cause cough is controversial.[13,14] Cough can also be induced by stimulation of other sites innervated by the vagus nerve such as the external auditory canal and the tympanic membrane (Arnold's nerve).

Cough can be mechanically or chemically stimulated by a variety of endogenous or exogenous stimuli (Table 13–1). Citric acid, capsaicin, distilled water, and hypertonic saline have been used to measure cough receptor sensitivity in both normal children and children with various diseases.[1,15] The mediators that normally are involved following stimulation by a foreign body or mucus are not known, but they presumably involve tachykinins such as neurokinin A, bradykinin, substance P, or calcitonin gene-related peptide (CGRP).

TABLE 13–1. Some Exogenous and Endogenous Cough Stimuli

Mechanical	Chemical	Inflammatory Mediators
Foreign body	Capsaicin	Histamine
Dust particle	Tartaric acid	Bradykinin
Mucus	Citric acid	Prostaglandins (E_2, $F_{2\alpha}$)
Inflation/deflation	Acetic acid	
	Nicotine	
	Hypertonic solution	
	Smoke	

Afferent Vagal Nerves

The afferent pathways for cough involve the vagal nerve and those structures that have vagal innervation, including the larynx, tracheobronchial tree, external auditory canal and tympanic membrane, esophagus, and intra-abdominal viscera. In the lung, the larynx and large airways appear to be more sensitive to mechanical stimulation, whereas the more distal airways are less mechanosensitive and more chemosensitive.[13] Presumably this is related to different sensory innervation by vagal pathways.

The Cough Center

The so-called cough center is probably located in the dorsal medulla in the nucleus tractus solitarius and is activated by vagal afferents that synapse in this area.[16] Cough may be suppressed voluntarily, presumably by cortical mechanisms.[17,18]

Effectors

The efferent limb involves expiratory muscles that create elevated intrathoracic pressures and are essential for the production of an effective cough.[19,20] The efferent limb involves the recurrent laryngeal nerve (vagus), which is responsible for glottic closure, and spinal nerves from C3 to S2. The muscles of expiration include the abdominal muscles, which contract as a unit during cough, and the intercostal muscles.[21] Muscles of the pelvic floor also are activated.

Development of the Cough Reflex

Little is known about the developmental aspects of the cough reflex. In fetal lambs a laryngeal sphincter has been described that periodically opens to allow the rapid release of lung liquid, resembling a cough.[22,23] However, this observation has not been investigated further. Few studies have been done in the human newborn infant. Prematurely born infants less than 35 weeks' gestation have "immature" responses to mechanical stimulation of the bronchial mucosa (which presumably stimulates irritant receptors), possibly because of lack of myelination of vagal afferent fibers.[24] Cough is also absent in most premature infants when saline is injected into the trachea. By 1 month postnatal age, only 25% of preterm infants cough in response to saline, whereas 90% of full-term babies respond with cough.[25] This is in contrast to newborn kittens who have a well developed cough reflex when the larynx is mechanically stimulated. However, even in this species, stimulation of the tracheobronchial tree to produce cough remains ineffective for at least the first week of life.[26] In a study of puppies from 1 to 17 days of age, spontaneous activity of rapidly adapting (irritant) vagal receptor activity was only about one-quarter of that seen in the adult dog.[27] Whether this was secondary to reduced numbers of receptors or to a reduced myelination of vagal fibers at this age remains unknown. Unfortunately neither mechanical nor chemical stimulation of the tracheobronchial tree was done in this study. In a theoretic analysis Leith suggested that the low lung recoil and compliant trachea of the newborn infant could make upstream cough clearance less effective than it is in adults.[28] Clearly, the precise maturation of peripheral, central, and effector pathways remains unknown.

Mechanism of Airway Clearance

Two major mechanisms have been thought to be responsible for the effectiveness of cough in clearing mucus from the lung. The first is referred to as the two-phase gas-liquid flow theory.[3,5] This theory proposes that there are four primary types of airflow through a liquid, depending on gas velocity: (1) At low velocity (< hr 60 cm/s) air flows through mucus as small bubbles. These bubbles do not enhance the clearance of mucus. (2) At velocities between 60 and 1,000 cm/s bubbles increase in size and coalesce within the mucus to produce "slug flow," which has the ability to be effective in moving mucous plugs cephalad. (3) At greater air velocity, between 1,000 and 2,500 cm/s, there is a continuous gas channel through the mucus such that the mucus occupies an annular sleeve along the side of the airways and is transported cephalad in a wavelike motion. (4) At very high gas velocity (> hr 2,500 cm/s), which occurs in large airways during cough, so-called misty flow occurs in which mucus is blown off the surface as plugs or aerosolized droplets. The efficiency of mucus clearance depends on surface velocity, liquid layer of thickness, and viscosity of the mucus. Lower airflow velocity (as occurs during huffing) may be effective, because annular flow of liquid can be achieved.

Of interest is the observation that in normal subjects, cough appears to enhance mucus clearance by stimulation of the mucociliary apparatus rather than by a two-phase gas-liquid flow mechanism.[2]

Productive versus Nonproductive Cough

In both children and adults, increased cough receptor sensitivity (CRS), as measured by inhalation of cough triggering agents, is enhanced in subjects with nonproductive ("dry") cough, but not in patients with a productive cough.[1,29] Why CRS increases in some subjects and not in others remains unclear. Possible mechanisms include an increased CGRP nerve density, persistent inflammation, and surfactant abnormalities. Damage to airway epithelium as may be caused by viral infections may enhance exposure of cough receptors to noxious stimuli. In addition, animal data clearly show that exposure to cigarette smoke increases CRS which stimulates vagally activated neurons in the nucleus tractus solitarius of the medulla.[30] The mechanism for this increased sensitivity is unknown but might be secondary to the release of compounds such as neuropeptides, serotonin, bradykinin, or arachidonic acid metabolites resulting in neurogenic inflammation.[31] Another possibility involves the complex interaction between rapidly adapting receptors, release of tachykinins from C fiber endings, and the central inhibition of cough by C fiber reflex action.[13,32] Nonproductive cough also may arise from stimulation of sites that are remote from the larynx and lung, for example, the external auditory canal and distal esophagus.[33,34] Gastroesophageal reflux may cause chronic cough, presumably via a vagal reflex.

Pharmacology of Cough

Patients with excessive production of pulmonary secretions need to be encouraged to cough, since this is an important pulmonary defense mechanism. On the other hand frequent nonproductive or irritative cough may lead to fatigue and interfere with sleep and other vital functions such as eating. In general, treatment of cough requires that the primary disorder be treated effectively to alleviate cough.

Drugs used in the control of cough have either a predominant central action or a predominant peripheral action.[29] Parenteral administration of opiates clearly is effective in reducing the sensitivity of the cough reflex, presumably through a central mechanism.[29] Opiates act through mu2 and kappa opiate receptors but not via delta receptors.[35] The oral administration of codeine or dextromethorphan causes only a marginal decrease in cough sensitivity when administered in dosages that are free of central nervous system side effects. Nonopioid cough suppressing drugs that do not act through opioid receptors include dextromethorphan, levopropoxyphene napsylate, and pholcodine.[36] Benzonatate is a drug related to procaine, and it acts on both cough receptors and the cough center.[36] In adults nebulized lidocaine also will reduce cough at a dose that does not inhibit reflex bronchoconstriction.[37] Similar studies have not been done in children.

Recently, it has been demonstrated that low doses of the γ-aminobutyric acid (GABA) agonist baclofen are effective in inhibiting cough in normal adults, when taken for a prolonged period of time.[38] This may be a useful therapy for chronic (>3 weeks) nonproductive cough.

Finally, it has been noted that some patients who take angiotensin converting enzyme inhibitors may develop cough.[39] This phenomenon also has been noted in patients who have undergone heart-lung transplantation, thereby implicating local release of tachykinins. These patients may be a useful model for the study of antitussive drugs in the human, rather than relying on data from animal studies.

TABLE 13–2. Some Drugs and Agents Important in Cough

Antitussives*	Protussives
Codeine	Hypertonic saline*
Dextromethorphan	Terbutaline plus chest physiotherapy*
Ipratropium bromide	Amiloride*
Dexbrompheniramine	Carbocysteine†
Pseudoephedrine	Bromhexine†
Diphenhydramine	Guaifenesin†
Caramiphen	

* Proven efficacy
† Not efficacious.

Adapted from Reisine T, Pasternak G. Opioid analgesics and antagonists. In: Hardman JG, Limbird LE, eds. Goodman and Gilman's the pharmacological basis of therapeutics. 9th ed. New York: McGraw Hill, 1996:521–55.

Little is known about the management of productive and nonproductive cough.[40] Progressive therapy is aimed at enhancing the effectiveness of cough, with or without an increase in cough frequency.[41] Only a few drugs have been evaluated adequately with respect to enhanced cough clearance, and their clinical relevance remains to be tested (Table 13–2).

References

1. Chang AB. Cough receptors and asthma in children. Pediatr Pulmonol 1999,28:59–70.
2. Bennett WD, Fisher WM, Chapman WF. Cough-enchanced mucus clearance in the normal lung. J Appl Physiol 1990;65:1670–5.
3. Bouros N, Scafakos N, Green M. Cough: physiological and pathophysiological considerations. In: Roussos C, ed. Lung biology in health and disease. 2nd ed. Vol. 85. New York: Marcel Dekker Inc., 1995.
4. Yamagihara N, VonLeden H, Werner-Kukuk E. The physical parameters of cough: the larynx in a normal single cough. Acta Otolaryngol 1966;61:495–510.
5. Leith DE. Cough. In: Brain JD, Proctor D, Reid LM, eds. Respiratory defense mechanisms. Vol. 5. New York: Marcel Dekker Inc., 1977:545–92.
6. Kim CS, Iglesia AJ, Sackner MA. Mucus clearance by two-phase gas-liquid flow mechanism: asymmetric periodic flow model. J Appl Physiol 1987;62:959–71.
7. McCool FD, Leith DE. Pathophysiology of cough. Clin Chest Med 1987;8:189–95.
8. Rayl JE. Tracheobronchial collapse during cough. Radiology 1965;85,87–92.
9. Fontana GA, Pantaleo T, Lavorni F, et al. Coughing in laryngectomized patients. Am J Resp Crit Care Med 1999;160:1578–84.
10. Rossman CM, Waldes R, Sampson D, Newhouse MT. Effect of chest physiotherapy on the removal of mucus in patients with cystic fibrosis. Am Rev Respir Dis 1982; 126:131–5.
11. Young S, Abdul-Sattar N, Caric D. Glottic closure and high flows are not essential for productive cough. Bull Eur Physiopathol 1987;23 Suppl 10:115–75.
12. Leith DE, Butler JP, Sneddon SL, Brain JD. Cough. In: Macklem P, ed. Handbook of physiology 3. American Physiological Society, Washington, DC, 1986:315–36.
13. Widdicombe JG. Sensory neurophysiology of the cough reflex. J Allergy Clin Immunol 1996;98:84–90.
14. Fox AJ, Barnes PJ, Urban L, Dray A. An in vitro study of the properties of single vagal afferents innervating guinea pig airways. J Physiol 1998;469:21–35.
15. Chang AB, Phelen PD, Sawyer SM, Robertson CF. Airway hyperresponsiveness and cough receptor sensitivity in children with recurrent cough. Am J Respir Crit Care Med 1997;155:1935–9.
16. Bolser DC, Balky DM, Moriss KF, et al. Responses of putative nucleus tractus solitarius (NTS) interneurons in cough reflex pathways during laryngeal and tracheobronchial cough. FASEB J 2000;14:A644.
17. Hutchings HA, Eccles R. The opioid agonist codeine and antagonist naltrexone do not affect voluntary suppression of capsaicin induced cough in healthy subjects. Eur Respir J 1994;7:715–9.
18. Hutchings HA, Eccles R, Smith AP, Jawad MSM. Voluntary cough suppression as an indication of symptom severity in upper respiratory tract infections. Eur Respir J 1993; 6:1949–1954.
19. Fontana GA, Pantaleo T, Lavorini F, et al. Coughing in laryngectomized patients. Am J Respir Crit Care Med 1999;160:1578–84.
20. Dicpinigaitis PV, Grimm DR, Lesser M. Cough reflex sensitivity in subjects with cervical spinal cord injury. Am J Respir Crit Care Med 1999;159:1660–2.
21. Bolser DC, Reir PJ, Davenport PW. Responses of the anterolateral abdominal muscles during cough and expiratory threshold loading in the cat. J Appl Physiol 2000; 88:1207–14.
22. Adams FH, Desilets DT, Towers B. Control of flow of fetal lung fluid at the laryngeal outlet. Respir Physiol 1967; 2:302–9.
23. Adams FH, Desilets DT, Towers B. Physiology of the fetal larynx and lung. Ann Otol Rhinol Laryngol 1967; 76:735–45.
24. Fleming PJ, Bryan AC, Bryan MH. Functional immaturity of pulmonary irritant receptors and apnea in newborn preterm infants. Pediatrics 1978;61:515–8.
25. Miller HC, Proud GO, Behrle FC. Variation in the gag, cough and swallow reflexes and tone of the vocal cords as determined by direct laryngoscopy in newborn infants. Yale J Biol Med 1952;24:284–91.
26. Karlsson JA, Sant'Ambrogio G, Widdicombe J. Afferent neural pathways in cough and reflex bronchoconstriction. J Appl Physiol 1988;65:1007–23.
27. Fisher JT, Sant'Ambrogio G. Location and discharge properties of respiratory vagal afferents in the newborn dog. Respir Physiol 1982;50:209–20.
28. Leith DE. The development of cough. Am Rev Respir Dis 1985;131 Suppl: S39–42.
29. Fuller RW. Cough. In: Crystal RG, West JB, eds. The lung: scientific foundations. New York: Raven Press Ltd., 1991: 1861–7.
30. Mutoh T, Joad JP, Bonham AC. Chronic passive cigarette smoke exposure augments bronchopulmonary C-fibre inputs to nucleus tractus solitarii neurons and reflex output in young guinea pigs. J Physiol 2000; 523:223–33.

31. Nadel JA, Borson DB. Modulation of neurogenic inflammation by neutral endopeptidases. Am Rev Respir Dis 1991;143:533–6.
32. Widdicombe JG. Neurophysiology of the cough reflex. Eur Respir J 1995;8:1193–202.
33. Ing AJ, Ngu MC, Breslin ABX. Pathogenesis of chronic cough associated with gastroesophageal reflux. Am J Respir Crit Care Med 1994;149:160–7.
34. Laloo UG, Barnes PJ, Chung KF. Pathophysiology and clinical presentation of cough. J Allergy Clin Immunol 1996; 98:591–7.
35. Kamei J. Role of opioidergic and serotonergic mechanisms in cough and antitussives. Pulm Pharmacol 1996;9: 349–56.
36. Reisine T, Pasternak G. Opioid analgesic and antogonists. In: Hardman JG, Limbird LE, eds. Goodman and Gilman's The pharmacological basis of therapeutics. 9th ed. New York: McGraw-Hill, 1996:521–55.
37. Choudry NB, Fuller RN, Anderson N, Karlsson JA. Separation of cough and reflex bronchoconstriction by inhaled anaesthetic. Eur Respir J 1990:140:137–41.
38. Dicpinigaitis PV, Dobkin JB, Rauf K, Aldrich TK. Inhibition of capsaicin-induced cough by the gamma-aminobutyric acid agonist baclofen. J Clin Pharmacol 1998; 38:364–7.
39. Gabbay R, Small T, Corris PA. Angiotensin converting-enzyme inhibitor cough: lessons from heart-lung transplantation. Respirology 1998;3:39–40.
40. Irwin RS, Boulet RF, Cloutier MM, et al. Managing cough as a defensive mechanism and as a symptom. A concensus panel report of the American College of Chest Physicians. Chest 1998;114:133–81S.
41. Irwin RS, Curley FJ. The treatment of cough: a comprehensive review. Chest 1991;99:1477–84.

CHAPTER 14

Oxygen Transport

George Lister, MD, John Fahey, MD

The transport of oxygen (O_2) from the ambient environment to the tissues requires a series of steps that depend on the integration of three systems: the lungs, the circulation, and the blood. Under resting conditions O_2 transport to the tissues is normally in great excess of O_2 consumption. However, little O_2 is stored in the body, so when O_2 supply decreases or demands increase significantly, a mismatch between supply and demands can quickly result in hypoxia and threaten survival, unless these systems can respond rapidly to restore the balance.[1,2] Furthermore, if any of the systems is compromised, the other two must adapt both acutely and chronically to compensate for the disrupted O_2 transport.

The response to limitations in O_2 supply and the mechanisms for adaptation are central features of virtually all forms of cardiorespiratory disease in children. The aim here is to review the general principles governing the relationship between O_2 supply and consumption under normal and pathologic conditions. We focus on the integration of processes that maintain metabolic homeostasis during both acute and chronic reductions of O_2 transport, and discuss various approaches that have been used in patients to detect an inadequate O_2 supply. When possible, we draw from experimental data derived from or specifically related to newborns, infants, or children; however, of necessity, much of the information has been obtained from studies in more mature individuals.

Relationship Between Oxygen Consumption and Transport

Quantitative Relationship

Oxygen transport to the tissues can be quantified as the systemic O_2 transport (often written as SOT, TO_2, or QO_2), the product of systemic blood flow rate (Q) and arterial O_2 content (Ca_{O_2}):

$$SOT = Q \times Ca_{O_2} \qquad (14\text{–}1)$$

Arterial O_2 content is a function of arterial hemoglobin concentration (Hb), hemoglobin O_2 saturation (Sa_{O_2}), and O_2 pressure (Pa_{O_2}), as follows:

$$Ca_{O_2} = [(1.34 \times Hb\ (Sa_{O_2}) + (Pa_{O_2} \times 0.003)]/100 \qquad (14\text{–}2)$$

By substitution,

$$SOT = Q\ [(Hb \times 1.34 \times Sa_{O_2}) + (Pa_{O_2} \times 0.003)]/100 \qquad (14\text{–}3)$$

where SOT is expressed in mL O_2/min; Q is in mL blood/min; Hb is in g/dL blood; Pa_{O_2} is in mm Hg; 1.34, the O_2 carrying capacity of Hb, is in mL O_2/g Hb; and 0.003, the solubility of O_2 in blood, is in mL O_2/dL blood mm Hg.

More than 80 years ago Sir Joseph Barcroft, one of the fathers of fetal physiology, recognized that tissue oxygenation could be endangered by "stagnant anoxemia," "anemic anoxemia," and "hypoxic anoxemia."[3] Equation 14–3 quantifies these relationships by showing that systemic O_2 transport may be compromised by reductions in systemic perfusion, hemoglobin concentration, or oxygenation of blood (low P_{O_2} or hemoglobin O_2 saturation).

The rate of O_2 uptake ($\dot{V}_{O_2}$) by the lungs, which in steady state must be equivalent to O_2 consumption by the tissues, can be derived as the difference between the volume flow of O_2 into and out of the lungs. Oxygen consumption can then be related directly to the SOT as follows (Figure 14–1):

$$\dot{V}_{O_2} = SOT \times E_{O_2} \qquad (14\text{–}4)$$

where E_{O_2} represents extraction of O_2.

This relationship demonstrates that adjustments in O_2 extraction (a dimensionless term that is to be distinguished from the arteriovenous O_2 content difference) can help maintain O_2 consumption if O_2 transport is disturbed. Before discussing specific disturbances in transport, it is important to consider normal factors that influence O_2 consumption.

Oxygen Consumption Rate

Owing to the usual abundance of SOT relative to consumption, the O_2 consumption rate is normally dictated by metabolic demands and is not influenced by modest alterations in O_2 transport.[4,5] For example, the resting O_2 consumption for a human newborn is approximately 7 mL/min/kg, whereas the SOT is approximately 30 mL/min/kg. Systemic O_2 transport varies in response to changes in O_2 consumption and metabolic demands.

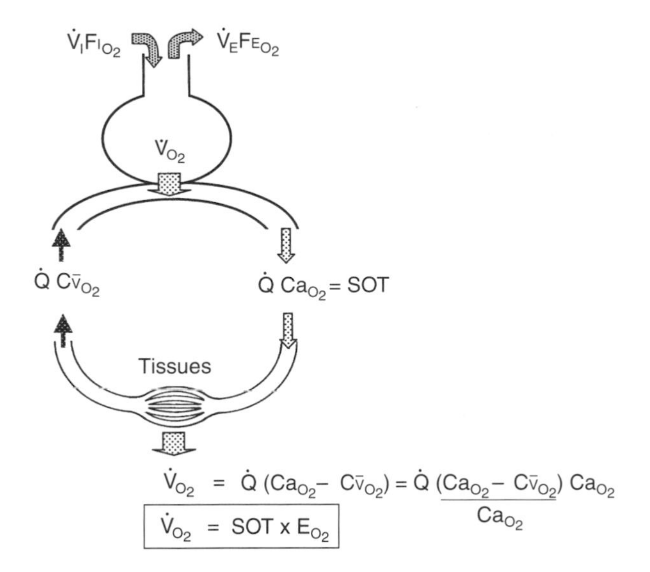

FIGURE 14–1. Relationship between systemic oxygen transport (SOT) and oxygen consumption. This figure shows a mass balance for O_2, where pulmonary O_2 uptake is equivalent to tissue O_2 consumption. Uptake of O_2 can be derived from the difference between O_2 in inspired and expired gas, where $\dot{V}_I$ and $\dot{V}_E$ represent inspired and expired gas volumes per unit of time, and $F_{I_{O_2}}$, and $F_{E_{O_2}}$ are the concentrations of O_2 in inspired and expired gas. Systemic O_2 transport, by definition, is the product of systemic blood flow ($\dot{Q}$) and arterial O_2 content. The rate of O_2 consumption ($\dot{V}_{O_2}$), by the Fick equation, is the product of systemic blood flow and arteriovenous oxygen content difference. After multiplying the numerator and denominator by Ca_{O_2} (arterial O_2 content) and regrouping terms, oxygen consumption is the product of SOT and fractional O_2 extraction (arterial O_2 content/arteriovenous O_2 content difference) where E_{O_2} is extraction, and Ca_{O_2}-$C\bar{v}_{O_2}$ is the arteriovenous difference.

Consumption of O_2 differs widely among mammals at rest, being a function of size and maturity. In general, smaller mammals have a higher metabolism normalized to mass, because their higher surface-to-mass ratio increases heat loss per volume or mass of tissue. However, even when metabolism is normalized to surface area ($\sim$ mass$^{\cdot 67}$), it is not constant throughout the animal kingdom. Rather, Weibel[6] has shown that when metabolism is related to mass$^{\cdot 75}$, it is relatively constant over homeothermic species of widely disparate size, which suggests that factors other than heat conservation are important for differences in metabolic demand.

Metabolic rate also varies as a function of environment and activity, two issues of particular importance for the very small infant. When environmental temperature is varied systematically and O_2 consumption measured, a thermoneutral range of temperature can be determined in which O_2 consumption is minimal. This range is narrower and the thermoneutral temperature higher for the very small compared to the larger infant.[7] For this reason, maintaining normal body temperature in a cool environment can impose a large metabolic cost. Alternatively, when demands are increased systematically, such as with graded exercise, one can determine the upper limit of aerobic metabolism. For adults the maximal O_2 consumption is in the range of 35 to 45 mL O_2/kg/min, and O_2 transport may exceed this value by three- to fourfold (see Chapter 31, "Exercise Physiology"). Values for children vary as a function of size.[8] Whole-body O_2 consumption also varies in proportion to body temperature over the physiologic range;[9,10] there is a 10 to 13% increase in $\dot{V}_{O_2}$ per degree centigrade elevation above normal body temperature (the Q_{10} effect). However, because we are homeothermic, lowering of body temperature below 37°C will not reduce demands, unless homeostatic responses to maintain body temperature such as shivering are blocked. This is an important clinical consideration, for example, for very small infants, those patients who recover from hypothermia-induced during surgery, or children with burns.

Finally, growth rate is also an important determinant of metabolic demands. Healthy infants and young children have higher metabolic rates than do adults when indexed to body weight or surface area.[11] A significant proportion of the O_2 demands in infants is required for growth. In newborn lambs, growth accounts for 30 to 35% of the metabolic demands.[10] This figure is difficult to obtain for humans, but estimates suggest that 3 to 13% of the O_2 consumption is used for growth and growth-related processes in very young infants.[12] Thus, growth represents an added metabolic burden for infants and children. Conversely, poor growth may represent an adaptation for the infant with compromised O_2 delivery.

Stresses such as traumatic injury, infection, or burns have been associated with increases in metabolic demands as much as twofold, depending on specific conditions. In addition O_2 requirements can be raised or lowered by medications. Catecholamines with β_2 effects can increase metabolic rate by more than 10%.[13] Sedatives and anesthetic agents can lower O_2 demands by reducing movement, agitation, or pain. Muscle relaxants in combination with mechanical ventilation can alleviate the work of breathing, which is usually $\leq 2\%$ of metabolic expenditure.[14] However, with some pathologic circumstances, for example, weaning of patients with cardiorespiratory disease from mechanical ventilation, work of breathing can represent over 50% of metabolic rate.[15] While it is widely accepted that infants with bronchopulmonary dysplasia have an elevated work of breathing, it is less clear how much of resting energy expenditure is devoted to this work.[16,17] Part of the difficulty in obtaining such estimates arises from the technical obstacles, for example, the inability to control nonrespiratory metabolic expenditure as respiration is altered.

Response to Reductions in Oxygen Transport

In contrast to conditions when demands change, when O_2 transport is systematically decreased, one can derive the

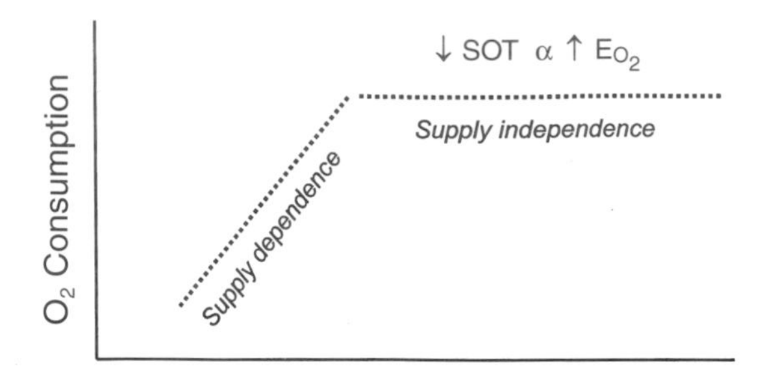

FIGURE 14–2. The relationship between O_2 consumption and systemic O_2 transport (SOT) as transport is progressively reduced. Note that O_2 consumption is initially "supply independent," and reduction in SOT is offset by an increase in extraction of O_2 (E_{O_2}). The point at which O_2 consumption becomes supply limited often is viewed as a critical O_2 transport.

limits of O_2 transport. Equation 14–4 demonstrates that any reductions in SOT must be accompanied by comparable increases in O_2 extraction, if O_2 consumption is to remain constant. When O_2 transport has been progressively reduced in mammals under acute experimental conditions in which demands were kept relatively constant, there is a biphasic response in whole body O_2 consumption. Initially, O_2 consumption remains constant and is independent of O_2 transport. Then, as O_2 transport is decreased further, there appears to be a "critical point" below which O_2 consumption becomes dependent on O_2 transport; further reductions in O_2 transport are attended by progressive decreases in O_2 consumption (Figure 14–2).[18–20] Subjects that follow this pattern have been described as O_2 regulators and are distinguished from O_2 conformers (eg, many fish), who decrease O_2 consumption when O_2 transport is reduced.[21]

Studies comparing the effect of different types of hypoxic disturbances on a subject or homogeneous group of subjects have shown that there is generally a single critical O_2 transport that is independent of whether the hypoxia is produced by anemia, hypoxemia, low cardiac output, or combinations of these.[20,22–24] When, as just described, O_2 consumption appears to be limited by transport or convection rather than by diffusion of O_2, and fractional O_2 extraction is near maximal, the relationship has been described as physiologic supply dependency. Using the Krogh tissue cylinder model to describe diffusion of O_2 from capillaries, Schumacker and Samsel have demonstrated that the experimental observations are in accord with predictions only if intercapillary distances are $\leq 80\,\mu$ and there are functional arteriovenous shunts;[25] alternatively there may be considerable heterogeneity of effective diffusion distances. As O_2 transport is reduced below a critical level, some tissues must suffer acutely a mismatch between O_2 supply and demand, that is, hypoxia. The hypoxic tissues must sustain metabolism by anaerobiosis, reduce their metabolic rate, or both. Thus, when O_2 consumption decreases, there also may be evidence of increased anaerobic metabolism such as lactic acidemia. In addition to studies using intact experimental animals, this general relation between O_2 consumption and transport has been demonstrated in isolated tissues or cells when O_2 supply has been reduced by decreasing ambient P_{O_2}, as well as in humans when O_2 transport has been decreased progressively with no intended change in O_2 demands.[26,27] Clearly, it is more straightforward to ensure that O_2 demands are not altered in isolated systems in contrast to the intact state. Therefore, much caution is needed when interpreting the response to a change in O_2 supply in patients. Both cardiac and respiratory work may change in response to alterations in O_2 supply. For example, ventilation and cardiac output usually increase when hypoxemia is induced. Although the metabolic cost of such changes can be estimated from knowledge of pressure-volume work of the heart and respiratory system, there are also responses that cannot be quantified easily. There may be release of catecholamines that stimulate thermogenesis and a marked redistribution of blood flow that alters heat loss[28,29] or metabolic demands of organs such as the liver and kidney. For example, Schlichtig et al[30] demonstrated that progressive reduction in renal perfusion was accompanied by a decrease in renal $\dot{V}_{O_2}$ before there were any changes in whole body $\dot{V}_{O_2}$. An earlier study by Lassen and Thaysen[31] showed that the renal $\dot{V}_{O_2}$ varied with metabolic work (Na transport) that diminished as perfusion declined. In addition, an increase in ventilation with alkalemia (respiratory alkalosis) has been shown to increase whole body O_2 uptake,[32] an effect not related to respiratory work because it occurs with mechanical as well as spontaneous ventilation. Despite these important disclaimers, the response of O_2 consumption to experimental reductions in O_2 transport has been remarkably consistent among healthy subjects of different species or ages. The major differences relate to the initial O_2 consumption rate and the value at which O_2 transport becomes critical.

Although there are few data in adults and none in children defining critical levels of SOT, some estimates can be derived by inference. It is known that the normal resting O_2 consumption rate for neonates is nearly twice that of adults when normalized to body mass. The critical O_2 transport has been reported to be close to 6 to 8 mL/min/kg for anesthetized adult humans,[27] and it is probably close to twice that value for neonates under similar conditions.[11] For the older child, values presumably can be scaled on the basis of normal resting O_2 consumption.[19] However, these values for critical SOT should be taken only as crude estimates, because there are no experimental data for confirmation, and because the level to which extraction can increase in human subjects in response to a limited O_2 transport is unclear (see later discussion). As there are large differences in metabolic demands between subjects under apparently similar conditions, it is much more useful clinically to make judgments regarding the adequacy of oxygenation based on data from the specific subject rather than on a preconceived notion of a critical value. There are also important differences in both the acute and chronic compensation to the various forms of hypoxia that influence the response to supply limitation.

It is also important to stress that when O_2 supply is reduced, changes in demands can be of critical importance for organ function and can even influence whether injury results. The kidney provides a useful example. When renal blood flow is diminished, the potential for ischemic damage may be tempered somewhat by the simultaneous reduction in demands caused by reduced glomerular filtration and resultant decreased ion transport. By contrast, if the demands of the kidney are raised when O_2 is in short supply, the onset or degree of damage can be amplified. This has been shown in studies in which ischemic or hypoxic injury was increased by agents that raised Na-K pump activity and was reduced by ouabain, a drug that blocks Na-K adenosinetriphosphatase.[33,34] Although it may not be possible to rest organs, it is worth restricting factors that elevate demands. Interestingly, when there is a diminution of metabolic demands by processes that limit O_2 supply, it may be virtually impossible to determine whether the diminished O_2 consumption is a result of or a contributor to the decreased O_2 supply without some independent assessment of tissue oxygenation.

Regulation of Peripheral Oxygen Extraction

Matching of Perfusion and Metabolism

The body's major compensation for a declining O_2 transport is an increase in O_2 extraction (see Equation 14–4), which occurs reflexively and uses a variety of systemic and local organ hemodynamic and metabolic alterations. These mechanisms are essential to understanding both normal and abnormal O_2 transport. Blood flow, and thereby O_2 flow, normally is distributed to regions to match the nutritional demands of the tissue.[1,35,36] Such apportionment of blood flow occurs at rest or when there is increased metabolic demand. For example, gut blood flow increases following enteric feeding,[37] just as muscle blood flow increases during exercise. There are some exceptions for tissues or organs performing specialized tasks when blood flow regulation may be subservient to other factors.[38] The kidney requires high blood flow for efficient filtration and, therefore, has a very low O_2 extraction under normal conditions. The skin also has a high blood flow rate relative to metabolism, owing to its role in heat exchange with the environment for thermoregulation.

The overall O_2 extraction for the whole body is the average of the extractions for each organ, weighted in proportion to their respective blood flows. In conditions of reduced O_2 transport or elevated O_2 demands, the whole body fractional O_2 extraction is a measure of the distribution of O_2 flow to the tissues relative to demands, and would be expected to increase in response to such disturbances. In hypoxic states, a low O_2 extraction (high mixed venous O_2 saturation or P_{O_2}), despite evidence of tissue O_2 insufficiency, has been used as evidence that there is mismatching of O_2 supply to consumption.[39]

When O_2 transport is reduced there are normally changes in the distribution of blood and O_2 flow, regulated at the resistance vessels and at the capillaries, and alterations in hemoglobin O_2 affinity that acutely serve to increase peripheral O_2 extraction and to help preserve O_2 metabolism at its previous level. These also may be coupled with more chronic adaptations, if the disturbance in O_2 transport is sustained.

Control of Resistance Vessels

When O_2 transport is reduced, any responses that alter organ vascular resistance will potentially change organ blood flow (flow = pressure × vascular resistance). A change in the total cross-sectional area of the resistance vessels, effected by both local and systemic factors, is a potent mechanism for altering organ perfusion, because vascular resistance is roughly proportional to $1/\text{radius}^4$ (from Poiseuille's law).

Some organs, particularly the heart, brain, and kidney, decrease their input resistance in response to a decrease in organ perfusion pressure.[40,41] This ability to sustain blood flow locally (autoregulation) is important when blood pressure is reduced in conjunction with the limitation in O_2 transport. Organ resistance also can be increased by systemic responses to reduced O_2 transport, which include both nervous and humoral stimulation.

With low cardiac output there is local release of norepinephrine from sympathetic nerve fibers in response to stimulation of "low-pressure" stretch receptors or mechanoreceptors across the wall of the right atrium and the pulmonary artery and "high-pressure" baroreceptors in the carotid sinus and aortic arch.[42–44] The reduced cardiac filling decreases atrial stretch and thereby diminishes the rate of firing of vagal afferent nerves, which normally sustain tonic inhibition of sympathetic outflow. The increased sympathetic activity causes arterial and venous constriction. Stimulation of arterial baroreceptors increases sympathetic outflow to the heart (tachycardia, increased contractility) and peripheral circulation (arterial vasoconstriction). In all forms of hypoxia there is an increase in circulating norepinephrine and epinephrine concentrations, in response to chemoreceptor stimulation during anemia or hypoxemia[45] or baroreceptor stimulation during low cardiac output.[42] The sympathetic response also causes afferent vasoconstriction in the kidney, decreasing effective renal plasma flow. Renin, which is released from the kidney in response to decreased perfusion of the macula densa, catalyzes conversion of angiotensinogen to angiotensin I. Angiotensin I is then converted to angiotensin II by angiotensin converting enzyme, located on the luminal surface of endothelial cells. Because of the large surface area in the pulmonary vascular bed, the lungs are the primary site for production of angiotensin II, which stimulates the release of aldosterone from the adrenal gland and can cross the blood-brain barrier to promote the release of arginine vasopressin from the pituitary gland. Vasopressin release also is stimulated by decreased aortic or atrial pressure.[46,47] Angiotensin II, aldosterone, and vasopressin each cause vasoconstriction and potentiate the effects of the sympathetic nervous system in low perfusion states. Aldosterone and vasopressin also increase salt and water retention, respectively, which helps restore perfusion. In general, these humoral and nervous responses increase regional vascular resistance and thereby divert blood flow away from organs that respond. Therefore, perfusion of a given organ during a reduction in O_2 transport depends strongly on the interplay between autoregulation, which serves to sustain flow, and autonomic and humoral factors, which serve to curtail flow. The heart and the brain, but not the kidney, have sparse sympathetic innervation and are relatively resistant to sympathetic control, whereas organs with poor ability to autoregulate usually are richly innervated and subject to sympathetic influence.[42,48,49] In this manner, organs with low resting O_2 extraction (kidney, gut, and skin) and rich sympathetic innervation may have a reduction in relative O_2 flow in the presence of limited SOT. However, by increasing O_2 extraction in response, these organs may be able to sustain oxidative metabolism. In addition, the sympathetic vasoconstriction may be overcome with time in hypoxic regions, presumably as a result of the local accumulation of metabolites.[50]

Control of Capillary Perfusion

Despite any decrement in blood flow, all organs can enhance extraction locally by redistributing capillary perfusion. As O_2 is unloaded from blood in exchange vessels (predominantly capillaries), it diffuses along a pressure gradient from blood to cells and mitochondria. As mentioned, the geometric arrangement by which this diffusion occurs does not fully account for the data observed in vivo, and it is quite possible that the arrangement varies depending on the tissue. The determinants of capillary O_2 extraction and factors that render the tissues susceptible to hypoxia have been reviewed extensively.[51] Without over simplifying a complex topic, it has been proposed that whenever there is a reduction in O_2 supply or an increase in O_2 demand, both of which would decrease the driving pressure for O_2, recruitment of more capillaries can serve to enhance O_2 extraction.[36,52] Precapillary sphincters are located at the arterial end of each capillary and serve to keep the capillary either open or closed to blood flow at any given time. The sphincter tone, which is thought to be regulated by local metabolic factors (and possibly tissue P_{O_2}), effectively determines capillary density. In addition, while it is well recognized that some tissues have the capacity to sense O_2 (eg, the kidney and carotid and aortic bodies), it long has been the suggested and more recently confirmed that vascular smooth muscle also has the machinery to sense changes in O_2.[53,54] When organ O_2 flow is decreased, capillaries that previously were closed become perfused (Figure 14–3). This serves to enhance O_2 extraction by at least three mechanisms: (1) the surface area for diffusion is increased; (2) the distance for diffusion between capillary and cell is reduced; and (3) the transit time for blood flow is increased because flow = velocity × cross-sectional area.[51] These responses permit very high levels of O_2 extraction acutely, consistently ≥ 0.65 in intact animals at the critical O_2 transport, and as high as 0.90 during reversible reductions in cardiac output.[18]

It is recognized that there is a decrease in capillary density relative to cross-sectional area in certain peripheral muscles (eg, diaphragm, soleus, extensor digitorum longus) with postnatal development.[55] The importance of this observation for peripheral O_2 extraction is unclear, but it potentially facilitates O_2 uptake in younger animals. Chronic changes also occur in the peripheral capillaries in response to more sustained stresses in O_2 transport; for example, myocardial diffusion capacity can increase with exercise training.[56] Whether similar potentially important forms of adaptation are available to children with sustained reductions in O_2 transport has not been explored.

The precise mechanism(s) by which peripheral vascular smooth muscle relaxes in response to decreases in O_2 tension has not been resolved. In fact, the mechanism by which biologic tissues in general sense O_2 is a topic of considerable interest and current investigation. There are many reports of K^+ channels that are sensitive to local hypoxia and change their conductance in response to changes in P_{O_2}.[57] For example, vascular smooth muscle can respond because of O_2-sensitive voltage-dependent Ca^{2+} channels that may regulate regional flow or because of a cytochrome aa_3 O_2 sensor, which transduces its response via changes in [Pi].[53,54] In addition, mitochondria also have been implicated as a site for O_2 tension, because they lie at the end of the electron transport chain and in ideal position to detect functional responses. Chandel and Schumacker and colleagues have made a compelling argument that cytochrome oxidase, through a reduction in maximum velocity during hypoxia, serves as the

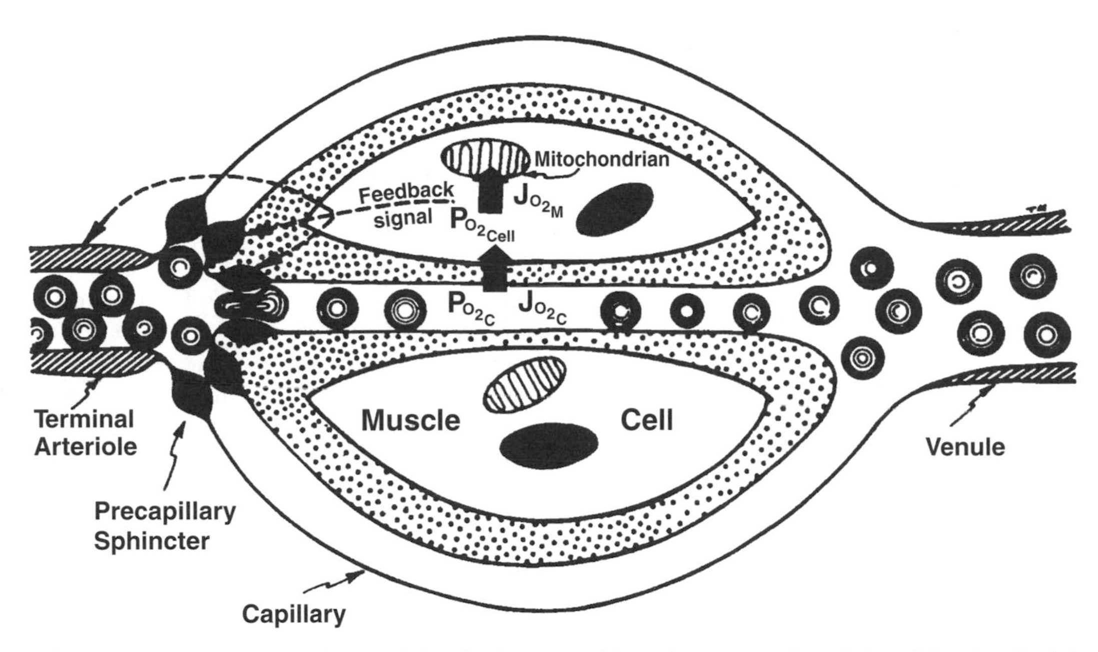

FIGURE 14–3. Schematic diagram of the microcirculation. As shown, arteriolar resistance controls perfusion of the microcirculation, and precapillary sphincters control the distribution of microcirculatory blood flow. P_{O_2} = partial pressure of O_2; $P_{O_{2C}}$ = capillary P_{O_2}, $J_{O_{2C}}$ = flux of oxygen out of the capillary; $J_{O_{2M}}$ = flux of oxygen into the mitochondrion. (Reproduced with permission from Granger HJ et al.[36])

functional sensor of P_{O_2} in some tissues.[58,59] Discussion is beyond the scope of this chapter, but there are a number of interesting reviews on the topic of cellular oxygen sensing.[57,59,60]

Alterations in Hemoglobin Oxygen Affinity

In conjunction with the aforementioned changes in diffusion, the local increase in H^+ that occurs when O_2 transport is reduced produces a rightward shift of the O_2 dissociation curve (ODC), which acutely permits more unloading of O_2 from hemoglobin (ie, a lower venous O_2 saturation) for any given venous P_{O_2}.[61] This is an exaggeration of the usual difference in hemoglobin O_2 affinity between arterial and venous blood that occurs in response to differences in H^+ concentrations. Owing to interorgan differences in blood flow relative to metabolism, the shift in the ODC may vary depending on regional venous pH, and it does not necessarily interfere with O_2 loading at the arterial level if arterial pH remains normal.[62] There is also a more chronic response that can increase tissue O_2 extraction. Hemoglobin O_2 interaction is affected by the concentration of phosphate in red blood cells, the most important source of which is 2,3-diphosphoglycerate (DPG), a product of the Rapoport-Luebering shunt peculiar to erythrocyte glycolysis.[63] By binding with hemoglobin, DPG reduces the affinity of hemoglobin for O_2 and thereby shifts the ODC to the right, that is, it increases the P50, the P_{O_2} at which hemoglobin is 50% saturated.[64] Red cell DPG concentration is regulated primarily by red blood cell H^+ concentration, because the activity of the rate-limiting enzyme is pH sensitive.[65] With low O_2 transport, there is a low venous O_2 concentration; this decreases red cell H^+ concentration because of the improved buffering of deoxyhemoglobin, so that DPG synthesis is stimulated—a response that is maximal within about 24 hours.[66] Of importance for neonates and infants, fetal hemoglobin binds DPG much less effectively than does adult hemoglobin, and this is the reason that fetal hemoglobin has a relatively low P50 (high affinity for O_2) in vivo.[67] The reduced binding to hemoglobin causes end-product inhibition of DPG synthesis. Therefore, a shift in the ODC is not a significant mechanism for very young infants in response to a limited O_2 supply.[68] As the proportion of fetal hemoglobin decreases from about 77% at birth to less than 2% by 8 months and the concentration of 2,3-DPG increases, the P50 progressively increases in the normal infant (from 20 to 30 mm Hg), and the capacity to respond by altering hemoglobin O_2 affinity improves.[69] (After adolescence, P50 decreases to 27 mm Hg, the normal adult value.)

How effective a particular change in P50 is in improving tissue oxygen unloading depends on how much O_2 loading at the arterial side of the circulation is simultaneously affected. When pulmonary capillary and arterial P_{O_2} are normal, as with anemia or low cardiac output, O_2 loading occurs on the relatively flat part of the ODC, so that there is a negligible decrease in arterial O_2 saturation with a rightward shift of the ODC (Figure 14–4).[70] However, with arterial hypoxemia the effects of a shift in the ODC are more complex and depend on whether the hypoxemia is caused by true right-to-left shunt or by alveolar hypoxia. Turek and colleagues[62,71] analyzed in

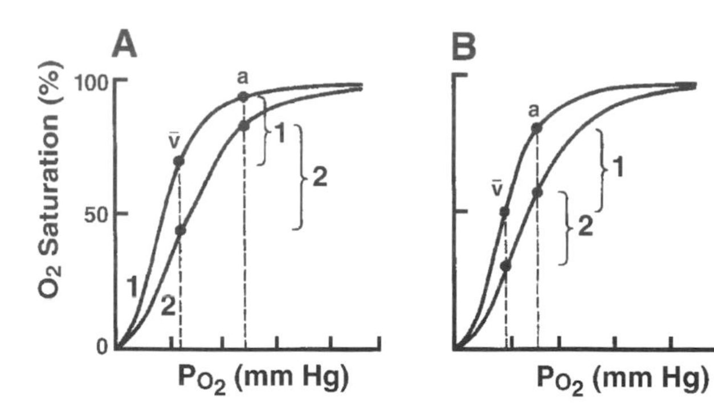

FIGURE 14–4. The effect of a shift in the O_2 dissociation curve on O_2 unloading with alveolar hypoxia. The height of the brackets indicates the quantity of O_2 unloaded by hemoglobin. *A*, With mild alveolar hypoxia, a shift to the right enhances O_2 unloading, while it produces less impairment of O_2 loading. The reason is that the partial pressure of arterial O_2 (Pa_{O_2}) is fixed by the alveolar P_{O_2}, which is on a less steep part of the curve than is the mixed venous point (v). Therefore, the arteriovenous O_2 saturation difference is greater with curve 2 than with curve 1. *B*, With more severe alveolar hypoxia, both alveolar and arterial P_{O_2} are very low, and both the arterial and mixed venous points are on a steep part of the curve. Hence, in this case the arteriovenous O_2 saturation difference is smaller with the right-shifted curve. (Reproduced with permission from Lister G.[70])

detail the effects of hemoglobin O_2 affinity on O_2 extraction during alveolar hypoxia. They showed that a line can be constructed for any given ODC connecting the arterial and venous points. For any given arterial and venous P_{O_2}, the steeper the line, the greater will be the arteriovenous O_2 saturation or content difference. The highest arteriovenous O_2 content difference is attained when the P50 is between the arterial and venous P_{O_2}. In general, a rightward shift of the ODC enhances O_2 extraction with mild arterial hypoxemia, whereas a leftward shift is more beneficial with very severe arterial hypoxemia. As such, it has been observed that individuals living at a high altitude may have a right or left shift in the ODC (decrease or increase in DPG concentration), depending on the degree of alveolar hypoxia.[72] The analysis of the effects of a change in P50 is even more complex when there is marked heterogeneity of ventilation-perfusion, although a rightward shift of the ODC is generally beneficial.[73] When there is an intracardiac shunt producing hypoxemia, rightward shift of the ODC enhances O_2 unloading, because the pulmonary capillary P_{O_2} is high and O_2 loading is relatively unperturbed, while unloading at the venous side of the circulation is improved. Thus, children with chronic cyanosis from congenital cardiac disease usually have an increase in P50. The exception to this is seen in young infants, because DPG that binds poorly to fetal hemoglobin has relatively less effect on hemoglobin-O_2 affinity than when there is predominantly adult hemoglobin.

Disturbances in Oxygen Extraction

The responses to reductions in O_2 transport described above are in contrast to some observations that have been made on certain pathologic states, most notably the adult respiratory distress syndrome (ARDS), sepsis, and pulmonary hypertension.[74–77] In these conditions some investigators have observed an apparent dependence of O_2 consumption on systemic O_2 transport over a wide range throughout which O_2 extraction is low (less than 0.30).[74,75] This type of response has been referred to as pathologic supply dependence, because it is believed to represent a failure of the peripheral circulation to extract O_2 appropriately. However, the interpretation of the data is controversial.[78–82] Some studies of patients with ARDS have shown that there is a range of O_2 transport for which O_2 consumption is not dependent, whereas other studies have not; however, no investigators have found high O_2 extraction in these patients. One source of disparity between studies has been the use of coupled variables: calculation of both the dependent variable, O_2 consumption, and the independent variable, SOT, using the same measured cardiac output; the coupling creates a dependence owing to shared variance. In studies by Ronco et al[80] of patients with sepsis or ARDS, where O_2 consumption was measured by expired gas analysis, there was no oxygen supply dependence of oxygen consumption throughout a wide range of O_2 transport. The investigators actually demonstrated that using cardiac output to calculate the variables produced dependence when it did not exist. Thus, it remains to be proven whether impaired extraction is an important factor in critically ill patients.

On the other hand, the findings in patients with ARDS and sepsis strongly suggest that impaired O_2 extraction may have clinical importance, and this issue has been reviewed in detail.[77,83] Some laboratory observations also support this thesis. For example, peripheral microembolism and loss of autoregulation[84–86] have both been shown to produce O_2 supply dependence in peripheral muscle in a range of O_2 transport that should be O_2 supply independent. In addition, the use of 100% inspired O_2 or positive end-expiratory pressure (PEEP) decreased whole body O_2 extraction in dogs after oleic acid-induced lung injury.[87] These injuries could potentially increase capillary diffusion distances owing to endothelial damage and edema, reduce capillary surface area, or maldistribute blood flow, which would then reduce O_2 extraction in the peripheral circulation. Although no single mechanism has been identified, the types of experimental injuries implicate common therapies such as high O_2 concentrations, positive-pressure breathing, and vasoactive drugs as potential contributing factors to pathologic O_2 supply dependence, an important consideration for the management of children with severe pulmonary disease.

Specific Disturbances in Oxygen Transport

The following discussion is derived directly from observations in experimental animals or in adult humans. For the most part, there is little direct evidence about responses in infants and children. However, experiments in immature animals suggest that inference from other subjects is reasonable.

Low Systemic Perfusion

With an acute reduction in cardiac output, SOT declines proportionately. There might be a small increase in arterial O_2 content, because the stimulation of ventilation with acidemia will cause arterial P_{CO_2} to decrease, and the respiratory exchange ratio may increase, both of which increase alveolar and arterial P_{O_2}; however, these effects are usually quite small and inconsequential. An increase in O_2 extraction provides the only acute mechanism for sustaining oxidative metabolism. Under certain circumstances, a reduction in blood flow may be more disruptive to metabolism than is anemia or hypoxia. This is because there is potential for limitations in supply of substrates other than oxygen, and there may be accumulation of metabolites that, in turn, can alter substrate use.[88]

In experiments with young lambs, cardiac output can be reduced by about 50% before there are signs of hypoxemia.[19] However, owing to differences in hemoglobin concentration with postnatal development, the tolerance to a reduction in cardiac output can vary widely, as has been shown in lambs during experimental anemia or polycythemia.[23] For example, with a hemoglobin concentration of 7.4 g/dL, cardiac output could be decreased by only 33% before a critical O_2 transport was reached, whereas with a concentration of 16.5 g/dL, cardiac output could be reduced by 60%. Similarly, arterial hypoxemia reduces the tolerance to decreased cardiac output. These observations have obvious practical implications for children who have a low cardiac output and become either anemic or hypoxemic.

With chronic reductions in cardiac output, hematologic adjustments tend to maintain an enhanced O_2 extraction while restoring mixed venous P_{O_2} toward normal. An increase in 2,3-DPG and a consequent rise in P50 has been observed in patients with low cardiac output,[89] although, if acidemia persists, DPG synthesis is not stimulated. A low cardiac output does not provoke an increase in hemoglobin concentration or erythropoietin concentration, even though erythropoietin production presumably is stimulated by low renal venous P_{O_2}.[90] It has been suggested that the reduced renal blood flow would reduce renal O_2 consumption, thereby restoring venous P_{O_2} toward normal. Despite these adaptations, infants or children with persistently low cardiac output still may have an insufficient O_2 transport, as manifested by markedly reduced exercise tolerance and growth.

Anemia

With an acute reduction in hemoglobin concentration without a change in blood volume, cardiac output increases, as does O_2 extraction.[5,24,91,92] Thus, O_2 transport does not decrease in proportion to the decline in hemoglobin concentration. In controlled studies of experimental animals, a critical O_2 transport has been reached when hematocrit was in the range of 10 to 15%, as detected by either a decrease in O_2 consumption or an increase in arterial lactate concentration.[22,23,92] The opposing effects of increased blood flow (from diminished viscosity and increased contractility) and decreased O_2 content on O_2 transport during anemia (and during polycythemia) yield a curvilinear relationship, shaped like an inverted U between systemic O_2 transport (y-axis) and hemoglobin concentration or hematocrit (x-axis).[93] The hematocrit at which O_2 transport is maximal usually has been found to be in the range of 35 to 50%, although this is affected by the metabolic demands of the tissue under study.[94]

With chronic anemia, there is a right shift of the O_2 dissociation curve that enhances O_2 extraction.[1] The increased P50 permits cardiac output to decrease toward normal at rest, but such compensation provides no particular benefit during stress, such as exercise.[91] However, with chronic anemia, there also may be plasma volume expansion, which increases cardiac output by increasing stroke volume. This causes O_2 transport at rest to be higher than that with acute anemia and improves tolerance to exercise. In a study of chronic anemia sustained for 2 weeks in young lambs, Bernstein and colleagues found that cardiac output and O_2 extraction both were increased sufficiently above control values to keep O_2 transport in the low-normal range and O_2 consumption normal, despite an induced reduction in hemoglobin concentration to 60% of control.[95] Although there was decreased O_2 transport to the splanchnic circulation, somatic growth was similar to that of controls. However, the mechanisms for growth failure in anemic children may be complex and not simply related to reduced O_2 transport, because caloric intake often is affected also. It is also important to note that many of the adverse effects of anemia may be amplified if red blood cell deformability is abnormal. Two important examples of this are iron deficiency and sickle cell disease, both of which impair transit through the microcirculation and have been implicated as a cause of vascular occlusion and strokes.[96]

Hypoxemia

A commonly studied disturbance in O_2 transport has been hypoxemia produced by alveolar hypoxia. With acute hypoxemia, O_2 extraction increases, while the cardiac output response is variable and there is a net decrease in SOT.[5,24,97] Cardiac output usually does not increase as much when arterial O_2 content is reduced by hypoxemia than it does with anemia, because the viscosity is not reduced.[24] In addition, depending on the method used to induce hypoxemia, there may be some limitation of systemic blood flow. For example, with alveolar hypoxia, the increased pulmonary vascular resistance can limit right ventricular output. In addition to the circulatory changes, hypoxemia also stimulates ventilation,[98] which seems to be important for the augmentation in cardiac output.[99] However, with either shunt or alveolar hypoxia, this ventilatory response affords little improvement in arterial O_2 content. The critical inspired O_2 concentration (or arterial P_{O_2}) varies widely depending on age, species, size, and ambient environment, but in young subjects O_2 consumption usually decreases when inspired O_2 is near 0.10 (Pa_{O_2} of 25 to 30 mm Hg).[97,100] It also has been shown that the effect of alveolar hypoxia may be magnified if demands are increased. For example, when neonates are placed in a cool environment, even mild alveolar hypoxia may induce a decrease in O_2 consumption, in contrast to results in a neutral thermal environment.[101]

With chronic hypoxemia, there are two major hematologic adjustments that potentially can improve tissue oxygenation. However, it is important to stress that the effects of and adaptations to chronic hypoxemia are dependent on the nature of the disturbance, the experimental model, and the species studied. The widely held view is that hypoxemia, by decreasing renal venous P_{O_2}, increases erythropoietin transcription, which stimulates hemoglobin synthesis. Current evidence suggests that hypoxia-inducible factor 1 binds to erythropoietin during O_2 deprivation and causes a marked increase in messenger ribonucleic acid (mRNA) primarily related to increased transcription.[60] In the presence of hypoxemia from alveolar hypoxia or congenital cardiac disease, there is almost an inverse relation between the hemoglobin concentration and the arterial O_2 saturation, keeping arterial O_2 content nearly constant.[102] Similarly, in experimental chronic hypoxemia in young lambs, arterial O_2 content was normal owing to the polycythemia.[103] Blood viscosity also increases as hemoglobin concentration rises; the polycythemia may become maladaptive, and with some conditions O_2 transport has been improved by hemodilution.[104] As discussed earlier, any benefit from changes in hemoglobin O_2 affinity with hypoxemia depends on the severity and type of hypoxemia. The circulatory response with chronic hypoxemia also is varied and may be limited if there are chronic changes in the pulmonary vascular bed that restrict blood flow, as might be anticipated with alveolar hypoxia. As with the other chronic disturbances in O_2 transport, interference with growth and activity can be anticipated,[103,105–107] although the exact cause is not determined and also may be a function of the cause of the hypoxemia.

Combinations of Disturbances

As is apparent from the discussion, compensation for one type of disruption in O_2 supply requires adaptive changes in other parts of the system. When these adaptations are thwarted, reserve is exhausted rapidly. For example, infants with cyanotic congenital cardiac disease may maintain sufficient O_2 transport to grow and be active owing to an increased cardiac output, increased O_2 extraction, and (to some extent) increased hemoglobin concentration. In this setting tissue hypoxia rapidly ensues when cardiac output is reduced or when metabolic demands increase (eg, with dehydration or fever). Furthermore, even the "normal" postnatal changes can help precipitate a mismatch of O_2 supply and demand in the presence of a limited but compensated disturbance in O_2 transport. The "physiologic" decline in hemoglobin concentration can contribute substantially to the genesis of circulatory failure in the presence of a large interventricular communication.[108] Thus, the particular level of O_2 transport often is less relevant than is a recognition of the interplay between each of the factors responsible for providing O_2 transport to the tissues. Moreover, without some reference to metabolic demands or some independent measure that is sensitive to hypoxia, it is difficult to predict the adequacy of O_2 transport in a given subject.

Determination of Insufficient Oxygen Transport

General Considerations

As described above, it is clear that when whole body O_2 consumption decreases because of a critical limitation in O_2 supply, some tissues must be consuming less O_2 than under resting conditions. It is also possible that demands may decrease as O_2 transport is reduced under certain conditions. It has been proposed that certain O_2-consuming processes, described as "facultative metabolism," may be reduced in response to limited O_2 supply without threatening immediate survival. Such metabolism might involve growth or thermoregulation. The fraction of an O_2 deficit incurred during an hypoxic period that is not subsequently "repaid" during reoxygenation has been used as a measure of facultative metabolism. When defined in this manner, facultative metabolism has been found to be a relatively large proportion of total metabolism in animals that tolerate long periods of hypoxia, such as the freshwater turtle or seal.[109,110] In light of the large fraction of metabolism devoted to growth during fetal and early postnatal life, it has been suggested that immature subjects also have a relatively large proportion of facultative metabolism, and this may help confer some of the apparent tolerance to acute hypoxia in contrast to adults.[10]

Despite all the factors that potentially alter demands for O_2 during physiologic O_2 supply dependence, the critical O_2 transport for the whole body has been found to be surprisingly close to that for individual tissues, including limb, gastrointestinal tract, and liver.[26] This suggests that the distribution of O_2 flow during periods of supply limitation is remarkably equitable, and that useful information can be derived from examining systemic responses. There is no a priori means of estimating metabolic demands (with the possible exception of working muscle). Furthermore, there is wide variation in O_2 consumption among subjects, so that it rarely is possible to interpret whether O_2 transport is sufficient on the basis of a single measurement of O_2 consumption. Therefore, for the whole body or for isolated tissue as well, there are only two general strategies for determining the adequacy of O_2 transport or the presence of hypoxia: (1) manipulating O_2 transport without altering demands and measuring the response of O_2 consumption, and (2) measuring a marker of tissue oxygenation. Both of these strategies are addressed below.

Measurement of Oxygen Consumption

In experimental studies with animals, the critical O_2 transport can be determined under controlled conditions, but there are a number of important technical and ethical constraints for patients, especially children. First, the measurement of O_2 consumption in ventilated patients or in patients breathing a high inspired O_2 concentration has potential error or artifact. If the subject is breathing 100% O_2 using a closed circuit with removal of carbon dioxide, O_2 consumption can be quantified from the change in the volume of gas in the circuit with respect to time. However, the use of 100% O_2 may not be desirable and may change metabolic rate as well as other cardiorespiratory functions that may be of interest, such as systemic or pulmonary blood flow. Alternatively, if a subject is breathing an inspired gas mixture that contains some nitrogen, O_2 consumption can be measured from knowledge of inspired and expired gas volumes and concentrations of oxygen, carbon dioxide, and nitrogen. Usually the volume of inspired gas can be calculated during steady state from the expired gas volume (generally easier to measure than is inspired volume) and the difference in nitrogen concentrations between inspired and expired gas. Therefore, O_2 consumption can be quantified by one of the variations of the following formulas (see Figure 14–1):[111,112]

$$V_{O_2} = (V_I\,(FI_{O_2}) - (V_E\,(FE_{O_2}) \qquad (14\text{–}5)$$

because $V_I \times FI_{N_2} = V_E \times FE_{N_2}$, or

$$V_I\,(1 - FI_{O_2} - FI_{CO_2}) = V_E\,(1 - FE_{O_2} - FE_{CO_2}), \qquad (14\text{–}6)$$

Therefore,

$$V_{O_2} = V_E\,(FI_{O_2}\,[(1 - FE_{O_2} - FE_{CO_2})/(1 - FI_{CO_2} - FI_{O_2})] - FE_{O_2}), \qquad (14\text{–}7)$$

where V_I and V_E are the flows of inspiratory and expiratory gas, and FI_{N_2}, FI_{O_2}, FI_{CO_2}, FE_{N_2}, FE_{O_2} and FE_{CO_2} are the fractional concentrations of nitrogen, O_2, and carbon dioxide in inspiratory and expiratory gas. Usually FI_{CO_2} is negligible and can be ignored, thereby simplifying the equation.

As is clear from Equation 14–7, when FI_{O_2} approaches 1.0 and $FI_{CO_2} = 0$, there is potential for considerable error owing to the inability to correct for the difference between inspired and expired gas volumes. Measurement of O_2 consumption also is difficult in children who are intubated, because of potential losses of expired gas from the circuit. This is a particular concern when there is positive-pressure breathing, especially if an uncuffed endotracheal tube is used. Despite the many constraints, a number of systems have been devised for measuring O_2 consumption in infants during spontaneous or assisted respiration and at various inspired O_2 concentrations.[113,114] However, it is important to be aware of the potential sources for error.

Second, demands must not be altered simultaneously. The use of sedation and control of respiration simplify this concern, but there are other factors (discussed above) that cannot be controlled. It is important to recognize that when O_2 demands are altered as O_2 transport is manipulated, a relationship that artifactually shows O_2 supply dependence is yielded; it is analogous to exercise in which both O_2 consumption and transport increase.

Third, resting O_2 consumption and O_2 transport vary over time for a given subject. When O_2 consumption increases, O_2 transport also rises, again producing the appearance of supply dependence when it does not exist.

Fourth, to determine a critical point, it usually is necessary to have some points on the descending limb to define a line or determine a threshold, and to have sufficient time for steady state to be reached and O_2 extraction to become maximized. This may not be safe in many subjects because of the potential for deterioration during the hypoxia. Thus, despite the usefulness in the laboratory of manipulation of O_2 transport, there are often hurdles to overcome that render this approach impractical for clinical use.

Measures of Tissue Hypoxia

Because of the many difficulties cited above, it has been appealing to use a metabolic marker to detect hypoxia. Many such markers have been proposed, and the rationale for their use follows directly from the biochemical events that occur as hypoxia ensues, as described briefly below. With severe decrements in O_2 transport, there is insufficient O_2 for oxidative phosphorylation by mitochondria. Consequently, the electron transport chain slows, and there is failure to phosphorylate adenosine diphosphate (ADP) to adenosine triphosphate (ATP) and to reoxidize the cytochromes, which remain in the reduced state. There is also an increase in the concentration of adenosine monophosphate (AMP), which is

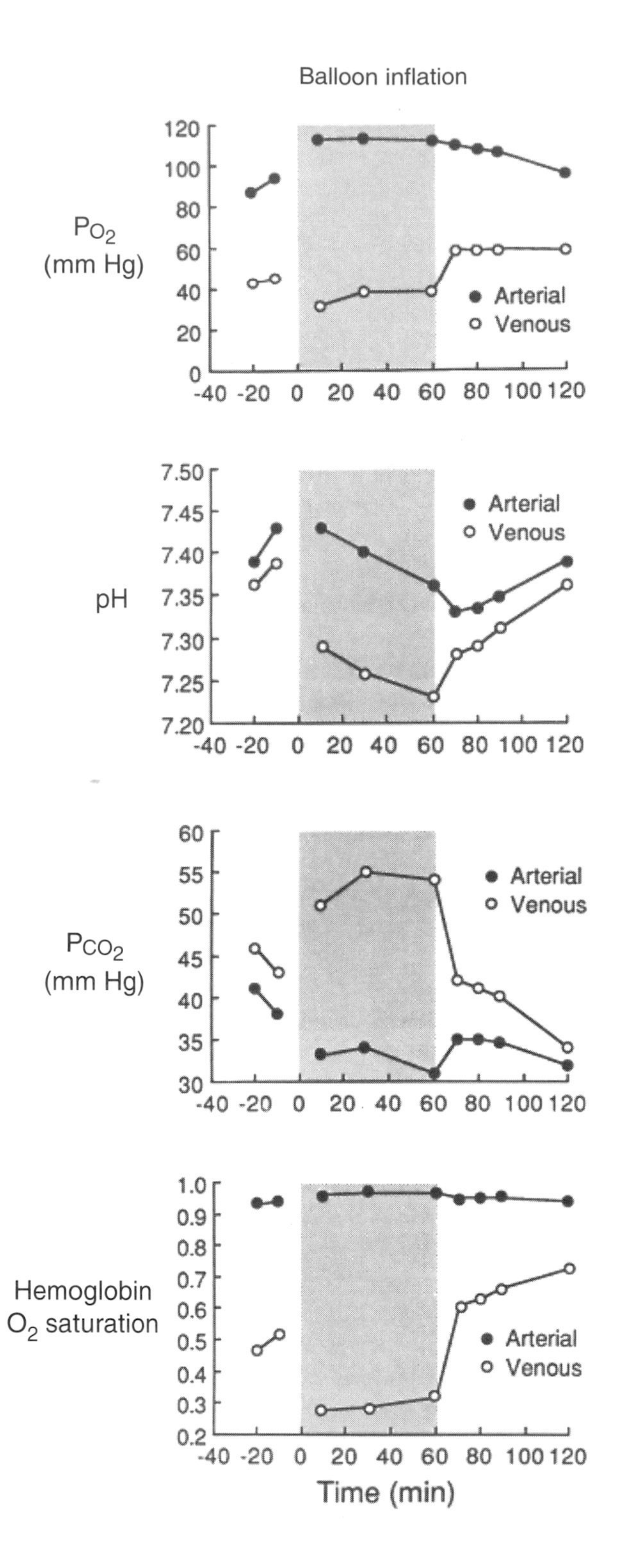

FIGURE 14–5. Changes in arterial and mixed venous blood gases, pH, and hemoglobin O_2 saturation during a 60-minute period of low cardiac output in an intact 2-month-old lamb. Note that arteriovenous differences for all variables increase during low cardiac output and that arterial pH and partial pressure of CO_2 are near normal despite the venous acidosis. P_{O_2} = partial pressure of O_2. (Reproduced with permission from Fahey JT and Lister G.[115])

catabolized rapidly during hypoxia to inosine and hypoxanthine. Accordingly, the state of phosphorylation of the nucleotides, the presence of products of catabolism, and the redox state of one or more of the cytochromes all enable inferences to be made regarding oxygenation.

Some tissues, particularly skeletal muscle and to a lesser extent brain and heart, can resynthesize ATP for brief periods by transferring a high-energy phosphate from creatine phosphate to ATP creatine phosphate, in the presence of the enzyme creatine kinase; this serves as an energy reservoir during hypoxic stress, but this source rapidly becomes depleted.

As O_2 supply is reduced, ADP can be phosphorylated anaerobically during glycolyis, although this is considerably less efficient than aerobic metabolism in terms of ATPs produced per mole of glucose. With anaerobic metabolism, lactic acid, the end product, accumulates in cells and diffuses into venous blood. If perfusion remains relatively intact, lactate concentration increases in venous and arterial blood. With the increase in blood lactate concentration, there is also an increase in H^+ and base deficit. With the marked reduction in O_2 transport relative to O_2 consumption, fractional O_2 extraction increases and mixed venous P_{O_2} decreases, as discussed earlier (Figure 14–5). The above summary of some of the changes in response to hypoxia is by no means complete and is intended only to highlight the biochemical events that have been most useful clinically for detecting O_2 supply insufficiency. Many exhaustive reviews of the topic are available. What follows is a brief critique of common nonexperimental markers as they apply to the assessment of hypoxia.

Arterial blood pH

With tissue hypoxia, there is local acidosis and eventually systemic acidemia. However, because of the large capacity of blood to buffer H^+ and the simultaneous changes in P_{CO_2} in response to the acidemia or hypoxia, pH is a relatively insensitive measure of hypoxia, and it increases relatively late. Although venous pH also may be a sign of tissue hypoxia, it is very sensitive to the flow rate in the circulation from which it is sampled, because arteriovenous pH increases as flow decreases. Therefore, a peripheral venous blood sample may not reflect arterial pH. It has been suggested that a decrease in mixed venous pH may be more reflective of tissue hypoxia than arterial pH; this is particularly true when arterial pH is specifically controlled, as with ventilatory support or buffer infusion. There is no specific advantage to using arteriovenous difference for H^+ than that for O_2 or CO_2, each of which increases whenever systemic blood flow is low[115] (Figure 14–6).

Base excess

The concept of base excess (or deficit) was developed as a construct that can separate the change in acid-base

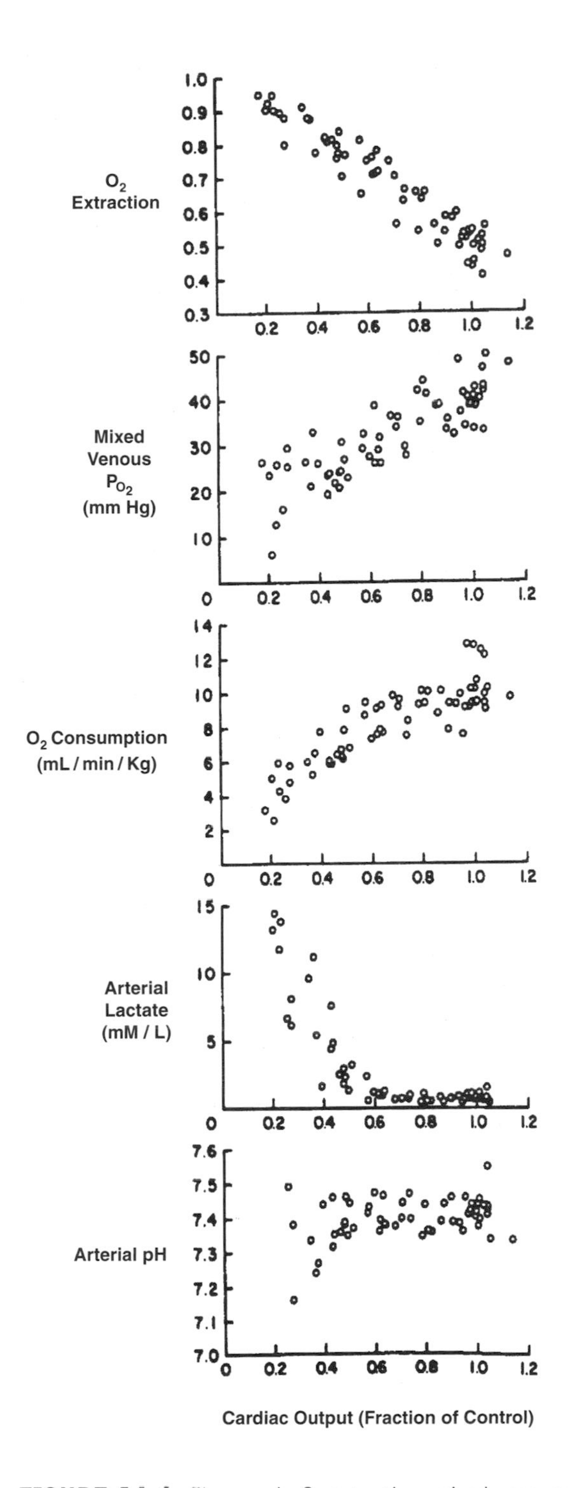

FIGURE 14–6. Changes in O_2 extraction, mixed venous partial pressure of O_2 (P_{O_2}), O_2 consumption, arterial lactate concentration, and arterial pH as a function of cardiac output expressed as a fraction of a control value (in a group of lambs). Because arterial O_2 content was constant, the curves would be exactly the same if data were expressed as a fraction of systemic O_2 transport. The critical cardiac output was approximately 0.65 of control. Note that O_2 extraction increased to levels in excess of 0.90. Note also that arterial pH is widely scattered and is often in the normal range below a critical cardiac output. (Reproduced with permission from Fahey JT and Lister G.[18])

balance caused by respiratory changes from that caused by metabolic changes.[116,117] Its calculation is based on pH, P_{CO_2}, and hemoglobin. It is intended to be used to interpret acute changes and should therefore be sensitive to changes in metabolism even when there is simultaneous respiratory compensation. However, if a subject has an abnormal base excess prior to an hypoxic disturbance (eg, with chronic diuretic usage or chronic hyper- or hypoventilation), it is not possible to interpret the base excess without reference to the previous state. Despite the theoretic appeal of this measure, it is somewhat insensitive to experimental changes in metabolism induced over a period of hours,[97] and Shibutani et al found it did not consistently detect critical O_2 transport in adults during anesthesia,[27] although others have found it valid experimentally,[10,118] and it has wide clinical use.

Arterial blood lactate concentration

It has been well documented that arterial blood lactate concentration increases in response to various forms of hypoxia, as a manifestation of increased anaerobic metabolism.[5,119] However, stimuli (eg, hyperventilation or catecholamine infusion) not thought to cause hypoxia also may account for modest increases in lactate concentration.[119–122] For this reason, the ratio of lactate to pyruvate (or some variation of this, such as excess lactate) often has been used to distinguish hypoxic from non-hypoxic processes, because the ratio increases only with the former.

Arterial lactate concentration has been found to be quantitatively related to the magnitude and duration of hypoxia over relatively short periods under experimental states. With various forms of sustained hypoxia, blood lactate concentration progressively increases, and the rate of lactate accumulation is directly proportional to the rate of O_2 deficit accumulation, that is, the difference between O_2 consumption at rest and during hypoxia, integrated with respect to time.[2,123,124] However, it is important to remember that blood lactate concentration represents the balance between production and use. If lactate removal and production both increase, there may be no net increase in concentration. For example, during relatively mild hypoxia, O_2 consumption can decrease without an increase in lactate concentration. Some have proposed that lactate never increases unless hepatic perfusion is reduced, arguing that the capacity to metabolize lactate is not exceeded unless the delivery to the liver is diminished. Studies of hepatic perfusion during hypoxia lend support to this notion.[26] In practice, however, lactate provides a sensitive marker of acute hypoxia, and under most conditions an increase in blood lactate concentration will reveal the threshold for hypoxia. Although there are problems with the use of lactate as a marker for tissue hypoxia, it remains the gold standard for in vivo experiments and clinical medicine.

Fractional oxygen extraction

As outlined previously, fractional extraction increases progressively as transport is compromised progressively. If there were a theoretic maximal extraction, this would provide a sensitive and specific sign of hypoxia. However, there are very few data from humans to provide such a maximum, and some investigators have argued using data from multiple studies that extraction does not increase much.[78] In another study,[125] O_2 extraction was as high as 0.68 (calculated from the data in that study). There are a number of possible explanations for such discrepancies between studies of humans and laboratory animals: (1) there may be relatively rapid changes in metabolic demands in response to a low O_2 transport in humans, so that extraction remains high only transiently; (2) there may be true differences in the capacity to extract oxygen; (3) the grouped data reported in some studies obscure the possibility that a critical O_2 transport may not have been attained in any individual subject; or (4) there may not have been sufficient time at a particular O_2 transport for extraction to become maximized. Whatever the reasons, there have not been extensive reports to demonstrate the capacity of humans to increase O_2 extraction to the range that has been seen in experimental animals, even when there is an increase in lactate concentration. Therefore, further studies are needed to discern whether fractional O_2 extraction is reliable to detect hypoxia for clinical purposes.

Mixed venous partial pressure of oxygen

Venous P_{O_2} represents the lowest driving pressure for diffusion of O_2 from blood to tissue, and as such should reflect the tissue P_{O_2}. For this reason, it has been used as a signal for tissue hypoxia. However, as described earlier, O_2 consumption becomes perfusion rather than diffusion limited with physiologic limitation in O_2 transport. Thus, the specific critical mixed venous P_{O_2} depends on the type of disturbance in O_2 transport,[5,23] which is not widely recognized. The reason for this is as follows. If, for a given subject, there is a single critical SOT independent of whether the disturbance is caused by anemia, hypoxemia, low perfusion, or combinations of these, there also will be a single fractional O_2 extraction. Furthermore, the fractional O_2 extraction $(Ca_{O_2} - C\bar{v}_{O_2})/Ca_{O_2}$ is virtually equivalent to $(Sa_{O_2} - Sv_{O_2})/Sa_{O_2}$ (except under conditions in which there is a large fraction of dissolved oxygen, eg, in hyperoxia or very severe anemia). Therefore, when arterial blood remains well oxygenated, as with anemic or stagnant hypoxia, there will be a higher Sv_{O_2} (saturation of venous O_2) than during conditions with arterial hypoxemia. Because critical Pv_{O_2} depends on the Sv_{O_2}, one would predict a single critical Pv_{O_2} for anemia, low cardiac output, and combinations of these, whereas the critical Pv_{O_2} would be lower with hypoxemia; furthermore, when transport is reduced by hypoxemia in combination with anemia or low cardiac output, Pv_{O_2} at the critical point should be an intermediate value. The relationship between Pv_{O_2} and Sv_{O_2} is influenced by the position of the O_2 dissociation curve. Hence, a change in P50 should predictably alter the critical Pv_{O_2}, and, as demonstrated experimentally, a right-shifted curve produces a higher critical Pv_{O_2}.[126] For these reasons, mixed venous P_{O_2} can be misleading as a marker for hypoxia when arterial P_{O_2} is changing, even though it is well established that a low Pv_{O_2} is usually a sign of hypoxia.

Conclusion

It has been our intention to provide the background necessary to understand disturbances in O_2 transport in patients or in experimental subjects. We have tried to present appropriate information describing the integrated responses to acute and chronic limitations in O_2 supply, and to suggest how interference with the normal adaptation might further compromise tissue oxygenation. We also have highlighted some of the important constraints related to unanticipated or unpredictable changes in metabolic demands that can influence the understanding of experimental results or clinical observations. It should be clear from the discussion that there is no universal measure of hypoxia available for clinical use. Therefore, the clinician must be aware of the variety of approaches for detecting insufficient O_2 transport and be armed with caution when interpreting laboratory data.

References

1. Finch CA, Lenfant C. Oxygen transport in man. N Engl J Med 1972;286:407–15.
2. Cain SM. Oxygen deficit incurred during hypoxia and its relation to lactate and excess lactate. Am J Physiol 1967;213:57–63.
3. Barcroft J. On anoxaemia. Lancet 1920;ii:485–9.
4. Fahey J, Lister G. Oxygen transport in low cardiac output states. J Crit Care 1987;2:288–305.
5. Cain SM. Appearance of excess lactate in anesthetized dogs during anemic and hypoxic hypoxia. Am J Physiol 1965; 209:604–10.
6. Weibel E. The body's need for oxygen. In: Weibel E, ed. The pathway for oxygen. Cambridge, MA: Harvard University Press, 1984:30–48.
7. Adams FH, Fujiwara T, Spears R, Hodgman J. Gaseous metabolism in premature infants at 32–34° ambient temperature. Pediatrics 1964;33:75–82.
8. Godfrey S. Exercise testing in children. Philadelphia: WB Saunders, 1974.
9. Sidi D, Kuipers J, Heymann M, Rudolph A. Effects of ambient temperature on oxygen consumption and the circulation in newborn lambs at rest and during hypoxemia. Pediatr Res 1983;17:254–8.
10. Sidi D, Kuipers J, Teitel D, et al. Developmental changes in oxygenation and circulatory responses to hypoxemia in lambs. Am J Physiol 1983;245:H674–82.

11. Lister G, Moreau G, Moss M, Talner N. Effects of alterations of oxygen transport on the neonate. Semin Perinatol 1984;8:192–204.
12. Sauer PJ, Dane HJ, Visser HK. Longitudinal studies on metabolic rate, heat loss, and energy cost of growth in low birth weight infants. Pediatr Res 1984;18:254–9.
13. Cain SM. Diminution of lactate rise during hypoxia by P_{CO_2} and beta-adrenergic blockade. Am J Physiol 1969; 217:110–6.
14. Roussos CCE. Respiratory muscle energetics. In: Macklem PT, Mead J, eds. Handbook of physiology: the respiratory system. Bethesda (MD): American Physiology Society, 1986:481–510.
15. Field S, Kelly SM, Macklem PT. The oxygen cost of breathing in patients with cardiorespiratory disease. Am Rev Respir Dis 1982;126:9–13.
16. Kalhan SC, Denne SC. Energy consumption in infants with bronchopulmonary dysplasia. J Pediatr 1990;116:662–4.
17. Kurzner SI, Garg M, Bautista DB, et al. Growth failure in bronchopulmonary dysplasia: elevated metabolic rates and pulmonary mechanics. J Pediatr 1988;112:73–80.
18. Fahey JT, Lister G. A simple method for reducing cardiac output in the conscious lamb. Am J Physiol 1985; 249:H188–92.
19. Fahey JT, Lister G. Postnatal changes in critical cardiac output and oxygen transport in conscious lambs. Am J Physiol 1987;253:H100–6.
20. Adams RP, Dieleman LA, Cain SM. A critical value for O_2 transport in the rat. J Appl Physiol 1982;53:660–4.
21. Dejours P. Oxygen demand and gas exchange. In: Wood SC, Lenfant C, eds. Evolution of respiratory process. Vol. 13. New York: Marcel Dekker, 1979:1–50.
22. Cain SM. Oxygen delivery and uptake in dogs during anemic and hypoxic hypoxia. J Appl Physiol 1977; 42:228–34.
23. Heusser F, Fahey JT, Lister G. Effect of hemoglobin concentration on critical cardiac output and oxygen transport. Am J Physiol 1989;256:H527–32.
24. Schwartz S, Frantz RA, Shoemaker WC. Sequential hemodynamic and oxygen transport responses in hypovolemia, anemia, and hypoxia. Am J Physiol 1981; 241:H864–71.
25. Schumacker PT, Samsel RW. Analysis of oxygen delivery and uptake relationships in the Krogh tissue model. J Appl Physiol 1989;67:1234–44.
26. Fahey JT, Lister G, Sanfillippo DJ, Edelstone DIE. Hepatic and gastrointestinal oxygen and lactate metabolism during low cardiac output in lambs. Pediatr Res 1997; 41:842–51.
27. Shibutani K, Komatsu T, Kubal K, et al. Critical level of oxygen delivery in anesthetized man. Crit Care Med 1983;11:640–3.
28. Cain SM. Peripheral oxygen uptake and delivery in health and disease. Clin Chest Med 1983;4:139–48.
29. Landsberg L, Saville ME, Young JB. Sympathoadrenal system and regulation of thermogenesis. Am J Physiol 1984;247:E181–9.
30. Schlichtig R, Kramer DJ, Boston JR, Pinsky MR. Renal O_2 consumption during progressive hemorrhage. J Appl Physiol 1991;70:1957–62.
31. Lassen NA, Munk O, Thaysen JH. Oxygen consumption and sodium reabsorption in the kidney. Acta Physiol Scand 1961;51:371–84.
32. Cain SM. Increased oxygen uptake with passive hyperventilation of dogs. J Appl Physiol 1970;28:4–7.
33. Brezis M, Rosen S, Silva P, et al. Polyene toxicity in renal medulla: injury mediated by transport activity. Science 1984;224:66–8.
34. Brezis M, Rosen S, Spokes K, et al. Transport-dependent anoxic cell injury in the isolated perfused rat kidney. Am J Pathol 1984;116:327–41.
35. Guyton A, Jones C, Coleman T. Circulatory physiology: cardiac output and its regulation. Philadelphia: WB Saunders, 1973:334–43.
36. Granger HJ, Goodman AH, Cook BH. Metabolic models of microcirculatory regulation. Fed Proc 1975;34:2025–30.
37. Edelstone DI, Holzman IR. Oxygen consumption by the gastrointestinal tract and liver in conscious newborn lambs. Am J Physiol 1981;240:G297–304.
38. Wade O, Bishop J. Cardiac output and regional blood flow. Blackwell: Oxford, 1962.
39. Cain SM. Acute lung injury. Assessment of tissue oxygenation. Crit Care Clin 1986;2:537–50.
40. Lassen N. Cerebral blood flow and oxygen consumption in man. Physiol Rev 1959;39:183–238.
41. Selkurt E. The relation of renal blood flow to effective arterial pressure in the intact kidney of the dog. Am J Physiol 1946;147:537–49.
42. Abboud FM, Heistad DD, Mark AL, Schmid PG. Reflex control of the peripheral circulation. Prog Cardiovasc Dis 1976;18:371–403.
43. Johnson JM, Rowell LB, Niederberger M, Eisman MM. Human splanchnic and forearm vasoconstrictor responses to reductions of right atrial and aortic pressures. Circ Res 1974;34:515–24.
44. Rothe CF. Physiology of venous return. An unappreciated boost to the heart. Arch Intern Med 1986;146:977–82.
45. Sylvester JT, Scharf SM, Gilbert RD, et al. Hypoxic and CO hypoxia in dogs: hemodynamics, carotid reflexes, and catecholamines. Am J Physiol 1979;236:H22–8.
46. Shoji M, Kimura T, Matsui K, et al. Role of intracerebral angiotensin receptors in the regulation of vasopressin release and the cardiovascular system. Neuroendocrinology 1986;43:239–44.
47. Share L. Control of plasma ADH titer in hemorrhage: role of atrial and arterial receptors. Am J Physiol 1968;215:1384–9.
48. Belloni FL. The local control of coronary blood flow. Cardiovasc Res 1979;13:63–85.
49. Heistad DD, Marcus ML. Evidence that neural mechanisms do not have important effects on cerebral blood flow. Circ Res 1978;42:295–302.
50. Berne R. Regulation of coronary blood flow. Physiol Rev 1964;44:1–29.
51. Kreuzer F, Cain SM. Regulation of the peripheral vasculature and tissue oxygenation in health and disease. Crit Care Clin 1985;1:453–70.
52. Granger HJ, Goodman AH, Granger DN. Role of resistance and exchange vessels in local microvascular control of skeletal muscle oxygenation in the dog. Circ Res 1976; 38:379–85.

53. Katayama Y, Coburn RF, Fillers WS, Baron CB. Oxygen sensors in vascular smooth muscle. J Appl Physiol 1994; 77:2086–92.
54. Franco-Obregon A, Urena J, Lopez-Barneo J. Oxygen-sensitive calcium channels in vascular smooth muscle and their possible role in hypoxic arterial relaxation. Proc Natl Acad Sci U S A 1995;92:4715–9.
55. Smith D, Green H, Thomson J, Sharratt M. Capillary and size interrelationships in developing rat diaphragm, EDL, and soleus muscle fiber types. Am J Physiol 1989; 256:C50–8.
56. Laughlin MH, Tomanek RJ. Myocardial capillarity and maximal capillary diffusion capacity in exercise-trained dogs. J Appl Physiol 1987;63:1481–6.
57. Haddad GG, Jiang C. O_2-sensing mechanisms in excitable cells: role of plasma membrane K+ channels. Annu Rev Physiol 1997;59:23–42.
58. Chandel NS, Maltepe E, Goldwasser E, et al. Mitochondrial reactive oxygen species trigger hypoxia-induced transcription. Proc Natl Acad Sci U S A 1998;95:11715–20.
59. Chandel NS, Schumacker PT. Cellular oxygen sensing by mitochondria: old questions, new insight. J Appl Physiol 2000;88:1880–9.
60. Semenza GL. Regulation of mammalian O_2 homeostasis by hypoxia-inducible factor 1. Annu Rev Cell Dev Biol 1999;15:551–78.
61. Cain SM, Adams RP. O_2 transport during two forms of stagnant hypoxia following acid and base infusions. J Appl Physiol 1983;54:1518–24.
62. Turek Z, Kreuzer F, Ringnalda BE. Blood gases at several levels of oxygenation in rats with a left-shifted blood oxygen dissociation curve. Pflugers Arch 1978;376:7–13.
63. Sacks LM, Delivoria-Papadopoulos M. Hemoglobin-oxygen interactions. Semin Perinatol 1984;8:168–83.
64. Benesch R, Benesch RE. The effect of organic phosphates from the human erythrocyte on the allosteric properties of hemoglobin. Biochem Biophys Res Commun 1967 26:162–7.
65. Versmold H, Seifert G, Riegel KP. Blood oxygen affinity in infancy: the interaction of fetal and adult hemoglobin, oxygen capacity, and red cell hydrogen ion and 2,3-diphosphoglycerate concentration. Respir Physiol 1973; 18:14–25.
66. Lenfant C, Torrance JD, Reynafarje C. Shift of the O_2-Hb dissociation curve at altitude: mechanism and effect. J Appl Physiol 1971;30:625–31.
67. Bauer C, Ludwig M, Ludwig I, Bartels H. Factors governing the oxygen affinity of human adult and foetal blood. Respir Physiol 1969;7:271–7.
68. Versmold HT, Linderkamp C, Dohlemann C, Riegel KP. Oxygen transport in congenital heart disease: influence of fetal hemoglobin, red cell pH, and 2,3-diphosphoglycerate. Pediatr Res 1976;10:566–70.
69. Oski FA, Delivoria-Papadopoulos M. The red cell, 2,3-diphosphoglycerate, and tissue oxygen release. J Pediatr 1970;77:941–56.
70. Lister G. Oxygen transport. In: Gluckman PD, Heymann MA, eds. Perinatal and pediatric pathophysiology: a clinical perspective. London: Edward Arnold Publishers, 1993:547–555.
71. Turek Z, Kreuzer F, Hoofd LJ. Advantage or disadvantage of a decrease of blood oxygen affinity for tissue oxygen supply at hypoxia. A theoretical study comparing man and rat. Pflugers Arch 1973;342:185–97.
72. Banchero N, Grover RF, Will JA. Oxygen transport in the llama (*Lama glama*). Respir Physiol 1971;13:102–15.
73. Turek Z, Kreuzer F. Effect of shifts of the O_2 dissociation curve upon alveolar-arterial O_2 gradients in computer models of the lung with ventilation-perfusion mismatching. Respir Physiol 1981;45:133–9.
74. Danek SJ, Lynch JP, Weg JG, Dantzker DR. The dependence of oxygen uptake on oxygen delivery in the adult respiratory distress syndrome. Am Rev Respir Dis 1980; 122:387–95.
75. Powers SR Jr, Mannal R, Neclerio M, et al. Physiologic consequences of positive end-expiratory pressure (PEEP) ventilation. Ann Surg 1973;178:265–72.
76. Brent BN, Matthay RA, Mahler DA, et al. Relationship between oxygen uptake and oxygen transport in stable patients with chronic obstructive pulmonary disease. Physiologic effects of nitroprusside and hydralazine. Am Rev Respir Dis 1984;129:682–6.
77. Cain SM. Supply dependency of oxygen uptake in ARDS: myth or reality? Am J Med Sci 1984;288:119–24.
78. Dantzker DR, Foresman B, Gutierrez G. Oxygen supply and utilization relationships. A reevaluation. Am Rev Respir Dis 1991;143:675–9.
79. Ronco JJ, Phang PT, Walley KR, et al. Oxygen consumption is independent of changes in oxygen delivery in severe adult respiratory distress syndrome. Am Rev Respir Dis 1991;143:1267–73.
80. Ronco JJ, Fenwick JC, Wiggs BR, et al. Oxygen consumption is independent of increases in oxygen delivery by dobutamine in septic patients who have normal or increased plasma lactate. Am Rev Respir Dis 1993;147:25–31.
81. Phang PT, Cunningham KF, Ronco JJ, et al. Mathematical coupling explains dependence of oxygen consumption on oxygen delivery in ARDS. Am J Respir Crit Care Med 1994;150:318–23.
82. Schumacker PT, Cain SM. The concept of a critical oxygen delivery. Intensive Care Med 1987;13:223–9.
83. Schumacker PT. Oxygen supply dependency in critical illness: an evolving understanding. Intensive Care Med 1998;24:97–9.
84. Landau SE, Alexander RS, Powers SR Jr, et al. Tissue oxygen exchange and reactive hyperemia following microembolization. J Surg Res 1982;32:38–43.
85. Ellsworth ML, Goldfarb RD, Alexander RS, et al. Microembolization induced oxygen utilization impairment in the canine gracilis muscle. Adv Shock Res 1981;5:89–99.
86. Duran WN, Renkin EM. Oxygen consumption and blood flow in resting mammalian skeletal muscle. Am J Physiol 1974;226:173–7.
87. Long GR, Nelson, Sznajder. Systemic O_2 delivery and consumption during acute lung injury in dogs. J Crit Care 1988;3:249–55.
88. Maker HS, Nicklas WJ. Biochemical response of body organs to hypoxia and ischemia. In: Robin ED, ed. Extrapulmonary manifestations of respiratory disease. Vol. 8. New York: Marcel Dekker, 1978:107–49.

89. Metcalfe J, Dhindsa DS, Edwards MJ, Mourdjinis A. Decreased affinity of blood for oxygen in patients with low-output heart failure. Circ Res 1969;25:47–51.
90. Jelkmann W. Renal erythropoietin: properties and production. Rev Physiol Biochem Pharmacol 1986;104:139–215.
91. Woodson RD, Wills RE, Lenfant C. Effect of acute and established anemia on O_2 transport at rest, submaximal and maximal work. J Appl Physiol 1978;44:36–43.
92. Berman W Jr, Lister G Jr, Alverson D, Olsen S. Ouabain effects on oxygen physiology in anemic lambs. Pediatr Res 1987;21:447–52.
93. Crowell JW, Smith EE. Determinant of the optimal hematocrit. J Appl Physiol 1967;22:501–4.
94. Shepherd AP, Riedel GL. Optimal hematocrit for oxygenation of canine intestine. Circ Res 1982;51:233–40.
95. Bernstein D, Teitel DF, Rudolph AM. Chronic anemia in the newborn lamb: cardiovascular adaptations and comparison to chronic hypoxemia. Pediatr Res 1988; 23:621–7.
96. Linderkamp O, Mayr S, Sengespeik C, et al. Eisenmangel bei Vorliegen von cyanotischen Herzvitien: Eine Ursache fur cerebrale Komplikationen. Monatsschr Kinderheilkd 1976;124:301–2.
97. Moss M, Moreau G, Lister G. Oxygen transport and metabolism in the conscious lamb: the effects of hypoxemia. Pediatr Res 1987;22:177–83.
98. Lahiri S, Mulligan E, Nishino T, et al. Relative responses of aortic body and carotid body chemoreceptors to carboxyhemoglobinemia. J Appl Physiol 1981;50:580–6.
99. Kontos HA, Mauck HP Jr, Patterson JL Jr. Mechanism of reactive hyperemia in limbs of anesthetized dogs. Am J Physiol 1965;209:1106–14.
100. Levison H, Delivoria-Papadopoulos M, Swyer PR. Variations in oxygen consumption in the infant with hypoxaemia due to cardiopulmonary disease. Acta Paediatr Scand 1965;54:369–74.
101. Oliver TK. Gaseous metabolism in newly born human infants. Am J Dis Child 1963;105:427–34.
102. Berman W Jr, Wood SC, Yabek SM, et al. Systemic oxygen transport in patients with congenital heart disease. Circulation 1987;75:360–8.
103. Teitel D, Sidi D, Bernstein D, et al. Chronic hypoxemia in the newborn lamb: cardiovascular, hematopoietic, and growth adaptations. Pediatr Res 1985;19:1004–10.
104. Rosenthal A, Nathan DG, Marty AT, et al. Acute hemodynamic effects of red cell volume reduction in polycythemia of cyanotic congenital heart disease. Circulation 1970;42:297–308.
105. Linde LM, Dunn OJ, Schireson R, Rasof B. Growth in children with congenital heart disease. J Pediatr 1967; 70:413–9.
106. Naeye RL. Anatomic features of growth failure in congenital heart disease. Pediatrics 1967;39:433–40.
107. Feldt RH, Strickler GB, Weidman WH. Growth of children with congenital heart disease. Am J Dis Child 1969;117:573–9.
108. Lister G, Hellenbrand WE, Kleinman CS, Talner NS. Physiologic effects of increasing hemoglobin concentration in left-to-right shunting in infants with ventricular septal defects. N Engl J Med 1982;306:502–6.
109. Robin ED. Of men and mitochondria: coping with hypoxic dysoxia. The 1980 J. Burns Amberson Lecture. Am Rev Respir Dis 1980;122:517–31.
110. Robin ED, Lewiston N, Newman A, et al. Bioenergetic pattern of turtle brain and resistance to profound loss of mitochondrial ATP generation. Proc Natl Acad Sci U S A 1979;76:3922–6.
111. Stanek KA, Nagle FJ, Bisgard GE, Byrnes WC. Effect of hyperoxia on oxygen consumption in exercising ponies. J Appl Physiol 1979;46:1115–8.
112. Welch HG, Mullin JP, Wilson GD, Lewis J. Effects of breathing O_2-enriched gas mixtures on metabolic rate during exercise. Med Sci Sports 1974;6:26–32.
113. Lister G, Hoffman JI, Rudolph AM. Oxygen uptake in infants and children: a simple method for measurement. Pediatrics 1974;53:656–62.
114. Abdul-Rasool IH, Chamberlain JH, Swan PC, Mitchell FT. Measurement of respiratory gas exchange during artificial respiration. J Appl Physiol 1981;51:1451–6.
115. Fahey JT, Lister G. Response to low cardiac output: developmental differences in metabolism during oxygen deficit and recovery in lambs. Pediatr Res 1989;26:180–7.
116. Bunker JP. The great trans-atlantic acid-base debate. J Anesthesiol 1965;26:591–4.
117. Severinghaus JW. Letter to the editor. Anesthesiology 1977;47:233–4.
118. Edelstone DI, Darby MJ, Bass K, Miller K. Effects of reductions in hemoglobin-oxygen affinity and hematocrit level on oxygen consumption and acid-base state in fetal lambs. Am J Obstet Gynecol 1989;160:820–6.
119. Huckabee W. Relationships of pyruvate and lactate during anaerobic metablism. II. Exercise and formation of O_2 debt. J Clin Invest 1958;37:255–63.
120. Takano N. Blood lactate accumulation and its causative factors during passive hyperventilation in dogs. Jpn J Physiol 1966;16:481–96.
121. Eldridge F, Salzer J. Effect of respiratory alkalosis on blood lactate and pyruvate in humans. J Appl Physiol 1967; 22:461–8.
122. Oliva PB. Lactic acidosis. Am J Med 1970;48:209–25.
123. Moss M, Kurzner S, Razlog Y, Lister G. Hypoxanthine and lactate concentrations in lambs during hypoxic and stagnant hypoxia. Am J Physiol 1988;255:H53–9.
124. Saltiel A, Sanfilippo DJ, Hendler R, Lister G. Oxygen transport during anemic hypoxia in pigs: effects of digoxin on metabolism. Am J Physiol 1992;263: H208–17.
125. Lutch JS, Murray JF. Continuous positive-pressure ventilation: effects on systemic oxygen transport and tissue oxygenation. Ann Intern Med 1972;76:193–202.
126. Schumacker PT, Long GR, Wood LD. Tissue oxygen extraction during hypovolemia: role of hemoglobin P50. J Appl Physiol 1987;62:1801–7.

CHAPTER 15

PULMONARY GAS EXCHANGE

J. JULIO PÉREZ FONTÁN, MD

During their adaptation to air breathing, terrestrial vertebrates adopted an invaginated arrangement for their gas exchanging organs. The internalization of the large pulmonary surface needed to support their levels of activity minimized water and heat losses while allowing for a tight regulation of blood partial pressure of carbon dioxide (P_{CO_2}) and P_{O_2} through adjustments in the depth and rate of breathing. An invaginated lung, however, also imposed some limitations. For instance, unlike the countercurrent system that operates in fish gills, inflowing and outflowing gases share the same pathway and must mix, reducing the efficiency of the exchanger. Also, the transport of these gases in and out of the alveoli through relatively narrow air passages requires a muscle-powered convection mechanism, which demands considerably more energy than the passive mechanisms used by less evolved animals. To reconcile the need for a large surface area with the limited size of the organism, the lung had to become divided into millions of alveoli (300 million in a developed human) supplied by a network of airways and blood vessels. The branching organization of this network facilitates both ventilation and perfusion by increasing total cross-sectional area and reducing viscous resistance to the movement of air and blood. However, the fact that each branch constitutes a unique pathway for gas exchange creates an opportunity for shunting of venous blood to the arterial side of the circulation in poorly ventilated alveoli, causing arterial hypoxemia. Finally, under the humid conditions dictated by their proximity to the blood stream, alveoli are inherently unstable and require a surfactant system to reduce surface tension. These drawbacks of the invaginated lung become relevant in two situations of interest for pediatricians and developmental physiologists. The first occurs at the time of birth; over a short period of time the fetus has to recapitulate the evolution from liquid to atmospheric breathing while retaining the ability to increase oxygenation and ventilation in response to rapidly changing metabolic needs.[1–3] The second occurs when disease processes disrupt the structure of the gas exchanging units or limit their ability to exchange gases effectively. In this chapter, we analyze the foundations of both normal and abnormal pulmonary gas exchange, highlighting (when data are available) how the developing respiratory system differs from that of the adult.

Components

The theoretic and experimental analysis of gas exchange has provided fundamental insights into the function of the lungs, generating useful tools to (1) measure metabolic activity, (2) estimate pulmonary blood flow, (3) judge the progression of disease from its effects on the efficiency of the gas exchanging system, and (4) assign the manifestations of pulmonary illness to their appropriate origin within the structure of the lungs. Much of what is known today has been learned by using the respiratory gases, CO_2 and O_2, as probes to study the relationship between ventilation and circulation. The general strategy has been to derive mass balances for one or both gases in concert with some idealized model of the lung. Two important features of respiration have aided in these derivations. In the steady state, the quantities of CO_2 and O_2 exchanged in the lung are equivalent to those exchanged in the metabolizing tissues. In addition, there is no net exchange of N_2 between the body and the atmosphere, and, therefore, differences in inspired and expired gas volumes can be corrected from knowledge of the N_2 concentrations. In the past five decades, these simple principles have been applied elegantly to derive formulations for CO_2 production and O_2 consumption (and their relationship), alveolar ventilation and capillary perfusion (and their relationship), dead space, and venous admixture.

Ventilation and Composition of Alveolar Gas

ALVEOLAR AND DEAD SPACE VENTILATION

Ventilation is a process of mass transport that typically involves a reciprocating movement of atmospheric gas to the alveoli and of alveolar gas to the atmosphere. It is regulated by a feedback reflex activated by chemoreceptors sensitive to pH and P_{O_2} located in the medulla and carotid arteries. Stimulation of these chemoreceptors initiates a multineuronal response that ultimately changes the neural outflow to the respiratory muscles.[4] Additional sensory inputs from lung and chest wall mechano- and nociceptive receptors and descending regulatory inputs from brain stem and supratentorial centers help shape the specific breathing pattern (defined by the combination of tidal volume, inspiratory time, and breathing

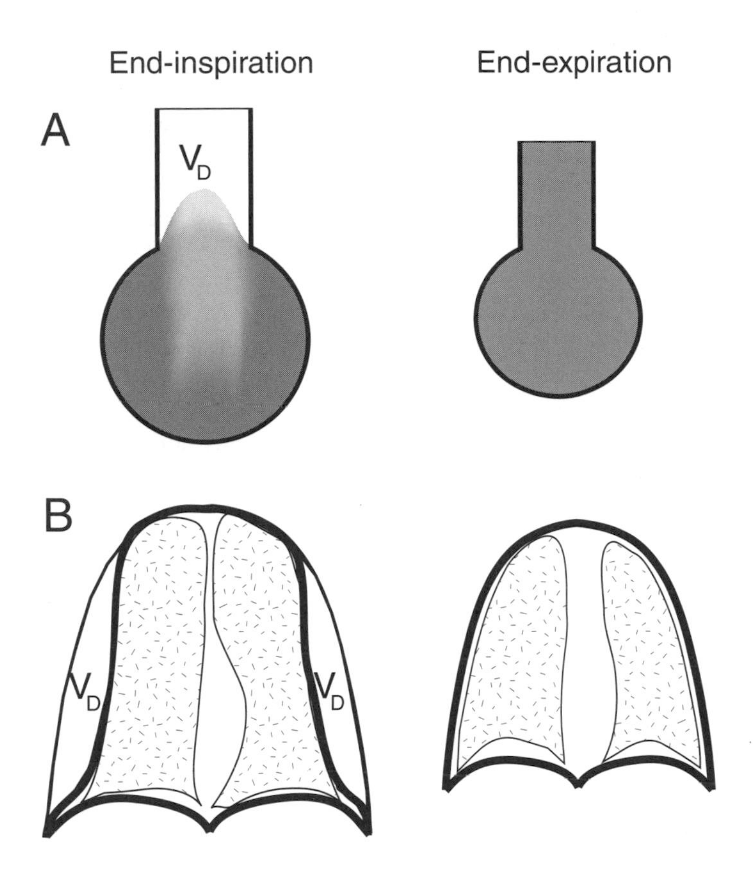

FIGURE 15–1. Two examples of wasted ventilation. *A*, The conducting airways act as an anatomic dead space (V_D). During inspiration the gas contained in this space retains the composition of the inspired gas (in reality, there is some diffusion of alveolar gas into the neighboring bronchi and inspired gas into the alveoli as shown by the differences in the intensity of the shading). Thus energy used in transporting this gas from the atmosphere is wasted in terms of gas (CO_2) exchange. During expiration, the space becomes filled with alveolar gas, which then enters the alveoli once again during the following inspiration. *B*, Chest wall retractions during inspiration are common in infants with lung disease and have effects comparable to those of the anatomic dead space. This occurs because, to maintain minute alveolar ventilation, the volume displacement of the diaphragm must increase to compensate for the volume loss caused by the inward wall distortion of the rib cage (V_D).

frequency[5–8]). The chemoreceptor reflex is particularly sensitive to variations in arterial P_{CO_2}, which, as we will see below, is considerably more responsive than P_{O_2} to changes in ventilation.

Minute ventilation can be defined as the product of tidal volume and breathing frequency. Because of ease of measurement, the exhaled tidal volume is almost always used in this calculation, and the symbol $\dot{V}_E$ is then applied to represent minute ventilation. In this nomenclature, $\dot{V}$ is the notation for gas flow, the subscript E indicates that the measurement was done during both expiration and the gas phase (liquid phase measurements are indicated by lowercase subscripts). Typically, when corrections are made for temperature and humidity, $\dot{V}_E$ is slightly less than the inspiratory minute ventilation ($\dot{V}_I$) because, under most conditions, O_2 consumption exceeds CO_2 production by a small amount.

Minute ventilation is a well-defined quantity, that can be determined accurately using widely available equipment. Its value informs the clinician of the minimum mechanical and energetic demands placed on the respiratory muscles. However, the value of $\dot{V}_E$ does not bear a direct relationship with the net volumes of CO_2 and O_2 transferred across the lungs or with the partial pressures of either gas in the alveoli or in the arterial blood. This arises from two important features of the gas exchanging system: first, gas that enters the lungs with each breath undergoes equilibration with the pulmonary capillary blood; and, second, the relationship between the volumes of gas and blood that equilibrate in each alveolar-capillary unit can vary widely.

A substantial portion of the ventilatory effort is wasted. Although the mechanisms for the wasted ventilation are multiple, since the turn of the last century, physiologists have focused their attention on the role of the conducting airways as a source of ventilatory inefficiency.[9–11] The series arrangement of the airways and gas exchanging spaces makes it inevitable that, at the end of an inspiration, a portion of the inhaled tidal volume will remain in the conducting airways where it has no contact or proximity with the pulmonary capillary blood and from where it is exhaled unchanged at the beginning of the subsequent expiration (Figure 15–1). In this regard, the trachea and bronchi constitute an *anatomic or series dead space* (V_D), which adds to the ventilatory burden of the respiratory muscles without participating in the gas exchanging functions of the lungs. By the same principle, inspiratory retractions of the chest wall, a common manifestation of lung mechanical dysfunction especially in newborns and small infants, also represent a form of wasted ventilatory effort because they add substantially to the volume displaced by the diaphragm without contributing to alveolar ventilation.[12]

Bohr[9] was the first to derive equations to quantify the relationship between anatomic dead space and overall ventilation by applying a simple mass balance to the movement of CO_2 in and out of the alveolar spaces (CO_2 is practically absent from the inspired gas, which simplifies the computations). In the steady state, the volume of CO_2 that exits the lungs in the expired gas must be equal to the volume of CO_2 eliminated from the blood. (Note that, by convention, CO_2 specifically rather than O_2 is used to define the gas exchanging space.) If we divide $\dot{V}_E$ into two idealized portions, one consisting of the gas volume that equilibrates its P_{CO_2} with the capillary blood over a period of time (minute alveolar ventilation or $\dot{V}_A$) and the other encompassing the gas volume that, over the same period, undergoes no CO_2 exchange with the blood (dead space ventilation or $\dot{V}_D$), we can write the following three-term equation:

$$\dot{V}_E \, F_{E_{CO_2}} = \dot{V}_A \, F_{A_{CO_2}} = (\dot{V}_E - \dot{V}_D) \, F_{A_{CO_2}} \qquad (15\text{–}1)$$

where $F_{E_{CO_2}}$ and $F_{A_{CO_2}}$ are the fractional concentrations of CO_2 in the mixed expired gas and in the alveolar gas, respectively. By manipulating arithmetically the first and third terms of the equation, we arrive to the common expression of Bohr's equation for CO_2:

$$\dot{V}_D / \dot{V}_E = (F_{A_{CO_2}} - F_{E_{CO_2}}) / F_{A_{CO_2}} \qquad (15\text{–}2)$$

which defines $\dot{V}_D$ relative to $\dot{V}_E$, a formulation that conveys the idea of an efficiency ratio (or, more precisely, an "inefficiency ratio"). Because $\dot{V}_D$ and $\dot{V}_E$ are the respective products of V_D and tidal volume (V_T) by the breathing frequency, the value of V_D can be calculated as

$$V_D = V_T \, (F_{A_{CO_2}} - F_{E_{CO_2}}) / F_{A_{CO_2}} \qquad (15\text{–}3)$$

Similarly, because Dalton's law states that the fractional concentration of a gas in a mixture of gases is equivalent to the ratio of its partial pressure to the total pressure of the gas mixture (in this case the atmospheric pressure), $F_{A_{CO_2}}$ and $F_{E_{CO_2}}$ can be replaced in Equations 15–2 and 15–3 by the partial pressures of CO_2 in the alveolar gas ($P_{A_{CO_2}}$) and in the expired gas ($P_{E_{CO_2}}$). $F_{E_{CO_2}}$ or $P_{E_{CO_2}}$ is determined empirically. However, $F_{A_{CO_2}}$ or $P_{A_{CO_2}}$ cannot be measured directly and is therefore estimated by measuring the fractional concentration ($F_{ET_{CO_2}}$) or the partial pressure of CO_2 ($P_{ET_{CO_2}}$) in the end-tidal gas (the last gas to exit the airway opening during expiration).

Both direct measurements of airway volume[10,11,13,14] and indirect physiologic estimates based on expired CO_2 analysis[15,16] have yielded reasonably similar values for the anatomic dead space, ranging between one-quarter and one-third of a normal tidal volume. Approximately 30 to 50% of this space resides in the extrathoracic airway (nose, pharynx, larynx, and extrathoracic trachea) as shown by measurements performed before and after tracheostomy.[17] When normalized for lung volume, dead space is slightly smaller in newborn than in adult humans,[18] perhaps because of the relatively small size of the newborn's trachea; however, it remains relatively constant during postnatal development[19] and aging and is not affected substantially by the presence of lung disease. Not surprisingly, the anatomic dead space volume increases in proportion to transpulmonary pressure,[20] which, for the intrapulmonary airways, bears a close relationship with airway transmural pressure. As a result, dead space is related to lung volume also, although the relationship is not as linear.[21] Both anatomic and physiologic dead space increase with ventilatory frequency, a finding that has been attributed to decreased diffusion of CO_2 from the alveolus to the conducting airways.[22]

Even when measured accurately, $F_{ET_{CO_2}}$ tends to underestimate $F_{A_{CO_2}}$ during exercise or in the presence of ventilation inequalities in diseased lungs. Thus, as a simpler alternative, Enghoff[23] introduced the idea of using the arterial P_{CO_2} (Pa_{CO_2}) to replace $P_{A_{CO_2}}$ in the Bohr equation. However, the resultant value, known as the *physiologic dead space*, consistently overestimates the anatomic dead space. Far from being a simple calculation artifact, the difference between physiologic and anatomic dead space, usually referred to as the *alveolar or parallel dead space* (V_{DA}), highlights some of the inefficiencies of the gas exchanging process in the alveoli. Its formula can be deduced easily from Equation 15–3:

$$V_{DA} = V_T \, P_{E_{CO_2}} \, (Pa_{CO_2} - P_{ET_{CO_2}}) / (Pa_{CO_2} \, P_{ET_{CO_2}}) \qquad (15\text{–}4)$$

Unlike the anatomic dead space, the alveolar dead space is influenced by the distribution of ventilation-perfusion ratios ($\dot{V}_A/\dot{Q}$) in the lungs (see below). The $P_{A_{CO_2}}$ of alveolar units with low ($\dot{V}_A/\dot{Q}$) ratios (usually resulting from underventilation) cannot exceed the P_{CO_2} of the blood entering the lungs through the pulmonary arteries, which is only a few millimeters of mercury greater than that of the blood exiting the lungs through the pulmonary veins. Consequently, these units have a small effect on the alveolar dead space, because their contribution to the expired gas does not raise the values of $P_{E_{CO_2}}$ and $P_{ET_{CO_2}}$ substantially. In contrast, alveolar units with high $\dot{V}_A/\dot{Q}$ ratios (usually from underperfusion) have considerably lower $P_{A_{CO_2}}$ values and are therefore overrepresented in the calculation.[22] Accordingly, the alveolar dead space, or, in more simple terms, the difference between Pa_{CO_2} and PET_{CO_2}, provides the clinician with a basic tool to judge the effects of disease or therapeutic interventions that may reduce regional perfusion in the lungs. The effect of positive end-expiratory pressure is a good example. When this pressure is increased, alveolar capillaries become compressed, especially in compliant areas of the lung, reducing blood flow and CO_2 elimination in those areas. As a result, the difference between Pa_{CO_2} and PE_{CO_2} widens.

Composition of Alveolar Gas

The above discussion introduces the idea that the fractional concentrations (or partial pressures) of CO_2 in the inspired, alveolar, and expired gases are linked by a relationship that defines the efficiency of the gas exchanging process. Although the formulations shown in Equations 15–1 to 15–4 are for CO_2, a similar mass balance analysis can be applied to derive the efficiency of O_2 exchange based on the relationship between inspired and expired volumes of O_2 and the volume of O_2 taken up by the blood.

Whether we are considering a single alveolar unit or the whole lung as a homogeneous ensemble of many alveolar units, predicting the composition of the alveolar gas requires knowing both the rate at which this gas is renewed through ventilation and the rates at which the individual gases contained in the alveolar mixture are removed or added by the pulmonary capillary blood. In the steady state, there is no net exchange of N_2 between the body and the atmosphere. Under such circumstances, the problem is therefore reduced to understanding how the concentrations of CO_2 and O_2 in the alveolar gas are affected by the flux of these two gases across the alveolar-capillary membrane.

The volume of CO_2 returned to the alveoli by the pulmonary blood vessels is represented by the symbol $\dot{V}_{CO_2}$, using the same notation described for other ventilation variables. Except for the rare circumstances in which O_2 is exchanged outside the lungs, for example during extracorporeal membrane oxygenation or cardiopulmonary bypass, $\dot{V}_{CO_2}$ is equivalent to the body's CO_2 production. Similarly, the volume of O_2 removed from the air spaces by the pulmonary blood vessels is represented by the symbol $\dot{V}_{O_2}$ and is, under most conditions, equivalent to the body's O_2 consumption. $\dot{V}_{CO_2}$ and $\dot{V}_{O_2}$ can be calculated as follows:

$$\dot{V}_{CO_2} = V_E\, FE_{CO_2} \tag{15–5}$$

and

$$\dot{V}_{O_2} = V_I\, FI_{O_2} - V_E\, FE_{O_2} \tag{15–6}$$

where FI_{O_2} and FE_{O_2} are the fractional concentrations of O_2 in the inspired and expired gases, respectively. Because no further exchange occurs after gas leaves the alveoli, the volume of expired CO_2 or O_2 ($V_E\, F_E$) must be equal to the volume of the same gas removed from the alveoli by the effective alveolar ventilation ($\dot{V}_A\, F_A$). Accordingly, Equations 15–5 and 16–6 can also be written as follows:

$$\dot{V}_{CO_2} = \dot{V}_A\, FA_{CO_2} \tag{15–7}$$

and

$$\dot{V}_{O_2} = \dot{V}_I\, FI_{O_2} - \dot{V}_A\, FA_{O_2} \tag{15–8}$$

By applying Dalton's law once again and substituting FA_{CO_2} with $PA_{CO_2}/(P_B - P_{H_2O})$, where P_B represents the atmospheric pressure and P_{H_2O} represents the water vapor pressure at body temperature, we obtain the following equation:

$$PA_{CO_2} = (P_B - P_{H_2O})\, \dot{V}_{CO_2} / \dot{V}_A \tag{15–9}$$

which shows that PA_{CO_2} and, by extension, Pa_{CO_2} are directly and inversely related to $\dot{V}_{CO_2}$ and $\dot{V}_A$, respectively.

The relationship between PA_{O_2}, $\dot{V}_{O_2}$, and $\dot{V}_A$ is considerably more complex, not only because O_2 is present in the alveolar gas, but also because CO_2 and O_2 are not necessarily exchanged in equal volumes between the alveoli and pulmonary capillaries. As a result, excess O_2 may enter the alveoli to replace volume lost when CO_2 elimination is less than O_2 uptake or, alternatively, O_2 may be displaced out of the alveoli by an excess of CO_2 when the opposite is true. In trying to solve the arithmetic problem created by this inequality, respiratory physiologists realized that by introducing into their derivations the ratio $\dot{V}_{CO_2}/\dot{V}_{O_2}$, known as the *respiratory exchange ratio* or *respiratory quotient* (R), they circumvented the need to include $\dot{V}_{CO_2}$ or $\dot{V}_{O_2}$ in their calculation.[24,25] In the steady state, the value of R for the whole lung depends on the pathways for fuel use by the tissues. When considered for individual alveolar units, however, R is influenced also by the specific unit's $\dot{V}_A/\dot{Q}$ ratio. Because the relationships between blood content and partial pressure are different for CO_2 and O_2, CO_2 elimination exceeds O_2 uptake in alveoli with high $\dot{V}_A/\dot{Q}$ ratios, which therefore have a high R value. In contrast, O_2 uptake is greater than CO_2 elimination in alveoli with low $\dot{V}_A/\dot{Q}$ ratios, and, thus, these alveoli have a lower R value.

As noted above, another important point in the derivation of an alveolar gas equation came from the recognition that, as long as the body's N_2 content is constant, N_2 uptake and elimination in the lungs must be equal:

$$\dot{V}_I\, FI_{N_2} = \dot{V}_E\, FE_{N_2} = \dot{V}_A\, FA_{N_2} \tag{15–10}$$

where FI_{N_2}, FE_{N_2}, and FA_{N_2} are the fractional concentrations of N_2 in the inspired, expired, and alveolar gas, respectively. By substituting for $\dot{V}_I$ and replacing FI_{N_2} with $(1 - FI_{O_2})$ and FA_{N_2} with $(1 - FA_{O_2} - FA_{CO_2})$, the following equation can be written for R:

$$R = FA_{CO_2}\,(1 - FI_{O_2}) \,/\, (FI_{O_2} - FI_{O_2}\, FA_{CO_2} - FA_{O_2}) \tag{15–11}$$

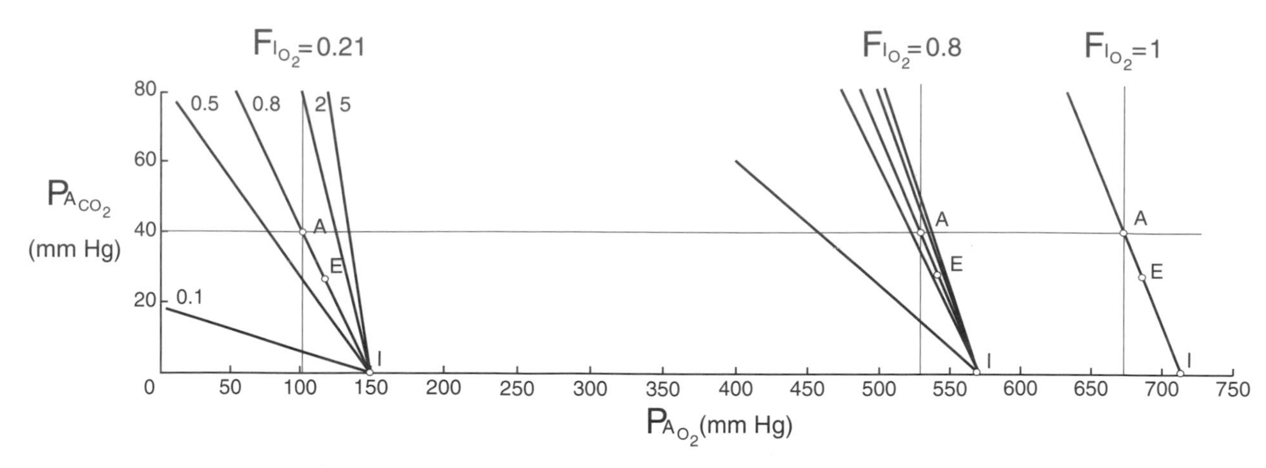

FIGURE 15–2. Graphic solution of the alveolar gas equation after reaching the steady state in three different inspired O_2 concentrations at sea level (F_{IO_2}): room air ($F_{IO_2} = 0.21$), 80% O_2, and 100% O_2. When N_2 is present in the inspired gas, the relationship between P_{CO_2} and P_{O_2} (P_{AO_2}) is defined by a family of isopleths, each representing a different respiratory exchange ratio (R). The points representing the compositions of the alveolar (A), mixed-expired (E), and inspired (I) gases must lie on the same R line. The ratio of the distances AE/AI is equivalent to the dead space–to–tidal volume ratio (V_D/V_T in Equation 15–3). As the F_{IO_2} increases, the isopleths become steeper and come closer together, because the disappearance of N_2 makes it impossible for the CO_2-O_2 exchange to remain uneven. When the inspired gas is 100% O_2, the exchange of O_2 and CO_2 must be isovolumic, because any exchange-related change in volume will be compensated by an inflow or outflow of 100% O_2. Therefore, there is a single R line of slope −1.

From this, F_{AO_2} can then be derived as:

$$F_{AO_2} = F_{IO_2} - F_{ACO_2} / R + F_{ACO_2}\, F_{IO_2}\, [(1-R)/R] \quad (15\text{–}12)$$

or, by multiplying both sides of the equation by $(P_B - P_{H_2O})$:

$$P_{AO_2} = F_{IO_2}(P_B - P_{H_2O}) - P_{ACO_2}/R + P_{ACO_2}\, F_{IO_2}\,[(1-R)/R] \quad (15\text{–}13)$$

P_{AO_2} is also the highest or "ideal" end-capillary P_{O_2} ($P_{c'O_2}$) that could be expected if gas exchange were homogeneous and alveolar and capillary P_{O_2} reached equilibrium throughout the lung. The common formulation of the alveolar gas equation shown in Equation 15–13 defines the value of P_{AO_2} in relationship to both the P_{O_2} of the gas entering the alveoli and the decline in alveolar O_2 volume as this gas diffuses into the capillary blood. The P_{O_2} of the inspired gas is determined by the F_{IO_2} and the total pressure of dry gas ($P_B - P_{H_2O}$). The quantitative effect of O_2 diffusion on the alveolar P_{O_2} is, in turn, inferred from the P_{ACO_2} which is divided by R to acknowledge that CO_2 and O_2 are not exchanged evenly. The last element of the equation, which is small and often omitted for simplicity, provides an additional correction to account for the gas that may enter or exit the alveoli to keep total gas pressure constant when the volume of CO_2 eliminated does not equal the volume of O_2 taken up by the blood. This correction assumes that the displaced gas has the same composition as the inspired gas, ignoring the fact that there is considerable contamination by alveolar gas contained in the anatomic dead space. (Although appropriate mathematic and graphic strategies to deal with this complication have been published,[26] their details are beyond the scope of the present review.) Inherent in these discussions is the notion that, ventilation being a cyclic process, the values of P_{AO_2} and P_{ACO_2} must fluctuate during the respiratory cycle. However, calculations based on several model representations indicate that the fluctuation is small, not usually exceeding 5 mm Hg for the partial tensions of either gas.[27]

Equations 15–12 and 15–13 illustrate a basic underpinning of the ventilation process: the alveolar concentrations or partial pressures of CO_2 and O_2 are linked to each other and to R in such a way that, when two of these variables are specified, only one value can exist for the third one. This notion is most evident in a graphic format (Figure 15–2). When P_{ACO_2} is plotted against P_{AO_2}, a family of lines or *isopleths* can be drawn for a given F_{IO_2}, each isopleth representing a different R. The coordinates defining the P_{CO_2}-P_{O_2} combinations found in the alveolar, mixed-expired, and inspired gas must fall on the same R line. The principles contained in the alveolar gas equation also can be enunciated by saying that P_{AO_2} is directly related to the rate at which the alveolar gas is renewed with inspired gas (defined by $\dot{V}_A$) and reciprocally related to the rate at which O_2 is removed from the alveoli by the blood ($\dot{V}_{O_2}$). P_{AO_2} is influenced also by the rate at which CO_2 is returned to the alveolar space ($\dot{V}_{CO_2}$) through the effect that this variable has on P_{ACO_2}. Such principles apply both to a single alveolar unit and to the lung as a whole. When the whole lung is considered in the steady state, $\dot{V}_{CO_2}$ and $\dot{V}_{O_2}$ represent both the ventilation-weighted average of all the alveoli and the CO_2 consumption and O_2 production of the body. When a single alveolus is examined, however, $\dot{V}_{CO_2}$ and $\dot{V}_{O_2}$ reflect primarily the $\dot{V}_A/\dot{Q}$ ratio of that alveolus. This concept is particularly important when alveolar or regional $\dot{V}_A/\dot{Q}$

ratios become more heterogeneous in the presence of lung disease.

Hypoventilation and Hyperventilation

Decreases (hypoventilation) and increases (hyperventilation) in alveolar ventilation resulting in blood gas abnormalities are encountered commonly in clinical practice, often coexisting with other anomalies of pulmonary gas exchange. Hypoventilation is seen in three types of circumstances: decreased neural output, impaired conduction, and insufficient muscle strength. Neural output to the respiratory muscles may be decreased as a consequence of congenital or acquired abnormalities of the respiratory neuronal network in the medulla (eg, central nervous system malformations, Ondine's curse, or head trauma) or intoxication by substances that depress the respiratory drive (eg, opioids). Impaired conduction may be present when the translation of the neural into mechanical breaths is prevented by dysfunction of the spinal respiratory motoneurons or their nerve fibers (eg, polyneuritis) or by anomalies of the neuromuscular junctions (eg, myasthenia gravis). Finally, muscle strength may be insufficient due to intrinsic abnormalities of the respiratory muscles themselves (eg, inherited myopathy) or, more commonly, muscle fatigue occurring when alterations of the mechanical function of the lungs or chest wall cannot be compensated by increasing respiratory muscle activity. Hyperventilation usually develops as a response to activation of the respiratory drive by hypoxemia (high altitude or intrapulmonary shunting) or metabolic acidosis, increased mechanoreceptor inputs (pulmonary edema or fibrosis), supratentorial influences (eg, agitation), or direct irritation by intracranial injuries (cerebral edema or inflammation).

Hypoventilation causes an increase in PA_{CO_2} and a decrease in PA_{O_2}, which, once the steady state is reached, are both predictable from the alveolar gas equation (Equation 15–13). Because ventilation anomalies interfere only with the composition of the alveolar gas, the alveolar-arterial (A-a) P_{O_2} or P_{CO_2} gradient is preserved—a distinctive characteristic of these anomalies. In the absence of associated diffusion-related defects or right-to-left shunts, end-capillary P_{CO_2} and P_{O_2} remain close to PA_{CO_2} and PA_{O_2}, respectively. The severity of the hypercapnia often is limited by the individual's ability to tolerate the associated arterial hypoxemia. This limitation is removed by administration of supplemental O_2, allowing the Pa_{CO_2} to increase further—a finding that often is interpreted as iatrogenic suppression of the hypoxic or peripheral chemoreceptor drive. The rapidity with which Pa_{CO_2} and PA_{O_2} change is affected greatly by the distribution volumes of each gas. Carbon dioxide is very soluble in fat and is therefore stored in a variety of tissues. Interestingly, hypoventilation-induced hypercapnia develops considerably more slowly than hyperventilation-induced hypocapnia. When $\dot{V}_A$ decreases, the rate of Pa_{CO_2} increase is limited by the whole-body $\dot{V}_{CO_2}$ and does not exceed 3 to 6 mm Hg/min at rest, even in an apneic subject.[28] However, when $\dot{V}_A$ increases, it is $\dot{V}_A$ that determines the speed with which Pa_{CO_2} decreases, and, thus, the decrease can be rapid.[29] Oxygen has a volume of distribution 100-fold smaller than CO_2. As a result, when hypoventilation ensues, $\dot{V}_{O_2}$ is maintained relative to $\dot{V}_{CO_2}$, R decreases, and hypoxemia develops rapidly. For this reason, in a patient breathing room air, monitoring of O_2 levels in blood provides an earlier warning of hypoventilation than does monitoring of CO_2 levels in blood or expired gas.

Diffusion

One of the most striking turns in the development of the prenatal lung is the transformation of the acini from coarse pseudoglandular structures (soon after the airways complete their branching morphogenesis) to a delicate lattice of interalveolar membranes and septa (at the time of birth). This transformation results not only from a process of septation and growth but also from a progressive reduction of the components of the lung interstitium. At completion, the mature alveolar wall contains a single network of capillaries and a sparse matrix arranged to minimize the barrier for gas exchange. Even though the membranes and cytoplasm of two cells (the alveolar epithelial and capillary endothelial cells) always separate the alveolus from the capillary lumen, the distance from air to blood may be as short as 0.2 μm in man and even shorter in small mammals.[30]

Carbon dioxide and oxygen molecules travel this distance and any additional space between their origin in the alveoli and their destination in the bloodstream by a process of diffusion. Unlike convective gas flow, which follows a hydraulic pressure gradient, the movement of diffusing molecules is caused by a difference in the partial pressure of the gas between two points. The progress of the diffusion process is influenced both by the characteristics of the moving gas molecules and by the media through which the molecules move. For example, gases with a small molecular size diffuse more easily than do gases that consist of larger molecules, the rate of diffusion being inversely proportional to the square root of the gas density (Graham's law). Membranes or spaces, such as the plasma and cytoplasm, that have a high water content, speed up the diffusion of water-soluble gases which, like CO_2 (24 times more water soluble than O_2), can enter the liquid phase in greater molecular numbers.

Described in these terms, gas diffusion is undeniably similar to the passage of electricity through a conductor. Physiologists have extended the analogy by describing the diffusion of each gas in terms of a conductance or, in the less precise but more common terminology, *diffusing capacity*. Diffusing capacity defined as the result of dividing the net flow of molecules being transported by the pressure driving the diffusion (the difference of partial pressures of the gas at the origin and destination points). The O_2 diffusing capacity of the whole lung (DL_{O_2}), for instance, is calculated as follows:

$$DL_{O_2} = \dot{V}_{O_2} / (PA_{O_2} - \bar{P}c'_{O_2}) \quad (15\text{–}14)$$

where $\bar{P}c'_{O_2}$ represents the mean capillary P_{O_2}. This representation implies that there is a direct proportionality between gas flow and the pressure driving it—an assumption that has been borne out experimentally under some conditions.

Oxygen Diffusion

Because O_2 is transported bound to hemoglobin, O_2 molecules must diffuse not only across the alveolar gas, the alveolar epithelium, the interstitial matrix, and the capillary endothelium, but also across a layer of plasma and the erythrocyte's membrane and cytoplasm. This trajectory involves transitions through markedly different media and ends in a chemical reaction (binding to hemoglobin) that, in itself, influences the pressure difference that drives the diffusion process. Thus, the O_2 diffusing capacity of the lung (DL_{O_2}) may describe well the relationship between the involved variables, but it lacks ultimate physical representation. Furthermore, because of the high diffusiveness of O_2 (the P_{O_2} of the capillary blood and alveolar gas equilibrates almost completely in the passage through the alveolar capillary), the difference between PA_{O_2} and $\bar{P}c'_{O_2}$ is very small (it is the average or $\bar{P}c'_{O_2}$ that counts, not the final capillary P_{O_2}). Consequently, even modest errors in the calculation of $\bar{P}c'_{O_2}$ produce a large error in DL_{O_2}. The error is compounded further by the fact that $\bar{P}c'_{O_2}$ cannot be measured directly and is difficult to estimate because the P_{O_2} of the capillary blood changes quickly and nonlinearly relative to time or distance as blood travels through the alveolar wall.

Respiratory physiologists have devised several strategies to circumvent these limitations and assess O_2 diffusion. The most common method is to use CO as a tracer gas. Because of its extremely high affinity for the heme site in the hemoglobin molecule, CO can diffuse into the blood in relatively large amounts without increasing its capillary partial pressure perceptibly. As a result, its diffusion capacity can be simply approximated as $\dot{V}_{CO}/PA_{CO}$, where $\dot{V}_{CO}$ represents the uptake of CO, and PA_{CO} represents the partial pressure of CO in the alveolar gas. All the information needed in the calculations can be obtained by measuring CO concentrations in the inspired and expired gas while the individual takes and holds a single breath from a gas mixture containing CO (single breath method[31,32]) or breathes from a dilute CO mixture until reaching steady state concentrations in the expired gas (steady state method[33]). Because of differences in solubility and diffusiveness in water, DL_{O_2} is greater than CO diffusing capacity by a factor of 1.23.[30] A more direct alternative is to determine DL_{O_2} under conditions in which the P_{O_2} gradient between the alveolar gas and the capillary blood is increased. This can be accomplished either by reducing the FI_{O_2} below atmospheric levels[34] or during exercise (Figure 15–3), both are circumstances that delay and may even prevent the complete equilibration between the P_{O_2} of the capillary blood and alveolar gas.

In a resting individual, the high diffusiveness of O_2 and the steep incline of the hemoglobin dissociation curve at the P_{O_2} levels of the pulmonary venous blood ($\approx$ 40 mm Hg) promote the rapid loading of O_2 into the capillary blood. The Bohr effect facilitates O_2 loading even further by increasing the O_2 saturation of hemoglobin as CO_2 is unloaded, thereby limiting the rise in capillary P_{O_2} and, in the process, raising the diffusion gradient. The common wisdom is that by the time an erythrocyte has traveled a third of its path through the intra-alveolar segment of the capillary, its hemoglobin is already saturated with O_2. This can be interpreted as an indication that the "true capacity" for O_2 diffusion cannot possibly be tested at rest. Consistent with this view is the fact that exercise can cause a several-fold increase in DL_{O_2}. Although the increase may in part be related to parallel capillary recruitment,[35,36] it usually is interpreted as a result of the participation of a larger portion of the capillary in the diffusion process.[30]

It has been known for a long time that anemic individuals have decreased O_2 and CO diffusing capacities.[34] This observation is a reminder of the importance that the kinetics of the incorporation of both gases into the hemoglobin molecule has for their apparent diffusiveness. Roughton and Forster[37] developed this idea into the proposal that because diffusion encompasses two conductive processes in series (one the transfer across the alveolar-capillary membrane and plasma, and the other the passage into the erythrocyte and reaction with hemoglobin), whole lung diffusing capacity could be calculated as the combined conductance of two electrical elements in series. The diffusing capacity of the first element often is represented as DM; the diffusing capacity of the second element is determined by multiplying the volume of blood contained in the capillary bed (Vc) by a coefficient θ, which is the rate at which the pertinent gas becomes bound to one volume unit of blood. For O_2,

$$1/DL_{O_2} = 1/DM_{O_2} + 1/(Vc\ \theta_{O_2}) \quad (15\text{–}15)$$

where the use of O_2 as a suffix indicates that the coefficient in question is specific for that gas. To resolve the equation, θ_{O_2} and DL_{O_2} are determined empirically in vitro and in vivo, respectively.[34] This leaves two variables, which can be isolated by performing measurements of DL_{O_2} and θ_{O_2} at different O_2 concentrations. More than a tool to assess pulmonary function, Equation 15–15 provides a conceptual frame to analyze the physiologic factors that alter O_2 diffusion in the lungs. For example,

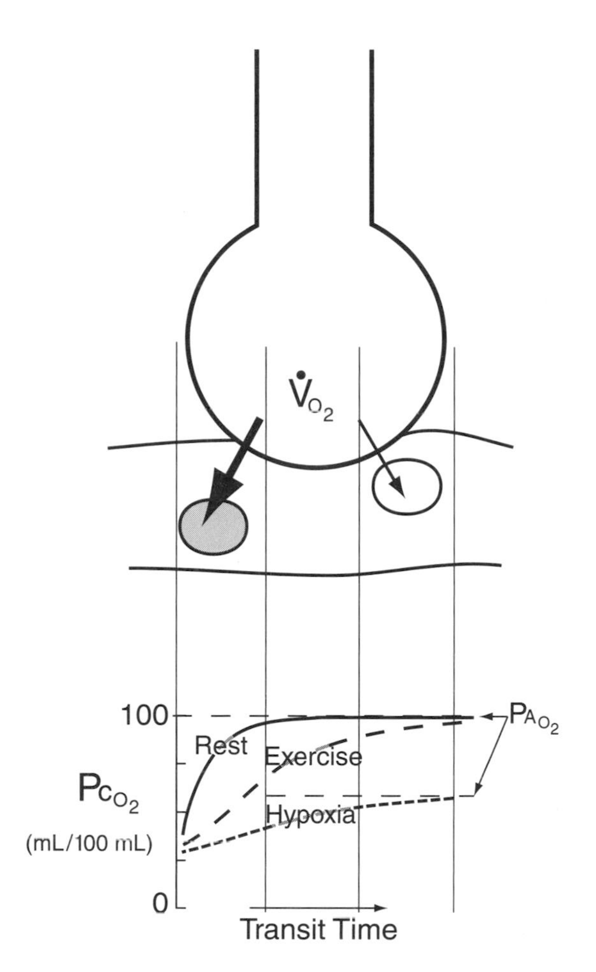

FIGURE 15–3. Schematic representation of alveolar-capillary diffusion of O_2. A single alveolus and capillary arc represented (*top*). Because hemoglobin has a greater capacity for O_2 at low P_{O_2} values and there is a greater difference between $P_{A_{O_2}}$ and $\bar{P}c'_{O_2}$, O_2 uptake ($\dot{V}_{O_2}$) takes place more rapidly in the first portion of the capillary (*thicker arrow*). Under resting conditions, the majority of $\dot{V}_{O_2}$ is believed to occur in the first third of the pulmonary capillary's trajectory (*bottom*). During exercise, however, blood flow through the capillary is faster, and equilibration between capillary P_{O_2} ($\bar{P}c'_{O_2}$) and alveolar P_{O_2} ($P_{A_{O_2}}$) does not occur until the end of the capillary, or is incomplete. During alveolar hypoxia (for instance, at high altitude), loading of O_2 into the hemoglobin molecule occurs entirely on the steep portion of the O_2 hemoglobin dissociation relationship. As a result of the decreased driving pressure for diffusion, the increase in $\bar{P}c'_{O_2}$ is slowed down considerably. The delay in alveolar-capillary P_{O_2} equilibration caused by exercise or alveolar hypoxia may render otherwise inadvertent diffusion defects evident as hypoxemia. In addition, under these conditions, the mean capillary P_{O_2} becomes discernibly lower than $P_{A_{O_2}}$, making the calculation of O_2 diffusion capacity possible (see text).

thickening of the alveolar-capillary membrane by pulmonary edema or fibrosis increases the diffusion distance and reduces the value of $D_{M_{O_2}}$. In contrast, increases in alveolar volume and pulmonary blood flow expand Vc and, under most circumstances, enlarge the alveolar and capillary surface area for diffusion, increasing $D_{M_{O_2}}$ simultaneously.[34,38] Decreases in temperature to the range used in cardiopulmonary bypass, anemia, and macrocytosis reduce θ_{O_2} alone.[39,40]

Carbon Dioxide Diffusion

Because of its high solubility in water, CO_2 is considered to diffuse 20 times faster than O_2 from the pulmonary capillary lumen to the alveolar gas. Although this view has been challenged on the basis of the effective solubility of CO_2 being much lower[41] (one of the reasons being that the actual diffusion of CO_2 in the gas phase of the alveolus is slower than that of O_2), it is reasonable to state that CO_2 diffusion impairments are of little clinical relevance. As blood enters the alveolar capillaries, CO_2 begins to transfer immediately from its dissolved state in the plasma to the alveolar gas. Simultaneously, dissolved CO_2 is replenished with CO_2 molecules liberated from two sources: (1) the carbamino compounds formed with plasma proteins and hemoglobin and (2) plasma bicarbonate ions that move into the erythrocyte (Hamburger's phenomenon), where they undergo combination with protons to form carbonic acid; this is rapidly dehydrated into CO_2—a reaction catalyzed by carbonic anhydrase. As a result of the interactive nature of these chemical reactions and the relatively gradual slope of the CO_2 dissociation curve, CO_2 is downloaded more uniformly along the pathway of the pulmonary capillary than is O_2. Diffusion of CO_2 is delayed further by the Haldane effect, which renders both the release of CO_2 bound to the hemoglobin and the availability of protons for combination with bicarbonate contingent upon hemoglobin oxygenation.

Although under most circumstances $\dot{V}_{CO_2}$ and $\dot{V}_{O_2}$ are similar in magnitude, the partial pressure gradient driving CO_2 diffusion is considerably lower than is the pressure driving O_2 diffusion, a reflection of the relatively steep relationship between CO_2 content and P_{CO_2}. The difference between mixed-venous P_{CO_2} and $P_{A_{CO_2}}$ is usually only 5 to 6 mm Hg. Because end-capillary P_{CO_2} equilibrates with $P_{A_{CO_2}}$, the effective driving pressure for CO_2 diffusion is small, and, therefore, the diffusing capacity for this gas cannot be measured in a practical way.

Abnormalities

It is widely accepted that diffusion abnormalities contribute little to the alterations in pulmonary gas exchange observed in adults at rest and even less in those in children with lung disease. It is less certain whether hidden diffusion defects may be made apparent by exercise, fever, or alveolar hypoxemia, especially in the newborn or premature infant whose pulmonary blood flow is relatively high. Regardless of these considerations, $D_{L_{O_2}}$ measurements are used frequently as a clinical tool in the evaluation of the progression of respiratory illness, particularly if it involves the interstitium of the lung, as in the case of those resulting in pulmonary fibrosis. However, the interpretation of the results is fraught with ambiguities caused by a large number of factors unrelated to the structure of the alveolar-capillary membrane. One area in which the potential usefulness of DL_{O_2} determinations has not been explored sufficiently is the appraisal of changes of capillary surface area.[42] Diffusion capacity measurements (O_2 or CO) correlate well with this surface area and may therefore provide a reasonable estimate of how diseases of the pulmonary vasculature or the lung parenchyma affect capillary development.[43]

Perfusion

Ventilation and diffusion define in great part the conditions for the transfer of CO_2 and O_2 between the atmosphere and the blood, and, hence, they establish the potential for $\dot{V}_{CO_2}$ and $\dot{V}_{O_2}$. Whether this potential can be reached, however, depends critically on blood flow. Compared to other viscera, the lungs have a highly specialized vascular supply. Not only does the pulmonary vascular network accommodate the entirety of the cardiac output, but it does so in vessels that are exposed to constantly changing stresses and strains during breathing. After the adaptations that take place in the perinatal period are complete, pulmonary vessels offer considerably less resistance to the passage of blood than do systemic vessels. However, the tone of their smooth muscle is sensitive to changes in the local pH, P_{CO_2}, and P_{O_2}, a feature that allows a fine regional optimization of the $\dot{V}_A/\dot{Q}$ ratios.

The equations that define the relationship between gas elimination or uptake by the entire lung circulation or by a single alveolar-capillary unit are contained in the Fick principle, which is the mathematic formulation of a simple mass balance between an organ's inflow and outflow:

$$\dot{V}_{CO_2} = \dot{Q}\,(C\bar{v}_{CO_2} - Ca_{CO_2}) \qquad (15\text{–}16)$$

and

$$\dot{V}_{O_2} = \dot{Q}\,(Ca_{O_2} - C\bar{v}_{O_2}) \qquad (15\text{–}17)$$

where the abbreviations Ca and $C\bar{v}$ represent the content or total volume of CO_2 or O_2 present in a volume unit of arterial or mixed-venous blood (both dissolved and bound to hemoglobin or other proteins). For the whole lung, $\dot{V}_{CO_2}$, $\dot{V}_{O_2}$, and $\dot{Q}$ are determined by the body's metabolic activity and the reflex circulatory and respiratory adjustments that facilitate the fulfillment of this activity. Arterial and mixed-venous contents are interdependent variables whose values are influenced by clinical changes or therapeutic manipulations that alter a patient's metabolic rate and cardiac output. For a single alveolar-capillary unit, venous content is presumably the same as for all other units, and it therefore can be considered independent of that particular unit's performance as a gas exchanger. Arterial or, more appropriately, end-capillary content (Ca_{CO_2} or Ca_{O_2}) is a function of the equilibration of partial pressures of the pertinent gas across the alveolar-capillary membrane. Barring severe diffusion abnormalities, it is determined by the partial pressures in the alveolar gas (PA_{CO_2} or PA_{O_2}). Consequently, for most alveolar-capillary units, $\dot{Q}$ is the main determinant of $\dot{V}_{CO_2}$ or $\dot{V}_{O_2}$.

Venous Admixture and Shunt

The terms "venous admixture" and "shunt" are used to describe a situation in which a portion of the blood that reaches the arterial side of the circulation does not reach P_{O_2} equilibrium with the alveolar gas. In a strict sense, venous admixture is an index or calculated value computed as the amount of mixed-venous blood that would have to be added to ideal end-capillary blood (usually assumed to have a P_{O_2} identical to the PA_{O_2}) to reproduce the observed Pa_{O_2}. Defined in such terms, venous admixture can be caused by three general processes: (1) shunt, whereby blood bypasses exchange with the alveolar gas in abnormal vascular pathways outside the lung or in consolidated, collapsed, or otherwise unventilated alveoli; (2) diffusion impairment, which prevents the pulmonary capillary blood from attaining equilibrium with the alveolar gas; and (3) ventilation-perfusion inequality, as discussed below. All three of these processes contribute to create a difference between the calculated PA_{O_2} (or $\bar{P}c'_{O_2}$) and Pa_{O_2}, and, therefore, they often are loosely lumped together under the term shunt. However, there is at least one important feature that distinguishes them: the apparent amount of venous admixture caused by diffusion abnormalities or ventilation-perfusion inequality decreases as the FI_{O_2} is increased. In contrast, true shunt is unaltered by FI_{O_2}, unless the administration of supplemental O_2 has an indirect effect on the distribution of blood flow in the lungs. This may happen when O_2-induced pulmonary vasodilation increases pulmonary blood flow at the expense of a cardiac right-to-left shunt (reducing the shunt), or when O_2-induced release of hypoxic vasoconstriction diverts blood flow from ventilated to nonventilated areas of the lung (increasing the shunt).

There are obvious similarities between the concepts of venous admixture and dead space. Both involve simplifying assumptions to divide blood or gas flow into absolute compartments, generating, in the process, a quantitative appraisal of the efficiency of oxygenation or CO_2 removal. In dead space, one compartment is composed of alveolar gas that undergoes ideal exchange (by convention for CO_2) with the capillary blood ($\dot{V}_A$, see Equation 15–1); the other compartment ($\dot{V}_D$) does not participate in gas exchange at all. In venous admixture, one compartment is composed of capillary blood that undergoes ideal gas exchange (by convention for O_2) with the alveolar gas ($\dot{Q}p$); the other compartment ($\dot{Q}s$) does not participate in gas exchange at all. Thus, blood exiting the first compartment has an O_2 content that would be predicted from the $\bar{P}c'_{O_2}$ and the hemoglobin concentration; blood exiting the second compartment has the same O_2 content as the mixed-venous blood. Knowing that the total systemic arterial or venous blood flow, ($\dot{Q}t$) is equivalent to $\dot{Q}p + \dot{Q}s$, the classic shunt equation can be derived easily:

$$\dot{Q}s/\dot{Q}t = (Cc'_{O_2} - Ca_{O_2}) / (Cc'_{O_2} - C\bar{v}_{O_2}) \qquad (15\text{–}18)$$

where Cc'_{O_2} represents the end-capillary oxygen content, which usually is estimated from the PA_{O_2} and the O_2-hemoglobin dissociation relationship. By rearranging the terms, it is possible to define Ca_{O_2} as a function of the ratio $\dot{Q}s/\dot{Q}t$:

$$Ca_{O_2} = Cc'_{O_2}\ (1 - \dot{Q}s/\dot{Q}t) + Cv_{O_2}\ (\dot{Q}s/\dot{Q}t) \qquad (15\text{–}19)$$

This formulation illustrates well the apportionment of Ca_{O_2} into its two components. It also makes evident the importance of $C\bar{v}_{O_2}$ (and, by extension, cardiac output, hemoglobin concentration, and Ca_{O_2} itself) in determining arterial oxygenation in the presence of venous admixture.

To carry further the conceptual similarities between venous admixture and dead space, a distinction must be made between true or anatomic shunt and venous admixture, as defined above. The anatomic shunt is the flow of venous blood that mixes with the pulmonary capillary blood. There are several forms of anatomic shunt. In healthy humans a small proportion (usually less than 3%) of the systemic venous return bypasses the alveolar circulation through bronchial vessels that drain into the pulmonary veins or by small coronary veins (known as thebesian veins) that drain directly into the left ventricle.[44] This is sometimes referred to as the physiological shunt. In the presence of lung disease, venous blood may enter the arterial side of the circulation through nonventilated alveoli, which behave as an often variable but true anatomic shunt. Finally, patients with congenital heart anomalies can develop increased venous admixture by a variety of mechanisms. These include right ventricular inflow or outflow obstructions, where the venous blood is shunted into the left side of the heart through an atrial or ventricular septal defect; lesions where venous and pulmonary capillary blood mix in a common heart chamber; and D-transposition of the great vessels, in which pulmonary and systemic circulations are separate and venous and arterial blood mix only through a balanced atrial, ventricular, or ductal bidirectional shunt.

As mentioned above, unlike diffusion defects and $\dot{V}_A/\dot{Q}$ inequality, the arterial hypoxemia observed in the presence of a large anatomic right-to-left shunt is relatively insensitive to O_2 supplementation.[45] This fact has served as the basis for the common misconception that a substantial increase in Pa_{O_2} during 100% O_2 breathing rules out a cyanotic anomaly of the heart. Assuming that the shunt is not affected by O_2 breathing, an increase in the FI_{O_2} can only raise Ca_{O_2} by increasing Cc'_{O_2} (Figure 15–4). If the hemoglobin in the pulmonary end-capillary blood is already fully saturated with O_2, the increase of Cc'_{O_2} involves exclusively the dissolved O_2 fraction of Cc'_{O_2}. As arterial blood circulates through the body, the increase in Ca_{O_2} brings about a similar increase in $C\bar{v}_{O_2}$, which contributes to establish a new equilibrium. The relatively small additional volume of O_2 (≈ 1.5 mL/100 mL) that can be dissolved in capillary blood limits the increase in Ca_{O_2}. How much the Pa_{O_2} rises in response to this increase in Ca_{O_2} depends on the hemoglobin dissociation curve. If the initial O_2 saturation is high (relatively small shunt), the Ca_{O_2} increase will fully saturate the hemoglobin and may drive Pa_{O_2} to a high level. On the other hand, if the initial O_2 saturation is low (relatively large shunt), as is frequently the case for infants with cyanotic congenital heart defects, the Pa_{O_2} is not likely to rise much despite the increase in Ca_{O_2}. However, to avoid costly mistakes, clinicians must understand that Pa_{O_2} values well above 100 mm Hg are not uncommon in infants with certain forms of cyanotic heart disease while breathing supplemental O_2,[46] especially when the initial net right-to-left shunt is not large or when the shunt decreases as a result of O_2 administration. Two distinctive characteristics of the newborn contribute to this finding. One is the presence of high concentrations of fetal hemoglobin, which remains well saturated with O_2 even at low P_{O_2} values. The other is the polycythemia typical of the newborn period, which results in a larger than usual increase in Cc'_{O_2} and, by extension, in Ca_{O_2}.

Ventilation-Perfusion Inequality

The recognition that regional differences in $\dot{V}_A/\dot{Q}$ relationships are the main reason for both the hypoxemia and hypercapnia observed in subjects with lung disease appears for the first time in the writings of Krogh and Lindhard in 1917.[47] However, the understanding and quantification of the mechanisms underlying $\dot{V}_A/\dot{Q}$ inequality or "mismatch" is relatively recent.[48,49]

Fundamental to the understanding of $\dot{V}_A/\dot{Q}$ inequality is the idea that gas exchange in each of the alveolar units that form the lung really has not one, but two final products: the compositions of the alveolar gas and the end-capillary blood. Even though there is P_{CO_2} and P_{O_2} equilibration between alveolar gas and blood, their respective CO_2 and O_2 contents differ in a manner that depends on the relationships between $\dot{V}_A$ and $\dot{Q}$. Alveolar units with a high $\dot{V}_A/\dot{Q}$, for instance, have a low PA_{CO_2} (see Equation 15–9). Because the relationship between CO_2 content and P_{CO_2} is relatively steep (although not linear), these units are capable of removing large amounts of CO_2 from the capillary blood. The same units also have an increased P_{O_2}, as predicted by the alveolar gas equation (see Equation 15–13), but their ability to take up O_2 is limited because the O_2 hemoglobin dissociation curve is

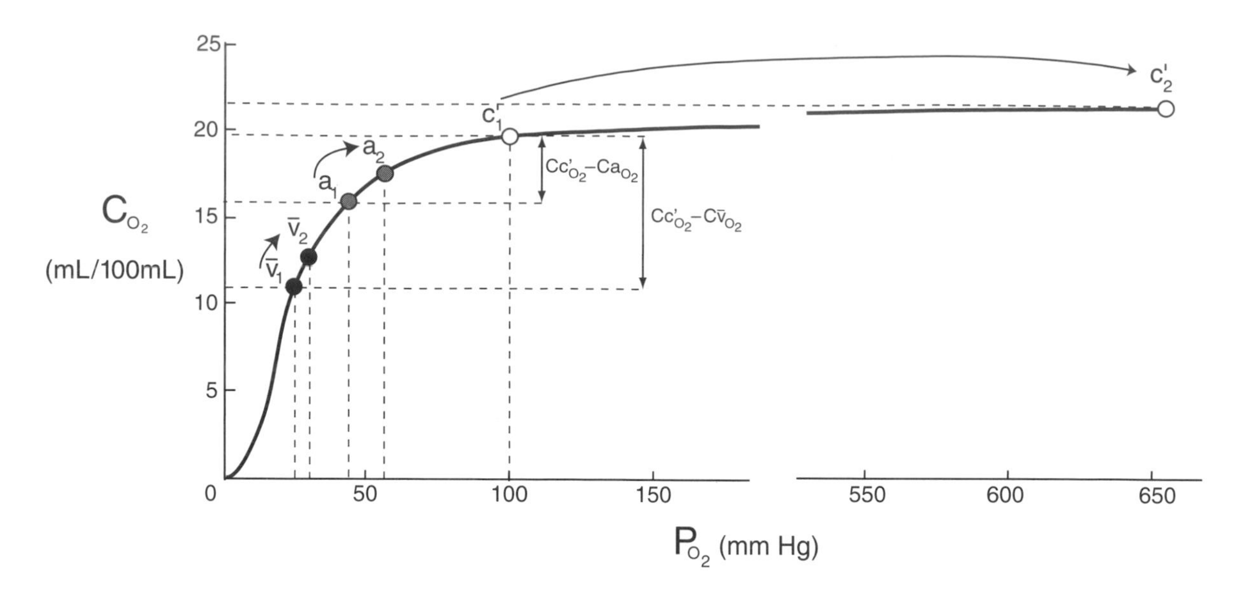

FIGURE 15–4. Schematic representation of the effects of breathing 100% O_2 on the end-capillary (c'), arterial (a), and mixed venous (v) oxygen content (C_{O_2}) in the presence of an ≈ 45% anatomic shunt. If the shunt ratio $[(Cc'_{O_2}-Ca_{O_2}) / (Cc'_{O_2}-C\bar{v}_{O_2})]$ remains constant, the increase in dissolved O_2 fraction at the pulmonary capillaries (c'_1 to c'_2) must be matched by a similar increase in both arterial (a_1 to a_2) and mixed-venous ($\bar{v}_1$ to $\bar{v}_2$) C_{O_2}. If the shunt is large (as in this case), the increase in arterial P_{O_2} is limited by the small volume of additional O_2 that can be accommodated in solution and by the steep slope of the C_{O_2}-P_{O_2} relationship. However, when the shunt is smaller or the venous and arterial points are higher in the curve (eg, in the presence of fetal hemoglobin or when the O_2 hemoglobin dissociation curve is shifted to the left), the small increase in end-capillary C_{O_2} may drive the arterial point over to the flat portion of the C_{O_2}-P_{O_2} relationship. Contrary to widespread belief, arterial P_{O_2} values greater than 100 mm Hg may therefore be reached in infants with cyanotic heart disease during hyperoxic breathing. Hemoglobin concentration was assumed to be 15 g/100 mL.

almost flat at normal PA_{O_2} levels, and, thus, capillary O_2 content can increase only by raising the volume of dissolved O_2. Conversely, alveolar units with a low $\dot{V}_A/\dot{Q}$ cannot increase their PA_{CO_2} above the mixed-venous P_{CO_2} (which is only a few millimeters of mercury above the PA_{CO_2}). Accordingly, they remove only a small volume of CO_2 from the capillary blood. However, in the presence of $\dot{V}_A/\dot{Q}$ inequality, the PA_{O_2} of low $\dot{V}_A/\dot{Q}$ units decreases to a range where the O_2 hemoglobin dissociation curve is steep, thereby generating a substantial venous admixture. (Note that this is in distinction to global hypoventilation in which the decrease in PA_{O_2} is proportional to the increase in PA_{CO_2}, producing no venous admixture.)

The preceding discussion can be summarized by saying that alveolar units with a high $\dot{V}_A/\dot{Q}$ have an increased R value (high $\dot{V}_{CO_2}$ and low $\dot{V}_{O_2}$), whereas alveolar units with a low $\dot{V}_A/\dot{Q}$ have a decreased R value (low $\dot{V}_{CO_2}$ and higher $\dot{V}_{O_2}$). The overall $\dot{V}_{CO_2}$ and $\dot{V}_{O_2}$ (and hence, R) are determined by the fuels being consumed by the body. The aggregate R of all the alveolar-capillary units must be equal to the overall R. Thus, the $\dot{V}_A$ and $\dot{Q}$ of individual units also depend on metabolism. Furthermore, the distribution of these units must be such that all the CO_2 produced and all the O_2 consumed by the body are accommodated. Because there are many ways in which this can happen, physiologists have derived compartmental models for gas exchange whereby a specific distribution of $\dot{V}_A$ and $\dot{Q}$ is presumed for each compartment. For some purposes, it is quite sufficient to consider just two compartments. For other purposes, more complex multicompartment models have been considered.[50,51] Although cumbersome for clinical use, standardized analyses of the arterial and expired concentrations of inert gases in conjunction with the mathematic formulations of these models can provide a helpful quantitative assessment of the continuous distribution of $\dot{V}_A/\dot{Q}$ ratios in normal and diseased lungs.[52]

Calculation of Ventilation-Perfusion Ratios

If we assume that all alveolar units are supplied with the same alveolar gas and venous blood and that end-capillary blood equilibrates perfectly with alveolar gas, we can write the following equality (from Equations 15–9 and 15–16):

$$\dot{V}_{CO_2} = (\dot{V}_A\ PA_{CO_2}) / (P_B - P_{H_2O}) = \dot{Q}\ (C\bar{v}_{CO_2} - Cc'_{CO_2}) \quad (15\text{–}20)$$

Because here the equality applies to a single alveolar unit, the last term of the equation differs from that in Equation 15–16 in that the arterial CO_2 content (Ca_{CO_2}) is replaced by the end-capillary CO_2 content (Cc'_{CO_2}). By rearranging terms, we can obtain an expression for the $\dot{V}_A/\dot{Q}$ ratio for CO_2:

$$\dot{V}_A/\dot{Q} = (P_B - P_{H_2O})\ (C\bar{v}_{CO_2} - Cc'_{CO_2}) / PA_{CO_2} \quad (15\text{–}21)$$

A similar equation can be written for O_2:

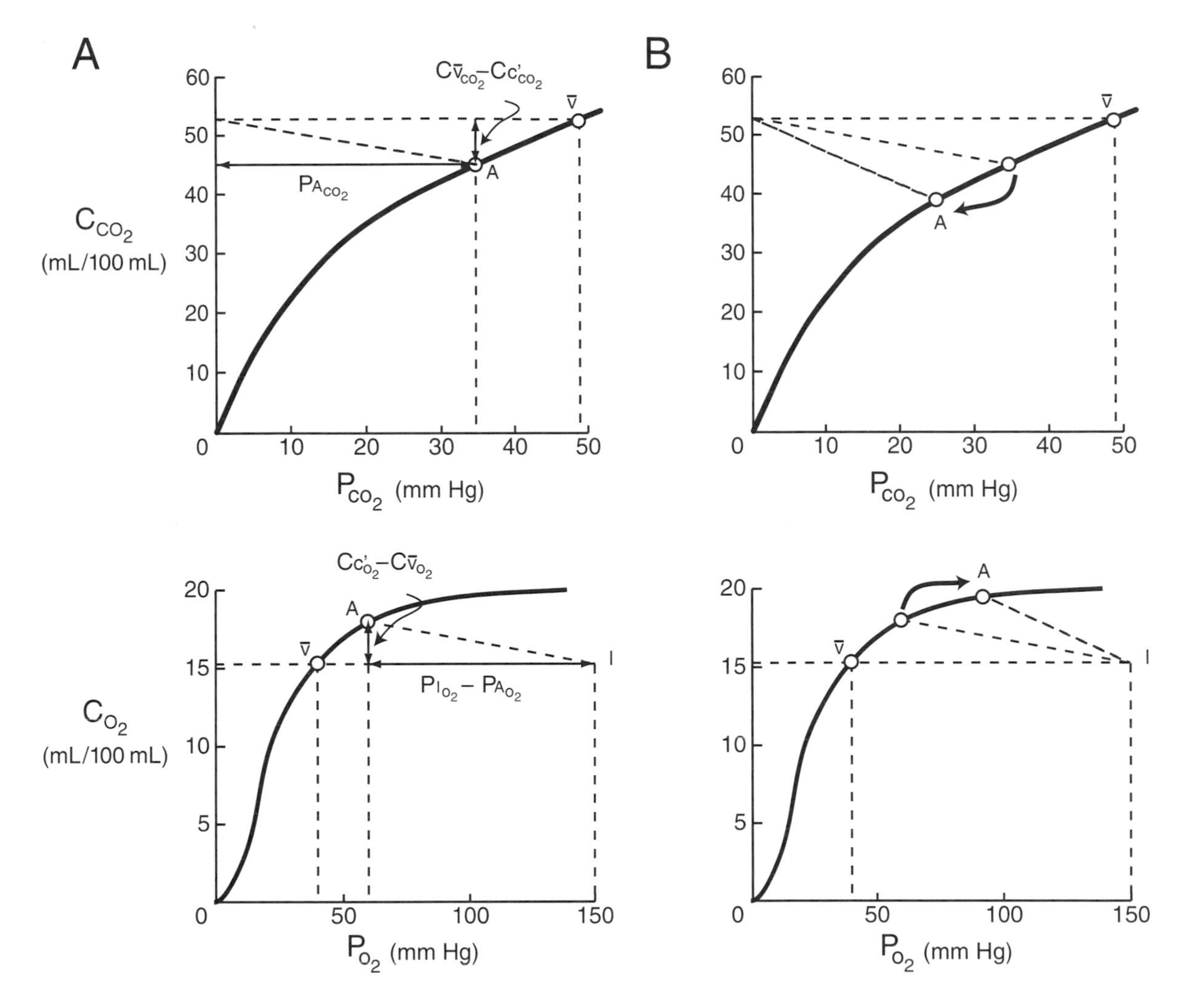

FIGURE 15–5. Graphic demonstration of the effect of ventilation-perfusion ($\dot{V}_A/\dot{Q}$) inequality on CO_2-O_2 exchange in a single alveolar unit during air breathing at sea level. *A*, For each gas, the position of the alveolar (A) point on the content (C_{CO_2} or C_{O_2})-P_{CO_2} or P_{O_2} relationship must satisfy the $\dot{V}_A/\dot{Q}$ equation (Equation 15–21). Consequently, the quotients $(C\bar{v}_{CO_2}-Cc'_{CO_2})$ / PA_{CO_2} and $(Cc'_{O_2}-C\bar{v}_{O_2})$ / $(PI_{O_2}-PA_{O_2})$ must equal the product of $(\dot{V}_A/\dot{Q})$ by the constant $(P_B-P_{H_2O})$. These ratios are equivalent to the slope of the discontinuous lines connecting the alveolar or end-capillary point (A,c') to the C_{CO_2} axis at the mixed venous point ($\bar{v}$) for CO_2 and the same point to the intersection of the mixed-venous C_{O_2} and the inspiratory P_{O_2} (I) for O_2 (see West[51]). *B*, An increase in $\dot{V}_A$ relative to $\dot{Q}$ augments this slope, causing the alveolar points to move away from the mixed-venous points along the corresponding curve (*arrows*). However, the relative flat incline of the C_{O_2}-P_{O_2} curve limits the increase in C_{O_2}. This is why increases in ventilation can decrease arterial P_{CO_2} but cannot compensate the hypoxemia of patients with $\dot{V}_A/\dot{Q}$ mismatch.

$$\dot{V}_A/\dot{Q} = (P_B - P_{H_2O})\,(Cc'_{O_2} - C\bar{v}_{CO_2})\,/\,(PI_{O_2} - PA_{O_2}) \qquad (15–22)$$

by combining Equations 15–21 and 15–22, the following can be derived:

$$\dot{V}_A/\dot{Q} = R\,(P_B - P_{H_2O})\,(Cc'_{O_2} - C\bar{v}_{CO_2})\,/\,PA_{CO_2} \qquad (15–23)$$

Equations 15–21 and 15–22 can be resolved graphically.[53] The result illustrates well the effect of $\dot{V}_A/\dot{Q}$ on CO_2 and O_2 exchange by a single alveolar unit (Figure 15–5). Provided that the mixed-venous blood composition does not change, an increase in $\dot{V}_A$ relative to $\dot{Q}$ causes the point that defines end-capillary CO_2 content and PA_{CO_2} to slide down along the CO_2 dissociation curve. At the same time, the point that defines end-capillary O_2 content and PA_{O_2} is forced to slide up along the O_2 dissociation curve. As long as the PA_{O_2} is sufficiently high for the O_2 hemoglobin dissociation curve to be in its flat portion, the result is, once again, a greater decrease in Cc'_{CO_2} than in Cc'_{O_2}. A decrease in $\dot{V}_A$ relative to $\dot{Q}$ will have the opposite effect. However, Cc'_{O_2} decreases more than Cc'_{CO_2}, because the O_2-hemoglobin dissociation curve is steeper at lower PA_{O_2} values. An increase in the FI_{O_2} will augment PI_{O_2} and move the $Cc'_{O_2} = PA_{O_2}$ point up in the O_2 dissociation curve.

Neither these equations nor their graphic solution take into account the interactions between CO_2 and O_2 transport by hemoglobin (the Bohr and Haldane effects). The

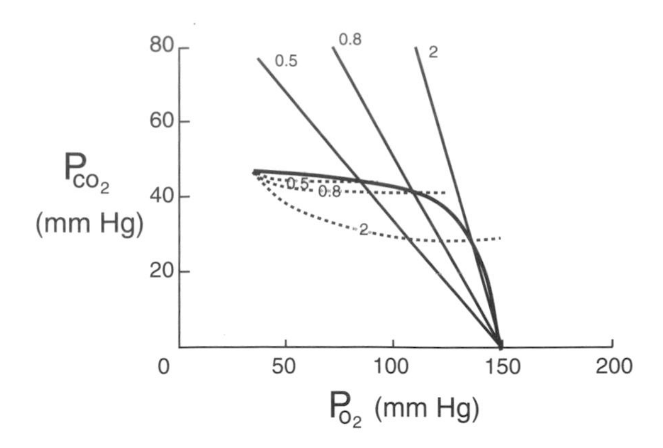

FIGURE 15–6. Diagram of P_{CO_2}-P_{O_2} demonstrating the effect of changes in $\dot{V}_A/\dot{Q}$ ratio on the relationship between alveolar P_{CO_2} and P_{O_2} for a single alveolar unit. The curve is anchored by the mixed-venous ($\bar{v}$) and inspiratory points (shown here for air at sea level). The alveolar and blood R isopleths are superimposed (see Figure 15–2 and text). In the steady state, the R values for alveolar gas and blood must be the same, and, therefore, the lines converge on the same point of the $\dot{V}_A/\dot{Q}$ curve.

computations involved in such an exercise are complex and require an iterative approach.[53] To simplify the analysis, it has become customary to represent all the possible $\dot{V}_A/\dot{Q}$ ratios on a relationship between P_{CO_2} and P_{O_2}.[24,54] The resultant curve (Figure 15–6) spans the two extremes of $\dot{V}_A/\dot{Q}$: 0 at the mixed-venous point, where the alveolar unit behaves as a pure shunt; and ∞ at the inspiratory point, where the alveolar unit behaves as a pure dead space. Between these two points, which are fixed by factors outside the lung, the curve describes a continuous spectrum of PA_{CO_2}-PA_{O_2} values, each defined by a $\dot{V}_A/\dot{Q}$ ratio and the R values for alveolar gas and blood (in a steady state, blood and alveolar gas must have the same R value). There is a sharp decrease in PA_{O_2} as the $\dot{V}_A/\dot{Q}$ ratio diminishes towards the mixed-venous point, but PA_{CO_2} changes little. Conversely, PA_{CO_2} decreases more than PA_{O_2} increases as the $\dot{V}_A/\dot{Q}$ ratio increases towards the inspiratory point.

Effects on Gas Exchange

Ventilation-perfusion inequality is one of the servitudes imposed by gravity on the lungs of terrestrial animals. It is exacerbated in the standing position, whereby the weight of the blood column alone forces an increase in the perfusion of the lung bases several-fold relative to the lung apexes. Because the presence of air in the airways and alveolar spaces attenuates the gravitational influences on the lung tissue itself, ventilation is less affected by height than perfusion, and, thus, although the bases are still ventilated more than the apexes in absolute terms, the overall $\dot{V}_A/\dot{Q}$ ratio decreases from top to bottom of the lungs. The smaller size of the lungs in infants and children tends to reduce the inequality, rendering the relative distributions of gas and blood flows less dependent on position.[55]

In the absence of intracardiac shunting, the alveolar gas and the arterial blood are the composite products of the gas and end-capillary blood from millions of alveolar units. Accordingly, the P_{O_2} of the mixed-alveolar gas could be calculated as the sum of the products of $\dot{V}_A$ and PA_{O_2} for each unit. The Ca_{O_2} could also be determined from the sum of the products of $\dot{Q}$ and Cc'_{O_2} for each of the same units (the calculations for O_2 have to be made in terms of content not partial pressure). Because the dependent areas of the lungs (the bases in a standing individual) receive a disproportionately large amount of blood flow and have a low $\dot{V}_A/\dot{Q}$ ratio, they tend to drag down the Ca_{O_2} and Pa_{O_2} (the effect on Ca_{CO_2} and Pa_{CO_2} is smaller because the CO_2 dissociation curve has a more linear profile than the O_2 dissociation curve through the range normally encountered in clinical practice). The result is the development of a small gradient between the P_{O_2} of the mixed-alveolar gas and the Pa_{O_2}. Under normal circumstances this gradient does not exceed 4 or 5 mm Hg in both children and young adults. However, considerably greater gradients have been reported in premature newborns, a finding that has been attributed to decreased stability of the immature air spaces and underdevelopment of the collateral ventilation system.[56,57]

The alveolar-arterial P_{O_2} gradient is evident in the relative positions of the arterial and mixed-alveolar points on the P_{O_2}-P_{CO_2} relationship (Figure 15–7). The arterial point is located on the blood R curve but displaced to the left of the ideal alveolar point on the $\dot{V}_A/\dot{Q}$ curve. The mixed-alveolar point is located on the alveolar R line but displaced to the right. The distance between these points is the measure of the alveolar-arterial gradient and the best indication of the efficiency of the lung as a multialveolar gas exchanger.

Inequality of $\dot{V}_A/\dot{Q}$ is the inevitable consequence of airway and parenchymal lung disease. With increased severity and distribution of the inequality, the arterial point becomes displaced further to the left of the ideal alveolar point on the blood R curve (generating a venous admixture), while the mixed-alveolar point is displaced further to the right on the corresponding alveolar R line (creating a dead space effect; see Figure 15–7). The result is the widening of the alveolar-arterial P_{O_2} gradient and the appearance of a noticeable alveolar-arterial P_{CO_2} gradient. Typically, the Pa_{O_2} decreases, often severely, unless the inspired gas is enriched with supplemental O_2. Administration of O_2 is highly effective in ameliorating the hypoxemia induced by $\dot{V}_A/\dot{Q}$ inequality. The mechanism is an increase in the PA_{O_2} in alveolar units with a low $\dot{V}_A/\dot{Q}$. Because of the shape of the O_2 hemoglobin dissociation curve, the PA_{O_2} increase is smaller at low than at high FI_{O_2} levels. As a consequence, the alveolar-arterial P_{O_2} difference tends to increase and then decrease as more O_2 is added to the inspired gas.

Because $\dot{V}_A/\dot{Q}$ inequality also displaces the mixed-alveolar point downward, there is as much an impedi-

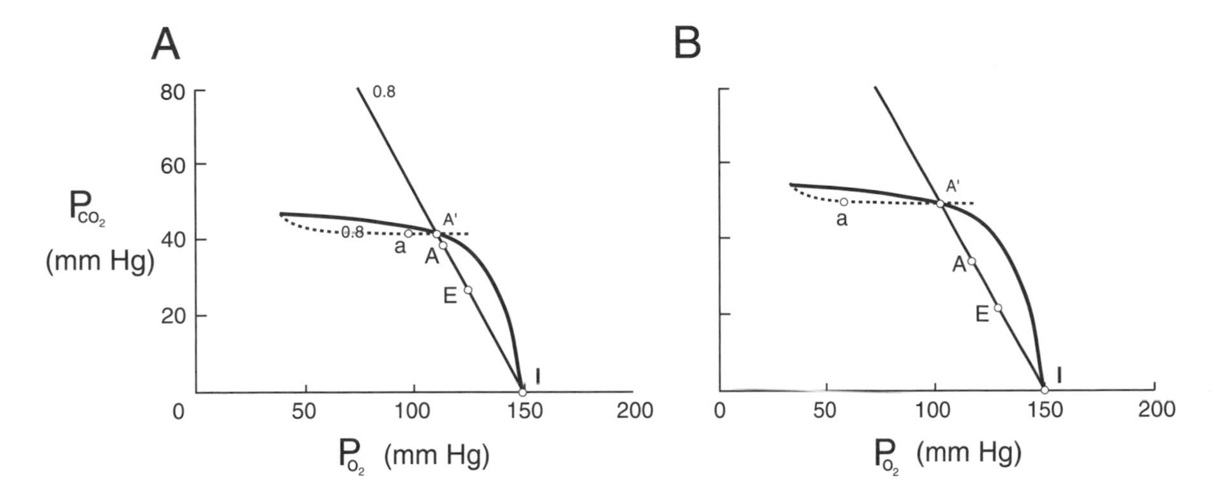

FIGURE 15–7. Diagrams of P_{CO_2}-P_{O_2} demonstrating the effects of $\dot{V}_A/\dot{Q}$ inequality on arterial and alveolar P_{CO_2} and P_{O_2} for the whole lung. *A*, The small degree of $\dot{V}_A/\dot{Q}$ inequality present in the normal lung causes the arterial (a) and alveolar (A) points to become displaced, each along the corresponding blood and alveolar R line (0.8 in the example), away from the ideal alveolar point (A′). The result is a small alveolar-arterial P_{O_2} gradient (there is a smaller P_{CO_2} gradient that is abolished by the normal chemoreceptor response). The mixed-expiratory (E) and inspiratory (I) points are also represented. *B*, When $\dot{V}_A/\dot{Q}$ inequality increases in the presence of disease, the arterial and alveolar points become more widely separated, their exact position being determined by the distribution of $\dot{V}_A/\dot{Q}$ ratios in the lung. The alveolar-arterial P_{O_2} gradient increases, and a P_{CO_2} gradient may develop, raising the arterial and mixed venous P_{CO_2}s.

ment to CO_2 exchange as there is for O_2 exchange. However, the lung is better equipped to deal with the ensuing increase in Pa_{CO_2}. The response to any elevation of the blood CO_2 content is initiated by medullary chemoreceptors, which trigger an immediate increase in ventilation. It is traditionally accepted that if the new $\dot{V}_A$ is sufficient and can be sustained, the Pa_{CO_2} does not increase, even though a substantial portion of the ventilatory effort is wasted as dead space ventilation. On the other hand, if the respiratory muscles are unable to carry the new load, then hypercapneic respiratory failure develops. Contrary to this view, West[49] has proposed that, although hypercapnia is indeed an indication of advanced lung disease, $\dot{V}_A/\dot{Q}$ inequality can increase the Pa_{CO_2} without failure of the respiratory muscles. The reason is the shape of the blood's CO_2 dissociation relationship, which is more hyperbolic than rectilinear. As a result, increases in CO_2 content in very low $\dot{V}_A/\dot{Q}$ areas cannot be compensated completely by higher $\dot{V}_A/\dot{Q}$ areas in a manner similar to that discussed above to explain the hypoxemia of $\dot{V}_A/\dot{Q}$ mismatch. Nevertheless, the Pa_{CO_2} elevation is always less prominent than is the decrease in Pa_{O_2}, simply because the slope of the blood's CO_2 dissociation curve is less steep than that of the O_2 dissociation curve.

Summary

This chapter provides a step-by-step view of the processes involved in pulmonary gas exchange. The processes involved are complex and interactive, yet highly predictable. Understanding how each step can be altered by disease is fundamental to the clinician caring for infants or children with lung illnesses. By recognizing the characteristics of each alteration, it becomes possible not only to recognize the origin of most gas exchange abnormalities, but also to devise more rational therapeutic strategies to treat them. In no place is this more important than in intensive care units, where the correlation between the findings of the physical examination and the blood gas analysis can provide useful insights into the changing nature and course of respiratory illnesses.

References

1. Lister G, Walter TK, Versmold HT, et al. Oxygen delivery in lambs: cardiovascular and hematologic development. Am J Physiol 1979;237:H668–75.
2. Sidi D, Kuipers JRG, Teitel D, et al. Developmental changes in oxygenation and circulatory responses to hypoxemia in lambs. Am J Physiol 1983;245:H674–82.
3. Teitel D, Rudolph AM. Perinatal oxygen delivery and cardiac function. Adv Pediatr 1985;32:321–47.
4. Berger AJ, Mitchell RA, Severinghaus JW. Regulation of respiration. N Engl J Med 1977;297:92–7.
5. Mead J. Control of respiratory frequency. J Appl Physiol 1960;15:325–36.
6. Haddad GG, Lai TL, Mellins RB. Determination of ventilatory pattern in REM sleep in normal infants. J Appl Physiol 1982;53:52–6.
7. Luijendijk SCM, Milic-Emili J. Breathing patterns in anesthetized cats and the concept of minimum respiratory effort. J Appl Physiol 1988;64:31–41.
8. Clark FJ, von Euler C. On the regulation of depth and rate of breathing. J Physiol 1972;222:267–95.
9. Bohr C. Ueber die Lungenathmung. Skand Arch Physiol 1891;2:236–68.

10. Loewy A. Ueber die Bestimmung der Grosse des "Schadlichen Luftraumes" im Thorax und der alveolaren Sauerstoffspannung. Pfluegers Arch. Gesamte Physiol. Menschen Tiere 1894;58:416–27.
11. Rohrer F. Der Strömungswiderstand in den menschlichen Atemwegen und der Einfluss der unregelmässigen Verzweigung des Bronchialsystems auf den Atmungsverlauf in verschiedenen Lungenbezirken. Pfluegers Arch. Gesamte Physiol. Menschen Tiere 1915;162:225–99.
12. Heldt GP, McIlroy MB. Distortion of chest wall and work of diaphragm in preterm infants. J Appl Physiol 1981; 62:164–9.
13. Horsfield K, Cumming G. Morphology of the bronchial tree in man. J Appl Physiol 1968;24:373–83.
14. Weibel RR. Morphometry of the human lung. Berlin: Springer-Verlag, 1963.
15. Fowler WS. Lung function studies. II. The respiratory dead space. Am J Physiol 1948;154:405–16.
16. Folkow B, Pappenheimer JR. Components of the respiratory dead space and their variation with pressure breathing and bronchoactive drugs. J Appl Physiol 1955;8:102–10.
17. Bohn DJ, Miyasaka K, Marchak BE, et al. Ventilation by high-frequency oscillation. J Appl Physiol 1980;48:710–6.
18. Mortola JP. Dysanaptic lung growth: an experimental and allometric approach. J Appl Physiol 1983;54:1236–41.
19. Kerr AA. Dead space ventilation in normal children and children with obstructive airway disease. Thorax 1976; 31:63–9.
20. Shepard RH, Campbell EJM, Martin HB, Enns T. Factors affecting the pulmonary dead space as determined by single breath analysis. J Appl Physiol 1957;11:241–4.
21. Birath G. Respiratory dead space measurements in a model lung and healthy human subjects according to the single breath method. J Appl Physiol 1959;14:517–20.
22. Anthonisen NR, Fleetham JA. Ventilation: total, alveolar, and dead space. In: Farhi LE, Tenney SM, eds. Gas exchange. Bethesda (MD): American Physiological Society, 1987:113–29.
23. Enghoff H. Volumen unefficax. Bemerkungen zur Frage des schadlichen Raumes. Uppsala Läkarefoeren. Förh 1938;44:191–218.
24. Rahn H, Fenn WO. A graphical analysis of the respiratory gas exchange. Washington (DC): American Physiological Society, 1955.
25. Fenn WO, Rahn H, Otis AB. A theoretical study of the composition of the alveolar air at altitude. Am J Physiol 1946;146:637–53.
26. Ross BB, Fahri LE. Dead-space ventilation as a determinant in the ventilation-perfusion concept. J Appl Physiol 1960;15:363–71.
27. Hlastala MP. A model of fluctuating alveolar gas exchange during the respiratory cycle. Respir Physiol 1972;15: 214–32.
28. Ivanov SD, Nunn JF. Methods of elevation of P_{CO_2} for restoration of spontaneous breathing after artificial ventilation of anaesthetised patients. Br J Anaesth 1969; 41:28–37.
29. Ivanov SD, Nunn JF. Influence of duration of hyperventilation on rise time of P_{CO_2} after step reduction of ventilation. Respir Physiol 1968;4:243–9.
30. Weibel ER. The pathway for oxygen. Structure and function in the mammalian respiratory system. Cambridge (MA): Harvard University Press, 1984.
31. Krogh A, Krogh M. Rate of diffusion of CO into the lungs of man. Scand Arch Physiol 1909;23:236–47.
32. Forster RE. The single-breath carbon monoxide transfer test 25 years on: a reappraisal. 1. Physiological considerations. Thorax 1983;38:1–5.
33. Forster RE. Diffusion of gases. In: Fenn WO, Rahn H, eds. Handbook of physiology. Respiration. Vol. I. Washington (DC): American Physiological Society, 1984:839–72.
34. Forster RE. Diffusion of gases across the alveolar membrane. In: Fahri LE, Tenney SM, eds. Gas exchange. Bethesda (MD): American Physiological Society, 1987: 71–88.
35. Maseri A, Caldini P, Haward P, et al. Determinants of pulmonary vascular volume: recruitment versus distensibility. Circ Res 1972;31:218–28.
36. Capen RL, Latham LP, Wagner WW. Diffusing capacity of the lung during hypoxia: role of capillary recruitment. J Appl Physiol 1981;50:165–71.
37. Roughton FJW, Forster RE. Relative importance of diffusion and chemical reaction rates in determining rate of exchange of gases in the human lung, with special reference to true diffusing capacity of pulmonary membrane and volume of blood in the lung capillaries. J Appl Physiol 1957;11:290–302.
38. Gong H Jr, Kurpershoek CJ, Meyer DH, Cross CE. Effects of cardiac output on $^{18}O_2$ lung diffusion in normal resting man. Respir Physiol 1972;16:313–26.
39. Holland RAB, Forster RE. The effect of size of red cells on the kinetics of their oxygen uptake. J Gen Physiol 1966;49:727–42.
40. Power GG, Aoki VS, Lawson WH Jr, Gregg JB. Diffusion characteristics of pulmonary blood-gas barrier at low temperatures. J Appl Physiol 1971;31:438–46.
41. Wagner PD, West JB. Effects of diffusion impairment on O_2 and CO_2 time courses in pulmonary capillaries. J Appl Physiol 1972;33:62–71.
42. Weibel ER, Taylor CR, O'Neil JJ, et al. Maximal oxygen consumption and pulmonary diffusing capacity: a direct comparison of physiologic and morphometric measurements in canids. Respir Physiol 1983;54:177–88.
43. Pitt BR, Lister G, Davies P, Reid L. Correlation of pulmonary ACE activity and capillary surface area during postnatal development. J Appl Physiol 1987;62:2031–41.
44. Nunn JF. Applied respiratory physiology. Cambridge: University Press, 1993.
45. Petros AJ, Doré CJ, Nunn JF. Modification of the iso-shunt lines for low inspired oxygen concentrations. Br J Anaesth 1994;72:515–22.
46. Yabek SM. Neonatal cyanosis. Reappraisal of response to 100% oxygen breathing. Am J Dis Child 1984;138:880–4.
47. Krogh A, Lindhard J. The volume of the dead space in breathing and the mixing of gases in the lungs of man. J Physiol 1917;51:59–90.
48. West JB. State of the art. Ventilation-perfusion relationships. Am Rev Respir Dis 1977;116:919–43.
49. West JB. Causes of carbon dioxide retention in lung disease. N Engl J Med 1971;284:1232–6.

50. Lenfant C, Okubo T. Distribution function of pulmonary blood flow and ventilation-perfusion ratio in man. J Appl Physiol 1968;24:668–79.
51. West JB. Pulmonary pathophysiology—the essentials. Baltimore: Williams & Wilkins, 1987.
52. Wagner PD, Saltzman HA, West JB. Measurement of continuous distributions of ventilation-perfusion ratios: theory. J Appl Physiol 1974;36:588–99.
53. Fahri LE. Ventilation-perfusion relationships. In: Farhi LE, Tenney SM, eds. Gas exchange. Bethesda (MD): American Physiological Society, 1987:199–215.
54. West JB. Ventilation/blood flow and gas exchange. Oxford: Blackwell, 1990.
55. Heaf DP, Helms P, Gordon I, Turner HM. Postural effects on gas exchange in infants. N Engl J Med 1983;308:1505–8.
56. Parks CR, Woodrum DE, Alden ER, et al. Gas exchange in the immature lung. I. Anatomical shunt in the premature infant. J Appl Physiol 1974;36:103–7.
57. Woodrum DE, Oliver TK, Hodson WA. The effect of prematurity and hyaline membrane disease on oxygen exchange in the lung. Pediatrics 1972;50:380–6.

CHAPTER 16

Tissue and Cellular Carbon Dioxide Transport and Acid-Base Balance

Erik R. Swenson, MD

The oxidation of carbohydrates, proteins, and fats to carbon dioxide (CO_2) is one aspect of adenosine triphosphate (ATP) generation by aerobic metabolism. Carbon dioxide itself is not an acid, but it can combine with water to form a relatively nontoxic weak acid, H_2CO_3. Compared with glycolysis or other anaerobic pathways, the quantity of potential H^+s (1 CO_2 per 6 ATPs) in aerobic metabolism is smaller by an order of magnitude. Nevertheless, the constant elimination of CO_2 is crucial to ensure a stable intra- and extracellular pH, which is vital for optimal functioning of cell proteins, enzymes, and membranes. The integrated functioning of blood, lungs, circulation, and the nervous system permits the excretion of vast amounts of potential acid (200 to 300 mEq/kg/d) without development of tissue and cellular acidosis. However, many diseases and drugs may adversely affect normal cell and organ acid-base regulation. Conditions affecting ventilatory control and cardiopulmonary, renal, endocrine, or hematologic function may create or exacerbate acidotic and/or alkalotic states. The great majority of studies defining the physiology and pathophysiology of CO_2 transport and acid-base balance have been performed in adults, and, in large part, precepts derived from these studies apply both qualitatively and quantitatively to pediatric age groups. In this chapter data generated in children and infants are highlighted whenever possible, and any pertinent differences between adults and children are emphasized.

Physiology of Carbon Dioxide Transport and Exchange

Carbon dioxide is produced within the cells of the body principally by aerobic metabolism but also from the generation of CO_2 when intra- and extracellular bicarbonate stores are used to buffer organic acids generated by anaerobic metabolism, starvation, uncontrolled diabetes, or inherited disorders of intermediary metabolism. Elimination occurs mainly via the lungs, although a small fraction can be excreted by the kidney in an alkaline urine or across the skin in premature infants.[1] Resting production of CO_2 by adults is 3 mL/min/kg; in infants and premature newborns, this production rate is approximately doubled. Normal children and adolescents have values intermediate to these.

Carbon dioxide diffuses from tissue cells into the capillary blood and is carried in chemical combination and physical solution in the venous blood to the lungs, where a portion of it diffuses into alveolar gas and is eliminated in the expired breath. As with the transport of O_2 by blood, most CO_2 is not carried as the gas itself but, rather, in several chemical forms directly or indirectly dependent on hemoglobin (Hb). However, crucial chemical and kinetic differences exist between O_2 and CO_2 transport that relate to our understanding of pathophysiologic gas exchange and acid-base disturbances.[2]

Not only is CO_2 a waste product of metabolism, but, in most tissues and organs with acid-base translocating epithelia, CO_2 and water provide a limitless source of hydrogen and bicarbonate ions for cellular and systemic acid-base regulation. In addition, various processes such as digestion, bone remodeling, and fluid secretion or absorption depend on CO_2 as a source of acid-base equivalents.[3]

Carbon Dioxide Equilibrium and Buffer Chemistry

The CO_2-bicarbonate (HCO_3^-) buffer system occupies a dominant position among the numerous intra-and extracellular buffers. Its pre-eminence rests on its ready availability and early evolutionary use in a variety of physiologic functions. The basic chemistry of buffers and pH in simple solutions is discussed well in Cohen and Kassirer,[4] to which the reader is referred for further detail.

Three features of the CO_2-HCO_3^- system distinguish it from all other physiologic buffers: (1) one member of the pair is a gas, (2) the concentration of each of the pair can be manipulated independently to resist an acid-base perturbation, and (3) the rate of one of the chemical reactions involved is extremely slow. The relevance of the first two features is that since CO_2 is a highly diffusible gas; its excretion by the lungs can vary rapidly to lower or raise its concentration. In parallel fashion, but with a slower response, renal HCO_3^- reabsorption and excretion can be adjusted to alter the HCO_3^- of body fluids. This can be appreciated more easily by examining the equilibrium reaction:

$$CO_2 + H_2O \leftrightarrow H_2CO_3 \leftrightarrow H^+ + HCO_3^- \qquad (16\text{–}1)$$

whose pK_a (or apparent equilibrium constant) is 6.1 at 37°C and normal body tonicity.

The Henderson-Hasselbalch equation, from which pH can be determined is as follows:

$$pH = pK_a + \log \frac{[HCO_3^-]}{[CO_2]} \qquad (16\text{–}2)$$

This equation demonstrates that by independently manipulating either the CO_2 or HCO_3^- concentration, changes in pulmonary or renal function can alter systemic pH. Thus, in contrast to all other body buffers, this pair can be considered an open system. If the system were closed, a shift from equilibrium in either direction would be limited by the change in the concentrations of the reactant. The open nature of this buffer system helps to explain an apparent contradiction to the rule that a buffer pair is effective only if its pK is near that of the pH of the system. This is true for a closed system, but the rapidity with which the concentration of CO_2 can be altered by pulmonary ventilation makes this buffer pair effective even at a pH more than a log unit different from its pK_a.

The third unique feature of the CO_2-HCO_3^- buffer system is that an enzyme is necessary for it to operate in vivo. Although both reactions in Equation 16–1 above are reversible, the first is extremely slow but can be accelerated many thousand-fold by the enzyme carbonic anhydrase (CA), which exists in red cells and almost all tissues of the body.[5] The magnitude of physiologic catalysis is such that CO_2 hydration is essentially instantaneous and almost as rapid as the diffusion of CO_2 and the ionization of carbonic acid.

The extent to which CO_2 can be hydrated to yield bicarbonate is dependent on the temperature, concentrations of CO_2, and all non-HCO_3^- buffers of appropriate pK_a. In red cells, Hb is by far the most important buffer, with albumin and inorganic phosphates the most important in plasma. Phosphates and a variety of other proteins and small peptides constitute the chemical intracellular nonbicarbonate buffering capacity.

The foregoing description is that of CO_2 in simple biologic media. It does not take into account certain time-dependent aspects of gas exchange, such as red cell and plasma transit time through tissue and lung capillaries and rates of CO_2 diffusion and chemical reaction and linkage to O_2 exchange, which are relevant to a complete understanding of CO_2 transport and acid-base balance.

Transfer of Carbon Dioxide to and from Blood

In metabolically active cells, tissue carbon dioxide partial pressure (P_{CO_2}) is greater than the P_{CO_2} of arterial blood flowing into systemic capillaries. Therefore, CO_2 diffuses from the cells into the interstitial space and plasma. Some dissolves in the plasma. A small amount reacts with amino groups of plasma proteins to form carbamino compounds. Another small portion combines with water to yield carbonic acid, which then dissociates into H^+ and HCO_3^- (see Equation 16–1), and the H^+ is buffered by plasma buffers. The vast majority of the CO_2 diffuses into erythrocytes, where it reacts as it does in plasma but to a much greater extent. Some remains in the dissolved form; more combines with Hb to form carbamino compounds of the following general form:

$$R\text{-}NH_2 + CO_2 \leftrightarrow R\text{-}NHCOO\text{-} + H^+ \qquad (16\text{–}3)$$

The greatest amount of CO_2, however, combines with H_2O in the presence of high concentrations of carbonic anhydrase to form carbonic acid, which dissociates to H^+ and HCO_3^-. Much of the H^+ generated by both reactions is buffered by other titratable amino acids in Hb. A rate-limiting buildup of HCO_3^-, which might otherwise slow and decrease the overall uptake of CO_2, is prevented by a one-for-one electroneutral exchange of HCO_3^- for Cl^- across the red cell membrane (Hamburger's phenomenon), mediated by band 3 protein, an integral membrane glycoprotein. The important diffusion steps, chemical reactions, and exchange processes are shown in Figure 16–1. When venous blood reaches the lung capillaries, CO_2 diffuses from the blood down its concentration gradient into the alveolar gas space whose P_{CO_2} is determined by the level of alveolar ventilation. The resulting disequilibrium as molecular CO_2 diffuses away initiates a reversal of all the reactions and events described above.

Carbon Dioxide Transport in the Blood

In quantitative terms, the contributions of plasma and red cells to total CO_2 transport are nearly equal. Table 16–1 lists normal values for the concentrations of the three forms of CO_2 carried in blood: physically dissolved CO_2, bicarbonate CO_2, and carbamino-bound CO_2. Concentrations are given for plasma and red cells of arterial and mixed venous blood. The relative contributions of each form of CO_2 transport to total CO_2 exchange also are shown.

The solubility of CO_2 in blood is about 24 times greater than that of O_2. The amount of CO_2 dissolved in blood is calculated as shown:

$$C_{CO_2} = CO_2 \times P_{CO_2} \qquad (16\text{–}4)$$

where CO_2 is 0.072 mL/100 mL-mm Hg and P_{CO_2} is the partial pressure of dissolved CO_2 in mm Hg. This amount of CO_2 at physiologic P_{CO_2} represents only about 6% of the total CO_2 content. Were this the only form of CO_2 transport, its modest solubility would require higher rates of ventilation and cardiac output to keep pace with resting metabolic production than those measured with maximal exercise.

The second form of carriage is in combination with blood proteins. By far the greatest quantity of protein

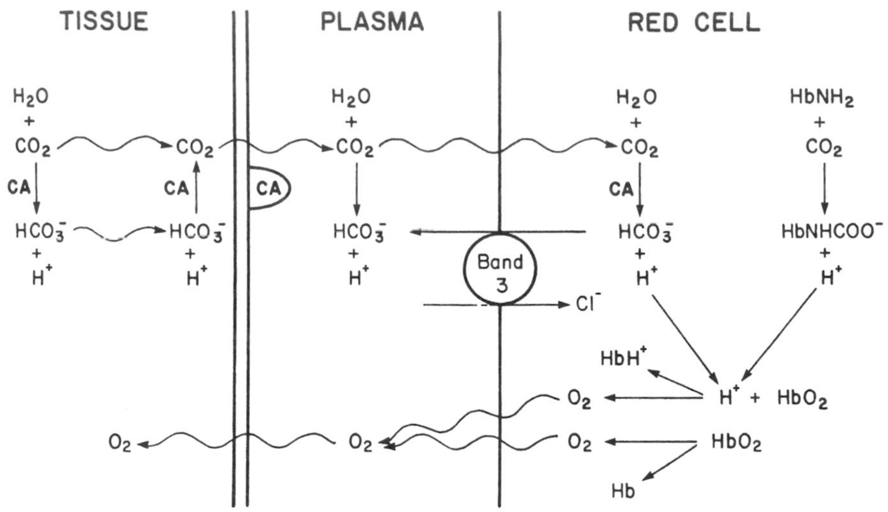

FIGURE 16–1. Reactions of CO_2 and O_2 in blood during tissue gas exchange. At the lungs, reactions proceed in the opposite direction to evolve CO_2 into the alveoli. The linkage between CO_2 and O_2 exchange (Bohr/Haldane effect) is illustrated by the hydrogen ion binding and release reactions of hemoglobin and CO_2. CA = carbonic anhydrase either cytoplasmic in tissues and red cells or membrane bound, as is the case for the capillary endothelium with enzyme activity available to plasma; band 3 = the anion exchange protein within the red cell membrane; ⁓ = diffusion; → = chemical reaction (including the binding and translocation of anions by band 3 protein); Hb = hemoglobin; $HbNHCOO^-$ = hemoglobin carbamate. (Reproduced with permission from Swenson ER.[2])

participating in this transport is Hb. At normal P_{CO_2} and hematocrit, CO_2 stored as carbamino compounds amounts to 4 to 6% of total CO_2 content. The vast majority of CO_2 carriage is in the form of bicarbonate. The amount of CO_2 stored as bicarbonate in blood at normal hematocrit is about 42 mL/100 mL at a P_{CO_2} of 40 mm Hg. This accounts for the remaining 90% of the total CO_2 carried in blood.

The relationship between CO_2 content and P_{CO_2} is curvilinear, but it is much closer to a straight line than the O_2 equilibrium curve (Figure 16–2). Over the normal physiologic range (35 to 50 mm Hg) the CO_2 equilibrium

TABLE 16–1. Normal Values* for Blood Carbon Dioxide Transport

	Unit	Arterial	Venous	Venoarterial Difference
Whole blood				
HCT	%	45	45	—
Hb saturation	%	95	70	—
P_{CO_2}	mm Hg	40	46	6
	kPa	5.3	6.1	0.8
	mM	1.3	1.5	0.2
HCO_3^-	mM	15.9	17.3	1.4
Carbamino-CO_2	mM	1.2	1.4	0.2
Total CO_2	mM	18.4	20.2	1.8
	vol %	48	52	4
Plasma				
pH		7.4	7.37	−0.03
P_{CO_2}	mm Hg	40	46	6
HCO_3^-	mM	24.4	26.2	1.8
Carbamino-CO_2	mM	0.3	0.3	0.0
Red cell				
pH		7.22	7.20	−0.02
P_{CO_2}	mm Hg	40	46	6
HCO_3^-	mM	5.6	6.2	0.6
Carbamino-CO_2	mM	2.2	2.6	0.4

*For adults and children over 2 years old.
HCT = hematocrit; Hb = hemoglobin; P_{CO_2} = partial pressure of carbon dioxide; HCO_3^- = bicarbonate.

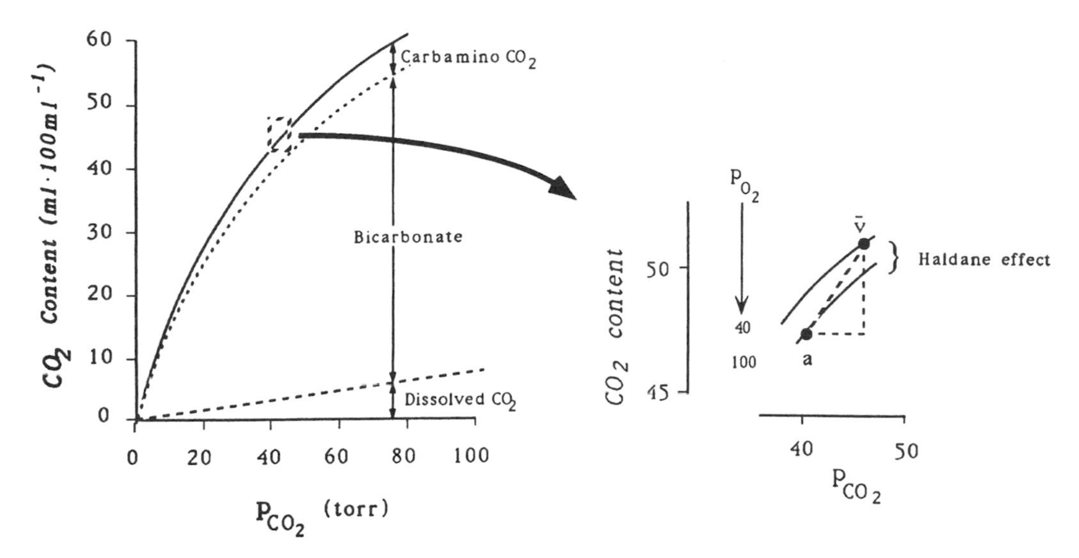

FIGURE 16–2. Components of the CO_2 dissociation curve for whole blood. Although the curve in nonlinear over the entire range of P_{CO_2} values, it can be considered virtually linear within the bound of normal P_{CO_2} fluctuations—even within the pathophysiologic extremes of hypocapnia and hypercapnia. This, of course, is in marked contrast to the O_2 dissociation curve over the normal P_{CO_2} range. The oxylabile buffer capacity of hemoglobin effectively increases the slope of the CO_2 dissociation curve during normal gas exchange (*inset*). This enhancement of CO_2 exchange, or Haldane effect, is the added effect of increased hemoglobin carbamino CO_2 formation and buffer capacity (increased hemoglobin p*K*) as O_2 is released.

curve is virtually straight. The CO_2 content in blood is much higher than is the O_2 content, because of the large bicarbonate pool that results from the strong buffering capacity of Hb and its lesser direct binding of CO_2 as carbamino-CO_2. In this regard, it is somewhat curious that Hb usually is considered only in light of its O_2-carrying function.

The physiologic CO_2 equilibrium curve has a steeper slope because of the Haldane effect (see Figure 16–2). The mixed venous point lies on a CO_2 equilibrium curve appropriate for a 75% oxygen saturation. The arterial point lies on another curve appropriate for a 97% oxygen saturation. During gas exchange both CO_2 and O_2 are transferred simultaneously. As CO_2 is given up in the lung and the level of CO_2 in the blood moves down the CO_2 equilibrium curve, the curve shifts to the right because of O_2 uptake. The vertical distance between the two CO_2 curves then represents the CO_2 content exchanged by virtue of the Haldane effect. The importance of this O_2-linked CO_2 exchange is considered further below.

The relative contribution of each of the three CO_2 transport forms to CO_2 transfer from tissues to blood and blood to lungs is not necessarily proportional to their concentrations in whole blood or partitioning between red cells and plasma. As shown in the arteriovenous differences listed in Table 16–1, changes in plasma and red cell concentrations contribute equally to total CO_2 transfer. However, most of CO_2 transfer (90%) arises from HCO_3^- (90%), which first must be generated within the red cell and then transferred to the plasma. Thus, in a sense, the majority of CO_2 entering or leaving blood is dependent on the presence of erythrocytes, because they contain 10 times the buffering capacity of plasma and the overwhelming catalytic activity of carbonic anhydrase. Although it has been demonstrated recently that certain capillary beds (eg, brain, skeletal muscle, GI tract, and lung) have carbonic anhydrase in their plasma-facing endothelial membranes, the catalytic activity here is less than 1% of that in red cells. The low carbonic anhydrase activity available and poor buffer capacity of plasma relative to red cells means that little extracellular (plasma) HCO_3^- formation or dehydration occurs physiologically.

The combined contribution of HCO_3^- and, thus, of carbonic anhydrase to total CO_2 transfer amounts to about 80 to 85%. Although red cell carbonic anhydrase is expressed late in fetal gestation only, and levels in newborns are only 10 to 20% of those in adults,[6] it still represents a vast excess over that required for physiologic purposes (see below), so that, even in newborns, HCO_3^- is the main transport form and precursor of eliminated CO_2. The contribution of red cell membrane anion exchange has been calculated to be responsible for about 30% of total CO_2 exchange. It has been demonstrated recently that even human fetal red cells have anion exchange capacity equal to that of adult cells;[7] thus, it is certain that the contribution of the HCO_3^--Cl^- exchange does not vary with age. In the past, the fraction of total CO_2 exchange attributable to carbamino-CO_2 was thought to be as high as 30%, but this has been adjusted to between 5 and 10% in adults on the basis of in vitro studies in which physiologic conditions were more carefully addressed—principally 2,3-diphosphoglycerate

(DPG) concentration and Hb saturation. However, in infants and children with persisting fetal Hb, the contribution of carbamino-CO_2 may be 15 to 20%.[8] Last, the contribution of dissolved CO_2 is 5%, but it increases of necessity if the contributions of HCO_3^- and carbamino-CO_2 are diminished by drugs, anemia, or other disease conditions.

Determinants of Arterial and Venous Carbon Dioxide Content

Table 16–1 gives normal values for arterial and venous whole blood P_{CO_2}, pH, and HCO_3^- in adults and children above the age of 2 years. In infants, arterial P_{CO_2} averages about 35 mm Hg, and HCO_3^- is about 20 mM. The determinants of arterial P_{CO_2} are alveolar ventilation and CO_2 production ($\dot{V}_{CO_2}$). Arterial CO_2 content is then determined by the Pa_{CO_2} and the CO_2 equilibrium curve. Mixed venous CO_2 content ($C\bar{v}_{CO_2}$) is determined by the balance between CO_2 production and cardiac output ($\dot{Q}$) added to arterial CO_2 content (Ca_{CO_2}), as dictated by Fick's principle:

$$C\bar{v}_{CO_2} = Ca_{CO_2} + \dot{V}_{CO_2}/\dot{Q} \qquad (16\text{–}5)$$

The mixed venous P_{CO_2} is then determined by the CO_2 equilibrium curve and $C\bar{v}_{CO_2}$. If cardiac output increases or CO_2 production decreases, both $C\bar{v}_{CO_2}$ and $P\bar{v}_{CO_2}$ decrease. The opposite occurs with a decrease in cardiac output or an increase in CO_2 production.

Under normal circumstances the respiratory quotient (RQ) is around 0.8:

$$RQ = \frac{\dot{V}_{CO_2}}{\dot{V}_{O_2}} = \frac{\dot{Q}(Cv_{CO_2} - Ca_{CO_2})}{\dot{Q}(Ca_{O_2} - Cv_{O_2})} = 0.8 \qquad (16\text{–}6)$$

so the normal (arterial – venous) O_2 content difference of 5 mL/100 mL results in a (venous – arterial) CO_2 content difference of 4 mL/100 mL. If the balance between $\dot{V}_{CO_2}$ and $\dot{Q}$ changes, there will be a change in both ($Cv_{CO_2} - Ca_{CO_2}$) and ($Ca_{O_2} - Cv_{O_2}$). However, the ratio of the two differences will be affected only by a change in metabolic substrate use or by transient changes in acid-base state.

Carbon Dioxide-Oxygen Interactions

To differing degrees, each gas in the course of its own transfer enhances the quantitative exchange of the other.[9] Because the transport of both CO_2 and O_2 depends largely on Hb, and each gas affects the Hb binding to and/or buffering of the other, there is a significant linkage between CO_2 and O_2 exchange.

The Bohr effect, or the influence of CO_2 on the O_2-Hb equilibrium curve, occurs by two mechanisms. The binding of CO_2 to Hb as carbamino-CO_2 generates a proton (Equation 16–3), as does the hydration of CO_2 directly (Equation 16–1). The binding of H^+ to certain amino acids in Hb causes conformational changes in the tertiary structure of the protein, the result of which is a decrease in Hb's affinity for oxygen or a higher P-50 (a right-shifted Hb-O_2 equilibrium curve). The greater the degree of Hb desaturation, the greater the effect of any given P_{CO_2} change. Under resting normoxic conditions, the Bohr effect is responsible for less than 5% of O_2 uptake in the lung,[10] because the mixed venous-arterial pH and P_{CO_2} differences are small, and the upper part of the Hb-O_2 equilibrium curve is relatively flat and insensitive to changes in pH and P_{CO_2}. In contrast, the physiologic significance of the Bohr effect is important for O_2 unloading in tissues and for placental O_2 transfer. In working muscles it may contribute about 20% to O_2 delivery.[11] In the placenta, where both fetal and maternal blood make contact, it has been estimated that 8 to 10% of O_2 exchange may be facilitated by the Bohr effect.[12]

The effect of O_2 on CO_2 transport and exchange (the Haldane effect) is considerably larger than that of the Bohr effect on O_2 exchange. The binding of oxygen to Hb alters both Hb's binding of CO_2 directly as carbamino-CO_2 and its overall p*K* (its buffering capacity for H^+). The first effect accounts for virtually all of the contribution of carbamino-CO_2 to CO_2 transfer between blood and tissues or lungs, that is, all carbamino-CO_2 contribution is O_2 linked. It probably accounts for about one-third of the Haldane effect. The other two-thirds derive from the reduced buffering capacity of Hb as it is fully oxygenated. Model calculations and in vitro data suggest that the Haldane effect accounts for 35 to 40% of CO_2 exchange under normal postnatal conditions,[8] and as much as 46% in the placenta.[12]

Kinetic Aspects of Carbon Dioxide Exchange

It is conventionally thought that there is early CO_2 equilibration during capillary gas exchange, because CO_2 is some 20 times more diffusible than O_2.[13] If CO_2 transport by blood occurred solely by its carriage as dissolved CO_2, this would be correct. However, as with oxygen, the transport of CO_2 is critically dependent on its interactions directly and indirectly with Hb. Whereas oxygen binding to and release from Hb is essentially instantaneous, several chemical reaction and exchange rates of CO_2 are much slower. Although controversy persists about the true magnitude and physiologic significance of end-capillary CO_2 disequilibrium, it is increasingly clear that CO_2 exchange cannot be considered fully complete in the time of normal capillary transit.[14]

Table 16–2 lists the times for 90 percent completion of all the diffusion and reaction steps in CO_2 exchange. The critical value to be considered is the average transit time of blood through capillaries, which, depending on the tissue and its metabolic rate, blood flow, and capillary density, ranges between 0.4 and 1.0 second. It is immediately apparent that the uncatalyzed rates of CO_2 hydration and HCO_3^- dehydration are exceedingly slow but are

TABLE 16–2. Rates of Carbon Dioxide Exchange Processes

Reaction	Time to 90% Completion (ms)
Diffusion of CO_2	1–3
Carbamino-CO_2 binding/release*	250–300
Chloride-bicarbonate exchange	400–500
Bohr/Haldane effects	250
CO_2 hydration/HCO_3^- dehydration	
Uncatalyzed	$>4 \times 10^4$
Catalyzed by carbonic anhydrase	5

*This value reflects the predominant rate-limiting effect of O_2 diffusion because all the carbamino-CO_2 contribution is O_2-exchange dependent.

accelerated sufficiently by carbonic anhydrase. The degree of catalysis by carbonic anhydrase is so extraordinarily in excess that more than 99 percent inhibition is necessary before CO_2 hydration becomes a limiting factor in CO_2 exchange.[15] Thus, although red cell carbonic anhydrase concentrations vary from 5% of adult values in premature infants to 10 to 20% at term and 30 to 40% in children below the age of 2 to 3 years,[6] these variations have no physiologic relevance, even to gas exchange insufficiency in the infant respiratory distress syndrome.[16]

However, the rate of red cell anion exchange, on which 30% of CO_2 exchange depends, may be rate limiting, even at rest. As capillary transit times fall with increased cardiac output, especially if capillary reserve is limited (as may occur in many disease conditions), the potential exists for significant CO_2 disequilibrium between arterial blood and alveolar gas and between tissue and venous blood. To further compound the problem, end-capillary O_2 equilibration may not occur under these conditions. Since the Haldane effect plays a large role in CO_2 exchange, end-capillary O_2 disequilibrium magnifies further the CO_2 disequilibrium.

The physiologic consequences of any in vivo CO_2 end-capillary disequilibrium in a healthy person at rest are minimal. This is because CO_2 is such a soluble gas that P_{CO_2} gradients across tissues and the lungs are fairly small (about 4 to 8 mm Hg). Any failure of equilibration that would cause CO_2 retention and therefore raise P_{CO_2} can be countered easily by slight increases in ventilation and cardiac output. At rest, lung CO_2 equilibration is roughly 97% complete, which would lead to less than a 1-mm Hg difference between arterial and alveolar P_{CO_2}. With maximal exercise, comparable values would be 87% equilibration and a 6-mm Hg arterial-alveolar P_{CO_2} difference.[17] However, if normal ventilatory and cardiac responses are limited, and/or parenchymal lung disease exists, significant CO_2 retention and respiratory acidosis could develop. It should also be noted that with severe $\dot{V}_A/\dot{Q}$ mismatching and reduction in diffusing capacity, large arterial-alveolar P_{CO_2} differences can develop, which have been ascribed to these factors alone and not to end-capillary CO_2 disequilibrium.[18] Probably all three factors are important. Drugs interfering with either carbonic anhydrase or red cell anion exchange clearly cause end-capillary CO_2 disequilibrium. In healthy individuals this can be tolerated with minimal problems, but these agents may be toxic in patients with cardiopulmonary insufficiency.[14]

Respiratory Acid-Base Balance

Control of Ventilation

Alveolar ventilation is controlled primarily to ensure adequate tissue oxygenation, CO_2 removal, and pH homeostasis. Under normal conditions, monitoring of CO_2 (via changes in H^+ concentration) by central and peripheral chemoreceptors provides the dominant signal by which gas exchange is assessed and ventilation regulated. As a consequence, arterial P_{CO_2} and pH are maintained within narrow ranges and Hb is kept fully saturated. This efficiency depends on normal central nervous system (CNS) function, respiratory muscle strength, cardiovascular status, and pulmonary parenchymal integrity. Age, sleep state, endocrine status, level of anxiety or stress, and voluntary cortical input influence overall function. The ventilatory response to changes in HCO_3^- caused by nonvolatile acid or base is considered briefly in the discussion of compensation to metabolic acidosis and alkalosis. A full discussion of neurophysiologic control is beyond the scope of this chapter, but can be found in Chapters 29 and 30.

Tissue Responses to Carbon Dioxide and Acid-Base Changes

Tissue responses to changes in the acid-base milieu include simple passive chemical buffering in both the extra- and intracellular compartments as well as active intracellular pH regulation. A change in pH caused by primary changes in CO_2 is resisted but not totally corrected by binding or release of protons from non-HCO_3^- buffers. Primary changes in H^+ and/or OH^- not caused by CO_2 changes (metabolic acid-base disturbances) are buffered by both HCO_3^- and non-HCO_3^- buffer stores.

Within minutes of a rise or fall in CO_2, intra- and extracellular buffers are titrated. Although large changes in plasma bicarbonate occur with in vitro CO_2 titration of blood (see Figure 16–2), considerably smaller changes occur in vivo. The discrepancy between in vitro blood and total body CO_2 dissociation curves can be explained largely by the differences in the space through which newly generated HCO_3^- distributes. Bicarbonate generated by Hb and other nonbicarbonate buffers has access only to the plasma phase during in vitro CO_2 titration, but it can freely diffuse into the much larger (approximately twofold) poorly buffered interstitial space. In addition, active intracellular pH regulation (see below) results in a further apparent lowering of the buffer capacity of the extracellular space. The net result of these processes is to reduce the slope of the in vivo blood CO_2 dissociation curve by 30 to 50%, depending on the size of the extra- and intracellular fluid compartments. Measurement of extracellular pH as is usually done by arterial blood gas sampling reveals that blood (with its intracellular Hb), plasma, and interstitial body fluids make up about 30% of the total body buffering capacity. The remaining 70% is provided by tissue intracellular buffers. Beyond simple chemical buffering, there are also small changes in intermediary metabolism that alter the production of lactic acid and other ketoacids. Thus, with hypocapnia, lactate concentrations in blood rise 2 to 3 mM, and with hypercapnia, they fall slightly.

Of considerable importance, but not easily assessed clinically, are the responses by many tissues to further defend intracellular pH (pH_i). In view of the marked pH sensitivity in virtually all cellular processes,[19] the importance of pH_i regulation is hardly surprising. With the exception of red cells, all cells appear to have pH_i values that are appreciably more alkaline than would be predicted if H^+ and HCO_3^- were passively distributed across the plasma membrane. Transmembrane pH differences vary among tissues but range between 0.2 and 0.5 units,[20] in contrast to the 0.8 to 1.5 unit difference that would occur in the face of no pH_i regulation. The same transmembrane ion exchanges, directly and secondarily linked to the Na^+-K^+ gradient, that are used in normal ionic regulation can also be stimulated selectively in the face of endogenous or exogenous acid-base disturbances.[21] In acidosis these include exchange of extracellular Na^+ for intracellular H^+ via the Na^+-H^+ membrane antiporter, and active H^+ extrusion by proton translocating ATPases. In alkalosis these include exchange of extracellular $C1^-$ for intracellular HCO_3^- or $NaCO_3^-$ via membrane anion exchangers similar to red cell band 3 protein. Certain critical tissues and organs such as the heart,[22] brain,[23–25] liver,[26] respiratory muscles,[27] and kidneys[28] have a remarkable capacity to defend their pH. The rate and magnitude of these responses help to explain the surprising tolerance to acidosis and alkalosis in otherwise healthy children and adults, without underlying circulatory insufficiency or hypoxemia.[29] Because these mechanisms are linked to continuous maintenance of normal ion gradients by Na^+-K^+ ATPase or they consume ATP directly, the requirement for adequate O_2 and substrate delivery is obvious.

The time course of adjustment to acute hypo- or hypercapnia is quite fast (10 to 20 minutes), and a new steady state is reached in which plasma bicarbonate remains fairly constant at slightly reduced or slightly raised levels, respectively, for about 6 hours. In this period the impact of early changes in renal acid excretion and HCO_3^- reabsorption are minimal, so it is possible to define the normal responses to acute hypo- and hypercapnia. Plasma pH and bicarbonate concentration appear to vary proportionally with the P_{CO_2} over a range of 15 to 90 mm Hg. The relationship between arterial H^+ concentration and P_{CO_2} is about 0.7 mEq/L • mm Hg^{-1} (or 0.01 pH unit/mm Hg), and that for plasma HCO_3^- is 0.2 mmol/L • mm Hg. A graphic depiction of these steady state relationships for acute respiratory acidosis and alkalosis is shown in Figure 16–3, an acid-base nomogram that incorporates these values and the 95 percent confidence limits for a variety of acute and chronic acid-base disturbances in adults. The only data relating to children are those of Engel and colleagues[30] in children with cystic fibrosis in a chronic steady state of hypercapnia, and those of Albert and colleagues[31] and Edelman and colleagues[32] in children with uncomplicated metabolic acidosis. In these studies, no significant differences exist between these data and those for adults. Data such as these have not been established in neonates, but a slightly altered nomogram for neonates, taking into account their normally lower P_{CO_2} and HCO_3^-, has been developed by Carlo and associates.[33] A significant difference between neonates and adults and older children is the considerably larger extracellular volume of the term and preterm newborn. The almost twofold greater extracellular water space (about 50% of total body water) will clearly alter the distribution of HCO_3^- in response to acute changes in CO_2. Although standard equations have been developed for adults that reflect the smaller extracellular water space (about 25% of total body water), no such equations have been tested fully in neonates. Qualitatively, the clinical consequence of using standard (ie, adult) equations to evaluate plasma HCO_3^- changes occurring solely as the result of nonrespiratory acid-base imbalance in the neonate is to overstate the severity of either a metabolic acidosis or alkalosis, or to falsely diagnose its presence.

The foregoing discussion of acute respiratory acidosis and alkalosis rests on the usual clinical situation that a change in P_{CO_2} results from altered ventilation or an inappropriate ventilatory response to a change in CO_2 production. Thus, consideration of a physiologic ventilatory response is not germane. The possible exceptions to this are conditions in which low cardiac output, severe anemia, or chemical reaction limitation cause tissue hypercapnia without arterial hypercapnia (see "Respiratory Acidosis"). The appropriate ventilatory response under these conditions is not known.

The time course of adjustment to a primary acute changes in HCO_3^- caused by either acid gain/loss or base gain/loss is also quite rapid. The simple chemical buffering by intra- and extracellular buffers is accomplished within minutes. Active intracellular pH regulation similarly occurs in several minutes. The buffering by CO_2/HCO_3^- stores either generates CO_2 (metabolic acidosis) or consumes CO_2 (metabolic alkalosis), and so leads to a transient increase or decrease in CO_2 excretion by the lung. In the subsequent first several hours after the onset

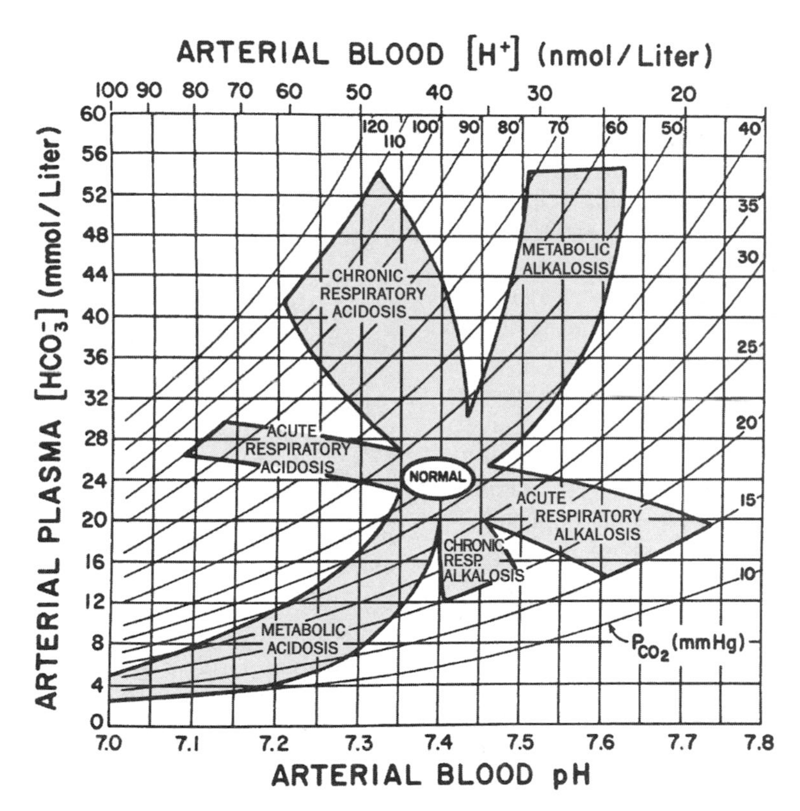

FIGURE 16–3. Acid-base nomogram showing 95% confidence limits for diagnosis of primary uncomplicated respiratory and metabolic acid-base disturbances. Values outside these "bands" indicate mixed disorders or single disorders in a non–steady state situation. (Reproduced with permission from Cogan MG, Rector FC. Acid-base disorders. In: Brenner BM, Rector FC, eds. The kidney. 3rd ed. Philadelphia: WB Saunders, 1986.)

of a metabolic acid-base disturbance, secondary hyper- or hypoventilation is evoked to further compensate the acid-base imbalance.[34,35] The net effect of acute chemical and slightly slower ventilatory adjustments yields the relationships plotted in Figure 16–3 for metabolic acidosis and alkalosis. On average, each milliequivalent-per-liter decrement in plasma HCO_3^- concentration evokes a 1.1– to 1.3–mm Hg fall in P_{CO_2}, and for each milliequivalent-per-liter increment in plasma HCO_3^- there is a 0.7– to 0.9–mm Hg rise in P_{CO_2}. Extrapolating to extreme metabolic acidosis (< 5 mEq/L HCO_3^-) yields values of P_{CO_2} (8 to 10 mm Hg) at the physiologic maximum of hyperventilation. In the opposite direction, the degree of hypoventilation is somewhat blunted by the eventual development of arterial hypoxemia.

Renal Responses to Carbon Dioxide and Acid-Base Changes

The response of the kidneys in regulating systemic acid-base balance is of slower onset, so that there is little compensation by the kidney until many hours after the onset of a pH disturbance. The time course and response of the kidneys to metabolic acidosis or alkalosis of nonrenal origin is beyond the scope of this chapter; the reader is referred to Cohen and Kassirer[4] for more information.

Respiratory acidosis and respiratory alkalosis elicit considerable changes in tubular acid secretion and HCO_3^- reabsorption. Principally, the kidneys appear to respond directly to the changes in P_{CO_2}, rather than acidemia or alkalemia per se.[36] Although it is possible to detect changes in urine pH within 1 hour, quantitative loss of H^+ or HCO_3^- does not occur appreciably for at least 6 hours. The full expression of renal adaptation may take several days and depends on a normal extracellular volume status and renal function.

In hypercapnia proximal tubular intracellular acidosis promotes more HCO_3^- reabsorption by an increase in the number and activity of the Na^+-H^+ antiporter at the luminal membrane and by an increase in the basolateral (contraluminal) membrane Na^+-HCO_3^- cotransport.[37] The proximal tubule also has an H^+ translocating ATPase pump that contributes to the reabsorption of HCO_3^-. This activity is stimulated early and likely helps to conserve the newly generated HCO_3^- (from earlier body chemical buffering) that might otherwise escape in the urine. There is additional increased HCO_3^- reclamation in the loop of Henle by H^+ secretion, so that by the time tubular urine reaches the distal nephron, all filtered HCO_3^- has been recovered. In the distal tubule and collecting duct, there is a further hypercapnia-stimulated H^+ secretion that titrates all other filtered buffers. This enhanced H^+ secretion appears to be mediated principally by activation and insertion into the luminal membranes of new H^+-ATPase pumps.[38] However, the majority of net H^+ secretion (ie, new HCO_3^- synthesis) comes largely from enhanced NH^{4+} secretion occurring in the first few days.[39]

Renal adaptation to hypocapnia entails suppression of renal acidification expressed as a transient decrease in net acid excretion and a persistent reduction in HCO_3^- reabsorption. Less is known about the mechanisms involved than about compensation to hypercapnia. Reduced luminal membrane Na^+-H^+ exchange activity has been demonstrated in both the proximal and distal tubules,[40] which probably accounts for the decreased rate of HCO_3^- reabsorption. Endocytic retrieval of H^+-APTase pumps from luminal membranes of the collecting duct also may play a role.[41] Direct HCO_3^- secretion by collecting duct cells has been shown in some animals[42] in metabolic alkalosis, but has not been studied in respiratory alkalosis. Loss of HCO_3^- in the urine accounts for only a fraction of the observed fall in plasma HCO_3^-; the remainder represents decreased acid secretion (NH_4^+ and titratable acid).[43] In fact, if the reduction in P_{CO_2} is gradual, loss of HCO_3^- in the urine is trivial, and virtually all the reduction in plasma HCO_3^- is secondary to decreased acid excretion.[44] Responses to acute and chronic respiratory acidosis or alkalosis have not been well studied in human infants. Considerable controversy still remains over whether the early mild hypobicarbonatemia is due to renal immaturity or to extra-renal factors (such as relative volume expansion) that cause HCO_3^- reabsorption to be depressed, as in the adult. Both are probably important factors.[45,46] However, in terms of the magnitude of response to acid-base stresses, the reduced capacity of newborn animals to increase NH_4^+ and titratable acid secretion during acid loading,[47] and a decreased proximal tubular capacity for tubular acid secretion[48] due to lesser Na^+-H^+ antiporter and basolateral membrane HCO_3^- transport activity, suggest that some limitation in pH defense may occur. Although renal carbonic anhydrase is intimately involved in acid secretion, and red cell carbonic anhydrase levels do increase in the first months of life, there appear to be no differences in renal carbonic anhydrase activity among premature newborns, term infants, and adults.[49] By 1 month of age, no apparent immaturity of renal acid-base adaptation is detectable.[47]

It has been proposed that the rate of liver urea synthesis may influence the concentration of HCO_3^- and thus contribute to acid-base regulation. This controversial theory[50] posits that the metabolism of protein yields nearly stoichiometric amounts of NH_4^+ and HCO_3^-. In humans, the daily protein ingestion of 1 to 2 g/kg leads to the formation of about 10 to 20 mmol/kg of HCO_3^- and NH_4^+. Excretion of this amount of HCO_3^-, by the kidneys would require rates of water excretion incompatible with other aspects of renal function. The major pathway for the elimination of this metabolically generated HCO_3^- is hepatic urea synthesis, which consumes NH_4^+ and HCO_3^- in equal amounts:

$$2NH_4^+ + 2HCO_3^- \ \text{urea} + CO_2 + H_2O \qquad (16\text{–}7)$$

This important dual role of urea synthesis for disposal of HCO_3^- and NH_4^+ has some supporting evidence. In vitro, extracellular pH modulates normal hepatic urea synthesis in an apparent compensatory fashion.[50] That is, during acidosis, urea synthesis is depressed slightly, thus sparing metabolically produced HCO_3^- for repletion of decreased base stores. The remaining NH_4^+ is detoxified by the liver in the formation of glutamine, which is then carried to the kidneys to be liberated as NH_4^+ by tubular deamination of glutamine. Support for this concept comes from recent studies showing that mild liver failure (with demonstrable reductions in the capacity for hepatic urea synthesis) is associated with metabolic alkalosis.[51] Others have argued, however, that acid-base-related alterations in urea synthesis only reflect pH-mediated changes in NH_3 concentration, the true nitrogen substrate for the rate-limiting urea cycle enzyme, carbamoyl-phosphate synthase.[52,53] Moreover, more recent whole animal and human studies, rule out the liver as a major organ subserving acid-base regulation. If urea formation were critical to acid-base regulation as depicted in Equation 16–7, then metabolic alkalosis should be an integral feature of hepatic failure. However, it is a rare acid-base disturbance in hepatic failure and can usually be attributed to iatrogenic interventions or electrolyte abnormalities. An 85% hepatectomy in rats does not cause metabolic alkalosis or alter the ability to handle normally an HCO_3^- infusion, despite a 60% reduction in urea synthesis.[54] In humans directly measured impaired urea synthesis rates in patients prior to liver transplantation were not associated with metabolic alkalosis, nor was metabolic acidosis apparent following transplantation with normalization of urea synthetic capacity.[55]

Respiratory Acid-Base Disorders

A variety of pulmonary and nonpulmonary disorders cause primary deviations from normal P_{CO_2} and pH. The diagnosis and treatment of respiratory acid-base disturbances are best approached through an understanding of the fundamental relationships between lung function, tissue and renal acid-base metabolism, and control of ventilation. In this chapter, only primary respiratory acidosis and alkalosis are discussed, but it is important to realize that respiratory acidosis (hypercapnia) and respiratory alkalosis (hypocapnia) can be secondary physiologic responses to primary metabolic or renal acid-base disturbances. Indeed, the absence of compensatory hypo- and hypercapnia in metabolic derangements of acid-base homeostasis should suggest the possibility of unrecognized abnormalities in ventilatory control, neuromuscular dysfunction, or parenchymal lung disease. A discussion of the even larger number of conditions causing metabolic acidosis and alkalosis is beyond the scope of this chapter; the reader is referred to standard nephrology texts or Cohen and Kassirer.[4]

The diagnosis of respiratory acid-base disorders is based traditionally on arterial blood gases, for several reasons. First, they provide direct data on pulmonary gas exchange efficiency and arterial oxygenation. Second, overall tissue acid-base status, can be assessed, because arterial blood is, in effect, a mixed sample of blood from all the tissues, and the usual (arterial – venous) P_{CO_2} difference is only 4 to 6 mm Hg. In most cases this is true, with the caveat that all species of CO_2 are in equilibrium (ie, there is no significant end-capillary CO_2 disequilibriums) and that cardiac output and tissue perfusion are adequate. If one or both cannot be assumed, the (venous–arterial) P_{CO_2} difference can increase markedly, rendering arterial blood gas acid-base analysis either a poor indicator of tissue acid-base status, or even incorrect as to whether acidosis or alkalosis exists in the tissues.[56] Last, it has been a point of controversy whether the dissociation constant for CO_2 is constant during acute changes in acid-base state so that the calculation of HCO_3^- can be made accurately on the basis of arterial (venous) P_{CO_2} and pH. Data in newborns and adults support the constancy of the p*K* for CO_2 under a variety of situations.[57,58]

Respiratory Alkalosis

Pathophysiology

Hypocapnia develops whenever a sufficiently strong ventilatory stimulus transiently causes CO_2 output in the lungs to exceed its metabolic production by tissues. The subsequent alkalinization evokes a number of chemical and physiologic adjustments whose mechanisms differ in their quantitative magnitude and time course. Despite the fact that these mechanisms somewhat overlap in time, it has proved useful for diagnostic and therapeutic purposes to separate respiratory alkalosis into acute (chemical and active tissue buffering) and chronic (renal compensation) phases, as discussed above.

Clinical features

The effects of respiratory alkalosis vary according to its duration and severity but, in general, are primarily those of the underlying disease causing the alkalosis.[59] Acute hypocapnia presents with more profound manifestations than does chronic hypocapnia, presumably because of the further compensation afforded by renal adjustments and active intracellular adaptation. Rapid lowering of P_{CO_2} causes dizziness, mental confusion, and rarely seizures, even in the absence of hypoxemia, as a consequence of reduced cerebral blood flow. Cerebral perfusion may fall as much as 40% with a drop in P_{CO_2} below 20 mm Hg. The cardiovascular effects of acute hypocapnia in the awake child are generally minimal; usually, only an increase in heart rate is reported. In anesthetized or mechanically ventilated patients, however, cardiac output and blood pressure may fall because of the depressant effects of anesthesia and positive-pressure ventilation on heart rate, systemic resistance, and venous return. Respiratory alkalosis does not induce cardiac rhythm disturbances in healthy children but may do so in patients with heart disease owing to changes in oxygen unloading by blood from a left shift in the hemoglobin-oxygen dissociation curve (Bohr effect) and changes in extracellular potassium, sodium, and calcium concentration. Acute respiratory alkalosis causes minor intracellular shifts of sodium, potassium, and phosphate and reduces serum-free calcium by increasing the protein-bound fraction. Hypocapnia-induced hypokalemia is usually minor (approximately 0.2 mEq/L with a 10– to 15–mm Hg drop in P_{CO_2}). Changes in chronic hypocapnia have been studied adequately only in normal humans ascending to real or simulated high altitude, and so are necessarily complicated by the attendant hypoxia. Plasma and extracellular fluid volume falls by about 10% in chronic hypocapnia as a result of the urinary sodium loss that accompanies the excretion of HCO_3^-. The small changes in plasma electrolytes noted in acute respiratory alkalosis generally are not detectable in sustained hypocapnia. However, the anion gap is raised by 4 to 5 mmol/L as a result of increases in lactate and titration of plasma proteins.

Etiology

The causes of respiratory alkalosis are presented in Table 16–3. With the exception of controlled mechanical ventilation, hypocapnia stems from either an excessive non-metabolic signal or a reduced oxygen supply. Hypoxia stimulates ventilation with ever-increasing strength as the arterial P_{CO_2} falls below 5 to 65 mm Hg, whether from lung disease, high altitude, or inspiration of air with a reduced concentration of oxygen ($F_{IO_2} < 0.21$). Anemia and hypotension are associated with hyperventilation and may be partly the result of reduced oxygen delivery to tissues in general or, more specifically, to critical areas such as the carotid body or brain. However, parallel changes in CO_2 transport (see "Respiratory Acidosis") also must take place and will stimulate ventilation. This may be most clinically important in a child with severe anemia and lung disease, particularly in efforts to wean the child from mechanical ventilation.[60] In the case of acute hypotension, part of the hypocapnia may be the result of aortic baroreceptor stimulation. Despite its considerable interference with oxygen uptake and delivery, acute carbon monoxide poisoning usually is not associated with hyperventilation, because peripheral chemoreceptors respond to arterial P_{O_2} (usually normal) and not to oxygen content. Carbon monoxide may depress directly central ventilatory control.[61]

TABLE 16–3. Causes of Respiratory Alkalosis

Hypoxia and hypoxemia
- Altitude/low F_{IO_2}
- Anemia
- Hypotension
- Lung disease

Pulmonary disorders
- Edema (hydrostatic or permeability)
- Embolism
- Airway obstruction/inflammation
- Pneumonia
- Interstitial lung disease/pneumonitis

Mechanical ventilation

Extrapulmonary disorders
- Hyperventilation: anxiety/idiopathic
- Neurologic disease
  - Cerebrovascular accident, hemorrhage
  - Infection (meningitis, encephalitis)
  - Trauma
  - Tumor
- Hormones/drugs
  - Catecholamines
  - Progesterone
  - Methylxanthines
  - Nicotine
  - Salicylates, almitrine, doxapram
- Pregnancy
- Hyperthermia
- Liver failure
- Sepsis
- Recovery from metabolic acidosis

F_{IO_2} = fractional concentration of O_2 in inspired gas.

A great number of cardiopulmonary disorders often result in respiratory alkalosis in their early to intermediate stages. Because right-to-left shunting and ventilation-perfusion inequality affect oxygen uptake to a far greater extent than does CO_2 output, hyperventilation usually results in hypocapnia.[62] However, hypoxemia is not the sole cause, because correction of arterial P_{O_2} does not always relieve the hyperventilation and alkalosis. Hyperventilation also results from stimulation of airway and parenchymal irritant receptors with inflammation and edema. A finding of normocapnia and hypoxemia may herald the onset of rapid respiratory failure and should prompt the physician to assess whether the child is becoming fatigued. Respiratory alkalosis is not uncommon during mechanical ventilation when overestimates in tidal volume and frequency are made, or when patients trigger an excessive number of additional breaths by the ventilator.

The remaining large number of conditions causing respiratory alkalosis all have in common an over-riding ventilatory stimulus of a nonmetabolic nature coupled with normal pulmonary function. Thus, it is in these disorders that the most severe respiratory alkalosis can be observed. Hyperventilation is a usual feature of stress, such as anxiety and drug or alcohol withdrawal, and is in part catecholamine mediated. When extreme and symptomatic, the hyperventilation syndrome may mimic a number of serious conditions and be quite disabling. Paresthesias, circumoral numbness, chest wall tightness or pain, dizziness, inability to take an adequate breath, and rarely tetany may themselves be sufficiently stressful to perpetuate a vicious cycle. Examination sometimes reveals conspicuous overbreathing but often shows only frequent sighing and thoracic breathing. Tachycardia and overt anxiety may be present. Arterial blood gas analysis will demonstrate an acute or chronic respiratory alkalosis, often with hypocapnia in the range of 15 to 30 mm Hg and no hypoxemia. Diseases or injury within the CNS can produce several patterns of hyperventilation with sustained arterial P_{CO_2} levels of 20 to 30 mm Hg. The site or injury is probably more critical than its nature in establishing the abnormal pattern of breathing. Many drugs and hormones provoke hyperventilation, either by direct peripheral or central stimulation or by alterations in basal cellular metabolism. Conditions such as hyperthyroidism, very high caloric loads, and exercise raise the basal metabolic rate, but ventilation usually rises in proportion, so that arterial blood gases are unchanged and respiratory alkalosis does not develop. Salicylates are the most common cause of drug-induced respiratory alkalosis. The actions of salicylates are multiple and include direct medullary chemoreceptor stimulation, uncoupling of oxidative phosphorylation, inhibition of red-cell chloride-bicarbonate exchange, and metabolic acidosis. For these reasons, salicylate toxicity can be associated with severe hypocapnia and arterial P_{CO_2} of 10 mm Hg or less. The methylxanthine drugs such as theophylline stimulate ventilation and increase the ventilatory response to CO_2. Catecholamines and various other vasoactive agents are capable of stimulating ventilation, but probably only to a minor degree at their usual physiologic and pharmacologic levels. Progesterone increases ventilation and lowers arterial P_{CO_2} by as much as 5 to 10 mm Hg. Other respiratory stimulants such as almitrine and doxapram acting at the carotid body may have sufficient potency to be used clinically to treat hypoventilation.

Hyperthermia from any cause provokes hyperventilation. Often the hyperventilation exceeds the temperature-induced rise in metabolic rate so that respiratory alkalosis can develop. The complex effects of changes in temperature on the dissociation constant of H_2O and on the p*K*a of buffers makes interpretation of changes in acid-base status difficult. Clinical blood gas analyzers are calibrated and measured at 37°C, and when the patient's temperature differs, the values are adjusted to the correct temperature. Underlying this approach is the assumption that normal values at 37°C are temperature independent, but recent work in animals suggests that pH apparently is regulated to maintain a constant alkalinity relative to water, whose neutral point (pN) varies with temperature; that is, pH-pN does not change appreciably with temperature. For practical purposes, it may be more useful to measure all blood samples at 37°C and use standard criteria at this temperature to ascertain qualitative deviations from normal acid-base balance in hyperthermia and hypothermia. Analysis of P_{O_2} and P_{CO_2} above or below 37°C, however, does require a temperature correction to obtain in vivo values for assessment of gas exchange efficiency in the lung.

Respiratory alkalosis is a prominent feature in liver failure, and its severity correlates well with the degree of hepatic insufficiency and mortality. The factors stimulating ventilation are unknown, but it is doubtful whether ammonia is the sole mediator. Glutamate, a known excitatory neurotransmitter, also rises with liver failure and may be responsible. Respiratory alkalosis is common in patients with gram-negative septicemia and is often an early finding—before fever, hypoxemia, and hypotension develop and further compound the hypocapnia. It is presumed that some bacterial product or toxin acts as a stimulant, but the mechanism remains unknown.

In the early stages of rapid recovery from chronic metabolic acidosis, the former compensating respiratory alkalosis continues unabated and can result in true alkalemia for several hours. This is commonly observed after hemodialysis when HCO_3^- is quickly increased. It has been proposed that there is a delay in the correction of the acidosis surrounding the medullary respiratory center. However, data suggest that brain extracellular fluid acid-base status is adjusted quite quickly. More likely, changes in oxygen delivery resulting from the acute left shift in the Hb-O_2 dissociation may cause a transient degree of intracellular cerebral hypoxia and acidosis that briefly sustains the hyperventilation.

Diagnosis

The diagnosis of respiratory alkalosis rests ultimately on measurement of arterial pH and P_{CO_2} or transcutaneous P_{CO_2}, if skin perfusion is adequate. End-tidal P_{CO_2} may substitute for an arterial sample if lung function is normal and no other acid-base disturbance is suspected. A low serum HCO_3^- level is consistent with a diagnosis of chronic respiratory alkalosis but cannot substitute for arterial pH and P_{CO_2}. A detailed history and careful physical examination provide important clues to the nature and duration of any acid-base derangement. Standard nomograms (see Figure 16–3) are helpful in supporting the diagnosis of a single acid-base disturbance or in directing attention to the possibility of a combined disorder. Their limitations should be recognized; they describe the acid-base status in steady-state conditions; thus, their use is limited if the patient's condition is changing rapidly. Second, the extremes are less well defined and, in most studies, probably include data that are the summation of several acid-base disorders. Last, values falling within the respiratory alkalosis confidence bands also may occur with a combination of disorders, and the need for clinical judgment remains paramount.

When a diagnosis of hyperventilation or respiratory alkalosis is made, the cause should be investigated. Diagnosis of the hyperventilation syndrome is made by exclusion and by testing whether a patient's symptom complex can be reproduced by a 3- to 5-minute session of hyperventilation and relieved by rebreathing from a small-volume paper bag. In difficult cases it may be important to rule out other conditions such as pulmonary embolism, heart disease, and hyperthyroidism. Occult airway disease may require such tests as response to bronchodilators, bronchoconstrictor provocation, and skin tests to common allergens, in addition to routine pulmonary function studies.

Treatment

The treatment of respiratory alkalosis is primarily directed to its underlying cause. Respiratory alkalosis is rarely life threatening, and direct measures to correct it are usually unnecessary and often unsuccessful if the stimulus remains unchecked. If hypoxemia coexists with respiratory alkalosis, supplemental inspired oxygen obviously is indicated. If respiratory alkalosis complicates ventilator management, changes in dead space, tidal volume, and frequency or addition of CO_2 in inspired gas can minimize the hypocapnia, but temporary controlled sedation and paralysis may be required. Patients with the hyperventilation syndrome can be benefited by sympathetic explanation, rebreathing from a paper bag during symptomatic attacks, and attention to underlying psychologic stress.

Respiratory Acidosis

Pathophysiology

Respiratory acidosis develops from an imbalance between metabolic CO_2 production and pulmonary CO_2 excretion. This most often arises from decreased efficiency of CO_2 elimination in the lungs. Alveolar hypoventilation results in CO_2 retention and hypercapnia, which eventually raise the gradient of CO_2 from tissues to inspired air, so that a new balance between CO_2 production and removal is restored. The subsequent acidification of body fluids is resisted and partially corrected by short-term chemical buffering and more long-term renal adaptation. Usually a degree of hypoxemia coexists with respiratory acidosis, unless the patient is receiving supplemental inspired oxygen. As far as is known, hypoxemia does not impair these compensatory processes unless it is so severe that anaerobic metabolism (lactic acidosis) ensues in tissues whose oxygen delivery becomes limited.

Clinical features

The clinical features of respiratory acidosis vary according to its severity, its duration, the underlying disease, and whether there is accompanying hypoxemia.[63] In general, manifestations of hypercapnia are most marked when the P_{CO_2} rises quickly and are less profound in chronic respiratory acidosis. The most important effects of hypercapnia are those in the CNS. Rapidly increasing P_{CO_2} can cause anxiety, severe dyspnea, confusion, psychosis, and hallucinations and can even progress to coma. Lesser degrees of dysfunction in chronic severe hypercapnia include sleep disturbances, loss of memory, daytime somnolence, and personality changes. Coordination may be impaired, and motor disturbances such as tremor, myoclonic jerks, and asterixis can develop. The exquisite sensitivity of the normal cerebral vasculature to the vasodilating effects of CO_2 helps to explain the headaches and other signs that mimic raised intracranial pressure, such as papilledema, abnormal reflexes, and focal muscle weakness. Acute hypercapnia also causes tachycardia, vasodilation in the systemic circulation, and vasoconstriction in the pulmonary circulation, but may be modified significantly in the face of hypoxemia, metabolic acidosis, cardiac insufficiency, and β-adrenergic blockade. Hypercapnia may play a contributory role in pulmonary hypertension secondary to hypoxemic lung disease. Cardiac arrhythmias occur in many patients with respiratory acidosis, but it is more likely that concomitant disorders such as pre-existing heart disease, electrolyte imbalance, and hypoxia are responsible.

Etiology

Respiratory acidosis may arise from disease or dysfunction at any point in the transport of CO_2 from respiring cells to the atmosphere. Carbon dioxide homeostasis and its regulation require normal lung mechanics, circulation, and ventilatory drive. When the neuromuscular limb of the respiratory system remains intact and is operating below its maximal capacity, defects elsewhere may be totally or partially compensated by increased ventilation. Table 16–4 is an extensive list of causes of respiratory acidosis. It is not uncommon, especially in severely ill patients, to find more than one cause. Acute alveolar hypoventilation rarely causes life-threatening CO_2 retention before critical hypoxemia supervenes. However, when alveolar hypoventilation occurs with provision of supplemental oxygen, severe respiratory acidosis can develop in as little as 10 to 15 minutes.

Carbon dioxide retention and respiratory acidosis secondary to intrinsic acute and chronic lung disease of any cause signify rapid deterioration or end-stage disease, and often have a poor prognosis. Indeed, patients with earlier

TABLE 16–4. Causes of Respiratory Acidosis

- **Hypoventilation**
  - Depression of ventilatory drive
    - Drugs
      - General anesthetics
      - Overdosage: sedatives, alcohol, narcotics, ß-blockers
    - Brain-stem lesions
    - Sleep-disordered breathing syndromes
    - Idiopathic hypoventilation syndromes
  - Neuromuscular disease
    - High cervical cord trauma
    - Disorders of neuromuscular junction
      - Botulism
      - Tetanus
      - Myasthenia gravis
      - Paralyzing drugs
    - Demyelinating diseases
      - Guillain-Barré syndrome
      - Multiple sclerosis
      - Amyotrophic lateral sclerosis
      - Poliomyelitis
    - Abnormalities of skeletal muscle
      - Electrolyte disorders
        - Hypokalemia
        - Hypophosphatemia
      - Myxedema
      - Myositis
        - Dermatopolymyositis
        - Lupus
      - Disorders of muscle metabolism
      - Myopathies
        - Muscular dystrophy
        - Spinal muscle atrophy
    - Respiratory muscle fatigue
  - Mechanical ventilation

- **Ventilation-perfusion mismatch**
  - Obstructive disorders
    - Upper airway obstruction
    - Asthma/diffuse bronchoconstriction
    - Chronic obstructive pulmonary disease
  - Restrictive disorders
    - Intrapulmonary
      - Extensive pneumonia
      - Adult respiratory distress syndrome
      - Cardiogenic pulmonary edema
      - Interstitial fibrosis and pneumonitis
    - Extrapulmonary
      - Pneumothorax, hydrothorax, hemothorax
      - Diffuse pleural thickening
      - Chest wall/spinal abnormalities
      - Severe obesity

- **Abnormalities in blood CO_2 transport**
  - Decreased perfusion
    - Heart failure
    - Cardiac arrest/cardiopulmonary resuscitation
    - Extensive pulmonary embolism
  - Severe anemia
  - Carbonic anhydrase inhibition
  - Red cell anion exchange inhibition

stages of lung damage are usually normocapnic or hypocapnic. The small degree of hypercapnia that can otherwise result from mild-to-moderate ventilation-perfusion mismatch is offset easily by increased ventilation, because lung units with high ventilation-perfusion values compensate for the decreased efficiency of low ventilation-perfusion units in CO_2 elimination but not oxygen uptake.

Reduction in ventilatory drive from depression of the respiratory center by a variety of drugs, injury, or disease can produce respiratory acidosis. Acutely, this may occur with general anesthetics, sedative and β-adrenergic blocker overdosage, and head and brain-stem trauma, and rarely during normal sleep. Chronic causes of respiratory center depression include sedatives, alcohol, intracranial tumors, bulbar poliomyelitis, the several syndromes of sleep-disordered breathing, and the primary alveolar and obesity-hypoventilation syndromes. A discussion of the pathophysiology, diagnosis, and treatment of disorders in ventilatory control and sleep-disordered breathing can be found elsewhere in this text. Neuromuscular disorders involving abnormalities or disease in the motor neurons, neuromuscular junction, and skeletal muscle can cause acute respiratory acidosis due to hypoventilation. Although a number of diseases should be considered in the differential diagnosis, drugs and electrolyte disorders should always be ruled out. Mechanical ventilation, when not properly adjusted and supervised, may result in respiratory acidosis. This will occur if CO_2 production suddenly rises (because of fever, agitation, sepsis, or overfeeding), or if alveolar ventilation falls because of worsening pulmonary function, and the patient is unable to trigger an adequate increase in respiratory frequency. The patient's failure to increase the level of assisted ventilation spontaneously may be the result of controlled mechanical ventilation, paralysis, or loss of normal ventilatory drives from disease or sedation. Leaks, disconnections, or obstructions anywhere in the ventilatory circuit are obvious causes for reduced alveolar ventilation. High levels of positive end-expiratory pressure in the presence of reduced cardiac output may cause hypercapnia as a result of large increases in alveolar dead space. Overproduction of CO_2 in and of itself is never a cause of respiratory acidosis, because the normal respiratory system is able to respond to as much as a 20-fold increase in metabolism (heavy exercise) without the development of hypercapnia. However, it can complicate ventilator management and should always be considered as a cause of further deterioration in a patient receiving mechanical ventilation.

Disease and obstruction of the airways are marked by respiratory acidosis when it is severe or long standing. Acute hypercapnia follows sudden occlusion of the upper airway or, with the more generalized bronchospasm that occurs with severe asthma, anaphylaxis, and inhalational burn or toxin injury. Chronic hypercapnia and respiratory acidosis occur in end-stage chronic obstructive pulmonary disease (COPD; emphysema, chronic bronchitis, bronchiolitis, and cystic fibrosis). Untreated severe reversible airway obstruction such as asthma and occult functional and anatomic upper airway obstructive lesions are encountered much less commonly, but they may present with CO_2 retention. Sustained hypercapnia in COPD eventually can engender a decreased ventilatory responsiveness to CO_2 as measured by changes in ventilation per unit rise in CO_2. This occurs for several reasons. First, there may be normal sensitivity but chronic muscle fatigue from the increased work of breathing, which prevents full expression of this drive, as can be shown in normal subjects breathing against an external resistance. In some patients there may be true reduced neural output from the respiratory controller in response to an elevated CO_2 level. This phenomenon is poorly understood and in some cases may be an inherited trait, since some healthy family members of patients with COPD and CO_2 retention have reduced ventilatory responsiveness to CO_2. Furthermore, long-standing hypercapnia elicits compensatory renal bicarbonate generation and changes in cerebrospinal fluid and brain extracellular fluid hydrogen ion concentration that almost normalize the pH bathing the respiratory centers in the medulla. Thus, the effect on brain pH of an incremental rise in P_{CO_2} is less when the HCO_3^- value is already raised. The interplay of ventilatory muscle strength, inherent CO_2 sensitivity, and compensatory acid-base adjustments in the CNS probably help to explain the lack of any strong correlation between the degree of airway obstruction and the onset of eventual CO_2 retention in these patients.

Restrictive disorders involving both the chest wall and the lungs can cause acute and chronic respiratory acidosis. Acute hypercapnia may complicate any form of extraparenchymal restriction, especially if the patient's underlying lung function is limited. Rapidly progressing restrictive processes in the lung can lead to respiratory acidosis, because the high cost of breathing causes ventilatory muscle fatigue. Restrictive diseases that lead to replacement of normal alveolar space by scarring and exudate will manifest CO_2 retention when the loss in lung compliance and extent of ventilation-perfusion mismatch become severe. In contrast to patients with COPD, these individuals rarely show decreased CO_2 sensitivity and thus can be profoundly dyspneic.

Respiratory acidosis may develop when the ability of the cardiovascular system and blood to transport CO_2 is compromised greatly. In contrast to all other forms of metabolic and respiratory acid-base derangements, arterial blood measurements in these conditions may not reflect the true tissue acid-base status. Thus, in such situations a respiratory acidosis will not yield a respiratory arterial acidemia. This dissociation between arterial and tissue acid-base status occurs either as a consequence of reduced pulmonary blood flow or when the total CO_2-carrying capacity of blood or the kinetics of CO_2 exchange are decreased severely. Compensatory hyperventilation can result in no detectable arterial hypercapnia if lung function, respiratory muscle strength, and ventilatory drive are adequate, or if ventilation is supported mechanically. In cardiac resuscitation and high-grade pulmonary vascular obstruction (embolism or destruction), low cardiac output and poor perfusion of the tissues and lung will result in decreased CO_2 elimination (as well as decreased oxygen uptake) and CO_2 retention. If ventilation is stimulated greatly or supported mechanically, the extent, or even presence, of a respiratory acidosis may be obscured, because enough CO_2 is cleared from the reduced pulmonary blood flow to yield frank arterial normocapnia or hypocapnia (and alkalemia).

Anemia decreases both the oxygen and the CO_2-carrying capacity of blood and can cause a degree of tissue respiratory acidosis, both from loss of the buffering capacity provided by Hb and from reduction in the total red cell surface area available for bicarbonate-chloride exchange with plasma. The ensuing CO_2 retention (and lactic acidosis if oxygen delivery also is critically compromised) stimulates compensatory hyperventilation. Analysis of arterial blood, however, will not mirror accurately the tissue acid-base status. In a similar fashion, inhibitors of red cell anion (bicarbonate-chloride) exchange, such as salicylates, furosemide, probenecid, and certain nonsteroidal anti-inflammatory drugs in high concentration (rarely problematic in their therapeutic ranges in patients with normal lung function), can impair the efficiency of CO_2 elimination and potentially cause respiratory acidosis. Inhibitors of carbonic anhydrase such as acetazolamide also cause a variable degree of respiratory acidosis. Again whether this is reflected in arterial blood depends on the magnitude of compensatory hyperventilation. The constant state of in vivo disequilibrium between CO_2 and bicarbonate during carbonic anhydrase inhibition, and between plasma and red cell bicarbonate during anion exchange inhibition, renders analysis of arterial blood gases (measured at equilibrium ex vivo) difficult, because there is no simple means by which to calculate in vivo values retroactively. These hemocirculatory disorders thus constitute a special category of respiratory acidosis whose presence may be hidden if arterial blood gas values are analyzed in ignorance of the true pathophysiologic state. It should be understood that any observed hyperventilation and lack of arterial hypercapnia are secondary and should not to be interpreted as evidence of a primary respiratory alkalosis. Although difficult to obtain, some indicator of tissue P_{CO_2} (such as mixed venous P_{CO_2}) will reflect more accurately the actual systemic acid-base status.

Diagnosis

The diagnosis of respiratory acidosis cannot be made reliably on the basis of clinical assessment of the level of ventilation. It is difficult to judge the depth of ventilation accurately; even if ventilation is increased, it may not be sufficient to counter adverse changes in dead space or rates of CO_2 production. Thus, diagnosis rests principally on measurement of arterial P_{CO_2} and pH, keeping in mind the few situations when arterial values no longer closely parallel tissue acid-base status. Detailed history and physical examination often provide important diagnostic clues to the nature and duration of the acidosis. The use of standard nomograms and the 95% confidence intervals for acute and chronic respiratory acidosis supports the diagnosis of a single disturbance, or can draw attention to other acid-base disturbances, if the patient is in a steady state. Frequent assessment over time, especially in response to therapy, can be helpful. To investigate the cause of respiratory acidosis, pulmonary function studies (including spirometry, diffusing capacity for carbon monoxide, lung volumes, and arterial P_{O_2} and saturation) usually provide adequate assessment of whether respiratory acidosis is secondary to lung disease. Workup for nonpulmonary causes should include a detailed drug history, measurement of hematocrit, and assessment of upper airway, chest wall, pleural, and neuromuscular function. Rarely, it may be necessary to monitor breathing during sleep or to measure ventilatory drives.

Treatment

The treatment of respiratory acidosis depends on its severity and rate of onset. Acute respiratory acidosis can be life threatening, and measures to reverse the underlying cause should be simultaneous with restoration of adequate alveolar ventilation to relieve severe hypoxemia and acidemia. Temporarily, this may necessitate tracheal intubation and assisted mechanical ventilation. Severe respiratory acidosis unresponsive to modern techniques of mechanical ventilation is rare but may be encountered in status asthmaticus, major pulmonary barotrauma, and severe end-stage restrictive and obstructive pulmonary disease. In these situations alkali therapy (intravenously infused sodium bicarbonate, Carbicarb, or other basic equivalents such as tromethamine [THAM]) may be used as a temporary measure to raise arterial pH. A range of 7.10 to 7.20 is a good compromise between tolerable acidemia and problems with volume overload and subsequent posthypercapnic alkalosis. As mentioned earlier, if oxygenation and tissue perfusion are not compromised and intracranial pressure is normal, tolerance to severe hypercapnia is remarkable, and strict maintenance of pH may not be necessary for a satisfactory outcome as primary therapy is instituted. This applies to the difficult-to-ventilate patient with status asthmaticus[64] and in those with acute respiratory distress syndrome[65] in which low tidal volumes and permissive hypercapnia have been used. Sedation and paralysis may be helpful when severe agitation increases CO_2 production and causes the patient to struggle against the ventilator. Extracorporeal venovenous CO_2 removal has been tried successfully in severe adult respiratory distress syndrome with respiratory acidosis, but a recent randomized trial in adults showed no mortality difference when compared with standard protocol-based ventilation strategy.[66]

Oxygen should always be provided, but very carefully titrated, in patients with severe COPD and chronic CO_2 retention who are still breathing spontaneously. When oxygen is used injudiciously, ($F_{IO_2} > 0.4$), these patients may experience further respiratory acidosis. The basis for this is multifactorial and controversial. Classically, it has been believed to be a consequence of further alveolar hypoventilation attendant on suppression of the hypoxic ventilatory drive; however, further ventilation-perfusion mismatch secondary to release of hypoxic vasoconstriction in poorly ventilated lung units may be equally important. To a lesser extent, decreased solubility of CO_2 in already hypercapnic but better oxygenated blood (the Haldane effect) may further elevate the P_{CO_2}.

Aggressive and rapid correction of hypercapnia should be avoided; otherwise the falling P_{CO_2} may provoke the same complications noted with acute respiratory alkalosis (ie, cardiac arrhythmias, reduced cerebral perfusion, and seizures). It is advisable to lower the P_{CO_2} gradually in chronic respiratory acidosis while simultaneously providing sufficient chloride and potassium to enhance the renal excretion of bicarbonate. If these measures fail to prevent post-hypercapnic metabolic alkalosis, further reduction in bicarbonate can be accomplished by the use of acetazolamide (5 mg/kg) or dilute (0.1 N) hydrochloric acid infusion via a central vein.

Chronic respiratory acidosis is frequently difficult to correct, but general measures aimed at maximizing lung function with antibiotics, oxygen, bronchodilators, corticosteroids, diuretics, and physiotherapy can help some patients and can forestall further deterioration in most. The use of respiratory stimulants may prove helpful in selected cases, particularly if the patient appears to have hypercapnia out of proportion to the level of lung function, or suffers from sleep-disordered breathing or one of the hypoventilation syndromes. These stimulants include progesterone, protriptyline, acetazolamide, theophylline, doxapram, and almitrine. Sedatives and alcohol generally should be avoided, although low doses of codeine and other narcotics may help to relieve disabling dyspnea in a few patients, for whom nothing else can be offered.

References

1. Evans NJ, Rutter N. Percutaneous respiration in the newborn infant. J Pediatr 1986;108:282–6.
2. Swenson ER. Kinetics of oxygen and carbon dioxide exchange. In: Boutilier RG, ed. Advances in comparative and environmental physiology. Vol. 6. Berlin-Heidelberg: Springer-Verlag, 1990:163–209.
3. Haussinger D. pH homeostasis: mechanisms and control. London: Academic Press, 1988.
4. Cohen JJ, Kassirer JP. Acid-base. Boston: Little, Brown, 1982.
5. Maren TH. Carbonic anhydrase: chemistry, physiology and inhibition. Physiol Rev 1967;47:595–708.
6. Kleinman LI, Petering HG, Sutherland JM. Blood carbonic anhydrase activity and zinc concentration in infants with respiratory-distress syndrome. N Engl J Med 1967;277:1157–61.
7. Brahm J, Wimberley PD. Chloride and bicarbonate transport in fetal red cells. J Physiol 1989;419:141–56.
8. Bauer C. Schroeder E. Carbamino compounds of hemoglobin in human adult and fetal blood. J Physiol 1972;227:457–71.
9. Tyuma I. The Bohr effect and the Haldane effect in human hemoglobin. Jpn J Physiol 1984;34:204–16.
10. Hlastala MP. Significance of the Bohr and Haldane effects in the pulmonary capillary. Respir Physiol 1973;17:81–92.
11. Bauer C. On the respiratory function of hemoglobin. Rev Physiol Biochem Pharmacol 1974;70:1–31.
12. Hill EP, Power GG, Longo LD. A mathematical model of carbon dioxide transfer in the placenta and its interaction with oxygen. Am J Physiol 1973;224:283–99.
13. Piiper J. Pulmonary and circulatory carbon dioxide transport and acid-base homeostasis. In: Haussinger D, ed. pH homeostasis: mechanisms and control. London: Academic Press, 1988:181–202.
14. Bidani A, Crandall ED. Quantitative aspects of capillary CO_2 exchange. In: Chang M, Paiva M, eds. Respiratory physiology: an analytical approach. New York: Marcel Dekker, 1989:371–420.
15. Swenson ER. The respiratory aspects of carbonic anhydrase. Ann N Y Acad Sci 1984;429:547–60.
16. Maren TH. Carbonic anhydrase and respiratory distress. N Engl J Med 1968;278:398–9.
17. Johnson RL, Ramanathan M. Buffer equilibria in the lungs. In: Seldin GW, Giebisch G, eds. The kidney: physiology and pathophysiology. New York: Raven Press, 1985:149–71.
18. Wagner PD, West JB. Effects of diffusion impairment on O_2 and CO_2 time courses in pulmonary capillaries. J Appl Physiol 1972;33:62–71.
19. Somero GN. Protons, osmolytes, and fitness of internal milieu for protein function. Am J Physiol 1986;251:R197–213.
20. Roos A, Boron WF. Intracellular pH. Physiol Rev 1982;61:296–434.
21. Hoffman EK, Simonsen LO. Membrane mechanisms in volume and pH regulation in vertebrate cells. Physiol Rev 1989;69:315–82.
22. Bettice JA, Wang BC, Brown EB Jr. Intracellular buffering of heart and skeletal muscles during the onset of hypercapnia. Respir Physiol 1976;28:89–98.
23. Lih L, Gonzalez-Mendez R, Severinghaus JW. Cerebral intracellular changes during supercarbia: a in vivo ^{31}P

nuclear magnetic resonance study in rats. J Cereb Blood Flow Metab 1985;5:537–42.

24. Javaheri S, Glendening A, Papadakis N, Brody JS. Changes in brain surface pH during acute isocapnic metabolic acidosis and alkalosis. J Appl Physiol 1981;51:276–81.
25. Arieff AI, Kerian A, Massry SG, Delima J. Intracellular pH of brain: alterations in active respiratory acidosis and alkalosis. Am J Physiol 1976;230:804–12.
26. Weintraub WH, Machen TE. pH regulation in hepatoma cells: roles of Na-H exchange, CI-HCO_3 exchange and Na-HCO_3 cotransport. Am J Physiol 1989;257:G317–27.
27. Wood SC, Schaefer KE. Regulation of intracellular pH in lungs and other tissues during hypercapnia. J Appl Physiol 1978;45:115–8.
28. Jentsch TJ, Janicke I, Sorgenfrei S, et al. Regulation of intracellular pH in monkey kidney epithelial cells. Am J Physiol 1986;252:6109–13.
29. Goldstein B, Shannon DC, Todres ID. Supercarbia in children: clinical course and outcome. Crit Care Med 1990; 18:166–8.
30. Engel K, Dell RB, Rahill WJ, et al. Quantitative studies of acid-base displacement in respiratory acidosis. J Appl Physiol 1986;24:288.
31. Albert MS, Dell RB, Winters RW. Quantitative displacement of acid-base equilibrium in metabolic acidosis. Ann Intern Med 1967;66:312.
32. Edelman CM Jr, Boichis H, Soriano JR, Start H. The renal response of children to acute ammonium chloride acidosis. Pediatr Res 1967;1:452–6.
33. Carlo WA, Pacifico L, Charburn RL, et al. Efficacy of computer assisted management of respiratory failure in neonates. Pediatrics 1986;78:139–42.
34. Asch MD, Dell RB, Williams GS. Time course for development of respiratory compensation in metabolic acidosis. J Lab Clin Med 1969;73:610–7.
35. Pierce NF, Fedoon DS, Brigham KL. The ventilatory response to acute base deficit. Ann Intern Med 1970; 72:663–6.
36. Madias NE, Wolf CJ, Cohen JJ. Regulation of acid-base equilibrium in chronic hypercapnia. Kidney Int 1985; 27:538–43.
37. Ruiz OS, Arruda JAL, Talor Z. Na-HCO_3 cotransport and Na-H antiporter in chronic respiratory acidosis and alkalosis. Am J Physiol 1989;256:F414–20.
38. Madsen KM, Tisher CC. Cellular responses to acute respiratory acidosis in rat medullary collecting duct. Am J Physiol 1983;245:F670–9.
39. Rodriguez-Nichols F, Laughrey E, Tannen RL. Response of renal NH_3 production to chronic respiratory acidosis. Am J Physiol 1984;247:F896–903.
40. Hilden SA, Johns CA, Madias NE. Adaptation of rabbit renal cortical Na^+-H^+ exchange activity in chronic hypocapnia. Am J Physiol 1989;257:F615–22.
41. Al-Awqati Q. The cellular renal response to respiratory acid-base disorders. Kidney Int 1985;28:845–55.
42. Star RA, Burg MB, Knepper MA. Bicarbonate secretion and chloride reabsorption by rabbit cortical collecting ducts. Role of chloride/bicarbonate exchange. J Clin Invest 1985;76:1123–30.
43. Gledhill N, Beirne GJ, Dempsey JA. Renal response to short term hypocapnia in man. Kidney Int 1975;8:376–81.
44. Gennari FJ, Goldstein MB, Schwartz WB. The nature of the renal response to chronic hypocapnia. J Clin Invest 1972;51:1722–9.
45. Moore ES, Fine BP, Statrasook SA, et al. Renal reabsorption of bicarbonate in puppies: effect of extracellular volume contraction on the renal threshold for bicarbonate. Pediatr Res 1972;6:859–67.
46. van der Heijden AJ, Guignard J-P. Bicarbonate reabsorption by the kidney of the newborn rabbit. Am J Physiol 1989;256:F29–34.
47. Edelman CM, Rodriquez-Soriano J, Boichis A, et al. Renal bicarbonate reabsorption and hydrogen ion excretion in normal infants. J Clin Invest 1967;46:1309–17.
48. Baum M. Neonatal rabbit juxtamedullary proximal convoluted tubule acidification. J Clin Invest 1991;85: 499–506.
49. Lorenz JM, Kleinman LT. Effects of euvolemic and hypervolemic hyperbicarbonatemia on segmental nephron HCO_3 reabsorption. Pediatr Res 1990;27:604–11.
50. Atkinson DE, Bourke E. Metabolic aspects of the regulation of systemic pH. Am J Physiol 1987;252:F947–56.
51. Haussinger D, Steeb R, Gerok W. Ammonium and bicarbonate homeostasis in chronic liver disease. Kline Wochenschr 1990;68:175–82.
52. Walzer M. Roles of urea production, ammonia excretion and amino acid oxidation in acid-base balance. Am J Physiol 1986:250:F181–8.
53. Cheema-Dhadli S, Jungas RL, Halperin ML. Regulation of urea synthesis by acid-base balance in vivo: role of NH_3 concentration. Am J Physiol 1987;252:F221–5.
54. Ahmdal T, Vilstrup H, Bjerrum K, Kristensen L. Decrease in ureagenesis by partial hepatectomy does not influence acid-base balance. Am J Physiol 1989;257:F696–9.
55. Shangraw RE, Jahoor F. Effect of liver disease and transplantation on urea synthesis in humans: relationship to acid-base status. Am J Physiol 1999;276:G1145–52.
56. Androgue JH, Rashad MN, Gorin AB, et al. Arteriovenous acid-base disparity in circulatory failure: studies on mechanisms. Am J Physiol 1980;257:F1087–93.
57. Karlowicz MG, Simmons MA, Brusilow SW, Jones MD Jr. Carbonic acid dissociation constant (pK_1) in critically ill newborns. Pediatr Res 1984;18:1287–9.
58. Kruse JA, Kukku P, Carlson RW. Relationship between the apparent dissociative constant of blood carbonic acid and severity of illness. J Lab Clin Med 1989;114:568–74.
59. Slutsky AS, Rebuck AS. Respiratory alkalosis: physiological implications and clinical consequences. Acute Care 1986;12:34–48.
60. Schonhofer B, Bohrer H, Kohler D. Blood transfusion facilitating difficult weaning from the ventilator. Anesthesia 1998;53:181–4.
61. Cobun RF, Forman HJ. Carbon monoxide toxicity. In: Farhi LE, Tenney SM, eds. The respiratory system. Vol. IV. Gas exchange. Bethesda (MD): American Physiological Society, 1987:439–56.
62. West JB. Pulmonary pathophysiology—the essentials. Baltimore, Williams & Wilkins, 1977:20–41.

63. Weinberger SE, Schwartzstein M, Weiss JW. Hypercapnia. N Engl J Med 1989;321:1223–30.
64. Darioli R, Perret C. Mechanical controlled hypoventilation in status asthmaticus. Am Rev Respir Dis 1984;129:385–9.
65. ARDS Network. Ventilation with lower tidal volumes as compared with traditional tidal volumes for acute lung injury and the acute respiratory distress syndrome. N Engl J Med 2000; 342:1301–6.
66. Morris A, Wallace CJ, Menlove RL, et al. Randomized clinical trial of pressure-controlled inverse ratio ventilation and extracorporeal CO_2 removal for adult respiratory distress syndrome. Am J Respir Crit Care Med 1994; 149:295–305.

CHAPTER 17

HEART-LUNG INTERACTIONS

STEVEN M. SCHARF, MD, PHD, ANTHONY S. SICA, PHD

The cardiovascular and respiratory systems work in concert toward a common goal—the delivery of oxygen and metabolites to peripheral tissues, and the delivery of metabolic byproducts such as carbon dioxide to the lungs. The integration between these systems occurs at mechanical and neurophysiologic levels. The mechanical interactions relate to the effects of altered pulmonary mechanics on pulmonary hemodynamics, the effects of intrathoracic pressure on pulmonary and cardiac hemodynamic function, and the effects of lung volume and intrathoracic pressure on cardiac and circulatory function. Neurophysiologic interactions are also quite complex. These include interactions between respiratory- and circulatory-related neurons at the level of the central nervous system (central integration), reflex effects of altered respiratory mechanics on cardiocirculatory function, and reflex effects of altered circulatory function on ventilatory control (eg, congestive heart failure).

It is beyond the scope of this chapter to review in detail all of the possible interactions that are important for the care of the newborn and child. We have chosen to write this chapter in two parts. The first part overviews some of the important mechanical interactions whereby altered respiratory mechanics can influence peripheral circulatory and cardiac function. The principles outlined here are of importance to understanding the influence of respiratory loading, as in airways obstruction, and mechanical ventilation on cardiocirculatory function. The second part reviews the development of central nervous system respiratory-circulatory interactions at the level of respiratory and cardiac pattern generators. This is of particular importance for understanding the pathophysiology of sudden infant death syndrome (SIDS) and other conditions in which the cardiorespiratory response to ventilatory loading is inadequate. No attempt has been made to be exhaustive in this chapter. Rather, the authors hope to elucidate some of the essential vocabulary and theoretic framework that will enable the reader to understand the current clinical literature.

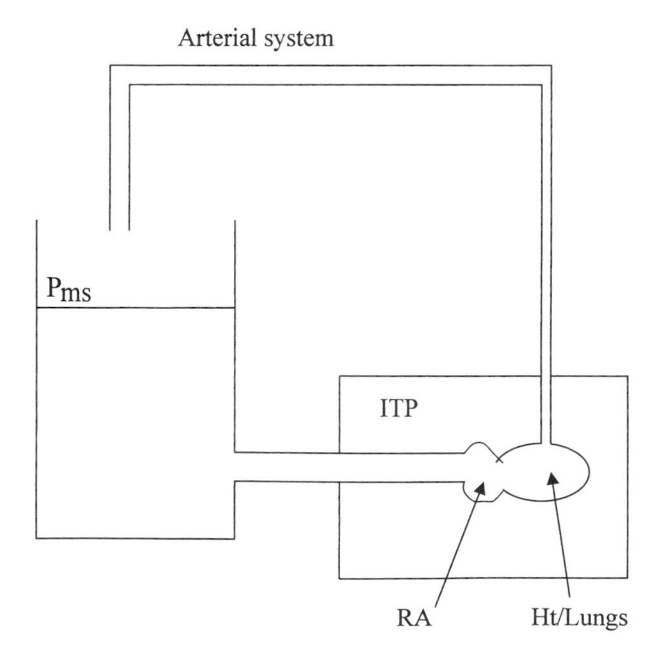

FIGURE 17–1. Simplified scheme of the circulatory system. See text for explanation. P_{ms} = mean systemic pressure; ITP = intrathoracic pressure; RA = right atrium.

Mechanical Principles of Heart-Lung Interactions

VENOUS RETURN AND THE CONTROL OF CARDIAC OUTPUT

Venous return and the determination of cardiac output

Changes in cardiac output (CO) with ventilatory maneuvers, especially those associated with increased airway pressure, may be understood in terms of the interaction between venous return (VR) and cardiac function according to the classic theory of Guyton et al,[1,2] the basic principles of which remain valid today, in spite of numerous modifications. Figure 17–1 shows a simplified scheme of the circulatory system, including a lumped peripheral circulatory reservoir. This reservoir is primarily venous, since most blood volume is contained in the veins. The reservoir drains via a resistance (called the resistance to venous return) into the right atrium, which is located in the chest and is subject to changes in intrathoracic pressure. The right atrium can be considered to be the priming chamber for the heart and lungs, which for this analysis are lumped. The heart then generates pressure in the arterial resistance, which allows blood to flow back into the peripheral reservoir. The pressure in

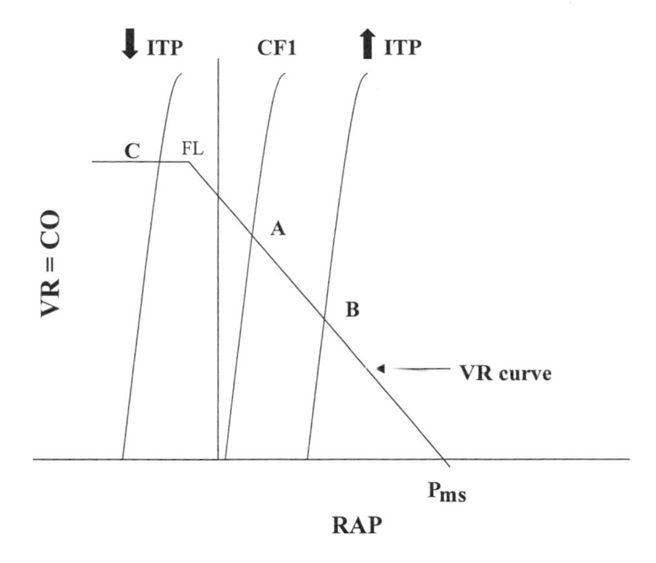

FIGURE 17–2. Venous return and cardiac function curves. Points of intersection of different cardiac function curves with the venous return curve are shown (*A, B, C*). The slope of the VR curve = 1/(resistance to venous return). Shift of cardiac function curves with increasing or decreasing ITP also is shown. See text for further explanation. RAP = right atrial pressure; VR = venous return; CO = cardiac output; ITP = intrathoracic pressure; CF1 = baseline cardiac function curve; FL = point of flow limitation; P_{mc} = mean systemic pressure.

the lumped common circulatory reservoir, called mean systemic pressure (P_{ms}), is determined by the stressed volume in the chamber and its compliance. Venous return is determined by the pressure gradient between P_{ms} and right atrial pressure (RAP), which acts as the back pressure to VR as well as an index of the diastolic filling (preload) of the heart. Mathematically, the equation describing VR may be described as follows:

$$VR = \frac{P_{ms} - RAP}{R_{VR}}$$

where R_{VR} is resistance to VR.

Figure 17–2 demonstrates how a change in RAP affects VR. The curve describing the relationship between RAP and VR is called a *venous return curve*. Note that as RAP increases, VR decreases until flow is zero. At the point of zero flow, RAP is equal to P_{ms}, and the gradient for VR is zero. Decreasing RAP leads to increases in VR until RAP falls below the point of *flow limitation*. Below this point further decreases in RAP fail to elicit increases in VR. Flow limitation is thought to be due to collapse of the great veins at or near the thoracic inlet and is influenced by abdominal pressure, tissue pressure, and critical closing pressure of certain abdominal organs, notably the liver. Since RAP is also an index of cardiac preload, a curve describing the relationship between RAP and CO can be described—the classic *Starling function curve*. Three cardiac function curves are shown in Figure 17–2. The curves plot CO as a function of RAP. For now we concentrate on CF1, the "normal" cardiac function curve. Since, at equilibrium, VR must equal CO, under steady state conditions the system exists at the point of intersection of the VR and cardiac function curves, indicated as point A in Figure 17–2. The slope of the venous return curve is equal to the inverse of the resistance to venous return ($1/R_{VR}$). This term includes simple venous ohmic resistance, and also the distribution of arterial blood to vascular beds with different drainage characteristic changes.[3]

The value of P_{ms} is not precisely known under most clinical situations. In anesthetized dogs undergoing right heart bypass it is approximately 7 mm Hg.[1–3] In closed-chest animals (REF) and in anesthetized humans, P_{ms} is somewhat greater[4,5]—10 to 12 mm Hg. Respiratory maneuvers can translocate blood volume into or out of the thorax, thus changing the volume in the peripheral reservoirs and hence changing P_{ms}. For example, positive pressure ventilation, by raising intrathoracic pressure (ITP), can translocate blood volume from intrathoracic reservoirs (the heart and lungs) into the periphery, raising P_{ms} and partially compensating for decreased VR (see below). Similarly, respiratory maneuvers can change the pressure surrounding the great veins and change the point of flow limitation as well.

Unfortunately, the simple model depicted in Figure 17–1 fails when one considers the relationships between VR from different areas in the body. For example, VR through the inferior vena cava from abdomen and legs is approximately three times that through the superior vena cava. The abdominal vascular compartment is a major reservoir of blood, and changes in abdominal mechanics can have substantial influence on VR and CO. Raising abdominal pressure tends to empty the abdominal capacitance bed toward the right atrium. Under the right conditions, this can lead to increased VR.[6] In the steady state, after the abdominal capacitance bed has been emptied, increased back pressure to VR from the extra-abdominal compartments is still present, potentially reducing steady-state VR from the legs. Takata et al[6] developed a model for understanding abdominal VR produced by changes in respiration that can also be used to understand the variable and confusing reports in the literature that an increase in abdominal pressure can either decrease, increase, or produce no change in CO. With low abdominal pressure and high intravascular volume, raising abdominal pressure shifts blood volume from the abdomen to the thorax, and VR and CO increase. On the other hand, with hypovolemia or increased abdominal pressure (eg, with ascites), further increases in abdominal pressure cannot translocate volume from the abdomen into the thorax. This is because, under these conditions, abdominal pressure is greater than intravascular pressure and leads to collapse of the inferior vena cava at the thoracic inlet. Thus, increasing abdominal pressure may actually decrease VR and CO. Recently Tarasiuk et al[7] applied these principles to understand the effects of periodic obstructive apneas on abdominal VR. Obstructive sleep apnea is associated with large swings in intrathoracic and probably intra-abdominal pressures. In anesthetized dogs, these authors demonstrated an elimination of inspiratory flow limitation when the animals were made hypervolemic. This finding suggests that hypervolemia in sleep apnea patients is an adaptive mechanism for preserving VR during apneas.

Effects of changes in intrathoracic pressure on venous return

If airway pressure increases, lung volume increases. This leads to an increase in ITP as determined by lung and chest wall compliance in addition to the increase in airway pressure. If there were no effect on cardiac function, then the cardiac function curve would shift to the right along the x-axis by an amount equal to the increase in ITP, as shown in Figure 17–2. Because increases in ITP are transmitted through to the right atrium raising RAP and reducing the gradient for VR (P_{ms}–RAP), the steady state point of intersection of the VR and cardiac function curves moves to point B. Effectively, the point of intersection between VR and cardiac function curves "slides" down the VR curve, increasing RAP and decreasing steady state CO and VR. Thus, with increased airway pressure, VR decreases—at least when cardiac function is normal. If, as discussed below, cardiac function is improved by the increase in ITP, this would have little effect on the changes in CO in normal hearts, because normal cardiac function curves are steep, and further increases in the slope of the cardiac function curve, whose theoretic maximum limit is a vertical line, are small. Thus, with normal hearts, when ITP is increased, VR effects prevail over the cardiac function effects, and CO decreases.

Figure 17–2 also illustrates the effects of decreased ITP. If there were no change in cardiac function with decreased ITP (see below), then because of transmission of ITP to the right atrium, there would be a parallel leftward shift in the cardiac function curve. This would result in a shift in the point of intersection of the VR and cardiac function curves such that VR would increase and RAP would decrease. Just as there are limits on the amount by which VR can decrease with increased ITP (ie, zero flow), there are limits on the amount by which VR can increase with decreases in ITP—because of the flow limiting point. Decreases in ITP that decrease RAP below the point of flow limitation (which is likely around –4 to –10 mm Hg,[2,7] although little is known about this value in most clinically relevant situations) fail to elicit further increases in VR.

Finally, as with the heart, the peripheral circulatory system is subject to external influences. Figure 17–3 shows the effects of sympathetic stimulation and administration of volume to the peripheral circulatory reservoir. Venous return curve 1 and cardiac function curve 1 illustrate the normal situation and intersect at point A. Sympathetic stimulation shifts the VR curve to the right in parallel (increased P_{ms} with little change in resistance to VR). However, because of inotropic effects, the cardiac function curve becomes more steep. Thus, CO and VR in a steady state increase, with little change in RAP (point B). With volume infusion into the peripheral circulatory reservoir, either external or by shifting blood from "unstressed" compartments, P_{ms} increases and the VR curve shifts to the right as in sympathetic stimulation, but the cardiac function curve does not change (ignoring possible reflex effects). Thus, CO and VR increase with an increase in RAP. Finally, if there is a poorly functioning heart, the cardiac function curve shifts to curve 2, and the point of intersection also shifts rightward (point C). In this scenario CO has decreased although RAP has increased. If cardiac dysfunction is long standing, then compensatory mechanisms, including fluid retention and sympathetic stimulation,[8,9] come into play, which lead to rightward shifts in the venous return curve as in curve 2. However, because of the flat cardiac function curve, the expected increase in cardiac output is blunted (point D) with a poorly functioning heart, and little increase in output occurs by progressively raising P_{ms} (shifting the venous return curve rightward).

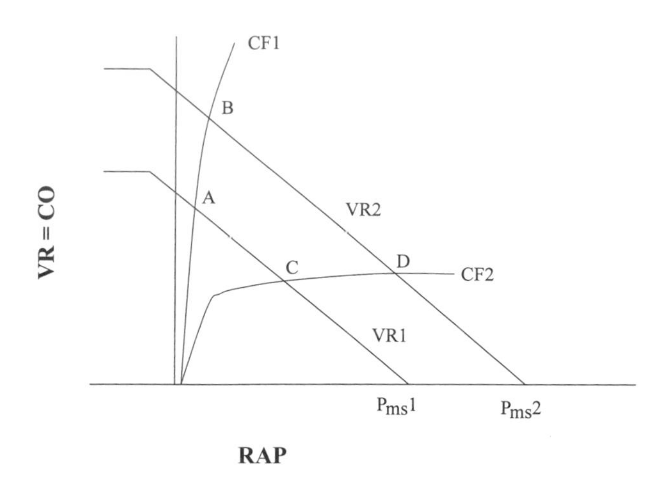

FIGURE 17–3. Further manipulation of the venous return and cardiac function curves. $P_{ms}1$ = mean systemic pressure under baseline conditions; $P_{ms}2$ = mean systemic pressure following infusion of volume into the peripheral reservoir or sympathoadrenal stimulation. No change in the resistance to VR is postulated; hence, no change in the slope of the VR curve is seen. VR1 = venous return curve under normal or baseline conditions. VR2 = venous return curve after volume infusion or sympathetic stimulation. CF1 = normal or baseline cardiac function curve. CF2 = severely depressed cardiac function curves. *Point A* is the normal intersection of the VR and CF curves; *point B* is the change in intersection following infusion of volume; *point C* is the change in intersection with acute decompensation of cardiac function; and *point D* is the change in intersection with a poorly functioning heart but an increase in P_{ms} due either to sympathetic stimulation or to fluid retention. RAP = right atrial pressure.

The cardiac function curves depicted essentially illustrate the pump function of the heart. Thus, anything that adversely affects cardiac function, such as myocardiopathy, ischemia, valvular disease, intracardiac shunting, and pericardial effusion, will have similar effects on the cardiac function curve to those depicted. Finally, similar analysis for left ventricular function can be made. However, in this case, the appropriate VR curves are pulmonary VR curves. At any rate, changes in left ventricular function will only affect CO and VR through their effects on RAP.

Effects of changes in intrathoracic pressure on cardiac function

In the last century, Donders[10] recognized that decreasing ITP during inspiration aids the entrance of blood into the chest from the periphery but impedes the egress of blood from the chest to the periphery. This is because the heart and great vessels are exposed to ITP. Figure 17–4 presents a simplified scheme of the left ventricle (LV). At "baseline" during systole, LV pressure is shown as 100 units and ITP is –3 units. The LV, thus "sees" a pressure across its wall of 103 units. Hence, the stress on the LV is properly expressed as the pressure gradient, called the transmural pressure, across its wall. Without knowledge of ITP, measurements of intracavitary pressure alone will give incomplete assessments of LV wall stress.

During normal quiet breathing, changes in ITP are small, and errors introduced by not measuring ITP also are therefore small. However, with abnormal respiration (eg, with airways obstruction or positive pressure ventilation), the stress across the LV wall cannot be assessed using measurements of intracavitary pressure alone. For example, if there is a large sustained decrease in ITP (Müller maneuver), decreasing ITP to –30 units as in Figure 17–4, then at systole, for the same intracavitary LV pressure of 100 units, the LV actually is contracting against a pressure of 130 units across its wall. This is sensed by the LV as an increase in LV afterload, and the ventricle dilates. Conversely, if there is an increase in ITP (as during the performance of a Valsalva maneuver or with the application of positive airways pressure) to +30 units as in Figure 17–4, for the same LV intracavitary pressure of 100 units, LV transmural systolic pressure decreases to 70 units, and the LV senses this as a decrease in afterload with improved ventricular ejection. Thus, under particular circumstances, changing ITP could aid or hinder ventricular ejection. Numerous studies in humans and animals have confirmed the basic principles of the effects of changes in ITP on ventricular function.[11–13] In fact, the afterload effects produced during sustained decreases in ITP (Müller maneuver) are severe enough to lead to regional myocardial wall akinesia.[14]

Clinical conditions that lead to increases in ITP include expiratory obstruction (grunting respiration), application of mechanical ventilation, and application of continuous positive airway pressure (CPAP). Conditions leading to decreased ITP include any obstructive airways disease (eg, asthma, bronchiolitis), pulmonary edema, pneumonia or respiratory distress syndrome, upper airway obstruction (eg, croup), and obstructive sleep apnea. In the latter conditions, the inspiratory negative swings in ITP are exaggerated greatly, whereas the positive expiratory swings are less affected. Thus, the overall change in ITP is negative.[15–18]

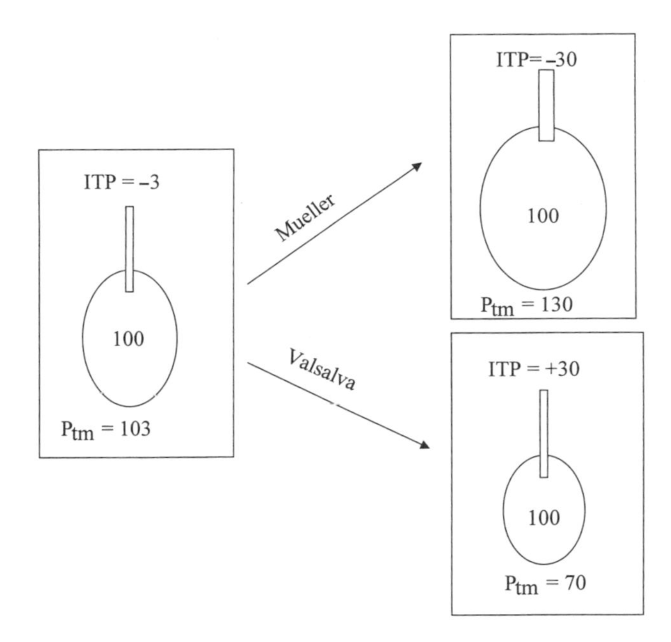

FIGURE 17–4. Illustration of effects of changes in intrathoracic pressure (ITP) on left ventricular (LV) systolic transmural pressure. Normally ITP is around –3 mm Hg. With a Valsalva maneuver, ITP is shown to increase to +30. For the same LV systolic pressure, the effective afterload has decreased to 70 mm Hg. For a Müller maneuver generating ITP of –30, LV systolic transmural pressure P_{tm} has increased to 130. Thus, the LV senses the change in ITP as an increase in the afterload.

Cardiac chamber interactions: ventricular interdependence

The outputs of the ventricles are linked. First, the LV cannot pump out more or less (unless circulatory failure occurs) than does the right ventricle (RV). In a sense, the LV is a slave to the RV. This type of interaction is called a *series interaction*. Second, the ventricles share a common septum and common fiber bundles and are surrounded by a common pericardium. Finally, the surrounding lungs could act to stiffen the pericardium and add to its effect on mediating interactions between the cardiac chambers. These anatomic facts lead to *parallel interactions* between the ventricles. The subject of interactions between cardiac chambers has been reviewed extensively elsewhere.[19] It is well known, however, that dilation of one ventricle leads to stiffening or decreased compliance of the opposite

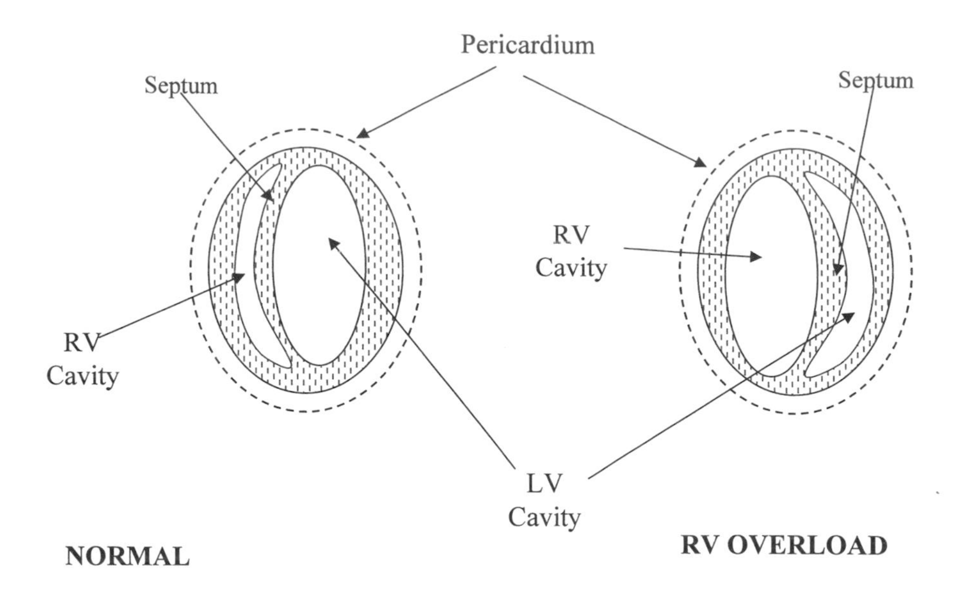

FIGURE 17–5. Schematic of effects of right ventricular (RV) overload on the normal RV–left ventricular (LV) volume relations. Note that with RV volume overload, as might be caused by increasing venous return during exaggerated inspirations, there is an increase in RV and a decrease in LV diastolic volume. The interventricular septum appears "shifted" to the left, resulting in a decrease in LV preload.

ventricle. This effect is largely, but not entirely, mediated through the interventricular septum. The stiffer the septum, the less one cardiac chamber affects the other and vice versa. Maughan et al[20] have modeled interventricular interactions in terms of three elastances; the elastance of the septum (E_S), the elastance of the RV free wall (E_{RF}), and the elastance of the LV free wall (E_{LF}). Ventricular interaction may be expressed as the degree of "cross-talk" gain, defined as the ratio of change of pressure in one chamber following a pressure change in the other, for isovolumic conditions. According to the model, when RV pressure is increased, the ratio of pressure change in the left ventricle (ΔLVP) to that of the RV (ΔRVP) is:

$$\frac{\Delta LVP}{\Delta RVP} = \frac{E_{LF}}{E_S + E_{LF}}$$

Similarly, when pressure is increased in the LV, the ratio of change in RV to LV pressure is:

$$\frac{\Delta RVP}{\Delta LVP} = \frac{E_{RF}}{E_S + E_{RF}}$$

It can be seen that the elastance of the septum is an important component of the degree of interaction between the ventricles. The stiffer the septum, the less the interaction. However, free wall elastance is also important. The stiffer the free wall of the opposite ventricle, the more pressure swings in one ventricle lead to pressure swings in the other. The elastance of the ventricular free walls can be increased by stiffening the myocardium (as with hypertrophy or ischemia), stiffening the pericardium (as with tamponade), or stiffening the lungs adjacent to the ventricular free wall (considered below). Hence, although "septal shift" (Figure 17–5) is often taken as a sign of ventricular interactions (especially with RV overload), the surrounding myocardium, pericardium, or lung acts as an amplifier for these interactions.

Respiratory maneuvers can change ventricular volumes independently. For example, as ITP decreases, VR increases. This can lead to increased RV diastolic volume and transmural pressure. This, in turn, stiffens the LV and leads to decreased LV diastolic volume, as shown in Figure 17–5. The importance of this phenomenon will be considered below. The stiffer the septum, the less important are these interactions.[20] Similar considerations may be applied for severe RV overload due to severe pulmonary hypertension.

It also may be deduced that during systole, pressure generation in one ventricle aids pressure generation in the other. In fact, during systole, approximately 40 to 60% of the pressure generated by the RV actually is due to contraction of the LV.[21] This finding has been used to explain the observations that the afterload tolerance of the RV during pulmonary arterial occlusion is increased if aortic pressure is increased.[22] However, during respiratory maneuvers, systolic interaction probably plays little role—the more important interactions being those during diastole as described above.

Transmural Pressure and Mechanical Heart-Lung Interactions

Critically ill patients frequently require monitoring of intravascular pressure. This is used especially for measuring the preload of any given cardiac chamber–central venous pressure for the RV and pulmonary artery occlusion or "wedge" pressure for the LV. If intravascular pressure is referenced to atmospheric pressure, as is usual for most critical care units and cardiac catheterization laboratories, then changes in ITP that are transmitted to the heart also are included in the measurement. In normal subjects at rest this leads to small errors only; however, with respiratory distress, when ITP decreases substantially during inspiration, or with positive pressure ventilation with high levels of positive end-expiratory pressure (PEEP), this error can be large. The state of "filling" of a cardiac structure is reflected best by referencing the intracardiac pressure to the pressure on the cardiac surface. This *transmural* pressure reflects the stress across the wall of the chamber during both systole and diastole.

Many studies of cardiac function during respiratory failure attempt to estimate transmural end-diastolic (filling of RV and LV) and end-systolic pressures. Often esophageal pressure is subtracted from intracardiac pressure to yield an estimate of transmural filling pressure. Although this simple approach may yield valuable insight under many circumstances, it ignores a number of factors. First, changes in body position and the weight of mediastinal contents on the esophagus can change baseline esophageal pressure.[23] It is often assumed that changes in cardiac surface pressure with respiration are adequately represented by changes in esophageal pressure, even if the baseline is shifted with changes in body position. Unfortunately this assumption is not always valid, because the heart is located within a potential space between the lungs, the pericardial fossa. At large lung volumes the heart is mechanically compressed by the expanding lung, and there are mechanical interactions between the heart and lungs producing changes in cardiac surface pressure that are not reflected by esophageal pressure.[24–26] As lung volume increases, cardiac fossa and cardiac surface (pericardial) pressures may increase more than does esophageal pressure. Using esophageal pressure as the reference for calculation of transmural pressure under these circumstances will actually lead to an overestimate of cardiac transmural pressure.[25] This type of interaction is well known in patients with hyperinflation of the lungs due to gas trapping and emphysema.[27] Similarly with high levels of PEEP, pulmonary artery occlusion (wedge) pressures may be elevated due to the mechanical compressive effects of surrounding lung.

A second factor influencing cardiac surface pressure that is not reflected in esophageal pressure is the elasticity of the pericardium. Although the pericardium normally is thought of as a relaxed membrane transmitting all pressure changes, the pericardium normally limits cardiac expansion, even at physiologic cardiac volumes.[28,29] Thus, cardiac surface or pericardial pressure is equal to the arithmetic sum of two pressures–cardiac fossa (intrathoracic) pressure and transpericardial pressure.[30]

$$\text{CSP} = \text{ITP} + \text{TP}$$

where CSP = cardiac surface (pericardial) pressure, ITP = intrathoracic or cardiac fossa pressure, and TP = transpericardial or cardiac elastic recoil pressure. At low cardiac volumes, TP is small, and the pericardial contribution to CSP is small. However, with cardiac dilation, pericardial fibrosis, or tamponade, the pericardial component CSP can be large. This would not be measured by changes in esophageal pressure.

It is clear that estimates of changes in preload or afterload made from estimates of filling pressure can be difficult to interpret, even if esophageal pressure is used as the reference point for intracavitary pressure. However, a sophisticated knowledge of the relevant conditions will allow the clinician to interpret the readings obtained in the light of the physiologic and clinical circumstances. For example, in patients on mechanical ventilation with high positive airway pressures, mechanical cardiac-pulmonary interactions could contribute to a measured elevation in pulmonary artery occlusion pressure. To estimate the degree to which pericardial pressure, as opposed to LV preload, contributes to a measured elevation in pulmonary artery occlusion pressure, the measurement of the "nadir" pulmonary arterial occlusion (wedge) pressure has been suggested.[31] For this, one can briefly discontinue the PEEP. Pressure measured by the wedged pulmonary arterial catheter will drop immediately by the amount that the PEEP increased the CSP. After a few more seconds the pulmonary arterial occlusion pressure will begin to increase again as VR increases. However, the nadir value for the wedge pressure can be used to predict LV end-diastolic filling pressure, and the difference between pulmonary arterial wedge pressure and the nadir pressure equals the amount by which CSP is influenced by the PEEP.

Effects of Lung Volume

Many clinically relevant conditions are associated with pulmonary hyperinflation. These include asthma, chronic obstructive pulmonary disease, congenital emphysema, and ventilation with high airway pressures. As discussed, pulmonary hyperinflation can be associated with decreased ventricular diastolic compliance and can be an impediment to diastolic filling. Changes in lung volume also affect the pulmonary vascular bed. There is a biphasic relationship between lung volume and pulmonary vascular resistance and capacitance.[32] In the normal lung, as lung volume increases from residual volume to functional residual capacity (FRC), pulmonary vascular resistance decreases and vascular capacitance increases. Then, as lung volume increases from FRC to total lung capacity, pulmonary vascular resistance increases and capacitance decreases. Thus, lung volume above the FRC leads to increased pulmonary vascular resistance and decreased capacitance. The biphasic behavior of pulmonary vasculature with increasing lung volume has been explained by assuming that different parts of the pulmonary microvasculature are connected in series and behave differently with changes in lung volume.[33] Microvasculature located within interalveolar septa (intra-alveolar vessels) are exposed to alveolar pressure and are constricted or closed as lung volume increases. Extra-alveolar vessels located in alveolar corners or within peribronchial spaces are exposed to expanding forces as lung volume increases. The overall effect on pulmonary vascular resistance is the arithmetic sum of the effects on these two classes of vessels. Thus, as lung volume increases from residual volume to FRC, effects on extra-alveolar vessels predominate, and pulmonary vascular resistance decreases. As lung volume increases from FRC to total lung capacity, the effects on intra-alveolar vessels predominate and pulmonary vascular resistance increases. Lung volume–related increases in pulmonary vascular resistance are compounded by the presence of edema fluid around pulmonary microvasculature, hypoxia- and acidosis-mediated vasoconstriction, and thrombi/emboli within the pulmonary vasculature. All of these conditions are associated with respiratory failure in the critical care unit.

Effects of Changes in Blood Gas Tensions

Many of the effects of abnormal respiration are mediated through changes in blood gas tensions. These may be thought of as *indirect* heart-lung interactions. A thorough review of this complicated field is beyond the scope of this chapter. However, here we note that hypoxemia is associated particularly with enhanced sympathetic and parasympathetic tones. The circulatory response to hypoxia depends on the level of hypoxia, pulmonary/chest wall afferent input on vasomotor and respiratory control centers, arterial P_{CO_2}, and the balance between carotid and aortic body stimulation.[34,35] The response to a particular set of circumstances also depends on the maturation of the ventilatory controller. For example, with constant ventilation or during apneas, hypoxic stimulation of peripheral chemoreceptors produces a parasympathetic-mediated bradycardia. However, if ventilation is allowed to increase (hyperpnea), heart rate increases.[36] Further, the parasympathetic component of hypoxic stimulation increases as the severity of hypoxemia increases. There is a well-documented coupling between respiratory and autonomic activity.[35] One manifestation is the well-known sinus arrhythmia, which reflects alterations in parasympathetic tone coupled to respiration. There is also a coupling between respiratory activity and sympathetic tone, which is coordinated at the level of the brain stem and is not dependent on mechanical factors per se, although it may be modulated by them. Chronic disease conditions such as obstructive airways disease, upper airway obstruction, and chronic heart failure are associated with alterations in autonomic tone and its coupling to respiration. These chronic changes in indirect heart-lung interactions can act to buffer or enhance the pathophysiologic consequences of the disease.

Pulsus paradoxus and the interaction of left ventricle afterload and preload

Left ventricle stroke volume and arterial pressure decrease during inspiration. If inspiration is prolonged, stroke volume returns to its preinspiratory level even during the inspiratory effort. Further, during the first few beats of expiration, stroke volume and arterial pressure increase above the preinspiratory baseline.[16,37] The difference between maximum and minimum systolic arterial pressure normally is not more than 10 torr. When the arterial pressure varies by more than 10 mm Hg, the phenomenon is called *pulsus paradoxus*. This term was first coined by Kussmaul.[38] He reported that in patients with fibrosing mediastinitis and pericarditis, the peripheral pulse disappeared during inspiration, whereas heart sounds continued. He considered this a "paradox." Pulsus paradoxus was later described in patients with severe airway obstruction[39] and was shown to be a good correlate of the severity of airway obstruction.[40]

Although a number of mechanisms have been proposed to explain pulsus paradoxus,[40] the interaction between LV preload and afterload during inspiration appears to be largely responsible, with some modulation by direct transmission of intrathoracic pressure to the arterial system.[41] During inspiration, RV filling increases. Because of diastolic interaction, this leads to stiffening of the LV and decreased LV preload (see Figure 17–5). Many studies have demonstrated increased RV and decreased LV end-diastolic volume during normal and obstructed inspiration in animals and man.[40] Thus, decreased LV preload plays a role in decreasing LV stroke output during inspiration.

With increasing respiratory distress, inspiratory swings in ITP become increasingly negative. This brings into play the effects of decreasing ITP on LV afterload as well as preload. The interaction between preload (interdependence) and afterload (ITP) during inspiration was investigated by Peters et al,[42,43] who timed decreases ITP to ventricular systole and diastole. These authors demonstrated decreases in LV preload when ITP decreased during LV diastole, and increases in LV afterload when ITP decreased during LV systole. Thus, there is an interaction between VR related decreases in LV preload (ventricular interdependence) and inspiratory increases in LV afterload that produce the pulsus paradoxus observed in patients with airway obstruction. Figure 17–6 shows the effects of an obstructed inspiration on stroke volume and blood pressure. Note the decrease in stroke volume, which parallels the decrease in arterial pressure during the inspiration. There is a clear decrease in LV end-diastolic dimension, consistent with a decrease in LV preload (probably interdependence effects). Further, immediately following the end of the inspiratory effort, there is an immediate rise in both stroke volume and blood pressure. The degree of pulsus paradoxus recorded

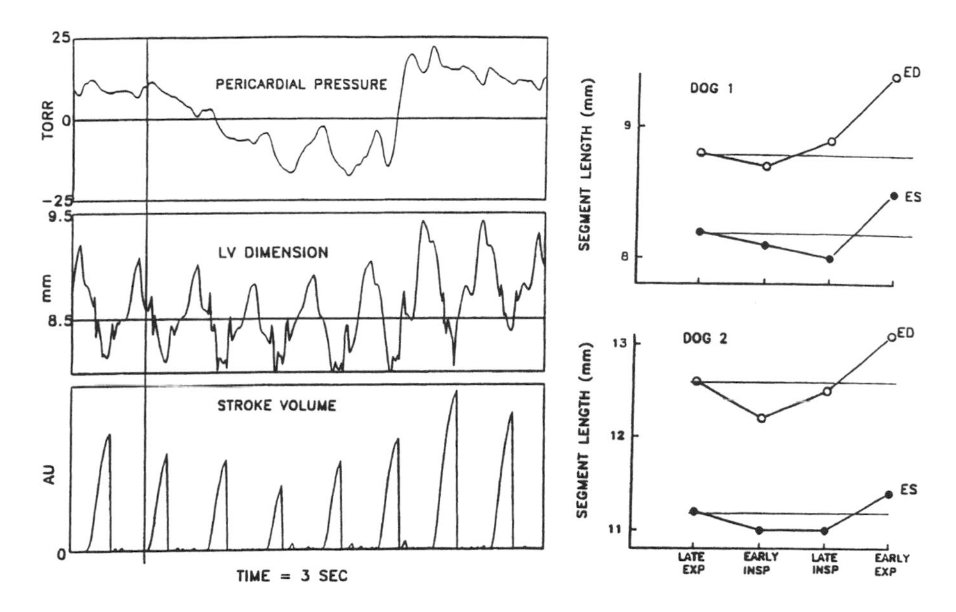

FIGURE 17–6. Changes in pericardial pressure, left ventricle (LV) dimension (on the free wall), and LV stroke volume during an inspiration. The animals are vagotomized to decrease respiratory rate and increase cycle time for better visualization of events. The *left panel* illustrates raw tracings in one dog. The *right panel* shows end-diastolic (ED) and end-systolic (ES) segment lengths during various phases of the respiratory cycle. Note that, in these cases, during inspiration there is a decrease in preload (as shown by ED level) and afterload (as shown by ES level). Immediately following inspiration (early expiration) there is an increase in preload and afterload flow. These findings suggest that, under these circumstances, the decrease in stroke volume during inspiration, which was matched by changes in arterial pressure (not shown), was due to changes in LV preload, probably related to interdependence effects. (Reproduced with permission from Scharf SM et al.[37])

by the clinical observer would therefore be the difference between the postinspiratory high blood pressure and the inspiratory low blood pressure.

Finally, there are numerous factors that modulate the degree of pulsus paradoxus with airway obstruction. For example, Federici et al[44] compared the effects of sympathetic, vagal, and total autonomic blockade on aortic pressure during inspiration. With sympathetic blockade, aortic pressure actually rose during inspiration—a finding attributed to vagal withdrawal during inspiration. These studies demonstrate the breath-by-breath changes in autonomic tone that can accompany changes in airway resistance. Lung volume increases during most clinical situations with increased airway resistance. This can influence VR both by moderating expiratory pressure and pulmonary vascular resistance, and by closing off flow through the inferior vena cava (see below). Increased lung volume can also modify flow by limiting ventricular filling on the basis of direct mechanical cardiopulmonary interactions. Finally, increased intrathoracic blood volume decreases the degree of pulsus paradoxus[45] in asthma. This may be due to better maintenance of LV preload and, hence, better maintenance of stroke volume with airway obstruction.

Effects of positive end-expiratory pressure on venous return

It is well known that ventilation with increased PEEP can lead to decreased CO and blood pressure, usually attributed to the transmission of increased ITP to the right atrium and increased RAP (see Figure 17–4). It also is recognized that at very high levels of airway pressure, with pulmonary hyperinflation, pulmonary vascular resistance can increase sufficiently to lead to circulatory failure on the basis of increased RV afterload. This is especially true if baseline pulmonary arterial pressure is increased, as is often the case with respiratory distress syndromes. However, in their initial studies Scharf et al[46] felt that the degree to which CO (and hence VR) decreased with PEEP was less than expected if only transmission of increased ITP to the right atrium were involved with PEEP. They suggested that PEEP-induced increases in abdominal pressure and/or sympathetic stimulation with increases in P_{ms} could be responsible for buffering the adverse effects of PEEP. In a subsequent paper, Scharf and Ingram demonstrated that abdominal pressure changes were small with PEEP, at least in anesthetized dogs,[47] and that sympathoplegia exacerbated the adverse effects of PEEP on the circulation. Fessler et al[48] extended these studies. They demonstrated in a series of studies that, indeed, sympathetic response to PEEP increased P_{ms}, tending to buffer the effects of decreased CO. It is expected that the effects of PEEP would therefore be worse with hypovolemia and with sympathoplegia, and, indeed, this has been the case clinically. Finally, Fessler et al[49] demonstrated that there was a rightward shift in the point of flow limitation on the VR curve,

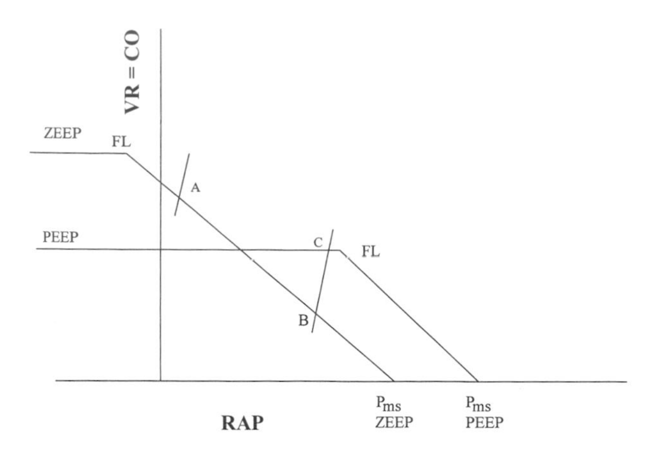

FIGURE 17–7. Effects of positive end-expiratory pressure (PEEP) on venous return (VR)–cardiac function relations. Note, with PEEP there is a sympathetic-mediated increase in mean systemic pressure (P_{ms}) and a rightward shift in the point of flow limitation (FL). Only segments of the cardiac function curves are shown. *Point A* is the normal intersection of cardiac function and VR curves; *point B* illustrates the change in intersection with PEEP, if there were no compensation—the intersection point would merely "slide" down the venous return curve; *point C* is the intersection of VR and cardiac function curves when there is a compensatory increase in P_{ms} mediated by sympathetic stimulation and/or translocation of intrathoracic blood volume into the peripheral venous reservoir. ZEEP = zero end-expiratory pressure; RAP = right atrial pressure.

which tends to limit flow at higher RAP. Figure 17–7 demonstrates the effects of PEEP on the VR relationships. The rightward shift of the flow limiting point leads to greater decreases in CO than would be expected, whereas the rightward shift of the VR curve (increased P_{ms}) buffers the effects of PEEP. In fact, there is a circumstance when PEEP could lead even to an increase in CO (we will leave this as an exercise for the reader). The shift of the flow limiting point was demonstrated in the studies of Fessler et al to be due most likely to direct mechanical effects of the expanding lungs on the inferior vena cava (thus, effectively increasing the surrounding pressure).[48,49] The extent to which this finding in dogs, which have a long intrathoracic inferior vena cava, is applicable to humans, who have relatively short intrathoracic vena cava, is still speculative.

Central Regulation of Sympathetic Discharge

Central cardiopulmonary interactions are the end-product of complex processes that reflect the integrated activity of central autonomic and respiratory structures. Multiple inputs from chemoreceptors, baroreceptors, mechanoreceptors in skeletal (including respiratory) muscles, mechanoreceptors in the lung, other brain-stem structures, and cortical/voluntary inputs impinge on the respiratory motoneurons. This integration is readily apparent in the discharges of sympathetic preganglionic neurons of the thoracic spinal cord and in peripherally located preganglionic nerves, which are synchronized (locked in) with respiratory motoneuron discharge. Figure 17–8 displays phrenic and cervical sympathetic nerve activities simultaneously with action potentials recorded extracellularly from a spinal preganglionic neuron (T4 spinal level). An increase in cervical sympathetic discharge is evident during inspiration. Neuronal activity is actually phase spanning-discharging during early to mid-inspiration, with a secondary increase in frequency during early to mid-expiration. The inspiratory-triggered histograms of Figure 17–9 show sympathetic neuronal activity averaged over 25 inspiratory cycles, thereby giving a better demonstration of the pattern of respiratory modulation. Indeed, manipulations that affect the central respiratory pattern generator are transmitted readily to neural circuits generating central sympathetic activity. Such tight coupling is illustrated clearly in Figure 17–10. Systemic application of the γ-aminobutyric acid $(GABA)_A$ receptor antagonist bicuculline affects both the amplitude and rate of phrenic discharge—an effect clearly observable in cervical sympathetic activity. A second type of modulation is observable in sympathetic activity and appears as bursts that are more apparent during expiration (see Figure 17–10, *left*). This expiratory activity is not respiratory related; rather, it is a peripheral reflection of the effect of baroreceptor afferent input on central sympathetic neurons. Baroreceptor input is maximal during systole, producing sympathetic inhibition, and minimal during diastole, when sympathetic discharge reflexively increases; hence, bursts have a pulse-like appearance in sympathetic discharge. Baroreceptor activity modulates and is modulated by respiratory output. The role of

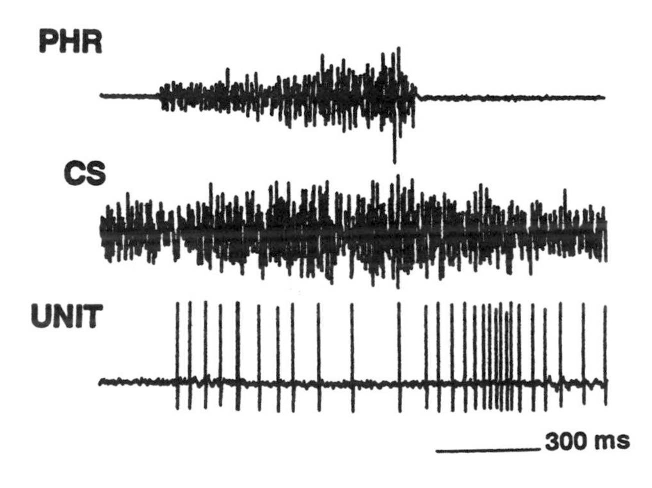

FIGURE 17–8. Neural activities recorded from a vagotomized newborn kitten. Digital traces (at a sample rate of 5 kHz) of C5 phrenic (PHR) and preganglionic cervical sympathetic (CS) nerves along with extracellularly recorded activity of preganglionic sympathetic neuron (UNIT) of the thoracic spinal cord (fourth thoracic segment).

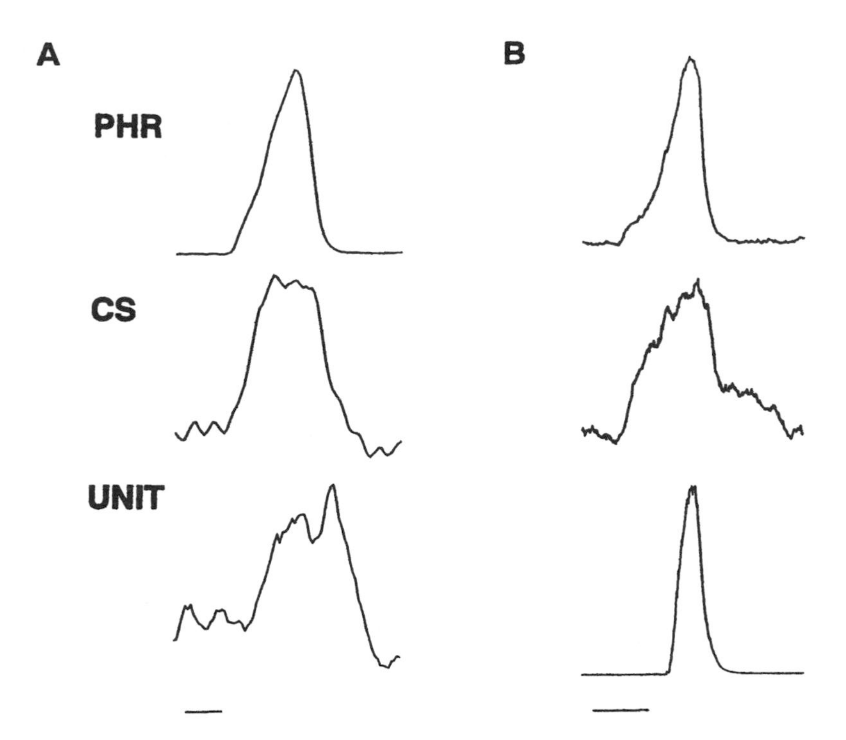

FIGURE 17–9. Inspiratory triggered histograms (N = 25 to 30 inspiratory phases) of activities of integrated (100-ms time constant) C5 phrenic nerve (PHR), preganglionic cervical sympathetic nerve (CS), and extracellularly recorded activity of preganglionic sympathetic neuron (UNIT) of the thoracic spinal cord (fourth thoracic segment). Signal were sampled at 128 Hz. *A*, The same signals as are depicted in Figure 17–8. *B*, Neural activities taken from a different newborn animal. The UNIT activity in *B* occurs only during the inspiratory phase (actually with a late onset relative to phrenic discharge), whereas neuronal activity in *A* is present in both respiratory phases. *Horizontal bars* beneath traces represent 300 ms.

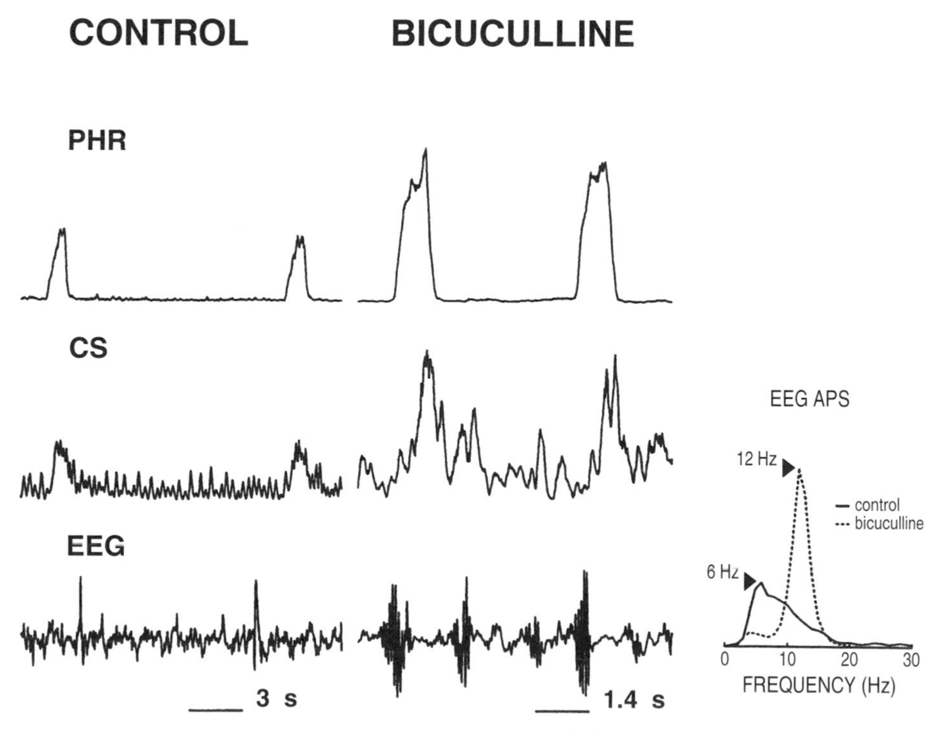

FIGURE 17–10. Neural activities recorded from vagotomized newborn kitten. Digital traces (at a 128-Hz sample rate) representing discharges of integrated (100-ms time constant) C5 phrenic (PHR) and preganglionic cervical sympathetic (CS) nerves along with an electroencephalogram (EEG) during a control period (*left*) and immediately after cessation of systemic application of bicuculline (*right*). Note the appearance of activity in the α band after bicuculline infusion, indicated in EEG autopower spectra (APS) as a shift from primarily θ activity (6 Hz) to 12 Hz activity.

baroreceptor afferents in helping to sculpt sympathetic discharge as well as forebrain structures that may modulate neurons of the baroreceptor reflex arc are the subject of the remainder of this section.

The autonomic nervous system exerts a relatively fine degree of control on vasomotor tone, mainly through the activity of lower brain-stem neurons that form the networks shaping central sympathetic discharge. It is precisely such activity that is transmitted to sympathetic preganglionic neurons of the thoracic spinal cord and, from there, to peripherally located target organs via intercalated synapses in sympathetic ganglia. Thus, while brain-stem neurons may be considered the basic elements involved in the generation of basal sympathetic discharge, this core activity is subject to modulation by peripheral afferent inputs as well as by central afferents that may originate in a number of different supramedullary sites including the cerebral cortex. The role that baroreceptor afferent inputs play in altering ongoing sympathetic activity provides an excellent example of such widespread influences on the sympathetic controller circuits, which modulate and are modulated by respiratory activity. Some of this modulation is central, and some stems from alterations in blood pressure due to respiratory activity (eg, pulsus paradoxus). Hence, this review initially presents a brief overview of the role of baroreceptor afferent inputs and their ability to alter basal sympathetic outflow directly at the level of the brain stem. Next, we discuss the role of the cerebral cortex in modulating downstream structures involved in the sympathetic response to baroreceptor activation. Finally, we describe some of the aspects of sympathetic activation that result from periodic hypoxemia of the type seen with disordered breathing during sleep as a paradigm for chronic effects of abnormal respiration on sympathetic activity.

Barosensory Neurons of the Brain Stem

Stimulation of baroreceptor endings in the aortic arch and/or the carotid sinus by elevation of arterial blood pressure will activate brain-stem neurons to return blood pressure to within normal levels by reflexive bradycardia and decreases of vasoconstrictive sympathetic nerve activity. The baroreceptor reflex is dependent upon afferents that traverse the carotid sinus and aortic depressor nerves to terminate in the dorsal, medial, and commissural subdivisions of the medullary nucleus of the solitary tract (NTS). In turn, afferents emerging from the NTS terminate in the rostral ventrolateral medulla (RVLM), a region consisting of neurons that participate in the tonic and reflex control of sympathetic discharge and blood pressure and that provide excitation to spinal preganglionic neurons via monosynaptic projections.[50–54] The importance of the RVLM as a locus of sympathoexcitatory neurons was highlighted by the finding of a markedly diminished or no response to baroreceptor activation following placement of either neurotoxic lesions placed in the RVLM or electrolytic lesions that disrupted spinal pathways emerging from the RVLM.[55] Such results demonstrate the importance of the NTS-RVLM circuit in the maintenance of basal sympathetic discharge. However, complete identification of the baroreceptor circuit required the finding of a site that could mediate baroreceptor-related inhibition. A clue was given by the finding that $GABA_A$ receptors exerted a tonic inhibitory influence on RVLM neurons. For example, injections of the $GABA_A$-receptor antagonist bicuculline were associated with increased blood pressure, whereas GABA injections into the RVLM led to decreased blood pressure.[56–60] Thus, a likely source of inhibition would be medullary neurons that project to the RVLM and synthesize GABA. In fact, such a population was described in a region of the brain stem designated as the caudal ventrolateral medulla (CVLM). Caudal ventrolateral neurons make presumptive inhibitory synapses on sympathoexcitatory neurons of RVLM,[52,59,60] reducing the gain of sympathetic spinal efferent activity and thereby helping to lower blood pressure.

Although neurons of the NTS, RVLM, and CVLM form essential components of the sympathetic controller circuitry, other regions participate in the shaping of central sympathetic discharge. Identification of such neurons often is made on the basis of common periodicities present in spike potentials: the 2 to 6 Hz (related to the cardiac rhythm) and 10 Hz (range, 8 to 13 Hz) rhythms have been reported upon extensively.[61] The 2 to 6-Hz periodicity in sympathetic discharge was shown to be an endogenous brain-stem rhythm, entrained by phasic baroreceptor afferent inputs, and was prominent in the activities of caudal and rostral ventrolateral medullary neurons.[62–66] Recent studies have shown that neurons of the CVLM and RVLM, caudal medullary raphe, the para-ambiguual area, and caudal ventrolateral pons had activities in the 2 to 6-Hz and 10-Hz frequency bands, and that a subpopulation of neurons in each structure had axonal projections to sites in the thoracic spinal cord containing sympathetic preganglionic neurons.[67–69] These findings provide additional support for the concept that the sympathetic controller system is organized diffusely, with a number of different regions having the ability to modulate central sympathetic discharge.

Modulation of Sympathetic Discharge by Medial Prefrontal and Insular Cortices

Both the medial prefrontal cortex (MPFC) and the insular cortex (IC) are regions of the cerebral cortex that have been shown to be important for modulating cardiovascular activity during conditions of stress.[70–79] The MPFC is related synaptically to sympathetic-related structures of the brain stem and possibly to sympathetic preganglionic sympathetic neurons in the thoracic spinal cord.[80,81]

Within the brain stem, however, axons of MPFC neurons are known to terminate in the NTS, near neurons that may be involved in processing visceral afferent information and also in the caudal intermediate depressor region.[81–84] Furthermore, the finding that activation of the MPFC induces expression of Fos, the protein product of the immediate-early gene *c-fos* in the NTS, supports the idea of an excitatory projection.[79] Such a termination pattern raises the possibility that the MPFC may synaptically modulate neurons involved in processing baroreceptor afferent inputs.[85,86] The finding of a projection to the RVLM suggests direct modulation of premotor sympathoexcitatory neurons.[87–89] Such a pathway would bypass the proposed intramedullary baroreflex circuit (NTS → CVLM →RVLM).

Physiologic studies using electrical stimulation or glutamate injection in the MPFC showed that activation was associated with Fos expression in the NTS, a depressor response, reduction of sympathetic nerve activity (SNA), attenuation of the baroreceptor reflex, and decrease in discharge of barosensitive RVLM neurons.[80,87–90] Such widespread effects, however, were not noted in studies of awake rats that had received bilateral MPFC excitotoxic lesions several weeks earlier: baseline arterial pressure and heart rate were unaffected by lesions, but a reduction in the sensitivity of the baroreflex was noted.[91] This finding supports the hypothesis that MPFC outflows act to maintain blood pressure within normal limits by facilitating neuronal activity of the medullary baroreflex circuitry.

Unlike the MPFC, projections from the IC to the ventral lateral medulla have not been described.[92] The caudal NTS and the dorsal vagal motor nucleus receive projections from the IC.[93] Furthermore, the IC may be related synaptically to NTS second-order baroreceptor sensory neurons, thereby supporting the hypothesis that the IC directly modulates the baroreflex.[94] However, studies of humans undergoing surgical procedures for the treatment of epilepsy, as well as experimental studies in rats, have provided data supporting hemispheric specialization for the IC;[95–98] furthermore, there is electrophysiologic evidence of a larger population of sympathoexcitatory neurons in right posterior IC than in the entire left IC.[99] The precise role of the IC in cardiovascular regulation, especially under conditions of stress, remains largely unresolved. The few studies that have attempted to address the role of the IC in cardiovascular function were mainly conducted in anesthetized rats,[70–72,94,98] although one study was carried out on unanesthetized animals.[71] The findings of those studies indicated that lesions of the right IC elicited increases of blood pressure; however, bilateral inactivation of the IC with lidocaine did not increase either mean arterial pressure or heart rate.[94] Whether blood pressure increased and, if so, to what extent was dependent on the state of the animal (anesthetized or not), the type of lesion (electrical, excitotoxic, or reversible using lidocaine), and the extent (ie, right IC versus bilateral IC). Despite different experimental conditions, it can be concluded reasonably from the data that right IC lesions produce increased mean arterial pressure, as demonstrated in awake rats.[70] These data support also the hypothesis that outflows from the right IC are tonic and sympathoinhibitory. On the other hand, lesions studies of the left IC indicate that the left side is primarily involved in parasympathetic function.[98] However, conflicting results were reported depending on whether a lesion was placed in the left IC or bilaterally: in the former case the gain of the baroreflex was increased,[98] whereas an attenuation of the reflex was noted in the latter case.[94] The aforementioned findings strongly suggest that autonomic modulation is not lateralized entirely, and that bilateral lesions of the IC may mask the predominant role of each side. These studies suggest that both the MPFC and IC are involved in the modulating sympathetic discharge, although each of these cortical regions may do so differently. The role of the MPFC seems to be one of dampening increases of blood pressure by modulating the baroreflex, whereas the IC may actually exert a tonic sympathoinhibition.

The sympathetic system seems to be best categorized as rather diffusely organized, wherein cardiovascular reflexes, dependent upon the integrity of lower brainstem structures, are capable of modulation by distant forebrain structures. Hence, the final common output of central sympathetic circuits that emerges from the spinal cord is encoded in the nerve traffic of preganglionic axons that form preganglionic nerves. Such output undergoes additional alteration within the local networks of sympathetic ganglia. The nerve traffic that finally is carried to target organs by postganglionic nerves contains the neural code that ensures homeostasis. The same code emerges in reflex changes in cardiopulmonary mechanics.

Sympathetic Effects of Chronic Intermittent Hypoxia

Patients with apneas during sleep, as well as those with chronic lung disease, may experience periodic desaturation during sleep. They also develop chronic hypertension, even during the daytime when oxygenation and breathing are normal.[18] In addition, there are acute elevations of systemic arterial pressure at apnea termination associated with arousal.[18] Sympathetic neuronal activity is elevated in sleep apnea patients; levels during the day are correlated to the degree of nocturnal hypoxemia.[100] Baroreceptor activity also is blunted in sleep apnea patients.[101] These findings are indicative of an open-loop condition with abnormally high resting sympathetic nerve activity, untethered by the baroreceptor reflex that would normally lower both sympathetic activity and arterial pressure. Thus, hypertension is maintained even during wakefulness in patients, and it increases the risk of cardiovascular morbidity and mortality. The development of hypertension may involve not only brain-stem dysregulation, but also abnormalities in cortical areas involved in sympathetic regulation (see above).

In order to facilitate studies into the relation between intermittent hypoxia, sympathetic activation, and hypertension, animal models have been developed. Fletcher et al[102] first reported the chronic hypertensive response to chronic intermittent hypoxia (CIH) in rats. Animals were placed in chambers for 7 hours per day during the sleep period for 35 days. The chamber was flushed alternately with nitrogen and room air to achieve a nadir of ambient oxygen concentration of 3 to 5%, returning to 21% with a periodicity of approximately 1 minute. Animals thus treated developed systemic hypertension even when not exposed to hypoxia. Subsequent experiments by the same group investigated peripheral mechanisms for development of hypertension. It was found that hypertension depended on peripheral afferent inputs from the carotid sinus.[103] Chemical sympathectomy with 6-OH dopamine also eliminated this response, demonstrating the role of the peripheral sympathetic nervous system.[104]

Using a similar model our group[105] demonstrated that CIH increases the gain of sympathetic circuits to subsequent hypoxia and hypercapnia, even though animals were not exposed to a stimulus of hypercapnia. Baroreceptor function, as determined by the slope of the arterial pressure–heart rate regression line during phenylephrine infusion, was not changed. We then went on to identify the neural circuits involved with the response to CIH. We used the *c-fos* gene expression as a marker for genetic and morphologic changes following CIH and to map neuroanatomic substrates for the CIH response. First, we determined whether CIH activated brain-stem regions: the RVLM, the CVLM, and the NTS involved in regulating sympathetic neural activity. We demonstrated that 30 days of CIH elicited a greater Fos expression in these well-defined regions of the medulla involved in tonic and reflex control of sympathetic neural discharge compared to controls.[106] Greater Fos expression also was observed in experimental animals in the C1 adrenergic area of the RVLM. Activation of this area is consistent with the known importance of this vasomotor area in integration of afferent information processed by the NTS and other areas, providing synaptic excitation to spinal sympathetics.[107]

Recent studies in our laboratory have focused on cortical areas activated by CIH. We have demonstrated that neurons of the MPFC and IC show Fos expression following 30 days of CIH (unpublished data). These findings are consistent with the known importance of these cortical structures in modulation of sympathetic tone (see above). Thus, our studies are consistent with the idea that arterial chemoceptive stimuli associated with CIH reach the forebrain, in part, by way of ascending parallel pathways originating in the NTS and intermediary neurons distributed along the medullary chemoreceptor reflex arc.[102,108] The observation of CIH-induced expression of the *c-fos* gene in cortex implicates a role for the transcription regulator Fos in long-term adaptations to chemoreceptor and baroreceptor activation. Our studies and those of others indicate that persistent activation of lower brain-stem autonomic regions combines with activation of key cortical areas to shape the cardiovascular responses to CIH, and should be taken into account when considering the genesis of cardiovascular morbidity in obstructed breathing and in diseases producing CIH such as sleep apnea.

Conclusion

The respiratory and cardiovascular systems interact on multiple levels from simple mechanics to complex central neural interactions. The relative importance of the different types of interaction depends on the disease process, the chronicity of the illness, and on the mechanoneural milieu of the patient. One cannot consider the mechanical effects of loading, for example, without considering the neurophysiologic implications of the consequent baroreceptor and chemoreceptor inputs resulting from abnormal respiration. Advances in this field, especially those with the implications for neonatal and pediatric clinicians, will need to take these complexities into account.

References

1. Guyton AC, Jones CE, Coleman TG. Circulatory physiology: cardiac output and its regulation. Philadelphia (PA): W.B. Saunders, 1973.
2. Guyton AC, Adkins LH. Quantitative aspects of the collapse factor in relation to venous return. Am J Physiol 1954;177:523–7.
3. Caldini P, Permutt S, Wadell JP, Riley RL. Effect of epinephrine on pressure, flow and volume relationships in the systemic circulation of dogs. Circ Res 1974;34:606–23.
4. Beloucif S, Bizot J, Leenhardt A, Payen D. PEEP increases mean systemic pressure in humans [abstract]. Am J Respir Crit Care Med 1995;151:A708.
5. Tarasiuk A, Scharf SM. Venous return in obstructive apneas. Am Rev Respir Dis 1993;148:323–9.
6. Takata M, Wise RA, Robotham JL. Effects of abdominal pressure on venous return: abdominal vascular zone conditions. J Appl Physiol 1990;69:1961–72.
7. Tarasiuk A, Chen L, Scharf SM. Effects of periodic obstructive apnoeas on superior and inferior venous return in dogs. Acta Physiol Scand 1997;161:187–94.
8. Kaye DM, Lambert GW, Lefkovits J, et al. Neurochemical evidence of cardiac sympathetic activation and increased central nervous system norepinephrine turnover in severe congestive heart failure. J Am Coll Cardiol 1994; 23:570–8.
9. Cohn JN, Levine TB, Oliveri MT, et al. Plasma norepinephrine as a guide to prognosis in patients with chronic congestive heart failure. N Engl J Med 1984;311:819–23.

10. Donders FC. Contribution to the mechanism of respiration and circulation in health and disease, 1853. In: West JB, ed. Translations in respiratory physiology. Stroudsburg (PA): Dowden, Hutchinson and Ross, 1975: 298–318.
11. Scharf SM, Brown R, Tow DE, Parisi AF. Cardiac effects of increased lung volume and decreased pleural pressure. J Appl Physiol 1979;47:257–62.
12. Buda AJ, Pinsky MR, Ingels NB, et al. Effect of intrathoracic pressure on left ventricular performance. N Engl J Med 1979;301:453–9.
13. Charlier AA. Beat to beat hemodynamic effects of lung inflation and normal respiration in anesthetized and conscious dogs. Brussels, Belgium: Editions Arscia, 1967.
14. Scharf SM, Woods B O'B, Brown R, et al. Effects of the Müller maneuver on global and regional left ventricular function in angina pectoris with or without previous myocardial infarction. Am J Cardiol 1987;59:1305–9.
15. Stalcup A, Mellons RB. Mechanical forces producing pulmonary edema in acute asthma. N Engl J Med 1977; 297:592–6.
16. Strohl KS, Scharf SM, Brown R, Ingram RH Jr. Cardiovascular performance during bronchospasm in dogs. Respiration 1987;51:39–48.
17. Woolcock AJ, Read J. Lung volumes in exacerbations of asthma. Am J Med 1966;41:259–73.
18. Podszus TE, Greenberg H, Scharf SM. Influence of sleep state and sleep-disordered breathing on cardiovascular function. In: Sullivan CE, Saunders NA, eds. Sleep and breathing II. New York: Marcel Dekker, 1993: 257–310.
19. Janicki JS, Shroff SG, Weber KT. Ventricular interdependence. In: Scharf SM, Cassidy SS, eds. Heart lung interactions in health and disease. New York: Marcel Dekker, Inc., 1989:285–308.
20. Maughan WL, Sunagawa K, Sagawa K. Ventricular systolic interdependence: volume elastance model in isolated canine hearts. Am J Physiol 1987;253:H1381–90.
21. Yamaguchi S, Li KS, Harasawa H, et al. The left ventricle affects the duration of right ventricular ejection. Cardiovasc Res 1993;27:211–5.
22. Scharf SM. Right ventricular load tolerance: role of left ventricular function. Perspectives en réanimation, les interactions cardio-pulmonaires. Arnette, Paris: Societé de Réanimation de Langue Français, 1994: 17–28.
23. Marini JJ, O'Quinn R, Culver BH, Butler J. Estimation of transmural cardiac pressures during ventilation with PEEP. J Appl Physiol 1982;53:384–91.
24. Takata M, Robotham JL. Ventricular external constraint by the lung and pericardium during positive end-expiratory pressure. Am Rev Respir Dis 1991;143:872–5.
25. Scharf SM, Brown R, Warner KG, Khuri S. Esophageal and pericardial pressures and left ventricular configuration with respiratory maneuvers. J Appl Physiol 1989; 66:481–91.
26. Cabrera MR, Nakamura GE, Montague DA, Cole RA. Effect of airway pressure on pericardial pressure. Am Rev Respir Dis 1989;140:659–67.
27. Butler J, Schrijen F, Henriquez A, et al. Cause of the raised wedge pressure on exercise in chronic obstructive pulmonary disease. Am Rev Respir Dis 1988;138:350–4.
28. Glantz SA, Misbach GA, Moores WY, et al. The pericardium substantially affects the left ventricular diastolic pressure–volume relationship in the dog. Circ Res 1978; 42:433–41.
29. Dauterman K, Pak PH, Maughan WL, et al. Contribution of external forces to left ventricular diastolic pressure: implications for the clinical use of the Starling Law. Ann Intern Med 1995;122:737–42.
30. Huberfeld S, Genovese J, Tarasiuk A, Scharf SM. Effects of CPAP on pericardial pressure, transmural left ventricular pressures and respiratory mechanics in hypervolemic unanesthetized pigs. Am J Respir Crit Care Med 1995; 152:142–7.
31. Pinsky MR, Vincent JL, DeSmet JM. Estimating left ventricular filling pressure during positive end-expiratory pressure in humans. Am Rev Respir Dis 1991;143:25–31.
32. Whittenberger JL, MacGregor M, Berglund E, Borst MC. Influence of state of inflation of the lung on pulmonary vascular resistance. J Appl Physiol 1960;15:878–82.
33. Howell JBL, Permutt S, Proctor D, Riley RL. Effect of inflation of the lung on different parts of the pulmonary bed. J Appl Physiol 1961;16:71–6.
34. Heistad DD, Abboud FM. Circulatory adjustments to hypoxia. Circulation 1980;61:463–9.
35. De Burgh DM. Interactions between respiration and circulation. In: Cherniack N, Fishman AP, eds. Handbook of physiology. Vol. II. Pt. II. Bethesda (MD): Williams & Wilkins, 1986:529–94.
36. Angell JJE, De Burgh DM. Cardiovascular responses in apnoeic asphyxia: role of arterial chemoreceptors and the modification of their effects by a pulmonary vagal inflation reflex. J Physiol 1967;201:87–104.
37. Scharf SM, Graver LM, Khilnani S, Balaban K. Respiratory phasic effects of inspiratory loading in left ventricular hemodynamics in vagotomized dogs. J Appl Physiol 1992;73:995–1003.
38. Kussmaul A. Weber schwielige Mediastino-pericardities und den paradoxen puls. Klin Wochenschr 1873;10:433–8. [Translated in Shapir E, Salick AL. A clarification of the paradoxic pulse. Am J Cardiol 1965;16:426–31.]
39. Dornhorst AC, Howard P, Lethar GL. Pulsus paradoxus. Lancet 1952;i:746–8.
40. Scharf SM. Cardiovascular effects of airways obstruction. Lung 1991;169:1–23.
41. Viola AR, Puy RMJ, Goldman E. Mechanisms of pulsus paradoxus in airway obstruction. J Appl Physiol 1990; 68:1927–31.
42. Peters J, Kindred MK, Robotham JL. Transient analysis of cardiopulmonary interactions I. Diastolic events. J Appl Physiol 1988;64:1506–17.
43. Peters J, Kindred MK, Robotham JL. Transient analysis of cardiopulmonary interactions II. Systolic events. J Appl Physiol 1988;64:1518–26.
44. Federici A, Dambrosio M, Sorrentino G, Fiore T. Aortic pressure and heart rate patterns during the respiratory cycle in different autonomic conditions in conscious dogs. Boll Soc Ital Biol Sper 1984;40:1119–25.
45. Squara P, Dhainaut JF, Schremmer B, et al. Decreased paradoxic pulse from increased venous return in asthma. Chest 1990;97:377–83.

46. Scharf SM, Caldini P, Ingram RH. Cardiovascular effects of positive airway pressure in dogs. Am J Physiol 1977; 232:H35–40.
47. Scharf SM, Ingram RH. Influence of abdominal pressure and sympathetic vasoconstriction on the cardiovascular response to PEEP. Am Rev Respir Dis 1977;116:661–70.
48. Fessler HE, Brower RG, Wise RA, Permutt S. Effects of positive end-expiratory pressure on the gradient for venous return. Am Rev Respir Dis 1991;143:19–24.
49. Fessler HE, Brower RG, Wise RA, Permutt S. Effects of positive end-expiratory pressure on the canine venous return curve. Am Rev Respir Dis 1992;146:4–10.
50. Haselton JR, Guyenet PG. Central respiratory modulation of medullary sympathoexcitatory neurons in the rat. Am J Physiol 1989;30:R739–50.
51. Haselton JR, Guynet PG. Electrophysiological characterization of putative C1 adrenergic neurons in the rat. Neuroscience 1989;30:199–214.
52. Ruggiero DA, Meeley MP, Anwar M, Reis DJ. Newly identified GABAergic neurons in regions of the ventrolateral medulla which regulate blood pressure. Brain Res 1985; 339:171–7.
53. Ruggiero DA, Anwar M, Gootman PM. Presumptive adrenergic neurons containing phenylethanolamine N-methyltransferase immunoreactivity in the medulla oblongata of neonatal swine. Brain Res 1992;583:105–19.
54. Ruggiero DA, Cravo SL, Golanov EV, et al. Adrenergic and non-adrenergic spinal projections of a cardiovascular-active pressor area of medulla oblongata: quantitative topographic analysis. Brain Res 1994;663:107–20.
55. Granata AR, Ruggiero DA, Park DH, et al. Brain stem area with C1 epinephrine neurons mediates baroreflex vasodepressor responses. Am J Physiol 1985;248:H547–67.
56. Benarroch EE, Granata AR, Ruggiero DA, et al. Neurons of C1 area mediate cardiovascular responses initiated from ventral medullary surface. Am J Physiol 1986;250:R932–45.
57. Ross CA, Ruggiero DA, Park DH, et al. Tonic vasomotor control by the rostral ventrolateral medulla: effect of electrical or chemical stimulation of the area containing C1 adrenaline neurons on arterial pressure, heart rate, and plasma catecholamines and vasopressin. J Neurosci 1984;4:474–94.
58. Urbanski R, Sapru H. Putative neurotransmitters involved in medullary cardiovascular regulation. J Auton Nerv Syst 1988;25:181–93.
59. Jeske I, Reis DJ, Milner TA. Neurons in the barosensory area of the caudal ventrolateral medulla project monosynaptically onto sympathoexcitatory bulbospinal neurons in the rostral ventrolateral medulla. Neuroscience 1995; 65:343–53.
60. Ross CA, Ruggiero DA, Reis DJ. Connections between the nucleus of the tractus solitarii and the rostral ventrolateral medulla: a possible anatomical substrate of baroreceptor and other visceral reflexes. J Comp Neurol 1986; 242:511–34.
61. Malpas SC. The rhythmicity of sympathetic nerve activity. Prog Neurobiol 1998;56:65–96.
62. Barman SM, Gebber GL. Sympathetic nerve rhythm of brain stem origin. Am J Physiol 1980;239:R42–7.
63. Barman SM, Gebber GL. Brain stem neuronal types with activity patterns related to sympathetic nerve discharge. Am J Physiol 1981;240:R335–47.
64. Gebber GL. Central oscillators responsible for sympathetic nerve discharge. Am J Physiol 1980;239:H143–55.
65. Gebber GL, Barman SM. Basis for 2–6 cycles rhythm in sympathetic nerve discharge. Am J Physiol 1980;239:R48–56.
66. McCall RB, Gebber GL. Brainstem and spinal synchronization of sympathetic nervous discharge. Brain Res 1975; 89:139–43.
67. Barman SM, Gebber GL. Subgroups of rostral ventrolateral medullary and caudal medullary raphe neurons based on patterns of relationship to sympathetic nerve discharge and axonal projections. J Neurophysiol 1997; 77:65–75.
68. Barman SM, Gebber GL. Classification of caudal ventrolateral pontine neurons with sympathetic nerve-related activity. J Neurophysiol 1998;80:2433–45.
69. Dempsey CW, Richardson DE, Kocsis B, et al. Neurons of the rostral para-ambiguual field have activity correlated to the 10-Hz rhythm in sympathetic nerve discharge of urethane-anesthetized cat. Brain Res 1997;768:102–10.
70. Butcher KS, Cechetto DF. Insular lesion evokes autonomic effects of stroke in normotensive and hypertensive rats. Stroke 1995;26:459–65.
71. Butcher KS, Cechetto DF. Receptors in the lateral hypothalamus area involved in insular cortex sympathetic responses. Am J Physiol 1998;275:H689–96.
72. Butcher KS, Cechetto DF. Neurotransmission in the medulla mediating insular cortical and lateral hypothalamic sympathetic responses. Can J Physiol Pharmacol 1998;76:737–46.
73. Cechetto DF, Saper CB. Evidence for a viscerotropic sensory representation in the cortex and thalamus in the rat. J Comp Neurol 1987;262:27–45.
74. Cechetto DF, Chen SJ. Subcortical sites mediating sympathetic responses from the insular cortex in the rat. Am J Physiol 1990;258:R245–55.
75. Gray TS, Piechowski RA, Yracheta JM, et al. Ibotenic acid lesions of the rat stria terminalis attenuate conditioned stress-induced increases in prolactin, ACTH, and corticosterone. Neuroendocrinology 1993;57:517–24.
76. Jaskiw GE, Karoum F, Freed WJ, et al. Effect of ibotenic acid lesions of the medial prefrontal cortex on amphetamine-induced locomotion and regional brain catecholamine concentrations in the rat. Brain Res 1990;534:263–72.
77. Jaskiw GE, Weinberger DR. Ibotenic acid lesions of the medial prefrontal cortex potentiate FG-7142-induced attenuation of exploratory activity in the rat. Pharmacol Biochem Behav 1990;36:695–7.
78. Jinks AL, McGregor IS. Modulation of anxiety-related behaviors following lesions of the prelimbic or infralimbic cortex in the rat. Brain Res 1997;772:181–90.
79. Verberne AJM, Owens NC. Cortical modulation of the cardiovascular system. Prog Neurobiol 1998;54:149–68.
80. Bacon SJ, Smith AD. A monosynaptic pathway from an identified vasomotor centre in the medial prefrontal cortex to an autonomic area in the thoracic spinal cord. Neuroscience 1993;54:719–28.

81. Hurley KM, Herbert H, Moga MM, Saper CB. Efferent projections of the infralimbic cortex of the rat. J Comp Neurol 1991;308:249–76.
82. Ba M'hamed S, Sequeira H, Poulain P, et al. Sensory motor cortex projections to the ventrolateral and dorsomedial medulla oblongata in the rat. Neurosci Lett 1993; 164:195–8.
83. Buchanan SL, Thompson RH. Neuronal activity in the midline thalamic nuclei during Pavlovian heart rate conditioning. Brain Res Bull 1994;35:237–40.
84. Yasui Y, Itoh K, Shigemoto R, Mizuno N. Topographical projections from the cerebral cortex to the nucleus of the solitary tract in the cat. Exp Brain Res 1991;85:75–84.
85. Chalmers J, Arnolda L, Llewellynsmith I, et al. Central neurons and neurotransmitters in the control of blood pressure. Clin Exp Pharmacol Physiol 1994;21:819–29.
86. Guyenet PG, Filtz TM, Donaldson SR. Role of excitatory amino acids in rat vagal and sympathetic baroreflexes. Brain Res 1987;407:272–84.
87. Owens NC, Sartor DM, Verberne AJM. Medial prefrontal cortex depressor response role of the solitary tract nucleus in the rat. Neuroscience 1999;89:1331–46.
88. Owens NC, Verberne AJM. Medial prefrontal depressor response: involvement of the rostral and caudal ventrolateral medulla in the rat. J Auton Nerv Syst 2000;78:86–93.
89. Verberne AJM. Medullary sympathoexcitatory neurons are inhibited by activation of the medial prefrontal cortex in the rat. Am J Physiol 1996;270:R713–9.
90. Buchanan SL, Valentine J, Powell DA. Autonomic responses are elicited by electrical stimulation of the medial but not lateral frontal cortex in rabbits. Behav Brain Res 1985;18:51–62.
91. Verberne AJM, Lewis SJ, Worland PJ, et al. Medial prefrontal cortical lesions modulate baroreflex sensitivity in the rat. Brain Res 1987;26:243–9.
92. Yasui Y, Breder CD, Saper CB, Cechetto DF. Autonomic responses and efferent pathways from the insular cortex in the rat. J Comp Neurol 1991;303:355–74.
93. Ruggiero DA, Marovitch S, Granata AR, et al. A role of insular cortex in cardiovascular function. J Comp Neurol 1987;257:189–207.
94. Saleh TM, Connell BJ. Role of the insular cortex in the modulation of baroreflex sensitivity. Am J Physiol 1998;43:R1417–24.
95. Oppenheimer SM, Gelb A, Girvin JP, Hachinski VC. Cardiovascular effects of human insular cortex stimulation. Neurology 1992;42:1727–32.
96. Yoon B-Y, Morillo CA, Cechetto DF, Hachinski V. Cerebral hemispheric lateralization in cardiac autonomic control. Arch Neurol 1997;54:741–4.
97. Zamrini EY, Meador KJ, Loring DW, et al. Unilateral cerebral inactivation produces different left/right heart responses. Neurology 1990;40:1408–11.
98. Zhang ZH, Rashba S, Oppenheimer SM. Insular cortex lesions alter baroreceptor sensitivity in the urethan-anesthetized rat. Brain Res 1998;813:73–81.
99. Zhang ZH, Oppenheimer SM. Characterization, distribution and lateralization of baroreceptor-related neurons in the rat insular cortex. Brain Res 1997;760:243–50.
100. Peled N, Greenberg A, Pillar G, et al. Contributions of hypoxia and respiratory disturbance index to sympathetic activation and blood pressure in obstructive sleep apnea syndrome. Am J Hypertens 1998;11:1284–9.
101. Parati G, diRienzo M, Bonsignore MR, et al. Autonomic cardiac regulation in obstructive sleep apnea: evidence from spontaneous baroreflex analysis during sleep. J Hypertens 1997;15:1621–6.
102. Fletcher EC, Lesske J, Qian W, et al. Repetitive episodic hypoxia causes diurnal elevations of systemic blood pressure in rats. Hypertension 1992;19:555–61.
103. Fletcher EC, Lesske J, Behm R, et al. Carotid chemoreceptors, systemic blood pressure and chronic episodic hypoxia mimicking sleep apnea. J Appl Physiol 1992; 72:1978–84.
104. Fletcher EX, Lesske J, Culman J, et al. Sympathetic denervation blocks blood pressure elevation in episodic hypoxia. Hypertension 1992;20:612–9.
105. Greenberg HE, Sica A, Batson D, Scharf SM. Chronic intermittent hypoxia increases sympathetic responsiveness to hypoxia and hypercapnia. J Appl Physiol 1999; 86:298–305.
106. Greenberg HE, Sica AL, Scharf SM, Ruggiero DA. Expression of c-fos in the rat brainstem after chronic intermittent hypoxia. Brain Res 1999;816:638–45.
107. Reis DJ, Golanov E, Ruggiero DA, Sun MK. Sympathoexcitatory neurons of the rostral ventrolateral medulla are oxygen sensors and essential elements in the tonic and reflex control of the systemic and cerebral circulation. J Hypertens 1994;12 Suppl 10: S159–80.
108. Ruggiero DA, Anwar M, Kim J, Glickstein S. Visceral afferent pathways to the thalamus and olfactory tubercle: behavioural implications. Brain Res 1998;799:159–71.

CHAPTER 18

Respiratory Muscle Function: Implications for Ventilatory Failure

Alia Bazzy-Asaad, MD

Maintenance of normal ventilation requires that the respiratory system be capable of adjusting its output in response to changes in metabolic demand. In other words, to overcome the consequences of lung pathology that could potentially interfere with gas exchange, tidal volume and/or respiratory rate must be increased to ensure that the appropriate amount of air reaches the gas exchanging units in the alveoli. Failure to do so will result in hypoxemia, hypercapnia, and ventilatory failure. Accomplishing this goal involves a complex process that includes the central nervous system (CNS), the peripheral nervous system, the respiratory muscles, and the chemoreceptors that provide feedback to the central controller, that is the CNS. The respiratory muscles perform the function of the mechanical pump that is responsible for moving gas in and out of the lungs. Thus, their role is central to maintaining ventilation.

Ventilatory failure is an important cause of morbidity in children, especially in the newborn period. Failure is related most commonly to lung pathology, such as respiratory distress syndrome of the newborn; however, a variety of conditions that involve the airways, central and peripheral nervous systems, and the musculoskeletal system also may lead to ventilatory failure. The concept that failure under any of these circumstances may be, at least in part, related to respiratory muscle failure was not well appreciated until the late 1970s when pioneering work by Roussos and Macklem demonstrated that when the respiratory system is loaded, respiratory muscle fatigue can occur.[1] Since then many investigators have shown that respiratory muscle failure can contribute to ventilatory failure in both humans and animals when the work of breathing is increased. Increased work occurs not only when airway and parenchymal lung diseases exist but also may be found in conditions in which the ventilatory drive is increased because of metabolic derangements, as may occur in congestive heart failure, cardiogenic shock, or diabetic ketoacidosis.

Work to date on skeletal muscle, including the respiratory muscles, has shown that the newborn motor unit has different characteristics from that of the adult. The developmental biology of skeletal muscles in general, and the diaphragm in particular, is complex. This renders it difficult to predict the susceptibility of neonatal muscle to fatigue as compared to the mature muscle. This chapter reviews the current state of knowledge regarding mechanisms underlying respiratory muscle fatigue and highlights the differences between neonatal and adult motor units and how they affect respiratory muscle function.

Dynamics of Muscle Contraction

Failure to generate force by a muscle may be related to failure at one or more sites along the neuromuscular axis, that is, from the CNS to the contractile proteins in the muscle fibers. Hence, a brief review of the various steps that lead to force generation follows.

The command for voluntary muscle contraction originates in the motor regions of the CNS (Figure 18–1). The impulses, or action potentials, are conducted along axons in nerves until they reach a specialized synapse known as the neuromuscular junction (NMJ). The process of NM transmission involves propagation of an impulse from the motor neuron to the presynaptic nerve terminal, and transmission of this impulse across the NMJ to the muscle plasma membrane or sarcolemma. Because of an impedance mismatch between the small nerve fiber, which has high impedance, and the muscle fiber, which has low impedance, the amount of muscle membrane depolarization produced by the incoming electrical impulse is too small to bring the muscle fiber membrane from its resting potential to threshold potential. Hence, chemical amplification of the impulse is achieved via the neurotransmitter acetylcholine (ACh). Acetylcholine binds to its receptor on the postsynaptic muscle membrane in a specialized area known as the end plate. The receptor is, in fact, an ion channel, which then opens and allows for cationic nonspecific current flux leading to a depolarization of the postsynaptic membrane. This depolarization, known as the end plate potential or EPP, is of sufficient magnitude to open voltage-gated sodium (Na^+) channels expressed in the muscle membrane and allow current to flow through the muscle fiber and a muscle action potential to be generated. The action potential propagates and reaches the T tubular sarcoplasmic reticulum (SR) system, opening voltage-sensitive channels in the SR known as ryanodine receptors or calcium (Ca^{2+})-release channels, through which Ca^{2+} ions are released into the cytoplasm. Calcium then binds to troponin, a protein

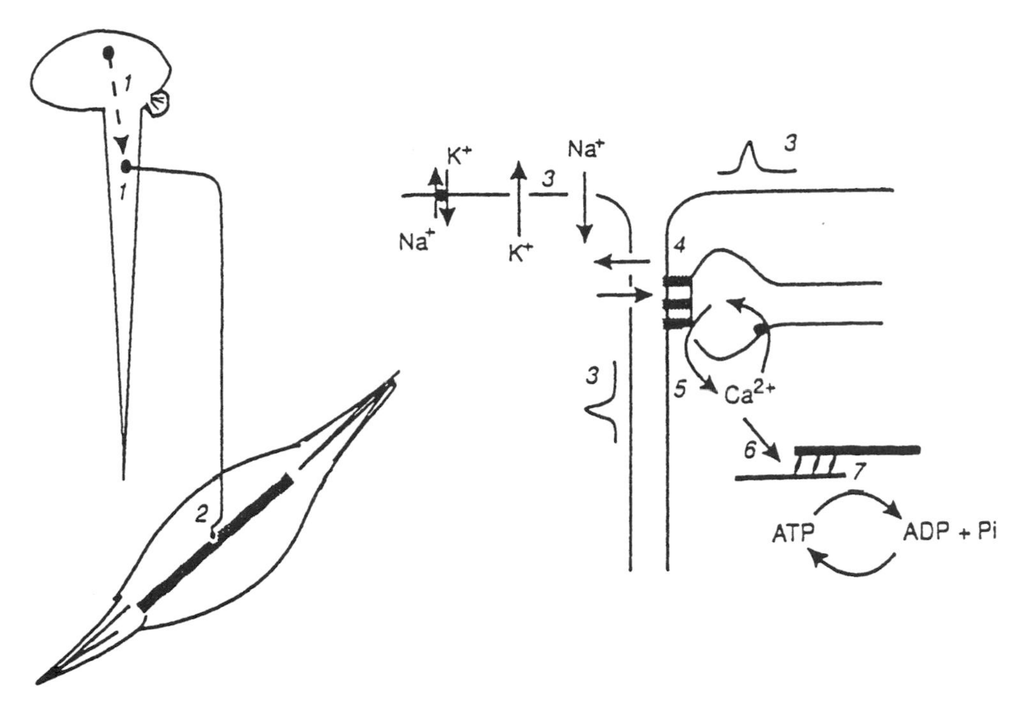

FIGURE 18–1. Schematic pathway involved in the generation of force and potential sites of failure. 1 = central sites; 2 = neuromuscular transmission; 3 = action potential propagation along sarcolemma and T tubule; 4 = depolarization of T tubule and sarcoplasmic reticulum system; 5 = opening of Ca^{2+} channels and release of Ca^{2+}; 6 = binding of Ca^{2+} to troponin; 7 = actin-myosin cross-bridge cycling. ATP = adenosine triphosphate; ADP = adenosine diphosphate; Pi = inorganic phosphate. (Reproduced with permission from Vollestad NK. Changes in activation, contractile speed, and electrolyte balance during fatigue of sustained and repeated contractions. In: Roussos C, ed. The thorax. Vol. 85. New York: Marcel Dekker, Inc., 1995:235–53.)

involved in regulating Ca^{2+}-activated actin and myosin interaction; this removes tropomyosin from the actin filaments and initiates cross-bridge cycling between actin and myosin, resulting in force generation.[2,3] Although much detail has been elucidated regarding the molecular mechanisms that underlie regulation of skeletal muscle contraction, it is beyond the scope of this chapter (for a review, see Gordon et al[4]).

Respiratory Muscle Fatigue

Although the respiratory muscles, in particular the diaphragm, consist of striated muscle, they differ from limb muscles in that they function all the time. Thus, from a functional standpoint, they are similar to the heart. It is surprising that interest in the diaphragm and mechanisms of its failure is relatively recent, considering that it is essential for sustaining life. Possible explanations include the fact that the respiratory muscles are capable of generating high force and swings in pressure for prolonged periods without evidence of failure.[5] In addition, there are a number of different respiratory muscles, such that during eupnea ventilatory function is maintained by recruiting one or more of these muscles. Therefore, the redundancy in the system appears to be protective and to provide a large safety margin. Hence, although the concept of skeletal muscle fatigue is not novel, it was not until the pioneering work of Roussos and Macklem in the late 1970s that respiratory muscle fatigue was demonstrated in adult humans.[1] Since then respiratory muscle fatigue has been demonstrated in a number of experimental and clinical settings, including weaning from mechanical ventilation,[6,7] cardiogenic shock,[8] resistive loading,[5,9] and in the newborn infant.[10] However, not everyone agrees that respiratory muscle fatigue is an entity that can be demonstrated in the clinical setting. Part of the reason for this may be that the term "fatigue" has been defined in many ways, depending on the type of task being performed and the method used to measure task failure. To resolve some of the controversy, the National Heart, Lung, and Blood Institute of the National Institutes of Health convened a workshop that proposed a definition of fatigue as "the loss of the capacity to develop force and/or velocity in response to a load that is reversible by rest."[11] The definition endeavored to distinguish fatigue from weakness, a situation in which reduced force generation is not reversed by rest. It is currently the accepted definition and has allowed easier comparison of data among studies.

Potential Sites

Based on the steps involved in the production of force by a muscle, it is conceivable that failure could occur in any of the processes involved in these steps, resulting in failure to produce force or in muscle fatigue. Thus, investigators have categorized these processes into two groups:

TABLE 18–1. Classification of Fatigue

Type of Fatigue	Mechanism
Central	Failure to sustain recruitment or decreased frequency of stimulation of motor units
Peripheral	
High frequency	Impaired neuromuscular transmission or action potential propagation
Low frequency	Impaired excitation-contraction coupling or cross bridge cycling

Adapted from Edwards RHT, Faulkner JA. Structure and function of respiratory muscles. In: Roussos C, ed.The thorax. Vol. 85. New York: Marcel Dekker, Inc., 1995;185–217.

central and peripheral. Central failure refers to the CNS up to the NMJ, whereas peripheral failure refers to failure from the NMJ onward (Table 18–1).

Central fatigue

Central fatigue refers to the condition in which loading or exercise induces a reduction in the voluntary activation of a muscle.[12] This *may* result in loss of force output by the muscle. Generally, increasing effort does not restore force, however, if the muscle can be stimulated electrically, force is restored to "prefatigue" levels. This has been demonstrated in limb skeletal muscle as well as in the diaphragm,[13–15] and is believed to be an adaptive mechanism to protect the diaphragm from injury secondary to prolonged increased contractile output. In the diaphragm the lack of a decrease in force has been attributed to recruitment of accessory muscles of respiration. For example, a lack of decrease in transdiaphragmatic pressure (P_{di}), an index of force generated by the diaphragm, has been shown to be associated with a progressive decrease in the activation of the diaphragm and the recruitment of rib cage and other accessory respiratory muscles.[14–16]

The neural mechanisms underlying central fatigue have been investigated by examining motor unit discharge frequencies during fatiguing exercise. In a study of fatigue in limb muscle, a decline in force was accompanied by a decline in the integrated electromyogram (EMG), an index of muscle activation. A drop in single muscle fiber spikes recorded with intramuscular electrodes also was noted but was not accompanied by a decline in the muscle mass action potential.[17,18] This result was interpreted as demonstrating a reflex decrease in the firing discharge of the motoneurons innervating the muscle, with a concomitant decline in muscle contractile speed. To determine the role of peripheral feedback from the muscle to the motor cortex in this process, blockade of peripheral afferent input was achieved by injecting local anesthetic into the nerve supplying intrinsic hand muscle[19] and the tibialis anterior muscle.[20] In these experiments, motor unit discharge rates did not decline, as in cases without nerve blockade, suggesting that input from the periphery contributes to this decline.[12] Although the stimulus for this reflex inhibition has not been fully elucidated, recent evidence supports a role for increasing interstitial potassium (K^+) as a factor that may activate nocioceptor or metaboreceptor fibers.[21] It is likely that similar mechanisms are operational in the respiratory muscles.

Peripheral fatigue

Peripheral fatigue refers to the failure of processes involved in neuromuscular transmission, excitation-contraction coupling, or cross-bridge cycling. Each one of these processes is complex and is discussed in some detail below.

NEUROMUSCULAR TRANSMISSION FAILURE. Successful propagation of an electrical impulse along an axon to a muscle fiber requires that the impulse reach the presynaptic nerve terminal and transmit across the NMJ to the muscle plasma membrane or sarcolemma. As mentioned earlier, the impedance mismatch necessitates chemical amplification of the impulse via ACh. The ACh receptor (AchR) allows for cationic nonspecific current flux, leading to a depolarization of the postsynaptic membrane. This depolarization, or EPP, opens voltage-gated Na^+ channels and current flows through the muscle fiber. The ACh then dissociates from the AChR, the ion channel closes, and the muscle plasma membrane repolarizes. Acetylcholine is hydrolyzed in the synaptic cleft by the enzyme ACh esterase, thus freeing the receptor. Choline is taken up into the nerve terminal for resynthesis of ACh and for packaging in synaptic vesicles.

Two potential sites of failure exist along this pathway. The first has been referred to as axonal branch-point failure, and the second is transmission failure across the NMJ. Branch-point failure refers to the inability of an action potential originating in a motoneuron to propagate along all points of axonal bifurcation. Hence, some action potentials are "lost" at branch points, do not reach muscle fibers, and do not participate in a contraction. This usually occurs when the firing frequency of the motoneuron is high, as has been demonstrated in limb skeletal muscle.[22–24] The probability of this event occurring may be dependent on the type of muscle fiber that is innervated. Recent work from Sieck and Prakash has shown that fast-fatiguing (FF) motor units (ie, units with a fast speed of contraction but rapid fatigability) have a large innervation ratio with more muscle fibers within a unit. These units will therefore have more axonal branches and likely a high probability of branch-point failure.[25] Such failure is demonstrated by the absence of EPPs or action potentials in the muscle fiber in response to nerve stimulation.

Transmission failure across the NMJ may involve either presynaptic or postsynaptic mechanisms. Presynaptic failure refers to decreased release of ACh in response to a nerve impulse secondary to depletion of this neurotransmitter. A decrease in ACh manifests electrically as a decrease in the size of the EPP. This, in turn, fails to depolarize the postsynaptic muscle sarcolemma to threshold and to trigger an action potential in the muscle fiber. Postsynaptic failure refers to either desensitization of the AChR to ACh or to decreased excitability of the postsynaptic membrane. Receptor desensitization has been shown to occur after prolonged exposure of the receptor to its ligand, as may occur if ACh accumulates in the synaptic cleft,[26] especially at high stimulation frequencies. Decreased sarcolemmic excitability may be secondary to accumulation of extracellular K^+, membrane depolarization with resulting Na^+ channel inactivation, and failure of action potential generation. There are studies in the literature to support and refute the existence of this mechanism, depending on the preparation used and the experimental paradigm.

The NMJ is not well developed at birth, and the immature synapse is less complex than the mature synapse. Most of the information available regarding the development of the NMJ has been obtained from experiments performed in rodents. In these animals NMJ development starts about a week before birth and continues until the fourth postnatal week.[27] During the prenatal week, motoneurons extend their axons into the regions where muscle will form. The skeletal muscle fibers form by fusion of mononucleated myogenic cells, a process that coincides with the arrival of the nerve axons.[27] The myotubules become innervated within 1 day, with one synapse forming at each contact site. However, initially, several axons innervate a single myotubule, a phenomenon known as polyneuronal innervation.[28] Associated with this synapse formation is the appearance of AChRs that spread over most of the surface of the immature muscle, gathering soon thereafter at the NMJ in the area of contact with the nerve terminal.[29] Following birth, and during the first postnatal month, the process of synaptic elimination takes place, transforming innervation from a polyneuronal to a mononeuronal pattern.[30,31] The remaining synapse begins to develop toward the mature form, with elaboration of synaptic folds and concentration of AChRs at the tops of the folds.[32,33] Electrophysiologic properties also change with maturation: the resting membrane potential, miniature EPP (MEPP) frequency, and EPP amplitude all increase with age, while MEPP amplitude and EPP rise time decrease,[34] indicating an increase in ACh release with age.[35] Safety factor for NM transmission also has been shown to be low in the newborn and to increase with maturation.[34,36,37]

Although the aforementioned data clearly demonstrate the developmental differences in the structure of the NMJ and the electrophysiologic properties of synaptic transmission, there are few studies that indicate that these differences are of any functional significance. Whereas the role of NM transmission failure in the development of muscle fatigue in the intact adult is controversial,[8,38–40] the limited data from newborn animals suggest that NM transmission is not impaired even under conditions of hypoxia and hypercapnia.[41,42] Hence, it would appear that the neuromuscular system in the newborn is functionally adapted to respond appropriately to stress, despite its immaturity. However, studies from our laboratory and others show that in the isolated rat diaphragm, NM transmission failure can be demonstrated in the newborn with brief stimulation periods of 1 s at frequencies above 20 Hz[37,43] (Figure 18–2). Because of the immaturity of many of the components of the NMJ, as described previously, several mechanisms could explain this failure, including axonal conduction failure, inadequate ACh quantal release, low safety factor, or desensitization of AChRs. Studies from our laboratory suggest that in the newborn diaphragm, neurotransmitter release is inadequate.[44] This is based on the pattern of EPP amplitude, which increases during the initial part of the train and then decreases toward the level of the first EPP in that train (Figure 18–3). This initial "facilitation" suggested that inadequate ACh release may be at the basis of the action potential failure—a situation similar to that seen when low Ca^{2+} levels

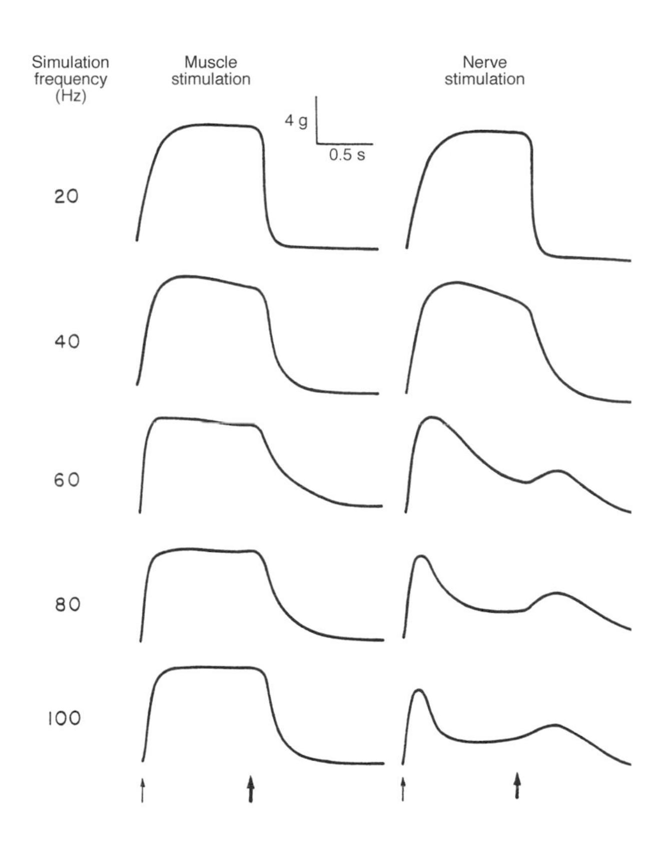

FIGURE 18–2. Force developed by the diaphragm of a neonatal rat in response to direct stimulation or stimulation via the phrenic nerve. Note that with nerve stimulation at ≥ 40 Hz, force is not maintained throughout the duration of stimulation (1 s), suggesting neuromuscular transmission failure. (Reproduced with permission from Feldman JD et al.[43])

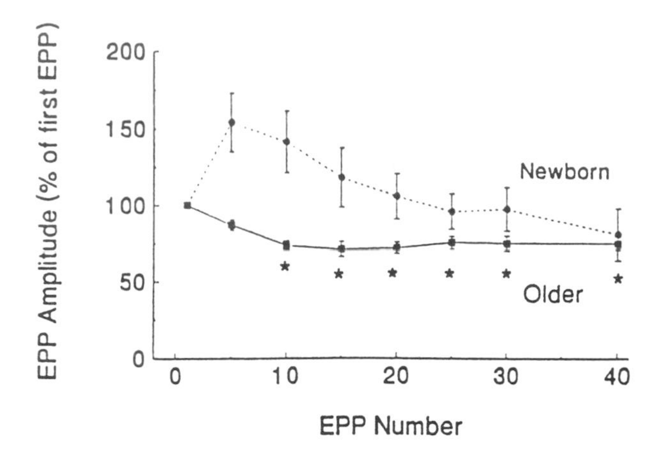

FIGURE 18–3. End-plate potential (EPP) amplitude during stimulation at 50 Hz as a function of EPP number within a 1-s train. Amplitude of EPP is expressed as percentage of the first EPP in the train. Note that in the newborn (•) amplitude initially increases then decreases, whereas in the older diaphragm (—•—) the amplitude decreases gradually to a plateau by the 10th spike. (Reproduced with permission from Bazzy AR.[44])

lead to decreased ACh release.[45] This raised the question as to whether Ca^{2+} influx is different in the newborn nerve terminal because of "immaturity" of presynaptic Ca^{2+} channels. Preliminary investigation suggests that although, in the mature NMJ, the P-subtype of the Ca^{2+} channel is the primary route of Ca^{2+} influx, the activity of this channel appears to be modulated by other factors—possibly by other Ca^{2+}channel subtypes.[46] Further investigation is currently underway.

Excitation-Contraction Coupling. Excitation contraction (E-C) coupling failure, or failure to activate the contractile system, is believed to occur when long duration fatigue occurs after completing a muscular task. This type of failure is also known as low-frequency fatigue, referring to the phenomenon in which during recovery force generation returns to prefatigue levels with high-frequency stimulation but not with low-frequency stimulation.[47] This is in contrast to high-frequency fatigue, which implies rapid recovery of force at low-stimulation frequencies, and is associated with neuromuscular transmission failure or failure of action potential propagation along the sarcolemma.[47] The complete mechanism underlying E-C coupling has not been elucidated fully, but it is clear that several proteins play an important role, with Ca^{2+} being the central ion in the process. The proteins are believed to regulate Ca^{2+} concentration in the muscle fiber; they include the inositol triphosphate (IP_3) receptor, the ryanodine receptor, and the dihydropyridine (DHP) receptor.[48] Depolarization of the T tubule leads to activation of phospholipase C, which, in turn, leads to the formation of IP_3. Inositol triphosphate then binds to the cytoplasmic amino terminal of the IP_3 receptor that is embedded within the SR membrane. This event triggers the opening of Ca^{2+} channels and the release of Ca^{2+} into the cytosol.[48] The ryanodine receptor is also in the SR membrane. Transgenic mice lacking this receptor are unable to release Ca^{2+}, thus confirming its central role in E-C coupling.[2] The DHP receptor forms an L-type Ca^{2+} channel but can also bind DHP and other antagonists. It is believed that the DHP receptor in the T tubule system serves as a voltage sensor.[49] The receptor consists of five subunits, some of which contain multiple phosphorylation sites that may be important for muscle contraction.[48] Other proteins, including triadin, FKBP12, calmodulin, calsequestrin, and junctin all have been shown to play important roles in E-C coupling and Ca^{2+} release. They do so by interacting with the DHP receptor and the SR Ca^{2+}-release channel (triadin), by modulating ryanodine-receptor function (FKBP12 and calmodulin), or by modifying Ca^{2+} release through interactions with triadin (calsequestrin), calsequestrin, and ryanodine receptor (junctin).[48]

Because of the complex nature of E-C coupling, it is conceivable that there are many potential sites of failure within this process and that a variety of mechanisms may contribute to the success or failure of this coupling. For example, levels of reactive oxygen species (ROS) or free radicals have been shown to increase with fatiguing exercise in the diaphragm and have been implicated in the pathogenesis of respiratory muscle dysfunction.[50,51] One proposed mechanism underlying this dysfunction is a change in the redox environment of the cell, affecting the redox-sensitive SR Ca^{2+}-release channel.[2] Metabolic changes both locally in the microenvironment of the triadic space and more globally within the muscle fiber comprise another mechanism that may be involved in impaired E-C coupling. There is evidence to suggest that microenvironmental concentrations of adenosine triphosphate (ATP), glycogen, and lactate, as well as ionic levels of Ca^{2+} and Mg^{2+}, may all be important in modifying the function of the SR.[2] From a developmental perspective, work in the baboon diaphragm suggests that the SR is poorly developed.[52] This finding was consistent with the slower contractile properties observed in the neonatal muscle. What effect the aforementioned modifying factors have on an immature system remains to be determined.

Cross-Bridge Cycling. Understanding the interaction between muscle contractile proteins and the regulation of contraction has advanced rapidly in recent years, owing to information derived from both structural and functional studies (for review see Gordon et al[4]). The contractile proteins can be visualized histologically and by electron microscopy as thin and thick filaments that are arranged in parallel to form a sarcomere. In skeletal muscle the sarcomere is the unit of contraction; muscle fibers are arranged in parallel, and each muscle fiber is composed of many sarcomeres arranged in series. The thin

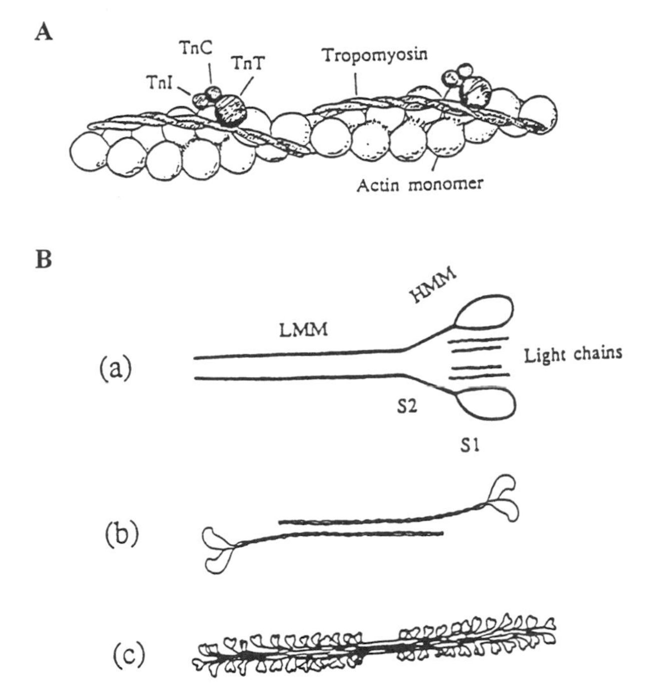

FIGURE 18–4. *A*, Actin thin filament with tropomyosin and troponin subunits (TnI, TnC, and TnT-see text for discussion). *B*, Myosin structure (*a*) and assembly into thick filaments. The tails of two molecules combine together to form a rod (*b*), and several rods combine to form a filament (*c*). S1 = head fragments; S2 = flexible region; LMM = L-meromyosin; HMM = H-meromyosin. (Reproduced with permission from Jones DA.[3])

filament is composed of three proteins: actin, tropomyosin, and troponin, the latter consisting of three subunits (Figure 18–4). The thick filament is a polymer of the protein myosin, which interacts with actin to produce sarcomere shortening and muscle contraction.

Actin is a globular protein consisting of monomers or subunits (G-actin) that polymerize into double helical strands (F-actin) and form the backbone of the thin filament. Each actin makes contact with four other actin strands, as well as with tropomyosin and troponin. The peripheral regions of the actin strand interact with myosin, whereas the more central regions are involved in actin-actin interactions.[4] Tropomyosin is a molecule of around 42 nm in length and is comprised of two α-helical chains arranged in a coiled coil. The expression of these chains is controlled by at least two genes, with variable expression depending on muscle type and species.[4] Each chain interacts with seven monomers of an F-actin strand. The binding of tropomyosin to actin is influenced by the interactions of contiguous proteins such as other actin and tropomyosin molecules, as well as troponin and myosin. Tropomyosin is believed to block sterically myosin binding sites on actin, with its effect being overcome by Ca^{2+} binding to troponin and movement of tropomyosin as a result to uncover these sites. Troponin consists of three interacting subunits: (1) TnC, which binds Ca^{2+}; (2) TnI, which binds to actin and inhibits actomyosin ATPase, an enzyme that plays a major role in the energetics involved in actin-myosin interaction and contraction-relaxation cycling; and (3) TnN, which is involved in linking troponin to tropomyosin.[4]

Myosin is the main motor protein constituting the thick filament. It consists of two identical heavy chains (MW ≅ 200 kD each) and four light chains (MW ≅ 20 kD each) or regulatory chains. The myosin heavy chain (MHC) has three fragments, the globular head, or S1 fragment, which combines with actin and has the enzymatic activity; the S2 region, which is the flexible region of the molecule; and the tail region, which forms the majority of the molecule's length (see Figure 18–4*B*). The tails from two molecules coil together to form a rod with the S1 head fragment projecting outward, and rods from multiple molecules combine to form the thick filament. The projecting heads are then available for interaction with actin.[3,4]

Both MHCs and light chains consist of a range of isoforms based on muscle type (ie, slow versus fast fibers) and developmental stage of the organism (eg, embryonic or neonatal). In the diaphragm, MHC_{slow}, MHC_{emb}, and MHC_{neo} predominate during late embryonic development; at the time of birth MHC_{neo} is the main isoform. With advancing age other isoforms including MHC_{slow}, MHC_{2A}, MHC_{2B}, and MHC_{2x} begin to appear in different fibers. These isoforms confer contractile properties to the fibers in which they are found. For example, fibers expressing MHC_{slow} have a slower velocity of shortening and generate less force than fibers expressing MHC_{2A} or MHC_{2B}. The transitions with age have been well studied in the diaphragm and limb muscle and are described in detail in Chapter 10 by Sieck and colleagues.

As mentioned earlier, muscle contraction is accomplished via the interaction of actin and myosin at specific binding sites forming cross-bridges. The interaction occurs in a cyclical manner, with the myosin head binding to actin, pulling the actin binding site toward a central equilibrium position, and generating force. This is an energy-consuming process that involves hydrolysis of ATP by an ATPase reaction located in the head region of the MHC. Recent work in cardiac muscle suggests that neonatal muscle may have less efficient cross-bridge cycling kinetics than does adult cardiac muscle.[53] Whether the same is true for the respiratory muscles remains to be determined.

Metabolic Properties and Fatigue

Skeletal muscles have been classified based on their contractile and fatigue properties and their metabolic profile. The functional unit of a skeletal muscle is the motor unit, which consists of a group of muscle fibers innervated by a single motoneuron. Using criteria such as contraction time, relaxation time, and maximum force, motor units have been classified into four types:[54] slow-twitch units and three types of fast-twitch units. Slow units are differentiated from fast units by the absence of a "sag" in the unfused tetanic response and a slow contraction time. Slow units also are fatigue resistant. Fast-twitch units are subdivided based on their fatigue resistance into fatigue resistant (FR), fatigue intermediate (FInt), and fatigable (FF). The greatest force is produced by FF units and the least by slow units. The larger force produced by these units is related to the larger cross-sectional area of the fibers, a higher innervation ratio (number of fibers per motoneuron), and a larger specific force (force per unit cross-sectional area).

The contractile properties of a muscle are determined by the specific contractile protein isoforms and the metabolic profile of the muscle fiber. Histochemically, muscle fibers have been classified depending on myofibrillar ATPase staining after alkaline preincubation. This staining distinguishes the two major fiber types: slow-twitch or type I and fast-twitch or type II. Type II fibers are subclassified with the nomenclature depending on the classification scheme used. In the scheme that uses the oxidative and glycolytic enzymatic activity of the fiber,[55] type II fibers are classified into fast-twitch glycolytic (FG) and fast-twitch oxidative glycolytic (FOG). If pH lability is used as the differentiating factor,[56] fibers are classified based on their ATPase staining following acid preincubation into type IIa, IIb, and IIc. In general, type IIa fibers correspond to FOG fibers and are fatigue resistant, while type IIb fibers correspond to FG fibers and are fatigable.

The diaphragm is a muscle with mixed fibers. Depending on the animal species, the composition of the diaphragm may range from almost exclusively type IIa fibers, as in small rodents, to about 40 to 45% type I and 55 to 60% type II fibers, as in medium-size animals such as dogs, monkeys, and sheep.[57,58] Large mammals over 500 kg in weight have about 80% type I fibers in the diaphragm. The human diaphragm falls in the category of medium-size mammals. However, the diaphragm undergoes changes in its fiber-type composition with development. Following birth the percentage of type I fibers increases from about 10% to reach adult proportions of around 45% over the first few years.[59] This low proportion of type I fibers is accompanied by a high proportion of type IIc fibers, which also have a high oxidative capacity.[52,60] The overall oxidative capacity of the diaphragm is low at birth, and the muscle has slower contractile properties than the mature muscle.[60] These properties are consistent with the MHC isoforms that are expressed in the muscle at the time. As has been shown in the rat, the postnatal increases in velocity of shortening and specific force correlate inversely with the expression of MHC_{neo} and directly with MHC_{2X}, a fast MHC isoform.[61] This can be explained by differences in myosin ATPase activity in the various isoforms.

The neural control of motor units generally is dictated by two important variables: synaptic drive of the motoneuron and the electrical activation of the motoneuron. For example, with tidal breathing at rest a certain number of motoneurons are active and activate muscle fibers to cause contraction and force generation. When the respiratory load is increased, as may occur with hypoxia or hypercapnia, the synaptic drive to the phrenic motoneurons increases and results in a greater motoneuron firing rate. This, in turn, leads to the depolarization of more muscle fibers and muscle contraction with a larger force than during eupnea. The number of motor units that are active during eupneic breathing appears to be only 10 to 15% of the available pool, with the number increasing with the intensity of the respiratory load—the highest being during expulsive maneuvers such as coughing.[62]

Reactive Oxygen Species and Diaphragmatic Dysfunction

In recent years it has become increasingly apparent that reactive oxygen species or free radicals play an important role in the development of respiratory muscle dysfunction, especially with strenuous contractions and with sepsis. These free radicals are molecules that have an unpaired electron in the outer orbit, and because they are energetically unstable, they are highly reactive and are capable of initiating a chain of reactions that generate more free radicals.[63] Oxygen radicals such as superoxide ($O_2^{\cdot}$), hydroxyl radicals ($OH^{\cdot}$), and hydrogen peroxide (H_2O_2) are produced from cellular metabolic activities such as electron transport in mitochondria, the conversion of hypoxanthine to xanthine, leukocyte NADPH (reduced nicotinamide adenine dinucleotide phosphate) oxidase activity, and the microsomal P450 system.[63] These reactions mediate cellular injury through lipid peroxidation and membrane damage. Lipid peroxides are inhibitors of many cellular enzymes and also may produce toxic substances that cause damage to proteins.[50] Oxygen free radicals also may damage nucleic acids, cause protein sulfhydryl oxidation, and lead to intracellular enzyme activation.[50] To prevent such events under physiologic circumstances, several natural substances exist in the body that are capable of inactivating free radicals and protecting tissues from injury. They include superoxide dismutase, catalase, α-tocopherol, and the glutathione-redox system, among others.[63] These antioxidants act either directly on a specific free radical or nonspecifically on many free radicals. For example, superoxide dismutase eliminates $O_2^{\cdot}$, and catalase catalyzes dismutation of H_2O_2 to H_2O_2 and molecular oxygen; on the other hand, α-tocopherol (vitamin E) acts as a nonspecific intracellular antioxidant that donates protons to free radicals that form in lipid membranes.[50]

The interest in the production by and effects of free radicals on the diaphragm stems from the observation that administration of an antioxidant to a diaphragm undergoing low-frequency fatiguing stimulation resulted in preservation of force as compared to untreated diaphragms.[64] This suggested that free radicals produced by the contracting diaphragm play a role in engendering fatigue. Further investigation in both human muscle and animal models has confirmed this finding and also has shown that free radical generation increases with fatiguing contractions,[65–67] in models of ischemia and reperfusion injury,[68] and with overwhelming infection or sepsis.[69,70] Interestingly, exposure of resting muscle to antioxidants results in less force generation at low-stimulation frequencies, suggesting a decrease in the Ca^{2+} available for cross-bridge cycling.[51] This is based on the observation that the SR Ca^{2+}-release channel is rich in sulfhydryl groups that are believed to play an important role in the regulation of the channel.[2] Oxidation of these groups appears to trigger opening of the channel, whereas reduction closes it.[2] Hence, the sensitivity of this channel to redox state may play a role in the regulation of contractile function.

Diagnosis

The diagnosis of respiratory muscle fatigue in vivo is not easy to make. As can be appreciated from the preceding discussion, failure can occur at multiple sites in the neuromuscular system, which is most likely the case in clinical situations. In addition there is a relatively large number of muscles that participate in the respiratory pump, the major ones being the diaphragm, intercostal muscles, and abdominal muscles. Thus, while eupneic breathing in an adult can be sustained with the activity of only one muscle, that is, the diaphragm, many muscles are recruited when the respiratory system is loaded as might occur with exercise, airway disease, or lung parenchymal disease. In addition, the respiratory control system can shift the work of breathing from one muscle to another or recruit several muscles simultaneously so that muscles may act synergistically and improve the overall muscular performance and output. For example, during inspiratory flow resistive breathing both inspiratory and expiratory muscles are recruited, including the abdominal muscles. The potential benefit of abdominal muscle contraction during expiration is the lengthening of fibers of the diaphragm by pushing the abdominal contents toward the thorax. This places the diaphragm at a mechanically advantageous position on the length tension curve, since more force is generated at a longer fiber length. Thus the respiratory muscles function in a cooperative fashion that helps delay the onset of respiratory pump failure and ultimate ventilatory failure.

Another factor that may contribute to precipitating or delaying the onset of fatigue is the pattern of breathing adopted by the subject in the face of a respiratory load. Studies have shown that the duration of the time spent in inspiration (Ti) out of the total respiratory cycle time (Ttot) (ie, Ti/Ttot), significantly influences the length of time loaded breathing can be sustained (endurance time).[71,72] The pressure reached and the energy expenditure in each breath are determined by Ti/Ttot. In addition, Ti/Ttot and inspiratory flow rate can be important regulators of blood flow. Studies have shown that when the diaphragm is exposed to large pressure swings and high transmural pressures, contraction of the muscle can alter the geometry of the microvasculature in relation to the arrangement of the muscle fibers and potentially can impede blood flow.[73,74]

Because of this complexity, it is difficult to identify one parameter that will unequivocally distinguish the presence of respiratory muscle fatigue. Measurements such as vital capacity and maximum inspiratory and expiratory pressures may be useful for assessing overall respiratory pump performance, including that of the rib cage, but they require subject cooperation and maximal effort. In addition, the presence of lung or rib cage pathology affects these parameters and thus renders them unreliable as indices of muscle function.[75] The electrical activity of a muscle, (seen on an EMG) also has been used to assess respiratory muscle activity. Diaphragmatic fatigue has been associated with changes in the EMG spectrum of frequencies expressed as a ratio of high frequencies to low frequencies, the centroid frequency, or median frequency. However, we and others have shown that the EMG may be affected by factors other than fatigue, including change in muscle fiber length and electrode position.[76,77] Also, the relatively complicated technical aspects of these recordings render EMG analysis impractical clinically.

A more reliable index of diaphragm function is transdiaphragmatic pressure or P_{di}. Transdiaphragmatic pressure is the difference in pressure above and below the diaphragm and is an index of the force generated by the diaphragm.[78] The pressure difference is measured by subtracting pleural pressure, represented by esophageal pressure, from abdominal pressure, represented by gastric pressure. This measurement has been used extensively in both humans and animals.[1,5,41,71] Despite its usefulness, an important drawback of P_{di} measurement is that it requires that an individual experienced in the proper positioning of a catheter in the esophagus insert two balloon catheters in the patient. In addition, it does not provide any information regarding the potential site(s) of fatigue. To separate central fatigue from peripheral fatigue, studies have been performed in which either P_{di} or the compound electrical activity (M wave) of the diaphragm is measured in response to external electrical stimulation of the phrenic nerve.[14,79–81] Thus, one can obtain direct information regarding the ability of the diaphragm to contract irrespective of CNS input. The success of this procedure depends on the ability to localize the phrenic nerve in the neck at the posterior border of the sternomastoid muscle, which may be difficult in an obese subject or a subject with hypertrophied neck muscles secondary to chronic lung disease. Phrenic nerve stimulation has been performed in children but mostly in the context of assessing and monitoring candidates for diaphragmatic pacing because of central alveolar hypoventilation syndrome or spinal cord injury.[82,83]

Chest Wall Mechanics and Diaphragm Fatigue in the Neonate

In addition to the factors discussed above, maturational state of the chest wall plays an important role in the mechanics of breathing and diaphragmatic performance in the neonate. Unlike the chest wall in the adult, the chest wall in the neonate is highly compliant, and expansion of the rib cage is limited during inspiration.[84] This becomes more prominent during rapid eye movement (REM) sleep, when intercostal muscle activity is inhibited and the rib cage is unstable and distorts easily.[10,84] An added load on the respiratory system is created, and the potential for diaphragmatic fatigue occurs. However, the question of whether the respiratory muscles and respiratory pump are more susceptible to fatigue and failure in the neonate in the clinical setting has not been resolved completely. For example, while some investigators have shown that neonatal diaphragmatic fibers are more resistant to fatigue in vitro,[60] others have demonstrated that the percentage of fatigue resistant fibers is small in this age group in humans.[59] The immature diaphragm appears to be more susceptible to neuromuscular transmission failure,[44,60] but the presence of polyneuronal innervation may be important in offsetting this susceptibility by allowing for recruitment of more muscle fibers. Reconciling these findings awaits further investigation not only at the cellular and molecular levels, but also at the level of the whole organism.

Conclusion

Demonstrating the presence of respiratory muscle fatigue and determining the site of failure has been possible and reproducible in the laboratory. The challenge has been to devise a relatively simple, reliable, and standardized method that would permit determination of the incidence and prevalence of respiratory muscle fatigue in the clinical setting. In addition, many questions regarding the cellular and molecular basis of muscle function under physiologic and pathophysiologic conditions remain unanswered. At the current rate of knowledge growth with the advent of highly sophisticated investigative tools, it is probable that these questions will be answered in the next few years.

References

1. Roussos CS, Macklem PT. Diaphragmatic fatigue in man. J Appl Physiol 1977;43:189–97.
2. Favero T. Sarcoplasmic reticulum Ca2+ release and muscle fatigue. J Appl Physiol 1999;87:471–83.
3. Jones DA. Skeletal muscle physiology: structure, biomechanics, and biochemistry. In: Roussos C, ed. The thorax. Vol. 85. New York: Marcel Dekker, Inc., 1995: 3–32.
4. Gordon AM, Homsher E, Regnier M. Regulation of contraction in striated muscle. Physiol Rev 2000;80: 853–924.
5. Bazzy AR, Haddad GG. Diaphragmatic fatigue in unanesthetized adult sheep. J Appl Physiol 1984;57:182–90.
6. Hubmayr RD, Rehder K. Respiratory muscle fatigue in critically ill patients. Semin Respir Med 1992;13:14–21.
7. Cohen CA, Zagelbaum G, Gross D, et al. Clinical manifestations of inspiratory muscle fatigue. Am J Med 1982; 73:308–16.
8. Aubier M, Trippenbach T, Roussos C. Respiratory muscle fatigue during cardiogenic shock. J Appl Physiol 1981; 51:499–508.
9. Aldrich TK. Transmission failure of the rabbit diaphragm. Respir Physiol 1987;69:307–19.
10. Muller NL, Gulston G, Cade D, et al. Diaphragmatic muscle fatigue in the newborn. J Appl Physiol 1979;46:688–95.
11. National Heart, Lung, and Blood Institute workshop: respiratory muscle fatigue. Report of the Respiratory Muscle Fatigue Workshop Group. Am Rev Respir Dis 1990; 142:474–80.
12. Gandevia SC, Allen GM, McKenzie DK. Central fatigue: critical issues, quantification and practical implications. In: Gandevia SC, Enoka RM, McComas AJ, Stuart DG, Thomas CK, eds. Fatigue: neural and muscular mechanisms. Vol. 384. New York: Plenum Press, 1995:281–94.
13. Bigland-Ritchie B, Jones DA, Hosking GP, Edwards RHT. Central and peripheral fatigue in sustained maximal voluntary contractions of human quadriceps muscle. Clin Sci Mol Med 1978;54:609–14.
14. Bellemare F, Bigland-Ritchie B. Central components of diaphragmatic fatigue assessed by phrenic nerve stimulation. J Appl Physiol 1987;62:1307–16.
15. McKenzie DK, Bigland-Ritchie B, Gorman RB, Gandevia SC. Central and peripheral fatigue of human diaphragm and limb muscles assessed by twitch interpolation. J Physiol (Lond) 1992;454:643–56.
16. Ward ME, Eidelman D, Stubbing DG, et al. Respiratory sensation and pattern of respiratory muscle activation during diaphragm fatigue. J Appl Physiol 1988;65: 2181–9.
17. Bigland-Ritchie B. Muscle fatigue and the influence of changing neural drive. Clin Chest Med 1984;5:21–34.
18. Bigland-Ritchie B, Woods JJ. Changes in muscle contractile properties and neural control during human muscle fatigue. Muscle Nerve 1984;7:691–9.
19. Gandevia SC, Macefield G, Burke D, McKenzie DK. Voluntary activation of human motor axons in the absence of muscle afferent feedback. The control of the deafferenated hand. Brain 1990;113:1563–81.
20. Macefield G, Gandevia SC, Bigland-Ritchie B, et al. The firing rates of human motoneurons voluntarily activated in the absence of muscle afferent feedback. J Physiol (Lond) 1993;471:429–43.

21. Sjogaard G, McComas AJ. Role of interstitial potassium. In: Gandevia SC, Enoka RM, McComas AJ, Stuart DG, Thomas CK, eds. Fatigue: neural and muscular mechanisms. Vol. 384. New York: Plenum Press, 1995:69–80.
22. Smith DO. Mechanisms of action potential propagation failure at sites of axon branching in the crayfish. J Physiol (Lond) 1980;301:243–59.
23. Sandercock TG, Faulkner JA, Albers JW, Abbrecht PH. Single motor unit and fiber action potentials during fatigue. J Appl Physiol 1985;58:1073–9.
24. Clamann HP, Robinson AJ. A comparison of electromyographic and mechanical fatigue properties in motor units of cat hindlimb. Brain Res 1985;327:203–19.
25. Sieck GC, Prakash YS. Fatigue at the neuromuscular junction: branch point vs. presynaptic vs. postsynaptic mechanisms. In: Gandevia SC, Enoka RM, McComas AJ, Stuart DG, Thomas CK, eds. Fatigue: neural and muscular mechanisms. New York: Plenum Press, 1995:83–100.
26. Katz B, Thesleff S. On the factors which determine amplitude of the "miniature end-plate potential." J Physiol (Lond) 1957;137:267–78.
27. Slater C, Vincent A. Structure and development of the neuromuscular junction. In: Vincent A, Wray D, eds. Neuromuscular transmission: basic and applied aspects. New York: Pergamon Press, Inc., 1992:1–26.
28. Redfern PA. Neuromuscular transmission in the newborn rat. J Physiol 1970;209:701–9.
29. Bevan S, Steinbach JH. The distribution of α-bungarotoxin binding sites on mammalian skeletal muscle developing in vitro. J Physiol 1977;267:195–213.
30. Bennett MR, Pettigrew AG. The formation of synapses in striated muscle during development. J Physiol 1974; 241:515–45.
31. Bixby JL. Ultrastructural observations on synapse elimination in neonatal rabbit skeletal muscles. J Neurocytol 1981;10:81–100.
32. Matthews-Bellinger JA, Salpeter MM. Fine structural distribution of acetylcholine receptors at developing mouse neuromuscular junctions. J Neurosci 1983;3:644–57.
33. Steinbach JH. Developmental changes in acetylcholine receptor aggregates at rat skeletal neuromuscular junctions. Dev Biol 1981;84:267–76.
34. Kelly SS, Roberts DV. The effect of age on the safety factor in neuromuscular transmission in the isolated diaphragm of the rat. Br J Anaesth 1977;49:217–22.
35. Kelly SS. The effect of age on neuromuscular transmission. J Physiol 1978;274:51–62.
36. Wilson DF, Cardaman RC. Age-associated changes in neuromuscular transmission in the rat. Am J Physiol 1979;237:C31–7.
37. Fournier M, Alula M, Sieck GC. Neuromuscular transmission failure during postnatal development. Neurosci Lett 1991;125:34–6.
38. Aldrich TK, Appel D. Diaphragm fatigue induced by inspiratory resistive loading in spontaneously breathing rabbits. J Appl Physiol 1985;59:1527–32.
39. Bigland-Ritchie B, Kukulka CG, Lippold OCJ, Woods JJ. The absence of neuromuscular transmission failure in sustained maximal voluntary contractions. J Physiol 1982;330:265–78.
40. Bazzy AR, Donnelly DF. Diaphragmatic failure during loaded breathing: role of neuromuscular transmission. J Appl Physiol 1993;74:1679–83.
41. Watchko JF, LaFramboise WA, Standaert TA, Woodrum DE. Diaphragmatic function during hypoxemia: neonatal and developmental aspects. J Appl Physiol 1986; 60:1599–604.
42. Watchko JF, Standaert TA, Woodrum DE. Diaphragmatic function during hypercapnia: neonatal and developmental aspects. J Appl Physiol 1987;62:768–75.
43. Feldman JD, Bazzy AR, Cummins TR, Haddad GG. Developmental changes in neuromuscular transmission in the rat diaphragm. J Appl Physiol 1991;71:280–6.
44. Bazzy AR. Developmental changes in rat diaphragm endplate response to repetitive stimulation. Dev Brain Res 1994;81:314–7.
45. Katz B, Miledi R. The role of calcium in neuromuscular facilitation. J Physiol 1968;195:481–92.
46. Breugelmans JG, Bazzy AR. Developmental differences in endplate response to P-type calcium channel blockade in the rat diaphragm. Dev Brain Res 1997;101:277–81.
47. Edwards RHT. Human muscle function and fatigue. In: Porter R, Whelan J, ed. Human muscle fatigue: physiological mechanisms. London: Pitman Medical Ltd., 1981:1–18.
48. Wingertzahn MA, Ochs RS. Control of calcium in skeletal muscle excitation-contraction coupling: implications for malignant hyperthermia. Mol Genet Metab 1998; 65:113–20.
49. Rios E, Pizarro G. Voltage sensor of excitation-contraction coupling in skeletal muscle. Physiol Rev 1991;71:849–908.
50. Anzueto A, Supinski GS, Levine SM, Jenkinson SG. Mechanisms of disease: are oxygen-derived free radicals involved in diaphragmatic dysfunction? Am J Respir Crit Care Med 1994;149:1048–52.
51. Clanton TL, Zuo L, Klawitter P. Oxidants and skeletal muscle function: physiologic and pathophysiologic implications. Proc Soc Exp Biol Med 1999;222:253–62.
52. Maxwell LC, McCarter JM, Keuhl TJ, Robotham JL. Development of histochemical and functional properties of baboon respiratory muscles. J Appl Physiol 1983; 54:551–61.
53. Prakash YS, Cody MJ, Housmans PR, et al. Comparison of cross-bridge cycling kinetics in neonatal vs. adult rat ventricular muscle. J Muscle Res Cell Motil 1999; 20:717–23.
54. Burke RE, Levine DN, Tsairis P, Zajac FE. Physiological types and histochemical profiles of motor units of cat gastrocnemius. J Physiol (Lond) 1973;234:723–48.
55. Peter JB, Barnard RJ, Edgerton VR, et al. Metabolic profiles of three fiber types of skeletal muscle in guinea pigs and rabbits. Biochemistry 1972;11:2627–33.
56. Brooke MH, Kaiser KK. Muscle fiber types: how many and what kind? Arch Neurol 1970;23:369–79.
57. Edwards RHT, Faulkner JA. Structure and function of the respiratory muscles. In: Roussos C, ed. The thorax. Vol. 85. New York: Marcel Dekker, Inc., 1995:185–217.
58. Bazzy AR, Kim YJ. Effect of chronic respiratory load on cytochrome oxidase activity in diaphragm fibers. J Appl Physiol 1992;72:266–71.

59. Keens TG, Bryan AC, Levison H, Ianuzzo CD. Developmental pattern of muscle fiber types in human ventilatory muscles. J Appl Physiol 1978;44:909–13.
60. Sieck GC, Fournier M. Developmental aspects of diaphragm muscle, structural and functional organization. In: Haddad GG, Farber J, eds. Developmental neurobiology of breathing. New York: Marcel Dekker, 1991:375–428.
61. Johnson BD, Wilson LE, Zhan WZ, et al. Contractile properties of the developing diaphragm correlate with myosin heavy chain phenotype. J Appl Physiol 1994;77:481–7.
62. Sieck GC, Fournier M. Diaphragm motor unit recruitment during ventilatory and nonventilatory behaviors. J Appl Physiol 1989;66:2539–45.
63. Supinski GS, Anzueto A. Oxygen-derived free radicals and the respiratory muscles. In: Roussos C, ed. The thorax. Vol. 85. New York: Marcel Dekker, Inc., 1995:349–95.
64. Shindoh CA, DiMarco A, Thomas A, et al. Effect of N-acetylcysteine on diaphragm fatigue. J Appl Physiol 1990;68:2107–13.
65. Reid MB, Haack KE, Franchek KM, et al. Reactive oxygen in skeletal muscle I. Intracellular oxidant kinetics and fatigue in vitro. J Appl Physiol 1992;73:1797–804.
66. Reid MB, Stokic DS, Koch SM, et al. N-Acetylcysteine inhibits muscle fatigue in humans. J Clin Invest 1994; 94:2468–74.
67. Travaline JM, Sudarshan S, Roy BG, et al. Effect of N-acetylcysteine on human diaphragm strength and fatigability. Am J Respir Crit Care Med 1997;156:1567–71.
68. Supinski G, Stofan D, DiMarco A. Effect of ischemia-reperfusion on diaphragm strength and fatigability. J Appl Physiol 1993;75:2180–7.
69. Hussain SN, Graham R, Rutledge F, Roussos C. Respiratory muscle energetics during endotoxic shock in dogs. J Appl Physiol 1986;60:486–93.
70. Van Surell C, Boczkowski J, Pasquier C, et al. Effects of N-acetylcysteine on diaphragmatic function and malondialdehyde content in *Escherichia coli* endotoxemic rats. Am Rev Respir Dis 1992;146:730–4.
71. Bellemare F, Grassino A. Effect of pressure and timing of contraction on human diaphragm fatigue. J Appl Physiol 1982;53:1190–5.
72. Sadoul N, Bazzy AR, Akabas SR, Haddad GG. Ventilatory response to fatiguing and nonfatiguing resistive loads in awake sheep. J Appl Physiol 1985;59:969–78.
73. Supinski GS, DiMarco AF, Altose MD. Effect of diaphragmatic contraction on intramuscular pressure and vascular impedance. J Appl Physiol 1990;68:1486–93.
74. Hussain SN, Magder S. Diaphragmatic intramuscular pressure in relation to tension, shortening, and blood flow. J Appl Physiol 1991;71:159–67.
75. Anzueto A. Muscle dysfunction in the intensive care unit. Clin Chest Med 1999;20:435–52.
76. Bigland-Ritchie BR, Donovan EF, Roussos CS. Conduction velocity and EMG power spectrum changes in fatigue of sustained maximal efforts. J Appl Physiol 1981; 51:1300–5.
77. Bazzy AR, Korten JB, Haddad GG. Increase in electromyogram low-frequency power in nonfatigued contracting skeletal muscle. J Appl Physiol 1986;61:1012–7.
78. Roussos C, Macklem PT. The respiratory muscles. N Engl J Med 1982;307:786–97.
79. Aubier M, Murciano D, Lecocguic Y, et al. Bilateral phrenic nerve stimulation: a simple technique to assess diaphragmatic fatigue in humans. J Appl Physiol 1985;58:58–64.
80. Criner GJ, Travaline JM, Holt GA, et al. Variability of electrophrenic diaphragm twitch stimulation over time in normal subjects. Respir Physiol 1999;118:39–47.
81. Rafferty GF, Lou Harris M, Polkey MI, et al. Effect of hypercapnia on maximal voluntary ventilation and diaphragm fatigue in normal humans. Am J Respir Crit Care Med 1999;160:1567–71.
82. Brouillette RT, Marzocchi M. Diaphragm pacing: clinical and experimental results. Biol Neonate 1994;65:265–71.
83. Similowski T, Straus C, Attali V, et al. Assessment of the motor pathway to the diaphragm using cortical and cervical magnetic stimulation in the decision-making process of phrenic pacing. Chest 1996;110:1551–7.
84. Mortola JP. Chest wall mechanics in newborns. In: Roussos C, ed. The thorax. New York: Marcel Dekker, Inc., 1995:617–31.

CHAPTER 19

Airway Smooth Muscle

Young-Jee Kim, MD, Julian Solway, MD, Marc B. Hershenson, MD

Development

By the end of the human embryonic period (53 days' gestation), the branching epithelial tubules in the primordial lung are covered with airway smooth muscle to the base of the terminal sacs.[1] Further, the primative airways are ensheathed in an extensive plexus of nerve bundles and forming ganglia. Thus, contrary to the traditional viewpoint that infants fail to respond to bronchodilators because of a deficiency in airway smooth muscle, airway narrowing due to smooth muscle contraction may occur early in fetal life.[2] Indeed, since tracheal obstruction has been demonstrated to induce pulmonary hyperplasia,[3] airway smooth muscle contraction might regulate lung growth by increasing intraluminal pressure.

It has long been suggested that airway smooth muscle force generation is altered in immature animals. In the pig, maximal stress generation in response to carbachol and histamine, normalized by myosin heavy chain cross-sectional area, appears to peak in 4-week-old (suckling) pigs, relative to either fetal or more mature animals.[4] This decrease in contractile response with maturation is independent of smooth muscle receptor distribution, cellularity, and myosin isoform distribution.[5] However, the use of physiologic studies has been limited by species differences, as well as differences in the normalization schemes used to compare airway tissues from animals of different ages.

Increasingly it has been recognized that smooth muscle shortening, rather than force generation, may be a more physiologic measure of airway function, as it correlates more closely with airway luminal cross-sectional area. Shortening velocity increases progressively with maturation in the pig[6] but decreases in the guinea pig.[7] The latter reduction is accompanied by a dramatic increase in the internal resistance to shortening, emphasizing the potential importance of smooth muscle viscoelastic properties in the determination of smooth muscle shortening and airway narrowing. Such factors have been implicated recently in the pathogenesis of asthma (see below).

Airway narrowing in response to methacholine is greater in immature rabbits compared to mature animals.[8] These observations are consistent with data suggesting that human airway responsiveness is increased in infants relative to adults.[9] Although maturational differences in airway responsiveness may relate to differences in smooth muscle function, it should be recognized that airway narrowing is not only a function of smooth muscle contraction but also of muscle afterload and airway-parenchymal interactions. For example, developmental increases in airway wall elastance and alveolar number tend to reduce airway narrowing and responsiveness with maturation.

Biochemistry of Smooth Muscle Contraction and Relaxation

Airway smooth muscle tone is primarily determined by the intracellular calcium ion concentration (Figure 19–1). Intracellular calcium binds to calmodulin, increasing its affinity for myosin light chain kinase (MLCK). Binding of the calcium-calmodulin complex to MLCK increases its activity, leading to phosphorylation of 20-kD regulatory myosin light chains (MLC20), which in combination with myosin heavy chains comprise the myosin thick filament. Phosphorylation of MLC20 induces binding of the myosin heavy chain to the actin thin filament and activates myosin heavy chain adenosine triphosphatase (ATPase). The energy derived from the splitting of ATP is used to cause rotation of the myosin head, sliding the thick myosin filament past the thin actin filament, resulting smooth muscle shortening.

Most bronchoconstrictors activate G protein–coupled surface receptors. These receptors are linked to the contractile apparatus via signal-transduction pathways. Bronchoconstrictor receptors are coupled via the Gq isoform to phospholipase C, which catalyzes the conversion of phosphoinositide 4,5-bisphosphate to inositol 1,4,5-trisphosphate (IP_3) and diacylglycerol. Binding of IP_3 to a specific receptor on endoplasmic/sarcoplasmic reticulum leads to release of Ca^{2+} from intracellular stores. Alternatively, calcium for contraction also may enter the cytosol from extracellular sites through receptor-operated and voltage-dependent calcium channels.

There is often a lack of correlation between intracellular calcium concentration and airway smooth muscle tension. An increase in the smooth muscle tension and/or phosphorylation of MLC20 at a constant calcium

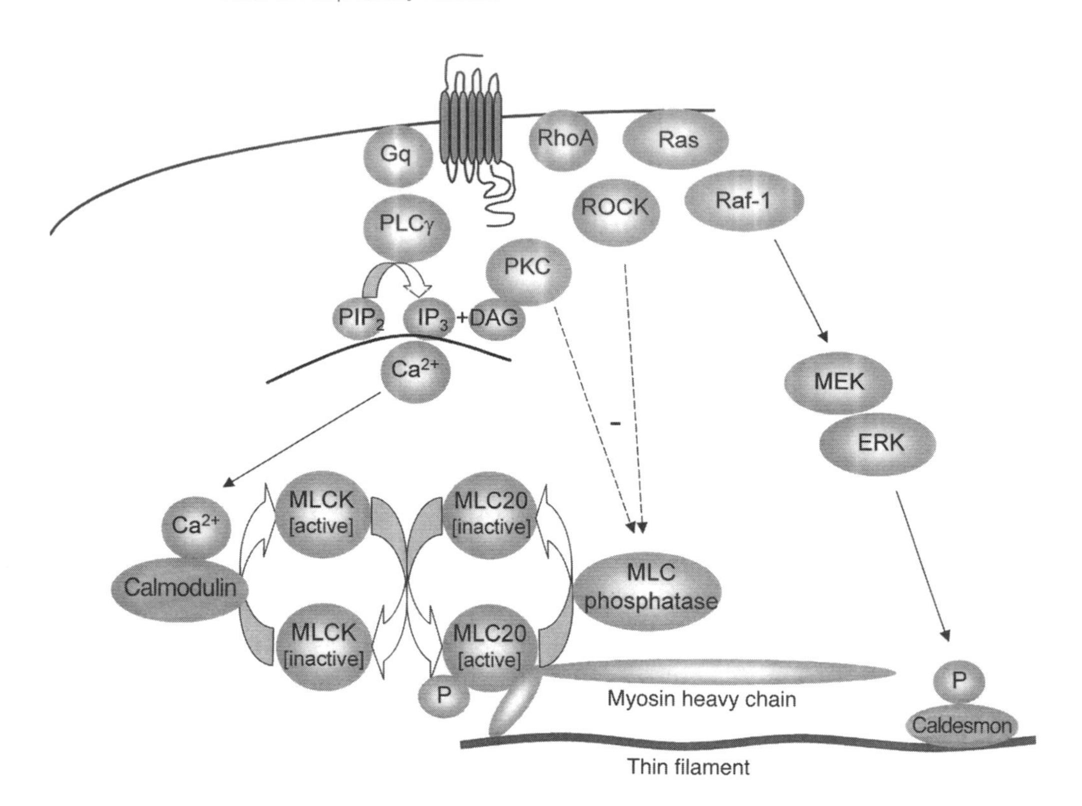

FIGURE 19–1. Biochemistry of smooth muscle contraction. Bronchoconstrictors activate G protein–coupled seven transmembrane surface receptors, which are coupled to calcium release from the sarcoplasmic reticulum via Gq and phospholipase Cγ PLCγ. Phospholipase Cγ catalyzes the conversion of phosphoinositide 4,5-bisphosphate (PIP_2) to inositol 1,4,5-trisphosphate (IP_3) and diacylglycerol (DAG). Intracellular calcium binds to calmodulin, ultimately leading to myosin light chain kinase (MLCK) activation, phosphorylation of 20-kD regulatory myosin light chains (MLC20), binding of myosin heavy chain to the actin thin filament, activation of the myosin heavy chain ATPase, rotation of the myosin head, sliding of the thick myosin filament past the thin actin filament, and smooth muscle shortening. Diacylglycerol activates protein kinase C (PKC), which may regulate calcium sensitivity via inhibition of an MLC phosphatase. RhoA and its downstream effector rho-associated coiled coil-forming protein kinase (ROCK) also may regulate calcium sensitivity. Finally, calcium sensitivity may be influenced by thin filament regulatory proteins such as caldesmon, which inhibit the ATPase activity of myosin. Caldesmon-actomyosin inhibitory activity is, in turn, regulated by phosphorylation by extracellular signal-regulated kinase (ERK), which is phosphorylated and activated via sequential activation of the 21-kD GTPase Ras, the serine/threonine kinase Raf-1, and the dual function kinase mitogen-activated protein kinase/ERK kinase (MEK).

concentration is referred to as calcium sensitization. Recently, substantial progress has been made at determining the signaling mechanisms by which this process might occur. Calcium sensitization is thought to be mediated primarily by a G protein-coupled inhibition of an MLC phosphatase.[10,11] Phosphatase inhibition may occur by protein kinase C–dependent[12] and RhoA-dependent pathways.[13] The Rho family of guanosine triphosphatases (including RhoA-C, Rac1 and 2, and Cdc42), through their regulation of the actin cytoskeleton[14] and interactions with multiple target proteins, may influence such diverse cellular activities as morphologic change, motility, adhesion, cell cycle progression, transformation, and apoptosis. It recently has been reported that inhibition of a RhoA target protein called rho-associated coiled coil-forming protein kinase (ROCK) by the chemical inhibitor Y-27632 relaxes human bronchial smooth muscle through inhibition of calcium sensitization.[15] Selective inhibition of this pathway may therefore represent a new strategy to resolve airflow obstruction in asthma.

Thin filament regulatory proteins such as caldesmon also may influence calcium sensitivity by virtue of their ability to inhibit the ATPase activity of myosin. Caldesmon-actomyosin inhibitory activity is, in turn, regulated by phosphorylation. Recent studies suggest that caldesmon is regulated by extracellular signal–regulated kinase (ERK),[16] a serine/threonine kinase of the mitogen-activated protein (MAP) kinase superfamily. These kinases participate in the transduction of growth- and differentiation-promoting signals to the cell nucleus (Figure 19–2). As discussed below, MAP kinases also have been demonstrated to play a significant role in the regulation of airway smooth muscle proliferation.[17]

β_2-Adrenergic receptor agonists, prostaglandin E_2, vasoactive intestinal peptide (VIP), nitric oxide, and other substances function as bronchodilators in human airways. Of these, only β_2-agonists are used currently in treatment of airways disease. β_2-Adrenergic, VIP, and EP (prostaglandin) receptors are coupled via the Gs isoform to membrane-bound adenylyl cyclase. Stimulation of

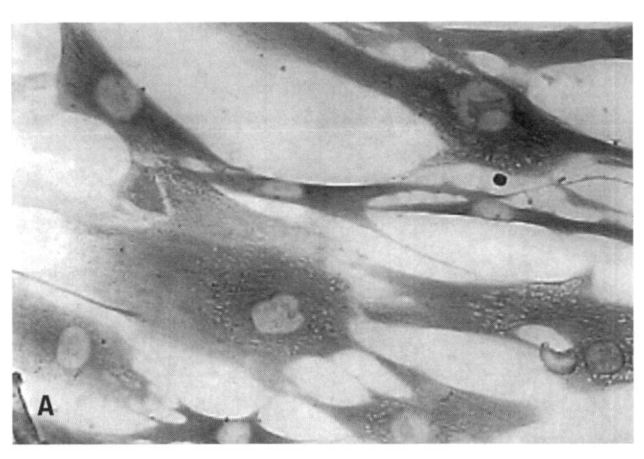

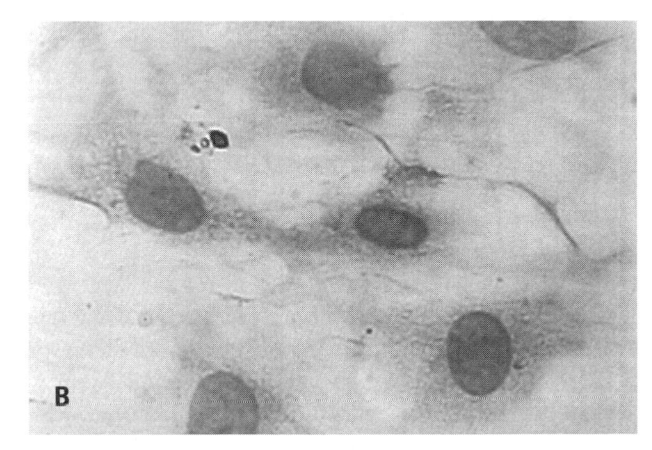

FIGURE 19–2. Translocation of extracellular signal–regulated kinase (ERK) to the cell nucleus. *A*, Unstimulated primary bovine tracheal myocytes. *B*, Cells treated with 10% fetal bovine serum for 10 minutes. Cells were fixed and immunostained using an antibody against ERK (diaminobenzidine plus nickel stain, original magnification X400; antibody purchased from Transduction Laboratories).

these receptors leads to an increase in the production of adenosine 3′,5′-cyclic monophosphate (cAMP). The formation of cAMP activates protein kinase A, which phosphorylates serine and threonine residues on specific regulatory proteins, activates potassium channels,[18,19] and inactivates MLCK,[20] leading to smooth muscle relaxation. On the other hand, nitric oxide activates guanylyl cyclase, which then induces the formation of cyclic guanosine monophosphate (cGMP) and activation of protein kinase G. Phosphodiesterases catalyze hydrolysis of cAMP and cGMP; therefore, inhibition of these enzymes results in bronchodilation.

Airway Smooth Muscle in Disease

Asthma

Changes in muscle function

Bronchial hyper-responsiveness—excessive airway narrowing caused by stimuli that normally elicit little or no response—is the physiologic hallmark of asthma. Investigators have therefore sought to identify a functional abnormality of asthmatic smooth muscle that can explain the bronchial hyper-responsiveness seen in asthma. Initial in vitro studies comparing the sensitivity and force generation of asthmatic airway smooth muscle tissue to that derived from control individuals has failed to discern a consistent difference between groups.[21–26]

Recent studies demonstrate more subtle abnormalities of airway smooth muscle function that could, indeed, underlie asthmatic constrictor hyper-responsiveness. Trachealis or bronchial smooth muscle from antigen-sensitized dogs shortens with elevated maximal velocity and to a greater total extent than do corresponding muscles from control animals, even though no differences in isometric force generation are evident.[27,28] Similar results have been found in normal human trachealis muscle incubated in serum from atopic subjects.[29] Tracheal smooth muscle strips isolated from ovalbumin-sensitized SJL mice, which exhibit hyper-responsiveness, also exhibit increased maximal shortening velocity and increased extent of total unloaded shortening when compared to nonsensitized SJL mice or to sensitized or nonsensitized mice of the ASW strain.[30] No differences in isometric force generation were found among sensitized or control mice of either strain. Finally, in the one study that evaluated the extent of unloaded shortening in asthma, airway smooth muscle strips from a single asthmatic patient did shorten excessively relative to controls.[31] Taken together, these data suggest that airway smooth muscle from asthmatic patients may differ from controls by virtue of its shortening velocity. The molecular mechanism underlying the increased maximal shortening velocity that accompanies antigen sensitization has been elucidated partially. Sensitization increases the quantity and total activity of MLCK within the trachealis muscle (though enzyme specific activity remains constant).[32,33]

How can excessive smooth muscle shortening lead to airways hyper-responsiveness in vivo? With each tidal breath the smooth muscle encircling each airway stretches.[34–37] Stretching could reduce muscle force generation substantially, due to intracellular remodeling of the contractile apparatus[38] and the slipping of actin and myosin filaments relative to each other, reversing the filament sliding that effected contraction and muscle shortening before the stretch.[39] After release of a tidal breath-induced muscle stretch, the smooth muscle encircling the airway shortens again. If the airway smooth muscle can shorten quickly, then the airway narrowing caused by muscle contraction and present prior to the tidal breath may be restored through most of exhalation. In contrast, if the airway smooth muscle shortens slowly relative to the time scale of the breathing cycle, then the lengthening (and bronchodilation) induced by each tidal breath could persist through much of the expiratory phase. Consistent with this model, normal subjects trained to avoid deep inhalations throughout methacholine responsiveness testing exhibit bronchoconstrictor responsiveness resembling that of asthmatic subjects.[40] Further, deep inspiration reduced the apparent methacholine responsiveness in control, but not asthmatic, subjects. Thus, differences in the response to bronchoconstrictor agonists could be due to disparate velocities of smooth muscle shortening in asthmatic and normal airways.

In addition to potential contractile dysfunction, reports suggest that smooth muscle from asthmatic airways does not relax normally in response to β-adrenergic agonists.[26] This abnormality stems from uncoupling of β-adrenergic receptor signaling, rather than a change in β-adrenergic receptor abundance.[41] In cultured human airway smooth muscle cells, interleukin-1 treatment impairs β-adrenergic relaxation by inducing cyclooxygenase-2 expression, which, in turn, provokes prostaglandin E_2 release.[42] The mechanism by which prostaglandin E_2 contributes to β-adrenergic hyporesponsiveness is unclear, but it is conceivable that prostaglandin E_2, a known activator of protein kinase A, induces phosphorylation of the β-adrenergic receptor, thereby inhibiting its ability to bind and activate Gs.

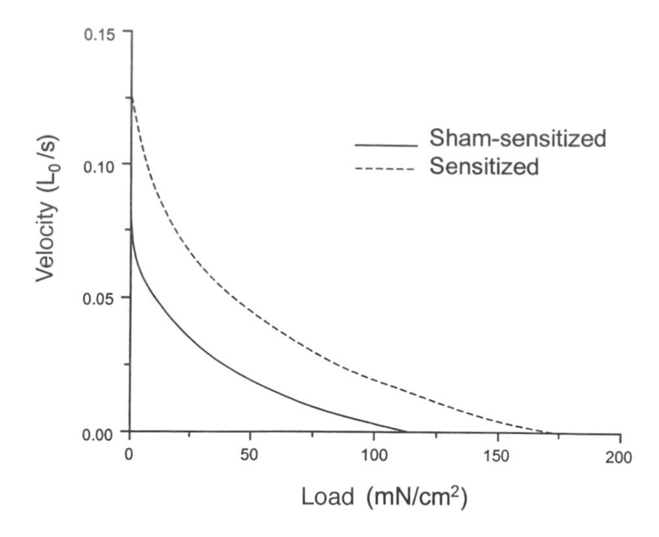

FIGURE 19–3. Schematic demonstrating force-velocity curves of sham-sensitized and sensitized human airway bronchial smooth muscle rings. (Adapted from Mitchell RW et al.[29])

Increased smooth muscle mass

Increased airway smooth muscle mass has been demonstrated in patients with nonfatal[43] and fatal asthma.[43–51] In the most convincing study to date, Ebina and colleagues[51] examined the airway thickness and smooth muscle cell in number of patients with fatal asthma using state-of-the-art stereologic techniques. Two subgroups of asthmatic airways were found: one in which smooth muscle mass was increased only in the central bronchi (Type I) and another in which smooth muscle thickness was increased throughout the airway tree (Type II). In Type I, smooth muscle hyperplasia was responsible for central airway smooth muscle thickening, whereas in Type II, cellular hypertrophy was present over the length of the airway tree.

Increased expression of epidermal growth factor (EGF), a mitogen for human airway smooth muscle,[52] has been noted in the airways of asthmatic patients.[53,54] In addition, when added to cultured human airway smooth muscle cells, bronchoalveolar lavage fluid from asthmatic airways increased the ERK activation, cyclin D_1 protein abundance, [^{3}H]-thymidine incorporation, and cell number relative to that from control subjects.[55] Finally, excess airway smooth muscle deoxyribonucleic acid (DNA) synthesis has been demonstrated in two animal models of airways disease, hyperoxic exposure and allergen sensitization.[56–58] Taken together, the above data strongly suggest that excess smooth muscle proliferation is present in the airways of patients with asthma, and they highlight the need for a precise understanding of the events involved in airway smooth muscle mitogenesis.

To that end, investigators have developed cell culture systems adopting tracheal and bronchial myocytes from different species. A growing body of literature suggests that common signal-transduction pathways regulate airway smooth muscle cell cycle entry across species lines (Figure 19–3). The ERK and phosphatidylinositol 3-kinase (PI 3-kinase)/Rac1 pathways appear to be major positive regulators of airway smooth muscle proliferation (Figure 19–4). It is conceivable also that growth factor stimulation of airway smooth muscle simultaneously elicits signaling through negative regulatory pathways such as the p38 MAP kinase pathway, perhaps as a safeguard against excessive growth. Finally, different protein kinase C isoforms may have distinct roles in the regulation of cell proliferation. These pathways are elucidated below.

Activation of ERK has been shown to be required for DNA synthesis in a wide variety of cell types, including airway smooth muscle from three different species.[59–63] The prototype route to ERK activation involves Ras, a 21-kD GTPase; Raf-1, a 74-kD cytoplasmic serine/threonine kinase; and MAP kinase/ERK kinase (MEK)-1, a 45-kD dual function kinase. Several studies confirm that Ras, Raf, and MEK function upstream of ERK in airway smooth muscle. Microinjection of anti-Ras neutralizing antibody inhibits DNA synthesis in human airway smooth muscle cells,[64] and overexpression of a dominant-negative H-Ras inhibits platelet-derived growth factor (PDGF)-mediated ERK activation in bovine tracheal myocytes.[65] Overexpression of a kinase-dead mutant of Raf-1 inhibits endothelin-induced ERK activation in rat airway smooth muscle.[66] Finally, inhibition of MEK-1 inhibits ERK activation and DNA synthesis in bovine, rat, and human airway smooth muscle cells.[59–63]

The precise transcription factor targets of ERK in airway smooth muscle cells are not known. However, as in

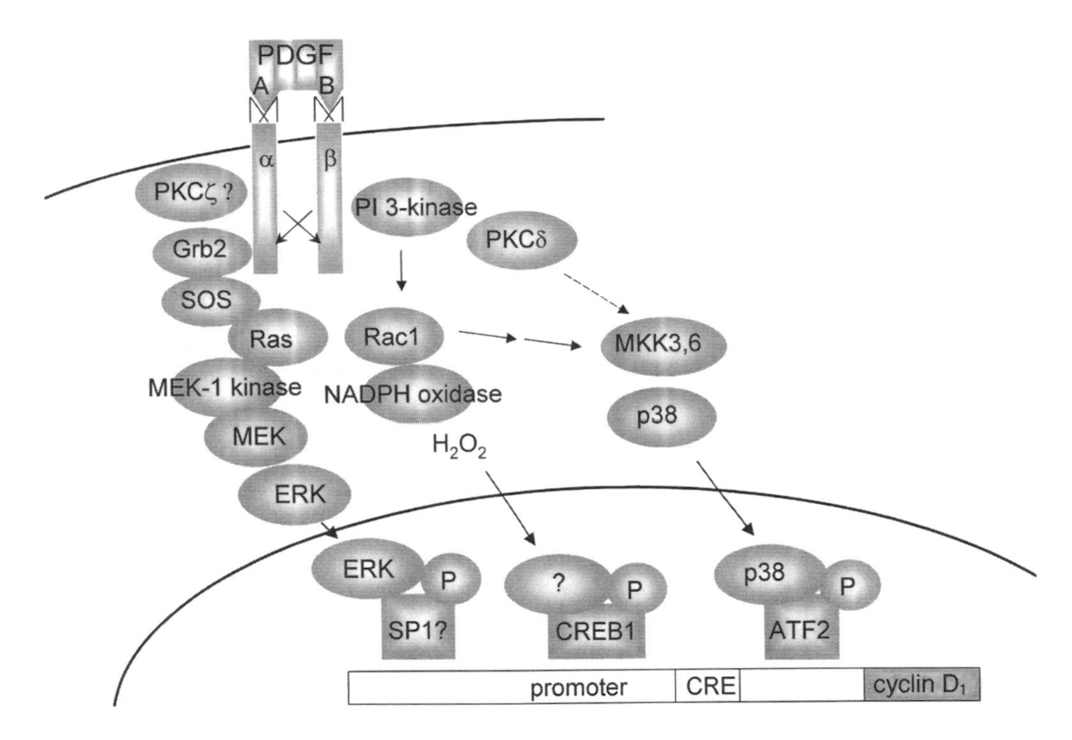

FIGURE 19–4. Signaling pathways regulating airway smooth muscle proliferation. The extracellular signal–regulated kinase (ERK) and phosphatidylinositol 3-kinase (PI 3-kinase)/Rac1 pathways positively regulate transcription from the cyclin D_1 promoter, whereas p38 mitogen-activated protein (MAP) kinase inhibits promoter activity. Protein kinase C (PKC)ζ and δ also may regulate cell cycle traversal. PDGF = platelet-derived growth factor; NADPH = reduced nicotinamide-adenine dinucleotide phosphate.

other cells,[67–69] it has been shown in bovine tracheal myocytes that ERK activation induces the expression of cyclin D_1,[70] a G_1 cyclin required for mammalian cell cycle progression.[71] However, ERK activation may not be sufficient for cell proliferation. In NIH 3T3 fibroblasts, constitutive activation of MEK-1, while sufficient to increase ERK activation and expression of cyclin D_1, is insufficient for maximal phosphorylation of the retinoblastoma protein, degradation of the cyclin-dependent kinase inhibitor p27, and cyclin A expression.[72] Furthermore Ras, but not ERK, is required for growth factor–induced degradation of p27 in IIC9 fibroblasts.[73] Thus, Ras may coordinate cell cycle progression by regulating signaling through both ERK-dependent and ERK-independent signaling pathways.

Phosphatidylinositol 3-kinase is a lipid kinase comprised of an 85-kD regulatory subunit and a 110-kD catalytic subunit, which phosphorylates phosphatidylinositol at the D-3 hydroxyl of the inositol ring, forming the phosphatidylinositides phosphatidylinositol 3-phosphate, phosphatidylinositol 3,4-diphosphate and phosphatidylinositol 3,4,5-triphosphate. At least three different isoforms of the 110-kD regulatory subunit of PI 3-kinase have been identified in man.[74] By virtue of its Src homology 2 (SH2)-containing regulatory subunit, PI 3-kinase may interact with a number of mitogenic signaling intermediates including the PDGF receptor,[75] Ras,[76] and Src family kinases.[77–80] Further, D-3 phosphorylated phosphoinositide products of PI 3-kinase may induce the translocation of additional intermediates to the cell membrane via their pleckstrin homology domains, including Akt (protein kinase B) and guanine nucleotide exchange factors, the upstream activators of GTPases.[81]

Growth factors activate PI 3-kinase in human airway smooth muscle cells.[82,83] Chemical inhibitors of PI 3-kinase, wortmannin and LY294002, inhibit airway smooth muscle DNA synthesis.[84–86] Overexpression of the catalytic subdomain of PI 3-kinase in bovine tracheal myocytes induces transcription from the cyclin D_1 promoter but fails to activate ERK,[86] suggesting that PI 3-kinase signaling occurs independently of ERK. Similarly, wortmannin and LY294002 markedly inhibit epidermal growth factor (EGF)-induced PI 3-kinase activation in human airway smooth muscle cells but have no effect on ERK activation.[85]

As noted above, phosphoinositide products of PI 3-kinase may influence the translocation of guanine nucleotide exchange factors, the upstream activators of GTPases.[81] Accordingly, Rac1[87] has been shown to function as an upstream activator of cyclin D_1 expression in bovine tracheal myocytes. Rac1 forms part of the reduced nicotinamide-adenine dinucleotide phosphate (NADPH)-oxidase complex that generates reactive oxygen species such as H_2O_2. Intracellular reactive oxygen intermediates

TABLE 19–1. Pharmacologic Agents for the Management of Acute Asthma in Children

Class	Generic Name	Indication	Dose
β_2 Agonists	Albuterol	Status asthmaticus	2.5–5 mg/dose by nebulizer, as needed; or continuous nebulization of 5 mg/mL
	Terbutaline	Status asthmaticus	Loading dose of 2 μg/kg IV over 5 min; continuous IV infusion of 0.075 μg/kg/min;[100] infusion rates of up to 10 μg/kg/min have been used[101]
Anticholinergics	Ipratropium bromide	Emergency room treatment	250 μg/dose by nebulizer, approx. every 20 min for three doses[102]
Magnesium	Magnesium sulfate	Emergency room treatment	25 mg/kg (maximum, 2 g) IV over 20 min[103]
Phosphodiesterase inhibitors	Aminophylline	Status asthmaticus	6 mg/kg IV over 20–30 min, continuous IV infusion of 1.0 mg/kg/h; titrate to serum level
Corticosteroids	Methylprednisolone	Status asthmaticus	2 mg/kg IV followed by 0.5–2 mg/kg (maximum, 60 mg) every 6 h[104]
	Prednisone/ prednisolone	Status asthmaticus	2 mg/kg PO followed by 1–2 mg/kg (maximum, 120 mg) every 12 h[104,105]

IV = intravenously; PO = per os (by mouth).

are increased following growth factor treatment of both bovine[87] and rat tracheal myocytes.[88] Further, treatment with antioxidants attenuates both growth factor–induced cyclin D_1 expression and DNA synthesis in these cells.[87,88] Finally, it has been shown recently in HepG2 cells that PDGF-induced H_2O_2 production requires activation of PI 3-kinase.[89] Taken together, these data suggest that, in the context of the cyclin D_1 promoter, PI 3-kinase is an upstream activator of Rac1.

Protein kinase C is a complex family of signaling intermediates including three types of eleven different isoenzymes. Different PKC isoforms may have distinct roles in the regulation of cell proliferation. PKCζ activity increases in proliferating human airway smooth muscle.[90] On the other hand, preliminary studies indicate that PKCδ is a negative regulator of bovine tracheal smooth muscle cyclin D_1 expression.[91]

Finally, growth factor treatment of airway smooth muscle cells has been shown to induce activation of the two stress-activated MAP kinases, p38 and Jun amino-terminal kinase (JNK),[65,92,93] consistent with the notion that these intermediates, like ERKs, play a role in the growth regulation. However, unlike ERK, selective activation of p38 inhibits airway smooth muscle cell cycle progression,[94] as it does in CCL39 hamster lung fibroblasts.[69] Paradoxically, p38 may be stimulated by Ras and Rac1,[65,95–97] suggesting that GTPases may simultaneously activate positive and negative growth regulatory pathways, perhaps as a safeguard against excessive growth.

Smooth muscle hypertrophy

As noted above, airway smooth muscle hypertrophy is present in at least a subgroup of patients with fatal asthma.[51] The signaling pathways regulating contractile protein expression have not been well studied, owing to the difficulty of establishing a cell culture model. However, it has been demonstrated recently that prolonged serum deprivation induces a subset of airway smooth muscle cells to express smooth muscle actin, myosin heavy chain, and SM22.[98] Development of this "contractile phenotype" appears to be regulated primarily by posttranscriptional mechanisms and is dependent on PI 3-kinase. On the other hand, transcription of contractile protein messenger ribonucleic acids (mRNAs) appears to be inhibited by activation of ERK (Hershenson M, Solway J, unpublished data, 1999). The involvement of PI 3-kinase and ERK in airway smooth muscle differentiation, as well as proliferation, suggests that signaling intermediates may be used in various combinations to achieve distinct biologic responses. A possible mechanism by which this occurs may involve scaffolding proteins, which may bind several signaling molecules to create multienzyme complexes or, conversely, sequester signaling proteins so they do not interact with other proteins.[99] Scaffolding also may control subcellular localization.

Pharmacology

Although a thorough review of asthma pharmacology is beyond the scope of this chapter, selected aspects in the management of acute asthma are considered here. It was once promulgated that wheezing infants fail to respond to bronchodilators because of a deficiency in airway smooth muscle. It is now clear, however, that normal infants may exhibit greater airway cholinergic responsiveness than adults, consistent with the notion that asthma may occur early in life. As in adults, the pharmacologic treatment of acute asthma in children primarily consists of β_2-agonists, anticholinergics, magnesium, phosphodiesterase inhibitors, corticosteroids, mast cell stabilizers, and leukotriene modifiers (Table 19–1).[100–105] As the latter two classes of agents do not directly regulate airway smooth muscle, they are not discussed here.

β_2-Agonists are the drugs of choice to treat bronchoconstriction in status asthmaticus. They may be delivered directly to the airways via nebulization, metered-dose inhaler, or dry powder inhaler, or systemically by oral or parenteral routes. In general, direct delivery to the airways is the preferred route of administration, as systemic administration causes more side effects and is no more effective than direct administration. Given the effectiveness of today's nebulizers and spacer devices for delivering β_2-agonists to infants and children, there is simply no justification for the use of oral β_2-agonists. Although selective β_2-agonists such as albuterol and terbutaline have been administered safely by continuous intravenous infusion, intravenous administration produces no greater bronchodilation than does aerosol delivery.[106,107] Nevertheless, the use of intravenous terbutaline might be tried in patients with impending or existing respiratory failure. Isoproterenol should be avoided, owing to the drug's nonselective cardiac effects.

In general, the addition of anticholinergics to β_2-agonist therapy appears to reduce airflow obstruction marginally in pediatric patients with acute asthma. Anticholinergics produce less bronchodilation at peak effect than do β_2-agonists, and they achieve a more variable clinical response, suggesting that cholinergic mechanisms play a variable role in patients with acute asthma. However, in patients with more severe obstruction, ipratroprium bromide may reduce the need for hospitalization.[102]

The precise mechanism by which magnesium sulfate relaxes smooth muscle remains unknown, but it may involve the inhibition of cellular calcium entry through voltage-dependent calcium channels.[108] In the one randomized trial of intravenous magnesium therapy in the treatment of children with asthma, patients who received magnesium had significantly greater improvement in short-term pulmonary function and were more likely to be discharged home from the emergency department.[103]

Intravenous administration of the phosphodiesterase inhibitor aminophylline has been shown in at least three reports to be of no additional benefit in the treatment of acute asthma in children when given with corticosteroids and β_2-agonists.[109–111] Thus, aminophylline treatment should no longer be included in the routine treatment of hospitalized children with status asthmaticus. The use of aminophylline in the treatment of children with impending respiratory failure may still be warranted, however, as these patients were excluded from the above studies. Indeed, a recent study of patients with severe acute asthma unresponsive to nebulized salbutamol showed that intravenous aminophylline, when added to a treatment regimen of inhaled salbutamol, inhaled ipratropium, and intravenous steroids, significantly increases expiratory flow while reducing the need for mechanical ventilation.[112] Thus, aminophylline may still have a place in the management of severe acute asthma in children unresponsive to initial treatment.

It generally is agreed now that suppression of airway inflammation with corticosteroids should be the mainstay of pharmacologic therapy in chronic and acute asthma. In addition, glucocorticoids may increase the gene expression of β_2-adrenergic receptors in airway smooth muscle and also prevent the downregulation that occurs with prolonged administration of a β_2-agonist.[113,114]

Bronchiolitis

It has long been debated whether the small airways obstruction observed in infants with viral bronchiolitis is responsive to bronchodilators, that is, whether airway smooth muscle tone is abnormal in this disease. Assessments of this problem have been plagued by the inability to measure pulmonary function in these patients. However, a new technique comprising passive inflation of the lungs followed by rapid thoracic compression has obtained forced expiratory maneuvers similar to those generated during spirometry in older children and adults.[115] It has been shown recently using this technique that a majority of infants with acute viral bronchiolitis respond to bronchodilators with improved expiratory flow.[116] These data are consistent with previous studies and provide a rationale for the application of bronchodilators in infants with acute bronchiolitis.

Bronchopulmonary Dysplasia

As with bronchiolitis, difficulties with pulmonary function testing in infants have hindered efforts to measure airway function in patients with bronchopulmonary dysplasia. Nevertheless, several studies indicate that β_2-agonists reduce airways resistance in infants with bronchopulmonary dysplasia.[117–119] Airway structural changes likely contribute to the observed airways responsiveness. It has been demonstrated that smooth muscle mass is increased abnormally in the airways of premature infants with bronchopulmonary dysplasia,[120–122] perhaps due, in part, to excess cell proliferation.

References

1. Sparrow MP, Weichselbaum M, McCray PB. Development of the innervation and airway smooth muscle in human fetal lung. Am J Respir Cell Mol Biol 1999;20:550–60.
2. McCray PBJ. Spontaneous contractility of human fetal airway smooth muscle. Am J Respir Cell Mol Biol 1993; 8:573–80.
3. Hooper SB, Han VK, Harding R. Changes in lung expansion alter pulmonary DNA synthesis and IGF-II gene expression in fetal sheep. Am J Physiol 1993;265:L403–9.
4. Sparrow MP, Mitchell HW. Contraction of smooth muscle of pig airway tissues from before birth to maturity. J Appl Physiol 1990;68:468–77.
5. Murphy TM, Mitchell RW, Halayko A, et al. Effect of maturational changes in myosin content and morphometry on airway smooth muscle contraction. Am J Physiol 1991;260:L471–80.
6. Ikeda K, Mitchell RW, Guest KA, et al. Ontogeny of shortening velocity in porcine trachealis. Am J Physiol 1992; 262:L280–5.
7. Chitano P, Wang J, Cox CM, et al. Different ontogeny of rate of force generation and shortening velocity in guinea pig trachealis. J Appl Physiol 2000;88:1338–45.
8. Shen X, Bhargava V, Wodicka GR, et al. Greater airway narrowing in immature than in mature rabbits during methacholine challenge. J Appl Physiol 1996;81:2637–43.

9. Montgomery GL, Tepper RS. Changes in airway reactivity with age in normal infants and young children. Am Rev Respir Dis 1990;142:1372–6.
10. Shirazi A, Iizuka K, Fadden P, et al. Purification and characterization of the mammalian myosin light chain phosphatase holoenzyme. The differential effects of the holoenzyme and its subunits on smooth muscle. J Biol Chem 1994;269:31598–606.
11. Kitazawa T, Masuo M, Somlyo AP. G protein-mediated inhibition of myosin light-chain phosphatase in vascular smooth muscle. Proc Natl Acad Sci U S A 1991; 88:9307–10.
12. Bremerich DH, Warner DO, Lorenz RR, et al. Role of protein kinase C in calcium sensitization during muscarinic stimulation in airway smooth muscle. Am J Physiol 1997; 273:L775–81.
13. Hirata K, Kikuchi A, Sasaki T, et al. Involvement of rho p21 in the GTP-enhanced calcium ion sensitivity of smooth muscle contraction. J Biol Chem 1992;267:8719–22.
14. Hall A. Rho GTPases and the actin cytoskelton. Science 1998;279:509–14.
15. Yoshii A, Iizuka K, Dobashi K, et al. Relaxation of contracted rabbit tracheal and human bronchial smooth muscle by Y-27632 through inhibition of Ca^{2+} sensitization. Am J Respir Cell Mol Biol 1999;20:1190–200.
16. Hedges JC, Oxhorn BC, Carty M, et al. Phosphorylation of caldesmon by ERK MAP kinases in smooth muscle. Am J Physiol 2000;278:C718–26.
17. Page K, Hershenson MB. Mitogen-activated signaling and cell cycle regulation in airway smooth muscle. Front Biosci 2000;5:D258–67.
18. Kume H, Takai A, Tokuno H, Tomita T. Regulation of Ca^{2+}-dependent K^+-channel activity in tracheal myocytes by phosphorylation. Nature 1989;341:152–4.
19. Lin YF, Jan YN, Jan LY. Regulation of ATP-sensitive potassium channel function by protein kinase A-mediated phosphorylation in transfected HEK293 cells. EMBO J 2000;19:942–55.
20. Gerthoffer WT. Calcium dependence of myosin phosphorylation and airway smooth muscle contraction and relaxation. Am J Physiol 1986;250:C597–604.
21. Bai TR. Abnormalities in airway smooth muscle in fatal asthma. A comparison between trachea and bronchus. Am Rev Respir Dis 1991;143:441–3.
22. de Jongste JC, Mons H, Bonta IL, Kerrebijn KF. In vitro responses of airways from an asthmatic patient. Eur J Respir Dis 1987;71:23–9.
23. Bjorck T, Gustafsson LE, Dahlen SE. Isolated bronchi from asthmatics are hyperresponsive to adenosine, which apparently acts indirectly by liberation of leukotrienes and histamine. Am Rev Respir Dis 1992;145:1087–91.
24. Black JL. Pharmacology of airway smooth muscle in chronic obstructive pulmonary disease and in asthma. Am Rev Respir Dis 1991;143:1177–81.
25. Whicker SD, Armour CL, Black JL. Responsiveness of bronchial smooth muscle from asthmatic patients to relaxant and contractile agonists. Pulm Pharmacol 1988;1:25–31.
26. Goldie RG, Spina D, Henry PJ, et al. In vitro responsiveness of human asthmatic bronchus to carbachol, histamine, beta-adrenoceptor agonists and theophylline. Br J Clin Pharmacol 1986;22:669–76.
27. Antonissen LA, Mitchell RW, Kroeger EA, et al. Mechanical alterations of airway smooth muscle in a canine asthmatic model. J Appl Physiol 1979;46:681–7.
28. Jiang H, Rao K, Halayko AJ, et al. Bronchial smooth muscle mechanics of a canine model of allergic airway hyperresponsiveness. J Appl Physiol 1992;72:39–45.
29. Mitchell RW, Ruhlmann E, Magnussen H, et al. Passive sensitization of human bronchi augments smooth muscle shortening velocity and capacity. Am J Physiol 1994; 267:L218–22.
30. Fan T, Yang M, Halayko A, et al. Airway responsiveness in two inbred strains of mouse disparate in IgE and IL-4 production. Am J Respir Cell Mol Biol 1997;17:156–63.
31. Bramley AM, Thomson RJ, Roberts CR, Schellenberg RR. Hypothesis: excessive bronchoconstriction in asthma is due to decreased airway elastance. Eur Respir J 1994; 7:337–41.
32. Jiang H, Rao K, Halayko AJ, et al. Ragweed sensitization-induced increase of myosin light chain kinase content in canine airway smooth muscle. Am J Respir Cell Mol Biol 1992;7:567–73.
33. Ammit AL, Armour CL, Black JL. Smooth muscle myosin light chain kinase content is increased in human sensitized airways. Am J Respir Crit Care Med 2000;161:257–63.
34. Vincent NJ, Knudson R, Leith DE, et al. Factors influencing pulmonary resistance. J Appl Physiol 1970;29:236–43.
35. Hoppin FG Jr, Green M, Morgan MS. Relationship of central and peripheral airway resistance to lung volume in dogs. J Appl Physiol 1978;44:728–37.
36. Brown RH, Mitzner WE. Effect of lung inflation and airway tone on airway diameter in vivo. J Appl Physiol 1996; 80:1581–8.
37. Ding DJ, Martin JG, Macklem PT. Effects of lung volume on maximal methacholine-induced bronchoconstriction in normal humans. J Appl Physiol 1987;62:1324–30.
38. Gunst SJ, Meiss RA, Wu MF, Rowe M. Mechanisms for the mechanical plasticity of tracheal smooth muscle. Am J Physiol 1995;268:C1267–76.
39. Fredberg JJ, Jones KA, Nathan M, et al. Friction in airway smooth muscle: mechanism, latch, and implications in asthma. J Appl Physiol 1996;81:2703–12.
40. Skloot G, Permutt S, Togias A. Airway hyperresponsiveness in asthma: a problem of limited smooth muscle relaxation with inspiration. J Clin Invest 1995;96:2393–403.
41. Bai TR, Mak JC, Barnes PJ. A comparison of beta-adrenergic receptors and in vitro relaxant responses to isoproterenol in asthmatic airway smooth muscle. Am J Respir Cell Mol Biol 1992;6:647–51.
42. Laporte JD, Moore PE, Panettieri RA, et al. Prostanoids mediate IL-1 beta-induced beta-adrenergic hyporesponsiveness in human airway smooth muscle cells. Am J Physiol 1998;275:L491–501.
43. Carroll N, Elliot J, Morton A, James A. The structure of large and small airways in nonfatal and fatal asthma. Am Rev Respir Dis 1993;147:405–10.
44. Dunhill MS The pathology of asthma, with special reference to changes in the bronchial mucosa. J Clin Pathol 1960;13:27–33.

45. Takizawa T, Thurlbeck WM. Muscle and mucous gland size in the major bronchi of patients with chronic bronchitis, asthma and asthmatic bronchitis. Am Rev Respir Dis 1971;104:331–6.
46. Heard BE, Hossain S. Hyperplasia of bronchial smooth muscle in asthma. J Pathol 1973;110:319–32.
47. Sobonya RE. Quantitative structural alterations in long-standing allergic asthma. Am Rev Respir Dis 1984; 130:289–92.
48. James AL, Pare PD, Hogg JC. The mechanics of airway narrowing in asthma. Am Rev Respir Dis 1989;139:242–6.
49. Ebina M, Yaegashi H, Chiba R, et al. Hyperreactive site in the airway tree of asthmatic patients revealed by thickening of bronchial muscles. A morphometric study. Am Rev Respir Dis 1990;141:1327–32.
50. Saetta M, Di Stefano A, Rosina C, et al. Quantitative structural analysis of peripheral airways and arteries in sudden fatal asthma. Am Rev Respir Dis 1991; 143:138–43.
51. Ebina M, Takahashi T, Chiba T, Motomiya M. Cellular hypertrophy and hyperplasia of airway smooth muscles underlying bronchial asthma. A 3-D morphometric study. Am Rev Respir Dis 1993;148:720–6.
52. Cohen MD, Ciocca V, Panettieri RA. Transforming growth factor-β1 modulates human airway smooth muscle cell proliferation induced by mitogens. Am J Resp Cell Mol Biol 1997;16:85–90.
53. Vignola AM, Chancz P, Chiappara G, et al. Transforming growth factor-β expression in mucosa biopsies in asthma and chronic bronchitis. Am J Resp Crit Care Med 1997;156:591–9.
54. Amishima M, Munakata M, Nasuhara Y, et al. Expression of epidermal growth factor and epidermal growth factor receptor immunoreactivity in the asthmatic human airway. Am J Respir Crit Care Med 1998;157:1907–12.
55. Naureckas ET, Ndukwu IM, Halayko AJ, et al. Bronchoalveolar lavage fluid from asthmatic subjects is mitogenic for human airway smooth muscle. Am J Respir Crit Care Med 1999;160:2062–6.
56. Hershenson MB, Kelleher MD, Naureckas ET, et al. Hyperoxia increases airway cell S-phase traversal in immature rats in vivo. Am J Respir Cell Mol Biol 1994; 11:296–303.
57. Wang ZL, Walker BA, Weir TD, et al. Effect of chronic antigen and beta 2 agonist exposure on airway remodeling in guinea pigs. Am J Respir Crit Care Med 1995;152(6 Pt 1):2097–104.
58. Panettieri RA, Murray RK, Eszterhas AJ, et al. Repeated allergen inhalations induce DNA synthesis in airway smooth muscle and epithelial cells *in vivo*. Am J Physiol 1998;274:L417–24.
59. Karpova AY, Abe MK, Li J, et al. MEK1 is required for PDGF-induced ERK activation and DNA synthesis in tracheal myocytes. Am J Physiol 1997;272:L558–65.
60. Whelchel A, Evans J, Posada J. Inhibition of ERK activation attenuates endothelin-stimulated airway smooth muscle proliferation. Am J Respir Cell Mol Biol 1997;16:589–96.
61. Walker TR, Moore SM, Lawson MF, et al. Platelet-derived growth factor-BB and thrombin activate phosphoinositide 3-kinase and protein kinase B: role in mediating airway smooth muscle proliferation. Mol Pharmacol 1998; 54:1007–15.
62. Lew DB, Dempsey BK, Zhao Y, et al. Beta-hexosaminidase-induced activation of p44/42 mitogen-activated protein kinase is dependent on p21Ras and protein kinase C and mediates bovine airway smooth-muscle proliferation. Am J Respir Cell Mol Biol 1999;21:111–8.
63. Orsini MJ, Krymskaya VP, Eszterhas AJ, et al. MAPK superfamily activation in human airway smooth muscle: mitogenesis requires prolonged p42/p44 activation. Am J Physiol 1999;277:L479–88.
64. Ammit AJ, Kane SA, Panettieri RAJ. Activation of K-p21ras and N-p21ras, but not H-p21ras, is necessary for mitogen-induced airway smooth muscle proliferation. Am J Respir Cell Mol Biol 1999;21:719–27.
65. Page K, Li J, Hershenson MB. Platelet-derived growth factor stimulation of mitogen-activated protein kinases and cyclin D_1 promoter activity in cultured airway smooth muscle cells: role of Ras. Am J Respir Cell Mol Biol 1999; 20:1294–302.
66. Vichi P, Whelchel A, Knot H, et al. Endothelin-stimulated ERK activation in airway smooth-muscle cells requires calcium influx and Raf activation. Am J Respir Cell Mol Biol 1999;20:99–105.
67. Albanese C, Johnson J, Watanabe G, et al. Transforming p21ras mutants and c-Ets-2 activate the cyclin D_1 promoter through distinguishable regions. J Biol Chem 1995; 270:23589–97.
68. Watanabe G, Howe A, Lee R, et al. Induction of cyclin D_1 by simian virus 40 small T tumor antigen. Proc Natl Acad Sci U S A 1996;93:12861–6.
69. Lavoie J, L'Allemain G, Brunet A, et al. Cyclin D_1 expression is regulated positively by $p42/p44^{MAPK}$ and negatively by $p38/HOG^{MAPK}$ pathway. J Biol Chem 1996;271:20608–16.
70. Ramakrishnan M, Musa NL, Li J, et al. Catalytic activation of extracellular signal-regulated kinases induces cyclin D_1 expression in airway smooth muscle. Am J Respir Cell Mol Biol 1998;18:736–40.
71. Xiong W, Pestell RG, Watanabe G, et al. Cyclin D_1 is required for S-phase traversal in bovine tracheal myocytes. Am J Physiol 1997;272:L1205–10.
72. Cheng M, Sexl V, Sherr CJ, Roussel MF. Assembly of cyclin D-dependent kinase and titration of p27Kip1 regulated by mitogen-activated protein kinase kinase (MEK1). Proc Natl Acad Sci U S A 1998;95:1091–6.
73. Weber JD, Hu W, Jefcoat SC Jr, et al. Ras-stimulated extracellular signal-related kinase 1 and RhoA activities coordinate platelet-derived growth factor-induced G1 progression through the independent regulation of cyclin D_1 and p27. J Biol Chem 1997;272:32966–71.
74. Keith CT, Schreiber SL. PIK-related kinases: DNA repair, recombination and cell cycle checkpoints. Science 1995; 270:50–1.
75. Claesson-Welsh L. Platelet-derived growth factor receptor signaling. J Biol Chem 1994;269:32023–6.
76. Marshall MS. Ras target proteins in eukaryotic cells. FASEB J 1995;9:1311–8.
77. Liu X, Marengere LE, Koch CA, Pawson T. The v-Src SH3 domain binds phosphatidylinositol 3'-kinase. Mol Cell Biol 1993;13:5225–32.

78. Corey S, Eguinoa A, Puyana-Theall K, et al. Granulocyte-macrophage colony-stimulating factor stimulates both association and activation of phosphoinositide 3OH-kinase and src-related tyrosine kinase(s) in human myeloid derived cells. EMBO J 1993;12:2681–90.
79. Yamanashi Y, Fukui Y, Wongsasant B, et al. Activation of Src-like protein-tyrosine kinase Lyn and its association with phosphatidylinositol 3-kinase upon B-cell antigen receptor-mediated signaling. Proc Natl Acad Sci U S A 1992;89:1118–22.
80. Pleiman CM, Hertz WM, Cambier JC. Activation of phosphatidylinositol-3' kinase by Src-family kinase SH3 binding to the p85 subunit. Science 1994;263:1609–12.
81. Lemmon MA, Ferguson KM, O'Brien R, et al. Specific and high-affinity binding of inositol phosphates to an isolated pleckstrin homology domain. Proc Natl Acad Sci U S A 1995;92:10472–6.
82. Krymskaya VP, Hoffman R, Eszterhas A, et al. EGF activates ErbB-2 and stimulates phosphatidylinositol 3-kinase in human airway smooth muscle cells. Am J Physiol 1999; 276:L246–55.
83. Krymskaya VP, Hoffman R, Eszterhas A, et al. TGF-1 modulates EGF-stimulated phosphatidylinositol 3-kinase activity in human airway smooth muscle cells. Am J Physiol 1997;273:L1220–27.
84. Scott PH, Belham CM, al-Hafidh J, et al. A regulatory role for cAMP in phosphatidylinositol 3-kinase/p70 ribosomal S6 kinase-mediated DNA synthesis in platelet-derived-growth-factor-stimulated bovine airway smooth-muscle cells. Biochem J 1996;318:965–71.
85. Krymskaya VP, Penn RB, Orsini MJ, et al. Phosphatidylinositol 3-kinase mediates mitogen-induced human airway smooth muscle cell proliferation. Am J Physiol 1999; 277:L65–78.
86. Page K, Li J, Liu P, et al. Phosphatidylinositol 3-kinase is required for cyclin D_1 promoter activity and S-phase traversal in bovine tracheal myocytes [abstract]. Am J Respir Crit Care Med 1999;159:A532.
87. Page K, Li J, Hodge JA, et al. Characterization of a Rac1 signaling pathway to cyclin D_1 expression in airway smooth muscle cells. J Biol Chem 1999;274:22065–71.
88. Brar SS, Kennedy TP, Whorton AR, et al. Requirement for reactive oxygen species in serum-induced and platelet-derived growth factor-induced growth of airway smooth muscle. J Biol Chem 1999;274:20017–26.
89. Bae YS, Sung G-Y, Kim O-S, et al. Platelet-derived growth factor-induced H_2O_2 production requires the activation of phosphatidylinositol 3-kinase. J Biol Chem 275:10527–31.
90. Carlin S, Yang KX, Donnelly R, Black JL. Protein kinase C isoforms in human airway smooth muscle cells: activation of PKC during proliferation. Am J Physiol 1999; 276:L506–12.
91. Page K, Corbit K, Li J, et al. Protein kinase C delta is an upstream activator of p38 MAP kinase and involved in the negative regulation of cyclin D_1 expression in bovine tracheal smooth muscle cells [abstract]. Am J Respir Crit Care Med 2000;161:A895.
92. Shapiro PS, Evans JN, Davis RJ, Posada JA. The seven-transmembrane-spanning receptors for endothelin and thrombin cause proliferation of airway smooth muscle cells and activation of the extracellular regulated kinase and c-Jun NH_2-terminal kinase groups of mitogen-activated protein kinases. J Biol Chem 1996;271:5750–4.
93. Pyne NJ, Pyne S. Platelet-derived growth factor activates a mammalian Ste20 coupled mitogen-activated protein kinase in airway smooth muscle. Cell Signal 1997; 9:311–7.
94. Page K, Li J, Liu P, et al. Inhibition of p38 MAP kinase increases cyclin D_1 expression in cultured airway smooth muscle cells [abstract]. Am J Respir Crit Care Med 1999;159:A532.
95. Minden A, Lin A, Smeal T, et al. c-Jun N-terminal phosphorylation correlates with activation of the Jnk subgroup but not the Erk subgroup of mitogen-activated protein kinases. Mol Cell Biol 1994;14:6683–8.
96. Zhang S, Han J, Sells MA, et al. Rho family GTPases regulate p38 mitogen-activated protein kinase through the downstream mediator Pak1. J Biol Chem 1995;270:23934–6.
97. Bagrodia S, Derijard B, Davis RJ, Cerione RA. Cdc42 and PAK-mediated signaling leads to Jun kinase and p38 mitogen-activated protein kinase activation. J Biol Chem 1995;270:27995–8.
98. Halayko AJ, Camoretti-Mercado B, Forsythe SM, et al. Divergent differentiation paths in airway smooth muscle culture: induction of functionally contractile myocytes. Am J Physiol 1999;276:L197–206.
99. Hershenson MB, Abe MK. Mitogen-activated signaling in airway smooth muscle. A central role for Ras. Am J Respir Cell Mol Biol 1999;21:651–4.
100. Fuglsang G, Pedersen S, Borgstrom L. Dose-response relationships of intravenously administered terbutaline in children with asthma. J Pediatr 1989;114:315–20.
101. Stephanopoulos DE, Monge R, Schell KH, et al. Continuous intravenous terbutaline for pediatric status asthmaticus. Crit Care Med 1998;26:1744–8.
102. Schuh S, Johnson DW, Callahan S, et al. Efficacy of frequent nebulized ipratropium bromide added to frequent high-dose albuterol therapy in severe childhood asthma. J Pediatr 1995;126:639–45.
103. Ciarallo L, Sauer AH, Shannon MW. Intravenous magnesium therapy for moderate to severe pediatric asthma: results of a randomized, placebo-controlled trial. J Pediatr 1996;129:809–14.
104. Becker JM, Arora A, Scarfone RJ, et al. Oral versus intravenous corticosteroids in children hospitalized with asthma. J Allergy Clin Immunol 1999;103:586–90.
105. Barnett PL, Caputo GL, Baskin M, Kuppermann N. Intravenous versus oral corticosteroids in the management of acute asthma in children. Ann Emerg Med 1997;29:212–7.
106. Pierce RJ, Payne CR, Williams SJ, et al. Comparison of intravenous and inhaled terbutaline in the treatment of asthma. Chest 1981;79:506–11.
107. Salmeron S, Brochard L, Mal H, et al. Nebulized versus intravenous albuterol in hypercapnic acute asthma. A multicenter, double-blind, randomized study. Am J Respir Crit Care Med 1984;149:1466–70.
108. Kumasaka D, Lindeman KS, Clancy J, et al. $MgSO_4$ relaxes porcine airway smooth muscle by reducing Ca^{2+} entry. Am J Physiol 1996;270:L469–74.

109. DiGiulio GA, Kercsmar CM, Krug SE, et al. Hospital treatment of asthma: lack of benefit from theophylline given in addition to nebulized albuterol and intravenously administered corticosteroid. J Pediatr 1993;122:464–9.
110. Carter E, Cruz M, Chesrown S, et al. Efficacy of intravenously administered theophylline in children hospitalized with severe asthma. J Pediatr 1993;122:470–6.
111. Strauss RE, Wertheim DL, Bonagura VR, Valacer DJ. Aminophylline therapy does not improve outcome and increases adverse effects in children hospitalized with acute asthmatic exacerbations. Pediatrics 1994; 93:205–10.
112. Yung M, South M. Randomised controlled trial of aminophylline for severe acute asthma. Arch Dis Child 1998; 79:405–10.
113. Mak JC, Nishikawa M, Shirasaki H, et al. Protective effects of a glucocorticoid on downregulation of pulmonary beta 2-adrenergic receptors in vivo. J Clin Invest 1995; 96:99–106.
114. Mak JCW, Nishikawa M, Barnes PJ. Glucocorticosteroids increase 2-adrenergic receptor transcription in human lung. Am J Physiol 1995;268:L41–6.
115. Feher A, Castile R, Kisling J, et al. Flow limitation in normal infants: a new method for forced expiratory maneuvers from raised lung volumes. J Appl Physiol 1996;80:2019–25.
116. Modl M, Eber E, Weinhandl E, et al. Assessment of bronchodilator responsiveness in infants with bronchiolitis. A comparison of the tidal and the raised volume rapid thoracoabdominal compression technique. Am J Respir Crit Care Med 2000;161:763–8.
117. Gomez-Del Rio M, Gerhardt T, Hehre D, et al. Effect of a beta-agonist nebulization on lung function in neonates with increased pulmonary resistance. Pediatr Pulmonol 1986;2:287–91.
118. Wilkie RA, Bryan MH. Effect of bronchodilators on airway resistance in ventilator-dependent neonates with chronic lung disease. J Pediatr 1987;111:278–82.
119. Stefano JL, Bhutani VK, Fox WW. A randomized placebo-controlled study to evaluate the effects of oral albuterol on pulmonary mechanics in ventilator-dependent infants at risk of developing BPD. Pediatr Pulmonol 1991;10:183–90.
120. Hislop AA, Haworth SG. Airway size and structure in the normal fetal and infant lung and the effect of premature delivery and artificial ventilation. Am Rev Respir Dis 1989;140:1717–26.
121. Sward-Comunelli SL, Mabry SM, Truog WE, Thibeault DW. Airway muscle in preterm infants: changes during development. J Pediatr 1997;130:570–6.
122. Johnson DE, Burke BA, Anderson WR. Alterations in airway epithelial and smooth muscle area in infants with bronchopulmonary dysplasia [abstract]. Am Rev Respir Dis 1990;141:A159.

CHAPTER 20

Pulmonary Edema and Injury to the Developing Lung

David P. Carlton, MD

Pulmonary edema is a significant cause of respiratory failure in patients with acute lung disease and is a consistent finding in almost all lung injury syndromes. Normal water balance in the lung requires that net transvascular fluid movement from the pulmonary circulation be matched by effective clearance pathways ultimately leading to the deposition of fluid back into the circulation. This chapter explores the normal pathways by which fluid moves into and out of the developing lung and examines at least some of the conditions that disrupt fluid balance in the newborn lung.

General Principles of Lung Fluid Balance

By definition, the portion of the pulmonary vascular bed that participates in fluid exchange is referred to as the microcirculation. Under normal conditions, fluid moves from the pulmonary microcirculation into the lung interstitium, a process that is governed by the sum of hydrostatic and osmotic pressures across the sites of fluid exchange.

Transvascular flow of liquid across the microcirculation of the lung is described in general terms by the Starling equation $Jv = LpS\,[(P_{mv}-P_i) - \sigma(\pi_{mv}-\pi_i)]$ wherein Jv represents net liquid movement, Lp is the hydraulic conductivity (the permeability to water), S is the surface area available for fluid exchange, P_{mv} and P_i represent the hydrostatic pressures of the microcirculation and interstitium, respectively, σ is the osmotic reflection coefficient (a term used to describe the permeability of the barrier to osmotically active solutes), and π_{mv} and π_i are the osmotic pressures in the microvascular and interstitial spaces, respectively. This equation allows that Jv will increase as permeability or surface area increases, if the difference between hydrostatic pressures in the microcirculation and interstitium increases, or if the difference between osmotic pressures in the microcirculation and interstitium decreases. Note that blood flow has no bearing on fluid filtration. However, conditions that increase pulmonary blood flow are likely to increase microvascular hydrostatic pressure or to increase the surface area available for fluid exchange. It is these two factors that account for the increase in transvascular fluid movement seen in conditions associated with increased pulmonary blood flow.[1]

Although the exact site of fluid filtration is uncertain, experimental evidence points to vascular sites somewhat distal to the arterioles, in the alveolar capillaries, and fluid exchange is probably restricted to only a portion of these capillaries.[2] There are no lymphatics in the alveolar septal wall, but fluid that traverses the circulation at this point moves to the loose connective tissue that surrounds the respiratory and terminal bronchioles and small pulmonary vessels as a result of a hydraulic pressure gradient favoring fluid movement in this direction. It is in the connective tissue of these bronchovascular structures that lymphatics arise.[3] The pressure gradient from the alveolar wall to these loose connective tissue spaces serves to minimize interstitial collections of fluid in the anatomic area responsible for gas exchange.[4] Once fluid enters the interstitial space, it is transported back to the systemic circulation by way of lung lymphatics. Assuming that lymphatic clearance is unimpeded, the resolution of pulmonary edema ultimately depends on the return to normal of those factors that accentuated transvascular fluid transport.

If the lymphatics are unable to clear effectively the transvascular fluid load, the alveolar septum begins to fill with fluid and widen.[5,6] After this, the alveolar space fills with fluid, causing loss of gas volume and alveolar collapse. Experimental studies have not made clear the exact site of transepithelial movement of fluid into the alveolus, and it is possible that leakage occurs at different sites along the respiratory epithelial barrier, depending on the mechanism of edema formation.[5,7–9]

Clearance of alveolar fluid into the interstitium is an important component of the resolution of pulmonary edema. Whereas interstitial edema may alter some elements of lung mechanics, it is alveolar edema that significantly disturbs gas exchange. Epidemiologic studies show that clearance of fluid from the air spaces is associated with clinical improvement in patients with acute lung injury.[10] Unlike the transvascular movement of fluid, the Starling equation does not fully explain transepithelial clearance of air-space fluid. When liquid solutions that contain protein are placed into the distal lung, these solutions become sufficiently concentrated over time that the osmotic pressure exerted by the protein remaining in the air space far exceeds any hydrostatic force in the interstitium that would act to move fluid out of the alveolus.[11,12] Thus, a model of "active, " that is, energy-requiring, fluid transport from the air space into the interstitium is necessary to explain the loss of alveolar liquid in the face of ever-increasing alveolar protein osmotic pressure. Such a mechanism is now well established and is characterized, at least in part, by the transmembrane movement of Na^+ across the apical surface of the respiratory epithelial cell.[13,14] The movement of Na^+ across the apical surface is considered "passive," occurring only because of the activity of the Na^+-K^+-ATPase, an enzyme that translocates three Na^+ ions to the interstitium in exchange for two K^+ ions on the basolateral surface of the respiratory epithelium. The normal function of this pump results in a low intracellular concentration of Na^+, thus providing the electrochemical driving force for Na^+ entry. Water follows the movement of Na^+ out of the air space, across the respiratory epithelium, and into the lung interstitium.

Lung Fluid Balance in the Fetus

Because the fetal lung is gasless, it is often considered to be atelectatic. In actuality, the fetal lung lumen is filled with liquid of rather unique composition that derives from the respiratory epithelium.[15–17] During the latter portion of gestation, at least in the fetal lamb (an animal of similar size to the human fetus), the lung is distended with a volume of fluid on the order of 20- to 30 mL/kg body weight.[18–20]

Fluid normally moves from the fetal pulmonary microcirculation into the lung interstitium.[21,22] However, unlike the mature lung, in which fluid entering the lung is subsequently cleared by lymphatics, most of the transvascular fluid in the fetal lung moves across the respiratory epithelium into the potential air spaces.[23] From there, the liquid then moves up the tracheobronchial tree and into the oropharynx, from which it either flows into the amniotic fluid or is swallowed. Although there remains uncertainty about when luminal lung liquid formation begins, it may occur quite early in gestation, perhaps by mid-first trimester in the human.[24] By the latter part of gestation, when quantitative measurements can be made more easily, the rate of lung liquid formation, at least as measured in fetal sheep, is on the order of 3 to 5 mL/kg body weight per hour.[17,25,26] Respiratory epithelium at all levels may contribute to lung liquid formation, but the respiratory epithelium of the distal lung probably makes the greatest contribution, if only because of the extensive surface area available for transepithelial fluid secretion.[20,27,28] Liquid in the interstitium that will ultimately fill the potential air spaces is thought to derive from the pulmonary circulation, rather than from the bronchial circulation, because pulmonary artery ligation reduces the formation of lung liquid.[29,30] Fetal lung liquid provides a dynamic template around which the fetal lung develops. Under conditions in which lumen volume is not maintained by fluid distension, the lung becomes hypoplastic, and its development is incomplete.[31,32]

The liquid that fills the lumen of the lung during fetal life is distinct in composition from amniotic fluid, lung interstitial fluid, and plasma, indicating that lung liquid is not simply "spill-over" from one of these compartments.[16,18] Of note, the Cl^- concentration of lung liquid is approximately 150 mEq/L, and it contains only scant amounts of protein, less than 0.03 g/dL, which is approximately 1% of the value measured in interstitial fluid. Pioneering experiments in fetal lambs nearly 25 years ago established by use of thermodynamic calculations the existence of an "active" process by which Cl^- is translocated from the basolateral surface of the respiratory epithelial cell into the lung lumen.[28]

At least in some animal models, compounds that inhibit the function of the Na^+-K^+-$2Cl^-$ cotransporter slow or stop completely the secretion of fluid into the fetal lung lumen.[33–35] The presumed mechanism by which fluid transport is inhibited under these conditions derives from the understanding of Cl^--linked fluid movement in other ion-transporting epithelia (Figure 20–1).[36] This model predicts that Cl^- enters the cell across the basolateral membrane by way of the Na^+-K^+-$2Cl^-$ cotransporter, accompanied by K^+ and Cl^-. Once intracellular, Cl^- exits across the apical membrane surface of the cell into the lung lumen down its electrochemical gradient. Water follows the transepithelial movement of Cl^- from the interstitium into the potential air spaces of the lung at a rate sufficient to account for the generation of nearly 500 mL of fluid each day in the fetal lamb.[17,25] In this model of Cl^--linked fluid transport, there is little, if any, influence of Starling-type forces on transepithelial fluid balance. The relative independence of transepithelial fluid transport from hydrostatic and protein osmotic pressure gradients is demonstrated by experiments in which saline infused intravenously into fetal lambs, in sufficient volume to increase pulmonary vascular pressures and double lung lymph flow, has no influence on luminal lung liquid secretion.[23]

In the absence of respiratory distress, incomplete development itself does not appear to have an independent effect on lung vascular permeability.[37] The protein sieving characteristics of the premature fetal pulmonary vasculature is similar to that measured in term newborn lambs. Moreover, an equivalent hydrostatic challenge administered to premature fetal lambs and to newborn term lambs results in similar increases in transvascular fluid filtration. These observations suggest that any change in lung vascular permeability in the immature lung that occurs after birth must be triggered directly or indirectly by interventions that occur postnatally.

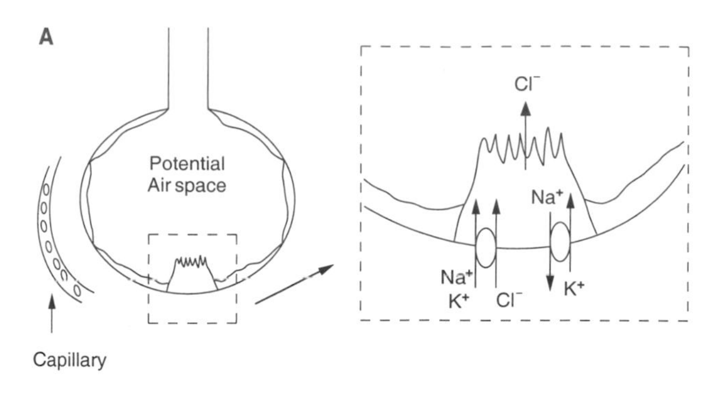

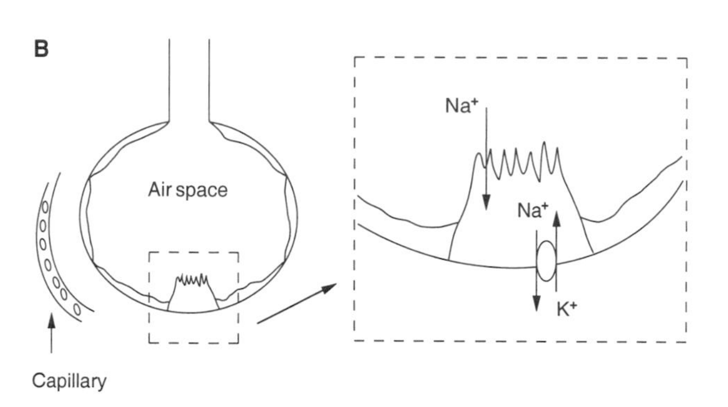

FIGURE 20–1. *A*, Representation of Cl^- secretion into the potential airs pace based on Na^+-K^+-$2Cl^-$ cotransport at the basolateral cell surface. *B*, Representation of Na^+ reabsorption pathway in the distal lung. The specific epithelial cell type responsible for either of these functions in vivo is unknown.

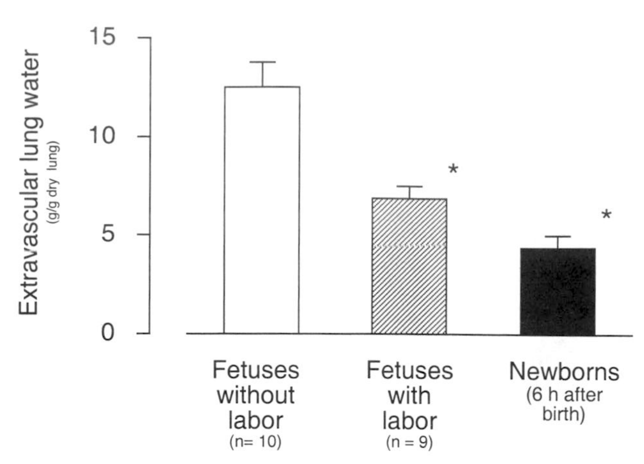

FIGURE 20–2. Postmortem extravascular lung water content (mean ± SD) in lambs during labor and after birth compared with lambs that were killed before labor. *Significantly different from fetuses without labor ($p < .05$). (Adapted from Bland RD and McMillan DD.[39])

Lung Fluid Balance around the Time of Birth

As important as it is for the lung to be distended by fluid in utero, it is crucial that this liquid leave the lung soon after birth so as not to interfere with postnatal gas exchange. Although it is impossible to exclude entirely a role for the efflux of luminal liquid by way of the upper airway, animal studies have clarified that this route need play little, if any, role in postnatal lung liquid clearance. Studies in animals have shown that extravascular lung water content is equivalent in those that are delivered vaginally or by cesarean section (thus foregoing chest or abdominal compression), as long as the fetus experiences labor (Figure 20–2).[21,38,39] Clearance of liquid from the lung after birth is thought to occur as a result of liquid reabsorption across the respiratory epithelium back into the lung interstitium. Once in the interstitium, liquid collects in the loose connective tissue surrounding the small vessels and airways, from which it is either reabsorbed back into the vessels of the lung, or is transported by way of lymphatics into the systemic circulation. The exact contribution of these two pathways to perinatal lung fluid clearance is uncertain, but lymphatics do not appear to clear more than 10 to 20% of the fetal lung liquid.[21]

Changes occur in lung fluid balance at the end of gestation that prepare the lung for air-breathing after birth. At least under some experimental conditions, luminal lung liquid volume and the rate of liquid secretion decrease beginning several days before delivery.[26,40] This process is accentuated near the time of birth such that in fetal lambs near term, extravascular lung water is reduced by nearly 50% during labor.[21] When the distribution of fluid is examined in animals in labor, there is a relative decrease in the proportion of liquid found in the potential air spaces compared with that found in the interstitium.

Although extravascular lung water content does not decrease immediately after birth, there is a redistribution of fluid within the lung that facilitates gas-filling of the alveoli. Clearance of fluid out of the air spaces into the interstitial spaces is rapid, consistent with the usual observation of normoxemia within minutes after birth.[41] The redistribution of fluid within the lung probably occurs as a result of two different mechanisms. First, when the newborn lung fills with air immediately after birth, there is a transient increase in permeability of the respiratory epithelium that allows for bulk movement of fluid out of the distal air space into the interstitium.[42] This process is one that could be driven by Starling forces whereby the combination of a relatively greater interstitial protein osmotic pressure and a relatively lower interstitial pressure facilitate fluid entry into the interstitium.

The other mechanism important in clearance of fetal lung fluid is the transepithelial reabsorption of Na^+ back into the interstitium. This process begins at least during labor and perhaps as early as a few days before birth.[41,43] Current understanding of this process allows that the Na^+-K^+-ATPase on the basolateral surface of the respiratory epithelium maintains a low intracellular Na^+ concentration and provides for an electrochemical driving force promoting transmembrane Na^+ entry into the cytoplasm, a process that occurs at the apical surface of the cell (see Figure 20–1). Once intracellular, Na^+ is then translocated across the basolateral surface into the lung interstitium. Water follows the osmotic change induced by the movement of Na^+ out of the air space and into the interstitium. Beginning around the same time, the Cl^- secretory process that provided the osmotic force for liquid secretion into the fetal lung lumen during development ceases to function, thus establishing a predominately Na^+-reabsorbing respiratory epithelium after birth.[44]

The importance of ion transport-linked fluid clearance after birth is demonstrated by experiments in which Na^+ reabsorption is impaired. If pathways for Na^+ reabsorption in the respiratory epithelium are either blocked pharmacologically or altered genetically in such a fashion as to inhibit their function, then water fails to leave the lung in a timely manner and respiratory distress occurs.[45–47] Studies in term and preterm infants within hours to days after birth show that patients who have respiratory difficulty have abnormalities in electrical potential across the nasal epithelium consistent with a disturbance in the expected pattern of Na^+ reabsorption across the respiratory epithelium.[48] The abnormalities in electrical potential across the nasal epithelium disappear as respiratory difficulty subsides.

The sequence of events that initiate Na^+-linked fluid reabsorption in the lung are not completely clear at this time, but circulating catecholamines and hormones are probably involved. In fetal lambs, β-adrenergic agents slow luminal liquid secretion or cause liquid reabsorption from the potential air spaces into the interstitium.[49–51] Either of these β-adrenergic-induced events can be inhibited by the instillation of agents that block Na^+ reabsorption.[50] Instillation into the lung of a cell-permeable form of cyclic adenosine monophosphate (cAMP) or increasing intracellular cAMP concentration replicates the effect of β-adrenergic agents, consistent with the hypothesis that β-adrenergic stimulation is transduced, at least in part, by way of cAMP signaling.[52,53] However, there are several observations that challenge the notion that catecholamines are the final common mediator of lung liquid removal around the time of birth. These include studies that show that lung water content decreases in the absence of changes in circulating epinephrine concentration,[21,43] studies that show that irreversible disruption of β-adrenergic signaling does not prevent the perinatal decline in lung water content,[54] and experiments in which pharmacologic blockade of β-adrenergic receptors with propranolol does not prevent absorption of luminal lung liquid.[43] Other perinatal hormones can also trigger luminal lung liquid reabsorption, adding to the confusion as to whether there is one final common pathway for luminal lung liquid reabsorption or whether this process has multiple physiologic mediators. Although there may be uncertainty about the specific hormonal influence responsible for luminal liquid reabsorption, there is more certainty that whatever the physiologic trigger, Na^+-linked fluid removal is a critical mechanism responsible for removal of luminal lung liquid around the time of birth.[41,43,46,47]

Lung Fluid Balance in the Normal Postnatal Lung

Transvascular fluid filtration in the developing lung is greater by about 50% per unit of lung mass compared with the mature lung.[39,55] This increase in fluid filtration is probably the result of hydrostatic pressure differences in the microcirculation and the surface area available for fluid exchange and not from a difference in lung vascular permeability. At sea level, pulmonary vascular pressures are greater in newborn lambs than they are in mature sheep.[39] Experiments suggests that hydrostatic pressure in the microcirculation may be as much as 50% greater in the newborn lung than in the adult lung. In addition, interstitial pressure measured by micropuncture techniques is less in the newborn lung than it is in the mature adult lung.[56] The higher microvascular pressure and lower interstitial pressure in the newborn lung increase the transmural hydrostatic pressure difference across the pulmonary microcirculation, a change that would increase fluid filtration. As well, the relative surface area available for fluid exchange is probably greater in the newborn lung compared with the adult lung. Because the newborn lung is comparatively smaller than the adult lung, the greater left atrial pressure in the newborn makes it likely that a larger fraction of the pulmonary microcirculation participates in fluid exchange compared with the adult lung. As is the case with an increase microvascular pressure, a relatively larger surface area available for fluid exchange increases transvascular fluid filtration.

Although the transmural hydrostatic pressure gradient tends to favor excess fluid filtration in the newborn lung, lung vascular permeability does not appear to be different from that of the adult.[39,57] Under conditions in which lung vascular permeability is increased and the protein-sieving characteristic of the endothelial barrier is disturbed, the ratio of low and high molecular weight proteins in the interstitium and plasma changes. There is no such difference measurable between newborn and adult sheep. Likewise, if lung vascular permeability is increased experimentally, a given increase in microvascular pressure results in a greater increase in transvascular fluid filtration across the more permeable vascular bed. In newborn and adult sheep, a similar change in lung microvascular pressure results in an equivalent change in lung lymph flow. These two observations indicate that lung vascular permeability in the pulmonary circulation is similar in the newborn and mature adult lung.

Conditions that Alter Fluid Balance in the Developing Lung

Respiratory Distress Associated with Premature Birth

Lambs that are delivered prematurely often develop respiratory distress that is similar to the acute respiratory failure characteristic of premature infants who have hyaline membrane disease.[22,58–60] Pulmonary edema is a consistent finding in this clinical situation. Inadequate pulmonary surfactant is central to the pathogenesis of hyaline membrane disease, and its absence leads to atelectasis and loss of lung volume at end-expiration.[61] However, at end inspiration lung volume is also reduced, owing in great part to the presence of protein-rich alveolar edema that fills the distal air spaces (Figure 20–3).[62] This observation helps to explain why supplemental oxygen often is required to treat hyaline membrane disease, even under conditions in which the lung is kept sufficiently inflated to prevent generalized atelectasis.

Pulmonary edema that complicates respiratory distress after premature birth is the result of excess fetal lung liquid at birth, an impaired ability to clear alveolar fluid, and excess transvascular fluid filtration. The lungs of animals born prematurely contain more extravascular lung water than do term animals because interrupting development by premature birth precludes the normal preparative processes that occur before term delivery, including a reduction in total extravascular lung water and a shift of liquid from the potential air spaces into the interstitium.[21,63]

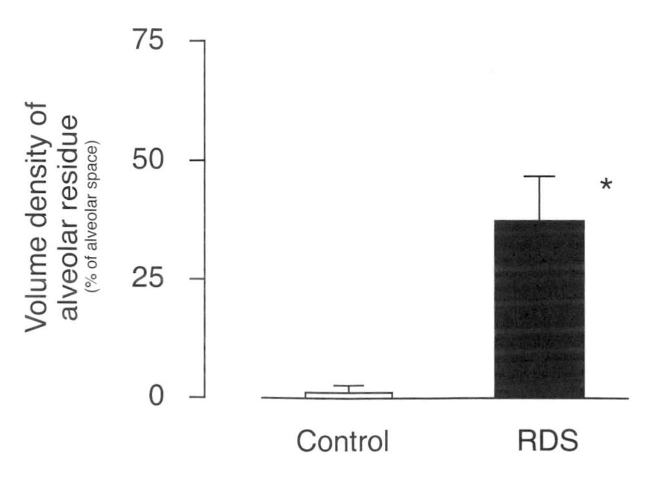

FIGURE 20–3. Quantitative assessment (mean ± SD) of protein-rich alveolar edema in premature control monkeys and in those premature monkeys with respiratory distress syndrome (RDS). *Significantly different from control ($p \leq .05$). (Adapted from Jackson JC et al.[62])

Whereas the lungs of term animals that have not experienced labor may also contain excess extravascular lung water at birth, the epithelial ion transport processes that are responsible for moving fluid from the lung lumen into the interstitium would nevertheless be expected to be mature and operative at term. However, there is reason to believe that these critical ion-transporting pathways may not participate effectively in luminal liquid translocation at the time of premature birth. For instance, the effectiveness of intravenous infusions of β-adrenergic agents on lung liquid movement is related to the gestational age of the animal.[50,51,53] In the premature lung, infusion of these agents may only slow secretion instead of triggering fluid reabsorption as they do in the near-term fetal lung. Although the maturational basis for the difference in response to β-adrenergic agents is uncertain, the normal increase in endogenous glucocorticoids near the end of gestation, in concert with thyroid hormone, may be necessary to provide the proper milieu for β-adrenergic agents to work effectively.[64]

The molecular basis of ion transport-linked luminal fluid removal is founded on the complementary functions of Na^+-transporting pathways and Na^+-K^+-ATPase activity. Sodium channel and Na^+-K^+-ATPase mRNA expression increase near the time of term birth and are accompanied by increases in Na^+-K^+-ATPase enzyme mass and activity.[65–70] Thus, if development is interrupted prematurely, the molecular mechanisms responsible for moving fluid from the potential air spaces into the interstitium may be less effective immediately after birth than would otherwise be expected at term. Indirect measures of respiratory epithelial ion transport in premature infants support this hypothesis.[48]

In addition to the burden of excess fetal lung liquid and an impaired ability of the lung to clear alveolar fluid, excessive transvascular fluid filtration also contributes to edema formation after premature birth. In premature lambs with respiratory distress, lung lymph and protein flow increase after birth by nearly three-fold compared with their values before birth, indicating that lung vascular permeability has increased.[22] Additional factors that increase transvascular fluid filtration in the premature lung include elevated pulmonary arterial pressure, decreased plasma protein oncotic pressure, and decreased lung interstitial pressure. Neutrophils disappear from the circulation immediately after birth in premature lambs with respiratory distress and subsequently accumulate in the lungs (Figure 20–4).[71–73] Their appearance in the air spaces is directly related to extravascular lung water

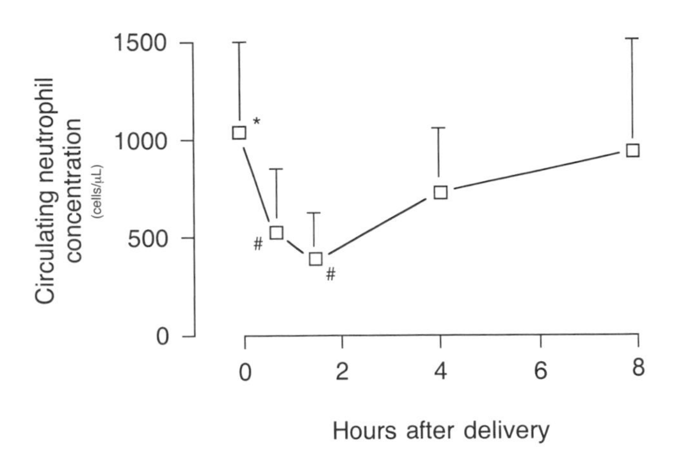

FIGURE 20–4. Circulating neutrophil concentration in chronically catheterized preterm lambs before and after birth. *Prenatal value 0 to 2 hours before birth; #significantly different from value before birth ($p < .05$). (Adapted from Carlton DP et al.[71])

accumulation and lung vascular injury, and eliminating them from the circulation before birth preserves lung vascular permeability after delivery.[71] Epidemiologic studies support a similar relation between neutrophils and respiratory distress in premature infants.[74]

In addition to the increase in lung vascular permeability, the respiratory epithelial barrier is also injured in the setting of respiratory distress after premature birth. Excess protein is recovered from the lungs of mechanically ventilated premature lambs with respiratory failure compared with control term lambs, and small solutes aerosolized into the lung of premature infants disappear more rapidly in the presence of respiratory distress than they do in patients without lung disease.[75–77]

Thus, the premature lung is disadvantaged by relatively too much fetal lung fluid at birth and an impaired ability to clear alveolar fluid. If respiratory distress complicates the postnatal course, excess transvascular fluid filtration adds to the burden of fluid already present in the lung and an increase in epithelial permeability allows protein-rich edema fluid to fill the distal air spaces.

Surfactant Therapy

The immature lung that contains an inadequate amount of surfactant is prone to edema formation. The edema formation derives primarily from the reduced interstitial pressure that accompanies a lower alveolar liquid pressure in the alveolar hypophase and from the effects of mechanical ventilation on lung vascular and respiratory epithelial permeability.[78]

If surfactant deficiency augments edema formation, does surfactant replacement reduce edema formation? Short-term studies of surfactant replacement in the premature lung show no influence of surfactant on lung water content, but studies of longer duration show that surfactant reduces extravascular lung water (Figure 20–5).[79–81] The reduction in edema is, at least in part, a result of less transvascular fluid filtration.[80] Surfactant replacement reduces the transmural hydrostatic pressure gradient by increasing interstitial pressure, without affecting pulmonary vascular pressures. Surfactant replacement also reduces transvascular fluid filtration by preserving the integrity of the vascular endothelial barrier. In the absence of surfactant, lung lymph and protein flow increase by threefold after delivery, but following surfactant replacement, lung lymph and protein flow are not significantly different from their values before birth, a response typically seen in healthy term lambs after birth.[21] Epithelial permeability is likewise preserved if surfactant is administered at the time of birth.[76] Surfactant likely preserves lung vascular and epithelial permeability because less inflation pressure is required to achieve targeted blood gas tensions.[76,82]

Hypoxia

The influence of hypoxia on lung fluid balance is generally assessed under conditions in which experimental animals breathe low concentrations of inspired oxygen, an admittedly atypical clinical situation. However, regional hypoxia, as occurs clinically with atelectasis or alveolar edema, is more difficult to replicate consistently in the laboratory and, thus, studied infrequently in experimental models. Therefore, observations from

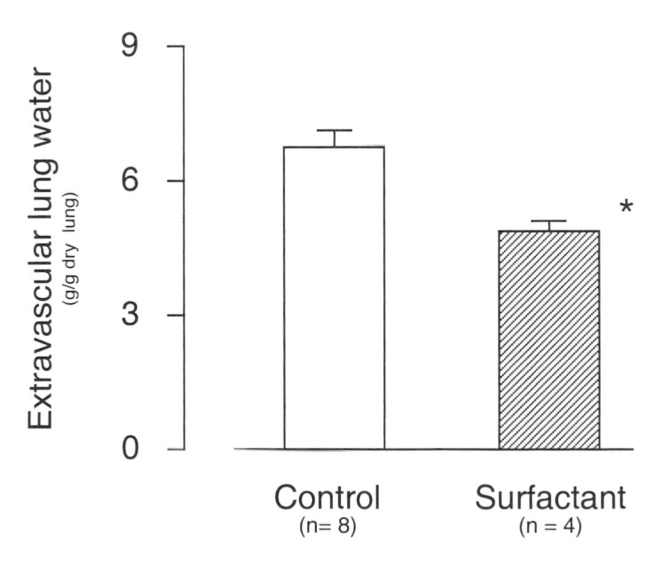

FIGURE 20–5. Pulmonary edema assessed as postmortem extravascular lung water 8 hours after birth (mean ± SD). Transvascular fluid filtration also was less in lambs that had received surfactant at the time of birth. *Significantly different from control ($p < .05$). (Adapted from Carlton DP et al.[80])

experiments performed under conditions of global hypoxia are used to provide insight into changes that would be expected to occur with regional hypoxia.

In the adult lung, hypoxia increases pulmonary arterial pressure, but it has no effect on transvascular fluid filtration.[83] In contrast, hypoxia increases both pulmonary arterial pressure and transvascular fluid filtration in the developing lung.[84,85] There are several potential mechanisms by which fluid filtration might increase in response to hypoxia. There is evidence that hypoxia causes pulmonary venular constriction, an effect that would increase hydrostatic pressure upstream in the microcirculation.[86] Other experiments suggest that redistribution of blood flow might explain the vascular changes responsible for enhanced transvascular fluid filtration.[87] Both mechanisms may be important. In hypoxia-induced transvascular fluid filtration, there is no evidence that the permeability of the lung endothelial barrier is altered, even when hypoxia is severe enough to cause asphyxia and asystole.[55,85,88,89]

Hyperoxia

Almost all patients who have respiratory failure require supplemental oxygen. Although increased concentrations of oxygen have protean effects on the developing lung, one prominent pathologic feature of hyperoxia-induced injury is the development of pulmonary edema. Extravascular lung water content is significantly greater in newborn lambs that breathe 100% oxygen for 3 to 5 days than it is in control lambs.[90] Radiolabeled albumin transport across the pulmonary vascular bed is accelerated and transvascular fluid and protein movement are increased after several days of hyperoxia, indicating that an increase in lung vascular permeability has occurred. Pulmonary vascular pressures do not increase in response to hyperoxia-induced lung injury in the newborn lung, suggesting that transmural hydrostatic pressure gradients do not contribute to edema formation in hyperoxia. Hyperoxia is associated with a decrease in the transmural protein oncotic difference, and such a change enhances transvascular fluid movement across the endothelial barrier.

The mechanism responsible for an increase in lung vascular permeability and pulmonary edema as a consequence of oxygen exposure is not clear. In some experimental models, neutrophils appear to be an important mediator of hyperoxia-induced pulmonary edema.[91,92] However, experiments in newborn lambs cast doubt on the importance of neutrophils in the pathogenesis of this condition.[93] Lambs treated with hydroxyurea to reduce circulating neutrophil concentration to less than 50 cells/μL develop severe respiratory failure within 3 to 5 days when exposed to 100% oxygen and have an increase in lung vascular permeability similar to that seen in lambs treated with hyperoxia that have a normal neutrophil concentration. Thus, at least in the developing lung, neutrophils are not critical in the pathogenesis of hyperoxia-induced lung vascular injury and edema.

Strategies that attempt to alter the unfavorable effect of oxygen on vascular permeability provide some insight into the pathogenesis of oxygen-induced injury, at least in the newborn lung. Specifically, intravenous injection of low concentrations of endotoxin delay the onset of lung vascular injury in response to hyperoxia in newborn lambs.[94] This response is not mediated by an increase in lung antioxidant content as is the case in mature adult lungs, but rather it seems to be the result of an inhibition of cytochrome P-450. In related studies, inhibition of cytochrome P-450 has been shown to delay the onset of hyperoxia-induced lung vascular injury.[95]

Infection

Infection is commonly associated with pulmonary edema and respiratory failure. Bacteremia causes an increase in lung water content and an increase in transvascular fluid movement from the pulmonary circulation.[96–99] The typical changes in lung fluid balance in this setting include an initial two- to threefold increase in pulmonary arterial pressure with little or no change in left atrial pressure, accompanied by an increase in transvascular filtration of fluid with low protein concentration. Within a few hours of infection, pulmonary arterial pressure returns to near baseline values, but transvascular fluid and protein movement remain elevated. Excessive transvascular fluid filtration that occurs hours after infection cannot be accounted for by hemodynamic alterations alone and is most consistent with an increase in lung vascular permeability. The initial pulmonary hypertensive phase of the reaction is prevented by inhibiting cyclooxygenase activity, suggesting that prostaglandin derivatives are instrumental to the increase in transvascular fluid filtration during the first hours of infection. If methylprednisolone is administered intravenously before the bacterial toxin is injected, the increase in lung vascular permeability is prevented.

Mechanical Ventilation

Although treatment of respiratory failure with mechanical ventilation is an essential element of respiratory support, mechanical ventilation can cause or aggravate injury to the lung and lead to pulmonary edema. Although air leak syndromes, such as pneumothorax or pulmonary interstitial emphysema are well-recognized examples of ventilator-associated injury, laboratory and clinical information now suggest that mechanical ventilation injures the lung in more subtle but equally serious ways.[100] Because mechanical ventilation may aggravate or cause lung injury and edema, no longer are maximizing arterial oxygenation or reducing the work of breathing sufficient goals in and of themselves in ventilator management. Currently, the goal now generally includes an attempt to minimize ventilator-associated lung injury. It is clear that at least one approach to minimizing mechanical ventilation improves outcome. In patients who have acute respiratory distress syndrome, limiting the magnitude of repetitive tidal excursions reduces mortality, and the improvement in survival is seen across all subgroups of patients.[101,102]

Experimental studies designed to elucidate those factors important in ventilator-associated injury show that the extent of tissue overdistension, not inflation pressure, is the critically injurious component of artificial ventilation.[101] Indeed, mechanical ventilation with normal tidal volume excursions, even for prolonged periods, does not injure the lungs, raising doubt that mechanical ventilation itself is noxious.[103] Studies in which peak inflation pressure is kept constant and lung volume is allowed to vary demonstrate that pulmonary edema and lung vascular injury occur only when high peak inflation pressures are accompanied by overdistension.[104–107] In a lung that has developed as expected and in which resistance and compliance are normal, application of positive pressure ventilation should have little deleterious effect. Harm occurs if otherwise normal lung units are overdistended. However, even if close attention is paid to factors important in ventilator-associated injury, judicious mechanical ventilation may be harmful, because in heterogeneous lung disease, compliance and resistance are nonuniform and local overdistension of lung units almost unavoidable.

Although overdistension, and not inflation pressure, is the critical element in the pathogenesis of ventilator-associated lung edema, in routine clinical use, an increase in inflation pressure almost always results in at least local overdistension if all other factors are kept constant. Only rarely does the clinical situation allow a distinction between "volutrauma" and "barotrauma," as can be made in the experimental setting. For this reason, under most clinical scenarios, the two terms can be used interchangeably to describe ventilator-associated lung injury. It would be unusual to increase inflation pressure without at least some portion of the lung becoming further distended, even if compliance is poor and an increase in overall lung volume cannot be detected. Conversely, inflation of the lung with more volume than necessary, even if only modest inflation pressures are necessary to do so, places the lung at greater risk of injury than the inflation pressure would otherwise indicate.

If overdistension is the trigger for pulmonary edema formation in ventilator-associated lung injury, which "volume" is most critical in determining injury? Experiments that alter end-expiratory volume, tidal volume, and total lung volume in animals point to end-inspiratory volume as the essential variable in ventilator-associated lung injury.[100] Translating this information to the clinical setting, it is less the mean airway pressure and more the peak inflation pressure that is related to injury. This may underlie the reduction in edema seen in experiments that compare extravascular lung water content between conventional mechanical ventilation and high frequency ventilation in the immature lung.[108–110] To achieve a similar degree of gas exchange, peak inflation pressures generated by a high frequency device always are less than those generated by tidal breaths by conventional ventilation. In premature infants, inspiratory capacity and total lung capacity are reduced by 50 to 75% in the setting of respiratory distress, narrowing the therapeutic index for even small tidal volume excursions.[111]

Lung vascular and respiratory epithelial cell permeability appears to be increased in most experimental models of ventilator-associated injury.[100] Epithelial injury occurs when the lung is expanded, and this phenomenon appears to be accentuated when applied to a smaller volume.[112–114] That is, the same distending pressure applied to a small lung appears to cause a greater transepithelial movement of solute than does the application of that same pressure to a larger lung.

Whether an increase in hydrostatic driving forces for transvascular fluid formation contributes to the excess lung water content in ventilator-associated lung injury is unclear. In newborn lambs, calculated transmural hydrostatic pressure difference increases only modestly with large tidal volume ventilation and would be unlikely to account for the nearly sevenfold increase in transvascular fluid movement observed in this model of ventilator-associated lung injury.[105]

The variable that contributes most to the increase in lung water content in overinflation injury is vascular permeability.[100] In newborn lambs, after several hours of large tidal volume ventilation, transvascular protein flow is increased sevenfold and the sieving characteristics of the endothelial barrier are damaged.[105] Extensive tissue damage is not responsible for this injury, as transvascular fluid and protein movement is similar to baseline within 6 hours after reducing tidal volume to normal. It is likely that both time and degree of lung expansion are important variables that determine whether fluid balance is disturbed with overinflation injury.

Most patients who are at risk from ventilator-associated lung injury have neither healthy lung architecture nor normal lung mechanics. More likely, the lung has suffered some degree of injury from the patient's primary disease process. This preexisting injury often results in heterogeneity with respect to compliance and airways resistance. Thus overinflation occurs more readily in an injured lung than in a normal lung and appears to cause more injury than would be expected if the lung was healthy.[115] Intuitively, the explanation for this finding would be that the heterogeneity in compliance causes a redistribution of gas to the most compliant areas of the lung. Indirect evidence to support this notion is found in studies that demonstrate an inverse relation between compliance and lung water accumulation in ventilator-associated injury.[115]

Whether the barrier function of the lung endothelium is altered directly or indirectly is unclear and may depend on the magnitude and duration of overexpansion. Lung edema can be induced in as short a time as 2 minutes under some experimental conditions, but in others, hours of overinflation are necessary to increase in lung vascular permeability.[100] Injury induced by moderate but sustained overexpansion is associated with leukocyte accumulation in the air space and pulmonary vasculature.[116–118] Pulmonary leukostasis may serve a central role in the initiation of overexpansion injury, or it may result in injury independent of that triggered by overdistension.

Lung Edema in Bronchopulmonary Dysplasia

Premature lambs that are mechanically ventilated for 3 to 4 weeks show histologic abnormalities in tissue sections of the lung that are similar to those seen in premature infants who die with bronchopulmonary dysplasia.[119,120] Premature lambs require no intervention other than routine neonatal intensive care to acquire these abnormalities. Extravascular lung water was significantly elevated in these animals at the end of study, but most of the excess fluid was contained in the interstitium, not in the alveolar space (Figure 20–6).[120,121] Lung lymph flow was elevated and the concentration of protein in lymph compared with that in plasma was low. These observations suggest that lung fluid filtration is increased as a result of an increase in microvascular filtration pressure and not an increase in lung vascular permeability.

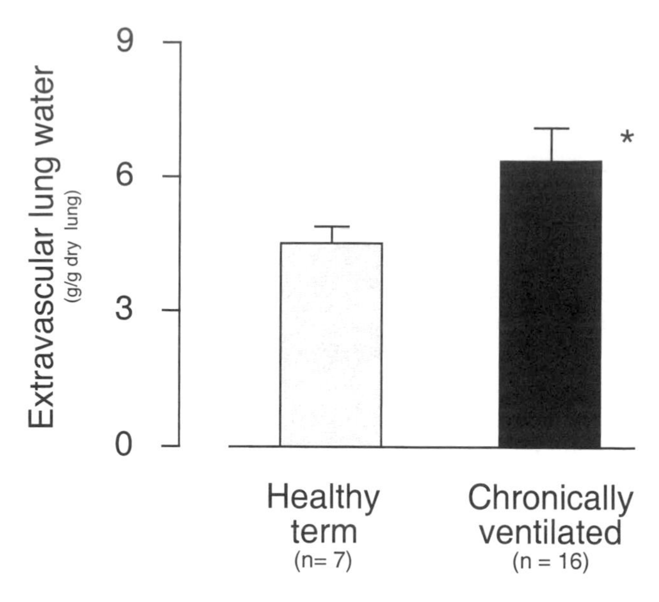

FIGURE 20–6. Postmortem extravascular lung water content (mean ± SD) in healthy term lambs at approximately 3 weeks after birth compared with preterm lambs that were mechanically ventilated for 3 weeks after birth. Term lambs weighed more than twice as much as the preterm lambs at a similar time after birth. *Significantly different from control ($p < .05$). (Adapted from Bland RD et al[120] and Cummings JJ et al.[121])

Summary

Liquid moves across the pulmonary microcirculation into the lung interstitium during fetal development just as it does in the mature postnatal lung. Fluid in the interstitium then either is carried back into the systemic circulation by way of lymphatics or moves across the respiratory epithelium into the potential air spaces. Transepithelial liquid movement into the lung lumen before birth is linked to the secretion of Cl^- ions across the respiratory epithelium into the potential air spaces. The presence of luminal liquid thus formed provides a dynamic template for lung development, and the absence of such a template prevents normal lung growth and differentiation. Around the time of birth, liquid secretion into the potential air spaces slows and ultimately ceases. Liquid then is reabsorbed from the lung lumen across the respiratory epithelium as a result of a temporary increase in respiratory epithelial permeability and the induction of Na^+-linked fluid movement. Once it has moved into the interstitium, the luminal liquid is cleared by lymphatic pathways and by reabsorption into the pulmonary circulation. A failure in postnatal adaptation that results in ineffective Na^+ reabsorption delays or prevents clearance of fetal lung liquid and results in impaired gas exchange and leads to respiratory distress. A variety of factors, including mechanical ventilation, surfactant deficiency, hypoxia or hyperoxia, and infection may influence lung fluid balance postnatally, predominately by increasing transvascular fluid filtration across the pulmonary microcirculation.

Acknowledgment

Supported in part by NIH grant HL 62491.

References

1. Teague WG, Berner ME, Bland RD. Effect of pulmonary perfusion on lung fluid filtration in young lambs. Am J Physiol 1988;255:H1336–41.
2. Ishikawa S, Tsukada H, Bhattacharya J. Soluble complex of complement increases hydraulic conductivity in single microvessels of rat lung. J Clin Invest 1993;91:103–9.
3. Gee MH, Havill AM. The relationship between pulmonary perivascular cuff fluid and lung lymph in dogs with edema. Microvasc Res 1980;19:209–16.
4. Glucksberg MR, Bhattacharya J. Effect of dehydration on interstitial pressures in the isolated dog lung. J Appl Physiol 1989;67:839–45.
5. Conhaim RL, Lai-Fook SJ, Eaton A. Sequence of interstitial liquid accumulation in liquid-inflated sheep lung lobes. J Appl Physiol 1989;66:2659–66.

6. Staub NC, Nagano H, Pearce ML. Pulmonary edema in dogs, especially the sequence of fluid accumulation in lungs. J Appl Physiol 1967;22:227–40.
7. Zumsteg TA, Havill AM, Gee MH. Relationships among lung extravascular fluid compartments with alveolar flooding. J Appl Physiol 1982;53:267–71.
8. Bachofen H, Schurch S, Weibel ER. Experimental hydrostatic pulmonary edema in rabbit lungs. Barrier lesions. Am Rev Respir Dis 1993;147:997–1004.
9. Bachofen H, Schurch S, Michel RP, Weibel ER. Experimental hydrostatic pulmonary edema in rabbit lungs. Morphology. Am Rev Respir Dis 1993;147:989–96.
10. Matthay MA, Wiener-Kronish JP. Intact epithelial barrier function is critical for the resolution of alveolar edema in humans. Am Rev Respir Dis 1990;142:1250–7.
11. Matthay MA, Landolt CC, Staub NC. Differential liquid and protein clearance from the alveoli of anesthetized sheep. J Appl Physiol 1982;53:96–104.
12. Matthay MA, Berthiaume Y, Staub NC. Long-term clearance of liquid and protein from the lungs of unanesthetized sheep. J Appl Physiol 1985;59:928–34.
13. Goodman BE, Fleischer RS, Crandall ED. Evidence for active Na^+ transport by cultured monolayers of pulmonary alveolar epithelial cells. Am J Physiol 1983;245:C78–83.
14. Schneeberger EE, McCarthy KM. Cytochemical localization of Na^+-K^+-ATPase in rat type II pneumocytes. J Appl Physiol 1986;60:1584–9.
15. Adams FH, Fujiwara T, Rowshan G. The nature and origin of the fluid in the fetal lamb lung. J Pediatr 1963;63: 881–8.
16. Adamson TM, Boyd RDH, Platt HS, Strang LB. Composition of alveolar liquid in the foetal lamb. J Physiol 1969;204:159–68.
17. Mescher EJ, Platzker ACG, Ballard PL, et al. Ontogeny of tracheal fluid, pulmonary surfactant, and plasma corticoids in the fetal lamb. J Appl Physiol 1975;39:1017–21.
18. Humphreys PW, Normand ICS, Reynolds EOR, Strang LB. Pulmonary lymph flow and the uptake of liquid from the lungs of the lamb at the start of breathing. J Physiol 1967;193:1–29.
19. Normand ICS, Reynolds EOR, Strang LB. Passage of macromolecules between alveolar and interstitial spaces in foetal and newly ventilated lungs of the lamb. J Physiol 1970;210:151–64.
20. Normand ICS, Olver RE, Reynolds EOR, Strang LB. Permeability of lung capillaries and alveoli to non-electrolytes in the foetal lamb. J Physiol 1971;219:303–30.
21. Bland RD, Hansen TN, Haberkern CM, et al. Lung fluid balance in lambs before and after birth. J Appl Physiol 1982;53:992–1004.
22. Bland RD, Carlton DP, Scheerer RG, et al. Lung fluid balance in lambs before and after premature birth. J Clin Invest 1989;84:568–76.
23. Carlton DP, Cummings JJ, Poulain FR, Bland RD. Increased pulmonary vascular filtration pressure does not alter lung liquid secretion in fetal sheep. J Appl Physiol 1992; 72:650–5.
24. McCray PB Jr, Bettencourt JD, Bastacky J. Developing bronchopulmonary epithelium of the human fetus secretes fluid. Am J Physiol 1992;262:L270–9.
25. Adamson TM, Brodecky V, Lambert TF, et al. Lung liquid production and composition in the "in utero" foetal lamb. Aust J Exp Biol Med Sci 1975;53:65–75.
26. Kitterman JA, Ballard PL, Clements JA, et al. Tracheal fluid in fetal lambs: spontaneous decrease prior to birth. J Appl Physiol 1979;47:985–9.
27. Krochmal EM, Ballard ST, Yankaskas JR, et al. Volume and ion transport by fetal rat alveolar and tracheal epithelia in submersion culture. Am J Physiol 1989;256:F397–407.
28. Olver RE, Strang LB. Ion fluxes across the pulmonary epithelium and the secretion of lung liquid in the foetal lamb. J Physiol 1974;241:327–57.
29. Shermeta DW, Oesch I. Characteristics of fetal lung fluid production. J Pediatr Surg 1981;16:943–6.
30. Wallen LD, Kulisz E, Maloney JE. Main pulmonary artery ligation reduces lung fluid production in fetal sheep. J Dev Physiol 1991;16:173–9.
31. Alcorn D, Adamson TM, Lambert TF, et al. Morphological effects of chronic tracheal ligation and drainage in the fetal lamb lung. J Anat 1977;123:649–60.
32. Moessinger AC, Harding R, Adamson TM, et al. Role of lung fluid volume in growth and maturation of the fetal sheep lung. J Clin Invest 1990;86:1270–7.
33. Carlton DP, Cummings JJ, Chapman DL, et al. Ion transport regulation of lung liquid secretion in foetal lambs. J Dev Physiol 1992;17:99–107.
34. Cassin S, Gause G, Perks AM. The effects of bumetanide and furosemide on lung liquid secretion in fetal sheep. Proc Soc Exp Biol Med 1986;181:427–31.
35. Thom J, Perks AM. The effects of furosemide and bumetanide on lung liquid production by in vitro lungs from fetal guinea pigs. Can J Physiol Pharmacol 1990;68: 1131–5.
36. Welsh MJ. Electrolyte transport by airway epithelia. Physiol Rev 1987;67:1143–84.
37. Carlton DP, Cummings DP, Scheerer R, Bland RD. Lung vascular protein permeability in preterm fetal and mature newborn sheep. J Appl Physiol 1994;77:782–8.
38. Bland RD, Bressack MA, McMillan DD. Labor decreases the lung water content of newborn rabbits. Am J Obstet Gynecol 1979;135:364–7.
39. Bland RD, McMillan DD. Lung fluid dynamics in awake newborn lambs. J Clin Invest 1977;60:1107–15.
40. Dickson KA, Maloney JE, Berger PJ. Decline in lung liquid volume before labor in fetal lambs. J Appl Physiol 1986;61:2266–72.
41. Brown MJ, Olver RE, Ramsden CA, et al. Effects of adrenaline and of spontaneous labour on the secretion and absorption of lung liquid in the fetal lamb. J Physiol 1983;344:137–52.
42. Egan EA, Olver RE, Strang LB. Changes in non-electrolyte permeability of alveoli and the absorption of lung liquid at the start of breathing in the lamb. J Physiol 1975;244: 161–79.
43. Chapman DL, Carlton DP, Nielson DW, et al. Changes in lung liquid during spontaneous labor in fetal sheep. J Appl Physiol 1994;76:523–30.
44. Nielson DW. Changes in the pulmonary alveolar subphase at birth in term and premature lambs. Pediatr Res 1988; 23:418–22.

45. Hummler E, Barker P, Gatzy J, et al. Early death due to defective neonatal lung liquid clearance in alpha-ENaC-deficient mice. Nat Genet 1996;12:325–8.
46. O'Brodovich H, Hannam V, Spear M, Mullen JBM. Amiloride impairs lung liquid clearance in newborn guinea pigs. J Appl Physiol 1990;68:1758–62.
47. O'Brodovich H, Hannam V, Rafii B. Sodium channel but neither Na^+-H^+ nor Na-glucose symport inhibitors slow neonatal lung water clearance. Am J Respir Cell Mol Biol 1991;5:377–84.
48. Barker PM, Gowen CW, Lawson EE, Knowles MR. Decreased sodium ion absorption across nasal epithelium of very premature infants with respiratory distress syndrome. J Pediatr 1997;130:373–7.
49. Lawson EE, Brown ER, Torday JS, et al. The effect of epinephrine on tracheal fluid flow and surfactant efflux in fetal sheep. Am Rev Respir Dis 1978;118:1023–6.
50. Olver RE, Ramsden CA, Strang LB, Walters DV. The role of amiloride-blockable sodium transport in adrenaline-induced lung liquid reabsorption in the fetal lamb. J Physiol 1986;376:321–40.
51. Walters DV, Olver RE. The role of catecholamines in lung liquid absorption at birth. Pediatr Res 1978;12:239–42.
52. Chapman DL, Carlton DP, Cummings JJ, et al. Intrapulmonary terbutaline and aminophylline decrease lung liquid in fetal lambs. Pediatr Res 1991;29:357–61.
53. Walters DV, Ramsden CA, Olver RE. Dibutyryl cyclic AMP induces a gestation-dependent absorption of fetal lung liquid. J Appl Physiol 1990;68:2054–9.
54. McDonald JV, Gonzales LW, Ballard PL, et al. Lung beta-adrenergic blockade affects perinatal surfactant release but not lung water. J Appl Physiol 1986;60:1727–33.
55. Bland RD, Hanson TA, Hazinski TA, et al. Studies of lung fluid balance in newborn lambs. Ann N Y Acad Sci 1982;384:126–45.
56. Fike CD, Lai-Fook SJ, Bland RD. Alveolar liquid pressures in newborn and adult rabbit lungs. J Appl Physiol 1988; 64:1629–35.
57. Brigham KL, Sundell H, Harris TR, et al. Lung water and vascular permeability in sheep: newborns compared with adults. Circ Res 1978;42:851–5.
58. Normand ICS, Reynolds EOR, Strang LB, Wigglesworth JS. Flow and protein concentration of lymph from lungs of lambs developing hyaline membrane disease. Arch Dis Child 1968;43:334–9.
59. Reynolds EOR, Jacobson HN, Motoyama EK, et al. The effect of immaturity and prenatal asphyxia on the lungs and pulmonary function of newborn lambs: the experimental production of respiratory distress. Pediatrics 1965;35:382–92.
60. Stahlman M, LeQuire VS, Young WC, et al. Pathophysiology of respiratory distress in newborn lambs. Am J Dis Child 1964;108:375–93.
61. Avery ME, Mead J. Surface properties in relation to atelectasis and hyaline membrane disease. Am J Dis Child 1959;97:517–23.
62. Jackson JC, Mackenzie AP, Chi EY, et al. Mechanisms for reduced total lung capacity at birth and during hyaline membrane disease in premature newborn monkeys. Am Rev Respir Dis 1990;142:413–9.
63. Bland RD. Dynamics of pulmonary water before and after birth. Acta Paediatr Scand Suppl 1983;305:12–20.
64. Barker PM, Walters DV, Markiewicz M, Strang LB. Development of the lung liquid reabsorptive mechanism in fetal sheep: synergism of triiodothyronine and hydrocortisone. J Physiol 1991;433:435–49.
65. Bland RD, Boyd CAR. Cation transport in lung epithelial cells derived from fetal, newborn and adult rabbits. Influence of birth, labor and postnatal development. J Appl Physiol 1986;62:507–15.
66. Chapman DL, Widdicombe JH, Bland RD. Developmental differences in rabbit lung epithelial cell Na^+-K^+-ATPase. Am J Physiol 1990;259:L481–7.
67. Ingbar DH, Weeks CB, Gilmore-Hebert M, et al. Developmental regulation of Na, K-ATPase in rat lung. Am J Physiol 1996;270:L619–29.
68. O'Brodovich H, Staub O, Rossier BC, et al. Ontogeny of alpha 1- and beta 1-isoforms of Na^+-K^+-ATPase in fetal distal rat lung epithelium. Am J Physiol 1993;264: C1137–43.
69. O'Brodovich H, Canessa C, Ueda J, et al. Expression of the epithelial Na^+ channel in the developing rat lung. Am J Physiol 1993;265:C491–6.
70. Talbot CL, Bosworth DG, Briley EL, et al. Quantitation and localization of ENaC subunit expression in fetal, newborn, and adult mouse lung. Am J Respir Cell Mol Biol 1999;20:398–406.
71. Carlton DP, Albertine KH, Cho SC, et al. Role of neutrophils in lung vascular injury and edema after premature birth in lambs. J Appl Physiol 1997;83:1307–17.
72. Jackson JC, Chi EY, Wilson CB, et al. Sequence of inflammatory cell migration into lung during recovery from hyaline membrane disease in premature newborn monkeys. Am Rev Respir Dis 1987;135:937–40.
73. Kinsella JP, Parker TA, Galan H, et al. Effects of inhaled nitric oxide on pulmonary edema and lung neutrophil accumulation in severe experimental hyaline membrane disease. Pediatr Res 1997;41:457–63.
74. Ferreira PJ, Bunch TJ, Albertine KH, Carlton DP. Circulating neutrophil concentration and respiratory distress in premature infants. J Pediatr 2000;136:466–72.
75. Jefferies AL, Coates G, O'Brodovich H. Pulmonary epithelial permeability in hyaline-membrane disease. N Engl J Med 1984;311:1075–80.
76. Jobe A, Ikegami M, Jacobs H, et al. Permeability of pre mature lamb lungs to protein and the effect of surfactant on that permeability. J Appl Physiol 1983;55:169–76.
77. Jobe A, Jacobs H, Ikegami M, Berry D. Lung protein leaks in ventilated lambs: effect of gestational age. J Appl Physiol 1985;58:1246–51.
78. Carlton DP, Bland RD. Surfactant and lung fluid balance. In: Robertson B, Taeusch HW, eds. Surfactant therapy for lung disease. New York: Marcel Dekker, Inc., 1995: 33–46.
79. Adams FH, Towers B, Osher AB, etal. Effects of tracheal instillation of natural surfactant in premature lambs. I. Clinical autopsy findings. Pediatr Res 1978;12:841–8.
80. Carlton DP, Cho SC, Davis P, et al. Surfactant treatment at birth reduces lung vascular injury and edema in preterm lambs. Pediatr Res 1995;37:265–70.

81. Notter RH, Egan EA, Kwong MS, et al. Lung surfactant replacement in premature lambs with extracted lipids from bovine lung lavage: effects of dose, dispersion technique, and gestational age. Pediatr Res 1985; 19:569–77.
82. Carlton DP, Cho S-C, Davis P, Bland RD. Inflation pressure and lung vascular injury in preterm lambs. Chest 1994; 105:115S–6S.
83. Bland RD, Demling RH, Selinger SL, Staub NC. Effects of alveolar hypoxia on lung fluid and protein transport in unanesthetized sheep. Circ Res 1977;40:269–74.
84. Bland RD, Bressack MA, Haberkern CM, Hansen TN. Lung fluid balance in hypoxic, awake newborn lambs and mature sheep. Biol Neonate 1980;38:221–8.
85. Bressack MA, Bland RD. Alveolar hypoxia increases lung fluid filtration in unanesthetized newborn lambs. Circ Res 1980;46:111–6.
86. Raj JU, Chen P. Micropuncture measurements of microvascular pressures in isolated lamb lungs during hypoxia. Circ Res 1986;59:398–404.
87. Hansen TN, LeBlanc AL, Gest AL. Hypoxia and angiotensin II infusion redistribute lung blood flow in lambs. J Appl Physiol 1985;58:812–8.
88. Hansen TN, Hazinski TA, Bland RD. Effects of asphyxia on lung fluid balance in baby lambs. J Clin Invest 1984; 74:370–6.
89. Hansen TN, Hazinski TA, Bland RD. Effects of hypoxia on transvascular fluid filtration in newborn lambs. Pediatr Res 1984;18:434–40.
90. Bressack MA, McMillan DD, Bland RD. Pulmonary oxygen toxicity: increased microvascular permeability to protein in unanesthetized lambs. Lymphology 1979;12:133–9.
91. Fox RB, Hoidal JR, Brown DM, Repine JE. Pulmonary inflammation due to oxygen toxicity: involvement of chemotactic factors and polymorphonuclear leukocytes. Am Rev Respir Dis 1981;123:521–3.
92. Shasby DM, Fox RB, Harada RN, Repine JE. Reduction of the edema of acute hyperoxic lung injury by granulocyte depletion. J Appl Physiol 1982;52:1237–44.
93. Raj JU, Hazinski TA, Bland RD. Oxygen-induced lung microvascular injury in neutropenic rabbits and lambs. J Appl Physiol 1985;58:921–7.
94. Hazinski TA, Kennedy KA, France ML, Hansen TM. Pulmonary O_2 toxicity in lambs: physiological and biochemical effects of endotoxin infusion. J Appl Physiol 1988;65:1579–85.
95. Hazinski TA, France ML, Kennedy KA. Cimetidine reduces hyperoxic lung injury in lambs. J Appl Physiol 1989; 67:1586–92.
96. Rojas J, Green RS, Hellerqvist CG, et al. Studies on group B β-hemolytic *Streptococcus*. II. Effects on pulmonary hemodynamics and vascular permeability in unanesthetized sheep. Pediatr Res 1981;15:899–904.
97. Rojas J, Larsson LE, Ogletree ML, et al. Effects of cyclooxygenase inhibition on the response to group B streptococcal toxin in sheep. Pediatr Res 1983;17:107–10.
98. Rojas J, Larsson LE, Hellerqvist CG, et al. Pulmonary hemodynamic and ultrastructural changes associated with group B streptococcal toxemia in adult sheep and newborn lambs. Pediatr Res 1983;17:1002–8.
99. Rojas J, Palme C, Ogletree ML, et al. Effects of methylprednisolone on the response to group B streptococcal toxin in sheep. Pediatr Res 1984;18:1141–4.
100. Dreyfuss D, Saumon G. Ventilator-induced lung injury. Lessons from experimental studies. Am J Respir Crit Care Med 1998;157:294–323.
101. Eisner MD, Thompson T, Hudson LD, et al. Efficacy of low tidal volume ventilation in patients with different clinical risk factors for acute lung injury and the acute respiratory distress syndrome. Am J Respir Crit Care Med 2001;164:231–6.
102. Group TARDS. Ventilation with lower tidal volumes as compared with traditional tidal volumes for acute lung injury and the acute respiratory distress syndrome. N Engl J Med 2000;342:1301–8.
103. Nash G, Bowen JA, Langlinais PC. "Respirator lung": a misnomer. Arch Pathol 1971;21:234–40.
104. Adkins WK, Hernandez LA, Coker PJ, et al. Age affects susceptibility to pulmonary barotrauma in rabbits. Crit Care Med 1991;19:390–3.
105. Carlton DP, Cummings JJ, Scheerer RG, et al. Lung overexpansion increases pulmonary microvascular protein permeability in young lambs. J Appl Physiol 1990;69: 577–83.
106. Dreyfuss D, Soler P, Basset G, Saumon G. High inflation pressure pulmonary edema. Respective effects of high airway pressure, high tidal volume, and positive end-expiratory pressure. Am Rev Respir Dis 1988;137: 1159–64.
107. Hernandez LA, Peevy KJ, Moise AA, Parker JC. Chest wall restriction limits high airway pressure-induced lung injury in young rabbits. J Appl Physiol 1989;66:2364–8.
108. Jackson JC, Truog WE, Standaert TA, et al. Reduction in lung injury after combined surfactant and high-frequency ventilation. Am J Respir Crit Care Med 1994;150:534–9.
109. Jackson JC, Truog WE, Standaert TA, et al. Effect of high-frequency ventilation on the development of alveolar edema in premature monkeys at risk for hyaline membrane disease. Am Rev Respir Dis 1991;143:865–71.
110. deLemos RA, Coalson JJ, Meredith KS, et al. A comparison of ventilation strategies for the use of high-frequency oscillatory ventilation in the treatment of hyaline membrane disease. Acta Anaesthesiol Scand Suppl 1989;90:102–7.
111. Vilstrup CT, Bjorklund LJ, Werner O, Larsson A. Lung volumes and pressure-volume relations of the respiratory system in small ventilated neonates with severe respiratory distress syndrome. Pediatr Res 1996;39:127–33.
112. Egan EA, Nelson RM, Olver RE. Lung inflation and alveolar permeability to non-electrolytes in the adult sheep in vivo. J Physiol 1976;260:409–24.
113. Egan EA. Response of alveolar epithelial solute permeability to changes in lung inflation. J Appl Physiol 1980; 49:1032–6.
114. Egan EA. Lung inflation, lung solute permeability, and alveolar edema. J Appl Physiol 1982;53:121–5.
115. Dreyfuss D, Soler P, Saumon G. Mechanical ventilation-induced pulmonary edema. Am J Respir Crit Care Med 1995;151:1568–75.

116. Sugiura M, McCulloch PR, Wren S, et al. Ventilator pattern influences neutrophil influx and activation in atelectasis-prone rabbit lung. J Appl Physiol 1994;77:1355–65.
117. Tsuno K, Miura K, Takeya M, Kolobow T, Morioka T. Histopathologic pulmonary changes from mechanical ventilation at high peak airway pressures. Am Rev Respir Dis 1991;143:1115–20.
118. Woo SW, Hedley-Whyte J. Macrophage accumulation and pulmonary edema due to thoracotomy and lung overinflation. J Appl Physiol 1972;33:14–21.
119. Albertine KH, Kim BI, Kullama LK, et al. Chronic lung injury in preterm lambs. Disordered respiratory tract development. Am J Respir Crit Care Med 1999;159:945–58.
120. Bland RD, Albertine KH, Carlton DP, et al. Chronic lung injury in preterm lambs: abnormalities of the pulmonary circulation and lung fluid balance. Pediat Res 2000;48:64–74.
121. Cummings JJ, Carlton DP, Poulain FR, et al. Hyperproteinemia slows lung liquid clearance in young lambs. J Appl Physiol 1993;74:153–60.

CHAPTER 21

Ion Flux and Homeostasis in the Lung

Marie E. Egan, MD

This chapter reviews ion transport and homeostasis of the lung. It is limited to epithelial ion transport, which is responsible for the composition and volume of airway surface fluid. The unique structure of the lung that allows for vectorial ion movement is examined and regional differences are reviewed; the pathways involved in the vectorial movement are described and the agents and conditions that modify and regulate ion transport are discussed. Last, the transition from the fetal fluid-secreting lung to the adult fluid-absorbing lung is reviewed. Transepithelial ion transport plays important roles in many of the primary physiologic functions of the lung including the maintenance of relatively dry alveolar spaces, normal mucociliary clearance, and normal airway defenses.[1-5] Therefore, a basic understanding of these processes is essential for a complete understanding of lung physiology and pathology.

Although the last decade has been filled with numerous discoveries that have extended our understanding of transepithelial ion transport, there are still many areas that need further investigation to fill the gaps in our knowledge. Much of the data presented in this chapter have been obtained from laboratory studies performed on animals and/or cells derived from human airways. The scientists who carried out these investigations employed sophisticated electrophysiologic laboratory techniques, such as whole-cell voltage clamp and single-channel patch clamp techniques, in vivo epithelial potential difference assays, ion flux studies, ion selective microelectrode measurements, ion specific dye assays, short-circuit current studies, as well as whole animal studies to obtain these insights.

Structure of the Lung

There are numerous cell types found in airway epithelia including types 1 and 2 pneumocytes, ciliated cells, Clara cells, secretory cells, basal cells, and goblet cells.[1,3-5] Each cell type has a unique function. The predominance of certain cell types varies along the bronchial tree. Ultimately, these differences serve the regions well and allow for a specialized microenvironment.

The proximal airway is characterized by a pseudostratified epithelium that is populated with submucosal glands (Figure 21–1).[1,3-5] In this region the epithelial layer comprises predominantly ciliated cells. The cilia move in an organized wavelike pattern and are instrumental for mucociliary clearance.[5] The cilia are surrounded by the periciliary fluid layer, a liquid layer, that allows for free

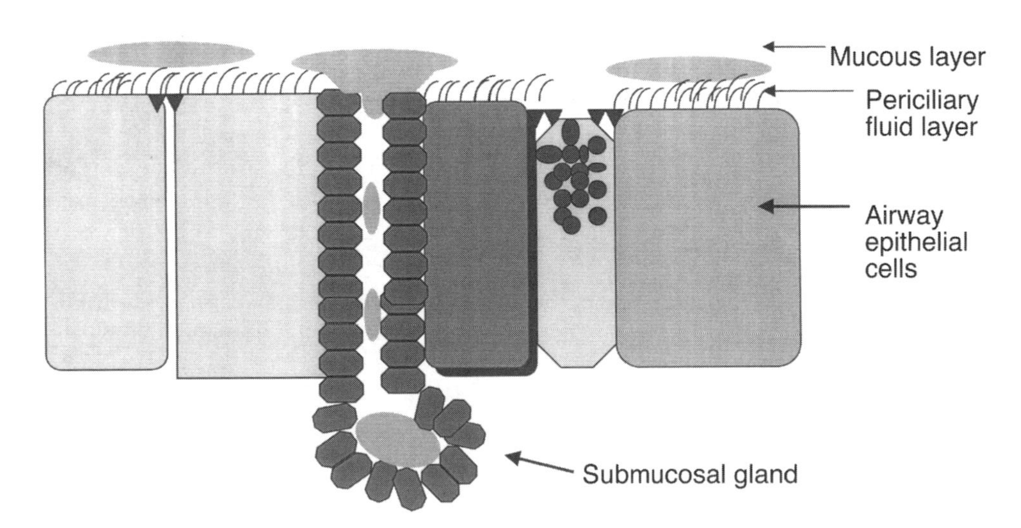

FIGURE 21–1. Schematic of proximal airway epithelia. The epithelial layer is populated with ciliated and nonciliated cells (basal and goblet cells) and submucosal glands. The periciliary fluid layer (sol) is produced by the epithelial cells and allows for normal ciliary movement and effective mucociliary clearance. The mucous layer (gel) is produced by the submucosal glands.

movement of the projections. This layer often is referred to as the "sol" portion of the airway surface fluid (ASF).[1,3–5] The second portion of the ASF is the mucous or gel layer, which is produced predominantly by the submucosal glands.[1,3–5] This gel layer is essential for capturing particles that reach the airway (see Figure 21–1). The particles are then removed from the airway via the mucociliary "escalator."[5] Direct measurements with ion selective microelectrodes, and short-circuit studies, have demonstrated that the ciliated cells actively transport ions, suggesting that they contribute to the ASF that is essential for ciliary movement.[4–6] The depth of this layer depends on numerous factors including the length of the cilia. Ideally, the periciliary fluid layer mirrors the length of the cilia. It has been postulated that alterations in this layer could lead to a mismatch of fluid and cilia and an uncoupling of cilia from the mucous "gel" layer, leading to abnormal mucociliary clearance.[1,2,4–6] The submucosal glands of the proximal airways comprise two cell types: mucous cells and serous cells. The serous cells reside in the distal portion of the gland, while the mucous cells lie in the proximal region. It is believed that the material secreted from the serous cells flushes the mucin from the more proximal portion of the gland. The secretions from the serous cells include substances such as lactoferrin and lysozmye, which are thought to contribute to the innate defense mechanisms of the lung.[1,4]

The more distal airways are populated with both ciliated cells and unciliated epithelial cells, known as Clara cells.[1,4] Clara cells appear to have a number of functions including immunomodulation and secretion. Most of the functions of Clara cells have been determined from animal studies.[7]

The alveolar region provides an extensive surface area (70 m^2) for gas exchange,[8] which is its major function. For the lung to accomplish adequate gas exchange, the alveolar space must not be filled with fluid. To maintain dryness in the air spaces, fluid must be transported into the interstitium and then into the microvasculature, where it is reabsorbed or transported to the lymphatics.[1] There are a number of transporters and channels that contribute to the fluid and ion transport of the region; however, many in the human lung have not been identified.

Epithelial Ion Transport

A general schema of airway epithelium shows an array of cells joined by tight junctions making a barrier that is somewhat impermeable to water (see Figure 21–1). Within the epithelial monolayer, each cell contains a number of transporters and ion channels that are localized to either the apical or basolateral membrane, allowing for vectorial ion movement (Figure 21–2).[1–5] Because there is localization of certain transporters and/or channels to specific membranes, vectorial movement of ions across the epithelial layer can occur.[1–5] Sodium (NA^+) and chloride (Cl^-) are the predominant ions involved in the transepithelial ion flux.[1–4]

Many different ion channels populate the apical membranes of airway epithelial cells: Cl^- channels such as ClC family members, the cystic fibrosis transmembrane conductance regulator (CFTR), and calcium-activated chloride channels, as well as epithelial sodium channels (ENaCs).[1–4,9–12] There is evidence that other nonspecific cation channels also are present on the apical surface.[13,14] The apical membrane also may contain potassium channels.[10] The basolateral membrane is populated by a number of potassium (K^+), Cl^-, and water channels.[15,16] In addition to ion channels, there are a number of energy-dependent transporters and exchangers in the respiratory epithelial layer, including the bicarbonate-chloride exchanger, a sodium-hydrogen exchanger, sodium-potassium-adenosinetriphosphatase (ATPase pump), and the Na^+-K^+-Cl^- cotransporter.[17–19]

Unlike the renal epithelial layer, the respiratory epithelial layer is not a classically "tight epithelia." Tight epithelial layers are essentially impermeable to water; they allow for the transport of ions through transcellular pathways, but there is little movement of ions, water, or solutes through paracellular pathways.[1–4,20] Because the respiratory epithelial layer is not as tight, there is some space that allows for paracellular movement of water and some passive movement of ions.[1–4,20] This space allows for the coupling of sodium and chloride across the epithelia and electrochemically neutral movement of ions and fluid (see Figure 21–2). It is clear that the net ion flux is tied intimately to fluid movement; therefore, whatever forces govern ion homeostasis also have profound effects on fluid movement and vice versa.[21]

Chloride Movement

Chloride secretion is a multistep active process (see Figure 21–2*A*). Initially, Cl^- enters the cell from the basolateral surface via the Na^+-K^+-Cl^- cotransporter. Because the cotransporter moves both sodium and potassium with chloride, the process is electroneutral, allowing the movement of Cl^- into the cell against its electrochemical gradient. The driving force for this reaction is the Na^+ movement. Sodium moves into the cell down its electrical and chemical gradient. Once in the cell, Cl^- can be secreted from the apical membrane of the cell through Cl^- channels.[4] There are several types of Cl^- channels present in the membrane that can be activated by a number of secretagogues via second- and third-messenger pathways. Once the channels are activated and open, the movement of Cl^- from the cell into the lumen of the airway is a passive process down chloride's electrochemical gradient. For this process to continue, Na^+ needs to be transported back out of the cell. This is accomplished by the Na^+-K^+-ATPase pump located on the basolateral

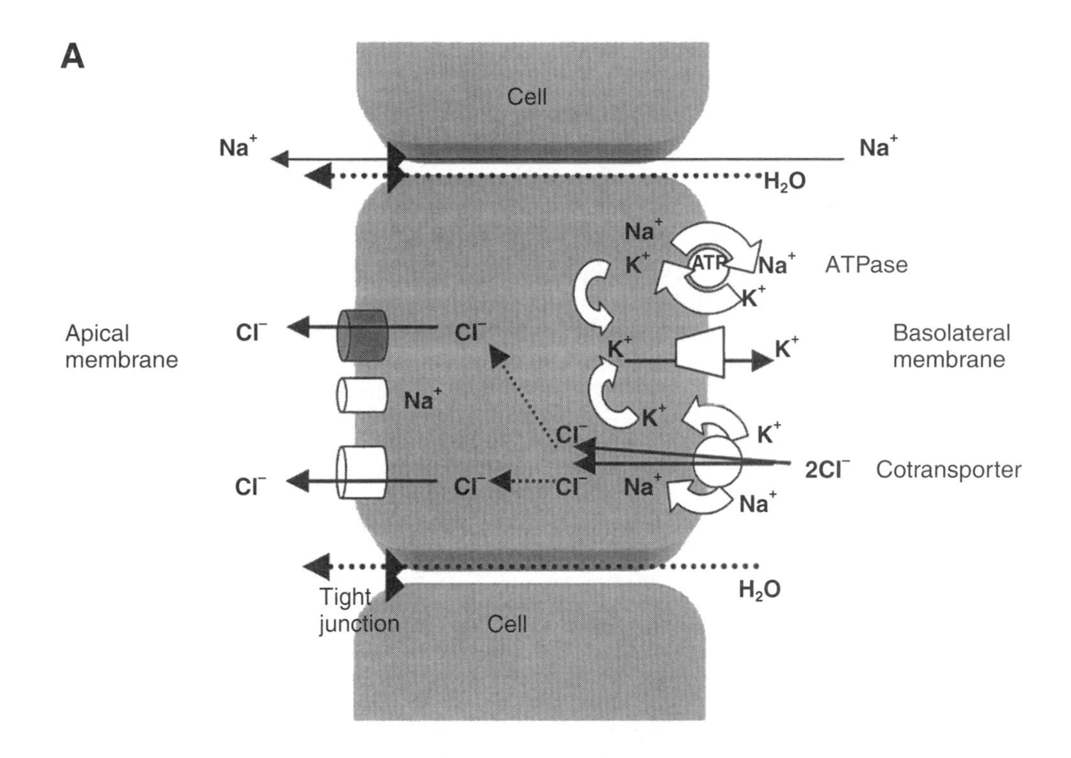

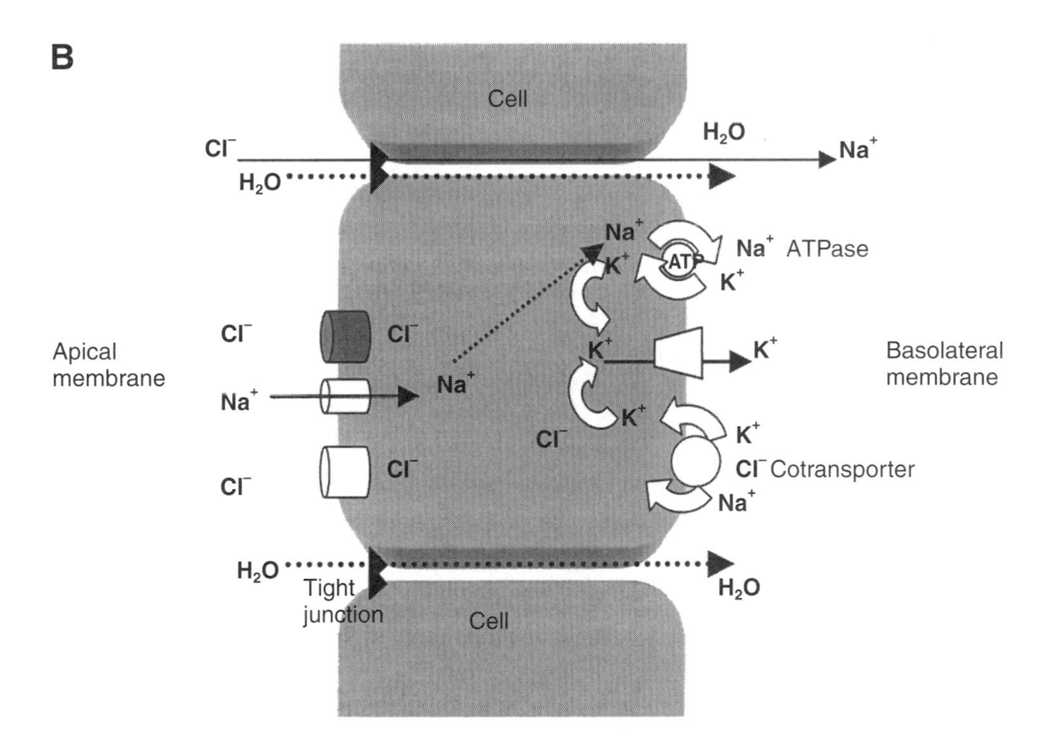

FIGURE 21–2. A model depicting transepithelial ion transport in the airway. *A*, The secretory model. Chloride enters the cell from the basolateral surface via the Na^+-K^+-$2Cl^-$ cotransporter. Then, chloride can be secreted from the apical membrane of the cell through chloride channels. For this process to continue, sodium needs to be transported back out of the cell via the Na^+-K^+-adenosinetriphosphatase (ATPase) pump located on the basolateral membrane. In addition, potassium channels allow potassium to move out of the cell. *B*, The absorptive model. Sodium enters cells from the apical membrane through amiloride-sensitive sodium channels such as epithelial sodium channel (ENaC). After entering the cell, sodium moves into cells down a favorable electrochemical gradient. At the basolateral membrane sodium exits the cell against its chemical and electrical gradient. This requires the activity of the Na^+-K^+- ATPase pump, whose activity generates the favorable gradient that allows Na^+ to enter the cell at the apical membrane.

membrane. This transporter exchanges Na^+ for K^+, thus maintaining a low intracellular NA^+ concentration and a negative intracellular voltage.[3,4,20] The basolateral membrane also contains K^+ channels that allow for the movement of K^+ out of the cell.[4,16,20] The movement of K^+ is particularly important in maintaining the resting potential of the cell membrane and preserving the negative intracellular potential. Maintenance of a negative intracellular potential provides the driving force for the movement of chloride out of the cell via the apical channels, and fluid secretion.[1,4,16,20]

Several Cl^- channels have been identified in respiratory epithelium.[1,2,22–26] The most intensely investigated Cl^- channel is the CFTR. Collins, Riordan, and Tsui[26–28] identified the gene that encodes for this protein in 1989. Mutations in this gene are the molecular basis for cystic fibrosis.[26–29] A thorough discussion of this disease is presented in Chapter 22. The CFTR is a member of the ATP-binding cassette transporter superfamily. All of the members of this superfamily require ATP for activation. They have a common motif referred to as a nucleotide-binding fold—the region of the protein where ATP is believed to act. The CFTR functions as a Cl^- channel.[29–31] Extensive patch clamp studies have demonstrated that the single-channel conductance of the channel is 8 to 10 pS. Conductance can be stimulated by cyclic adenosine monophosphate (cAMP)-dependent protein kinase A and regulated by protein kinase C.[29,31] A variety of phosphatases, enzymes that dephosphorylate proteins, can deactivate the CFTR protein, thus decreasing Cl^- channel activity[29,31] The CFTR is located on the apical membrane of a variety of airway cell types, including the superficial epithelial cell and certain ductal cells of submucosal glands.[29] In addition to its Cl^- channel activity, the CFTR can regulate other ion channels such as the ENaC and the outwardly rectifying Cl^- channel.[32] It is unknown whether the CFTR exerts its influence via direct interaction with these other channel proteins or if it occurs through interactions with associated proteins and signaling pathways.[32] Further studies are needed to elucidate the exact mechanism of action.

Although CFTR is clearly the most studied Cl^- channel, other chloride channels exist. Investigators have identified alternative Cl^- channels such as the outwardly rectifying Cl^- channel (ORCC)[33–35] and a calcium-activated chloride conductance.[1,33,35] Cyclic AMP-activated protein kinase A, protein kinase C, and extracellular ATP[1,2,32–35] can activate the ORCC. In addition, recent reports have identified messenger ribonucleic acid (mRNA) from members of the ClC Cl^- channel family in lung parenchyma.[36,37] Their expression appears to decrease from fetal to adult life. Activity of the ClC Cl^- channel appears to be increased in an acidic environment.[36] The functional importance of these non-CFTR channels in normal lung physiology is unknown, and further studies are necessary to determine their roles in Cl^- secretion and fluid movement. Given that children with cystic fibrosis are born with essentially "normal" lungs,[38] these alternative Cl^- channels likely play an important role in fluid secretion, at least during fetal life.

Although most of the Cl^- channels are believed to be located on the apical surface of epithelial cells, there are reports of Cl^- channels located on the basolateral membrane.[39] Using the patch clamp technique, Fischer and colleagues have identified at least two distinct Cl^- channels on the basolateral membrane of ciliated human airway epithelial cells.[39] One channel is believed to be an inwardly rectifying channel, whereas the second is an outwardly rectifying Cl^-; a third conductance was noted to be a 10-pS linear conductance channel. The channels appear to be activated by a number of factors including changes in cell Cl^-, cell volume, and cell potentials.[39]

Sodium Movement

Sodium absorption consists of multiple steps (see Figure 21–2*B*). Sodium can enter cells from the apical membrane through amiloride-sensitive Na^+ channels such as ENaC.[11,12,40,41] The majority of the Na^+ channels on the apical membrane are amiloride sensitive. (There is a residual Na^+ current component, which is amiloride insensitive.[1,40,41] This current may derive from the expression of another NA^+ channel that has not yet been identified.) Sodium also may move through a nonselective cation channel. Alternately, transport may be secondary to a pump or exchanger such as a Na^+-$2Cl^-$-K^+ cotransporter[1–3,19] or Na^+-H^+ exchangers.[18] Both the transporter and the exchanger have been identified in respiratory epithelium, but their exact location or role in epithelial transport has not been established.

After entering the cell, NA^+ moves further into the cell down a favorable electrochemical gradient; it therefore requires no expenditure of energy. At the basolateral membrane, NA^+ exits the cell against its chemical and electrical gradient. The activity of the Na^+-K^+-ATPase pump generates the favorable gradient that allows Na^+ to enter the cell at the apical membrane.[1–4,42]

Potassium Movement

Under normal circumstances it is clear that Na^+ and Cl^- movement predominate in the airway epithelia; however, there are other ions that contribute to the ion flux across the airway epithelia, including potassium and bicarbonate.[16,42–44] Not much is known about the net movement of potassium across the epithelial layer. There is a modest concentration of K^+ in the ASF (20 mEq/L).[1,2] It is unclear whether K^+ movement to the apical surface occurs through apically located K^+ channels or through paracellular flux. However, the transepithelial secretion appears to be nominal compared to the recycling that occurs across the basolateral membrane.[1–4,16,42] The recycling and movement of K^+ across the basolateral membrane, which maintains the resting membrane potential, has been studied thoroughly. This recycling is necessary for maintaining the negative cell voltage that is required to effect chloride secretion.[1–4,16,42] Potassium enters the cell through the Na^+-K^+-ATPase pump and Na^+-$2Cl^-$-K^+ cotransporter.[1–4,16,42] It exits the cell passively through basolateral K^+ channels. At least two channel types have been identified in airway epithelial cells. One channel has a large conductance of 150 pS. It is calcium sensitive and is stimulated by epinephrine.[43,44] Welsh and others have identified another K^+ channel with a 20-pS conductance. It is highly selective for potassium, inwardly rectifying, and the current-voltage relationship rectifies in symmetric solutions. Also, it is barium sensitive, that is, barium blocks the movement of K^+ through the channels.[16,42]

Bicarbonate Movement

Not much is known about what governs bicarbonate secretion and absorption. It is believed that the movement of bicarbonate may be important because of its buffering capacity and the effects pH can have on ion channels and transporters.[1,2,45] For instance, it has been shown that pH can alter chloride channel activity by increasing or decreasing a channel's open and closed times. This can alter the concentration of ions in ASF. Alterations in the salt concentration of ASF have been implicated in certain disease states such as cystic fibrosis. In addition, bicarbonate can alter the rheology of mucus. Recently it has been proposed that CFTR plays a role in bicarbonate transport.[45] Further studies are needed to elucidate the pathways important for bicarbonate secretion.

Water Movement

Until recently it was believed that most airway water movement occurs through osmosis.[1–4] As ions move across epithelial layers, an osmotic gradient/pressure is created, and water follows the ions. The movement of water is believed to occur through a paracellular pathway that exists between the cells. Recently, a family of water channels, aquaporins (AQPs), have been identified.[15,41,46–48] These channels or pores allow for water movement through cells[15,46–48] and may provide an alternative pathway for water movement across the airway epithelial layer. A number of water channels, AQPs 1 to 4, are located in various regions of the lung.[15,46,47] Aquaporin 1 is located on the endothelial cells of the microvasculature,[46] AQP3 is located on the basolateral membrane of basal epithelial cells in the trachea and nasopharynx,[46] and AQP4 is located on the basolateral membrane of ciliated columnar cells of the bronchi, trachea, and nasopharnyx.[46] There is some evidence to suggest that the expression of AQP4 correlates with CFTR expression[46–48]—the CFTR may act as an osmotic sensor for the apical epithelial membrane. Last, AQP5 is located on the apical membrane of type 1 pneumocytes and on acinar cells of submucosal glands.[46]

The expression of water channels varies depending on the developmental state, and the exposure to hormones, such as corticosteroids, and β-agonists. Prior to the identification of water channels, all fluid movement was believed to occur through the paracellular pathway. Today, it appears that there may be a combination of events and pathways that control the movement; further studies will need to be carried out to determine which pathway is most important. The predominant pathway for water movement may vary depending on stimuli such as hormones or inflammatory mediators.

Regulation and Modulation of Ion Transport

There are many factors that alter ion transport processes such as pH, nitric oxide, fatty acids, steroids, neurotransmitters, vasoactive intestinal peptide (VIP), substance P, bradykinin, calcium, cAMP, protein kinases A and C, ATP, prostaglandins, leukotrienes, adenosine, and β-adrenergic agonists. In this section the regulation of Na^+ and Cl^- transport is reviewed in detail.

Regulation of Chloride Secretion

In the mature airway (ie, the air-breathing lung), there is no detectable chloride secretion under basal conditions.[1] Chloride secretion can be stimulated in response to a number of stimuli and is regulated by a number of neural transmitters and hormonal agents. The stimulation of Cl^- secretion in response to an agonist increases the movement of Cl^- into the airway lumen; water follows passively through the paracellular pathway. The result is an increase in ASF, which optimizes mucociliary clearance.[1–5] Many of the agents that affect Cl^- secretion do so by activating or stimulating cAMP and then activating a cAMP-dependent protein kinase.[1–4] These agents include isoproterenol, epinephrine, VIP, and prostaglandins.[1–4,49] In addition, there are a number of agents that stimulate Cl^- secretion via calcium-dependent pathways. These pathways often rely on protein kinase C as well as phospholipase C activation.[2] Alternatively, extracellular nucleotides, such as ATP and uridine triphosphate (UTP) have been noted to increase Cl^- secretion. Nucleotide activation is believed to occur through activation of purinergic receptors,[2,32,50] of which there are a number of types. Each subclass has a different affinity for certain nucleotides.[2,32,50] After these purinergic receptors are activated, there may be multiple intracellular signaling pathways that are activated including cAMP-dependent and $Ca2^+$-dependent pathways.[2,32,50] Recently, nitric oxide has been shown to activate Cl^- secretion via activation of a cGMP-dependent pathway.[51,52] Last, Blaisdell et al have reported that pH can effect Cl^- secretion in fetal airway epithelial monolayers.[36]

This may be an important trigger for the change from secreting epithelia to absorbing epithelia.

There are also a number of agents that have been shown to inhibit Cl^- secretion. A number of drugs such as furosemide inhibit Cl^- secretion by decreasing the chemical driving force of Cl^-. These drugs affect the Na^+-K^+-$2Cl^-$ cotransporter. If Cl^- cannot enter the cell, there is no drive to then secrete it from the apical membrane.[1–4] Certain unsaturated fatty acids are reported to affect Cl^- channel activity.[53–55] Arachidonic acid has been shown to inhibit ORCC in patch clamp studies and short-circuit current experiments.[53–55] It is unclear whether the elaboration of such fatty acids from cell membranes in response to certain stimuli can contribute to lung pathophysiology; however, it has been suggested that increases in cell membrane arachidonate contribute to the proinflammatory environment of the cystic fibrotic airway and may play a role in the pathophysiology of cystic fibrosis.[56]

Regulation of Sodium Absorption

Although transport of NA^+ predominates in the airways, little is known about its short-term regulation. Much more is known about its long-term regulation by hormones such as aldosterone and glucocorticoids.[2,41,49] Often, agents that stimulate Cl^- secretion decrease Na^+ absorption. This may be an indirect effect, as the driving force for sodium movement is dissipated.[2–4] An exception to the rule is cAMP. It has been shown that cAMP-dependent pathways can effect Na^+ transport as well as Cl^- secretion. Elevation of cAMP levels results in increased Na^+ transport.[2–4,40,41] This alteration is believed to be related to changes in ENaC channel activity.

Inflammatory mediators such as bradykinin can increase Na^+ absorption. These agents bind to receptors located on the basolateral membrane of the cell. The receptors are linked to phospholipase C. The result of the coupling of the inflammatory mediator to the receptor is an increase in Na^+ absorption. It is not clear how the activation of phospholipase C results in the stimulation of Na^+ absorption.[57] There is evidence to support three different mechanisms. One possibility is that the activation of phospholipase C can increase in basolateral K^+-channel activity, which, in turn, increases the driving force for Na^+ movement.[2,57] Alternatively, there are data to suggest that phospholipase C has a direct effect on the Na^+-channel activity.[2,57] Last, there is indirect evidence of $Ca2^+$-dependent signaling pathway involvement.[2,57] Any one mechanism or a combination of these mechanisms would result in the increase in Na^+ transport; however, the effect would be quite short lived.

Hormones such as aldosterone, glucocorticoids, or thyroid hormone have longer-lasting effects on Na^+ transport.[58,59] Until recently little was known about how these substances affected Na^+ transport; however, investigation into the fetal lung has provided insight into their modes of action. It has been known that there is a change in net ion transport in the fetal lung from secretion to absorption that occurs during the last 10 weeks of gestation.[2,60–62] This change in ion transport coincides with higher levels of both thyroid and steroid hormones.[2,41] These observations led scientists to examine cultured fetal rat alveolar type II cells to determine the hormonal mechanism of action. These examinations revealed that there is an increase in expression of the α subunit of EnaC.[42] In addition, these hormones appear to enhance tonically the Na^+-K^+-ATPase.[41] These data suggest that these hormones may effect the transcription and expression of a number of transporter and channel proteins. By upregulating their expression, there is an increase in their activity and an increase in net Na^+ absorption.

Last, oxygen tension also can effect the expression and the function of the α subunit of ENaC. When the oxygen tension increases at birth there is an increase in amiloride-sensitive NA^+ absorption that correlates with this increase in expression. To date there is no oxygen response element identified.[41] Taken together, it appears there are a number of triggers that affect epithelial Na^+ channel subunit expression and may have long-term effects on NA^+ absorption.

Secretion versus Absorption

As stated earlier, the magnitude of secretion versus absorption varies depending on the region and the environmental state or experimental conditions of the respiratory epithelium. In the air-breathing lung, the major epithelial ion transport process needs to be net absorption. The surface area of the alveolar surface (70 m^2) is extremely large when compared to the airways (60 cm^2); therefore there needs to be a process that allows for the majority of the fluid generated by the alveolar epithelium (believed to be 1.5L/d) to be absorbed.[1,8] A nominal amount of secretion of Cl^- into the airway is necessary to maintain the periciliary fluid layer, which allows for normal mucociliary clearance. The ASF in the airways is only microns in height and varies depending on the length of cilia.[1,3–5]

The Secretory Model: The Fetal Lung and Perinatal Changes

A secretory airway epithelial layer is believed to be essential in the developing fetal lung. It is the movement of fluid that allows for proper airway and alveolar growth.[1–4,40,41] The production of fluid is believed to be due to active Cl^- secretion.[63] Investigators have established a body of evidence to support this theory. For instance, radiotracer flux experiments have demonstrated that the measured Cl^- flux is three times that expected with passive distribution.[60,61] In addition, the concentration of Cl^- is higher than that of serum, suggesting an accumulation of Cl^- in fetal fluid against its electrochemical gradient[60,61]—a situation that requires energy. The addition of cyanide abolishes fluid secretion, which supports the theory of energy-dependence.[62] The exact pathways responsible for the active Cl^- secretion are not well defined. What is known is that they may include the activity of chloride channels such as ClC2 and ClC5.[36,37,40] The ClC channels have been identified in the lung. It has been suggested that fetal Cl^- secretion is independent of the CFTR chloride channel, because infants born with cystic fibrosis do not have problems with lung development or fluid production.[38,41] At birth the lungs of infants with cystic fibrosis are relatively normal.[38,41] This suggests that there is function of the CFTR protein in utero that abruptly ends at birth or, more likely, that there are alternative pathways that are important in prenatal Cl^- secretion. It has been shown that there are differences in Cl^- channel expression during development. Tizzano and colleagues have demonstrated through comprehensive studies that the expression of CFTR is regulated developmentally in a fashion similar to that of the Na^+-K^+-ATPase.[64] The fact that bicarbonate is lower than expected for the electrochemical equilibrium might suggest that it is involved in Cl^- secretion and might be exchanged for Cl^- (for more details, see Chapter 22).

As delivery approaches there is a decrease in Cl^- secretion.[1–4,58] The dramatic transition from the "secretory lung" to the "absorptive lung" that occurs at the time of birth actually starts prenatally.[1–4] As the end of pregnancy approaches there is an increase in fluid absorption in the fetal lung.[1–4] Several investigators have shown that in the fetal lamb the rate of fluid production decreases and the rate of absorption increases.[1–4,40,60] Increases in the absorptive process occur at least 1 month prior to delivery, and the fluid production decreases at 1 week prior to delivery.[40] These changes appear to be due to a number of factors, including hormonal factors, neural input, and changes in the expression of certain transporters such as ENaC and the Na^+-K^+-ATPase pump.[40,64–68]

The Na^+-K^+-ATPase is comprised of three subunits, which are differentially expressed throughout development. The subunits that are important with regard to lung fluid are the α and β subunits.[40,41] The α subunit contains the catalytic site, whereas the β subunit is believed to have regulatory function. Both units are expressed at low levels early in gestation.[4,41] Investigators have shown that mRNA expression increases toward the end of gestation and that the regional distribution differs developmentally as well.[40,41] For instance, the expression of both subunits is diffuse throughout fetal life; as term approaches, the expression is intensified throughout. However, by 1 week of postnatal life, the expression pattern changes so that the expression is localized to small airways and lung parenchyma.[40,41] In addition, the distribution of Na^+-K^+-ATPase is isolated to the basolateral surface of the alveolar type II cell but not the alveolar type I cell.[41] Clearly, the changes in expression of this transporter mirror changes in Na^+ movement.

Expression of ENaC changes throughout development.[10,66] It is believed that ENaC is essential to the process of Na^+ absorption when transitioning from fetal to adult life. As with CFTR the expression of ENaC is diffuse early in gestation. The Na^+ channel is comprised of multiple subunits including α, β, and γ subunits.[11] Early in gestation all three ENaC subunits are expressed equally.[4,65,66] Later in gestation, expression of the α subunit increases dramatically, suggesting that it is essential for Na^+ channel activity and correlates to lung fluid clearance.[65,66] Mutations in the genes that encode for ENaC subunits can alter ENaC activity and delay fluid clearance at the time of birth.[40,65] Such genetic alterations have been associated with case reports of respiratory distress in the newborn (as discussed in Chapter 22).[40,66] Although ENaC provides the predominant pathway for Na^+ movement in the lung, there is a portion of Na^+ transport that is insensitive to amiloride, suggesting that there are alternative Na^+ pathways that have not yet been identified genetically.[41] Further studies are needed.

In addition to alterations in channel and transporter protein expression, ion and fluid homeostasis can be affected by hormonal regulation. There are many changes in hormone levels throughout prenatal life. One hormonal factor that influences fluid homeostasis is epinephrine. Epinephrine affects both fluid secretion and absorption through stimulation of β-adrenergic receptors. The effects of β-adrenergic stimulation on ion transport and fluid movement are multifold—it can affect directly a variety of channels and transporters including Cl^- and Na^+ channels.[2,3,4,69] However, the net effect of β-adrenergic stimulation on fluid movement depends on the level of expression of each transport protein and the proteins involved in the signaling pathways.

There are a number of other factors believed to be essential to allow the fetal lung to respond to the catecholamine/epinephrine surge that occurs at the time of birth. In the final 10 weeks of gestation there is an increase in both active thyroid hormone concentrations and steroid hormones.[40,41] The levels of these hormones early in pregnancy are very low, because the maternal hormones do not cross the placenta and fetal production is extremely low.[41] In animal models it has been shown that the timing of this increase in thyroid and steroid hormone production coincides with an absorptive response to epinephrine as opposed to a secretory response.[2,41] In addition, if a thyroidectomy is performed early in fetal life, the absorptive response to epinephrine is abolished.[68] Simultaneous infusion of cortisol and thyroid hormones[69] can restore the absorptive process.

Last, alterations in oxygen tension have been shown to affect the expression of a number of transport and channel proteins. Oxygen can effect the expression of the alpha subunit of ENaC.[41] This increase in expression correlates functionally with an increase in Na^+ absorption. To date, the oxygen response element of the α ENaC gene has not been identified. It has been shown that oxygen can increase the mRNA expression of both the α and β subunits of Na^+-K^+-ATPase.[41]

ABSORPTIVE MODEL: THE HEALTHY ADULT LUNG

When one begins to breathe air, the lung undergoes a transition to a predominantly absorptive tissue whose major goal is to reabsorb the fluid from the airway surface to maintain a dry airway. A dry airway allows for the greatest airway diameter, thus decreasing airway resistance and ensuring efficient gas exchange.[1–4] Fluid absorption is accomplished by optimizing Na^+ absorption. The normal Na^+-absorption pathways have been outlined in detail above. It is essential that the switch from net Cl^- secretion to net Na^+ absorption occurs in a timely fashion. If it does not occur, the neonatal lung may not be prepared for its most difficult task—"gas exchange." Abnormalities in the Na^+ pathways have been implicated in a number of noninfectious neonatal respiratory distress syndromes such as hyaline membrane disease[40] and transient tachypnea of the newborn.[40] These conditions are discussed in Chapter 22.

References

1. Boucher RC. Human airway ion transport, Part 1. Am J Respir Crit Care Med 1994;150:271–81.
2. Boucher RC. Human airway ion transport, Part 2. Am J Respir Crit Care Med 1994;150:581–93.
3. Welsh MJ. Mechanisms of airway epithelial ion transport. Clin Chest Med 1986;7:273–83.
4. Welsh MJ. Electrolyte transport by airway epithelia. Physiol Rev 1987;67:1143–84.
5. Wanner A, Salathe M, O'Riordan G. Mucociliary clearance in the airways. Am J Respir Crit Care Med 1996; 154:1868–902.
6. Cotton CU, Stutts MJ, Knowles MR, Boucher RC. Abnormal apical cell membrane in respiratory epithelium. An in vitro electrophysiologic analysis. J Clin Invest 1987;79:80–5.
7. Van Scott MR, Hester S, Boucher RC. Ion transport by rabbit nonciliated bronchiolar epithelial cells (Clara cells) in culture. Proc Natl Acad Sci U S A 1987;84:5496–500.
8. Kilburn KH. A hypothesis for pulmonary clearance and its implications. Am Rev Respir Dis 1968;98:449–63.
9. Jentsch TJ. Chloride channels. Curr Opin Neurobiol 1993; 3:316–21.
10. Zhou H, Tate S, Palmer L. Primary structure and functional properties of an epithelial K channel. Am J Physiol (Cell Physiol) 1994;266:C809–24.
11. O'Brodovich HM, Canessa C, Ueda J, et al. Expression of the epithelial Na^+ channel in the developing rat lung. Am J Physiol 1993;265:C491–6.
12. Canessa CM, Schild L, Buell G, et al. Amiloride-sensitive epithelial Na^+ channel is made of three homologous subunits. Nature 1994;367:463–7.
13. Xu W, Leung S, Wright J, Guggino SE. Expression of cyclic nucleotide-gated cation channels in airway epithelial cells. J Membr Biol 1999;171:117–26.
14. Jorissen M, Vereecke J, Carmeliet E, et al. Identification of a voltage-dependent non-selective cation channel in cultured adult and fetal nasal epithelial cells. Pflugers Arch 1990;425:617–23.
15. Verkman AS. Role of aquaporin water channels in kidney and lung. Am J Med Sci 1998;316:310–20.
16. McCann JD, Welsh MJ. Regulation of Cl^- and K^+ channels in airway epithelium. Annu Rev Physiol 1990;52:115–35.
17. Wheat VJ, Shumaker H, Burnham C, et al. CFTR induces the expression of DRA along with Cl^-/HCO_3^- exchange activity in tracheal epithelial cells. Am J Physiol Cell Physiol 2000;279:C62–71.
18. Paradiso AM. Identification of Na^+/H^+ exchange in human normal and cystic fibrosis ciliated airway epithelium. Am J Physiol 1991;261:L63–9.
19. Haas M, McBrayer DG, Yankaskas JR. Dual mechanisms for Na-K-Cl cotransporter regulation in airway epithelial cells. Am J Physiol 1993;264:C189–200.
20. Bazzaz FJ. Regulation of salt and water transport across airway mucosa. Clin Chest Med 1986;7:259–72.
21. Matsui H, Grubb BR, Tarran R, et al. Evidence for periciliary liquid layer depletion, not abnormal ion composition, in the pathogenesis of cystic fibrosis airways disease. Cell 1998;95:1005–15.
22. Duszyk M, French AS, Man SFP. Noise analysis and single-channel observations of 4 pS chloride channels in human airway epithelia. Biophys J 1992;61:583–7.
23. Duszyk M, French AS, Man SFP. The 20 pS chloride channel of human airway epithelia. Biophys J 1992; 57:223–30.
24. Cid LP, Montrose-Rafizadeh C, Smith DI, et al. Cloning of a putative human voltage-gated chloride channel (ClC-2) cDNA widely expressed in human tissues. Hum Mol Genet 1995;4:407–13.
25. Kemp PJ, MacGregor GG, Olver RE. G protein-regulated large-conductance chloride channels in freshly isolated fetal type II alveolar epithelial cells. Am J Physiol 1993; 265:L323–9.
26. Riordan JR, Rommens JM, Kerem BS, et al. Identification of the cystic fibrosis gene: cloning and characterization of complementary cDNA. Science 1989;245:1066–73.
27. Rommens JM, Iannuzzi M, Kerem BS, et al. Identification of the cystic fibrosis gene: chromosome walking and jumping. Science 1989;245:1059–65.
28. Kerem BS, Rommens JM, Buchanan JA, et al. Identification of the cystic fibrosis gene: genetic analysis. Science 1989;245:1073–80.
29. Davis PB, Drumm, M, Konstan MW. Cystic fibrosis. Am J Respir Crit Care Med 1996;154:1229–56.
30. Anderson MP, Gregory RJ, Thompson S, et al. Demonstration that CFTR is a chloride channel by alteration of its anion selectivity. Science 1991;253:202–53.
31. Welsh MJ, Anderson MP, Rich DP, et al. CFTR: a chloride channel with novel regulation. Neuron 1992;8:821–9.
32. Schweibert EM, Benos DJ, Egan ME, et al. CFTR is a conductance regulator as well as a chloride channel. Physiol Rev 1999;79:S145–66.

33. Anderson MP, Sheppard DN, Berger HA, Welsh MJ. Chloride channels in the apical membrane of normal and cystic fibrosis airway and intestinal epithelia. Am J Physiol 1992;263:L1–14.
34. Frizzell RA, Rechkemmer G, Shoemaker RL. Altered regulation of airway epithelial cell chloride channels in cystic fibrosis. Science 1986;233:558–60.
35. Welsh M. Abnormal regulation of ion channels in cystic fibrosis epithelia. FASEB J 1990;4:2718–25.
36. Blaisdell CJ, Edmonds RD, Wang X-T, et al. pH-regulated chloride secretion in fetal lung epithelia. Am J Physiol Cell Mol Physiol 2000;278:L1248–55.
37. Murray CB, Morales MM, Flotte TR, et al. ClC-2: a developmentally dependent chloride channel expressed in the fetal lung and downregulated after birth. Am J Respir Cell Mol Biol 1995;12:597–604.
38. McCray PJ, Reenstra WW, Louie E, et al. Expression of CFTR and presence of cAMP mediated fluid secretion in human fetal lung. Am J Physiol 1992;262:L472–81.
39. Illek B, Fischer H, Choi HK, et al. Regulation of chloride exit across the basolateral membrane in airways. Pediatr Pulmonol 1999;S19:195.
40. Pitkanen OM, O'Brodovich HM. Significance of ion transport during lung development and in respiratory disease of the newborn. Ann Med 1998;30:134–42.
41. Barker P. Genes that control lung liquid. Chest 1997; 111:105–10S.
42. Cotton C. Basolateral potassium channels and epithelial ion transport. Am J Respir Cell Mol Biol 2000;23:270–2.
43. Kunzelman K, Pavenstaedt H, Beck C, et al. Characterization of potassium channels in respiratory cells. I General properties. Pflugers Arch 1989;414:291–6.
44. Kunzelman K, Pavenstaedt H, Gregor R. Characterization of potassium channels in respiratory cells. II. Inhibitors and regulation. Pflugers Arch 1989;414:297–303.
45. Illek B, Yankaskas JR, Machen TE. cAMP and genistein stimulate HCO_3^- conductance through CFTR in human airway epithelia. Am J Physiol 1997;272:L752–61.
46. Lee MD, King LS, Nielson S, Agre P. Genomic organization and developmental expression of aquaporin-5 in lung. Chest 1997;111:111–3S.
47. Yasui M, Serlachius E, Lofgren M, et al. Perinatal changes in expression of aquaporin-4 and other water and ion transporters in rat lung. J Physiol 1997;505.1:3–11.
48. Umenishi F, Carter EP, Yang B, et al. Sharp increase in rat lung water channel expression in the perinatal period. Am J Respir Cell Mol Biol 1996;15:673–9.
49. Zeitlin PL, Loughlin GM, Guggino WB. Ion transport in cultured fetal and adult rabbit tracheal epithelia. Am J Physiol Cell Physiol 1988;254:C691–8.
50. Stutts MJ, Fitz JG, Paradiso AM, Boucher RC. Multiple modes of regulation of airway epithelial chloride secretion by extracellular ATP. Am J Physiol 1994;267:C1442–51.
51. Kamosinska B, Radomski MW, Duszyk M, et al. Nitric oxide activates chloride currents in human lung epithelial cells. Am J Physiol 1997;272:L1098–104.
52. Steagell WK, Elmer HL, Brady KG, Kelley TJ. CFTR-dependent regulation of epithelial inducible nitric oxide synthase expression. Am J Respir Cell Mol Biol 2000; 22:45–50.
53. Hwang TC, Guggino SE, Guggino WB. Direct modulation of secretory chloride channels by arachidonic acid and other cis unsaturated fatty acids. Proc Natl Acad Sci U S A 1990;87:5706–9.
54. Anderson MP, Welsh MJ. Fatty acids inhibit apical membrane chloride channels in airway epithelia. Proc Natl Acad Sci U S A 1990;87:7334–8.
55. Lindsell P. Inhibition of CFTR chloride currents by arachidonic acid. Can J Physiol Pharmacol 2000;78:490–9.
56. Freedman SD, Katz MH, Parker EM, et al. A membrane lipid imbalance plays a role in the phenotypic expression of cystic fibrosis in CFTR (-/-) mice. Proc Natl Acad Sci U S A 1999;96:13995–4000.
57. Clarke LL, Paradiso AM, Mason SJ, Boucher RC. Effects of bradykinin on Na^+ and Cl^- transport in human nasal epithelium. Am J Physiol 1992;262:C644–55.
58. Zeitlin PL, Wagner M, Markakis D, et al. Steroid hormones: modulators of Na^+ absorption and Cl^- secretion in cultured tracheal epithelia. Proc Natl Acad Sci U S A 1989; 86:2502–5.
59. Tchepichev S, Ueda J, Canessa C, et al. Lung epithelial Na^+ channel subunits are differentially regulated during development and by steroids. Am J Physiol 1995; 269:C805–12.
60. Mescher EJ, Platzker ACG, Ballard PL, et al. Ontogeny of tracheal fluid, pulmonary surfactant, and plasma corticoids in the fetal lamb. J Appl Physiol 1975;39:1017–21.
61. Krochmal EM, Ballard ST, Yankaskas JR, et al. Volume and ion transport by fetal rat alveolar and tracheal epithelia in submersion culture. Am J Physiol 1989;256:F397–407.
62. Olver RE, Strang LB. Ion fluxes across the pulmonary epithelium and the secretion of lung liquid in the foetal lamb. J Physiol 1974;241:327–57.
63. Parker PM, Boucher RC, Yankaskas JR. Bioelectric properties of cultured monolayers from epithelium of distal human fetal lung. Am J Physiol Lung Cell Mol Physiol 1995;268:L270–7.
64. Tizzano EF, Chitayat D, Buchwald M. Cell-specific localization of CFTR mRNA shows developmentally regulated expression in human fetal tissues. Hum Mol Genet 1993;2:219–24.
65. Hummler E, Barker P, Beerman F, et al. Role of epithelial sodium channel in lung liquid clearance. Chest 1997; 111:113S.
66. Smith DE, Otulakowski G, Yeger H, et al. Epithelial Na^+ channel (ENaC) expression in the developing normal and abnormal human perinatal lung. Am J Respir Crit Care Med 2000;161:1322–31.
67. Walters DV, Olver RE. The role of catecholamines in lung liquid absorption at birth. Pediatr Res 1978;12:239–42.
68. Barker PM, Brown MJ, Ramsden CA, et al. The effect of thyroidectomy in fetal sheep on lung liquid reabsorption induced by adrenaline or cyclic AMP. J Physiol (Lond) 1988;407:373–83.
69. Barker PM, Markiewicz M, Parker KA, et al. Synergistic action of triiodothyronine and hydrocortisone on epinephrine induced reabsorption of fetal lung liquid. Pediatr Res 1990;27:588–91.

CHAPTER 22

Disorders of Ion Transport

Hugh O'Brodovich, MD

The lung is a complex organ containing more than 40 different cell types. Over the past two decades much has been learned in regard to the function of individual cells, how they maintain lung homeostasis, and how their function is altered or lost during disease processes. The respiratory epithelium provides an excellent example of how our improved understanding of cellular and molecular biology has enhanced our ability to understand some common pulmonary diseases. Until the latter part of the 20th century, the respiratory epithelium was viewed largely as a passive barrier, much like a piece of plastic wrap, although it had been known that type II epithelium played a role in surfactant homeostasis, and that the cilia of pseudostratified columnar epithelium protected the lungs by propelling mucus. In the 1980s the expertise to culture lung epithelium became widely available, and the resultant studies provided much insight into respiratory epithelial cell function. For example, scientists discovered that some respiratory epithelial cells could secrete Cl^- (with Na^+ and water following) or absorb Na^+ (with Cl^- and water following). These observations led us to a better understanding of the pathogenesis of lung hypoplasia, transient tachypnea of the newborn, neonatal respiratory distress syndrome, and the underlying mechanism of cystic fibrosis (CF) lung disease. The purpose of this chapter is to build upon information outlined in Chapter 21, "Ion Flux and Homeostasis in the Lung," and to provide an improved understanding of how developmental immaturity or disease processes result in lung diseases, based on inadequate or inappropriate active ion transport.

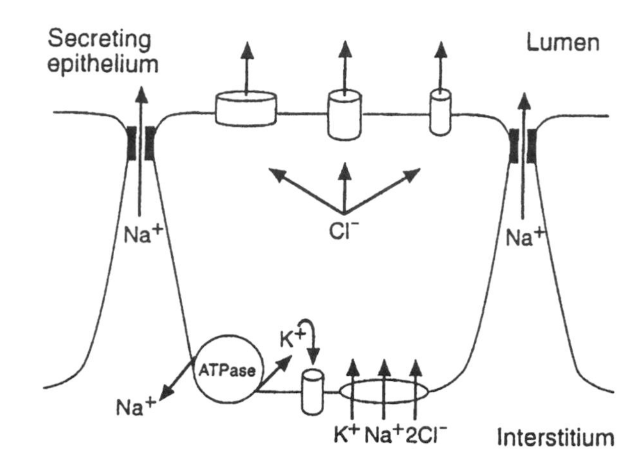

FIGURE 22–1. A model for Cl^- secretion can be developed from data from fetal lung liquid secretion.[1,2] Na^+/K^+ adenosinetriphospatase (ATPase)[3–6] maintains a high intracellular [K^+] and low [Na^+]. Cl^- entry relies, directly or indirectly, on Na^+ entering the cell down its electrochemical gradient. One path is via a basolateral bumetanide-sensitive $Na^+/K^+/2Cl^-$ co-transporter;[7] K^+ leaves the cell via K^+ channels,[8] Na^+ exits via the Na^+/K^+ ATPase, and intracellular [Cl^-] increases. Another model for Cl^- entry uses a basolateral Na^+-HCO_3^- symport that increases intracellular [HCO_3^-], and an adjacent Cl^- - HCO_3^- exchanger sends Cl^- into the cell. A sufficiently negative intracellular membrane potential results in Cl^- being above its electrochemical equilibrium, so that it exits the cell across the apical membrane against an unfavorable chemical gradient (in fetal distal lung epithelium the intracellular-to-extracellular [Cl^-] is ~40:110 mM,[9] usually through various Cl^- permeant ion channels. Sodium follows Cl^-, presumably by a paracellular route, with water passing between or through the cells via aquaporins.[10–15] (Reproduced with the permission of Blackwell Science, Inc. from O'Brodovich H.[16])

Basic Mechanisms of Ion Transport

There are three essential factors that are required for epithelium to actively transport salt and water. First, the epithelium must be polarized, which means specific proteins are localized to specific regions of the cytoplasmic membrane. For example, in Cl^- secreting epithelia, Cl^- permeant ion channels are present on the apical membrane of the cell. The second essential component is an energy-dependent process that is capable of directly or indirectly driving ions uphill against their electrochemical gradient. The third component is the presence of intercellular tight junctions, which greatly restrict the movement of ions, or at least some ions, across the epithelial cell layer. These three features are illustrated in Figures 22–1[1–16] and 22–2,[3–6,10–19] which respectively provide models for Cl^- (fluid) secretion and Na^+ (fluid) absorption.

Ion Transport in the Lung

Period of Fetal Life

Jost and Policard[20] first proved that the fluid within the fetal or newborn lung arises from the lung and does not merely represent aspirated amniotic fluid. Initially, it was believed that the intrapulmonary fluid represented a

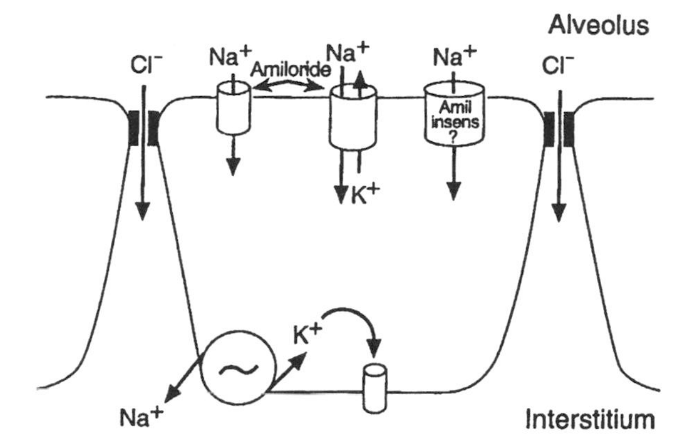

FIGURE 22–2. Vectorial Na^+ transport by fetal distal lung epithelium (FDLE) requires an Na^+/K^+ adenosinetriphosphatase (ATPase)[3–6] which, in concert with K^+ channels generates an electrochemical gradient (in lung epithelia the intracellular Na^+ is ~ 10 mM and the electrical potential is negative) for Na^+ entry into the epithelial cell. If there are open Na^+ conductive channels on the apical membrane, there is an apical-to-basal pathway for Na^+ transport, which generates a transepithelial potential difference. In vivo and in vitro experiments show that other Na^+ entry pathways (eg, Na^+/H^+ antiport, Na^+-glucose symport) are not involved in transepithelial Na^+ transport in normal FDLE.[4,17–19] Na^+ transport results in Cl^- and water movement, the latter via a paracellular or transcellular route via aquaporins.[10–15] Usually the apical membrane entry pathway for Na^+ is the rate limiting step in epithelial Na^+ transport. (Reproduced with the permission of Blackwell Science, Inc. from O'Brodovich H.[16])

transudate arising from the vasculature. However, critical experiments in the 1960s by Adamson and colleagues[21] demonstrated that this fetal lung liquid secretion required active ion transport and that it occurred secondary to the active secretion of Cl^- into the lumen of the developing lung. The presence of fluid within the developing lung is critical for normal lung development (see "Fetal Lung Hypoplasia"). The proposed mechanism for fetal lung liquid production is illustrated in part in Figure 22–1. This mechanism, however, does not totally explain the unique ion concentrations within the lung liquid where the [K] and [Cl] are much higher than in the plasma (Table 22–1).[22–24] The reason for the marked difference in the bicarbonate concentrations of the fetal lung liquid from fetal lambs and guinea pigs versus dogs and primates is unknown[22,23] (see Table 22–1).

Perinatal Period

To enable a successful transition to postnatal life, the Cl^- secretion by the fetal lung must either be markedly decreased or be overwhelmed by a much greater Na^+ (fluid) absorptive process. In the early 1980s, it was shown[25] that the lung liquid secretion in fetal lambs could be converted within minutes to a fluid absorptive process with the infusion of catecholamines or β-agonists at concentrations normally seen during birth. It was also demonstrated that this conversion from fluid secretion to fluid absorption could be blocked by the Na^+-transport inhibitor amiloride.[3] Subsequent studies by Walters et al[26] and Chapman et al,[27] respectively, showed that membrane permeant analogs of cyclic adenosine monophosphate (cAMP) and phosphodiesterase inhibitors similarly induce the fetal lung fluid absortive response. Other mediators that normally circulate at birth, such as antidiuretic hormone (ADH), similarly can induce the fluid absorptive response.[28,29] However, the mechanism of the ADH effect is controversial, as it is unknown whether this is a direct effect of ADH or if it occurs indirectly through stimulation of the sympathetic nervous system.[30,31]

Although circulating hormones may abruptly convert the intrauterine fetal lung from fluid secretion to fluid absorption, it is possible that these mediators are not responsible for the permanent switch from fluid secretion

TABLE 22–1. Mean Values for Solutes within Liquids Obtained from the Fetal Lung Lumen's Alveolar Fluid and Plasma of Different Species

Species and Fluids	Na^+ (mmol/kg H2O)	K^+ (mmol/kg H2O)	Cl^- (mmol/kg H2O)	HCO_3^- mmol/kg H2O	pH	Protein (g/dL)
Lamb*						
AF	150	6.3	157	2.8	6.27	0.027
Plasma	150	4.8	107	24	7.34	4.09
Guinea Pig†						
AF	135	11.8	145	1.9	N/A	N/A
Plasma	130	8.9	95	24	N/A	N/A
Dog‡						
AF	137	9	129	22	N/A	N/A
Plasma	140	6	111	25	N/A	N/A
Monkey‡						
AF	161	5.5	138	29	N/A	N/A
Plasma	144	3.5	109	22	N/A	N/A

AF = alveolar fluid; N/A = not available.
Data from: *Olver and Strang;[24] †O'Brodovich and Merritt;[22] and ‡Cotton et al.[23]

to absorption. The levels of these hormones increase only during the latter part of the birth process and rapidly decline shortly after birth. Similarly, when the intravenous infusions of β-agonists are discontinued, the lung immediately returns to its fluid secretory state.[25] Recent work has demonstrated that the increase in ambient oxygen concentration ($[O_2]$) at birth may be responsible, at least in part, for the permanent conversion from fluid secretion to absorption. The fetal alveolar epithelium is exposed to an $[O_2]$ of approximately 3%, whereas the postnatal lung is exposed to 21% O_2—a sevenfold increase in P_{O_2}. Barker and Gatzy[32] reported that such a change in P_{O_2} decreased the ability of late gestation fetal distal lung explants to form fluid-filled cysts in organ culture. Our laboratory has shown that primary cultures of mature rat fetal distal lung epithelium (FDLE) grown under fetal $[O_2]$ had only minimal amounts of amiloride-sensitive Na^+ transport and low levels of messenger ribonucleic acid (mRNA) coding for the epithelial Na^+ channel (ENaC). However, if these same cells were grown under postnatal $[O_2]$, there was a marked induction of amiloride-sensitive current and increases in the α, β, and γ ENaC mRNA levels. Subsequent studies have demonstrated that this is a reversible process in the FDLE[33] and that the "trigger level" for this induction is 7% $[O_2]$. This effect of O_2 on the ability of lung epithelia to transport Na^+ was demonstrated subsequently in adult type II cells.[34] In addition, studies in rats[35] exposed to hypobaric hypoxia demonstrated decreases in the amiloride-sensitive potential difference (PD) across their nasal respiratory epithelium, a surrogate measure for Na^+ transport (see below). This indicates that the $[O_2]$ effect, if present in humans, may have relevance to the pathophysiologic characteristics of pulmonary edema where the air spaces are fluid filled and to high-altitude pulmonary edema. This O_2 induction of amiloride-sensitive transport in lung epithelia requires heme-binding proteins[36] and may be mediated, at least in part, through reactive oxygen intermediates and NFκB signaling.[33]

Postnatal Period

After birth and throughout life, the respiratory epithelium continues to regulate the amount of fluid present in the alveolar space through its ability to actively transport Na^+ through Na^+-permeant ion channels. The amount of amiloride-sensitive Na^+ transport by the intact lung is comparable both at 7 and 30 days after birth in the guinea pig lung,[37] and similarly primary cultures of distal lung epithelium from the fetal[4] and adult[38] lung have comparable amounts of amiloride-sensitive Na^+ transport. Matthay and colleagues first showed that the adult lung could concentrate air space edema fluid to a greater extent than could be explained by classic Starling forces.[39,40] This work, combined with studies of adult type II epithelia,[38,41] demonstrated that type II epithelium from the adult lung used Na^+-transport pathways comparable to those used by many other Na^+-absorbing epithelia. Similarly, β-agonists and membrane-permeant analogs of cAMP could augment the Na^+ absorptive capabilities of lung epithelia.[4,38]

Sodium Transport in the Human Lung

Studies in the adult lung[42,43] show that the fluid clearance rate in the human (18%/h) is one of the most rapid of all mammals (dog, 4%/h; sheep, 8%/h; rabbit, 15%/h; mouse, 27%/h). Thus lung Na^+ transport is highly relevant to human lung disease when fluid fills the alveolar air space.

The epithelium lining the upper and conducting airways of the lung actively transport ions, thereby maintaining the appropriate amount of fluid bathing respiratory cilia, so that effective mucociliary transport can be undertaken. Simplified versions of these ion-transport pathways are outlined in Figures 22–1 and 22–2, and the reader is referred to reviews related to Na^+ transport by the fetal[1] and adult[44,45] airways and to Chapter 21 for further details.

It is difficult to study in vivo respiratory epithelial ion transport in humans. Although one must be cautious in extrapolating to the more distal regions of the lung, we now can make measurements of the amiloride-sensitive PD across the nasal epithelium, a surrogate for active Na^+ transport in the human.[44–50] It also is known that these measurements in the nasal respiratory epithelium reflect ion-transport patterns in more distal regions of the airways.[44,45,48,50] To allow a better understanding of human respiratory epithelial Na^+ transport, we developed a competitive quantitative reverse-transcriptase polymerase chain reaction (RT-PCR) method to measure ENaC mRNA levels in human subjects. This technology allowed us to make the first direct correlations of α, β, and γ human ENaC (hENaC) mRNA levels with amiloride-sensitive respiratory epithelia PD.[51] We found a negative correlation between the amount of γ hENaC mRNA and amiloride-sensitive PD of the nasal respiratory epithelium.[51] Similarly, this technique allowed us to demonstrate that the relative amounts of α, β, and γ hENaC mRNA differ significantly in the nasal, bronchial, and most distal regions of the human lung (Figure 22–3).[52] These latter studies suggest that Na^+ transport and Na^+ channel characteristics may vary between different regions of the lung, since experiments in oocyte expression systems show that ENaC biologic activity is influenced by varying amounts of α, β, and γ hENaC mRNA.[53]

Fetal Lung Hypoplasia

There are many factors that influence the development of the lung from the time of its first appearance, as it buds off the developing gastrointestinal tract, through to postnatal life. Lung development is a complex process involving many factors including growth factors and

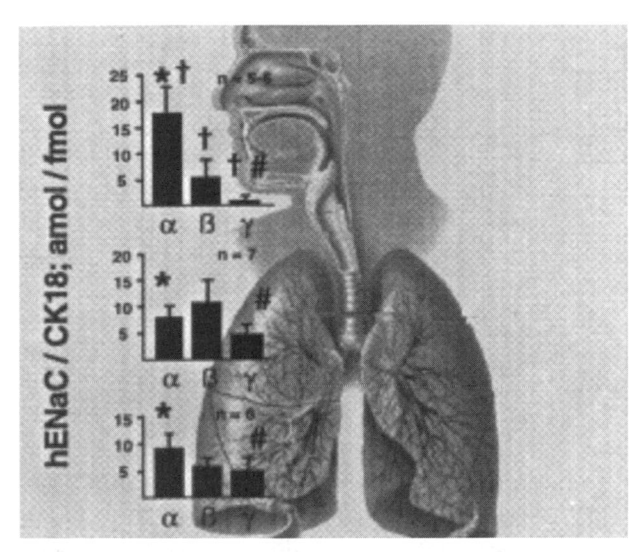

FIGURE 22–3. Small quantities of respiratory epithelium were obtained from the nasal, bronchial, and distal lung regions and were analyzed using quantitative reverse-transcriptase polymerase chain reaction to determine the relative amounts of human epithelial Na^+ channel (hENaC) subunit messenger ribonucleic acid (mRNA). Marked differences in the absolute and relative amounts α, β, and γ hENaC mRNA were found. (Adapted from Pitkänen O et al.[52])

mesenchymal-epithelial interactions; diverse mechanisms are likely involved in congenital lung defects, such as lung agenesis, lung aplasia, and dysplastic lung growth. For example, lung development can be perturbed through a variety of experimental approaches, including the use of genetic knockout models for growth factors. Similarly, mechanical compression of the lungs, which occurs with the clinical conditions of oligohydramnios or congenital diaphragmatic hernia, is associated with significant hypoplasia and dysplasia of the lungs. However, it is reasonable to speculate that at least some cases of fetal lung hypoplasia result from abnormalities in normal fetal respiratory epithelial ion transport. As described above, the fetal lung continuously secretes fluid into the developing air spaces of the lung at a rate of approximately 5 mL/kg/h (based upon fetal lamb studies).[3,21,24] The amount of liquid present in the developing lung air spaces has a dramatic effect on lung morphogenesis. Indeed, Alcorn et al[54] showed that increasing the amount of fluid within the fetal lamb lungs caused lung hyperplasia, whereas decreased fluid caused hypoplasia. This was confirmed in subsequent studies where the trachea or a bronchus was ligated resulting in a "hyperplastic" lung with an increased deoxyribonucleic acid (DNA) content per milligram of tissue.[55] In human lung development, a similar situation occurs in the syndrome of congenital laryngeal atresia, which is associated with hyperplastic lungs that are overdistended with fluid.[56] The time during gestation when the intervention takes place can have a significant effect on the severity of lung hypoplasia.[57] In vitro studies support these findings, since it has been shown that fetal lung explants from the pseudoglandular stage of lung development exposed to inhibitors of Cl^- (fluid) secretion have a reduction in the intraluminal fluid volume and decreased lung growth.[58]

Newborn Infants with Noninfective Respiratory Distress

Before the existence of neonatal intensive care units, the occurrence of significant respiratory distress in a newborn infant carried a grave prognosis. The majority of infants died from their acute lung disease.The discovery that a relative deficiency of air space surface active material was responsible for the pathogenesis of what was then termed "idiopathic respiratory distress syndrome"[59] and the advent of artificial ventilatory support for neonates led to dramatically improved survival. Physicians soon recognized two common forms of noninfective respiratory distress in the newborn human infant. One became known as "hyaline membrane disease" (HMD) or neonatal respiratory distress syndrome (nRDS); the other became known as "transient tachypnea of the newborn" (TTN). As described below, there is increasing evidence that immature ineffective active Na^+ transport plays an important pathophysiologic role in the initiation of both of these disorders.

Importance of Respiratory Epithelial Sodium Transport at Birth

The essential contribution of amiloride-sensitive epithelial Na^+ transport to the clearance of fetal lung liquid at the time of birth has been demonstrated by pharmacologic and genetic experiments. Studies in newborn guinea pigs, where amiloride or other inhibitors of Na^+ transport were instilled into the fluid-filled air spaces prior to the first breath, revealed that the amiloride-treated newborns developed respiratory distress and hypoxemia and failed to clear their lung liquid normally.[60] Since amiloride can block both Na^+ channels and other Na^+ entry pathways such as the Na^+/H exchanger and Na^+/glucose symport, additional experiments[17] were needed to demonstrate that these latter two mechanisms of Na^+ entry were not involved in fetal lung clearance. The functional cloning[61,62] of the amiloride-sensitive ENaC permitted the generation of mice in whom the α subunit of ENaC was knocked out.[63] The newborn mice that lacked the α subunit of ENaC did not have any detectable amiloride-sensitive transepithelial PD in lung cysts grown from their trachea, and they developed respiratory distress and hypoxemia and failed to clear their lung liquid. Death occurred shortly after birth. Postmortem examination demonstrated that, at both gross and microscopic levels, the lungs were morphologically normal. The subsequent cloning of the β and γ subunits of ENaC[53] permitted additional genetic experiments to look at the relative biologic importance of these other subunits in the lung during the perinatal period. Although the β and γ knockout models showed some minor delays in lung liquid clearance, newborn mice deficient in these subunits did not die from respiratory distress syndrome.[64–66] Rather, the mice died from metabolic disorders arising from the inability of the kidney to appropriately regulate Na^+ and other electrolytes.

The above experiments highlighted the relative importance of the α, β, and γ subunits of ENaC and emphasized the differences in their expression between different organ tissues. Since that time it has been recognized that the abundance of mRNA encoding the three subunits of ENaC varied significantly between tissues both in the basal state[53,61,62,67,68] and in response to stimuli known to alter gene expression.[67–72] How these differences in steady state mRNA levels correlate with different subunit protein contents is poorly understood. However, it is feasible that the stoichiometry of ENaC varies between tissues, thereby giving a different biologic effect. For example, experiments have shown that cells transfected with only the α subunit have amiloride-sensitive nonselective cation channels,[73] whereas cells transfected with all three subunits have the classic highly Na^+-selective amiloride-sensitive ENaC.[74] Differences in ENaC subunit stoichiometry also may provide an explanation for differences observed between epithelium cultured from immature fetal versus adult lung, where the fetal epithelium expresses at least two Na^+ channels with different biophysical properties, while the adult only expresses one under normal conditions.[75,76]

Hyaline Membrane Disease

One common form of respiratory distress in the newborn is the nRDS, or HMD.[77,78] It is characterized by diffuse microatelectasis with accompanying acute lung injury, air space fluid, hyaline membranes that are composed of fibrin and desquamated epithelium, and proteinaceous exudate that arises from the increase in alveolar capillary permeability.[79] Hyaline membrane disease had a high mortality rate until intermittent and continuous positive airway pressure became feasible and regularly used modalities in the newborn intensive units. These advances, combined with exogenous surfactant replacement therapy and modern support, dramatically changed the prognosis of this disease.

Prematurely born infants who develop HMD have two consistent findings at the time of birth. First, relative to other newborn infants, their lungs are deficient in surface active material[59] and do not have the usually seen 10-fold increase in abundance of air space surfactant relative to adult lungs.[80] Second, their nasal respiratory epithelium has significantly less amiloride-sensitive transepithelial PD,[47] presumably reflecting deficient ENaC expression in their respiratory epithelium. Studies in the rodent have illustrated that the mRNA encoding α rat ENaC (rENaC) starts increasing prior to birth, whereas β and γ rENaC mRNA is regulated differentially with maximal expression shortly after birth.[68] During the pseudoglandular and canalicular fetal lung development stages, all three subunit mRNAs are significantly less abundant than they are in the postnatal lung.

Experiments performed in nonprimate mammals provide some insights into the mechanisms whereby the mature, but not the immature, fetal lung can convert from liquid secretion to amiloride-sensitive fluid absorption. The fact that mature, but not immature, fetal lambs undergo this conversion in response to β-agonists and cAMP suggests that the defect must be distal to the β-adrenergic receptor in the cellular signal transduction pathway. However, at the present time, it is unknown whether the deficiency lies in the signal transduction pathway responsible for ENaC activation, or whether there is inadequate synthesis of ENaC or inadequate amounts of the ENaC channel that have been "trafficked" to the cytoplasmic membrane. The cellular production of ENaC membrane channels is markedly inefficient. Approximately 95% of the ENaC subunits that are synthesized in the endoplasmic reticulum are directed for degradation and fail to appear at the apical membrane.[81,82] This inefficiency provides a potential explanation for the large abundance of ENaC mRNA yet extremely scarce amount of ENaC protein at the apical membrane. These experiments and others highlight the multiple control sites for the expression of the active epithelial Na^+ channel (Figure 22–4).

Much of the information regarding the regulation of ENaC expression has been derived from animal experiments or cell transfection studies. One must extrapolate to the human with care, since recent work illustrates that there may be a significant difference between the human respiratory epithelium and that of the rodent, from which most of our information is derived. When developing fetal mouse lungs are evaluated by in situ hybridization, the α, β, and γ mENaC subunits are not evident in the developing respiratory epithelium until mid-to-late gestation.[83] In contrast, when we studied human fetal lungs it was evident that hENaC mRNA could be detected at the earlier stages of lung development; indeed α ENaC mRNA was detected already during the embryonic stage where the lung is but an early offshoot of the gastrointestinal tract.[84] Although in situ hybridization does not permit quantitative assessment, these two apparently contradictory studies provide a potential and intriguing mechanism for ENaC regulation in the developing fetal lung that is continuously secreting Cl^- and fluid. It is well known from other early embryonic development systems that mRNA can be synthesized and stored to await the

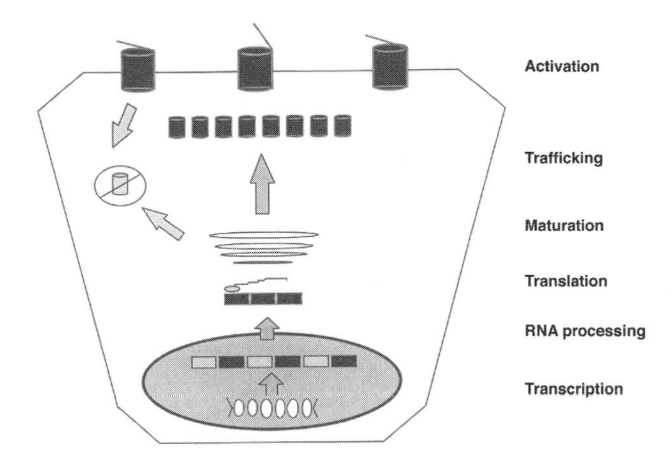

FIGURE 22–4. There are many potential sites for the regulation of apical membrane Na^+ channel activity, the rate-limiting step in Na^+ transport. These include the rate of transcription of ribonucleic acid (RNA) and its processing into mature messenger RNA (mRNA), the stability and, hence, half-life of the mRNA, and the efficiency of translating mRNA into proteins by the ribosomes within the rough endoplasmic reticulum. Regulation also may occur as the nascent protein undergoes maturation within the Golgi bodies and is "trafficked" to the membrane or undergoes degradation. After arriving at the membrane the Na^+ channel must be activated so that it can allow Na^+ to flow through its open pore. The rate at which the channel is removed from the membrane and whether it undergoes recycling to the membrane or immediately undergoes degradation have major effects on plasma membrane epithelial Na^+ channel activity.

appropriate signal to be immediately transformed into protein.[85,86] This would seem to be an excellent strategy for the developing lung. At birth, the lung must immediately increase its ENaC protein concentrations, and if one had to rely upon the entire synthetic pathway from gene transcription through translation and intracellular trafficking to the membrane, there possibly would not be sufficient time for one to survive the birth process. Rather, with abundant presynthesized mRNA localized near the protein synthetic machinery of the cell, one could, with an appropriate signal such as catecholamines and increased $[O_2]$, meet the challenge of the birth process in a rapid and timely fashion.

Steroid hormonal modulation of various synthetic pathways in the developing lung can have profound effects on lung morphogenesis. For example, thyroid and glucocorticoids dramatically alter the surfactant synthetic pathways and remodel the lung interstitium and distal lung unit.[80] Similarly these and other hormones can modulate the gene expression of ENaC and the in vivo ability of the lung to convert from fluid secretion to absorption. Earlier studies in the intact and thyroidectomized fetal lamb have demonstrated that exogenous thyroid and glucocorticoid hormone therapy can induce these otherwise premature lungs' capacity to convert from secretion to absorption in response to a β-agonist stimulus.[87,88] Glucocorticoids increase α ENaC mRNA in primary cultures of fetal distal lung epithelium in vitro[67,70] and experiments have demonstrated a differential regulation of ENaC subunits by glucocorticoids, where α but neither β or γ ENaC mRNA increase within 8 hours of treatment.[68] Another intriguing observation is that when FDLE are grown on top of the matrix secreted from fetal mixed lung cells grown under a fetal P_{O_2} environment,[89] they maintain an immature respiratory epithelial ion transport phenotype. Since glucocorticoids are known to modify the architecture of the distal lung unit, perhaps some of the in vivo response to glucocorticoids is secondary to a mesenchymal-epithelial interaction. Finally, female gender hormones increase ENaC expression[69] and may play an important role in the susceptibility to immature Na^+-transport pathways. It has been well recognized that female infants have a lower incidence of nRDS, and in the past this was largely attributed to differences in the maturation of the surfactant pathways.[78] However, it is possible that female newborn infants have a gender-related advantage in their ability to clear lung liquid through amiloride-sensitive Na^+-transport pathways.

Transient Tachypnea of the Newborn

As clinicians improved their ability to diagnose HMD, they recognized another group of infants who suffered from noninfective respiratory distress at birth. These infants developed tachypnea, hypoxemia, and respiratory distress but had a much different clinical and radiographic presentation and natural history. Infants with RDS type II, or what became known as transient tachypnea of the newborn (TTN), were more frequently full-term infants and often the product of cesarian section delivery. Clinically, infants with TTN have hyperinflated chests with associated chest radiographs illustrating marked overinflation with evidence of peribronchial interstitial and some air space edema. These infants have mature surfactant systems, which differentiates them from infants with HMD. It was hypothesized that TTN arose from residual excess fetal lung liquid within their lungs.[90] The symptoms arose from residual air space filling and interstitial edema in the interstitium and around the airways, the latter causing flow limitation, air trapping, and overinflation of the lungs. It also was noted that these infants required only relatively modest respiratory support and that, as a general rule, they did well, with full recovery within 48 to 72 hours. There were no long-term sequelae, such as chronic lung disease, as frequently occurred in preterm infants with severe HMD.[77] Studies in animals showed that the association with cesarian section delivery likely related to the larger amount of lung liquid to be cleared at the time of birth.[91] The infants born by cesarian section had not benefited from both the labour process, during which time fluid could be absorbed, and the associated stressful stimuli that can promote liquid absorption.[92]

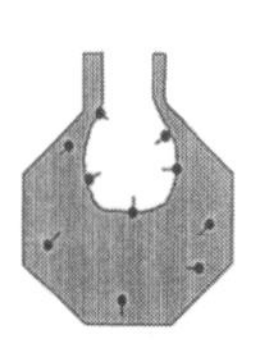
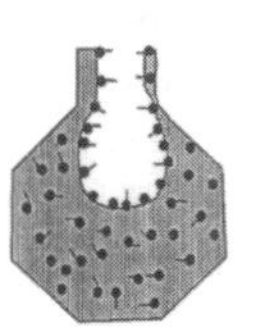
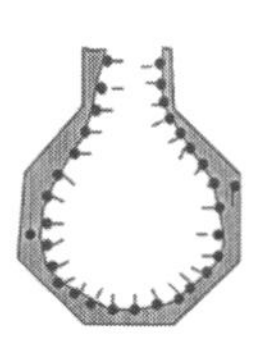

FIGURE 22–5. Data from in vitro and in vivo experiments strongly suggest that the defective Na^+ transport is a mechanism that, in addition to relative surfactant deficiency, leads to the development of respiratory distress syndrome (RDS) in the prematurely born infant. In mature-term infants, the "normal" amount of surfactant is approximately 10-fold greater than that in preterm fetuses or adults. This difference enables the infant to survive its "neonatal salt water drowning" that results from its fluid-filled lungs. A normal fluid (Na) reabsorptive capacity then clears the lung liquid. In transient tachypnea of the newborn, an abnormally slow clearance of lung liquid occurs; however, the large amount of surfactant still results in normal surface tension at the air-liquid interface. This results in mild to moderate respiratory distress that resolves within 24 to 48 hours, as Na^+-transport rapidly matures. In contrast, if both inadequate fluid (Na^+) reabsorption and a relative surfactant deficiency occur, the premature infant develops a severe RDS (hyaline membrane disease) that typically is characterized by severe lung injury. (Reproduced with the permission of Blackwell Science, Inc. from O'Brodovich H.[16])

The observations that TTN was associated with and caused by excess residual fetal lung liquid combined with the observation that, in contrast to previously held beliefs, the lymphatics cleared only minimal amounts of air space fluid at birth,[92] suggested that other mechanisms for "retained fetal lung liquid" might be involved. It was discovered[49] that infants with TTN had significantly lower amiloride-sensitive PD across the nasal epithelium relative to control infants without TTN, and that this amiloride-sensitive PD increased as the infants recovered from their disease (see above for discussion on nasal PD measurements). These observations suggested that TTN resulted from immaturity in the capacity of the respiratory epithelium to actively transport Na^+ (with Cl^- and water following). Since infants with TTN have the same amounts of surfactant as other newborn infants (ie, approximately 10-fold more than the amount present in premature or adult lungs,[80] these infants had sufficient surface active material in the distal regions of the lung, so that acute lung injury and increases in alveolar capillary permeability did not occur. The excess fluid would then slowly be transported out of the lungs, both by the relatively inefficient Na^+-transport system and by transepithelial forces likely arising from the miniscule protein content of the fetal lung liquid (see Table 22–1). The protein concentration of fetal lung liquid is approximately the same as that in cerebral spinal fluid.[21] The approximately 100-fold difference in protein concentration between the fetal lung liquid and interstitial fluid would result in a significant protein-generated transepithelial osmotic pressure. This also could explain the two phases of fetal lung liquid clearance that occur at birth, one of which is amiloride sensitive while the other is amiloride insensitive.[16]

Proposed Model for the Etiology of Respiratory Distress at Birth

All newborn infants have significant amounts of salt-containing fluid within the air spaces of the lungs. The more immature the newborn infant, the greater the lung water burden.[93] Some of these infants, especially those who are preterm, have insufficient amounts of surface active material within their air spaces. These two observations, along with our improved understanding of the ability of the human respiratory epithelium to transport Na^+,[47] permits one to speculate on pathogenesis of non-infective respiratory distress syndromes in the newborn infant (Figure 22–5).[16]

Cystic Fibrosis

Cystic fibrosis (CF), the most common fatal genetic disease in Caucasians, occurs in approximately 1 of 2,000 Caucasian births. The median survival of patients treated in Canadian and US CF clinics is approximately 30 years, despite advances in our understanding of the disease and new therapeutic modalities. Although abnormalities are seen in other exocrine organs of the body (eg, the pancreas, sweat glands, vas deferens, and liver), death results from a progressive chronic suppurative pulmonary disease in more than 95% of patients. The reader is referred to a detailed review of the fundamental mechanisms of CF and its clinical manifestations and treatment.[94]

Historic Overview

Cystic fibrosis was recognized as a distinct disease during the early part of this century; however, in retrospect, there are references to this disorder several hundreds of years ago. Cystic fibrosis was thought to be a "curse," and folklore from the middle ages predicted early death for infants who tasted salty when kissed. During the early 1900s, clinicians and pathologists recognized that there were groups of Caucasian infants who died from various disorders in different organ systems that had a common feature of exocrine gland dysfunction. The disorder was referred to by different names including cystic fibrosis of the pancreas, mucoviscidosis, and ultimately CF. It was recognized that the major clinical symptoms of CF resulted, in large part, from the involvement of two organs where there were abnormalities in both the amount and characteristics of the organ's mucus secretions. In the lung there was excess tenacious mucus and bronchiectasis, with associated acute and chronic bacterial infection. The gastrointestinal tract was unable to absorb food normally and the abnormal intraluminal secretions frequently led to obstruction either at birth (meconium ileus) or during later life (distal intestinal obstructive syndrome). The primary abnormality leading to the gastrointestinal manifestations of CF is the abnormal pancreatic secretions that destroy the exocrine function of the pancreas. Another key characteristic of CF was identified in the 1940s during a heat wave in New York City, when many infants presented to the hospital with heat prostration. Astute clinical investigators discovered that the cause was excess salt and water loss from the sweat glands rather than from the kidneys or gastrointestinal tract. Their observations ultimately led to the development of the principal diagnostic test for CF, the "sweat test," where pharmacologic and electrical stimulation of the skin's sweat glands produces fluid with abnormally high Cl^- and Na^+ concentrations.

Between 1960 and 1980 there was an ever-improving understanding of the functional abnormalities of the affected organs, which in turn, led to new approaches to care (eg, improved nutrition, regular physiotherapy, and aggressive use of antibiotics) with an associated dramatic improvement in survival. However, the survival rates have been largely unchanged over the past decade, despite the appearance of new therapies, including new mucus-thinning agents and anti-inflammatory drugs, and primitive attempts at transferring a functional "wild-type" CF gene to the respiratory epithelium.

Cystic fibrosis is not only the most frequent lethal genetic disease in the Caucasian population, but it is also the archetypical pulmonary disease identified with primary defects in transepithelial ion transport. Our present detailed understanding of the cellular and molecular mechanisms underlying or associated with cystic fibrosis reflects the tremendous effort made by fundamental science and patient-based researchers. A complete review of the aberrations of cellular function associated with CF is beyond the scope of this chapter. The reader is referred to several recent reviews[94–100] and Chapter 21 of this book.

Cystic Fibrosis Lung Disease

Approximately 95% of patients with CF ultimately die from their CF lung disease. The clinical presentations, tests of pulmonary function, and pathology demonstrate that the disease begins in the small airways.[101,102] As the disease progresses, bronchioles and bronchi become increasingly inflamed, infected, and ultimately destroyed in a chronic suppurative disorder. In Western industrialized nations, CF represents the most common cause of bronchiectasis in the pediatric age group and is characterized by a relentless progression through its cylindrical, fusiform, and saccular stages.

Early research suggested that the mucins of the infected lung were more highly sulfated[103] and that the CF sputum was abnormally thick and viscid. However, these observations were found to be secondary to the chronic inflammation/infection with associated cellular (eg, leukocyte) and bacterial debris and, most importantly, the tenacious DNA from dead cells. When compared with other diseases characterized by bronchiectasis, it is uncertain whether the abnormal nature of the sputum is a cause of, or is merely the result of, the chronic inflammation and infection within the lung.

Early studies showed that infants with CF who died shortly after birth for nonpulmonary reasons had slight, but significant, dilation of the acini of their tracheal mucous glands.[104] This observation has become more important since the cloning of the CF gene, because it is now known that certain epithelia within the mucous glands have very high expression of the CF gene. A CF-gene knockout mouse also has demonstrated changes in mucus and an increased number of airway mucus-producing cells prior to clinical infection.[105] These studies support the speculation that there is a primary abnormality in CF mucus or in its secretion. Although it has been suggested that CF cells cannot normally acidify intracellular vesicles,[106,107] thereby causing abnormal glycosylation of proteins, other studies[108,109] have subsequently refuted these observations.

Prior to the cloning of the CF gene, researchers discovered that there were abnormalities in the active transport of ions by the epithelia of some CF organs. In 1981, Knowles et al[110] measured the nasal respiratory transepithelial PD and demonstrated that it was abnormally high in CF and that the abnormal elevation was due to a marked increase in the amiloride-sensitive PD. These observations,[110] along with the identification of Cl^- impermeability in CF sweat glands by Quinton and Bijman,[111,112] solidified the two predominant characteristic defects in CF epithelial ion transport, specifically Na^+ hyperabsorption and apical membrane Cl^- impermeability in the respiratory epithelium, and Cl^- impermeability of the sweat gland.

Identification of the Genetic Defect

The search for the genetic cause of CF took place over many years. The initial breakthrough came when Tsui and co-workers localized the gene to chromosome 7 using restriction fragment length polymorphisms.[113,114] Several research groups around the world intensified their efforts to identify the gene within this vast area of genomic DNA. In 1989, the research group led by Tsui and Riordan, in collaboration with Collins' group at the University of Michigan, published three papers[115–117] outlining the normal (wild-type) and defective CF gene. The

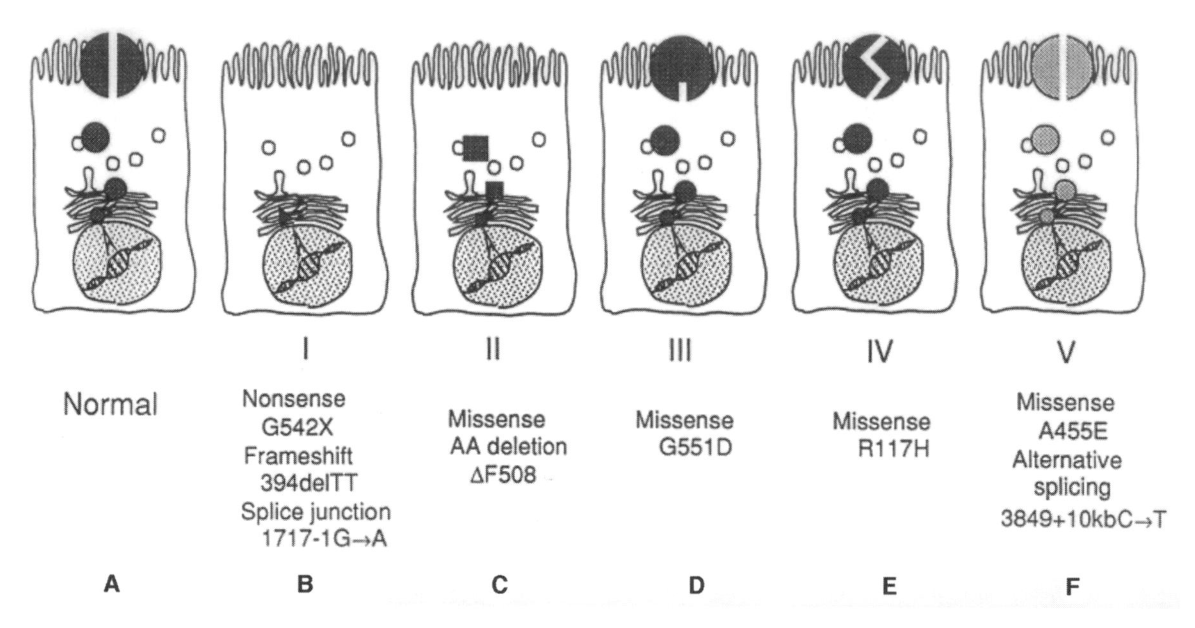

Figure 22–6. Molecular consequences of *CFTR* mutations. *A*, CFTR correctly positioned at the apical membrane of an epithelial cell, functioning as a chloride channel. *B*, Class I: no *CFTR* messenger ribonucleic acid or no CFTR protein formed (eg, nonsense, frameshift, or splice site mutation). *C*, Class II: trafficking defect. *CFTR* messenger ribonucleic acid formed, but protein fails to traffic to cell membrane. *D*, Class III: regulation defect. CFTR reaches the cell membrane but fails to respond to cAMP stimulation. *E*, Class IV: channel defect. CFTR functions as an altered chloride channel. *F*, Class V: synthesis defect. Reduced synthesis or defective processing of normal CFTR. Chloride channel properties are normal. (Reproduced with permission from Wilschanski M et al.[21])

investigators used the DNA sequence to develop a theoretic model for the structure of the protein encoded by the CF gene. As a result of the analysis of this predicted model, the gene became known as the cystic fibrosis transmembrane regulator (*CFTR*). Although there has now been more than 10 years of intensive research since the identification of the *CFTR* gene, the critical in vivo biologic function remains unknown. In other words, we still do not know how the loss of *CFTR* function causes the clinical manifestations of CF. Is it a result of its inability to function as a Cl^--permeant ion channel in either cytoplasmic or intracellular membranes? Is it because it no longer functions as a membrane transporter? Or is it because it fails to normally regulate the function of other intracellular or extracellular proteins? Perhaps there is a biologic function of *CFTR* that has yet to be discovered.

Initial Observations of the Function of the Protein Encoded by *CFTR*

After *CFTR* was identified, Rich and co-workers[118] demonstrated that transfecting wild-type *CFTR* cDNA into CF cells could correct the electrophysiologic abnormalities of the cytoplasmic membrane of the CF epithelial cell. Specifically, Cl^- channel activity could be detected; however, it was unknown if this was due to CFTR functioning as a Cl^- channel or whether CFTR was carrying out its regulatory function and inducing the insertion or activation of a pre-existing non-CFTR Cl^- channel into the cytoplasmic membrane. This question was answered by work by Bear et al[119] who provided direct proof that the protein encoded by *CFTR* could function as a Cl^--permeant ion channel. They demonstrated that CFTR could function as an ion channel with relative anion permeabilities of $NO_3 > Br \geq Cl^- > I >>$ gluconate and possessed a nonrectifying conductance of approximately 6 to 8 pS. The first insight as to how the most common *CFTR* mutation (ΔF508) affects CFTR was made by Kartner et al.[120] They demonstrated that, in contrast to wild-type CFTR, virtually no ΔF508 *CFTR* reached the cytoplasmic membrane of CF cells. At that time, it was clear that the ΔF508 mutation in *CFTR* was a "protein trafficking disorder" in which the CFTR protein was synthesized in the endoplasmic reticulum but was not normally "trafficked" to the cytoplasmic membrane.

Genetic Defects in *CFTR*

As of July 2000 there have been 913 different mutations identified in the *CFTR* gene of CF patients. The ever-increasing number and the characteristics of the mutations have been generated by the 130 groups representing the Cystic Fibrosis Genetic Analysis Consortium and are accessible on its web site <http://www.genet.sickkids.on.ca/cftr/>. The identification of the various mutations allowed clinicians and basic scientists to work together to correlate the genotype with the subsequent abnormalities in CFTR protein.

Cystic fibrosis gene mutations are classified into one of five different families (Figure 22–6).[121] Class I CF mutations reflect synthetic defects and result from premature stop codons or nonsense mutations in the CF gene. As a result the mRNA, which is unstable, is rapidly degraded and no CFTR protein is made. Common nonsense mutations include W1282X and G542X, the former of which is present in 60% of all CF chromosomes of the Ashkenazi Jewish population.[122] This is an interesting class of mutations, as it has been discovered[123,124] that aminoglycoside antibiotics can decrease the efficiency of the premature translation termination at the nonsense mutations, thereby augmenting the amount of full-length CFTR protein synthesized. These findings are now being pursued in clinical trials.[125]

Class II *CFTR* mutations are best termed "processing" or "trafficking" mutations. In this group the mRNA is synthesized and the CFTR protein is translated and synthesized in the endoplasmic reticulum; however, less than 1% of the defective CFTR protein is trafficked to the plasma membrane.[120] The commonest CF gene defect, termed ΔF508-CFTR, is a class II mutation in which a phenylalanine residue is missing in the defective CFTR protein. The intracellular trafficking of CFTR can be modulated by several approaches. CFTR chaperone proteins (eg, calnexin[126] and heat shock protein 70[127]) can enhance the biosynthetic pathway and trafficking to the cytoplasmic membrane. Similarly, lowering ambient temperatures to between 23°C and 27°C can increase the amount of ΔF508-CFTR trafficked to the plasma membrane temperature.[128,129] Compounds such as 8-cyclopentyl-1,3-dipropylxanthine (CPX) can improve the intracellular trafficking of ΔF508-CFTR, thus inducing Cl^- transport across the apical membrane of ΔF508-CFTR cells.[130]

Class III *CFTR* mutations can be termed "regulatory" mutations of *CFTR*. The class III CFTR proteins are synthesized normally and are trafficked to the cytoplasmic membrane; however, cAMP cannot activate the CFTR Cl^- channel and increase transmembrane Cl^- transport. The most common class III mutant is G551D, and it is associated with a severe clinical phenotype.

Class IV *CFTR* mutations, such as R117H, are associated with a relatively mild clinical phenotype. Patients with R117H-CFTR frequently have pancreatic sufficiency.[131] Class IV mutations can be termed "conduction" defects; they have reduced Cl^- transport in response to cAMP. It has been shown that although ΔF508-CFTR is predominately a class II mutation, it also has a mild conduction defect. The open probability (P_O) of a ΔF508-CFTR Cl^- channel is only about half that of wild-type CFTR.[129]

Class V *CFTR* mutations have decreased efficiency in mRNA transcription and subsequent RNA processing and splicing. Splicing of RNA refers to the removal of the introns from the initial RNA transcript and the attaching of the various exons together in the correct order, so that a normal *CFTR* mRNA is made. Two of the best known class V *CFTR* mutations are the 3849+10kbC→T, and the polythymidine mutations, in which there are only five thymidines as opposed to the usual seven thymidines at the intron-exon splice site.[132,133] Both of these mutations, as with other class V mutations, have impaired RNA-splicing efficiency and/or they use alternative splice sites. These class V RNA-processing defects decrease the amount of CFTR protein to varying degrees. For the 3849+10kbC→T mutation, the mRNA levels are only 5 to 10% of those found in comparable cells from normal subjects. This amount of mRNA appears to be near the threshold for the manifestations of clinical disease. Small differences in the mRNA levels lead to markedly different phenotypic expressions, ranging from isolated congenital bilateral absence of the vas deferens[132,133] to typical CF lung and pancreatic disease.

Biologic Mechanism of Cystic Fibrosis Lung Disease

Although it is beyond question that mutations of *CFTR* ultimately result in the clinical manifestations of CF, the actual pathophysiologic mechanisms are unknown. There are several competing theories that separately or together may explain the clinical phenotype. One of the favored theories for CF lung disease is that the absence of a normally functioning apical membrane CFTR Cl^- channel decreases the amount of Cl^- (with Na^+ and water following) being secreted into the airway lumen. This, combined with the inability of CFTR protein to regulate ENaC activity with concomitant Na^+ hyperabsorption,[110,134] an increased number of electrically active Na^+ channels,[135] and fluid hyperabsorption by CF epithelium[136] decreases the amount of fluid bathing the lower parts of the cilia (Figure 22–7). This presumably leads to an inability of the cilium to normally transport the overlying mucus, with resultant infection, epithelial damage, and inflammatory cell influx. However, there are several interesting caveats to this argument. For example, the highest *CFTR* mRNA expression is found in the mucous glands of the trachea. However, the initial lesion in CF lung disease occurs in the small bronchioles,[101,102] and these airways are devoid of mucous glands. This theory of inadequate airway surface liquid film has been reviewed recently in detail by Boucher.[137]

The Boucher model for CF lung disease assumes an isotonic absorption of the airway luminal fluid; however, Smith and co-workers have data suggesting that the absorption of electrolytes and water does not occur on a one-to-one basis, resulting in hypotonic ASL in normal (ie, non-CF) individuals.[138,139] In this latter model (Figure 22–8), the fluid overlying the CF epithelium has much higher Na^+ and Cl^- concentrations relative to fluid overlying normal respiratory epithelia.[138,139] In cell culture systems the elevated Na^+ and Cl^- concentrations have been

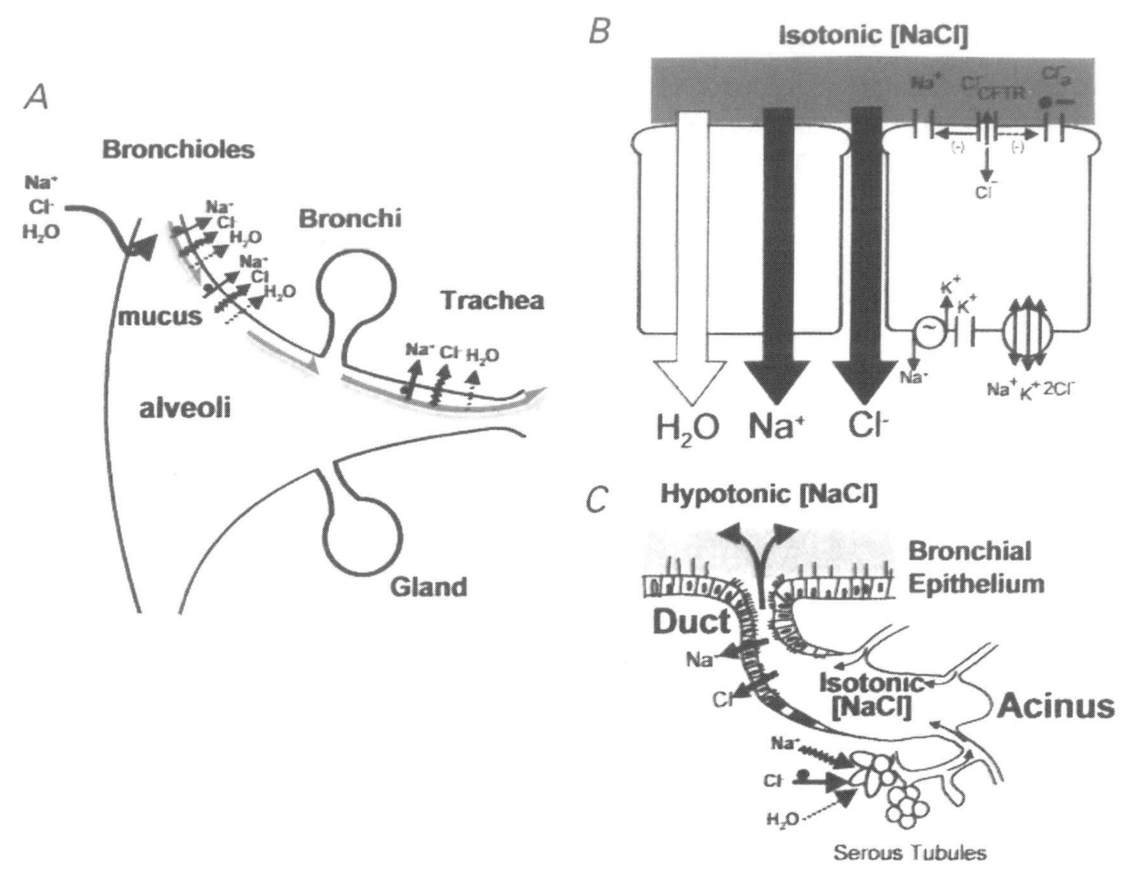

Figure 22–7. The isotonic volume transport model. *A*, Organ-level description. The relative surface areas (not to scale) of the different regions are shown. Both components (isotonic perciliary liquid and mucus) of airway surface liquid (ASL) are represented as being transported cephalad on pulmonary surfaces. In the airways, the mechanisms for absorption from the ASL are driven by active Na^+ absorption, with Cl^- and water accompanying passively. The bronchioles are shown as absorptive. Liquid could be secreted in either very distal bronchiolar regions or, as depicted, on alveolar surfaces. *B*, Model of superficial airway epithelial cells mediating isotonic volume transport. The basolateral Na^+-K^+ adenosinetriphosphatase generates the driving force for Na^+ entry across the apical membrane, which is mediated by epithelial Na^+ channel (ENaC). Both functions of *CFTR*, as a Cl^- channel (Cl_{CFTR}) and as a regulator of ENaC (Na^+), and the alternative (Ca-activated) Cl^- channel (Cl^-_a) are depicted on the apical membrane. Active Na^+ absorption is transcellular, whereas anion flow is partly cellular but largely transcellular. The epithelium is quite permeable to water, permitting isosmotic volume transport. Hence, the ASL is designated as isotonic [NaCl]. C, Submucosal gland. Isotonic volume secretion, which probably reflects a significant contribution from serous tubules expressing *CFTR* located in the acinar region. The gland ducts are represented as absorbing NaCl but not water, resulting in a hypotonic secretion. (Reproduced with permission from Boucher RC.[137])

shown to impair the function of key innate defense mechanisms against infection, specifically the function of defensins. The hypertonic model of CF ASL is attractive from a mechanistic point of view, as it links an electrolyte transport dysfunction with a propensity for infection. However, there are also major limitations to this model. The model does not take into account the fact that the major innate defense mechanisms of the surface lining fluid of the lung are larger proteins, such as lysozymes and surfactant protein A, and not defensins. The defensin theory also does not consider the unique predilection of the CF lung for infection by unusual (*Pseudomonas aeruginosa* and *Burkholderia cepacia*) and common (*Staphylococcus aureus*) bacteria that characterize CF lung disease. Whether inhibition of defensins by abnormal surface fluid electrolyte concentrations plays a predominant or a synergistic role with other phenomena (eg, enhanced adherence of *Pseudomonas* to the respiratory epithelia pili and respiratory epithelia cells,[140–143] abnormalities in cytokine and inflammatory mediator release,[144–150] or an intracellular epithelial defect in resisting infection[151]) requires further study. The reader is referred to a review article[99] for more discussion.

Whether either the isotonic or hypertonic model of CF airway surface lining fluid is correct is unknown. Regrettably, one cannot rely on studies from other organs. In some epithelia, such as toad skin,[152] the net transport of Na^+ is associated with isosmotic fluid transport. In contrast, the epithelium of the sweat duct absorbs more Na^+ and Cl^- than water and generates hypotonic sweat.[153] Experiments attempting to directly measure the relation between Na^+ and fluid transport by

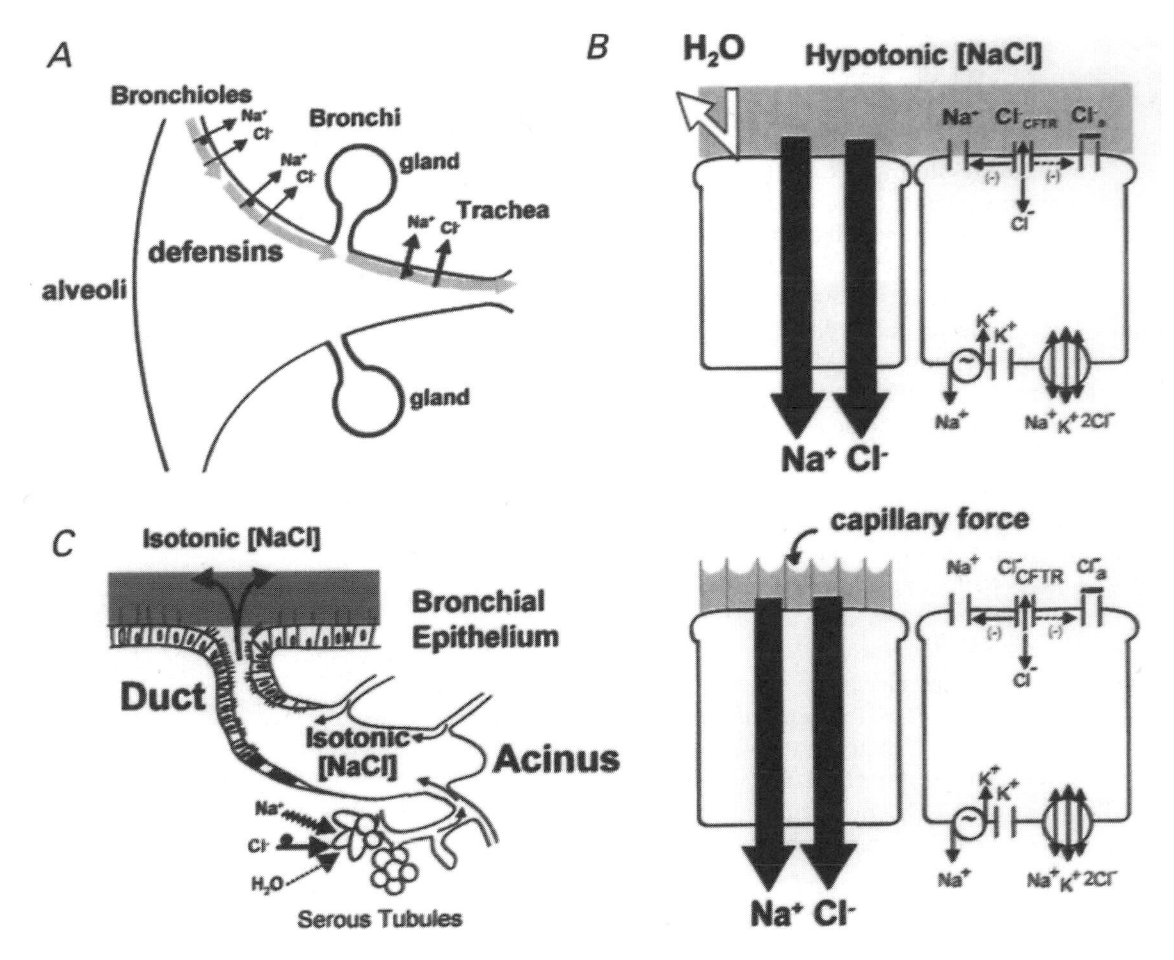

Figure 22–8. The hypotonic airway surface liquid physiology. *A*, Organ-level description. The epithelium lining airway surfaces is represented as absorbing $NaCl^-$ but not water from the airway surface liquid (ASL). Antimicrobial substances (defensins) are shown, which are active in the "low salt" environment. No arrows depicting surface liquid clearance are shown, due to the inability of the cell models to deal with volume absorption or a mucous layer. *B*, Cell models postulated to explain the production of hypotonic ASL. *Top*: The "sweat ductal" model. The key elements are the transcellular absorption of Na^+ (via epithelial Na^+ channel [ENaC]) and Cl^- (via CFTR) and epithelial water impermeability (*deflected arrow*). *Bottom:* The "surface forces" model. Outstretched cilia are depicted on the left cell that generate small radius (<0 to 1 μm) menisci at an air-water interface of high surface tension. NaCl is absorbed transcellularly, and osmotic force generated to absorb H_2O from the airway surface is balanced by "capillary" forces generated by the menisci, resulting in a low [NaCl] ASL. *C*, Submucosal glands. This model might predict isotonic gland secretion. Presumably, this process adds volume to the surface, and compositional modification (lowering [NaCl]) is performed by the superficial epithelium. (Reproduced with permission from Boucher RC.[137])

the airway and air space epithelial membranes have not yielded consistent results; authors have concluded that the human airway surface fluid's ion concentrations is hypotonic, isotonic, or hypertonic.[139,153–156]

There is incontrovertible evidence that mutations in *CFTR* cause the ultimate manifestations of CF lung disease. However, it is uncertain whether it is directly due to a loss of function of the CFTR protein (eg, inability to conduct Cl^- ions through the apical membrane) or whether it arises from some indirect secondary effect (eg, through the lack of the normal regulation of another critical cell function). Examples of indirect effects would be the modulation of *Pseudomonas* adherence to pili, the cellular inflammatory response, and inability to appropriately regulate Na^+ or bicarbonate transport. A lack of normal CFTR function also may be responsible for the findings that the outwardly rectifying chloride channel (ORCC) is uniformly absent in CF epithelium.[157–159] Since the ORCC has yet to be cloned, it is uncertain how the functions of *CFTR*-encoded transporters/channels and the ORCC are linked. However, it is known that changes in temperature[128,129] or cAMP concentrations[160] modulate both the CFTR channel and the ORCC. Similarly, changes in adenosine nucleotides can modulate Cl^- currents in cells, a process likely involving the ORCC.[161–163] More work is required to identify any pathogenic role of the lack of ORCC function in CF lung disease. In contrast to the abnormal regulation of ORCC and ENaC in CF epithelium, the calcium-activated Cl^- channel normally present in respiratory epithelium is present and functions normally in CF epithelium,[50,110] and studies are underway to assess whether pharmacologic manipulation of the calcium-activated Cl^- channel can alter the CF phenotype.[164,165]

At present it is unknown how the absence of a functional CFTR molecule results in increased Na^+ absorption by the respiratory epithelium of humans with CF[110] or *CFTR*-knockout transgenic mice.[166] It has yet to be proved that there is a direct molecule-to-molecule interaction of CFTR with ENaC. However, it is known that the presence of a normal CFTR molecule markedly alters the epithelium's Na^+ absorptive response to cAMP.[167] The only available study from humans, in which samples from several CF patients were pooled into a single sample, showed that the mRNA encoding ENaC is actually downregulated in CF relative to normal epithelium.[168]

It has now been more than a decade since the CF gene has been identified and, despite optimistic predictions at the time, regrettably there has been extremely little impact on the clinical care of patients with this lethal disorder. We can now provide improved genetic screening and counseling, and there has been some genotype-phenotype information in regard to the manifestations of pancreatic[169,170] and sweat Cl^- concentrations.[121] Another advance is that we can identify the 1 to 2% of all CF patients who have a sweat Cl^- concentration within the "normal range." For decades physicians had been puzzled by the rare patient who appeared to have the CF phenotype, yet, upon repeated sweat Cl^- analysis, had shown only mild elevations (40 to 60 mEq/L) or what had been believed to be entirely normal sweat Cl^- concentrations (< 40 mEq/L). It is now recognized that many of these patients have the class V mutation in their *CFTR* gene.

A slow pace of progress in the clinical arena following the discovery of a fundamental cause of a pediatric disease is not without precedent. Avery and Mead identified a relative deficiency in surface active material in premature infants dying of HMD in 1959.[59] However, it took approximately 30 years of fundamental science research before Fujiwara et al[171] conducted the critical clinical pilot study that culminated in today's successes related to exogenous surfactant therapy of HMD.[80] Hopefully a similar but more rapid scenario will unfold in response to our improved understanding of CF lung disease.

References

1. O'Brodovich H. Epithelial ion transport in the fetal and perinatal lung. Am J Physiol 1991;261:C555–64.
2. Strang LB. Fetal lung liquid: secretion and reabsorption. Physiol Rev 1991;71:991–1016.
3. Olver RE, Ramsden CA, Strang LB, Walters DV. The role of amiloride-blockade sodium transport in adrenaline-induced lung liquid reabsorption in the fetal lamb. J Physiol (Lond) 1986;376:321–40.
4. O'Brodovich H, Rafii B, Post M. Bioelectric properties of fetal alveolar epithelial monolayers. Am J Physiol 1990; 258:L201–6.
5. O'Brodovich H, Staub O, Rossier B, et al. Ontogeny of alpha1- and beta1- isoforms of Na/K ATPase in fetal distal lung epithelium. Am J Physiol 1993;264:C1137–43.
6. Bland RD, Boyd CAR. Cation transport in lung epithelial cells derived from fetal, newborn, and adult rabbits. J Appl Physiol 1986;61:507–15.
7. Cassin S, Gause G, Perks AM. The effects of bumetanide and furosemide on lung liquid secretion in fetal sheep. Proc Soc Exp Biol Med 1986;181:427–31.
8. O'Brodovich H, Rafii B. Effect of K channel blockers on basal and beta agonist stimulated ion transport by fetal lung epithelium. Can J Physiol Pharmacol 1993;71:54–7.
9. Tohda H, Foskett JK, O'Brodovich H, Marunaka Y. Cl^- regulation of a Ca^{2+} activate non selective cation channel in β agonist treated fetal lung alveolar epithelium. Am J Physiol 1994;266:C104–9.
10. Matthay MA, Folkesson HG, Verkman AS. Salt and water transport across alveolar and distal airway epithelia in the adult lung. Am J Physiol 1996;270:L487–503.
11. Hasegawa H, Ma TH, Skach W, et al. Molecular cloning of a mercurial-insensitive water channel expressed in selected water-transporting tissues. J Biol Chem 1994; 269:5497–500.
12. Frigeri A, Gropper MA, Turck CW, Verkman AS. Immunolocalization of the mercurial-insensitive water channel and glycerol intrinsic protein in epithelial cell plasma membranes. Proc Natl Acad Sci U S A 1995; 92:4328–31.
13. Ruddy MK, Drazen JM, Pitkänen O, et al. Modulation of aquaporin 4 and the amiloride-inhibitable Na^+ channel in perinatal rat lung epithelial cells. Am J Physiol 1998; 274:L1066–72.
14. Yasui M, Serlachius E, Lofgren M, et al. Perinatal changes in expression of aquaporin-4 and other water and ion transporters in rat lung. J Physiol (Lond) 1997;505:3–11.
15. Raina S, Preston GM, Guggino WB, Agre P. Molecular cloning and characterization of an aquaporin cDNA from salivary, lacrimal, and respiratory tissues. J Biol Chem 1995;270:1908–12.
16. O'Brodovich H. Immature epithelial Na^+ channel expression is one of the pathogenic mechanisms leading to human neonatal respiratory distress syndrome. Pro Assoc Am Physicians 1996;108:345–55.
17. O'Brodovich H, Hannam V, Rafii B. Sodium channel but neither Na^+-H^+ nor Na-glucose symport inhibitors slow neonatal lung water clearance. Am J Respir Cell Mol Biol 1991;5:377–84.
18. Wang X, Kleyman T, Tohda H, et al. 5-(N-Ethyl-N-isopropyl) amiloride-sensitive Na^+ currents in intact fetal distal lung epithelial cells. Can J Physiol Pharmacol 1993;71:58–62.
19. Barker PM, Boyd CAR, Ramsden CA, et al. Pulmonary glucose transport in the fetal sheep. J Physiol (Lond) 1989; 409:15–27.
20. Jost PA, Policard A. Contribution experimentale a l'étude du developpement prenatal du poumon chez le lapin. Arch D'Anatomie Microscopique 1948;37:323–32.
21. Adamson TM, Boyd RDH, Platt HS, Strang LB. Composition of alveolar liquid in the foetal lamb. J Physiol (Lond) 1969;204:159–68.

22. O'Brodovich H, Merritt TA. Bicarbonate concentration in rhesus monkey and guinea pig fetal lung liquid. Am Rev Respir Dis 1992;146:1613–4.
23. Cotton CU, Boucher RC, Gatzy JT. Bioelectric properties and ion transport across excised canine fetal and neonatal airways. J Appl Physiol 1988;65:2367–75.
24. Olver RE, Strang LB. Ion fluxes across the pulmonary epithelium and the secretion of lung liquid in the fetal lamb. J Physiol (Lond) 1974;241:327–57.
25. Brown MJ, Olver RE, Ramsden CA, et al. Effects of adrenaline and of spontaneous labour on the secretion and absorption of lung liquid in the fetal lamb. J Physiol (Lond) 1983;344:137–52.
26. Walters DV, Ramsden CA, Olver RE. Dibutyryl cAMP induces a gestation-dependent absorption of fetal lung liquid. J Appl Physiol 1990;68:2054–9.
27. Chapman DL, Carlton DP, Cummings JJ, et al. Intrapulmonary terbutaline and aminophylline decrease lung liquid in fetal lambs. Pediatr Res 1991;29:357–61.
28. Perks AM, Cassin S. The effects of arginine vasopressin and other factors on the production of lung liquid in fetal goats. Chest 1982;81:63–5S.
29. Hooper SB, Wallace MJ, Harding R. Amiloride blocks the inhibition of fetal lung liquid secretion caused by AVP but not by asphyxia. J Appl Physiol 1993;74:111–5.
30. O'Brodovich H, Rafii B, Perlon P. Arginine vasopressin and atrial natriuretic peptide do not alter ion transport by cultured fetal distal lung epithelium. Pediatr Res 1992; 31:318–22.
31. Strang LB, Barker PM. Invited editorial on "Amiloride inhibitis arginine vasopressin-induced decrease in fetal lung liquid secretion". J Appl Physiol 1993;75:1923–4.
32. Barker PM, Gatzy JT. Effect of gas composition on liquid secretion by explants of distal lung of fetal rat in submersion culture. Am J Physiol 1993;265:L512–7.
33. Rafii B, Tanswell AK, Otulakowski G, et al. O_2-induced Na^+ channel expression is associated with Nf-κB activation and blocked by superoxide scavenger. Am J Physiol 1998; 275:L764–70.
34. Planes C, Escoubet B, Blot-Chabaud M, et al. Hypoxia downregulates expression and activity of epithelial sodium channels in rat alveolar epithelial cells. Am J Respir Cell Mol Biol 1997;16:1–11.
35. Tomlinson LA, Carpenter TC, Baker EH, et al. Hypoxia reduces airway epithelial sodium transport in rats. Am J Physiol Lung Cell Mol Physiol 1999;277:L881–6.
36. Rafii B, Coutinho C, Otulakowski G, O'Brodovich H. Oxygen induction of epithelial Na^+ transport requires heme proteins. Am J Physiol Lung Cell Mol Physiol 2000;278:L399–406.
37. O'Brodovich H, Mullen JBM, Hannam V, Goodman BE. Active $^{22}Na^+$ transport by the intact lung during early postnatal life. Can J Physiol Pharmacol 1997;75:431–5.
38. Mason R, Williams MC, Widdicombe JH, et al. Transepithelial transport by pulmonary alveolar type II cells in primary culture. Proc Natl Acad Sci U S A 1982; 79:6033–7.
39. Matthay MA, Landolt CC, Staub NC. Differential liquid and protein clearance from the alveoli of anesthetized sheep. J Appl Physiol 1982;53:96–104.
40. Berthiaume Y, Staub NC, Matthay MA. Beta-adrenergic agonists increase lung liquid clearance in anesthetized sheep. J Clin Invest 1987;79:335–43.
41. Goodman BE, Fleischer RS, Crandall ED. Evidence for active Na^+ transport by cultured monolayers of pulmonary alveolar epithelial cells. Am J Physiol 1983;245:C78–83.
42. Garat C, Carter EP, Matthay MA. New in situ mouse model to quantify alveolar epithelial fluid clearance. J Appl Physiol 1998;84:1763–7.
43. Matthay MA, Wiener-Kronish JP. Intact epithelial barrier function is critical for the resolution of alveolar edema in man. Am Rev Respir Dis 1990;142:1250–7.
44. Boucher RC. Human airway ion transport. Am J Respir Crit Care Med 1994;150:271–81.
45. Boucher RC. Human airway ion transport. Am J Respir Crit Care Med 1994;150:581–93.
46. Knowles M, Carson JL, Collier AM, et al. Measurements of nasal transepithelial electric potential difference in normal human subjects *in vivo*. Am Rev Respir Dis 1981; 124:484–90.
47. Barker PM, Gowen CW, Lawson EE, Knowles M. Decreased sodium ion absorption across nasal epithelium of very premature infants with respiratory distress syndrome. J Pediatr 1997;130:373–7.
48. Boucher RC, Bromberg PA, Gatzy JT. Airway transepithelial electric potential in vivo: species and regional differences. J Appl Physiol 1980;48:169–76.
49. Gowen CW, Lawson EE, Gingras J, et al. Electrical potential difference and ion transport across nasal epithelium of term neonates: correlation with mode of delivery, transient tachypnea of the newborn, and respiratory rate. J Pediatr 1988;113:121–7.
50. Knowles M, Paradiso AM, Boucher RC. In vivo nasal potential difference: techniques and protocols for assessing efficacy of gene transfer in cystic fibrosis. Hum Gene Ther 1995;6:445–55.
51. Otulakowski G, Flueckiger-Staub S, Ellis L, et al. Relation between α, β, and gamma human amiloride-sensitive epithelial Na^+ channel mRNA levels and nasal epithelial potential difference in healthy men. Am J Respir Crit Care Med 1998;158:1213–20.
52. Pitkänen O, Smith D, O'Brodovich H, Otulakowski G. Expression of α, β, and γ = hENaC mRNA in the human nasal, bronchial, and distal lung epithelium. Am J Respir Crit Care Med 2001;163:273–6.
53. Canessa CM, Schild L, Buell G, et al. Amiloride-sensitive epithelial Na^+ channel is made of three homologous subunits. Nature 1994;367:463–7.
54. Alcorn D, Adamson TM, Lambert TF, et al. Morphological effects of chronic tracheal ligation and drainage in the fetal lamb lung. J Anat 1977;123:649–60.
55. Moessinger AC, Harding R, Adamson TM, et al. Role of lung fluid volume in growth and maturation of the fetal sheep lung. J Clin Invest 1990;86:1270–7.
56. Wigglesworth JS, Desai R, Hislop A. Fetal lung growth in congenital laryngeal atresia. Pediatr Pathol 1987;7:515–25.
57. Moessinger AC, Collin MH, Blanc WA, et al. Oligohydramnios-induced lung hypoplasia: the influence of timing and duration in gestation. Pediatr Res 1986; 20:951–4.

58. Souza P, O'Brodovich H, Post M. Lung fluid restriction affects growth but not airway branching of embryonic rat lung. Int J Dev Biol 1995;39:629–37.
59. Avery ME, Mead J. Surface properties in relation to atelectasis and hyaline membrane disease. Am J Dis Child 1959;97:517–23.
60. O'Brodovich H, Hannam V, Seear M, Mullen JBM. Amiloride impairs lung water clearance in newborn guinea pigs. J Appl Physiol 1990;68:1758–62.
61. Canessa CM, Horisberger JD, Rossier BC. Epithelial sodium channel related to proteins involved in neurodegeneration. Nature 1993;361:467–70.
62. Lingueglia E, Voilley N, Waldmann R, et al. Expression cloning of an epithelial amiloride-sensitive Na^+ channel: a new channel type with homologies to *Caenorhabditis elegans* degenerins. FEBS Lett 1993;318:95–9.
63. Hummler E, Barker P, Gatzy J, et al. Early death due to defective neonatal lung liquid clearance in α*ENaC*-deficient mice. Nat Genet 1996;12:325–8.
64. McDonald FJ, Yang BL, Hrstka RF, et al. Disruption of the β subunit of the epithelial Na^+ channel in mice: hyperkalemia and neonatal death associated with a pseudohypoaldosteronism phenotype. Proc Natl Acad Sci U S A 1999;96:1727–31.
65. Padervand S, Barker PM, Wang Q, et al. Salt restriction induces pseudohypoaldosteronism type 1 in mice expressing low levels of the β-subunit of the amiloride-sensitive epithelial sodium channel. Proc Natl Acad Sci U S A 1999;96:1732–7.
66. Barker PM, Nguyen MS, Gatzy JT, et al. Role of gammaENaC subunit in lung liquid clearance and electrolyte balance in newborn mice. J Clin Invest 1998;102:1634–40.
67. O'Brodovich H, Canessa CM, Ueda J, et al. Expression of the epithelial Na^+ channel in the developing rat lung. Am J Physiol 1993;265:C491–6.
68. Tchepichev S, Ueda J, Canessa CM, et al. Lung epithelial Na^+ channel subunits are differentially regulated during development and by steroids. Am J Physiol 1995; 269:C805–12.
69. Sweezey N, Tchepichev S, Gagnon S, et al. Female gender hormones regulate mRNA levels and function of the rat lung epithelial Na^+ channels. Am J Physiol 1998; 274:C379–86.
70. Champigny G, Voilley N, Lingueglia E, et al. Regulation of expression of the lung amiloride-sensitive Na^+channel by steroid hormones. EMBO J 1994;13:2177–81.
71. Lingueglia E, Renard S, Waldmann R, et al. Different homologous subunits of the amiloride-sensitive Na^+ channel are differently regulated by aldosterone. J Biol Chem 1994;269:13736–9.
72. Renard S, Voilley N, Bassilana F, et al. Localization and regulation by steroids of the α, β and γ subunits of the amiloride-sensitive Na^+ channel in colon, lung and kidney. Pflugers Arch 1995;430:299–307.
73. Kizer N, Guo XL, Hruska K. Reconstitution of stretch-activated cation channels by expression of the α-subunit of the epithelial sodium channel cloned from osteoblasts. Proc Natl Acad Sci U S A 1997;94:1013–8.
74. Ishikawa T, Marunaka Y, Rotin D. Electrophysiological characterization of the rat epithelial Na^+ channel (rENaC) expressed in MDCK cells—effects of Na^+ and Ca^{2+}. J Gen Physiol 1998;111:825–46.
75. Matalon S, Bauer M, Benos D, et al. Fetal lung epithelial cells contain two populations of amiloride-sensitive Na^+ channels. Am J Physiol 1993;264:L357–64.
76. Matalon S, O'Brodovich H. Sodium channels in alveolar epithelial cells: molecular characterization, biophysical properties, and physiological significance. Annu Rev Physiol 1999;61:627–61.
77. O'Brodovich H, Mellins RB. Bronchopulmonary dysplasia: unresolved neonatal acute lung injury. Am Rev Respir Dis 1985;132:694–709.
78. Farrell PM, Avery ME. State of the art: hyaline membrane disease. Am Rev Respir Dis 1975;111:657–8.
79. Jefferies AL, Coates G, O'Brodovich H. Pulmonary epithelial permeability in hyaline-membrane disease. N Engl J Med 1984;311:1075–80.
80. Jobe A, Ikegami M. State of the art: surfactant for the treatment of respiratory distress syndrome. Am Rev Respir Dis 1987;136:1256–75.
81. Staub O, Dho S, Henry PC, et al. WW domains of Nedd4 bind to the proline-rich PY motifs in the epithelial Na^+ channel deleted in Liddle's syndrome. EMBO J 1996;15:2371–80.
82. Staub O, Abriel H, Plant PR, et al. Regulation of the epithelial Na^+ channel by Nedd4 and ubiquitination. Kidney Int 2000;57:809–15.
83. Talbot CL, Bosworth DG, Briley EL, et al. Quantitation and localization of ENaC subunit expression in fetal, newborn and adult mouse lung. Am J Respir Cell Mol Biol 1999;20:398–406.
84. Smith DE, Otulakowski G, Yeger H, et al. Epithelial Na^+ channel (ENaC) expression in the developing normal and abnormal human perinatal lung. Am J Respir Crit Care Med 2000;161:1322–31.
85. Curtis D, Lehmann R, Zamore PD. Translational regulation in development. Cell 1995;81:171–8.
86. Wickens M, Kimble J, Strickland S. Translational control of developmental decisions. In: Hershey JWB, Mathrews MB, Sonenberg N, ed. Translational control. Cold Spring Harbor: Cold Spring Harbor Laboratory Press, 1996: 411–50.
87. Barker PM, Brown MJ, Ramsden CA, et al. The effect of thyroidectomy in the fetal sheep on lung liquid reabsorption induced by adrenaline or cyclic AMP. J Physiol (Lond) 1988;407:373–83.
88. Barker PM, Markiewicz M, Parker A, et al. Synergistic action of triiodothyronine and hydrocortisone on epinephrine-induced reabsorption of fetal lung liquid. Pediatr Res 1990;27:588–91.
89. Pitkänen O, Tanswell AK, O'Brodovich H. Fetal lung cell-derived matrix alters distal lung epithelial ion transport. Am J Physiol 1995;268:L762–71.
90. Avery ME, Gatewood O, Brumley G. Transient tachypnea of newborn. Am J Dis Child 1966;111:380–5.
91. Bland RD, Bressack MA, McMillan DD. Labor decreases the lung water content of newborn rabbits. Am J Obstet Gynecol 1979;135:364–7.
92. Bland RD, Hansen TN, Haberkern CM, et al. Lung fluid balance in lambs before and after birth. J Appl Physiol 1982;53:992–1004.

93. deSa DJ. Pulmonary fluid content in infants with respiratory distress. J Pathol 1969;97:469–79.
94. Davis PB, Drumm ML, Konstan MW. Cystic fibrosis. Am J Respir Crit Care Med 1996;154:1229–56.
95. Welsh MJ, Smith AE. Cystic fibrosis. Sci Am 1995;273:52–9.
96. Quinton P. Physiological basis of cystic fibrosis: a historical perspective. Physiol Rev 1999;70(1):S3–22.
97. Rubenstein RC, Zeitlin P. Use of protein repair therapy in the treatment of cystic fibrosis. Curr Opin Pediatr 1998;10:250–5.
98. Gugginio WB. Cystic fibrosis and the salt controversy. Cell 1999;96:607–10.
99. Tummler B, Kiewitz C. Cystic fibrosis: an inherited susceptibility to bacterial respiratory infections. Mol Med Today 1999;5:351–8.
100. Tizzano EF, Buchwald M. *CFTR* expression and organ damage in cystic fibrosis. Ann Intern Med 1995; 123:305–8.
101. Oppenheimer EJ, Esterly JR. Pathology of cystic fibrosis. Review of the literature and comparison of 146 autopsied cases. Perspective Pediatr Pathol 1975;2:241–78.
102. Lamarre A, Reilly BJ, Bryan AC, Levison H. Early detection of pulmonary function abnormalities in cystic fibrosis. Pediatrics 1972;50:291–8.
103. Lamb D, Reid L. The tracheobronchial submucosal glands in cystic fibrosis: a qualitative histochemical study. Br J Dis Chest 1972;66:239–47.
104. Sturgess J, Imrie J. Quantitative evaluation of the development of tracheal submucosal glands in infants with cystic fibrosis and control infants. Am J Pathol 1982;106:303–11.
105. Kent G, Iles R, Bear CE, et al. Lung disease in mice with cystic fibrosis. J Clin Invest 1997;100:3060–9.
106. Barasch J, Kiss B, Prince A, et al. Defective acidification of intracellular organelles in cystic fibrosis. Nature 1991; 352:70–3.
107. Barasch J, Al-Awqati Q. Defective acidification of the biosynthetic pathway in cystic fibrosis. J Cell Sci 1993; 106 Suppl 17:229–33.
108. Lukacs G, Chang X-B, Kartner N, et al. The cystic fibrosis transmembrane regulator is present and functional in endosomes. Role as a determinant of endosomal H. J Biol Chem 1992;267:14568–72.
109. Biwersi J, Verkman AS. Functional CFTR in endosomal compartment of CFTR-expressing fibroblasts and T84 cells. Am J Physiol Cell Physiol 2000;266:C149–56.
110. Knowles M, Gatzy J, Boucher R. Increased bioelectric potential difference across respiratory epithelia in cystic fibrosis. N Engl J Med 1981;305:1489–95.
111. Quinton PM, Bijman J. Higher bioelectric potentials due to decreased chloride absorption in the sweat glands of patients with cystic fibrosis. N Engl J Med 1983; 308:1185–9.
112. Quinton PM. Chloride impermeability in cystic fibrosis. Nature 1983;301:421–2.
113. Knowlton RG, Cohen-Haguenauer O, Nguyen VC, et al. A polymorphic DNA marker linked to cystic fibrosis is located on chromosome 7. Nature 1985;318:380–2.
114. Tsui L-C, Buchwald M, Barker D, et al. Cystic fibrosis locus defined by a genetically linked polymorphic DNA marker. Science 1985;230:1054–7.
115. Rommens JM, Iannuzzi MC, Kerem B-S, et al. Identification of the cystic fibrosis gene: chromosome walking and jumping. Science 1989;245:1059–65.
116. Riordan JR, Rommens JM, Kerem B-S, et al. Identification of the cystic fibrosis gene: cloning and characterization of complementary DNA. Science 1989;245:1066–73.
117. Kerem B-S, Rommens JM, Buchanan JA, et al. Identification of the cystic fibrosis gene: genetic analysis. Science 1989;245:1073–80.
118. Rich DP, Anderson MP, Gregory RJ, et al. Expression of cystic fibrosis transmembrane conductance regulator corrects defective chloride channel regulation in cystic fibrosis airway epithelial cells. Nature 1990;347:358–63.
119. Bear CE, Li C, Kartner N, et al. Purification and functional reconstitution of the cystic fibrosis transmembrane conductance regulator (CFTR). Cell 1992;68:809–18.
120. Kartner N, Augustinas O, Jensen T, et al. Mislocation of delta F508 CFTR in cystic fibrosis sweat gland. Nat Genet 1992;1:321–7.
121. Wilschanski M, Zielenski J, Markiewicz D, et al. Correlation of sweat chloride concentration with classes of the cystic fibrosis transmembrane conductance regulator gene mutations. J Pediatr 1995;127:705–10.
122. Shoshani T, Augarten A, Gazit E, et al. Association of a nonsense mutation (W128X), the most common mutation in the Ashkenazi Jewish cystic fibrosis patients in Israel, with presentation of severe disease. Am J Hum Genet 1992;50:222–8.
123. Howard M, Frizzell RA, Bedwell DM. Aminoglycoside antibiotics restore CFTR function by overcoming premature stop mutations. Nat (Med) 1996;2:467–9.
124. Bedwell DM, Kaenjak A, Benos DJ, et al. Suppression of a CFTR premature stop mutation in a bronchial epithelial cell line. Nat (Med) 1998;3:1280–4.
125. Wilschanski M, Famini C, Blau H, et al. A pilot study of the effect of gentamicin on nasal potential difference measurements in cystic fibrosis patients carrying stop mutations. Am J Respir Crit Care Med 2000;161:860–5.
126. Pind S, Riordan JR, Williams DB. Participation of the endoplasmic reticulum chaperone calnexin (p88 IP90) in the biogenesis of the cystic fibrosis transmembrane conductance regulator. J Biol Chem 1994;269: 12784–8.
127. Yang Y, Janich S, Cohn JA, Wilson JM. The common variant of cystic fibrosis transmembrane conductance regulator is recognized by hsp70 and degraded in a pre-Golgi nonlysosomal compartment. Proc Natl Acad Sci U S A 1993;90:9480–4.
128. Egan ME, Schwiebert EM, Guggino WB. Differential expression of ORCC and CFTR induced by low temperature in CF airway epithelial cells. Am J Physiol 1995;268:C243–51.
129. Denning GM, Anderson MP, Amara JF, et al. Processing of mutant cystic fibrosis transmembrane conductance regulator is temperature-sensitive. Nature 1992;358:761–4.
130. Arispe N, Ma JJ, Jacobson KA, Pollard HB. Direct activation of cystic fibrosis transmembrane conductance regulator channels by 8-cyclopentyl-1,3-dipropylxanthine (CPX) and 1,3-diallyl-8-cyclohexylxanthine (DAX). J Biol Chem 1998;273:5727–34.

131. Sheppard DN, Rich DR, Ostergaard LS, et al. Mutations in CFTR associated with mild-disease-form Cl^- channels with altered pore properties. Nature 1993;362:160–4.
132. Chillon M, Cassals T, Mercier B, et al. Mutations in the cystic fibrosis gene in patients with congenital absence of the vas deferens. N Engl J Med 1995;332:1475–80.
133. Kieswetter S, Macek M Jr, Davis C, et al. A mutation in CFTR produces different phenotypes depending on chromosomal background. Nat Genet 1993;5:274–8.
134. Cotton CU, Stutts MJ, Knowles M, et al. Abnormal apical cell membrane in cystic fibrosis respiratory epithelium. An in vitro electrophysiologic analysis. J Clin Invest 1987;79:80–5.
135. Duszyk M, French AS, Man SFP. Cystic fibrosis affects chloride and sodium channels in human airway epithelia. Can J Physiol Pharmacol 1989;67:1362–5.
136. Matsui H, Grubb BR, Tarran R, et al. Evidence for periciliary liquid layer depletion, not abnormal ion composition, in the pathogenesis of cystic fibrosis airways disease. Cell 1998;95:1005–15.
137. Boucher RC. Molecular insights into the physiology of the 'thin film' of airway surface liquid. J Physiol (Lond) 1999;516:631–8.
138. Smith JJ, Travis SM, Greenberg EP, Welsh MJ. Erratum. Cell 1996;87:100.
139. Smith JJ, Travis SM, Greenberg EP, Welsh MJ. Cystic fibrosis airway epithelia fail to kill bacteria because of abnormal airway surface fluid. Cell 1996;85:229–36.
140. Saiman L, Prince A. *Pseudomonas aeruginosa* pili bind to asialoGM1 which is increased on the surface of cystic fibrosis epithelial cells. J Clin Invest 1993;92: 1875–80.
141. Zar H, Saiman L, Quittell L, Prince A. Binding of *Pseudomonas aeruginosa* to respiratory epithelial cells from patients with various mutations in the cystic fibrosis transmembrane regulator. J Pediatr 1995;126:230–3.
142. Imundo L, Barasch J, Prince A, Al-Awqati Q. Cystic fibrosis epithelial cells have a receptor for pathogenic bacteria on their apical surface. Proc Natl Acad Sci U S A 1995;92:3019–23.
143. Saiman L, Cacalano G, Gruenert D, Prince A. Comparison of adherence of *Pseudomonas aeruginosa* to respiratory epithelial cells from cystic fibrosis patients and healthy subjects. Infect Immunol 1992;60:2808–14.
144. DiMango E, Zar H, Bryan R, Prince A. Diverse *Pseudomonas aeruginosa* gene products stimulate respiratory epithelial cells to produce interleukin-8. J Clin Invest 1995;96:2204–10.
145. Francoeur C, Denis M. Nitric oxide and interleukin-8 as inflammatory components of cystic fibrosis. Inflammation 1995;19:587–98.
146. Khan TZ, Wagener JS, Bost T, et al. Early pulmonary inflammation in infants with cystic fibrosis. Am J Respir Crit Care Med 1995;151:1075–82.
147. Dai Y, Dean TP, Church MK, et al. Desensitisation of neutrophil responses by systemic interleukin-8 in cystic fibrosis. Thorax 1994;49:867–71.
148. Ruef C, Jefferson DM, Schlegal-Haueter SE, Suter S. Regulation of cytokine secretion by cystic fibrosis airway epithelial cells. Eur Respir J 1993;6:1429–36.
149. Bedard M, McClure CD, Schiller NL, et al. Release of interleukin-8, interleukin-6, and colony-stimulating factors by upper airway epithelial cells. Am J Respir Cell Mol Biol 1993;9:455–62.
150. Dean TP, Dai Y, Shute JK, et al. Interleukin-8 concentrations are elevated in bronchoalveolar lavage, sputum, and sera of children with cystic fibrosis. Pediatr Res 1993;34:159–61.
151. Davidson DJ, Dorin JR, McLachlan G, et al. Lung disease in the cystic fibrosis mouse exposed to bacterial pathogens. Nat Genet 1995;9:351–7.
152. Nielsen R. Correlation between transepithelial Na^+ transport and transepithelial water movement across isolated frog skin (*Rana esculenta*). J Membrane Biol 1997; 159(1):61–9.
153. Quinton PM. Cystic fibrosis: a disease in electrolyte transport. FASEB J 1990;4:2709–17.
154. Joris L, Dab I, Quinton PM. Elemental composition of human airway surface liquid in healthy and diseased airways. Am Rev Respir Dis 1993;148:1633–7.
155. Gilljam H, Ellin A. Increased bronchial chloride concentration in cystic fibrosis. Scand J Clin Lab Invest 1989; 49:121–4.
156. Knowles MR, Robinson JM, Wood RE, et al. Ion composition of airway surface liquid of patients with cystic fibrosis as compared to normal and disease-control subjects. J Clin Invest 1997;100:2588–95.
157. Li M, McCann JD, Liedtke CM, et al. Cyclic AMP-dependent protein kinase opens chloride channels in normal but not cystic fibrosis airway epithelium. Nature 1988;331:358–60.
158. Li M, McCann JD, Anderson MP, et al. Regulation of chloride channels by protein kinase C in normal and cystic fibrosis airway epithelia. Science 1989;244:1353–6.
159. Welsh MJ. Abnormal regulation of ion channels in cystic fibrosis epithelia. FASEB J 1990;4:2718–25.
160. Schwiebert EM, Flotte T, Cutting GR, Guggino WB. Both CFTR and outwardly rectifying chloride channels contribute to cAMP-stimulated whole cell chloride currents. Am J Physiol 1994;266:C1464–77.
161. Schwiebert EM, Egan ME, Hwang T-H, et al. CFTR - regulates outwardly rectifying chloride channels through an autocrine mechanism involving ATP. Cell 1995;81:1063–73.
162. Zeitlin PL, Lu L, Rhim J, et al. A cystic fibrosis bronchial epithelial cell line: immortalization by adeno-12-SV40 infection. Am J Respir Cell Mol Biol 1995;4:313–9.
163. Gabriel SE, Clarke LL, Boucher RC, Stutts MJ. CFTR and outward rectifying chloride channels are distinct proteins with a regulatory relationship. Nature 1993;363:263–6.
164. Knowles M, Clarke LL, Boucher RC. Activation by extracellular nucleotides of chloride secretion in the airway epithelia of patients with cystic fibrosis. N Engl J Med 1991;325:533–8.
165. Bennett W, Olivier KN, Zeman KL, et al. Effect of uridine 5′-triphosphate plus amiloride on mucociliary clearance in adult cystic fibrosis. Am J Respir Crit Care Med 1996;153:1796–801.
166. Grubb BR, Boucher RC. Enhanced colonic Na^+ absorption in cystic fibrosis mice versus normal mice. Am J Physiol 1997;272:G393–400.

167. Stutts MJ, Rossier BC, Boucher RC. Cystic fibrosis transmembrane conductance regulator inverts protein kinase A-mediated regulation of epithelial sodium channel single channel kinetics. J Biol Chem 1997; 272:14037–40.
168. Burch LH, Talbot CR, Knowles M, et al. Relative expression of the human epithelial Na^+ channel subunits in normal and cystic fibrosis airways. Am J Physiol 1995; 269:C511–8.
169. Kristidis P, Bozon D, Corey M, et al. Genetic determination of exocrine pancreatic function in cystic fibrosis. Am J Hum Genet 1992;50:1178–84.
170. Kerem E, Corey M, Kerem B-S, et al. The relation between genotype and phenotype in cystic fibrosis—analysis of the most common mutation (ΔF_{508}). N Engl J Med 1990;323:1517–22.
171. Fujiwara T, Maeta H, Chida S, et al. Artificial surfactant therapy in hyaline-membrane disease. Lancet 1980; i:55–9.

CHAPTER 23

Cellular and Molecular Mechanisms in Hypoxic Injury or Adaptation

Gabriel G. Haddad, MD

One of the major problems in surgical and medical specialties is the morbidity and mortality that can ensue from delivery of low O_2 to tissues. In the intensive care setting, whether adult, pediatric, or neonatal, hypoxia is seen frequently, and the consequent morbidity is often devastating. In the surgical theater, it is often a main determinant of surgical success. In transplantation surgery, tissue preservation is crucial in the ultimate performance of the transplanted organ. Whether the condition is medical or surgical, in general, the three most sensitive organs in mammals and humans are the brain, heart, and kidney. This is why patients who suffer from hypoxic injury are often comatose and in renal and heart failure.

The inadequate delivery of O_2 to tissues and cells can be a consequence of a variety of etiologies, including those stemming from cardiac, respiratory, or vascular pathologies. Irrespective of etiology, a considerable amount of work has been performed and has focused mostly on the vascular component to try to understand the pathophysiology that limits the delivery of O_2 to tissues. For example, many investigators in the past 2 to 3 decades have studied the risk factors of atherosclerosis and the consequences that these have on vessel disease and on O_2 supply to tissues.

Although there has been a considerable amount of literature in this important area of research, at present we do not have a full understanding of the cascade of events that occur in or outside cells when such cells are deprived of O_2. So far most research has centered on blood vessels and clotting mechanisms—justifiably so, since ischemia and hypoxia often result from clotting problems and embolic phenomena. Although studies related to the inherent responses of tissues to the lack of O_2 are clearly important, they have been comparatively scarce. In fact, there are many gaps in our knowledge. For example, we do not have a good understanding of the O_2-sensing pathways. We do not know the importance of a variety of mechanisms that are activated or inactivated in the cell in response to lack of O_2. We do not know why neonatal mammals are much more tolerant to lack of O_2 than are more mature ones. We also do not have a good appreciation of the changes that occur after long-term versus short-term low-O_2 states. Many laboratories have contributed, however, to our current state of understanding of the cellular and molecular responses to lack of O_2. In this chapter, some of the salient features regarding the cellular and basic mechanisms when O_2 is depleted in the microenvironment of cells are summarized. Data that we obtained in our laboratory and from others are reviewed, including data gathered from a variety of cells, such as nerve, myocardial, endothelial, and epithelial cells. Issues pertaining to ontogeny as well as phylogeny are addressed. Last, some of the exciting new discoveries in this research area are highlighted conceptually with an emphasis on recent data obtained in both vertebrate and invertebrate animals. The chapter is divided into three sections: the first summarizes the effects of acute hypoxic stress on cells, the second addresses some of the chronic effects, and the third highlights some of the newer findings from an evolutionary perspective. Although a number of issues related to cell injury and cell tolerance to lack of O_2 are reviewed, the process of necrosis and apoptosis are not reviewed in detail.

Acute Hypoxic Stress

Whether epithelial or excitable cells, most cells in the body respond in the early phases of acute hypoxia by altering their ionic homeostasis and their membrane properties, such as membrane potential and input resistance. Furthermore, a wide range of intracellular events takes place, including gene regulation and protein expression. These latter changes, however, usually are not observed acutely or when the stress is of short term. If cells survive the hypoxic stress over a prolonged period of time, gene regulation and expression becomes, as is seen below, an important contributor to the overall survival or, in some instances, demise of cells and tissues when they are deprived of O_2. In this section, some of the membrane changes that have major impact on function in excitable cells when hypoxia is of short duration and acute are illustrated.

Overall Responses

Most data accumulated in the literature have focused on either nerve or myocardial cells, although muscle cells from the pulmonary arteries and renal tubular cells also have been studied under hypoxic and ischemic conditions.

Some of the changes that occur in the pulmonary vasculature are addressed in subsequent chapters (see Chapters 24 and 26). For simplicity, the focus here is on neurons, albeit not exclusively, since the signal-to-noise ratio is large, and since we understand in considerable detail the overall cellular responses to lack of oxygenation.

Passive properties of nerve cells and excitability

In response to hypoxia, all central neurons, whether from the brainstem (such as hypoglossal or vagal neurons) or from rostral areas (such as neocortical or hippocampal neurons), depolarize after a certain latency.[1–5] This latency is usually a few minutes in duration but can vary from about 30 to 60 seconds in hypoglossal neurons to several minutes in neocortical or vagal motoneurons.[1–3] During this latency period, membrane potential (V_m) may become more negative in some cells such as in vagal motoneurons. By 5 to 10 minutes after the initiation of low-O_2 conditions, V_m in nerve cells generally has become more positive and, in some neurons such as hypoglossal motoneurons, V_m has almost reached a nil potential. Indeed, hypoglossal motoneurons are inherently very sensitive to a lack of O_2. After about 10 minutes of hypoxia, these neurons can become injured and may not recover from the hypoxic stress.

Another important overall indicator of major ionic changes is the input resistance (R_m). Generally, and especially after the latent period, R_m decreases substantially during acute hypoxia.[1–5] The time course of this decrease varies, but it can be remarkably fast in some cells (eg, hypoglossal cells). Interestingly, even in cells that do not change their V_m or hyperpolarize during the latent period, R_m starts to decrease before V_m moves toward 0. Both R_m and V_m changes in hypoxia have major effects on excitability and on cell-to-cell communication in the central nervous system.[4]

With changes in V_m and R_m, it is predicted that neuronal excitability would be altered. Since cells depolarize with hypoxia, they first tend to be more excited and to fire action potentials at a higher rate. If the hypoxic stress persists and the depolarization continues, an anodal blockade ensues, and cells cease to fire and communicate electrically with others.[1–3] This blockade is due not only to the decrease in V_m toward 0 but also to the decrease in R_m. Interestingly, the decrease in excitability that occurs in hypoxia is not related only to the changes in these properties but also to changes in the kinetics and magnitude of the Na^+ current through the voltage-sensitive channels.[3,4] The Na^+ current peak decreases readily at the outset of hypoxia. We have demonstrated previously that it becomes reduced by 60% by 3 minutes of hypoxia. Indeed, this decrease is the main reason for the decrease in neuronal excitability at the outset, even before the change in V_m and R_m. The decrease in this current is due most likely to the activation of protein kinase C (PKC) activity.[6] This increase in kinase activity with hypoxia modulates the steady state inactivation of the Na^+ channels in such a way that the availability of these channels decreases. Does this decrease in excitability have an impact on cell survival? What are the functional roles of this decrease in the Na^+ current and in excitability? We believe that the decrease in excitability that is due to the decrease in the Na^+ current is related to a potential decrease in energy consumption and a decrease in the mismatch between supply and demand at a time when energy production is limited. Therefore, it is the activation of PKC that decreases the recruitment of Na^+ channels during hypoxia, which, in turn, decreases firing, excitability and energy expenditure. How PKC increases its activity during hypoxia is not known at the present time.

Adenosine triphosphate and metabolism

That steady state adenosine triphosphate (ATP) levels decrease in neurons during hypoxia is not surprising. However, it is well known from in vivo experiments that the fractional inspired O_2 concentration (FI_{O_2}) has to drop to very low levels before ATP starts to be reduced.[7] Since these experiments often are done on whole regions or on homogenates and ATP is measured in whole regions (ie, including nerve cells, glia, and processes at the same time), and since it is well known that glial elements are much more tolerant to the lack of O_2 and can maintain ATP levels much longer than can neurons, it is possible that the neurons in these studies lose their ability to maintain ATP much earlier and at a higher level of O_2 than was previously appreciated.[8] Adenosine diphosphate (ADP), ATP, and other metabolic products have a major impact on reactions that depend on them (eg, membrane pumps) and events that are affected by these reactions (eg, ATP-dependent or pH-dependent channel activity). Therefore, it is not difficult to envision the importance of metabolism on cell function, especially nerve cell function. However, the relationship between the various metabolic factors and neuronal excitability and function has not been well established and investigated. For example, the overall effect of kinase activity on various processes of cell function during hypoxia is not clear. Specifically, while increased PKC can inhibit the Na^+ current, it can activate other membrane proteins, such as the Na-H exchanger, which can have the opposite effect and increase Na^+ influx.[9] Hence, the overall cellular function of increased PKC activity is not fully delineated in hypoxic conditions. Furthermore, the upstream events leading to the activation of kinase activity are not known.

Regions, cell groups, and cell types

Another important general consideration is that various cell types respond differently to hypoxia depending on many variables.[7] Muscle and liver cells have been known to resist hypoxia and respond with little change, even

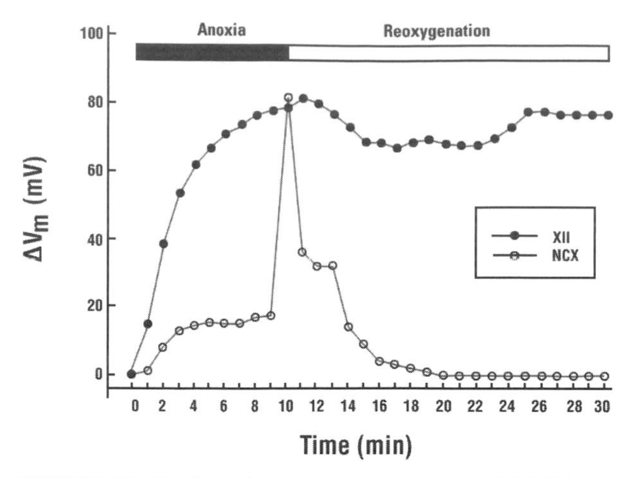

FIGURE 23–1. Mean change in membrane potential (ΔV_m) as a function of time in neocortical (NCX) and hypoglossal (XII) neurons harvested and studies in tissue slices. Note that XII neurons are much less tolerant than NCX neurons.

after a prolonged period of O_2 deprivation.[10,11] However, even in the central nervous system, glia can maintain homeostasis for a much longer period than can neurons.[12,13] The inherent neuronal response itself can vary significantly: hypoglossal neurons respond extremely quickly (within 30 to 60 seconds) and loose their ionic homeostasis readily in comparison with vagal or neocortical cells, which can last longer.[1–3,7] Hypoglossal cells depolarize and increase their conductance more than do neocortical cells, in about half of the time needed for neocortical cells to show a few millivolts of depolarization (Figure 23–1).[1–3] The return of hypoglossal cells to baseline during reoxygenation also is delayed as compared with that of neocortical neurons.[1–3] Further, if the hypoxic stress is maintained for equal times in neocortical and hypoglossal neurons, the likelihood of hypoglossal cell injury is much greater than that for neocortical cells. This might seem to be paradoxical to the teaching dogma that neocortical and hippocampal cells usually are most sensitive to ischemia. While this may be valid and supported by experimental evidence in vivo,[1–3,8] these experiments showing the vulnerability of neocortical and hippocampal neurons do not shed light on the inherent responses of single cells to the lack of O_2 as such but, rather, to low blood flow, low O_2 levels, neurotransmitters released in quantities and, likely, to a number of other variables such as O_2 consumption of the tissue. It is clear from our results and the results of others that hypoglossal neurons are much more sensitive to the lack of O_2 per say than are vagal, hippocampal, and neocortical neurons.[1–3,8] This also is the case for moderate or severe O_2 deprivation.

The reasons for the differential sensitivities of O_2 deprivation between various regions, cell types, or cell groups are not clear from published data.[8] However, there have been, a number of ideas, supported by experimental evidence, to explain differences in response to hypoxia between cells. Some of these ideas include differences in intracellular glycogen, Ca^{++} response and buffering, neurotransmitters released and responses of cells to these transmitters, O_2 consumption and metabolism, membrane properties and proteins, ionic homeostasis, gene expression during hypoxia, and responses to apoptotic stimuli. At present, additional work is needed in this arca to delineate the pathways of cell survival and cell death in hypoxia.

Ontogeny and phylogeny

A large body of literature is available on the subject of ontogeny and phylogeny. One of the fascinating aspects of ontogeny is that, with maturation, the sensitivity to a lack of O_2 is increased, and adult mammals seem to loose the resistance to hypoxia that the new born enjoys (Figure 23–2).[1,14,15] The tolerance or lack thereof in neonatal or mature mammals seems to affect various organs in a similar fashion. For example, the resistance of the neonatal mammal is not limited to the brain, but various organs that have been tested, such as the kidney and heart, have shown a similar resistance to hypoxic injury.[16–18] In addition, it is clear from the literature that earlier vertebrates such as the turtle (Figure 23–3)[8,19,20] and insects such as the *Drosophila*[21,22] are very resistant to a lack of O_2. These animals that are older evolutionally, whether vertebrates or invertebrates, have an amazing response to the lack of O_2. For example, the turtle can sustain complete O_2 deprivation for days and weeks without any cellular injury. We have shown recently that the *Drosophila melanogaster*, whose total life span is only about 5 weeks, can remain in an environment of a total lack of O_2 for hours and subsequently see, mate, and fly—complex behaviors that necessitate an intact central nervous system.[21,22] How such organisms can be so tolerant of anoxia has interested many investigators, including ourselves. It appears almost certainly now that such tolerance is the result of many processes and genetic pathways that result in such an amazing phenomenon, as compared with mammalian tissues, which essentially, cannot be exposed to a period of more than 5 to 10 minutes of anoxia without irreversible tissue injury.[1,2,7,19,21,22] Although newborn mammals generally have more tolerance to hypoxic injury than do their adult counterparts, turtles and tolerant organisms are much more tolerant than relatively tolerant newborn mammals.

The mechanisms for anoxia tolerance in the turtle have been summarized in recent review articles.[23–32] These mechanisms are related to a variety of issues, including a number of electrophysiologic aspects of neurons, ionic and neurotransmitter mechanisms, metabolic considerations, and oxidative stress and response. We are investigating the mechanisms of anoxic survival and protection in the *Drosophila* by adopting a genetic approach (see

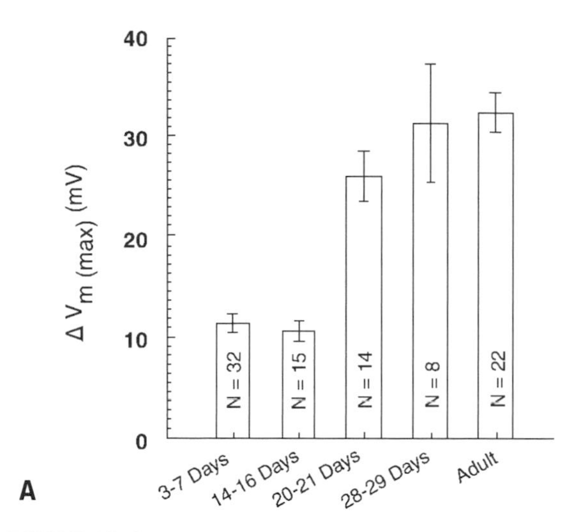

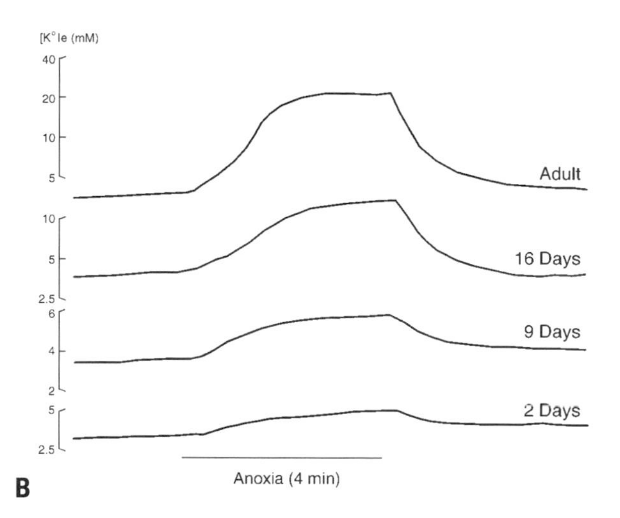

FIGURE 23–2. *A*, Maximum change in membrane potential (ΔV_m) as a function of age in rats. Numbers inside bars represent number of animals studied and used. Note that the depolarization that occurs during hypoxia increases as a function of age, reaching adult levels at about 3 to 4 weeks of life. *B*, Extracellular K^+ activity as a function of age before, during, and after anoxia in tissue slices. (Reproduced with permission from Haddad GG and Donnelly DF.[1])

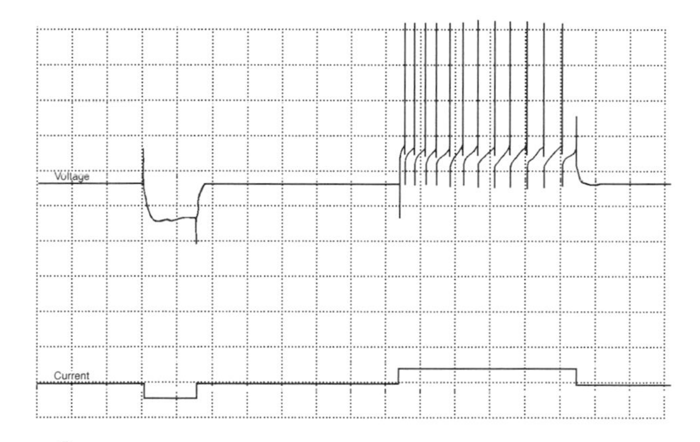

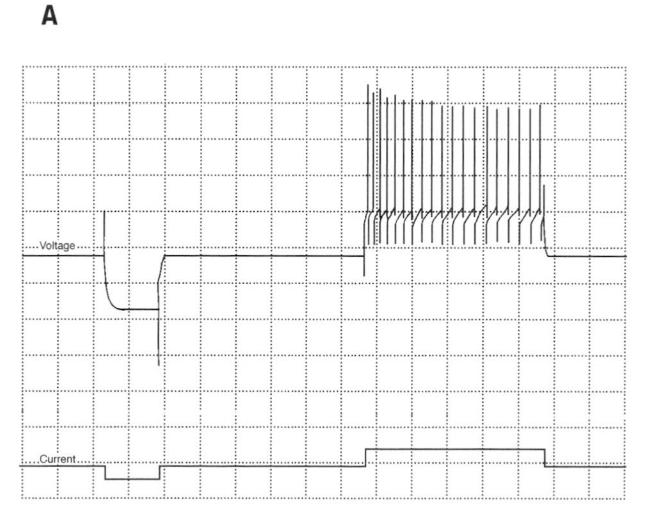

FIGURE 23–3. *A*, Voltage and current trace recorded from a turtle neuron in normoxia. *B*, The same recordings done after **2 hours** of anoxia. Note that firing is still occurring, and there may be a slightly higher input resistance after anoxia, since the voltage deflection is slightly larger with the same hyperpolarizing current.

below). Many questions remain to be answered, however, and it is likely that the answers will be forthcoming not from a single approach but from a variety of tools, approaches, and methodologies.

Specific Mechanisms in the Acute Cellular Response

In an acute setting, hypoxia induces a number of specific cellular responses that have been studied in a variety of cell types—mostly cardiac myocytes and neurons, although some data exist on epithelial cells from renal tubules and lung airways. A number of these mechanisms seem to play a role in all of these cell types but to different degrees and with different patterns. One example is the importance of heat shock proteins in both epithelial and excitable cells. A caveat should be mentioned here in relation to comparisons between studies. One major problem that has plagued this field is whether the given stimulus, that is, hypoxia, is similar in various studies. This is especially important when comparisons of similar outcome variables are desirable. In general, the majority of studies using in vitro preparations either do not measure the P_{O_2} used or they measure it at a location that is different from the source of the outcome variable. Hence, even those comparisons between studies using the same cell types have to be made with great caution from a quantitative point of view. In this section, the review is limited mostly to studies in nerve cells.

Ionic homeostasis: K^+ ion

In the first few to several minutes of acute hypoxic exposure, remarkable electrophysiologic changes occur. We and others have focused on K^+, Na^+, and Ca^{++} ions, and have studied the ionic changes and their regulation during low-O_2 states.[14,19,33–47] For example, K^+ ions largely determine V_m in nerve and other excitable cells. In addition, K^+ ion flux recently has been incriminated in cell fate determination (see below).[48–50]

One of the most dramatic events seen in adult mammalian brain tissue when hypoxia is instituted is that, within less than a minute, K^+ ion concentration increases in the extracellular space slowly but, at a later stage of the hypoxic period, K^+ efflux increases at an enormous rate (see Figure 23–2). We have shown previously that this increase is due not only to shrinkage of the extracellular space and a decrease in water content (albeit, this does happen) but is caused by an actual increase in the amount of K^+ ions.[33–35,50] This increase in extracellular K^+ is paralleled by a decrease in intraneuronal K^+ ions,[35] strongly suggesting that the efflux of K^+ into the extracellular space is neuronal in origin. With in vivo experiments, the concentration of K^+ in the extracellular space can reach more than 100 mM.[33–35,51] Even in tissue slice preparations in which there is constant perfusion, in some unstirred layers, the accumulation is substantial.[1,35]

In the past several years, we and others have examined the mechanisms of efflux of K^+ in cells.[1,2,19,35,41,42,46,47,52,53] There likely are a number of mechanisms that are responsible for this efflux, depending on the type of cells being studied and on their membrane channel endowment. For example, substantia nigra neurons have a high expression of ATP-dependent K^+ channels and a high level of glibenclamide-binding sites.[41,42,54] We have shown that, in these cells, a large percentage of the K^+ efflux takes place through these channels.[41,42,46,47] In contrast, neocortical cells have, in addition to these channels, a maxi-K type of channels, and we have demonstrated that such channels also participate in the efflux of K^+.[55] The efflux of K^+ also is dependent on the duration and severity of hypoxia.[2] The longer and more severe is the hypoxic stress, the larger is the increase in K^+ efflux.

Some of the interesting and intriguing questions at present relate to the regulation of these K^+ channels under conditions of O_2 deprivation: What triggers the opening and closing of these channels? Is O_2 itself interacting with the membrane and channel, or do the alterations that result from hypoxia modulate channel activity? How would a direct interaction with O_2, occur? If interaction is "indirect" through cytosolic changes, what are these changes that affect channel activity? These are some of the questions that we and others have tried to address in the past several years, with some success. For example, we know now that some species of ATP-sensitive K^+ channels are sensitive to the level of P_{O_2} in the microenvironment of the plasma membrane of neocortical and substantia nigra neurons (Figure 23–4).[41,42,46,47,54] These channels seem to reduce their open probability dramatically when the P_{O_2} is reduced below 20 torr. The idea that resulted from these experiments was that this reduction in channel activity occurred when the plasma membrane was excised, and, hence, the decrease in channel activity was obtained in the absence of any cytosolic factors. This suggested to us that there may be some important interactions between the P_{O_2} per se and the plasma membrane, which contains this ATP-sensitive K^+ channel as well as other membrane proteins that could interact with this channel. We also found that other factors do modulate this channel as well as other K^+ channels (with different characteristics), such as those of maxi-K channels.[55] These factors are cytosolic and, hence, could be related to the consequences of hypoxia.[55] For example, we have demonstrated that some of these factors are pH, reducing/oxidizing agents, and kinases (Figure 23–5). It is important to keep in mind that alterations of some of these factors (eg, kinases) can affect not only these ATP-sensitive K^+ channels but also other channels or exchangers during hypoxia (see below).

The importance of these studies stems from two ideas. The first is related to O_2-sensing mechanisms. Knowing how cells sense O_2 or the lack thereof is an important biologic question that may have many ramifications in animal life. For instance, knowing what starts the cascade of events that leads to injury or survival of cells when O_2 is lacking may have potential therapeutic implications. The second is related to a new concept—that of a link between ionic homeostasis and cell fate. There now are data that demonstrate in nerve cells and in T lymphocytes that K^+ flux is linked causally to apoptosis and cell death.[48,56,57] As a result, events that occur early during hypoxia across the plasma membrane may have implications on nuclear events downstream. If so, these events could then be linked to therapeutic modalities in conditions of low-O_2 states.

Ionic homeostasis: Ca^{++} and Na^+ ions

In the past decade, we and others have shown that Na^+ and Ca^{++} cations play a significant role in the cellular response to hypoxia and in hypoxic cell injury.[36,38,43–45,58–61] While intracellular Ca^{++} (Ca^{++}_i) level has been shown to be important, especially in relation to glutamate excitotoxicity, the relation between intracellular Na^+ and mechanisms of cell injury has not been well studied.

There is little doubt now that increases in Ca^{++}_i play a significant role in cell injury resulting from glutamate exposure. It is also well established that a number of mechanisms are activated as a result of this increase in Ca^{++}_i, such as the activation of proteases and lipases that can lead to injury.[5] Mechanisms that lead to this increase in Ca^{++}_i are well known.[38]

This increase in Ca^{++}_i may not be the main "culprit," however, during ischemia or hypoxia in vivo. Indeed, we demonstrated several years ago that the increase in Ca^{++}_i can be almost totally blocked, and cell injury still occurs in nerve cells when exposed to O_2 deprivation.[38,43,44] In parallel experiments from our laboratory, we also have

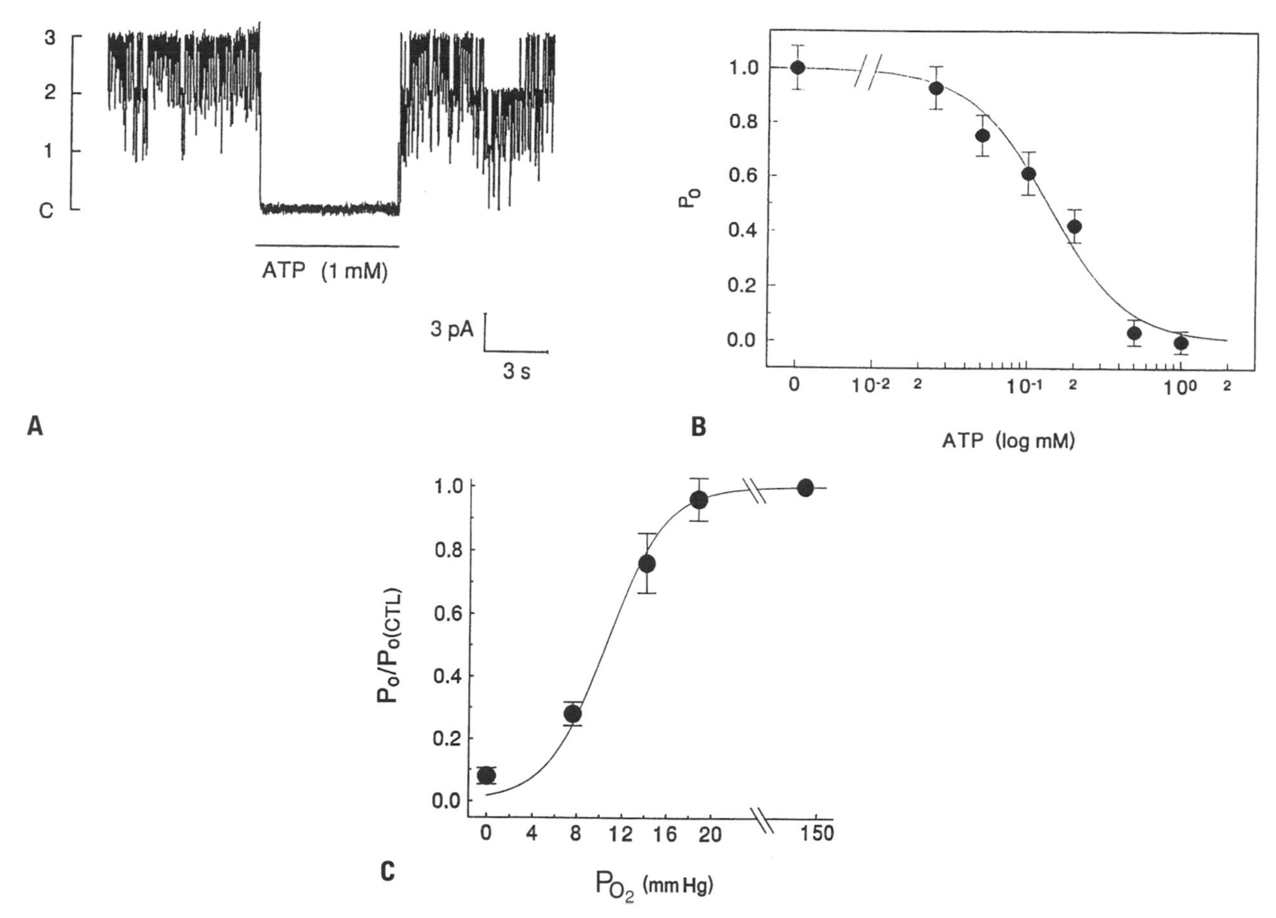

FIGURE 23–4. *A*, A K^+ channel that is exquisitely sensitive to adenosine triphosphate (ATP). Note how the three channels open are closed very quickly with ATP (1 mM). (Reproduced with permission from Jiang C, et al.[41] Copyright 1994 by the Society for Neurosciences.) *B*, Open probability (P_0) of this channel as a function of ATP concentration. (Reproduced with permission from Jiang C, et al.[41] Copyright 1994 by the Society for Neuroscience.) *C*, Normalized P_0 to control as a function of partial pressure of O_2 (P_{O_2}) in excised membrane patches expressing the same channels. Note that these channels respond to P_{O_2} without any cytosolic factors in excised membranes. (Reproduced with permission from Jiang C and Haddad GG.[54] Copyright 1994 National Acadamy of Sciences, USA.)

shown that the anoxia-induced depolarization in these same neurons is much attenuated when extracellular Na^+ (Na^+_o) is reduced to very low levels (5 mM).[5] Further, cell injury is totally eliminated when nerve cells are exposed to anoxia *if* Na^+_o is removed or markedly reduced (Figure 23–6).[38,43,44,45,58,60,61] Finally, we showed that Na^+_o is decreased in brain slices when they were deprived of O_2, suggesting again that cell injury is caused by the increase in Na^{++}_i, and that this injury is alleviated by removal or reduction in Na^+_o.[37,43–45,58,60,61] This is interesting since injury can be alleviated markedly even when the period of O_2 deprivation is much more prolonged (up to 20 to 30 minutes of anoxia). These data, lead to two main questions: (1) What is the mechanism for Na^{++} entry into nerve cells? and, perhaps more importantly, (2) How does this increase in Na^{++}_i lead to cell death? We believe that we have some answers to both of these questions.

Direct and indirect evidence has been acquired to indicate to us that Na^+ ions enter into neurons through a variety of mechanisms. For example, we have evidence that, although the voltage-gated Na^+ channels are less recruitable during hypoxia (shift of the steady state inactivation curve to the left) and the peak Na^+ current is reduced in a major way, these channels still play a role in Na^+ influx. Supporting this idea is the fact that tetrodotoxin, a specific blocker of the voltage-sensitive Na^+ channels, can alleviate injury in brain slices exposed to low O_2 conditions (Figure 23–7).[5,58,60–63] Other mechanisms also have been incriminated. We have shown for instance that exchangers, such as the Na-H and possibly the Na-Ca exchangers, can play a major role in Na^+ influx in neurons.[5,64,65] Interestingly, certain kinases (eg, PKC), which are important for the inhibition of the Na^+ current, activate the Na-H exchanger during hypoxia.[65] Therefore, with respect to Na^+ loading, PKC inhibits Na^+ entry through the inhibition of the Na^+ current via the voltage-sensitive Na^+ channels, but it dramatically increases Na^+ entry through the Na-H exchanger.[4,6,36,65] Influx of Na^+ ions through glutamate receptors/channels or transporters are also significant ways by which Na^+ can potentially enter neurons.

Evidence also has accumulated regarding the role of Na^+ influx in inducing injury during low-O_2 states in the

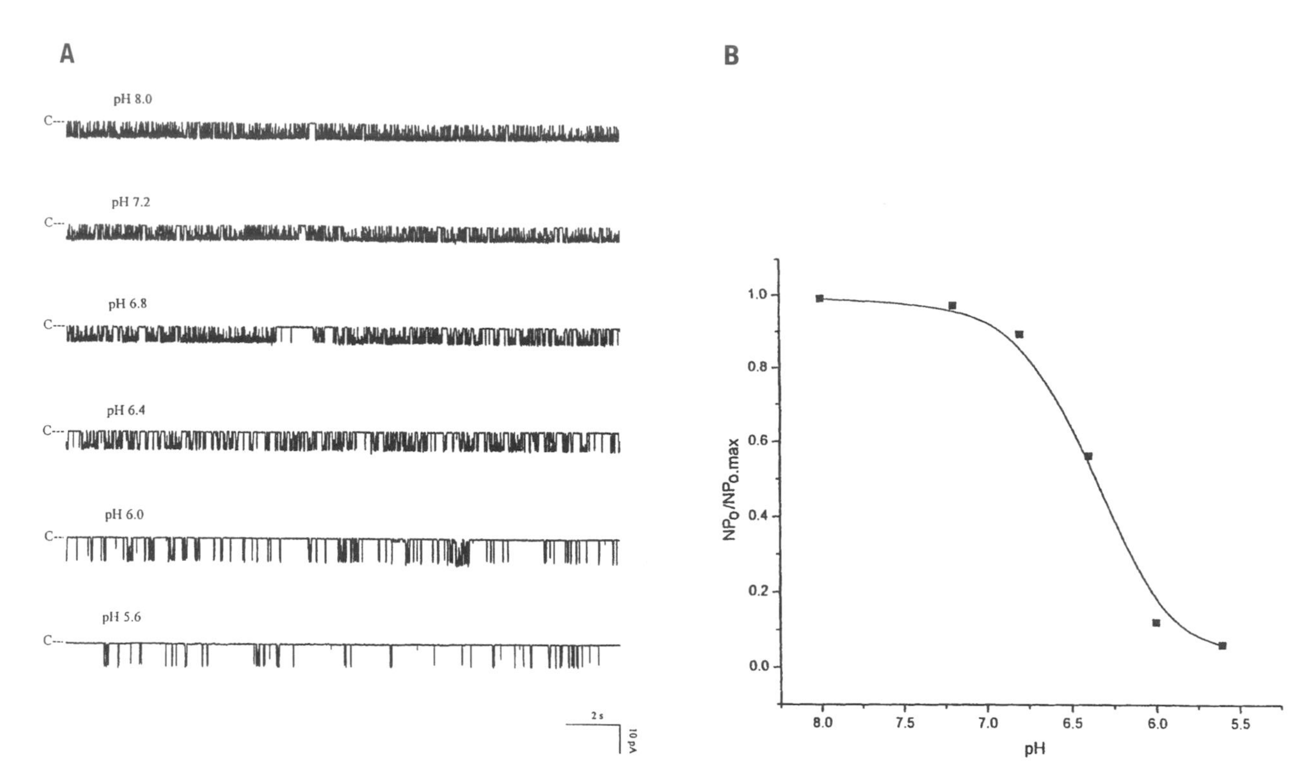

FIGURE 23–5. *A*, Single maxi-K channel activity (large-conductance, Ca^{++}-sensitive, and voltage-dependent channels) in inside/out membrane patches as a function of pH. Note that with a reduction in pH from 8 to 5.6, there is a dramatic drop in channel activity. *B*, The relation between the open probability as a function of control ($NP_O/NP_{O.max}$) and pH. (Reproduced with permission from Liu H et al.[55])

myocardium. Although it is clear now that Na^+ loading during hypoxia is potentially deleterious in the heart, it is not clear as to whether this is because of Na^+ loading per se or whether it is related to the ionic consequences of this Na^+ loading. For example, in the presence of high Na^+ concentration in the cytoplasm, the Na^+-Ca^{++} exchanger is activated, and Ca^{++} loading and its consequences set in. Recent evidence, however, has shown that Na^+ entry through both the voltage-sensitive Na^+ channel and the Na^+-H^+ exchanger are important. However, their significance depends on various factors such as the presence of acidity and the presence of a high concentration of K^+ in the extracellular fluid.[66,67]

Although it has been assumed that Na^+ entry into cells is followed by water, and the mechanism of cell death after Na^+ entry is related to swelling, blebbing, and membrane rupture, work in our laboratory and in that of others has shown that the mechanism(s) may not be that simple.[62,63] Indeed, there may be several pathways that can lead to cell death after Na^+ entry into cells. It is possible that acute swelling and necrosis may be an important

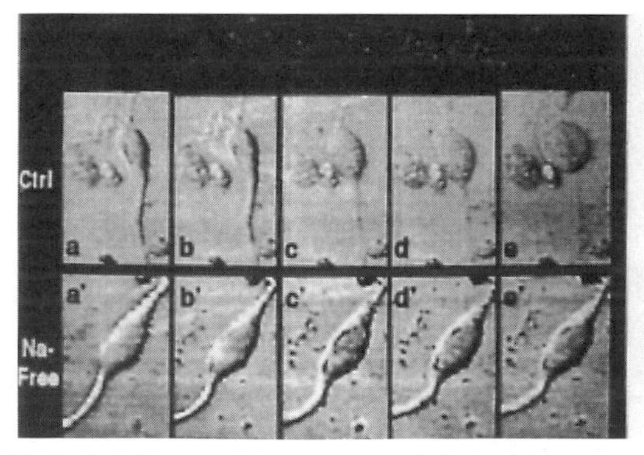

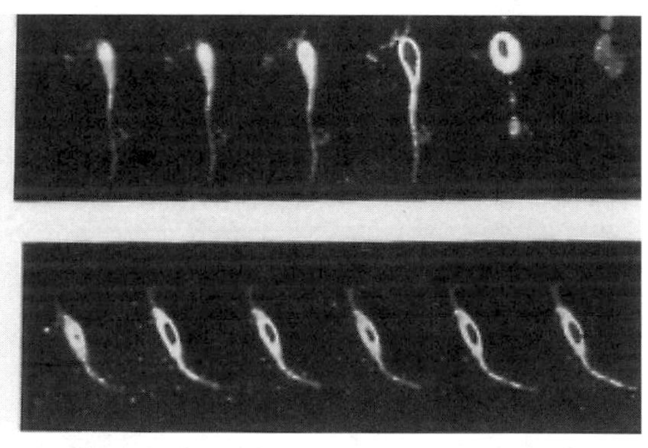

FIGURE 23–6. *Left, Top panel* shows the morphologic changes in rat nerve cells that occur before anoxia (*a*), during anoxia (*b, c, d*), and after anoxia or during reoxygenation (*e*). Note the severe changes such as rounding up of cells, blebbing, and degenerative changes that occur during a 10-minute anoxic period. *Bottom panel* shows the preservation of cell morphology when the same types of nerve cells are subjected to the same period of anoxia in the *absence* of extracellular Na^+. *Right,* The same types of cells, but in both *top* and *bottom* panels, intracellular Ca^{++} is measured with fluo-3. Note the lack of major changes in both intracellular Ca^{++} and in the morphology of cells when extracellular Na^+ is removed, indicating that influx of Na^+ is a major factor in neuronal injury.[38,43]

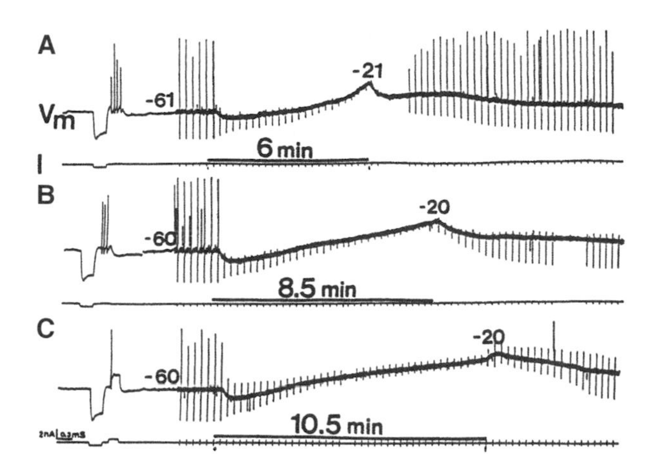

FIGURE 23–7. *A*, Membrane potential (V_m) trajectory before, during, and after 6 minutes of hypoxia in a brain-stem motoneuron. A current trace (I) is shown beneath every V_m trace in *A*, *B*, and *C*. Longer periods were required (*B*, 8.5 minutes: *C*, 10.5 minutes) to reach the same maximum Vm (20 mV) when tetrodotoxin bathed the cell at two different concentrations (0.1 and 0.5 μM). (Reproduced with permission from Fung M-L and Haddad GG.[58])

one, but we have new evidence that Na^+ entry can lead to apoptotic injury and cell death through the activation of caspases.[62,63] Here again, derangement in ionic homeostasis of Na^+ can lead to a change in cell fate and cell death.

Recently, interesting results related to Ca^{++} channels, in particular to the L-type Ca^{++} channels, have been implicated in sensing O_2 deprivation.[68,69] Fearon and colleagues have shown that a splice variant of the α_{1c} subunit was sensitive to hypoxia.[68] More importantly, perhaps, is the demonstration that this sensitivity was related to a structural motif on the proximal end of the 71–amino acid insert of that splice variant. Hence, not only do we have evidence that some Ca^{++} channels are sensitive to hypoxia, we now have additional data, at least with respect to this L-type Ca^{++} channel, indicating that part of the channel is responsible for this sensitivity. This opens up a research avenue related to the role of such channels in conditions such as pulmonary hypertension and their expression as a therapeutic target.

Chronic Hypoxic Stress

In an acute setting (time frame of minutes), it generally is difficult to determine whether a genetic regulation of certain processes has actually occurred or started to occur. During a chronic setting of hours and days, genetic regulation becomes prominent, especially when a stress such as hypoxia has set in. Discussed below are some important examples that are relevant to adaptation to the stress, implications for survival, and the potential for cell injury and, ultimately, cell death.

Protein Synthesis and Degradation

It has been shown numerous times and in a variety of tissues that metabolism is downregulated during chronic hypoxia.[7,70–72] Furthermore, overall protein synthesis also is reduced. In general cells, especially nerve cells, shut off activity and firing. We have discussed above the electrophysiologic correlates of this reduced metabolic activity.[4,6,36] It seems that the cellular response to hypoxia is coordinated within the cell, that is, between its various compartments. For example, the metabolic machinery is in sync with the activity of membrane proteins and ionic homeostasis.[5,73] Indeed, with a decrease in ATP generation after chronic hypoxia, the Na^+ channels, which are crucial for action potential generation and firing, are partially inhibited, reducing the ability of the cell to support its own actual activity.

Previously, we have coined the term "protein hierarchy" to describe the idea that, although overall protein synthesis is downregulated, some proteins actually are upregulated, illustrating the fact that there is a hierarchy in terms of cellular protein response to hypoxia.[5,23,53,71,73–77] This may be an important strategy for cells to adopt: the use of energy substrates in a targeted way to "fuel" only the needed processes. Examples of important proteins that are overexpressed in periods of hypoxia abound. These include stress or heat shock proteins (eg, HSP70 or 25) and the hypoxia-inducible factor (HIF; see below). While this differential regulation of protein synthesis can be an important mechanism for survival in periods of hypoxia, it is clear now that there are a number of potentially important mechanisms that allow cells to tolerate O_2 deprivation.

Role of Mitochondrial Enzymes

Since metabolic rate is decreased during chronic hypoxic states, one may question whether the level of mitochondrial enzyme activity changes. While this may be different from tissue to tissue, preliminary work from our laboratory has focused on α-ketoglutarate dehydrogenase complex (KGDHC). This enzyme complex plays a key role in regulating glucose flux in the tricarboxylic-acid (TCA) cycle. Like other mitochondrial enzymes, KGDHC changes in activity with age in early life and increases in all the brain regions examined, with most of the increase occurring between 10 and 30 days postnatally. With a hypoxic exposure to 9 to 10% F_{IO_2}, KGDHC activity was reduced throughout the brain of rats after 30 days but not after 10 days of exposure (Lai, Behar, and Haddad, unpublished observations, 2002). The rate of glutamate turnover found in these exposed rats also was decreased compared to control rats, indicating that the oxidative rate was lower in the brain of hypoxic rats. Although this is a key regulatory enzyme, which most likely affects oxidative flux, other enzymes may be modulated as well. If a number of mitochondrial enzymes are reduced, and if the TCA cycle activity is low, then this would seem to be consistent with a cellular survival strategy to decrease the rate of oxidation of glucose, since O_2, (a main substrate for this pathway) is lacking.

Stress Proteins: Mechanisms of Cytoprotection

While oxidative mitochondrial enzymes are reduced with chronic hypoxia, other proteins that can play a role in cytoprotection are upregulated. As mentioned above, one such family is the heat shock protein (HSP) family. This family has been shown to play a key role in minimizing or preventing injury of cells when they are subjected to a lack of O_2. In nerve cells, for example, a higher level of HSP70 is associated with increased tolerance to hypoxia or to glutamate excitotoxicity.[78–80] Cross-tolerance also has been described whereby heat shock, which increases HSP, increases the tolerance to hypoxia and glutamate toxicity.[78–80]

The role played by HSPs, often referred to as chaperones, is varied. For instance, the HSP molecules can participate in disassembling protein aggregates, translocating protein across intracellular compartments, and reconfiguring denatured or misfolded proteins. During the course of hypoxia and after reoxygenation, these processes to which HSPs contribute may prove to be essential for the survival of the tissues. The importance of these molecules has now been demonstrated in several tissues, including renal, cardiac, and nervous tissues.

Recent studies of renal tubular cells have shown that HSPs can preserve or restore cellular architecture and function following ischemia.[81–85] One way of preserving cellular integrity is via stabilization of the cytoskeleton, especially actin, and preservation of tight junctions. One of the membrane proteins that has been shown as a target for HSPs is the Na^+-K^+ ATPase, which is refolded and chaperoned to HSPs' native location during the reoxygenation phase.

The role of HSP70 in cytoprotection is relevant in this chapter for a different reason. It seems that HSP70 is more abundant in the immature nephron than in the mature one.[17,18] One hypothesis states that this increased constitutive expression of HSPs in the young confers the tolerance to hypoxia that the newborn enjoys. Although this increased tolerance to a lack of O_2 in the newborn is most likely multifactorial, the HSP upregulation could be a significant mechanism.

Coordination of Cellular Response

Is there a switch that helps coordinate the cellular response to hypoxia? One interesting development in this area in the past several years has been the discovery of the gene hypoxia-inducible factor 1 (*HIF1*).[72,86–97] *HIF1* was biochemically identified through the study of the expression of the erythropoietin reporter gene (*Epo*) in hepatoblastoma cell line–Hep3B and transgenic mice.[72,90–92] As a systemic physiological modulator, *Epo* regulates erythropoiesis and plays an important role in enhancing O_2-transport capacity in mammals in response to O_2 deprivation. By expressing different *Epo* reporter gene constructs in Hep3B cells under hypoxia (1% O_2), Semenza's group demonstrated that a deoxyribonucleic acid (DNA) fragment (5′TACGTGCT-3′) in the *Epo* gene is specific for *HIF1* binding and plays a key role in the control of the inducible transcription of the *Epo* gene during O_2 deprivation.[90–92] This DNA fragment, which is located in a 3′-flanking sequence in both human and mouse *Epo* genes and acts as a *cis*-acting hypoxia-inducible enhancer element, now has been shown to be located in many hypoxia-responsive genes. Detailed molecular analysis demonstrated that *HIF1* was a two-subunit complex, which guarantees its specific binding to this enhancer element.[86–89]

HIF1 is an α and β heterodimer. The α subunit is a recently discovered molecule, while the β subunit is a well-studied factor—aryl-hydrocarbon receptor nuclear translocator (*ARNT*)[72,86–89] which functions as a partner to many other molecules participating in various biologic and toxicologic processes.[72,76,86–89] Both *HIF1* subunits belong to a newly characterized basic helix-loop-helix-PAS (bHLH-PAS) family of transcription factors.[72,76,86–89] Each molecule from this family consists of three main domains: a very conserved bHLH domain, a moderately conserved PAS domain, and a nonconserved glutamine-rich domain. The bHLH domain promotes contiguous DNA binding and dimerization. The PAS domain is ~260 to ~310 amino acids in length and is named after the *Drosophila* Period (*Per*), the human *ARNT*, and the *Drosophila* Single-minded (*Sim*). This domain is therefore used for target gene specificity through dimerization of two proteins. The glutamine-rich domain is believed to be important for transcriptional activation.[72,76,86–89]

As major regulators of a homeostatic response to O_2 deprivation, both subunits of *HIF1* have been evolutionally conserved, at least from *Drosophila* to humans. Using a Gal4-fusion system, it was confirmed that *sima*[72,76] from *Drosophila* was a functional homologue of *HIF1*α and that it could confer O_2-regulated activities in mammalian cells.[72,76,86,88] Both *HIF1*α and *HIF1*β have been highly conserved from the fruit fly to human beings, not only at an amino acid level but also at a functional level. At a protein level, the identity of bHLH and PAS domains of fly *HIF1*α is 63% and 45% to the corresponding domains of human *HIF1*α; the identity of bHLH and PAS domains between human and fly *HIF1*β is 92% and 53%, respectively. The confirmation of *Drosophila sima* as an *HIF1*α homologue and the recent isolation and characterization of *Drosophila ARNT* (*HIF1*β) strongly suggests the existence of a conserved hypoxia signal–transduction system in wide variety of animals. No *HIF1* homologues in bacterium, yeast, and *Caenorhabditis elegans* have been found, possibly indicating that the O_2-sensing mechanisms in these organisms are different from those in higher animals.

As a transcription factor, *HIF1* is essential for the transcriptional response to O_2 deprivation. During hypoxia, this factor binds to a hypoxia-response element (HRE) to activate the transcription of several hypoxia-inducible genes. At a cellular level, *HIF1* induces the expression of many genes that participate in glycolysis for the maintenance of a minimum adenosine triphosphate (ATP) level for cellular function in a hypoxic environment.[72,76,86–89] In addition, *HIF1* activates transcription by recruiting the transcriptional adapter/histone acetyltransferase proteins (P300 and CREB-binding protein) to bind with a transcriptional complex. This is essential for the cellular response to hypoxia.[72,76,86–89] At a whole body level, this factor activates the transcription of many genes such as *Epo*, tyrosine hydroxylase, and the inducible nitric oxide synthase for a global response to hypoxia.[86–89] At a tissue/organ level, *HIF1* increases the transcription rate of the vascular endothelial growth factor (*VEGF*) and its receptor 1 (*VEGFR1*) genes for neovascularization and angiogenesis in a response to local O_2 deprivation.[86–89] Hence, *HIF1*'s importance derives from the fact that it is a switch mechanism for the coordinated cellular response to a lack of O_2. Of interest is that *HIF1* is also important in tumorigenesis and embryogenesis.[72,76,86–89] For example, complete deficiency of *HIF1α* (*HIF1α-/-*) results in developmental arrest and lethality by E11 in mouse embryos. These HIF1α-/- embryos manifest neural tube defects, cardiovascular malformations, and marked cell death within the cephalic mesenchyme.[72,76,86–98] Similarly, a targeted disruption of the *HIF1β/ARNT* locus in the mouse (*ARNT-/-*) leads to embryonic lethality by E10.5 due to defective angiogenesis of the yolk sac and branchial arches, and abnormal development of the vitello-embryonic circulation.[72,76,86,87,98] The lethality at about E11 in the *HIF1* knockout mice and a high level of *HIF1* mRNA expression at the same stage during normal development constitute further proof that *HIF1* plays a key role not only during hypoxic pathophysiologic conditions but also during normal embryonic development.

Maladaptive Mechanisms

Not every element of the response to hypoxia in cells is targeted to a beneficial effect that can contribute to cell survival. Indeed, there are events that are deleterious and contribute to sublethal injury and cellular dysfunction after the stress. Many examples can be cited. There are actually normal processes in the body that seem to be part of a natural response to environmental stimuli for example, that end up as diseases that afflict humans. A case in point is the inflammation in the airways that occurs as a response to an allergen and which is a natural response of the body to such a stress. Therefore, on the one hand, this process is a normal one, but on the other hand, it is tantamount to the pathophysiology of the condition of asthma.

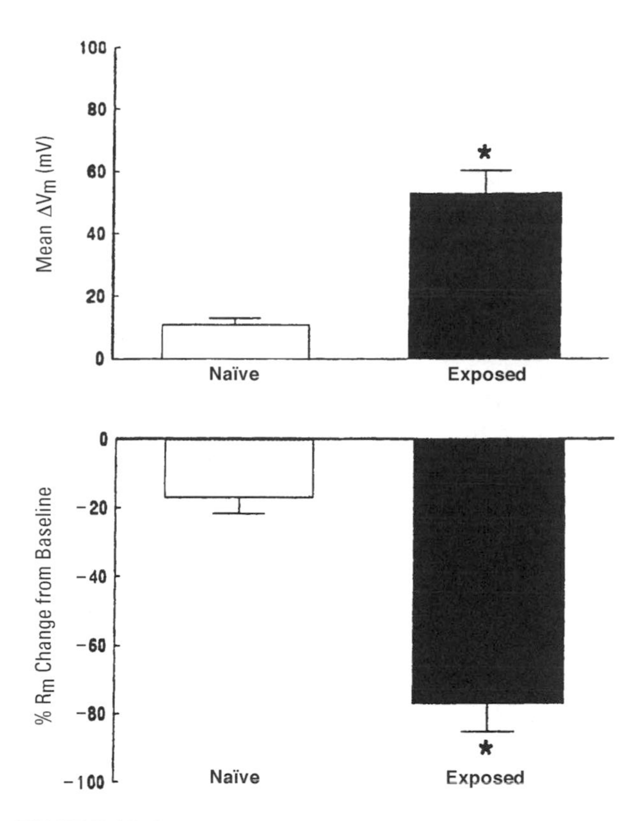

FIGURE 23–8. *Top*, Mean change in membrane potention (ΔV_m) in nerve cells in brain slices from naïve or hypoxia-exposed rats studied during an acute challenge of low O_2. Note the markedly increased ΔV_m in the exposed animals. *Bottom*, The same difference is found when input resistance (R_m) is recorded. (Reproduced from O'Reilly JP and Haddad GG.[99] Copyright 1996, page 205, with permission from Elsevier Science.)

With respect to chronic hypoxia, not all the events that take place are beneficial. For example, we have shown recently that previous exposure to hypoxia does not lead necessarily to tolerance. On the contrary, chronically exposed cells tolerate less well subsequent acute hypoxia.[61,99] Chronic hypoxia here is defined as sustained hypoxia over weeks. In a series of electrophysiologic studies on brain slices from animals exposed to chronic hypoxia (F_{IO_2}=9.5 to 10%), we have found that (1) resting V_m and R_m in cells from exposed animals were not different from those of naïve control in both neocortical and hypoglossal neurons; (2) acute hypoxia in vitro elicited dramatic differences between exposed and naïve neurons in that exposed neocortical neurons depolarized five times more than did naïve ones (ΔV_m=53 mV versus 10 mV); (3) exposed neurons showed anoxic depolarization much sooner than do the naïve ones when acute anoxia, a more severe O_2 deprivation, was used in vitro (Figure 23–8); and (4) exposed neurons showed a much less rapid recovery during reoxygenation than did those that were not exposed.[61,99] Therefore, we concluded from these studies that, while there was practically no major difference in electrophysiologic properties studied between both groups during baseline, there were marked differences between exposed and naïve neurons when they were stressed.

Apoptosis: Is Hypoxia a Stimulus?

To answer the question of whether hypoxia is a stimulus of apoptosis, investigators have used a number of models in the past few years. We have a reduced preparation and found that hypoxia, in a graded fashion, induces apoptosis in nerve cells in culture.[57,100,101] Although apoptosis and necrosis have overlapping phenotypes, at the molecular level, they are rather well defined and distinct. First, we have shown that hypoxia (1) increases annexin V staining, Tunel staining, and DNA laddering; (2) renders a large percentage of neurons shrunk in volume, with fragmented organelles and condensed nucleus at the electronmicroscopic level; and (3) increases *bcl*-2 and *p53*, both of which are important in apoptosis; antisense experiments demonstrated that both *bcl*-2 and *p53* have functional implications in our model, although *p53* probably has more of an effect during hypoxia (Figure 23–9). We have also shown that caspase-3 activation occurs during hypoxia.[57,62,63,100–102]

One important issue that we and others have been addressing is the relation between ionic homeostasis and programmed gene regulation and apoptosis.[49,50,57] We recently have shown, for example, that Na^+ influx during hypoxia is an important modulator of apoptosis and that this influx activates caspase-3. Interestingly, this apoptosis could be alleviated markedly by blocking certain routes of Na^+ ion entry such as the voltage-sensitive Na^+ channels.[102]

Protection against Cell Injury

It is clear that one major aim of the ongoing research that is related to hypoxia is aimed not only at understanding the normative biology of the hypoxic responses but also at discovering the pathogenetic mechanisms that lead to cell injury or death. Hence, it is not surprising that there have been a number of attempts at preclinical and clinical trials aimed at alleviating cell injury. Indeed, there have been many protective agents, such as antiglutamatergic agents, antioxidants, opioid-like agents, channel inhibitors or activators, growth factors, and caspase inhibitors, just to name a few. More recently, erythropoietin receptors have been found in the central nervous system, and erythropoietin itself was found to be neuroprotective.[103] Another interesting substance, a hormone—parathyroid hormone-related protein (ptrp)—also protects against excitotoxicity in the brain by regulating calcium flux.[104] This research has not yet resulted in a successful clinical trial. However, with the major advances that we are witnessing at present, it may be expected that a number of strategies may work in the near future and that major therapeutic advances will result.

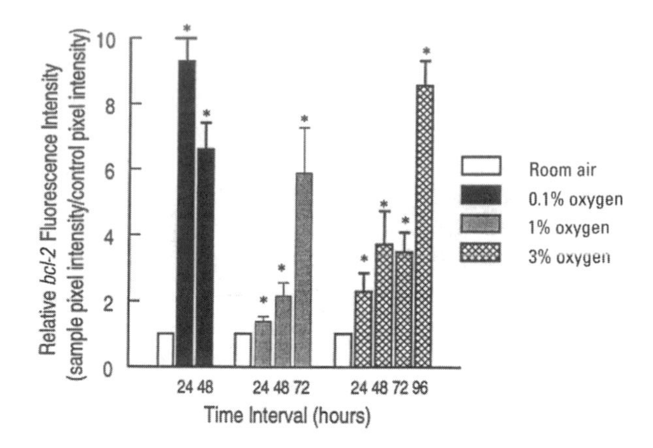

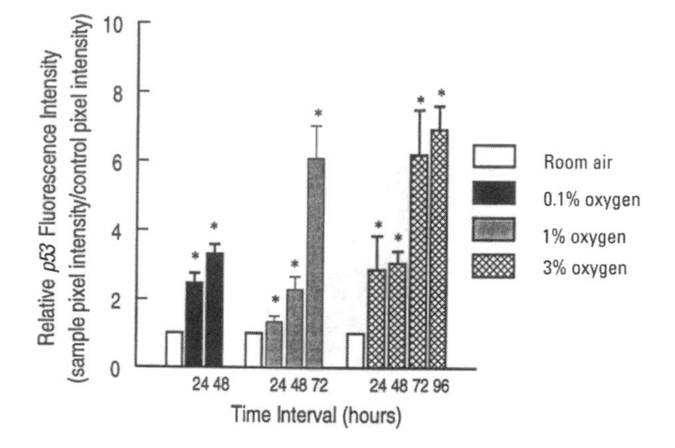

FIGURE 23–9. *Top, Bcl-2* fluorescence intensity plotted as a function of duration of hypoxic exposure and as a function of severity of hypoxia in cultured neurons. Note that *bcl-2* increases its expression with time or hypoxia severity. *Bottom,* Similar findings with *p53* expression in culture. *Significantly different from room air. (Reproduced with permission from Banasiak KJ and Haddad GG.[100] Copyright 1998, page 301, with permission from Elsevier Science.)

Novel Approaches to Understanding Hypoxic Responses at a Molecular Level

With the current revolution in biology and, in particular, molecular genetics, we have learned considerable amounts about the molecular and cellular basis of disease and about fundamental normal processes of growth and development, differentiation, and cell death. Central to this enhanced understanding of normal or pathologic processes are a number of technologic and conceptual advances that have taken place in the past few decades. These include, for example, the development and use of genetic model systems and, in particular, invertebrate models systems. Such systems have allowed investigators to uncover the genetic, molecular, and cell biologic nature and basis of normal and disease processes in efficient ways that could not have been possible otherwise. Furthermore, the enormous amount of information that is forthcoming from the various genome projects, whether in bacteria, yeast, *C. elegans*, *Drosophila*, or humans promises to yield extraordinary advances.

Although we have learned a great deal about the cellular and molecular responses to low-O_2 states, there are still many questions that are unanswered. For example, we do not know what is the exact role of each event in the overall scheme of the response to low O_2: What is the importance of the downregulation in metabolic rate during hypoxia in some individuals and species, and how does one assess its role? What is the importance of the increase in Ca^{++}_i during hypoxia? What is the importance of the opening of K^+ channels during hypoxia in nerve cells? All of these questions have elicited answers, mostly speculative, some based on evidence, sometimes teleologically reasonable, but often without hard evidence. Another interesting issue that remains a mystery is the basis of the wide heterogeneity in the response to lack of O_2 between organisms, between organs of the same individual, or between cell types of the same organ. Consider the vast difference between the rat and the turtle in terms of their cellular responses to hypoxia (see above). Consider the much greater resistance to the lack of O_2 in the newborn mammal versus the adult or mature animal (see above). While some of these questions are readily answerable in mammalian systems, others are not.

Several years ago, we elected to use a genetic model to try to answer some of the above questions in the *Drosophila melanogaster.* We had two major questions: (1) What is the genetic basis for the wide heterogeneity in the response to a lack of O_2? (2) Can we use anoxia-tolerant organisms to understand the basis of O_2 responsiveness? It was also clear to us at that time that the fresh water turtle that was considered the par excellence model for an anoxia-tolerant organism was not an optimal organism to examine, if cutting-edge molecular techniques were to be employed.

When *Drosophila* flies are subjected to extremely low oxygen concentrations ($\leq$0.01%) and their physiologic and behavioral responses are studied before, during, and after anoxia, they show an interesting phenomenon. They tolerate a complete N_2 atmosphere for 2 to 4 hours, following which they seem to recover totally without apparent injury and with the ability to mate, fly, and see normally. Of interest, mean O_2 consumption per gram of *Drosophila* tissue is substantially reduced in low-O_2 concentrations (20% of control).[21,22] It is interesting to note that the resistance to anoxia can be manifested differently in different organisms. For example, *Drosophila* definitely senses the lack of O_2, as it responds quickly in a similar way to that of mammals (ie, these flies develop anoxic stupor when the O_2 level is very low).[21,22,53] In addition, they show a physiologic response that is commensurate with this behavioral response. Indeed, extracellular recordings from flight muscles in response to Giant Fiber stimulation (a well-characterized nerve-muscle system and connections) reveal that, within a very short period, muscle evoked potentials (EPs) are totally silenced with anoxia,[21,22] and there is a complete recovery of muscle EPs with reoxygenation. This response in flies is different from that in turtles. Turtles do not seem to lose neuronal activity, even after prolonged anoxia,[5,21,22] extending to hours. From the point of view of sensing, flies seem to behave phenotypically in a manner that is similar to that of mammals, since they sense the low-O_2 conditions and respond to it like mammals.[21,22] However, flies do recover from prolonged anoxia, whereas mammalian organisms and tissues do not. Hence, the question arises, how can flies (and other organisms capable of tolerating anoxia) recover from anoxia and survive the severe stress?

Although some of the genetic models including *Drosophila* have been in use for many decades, the conservation of complements of genes with evolution, from prokaryotes to eukaryotes, and from yeast, *Drosophila, C. elegans*, and zebrafish to man, has strengthened the idea that these models can provide useful information, and they have become more appreciated in the past decade. Hence, with the important discovery of gene conservation, these models have become more timely in the efforts to solve problems relevant to human physiology, biology, and disease. Genes responsible for functions as varied as circadian rhythms, aging, alcohol intoxication, and development of tracheal buds, heart chambers, and central nervous system, all have been cloned first in model systems[22,77,101,105,106] and then studied in mammals as well as humans.

Assuming that there are genes in *Drosophila* that protect cells and tissues from anoxic injury, the main idea here is to mutagenize the fly genome and develop a mutagenesis screen to identify flies that have lost these genes, that is, flies that have loss-of-function mutations. These mutations are then mapped in detail using marker chromosomes and small deficiencies, and then cloned. The genes responsible for the abnormal phenotype are ascertained in various ways, including the use of transgenic techniques and rescue experiments. This approach has two main advantages: (1) the phenotype, which is an initial reference point, is relevant to the question asked; and (2) there is no bias in terms of the genes and molecules found.

At present, we have a number of mutations in various regions of the *Drosophila* genome that render flies susceptible to a lack of O_2. These flies have loss-of-function mutations and recover from anoxic stupor after a long latency. Electrophysiologic recordings from the Giant Fiber system in *Drosophila* have demonstrated that the recovery of the evoked potentials is much delayed (Figure 23–10). Therefore, these recordings have provided us with a correlate of the behavioral aspects of the prolonged recovery. Mapping of the induced mutations was performed with chromosomal markers and complementation tests.[22,106] Several markers were used

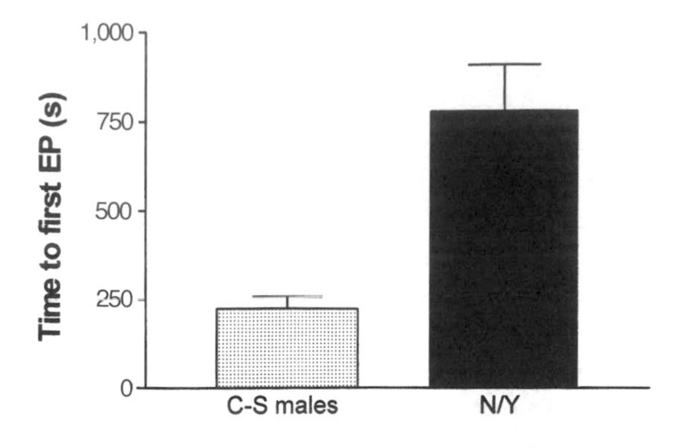

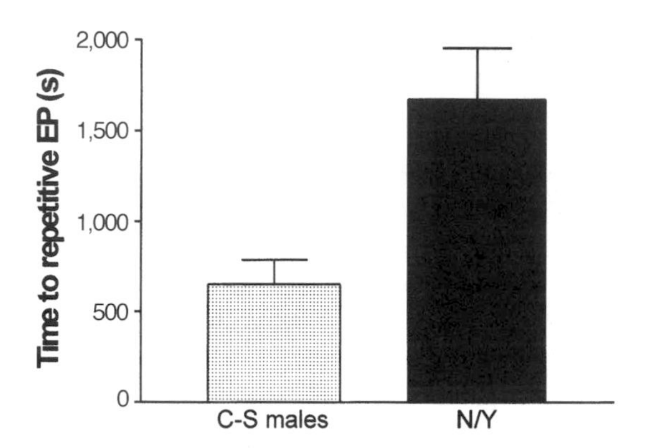

FIGURE 23–10. *Top*, Time to first evoked potential (EP) in both wild-type (C-S) and mutant male flies (N/Y) during the reoxygenation phase after having been exposed to anoxia. *Bottom*, Time to repetitive EP in both types of flies, in the same conditions as those represented in the top panel. Note that the mutant recovers from anoxia after a much longer latency.

and complementation testing was done on several recessive mutations obtained. Cloning of the first mutation is underway at present, taking advantage of the possibility that x-ray-induced mutations are usually sizeable.[22,106]

The current genetic screen has not been saturated. However, we had to screen more than 22,000 mutagenized flies to obtain the desired mutations.[22,106] This suggests that a limited number of genes could be mutated in *Drosophila* to produce similar phenotypes. Because these mutations profoundly disrupted the recovery from anoxia, we believe that this approach can be used effectively to dissect the genetic basis of resistance to anoxia, and to help delineate the genes responsible for protection against low O_2.

In our recent work, we have used other strategies. For example, we have cloned genes that seem to be important in mammals in *Drosophila*. The reason for cloning them in *Drosophila* is to study the genetic network between particular genes in the fly. These types of studies would be difficult to perform in mammals. For example, we have cloned the *Drosophila HIF1*β (*dHIF1*β) homologue and characterized it.[76] Our Northern analyses also showed that *HIF1*α and *dHIF1*β highest levels are expressed at an embryonic stage. Anoxic treatment upregulated the expression of the both α and β subunits in the fly. Overexpression of *dHIF1*α in transgenic embryos resulted in embryonic lethality, while overexpression of *dHIF1*β rendered flies significantly more sensitive to anoxic stupor and injury. Therefore, this type of work on the cloning and characterization of *dHIF1*β provides a framework for further genetic dissection of the *HIF1* complex and its role in the cellular or tissue response to O_2 deprivation.

Still another approach that may be useful is a differential display type of method. This polymerase chain reaction (PCR)-based method identifies the messenger ribonucleic acids that are over- or underexpressed when an organism is subjected to a stress or different condition, and a comparison between conditions is sought. This methodology probably will be replaced in the future by microchip arrays. Although the microchip array approach may not be driven by specific hypotheses, the result of such an approach would be a "global" view of the genes that are differentially expressed as a result of O_2 deprivation. Therefore, it may give investigators information on what is being expressed, and subsequent gene targeting at the functional level may be possible and useful insights, not only into the response of tissues to a lack of O_2, but also into potential targets for more specific and improved therapies that would enhance resistance to injury resulting from O_2 deprivation.

Summary and Future Directions

Cellular and molecular responses to hypoxia is an area of clinical and investigative importance. Although many questions have been solved, many are still unanswered. The recently developed methodologies, the novel approaches that can be harnessed well at present, and the various genomes of a number of microorganisms (*C. elegans, Drosophila,* and human) being completed or near completion, make this a prime time for research in this important area. Clinical implications forthcoming from this area of research can be tremendous, whether related to the susceptibility or tolerance of myocardial cells, neural cells, or renal tubular cells to a lack of O_2, in the elderly or in the young. Future directions should include research into (1) molecular genetics of hypoxia, (2) cell biology of injury and survival mechanisms, and (3) integration of the information obtained from the reduced preparations in all aspects of research, from cell physiology, molecular biology, and genetics to the role of various cellular elements in the overall function of the cell.

References

1. Haddad GG, Donnelly DF. O_2 deprivation induces a major depolarization in brainstem neurons in the adult but not in the neonatal rat. J Physiol (Lond) 1990;429:411–28.

2. Donnelly DF, Jiang C, Haddad GG. Comparative responses of brainstem and hippocampal neurons to O_2deprivation: in vitro intracellular studies. Am J Physiol 1992; 262:L549–54.
3. Jiang C, Haddad GG. Differential responses of neocortical neurons to glucose and/or O_2 deprivation in the human and rat. J Neurophysiol 1992;68:2165–73.
4. Cummins TR, Jiang C, Haddad GG. Human neocortical excitability is decreased during anoxia via sodium channel modulation. J Clin Invest 1993;91:608–15.
5. Haddad GG, Jiang C. Mechanisms of anoxia-induced depolarization in brainstem neurons: in-vitro current and voltage clamp studies in the adult rat. Brain Res 1993;625:261–8.
6. O'Reilly J, Cummins TR, Haddad GG. Oxygen deprivation inhibits Na^+ current in rat hippocampal neurones via protein kinase C. J Physiol (Lond)1997;503:479–88.
7. Haddad GG, Jiang C. O_2 deprivation in the central nervous system: on mechanisms of neuronal response, differential sensitivity and injury. Prog Neurobiol 1993;40:277–318.
8. Lipton P. Ischemic cell death in brain neurons. Physiol Rev 1999;79:1431–568.
9. Yao H, Gu XQ, Douglas RM, Haddad GG. The role of Na^+/H^+ exchanger during O_2 deprivation in mouse CA1 neurons. Am J Physiol Cell Physiol 2001;281:C1205–10.
10. Aw TY, Jones DP. Cyanide toxicity in hepatocytes under aerobic and anaerobic conditions. Am J Physiol 1989; 257:C435–41.
11. Aw TY, Andersson BS, Jones DP. Suppression of mitochondrial respiratory functions after short-term anoxia. Am J Physiol 1987;252:C362–8.
12. Ransom BR, Philbin DM Jr. Anoxia-induced extracellular ionic changes in CNS white matter: the role of glial cells. Can J Physiol Pharmacol 1992;70 Suppl:S181–9.
13. Fern R, Davis P, Waxman SG, Ransom BR. Axon conduction and survival in CNS white matter during energy deprivation: a developmental study. J Neurophysiol 1998; 79:95–105.
14. Hansen AJ. Extracellular potassium concentration in juvenile and adult rat brain cortex during anoxia. Acta Physiol Scand 1977;99:412–20.
15. Singer D. Neonatal tolerance to hypoxia: a comparative-physiological approach. Comp Biochem Physiol A Physiol 1999;123:221–34.
16. Gaudio KM, Thulin G, Siegel NJ. Immature tubules are tolerant of oxygen deprivation. Pediatr Nephrol 1997; 11:757–60.
17. Gaudio KM, Thulin G, Ardito T, et al. Immature renal tubules are resistant to prolonged anoxia. Pediatr Res 1994;35:152–6.
18. Ostadal B, Ostadalova I, Dhalla NS. Development of cardiac sensitivity to oxygen deficiency: comparative and ontogenetic aspects. Physiol Rev 1999;79:635–59.
19. Jiang C, Xia Y, Haddad GG. Role of ATP sensitive K^+ channels during anoxia: major differences between rat (newborn, adult) and turtle neurons. J Physiol (Lond) 1992; 448:599–612.
20. Xia Y, Jiang C, Haddad GG. Oxidative and glycolytic pathways in rat (newborn, adult) and turtle brain: role during anoxia. Am J Physiol 1992;262:R595–603.
21. Krishnan SN, Sun Y-A, Mohsenin A, et al. Behavioral and electrophysiologic responses of *Drosophila melanogaster* to prolonged periods of anoxia. J Insect Physiol 1997; 43:203–10.
22. Haddad GG, Sun Y-A, Wyman RJ, Xu T. Genetic basis of tolerance to O_2deprivation in *Drosophila melanogaster*. Proc Natl Acad Sci U S A 1997;94:10809–12.
23. Haddad GG. Study of anoxia tolerance: use of a novel genetic approach. In: Haddad GG, Xu T, eds. Genetic models in cardiorespiratory biology. Lung biology in health and disease series. New York: Marcel Dekker, 2001:139–51.
24. Wasser JS, Guthrie SS, Chari M. In vitro tolerance to anoxia and ischemia in isolated hearts from hypoxia sensitive and hypoxia tolerant turtles. Comp Biochem Physiol A Physiol 1997;118:1359–70.
25. Willmore WG, Storey WB. Antioxidant systems and anoxia tolerance in a freshwater turtle *Pseudemys scripta elegans*. Mol Cell Biochem 1997;170(1–2):177–85.
26. Arthur PG, Franklin CE, Cousins KL, et al. Energy turnover in the normoxic and anoxic turtle heart. Comp Biochem Physiol A Physiol 1997;117:121–6.
27. Willmore WG, Storey WB. Glutathione systems and anoxia tolerance in turtles. Am J Physiol 1997;273(1 Pt 2):R219–25.
28. Perez-Pinzon MA, Lutz PL, Sick TJ, Rosenthal M. Metabolic mechanisms of anoxia tolerance in the turtle brain. Adv Exp Med Biol 1997;411:75–81.
29. Hochachka PW, Buck LT, Doll CJ, et al. Unifying theory of hypoxia tolerance: molecular/metabolic defense and rescue mechanisms for surviving oxygen lack. Proc Natl Acad Sci U S A 1996;18:9493–8.
30. Lutz PL, Nilsson GE, Perez-Pinzon MA. Anoxia tolerant animals from a neurobiological perspective. Comp Biochem Physiol B Biochem Mol Biol 1996;113:3–13.
31. Jackson DC, Ramsey AL, Paulson JM, et al. Lactic acid buffering by bone and shell in anoxic softshell and painted turtles. Physiol Biochem Zool 2000;73:290–7.
32. Bickler PE, Donohoe PH, Buck LT. Hypoxia-induced silencing of NMDA receptors in turtle neurons. J Neurosci 2000;20:3522–8.
33. Hansen AJ. The extracellular potassium concentration in brain cortex following ischemia in hypo- and hyperglycemic rats. Acta Physiol Scand 1978;102:324–9.
34. Hansen AJ. Effect of anoxia on ion distribution in the brain. Physiol Rev 1985; 65:101–48.
35. Jiang C, Haddad GG. The effect of anoxia on intracellular and extracellular potassium activity in hypoglossal neurons in-vitro. J Neurophysiol 1991;66:103–11.
36. Cummins TR, Donnelly DF, Haddad GG. Effect of metabolic inhibition on the excitability of isolated hippocampal CA1 neurons: developmental aspects. J Neurophysiol 1991;66:1471–82.
37. Jiang C, Agulian S, Haddad GG. Cl^- and Na^+ homeostasis during anoxia in hypoglossal neurons: intracellular and extracellular in-vitro studies. J Physiol (Lond) 1992; 448:697–708.
38. Friedman JE, Haddad GG. Major differences in $Ca^{2+}{}_i$between neonatal and adult rat CA1 neurons in response to anoxia: role of $Ca^{+2}{}_O$ and $Na^+{}_O$. J Neurosci 1993;13:63–72.

39. Jiang C, Haddad GG. Short periods of hypoxia activate a K^+ current in central neurons. Brain Res 1993;64:352–6.
40. Xia Y, Haddad GG. Voltage-sensitive Na^+ channels increase in number in newborn rat brain after in utero hypoxia. Brain Res 1994;635:339–44.
41. Jiang C, Sigworth FJ, Haddad GG. O_2 deprivation activates an ATP-inhibitable K^+ channels in substantia nigra neurons. J Neurosci 1994;14:5590–602.
42. Jiang C, Haddad GG. Oxygen deprivation inhibits a K^+ channel independently of cytosolic factors in central neurons. J Physiol (Lond)1994;481:15–26.
43. Friedman JE, Haddad GG. Removal of extracellular sodium prevents anoxia-induced injury in rat CA1 hippocampal neurons. Brain Res 1994;641:57–64.
44. Friedman JE, Haddad GG. Anoxia induces an increase in intracellular sodium in rat central neurons. Brain Res 1994;663:329–34.
45. Chidekel AS, Friedman JE, Haddad GG. Anoxia-induced neuronal injury: role of Na^+ entry and Na^+-dependent transport. Exp Neurol 1997;146:403–13.
46. Haddad GG. K^+ions and channels: mechanisms of sensing O_2 deprivation in central neurons. Kidney Int 1997;51:467–72.
47. Jiang C, Haddad GG. Modulation of K^+ channels by intracellular ATP in human neocortical neurons. J Neurophysiol 1997;77:93–102.
48. Chin LS, Park CC, Zitnay KM, et al. 4-aminopyridine causes apoptosis and blocks an outward rectifier K^+ channel in malignant astrocytoma cell lines. J Neurosci Res 1997; 48:122–7.
49. Yu SP, Yeh CH, Sensi SL, et al. Mediation of neuronal apoptosis by enhancement of outward potassium current. Science 1997;278:114–7.
50. Yu SP, Yeh CH, Strasser U, et al. NMDA receptor-mediated K^+efflux and neuronal apoptosis. Science 1999;284:336–9.
51. Hansen AJ, Jounsgaard J, Hahnses H. Anoxia increases potassium conductance in hippocampal nerve cells. Acta Physiol Scand 1982;115:301–10.
52. Xia Y, Haddad GG. Major differences in CNS sulfonylurea receptor distribution between the rat (newborn, adult) and turtle. J Comp Neurol 1991;314:278–89.
53. Haddad GG, Liu H. Different O_2-sensing mechanisms by different K^+channels. In: Lahiri S, Prabhakar N, Foster RE, eds. Arterial chemoreceptors: oxygen sensing—from molecule to man. Vol. 475. Kluwer Academic/Plenum Publishers, 2000: 441–52.
54. Jiang C, Haddad GG. A direct mechanism for sensing low oxygen levels by central neurons. Proc Natl Acad Sci U S A 1994;91:7198–201.
55. Liu H, Moczydlowski E, Haddad GG. O_2 deprivation inhibits Ca^{2+}-activated K^+channels via cytosolic factors in mice neocortical neurons. J Clin Invest 1999;104:577–88.
56. Hida H, Takeda M, Soliven B. Ceramide inhibits inwardly rectifying K^+ currents via a Ras- and Raf-1-dependent pathway in cultured oligodendrocytes. J Neurosci 1998;18:8712–9.
57. Banasiak KJ, Xia Y, Haddad GG. Mechanisms underlying hypoxia-induced neuronal apoptosis. Prog Neurobiol 2000;62:215–49.
58. Fung M-L, Haddad GG. Anoxic-induced depolarization in CA1 hippocampal neurons: role of Na^+-dependent mechanisms. Brain Res 1997;762:97–102.
59. Xia Y, Haddad GG. Effect of prolonged O_2 deprivation on Na^+ channels: differential regulation in adult versus fetal rat brain. Neuroscience 1999;94:1231–43.
60. Fung M-L, Croning MDR, Haddad GG. Sodium homeostasis in hippocampal slices during oxygen and glucose deprivation: role of voltage-sensitive sodium channels. Neurosci Lett 1999;275(1):41–4.
61. Xia Y, Fung M-L, O'Reilly J, Haddad GG. Increased neuronal excitability after long term O_2 deprivation is mediated mainly by sodium channels. Mol Brain Res 2000;76:211–9.
62. Banasiak KJ, Haddad GG. Importance of sodium homeostasis during hypoxia-induced apoptosis [abstract]. Pediatr Res 1999;45:339A.
63. Banasiak KJ, Donnelly D, Haddad GG. Sodium flux during hypoxia-induced neuronal apoptosis [abstract]. Soc Neurosci 1999;25:754.
64. Yao H, Ma E, Gu XQ, Haddad GG. Intracellular pH regulation of CA1 neurons in Na^+/H^+ isoform 1 mutant mice. J Clin Invest 1999;104:637–45.
65. Yao H, Gu XQ, Haddad GG. Anoxia affects the pH regulation in mouse CA1 neurons [abstract]. Soc Neurosci 2000;26:1671.
66. Decking UKM, Hartmann M, Rose H, et al. Cardioprotective actions of KC 12291. Naunyn Schmiedebergs Arch Pharmacol 1998;358:547–53.
67. Eigel BN, Hadley RW. Contribution of the Na^+ channel and Na^+/H^+ exchanger to the anoxic rise of $[Na^+]$ in ventricular myocytes. Am J Physiol 1999;277:H1817–22.
68. Fearon IM, Varadi G, Koch S, et al. Splice variants reveal the region involved in oxygen sensing by recombinant human L-type Ca^{2+} channels. Circ Res 2000;87:537–9.
69. Yatani A, Kamp TJ. Tails of the L-type Ca^{2+} channel to sense oxygen or not. Circ Res 2000;87:535–6.
70. Haddad GG, Mellins RB. Hypoxia and respiratory control in early life. Annu Rev Physiol 1984;46:629–43.
71. Haddad GG. O_2 deprivation in tolerant and non-tolerant organisms: phylogeny and ontogeny. In: Haddad GG, Lister G, eds. Tissue oxygen: developmental, molecular and integrated function. Vol. 95. New York: Marcel Dekker, 1996:573–94.
72. Ma E, Haddad GG. Cell and molecular responses to hypoxic stress. In: Storey KB, Storey JM, eds. Environmental stressors and gene responses. Vol. 1. Stamford (CT): JAI Press, 2000:89–97.
73. Ma E, Xu T, Haddad GG. Gene regulation by O_2deprivation: an anoxia-regulated novel gene in *Drosophila melanogaster.* Mol Brain Res 1999;63:217–24.
74. Ma E, Haddad GG. Anoxia regulates gene expression in the central nervous system of *Drosophila melanogaster.* Mol Brain Res 1997;46:325–8.
75. Ma E, Haddad GG. A *Drosophila* Cdk5α-like molecule and its possible role in response to O_2 deprivation. Biochem Biophys Res Commun 1999;261:459–63.
76. Ma E, Haddad GG. Isolation and characterization of the hypoxia-inducible factor 1α in *Drosophila melanogaster.* Mol Brain Res 1999;73:11–6.
77. Haddad GG. Drosophila genes and anoxia. In: Fink G, ed. Encyclopedia of stress. California: Academic Press, 2000: 746–52.

78. Little E, Tocco G, Baudry M, et al. Induction of glucose-regulated protein (glucose-regulated protein 78/BiP and glucose-regulated protein 94) and heat shock protein 70 transcripts in the immature rat brain following status epilepticus. Neuroscience 1996;75:209–19.
79. Chen J, Graham SH, Zhu RL, Simon RP. Stress proteins and tolerance to focal cerebral ischemia. J Cereb Blood Flow Metab 1996;16:566–77.
80. Rordorf G, Koroschetz WJ, Bonventre JV. Heat shock protects cultured neurons from glutamate toxicity. Neuron 1991;7:1043–51.
81. Akcetin X, Pregla R, Darmer D, et al. Differential expression of heat shock proteins 70-1 and 70-2 mRNA after ischemia-reperfusion injury of rat kidney. Urol Res 1999;27:306–11.
82. Chien CT, Chen CF, Hsu SM, et al. Protective mechanism of preconditioning hypoxia attenuates apoptosis formation during renal ischemia/reperfusion phase. Transplant Proc 1999;31:2012–3.
83. Bush KT, George SK, Zhang PL, Nigam SK. Pretreatment with inducers of ER molecular chaperones protects epithelial cells subjected to ATP depletion. Am J Physiol 1999;277:F211–8.
84. Van Why SK, Siegel NJ. Heat shock proteins in renal injury and recovery. Curr Opin Nephrol Hypertens 1998; 7:407–12.
85. Van Why SK, Mann AS, Thulin G, et al. Activation of heat-shock transcription factor by graded reductions in renal ATP, in vivo, in the rat. J Clin Invest 1994;94:1518–23.
86. Semenza GL. HIF-1: mediator of physiological and pathophysiological responses to hypoxia. J Appl Physiol 2000; 88:1474–80.
87. Semenza GL. Surviving ischemia: adaptive responses mediated by hypoxia-inducible factor 1. J Clin Invest 2000;106:809–12.
88. Semenza GL. Regulation of mammalian O_2 homeostasis by hypoxia-inducible factor 1. Annu Rev Cell Dev Biol 1999; 15:551–78.
89. Semenza GL. Hypoxia-inducible factor 1: master regulator of O_2 homeostasis. Curr Opin Genet Dev 1998;8:588–94.
90. Semenza GL, Wang GL. A nuclear factor induced by hypoxia via de novo protein synthesis binds to the human erythropoietin gene enhancer at a site required for transcriptional activation. Mol Cell Biol 1992;12:5447–54.
91. Semenza GL. Roth PH, Fang HM, Wang GL. Transcriptional regulation of genes encoding glycolytic enzymes by hypoxia-inducible factor 1. J Biol Chem 1994; 269:23757–63.
92. Semenza GL, Jiang BH, Leung SW, et al. Hypoxia response elements in the aldolase A, enolase 1, and lactate dehydrogenase A gene promoters contain essential binding sites for hypoxia-inducible factor 1. J Biol Chem 1996; 271:32529–37.
93. Wang GL, Jiang BH, Rue EA, Semenza GL. Hypoxia-inducible factor 1 is a basic-helix-loop-helix-PAS heterodimer regulated by cellular O_2 tension. Proc Natl Acad Sci U S A 1995;92:5510–4.
94. Wang GL, Semenza GL. General involvement of hypoxia-inducible factor 1 in transcriptional response to hypoxia. Proc Natl Acad Sci U S A 1993;90:4304–8.
95. Wang GL, Semenza GL. Characterization of hypoxia-inducible factor 1 and regulation of DNA binding activity by hypoxia. J Biol Chem 1993;268:21513–8.
96. Wang GL, Semenza GL. Purification and characterization of hypoxia-inducible factor 1. J Biol Chem 1995; 270:1230–7.
97. Bergeron M, Gidday JM, Yu AY, et al. Role of hypoxia-inducible factor-1 in hypoxia-induced ischemic tolerance in neonatal rat brain. Ann Neurol 2000;48:285–96.
98. Iyer NV, Kotch LE, Agani F, et al. Cellular and developmental control of O_2 homeostasis by hypoxia-inducible factor 1 alpha. Genes Dev 1998;12:149–62.
99. O'Reilly JP, Haddad GG. Chronic hypoxia in vivo renders neocortical neurons more vulnerable to subsequent acute hypoxic stress. Brain Res 1996;711:203–10.
100. Banasiak KJ, Haddad GG. Hypoxia-induced apoptosis: effects of severity of hypoxia and role of p53 in neuronal cell death. Brain Res 1998;797:295–304.
101. Banasiak BJ, Cronin T, Haddad GG. bcl-2 prolongs neuronal survival in graded hypoxia. Mol Brain Res 1999; 72:214–25.
102. Banasiak K, Burenkova O, Haddad GG. Sodium influx during hypoxia induces neuronal apoptosis via activation of caspase-3 [abstract]. Soc Neurosci 2000;26:1880.
103. Brines, ML, Ghezzi P, Keenan S, et al. Erythropoietin crosses the blood-brain barrier to protect against experimental brain injury. Proc Nat Acad Sci U S A 2000; 97:10526–31.
104. Haddad GG. Use of genetic models in respiratory neurobiology and sleep. In: Strohl KP, ed. Current opinion in pulmonary medicine. Vol. 5. Philadelphia (PA): Lippincott Williams & Wilkins, 1999:349–54.
105. Brines ML, Ling Z, Broadus AE. Parathyroid hormone–related protein protects against kainic acid excitotoxicity in rat cerebellar granule cells by regulating L-type channel calcium flux. Neurosci Lett 1999;274:13–16.
106. Haddad GG. Enhancing our understanding of the molecular responses to hypoxia in mammals using *Drosophila melanogaster*. J Appl Physiol 2000;88:1481–7.

CHAPTER 24

Effects of Hypoxia on the Developing Pulmonary Circulation

Todd C. Carpenter, MD, Kurt R. Stenmark, MD

The pulmonary vascular bed is among the most sensitive tissues in the body to variations in oxygen levels. Changes in oxygenation are critical modulators of the physiology of the pulmonary circulation, starting with fetal lung development and continuing through the fetal-neonatal transition to include postnatal hypoxic pulmonary vasoconstriction. In addition, tissue hypoxia is an important factor in many disease states affecting the lung and its vessels, including infections, congenital heart lesions, pulmonary vascular lesions, and environmental exposures. The complex responses to hypoxia seen in the pulmonary vasculature have been the subject of intense study over the last decade. Through this work it has become increasingly clear that exposure to hypoxia has profound effects not only on vascular tone and structure in the developing lung but also on vascular development itself, on vascular permeability, and perhaps on the development and modulation of inflammatory responses in the lung as well.

Hypoxia in Early Pulmonary Vascular Development

The development of the pulmonary vascular bed in embryonic and fetal life is a complex and poorly understood process. Much has been learned in recent years, however, about the genes that appear to be critical for vascular development, primarily from studies of the effects of targeted deletions, or "knockouts," in those genes in experimental animals. As shown in Table 24–1, the deletion of any one of the genes critical for vascular development results in early embryonic lethality, often before any pulmonary vascular development takes place. Nonetheless, these studies have provided many important lessons for our understanding of lung vascular development. Among these concepts is the idea that, since fetal growth and development take place in a hypoxic environment, and since many of the genes that control fetal development are regulated by hypoxia, hypoxia itself may be a critical element in the process of vascular development.

Before discussing molecular mechanisms important in development and the role of hypoxia in this period, a brief review of the embryologic process of lung development is in order. The first intrapulmonary vascular structures to appear are vascular lakes of hematopoietic cells arising in embryos at approximately 4 weeks' gestational age. By 50 days' gestational age a vascular network with luminal connections to central pulmonary veins is present. Interestingly, at this time the airways have not yet reached these regions of the lung, and, thus, airway cells do not appear to direct the formation of the earliest vascular channels. At its first appearance, the pulmonary artery is small and thick walled, and it accompanies the airway tree only part of its distance, leaving many peripheral airways unaccompanied by a pulmonary artery branch. By contrast, the pulmonary veins have a peripheral and patent network well before the pulmonary arteries do. As airway branching continues in the pseudoglandular phase of lung development, the pulmonary artery catches up, so that small branches are found with all airways. By the canalicular phase, when lung development is compatible with viability in humans, continuity between pulmonary artery and the peripheral capillary network has been established. This combination of events lays the foundation for the formation and subsequent maturation of the vascular network into a system that ultimately allows blood flow from the heart, through the lungs, and back to the heart.[1,2]

Studies of the cellular processes responsible for embryonic lung development have given rise to the concept that multiple fundamental events are involved in blood vessel formation. Detailed reviews of this process are available elsewhere; here we briefly summarize the two primary processes: vasculogenesis and angiogenesis.[3–7] The de novo formation of endothelial cells from primitive mesenchymal precursors and the organization of these endothelial cells into vascular channels is termed "vasculogenesis." In contrast, vascularization as a result of the sprouting of new vessels from existing ones is termed "angiogenesis." This process is critical to the earliest stages of vascular development, is used in the remodeling of the primary capillary plexus formed by vasculogenesis, and, in some organs, can be used as the primary mechanism of blood vessel formation. Both vasculogenic and angiogenic processes appear to operate in human lung development, and, in addition, a lytic process may be used to establish connections between vascular channels derived from local vasculogenic

TABLE 24–1. Factors Involved in Vascular Development: Observations in Knockout Animals*

Gene Knockout	Stage of Embryonic Lethality	Vascular Phenotype
Receptor Tyrosine Kinases		
VEGFR1	E8.5–9.5	Failure of endothelial cell formation
VEGFR2	E8.5–9.5	Vascular channels disorganized, excess angioblasts, structures entering vessel lumens
VEGFR3	E9.5–12	Defective vessel remodeling and organization, irregular large vessels with defective lumens
Tie1	E13.5–P1	Edema, poor vessel integrity, and hemorrhage
Tie2	E10.5	Defective vessel remodeling, organization, and sprouting; heart trabeculation defects
Ephrin B2/B3	E10.5 (~30%)	Some defective vessel primordia; defective vessel remodeling, organization, and sprouting; heart trabeculation defects
PDGF-BR	P1	Failure of mesangial recruitment
Ligands		
VEGF-A†	E10.5	Absent dorsal aorta, defective endothelial cell development
Ang 1	E10.5	Vasculogenesis/angiogenesis intact; defective vessel remodeling, organization, and sprouting; heart trabeculation defects
Ang 2	E12.5–P1	Edema, poor vessel integrity, and hemorrhage
PDGF-BB	E10.5	Failure of glomerular development
TGF-β1	E10.5	Failure to remodel primary vascular plexus of yolk sac
Ephrin B2/B3	E10.5 (~30%)	Some defective vessel primordia; defective vessel remodeling, organization, and sprouting; heart trabeculation defects
Other factors		
HIF1α	≤ E10.5	Intact endothelial cell differentiation but defective yolk sac vascularization
VE-cadherin	E10.5	Failure to develop yolk sac vascular plexus
Tissue factor	E8.5	Embryonic vascular failure with failure of smooth muscle cell/pericyte recruitment

*Knockouts of *VEGF* and its receptors have yielded defects primarily in the early process of vasculogenesis, and, accordingly, these mutant embryos tend to die at early stages of development. In contrast, the *Tie2* and *Ang 1* knockout embryos die at later stages and exhibit defects similar to each other but with normal vasculogenesis and perturbed angiogenesis. Deletion of *Ang 2*, the putative natural antagonist of *Ang 1/Tie2* signaling, results in lethality at stages after the vascular system has undergone both vasculogenesis and angiogenesis. Ephrin B2/B3 and ephrin B2 knockout animals die primarily due to defects in angiogenesis similar to the *Tie2* and *Ang 1* knockout embryos, although some defects in vasculogenesis also were reported. Ephrin B4 mice die at similar stages.

†Because of the heterozygous lethality of heterozygous *VEGF* mutations, *VEGF* null (-/-) mice were generated by embryonic stem cell aggregation with tetraploid blastocysts resulting in contribution of the *VEGF* (-/-) cells to the embryo proper and not to extraembryonic tissues. This difference in technology makes direct comparison with the knockouts difficult. It might be predicted that contributions of *VEGF* from the extraembryonic (*VEGF* +/+ but tetraploid) tissues may have dampened the severity of the phenotype and allowed survival of the embryos to later stages of development.

VEGFR = vascular endothelial growth factor receptor; PDGF = platelet-derived growth factor; Ang = angiopoietin; TGF = transforming growth factor; *HIF* = hypoxia-inducible factor; VE = vascular endothelial; E = embryonic day; P = postnatal.

mechanisms and channels formed as a result of angiogenic mechanisms.[1,2]

Many of the genes required for the proper formation of blood vessels within the developing lung have been identified recently, and, to date, these genes appear to be identical to the genes critical for vascular formation in other organs throughout the body (see Table 24–1). Vascularization is clearly the result of the complex interplay of factors that act either as activators or inhibitors of the process and that are the products of numerous genes. The complexity of these events is evident in the fact that vascularization can be disrupted at multiple points with varying consequences. Molecules known to serve as inducers, or activators, of angiogenesis include vascular endothelial growth factor (*VEGF*), fibroblast growth factors (*FGFs*) 1 and 2, transforming growth factors (*TGFs*) α and β, tumor necrosis factor α (*TNF*-α), ephrins, angiogenin, and the angiopoietins. The negative regulators identified to date include angiostatin, endostatin, thrombospondin, platelet factor 4, and the 16-kD N terminal fragment of prolactin. Importantly, the expression of the genes coding for most of these regulatory factors is known to be modulated by hypoxia (Table 21–2).

Among the positive regulators of angiogenesis, *VEGF* occupies a particularly important place because of its potency and specificity for endothelial cells and because of the multitude of responses it can elicit in those cells.[3,6–8] *VEGF* is secreted by a variety of lung cell types, including airway epithelial cells, vascular smooth muscle cells, and fibroblasts. In adult animals, *VEGF* is known to induce increases in vascular permeability and to promote new blood vessel growth. Hypoxia has been shown to be a powerful signal stimulating *VEGF* expression, leading to the concept that low oxygen levels sensed by cells and tissues lead to the stimulation of new blood vessel development as a means of alleviating the hypoxia.[9,10] In the past few years, several additional members of the *VEGF* family have been discovered, including placenta growth factor (*PIGF*), *VEGF-B*, *VEGF-C*, *VEGF-D*, and viral homologues of *VEGF* termed *VEGF-E*, each of which may play specific roles in vascular development. The actions of the *VEGF* family members are mediated by a family of receptor tyrosine kinases (RTKs), whose members include *VEGFR1* (*Flt1*), *VEGFR2* (*KDR* or *Flk1*), and *VEGFR3* (*Flt4*). These receptors are expressed predominately, but not exclusively, on endothelial cells. In addition, neuropilin-1, a transmembrane protein involved in regulation of axonal guidance in neurons, has been described as a co-receptor for another *VEGF* family member, *VEGF-165*. Both *VEGF* and its receptors appear to be critical in early pulmonary vascular development. Numerous in vitro studies have demonstrated the importance of *VEGF*

TABLE 24–2. Regulators of Vascular Growth and the Effect of Hypoxia on Their Expression

Regulators	Effect of Hypoxia	Function
Activators		
VEGF family members*†	↑	Stimulate angiogenesis, vasculogenesis, permeability, leukocyte adhesion
VEGFR†, NRP-1	↑	Integrate angiogenic and survival signals
Ang 1 and *Tie2**†	↑	Stabilize vessels, inhibit permeability
Ephrins†	?	Regulate arterial/venous specification
PDGF-BB and receptors	↑	Recruit smooth muscle cells
FGF, HGF, MCP-1	↑	Stimulate angiogenesis, arterial development
TGF- β*1*‡, endoglin	↑	Stimulate extracellular matrix production
TGF-β receptors	?	Stimulate extracellular matrix production
Integrins α, β, $\alpha_v\beta_5$, $\alpha_3\beta_1$	↑	Receptors for matrix macromolecules and proteinases
VE-cadherin; PECAM (CD31)	↑	Endothelial junction molecules
Plasminogen activators, MMPs	↑	Remodel matrix, release and activate growth factors
PAI-1	↑	Stabilize nascent vessels
NOS, COX-2	↑	Stimulate angiogenesis and vasodilation
Id1/Id3	?	Determine endothelial plasticity
Inhibitors		
Angiostatin and related plasminogen kringles	?	Suppress tumor angiogenesis
Vasostatin, calreticulin	?	Inhibit endothelial growth
Endostatin (collagen XVII fragment)	?	Inhibit endothelial survival and migration
VEGFR1, soluble *VEGFR1*	?	Sink for *VEGF, VEGF-B* and *PIGF*
Soluble NRP-1	?	
Ang 2†‡	↑	Antagonist of *Ang 1*
TSP-1, -2	↓	Inhibit endothelial migration, growth, adhesion, and survival
Platelet factor 4	?	Inhibits binding of *bFGF* and *VEGF*
TIMPs, MMP inhibitors, PEX	?	Suppress pathologic angiogenesis
Prolactin (M, 16K)	?	Inhibits *bFGF/VEGF*
IFN-α, -β, -γ; IP-10; IL-4, IL-12, IL-18	?	Inhibit endothelial migration, downregulate bFGF

*Also present in or affecting nonendothelial cells.† Data from Yancopoulos GD, Davis S, Gale NW, et al. Vascular-specific growth factors and blood vessel formation. Nature 2000;407:242–8.
‡Opposite effect in some contexts.

VEGR = vascular endothelial growth factor receptor; NRP = neuropilin; *Ang* = angiopoietin; *PDGF* = platelet-derived growth factor; *FGF* = fibroblast growth factor; *HGF* = hematopoietic growth factor; MCP = monocyte chemoattractant protein; *TGF* = transforming growth factor; VE = vascular endothelial; PECAM = platelet-endothelial cell adhesion molecule; MMP = matrix metalloproteinase; PAI = plasminogen activator inhibitor; NOS = nitric oxide synthase; COX = cyclooxygenase; Id = inhibitor of differentiation; TSP = thrombospondin; TIMP = tissue inhibitor of MMP; PEX = proteolytic fragment of MMP2; IFN = interferon; IP = inducible protein; IL = interleukin; *PIGF* = placenta growth factor; *bFGF* = basic fibroblast growth factor; ↑ = increased function; ↓ = decreased function.

in endothelial cell proliferation, migration, and tube formation. Knockout studies have elegantly confirmed the critical importance of the *VEGF-A/VEGFR* system in the early stages of blood vessel formation in both vasculogenesis and angiogenesis (see Table 24–1). Recent work suggests that *VEGF* is also important in the process of alveolarization, which occurs later in lung development.[11]

In addition to the *VEGF/VEGFR* system, two other RTK systems have been described that act in an endothelial cell–specific manner and that are crucial for vascular development: the angiopoietins and their receptors, *Tie1* and *Tie2*, as well as the ephrins and their receptors, Eph β2 to β4.[3,6,7,12] As with *VEGF*, the specificity of the angiopoietins for the vascular endothelium results from the restricted distribution of the angiopoietin receptors, *Tie1* and *Tie2*, to these cells. The four known angiopoietins (*Ang 1* to *Ang 4*) all bind to *Tie2*. At present it is unclear whether these molecules also use the *Tie1* receptor. In addition, the angiopoietins provide an example of a growth factor family consisting of both receptor activators (*Ang 1* and *Ang 4*) and receptor blockers (*Ang 2* and *Ang 3*). The existence of both activators and blockers of the *Tie2* receptor suggests that turning off the receptor might be as important in some situations as turning it on in others. The actions of the angiopoietins are quite different than those of *VEGF*. *Ang 1* does not elicit mitogenic responses or induce vascular tube formation (vasculogenesis), but it does promote endothelial cell sprouting in vitro (angiogenesis). In vivo studies using knockout animals reveal that *Ang 1* seems to act in a coordinated fashion with *VEGF*, but that its critical role in vascular development occurs later than does the role of *VEGF*. Despite the above findings, the precise role of the angiopoietin/*Tie* system in lung development remains unclear at the present time.

Most recently, particular members of the large ephrin family have been identified as having important and unique roles in vascular development.[3,12,13] At least in some cases, these molecules appear to act via a receptor that is restricted not just to the vascular endothelium but even more precisely to the endothelium lining venous, as opposed to arterial, vessels. Ephrins act through the *Eph* receptors, which are the largest subfamily of RTKs. Interestingly, ephrins do not function as typical soluble ligands for their receptors; rather they must be membrane attached to activate their receptors. Like the angiopoietins, ephrins do not induce potent mitogenic responses from target cells. Recent studies in animals with targeted gene deletions, however, firmly establish *Eph* family members as key players in the process of embryonic vascular development (see Table 24–1). Perhaps most importantly, ephrin β2/Ephβ4 expression studies clearly demonstrate that there are molecular differences between arterial and venous endothelial cells even at very early stages of development; that these differences are, at least in part, programmed genetically; that these differences may be critical to the normal development of the vasculature; and that these differences may contribute to the differences in physiologic behavior between arteries and veins observed later in life (see below). Whether hypoxia affects ephrin signaling has not yet been established.

The factors described above act predominately in an endothelial-specific manner to initiate vascular tube formation and the processes of vasculogenesis and angiogenesis. Additional factors are necessary for the continued maturation and development of vessels in a process that includes the formation of extracellular matrix–rich basement membranes and the investment of new vessels with pericytes and smooth muscle cells. Platelet-derived growth factor B (*PDGF-B*) has been shown to be important in the recruitment of smooth muscle cells to new blood vessels, and signaling by *TGF-β1* and *Ang 1/Tie2* stabilizes the interaction between endothelial and smooth muscle cells. In addition, members of the coagulation cascade, including tissue factor (*TF*), factor V, and the thrombin receptor, also appear to play a critical role in vascular development.[6,14,15] Embryos rendered deficient for *TF* exhibit an early embryonic lethality. Although early blood vessel development occurs, the vessels exhibit decreased integrity due to a lack of pericytes and smooth muscle cells, which are the cell types that characteristically provide support for the vascular wall. *TF*, perhaps like *PDGF-B*, acts as a chemoattractant critical for vascular development, and this chemotactic activity appears independent of its role in blood coagulation. Importantly, both of these factors are regulated by hypoxia, and several studies suggest that hypoxia-induced upregulation of these genes contributes to pathophysiologic changes in the vasculature.

The exact role of the coagulation system in blood vessel development remains unclear. Growing vessels, however, are known to be highly permeable, a characteristic which may allow the extravasation of serum components triggering clot formation. These extracellular fibrin clots may act as provisional matrices that provide support for the growing vessels until the generation of extracellular matrix components by pericytes and smooth muscle cells provides a proper scaffolding. While these roles for the coagulation system remain speculative, the role of *TF* in recruiting supporting cells during vascular development seems clear, and it highlights the concept that a process that is active in the adult only in response to pathology (ie, generation of tissue factor and coagulation) also may play an important role during normal development.

Oxygen tension exerts significant effects on many of the genes known to be involved in vascular development.[10,14,16] Atmospheric levels of oxygen (ie, approximately 20%) are typically defined as "normoxia"; however, outside of the respiratory epithelium and the outer layer of the skin, few tissues are ever exposed to this level of oxygen. In fact, this level of oxygen has been shown to be detrimental to the development of embryos for many mammalian species. The optimum oxygen concentration for the proper development of mammalian embryos in vitro seems to be approximately 5%, not 20%.[17] The developing organism is well adapted to grow under these unique conditions. Much of the growth that occurs prior to the development of a true vasculature relies on glycolytic rather than oxidative phosphorylation mechanisms for cellular energy supplies. The switch to aerobic metabolism, which occurs at about embryonic day 11 and coincides with the formation of a complete chorioallantoic circulation in murine model systems, correlates with a marked increase in growth rate, which requires a much more efficient means of energy production. This change demands the ongoing development of an oxygen delivery system capable of supplying emerging metabolic demands and that most likely involves both genetic and environmental components.

Many of the genes involved in pulmonary vascular development respond either directly or indirectly to hypoxia, including *VEGF*, *flk1*, *flt1*, *PDGF-B*, *TF*, basic fibroblast growth factor (bFGF), angiopoietin-2, and *Tie2* (see Table 24–2).[10,14,16,18] The effects of hypoxia on the expression of these genes appear to be mediated wholly or in part via the transcription factor hypoxia-inducible factor 1 (HIF1),[19] which is a ubiquitous basic helix-loop-helix-PAS heterodimer that is activated by hypoxia. It is composed of two subunits, HIF1α and HIF1β or, ARNT (aryl-hydrocarbon receptor nuclear translocator). While HIF1β is a common subunit for several transcription factors, HIF1α is unique to HIF1 and is the subunit regulated by oxygen tension. Although HIF1 activity is controlled at many levels, a critical step appears to be the regulation of steady state levels of HIF1α protein, which increases exponentially as cellular oxygen concentration is decreased. Current data suggest that under normoxic conditions, HIF1 is subject to ubiquitination and proteosomal degradation, and that this process is inhibited under hypoxic conditions (Figure 24–1). It appears that a product of the tumor suppressor gene responsible for von Hippel-Lindau disease (VHL) is also critical in controlling HIF-sensitive genes. The VHL protein product, pVHL,

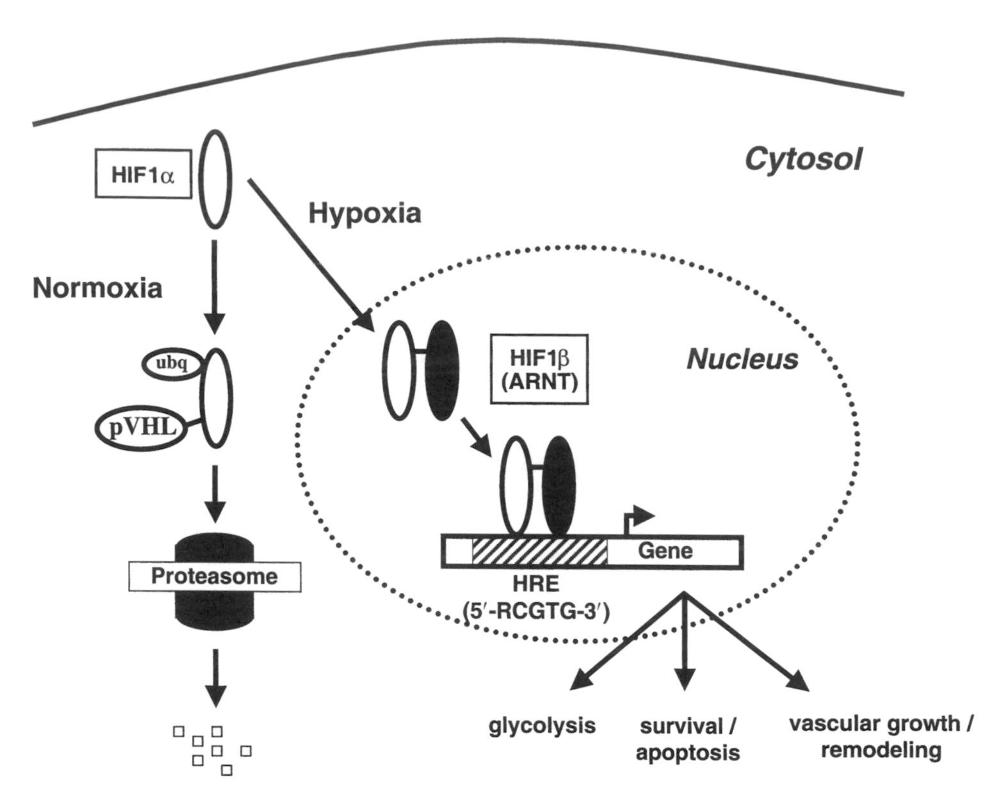

FIGURE 24–1. Activation of HIF1 (hypoxia-inducible factor 1) by hypoxia. Under normoxic conditions, HIF1α is rapidly ubiquinated (ubq) in the presence of the von Hippel-Lindau tumor suppressor gene product (pVHL) and then degraded. Under hypoxic conditions, ubiquitination is prevented, allowing HIF1α to translocate to the cell nucleus, where it binds HIF1β (ARNT). This dimeric protein binds to the hypoxia-response element (HRE) in both the 5′ and 3′ intronic sequences of genes and promotes the transcription of genes that have numerous cellular effects. (Adapted from D'Angio CT and Finkelstein JN.[9])

associates with *HIF1α* and *HIF2α* subunits and appears to target them for ubiquitination and rapid degradation under normoxic conditions. In hypoxic cells *HIF1α* is stabilized by an as yet unidentified oxygen-sensitive mechanism and is permitted to form an active complex with *HIF1β (ARNT)* that induces gene transcription. Once *HIF1α* has been stabilized by hypoxia and has dimerized with *HIF1β*, the molecule translocates to the nucleus and upregulates the transcription of certain genes by binding to specific *HIF1* binding domains with the consensus sequence 5′-RCGTG-3′. This sequence occurs within a structure known as a hypoxia-response element (HRE) present in the promoter, enhancer, or intervening regions of many genes (see Figure 24–1).

Experiments with targeted gene deletions have demonstrated the critical nature of the *HIF1α* transcription factor in embryogenesis.[20] Embryos lacking in *HIF1α* arrest in development by embryonic day 9 and die by embryonic day 10.5 with multiple major malformations, including cardiac, vascular, and neural tube defects as well as extensive cell death (see Table 24–1). Vasculogenesis appears to have initiated properly, but there is a later extensive regression of the developing vessels, apparently due to the death of migratory neural crest cells. Thus, *HIF1α* appears to be important in giving rise to the cells that stabilize the developing endothelial tubes, although it is not necessarily critical for the earliest stages of vasculogenesis. The phenotype is similar to that seen in *ARNT* knockout mice, where, again, there is embryonic lethality, mostly due to lack of development of vascular support structures.

Hypoxia, then, appears to be an essential element for normal pulmonary vascular development. Embryonic development proceeds normally only in a hypoxic environment, and this is likely due to the role of cellular oxygen levels in controlling the expression of the genes required for vasculogenesis, angiogenesis, and the further structural growth and development of the vasculature. Whether re-exposure to hypoxia in adult life can stimulate a reiteration of those processes that were observed in vascular development remains a question for further study, but this idea is strongly supported by observations that solid tumor growth is dependent on an angiogenic process initiated by hypoxia.

Effects on Pulmonary Vascular Tone

Changes in vascular tone in response to exposure to changes in oxygen tension are a defining characteristic of the pulmonary circulation. These effects of oxygen on pulmonary vascular tone are not only crucial to adult responses such as hypoxic pulmonary vasoconstriction but also appear to play a key role in the developing circulation as well. In late fetal life, oxygen tension and its effects on critical mediators help to control the changes in pulmonary vascular tone necessary for a successful transition to extrauterine life. The increase in oxygen levels at birth triggers pulmonary vascular dilation and allows the pulmonary circulation to shift from the constricted high-resistance vascular bed in utero to the dilated low-resistance circuit of the normal neonate. Interruptions, including hypoxic stresses, to that normal fetal-neonatal transition can lead to the development of neonatal pulmonary hypertension and may even lead to alterations in pulmonary vascular physiology that can extend into adult life.[21] Numerous mediators have been implicated in this process, but most recent attention has centered on the roles of nitric oxide, endothelin, and potassium channels in the vascular wall.

Nitric oxide (NO), originally described as "endothelium-derived relaxing factor" (EDRF) is the best known and probably the most important endogenous vasodilator in the lung. As the original name implies, NO is produced by the vascular endothelium and diffuses across to the vascular smooth muscle cell, where it triggers vasodilation by activation of soluble guanylate cyclase and cyclic guanosine monophosphate (cGMP) production. Nitric oxide is synthesized by the enzyme nitric oxide synthase (NOS), which exists in at least three isoforms in the pulmonary circulation: constitutive or endothelial NOS (eNOS), inducible NOS (iNOS), and neuronal NOS (nNOS). Whether NO plays a role in the maintenance of the normally low pulmonary vascular tone in mature animals remains uncertain. In most species, inhibition of NO synthesis does not lead consistently to significant increases in pulmonary vascular pressures under normoxic conditions.[22] Some human studies have shown a small effect of NOS inhibition on basal pulmonary vascular tone, but these results are quite variable. At the very least, the role of NO in the regulation of basal tone in the pulmonary vascular bed is not as great as it is in the systemic circulation, where NO inhibition more consistently leads to increases in vascular tone. These observations are consistent with immunohistochemical studies demonstrating little eNOS expression in resistance vessels in the lungs of adult animals.[22]

Exposure of the adult circulation to hypoxia appears in general to increase the expression of NOS and the production of NO, leading to the concept that increased NO synthesis is a protective response of the pulmonary vascular bed to higher pressures and higher shear stress.[22–24] Evidence also suggests that, in the adult circulation, hypoxia may stimulate NO production directly, in that hypoxia increases the expression of NOS in cultured pulmonary artery endothelial cells, and hypoxia leads to increases in NOS expression in the lungs of adult rats independent of increases in shear stress.[25,26]

The role of NO in the developing circulation appears to be quite different from the situation in the adult. Inhibition of NOS in the fetal animal tends to cause vasoconstriction, suggesting that NO plays a more significant role in controlling pulmonary vascular tone in the fetal animal than in the adult. In general, eNOS protein and messenger ribonucleic acid (mRNA) levels rise in late gestation, peaking in the perinatal period, and then following birth there is a time-dependent decrease in eNOS expression. For example, studies in normal piglets have found that pulmonary arterial eNOS levels at birth are several-fold higher than are those seen in adult animals. The amount of eNOS increases through postpartum day 3 and then slowly decreases to adult levels by day 10.[27,28] Interruption of the normal fetal-neonatal transition by exposing the animals to hypoxia immediately after birth leads to decreased expression of eNOS in the lung until the animals are reoxygenated.[28,29] Interestingly, exposing the animals to hypoxia after day 3 of life leads, as in the adult, to increased expression of eNOS, suggesting that a vulnerable window exists shortly after birth when the pulmonary vascular bed may be susceptible to decreases in endogenous vasodilators such as NO and, thus, be predisposed to the development of pulmonary hypertension.[28]

The pulmonary vasculature produces endogenous vasoconstrictor substances as well as vasodilators. The most widely studied of the endogenous vasoconstrictors are the endothelins (ETs), a family of small peptides synthesized predominantly in the vascular endothelium but also by vascular smooth muscle cells, airway smooth muscle cells, and airway epithelium. The ETs exert their activity via binding to cell membrane receptors, at least two of which exist in the pulmonary vasculature: the ET-A and ET-B receptors. The ET-A receptor is expressed predominantly by smooth muscle cells in blood vessels and airways. Activation of the ET-A receptor is associated consistently with smooth muscle contraction and thus with vasoconstriction. Activation of the ET-A receptor also may play a role in regulating lung inflammation, as pharmacologic blockade of the receptor ameliorates some inflammatory lung injuries. The ET-B receptor is expressed by endothelial cells and, to a lesser extent, by smooth muscle cells. In the pulmonary vasculature, the ET-B receptor is most consistently associated with a vasodilatory response elicited via increased release of NO from the endothelium, although some evidence suggests that ET-B receptor activation may cause vasoconstriction in smaller more distal pulmonary arteries. Evidence also suggests that the ET-B receptor plays a key role in the clearance of endothelin from the circulation.

Hypoxia can have significant effects on the endothelin system in the lung, but it remains unclear whether those effects differ between adult and fetal or neonatal animals. Exposure to hypoxia clearly increases ET production in the lung in adult animals, and even moderate levels of hypoxia may increase plasma ET levels in human adults.[30–33] Hypoxia also appears to increase the expression of both the ET-A and ET-B receptors, regardless of the age of the animal studied.[34,35] Interestingly, studies in both adult and neonatal animals suggest that hypoxia increases ET-A receptor expression to a greater extent than ET-B receptor expression, possibly leading to a more vasoconstrictive phenotype.[36,37] Endothelin clearly is present in the neonatal circulation, perhaps at levels greater than those typically seen in adults. Both ET-A and ET-B receptors are expressed in fetal and neonatal lung at levels greater than those seen in adult vessels, with an apparent predominance of the ET-A receptor.[38,39] Evidence from studies in late gestation fetal lambs also show that endothelin contributes to baseline pulmonary vascular tone in the fetus, and that the expression of both ET and its receptors change through development, increasing in late gestation and then decreasing to adult levels within several days after birth.[40] In addition, intrauterine pulmonary hypertension in this model is associated with no change in ET-A receptor expression but with a decrease in ET-B receptor expression, a shift that would seem to favor vasoconstriction.[41] Similar results have also been obtained in neonatal piglets exposed to hypoxia, although these investigators noted an increase in ET-A expression without a change in ET-B expression in the hypoxic animals.[37] The endothelin system in the lung, then, likely plays a significant role in controlling pulmonary vascular tone in both the neonate and the adult, and hypoxia is a not only a potent stimulus for ET production, but it also seems to consistently shift the balance of ET receptor patterns into a pattern favoring increased pulmonary vasoconstriction.

Another likely site of action of hypoxia on pulmonary vascular tone lies in the membrane potassium channels found in vascular smooth muscle cells. Depolarization of the vascular smooth muscle cell membrane leads to calcium influx and contraction. Potassium-channel activation counters that effect, leading to membrane hyperpolarization and vascular relaxation.[42] In addition, some work has suggested that cGMP, the intracellular mediator of NO effects in vascular smooth muscle, promotes vascular relaxation by activating potassium channels. Thus, potassium-channel activation in the vascular smooth muscle cell membrane may play a major role in determining pulmonary vascular tone, mediating the effects of NO and moderating the effects of endothelin. Several different subtypes of potassium channels have been described, each with slightly different effects and sensitivities to hypoxia.[42] Changes in the pattern of potassium-channel expression during vascular development may play a role in coordinating the transition to extrauterine life and in mediating the effects of hypoxia in the pulmonary circulation. In the adult circulation the predominant potassium channel is the voltage-gated potassium (K_v) channel. Acute hypoxia inhibits K_v-channel activity, leading to membrane depolarization and vasoconstriction.[43,44] In contrast, in the neonate and fetus, the calcium-gated potassium channel, the K_{Ca} channel, appears to be the predominant channel, and it responds to increased oxygen levels by causing membrane hyperpolarization and vasodilation.[45,46] Recent studies in sheep have shown that potassium-channel activation, particularly that of the K_{Ca} channel, plays a crucial role in the normal pulmonary vascular relaxation seen after birth. Adult pulmonary artery smooth muscle cells constrict in response to hypoxia more vigorously than do fetal or neonatal smooth muscle cells, and K_v-channel protein and mRNA levels have been shown to increase with maturation following birth.[47] The findings suggest that a perinatal shift from the K_{Ca} channel to the K_v channel as the predominant potassium channel in the pulmonary circulation determines the relative response of the pulmonary bed to hypoxia. In addition, pulmonary vascular smooth muscle cells from newborn piglets are relatively depolarized at birth and do not develop adult levels of membrane polarization until 3 days of age, a finding possibly related to diminished potassium-channel activity. Exposure to hypoxia during the fetal-neonatal transition prevents the development of the normal adult-level membrane potential in those cells, leaving the cells in a hypercontractile state.[48] Again, these results suggest that a vulnerable window exists in the neonate when exposure to hypoxia may profoundly affect the expression of a number of genes controlling the pulmonary vascular bed.

Finally, the site within the vasculature at which hypoxia exerts its effects on vascular tone deserves mention. The vessels responsible for the majority of the tone in the mature pulmonary vascular bed are the precapillary arterioles, the "resistance vessels." These vessels have long been thought to be the primary site of action of hypoxia in controlling pulmonary vascular tone, and no recent evidence exists to contradict that view of the adult circulation. However, evidence recently has been accumulated that the pulmonary veins, long thought to be relatively unimportant in determining overall pulmonary vascular resistance, may actually play a significant role in pulmonary responses to hypoxia, particularly in young animals. Studies in neonatal animals of several species have shown that about one-third of the total pulmonary vascular resistance is located in the venous circulation.[49,50] In response to either hypoxia or other vasoconstrictors, the pulmonary veins of newborn animals may actually constrict more vigorously than do the pulmonary arteries, in contrast to the adult pattern of greater arterial reactivity.[49,51,52] The particular genes responsible for these developmental changes in the site and vigor of the pulmonary vascular response to hypoxia are unknown, but recent studies raise the possibility that soluble guanylate cyclase, phosphodiesterases (PDEs), and protein kinase G

(PKG) may be involved. Current data support the possibility that the synthesis and concentration of vasodilating agents such as NO, prostacyclin, and atrial natriuretic peptide are increased during the fetal-neonatal transition, which results in increased intracellular cGMP levels. During development, there is an increase in the activity and expression of soluble guanylate cyclase and a decrease in the expression of PDEs that degrade cGMP, again consistent with the concept that increased cGMP is important in the relaxation observed in arteries and veins during the transition. Protein kinase G is important in mediating cGMP-induced vascular smooth muscle relaxation, and recent studies have demonstrated that PKG activity and mRNA expression is increased in arteries and veins of newborn animals as compared with fetal animals.[53] An interesting possibility is that, in response to hypoxia, PKG activity is decreased and that this leads to heightened venous tone, particularly in the newborn.

Effects on Pulmonary Vascular Structure

The histologic changes occurring in the pulmonary arterial wall in response to chronic hypoxia in both newborn and adult animals have been described extensively.[54–56] In general, there are extensive vascular wall thickening and fibroproliferative changes that occur at all segments of the pulmonary artery along its longitudinal axis. Intimal changes occur but are minimal compared with the medial and adventitial changes that result from both hypertrophy and hyperplastic responses in smooth muscle cells and fibroblasts as well as marked increases in the production and accumulation of numerous extracellular matrix proteins. Each cell type in the pulmonary arterial wall—endothelial cells, smooth muscle cells, and adventitial fibroblasts—exhibits a unique growth and matrix-producing response to hypoxia. Recent data also demonstrate that within each cell type there exist subpopulations of cells that exhibit dramatically different responses to hypoxia.[57–59] For each cell type, the magnitude of the growth or matrix response appears to be dependent on several variables, including the severity and duration of the hypoxic stimulus, the timing of the exposure (ie, the age), and the underlying genetic predisposition. Pathologic growth occurs when the delicate balance of proliferative and antiproliferative mechanisms that exists in the vessel wall is disrupted. In addition, the abnormal growth responses initiated by hypoxia can be amplified further by synergistic interactions between the hypoxic environment, mechanical stresses, newly synthesized growth factors, and numerous signal transduction pathways.

The magnitude of the hypoxic growth response in vivo is influenced significantly by the age and/or history of the animal at the time of exposure to hypoxia. The pulmonary circulation appears to be uniquely vulnerable to hypoxia-induced growth during periods of rapid cell growth, such as during development and following repair after injury.[55,60] This view has been supported by studies in a calf model of severe hypoxic pulmonary hypertension. Exposure of the neonatal calf to chronic hypoxia causes elevations in pulmonary artery pressure and structural changes in the vessels, particularly in the media and adventitia, that are far more severe than are those seen in adult animals exposed to the same conditions. Under these conditions, hypoxia appears to interrupt the normal differentiation of vascular cells, resulting in the persistence of a highly proliferative "fetal-like" phenotype.

The magnitude of hypoxic cellular growth in vivo is dependent on genetic factors as well. Stelzner et al have described the Fawn-hooded rat as a model of spontaneous pulmonary hypertension in which the rate of onset is accelerated by exposure to the relative hypoxia of the altitude in Denver compared with that of sea level ("normoxia" at both sites, but expected arterial P_{O_2} is 23 mm Hg lower in Denver).[61] Similar examples exist in other strains of rats and mice as well, but in these animals a greater hypoxic stress is required to elicit differences.[62] Even the bovine species, which normally exhibits a severe predisposition to hypoxic pulmonary hypertension, has been shown to lose that response through the breeding of animals successfully adapted to life at higher altitude. At the moment it is not clear which genes are overexpressed in those animals that are susceptible to hypoxia-induced pulmonary hypertension, or, on the other hand, which genes are not expressed in those animals who fail to develop severe pulmonary hypertension under hypoxic conditions. Several potential candidate genes exist. In the Fawn-hooded rat model, one potential contributor to the genetic predisposition to pulmonary hypertension is overexpression of the vasoconstrictor ET-1. In humans, the gene for familial pulmonary hypertension appears to be related to the bone morphogenetic protein receptor 2.[63] It is unknown at present whether the genetic predisposition to primary pulmonary hypertension in humans contributes to excessive responses to hypoxia.

A myriad of factors probably act in concert to regulate growth under hypoxic conditions. A complex network of proliferative and antiproliferative factors operates under both normal and pathologic conditions in the pulmonary arterial wall (Figure 24–2) to control growth.[16,54,55,64] Hypoxia-induced derangements in this balance result in abnormal vascular cell growth. In addition to the direct effects of hypoxia, low oxygen tension triggers indirect effects on the vasculature, such as mechanical stress and the leak of plasma proteins, that also act to initiate cell proliferation. It is difficult to identify the specific roles that each of these factors plays in hypoxia-induced remodeling of the pulmonary circulation, as many of the possible factors also trigger the activity or expression of

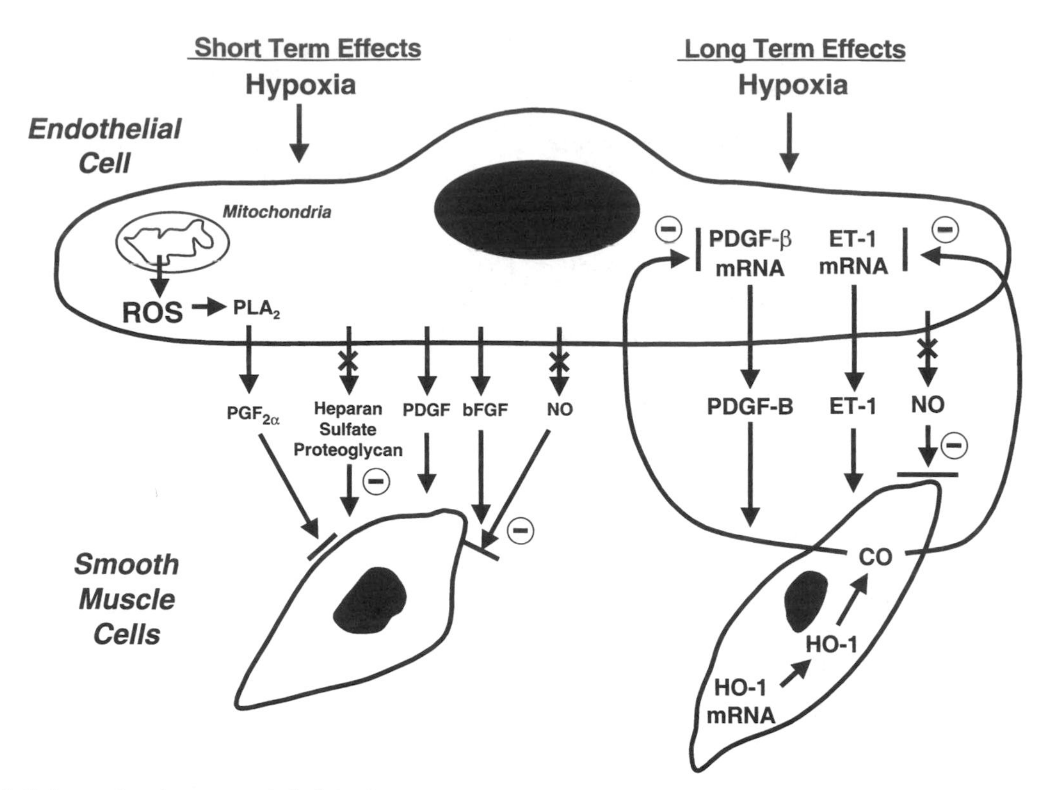

FIGURE 24–2. Interactions between endothelial cells and smooth muscle cells under hypoxic conditions in the neonatal lung circulation. X = blocked by hypoxia; ↓ = stimulation; – = inhibition of proliferation; ROS = reactive oxygen species ; PLA_2 = phospholipase A_2; $PGF_{2\alpha}$ = prostagladin $F_{2\alpha}$; *PDGF* = platelet-derived growth factor; *bFGF* = basic fibroblast growth factor; NO = nitric oxide; mRNA = messenger ribonucleic acid; ET = endothelin; CO = carbon monoxide; HO = heme oxygenase. (Adapted from Michiels CT et al.[64])

other confounding variables. Hypoxia alone, however, clearly disrupts the normal interactions between endothelial cells and smooth muscle cells, which are required for quiescence of both cell types in the intact vessel wall. Hypoxic exposure in and of itself also has significant effects on the release of mitogenic molecules from the endothelium. Short-term exposure of endothelial cells to hypoxia in vitro leads to the release of factors including prostagladin $F_{2\alpha}$, *bFGF*, *PDGF-BB*, *TGF-β*, *TF*, and ET-1 among others.[16,54,55,64] In addition, at least in the neonatal circulation, hypoxia may also downregulate certain molecules that are traditionally thought to inhibit smooth muscle cell proliferation, including NO and heparan sulfate proteoglycans. Thus, the acute release of promitogenic agents along with a decrease in antimitogenic agents may contribute to increases in the proliferation of smooth muscle cells.

During periods of prolonged hypoxia, other mechanisms may be "called on" to regulate the proliferative response. Findings from the Kourembanas laboratory suggest that one mechanism through which the proliferative response is modulated may be a negative-feedback loop involving smooth muscle cell–derived carbon monoxide (CO).[65] These investigators have observed increased CO production in smooth muscle cells under hypoxic conditions, a phenomenon thought to result from a transient induction of heme oxygenase-1 gene expression. Carbon monoxide released by the hypoxic smooth muscle cells appears to decrease the hypoxia-induced transcription of the mitogens *PDGF-BB* and ET-1 in endothelial cells by increasing their cGMP content. This cascade thus has the potential to eventually inhibit smooth muscle cell proliferation that is initiated under hypoxic conditions. In addition, increased CO release by smooth muscle cells under hypoxic conditions may act in an autocrine manner to inhibit smooth muscle cell proliferation. The most direct proof available of the validity of this concept may lie in the observation that hypoxia-induced pulmonary hypertension and structural remodeling in the rat was markedly attentuated by sustaining high levels of heme oxygenase expression.[65]

The mechanisms through which hypoxia exerts its effects on vascular wall cell gene expression have received much attention recently. Current evidence suggests that many, if not most, of the essential adaptive responses to hypoxia that are exhibited by endothelial, smooth muscle cell, and fibroblast populations in the vascular wall are mediated through the activation of the transcription factor, HIF.[19,66,67] Genes known to be regulated by HIF include several glycolytic enzymes, the glucose transporter *Glut-1*, adenylase, enolase, phosphoglycerate kinase, *VEGF*, ET, and *PDGF*, among others. Most evidence to

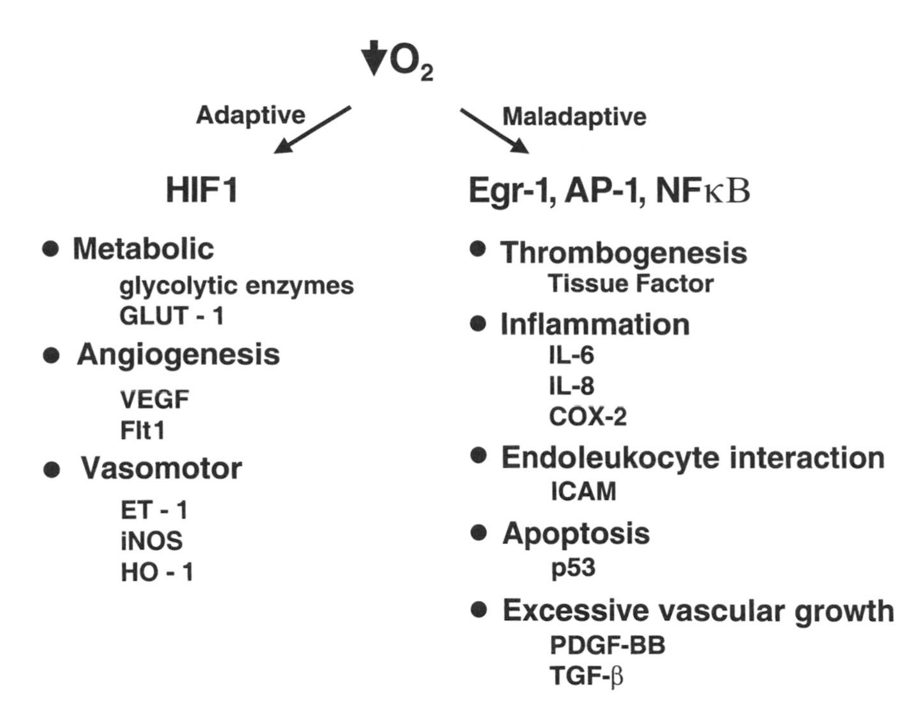

FIGURE 24–3. Vascular cell responses to hypoxia are mediated through both hypoxia-inducible factor (HIF)-dependent and HIF-independent (*Egr-1*, AP-1, NFκβ) transcription-factor pathways. These responses may be either adaptive or maladaptive depending on the physiologic context (see text). *VEGF* = vascular endothelial growth factor; ET = endothelin; iNOS = inducible nitric oxide synthase; HO = heme oxygenase; *Egr* = early growth response; IL = interleukin; ICAM = intercellular adhesion molecule; PDGF = platelet-derived growth factor; TGF = transforming growth factor.

date suggests that these gene products provide an adaptive mechanism to the cells under hypoxic conditions that presumably acts to re-establish cellular energy homeostasis. Some of the gene products act to initiate the glycolytic process, while others actually act to provide more blood flow and oxygen to hypoxic or ischemic areas. Under many hypoxic conditions these adaptive responses predominate, but it is clear that *HIF1* can contribute to pathophysiologic processes as well, including vascular remodeling. Evidence for this concept comes from heterozygous *HIF1α*-transgenic mice. These animals, which produce decreased amounts of *HIF1α,* demonstrate, in response to hypoxia, significantly increased right ventricular hypertrophy, increased pulmonary hypertension, and increased pulmonary vascular remodeling (as well as the delayed development of polycythemia) compared with wild-type animals with intact genes for *HIF1α*.[68]

Several other transcription factors also are upregulated under hypoxic conditions. This observation helps to explain how some of the genes observed to be induced under hypoxic conditions become activated, even though they do not contain a hypoxia-response element in their promoter sequence. Further, interest in these transcription factors is derived largely from the fact that hypoxic or ischemic conditions lead not only to adaptive responses but also sometimes to maladaptive responses (Figure 24–3). Prominent among these maladaptive responses is the deposition of fibrin in the ischemic lung vasculature, a consequence of the induction of the procoagulant protein *TF*. In addition, under certain circumstances hypoxic or ischemic conditions can create a proinflammatory state in the vasculature. These fibrotic and inflammatory responses appear to be mediated largely through transcription factors other than *HIF1*, most prominently early growth response gene-1 (*Egr-1*) and NFκB.[9,69,70] In general, experimental evidence supports the idea that hypoxia or ischemia can induce *Egr-1* expression and that *Egr-1* can then act as a master switch regulating a wide range of effector mechanisms. Gene targets of *Egr-1* under hypoxic conditions include interleukin (IL)-1β, *TF*, plasminogen activator inhibitor (PAI)-1, intercellular adhesion molecule 1 (ICAM-1), and *VEGF*. *Egr-1* and its targets may thus play a critical role in the pathologic responses observed in the chronically hypoxic pulmonary circulation.

Hypoxia is also known to stimulate NFκB activation and the transcription of many cytokine genes (eg, *TNF-α*, IL-6, IL-8) known to be regulated by this transcription factor.[9] The activated form of NFκB is a heterodimer that usually consists of two proteins, a p65 subunit and a p50 subunit, both of which are members of the NFκB/Rel family of transcription factors, which also includes c-Rel, Rel B, and p52. The activity of NFκB is regulated by an inhibitor, IκBα, which forms a complex with NFκB in the cytoplasm and inhibits the nuclear localization of the dimer. When cells receive signals that activate NFκB, IκBα is phosphorylated and degraded through a ubiquitin-proteasome pathway, resulting in translocation

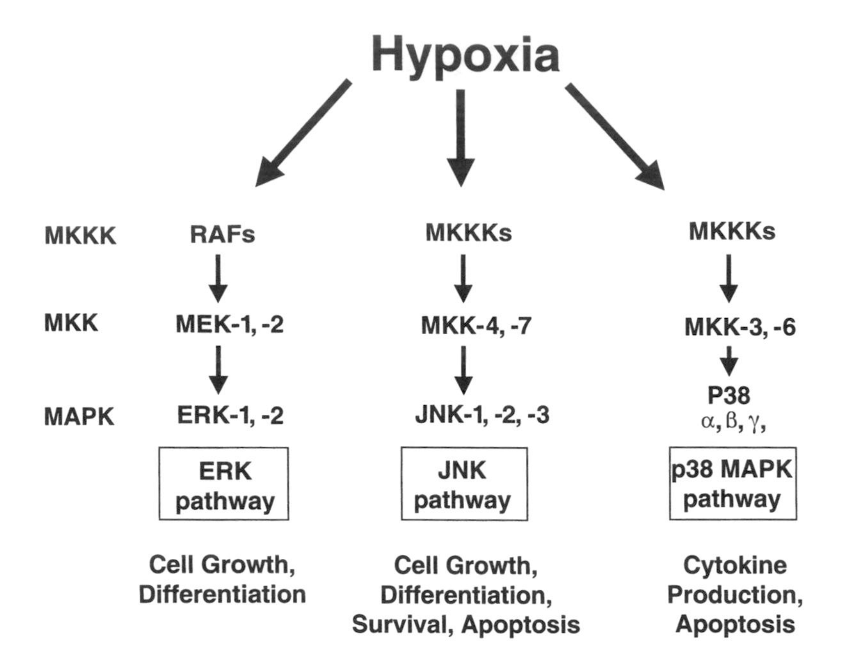

FIGURE 24–4. Hypoxia stimulates all members of the mitogen-activated protein kinase (MAPK) pathways. Each pathway (ERK, JNK, and *p38*) seems to be under the control of different upstream regulators, and the responses of each pathway to hypoxia are cell-type specific. For further review see Garrington and Johnson.[75] MKK = MAPK kinase; MKKK = MKK kinase; ERK = extracellular signal–regulated kinase; JNK = Jun amino-terminal kinase.

of NFκB to the nucleus, where it activates transcription of specific target genes. Recent information suggests that hypoxia-generated reactive oxygen species are critical in the activation process.[71] Thus, NFκB, like *Egr-1*, can elicit gene responses that contribute to vascular pathology under hypoxic conditions. Whether specific subsets of cells in the newborn animal are more prone than cells from the adult to hypoxic activation of these transcription factors remains unclear at present.

The pathways through which hypoxia increases transcription-factor expression are currently under intense investigation. Protein phosphorylation appears to be crucial for the expression of many hypoxic-inducible genes as inhibition of tyrosine kinase pathways has been shown to inhibit many HIF genes.[72] One important hypoxic target, perhaps crucial for proliferation, is the mitogen-activated protein kinase family of enzymes (MAPK). Several studies have demonstrated that the *p44* (extracellular signal–related kinase [ERK-1]) and *p42* (ERK-2) MAPK are crucial for proliferation in response to growth factors in a variety of cell types. Growth factors, via their surface receptors, initiate a series of events culminating in the phosphorylation of Ras guanine diphosphate to form the active form Ras guanine triphosphate. In turn, Ras then activates Raf which activates Mek; Mek very specifically activates ERK-1 and ERK-2 by tyrosine and threonine phosphorylation. Active ERKs are proline directed serine threonine kinases that can phosphorylate cytoplasmic proteins and/or translocate to the nucleus where they activate transcription factors which include *Egr*, HIF, and AP-1 as described above. There is good evidence that hypoxia, as well as sheer stress and reactive oxygen species, can directly initiate activation of the MAPK pathway, and that this activation can in some, but not all, cell types result in a proliferative response.[73,74]

In addition to the classic forms of MAPK described above, families of related MAPKs exist in cells and are referred to as the "stress-activated protein kinases" (Figure 24–4).[75] These kinases, such as Jun amino-terminal kinase (JNK) and *p38* MAPK, are known to be activated by many environmental stresses including heat shock, ultraviolet irradiation, cytokines, and toxins (eg, lipopolysaccharide). Recent studies demonstrate that hypoxia can activate both the JNK and *p38* MAPK pathways.[73,76] Evidence suggests that JNK family members can act in complicated ways to modulate the hypoxic response. At least in some vascular cells, it appears as though JNK-1 isoforms are important in the hypoxic proliferative response, whereas JNK-2 isoforms act to attenuate proliferative effects and may inhibit proliferation as well as induce apoptosis. The role of *p38* under hypoxic conditions remains unclear, although there is evidence that suggests that *p38* activation is necessary for the proliferative response in the adventitial fibroblast and may play a role in hypoxia-mediated apoptotic responses.

Another intracellular signaling pathway that appears to be critical for hypoxic responses is protein kinase C (PKC).[70,74,77] Numerous isozymes of PKC have been identified and demonstrated to be both developmentally regulated and cell specific. It is becoming increasingly clear

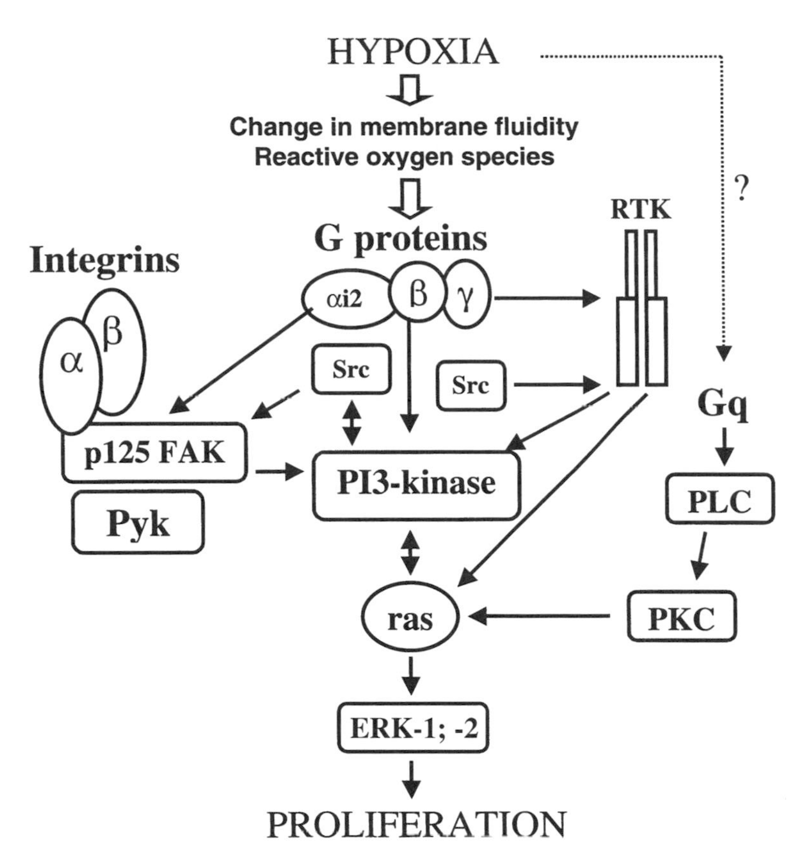

FIGURE 24–5. Hypothetic schema illustrating potential upstream events in hypoxia-initiated cell proliferation. Hypoxia acts via alterations in cell membrane fluidity or the generation of reactive oxygen species to activate G proteins (particularly those of the αi class but also potentially other classes including Gq). This activation initiates a kinase cascade that leads to cell proliferation. Key steps in this cascade include the activation of Src, PI3-kinase, Ras, and ERK-1 or -2. Other possible mechanisms leading to proliferation include G-protein initiated activation of *p125* focal adhesion kinase (FAK) and/or receptor tyrosine kinases (RTK).[76] Pyk = proline rich tyrosine kinase; PLC = phospholipase C; PKC = protein kinase C.

that the presence of specific PKC isozymes in different cell populations and their susceptibility to activation may confer unique properties to different cell types. Since PKC activation has been demonstrated to occur under hypoxic conditions and to contribute to a general pattern of overall enhanced growth capacity, recent experiments have tested the hypothesis that those populations of cells that reside in the vascular wall that demonstrate growth under hypoxic conditions exhibit different patterns of PKC isozyme expression than do those cells that are either growth inhibited or unresponsive to hypoxia. Data generated thus far raise the possibility that PKC-ζ and -β isoforms may play critical roles in hypoxia-induced proliferative responses. This finding is intriguing and is consistent with the idea that hypoxia-induced activation of PKC is critical for the induction of *Egr-1*, which, in turn, appears to be necessary for proliferative responses in specific cell populations under hypoxic conditions. Isozymes of PKC may act directly on targets within the nucleus or may interact at the level of Mek or ERK in stimulating transcription of hypoxia-inducible transcription factors. A current working hypothesis for how hypoxia may cause activation of critical intracellular signaling pathways is shown in Figure 24–5.[76]

Effects on Inflammation and Pulmonary Vascular Permeability

Returning to the paradigm of hypoxia as a trigger for angiogenesis and the finding that developing vessels tend to be leaky, it is perhaps not surprising that exposure to hypoxia also may have significant effects on pulmonary vascular permeability. In this view hypoxia is seen as the driving force in the development of new blood vessels, acting by increasing vascular permeability, by exposing normally quiescent tissues to circulating mitogens and vasoactive substances, and by stimulating the release of those mitogens and vasoactive substances via the activation of transcription factors such as *HIF1*, *AP-1*, *Egr-1*, and NFκB, as noted above.

In vitro studies using cultured endothelial cells support the idea that hypoxia increases vascular leak. Recent work has shown that the permeability of human endothelial cell monolayers increases after as little as 6 hours of exposure to hypoxia, and that those permeability changes are caused by reactive oxygen species and are mediated through the release of IL-6.[78] Studies with bovine aortic and pulmonary endothelial cells also have shown hypoxia to cause a time- and dose-dependent increase in monolayer permeability, which is associated with a decrease in adenylate cyclase activity and of cellular cyclic adenosine monophosphate (cAMP) levels.[79] Another mediator that has been implicated in the control of endothelial permeability is intracellular calcium. Increases in intracellular calcium lead to intercellular gap formation and increases in endothelial permeability to macromolecules. Increases in calcium can decrease cellular cAMP by altering the activity of a Ca^{+}-inhibited isoform of adenylate cyclase, and decreases in cAMP then lead to increases in permeability.[80]

In vivo work also supports the view that hypoxia can increase pulmonary vascular permeability. Studies in several species have shown increases in pulmonary vascular permeability associated with acute exposure to hypoxia.[81–84] Work in rodents consistently has shown increases in lung water content and in vascular leak occurring with acute exposure to hypoxia.[81,82,85] This accumulation of lung fluid develops gradually over 24 to 48 hours and may persist for up to 2 or 3 weeks. These increases in vascular leak associated with hypoxia also have been shown to decrease when the animals are treated with corticosteroids,[82] and corticosteroids have been shown to decrease pulmonary edema formation in climbers at altitude.[86] In addition, some studies in human subjects have suggested that a generalized increase in vascular permeability occurs with exposure to hypoxia, affecting all vascular beds including the pulmonary vessels.[87,88] Other studies suggest that humans may develop subclinical increases in lung water at altitude, particularly with exercise; thus, illnesses such as high-altitude pulmonary edema may be a more overt expression of a "normal" response to hypoxia.[89,90] These effects may not be consistent across all species, however, as work in adult sheep has failed to demonstrate an increase in lung lymph flow during hypoxia.[91]

The work cited above showing a link between hypoxia and cytokine release in altering endothelial permeability highlights the concept that the effects of hypoxia on vascular permeability in the lung also may be exaggerated by coexisting inflammation. In rabbits, for example, exposure to hypoxia alone or activation of complement by cobra venom factor alone does little to increase vascular leak, but exposure to both stimuli simultaneously causes large increases in albumin extravasation into the air spaces, and those increases can be blocked by neutrophil depletion.[92] Similar results have been obtained in adult rats exposed to endotoxin and hypoxia.[93] In weanling rats exposed to hypoxia shortly after recovery from a viral respiratory infection, neither exposure to hypoxia nor the recent virus alone altered lung leak, but exposure to both stimuli led to significant increases in vascular leak and lung water accumulation.[81] In this setting, the increased permeability in the animals exposed to both stimuli related, at least in part, to increases in lung endothelin content, as treatment with an endothelin-receptor blocker ameliorated the permeability and lung water changes.[94] Whether the age of the animal studied plays a role in these responses is unclear, although the magnitude of the permeability increases seen with equivalent hypoxic exposures may be larger in young animals as compared with adults.

As mentioned above, the concept that hypoxia can modulate inflammatory responses in the lung vasculature is also one that has gained a great deal of experimental support recently. Recent work by Bhattacharya et al has demonstrated that pulmonary hypertension generated by increases in left atrial pressure leads to the activation of mechanogated calcium channels on the endothelium of the pulmonary venules, resulting in increases in adhesion molecule expression (P-selectin) on the endothelial surface.[80,95,96] This study provides a link between the increases in vascular pressure known to occur with hypoxia and increases in lung inflammation. In addition, the same group has demonstrated that instillation of *TNF*-α into the alveolus leads to increases in intracellular calcium in the adjacent microvascular endothelium and subsequent increases in adhesion molecule expression at that site.[96] These findings suggest that direct alveolar-to-endothelial signaling allows an inflammatory stimulus directed at the alveolar epithelium to trigger local vascular responses that may affect vascular tone, increase vascular permeability, and promote further inflammation. Hypoxic environments also may promote inflammation by increasing the expression of adhesion molecules on the vascular endothelium.[97] Exposure of cultured aortic endothelial cells to hypoxia for 24 hours leads to a marked increase in adhesion molecule expression, with a 150% increase in vascular cell adhesion molecule expression and a 60% increase in ICAM-1 expression.[98]

Hypoxia also has been shown to trigger or modulate the production of a number of cytokines important in the regulation of pulmonary vascular tone and permeability. As mentioned above, IL-6 appears to play a key role in mediating the effects of hypoxia on cultured human endothelial cells. Cultured human lung fibroblasts and pulmonary artery smooth muscle cells exposed to hypoxia produce significant amounts of IL-6 and IL-8, an effect mediated, at least in part, via PDGF and platelet activating factor (PAF) receptors.[99] Exposure of cultured human pulmonary artery endothelial cells to hypoxia leads to increased production of endothelin and IL-8, both of which are exaggerated in the presence of proinflammatory cytokines such as IL-1 and *TNF*-α.[100] Endothelin expression also may be increased by IL-6 and *VEGF*, both of which are mediators that increase with exposure to hypoxia.[101,102] In addition, the combination of cytokines and hypoxia strongly inhibits NOS transcription and activity in cultured endothelial cells, again providing a potential link between inflammation and alterations in vascular tone.[100]

These studies taken together suggest that hypoxia may play a critical role in lung injury by both triggering and augmenting lung inflammation. Increases in pulmonary vascular pressures associated with hypoxia may incite inflammation, which, in turn, leads to changes in the balance of vasoconstrictors and vasodilators in the lung—leading perhaps to further elevations of pulmonary artery pressure, which then perpetuate the cycle. Adding these findings to the evidence discussed above, that hypoxia and inflammation can act together to alter vascular permeability, provides a compelling argument that these effects may contribute to lung injury and may, in fact, be relevant to a number of clinical situations. Whether these effects are consistent throughout the course of development, or whether they are more pronounced at particular ages as many of the other effects of hypoxia appear to be, awaits further study.

References

1. deMello DE, Reid LM. Embryonic and early fetal development of human lung vasculature and its functional implications. Pediatr Dev Pathol 2000;3:439–49.
2. Hall SM, Hislop AA, Pierce CM, Haworth SG. Prenatal origins of human intrapulmonary arteries: formation and smooth muscle maturation. Am J Respir Cell Mol Biol 2000;23:194–203.
3. Gale NW, Yancopoulos GD. Growth factors acting via endothelial cell-specific receptor tyrosine kinases: VEGFs, angiopoietins, and ephrins in vascular development. Genes Dev 1999;13:1055–66.
4. Carmeliet P, Jain RK. Angiogenesis in cancer and other diseases. Nature 2000;407:249–57.
5. Silverman ES, Collins T. Pathways of Egr-1-mediated gene transcription in vascular biology. Am J Pathol 1999; 154:665–70.
6. Yancopoulos GD, Davis S, Gale NW, et al. Vascular-specific growth factors and blood vessel formation. Nature 2000; 407:242–8.
7. Daniel TO, Abrahamson D. Endothelial signal integration in vascular assembly. Annu Rev Physiol 2000;62:649–71.
8. Petrova TV, Makinen T, Alitalo K. Signaling via vascular endothelial growth factor receptors. Exp Cell Res 1999; 253:117–30.
9. D'Angio CT, Finkelstein JN. Oxygen regulation of gene expression: a study in opposites. Mol Genet Metab 2000; 71:371–80.
10. Dachs GU, Tozer GM. Hypoxia modulated gene expression: angiogenesis, metastasis and therapeutic exploitation. Eur J Cancer 2000;36:1649–60.
11. Jakkula M, Le Cras TD, Gebb S, et al. Inhibition of angiogenesis decreases alveolarization in the developing rat lung. Am J Physiol Lung Cell Mol Physiol 2000; 279:L600–7.
12. Mellitzer G, Xu Q, Wilkinson DG. Control of cell behaviour by signaling through Eph receptors and ephrins. Curr Opin Neurobiol 2000;10:400–8.
13. Ilan N, Madri JA. New paradigms of signaling in the vasculature: ephrins and metalloproteases. Curr Opin Biotechnol 1999;10:536–40.
14. Maltepe E, Simon MC. Oxygen, genes, and development: an analysis of the role of hypoxic gene regulation during murine vascular development. J Mol Med 1998;76: 391–401.
15. Parry GC, Mackman N. Mouse embryogenesis requires the tissue factor extracellular domain but not the cytoplasmic domain. J Clin Invest 2000;105:1547–54.
16. Faller DV. Endothelial cell responses to hypoxic stress. Clin Exp Pharmacol Physiol 1999;26:74–84.
17. Bernardi ML, Flechon JE, Delouis C. Influence of culture system and oxygen tension on the development of ovine zygotes matured and fertilized in vitro. J Reprod Fertil 1996;106:161–7.
18. Marti HH, Risau W. Systemic hypoxia changes the organ-specific distribution of vascular endothelial growth factor and its receptors. Proc Natl Acad Sci U S A 1998; 95:15809–14.
19. Semenza GL. Expression of hypoxia-inducible factor 1: mechanisms and consequences. Biochem Pharmacol 2000;59:47–53.
20. Kotch LE, Iyer NV, Laughner E, Semenza GL. Defective vascularization of *HIF-1alpha*-null embryos is not associated with VEGF deficiency but with mesenchymal cell death. Dev Biol 1999;209:254–67.
21. Sartori C, Allemann Y, Trueb L, et al. Augmented vasoreactivity in adult life associated with perinatal vascular insult. Lancet 1999;353:2205–7.
22. Hampl, V, Herget J. Role of nitric oxide in the pathogenesis of chronic pulmonary hypertension. Physiol Rev 2000; 80:1337–72.
23. Tyler RC, Muramatsu M, Abman SH, et al. Variable expression of endothelial NO synthase in three forms of rat pulmonary hypertension. Am J Physiol 1999;276(2 Pt 1):L297–303.
24. Resta TC, Chicoine LG, Omdahl JL, Walker BR. Maintained upregulation of pulmonary eNOS gene and protein expression during recovery from chronic hypoxia. Am J Physiol 1999;276(2 Pt 2):H699–708.
25. Le Cras TD, Tyler RC, Horan MP, et al. Effects of chronic hypoxia and altered hemodynamics on endothelial nitric oxide synthase expression in the adult rat lung. J Clin Invest 1998;101:795–801.
26. Hampl V, Cornfield DN, Cowan NJ, Archer SL. Hypoxia potentiates nitric oxide synthesis and transiently increases cytosolic calcium levels in pulmonary artery endothelial cells. Eur Respir J 1995;8:515–22.
27. Hislop AA, Springall DR, Buttery LD, et al. Abundance of endothelial nitric oxide synthase in newborn intrapulmonary arteries. Arch Dis Child Fetal Neonatal Ed 1995;73:F17–21.
28. Hislop AA, Springall DR, Oliveira H, et al. Endothelial nitric oxide synthase in hypoxic newborn porcine pulmonary vessels. Arch Dis Child Fetal Neonatal Ed 1997; 77:F16–22.

29. Berkenbosch JW, Baribeau J, Perreault T. Decreased synthesis and vasodilation to nitric oxide in piglets with hypoxia-induced pulmonary hypertension. Am J Physiol Lung Cell Mol Physiol 2000;278:L276–83.
30. Aversa CR, Oparil S, Caro J, et al. Hypoxia stimulates human preproendothelin-1 promoter activity in transgenic mice. Am J Physiol 1997;273(4 Pt 1):L848–55.
31. Donahue DM, Lee ME, Suen HC, et al. Pulmonary hypoxia increases endothelin-1 gene expression in sheep. J Surg Res 1994;57:280–3.
32. Elton TS, Oparil S, Taylor GR, et al. Normobaric hypoxia stimulates endothelin-1 gene expression in the rat. Am J Physiol 1992;263(6 Pt 2):R1260–4.
33. Goerre S, Wenk M, Bartsch P, et al. Endothelin-1 in pulmonary hypertension associated with high-altitude exposure. Circulation 1995;91:359–64.
34. Li H, Chen SJ, Chen YF, et al. Enhanced endothelin-1 and endothelin receptor gene expression in chronic hypoxia. J Appl Physiol 1994;77:1451–9.
35. Soma S, Takahashi H, Muramatsu M, et al. Localization and distribution of endothelin receptor subtypes in pulmonary vasculature of normal and hypoxia-exposed rats. Am J Respir Cell Mol Biol 1999;20:620–30.
36. McCulloch KM, Docherty C, MacLean MR. Endothelin receptors mediating contraction of rat and human pulmonary resistance arteries: effect of chronic hypoxia in the rat [published erratum appears in Br J Pharmacol 1998;124:1586]. Br J Pharmacol 1998;123:1621–30.
37. Noguchi Y, Hislop AA, Haworth SG. Influence of hypoxia on endothelin-1 binding sites in neonatal porcine pulmonary vasculature. Am J Physiol 1997;272(2 Pt 2): H669–78.
38. Hislop AA, Zhao YD, Springall DR, et al. Postnatal changes in endothelin-1 binding in porcine pulmonary vessels and airways. Am J Respir Cell Mol Biol 1995;12:557–66.
39. Perreault T, Baribeau J. Characterization of endothelin receptors in newborn piglet lung. Am J Physiol 1995; 268(4 Pt 1):L607–14.
40. Ivy D, le Cras TD, Parker TA, et al. Developmental changes in endothelin expression and activity in the ovine fetal lung. Am J Physiol Lung Cell Mol Physiol 2000;278:L785–93.
41. Ivy DD, Le Cras TD, Horan MP, Abman SH. Increased lung preproET-1 and decreased ETB-receptor gene expression in fetal pulmonary hypertension. Am J Physiol 1998; 274(4 Pt 1):L535–41.
42. Standen NB, Quayle JM. K^+ channel modulation in arterial smooth muscle. Acta Physiol Scand 1998;164:549–57.
43. Wang J, Juhaszova M, Rubin LJ, Yuan XJ. Hypoxia inhibits gene expression of voltage-gated K^+ channel alpha subunits in pulmonary artery smooth muscle cells. J Clin Invest 1997;100:2347–53.
44. Hulme JT, Coppock EA, Felipe A, et al. Oxygen sensitivity of cloned voltage-gated K(+) channels expressed in the pulmonary vasculature. Circ Res 1999;85:489–97.
45. Cornfield DN, Saqueton CB, Porter VA, et al. Voltage-gated K(+)-channel activity in ovine pulmonary vasculature is developmentally regulated. Am J Physiol Lung Cell Mol Physiol 2000;278:L1297–304.
46. Cornfield DN, Reeve HL, Tolarova S, et al. Oxygen causes fetal pulmonary vasodilation through activation of a calcium-dependent potassium channel. Proc Natl Acad Sci U S A 1996;93:8089–94.
47. Reeve HL, Weir EK, Archer SL, Cornfield DN. A maturational shift in pulmonary K^+ channels, from $Ca2^+$ sensitive to voltage dependent. Am J Physiol 1998;275(6 Pt 1): L1019–25.
48. Evans AM, Osipenko ON, Haworth SG, Gurney AM. Resting potentials and potassium currents during development of pulmonary artery smooth muscle cells. Am J Physiol 1998;275(3 Pt 2):H887–99.
49. Raj JU, Hillyard R, Kaapa P, et al. Pulmonary arterial and venous constriction during hypoxia in 3- to 5-wk-old and adult ferrets. J Appl Physiol 1990;69:2183–9.
50. Raj JU, Chen P, Navazo L. Micropuncture measurement of lung microvascular pressure profile in 3- to 4-week-old rabbits. Pediatr Res 1986;20:1107–11.
51. Sheehan DW, Farhi LE, Russell JA. Prolonged lobar hypoxia in vivo enhances the responsivity of isolated pulmonary veins to hypoxia. Am Rev Respir Dis 1992; 145:640–5.
52. Arrigoni FI, Hislop AA, Haworth SG, Mitchell JA. Newborn intrapulmonary veins are more reactive than arteries in normal and hypertensive piglets. Am J Physiol 1999;277(5 Pt 1):L887–92.
53. Gao Y, Dhanakoti S, Tolsa JF, Raj JU. Role of protein kinase G in nitric oxide- and cGMP-induced relaxation of newborn ovine pulmonary veins. J Appl Physiol 1999; 87:993–8.
54. Durmowicz AG, Stenmark KR. Mechanisms of structural remodeling in chronic pulmonary hypertension. Pediatr Rev 1999;20:e91–102.
55. Stenmark KR, Mecham RP. Cellular and molecular mechanisms of pulmonary vascular remodeling. Annu Rev Physiol 1997;59:89–144.
56. Jones RM, Reid LM. Vascular remodeling in clinical and experimental pulmonary hypertensions. In: Bishop JE, Reeves JT, Laurent GJ, eds. Pulmonary vascular remodelling. London: Portland Press, 1995:47–115.
57. Frid MG, Dempsey EC, Durmowicz AG, Stenmark KR. Smooth muscle cell heterogeneity in pulmonary and systemic vessels. Importance in vascular disease. Arterioscler Thromb Vasc Biol 1997;17:1203–9.
58. Stenmark KR, Frid MG. Smooth muscle cell heterogeneity: role of specific smooth muscle cell subpopulations in pulmonary vascular disease. Chest 1998;114(1 Suppl): 82S–90S.
59. Stenmark KR, Frid M, Nemenoff R, et al. Hypoxia induces cell-specific changes in gene expression in vascular wall cells: implications for pulmonary hypertension. Adv Exp Med Biol 1999;474(1 Suppl):231–58.
60. Dempsey EC, Durmowicz AG, Stenmark KR, Stevens T. Hypoxia-induced changes in the contraction, growth, and matrix synthesis properties of vascular cells. In: Haddad GG, Lister G, eds. Tissue oxygen deprivation: from molecular to integrated function. New York: Marcel Dekker, 1996;225–74.
61. Stelzner TJ, O'Brien RF, Yanagisawa M, et al. Increased lung endothelin-1 production in rats with idiopathic pulmonary hypertension. Am J Physiol 1992;262(5 Pt 1): L614–20.

62. Underwood DC, Bochnowicz S, Osborn RR, et al. Chronic hypoxia-induced cardiopulmonary changes in three rat strains: inhibition by the endothelin receptor antagonist SB 217242. J Cardiovasc Pharmacol 1998;31(Suppl 1): S453–5.
63. Deng Z, Morse JH, Slager SL, et al. Familial primary pulmonary hypertension (gene PPH1) is caused by mutations in the bone morphogenetic protein receptor-II gene. Am J Hum Genet 2000;67:737–44.
64. Michiels C, Arnould T, Remacle J. Endothelial cell responses to hypoxia: initiation of a cascade of cellular interactions. Biochim Biophys Acta 2000;1497(1):1–10.
65. Christou H, Morita T, Hsieh CM, et al. Prevention of hypoxia-induced pulmonary hypertension by enhancement of endogenous heme oxygenase-1 in the rat. Circ Res 2000;86:1224–9.
66. Ratcliffe PJ, Pugh CW, Maxwell PH. Targeting tumors through the HIF system. Nat Med 2000;6:1315–6.
67. Semenza GL, Agani F, Feldser D, et al. Hypoxia, HIF-1, and the pathophysiology of common human diseases. Adv Exp Med Biol 2000;475:123–30.
68. Yu AY, Shimoda LA, Iyer NV, et al. Impaired physiological responses to chronic hypoxia in mice partially deficient for hypoxia-inducible factor 1alpha. J Clin Invest 1999; 103:691–6.
69. Khachigian LM, Collins T. Early growth response factor 1: a pleiotropic mediator of inducible gene expression. J Mol Med 1998;76:613–6.
70. Yan SF, Fujita T, Lu J, et al. Egr-1, a master switch coordinating upregulation of divergent gene families underlying ischemic stress. Nat Med 2000;6:1355–61.
71. Chandel NS, Trzyna WC, McClintock DS, Schumacker PT. Role of oxidants in NF-kappa B activation and TNF-alpha gene transcription induced by hypoxia and endotoxin. J Immunol 2000;165:1013–21.
72. Richard DE, Berra E, Gothie E, et al. p42/p44 mitogen-activated protein kinases phosphorylate hypoxia-inducible factor 1alpha (HIF-1alpha) and enhance the transcriptional activity of HIF-1. J Biol Chem 1999;274: 32631–7.
73. Jin N, Hatton N, Swartz DR, et al. Hypoxia activates jun-N-terminal kinase, extracellular signal-regulated protein kinase, and p38 kinase in pulmonary arteries. Am J Respir Cell Mol Biol 2000;23:593–601.
74. Stenmark KR, Bouchey D, Nemenoff R, et al. Hypoxia-induced pulmonary vascular remodeling: contribution of the adventitial fibroblast. Physiol Res 2000;49: 503–17.
75. Garrington TP, Johnson GL. Organization and regulation of mitogen-activated protein kinase signaling pathways. Curr Opin Cell Biol 1999;11:211–8.
76. Das M, Bouchey D, Moore MJ, et al. Hypoxia-induced proliferative response of vascular adventitial fibroblasts is dependent on G-protein mediated activation of MAP kinases. J Biol Chem. (In press)
77. Das M, Dempsey EC, Bouchey D, et al. Chronic hypoxia induces exaggerated growth responses in pulmonary artery adventitial fibroblasts: potential contribution of specific protein kinase C isozymes. Am J Respir Cell Mol Biol 2000;22:15–25.
78. Ali MH, Schlidt SA, Chandel NS, et al. Endothelial permeability and IL-6 production during hypoxia: role of ROS in signal transduction. Am J Physiol 1999;277(5 Pt 1): L1057–65.
79. Ogawa S, Koga S, Kuwabara K, et al. Hypoxia-induced increased permeability of endothelial monolayers occurs through lowering of cellular cAMP levels. Am J Physiol 1992;262(3 Pt 1):C546–54.
80. Stevens T, Garcia JG, Shasby DM, et al. Mechanisms regulating endothelial cell barrier function. Am J Physiol Lung Cell Mol Physiol 2000;279:L419–22.
81. Carpenter TC, Reeves JT, Durmowicz AG. Viral respiratory infection increases susceptibility of young rats to hypoxia-induced pulmonary edema. J Appl Physiol 1998;84:1048–54.
82. Stelzner TJ, O'Brien RF, Sato K, Weil JV. Hypoxia-induced increases in pulmonary transvascular protein escape in rats. Modulation by glucocorticoids. J Clin Invest 1988; 82:1840–7.
83. White P, Sylvester JT, Humphrey RL, et al. Effect of hypoxia on lung fluid balance in ferrets. Am J Respir Crit Care Med 1994;149:1112–7.
84. Welling KL, Sander M, Ravn JB, et al. Effect of alveolar hypoxia on segmental pulmonary vascular resistance and lung fluid balance in dogs. Acta Physiol Scand 1997; 161:177–86.
85. Tenney SM, Jones RM. Water balance and lung fluids in rats at high altitude. Respir Physiol 1992;87:397–406.
86. Wilson MD, Hart LL. Prophylaxis and treatment of altitude sickness with dexamethasone. Ann Pharmacother 1993; 27:733–5.
87. Hansen JM, Olsen NV, Feldt-Rasmussen B, et al. Albuminuria and overall capillary permeability of albumin in acute altitude hypoxia. J Appl Physiol 1994;76:1922–7.
88. Hansen JM, Kanstrup IL, Richalet JP, Olsen NV. High altitude-induced albuminuria in normal man is enhanced by infusion of low-dose dopamine. Scand J Clin Lab Invest 1996;56:367–72.
89. Ge RL, Matsuzawa Y, Takeoka M, et al. Low pulmonary diffusing capacity in subjects with acute mountain sickness. Chest 1997;111(1):58–64.
90. Podolsky A, Eldridge MW, Richardson RS, et al. Exercise-induced VA/Q inequality in subjects with prior high-altitude pulmonary edema. J Appl Physiol 1996;81: 922–32.
91. Landolt CC, Matthay MA, Albertine KH, et al. Overperfusion, hypoxia, and increased pressure cause only hydrostatic pulmonary edema in anesthetized sheep. Circ Res 1983;52:335–41.
92. Larsen GL, Webster RO, Worthen GS, et al. Additive effect of intravascular complement activation and brief episodes of hypoxia in producing increased permeability in the rabbit lung. J Clin Invest 1985;75:902–10.
93. Ono S, Westcott JY, Chang SW, Voelkel NF. Endotoxin priming followed by high altitude causes pulmonary edema in rats. J Appl Physiol 1993;74:1534–42.
94. Carpenter TC, Stenmark KR. Endothelin receptor blockade decreases lung water in young rats exposed to viral infection and hypoxia. Am J Physiol Lung Cell Mol Physiol 2000;279:L547–54.

95. Kuebler WM, Ying X, Singh B, et al. Pressure is proinflammatory in lung venular capillaries. J Clin Invest 1999; 104:495–502.
96. Kuebler WM, Parthasarathi K, Wang PM, Bhattacharya J. A novel signaling mechanism between gas and blood compartments of the lung. J Clin Invest 2000;105: 905–13.
97. Ishizuka T, Takamizawa-Matsumoto M, Suzuki K, Kurita A. Endothelin-1 enhances vascular cell adhesion molecule-1 expression in tumor necrosis factor alpha–stimulated vascular endothelial cells. Eur J Pharmacol 1999;369:237–45.
98. Setty BN, Stuart MJ. Vascular cell adhesion molecule-1 is involved in mediating hypoxia-induced sickle red blood cell adherence to endothelium: potential role in sickle cell disease. Blood 1996;88:2311–20.
99. Tamm M, Bihl M, Eickelberg O, et al. Hypoxia-induced interleukin-6 and interleukin-8 production is mediated by platelet-activating factor and platelet-derived growth factor in primary human lung cells. Am J Respir Cell Mol Biol 1998;19:653–61.
100. Ziesche R, Petkov V, Williams J, et al. Lipopolysaccharide and interleukin 1 augment the effects of hypoxia and inflammation in human pulmonary arterial tissue. Proc Natl Acad Sci U S A 1996;93:12478–83.
101. Okuda Y, Tsurumaru K, Suzuki S, et al. Hypoxia and endothelin-1 induce VEGF production in human vascular smooth muscle cells. Life Sci 1998;63:477–84.
102. Matsuura A, Yamochi W, Hirata K, et al. Stimulatory interaction between vascular endothelial growth factor and endothelin-1 on each gene expression. Hypertension 1998;32(1):89–95.

CHAPTER 25

Regulation of Cerebral Vascular Function by Oxygen

Michael Apkon, MD, PhD

It has been well recognized for more than a century that asphyxia causes a generalized dilation of pial arterioles on the surface of the brain. Asphyxia results in decreased oxygen delivery to the tissues, thereby creating a potential imbalance between metabolic rate and substrate delivery. Thus dilation in response to asphyxia may represent a mechanism to maintain transport of substrate at a time when blood flow is reduced or when the substrate concentration in the blood is limited. Roy and Sherrington[1] were the first to postulate that cerebral blood flow is matched to the tissue's metabolic demands by the vessels sensing changes in the partial pressure of CO_2 (Pa_{CO_2}), a main byproduct of cellular metabolism. Indeed, it is now well established that an increase in Pa_{CO_2} causes vasodilation, whereas a decrease in Pa_{CO_2} causes vasoconstriction. It is equally clear, however, that oxygen, the metabolic substrate, also regulates cerebral blood flow: hypoxia dilates cerebral blood vessels. Although this effect has been known for many years, the mechanisms by which the respiratory gases exert their vasomotor effects still are not completely understood. This chapter explores the possible mechanisms of cerebral vasoregulation by O_2 and identifies potential areas for future investigation.

Regulation of Vascular Tone by Oxygen

Brain blood flow changes little as arterial partial pressure of O_2 (Pa_{O_2}) falls near the normal physiologic range. However, once Pa_{O_2} falls below approximately 50 to 60 mm Hg, brain blood flow rises rapidly (Figure 25–1*A*).[2] The shape of the oxygen-hemoglobin dissociation curve may explain this apparent threshold effect. The relationship between cerebral blood flow and arterial oxygen content is hyperbolic, with blood flow varying linearly with the inverse of oxygen content (Figure 25–1*B*).[3,4] The effect of this vasodilation is that oxygen transport to the brain is relatively preserved as hypoxia becomes worse. The vasodilatory effect of hypoxia is long lasting. Sheep maintained in a hypoxemic environment (under conditions where blood Pa_{CO_2} is held constant) continue to have elevated cerebral blood flow for as long as 4 days.[5] Krasney et al[5] found a similar sustained elevation in cerebral blood flow for human subjects studied for over a week at altitudes of 5,000 m. It is important to note that these changes in cerebral blood flow are independent of changes in blood CO_2 tensions (Pa_{CO_2}) that might occur as a result of compensatory hyperventilation under conditions of hypoxia.

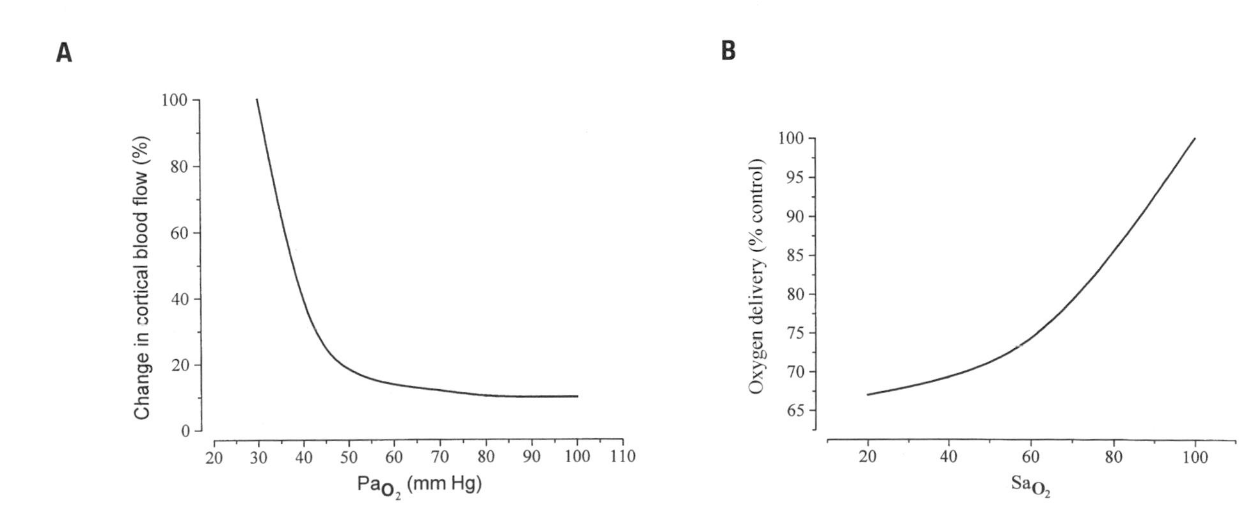

FIGURE 25–1. Changes in cortical blood flow as a function of partial pressure of arterial O_2 (Pa_{O_2}) (*A*) and saturation of arterial O_2 (Sa_{O_2}) (*B*). Data were derived by experiments in ventilated dogs under conditions of eucapnia. Note that blood flow changes little until the Pa_{O_2} falls below 60 mm Hg. (Adapted from McDowall DG.[2])

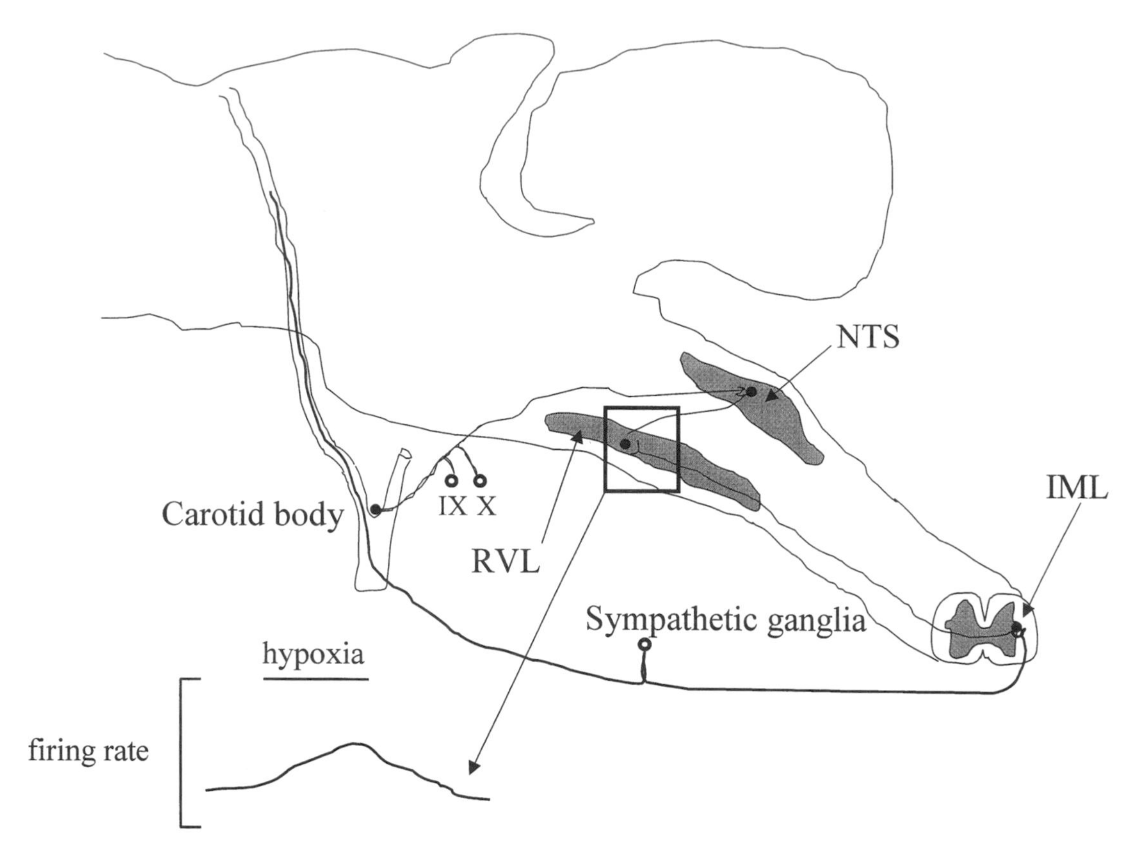

FIGURE 25–2. Anatomic basis for hypoxic regulation of sympathetic innervation to cerebral arteries. Nucleus tractus solitarii (NTS) receives afferent innervation from the carotid body via the IXth and Xth cranial nerves. Neurons of the NTS project to neurons in the nucleus reticularis rostroventrolateralis (RVL). These neurons increase their rate of firing during hypoxia. Intermediolateral neurons (IML) in the spinal cord project to the RVL and provide sympathetic input to the cervical sympathetic and stellate ganglia. Postganglionic sympathetic fibers follow the arterial supply to the brain. (Adapted from Reis DJ, Golanov EV, Ruggiero DA, et al. Sympatho-excitatory neurons of the rostral ventrolateral medulla are oxygen sensors and essential elements in the tonic and reflex control of the systemic and cerebral circulations. J Hypertens Suppl 1994;12:S159–80.)

The mechanism of this vasoregulation by oxygen is not clearly understood. Moreover, given the importance of preserving cerebral blood flow in the face of hypoxia, there may be parallel mechanisms subserving this vital function. The author considers those mechanisms mediated by neural or humoral signals originating outside the blood vessels as well as mechanisms that are intrinsic to the cerebral blood vessels.

Neural Regulation of Vasomotor Tone during Hypoxia

The cerebral vasculature is innervated by sympathetic neurons that originate primarily in the cervical sympathetic ganglia. These sympathetic nerve terminals contain catecholamine neurotransmitters as well as peptidergic neurotransmitters. They also may be capable of producing nitric oxide and other small signaling molecules. This apparatus for extrinsic control may provide a mechanism for regulation of cerebral vascular tone by oxygen. Cerebral blood vessels also receive innervation by parasympathetic nerve fibers. These fibers originate in the medulla. These parasympathetic ganglia that innervate cerebral vessels include the geniculate and the sphenopalatine ganglia.

Sympathoexcitatory neurons in the rostral ventrolateral medulla are stimulated by hypoxia.[6] This stimulation may be direct or mediated through afferent input from the carotid body through the nucleus tractus solitarii (Figure 25–2). Moreover, electrical stimulation of the ventral lateral medulla results in increases in cerebral blood flow throughout the cortex. The effect of hypoxia is not blunted by transection of the spinal cord, suggesting that this effect is not mediated by cervical sympathetic neurons. Hypoxia also continues to cause cerebral vasodilation when sympathetic nerve activity is ablated by sympathectomy or by inhibiting neuroexcitability. For example, newborn lambs continue to exhibit hypoxic-cerebral vasodilation even after surgical sympathectomy.[7]

However, bilateral lesions in the rostral ventrolateral medulla in adult rats diminish but do not prevent the increase in cerebral blood flow with hypoxia.[8] This suggests that changes in sympathetic nervous system activity may not be directly responsible for the response to hypoxia, but they may modulate the response of cerebral blood vessels to hypoxia. This is supported by the finding that sympathetic ganglionectomy causes no change in baseline cerebral blood flow but results in a greater increase in cerebral blood flow with hypoxia in rats.[9] Similarly, the sympathetic nervous system appears to limit the increase in blood flow with hypoxia in other species.[10–12] The fact that hypoxia vasodilates cerebral vessels independent of sympathetic nerve activity suggests that hypoxic vasodilation is primarily locally mediated and very intrinsic to the cerebral blood vessels.

Local Regulation of Vasomotor Tone during Hypoxia

The blood vessel is composed principally of two cells types: endothelial cells and vascular smooth muscle cells. Endothelial cells produce both vasoconstrictor and vasodilator substances that act on smooth muscle cells to alter vessel tone. It is therefore possible that either or both cell types are able to sense changes in Pa_{O_2} and thereby regulate vessel tone. It is also possible that the O_2-sensitive cells are close to, but not part of, the blood vessel itself. For example, either neurons or glia that are near the vessels may sense changes in Pa_{O_2} and release a diffusible substance that acts to regulate vasomotion. In examining potential mechanisms for hypoxic vasodilation, it is important to consider both the signal transduction cascade as well as the hypoxia-sensitive cell type. Characterizations of putative signal transduction cascades have relied generally on pharmacologic inhibition of either signaling molecule production or their action at their receptors. A number of signaling molecules have been examined for their role in hypoxic vasodilation. These include nitric oxide,[13–15] adenosine,[14,16,17] reactive oxygen species, eicosanoids,[18–20] and opioids.[18,21,22] Even if it were possible to determine with certainty which of these molecules are the critical messengers in the response to hypoxia (to date, this has not been possible), the challenge of determining the source of the molecules would remain, because many of the messengers considered can be produced by more than one cell type. For example, nitric oxide, although characterized as an endothelial-derived relaxing factor, can be produced by perivascular neurons[23,24] and glia,[25] as well as by vascular smooth muscle cells.[26] Reductionist approaches using in vitro preparations may not fully reveal the source, because it is not possible to replicate completely the in situ milieu around the blood vessel with the various cell types that may play a role in the response to hypoxia. The role of the principal systems is considered below.

Nitric Oxide

Nitric oxide causes vasodilation by stimulating the production of cyclic guanosine monophosphate (cGMP).[27] In isolated rabbit carotid and basilar arteries, hypoxia (to 15 torr) has caused an increase in cGMP levels, and this increase has been inhibited by the guanylyl cyclase inhibitor methylene blue.[28] Moreover, the increase in cGMP has depended on the integrity of the endothelium. Taken together, these results suggest that hypoxia-induced production of NO by endothelium contributes to hypoxic vasodilation. However, administration of methylene blue to live rabbits fails to inhibit increases in cerebral blood flow during hypoxia.[28] Other investigators have used inhibitors of NO synthase (NOS) to test whether NO production is required for hypoxic vasodilation. These studies have produced conflicting results. Systemic administration of NOS inhibitors has failed to inhibit cerebral hyperemia during hypoxia in rats,[13,29,30] and dogs.[31] One of these investigators, however, found that approximately half of vasodilation with more extreme hypoxia (to 33 torr) was inhibited by local application of the NOS inhibitor, N (nitro-L-arginine methylester).[14] Other investigators have found at least partial inhibition of hypoxic vasodilation by NOS inhibitors in rat,[32] cat,[33] adult[34] and fetal[35] sheep, and newborn piglets.[36]

The source of NO in hypoxic vasodilation is not clear. Besides vascular endothelial cells, parenchymal neurons, perivascular neurons, astrocytes, microglia, and oligodendrocytes all are capable of producing NO. A subset of neurons throughout the brain parenchyma contain NOS.[24,37] Experiments using cultured neurons, brain slices, and intact brain suggest that neuronal NO is produced and released in response to a number of stimuli, including activation of *N*-methyl-D-aspartate-type glutamate receptors,[38,39] acetylcholine,[40,41] and other neurotransmitters. Production of NO by neurons appears to be constitutive rather than inducible.[42] These neurons may modulate cerebral blood vessels by release of NO into the perivascular space. One specific group of NO-producing neurons may play a more direct vasoregulatory role. Neurons within the sphenopalatine ganglia stain intensely for NOS[43] and provide a major source of innervation to cerebral arteries.[44] Nitric oxide-containing nerve fibers presumably arising from this location are found within the walls of cerebral arteries. Glial cells appear to have both constitutive and inducible production of NO. In astrocytes NOS responds to a number of neurotransmitters, producing NO in sufficient quantities to relax cerebral arteries.[25] In microglia and astrocytes, induction of NOS also can occur in response to lipopolysaccharide and cytokines.[25,45]

It is not clear which of these sources of NO contributes to hypoxic vasodilation, if any. However, several investigators reporting an inhibitory effect of NOS inhibitors also found that hypoxic vasodilation is inhibited by local application of the Na^+-channel blocker, tetrodotoxin.[14,36] This suggests that the source of NO may be NOS-containing neurons, rather than endothelial cells. An alternative explanation, however, is that hypoxia is sensed by neuronal cells, but that they, in turn, cause

NO production from glial or endothelial cells via changes in the neuronal activity.

Adenosine

Winn and co-workers[46] showed that adenosine accumulates in the extracellular space during brain hypoxia and that this increase occurs within seconds of the onset of hypoxia. Moreover, adenosine is a cerebral vasodilator when applied topically to blood vessels studied using the closed cranial window technique.[47,48] Taken together, these data suggest that hypoxia causes the local release of adenosine, which then acts on its receptor to cause vasodilation. This hypothesis has been tested in two ways: (1) by examining the effect of accelerating or inhibiting the breakdown of adenosine; and (2) by testing the ability of adenosine receptor antagonists to inhibit the response to hypoxia.

Accelerating the breakdown of adenosine by topically applying adenosine deaminase attenuates (by greater than 50%) the response to hypoxia in rats.[17] Furthermore, adenosine receptor antagonists inhibit hypoxic vasodilation. For example, theophylline, a nonspecific adenosine receptor antagonist, inhibits hypoxic vasodilation in dogs,[49] rats,[47,50] and piglets.[48] Using more selective adenosine receptor antagonists, Coney and Marshall[51] demonstrated that adenosine acts through the adenos 2A receptor to dilate rat cerebral arterioles, and that inhibition of this receptor attenuates hypoxic vasodilation. These investigators found that local application (brain side of the blood-brain barrier) of a theophylline analog that does not permeate the blood-brain barrier inhibited vasodilation produced by similarly applied adenosine. However, hypoxic vasodilatation was inhibited only by analogs capable of penetrating the blood-brain barrier. Given that adenosine is not capable of crossing the blood-brain barrier, the investigators concluded that endothelial cells release adenosine in response to hypoxia. They suggested that abluminal increases in adenosine concentration caused by release from brain parenchymal are important in vasodilation only with severe hypoxia.

It is important to note that adenosine does not appear to underlie the response to hypoxia in all species or under all conditions. For example, Haller and Kuschinsky failed to find an inhibitory effect of theophylline on hypoxic vasodilation in cats.[52] However, these investigators tested the inhibitory effect of perivascularly applied theophylline under conditions of moderate hypoxia. The lack of response under these conditions might not be surprising if the endothelial cells are the important source of adenosine with hypoxia.

Experimental evidence pointing to the roles of NO and adenosine are not necessarily in conflict with each other. One way to explain this apparent paradox is to postulate that adenosine release leads to NO synthesis by endothelial cells, as has been demonstrated in umbilical endothelial cells.[53] However, there is no clear data to suggest that NO release with hypoxia derives from endothelial cells.

Eicosanoids

Metabolites of arachidonic acid are produced by cerebral blood vessels and brain parenchyma (Figure 25–3). These metabolites include prostaglandins (PGs), thromboxanes, leukotrienes, and eicosatetraenoic acids, and all have potent vasomotor effects in the cerebral vasculature. For example, topical application of arachidonic acid causes dilation of small cat pial arterioles, and this dilation is inhibited by the cyclooxygenase inhibitor indomethacin.[54] Hypoxia also may lead to increases in eicosanoid production, but the specific metabolites vary between species.[55] Hypoxia causes increases in prostaglandin production in dogs[56] and newborn pigs,[57] as well as increases in cerebrospinal fluid (CSF) thromboxane concentrations in mice.[58] However, indomethacin or other cyclooxygenase inhibitors do not block hypoxic vasodilation in cats[19,55] or newborn pigs.[57] These results suggest that prostaglandins do not play a direct role in hypoxic vasodilation in brain.

Recently, Harder and colleagues have provided evidence that a different arachidonate metabolite may be important in the vasomotor response to hypoxia. They have found that cerebral blood vessels produce 20-hydroxyeicosatetraenoic acid (20-HETE), a potent vasoconstrictor substance; 20-HETE is produced by ω-hydroxylation of arachidonic acid via a P450-dependent process. This P450-enzyme is a member of the extrahepatic 4A family of ω-hydroxylases that requires molecular oxygen and reduced nicotinamide-adenine dinucleotide phosphate (NADPH).[20] In rat renal and cremasteric vessels, P450-dependent production of 20-HETE is oxygen dependent, increasing as Pa_{O_2} is raised with half-maximal production at a Pa_{O_2} of 60 torr.[59] Reverse-transcription polymerase chain reaction experiments demonstrate that this P450 enzyme is contained within the vascular smooth muscle cells.[60] This enzyme is present in a number of blood vessels studies, and inhibition of this enzyme inhibits the vasodilatory response to hypoxia in some, but not all, segments of the circulation.[61]

In newborn pig, Leffler and Parfenova have demonstrated that specific light-dye-induced endothelial injury reduces the vasodilatory response to hypoxia in pial arterioles by approximately two-thirds.[57] The response to hypoxia in this preparation also was inhibited partially by two different inhibitors of P-450-dependent metabolism of arachidonic acid: 5,8,11,14-eicosatetraenoic acid and miconazole. This suggests that endothelial-dependent production of epoxygenase metabolites may contribute to hypoxic vasodilation in newborn pigs. Because the inhibitors attenuate the response to hypoxia, the metabolite is likely distinct from 20-HETE, which undergoes a decrease in production with hypoxia. Persistent, albeit

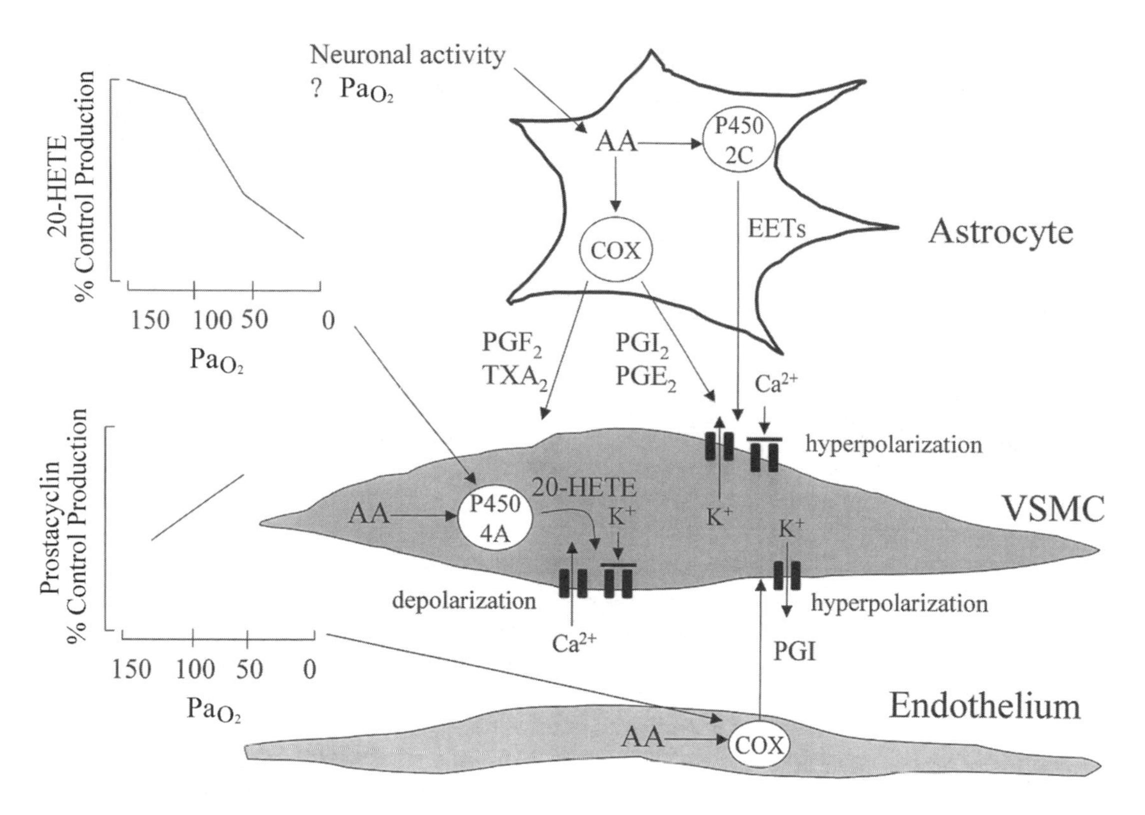

FIGURE 25–3. Schematic of arachidonic acid (AA) metabolism and its effects on cerebral vascular smooth muscle cells (VSMC). Arachidonic acid is metabolized by cyclooxygenase (COX) in astrocytes and endothelial cells. Both vasodilatory and vasocontricting substances are produced. Prostacyclin (PGI) released from endothelial cells activates K^+ channels on VSMCs to cause hyperpolarization and relaxation. Prostacyclin production increases with hypoxia (*lower inset*). Arachidonic acid also is metabolized by P450 to 20-HETE (20-hydroxyeicosatetraenoic acid) in VSMCs that acts to activate Ca^{2+} channels and inhibit K^+ channels, thereby leading to depolarization and vasoconstriction. The production of 20-HETE is reduced during hypoxia (*top inset*; adapted from Lombard JH, et al.[61]) Astrocytes use P450 to produce epoxyeicosatrienoacids that act to hyperpolarize and relax VSMCs. Metabolism of AA in astrocytes increases with neuronal stimulation and possibly with hypoxia. Pa_{O_2} = partial pressure of arterial O_2; PG = prostaglandin; TXA = thromboxane A.

reduced, hypoxic dilation suggests that there are also other mechanisms that contribute to this response.

Opioids

Just as hypoxia increases production or release of adenosine and eicosanoids, it also results in production or release of endogenous opioids including met- and leu-enkephalins and dynorphins.[62] Cerebral microvessels express opioid receptors,[63] and opiate-containing nerve fibers are found in large cerebral arteries of pigs and guinea pigs.[64,65] Glial cells also produce and release met-enkephalin in response to hypoxia.[66] Armstead and co-workers have examined the importance of opioid for the cerebral arterial response to hypoxia in newborn piglets. This group of investigators found that in newborn piglets, μ-opioid receptor antagonists attenuate hypoxic cerebral vasodilation.[62] The precise source of opioids in these experiments is unclear. Moreover, hypoxia may cause enkephalin release indirectly via the action of one or more other paracrine molecules. The rise in enkephalin with moderate and severe hypoxia, for example, is attenuated by inhibition of prostaglandin synthesis with indomethacin[18] and by antagonism of vasopressin receptors.[21] Hypoxia increases CSF concentrations of PGE_2 and arginine vasopressin. Moreover, local application of these substances causes vasodilation. It is not clear if the release of opioids is essential for this vasodilation.

The mechanism of dilation in response to opioids is not entirely known. Glibenclamide attenuates hypoxic vasodilation and also attenuates vasodilation in response to met-enkephalin,[67,68] suggesting that adenosine triphosphate (ATP) sensitive K^+-channel (K_{ATP})-channel activation plays an important role in this response. Vasodilation in response to opioids also is attenuated by specific endothelial NOS inhibitors, but not neuronal NOS inhibitors.[36,69] One way to integrate these individual findings is to consider a model in which hypoxia leads to the release of enkephalins from glia or neurons, because of hypoxia-induced increases of vasopressin, prostaglandins, neuronally derived NO, or other factors. These factors may act in series or in parallel to effect opioid release. Opioid release results in stimulation of endothelial NO production, which then results in increased smooth muscle cGMP levels leading, in turn, to activation of K_{ATP} channels and muscle relaxation.

Intrinsic Responses of Cerebral Arterioles to Hypoxia

One reductionist approach to examining the mechanism of hypoxic vasodilation is to examine the response of isolated blood vessels or the responses of single arterial smooth muscle cells. Isolated blood vessels have been studied by dissection and cannulation using fine glass micropipettes.[70] Vasomotor responses can then be measured using optical approaches to follow changes in vessel diameter. Flow through the vessel as well as the transmural pressure can be regulated independently. Isolated rabbit carotid and basilar arteries retain the capacity to dilate in response to hypoxia.[28] Feline middle cerebral arteries also retain vasodilatory responses ex vivo.[71] Thus it appears that cerebral arterial tissue has an intrinsic response to hypoxia. One difficulty with this interpretation is that isolated vessels may have preserved neural elements within the vessel wall.[72] However, hypoxic vasodilation of isolated vessels is not inhibited by tetrodotoxin,[71] which would be expected to block neurally mediated vasomotion.

Isolated arterioles are composed of both vascular smooth muscle cells and endothelial cells, and both of these cell types may be able to sense hypoxia independently. Light dye or mechanical injury to the endothelium reduces the dilatory response of isolated cerebral vessels to hypoxia,[73–75] demonstrating that endothelial cells have the capacity to sense hypoxia. However, isolated cerebral vascular smooth muscle cells also respond to hypoxia. Growing cerebral arterial smooth muscle cells on a flexible silicone substratum, Madden and co-workers[76] were able to demonstrate that these cultured cells developed spontaneous tone, and that this tone decreased when the P_{O_2} of the bathing solution was reduced.

Hypoxic vasodilation may occur as a result of a fall in the intracellular calcium concentration within the smooth muscle cells or a decrease in the calcium sensitivity of the contractile apparatus. Decreases in $[Ca^{2+}]_i$ have been observed in isolated rat cerebral arterial smooth muscle cells.[77] Such decreases might occur by decreases in Ca^{2+} influx, decreases in release from intracellular stores, or by more rapid Ca^{2+} extrusion and reuptake. Entry of Ca^{2+} occurs, in large part, via voltage-activated Ca^{2+} channels that open as the membrane potential becomes depolarized. Thus, Ca^{2+} entry may be reduced by direct modulation of voltage-activated Ca^{2+} channels or by regulation of other channels, so as to hyperpolarize the smooth muscle cell and reduce voltage-dependent opening of the Ca^{2+} channels. One important set of candidate regulatory targets is K^+ channels. Increasing the opening of K^+ channels would result in the hyperpolarization of the cell and this would result in a decrease in the opening of voltage-dependent Ca^{2+} channels.

The K_{ATP} channels are a particularly interesting potential target in hypoxia, because their activity appears to be regulated by the ATP-to-ADP (adenosine diphosphate) ratio within the cell; this ratio would be expected to change during hypoxia.[78] The K^+ channels are activated by hypoxia in isolated cat cerebral arterial smooth muscle cells, and these channels are blocked by glibenclamide, an inhibitor of K_{ATP} channels.[79] Glibenclamide also blocks hypoxia-induced vascular smooth muscle cell hyperpolarization in isolated rat cerebral arterioles,[75] suggesting that activation of K_{ATP} channels at least partly underlies hypoxic vasodilation. Indeed, glibenclamide inhibits hypoxic vasodilation in rat,[73] rabbit,[80] and gerbil[81] cerebral blood vessels but does not, itself, cause significant vasodilation. This suggests that K_{ATP} channels are normally quiescent but are activated by hypoxia.

The K_{ATP} channels also are activated by hypoxia in other systemic blood vessels including coronary artery.[82] However, these channels may not fully account for the response to hypoxia. In other vascular tissue, hyperpolarization may occur with hypoxia that is not marked enough to compromise cellular respiration, or when K_{ATP} channels are inhibited by glibenclamide.[83] It is possible that activation of other K^+ channels contributes to hyperpolarization and relaxation with hypoxia. Gebremedhin and co-workers have demonstrated that Ca^{2+}-activated K^+ (K_{Ca}) channels are activated by hypoxia in single cat cerebral arterial smooth muscle cells[84] (Figure 25–4). Interestingly, this activation by hypoxia does not appear to require an increase in $[Ca^{2+}]_i$. Inhibition of this channel by low concentrations of tetraethylammonium also blocks contraction of cat cerebral arterioles. This inhibitor has no effect on rat arterioles. Blockade of K_{Ca} channels using iberiotoxin also blocks hypoxic vasodilation in newborn pigs studied using the cranial window technique,[85] although later work by this group suggests that activation of these channels may be important in the response to hypoxia of moderate (10 to 20 minutes) duration but not shorter (< 5 minutes) or longer (40 minutes) durations.[86] In gerbils, both iberiotoxin and glibenclamide partially inhibited in vivo responses to hypoxia,[81] suggesting that both K_{ATP} and K_{Ca} channels may contribute to the hypoxic response.

Increasing the activity of K^+ channels would be expected to cause hyperpolarization, reducing activation of voltage-activated Ca^{2+} channels and thereby relaxing the smooth muscle cells. However, Ca^{2+} channels, also may be regulated directly. In rabbit cerebral arterial smooth muscle cells and in other systemic vascular smooth muscle cells[87] (Figure 25–5), hypoxia inhibits L-type Ca^{2+} channel activity by slowing the activation kinetics and by shifting the conductance-voltage relationship to positive membrane potentials.[88] It is not clear how to

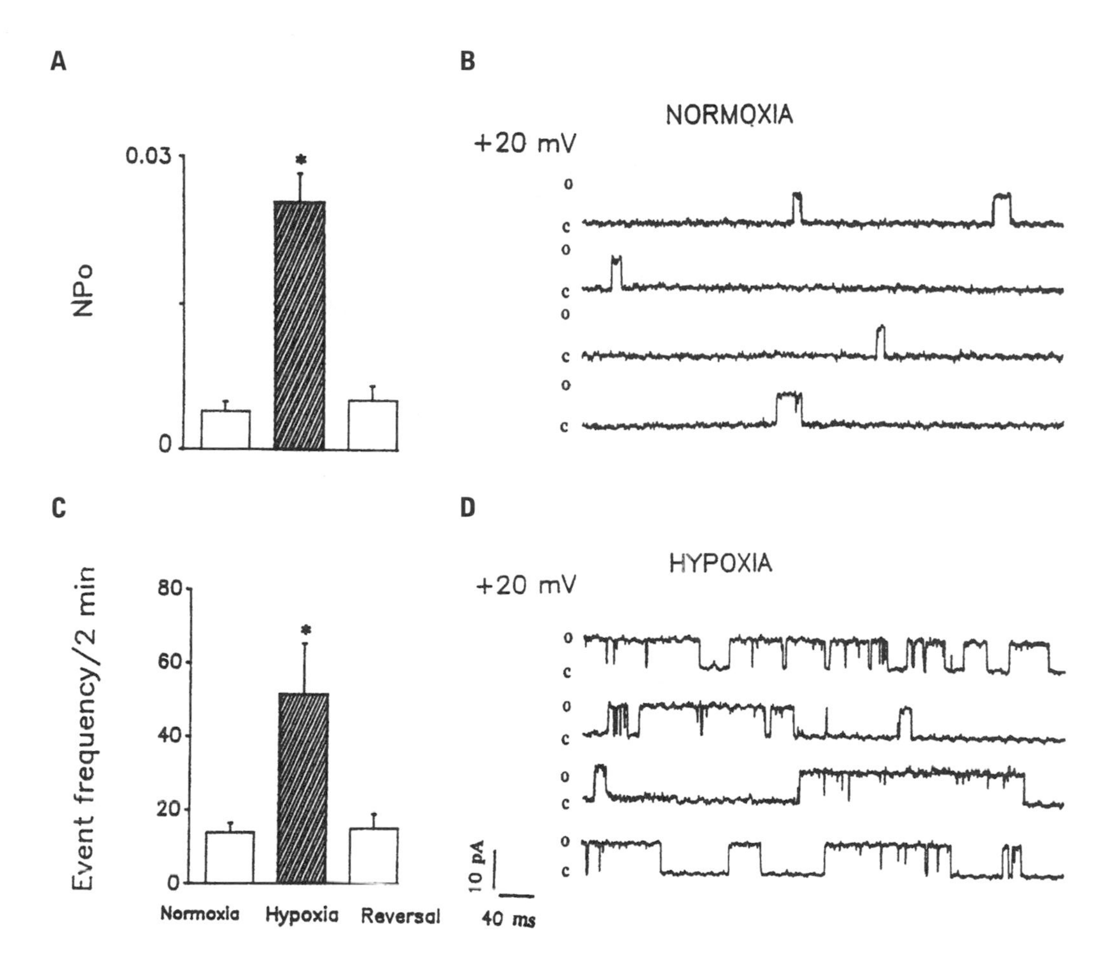

FIGURE 25–4. Effect of hypoxia on single channel K^+ currents in cat cerebral arterial smooth muscle cells studied using the cell-attached patch-clamp technique. *A* and *C* illustrate that the probability of the channel being open and the frequency of opening both increase reversibly with hypoxia. *B* and *D* illustrate representative traces of current recordings through a single channel under normoxic and hypoxic conditions. o = open; c = closed; NPo = open state probability. (Reproduced with permission from Gebremedhin D et al.[84])

reconcile this with the finding that glibenclamide, a K^+ channel inhibitor, inhibits the in vivo response to hypoxia in the same species.[80]

Summary

The nature of brain blood flow control by hypoxia is indeed a complex one. Multiple cell types including neurons, glia, vascular endothelial cells, and vascular smooth muscle cells have the capacity to sense and respond to changes in the local Pa_{O_2}. Moreover, each cell type has the ability to modulate vascular smooth muscle tone directly or indirectly through the synthesis and release of vasoactive molecules. Finally, the threat to tissue viability produced by hypoxia makes it likely that multiple mechanisms may contribute to defense by causing vasodilation. To fully understand the process of hypoxic vasodilation, it will be important to define not only which cells are critical to sensing changes in Pa_{O_2}, but also to determine how distinct mechanisms interact.

It will be important to describe whether mechanisms act in series, in parallel, or by one hypoxic response modulating another hypoxic response (Figure 25–6). For example, hypoxia-induced release of adenosine by neurons or glia may lead to release of NO by endothelial cells. This serial relationship could explain why both adenosine receptor antagonists and NOS inhibitors attenuate hypoxic vasodilation in some species. However, it is also possible that hypoxia causes the independent release of adenosine and NO, which then act in parallel to cause vasodilation. A third possibility is that hypoxia-induced release of adenosine acts to amplify hypoxia-induced release of NO. Alternatively, the hypoxia-sensing mechanism may allow modulation of another vasomotor pathway. This could potentially lead to the observation that a specific pathway is important under some, but not all, experimental conditions.

Parallel mechanisms may begin with a common origin. It is possible that a single O_2-sensing mechanism in

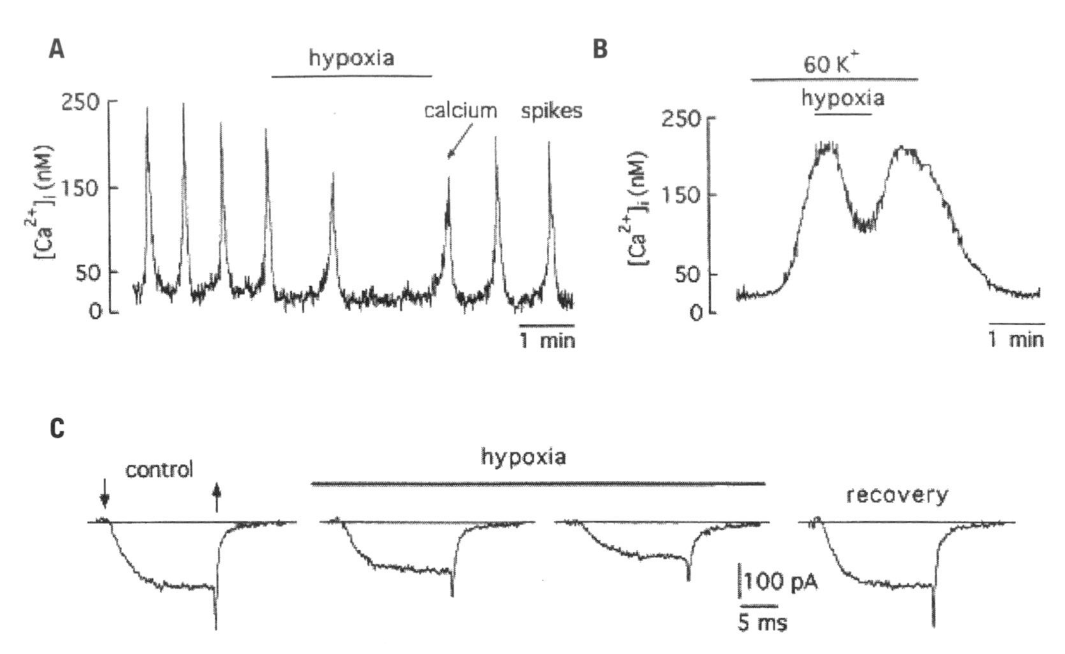

FIGURE 25–5. Alteration of Ca^{2+} homeostasis in arterial smooth muscle cells by hypoxia. *A*, Intracellular Ca^{2+} concentration in rabbit celiac arterial myocytes undergoes repetitive spikes that are inhibited reversibly by hypoxia. *B*, Depolarization of porcine coronary vascular smooth muscle cells causes a more sustained increases in $[Ca^{2+}]_i$, which are attenuated by hypoxia. *C*, Hypoxia reduces inward Ca^{2+} current in rabbit celiac arterial myocytes studied using the whole-cell patch-clamp technique. Currents (shown as downward deflections from the baseline) are activated by depolarization. Hypoxia to 20 mm Hg causes progressive but reversible reduction in the current. (Reproduced with permission from Lopez-Barneo J, Pardal R, Montoro RJ, et al. K^+ and Ca^{2+} channel activity and cytosolic $[Ca^{2+}]$ in oxygen-sensing tissues. Respir Physiol 1999;115:215–27.)

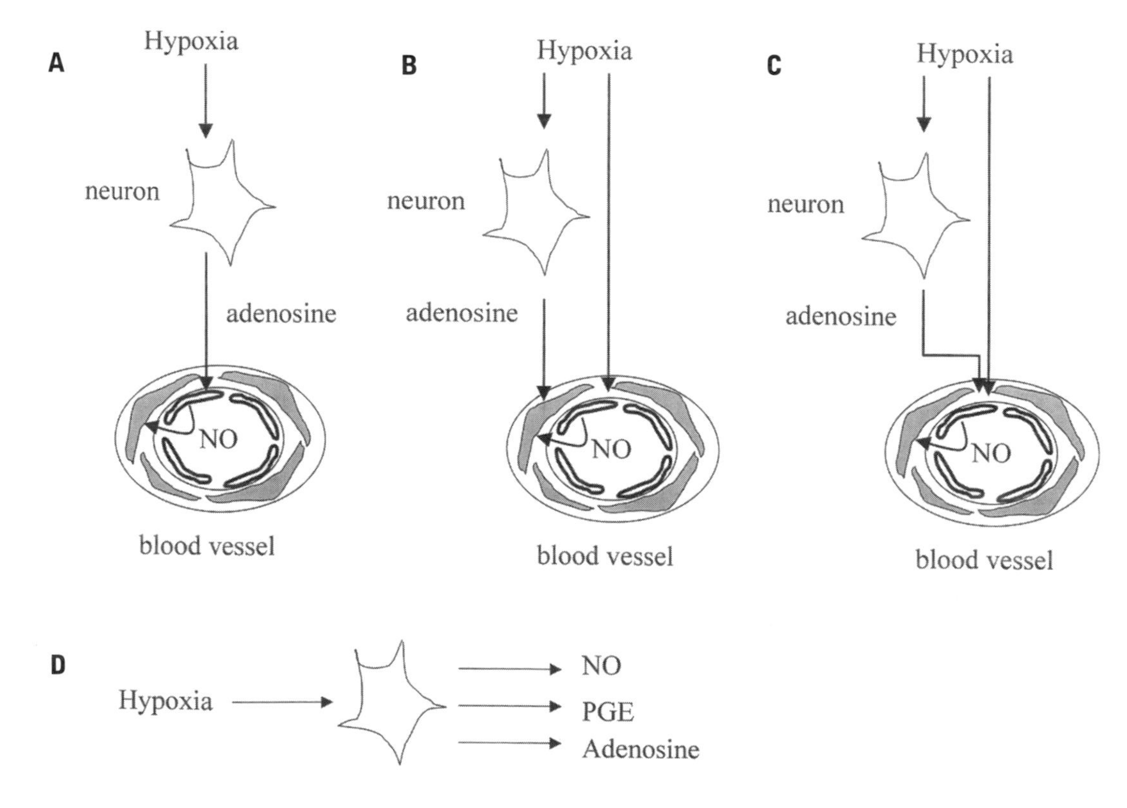

FIGURE 25–6. Schematic showing possible inter-relationships along and between oxygen-sensitive vasoregulatory pathways. Relationships between the action of adenosine and nitric oxide (NO) serve as examples. Signalling processes may act in series (*A*) or parallel (*B* and *D*). It is also possible that one oxygen-sensitive pathway modulates another (*C*). Parallel pathways may diverge from a common signaling point (*D*). PGE = prostaglandin E.

glial cells leads to production of both adenosine and NO, each of which is capable of causing cerebral vasodilation via distinct mechanisms. It is also possible that parallel processes converge to modulate vascular smooth muscle function through a common mechanism. Thus, activation of multiple receptors on vascular smooth muscle cell may lead to regulation of intracellular Ca^{2+} concentrations or Ca^{2+} sensitivity of the contractile apparatus. Similarly, multiple cascades may converge to regulate K_{Ca} or K_{ATP} channels.

The precise interplay between various mechanisms has great import with respect to pathophysiologic or pharmacologic manipulation of these processes. Specifically, serial or converging processes may be modulated by regulation of one or more targets. In contrast, parallel or diverging processes may require interaction at multiple targets to interfere with regulatory or maladaptive processes. The significant challenge moving forward is to develop a richer understanding of the complex interactions between the hypoxia-sensitive signaling pathways described above.

References

1. Roy CS, Sherrington CS. The regulation of the blood supply of the brain. J Physiol 1890;11:85.
2. McDowall DG. Interrelationships between blood oxygen tensions and cerebral blood flow. Int Anesthesiol Clin 1966;4:205–19.
3. McDowall DG. Interrelationships between blood oxygen tension and cerebral blood flow. In: Payne JP, Hill DW, eds. Oxygen measurements in blood and tissues. London: Churchill, 1966:205–14.
4. Jones MD Jr, Sheldon RE, Peeters LL, et al. Regulation of cerebral blood flow in the ovine fetus. Am J Physiol 1978;235:H162–6.
5. Krasney JA, Jensen JB, Lassen NA. Cerebral blood flow does not adapt to sustained hypoxia. J Cereb Blood Flow Metab 1990;10:759–64.
6. Sun MK, Reis DJ. Hypoxia selectively excites vasomotor neurons of rostral ventrolateral medulla in rats. Am J Physiol 1994;266:R245–56.
7. Massik J, Jones MD Jr, Miyabe M, et al. Hypercapnia and response of cerebral blood flow to hypoxia in newborn lambs. J Appl Physiol 1989;66:1065–70.
8. Underwood MD, Iadecola C, Reis DJ. Lesions of the rostral ventrolateral medulla reduce the cerebrovascular response to hypoxia. Brain Res 1994;635:217–23.
9. Kissen I, Weiss HR. Cervical sympathectomy and cerebral microvascular and blood flow responses to hypocapnic hypoxia. Am J Physiol 1989;256:H460–7.
10. Busija DW. Sympathetic nerves reduce cerebral blood flow during hypoxia in awake rabbits. Am J Physiol 1984; 247:H446–51.
11. Wagerle LC, Heffernan TM, Sacks LM, et al. Sympathetic effect on cerebral blood flow regulation in hypoxic newborn lambs. Am J Physiol 1983;245:H487–94.
12. Linder J. Effects of cervical sympathetic stimulation on cerebral and ocular blood flows during hemorrhagic hypotension and moderate hypoxia. Acta Physiol Scand 1982;114:379–86.
13. Kozniewska E, Oseka M, Stys T. Effects of endothelium-derived nitric oxide on cerebral circulation during normoxia and hypoxia in the rat. J Cereb Blood Flow Metab 1992;12:311–7.
14. Pelligrino DA, Wang Q, Koenig HM, et al. Role of nitric oxide, adenosine, N-methyl-D-aspartate receptors, and neuronal activation in hypoxia-induced pial arteriolar dilation in rats. Brain Res 1995;704:61–70.
15. Bari F, Thore CR, Louis TM, et al. Inhibitory effects of hypoxia and adenosine on N-methyl-D-aspartate-induced pial arteriolar dilation in piglets. Brain Res 1998;780:237–44.
16. Dora E, Koller A, Kovach AG. Effect of topical adenosine deaminase treatment on the functional hyperemic and hypoxic responses of cerebrocortical microcirculation. J Cereb Blood Flow Metab 1984;4:447–57.
17. Simpson RE, Phillis JW. Adenosine deaminase reduces hypoxic and hypercapnic dilatation of rat pial arterioles: evidence for mediation by adenosine. Brain Res 1991; 553:305–8.
18. Armstead WM. Relationship between opioids and prostaglandins in hypoxia-induced vasodilation of pial arteries in the newborn pig. Proc Soc Exp Biol Med 1996;212:135–41.
19. Wei EP, Ellis EF, Kontos HA. Role of prostaglandins in pial arteriolar response to CO_2 and hypoxia. Am J Physiol 1980;238:H226–30.
20. Harder DR, Gebremedhin D, Narayanan J, et al. Formation and action of a P-450 4A metabolite of arachidonic acid in cat cerebral microvessels. Am J Physiol 1994; 266:H2098–107.
21. Rossberg MI, Armstead WM. Relationship between vasopressin and opioids in hypoxia induced pial artery vasodilation. Am J Physiol 1996;271:H521–7.
22. Armstead WM. Role of opioids in hypoxic pial artery dilation is stimulus duration dependent. Am J Physiol 1998;275:H861–7.
23. Estrada C, Mengual E, Gonzalez C. Local NADPH-diaphorase neurons innervate pial arteries and lie close or project to intracerebral blood vessels: a possible role for nitric oxide in the regulation of cerebral blood flow. J Cereb Blood Flow Metab 1993;13:978–84.
24. Bredt DS, Hwang PM, Snyder SH. Localization of nitric oxide synthase indicating a neural role for nitric oxide. Nature 1990;347:768–70.
25. Murphy S, Simmons ML, Agullo L, et al. Synthesis of nitric oxide in CNS glial cells. Trends Neurosci 1993;16:323–8.
26. Iadecola C, Zhang F, Casey R, et al. Inducible nitric oxide synthase gene expression in vascular cells after transient focal cerebral ischemia. Stroke 1996;27:1373–80.
27. Moncada S, Palmer MJ, Higgs EA. Nitric oxide: physiology, pathophysiology, and pharmacology. Pharmacol Rev 1991;43:109–42.
28. Pearce WJ, Reynier-Rebuffel AM, Lee J, et al. Effects of methylene blue on hypoxic cerebral vasodilatation in the rabbit. J Pharmacol Exp Ther 1990;254:616–25.
29. Pelligrino DA, Koenig HM, Albrecht RF. Nitric oxide synthesis and regional cerebral blood flow responses to hypercapnia and hypoxia in the rat. J Cereb Blood Flow Metab 1993;13:80–7.
30. Buchanan JE, Phillis JW. The role of nitric oxide in the regulation of cerebral blood flow. Brain Res 1993; 610:248–55.
31. McPherson RW, Koehler RC, Traystman RJ. Hypoxia, alpha 2-adrenergic, and nitric oxide–dependent interactions on canine cerebral blood flow. Am J Physiol 1994; 266:H476–82.

32. Berger C, von Kummer R. Does NO regulate the cerebral blood flow response in hypoxia? Acta Neurol Scand 1998;97:118–25.
33. Ishimura N, Kitaguchi K, Tatsumi K, et al. Nitric oxide involvement in hypoxic dilation of pial arteries in the cat. Anesthesiology 1996;85:1350–6.
34. Iwamoto J, Yoshinaga M, Yang SP, et al. Methylene blue inhibits hypoxic cerebral vasodilation in awake sheep. J Appl Physiol 1992;73:2226–32.
35. van Bel F, Sola A, Roman C, et al. Role of nitric oxide in the regulation of the cerebral circulation in the lamb fetus during normoxemia and hypoxemia. Biol Neonate 1995; 68:200–10.
36. Wilderman MJ, Armstead WM. Role of neuronal NO synthase in relationship between NO and opioids in hypoxia-induced pial artery dilation. Am J Physiol 1997; 273:H1807–15.
37. Bredt DS, Snyder SH. Nitric oxide, a novel neuronal messenger. Neuron 1992;8:3–11.
38. Garthwaite J, Charles SL, Chess-Williams R. Endothelium-derived relaxing factor release on activation of NMDA receptors suggests role as intercellular messenger in the brain. Nature 1988;336:385–7.
39. Marin P, Quignard JF, Lafon-Cazal M, et al. Non-classical glutamate receptors, blocked by both NMDA and non-NMDA antagonists, stimulate nitric oxide production in neurons. Neuropharmacology 1993;32:29–36.
40. Hu J, el-Fakahany EE. Role of intercellular and intracellular communication by nitric oxide in coupling of muscarinic receptors to activation of guanylate cyclase in neuronal cells. J Neurochem 1993;61:578–85.
41. Reiser G. Mechanism of stimulation of cyclic-GMP level in a neuronal cell line mediated by serotonin (5-HT3) receptors. Involvement of nitric oxide, arachidonic-acid metabolism and cytosolic Ca2+. Eur J Biochem 1990; 189:547–52.
42. Galea E, Feinstein DL, Reis DJ. Induction of calcium-independent nitric oxide synthase activity in primary rat glial cultures. Proc Natl Acad Sci U S A 1992;89:10945–9.
43. Yamamoto R, Bredt DS, Snyder SH, et al. The localization of nitric oxide synthase in the rat eye and related cranial ganglia. Neuroscience 1993;54:189–200.
44. Toda N, Ayajiki K, Yoshida K, et al. Impairment by damage of the pterygopalatine ganglion of nitroxidergic vasodilator nerve function in canine cerebral and retinal arteries. Circ Res 1993;72:206–13.
45. Corradin SB, Mauel J, Donini SD, et al. Inducible nitric oxide synthase activity of cloned murine microglial cells. Glia 1993;7:255–62.
46. Winn HR, Rubio R, Berne RM. Brain adenosine concentration during hypoxia in rats. Am J Physiol 1981; 241:H235–42.
47. Morii S, Ngai AC, Ko KR, et al. Role of adenosine in regulation of cerebral blood flow: effects of theophylline during normoxia and hypoxia. Am J Physiol 1987; 253:H165–75.
48. Bari F, Louis TM, Busija DW. Effects of ischemia on cerebral arteriolar dilation to arterial hypoxia in piglets. Stroke 1998;29:222–8.
49. Emerson TE Jr, Raymond RM. Involvement of adenosine in cerebral hypoxic hyperemia in the dog. Am J Physiol 1981;241:H134–8.
50. Hoffman WE, Albrecht RF, Miletich DJ. The role of adenosine in CBF increases during hypoxia in young vs aged rats. Stroke 1984;15:124–9.
51. Coney AM, Marshall JM. Role of adenosine and its receptors in the vasodilatation induced in the cerebral cortex of the rat by systemic hypoxia. J Physiol 1998; 509:507–18.
52. Haller C, Kuschinsky W. Moderate hypoxia: reactivity of pial arteries and local effect of theophylline. J Appl Physiol 1987;63:2208–15.
53. Sobrevia L, Yudilevich DL, Mann GE. Activation of A2-purinoceptors by adenosine stimulates L-arginine transport (system y+) and nitric oxide synthesis in human fetal endothelial cells. J Physiol 1997;499:135–40.
54. Wei EP, Ellis EF, Kontos HA. Role of prostaglandins in pial arteriolar response to CO_2 and hypoxia. Am J Physiol 1980;238:H226–30.
55. Kontos HA, Wei EP, Ellis EF, et al. Prostaglandins in physiological and in certain pathological responses of the cerebral circulation. Fed Proc 1981;40:2326–30.
56. Herbaczynska-Cedro K, Truskolaski P, Ruszczewski P. Inhibitory effect of hydrocortisone on the release of prostaglandins from dog's brain in hypoxia and cerebral embolism. Acta Physiol Polonica 1978;29:501–7.
57. Leffler CW, Parfenova H. Cerebral arteriolar dilation to hypoxia: role of prostanoids. Am J Physiol 1997; 272:H418–24.
58. Shohami E, Gross J. Effects of hypoxia and anoxia on the ex vivo release of prostaglandins from mouse cortical slices. J Neurochem 1986;47:1678–81.
59. Harder DR, Narayanan J, Birks EK, et al. Identification of a putative microvascular oxygen sensor. Circ Res 1996; 79:54–61.
60. Gebremedhin D, Lange AR, Narayanan J, et al. Cat cerebral arterial smooth muscle cells express cytochrome P450 4A2 enzyme and produce the vasoconstrictor 20-HETE which enhances L-type Ca2+ current. J Physiol 1998; 507:771–81.
61. Lombard JH, Kunert MP, Roman RJ, et al. Cytochrome P-450 omega-hydroxylase senses O_2 in hamster muscle, but not cheek pouch epithelium, microcirculation. Am J Physiol 1999;276:H503–8.
62. Armstead WM. Opioids and nitric oxide contribute to hypoxia-induced pial arterial vasodilation in newborn pigs. Am J Physiol 1995;268:H226–32.
63. Peroutka SJ, Moskowitz MA, Reinhard JF Jr, et al. Neurotransmitter receptor binding in bovine cerebral microvessels. Science 1980;208:610–2.
64. Moskowitz MA, Brezina LR, Kuo C. Dynorphin B–containing perivascular axons and sensory neurotransmitter mechanisms in brain blood vessels. Cephalalgia 1986; 6:81–6.
65. Moskowitz MA, Saito K, Brezina L, et al. Nerve fibers surrounding intracranial and extracranial vessels from human and other species contain dynorphin-like immunoreactivity. Neuroscience 1987;23:731–7.
66. Armstead WM. Nitric oxide contributes to opioid release from glia during hypoxia. Brain Res 1998;813:398–401.
67. Armstead WM. Relationship among NO, the KATP channel, and opioids in hypoxic pial artery dilation. Am J Physiol 1998;275:H988–94.
68. Shankar V, Armstead WM. Opioids contribute to hypoxia-induced pial artery dilation through activation of ATP-sensitive K+ channels. Am J Physiol 1995; 269:H997–1002.
69. Wilderman MJ, Armstead WM. Role of endothelial nitric oxide synthase in hypoxia-induced pial artery dilation. J Cereb Blood Flow Metab 1998;18:531–8.

70. Duling BR, Gore RW, Dacey RG, et al. Methods for isolation, cannulation, and in vitro study of single microvessels. Am J Physiol 1981;241:H108–16.
71. Lombard JH, Smeda J, Madden JA, et al. Effect of reduced oxygen availability upon myogenic depolarization and contraction of cat middle cerebral artery. Circ Res 1986;58:565–9.
72. Yoshida K, Okamura T, Toda N. Histological and functional studies on the nitroxidergic nerve innervating monkey cerebral, mesenteric and temporal arteries. Jpn J Pharmacol 1994;65:351–9.
73. Fredricks KT, Liu Y, Rusch NJ, et al. Role of endothelium and arterial K+ channels in mediating hypoxic dilation of middle cerebral arteries. Am J Physiol 1994;267: H580–6.
74. Leffler CW, Smith JS, Edrington JL, et al. Mechanisms of hypoxia-induced cerebrovascular dilation in the newborn pig. Am J Physiol 1997;272:H1323–32.
75. Lombard JH, Liu Y, Fredricks KT, et al. Electrical and mechanical responses of rat middle cerebral arteries to reduced PO_2 and prostacyclin. Am J Physiol 1999; 276:H509–16.
76. Madden JA, Vadula MS, Kurup VP. Effects of hypoxia and other vasoactive agents on pulmonary and cerebral artery smooth muscle cells. Am J Physiol 1992;263: L384–93.
77. Vadula MS, Kleinman JG, Madden JA. Effect of hypoxia and norepinephrine on cytoplasmic free Ca2+ in pulmonary and cerebral arterial myocytes. Am J Physiol 1993;265:L591–7.
78. Davis NW, Standen NB, Stanfield PR. ATP-dependent potassium channels of muscle cells: their properties, regulation, and possible functions. J Bioenerg Biomembr 1991;23:509–35.
79. Bonnet P, Gebremedhin D, Rush NJ, et al. Effects of hypoxia on a potassium channel in cat cerebral arterial muscle cells. Z Kardiol 1991;80 Suppl 7:25–7.
80. Taguchi H, Heistad DD, Kitazono T, et al. ATP-sensitive K+ channels mediate dilatation of cerebral arterioles during hypoxia. Circ Res 1994;74:1005–8.
81. Messager T, de Bray JM, Jallet P, et al. Introduction of the closed cranial window technique in gerbils and verification by observation of the effects of specific drugs. Jpn J Pharmacol 1999;80:289–94.
82. Daut J, Maier-Rudolph W, von Beckerath N, et al. Hypoxic dilation of coronary arteries is mediated by ATP-sensitive potassium channels. Science 1990;247:1341–4.
83. Franco-Obregnon A, Urena J, Smani T, et al. Calcium channels, cytosolic calcium, and the vasomotor response to hypoxia. In: Lopez-Barneo J, Weir KS, eds. Oxygen regulation of ion channels and gene expression. New York: Futura Publishing, 1998:255–70.
84. Gebremedhin D, Bonnet P, Greene AS, et al. Hypoxia increases the activity of Ca(2+)-sensitive K+ channels in cat cerebral arterial muscle cell membranes. Pflugers Arch – Eur J Physiol 1994;428:621–30.
85. Armstead WM. Role of activation of calcium-sensitive K+ channels in NO- and hypoxia-induced pial artery vasodilation. Am J Physiol 1997;272:H1785–90.
86. Ben-Haim G, Armstead WM. Stimulus duration-dependent contribution of K(Ca) channel activation and cAMP to hypoxic cerebrovasodilation. Brain Res 2000; 853:330–7.
87. Franco-Obregon A, Urena J, Lopez-Barneo J. Oxygen-sensitive calcium channels in vascular smooth muscle and their possible role in hypoxic arterial relaxation. Proc Natl Acad Sci U S A 1995;92:4715–9.
88. Franco-Obregon A, Lopez-Barneo J. Low PO_2 inhibits calcium channel activity in arterial smooth muscle cells. Am J Physiol 1996;271:H2290–9.

CHAPTER 26

Cardiopulmonary Physiology at Altitude

Susan Niermeyer, MD

At high altitude the lung encounters an atmosphere of reduced density compared with the density at sea level. Although the fraction of inspired oxygen remains the same, lower barometric pressure decreases the density of gas molecules and thus lowers the oxygen content of inspired air. Hypoxia results when the compensatory increase in alveolar ventilation can no longer maintain alveolar oxygen partial pressure. Although many of the cardiopulmonary responses to high-altitude hypoxia are similar in adults and children, the unique developmental physiology of infancy and childhood sets the stage for different responses and mechanisms of disease. Variation in pathophysiology also arises from differences in altitude, length of exposure, and the population studied.

The following discussion focuses on the variability of response to hypoxia by examining cardiopulmonary physiology in neonates, older infants, and children at high altitude. Data from moderate to extreme high altitude are compared, and the differences in the pathophysiology of acute versus chronic high-altitude exposure are emphasized. Consideration of the variability of response to a given environment among different population groups provides insight into the process of adaptation to high altitude and the possible genetic mediation of cardiovascular/pulmonary responses.

Understanding the variety of problems arising from high-altitude hypoxia is important as children become increasingly mobile. Infants and children travel to high altitude with their families for recreation and employment reasons. The growth of urban and peri-urban population centers at high altitude in the United States, South America, and Asia means that more infants and children are residing at high altitude. Many of these children and their families are newcomers to high altitude. Other children, whose ancestors have lived for thousands of years in harsh, isolated high-altitude areas of the world, continue to suffer excess mortality and morbidity from respiratory and gastrointestinal infections due to the added stress of chronic hypoxia.[1]

In understanding all of these clinical settings, the importance of the effect of hypoxia on the developing pulmonary vascular system must be emphasized. At our institute we propose that pulmonary hypertension should be considered as a fourth major category of altitude-related illness in infants and children, in addition to the classic triad of acute mountain sickness (AMS), high-altitude cerebral edema (HACE), and high-altitude pulmonary edema (HAPE) that are recognized in adult medicine. Whether presenting as acute persistent pulmonary hypertension of the newborn, delayed normalization of pulmonary artery pressure in infancy, symptomatic high-altitude pulmonary hypertension, or subacute infantile mountain sickness (pulmonary hypertension with right ventricular failure), pathophysiologic changes in the pulmonary vascular bed are frequent in infants and children at high altitude and can be life threatening. Comparison of newcomer and adapted populations provides a unique opportunity to explore underlying mechanisms of disease, especially with respect to this aspect of cardiopulmonary physiology at altitude.

An orientation to the physical origin of high-altitude hypoxia and the general range of responses provides a framework for the specific physiologic responses of infants and children. The relationship between altitude and barometric pressure is displayed in Figure 26–1. Barometric pressure decreases more rapidly near the surface of the earth, as the upper atmosphere compresses the gas below it. Because temperature also affects the movement of gas molecules, the temperature decrease at extreme high altitudes contributes to the fall in barometric pressure. Latitude and season also influence the barometric pressure of high-altitude regions.[2]

The responses to hypoxia change with the degree and duration of exposure. Acute exposure (seconds to minutes) to an altitude sufficiently extreme to preclude acclimatization results in breathlessness, dizziness, paresthesias, and loss of consciousness. With more gradual exposure to moderately high altitude, acclimatization responses occur over a period of hours to months; these include increases in heart rate, ventilation, ventilatory response to CO_2, hemoglobin/hematocrit, and capillary density (Figure 26–2). The term "adaptation" often is used in reference to changes over decades or lifelong residence at high altitude. More precisely, the term adaptation refers to heritable (genetic) attributes—biochemical, physiologic, or anatomic—that are instrumental in living and reproducing successfully in a given environment.

The following material considers both acute high-

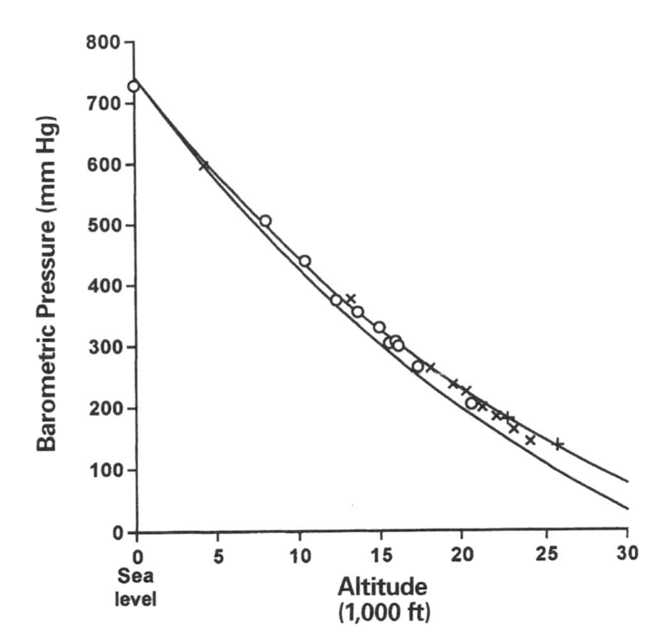

FIGURE 26–1. The relationship between barometric pressure and altitude as calculated from the formula of Zuntz (1906) using a mean air temperature of 15°C (*upper curve*) and the standard atmosphere equations (International Civil Aviation Organization, 1964) shown in the *lower curve*. The plotted points represent observations made on Mt. Everest and in the Andes (1,000 ft = 304.8 m). (Reproduced with permission from Ward MP et al.[2])

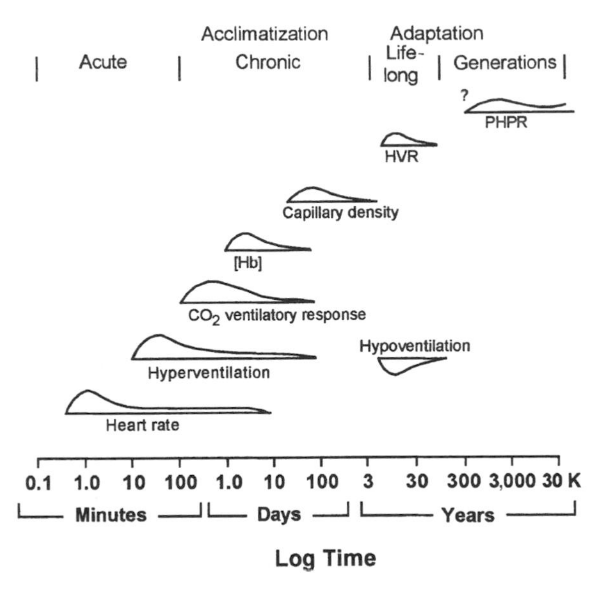

FIGURE 26–2. Chronology of the responses to hypoxia. (Reproduced with permission from Ward MP et al.[2])

altitude exposure, as experienced by infants and children who visit high altitude, and chronic high-altitude exposure, as experienced during fetal life, infancy, and childhood among populations resident at high altitude. In neonates and young infants, the spectrum of acute responses ranges from possible interruption of normal postnatal cardiopulmonary transition to clinically symptomatic high-altitude pulmonary hypertension. Certain underlying medical problems may be exacerbated by acute high-altitude exposure, and the question has been raised as to whether acute hypoxic exposure increases the risk of sudden infant death syndrome (SIDS). The classical altitude-related illnesses of AMS and HAPE occur with at least equal, and probably greater, frequency in children than in adults at high altitude. Consideration of chronic altitude exposure begins with fetal hypoxia and its relationships to subsequent pulmonary vascular development, lung liquid clearance, and alveolar structure. The link between perinatal pathophysiology and neonatal respiratory disorders commonly encountered at high altitude (delayed perinatal pulmonary vascular transition and retained fetal lung fluid) are emphasized. The clinical entity of subacute infantile mountain sickness is defined and related to the continuum of pathophysiology in the pulmonary vascular bed at altitude. Finally, SIDS and HAPE are reconsidered from the perspective of infants and children resident at high-altitude, and long-term differences in thoracic and pulmonary growth are identified.

Acute High-Altitude Hypoxia: Sojourners to High Altitude

Acute exposure to high-altitude hypoxia, such as that experienced by infants and children visiting the mountains, results in short- and medium-term acclimatization responses affecting ventilation, heart rate, oxyhemoglobin affinity, and hemoglobin concentration. Children exhibit increased susceptibility to disorders such as pulmonary hypertension and HAPE because of vulnerabilities during cardiopulmonary development. Certain underlying medical problems also predispose to illness at high altitude. It is clear that children experience AMS, the most common disorder resulting from acute exposure to high altitude, with a frequency equal to or greater than that in adults. The theoretic link also has been made between acute hypoxic exposure and SIDS.

Neonatal Period and Infancy

The fall in pulmonary artery pressures from very high intrauterine values to low near-adult values probably occurs completely in 1 to 3 days at sea level.[3] Closure of the fetal shunts (patent ductus arteriosus, patent foramen ovale) usually follows in the first week, but anatomic closure may not be complete for several more weeks (Figure 26–3). At moderately high altitude (2,000 to 3,000 m), changes in the circulation after birth may occur more slowly, and the stress of hypoxia upon exposure to higher altitudes may interrupt closure and elimination of fetal circulatory pathways. The principal concern in bringing a young baby to high altitude is that the postnatal cardiopulmonary transition process be completed successfully

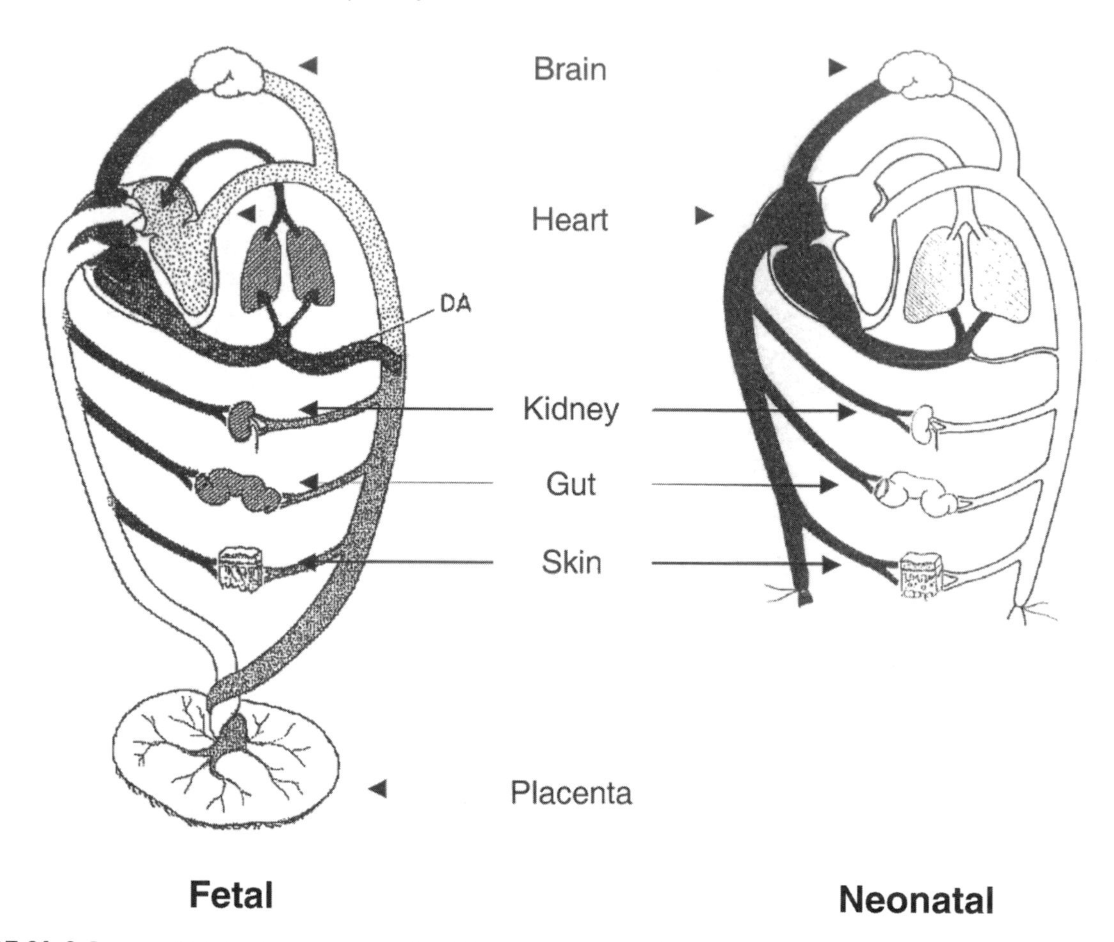

FIGURE 26–3. Patterns of fetal and neonatal circulation. DA = ductus arteriosus. (Reproduced with permission from Avery GB, ed. Neonatology: pathophysiology and management of the newborn. 1st ed. Philadelphia: JB Lippincott, 1975:112,113.)

at low altitude before exposure to high-altitude hypoxia. There is evidence that the hypoxia of 3,100 to 3,600 m and above can delay these physiologic processes or even reverse them if they are incomplete.[4–6]

Medical problems predisposing to altitude-related illness

Certain underlying medical conditions in infants increase the likelihood of problems at high altitude (Table 26–1). Infants with congenital heart disease (intracardiac shunts, abnormalities of the pulmonary artery, pulmonary hypertension) are at risk for right-to-left shunting, pulmonary edema, and/or profound hypoxemia at high altitude.[7] Valvular disease and consequences of cardiac arrhythmias also may be potentiated at high altitude. Primary pulmonary disorders that result in a requirement for supplemental oxygen at sea level predispose infants to difficulty at high altitude. Even brief disruptions in supplemental oxygen delivery, such as occur with crying or dislodgment of nasal cannula oxygen during sleep, can result in significant desaturation and more refractory hypoxemia if such conditions occur repetitively. Infants who have experienced respiratory distress as newborns, especially meconium aspiration, persistent pulmonary hypertension, or bronchopulmonary dysplasia, may once again develop respiratory distress and symptomatic pulmonary hypertension at high altitude. Infants experiencing lower respiratory infections such as pneumonia or bronchiolitis frequently experience significant hypoxemia at high altitude.[8] In young infants, such hypoxemia and other possible consequences of infection (pulmonary edema, arteriolar smooth muscle hypertrophy,[9] bronchoconstriction, airway blockage with secretions) may rapidly become synergistic and life threatening.

Pulmonary hypertension

The syndromes of acute altitude illness are commonly recognized as AMS, HACE, and HAPE. Pulmonary hypertension deserves consideration as a fourth major category of altitude-related illness in infants and children. This category should include disruption in the postnatal normalization of pulmonary artery pressures as well as recurrent or new-onset symptomatic pulmonary hypertension in response to high-altitude exposure. As noted above, pulmonary hypertension becomes the common pathway for expression of interrupted postnatal transition as well as a variety of underlying medical conditions. Considerable evidence in experimental animals supports the concept that hypoxic exposure during the neonatal period and

TABLE 26–1. Conditions Predisposing to Cardiopulmonary Problems at High Altitude

Cardiac
- Lesions that result in abnormal pulmonary blood flow
  - Patent ductus arteriosus
  - Patent foramen ovale
  - Ventricular septal defect
  - Atrial septal defect
  - Congenital absence of a pulmonary artery
- Congestive heart failure
  - Arrhythmias

Pulmonary
- Chronic lung disease
  - Oxygen requirement at sea level
  - Bronchopulmonary dysplasia
  - Cystic fibrosis
- Pulmonary hypertension

Infectious
- Upper respiratory tract infection
- Bronchiolitis
- Pneumonitis/pneumonia

Hematologic
- Sickle cell anemia

Adapted from Carpenter RC, Niermeyer S, Durmowicz AG. Altitude-related illness in children. Curr Probl Pediatr 1998;28:177–204.

infancy can interfere with the normal vascular changes that are an essential prerequisite for a normal postnatal fall in pulmonary vascular resistance.[10] Hypobaric hypoxia in newborn calves increases smooth muscle cell replication,[11] and similar findings were noted in the small muscular pulmonary arteries of hypoxic newborn piglets.[12] The consequences of vascular remodeling secondary to postnatal hypoxia may be subclinical under sea level conditions, but they may become clinically significant upon high-altitude exposure. Sartori et al identified young adults who had been treated for pulmonary hypertension in the neonatal period.[13] Upon exposure to high-altitude hypoxia at 4,559 m, these individuals showed a significantly greater mean increase in pulmonary artery pressure from 26.2 mm Hg (standard deviation [SD] 2.1) to 62.3 mm Hg (SD 7.3) as compared with control subjects whose pressure increased from 25.8 mm Hg (SD 2.3) to 49.7 mm Hg (SD 11.3).

Sudden infant death syndrome

Sudden infant death syndrome has been considered a risk mainly for populations resident at high altitude (see page 371); however, the observation that two deaths attributed to SIDS occurred within 2 days after intercontinental air travel raised the question of whether brief hypoxia increases the susceptibility to SIDS. Parkins et al[14] conducted a prospective trial to assess the response of healthy infants to airway hypoxia (15% oxygen for approximately 6 hours). They enrolled 34 infants (mean age 3.1 months), 13 of whom were siblings of SIDS victims. Baseline oxygen saturation fell from a median of 97.6% in room air to 92.8% in 15% oxygen, and periodic breathing increased 3.5-fold. Hypoxic exposure was ended early for 4 infants whose saturations fell below 80% for longer than 1 minute and for 2 others who were withdrawn at the request of a parent. None of the infants had prolonged pauses in their breathing during the trial or during the posthypoxic monitoring period (mean 4.5 hours). In fact, periodic breathing was significantly reduced during the posthypoxia period as compared with baseline. Although exposure to airway hypoxia produced predictable changes in saturation and breathing pattern, no conclusive link to sudden infant death was demonstrated.

Childhood

Acute mountain sickness

In adults, AMS is defined by the sine qua non of headache in the setting of altitude gain, plus one or more of the following signs: sleep disturbance, loss of appetite/nausea/vomiting, fatigue or weakness, and dizziness or lightheadedness (Table 26–2).[15] While AMS itself is not life threatening, it is uncomfortable, and further ascent may lead to serious complications of HACE. Diagnosis of AMS in preverbal and young school-aged children is difficult because of their inability to describe headache symptoms. We have therefore developed a set of criteria for evaluating AMS in children (Table 26–3) that relies on quantitation of the severity and prevalence of fussiness as a proxy for headache.[16] Likert scales for intensity and duration of fussiness were adapted from those developed for studies of infant colic. Assessment of appetite, amount of food consumed, and vomiting serves as an equivalent for gastrointestinal symptoms in the adult scale; playfulness stands as the equivalent for fatigue and/or dizziness; and ability to nap or sleep through the night indicates sleep disturbance. Twenty-three children between 3 and 36 months of age traveled from Denver to Fort Collins one weekend (no altitude change) and from Denver to 3,490 m in Keystone on the next weekend. After 4 hours at high altitude, 22% of the children exhibited signs of AMS as described previously (Figure 26–4). These signs normalized within 2 hours of return to Denver's altitude.

Awareness of the signs of AMS in young children is important for facilitating correct diagnosis and prompt treatment. Although HACE has not been well documented in children, it exists as a potential life-threatening possibility in the circumstance of further ascent with symptoms of AMS. The tool for assessing AMS in children is especially valuable for parents, who can more readily detect changes from baseline behavior in their own children than can a health professional. Moreover, parents most often in the position to decide about further ascent. A similar incidence (20%) of AMS occurred among adults and children ascending quickly to 3,490 m,[16] but

TABLE 26–2. Signs and Symptoms of Acute Mountain Sickness*

Sign or Symptom	Score	Description of Severity
Headache	0	None
	1	Mild
	2	Moderate
	3	Incapacitating
Gastrointestinal	0	Good appetite
	1	Poor appetite or nausea
	2	Nausea and vomiting
	3	Incapacitating
Fatigue/weakness	0	None
	1	Mild
	2	Moderate
	3	Incapacitating
Dizziness/lightheadedness	0	None
	1	Mild
	2	Moderate
	3	Incapacitating
Sleep	0	Slept well
	1	Slept not as well as usual
	2	Poor sleep
	3	No sleep
Overall effect on activities	0	None
	1	Mild reduction
	2	Moderate reduction
	3	Severe reduction
Change in mental status	0	None
	1	Lethargy
	2	Disoriented/confused
	3	Stupor
	4	Coma
Ataxia (heel-to-toe walking)	0	None
	1	Difficulty balancing
	2	Steps off line
	3	Falls down
	4	Unable to stand
Peripheral edema	0	None
	1	One location
	2	More than one location

*According to the Lake Louise scoring system, the first six categories are self-reported; the last three are assessed by medical personnel. A diagnosis of acute mountain sickness requires the presence of headache in the context of recent altitude gain, plus one of the following: fatigue, dizziness, gastrointestinal tract disturbance, or sleep disturbance.

Adapted from Hackett PH, Oelz O. The Lake Louise consensus on the definition and quantification of altitude illness. In: Sutton JR, Coates G, Houston CS, eds. Hypoxia and mountain medicine. Burlington (VT): Queen City Printers, 1992 p. 327–30.

other studies of AMS have suggested that the incidence of AMS actually may be higher in children and adolescents than in adults.[17,18]

Descent is the most effective remedy for AMS; however, oxygen administration and infant ibuprofen or acetaminophen may help relieve symptoms. Slow ascent, limited altitude gain, and avoidance of overnight stays at high altitude can help prevent severe AMS. The prophylactic use of acetazolamide remains controversial. Although diuretic dosages are established for infants to older children, it is likely that lower dosages remain effective as prophylaxis and minimize undesirable effects, such as paresthesias and dehydration. Definitive dosage recommendations await rigorous study of acetazolamide for prophylaxis of AMS in children.

TABLE 26–3. Modified Scoring Scale for Acute Mountain Sickness*

Category	Description and Score
Fussiness Score	
Amount of Unexplained Fussiness	
0	No fussiness
1	
2	
3	Intermittent fussiness
4	
5	
6	Constant fussiness when awake
Intensity of Fussiness	
0	No fussiness
1	
2	
3	Moderate fussiness
4	
5	
6	Hard crying and extreme fussiness
Pediatric Symptom Score	
How Well the Child has Eaten Today	
0	Normal
1	Slightly less than normal
2	Much less than normal
3	Vomiting or not eating
Playfulness of the Child Today	
0	Normal
1	Playing slightly less
2	Playing much less than normal
3	Not playing
Ability of the Child to Sleep Today	
0	Normal
1	Slightly less or more than normal
2	Much less or more than normal
3	Not able to sleep

*The Children's Lake Louise Scale. The diagnosis of acute mountain sickness requires a fussiness score ≥ 4, a pediatric symptom score ≥ 3, and a total Children's Lake Louise score ≥ 7.

Adapted from Yaron M, Waldman N, Niermeyer S, et al. The diagnosis of acute mountain sickness in preverbal children. Arch Pediatr Adolesc Med 1998;152:683–7.

High-altitude pulmonary edema

High-altitude pulmonary edema, the third element of the classic triad of acute complications resulting from high-altitude exposure (AMS, HACE, HAPE), also may occur more frequently in children than in adults (Figure 26–5). This observation likely relates to certain features of pathogenesis, such as exacerbation by antecedent viral infections, and also may reflect the inclusion of children who reside at high altitude and experience "re-entry" HAPE upon reascent to their home altitude after a stay at lower elevation (see page 371).

Elevated pulmonary artery pressure occurs almost without exception in cases of HAPE (Figure 26–6). However, the degree of pulmonary hypertension is quite

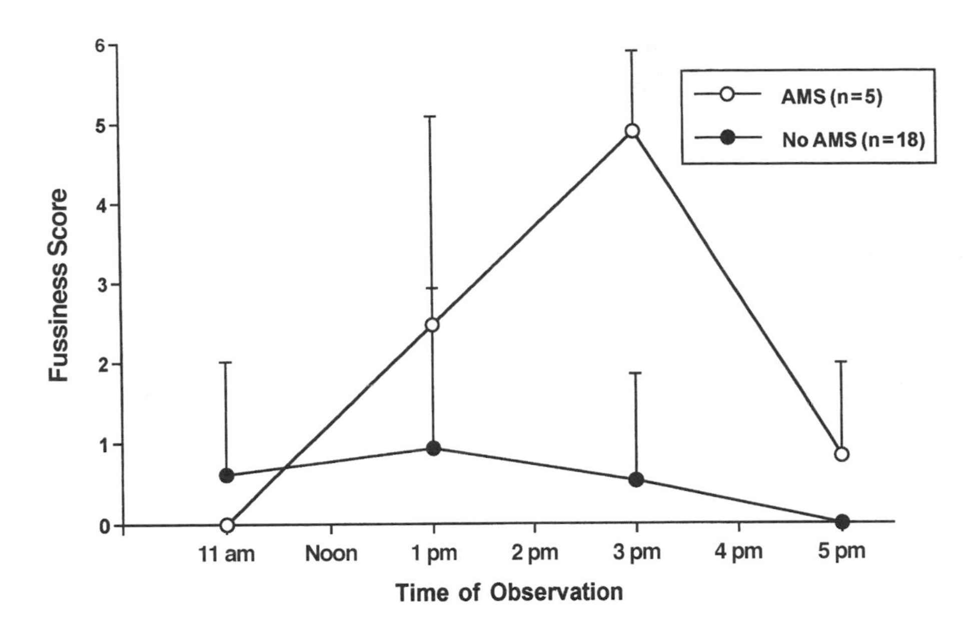

FIGURE 26–4. Fussiness scores on ascent to 3,488 m for subjects with and without acute mountain sickness (AMS). The 5:00 pm observations were made 2 hours after descent. (Adapted from Yaron M et al.[16])

variable from case to case.[19] Pulmonary capillary wedge pressures are normal in HAPE patients, indicating that left ventricular failure does not contribute to the pathogenesis. Several studies have examined the pulmonary vascular response to acute hypoxia in HAPE-susceptible individuals;[20–22] HAPE-susceptible persons showed an increase in pulmonary artery pressure with normal pulmonary capillary wedge pressure on re-exposure to hypoxia, even without signs of pulmonary edema. Seven children with re-entry HAPE showed that, upon hypoxic challenge, mean pulmonary artery systolic pressure increased to 56 mm Hg versus 18 mm Hg for control patients (Figure 26–7).[20] The increase varied from patient to patient, and the severity of hypoxia-induced pulmonary hypertension correlated poorly with the severity of HAPE.[20,21] Although pulmonary arterial hypertension is central to the pathogenesis of HAPE, it does not explain fully the development of this altitude-related illness.

Uneven vasoconstriction, with areas of underperfusion and overperfusion, may help explain the observed patchy distribution of pulmonary edema in HAPE patients and the microscopic disruption of the capillary wall leading to edema formation and alveolar hemorrhage.[23] Release and activation of inflammatory mediators with such "stress fractures" may amplify the initial mechanical injury. Lung perfusion scans in HAPE-susceptible persons taken to altitude support such a hypothesis of overperfusion.[24]

Alterations in vascular permeability also may play a role in the pathogenesis of HAPE. Studies of bronchoalveolar lavage fluid obtained at high altitude showed increased protein concentration in the lavage fluid from climbers with HAPE as opposed to the concentrations in those with AMS or without symptoms.[25,26] Increased protein in alveolar fluid, and the frequent findings of proteinuria and peripheral edema in persons exposed to altitude, raise the question of a link between hypoxia and a generalized increase in capillary permeability.[27,28] Studies in animal models and cell culture suggest that increased capillary permeability may result from exposure to hypoxia. Rats exposed to hypoxia demonstrate increased transvascular protein leak with increased lung water and histologic evidence of perivascular edema.[29] Endothelial cell monolayers exposed to hypoxia show a time-dependent increase in permeability.[30]

Considerable clinical evidence suggests that pre-existing inflammation increases the susceptibility to HAPE. Case reports from Peru and Colorado have pointed to an association between HAPE and recent minor respiratory infections.[20,31,32] A retrospective study in a Colorado mountain resort community at 2,800 m found that 79% of children diagnosed with HAPE had shown symptoms of an upper respiratory infection (cold, otitis, pharyngitis) in the 2 weeks preceding their arrival at altitude.[33] Only 17% of adults who developed HAPE had similar prior histories. Evidence from experimental animals also suggests a link between pre-existing inflammatory processes and development of HAPE. Young rats recovering from a mild parainfluenza viral infection were exposed to hypoxia. Despite showing few clinical symptoms of a viral illness at the time of hypoxic exposure, the animals experienced significant increases in lung water and lung lavage protein when compared with controls.[34] In other animal experiments, adult rats given small doses

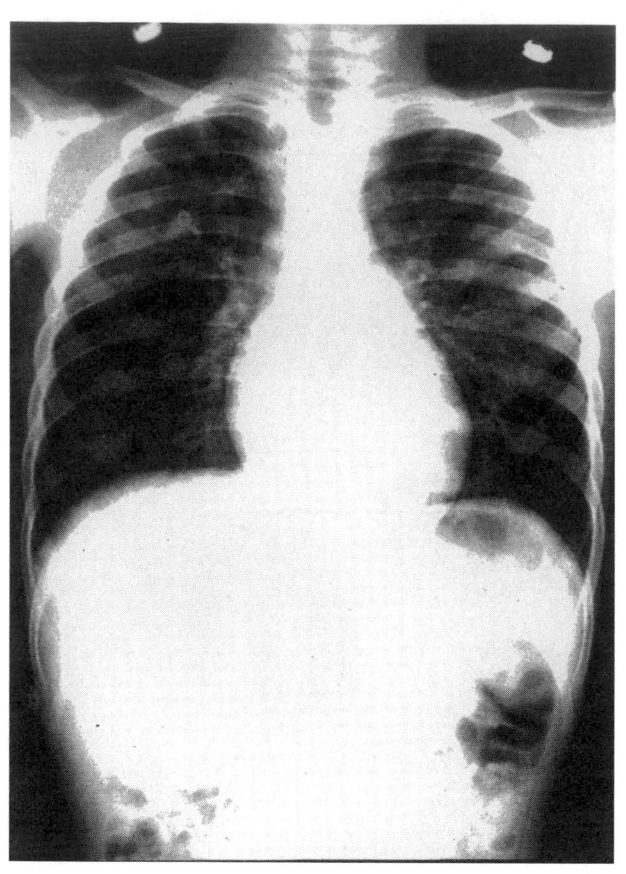

FIGURE 26–5. Chest radiograph showing high-altitude pulmonary edema.

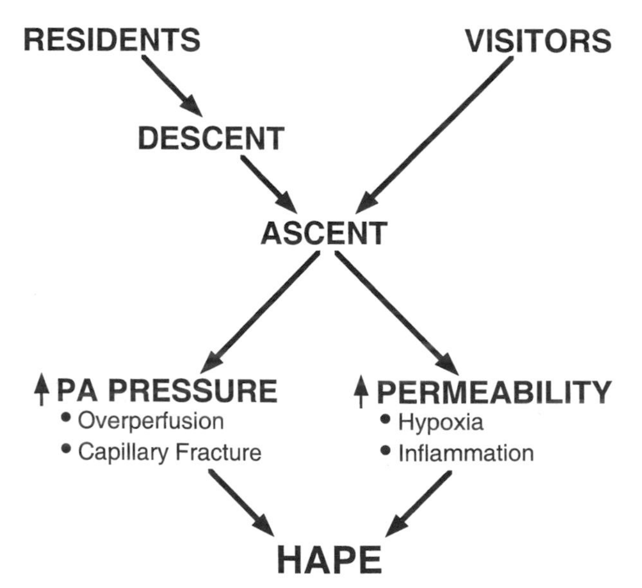

FIGURE 26–6. Proposed roles for increased pulmonary artery (PA) pressure and pulmonary capillary permeability in the pathogenesis of high-altitude pulmonary edema (HAPE). (Adapted from Carpenter RC, Niermeyer S, Durmowicz AG. Altitude-related illness in children. Curr Probl Pediatr 1998;28:177–204.)

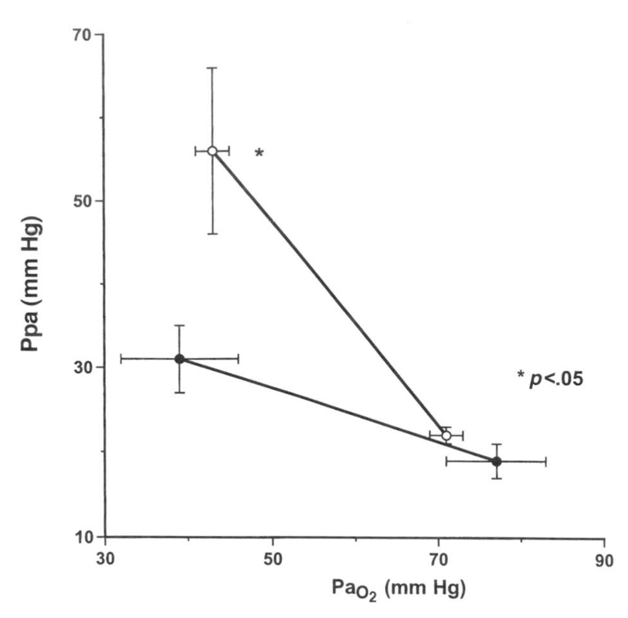

FIGURE 26–7. Exaggerated pulmonary arterial pressure (Ppa) response to hypoxia in high-altitude pulmonary edema–susceptible children at high altitude in Colorado. Pa_{O_2} = partial pressure of arterial oxygen. (Data from Fasules JW et al.[20]).

of endotoxin and exposed to hypoxia for 24 hours developed significant increases in lung edema. Control normoxic rats given endotoxin showed no detectable increase in lung water.[35] Thus, prior inflammatory insult to the lung may increase the likelihood of developing HAPE. The predilection for children to exhibit this association may relate to the greater frequency of respiratory infections in children or to specific pathophysiologic mechanisms yet to be defined.

Finally, the alveolar epithelium itself also may play a role in the development of HAPE. As discussed later (see section Lung Liquid Clearance), epithelial sodium channels actively regulate the movement of sodium and water out of air spaces. Laboratory evidence suggests that the function of epithelial sodium channels is impaired by exposure to hypoxia.[36,37] Recent studies suggest that subclinical dysfunction of epithelial sodium channels under normoxic conditions may predispose to development of pulmonary edema under hypoxic conditions.[38]

Chronic High-Altitude Hypoxia: Populations Resident at High Altitude

Fetal and Neonatal Periods

Evidence of fetal hypoxia

Reduction in birth weight with increasing altitude (Figure 26–8) is a well-documented effect of high-altitude residence.[39–42] Birth weight declines an average of 121 g/1,000 m altitude gain when altitude alone is considered, or 102 g/1,000 m when other factors such as gestational age, weight

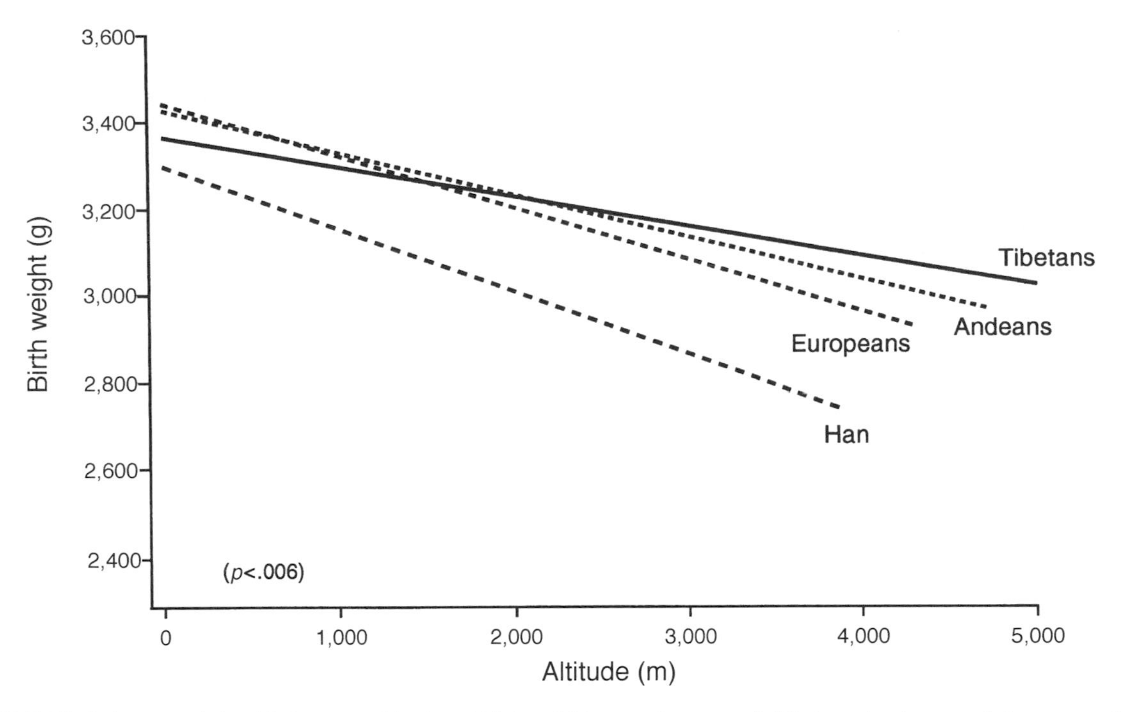

FIGURE 26–8. Inverse relationship between altitude and birth weight across the range of altitude and various population groups. Tibetan birth weight remains fairly constant at low altitude and 3,658 m. (Data from Niermeyer S et al.[42])

gain during pregnancy, and cigarette smoking are taken into account.[43] Above 2,000 m birth weight may decline as much as 65 g/500 m altitude gain.[44] Even at altitudes between 1,500 and 2,000 m, fetal growth appears sensitive to uterine oxygen delivery.[45] Reduction in birth weight can be attributed to the hypoxia and reduced fetal-placental oxygen delivery when other risk factors such as maternal age, parity, body size, nutrition, smoking, and prenatal care are controlled.[43]

The percentage of low-birth-weight babies also increases at high altitude compared to sea-level populations. Intrauterine growth restriction rather than prematurity accounts for the majority of the reduction in birth weight observed at high altitude.[46] Indeed, the first observation that small size at birth and prematurity were separable effects was made at high altitude,[47] leading to the classification of small-, appropriate-, and large-for-gestational age babies.[48] Babies born at high altitude are both lighter and shorter for gestational age.[49]

The higher hemoglobin and hematocrit observed in infants with lower birth weight at high altitude gives further support for the role of exaggerated hypoxia during fetal life.[50–52] This effect has been reported to have clinical significance in Colorado, where low birth weight was associated with a higher infant and neonatal mortality until 1980[53] and higher hemoglobin/hematocrit is associated with more intense neonatal jaundice.[54]

The impact of fetal growth restriction varies with relation to high-altitude ancestry; the longest-resident populations experience the smallest decline, and the shortest resident groups the greatest reduction in birth weight.[42] Thus, the reduction in birth weight is greatest among North Americans, intermediate in South Americans, and least among Tibetans. Specific comparisons between Tibetans and Han (Chinese) living at the same altitude, and among native Aymara, mestiza, and European women have further confirmed this generalization[54,55] (see Figure 26–8). Population differences in birth weight at high altitude reflect not only responses of increase in maternal hemoglobin and hyperventilation,[39,40] but also the proportion of common iliac blood flow directed to the uterine artery during pregnancy (Figure 26–9).[45,56] Again, comparison of long-resident (Tibetan) and newcomer (Han) populations resident at the same altitude support a role of genetic adaptation in modulating this effect, as well as that of growth restriction.[56]

Alterations of postnatal cardiopulmonary transition

Upon the backdrop of limited fetal oxygen supply, the hypoxia of high altitude continues to play a critical role in postnatal cardiopulmonary transition. At birth, dramatic changes occur in oxygen transport. The lungs change from being fluid-filled to air-filled, pulmonary blood flow increases dramatically, and fetal right-to-left shunts diminish and close. Oxygen serves as a powerful pulmonary vasodilator in this setting. At high altitude significant hypoxemia, persistent pulmonary hypertension, and persistence of fetal right-to-left shunts may occur acutely, especially with underlying pulmonary problems such as retained fetal lung fluid, surfactant

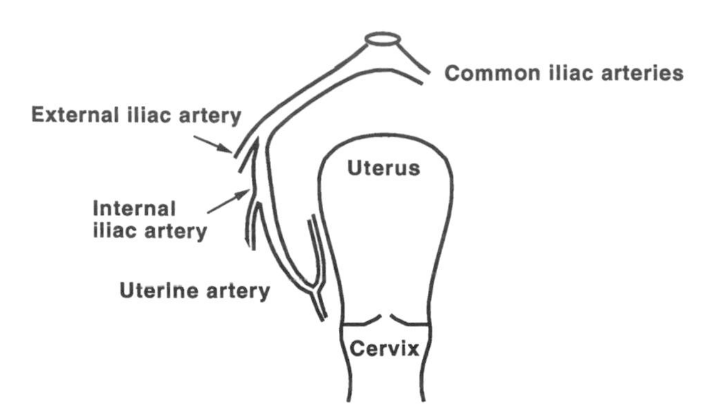

FIGURE 26–9. Schematic of lower extremity blood flow during pregnancy. Fetal oxygen delivery may be preserved by preferential direction of lower extremity blood flow to the internal iliac and uterine arteries. (Reproduced with permission from Moore LG et al.[56])

deficiency, or pneumonia. However, in the majority of infants, the reduction in oxygen availability with increasing altitude is reflected in moderately reduced arterial oxygen saturation during the neonatal period and infancy and possible subacute manifestations of pulmonary hypertension. At sea level, oxygen saturations during the first week of life average 91 to 96%, somewhat lower than the 94 to 98% range observed during the remainder of the neonatal period and infancy.[57] At 1,610 m in Denver, arterial oxygen saturation in healthy term infants averaged 92 to 94% from 24 to 48 hours through 3 months.[58] At 3,100 m in Leadville, Colorado, arterial oxygen saturation showed a different pattern, falling from 88 to 90% at 6 to 24 hours to 81 to 88% during the first week after birth, then rising gradually to attain values near those present shortly after birth by 2 to 4 postnatal months (Figure 26–10). The fall in arterial oxygen saturation at 1 week coincided with the occurrence of clinical signs of hypoxemia, for example, cyanosis, irritability, poor feeding, and failure to gain weight. At all ages, values during wakefulness were higher than those during active or quiet sleep, with intermediate values during feeding.[4] At 3,658 m in Lhasa, Tibet, arterial oxygen saturation of native Tibetan infants differed from that of Han infants whose families had recently arrived at high altitude. In both groups, arterial oxygen saturation was highest in the first 2 days after birth (90 to 94% in Tibetans and 86 to 92% in the Han), but then it declined, much like the pattern seen in infants in Leadville (see Figure 26–10). However, arterial oxygen saturation stabilized in the Tibetans, so that values remained similar to those in Leadville infants through 4 months of life (86 to 90%), but Han infants showed a progressive decline in mean arterial saturation, especially during sleep, through early infancy. Mean saturations in quiet sleep at 4 months among the Han infants were 76% versus 86% in the Tibetans.[52] At even higher altitudes (3,750 m) in Peru, arterial oxygen saturation in 2- to 5-month-old native Andean (Quechua) infants averaged 88 ± 3%.[8] At 4,540 m in Peru, directly measured arterial oxygen saturation ranged from 57 to 75% in newborn infants at 30 minutes to 72 hours of age,[6] and remained in the range of 74 to 80% throughout infancy.[59] From these examples, it is evident that arterial oxygen saturation in infants varies not only with altitude but also with postnatal age, behavioral

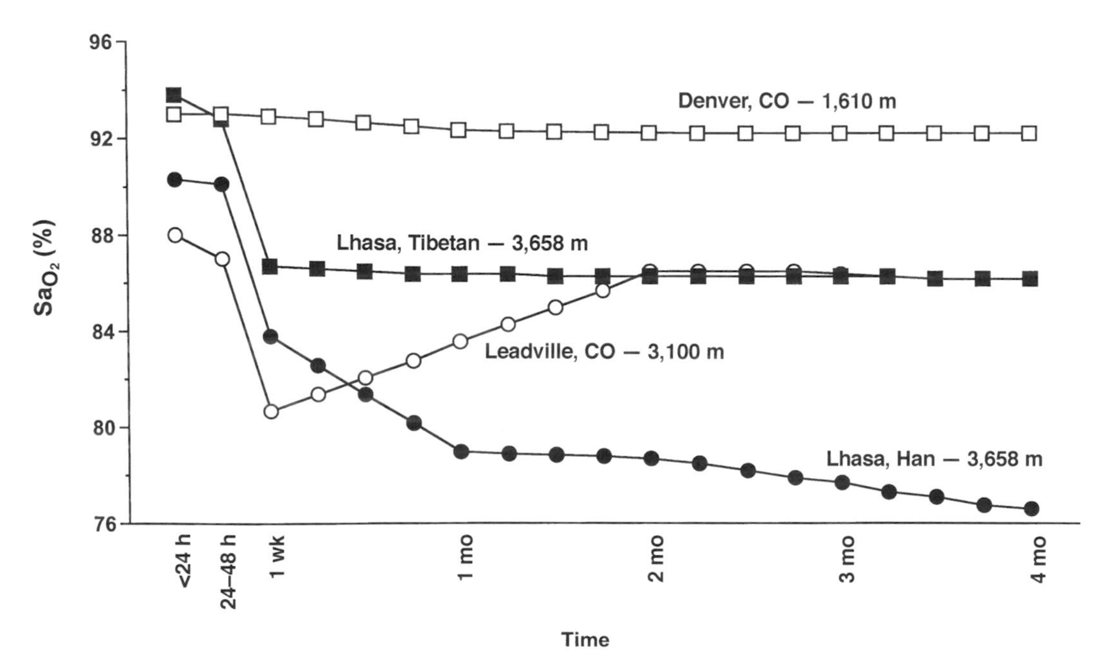

FIGURE 26–10. Comparison of arterial oxygen saturation (Sa_{O_2}) North American infants at 1,610 and 3,100 m, and native Tibetan and newcomer Han infants at 3,658 m. Saturations shown are representative of quiet sleep. (Data from Niermeyer et al[4] and Niermeyer et al.[52])

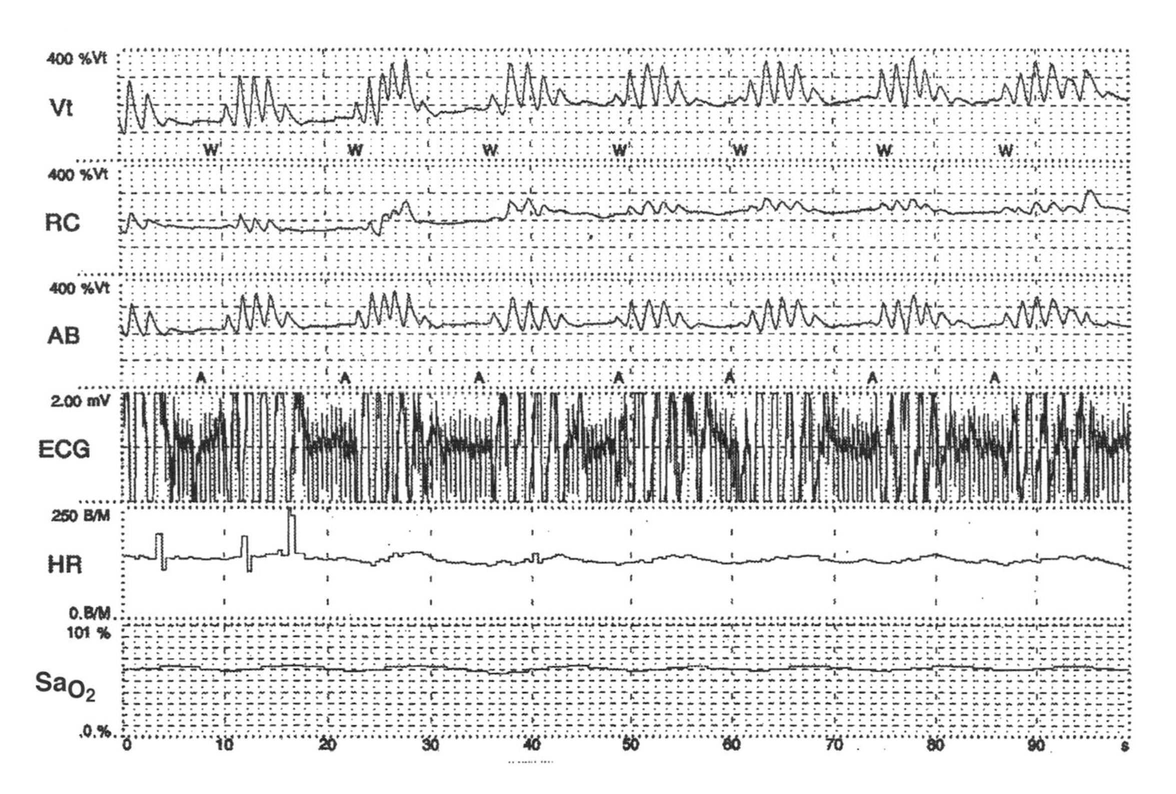

FIGURE 26–11. Periodic respiration and cyclic pattern of arterial oxygen saturation (Sa_{O_2}) in an infant at 3,100 m. Vt = tidal volume; RC = rib cage (thoracic excursion); AB = abdomen (abdominal excursion); ECG = electrocardiogram; HR = heart rate; B/M = breaths per minute. (Data from Niermeyer S et al.[5])

state/activity, and high-altitude ancestry. In general, populations with longstanding residence at high altitude have higher mean saturations than do non-native populations. Certain populations that do not historically reside at high altitude (such as the Han) may be uniquely predisposed to lower saturations and an increased incidence of clinical problems. At extreme high altitude, even native populations experience desaturation significant enough to interfere with normal development.

The interpopulational variation in arterial oxygen saturation clearly suggests a role for genetic adaptation. The dramatic differences in arterial oxygen saturation between Tibetan and Han infants residing at the same elevation, but differing in their high-altitude ancestry, likely result from differences in ventilation and/or pulmonary blood flow, which may be influenced by genetic factors. Increased ventilation not only serves to decrease the oxygen pressure gradient from the atmosphere to the alveoli and to raise arterial oxygen tensions, but the accompanying fall in arterial carbon dioxide tensions also may increase pH and shift the oxyhemoglobin dissociation curve to the left to raise saturation at a given oxygen pressure. Lower birth weight and higher hemoglobin and hematocrit in the Han infants suggest a greater degree of fetal hypoxia. This may influence development of the fetal pulmonary vascular bed as well as the pulmonary parenchyma (see below) and lead to differences in postnatal regulation of pulmonary blood flow and vascular resistance.

Breathing patterns during the neonatal period and infancy differ between high and low altitude. At sea level, periodic breathing occurs during sleep in the majority (78%) of full-term neonates.[60] The prevalence of periodic breathing declines as early as 1 month and certainly by 5 or 6 months in response to developmental changes in central and peripheral chemoreceptors.[61–64] Studies in Denver (1,610 m) suggested that periodic breathing was "much more frequent and less transitory…than has been previously described," but the prevalence (65%) was similar to that at sea level.[65,66] At higher altitude (3,100 m), the prevalence clearly increases, such that all neonates in Leadville at 3,100 m demonstrated a repetitive pattern of 4 to 6 breaths over 6 to 7 seconds followed by a pause of equal length.[65] More recent studies in Leadville confirmed this pattern and its association with cyclic declines in arterial oxygen saturation (Figure 26–11).[5]

Pulmonary artery pressure (Ppa) falls rapidly in the first days after birth at sea level. Normalization of Ppa is important for achieving first functional and then anatomic closure of the atrial and ductal shunts.[3] At 3,100 m in Leadville, healthy term infants had normal to moderately elevated echocardiographic indices of Ppa in the first week of life (Figure 26–12); measurements normalized fully by 2 to 4 months postnatal age.[4] However, all

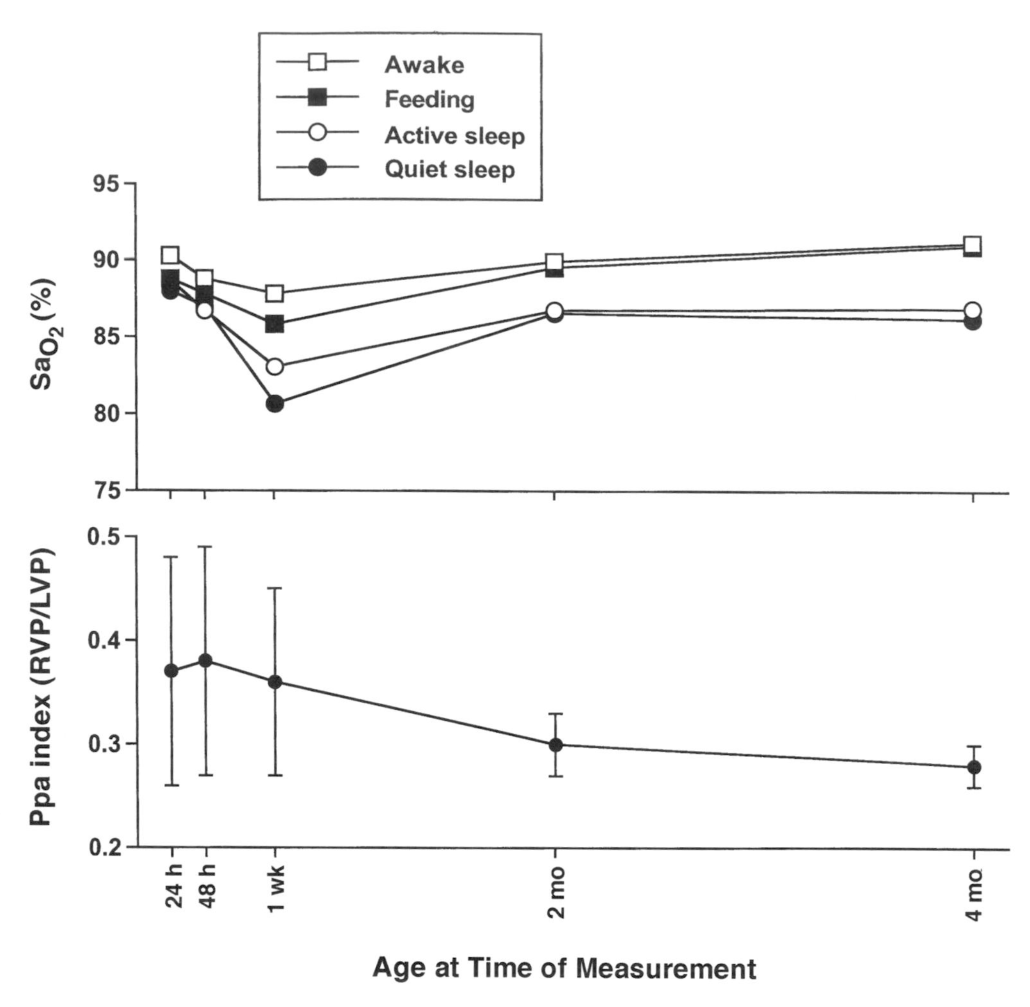

FIGURE 26–12. Temporal relationship of changes in arterial oxygen saturation (Sa_{O_2}) and estimates of pulmonary artery pressure (Ppa) among infants at 3,100 m in Leadville, Colorado. RVP = right ventricular pressure; LVP = left ventricular pressure. (Data from Niermeyer S et al.[4])

infants studied received routine supplemental oxygen during the first 24 to 48 hours. At higher altitudes where supplemental oxygen is not used, the postnatal fall in Ppa is prolonged or fails to occur. Newly born infants at 4,540 m in Peru with an alveolar P_{O_2} of approximately 50 mm Hg showed persistence of near-systemic Ppa for 72 hours following birth (Figure 26–13). Arterial oxygen saturation and Ppa showed an inverse relationship in this group of infants. Administration of 100% oxygen to three infants at this altitude at 72 hours resulted in normalization of Ppa to values near those at sea level.[6]

Both acute and subacute pulmonary hypertension occur at high altitude. The incidence of acute persistent pulmonary hypertension of the newborn has been estimated at 0.2% in sea-level populations.[67] Observations at 3,100 m in Leadville and at 3,600 to 3,800 m in La Paz, Bolivia suggest higher incidence rates. Among 35 consecutive term deliveries at 3,100 m, 17% (6 infants) demonstrated impaired cardiopulmonary transition during the first 3 months of life.[5] Impaired cardiopulmonary transition was defined as elevated pulmonary artery pressures or respiratory distress (cyanosis, dyspnea) necessitating supplemental O_2 and/or positive pressure ventilation. The observed rate represents roughly a 100-fold increase in complications of postnatal cardiopulmonary transition as compared with the described incidence of persistent pulmonary hypertension of the newborn at low altitude. Among the 6 infants, 1 was growth retarded and immediately developed progressive hypoxemia and pulmonary hypertension, requiring mechanical ventilation at 27 hours. Four others had periodic respirations with repetitive desaturations (< 60%, n=2 or < 70%, n=2) and were treated with supplemental O_2 during the first 10 days of life. The remaining infant had mean saturations of 82 to 87% and normal echocardiographic findings until 15 weeks when he developed systemic pulmonary artery pressures immediately preceding clinical signs of an upper respiratory infection. Thus, it appears that an impaired cardiopulmonary transition is more common at high altitude, and often is due

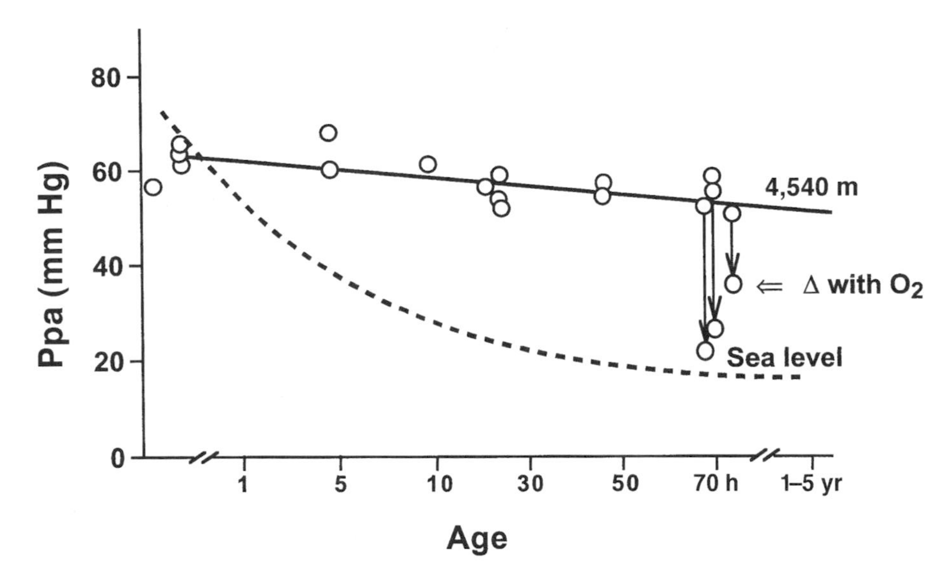

FIGURE 26–13. Persistence of near-systemic pulmonary artery pressures (Ppa) in newly born infants from birth to 70 hours of age at 4,540 m. Administration of supplemental oxygen at approximately 3 days of age resulted in a substantial fall in pulmonary artery pressures to near sea-level values. (Data from Gamboa R and Marticorena E.[6])

to a periodic respiratory pattern resulting in desaturation in the first week of life. However, acute persistent pulmonary hypertension of the newborn and more delayed subacute infantile pulmonary hypertension also contribute to neonatal and infant morbidity at high altitude.

Lung liquid clearance

Alterations in the normal clearance of fetal lung liquid surrounding the time of birth also may contribute to respiratory morbidity at high altitude. With the onset of labor, the fetal pulmonary fluid balance shifts from net production of lung liquid to net absorption of lung liquid, even before delivery.[68] After delivery, areas of gas exchange convert from being fluid- to air-filled. Absorption of fetal lung liquid continues, aided by physical expansion of the lungs and increased pulmonary blood and lymphatic flow.

Experimental animal data and clinical evidence from premature infants with respiratory distress syndrome suggest that epithelial sodium channels (ENaCs) play a central role in clearance of fetal lung liquid (Figure 26–14). Experimental data from the fetal lamb show that perinatal lung liquid absorption is mediated by amiloride-blockable sodium ion transport.[69–71] Mice homozygous for a mutation inactivating the α-ENaC subunit exhibit severe neonatal respiratory distress, which is fatal within hours of birth.[72] These animals show complete absence of amiloride-sensitive sodium transport in airway epithelia. Reintroducing the α-ENaC copy deoxyribonucleic acid (cDNA) under the control of a heterologous (cytomegalovirus) promoter results in alleviation of the respiratory distress syndrome, permitting approximately half of the transgenic animals to survive to adulthood.[73]

Data from premature human infants experiencing respiratory distress syndrome (RDS) suggest that decreased sodium ion transport across the immature respiratory epithelium contributes to the pathogenesis of RDS.[74] Transepithelial nasal potential difference was measured in preterm infants as a reflection of electrogenic transport of Na^+ and Cl^- across the epithelium of the both the upper

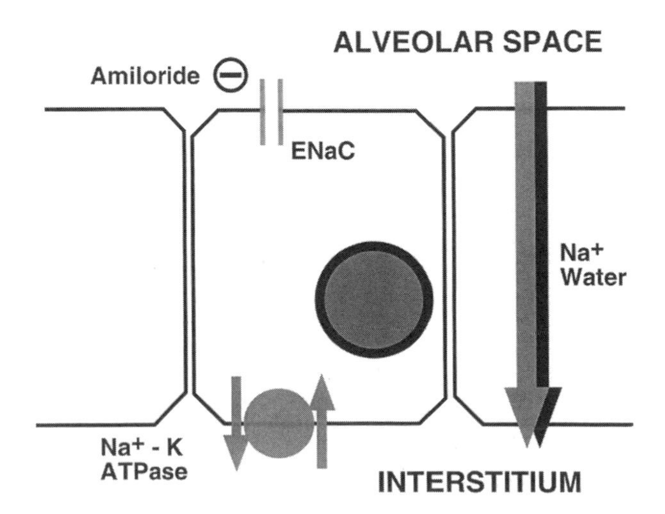

FIGURE 26–14. Schematic of the epithelial sodium channel (ENaC) and its role in fluid balance across the alveolar epithelium. ATPase = adenosinetriphosphatase. (Adapted from Scherrer U et al.[38])

and lower respiratory tracts. Thirty-one newborn infants ≤ 30 weeks' gestation were divided into those with and without RDS on the basis of clinical and radiographic criteria. Infants with RDS had lower maximal nasal epithelial potential difference than did those without RDS. Infants without RDS had potential differences similar to normal full-term infants. In an earlier study infants with transient tachypnea of the newborn and infants born by elective cesarean delivery exhibited a smaller fraction of amiloride-sensitive potential difference (30.9% and 31.8%, respectively) than did healthy infants (38.5%), consistent with submaximal activation of existing sodium channels.[75] The role of epithelial sodium ion transport has been well established as part of the pathogenesis of retained fetal lung fluid and RDS, both of which occur commonly in near-term infants at high altitude.

Several lines of evidence demonstrate that ENaCs may be inhibited by hypoxia. Hypoxia downregulates gene expression and activity of ENaC in rat alveolar epithelial cells.[37] In vitro experiments in resected human lung show decreased alveolar fluid clearance under hypoxic conditions.[76] In adults hypoxia may unmask subclinical dysfunction of ENaC and result in a predisposition to HAPE among affected individuals.[38] To date no controlled studies have been performed in newborns at high altitude. However, observations in Leadville, at 3,100 m and other Colorado mountain communities document the frequent occurrence of retained fetal lung fluid and RDS in near-term infants born at high altitude. Supplemental oxygen administration immediately after birth may attenuate the severity of illness, but it does not eliminate the problem. Postnatal supplemental oxygen administration can alleviate alveolar hypoxia and hypoxemia, but conditions of relative hypoxemia during fetal life may have altered the developmental profile of ENaC activity.

Alveolar development

Animal models of pulmonary development under hypoxia demonstrate alterations in the formation of the gas exchange unit. Such changes may contribute to altered pulmonary function among human infants born at high altitude. Pregnant rats were exposed to 10% oxygen for ≤ 9 hours on the last day of gestation. The dams and their pups were then again exposed to reduced oxygen for 1 to 2 hours immediately after birth.[77] This brief hypoxic stress resulted in significant changes in lung structure and development at 7 and 30 days. The changes included a slowed postnatal increase in lung volume, delayed septation of the gas exchange saccules, blunted increase in the gas exchange surface area, and accelerated thinning of the alveolar walls. Brief exposure prenatally and postnatally had the same effect as did prenatal exposure plus 7 days of postnatal hypoxia with 10% oxygen. The authors postulated that hypoxic exposure serves as a stimulus for the secretion of adrenal glucocorticoid hormones. Their findings are consistent with prior evidence that administration of a synthetic glucocorticosteroid (dexamethasone) impairs septation and the postnatal increase in lung volume, and also promotes alveolar wall thinning.[78,79] The findings of lower lung volume and delayed septation resemble those of Mortola et al,[80] who exposed rat pups postnatally to 5 to 7 days of 10% oxygen without prenatal exposure. However, the gas exchange surface area of these animals was not significantly reduced. Cunningham et al[81] reported greater alveolar volume and number, and greater gas exchange surface area in rats exposed postnatally to 12 to 13% oxygen. Thus, postnatal hypoxic exposure appears to result in variable effects as compared with combined prenatal and postnatal exposure.

A series of experiments explored the variability of alveolar development with differing timing and duration of postnatal exposure to moderate hypoxia. Female rats were exposed to 13% oxygen for ≥ 3 weeks before being bred and then throughout pregnancy as well as after birth of their pups.[82] Changes in gas exchange structures were examined at 2, 14, and 40 days (Figure 26–15). Between 2 and 14 days, hypoxic exposure resulted in impaired septation (gas exchange units remained larger, and fewer alveoli were formed). Rats kept in 13% oxygen had fewer alveolar attachments to bronchioles as compared with rats raised in normoxia. Gas-exchange volume in the hypoxia-exposed rats was equal to or greater than that in rats reared under sea-level conditions. Early moderate hypoxia appeared to irrevocably block alveolar septation. Diminished septation, in turn, decreased radial traction on conducting airways, leading to increased gas exchange volume. In another series of experiments, rats who had been reared in normoxia until 23 days were placed in 13% oxygen until 44 days.[83] These animals, exposed to hypoxia after the period of septation, increased the gas exchange surface area and average volume of alveoli, but the alveolar number was the same as that in rats reared in normoxia. Thus, the steps in alveolar formation and establishment of gas exchange surface area exhibited a complex response dependent on the timing and duration of exposure to moderate hypoxia.

These experimental findings may have direct relevance to differences in compliance of the respiratory system in human infants born at high altitude. Term healthy newborns in La Paz, (3,600 m, barometric pressure [Pb] 495 mm Hg) were compared with their counterparts in Santa Cruz, Bolivia (400 m, Pb 735 mm Hg).[84] Compliance of the respiratory system (Crs) was measured during tidal volume breathing by the multiple occlusion method. Compliance in the Santa Cruz infants was similar to that previously obtained in infants near sea level. However Crs was 33% greater and Crs per kilogram was 37% greater in the high-altitude group (Figure 26–16). Equal numbers of native Amerindians and mestizos of European ancestry

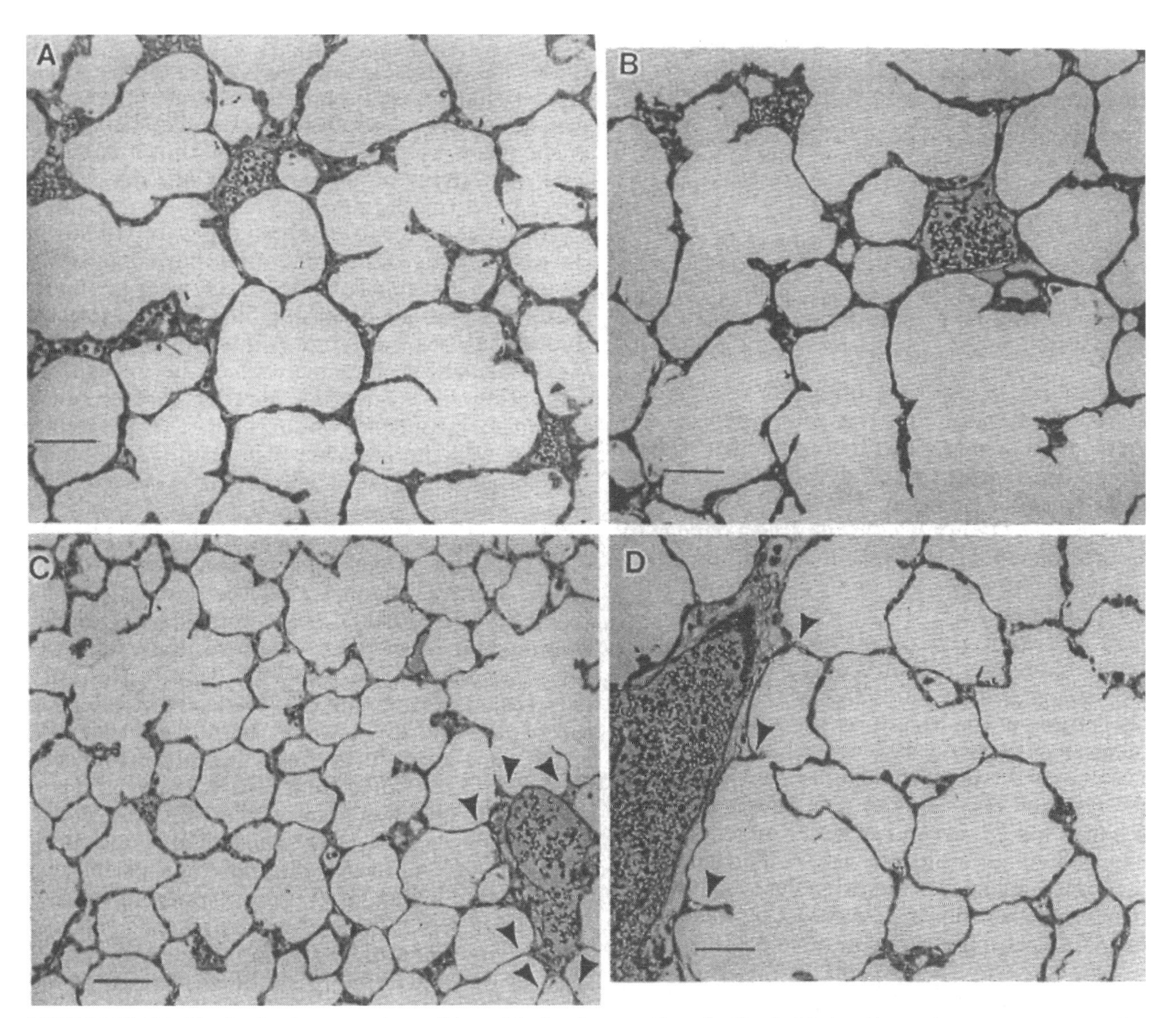

FIGURE 26–15. Alveolar development under conditions of fetal and neonatal hypoxia. Alveoli of 2-day-old pups that were never exposed to hypoxia (*A*) contrast with the impaired septation of the gas exchange saccules and accelerated thinning of the alveolar walls in pups of the same age exposed to pre- and postnatal hypoxia (*B*). *C* and *D*, The same exposure as in *A* and *B*, respectively, but animals were 40 days old. Arrowheads indicate alveolar attachments; scale marker = 50 microns. (1μm sections stained with teluidine blue. Corrections were made for shrinkage.) (Reproduced with permission from Massaro GD et al.[82])

made up the study groups at both sites. Such a comparison supports the hypothesis that the increase in compliance was a response to environmental conditions rather than the expression of a genetic trait. Of note the Crs per kilogram measurements of two infants born in La Paz after only a few days at high altitude were among the lowest values in the high-altitude group. Presumably, these fetuses experienced a relatively limited hypoxic exposure after considerable alveolar development had already taken place. The findings suggest that fetal hypoxia at high altitude plays a role in alterations in lung development. Futhermore, the findings in human infants are consistent with those in experimental animal literature, in that blunted alveolar septation could account for the greater compliance observed.

Later Infancy and Childhood

Persistent elevation of pulmonary artery pressure

The fall in Ppa and remodeling of the fetal vascular patterns to achieve adult norms may continue into infancy and childhood at high altitude. Persistently elevated Ppa and pulmonary vascular resistance were demonstrated by right heart catheterization in infants and children < 5 years at 4,330 m and 4,540 m in Peru.[59] High Ppa was associated with low arterial oxygen saturations in these children (Figure 26–17). Values of Ppa were higher in young children (1 to 5 years, Ppa systolic 58 ± 17 mm Hg and mean 45 ± 17 mm Hg) as compared with older children (6 to 14 years, Ppa systolic 41 ± 10 mm Hg and mean 28 ± 10 mm Hg). Evidence for delayed or absent postnatal regression of

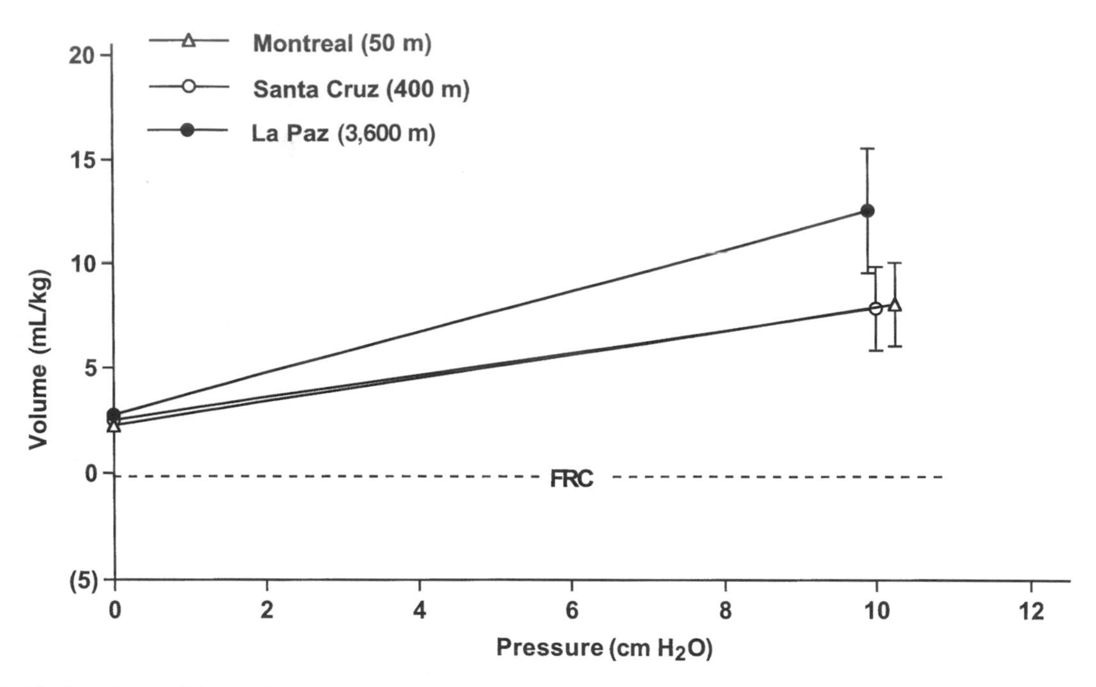

Figure 26–16. Compliance of the respiratory system as measured in term healthy newborns in Montreal, and Santa Cruz and La Paz, Bolivia. FRC = functional residual capacity. (Adapted from Mortola JP et al.[84])

the fetal pulmonary vascular pattern comes from pathologic observations of thickened pulmonary arteriolar muscle in South American children who died of nonpulmonary causes at high altitude.[85] An increased prevalence of patent ductus arteriosus can be ascribed to persistently elevated right-sided pressure, which maintains the fetal vascular pattern across the ductus.[86,87] Data from Han and Tibetan infants in the Qinghai Province of China (the northern portion of the Tibetan Plateau) corroborate an increased prevalence of atrial septal defect and patent ductus arteriosus, with the incidence increasing from near zero at sea level to more than 5% at 4,500 m.[88] The prolonged normalization of pulmonary artery structure and circulatory patterns presents a period of vulnerability to the development of symptomatic high-altitude pulmonary hypertension. A variety of stressors may serve as the trigger for clinical symptomatology. Recurrent hypoxemia, perhaps due to periodic desaturation during sleep or intercurrent viral infections, may ultimately lead to symptomatic high-altitude pulmonary hypertension or the full syndrome of subacute infantile mountain sickness. Symptomatic high-altitude pulmonary hypertension is characterized initially by lability in pulmonary artery pressures and oxygenation. Descent to lower altitude often results in resolution of symptoms in the early stage of the illness. However, once right ventricular hypertrophy and failure develop, the condition is poorly reversible.

Subacute infantile mountain sickness

The syndrome of subacute infantile mountain sickness (Table 26–4), as first described in Lhasa (3,658 m) in 15 infants or children who died between 3 and 16 months of age, is characterized by pulmonary hypertension and right heart failure.[89] All affected children were male; 14 were Han and 1 was Tibetan. All but 2 were born at low altitude and brought to Lhasa at an average of 2 months before the onset of disease symptoms. Clinical signs and symptoms included dyspnea, cough, cyanosis, sleeplessness and irritability, facial edema, hepatomegaly, and oliguria. Pathologic findings included medial hypertrophy of small pulmonary arteries, muscularization of

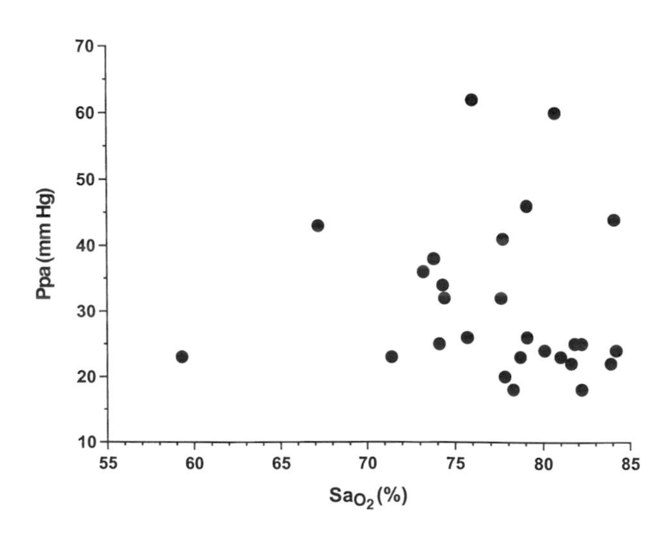

FIGURE 26–17. Inverse relationship of arterial oxygen saturation (Sa_{O_2}) and mean pulmonary artery pressure (Ppa) in children living at 4,330 m and 4,540 m in Peru. (Data from Sime F et al.[59])

TABLE 26–4. Clinical Signs and Symptoms and Pathologic Findings in Subacute Infantile Mountain Sickness

Clinical Signs and Symptoms
Dyspnea
Cough
Cyanosis
Sleeplessness/irritability
Hepatomegaly
Facial edema
Oliguria
Pathological Findings
Medial hypertrophy of small pulmonary arteries
Muscularization of pulmonary arterioles
Severe hypertrophy/dilation of the right ventricle

Criteria from Sui GJ, Liu YH, Cheng XS, et al. Subacute infantile mountain sickness. J Pathol 1988;155:161–70.

pulmonary arterioles, and severe right ventricular hypertrophy and dilation. A control group of native Tibetan infants and children who died from noncardiopulmonary causes showed normal thin-walled pulmonary arteries and arterioles after 4 months of age. A similar clinical syndrome was reported in 5 infants and 6 older children from Leadville (3,100 m), although the clinical condition was termed "primary pulmonary hypertension."[90] Three of these children had pulmonary hypertension at cardiac catheterization, and 1 was found to have medial hypertrophy and intimal thickening at autopsy. Thus, it is possible that repetitive desaturation episodes, intercurrent illness, or individual predisposition may be responsible for the development of clinically symptomatic pulmonary hypertension and right ventricular failure in certain children at altitude.

Sudden infant death syndrome

The possibility of an increased risk of SIDS in populations resident at high altitude has been raised on the basis of pathophysiologic and epidemiologic evidence. Breathing patterns in clinically healthy infants at high altitude share a number of features with those of infants who have experienced apparent life-threatening episodes, including greater amounts of periodic breathing and higher numbers of apneic pauses (defined as pauses > 3.6 seconds).[5,91] Data from experimental animals and humans indicate that exposure to chronic intermittent hypoxia during infancy can result in cardiorespiratory irregularity and depression.[92,93] Infants at high altitude exhibit lesser hypoxic ventilatory responsiveness as compared with adults.[62,94] A pathologic study by Naeye[95] drew parallels between the smooth muscle hypertrophy/hyperplasia of the pulmonary arteries in sea-level infants dying of SIDS or mild pulmonary inflammation and the increased pulmonary artery smooth muscle of age-matched infants living at high altitude. Of note, 8 of 10 high-altitude "hypoxic controls" in that series died of acute infectious processes, and 2 others had a history of apneic episodes preceding their deaths.

Epidemiologic studies have yielded mixed conclusions regarding the association between SIDS and altitude. A review of infant deaths using linked birth and death certificates in Colorado found no increase in the rate of SIDS for infants who were born, resided, or died at altitudes > 2,286 m.[96] A similar review of SIDS deaths in Nebraska found a statistically significant increase in SIDS incidence with increasing altitude of residence across the moderate altitude range of 300 m to 1,445 m.[97] Certain factors known to be associated with increased SIDS incidence rose in prevalence with increasing altitude: mean parity, decreased maternal age for parity, and decreased interval since last delivery. In Austria a positive association between altitude and the risk of SIDS in a county-by-county survey prompted a retrospective case-control study in the Tyrol.[98] The study compared 99 infants who died of SIDS with 136 randomly selected controls from the Tyrol (altitude range 500 m to 1,900 m). Altitude of residence emerged as a significant risk factor for SIDS among infants sleeping prone. Infants sleeping on their side or back showed only a marginal increase in SIDS risk across the altitude range. Variations in SIDS incidence could not be attributed to differences in social status or other risk conditions known to be associated with SIDS.

Although theoretic arguments for the role of fetal hypoxia or combined fetal/neonatal hypoxia have been advanced in explaining the observed links between SIDS and increasing altitude, these arguments remain untested. Alternative explanations for the observed associations include environmental factors of temperature and thermal insulation, which may prove critical for infants sleeping in the prone position, and demographic characteristics of families living at high altitude, in areas which are often more rural or isolated. Careful autopsy examination of SIDS cases at high altitude is important to detect instances of subclinical or unrecognized pulmonary hypertension or pneumonia.

Re-entry high-altitude pulmonary edema

A particular form of HAPE, re-entry HAPE, may occur in high-altitude residents as they return home after a sojourn at lower elevation. Children and young adults appear to have a higher incidence of re-entry HAPE than do older adults. Among residents of the Leadville area (3,100 m), the incidence of HAPE across the age range was estimated at 0.3%, but the incidence of re-entry HAPE was found to be almost three times higher (0.9%) among children younger than 14 years.[99] A series from Peru reported an incidence of HAPE in adolescents five times higher than that in the adult population studied (17% versus 3%).[31] The reasons underlying the predisposition of children and adolescents remain uncertain but likely include developmental differences in pulmonary vascular reactivity and

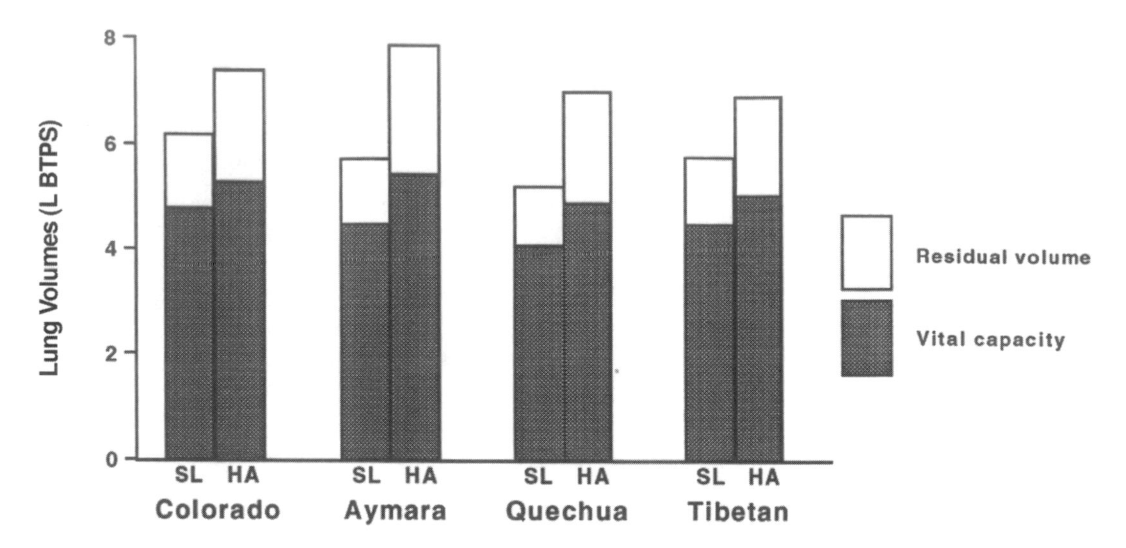

FIGURE 26–18. Comparative lung volumes among sea-level (SL) residents, newcomers to moderate altitude (Coloradans), and native high-altitude (HA) populations. Lung volumes are increased in all the populations living at high altitude. L BTPS = liters body temperature pressure standards. (Reproduced with permission from Niermeyer S et al.[42])

tone. A higher frequency of upper respiratory infections during childhood also may predispose to the development of re-entry HAPE.

Enlarged chest size and lung volumes

In populations native to high altitude, enlarged chest dimensions and accelerated thoracic development, despite generally smaller body size, are commonly regarded as signs of developmental response to high altitude in childhood and adolescence. This observation has fueled extensive debate over the role of genetic versus developmental factors. Chest shape appears to be influenced by altitude; both Andean and Himalayan populations demonstrate a phenotype of exaggerated chest depth as compared with chest width. Notably, however, persons of Quechua ancestry who are born and raised at low altitude also have enlarged chest dimensions.[100,101] Heritability of enlarged chest dimensions may be greater at high than at low altitude.[102] One explanation advanced that the action of natural selection increases the representation of genes increasing chest dimensions at high altitudes.[103] Preferential expression of genes coding for accelerated chest development also might occur in the high-altitude environment.

Chest dimensions do not necessarily reflect lung volumes or gas exchange area, although equivalence often is assumed. Despite the large number of studies of chest dimensions, few have documented complete lung volume measurements in children and adults at high altitude. Available data demonstrate that lung volumes are increased at high compared with low altitude across various populations, as compared with US standards or low-altitude newcomers from within the same population group. Residual volume increases most substantially, but vital capacity and total lung capacity also increase at high altitude (Figure 26–18). Adolescents of Aymara and mestizo ancestry (a mixture of Quechua and/or Aymara and Spanish) have modestly (~ 4%) larger vital capacity than do adolescents of European ancestry born and raised at high altitude, when measurements are controlled for body size.[101] Similar findings have been reported among Himalayan populations. Lung volumes are increased in young girls at high altitude in Ladakh, Jammu, and Kashmir states in India as compared with their lowland counterparts.[104] Boys aged 5 to 18 years in Himachal Pradesh state show similar differences.[105] Substantial interpopulational variation limits conclusions as to whether the magnitude of increase varies among Himalayan, Andean, and Rocky Mountain inhabitants. Nutrition also operates as a substantial confounder when interpreting changes in lung volume relative to body size across populations.

Evidence supports that infancy and childhood are critical periods for the development of lung volumes. Adult animals spending an equivalent amount of time at high altitude do not acquire increased lung volumes as do young animals.[106] In 11-to-19-year-old La Paz residents, an increase in lung volume was documented by early adolescence (age 11 years), and residual volume enlarged progressively with increasing age.[107] Frisancho and colleagues reviewed the environmental, developmental, and genetic influences on lung volumes among Bolivian high-altitude residents with varied population ancestry, altitude of birth, and duration of high-altitude residence. Growth and development at high altitude accounted for approximately 25% of the increase in vital capacity and residual volume among males but not among females.[108] Genetic factors accounted for an additional 25% of the variability, and occupational factors accounted for another 25% of the variability, increasing vital capacity but not residual volume.

Conclusion

The hypoxia of high altitude presents unique challenges to infants and children who either visit or reside in these areas worldwide. Understanding of the pathophysiology of acute altitude-associated illnesses and the developmental changes associated with chronic exposure can improve prevention, recognition, and treatment. With acute hypoxic exposure, underlying cardiopulmonary disorders, development of symptomatic high-altitude pulmonary hypertension, and development of HAPE pose the most serious threats to children. When transportation or access is limited, these conditions may become life threatening if not recognized early and responded to with descent or appropriate medical stabilization. Under conditions of chronic high-altitude hypoxia, symptomatic pulmonary hypertension, subacute infantile mountain sickness, and re-entry HAPE account for a portion of the excess morbidity and mortality experienced by children residing at high altitude.

Variation in response to the hypoxic environment of high altitude—among children of different ages and among different population groups—offers a key to defining pathophysiology at a cellular and molecular level. The model of fetal hypoxia at high altitude holds much promise for understanding the fetal antecedents not only of neonatal respiratory diseases, but also of cardiopulmonary conditions presenting in childhood, adolescence, and adulthood. In such a way, research questions and interventions at high-altitude may contribute to a better understanding of a variety of disorders mediated by hypoxia at low altitude.

References

1. Organización Panamericana de la Salud. Indicadoras Básicos. Boletín Epidemiológico 1999;201(3):14–15.
2. Ward MP, Milledge JS, West JB. High altitude medicine and physiology, 2nd ed. London: Chapman & Hall Medical, 1995.
3. Emmanouilides GC, Moss AJ, Duffie ER, Adams FH. Pulmonary artery pressure changes in human newborn infants from birth to 3 days of age. J Pediatr 1964; 65:327–33.
4. Niermeyer S, Shaffer E, Thilo E, et al. Arterial oxygenation and pulmonary arterial pressure in healthy neonates and infants at high altitude. J Pediatr 1993;123:767–72.
5. Niermeyer S, Moore LG, Shaffer E. Impaired cardiopulmonary transition at high altitude [abstract]. Pediatr Res 1998;43:292.
6. Gamboa R, Marticorena E. Presión arterial pulmonar en el recién nacido en las grandes alturas. Arch Inst Biol Andina 1971;4:55–66.
7. Hackett PH, Creagh CE, Grover RF, et al. High-altitude pulmonary edema in persons without the right pulmonary artery. N Engl J Med 1980;302:1070–3.
8. Reuland DS, Steinhoff MC, Gilman RH, et al. Prevalence and prediction of hypoxemia in children with respiratory infections in the Peruvian Andes. J Pediatr 1991; 119:900–6.
9. Simoes EA, Hayward AR, Ponnuraj EM, et al. Respiratory syncytial virus infects the Bonnet monkey, *Macaca radiata*. Pediatr Dev Pathol 1999;2:316–26.
10. Hall SM, Gorenflo M, Reader J, et al. Neonatal pulmonary hypertension prevents reorganisation of the pulmonary arterial smooth muscle cytoskeleton after birth. J Anat 2000;196:391–403.
11. Belknap JK, Orton EC, Ensley B, et al. Hypoxia increases bromodeoxyuridine labeling indices in bovine neonatal pulmonary arteries. Am J Respir Cell Mol Biol 1997; 16:366–71.
12. Tulloh RM, Hislop AA, Boels PJ, et al. Chronic hypoxia inhibits postnatal maturation of porcine intrapulmonary artery relaxation. Am J Physiol 1997;272:H2436–45.
13. Sartori C, Allemann Y, Trueb L, et al. Augmented vasoreactivity in adult life associated with perinatal vascular insult. Lancet 1999;353:2205–7.
14. Parkins KJ, Poets CF, O'Brien LM, et al. Effect of exposure to 15% oxygen on breathing patterns and oxygen saturation in infants: interventional study. BMJ 1998; 316:887–91.
15. Hackett PH, Oelz O. The Lake Louise consensus on the definition and quantification of altitude illness. In: Sutton JR, Coates G, Houston CS, eds. Hypoxia and mountain medicine. Burlington (Vt): Queen City Printers, 1992:327–30.
16. Yaron M, Waldman N, Niermeyer S, et al. The diagnosis of acute mountain sickness in preverbal children. Arch Pediatr Adolesc Med 1998;152:683–7.
17. Theis MK, Honigman B, Yip R, et al. Acute mountain sickness in children at 2835 m. Am J Dis Child 1993;147:143–5.
18. Honigman B, Theis MK, Koziol-McLain J, et al. Acute mountain sickness in a general tourist population at moderate altitudes. Ann Intern Med 1993;118:587–92.
19. Hultgren H. High-altitude pulmonary edema: current concepts. Ann Rev Med 1996;47:267–84.
20. Fasules JW, Wiggins JW, Wolfe RR. Increased lung vasoreactivity in children from Leadville, Colorado, after recovery from high altitude pulmonary edema. Circulation 1985;72:957–62.
21. Viswanathan R, Jain SK, Subramanian S, et al. Pulmonary edema of high altitude. II. Clinical aerodynamic, and biochemical studies in a group with a history of pulmonary edema of high altitude. Am Rev Respir Dis 1969;100:334–41.
22. Eldridge MW, Podolsky A, Richardson RS, et al. Pulmonary hemodynamic response to exercise in subjects with prior high-altitude pulmonary edema. J Appl Physiol 1996;81:911–21.
23. Podolsky A, Eldridge MW, Richardson RS, et al. Exercise-induced V/Q inequality in subjects with prior high-altitude pulmonary edema. J Appl Physiol 1996;81: 922–32.
24. Scherrer U, Vollenweider L, Delabays A, et al. Inhaled nitric oxide for high altitude pulmonary edema. N Engl J Med 1996;334:624–9.

25. Schoene RB, Swenson ER, Pizzo CJ, et al. The lung at high altitude: bronchoalveolar lavage in acute mountain sickness and pulmonary edema. J Appl Physiol 1988; 64:2605–13.
26. Schoene RB, Hackett PH, Henderson WR, et al. High altitude pulmonary edema: characteristics of lung lavage fluid. JAMA 1986;2256:63–9.
27. Richalet J-P. High altitude pulmonary oedema: still a place for controversy? Thorax 1995;50:923–9.
28. Severinghaus J. Hypothetical roles of angiogenesis, osmotic swelling, and ischemia in high-altitude cerebral edema. J Appl Physiol 1995;79:375–9.
29. Stelzner TJ, O'Brien RF, Sato K, Weil JV. Hypoxia-induced increases in pulmonary transvascular protein escape in rats. J Clin Invest 1988;82:1840–7.
30. Ogawa S, Koga S, Kuwabara K, et al. Hypoxia-induced increased permeability of endothelial monolayers occurs through lowering of cellular cAMP levels. Am J Physiol 1992;262:C546–54.
31. Hultgren H, Marticorena EA. High altitude pulmonary edema: epidemiologic observations in Peru. Chest 1978;74:372–6.
32. Alzamora-Castro V, Garrido-Lecca G, Battilana G. Pulmonary edema of high altitude. Am J Cardiol 1961; 7:769–78.
33. Durmowicz AG, Noordeweir E, Nicholas R, Reeves JT. Inflammatory processes may predispose children to high altitude pulmonary edema. J Pediatr 1997;130:838–40.
34. Carpenter TC, Reeves JT, Durmowicz AG. Viral respiratory infection increases the susceptibility of young rats to hypoxia-induced pulmonary edema. J Appl Physiol 1998;84:1048–54.
35. Ono S, Westcott JY, Chang SW, Voelkel NF. Endotoxin priming followed by high altitude causes pulmonary edema in rats. J Appl Physiol 1993;74:1534–42.
36. Planes C, Friedlander G, Loiseau A, et al. Inhibition of Na-K-ATPase activity after prolonged hypoxia in an alveolar epithelial cell line. Am J Physiol 1996;271:L71–8.
37. Planes C, Escoubet B, Blot-Chabaud M, et al. Hypoxia downregulates expression and activity of epithelial sodium channels in rat alveolar epithelial cells. Am J Respir Cell Mol Biol 1997;17:508–18.
38. Scherrer U, Sartori C, Lepori M, et al. High-altitude pulmonary edema: from exaggerated pulmonary hypertension to a defect in transepithelial sodium transport. Adv Exp Med Biol 1999;474:93–107.
39. Moore LG, Rounds SS, Jahnigen D, et al. Infant birth weight is related to maternal arterial oxygenation at high altitude. J Appl Physiol 1982;52:695–9.
40. Moore LG, Brodeur P, Chumbe O, et al. Maternal hypoxic ventilatory response, ventilation, and infant birth weight at 4300 m. J Appl Physiol 1986;60:1401–6.
41. Yip R. Altitude and birth weight. J Pediatr 1987;111:869–76.
42. Niermeyer S, Zamudio S, Moore LG. The people. In: Hornbein T, Schoene R, eds. High altitude. Vol. X of Lung biology in health and disease, L'enfant C (series ed.). New York: Marcel Dekker, 2001.
43. Jensen GM, Moore LG. The effect of high altitude and other risk factors on birthweight: independent or interactive effects? Am J Public Health 1997;87:1003–7.
44. Mortola JP, Frappell PB, Aguero L, Armstrong K. Birth weight and altitude: a study in Peruvian communities. J Pediatr 2000;136:324–9.
45. Zamudio S, Palmer SK, Droma T, et al. Effect of altitude on uterine artery blood flow during normal pregnancy. J Appl Physiol 1995;79:7–14.
46. McCullough RE, Reeves JT, Liljegren RL. Fetal growth retardation and increased infant mortality at high altitude. Obstet Gynecol Survey 1977;32:596–8.
47. Lichty JA, Ting RY, Bruns PD, Dyar E. Studies of babies born at high altitude. I. Relation of altitude to birth weight. Am Med Assoc J Dis Child 1957;93:666–9.
48. Lubchenco LO. Intrauterine growth as estimated from liveborn birth-weight data at 24 to 42 weeks of gestation. Pediatrics 1963;32:793–800.
49. Howard RC, Lichty JA, Bruns PD. Studies of babies born at high altitude. II. Measurement of birth weight, body length, and head size. Am Med Assoc J Dis Child 1957; 93:670–4.
50. Howard RC, Bruns PD, Lichty JA. Study of babies born at high altitude. III. Arterial oxygen saturation and hematocrit values at birth. Am Med Assoc J Dis Child 1957; 93:674–8.
51. Ballew C, Haas JD. Hematologic evidence of fetal hypoxia among newborn infants at high altitude in Bolivia. Am J Obstet Gynecol 1986;155:166–9.
52. Niermeyer S, Yang P, Shanmina, et al. Arterial oxygen saturation in Tibetan and Han infants born in Lhasa, Tibet. N Engl J Med 1995;333:1248–52.
53. Unger D, Weiser JK, McCullough RE, et al. Altitude, low birth weight and infant mortality in Colorado. JAMA 1988;259:3427–32.
54. Liebson C, Brown M, Thibodeau S, et al. Neonatal hyperbilirubinemia at high altitude. Am J Dis Child 1989;143:983–7.
55. Moore LG, Young D, McCullough RE, et al. Tibetan protection from intrauterine growth restriction at high altitude. Am J Hum Biol 2001;13:635–44.
56. Moore LG, Zamudio S, Zhuang J, et al. Oxygen transport in Tibetan women during pregnancy at 3658 m. Am J Phys Anthropol 2001;114:42–53.
57. Mok JY, McLaughlin FJ, Pintar M, et al. Transcutaneous monitoring of oxygenation: what is normal? J Pediatr 1986;108:365–71.
58. Thilo EH, Park-Moore B, Berman ER, Carson BS. Oxygen saturation by pulse oximetry in healthy infants at an altitude of 1610 m (5280 ft): what is normal? Am J Dis Child 1991;145:1137–40.
59. Sime F, Banchero N, Peñaloza D, et al. Pulmonary hypertension in children born and living at high altitudes. Am J Cardiol 1963;11:143–9.
60. Kelly DH, Stellwagen LM, Kaitz E, Shannon DC. Apnea and periodic breathing in normal full-term infants during the first twelve months. Pediatr Pulmonol 1985;1:215–9.
61. Glotzbach SF, Ariagno RL. Periodic breathing. In: Beckerman RC, Brouillette RT, Hunt CE, eds. Respiratory control disorders in infants and children. Baltimore (MD): Williams & Wilkins, 1992:142–60.
62. Matsuoka T, Mortola JP. Effects of hypoxia and hypercapnia on the Hering-Breuer reflex of the conscious newborn rat. J Appl Physiol 1995;78:5–11.

63. Lahiri S, Brody JS, Motoyama ED, Velasquez TM. Regulation of breathing in newborns at high altitude. J Appl Physiol 1978;44:673–8.
64. Barrington KJ, Finer NN, Wilkinson MH. Progressive shortening of the periodic breathing cycle duration in normal infants. Pediatr Res 1987;21:247–51.
65. Lubchenco LO, Ashby BL, Markarian M. Periodic breathing in newborn infants in Denver and Leadville, Colorado [abstract]. Soc Pediatr Res 1964;50.
66. Deming J, Washburn AH. Respiration in infancy. I. A method of studying rates, volume and character of respiration with preliminary report of results. Am J Dis Child 1935;49:108–24.
67. Walsh-Sukys MC, Tyson JE, Wright LL, et al. Persistent pulmonary hypertension of the newborn in the era before nitric oxide: practice variation and outcomes. Pediatrics 2000;105:14–20.
68. Bland RD, Nielson DW. Developmental changes in lung epithelial ion transport and liquid movement. Ann Rev Physiol 1992; 54:373–394.
69. Olver RE, Strang LB. Ion fluxes across the pulmonary epithelium and the secretion of lung liquid in the fetal lamb. J Physiol Lond 1973;241:327–57.
70. Olver RE, Ramsden CA, Strang LB, Walters DV. The role of amiloride-blockable sodium transport in adrenaline-induced lung liquid reabsorption in the fetal lamb. J Physiol (Lond) 1986;376:321–40.
71. Brown MJ, Olver RE, Ramsden CA, et al. Effects of adrenaline and spontaneous labour on the secretion and absorption of lung liquid in the foetal lamb. J Physiol (Lond) 1983;344:137–42.
72. Hummler E, Barker P, Gatzy J, et al. Early death due to defective neonatal lung liquid clearance in α-ENaC-deficient mice. Nat Genet 1996;12:325–8.
73. Hummler E, Barker P, Talbot C, et al. A mouse model for the renal salt-wasting syndrome pseudohypoaldosteronism. Proc Natl Acad Sci U S A 1997;94:11710–5.
74. Barker PM, Gowen CW, Lawson EE, Knowles MR. Decreased sodium ion absorption across nasal epithelium of very premature infants with respiratory distress syndrome. J Pediatr 1997;130:373–7.
75. Gowen CW, Lawson EE, Boucher RC, et al. Electrical potential difference and ion transport across nasal epithelium of term neonates: correlation with mode of delivery, transient tachypnea of the newborn, and respiratory rate. J Pediatr 1988;113:121–7.
76. Sakuma T, Okaniwa G, Nakada T, et al. Alveolar fluid clearance in the resected human lung. Am J Respir Crit Care Med 1994;150:305–10.
77. Massaro GD, Olivier J, Massaro D. Short-term perinatal 10% O_2 alters postnatal development of lung alveoli. Am J Physiol 1989;257:L221–5.
78. Massaro D, Massaro GD. Dexamethasone accelerates postnatal alveolar wall thinning and alters wall composition. Am J Physiol 1986;251:R218–24.
79. Massaro D, Teich N, Maxwell S, et al. Postnatal development of alveoli. Regulation and evidence for a critical period in rats. J Clin Invest 1985;76:1297–305.
80. Mortola JP, Morgan CA, Virgona V. Respiratory adaptation to chronic hypoxia in newborn rats. J Appl Physiol 1986; 61:1329–36.
81. Cunningham EJ, Brody JS, Jain BP. Lung growth induced by hypoxia. J Appl Physiol 1974;37:362–6.
82. Massaro GD, Olivier J, Dzikowsky C, Massaro D. Postnatal development of lung alveoli: suppression by 13% O_2 and a critical period. Am J Physiol 1990;258:L321–7.
83. Blanco LN, Massaro D, Massaro GD. Alveolar size, number, and surface area: developmentally dependent response to 13% O_2. Am J Physiol 1991;261:L370–7.
84. Mortola JP, Rezzonico R, Fisher JT, et al. Compliance of the respiratory system in infants born at high altitude. Am Rev Respir Dis 1990;142:43–8.
85. Arias-Stella J, Saldana M. The terminal portion of the pulmonary arterial tree in people native to high altitude. Circulation 1963;28:915–25.
86. Alzamora-Castro V, Battilana G, Abugattas R, Sialer S. Patent ductus arteriosus and high altitude. Am J Cardiol 1960;5:761–3.
87. Gamboa R, Marticorena E. The ductus arteriosus in the newborn infant at high altitude. Vasa 1972;1:192–5.
88. Miao CY, Zuberbuhler JS, Zuberbuhler JR. Prevalence of congenital cardiac anomalies at high altitude. J Am Coll Cardiol 1988;12:224–8.
89. Sui GJ, Liu YH, Cheng XS, et al. Subacute infantile mountain sickness. J Pathol 1988;155:161–70.
90. Khoury GH, Hawes CR. Primary pulmonary hypertension in children living at high altitude. J Pediatr 1963; 62:177–85.
91. Southall DP, Janczynski RE, Alexander JR, et al. Cardiorespiratory patterns in infants presenting with apparent life-threatening episodes. Biol Neonate 1990; 57:77–87.
92. Baker TL, McGinty DJ. Reversal of cardiopulmonary failure during active sleep in hypoxic kittens: implications for sudden infant death. Science 1977;198:419–21.
93. Rigatto H, Brady JP. Periodic breathing and apnea in preterm infants. II. Hypoxia as a primary event. Pediatrics 1972;50:219–28.
94. Cotton EK, Grunstein MM. Effects of hypoxia on respiratory control in neonates at high altitude. J Appl Physiol 1980;48:587–95.
95. Naeye RL. Pulmonary arterial abnormalities in the sudden-infant-death syndrome. N Engl J Med 1973; 289:1167–70.
96. Barkin RM, Hartley MR, Brooks JG. Influence of high altitude on sudden infant death syndrome. Pediatrics 1981;68:891–2.
97. Getts AG, Hill HF. Sudden infant death syndrome: incidence at various altitudes. Dev Med Child Neurol 1982; 24:61–8.
98. Kohlendorfer U, Kiechl S, Sperl W. Living at high altitude and risk of sudden infant death syndrome. Arch Dis Child 1998;79:506–9.
99. Scoggin CH, Hyers TM, Reeves JT, Grover RF. High-altitude pulmonary edema in the children and young adults of Leadville, Colorado. N Engl J Med 1977; 297:1269–72.
100. Melton TW. Comparison of growth and development in two Peruvian populations of high altitude ancestry. In: Eckhardt RB, Melton TW, eds. Population studies on human adaptation and evolution in the Peruvian Andes. No. 14. Occasional papers in anthropology.

University Park (PA): The Pennsylvania State University, 1992:192–241.

101. Greksa LP, Spielvogel H, Paz-Zamora M, et al. Effect of altitude on the lung function of high altitude residents of European ancestry. Am J Phys Anthropol 1988; 75:77–85.

102. Kramer AA. Heritability estimates of thoracic skeletal dimensions of a high-altitude Peruvian population. In: Eckhardt RB, Melton TW, eds. Population studies on human adaptation and evolution in the Peruvian Andes. No. 14. Occasional papers in anthropology. University Park (PA): The Pennsylvania State University, 1992:25–49.

103. Ahn YI. Heritability estimates of four anthropometric measurements on the thorax in a high altitude Peruvian population. In: Eckhardt RB, Melton TW, eds. Population studies on human adaptation and evolution in the Peruvian Andes. No. 14. Occasional papers in anthropology. University Park (PA): The Pennsylvania State University, 1992:113–37.

104. Malik SL, Pandey AK. Respiratory adaptation to high altitude in adolescent Bod girls of the Western Himalayas. Ann Hum Biol 1993;20:575–81.

105. Malhotra R. Thoracic adaptation to high altitude. Anthropol Anz 1986;44:355–9.

106. Johnson RL Jr, Cassiday SS, Grover RF, et al. Functional capacities of lungs and thorax in beagles after prolonged residence at 3100 m. J Appl Physiol 1985; 59:1773–82.

107. Greksa LP, Spielvogel H, Caceres E. Total lung capacity in young highlanders of Aymara ancestry. Am J Phys Anthopol 1994;94:477–86.

108. Frisancho AR, Frisancho HG, Albalak R, et al. Developmental, genetic, and environmental components of lung volumes at high altitude. Am J Hum Biol 1997; 9:191–203.

CHAPTER 27

Laryngeal Function and Respiratory System Neural Reflexes

Victor Chernick, MD, FRCPC, Sandra J. England, PhD, Gabriel G. Haddad, MD

The larynx is the most caudal segment of the upper respiratory tract. The activities of the intrinsic laryngeal muscle are an important determinant of both inspiratory and expiratory airflow resistance. These muscles also participate in a variety of nonrespiratory functions such as phonation, swallowing, and airway protection, which are not discussed in detail here. Several excellent reviews of the respiratory function of the larynx and other upper airway structures are available, and the reader is referred to these for a more detailed presentation.[1–3]

Laryngeal Muscles and Their Innervation

The laryngeal muscles can be divided into two groups, extrinsic and intrinsic, on the basis of the functional result of activation. Extrinsic muscles suspend and support the larynx. The pharyngeal constrictors are innervated by the glossopharyngeal nerve (IX) and the pharyngeal branch of the vagus (X). The stylopharyngeus, styloglossus, and sternothyroid muscles are innervated by cranial nerve XII and by the ventral ramus of C1. The intrinsic muscles are innervated by the recurrent laryngeal nerve and act to control the size of the glottis and vocal cord tension. The posterior cricoarytenoid (PCA) is the only laryngeal abductor; the adductors include the thyroarytenoid (TA), lateral cricoarytenoid, and interarytenoid muscles. One remaining muscle, the cricothyroid, innervated by the superior laryngeal nerve, has characteristics of both extrinsic and intrinsic muscles. It anchors the cricoid and thyroid cartilages together and, by rotating the thyroid cartilage forward, tautens and lengthens the vocal cords.

TABLE 27–1. Physiologic and Pathophysiologic Factors That Alter Laryngeal Muscle Activities

	Abductor		Adductor
	Inspiratory	Expiratory	Expiratory
REM sleep	+/–	–	–
Non-REM sleep	+/–	–	+/–
Maturation	?	?	–
Hypercapnia	+	+	–
Hypoxia	+	–	+
Increased resistance	+/–	–	+
Bronchoconstriction	+/–	–	+
Lung inflation	+	+	–
Lung deflation	–	–	+
Negative laryngeal pressure	+	+	–
Laryngeal cooling	–	–	–
Sedatives and anesthetics	–	–	–

See text for details. + = increased; – = decreased activity; +/– = no consistent effect.

Motoneurons supplying the intrinsic laryngeal muscles have been localized in the medulla throughout the rostral-caudal extent of the nucleus ambiguous, including the retrofacial nucleus.[4] The cricothyroid motoneurons are the most rostral, with the adductor neurons located more caudally. The motoneurons of the PCA muscle are coextensive with the above.

Respiratory Activity of Intrinsic Laryngeal Muscles

Activities and Mechanical Effects During Eupnea

It has been argued that laryngeal abduction during inspiration is achieved by extrinsic laryngeal muscles acting to rotate the cartilaginous structures and unfold the soft tissue,[5] but the general consensus is that abduction during inspiration is the result of activation of the PCA muscle (Table 27–1). When the PCA contracts, it rotates the arytenoid cartilages laterally on their articulations, with the cricoid cartilage pulling the posterior ends of the vocal cords outward.

Electromyograms of the PCA in animals and humans have shown that respiratory phasic activity is present (Figure 27–1).[6–9] The PCA begins contracting 50 to 500 msec before the onset of diaphragmatic contraction or inspiratory airflow. Electrical activity continues throughout inspiration. Thus, the glottis is actively widened during inspiration, as confirmed by direct visualization with fiber-optic laryngoscopy in humans.[10–12] The extent and timing of this widening varies considerably between individuals but is present in both adults and neonates.

The mechanical result of inspiratory glottic widening is a reduction in airflow resistance just before and during inspiratory effort.[10] Thus, the work of breathing is lower than would be the case if the glottis were narrow during inspiration. Because the larynx contributes a considerable portion (approximately 20%) of respiratory system resistance, the PCA plays an important role in actively reducing this resistance. The cricothyroid muscle is also active dur-

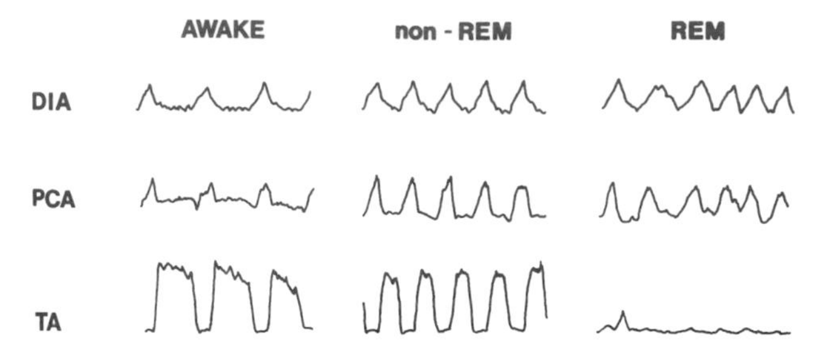

FIGURE 27–1. Moving time averages of the diaphragm (DIA) and posterior cricoarytenoid (PCA) and thyroarytenoid (TA) muscles during wakefulness and non-REM and REM sleep, recorded in a 28-day-old dog pup. An upward deflection reflects increased activity of the muscle. The PCA has an increased activity during inspiration coincident with diaphragmatic contraction, whereas the TA has phasic expiratory activity. Note the decrease in tonic or expiratory activity of the PCA during non-REM sleep as compared with wakefulness and the loss of phasic expiratory activity in the TA during REM.

ing inspiration and appears to act synergistically with the abductor.[8,13,14] If the vocal cords were not actively tautened and separated during inspiration, the negative pressure generated in the airway during diaphragmatic contraction would tend to suck the vocal cords toward the midline, resulting in increased resistance and inspiratory stridor.

During eupneic expiration, the vocal cords return to a more medial position because of the loss of active abduction. Further decreases in the glottic area occur if expiratory activity of adductor muscles is present. In newborn animals, direct evidence of active expiratory adduction has been reported.[7,15,16] Recordings of the electrical activity of the TA muscle (see Figure 27–1) show that activity begins as inspiratory airflow ceases and continues throughout expiration. This activity results in a substantial increase in airflow resistance and the time constant for lung emptying.[17] Evidence of active retardation of expiratory airflow in human infants has been obtained from examination of expiratory airflow patterns.[18] The degree to which airflow is retarded appears to decrease with maturation.

It has been postulated that lengthening of the expiratory time constant contributes to the elevation of end-expiratory lung volume above passive functional residual capacity in infants.[19] Without an active mechanism to slow expiratory airflow, the mechanical characteristics of the infant's respiratory system (ie, high chest wall compliance) would result in end-expiratory lung volume being only approximately 10% of total lung capacity compared with 40% in adults. This low lung volume would decrease oxygen stores and could result in atelectasis. In addition to active laryngeal adduction during expiration, the infant also uses postinspiratory diaphragmatic activity and a high breathing frequency to maintain an elevated end-expiratory lung volume. Postinspiratory diaphragmatic activity slows lung emptying and is also present in adults; short expiratory times limit the degree of lung emptying that can occur before the next inspiration.

Active laryngeal adduction is particularly prominent in newborns within the first few hours after birth (England, unpublished observations). During this time, the positive subglottic pressures generated with active adduction contribute to the establishment of lung air volume and promote fluid clearance.

Expiratory activity of laryngeal adductors in adults has been found in some, but not all, investigations. The discrepancies between studies may be partially explained by the use of anesthetics (see the section "Influence of Pharmacologic Agents and Alcohol"). Expiratory activity of the thyroarytenoid muscle is present in adult rats and humans during quiet breathing in wakefulness.[20,21] The mechanical effect of this activity is the same as in infants: an increased expiratory resistance and a slowing of expiratory airflow. Thus, expiration cannot be considered a totally passive process because both laryngeal adduction and postinspiratory diaphragmatic activity modulate the rate of lung emptying. However, these activities are far more prominent in infants than in adults.

In addition to the phasic activation of the PCA during inspiration and the TA during expiration, both muscles also exhibit tonic activity.[21] Thus, there is some tone in the PCA during expiration and in the TA during inspiration. These data suggest that the control, of laryngeal aperture at any time during the respiratory cycle is determined by the balance between activities of the abductor and adductors. Airflow resistance is finely tuned by this balance, with abduction normally predominating during inspiration and adduction during expiration. The larynx represents a rapidly variable and finely controlled resistance in the respiratory system. The laryngeal muscles are small and their activation does not impose large metabolic demands. Therefore, changes in airflow resistance and flow rates can be achieved at a much lower metabolic cost than would be required to achieve similar changes with contraction of the diaphragm or the intercostal or abdominal muscles.

Intrinsic Laryngeal Muscle Activities During Stimulated Breathing

The pattern of activation of the intrinsic laryngeal muscles at the time of inspiration and expiration is altered during hypercapnia, hypoxia, exercise, and voluntary hyperventilation. Hypercapnia and exercise are accompanied by an increase in phasic inspiratory activity in the PCA.[22,23] This results in increased glottic widening and decreased inspiratory airflow resistance.[24] This response decreases the inspiratory work of breathing under conditions that require high inspiratory flows. Furthermore, the PCA remains active during all, or a portion of, the expiratory phase during hypercapnia and exercise, leading to a substantial increase in the size of the glottis during expiration, a lowered expiratory airflow resistance, and increased expiratory flow rates without the necessity of activation of expiratory muscles such as those in the abdomen.

The pattern of changes in glottis aperture with voluntary hyperventilation and panting are similar to those described for hypercapnia.[25,26] The difference between the inspiratory and the expiratory size of the glottis is minimized under these conditions, but panting during bronchoconstriction may not result in minimizing laryngeal resistance (see the section "Influence of Resistance of Larynx During Pulmonary Function Testing").[17]

During hypoxia, the glottis is also widened with inspiration to a greater extent than during eupnea. However, the expiratory size of the glottis is not necessarily increased. If eucapnia is maintained during hypoxia, glottic narrowing to a greater extent than during eupnea is observed.[27] Posterior cricoarytenoid activity and active abduction do not continue into the expiratory phase during hypoxia, as is the case during hypercapnia, exercise, and hyperventilation. If hypocapnia accompanies hypoxia, a situation that exists at high altitude and during breathing of a hypoxic gas mixture without added CO_2, the glottis narrows to a greater extent during expiration than during normoxia. This is also the case in hypoxic patients with chronic obstructive pulmonary disease and presumably reflects a reflex mechanism for increasing lung volume.[28] Hyperinflation during hypoxia increases oxygen stores and prevents atelectasis, thereby minimizing arterial hypoxemia.

Laryngeal Muscle Activities with Increased Respiratory System Resistance

When an external resistance is added during inspiration, there is a compensatory increase in glottic widening and, presumably, abductor activity.[29] This increase in glottic size minimizes the total resistance during inspiration. However, addition of an expiratory external load results in what could be viewed as a noncompensatory response, increased expiratory glottic narrowing.[30–32] The mechanism by which this occurs is activation of laryngeal adductors during expiration. Rather than minimizing total resistance, this response results in a greater increase than can be attributed to the external load.

During histamine- or methacholine-induced bronchoconstriction, the glottis is slightly wider during inspiration in some individuals, but there is substantial narrowing of the glottis during expiration, as is the case with expiratory external loading.[17] This response results in an increased expiratory airflow resistance, a seemingly paradoxical reflex response.

Several explanations for this response have been suggested. Hyperinflation is known to occur during bronchoconstriction, and increased laryngeal adduction during expiration causes hyperinflation by the mechanism of increasing the time constant for lung emptying. Hyperinflation is beneficial to the extent that it maintains the patency of intrathoracic airways by increasing their distending volume and minimizes the inspiratory work of breathing. Thus, some degree of hyperinflation during bronchoconstriction may be advantageous. Furthermore, respiratory frequency is decreased because volume-time feedback from the lungs during expiration is important in determining the time of onset of the subsequent inspiration and slower lung emptying results in a longer expiratory time.[33] Expiratory airflow retardation during bronchoconstriction may thus limit the induced tachypnea.

Similar degrees of hyperinflation could be achieved by increasing postinspiratory diaphragmatic activity, that has been shown to be present during bronchoconstriction.[34] However, postinspiratory diaphragmatic activity imposes a large metabolic load on the already stressed diaphragm and could result in diaphragmatic fatigue and dyspnea.[33] Expiratory laryngeal adduction limits the necessity to use the diaphragm to achieve hyperinflation.

Laryngeal Muscle Activities During Sleep

The respiratory activities of the intrinsic laryngeal muscles during rapid eye movement (REM) and non-REM sleep have been studied in both newborns and adults.[7,8,15,16,20,21,35] The PCA is active during inspiration in non-REM sleep and, as in wakefulness, widens the glottis and minimizes inspiratory airflow resistance. Although there is some controversy as to whether inspiratory PCA activity increases or decreases during REM sleep, all investigators agree that phasic inspiratory activity is present while tonic activity during expiration decreases. Thus, the laryngeal abductor, like the diaphragm, is spared the generalized skeletal muscle atonia that occurs during REM sleep. A further implication of continued inspiratory laryngeal abduction during sleep is that the larynx is not normally a site of collapse in patients suffering from obstructive sleep apnea. The response of the PCA during hypercapnia and hypoxia is preserved during both non-REM and REM sleep.[23]

Thyroarytenoid muscle activity during expiration in non-REM sleep is present in newborn lambs and dogs and adult rats,[7,15,16,20] but not in adult humans.[21] In newborns, this increase in expiratory airflow resistance tends to increase end-expiratory lung volume, as discussed above. In contrast, TA activity all but disappears during REM sleep in both newborns and adults. The only activity observed is brief, non-respiratory-related bursts that are likely to represent the generalized twitching present intermittently during REM sleep. Unlike the PCA and diaphragm, respiratory TA muscle activity is abolished by the neural processes underlying the REM state.

The functional result of the loss of expiratory airflow retardation during REM sleep in infants is a decrease in

TABLE 27–2. Pulmonary Vagal Reflexes

Receptor	Location of Sensory Ending	Reflex
Slowly adapting (myelinated fiber)	Airway smooth muscle cells	Hering-Breuer Inflation and deflation limiting
Rapidly adapting irritant (myelinated) fiber	Airway epithelial cells	Hering-Breuer deflation reflex (with lung hyperinflation) Cough Mucus secretion Decreased laryngeal abduction, increased adduction
C fiber ending (unmyelinated)	Lung interstitial space	Apnea → rapid shallow breathing Bronchoconstriction Mucus secretion Laryngeal adduction

end-expiratory lung volume[19] and a decrease in arterial oxygenation.[36] The latter effect is minimal in healthy newborns (a decrease in arterial PO_2 of 3 to 4 mm Hg) but is of potentially much greater significance in infants and children with lung disease (see the section "Influence of Resistance of Larynx During Pulmonary Function Testing").[37]

Reflex Control of Laryngeal Muscles

The respiratory activity of the intrinsic laryngeal muscles is modified by afferent information reaching the respiratory control center in the medulla from mechanoreceptors in the lungs, peripheral and central chemoreceptors, and sensory inputs arising in the larynx. Also, the changes in laryngeal muscle activities that occur during REM sleep are likely to be mediated by neuronal activities arising in supramedullary brain structures, and the nonrespiratory movements of the vocal cords during phonation, defecation, and so forth are controlled by areas of the central nervous system that are not primarily involved in respiratory control.

Vagal Reflexes

There are three types of afferent feedback arising in the lungs and carried in the vagus nerve (Table 27–2). Slowly adapting, or stretch, receptors increase activity in response to increases in lung volume. Their activation results in increased abductor and decreased adductor activity.[38] This influence is important in decreasing laryngeal resistance during hyperpnea. During lung deflation, decreased activity of pulmonary stretch receptors promotes laryngeal adduction, a response that slows airflow out of the collapsing lungs.

Rapidly adapting, or irritant, receptors are activated when rapid changes in lung volume occur, under which circumstances a brief, rapid series of action potentials is observed in their vagal afferents. Little is known about the influence of this activity on the respiratory movements of the vocal cords, but it has been postulated to result in a decrease in abductor activity and an increase in active adduction.[39,40] Because these receptors are also activated during bronchoconstriction, they may contribute to the expiratory laryngeal adduction observed during bronchoprovocation and status asthmaticus.

The final group of receptors, C fiber afferents, have not been systematically studied in relation to laryngeal muscle activation, but the net result of their activation appears to be an increase in laryngeal resistance.[40,41] Functionally mature C fibers are present in the newborn and cause a sustained expiratory upper airway closure in response to pulmonary edema that could be of benefit in promoting positive pressures and fluid reabsorption.[42] The bronchoconstrictor response in the newborn to C fiber stimulation by lactic acid is complex, involving activation through the medullary respiratory centers of vagal cholinergic efferents, production of cyclooxygenase products, and perhaps release of tachykinins (such as substance P or neurokinin A) from pulmonary C fibers.[43]

Chemoreceptors

The effect on the larynx of central chemoreceptors is evident in the responses to hyper and hypocapnia. Hypercapnia causes an increase in the inspiratory activity of the PCA and results in continued activation of this abductor into the expiratory phase.[22] Peripheral, in particular carotid body, chemoreceptor activity increases in response to hypoxia and, to some extent, hypercapnia. As described earlier, hypoxia results in an increase in inspiratory PCA activity, but, unlike the situation with normoxic hypercapnia, the PCA does not always continue to dilate the glottis during expiration. Instead, active adduction of the vocal cords often accompanies hypoxia. Barrlett[44] showed that inhibition of PCA activity occurs during expiration with hypoxia when pulmonary stretch receptor activity is eliminated. Thus, peripheral chemoreceptor activity results in laryngeal narrowing during expiration, unless this response is overridden by the excitatory influence of pulmonary afferents.

Laryngeal Receptors

Three types of receptors located in the larynx and having afferents in the superior laryngeal nerve have been identified.[38] Their activation can alter the breathing pattern and the extent of contraction of upper airway muscles. They respond to changes in pressure, airflow, or temperature and the degree of contraction of laryngeal muscles. The upper airway is subjected to phasic pressure changes during inspiration and expiration. Negative pressures in the larynx promote abduction, both tonic and phasic, and also increase the latency between onset of contraction in the PCA and contraction of the diaphragm. Positive pressure pulses applied to the upper airway during inspiration partially inhibit inspiratory muscle activity and shorten inspiratory time. Thus, the laryngeal pressure sensors provide a positive feedback mechanism for controlling laryngeal airflow resistance both within and between breaths; the vocal cords will be abducted when exposed to negative pressure and adducted in response to positive pressure.

Airflow through or cooling of the larynx decreases adductor activity and expiratory laryngeal resistance.[45] PCA activity is also decreased when the larynx is cooled, resulting in an increased inspiratory resistance.[46] The latter response tends to decrease inspiratory airflow and provide time for greater warming and humidification of air to take place in the upper airway. Because cold air is known to induce bronchospasm, this mechanism may be useful in reducing exposure of the lower airways to cold air.

Active and passive movements of the larynx occur during breathing. Stretch reflexes in the laryngeal muscles are elicited when the muscles contract. Stretch facilitates muscle contraction in synergistic muscles and inhibits the activity of antagonistic muscles.[47] These receptors are probably more important in the fine coordination required for speech than in the respiratory movements of the vocal cords.

In addition to laryngeal mechanoreceptors that respond to pressure change or movement of the larynx discussed above, there are a large number of chemoreceptors (taste buds) present in the laryngeal surface of the epiglottis and in the larynx.[48] These receptors are involved in airway protective mechanisms, which have been reviewed in detail elsewhere.[49]

Influence of Pharmacologic Agents and Alcohol

The respiratory activities of the laryngeal muscles are altered by a variety of pharmacologic agents to a greater extent than is the diaphragm. Anesthetics, analgesics, sedatives, tranquilizers, and alcohol depress the activity of both the PCA and the adductors to a far greater extent than the respiratory depression they cause in diaphragmatic function.[50,51] This same phenomenon occurs in dilator muscles of the pharynx and nose. The consequence of differential decreases in upper airway muscle activity during anesthesia and sedation is that the airflow resistance of the entire upper airway increases during inspiration, and the active control of this resistance in response to various stimuli such as hypercapnia is reduced. In fact, much of the controversy about the activity of various upper airway muscles during eupnea and stimulated breathing arises from the use of anesthetics in experimental protocols. The decrease in inspiratory upper airway dilation after alcohol ingestion is believed to increase the incidence of snoring and obstructive sleep apnea in patients who are prone to such sleep disorders. Furthermore, inspiratory upper airway collapse and stridor may occur in patients who use such drugs.

Role of Laryngeal Sensory Afferents

Afferent sensory inputs from the larynx have major respiratory effects. Indeed, laryngeal afferents can trigger the most potent inhibitory reflex on respiration in mammals. In a chronically instrumented piglet model, Donnelly and Haddad[52] demonstrated that stimulation of the superior laryngeal nerve (SLN) decreased minute ventilation by 40 to 75%, induced apneas of 10 to 15 seconds, and decreased O_2 saturation and increased P_{CO_2} in a major way. In a separate work, Sanocka and colleagues[53] showed that the respiratory changes occur immediately and that these were followed by an immediate rise in blood pressure and, within 30 seconds, by a decrease in electroencephalographic (EEG) amplitude. Major cardiac slowing did not occur before 80 seconds of the start of the respiratory changes and apnea. The EEG became flat within 1 minute of the SLN stimulation. During prolonged and continuous SLN stimulation and during light anesthesia, these investigators also showed that piglets can autoresuscitate: every 1 to 2 minutes, the prolonged apnea induced by SLN stimulation was interrupted by a cluster of gasps increasing O_2 saturation, heart rate, and blood pressure.[54] The ability to "break through" the depression in cardiorespiratory status was dependent on arousal mechanisms as the presence of anesthesia impaired the mechanism responsible for initiating breathing during laryngeal reflex activation.[55]

Influence of Resistance of Larynx During Pulmonary Function Testing

There has been an increase in the use of various techniques to perform pulmonary function tests in infants and children. The aim of most tests is to assess the mechanical properties of the lungs and lower airways. However, unless the patient is intubated, the variable resistance of the larynx and other upper airway structures influences the measurements in a manner that is not necessarily predictable.

In most studies of respiratory system resistance, a higher expiratory than inspiratory resistance has been measured. Most of this difference can be accounted for by the fact that the larynx is actively abducted during inspiration and adducted during expiration. If laryngeal abduction and adduction were constant from breath to breath and when blood gases and bronchomotor tone are altered, laryngeal resistance would pose no problem in the interpretation of pulmonary function tests. However, the information already presented in this chapter indicates that this is certainly not the case. Several examples will be given of situations in which changes in laryngeal resistance influence the measured values of pulmonary function.

Panting has often been used to maximize the glottic aperture during inspiration and expiration and thereby minimize and standardize the effect of laryngeal resistance in measurements of respiratory system resistance.[26] However, after bronchoconstriction induced with histamine or methacholine, the laryngeal aperture is often smaller during panting than it was during the prebronchoconstriction measurements of resistance.[17] Thus, the increase in total airway resistance measured is the result of narrowing of the pulmonary airways and laryngeal constriction.

Two techniques for measuring pulmonary mechanics in infants and small children have received considerable attention. The passive flow-volume technique requires an end-inspiratory occlusion that elicits the Hering-Breuer inflation reflex and relaxes respiratory muscles, followed by release of the occlusion and measurements of the expiration immediately succeeding. However, laryngeal adduction may be present during the subsequent "passive" expiration, and results in slower expiratory flows than would be generated by a true passive collapse of the respiratory system to resting lung volume.[56] Thus, the respiratory system compliance and resistance calculated do not reflect the true characteristics of the lungs and chest wall.

The other technique that is often used is the compression or "squeeze" flow-volume method. The child is normally sedated for this measurement, and this fact alone may alter laryngeal muscle activities. For the measurement, a flow-volume curve is constructed from airflow during a rapid compression of the chest wall, a maneuver that stimulates maximal forced expiration. However, rapid decreases in lung volume and compression of the chest have been shown to increase laryngeal adduction in lambs.[16] Thus, the expiratory flow is reduced and does not exclusively reflect the mechanics of the lower respiratory system.

When either of these techniques is used to compare pulmonary function before and after administration of bronchoconstrictor agents, a change in flow reflects not only changes in bronchomotor tone in the lower airways but also the effect of bronchoconstriction on the activity of laryngeal adductors. Since bronchoconstriction normally results in increased laryngeal adduction during expiration, the increase in resistance of lower airways will be overestimated to an unpredicable degree. The use of the "squeeze" technique following pressure inflation of the lung to total lung capacity may lessen some of the problems associated with starting the squeeze at low lung volumes but does not obviate the problem associated with sedation.

In addition to influences on tests of pulmonary mechanics, the larynx may also contribute to changes in blood oxygenation in infants. As noted earlier, there is an absence of laryngeal adduction during expiration in REM sleep, and this loss in active retardation of airflow may result in a decreased lung volume at end expiration. Oxygenation may decrease as a result of decreases in oxygen stores and atelectasis in REM sleep. Thus, measurements of oxygen saturation, when used to assess pulmonary function in infants with lung diseases such as bronchopulmonary dysplasia, should be made in both quiet and REM sleep to reflect overall function accurately.

The Larynx in Disease

A description of all the anatomic and functional disorders that can affect normal laryngeal functioning in respiration is beyond the scope of this chapter, but some general concepts will be presented.

Pathophysiology of Laryngeal Structures

It is obvious that damage to the recurrent or superior laryngeal nerves will result in a decrease in the phasic respiratory control of laryngeal airflow resistance. Inspiratory laryngeal stridor often results from such damage. Likewise, pathology at the level of premotor control in the medulla affects laryngeal resistances during inspiration and expiration. Anatomic abnormalities of the cartilaginous or soft tissue structures of the larynx can alter airflow resistance and may result in an inability of laryngeal muscle activation to achieve appropriate levels of airflow resistance. Exercise intolerance and dyspnea may accompany any of these disorders if airflow limitation is severe enough.

Acute and Chronic Lung Disease

As noted earlier, bronchoconstriction is accompanied by an increased narrowing of the glottis during expiration. In bronchial asthma, Collett and colleagues observed pronounced narrowing of the glottis, vestibular folds (false cords), and pharynx.[57] The inspiratory dimensions of the larynx are also reduced in some individuals during bronchoconstriction.[17,32] As described earlier, enhanced expiratory adduction during bronchoconstriction probably represents a compensatory mechanism promoting hyperinflation.

Unlike this physiologic response, a syndrome in

which a primary adduction of the vocal cords produces glottic wheeze has been documented.[58,59] This syndrome may be differentiated from bronchial asthma by the fact that the wheeze is most pronounced at the level of the larynx, the patients breathe at low lung volumes using abdominal muscles during expiration, and no decreases in FEV_1 are evident with bronchial challenge. Although most cases appear to have a psychological basis, this may not always be true.[60]

An additional syndrome often misdiagnosed as asthma is active paradoxical movements of the vocal cords.[61] In this condition, inspiratory stridor and shortness of breath are present with no detectable anatomic abnormalities of the larynx and no obvious bronchoconstriction. It usually occurs after a respiratory tract infection and may represent a neurogenic reflex involving the superior laryngeal nerve. Active inspiration is accompanied by paradoxical adduction of the vocal cords, and, in fact, an attempt to perform rapid inspiration to total lung capacity usually results in glottic closure. The pathophysiology of this syndrome is poorly understood, but treatment with mechanical ventilation or continuous positive airway pressure (CPAP) breathing usually abolishes the transient respiratory distress.

Chronic obstructive lung disease accompanied by hypoxia in adults is accompanied by increased expiratory glottic narrowing. Although a systematic study of laryngeal resistances in infants with chronic lung disease has not been performed, the grunting that accompanies the respiratory distress syndrome in infants is the result of active laryngeal adduction during expiration. It is likely that expiratory laryngeal adduction is also pronounced in bronchopulmonary dysplasia. This appears to be a physiologic response promoting hyperinflation and increasing oxygen stores.

Tracheostomy and Intubation

When a tracheostomy is performed or a patient is intubated, there is a loss of dynamic control of inspiratory and expiratory airflow by the laryngeal muscles. In infants who use expiratory laryngeal adduction to elevate end-expiratory lung volume, lung volume may decrease when the larynx is effectively bypassed. In lambs, a switch from nasal to tracheostomy breathing results in a decrease in lung volume and respiratory dysrhythmia.[62] In dog pups, acute opening of a tracheostomy results in reflex activation of the TA muscle and tachypnea.[39] These responses are eliminated if continuous positive pressure is applied at the tracheostomy. It has long been recognized that intubated infants with respiratory distress are better oxygenated and have fewer apneic episodes when CPAP is provided. It should be noted that CPAP may replace the positive subglottic pressures that the infant normally generates with expiratory laryngeal adduction, but it does not replace the dynamic control of inspiratory and expiratory airflow generated with phasic changes in upper airway resistance.

This chapter is a revision of Chapter 6 from the first edition of this book, which was originally authored by Sandra J. England, PhD. It has been revised by Dr. Victor Chernick and Dr. Gabriel Haddad, editors of this current edition.

References

1. Mathew OP, Sant'Ambrogio G, eds. Respiratory function of the upper airway. New York: Marcel Dekker, 1988.
2. Bartlett D Jr. Upper airway motor systems. In: Cherniack NS, Widdicombe JG, eds. Handbook of physiology. Sect 3. The respiratory system II. Washington, DC: American Physiological Society, 1986:223–45.
3. Harding R. The upper respiratory tract in perinatal life. In: Johnston BM, Gluckman PD, eds. Respiratory control and lung development in the fetus and newborn. Ithaca, NY: Perinatology Press, 1986:331–76.
4. Iscoe SD. Central control of the upper airway. In: Mathew OP, Sant'Ambrogio G, eds. Respiratory function of the upper airway. New York: Marcel Dekker, 1988:125–92.
5. Fink BR. The human larynx. New York: Raven Press, 1975.
6. Brancatisano TP, Dodd DS, Engel LA. Respiratory activity of posterior cricoarytenoid muscle and vocal cord movements in humans. J Appl Physiol 1984;57:1143–9.
7. England SJ, Kent G, Stogryn HAF. Laryngeal muscle and diaphragmatic activities in conscious dog pups. Respir Physiol 1985;60:95–108.
8. Harding R, England SJ, Stradling JR, et al. Respiratory activity of laryngeal muscles in awake and sleeping dogs. Respir Physiol 1986;66:315–26.
9. Remmers JE, Bartlett D Jr. Reflex control of expiratory airflow and duration. J Appl Physiol 1977;4:80–7.
10. Baier H, Wanner A, Zarsecke S, Sackner MA. Relationships among glottis opening, respiratory flow, and upper airway resistance in humans. J Appl Physiol 1977;43:603–11.
11. Brancatisano TP, Collett PW, Engel LA. Respiratory movements of the vocal cords. J Appl Physiol 1983;54: 1269–76.
12. England SJ, Bartlett D Jr, Daubenspeck JA. Influence of human vocal cord movements on airflow and resistance during eupnea. J Appl Physiol 1982;52:773–9.
13. Woodson GE, Sant'Ambrogio FB, Mathew OP, Sant'Ambrogio G. Cricothyroid muscle response to respiratory stimuli. Physiologist 1985;28:304.
14. Konrad HR, Rattenborg CC. Combined action of laryngeal muscles. Acta Otolaryngol (Stockh) 1969;67:646–9.
15. Harding R, Johnson P, McClelland ME. Respiratory function of the larynx in developing sheep and the influence of sleep state. Respir Physiol 1980;40:165–79.
16. Harding R. State-related and developmental changes in laryngeal function. Sleep 1980;3:307–22.
17. England SJ, Ho V, Zamel N. Laryngeal constriction in normal humans during experimentally induced bronchoconstriction. J Appl Physiol 1985;58:352–6.
18. Kosch PC, Davenport PW, Wozniak JA, Stark AR. Reflex control of expiratory duration in newborn infants. J Appl Physiol 1985;58:575–81.

19. Henderson-Smart DJ, Read DJC. Reduced lung volume during behavioral active sleep in the newborn. J Appl Physiol 1979;46:1081–5.
20. Sherrey JH, Megirian D. Respiratory EMG activity of the posterior cricoarytenoid, cricothyroid and diaphragm muscles during sleep. Respir Physiol 1980;39:355–65.
21. Kuna ST, Insalaco G, Woodson GE. Thyroarytenoid muscle activity during wakefulness and sleep in normal adults. J Appl Physiol 1988;65:1332–9.
22. Bartlett D Jr. Effects of hypercapnia and hypoxia on laryngeal resistance to airflow. Respir Physiol 1979;37:293–302.
23. England SJ, Harding R, Stradling JR, et al. Laryngeal muscle activities during progressive hypercapnia and hypoxia in awake and sleeping dogs. Respir Physiol 1986;66:327–39.
24. England SJ, Bartlett D Jr. Changes in respiratory movements of the human vocal cords during hyperpnea. J Appl Physiol 1982;52:780–5.
25. Bartlett D Jr, Knuth SL. Human vocal cord movements during voluntary hyperventilation. Respir Physiol 1984;58:289–94.
26. Jackson AC, Gulesian PJ, Mead J. Glottal aperture during panting with voluntary limitation of tidal volume. J Appl Physiol 1975;5:834–6.
27. England SJ, Bartlett D Jr, Knuth SL. Comparison of vocal cord movements during isocapnic hypoxia and hypercapnia. J Appl Physiol 1982;53:82–6.
28. Higenbottam T, Payne J. Glottis narrowing in lung disease. Am Rev Respir Dis 1982;125:746–50.
29. Sekizawa K, Yanai M, Sasaki H, Takishima T. Control of larynx during loaded breathing in normal subjects. J Appl Physiol 1985;60:1887–93.
30. Brancatisano TP, Dodd DS, Collett PW, Engel LA. Effect of expiratory loading on glottic dimensions in humans. J Appl Physiol 1985;58:605–11.
31. Daubenspeck JA, Bartlett D Jr. Expiratory pattern and laryngeal responses to single-breath expiratory resistance loads. Respir Physiol 1983;54:307–16.
32. Higenbottam TN. Narrowing of glottis opening in humans associated with experimentally induced bronchoconstriction. J Appl Physiol 1980;49:403–7.
33. Brancatisano TP, Engel LA. Role of the upper airway in the control of respiratory flow and lung volume in humans. In: Mathew OP, Sant'Ambrogio G, eds. Respiratory function of the upper airway. New York: Marcel Dekker, 1988:447–518.
34. Muller N, Bryan AC, Zamel N. Tonic inspiratory muscle activity as a cause of hyperinflation in histamine induced asthma. J Appl Physiol 1980;49:869–74.
35. Orem J, Norris P, Lydic R. Laryngeal abductor activity during sleep. Chest 1978;73:300–1.
36. Martin RJ, Okken A, Rubin D. Arterial oxygen tension during active and quiet sleep in the normal neonate. J Pediatr 1979;94:271–4.
37. Zamel D, Revow M, England SJ. Expiratory airflow patterns and gas exchange in the newborn infant: results of model simulations. Respir Physiol 1989;75:19–28.
38. Mathew OP, Sant'Ambrogio FB. Laryngeal reflexes. In: Mathew OP, Sant'Ambrogio G, eds. Respiratory function of the upper airway. New York: Marcel Dekker, 1988:259–302.
39. England SJ, Stogryn HAF. Influence of the upper airway on breathing pattern and expiratory time constant in dog pups. Respir Physiol 1986;66:181–92.
40. Stransky A, Szereda-Przestaszewska M, Widdicombe JG. The effects of lung reflexes on laryngeal resistance and motoneuron discharge. J Physiol (Lond) 1973;231:417–38.
41. Jammes Y, Davies A, Widdicombe JG. Tracheobronchial and laryngeal responses to hypercapnia, histamine and capsaicin in dogs. Bull Eur Physiopathol Respir 1985; 21:515–20.
42. Diaz V, Dorion D, Renolleau S, et al. Effects of capsaicin pretreatment on expiratory laryngeal closure during pulmonary edema in lambs. J Appl Physiol 1999;86: 1570–7.
43. Marantz MJ, Vincent SG, Fisher JT. Role of vagal C-fiber afferents in the bronchomotor response to lactic acid in the newborn dog. J Appl Physiol 2001;90:2311–8.
44. Bartlett D Jr. Effects of vagal afferents on laryngeal responses to hypercapnia and hypoxia. Respir Physiol 1980;42:189–98.
45. Jammes J, Barthelemy P, Delpierre S. Respiratory effects of cold air breathing in anesthetized cats. Respir Physiol 1983;54:41–54.
46. Mathew OP, Sant'Ambrogio FB, Sant'Ambrogio G. Effects of cooling on laryngeal reflexes in the dog. Respir Physiol 1985;66:61–70.
47. Wyke BD, Kirchner JA. Neurology of the larynx. In: Hinchcliffe R, Harrison D, eds. Scientific foundations of otolaryngology. London: W Heinemann, 1976:546–74.
48. Bradley RM. Sensory receptors of the larynx. Am J Med 2000;108 Suppl 4a:S47–S500.
49. Isono S. Upper airway muscle function during sleep. Sleep and breathing in children: a developmental approach. In: Loughlin GM, Caroll JL, Marcus CL, eds. Lung biology in health research. Vol. 144. New York: Marcel Dekker, 2000;261–91.
50. Bonora M, Shields GI, Knuth SL, et al. Selective depression by ethanol of upper airway respiratory motor activity in cats. Am Rev Respir Dis 1984;130:156–61.
51. Hwang JC, St John WM, Bartlett D Jr. Respiratory-related hypoglossal nerve activity: influence of anesthetics. J Appl Physiol 1983;55:785–92.
52. Donnelly DF, Haddad GG. Respiratory changes induced by prolonged laryngeal stimulation in awake piglets. J Appl Physiol 1986;61:1018–24.
53. Sanocka UM, Donnelly DF, Haddad GG. Cardiovascular and neurophysiologic changes during graded duration of apnea in piglets. Pediatr Res 1988;23:402–7.
54. Sanocka UM, Donnelly DF, Haddad GG. Autoresuscitation: a survival mechanism in piglets. J Appl Physiol 1992;73:749–53.
55. Donnelly DF, Haddad GG. Effect of graded anesthesia on laryngeal-induced central apnea. Respir Physiol 1986;66: 235–45.
56. England SJ. Current techniques for assessing pulmonary function in the newborn and infant: advantages and limitations. Pediatr Pulmonol 1988;4:48–53.
57. Collett PW, Brancatisano AP, Engel LA. Upper airway dimensions and movements in bronchial asthma. Am Rev Respir Dis 1986;133:1143–9.

58. Downing ET, Braman SS, Fox MJ, Carrao WM. Factitious asthma: physiological approach to diagnosis. JAMA 1982;248:2878–81.
59. Christopher K, Wood RP, Eckert RC, et al. Vocal-cord dysfunction presenting as asthma. N Engl J Med 1983; 308:1566–70.
60. Cohen JI, ed. Upper airway obstruction in asthma. Johns Hopkins Med J 1980;147:233–7.
61. Collett PW, Brancatisano TP, Engel LA. Spasmodic croup in the adult. Am Rev Respir Dis 1983;128:719–23.
62. Johnson P. The development of breathing. In: Jones CT, Nathanielsz PW, eds. The physiological development of the fetus and newborn. London: Academic Press, 1985: 201–10.

CHAPTER 28

Fetal Respiratory Control and Changes at Birth

C.E. Blanco, MD, PhD, M.A. Hanson, MA, DPhil, Cert Ed, FRCOG

Rhythmic thoracic movements are present in utero from early in gestation in animals and human fetuses. This activity is sporadic early in gestation but becomes organized into clusters toward full term. Breathing must change from a periodic nonair intrauterine breathing pattern to a continuous air-breathing pattern during the transition from the intrauterine to the extrauterine environment.

The purpose of breathing activity after birth is to provide oxygenation and remove carbon dioxide by bringing fresh gas into contact with the alveolar membranes. Several physiologic changes must be met after birth to achieve adequate gas exchange. This clear, obligatory, and irreversible change occurs during the exclusion of the umbilical circulation and simultaneously with several other adaptations. In this chapter we discuss the origin of fetal breathing movements (FBMs), their function and responses to respiratory stimuli, and the changes that occur at birth. Understanding the prenatal impact of FBMs on lung growth and the mechanisms involved in the control of FBMs before and during the transition to continuous breathing at birth may give new insights into postnatal pathologic conditions, such as lung hypoplasia, apnea, congenital hypoventilation syndrome, and sudden infant death syndrome. Hence, the study of the physiologic mechanisms underlying the presence of FBMs and the processes occurring at birth is not only of interest to the physiologist but also is important for the neonatologist and pediatrician.

Characteristics of Fetal Breathing Movements

The study of FBMs has been performed almost exclusively using chronically instrumented fetal lambs at various gestational ages. The classic instrumentation is illustrated in Figure 28–1. This preparation has been used successfully because pregnant sheep tolerate fetal surgery without initiating preterm labor, and because fetal size allows for rather complicated instrumentation and procedures. Observations made in fetal sheep preparations have helped clinicians to study the characteristics of FBMs seen in the human fetus by ultrasonography.

Breathing activity in utero is present from early in gestation and is the consequence of rhythmic activation of

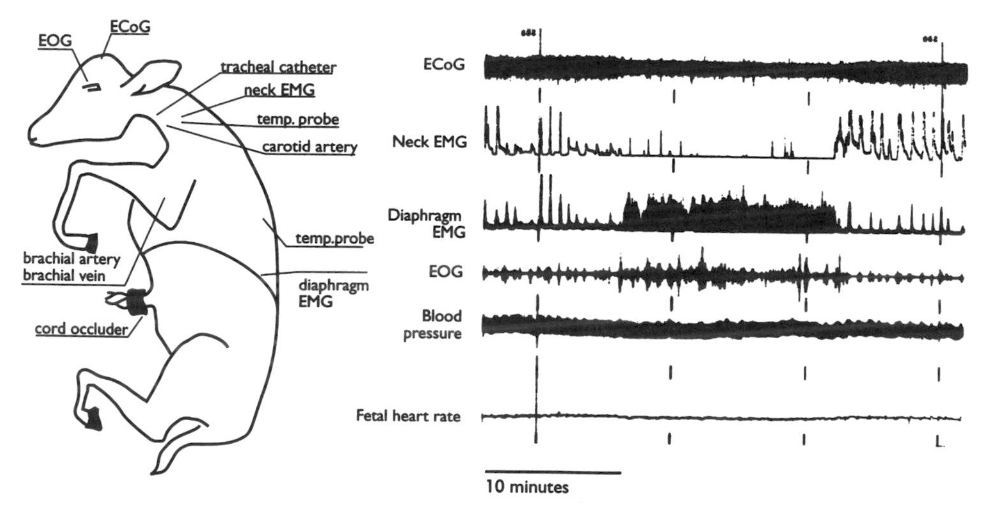

FIGURE 28–1. *Left,* Drawing of a fetal sheep instrumented for chronic recordings. *Right,* A 30-minute period of fetal recording showing from top to bottom: fetal electrocorticogram (ECoG), electromyogram (EMG) of the neck muscles, electromyographic activity of the diaphragm, eye movements recording electro-olfactogram-(EOG), blood pressure, and fetal heart rate. A cord occluder and temperature probe are also used. Neck and diaphragm EMGs and EOG are integrated signals. Note that the activity in diaphragm EMG appears when there is no activity in neck EMG, eyes movements are present, and ECoG voltage is low.

FIGURE 28–2. Simultaneous recording of electromyographic activity of the diaphragm and tracheal pressure. Note that muscle activity precedes the decrease in tracheal pressure.

respiratory neurons in the brain stem;[1,2] however, these breathing movements play no part in fetal gas exchange. The efferent activity of these respiratory neurons activates the respiratory motoneurons and, hence, the muscles (mainly the diaphragm), which generate a negative intrathoracic pressure. Figure 28–2 shows the association of the diaphragm electromyographic (EMG) activity and tracheal pressure in the sheep fetus; Figure 28–3 shows the movements of tracheal fluid with FBMs in the human fetus. Spasm of the diaphragm at 38 days of gestation (term, 147 days) and rhythmic movements of the diaphragm at 40 days of gestation have been described in the fetal lamb.[3] Chronic recordings from fetal lambs in utero performed at approximately 50 days of gestation showed two types of diaphragmatic activity: (1) unpatterned discharge, and (2) patterned, bursting discharge.[4] In the human fetus thoracic movements were observed from 10 to 12 weeks of gestation.[5] At this time in gestation there still is not a clear pattern, and FBMs appear to be uninhibited.

Later in gestation in the fetal lamb (75 to 110 days), movements of the diaphragm start to become periodic Figure 28–4. At this age they are often associated with nuchal muscle activity and rapid eye movements.[6,7] A more definitive pattern starts to appear at 108 to 120 days of gestation, when breathing movements become organized into a more complex state, now associated with the presence of rapid eye movements and nuchal muscle activity.[6–9] At this time in gestation the electroencephalographic activity, specifically, the electrocortical activity (ECoG), still does not show any signs of differentiation. However, by 120 to 125 days of gestation the ECoG shows a clear differentiation into low-voltage, high-frequency activity (range, 13 to 30 Hz; LVECoG) and high-voltage, low-frequency activity (range, 3 to 9 Hz; HVECoG).[6,10,11,12] At 130 days of gestation (Figure 28–5), breathing movements are rapid and irregular with a frequency of 0.1 to 4 Hz and an amplitude of 3 to 5 mm Hg and they produce small movements of tracheal fluid (<1 mL) (see Figure 28–3).[13] There are now two clearly defined fetal behavioral states in the fetal lamb: there is no nuchal muscle activity during LVECoG but rapid eye movements and FBMs are

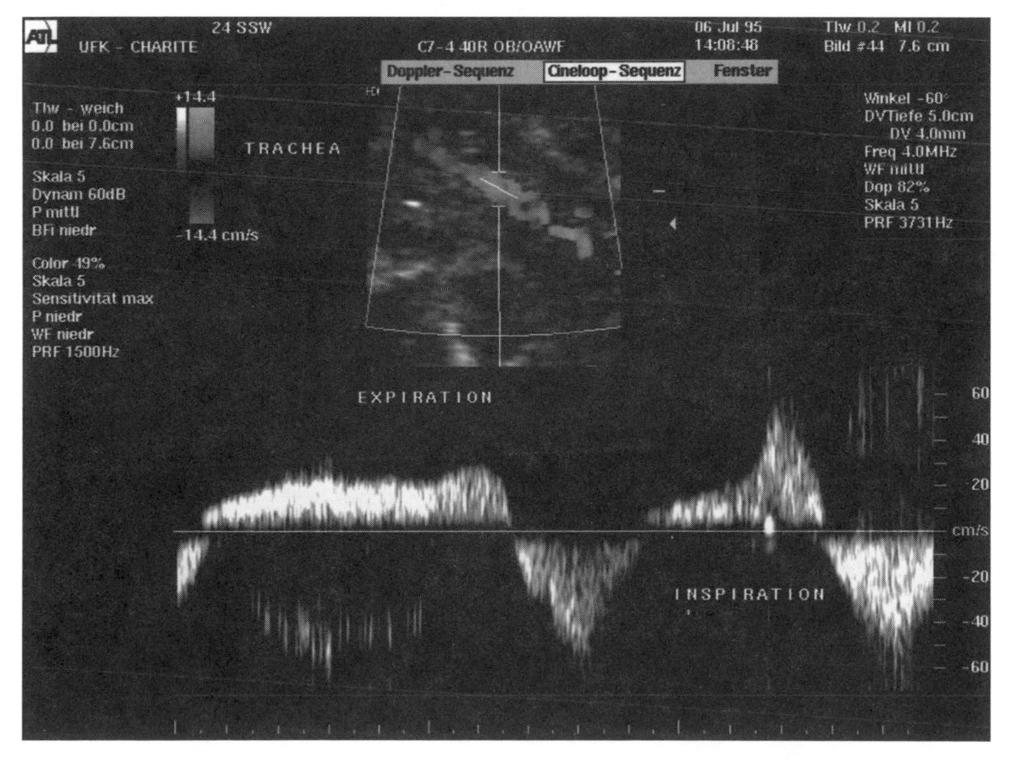

FIGURE 28–3. Velocity waveforms from the trachea in a normal human fetus at 30 weeks' gestation. During fetal breathing movements there is a succession of positive and negative signals corresponding respectively to expiration or inspiration. The pulsed-wave Doppler sample volume is placed over the color signal (red during expiration and blue during inspiration) related to tracheal fluid flow movements generated during breathing activity. The angle between the trachea and the ultrasound beam is kept as small as possible to allow further quantification of the volume displaced per breath. (Courtesy of Dr. Kalache.)

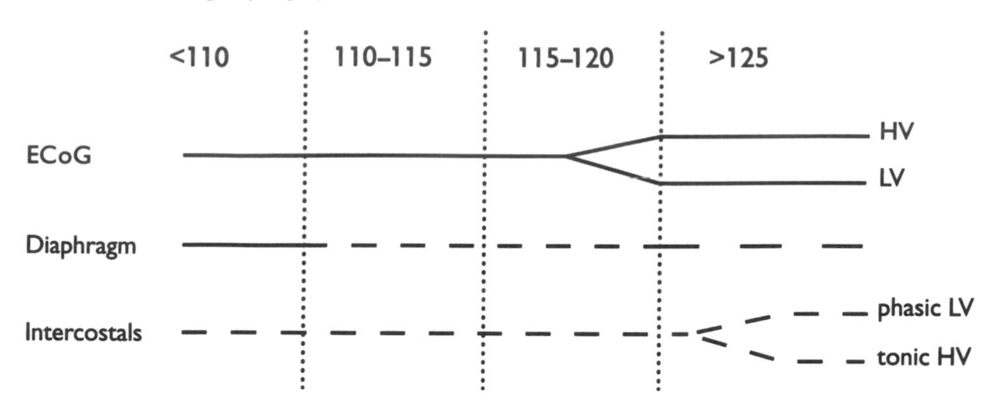

FIGURE 28–4. Diagram showing the activity of electrocorticogram (ECoG), the diaphragm, and intercostal muscles during maturation in the fetal sheep. Note that the ECoG activity is differentiated into low voltage (LV) and high voltage (HV) at between 115 and 120 days of gestation. Some days earlier diaphragmatic activity becomes more organized; these periods of activity become clearer still after the ECoG differentiation. Intercostal muscle activity is present in clusters from early in gestation; later in gestation this activity is differentiated into tonic (HV) and phasic (LV) depending on ECoG state.

present. Polysynaptic spinal reflexes are also relatively inhibited during the LVECoG state.[14] During HVECoG, there are no eye movements or FBMs, but nuchal muscle activity is present and polysynaptic reflexes are stronger (Figure 28–6).[14] The link between ECoG state and FBMs implies either that breathing activity is facilitated (or even stimulated) during LVECoG and/or that it is inhibited during HVECoG. During LVECoG there is more neural activity in cortical and subcortical structures, including the brain-stem reticular formation. This facilitatory state could increase the sensitivity for tonic stimuli, such as the level of arterial CO_2, and generate respiratory output. This hypothesis is supported by the observation that there are no breathing movements during fetal hypocapnia, even during the LVECoG state.[15] Extending this idea, the absence of FBMs during HVECoG could be due to a disfacilitation, as reported during quiet sleep in the adult, when slow waves appear in the electroencephalogram.[16,17] Other evidence also leads us to believe that during HVECoG there is an active inhibition of breathing activity—in fetal sheep FBMs and ECoG were dissociated after the brain stem was transected at the level of the colliculi.[18] Furthermore, FBM response to hypercapnia is limited to LVECoG activity in the intact fetus (Figure 28–7), but hypercapnia can produce continuous breathing in both LV and HVECoG after small bilateral lesions are made in the lateral pons.[19] The mechanisms, origin, and location for this inhibition are not clear, but it is known that it is of

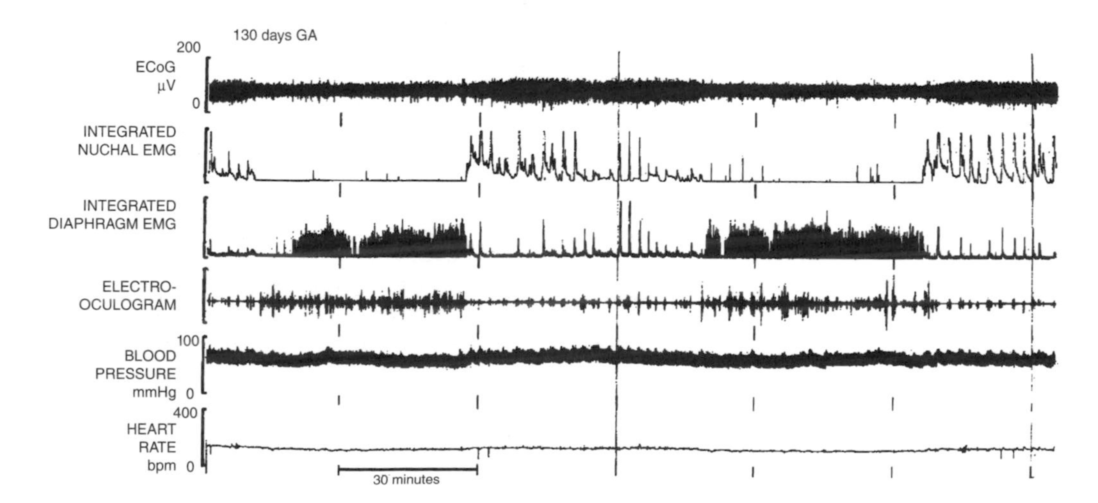

FIGURE 28–5. Chronic recording of a fetal sheep at gestational age (GA) of 130 days. There are two periods of fetal breathing activity represented by diaphragmatic activity associated to low-voltage electrocorticogram (ECoG), absence of neck muscle activity, and rapid eye movements. Note that with the appearance of high-voltage in the ECoG and sustained activity of the neck muscle there is a sudden stop of fetal breathing and eye movements. EMG = electromyogram.

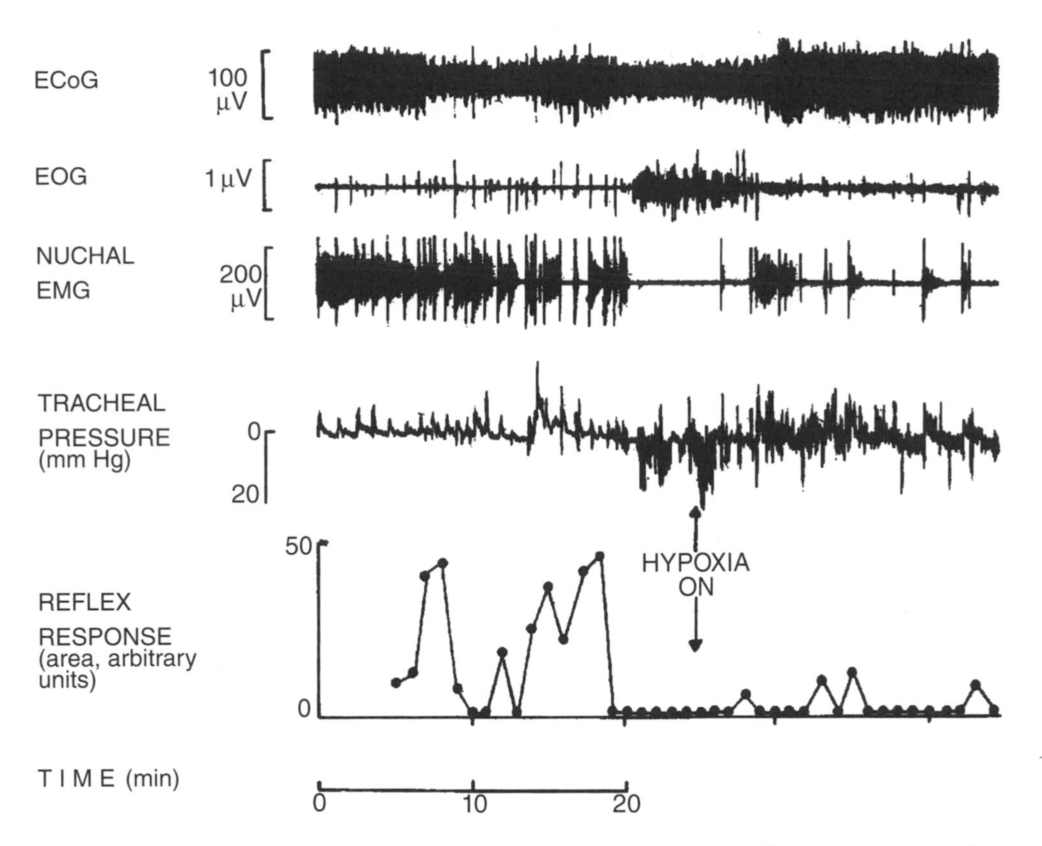

FIGURE 28–6. Association between polysynaptic reflux and fetal breathing movements. This recording shows from top to bottom: Electrocorticogram (ECoG), electro-oculogram (EOG), neck muscle electromyogram (EMG), tracheal pressure, and the amplitude of the polysynaptic reflex. The amplitude of the polysynaptic reflex reflects two types of inhibitory influences: (1) the amplitude of the reflex (expressed in arbitrary units) is decreased during low-voltage ECoG and (2) the amplitude of the reflex does not return to normal values during high-voltage ECoG as expected, due to the presence of fetal hypoxia (induced by exposing the ewe to low inspiratory oxygen indicated by ON in figure). For mechanisms, see text.

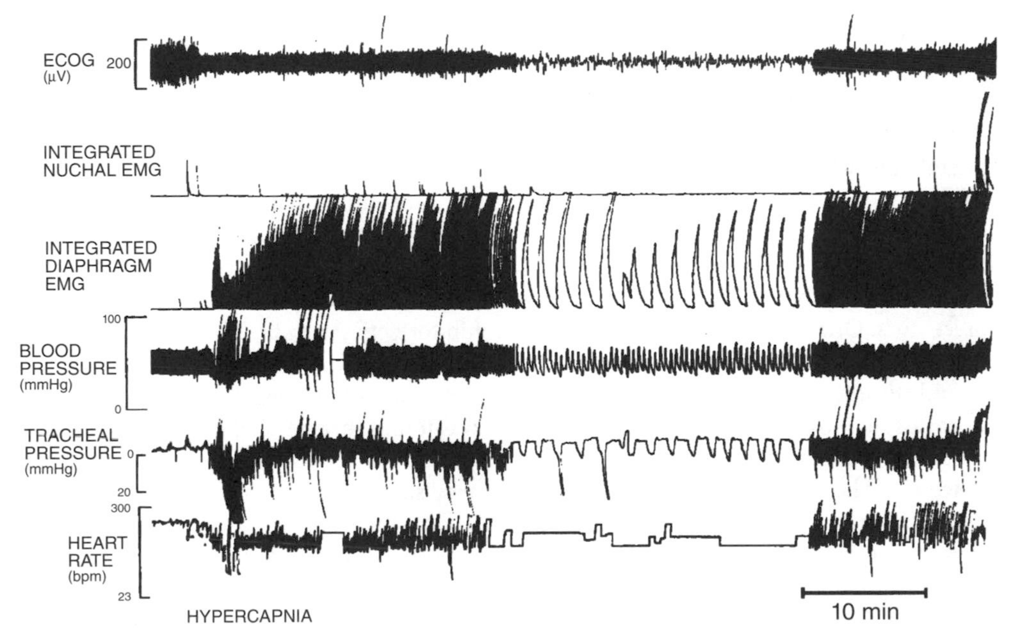

FIGURE 28–7. Fetal breathing movement response to hypercapnia. Fetal partial pressure of arterial CO_2 was 60 mm Hg from the beginning of the recording. Note the high activity in the diaphragm electromyogram (EMG) and the tracheal pressure channel. The recording was set to a high speed to show individual breaths. This response ends when the electrocorticogram (EcoG) switches to high-voltage activity (seen here in the last two minutes).

central origin, and that it can be over-ridden in utero and at the time of birth when breathing becomes continuous.

Central Neural Control of Fetal Breathing Movements

The work of Barcroft[20] gave rise to the concept that inhibitory mechanisms, which descend from higher centers, are involved in producing apneic periods in the fetus. This inhibitory control develops during the second half of gestation. This work also showed that the inhibition of FBMs by hypoxemia is not seen early in gestation, and that descending inhibitory processes develop later. Although the inhibition of FBMs in HVECoG and in hypoxia both involve descending inhibitory processes, they do not necessarily use the same neural mechanisms. Barcroft employed similar brain-stem transection techniques to those of Lumsden[21] to show that neural structures above the level of the pons do not exert significant control over FBMs. These studies were extended by Dawes and co-workers[22] who employed the technique of transection in the chronically instrumented late-gestation fetal sheep. They showed that transection at the level of the upper midbrain/caudal hypothalamus resulted in FBMs that were episodic but not related to the ECoG. These FBMs were still inhibited by hypoxia. These results clarify that the processes that mediate the inhibition of FBMs in HVECoG are different from those that produce the inhibition in hypoxia. Transection through the rostral pons/caudal midbrain produced FBMs that occurred almost continuously and were not inhibited by hypoxia. This focused attention on the upper pons for the inhibition of FBMs in hypoxia. Gluckman and Johnston[23] pursued this theory by making lesions in the rostrolateral pons, and they compiled a diagram showing areas not needed for the inhibition to be manifest, and the location of an area in the lateral pons which, if lesioned bilaterally, prevented the inhibition.

One of the key questions that emerged from these brain-stem studies was whether the descending inhibitory mechanism is capable of inhibiting the input from peripheral chemoreceptors. Once it had been established that the peripheral chemoreceptors are active in utero and respond to natural stimuli such as hypoxia or hypercapnia (see below), it was no longer necessary to view the effect of modest hypoxia in inhibiting FBMs as a direct depression of the medulla. The results of transection and lesion studies suggested that stimulation of FBMs occurred during hypoxia after the damage to the brain stem, as if a stimulatory effect of the peripheral chemoreceptors had been unmasked. Direct confirmation of this idea came from the study of Johnston and Gluckman[24] who conducted a two-stage procedure: first, lesions were placed in the brain stem as before to prevent the inhibition of FBMs in hypoxia or to give an overt stimulation; this was then prevented by chemodenervation at a second operation.

The nature (and indeed the location) of the inhibitory processes is not known. Because the inhibition occurs even in chemodenervated fetuses,[25] it is clear that the neurons involved do not receive an excitatory input from the chemoreceptors. They may therefore be chemoreceptors themselves or receive input from other cells thought to be sensitive to hypoxia, for example, those in the rostral ventrolateral medulla (RVLM).[26] The neural activity as a whole behaves as a chemoreceptor, because the chemoreceptor stimulant drug almitrine mimics the effects of hypoxia in inhibiting FBMs, irrespective of the integrity of the peripheral chemoreceptors.[27] As expected from the above discussion, the stimulatory effect of the drug on the peripheral chemoreceptors becomes manifest only when lesions were placed in the lateral pons,[28] unmasking its peripheral actions.

Chemoreceptor Function In Utero

The concept that peripheral chemoreceptors can produce effects on breathing can be traced to experiments conducted over 50 years ago,[20] in which breathing was shown to be stimulated in exteriorized midgestation animal fetuses by hypoxia or cyanide.[29] In late gestation, the dominant descending inhibitory effects on breathing arise from the fetal brain stem in hypoxia and with HVECoG (see above). It was perhaps the increasing interest in these processes that caused the scientific community to lose sight of the implications of the earlier observations. The idea became prevalent that the carotid chemoreceptors were quiescent in utero and were activated at birth, perhaps by the increase in sympathetic nervous activity. In addition, when it became clear that normal fetal arterial partial pressure of O_2 (P_{O_2}) in late gestation, both in the sheep and the human fetus, was about 25 mm Hg, it was thought that if the chemoreceptors were functional, they would be stimulated so intensely that powerful reflex effects would be induced continuously. This clearly was not the case, although it had been shown that brain-stem transection removed inhibitory effects on breathing[20,22] and permitted a stimulation in hypoxia. It was therefore essential to readdress the question of arterial chemoreceptor function in utero. It was found that both carotid[30] and aortic[31] chemoreceptors were active spontaneously at the normal arterial P_{O_2} in fetal sheep and that they responded with an increase in discharge if P_{O_2} fell or P_{CO_2} rose. There were several important implications of these findings. First, it was clear that the peripheral chemoreceptors would be able to stimulate fetal breathing under some circumstances but that it was the balance between this stimulatory input and the normally dominant inhibitory input from higher centers that determined the characteristics of fetal breathing (see above). Second, attention was redirected to the role that the carotid chemoreceptors play in initiating cardiovascular reflex responses to hypoxia.[32,33] Reflexes are the first-line defense of the fetus against reduced oxygen supply from the placenta, and understanding them is of clinical as well as scientific importance. Last, the observation that the fetal peripheral chemoreceptors discharge spontaneously (at ~5 Hz) at the normal fetal arterial P_{O_2} made it clear that the rise in P_{O_2} at birth would silence these chemoreceptors. Their sensitivity to P_{O_2} would then have to reset to the adult range postnatally, and this has generated research into the mechanisms of this resetting.[34,35]

Pharmalogic Control of Fetal Breathing Movements

A range of factors that would be expected to lower tissue P_{O_2} in the central nervous system (CNS) mimic hypoxia and inhibit FBMs, for example, CO poisoning,[36] oligomycin B,[37] and anemia.[38] Adenosine also is released in neural tissue during hypoxia; it stimulates the peripheral chemoreceptors but reduces respiratory output in the fetus and neonate. The stimulation of FBMs by adenosine after caudal brain-stem transection[39] is explicable in terms of the removal of descending inhibitory processes discussed earlier. In addition, the role of glutamate as an excitatory amino acid, recently has been addressed in the fetus and the neonate.[40,41]

Adrenergic agonists and antagonists also have been used to investigate catecholamines in the control of FBMs. Murata et al[42] showed that noradrenaline inhibits FBMs in the rhesus monkey, whereas isoproterenol, a β-adrenergic agonist, stimulates FBMs. However, Bamford et al[43] showed that the α_2-agonist clonidine increases FBMs and the α_2-antagonist idazoxan inhibits FBMs in fetal sheep. As α_2-adrenoreceptors exert a presynaptic inhibition on noradrenaline release, it has been suggested that noradrenaline stimulates rather than inhibits FBMs as indicated by Murata et al.[42] In a subsequent study, Bamford and Hawkins[44] showed that the α_2-adrenergic antagonist MSDL 657743 also stimulated FBMs in normoxia and maintained FBMs during hypoxia in the fetal sheep; a similar effect was reported by Giussani et al[45] after treatment with phentolamine, an α_1- and α_2-antagonist. Furthermore, Joseph and Walker[46] blocked the reuptake of noradrenaline from the synaptic cleft in fetal sheep and showed that FBMs were increased initially and then decreased, presumably owing to a depletion of presynaptic stores of noradrenaline. The conclusion is that noradrenaline stimulates FBMs, but that the predominant action of these drugs is on the presynaptic α_2-adrenergic receptor, which, when stimulated, inhibits endogenous release of noradrenaline.

Prostaglandins exert a powerful influence on FBMs and postnatal breathing. Prostaglandin E_2 (PGE_2) decreases the incidence of FBMs,[47] whereas meclofenamate and indomethacin, inhibitors of PG synthesis, increase FBMs.[48–50] The effect of prostaglandins appears to be central, as it is independent of the peripheral chemoreceptors[51] and because central administration of meclofenamate stimulates FBMs.[52,53] The same effects can be produced postnatally, with PGE_2 decreasing, and meclofenamate and indomethacin increasing, ventilation in lambs.[54,55] However, the change in the concentration of PGE_2 that occurs around birth cannot be solely responsible for either the decrease in FBMs seen immediately before birth,[50,56] or the onset of continuous breathing postnatally.[57] The well-established effects of ethyl alcohol to reduce the incidence of FBMs[58] are not mediated by prostaglandin[59] but by adenosine.[60]

Bennet et al[61] showed that large doses of thyroid-releasing hormone (TRH) can induce stimulation of FBMs. This effect may occur at the level of the respiratory neurons where TRH can be localized, but its physiologic significance is not known. This also may be true of the effects of the cholinergic agonist pilocarpine and serotonin (5-HT) precursor L-5-hydroxytryptophan (L-5-HTP).[62,63] Both of these agents stimulate FBMs, but pilocarpine induces LVECoG, and L-5-HTP induces HVECoG. This stresses again the coincidental rather than causal relationship between FBMs and LVECoG. Serotonin has been implicated in neural mechanisms controlling adult sheep, but the site of action in the fetus is not known. A range of opiates have effects on FBMs[64] but the physiologic localization of their effects have not been established.

The high rate of progesterone synthesis by the placenta in late gestation exposes the fetus to high concentrations of progesterone and its metabolites. Progesterone can influence fetal behavior, and normal progesterone production tonically suppresses arousal or wakefulness in the fetus.[65,66]

Finally, one of the striking aspects of FBMs is that FBMs cease 24 to 48 hours before parturition. The mechanism involved is not known. Kitterman et al[48] excluded a rise in plasma PGE_2, and Parkes et al[67] showed that the cease of FBMs did not occur if the fall in plasma progesterone was prevented.

Fetal Breathing Movements and Lung Growth

Fetal breathing movements are necessary for fetal lung growth and maturation. By opposing lung recoil, FBMs help to maintain the lung expansion that is known to be essential for normal growth and structural maturation of the fetal lungs. Fetal breathing movements induce complex and variable changes in thoracic dimensions; these induce small alterations in the shape of the lungs that may act as a stimulus to lung growth. The prolonged

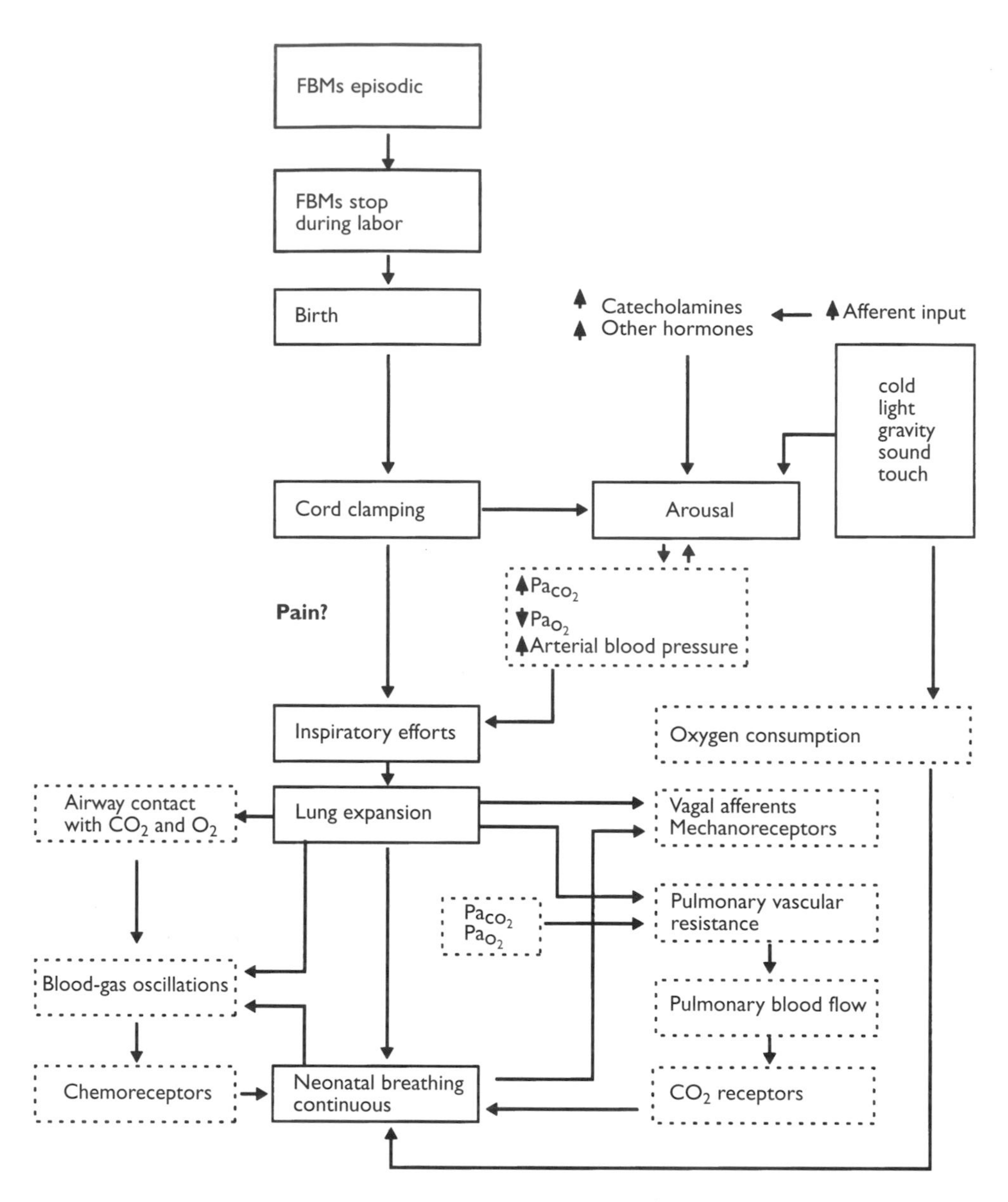

FIGURE 28–8. Diagram showing possible mechanisms involved in the changes on breathing activity during the transition at birth. (Reproduced with permission from Blanco C. Role of the brain stem in the changes at birth: initiation of continuous breathing and its maintenance. In the fetal and neonatal brain stem. In: Hanson MA, ed. Developmental and clinical issues. Cambridge: Cambridge University Press, 1991.)

absence or impairment of FBMs is likely to result in a reduced mean level of lung expansion, which can lead to hypoplasia of the lungs.[68] Moreover, static distension decreases steady state surfactant protein A (SP-A) and SP-B messenger ribonucleic acid (mRNA) levels in whole lung, whereas cyclic stretching increases SP-B and SP-A expression two- to fourfold and enhances 3H-choline incorporation into saturated phosphatidylcholine.[69]

Changes in Breathing and Behavior at Birth

At birth breathing activity must become continuous to fulfill its gas exchange function. After occlusion of the umbilical cord, the neonatal ECoG still cycles between low- and high-voltage states, which seem to have identical spectral characteristics to the fetal states. Low voltage ECoG activity is associated with the absence of nuchal muscle activity, the presence of rapid eye movements, and inhibition of polysynaptic reflexes, whereas HVECoG is associated with the presence of nuchal muscle activity, lack of rapid eye movements, and enhanced polysynaptic reflexes.[70] However, despite the fact that after birth the HVECoG state seems to be similar to the equivalent fetal state, breathing activity is present. The reason for this is not known, and its determination may require detailed spectral analysis of the ECoG from different areas of the brain before birth and during the first hours of postnatal life (Figure 28–8). It is worth noting that some mammals, such as the rat, cat, and rabbit, develop organized behavioral states 2 to 3 weeks after birth; however, they do not breathe continuously in utero and these species demonstrate the same transition to continuous breathing after birth as do more precocial species.

Studies of the mechanisms involved in the establishment of continuous breathing at birth have followed two lines: (1) attempts to induce continuous breathing in utero or (2) observation of establishment of continuous breathing during situations aimed at mimicking birth.

Induction of Continuous Breathing In Utero

It is well established that the inhibition of FBMs during HVECoG can be over-ridden, as demonstrated by the presence of continuous breathing during metabolic acidosis;[71,72] administration of prostaglandin synthetase inhibitors,[48,49,53] 5-HTP,[63,73] catecholamines,[74] pilocarpine,[62] TRH,[75] corticotropin-releasing factor,[61] central or peripheral fetal cooling;[76,77] and by lesions within the CNS (see above). These experiments show that FBMs can become continuous through the operation of various mechanisms including disinhibition during HVECoG, changes in the balance between stimulatory and inhibitory neuromodulators, increased arousability, and changes in chemoreceptor sensitivity.[78] Some, but not all, of these mechanisms are likely to play an important role at birth.

Establishment of Continuous Breathing during Simulated Birth

Experiments designed to observe changes in breathing activity after cord occlusion have led to two main hypotheses: (1) The exclusion of fetal-placental circulation leads to the disappearance of hormones or neuromodulators that exert continuous tonic inhibition (through the CNS) during fetal life; this allows continuous breathing postnatally.[79–82] There are reports indicating that an unidentified substance originating from placental tissue can inhibit fetal breathing activity.[83] Although this is a possible explanation, it is not yet demonstrated that such a substance is responsible for the modulation by ECoG of FBMs. Recently it was shown that breathing movements of goat fetuses maintained in an extrauterine incubation system for more than 24 hours were episodic, suggesting that intermittent breathing movements are intrinsic to the fetus, independent of placenta-derived factors.[84] (2) Breathing activity is dependent on the level of Pa_{CO_2} in utero and at birth.[15] It is known that during hypocapnia fetal and neonatal breathing is reduced.[15,77,79] Hypercapnia stimulates breathing activity, but this is inhibited in utero during quiet sleep.[80] However, this inhibition can be over-ridden if there are lesions in the lateral pons[19] or when hypercapnia is combined with cooling.[77] This over-ride might be explained by changes in the CO_2 sensitivity of central and/or peripheral chemoreceptors or by changes in the balance between central inhibitory and excitatory mechanisms caused by an increase in afferent input at birth. In this hypothesis, both changes in afferent input from chemo- and thermoreceptors to the CNS, and/or changes in CNS sensitivity to these inputs, are important in the transition from fetal to neonatal breathing. Changes in the plasma level of a placental neuromodulator at birth may then serve to maintain postnatal breathing after its initiation. More insight into these mechanisms may offer an explanation for the occurrence of apneic periods after birth.

Insights from Studies in the Neonate

Studies to identify brain-stem mechanisms that regulate breathing have been conducted in the neonate, in which hypoxia also inhibits breathing but after a transient chemoreceptor-mediated stimulation. It is theorized that the secondary fall in ventilation is produced by similar inhibitory processes to those that operate in the fetus. Transection of the brain stem through the rostral pons does, indeed, remove the secondary fall in ventilation,[85] as does placement of lesions in the lateral pons.[86] However, these studies did not identify any clear group of neurons involved in mediating the effect. Recent attention has focused on the red nucleus, located above the pons in the mesencephalon. The transection studies implicate structures in either the rostral pons or caudal mesencephalon, so it is likely that the red nucleus would be affected. In neonatal rabbits, electrical stimulation of the red nucleus produces a profound inhibition of respiratory output, and bilateral lesions in the red nucleus prevent the inhibition of respiratory output in hypoxia, while not affecting the cardiovascular responses. Evidence that neurons in the red nucleus are involved in this effect comes from the observation that chemical stimulation with glutamate also produces an inhibition of respiratory output.[87] Interestingly, the efferent pathway for these cells, the rubrospinal tract, runs in precisely the ventrolateral region of the pons lesioned by Gluckman and Johnston in their fetal studies.[23]

The observations on the red nucleus are interesting, because, in postnatal life, it has been implicated in producing the hypotonia of postural muscles, which occurs in rapid eye movement sleep. Such hypotonia also occurs in the fetus,[30] but it is associated with the presence, not absence, of FBMs. Once again, behaviorally related and hypoxia-induced inhibition of FBMs appears to be distinct. In addition, the brain-stem reticular formation and related nuclei associated with sleep and arousal have not been studied greatly in the postnatal period. In one study, Moore et al[88] reported that cooling the locus coeruleus by a few degrees, sufficient to reduce neuronal activity but not conducted action potentials, prevented the secondary

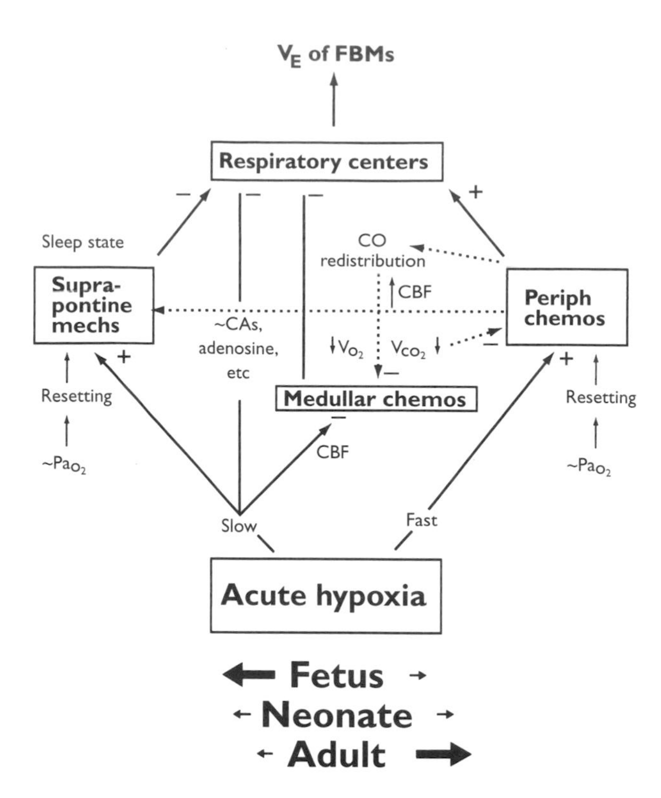

FIGURE 28–9. Simplified diagram presenting the different main mechanisms involved in the control of breathing in the fetus, neonate, and adult individual during acute hypoxia. Inhibitory mechanisms (mechs) originating in suprapontine areas are predominant in the fetus, whereas peripheral chemoreceptors (chemos) become progressively important postnatally. The structures or "centers" sensitive to the level of Pa_{O_2} in utero should reset their thresholds after birth when the level of Pa_{O_2} increases. V_E = minute ventilation; FBMs = fetal breathing movements; CA's = catecholamines; CO = cardiac output; CBF = cerebral blood flow; V_{O_2} = oxygen consumption; V_{CO_2} = carbon dioxide production.

fall in ventilation in hypoxia in neonatal lambs. The locus coeruleus has been implicated in producing arousal at birth.[89] There are also reports that structures as high in the brain as the thalamus are implicated in the descending inhibition of breathing during hypoxia.[90]

While the effects of acute hypoxia on FBMs have been studied widely, the effects of prolonged hypoxemia are quite different. Over a period of 6 to 12 hours, FBMs return to their control incidence, as does cycling of the EcoG.[91] Recent studies reveal that the peripheral chemoreceptors are necessary for the return of FBMs during sustained hypoxia produced by reduced uterine blood flow, but the mechanisms involved are not known.[92]

Conclusion

Spontaneous breathing movements are present during fetal life and they are important for normal development of the fetal lungs (Figures 28–9 and 28–10). Early in gestation they seem to represent free-running activity of the respiratory centers-not controlled by peripheral mechanisms but probably dependent on a tonic CO_2 drive. Maturation of sleep states brings into play powerful brain-stem inhibitory mechanisms that control this activity. Birth clearly involves some irreversible processes such as the transition to continuous breathing. However, breathing remains linked to behavioural and sleep states in the neonate as in the fetus, and clearly there is continuity of some control processes from late gestation to early postnatal life. Some of these processes mature relatively slowly after birth, such as the resetting of chemoreceptor hypoxia sensitivity and the diminishing influence of descending inhibitory effects on breathing in hypoxia. Understanding these effects is of vital importance to the prevention of SIDS and the care of newborn, especially preterm, babies.

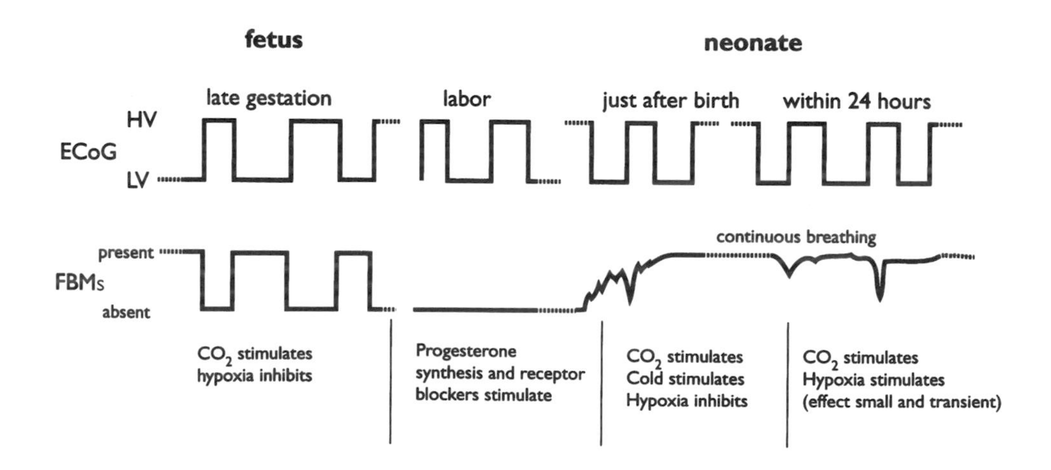

FIGURE 28–10. Summary of the main mechanisms involved in the control of fetal and early neonatal breathing. The roles of electrocorticography (ECoG) modulation, carbon dioxide, hypoxia, labor, and birth are emphasized. HV = high voltage; LV = low voltage; FBMs = fetal breathing movements. (Reproduced with permission from Gluckman PD, Heymann MA. Pediatrics and perinatology. Oxford: Arnold, 1996.)

References

1. Bystrzycka E, Nail B, Purves MJ. Central and peripheral neural respiratory activity in the mature sheep fetus and newborn lamb. Respir Physiol 1975;25:199–215.
2. Bahoric A, Chernick V. Electrical activity of phrenic nerve and diaphragm in utero. J Appl Physiol 1975;39:513–8.
3. Barcroft J. Researches on pre-natal life. Illinois: Charles C Thomas Publisher, 1946:261–6.
4. Cooke IRC, Berger PH. Precursor of respiratory pattern in the early gestation mammalian fetus. Brain Res 1990; 522:333–6.
5. Vries de JIP, Visser GHA, Prechtl HFR. The emergence of fetal behavior. 1. Qualitative aspects. Early Hum Dev 1982;7:301–22.
6. Clewlow R, Dawes GS, Johnston BM, Walker DW. Changes in breathing, electrocortical and muscle activity in unanaesthetized fetal lambs with age. J Physiol 1983; 341:463–76.
7. Ioffe S, Jansen AH, Chernick V. Maturation of spontaneous fetal diaphragmatic activity and fetal response to hypercapnia and hypoxemia. J Appl Physiol 1987; 62:609–22.
8. Bowes G, Adamson TM, Ritchie BC, et al. Development of patterns of respiratory activity in unanaesthetized fetal sheep in utero. J Appl Physiol 1981;50:693–700.
9. Szeto HH, Cheng PY, Decena JA, et al. Developmental changes in continuity and stability of breathing in the fetal lamb. Am J Physiol 1992;262:R452–8.
10. Dawes GS, Fox HE, Leduc BM, et al. Respiratory movements and rapid eye movements sleep in the fetal lamb. J Physiol (Lond) 1972;404:587–9.
11. Szeto HH, Vo TDH, Dwyer G, et al. The ontogeny of fetal lamb electrocortical activity: a power spectral analysis. Am J Obstet Gynecol 1985;153:462–6.
12. Szeto HH. Spectral edge frequency as a simple quantitative measure of maturation of electrocortical activity. Pediatr Res 1990;27:289–92.
13. Harding R, Bocking AD, Sigger JN. Influence of upper respiratory tract on liquid flow to and from fetal lungs. J Physiol 1986;61:68–71.
14. Blanco CE, Dawes GS, Walker DW. Effects of hypoxia on polysynaptic hind-limb reflexes of unanaesthetized fetal and new-born lambs. J Physiol 1983;39:453–4.
15. Kuipers IM, Maertzdorf WM, De Jong DS, et al. Effects of mild hypocapnia on fetal breathing and behavior in unanaesthetized normoxic fetal lambs. J Appl Physiol 1994;76:1476–80.
16. Steriade M, Contreras D, Amzica F. Synchronized sleep oscillations and their paroxysmal developments. Trends Neurosci 1994;17:199–208.
17. Phillipson EA, Bowes G, Townsend ER, et al. Carotid chemoreceptors in ventilatory response to changes in venous CO_2 load. J Appl Physiol 1981;51:1398–403.
18. Dawes GS, Gardner WN, Johnston BM, et al. Breathing in fetal lambs: the effects of brain stem section. J Physiol 1983;335:535–53.
19. Johnston BM, Gluckman PD. Lateral pontine lesion affects central chemosensitivity in unanaesthetized fetal lambs. J Physiol 1989;67:1113–8.
20. Barcroft J. The brain and its environment. New Haven: Yale University Press, 1938:44.
21. Lumsden T. Observations on the respiratory centers. J Physiol 1923;57:354–67.
22. Dawes GS. The central control of fetal breathing and skeletal muscle movements. J Physiol 1984;346:1–18.
23. Gluckman PD, Johnston BM. Lesions in the upper lateral pons abolish the hypoxic depression of breathing in unanaesthetized fetal lambs in utero. J Physiol 1987; 382:373–83.
24. Johnston BM, Gluckman PD. Peripheral chemoreceptors respond to hypoxia in pontine-lesioned fetal lambs in utero. J Appl Physiol 1993;75:1027–34.
25. Moore PJ, Parkes MJ, Nijhuis JG, et al. The incidence of breathing movements in fetal sheep in normoxia and hypoxia after peripheral chemodenervation and brain stem transection. J Dev Physiol 1989;11:147–51.
26. Nolan PC, Dillon GH, Waldrop TG. Central hypoxic chemoreceptors in the ventro-lateral medulla and caudal hypothalamus. Adv Exp Med Biol 1995;393:261–6.
27. Moore PJ, Hanson MA, Parkes MJ. Almitrine inhibits breathing movements in fetal sheep. J Dev Physiol 1989; 11:277–81.
28. Johnston BM, Moore PJ, Bennet L, et al. Almitrine mimics hypoxia in fetal sheep with lateral pontine lesions. J Appl Physiol 1990;69:1330–5.
29. Hanson MA. Peripheral chemoreceptor function before and after birth. In: Johnston BM, Gluckman P, eds. Respiratory control and lung development in the fetus and newborn. Ithaca, NY: Perinatology Press, 1986; 311–30.
30. Blanco CE, Dawes GS, Hanson MA, et al. The response to hypoxia of arterial chemoreceptors in fetal sheep and newborn lambs. J Physiol 1984;351:25–37.
31. Blanco CE, Dawes GS, Hanson MA, et al. The arterial chemoreceptors in fetal sheep and newborn lambs. J Physiol 1982;330:38P.
32. Bartelds B, Van Bel F, Teitel DF, et al. Carotid, not aortic, chemoreceptors mediate the fetal cardiovascular response to acute hypoxemia in lambs. Pediatr Res 1993;34:51–5.
33. Giussani DA, Spencer JAD, Moore PJ, et al. Afferent and efferent components of the cardiovascular reflex responses to acute hypoxia in term fetal sheep. J Physiol 1993;461:431–49.
34. Blanco CE, Hanson MA, McCoocke HB. Effects on carotid chemoreceptor resetting of pulmonary ventilation in the fetal lamb in utero. J Dev Physiol 1988;10:167–74.
35. Kumar P, Hanson MA. Re-setting of the hypoxic sensitivity of aortic chemoreceptors in the newborn lamb. J Dev Physiol 1989;11:199–206.
36. Koos BJ, Matsuda K, Power GG. Fetal breathing and sleep state responses to graded carboxyhemoglobinemia in sheep. J Appl Physiol 1988;65:2118–23.
37. Koos BJ, Sameshima H, Power GG. Fetal breathing movement, sleep state and cardiovascular responses to an inhibitor of mitochondrial ATPase in sheep. J Dev Physiol 1986;8:67–75.
38. Matsuda K, Ducsay C, Koos BJ. Fetal breathing, sleep state and cardiovascular adaptations to anaemia in sheep. J Physiol 1992;445:713–23.

39. Koss BJ, Chao A, Doany W. Adenosine stimulates breathing in fetal sheep with brain stem transection. J Appl Physiol 1992;72:94–9.
40. Bissonnette JM, Hohimer AR, Knopp SJ. Non-NMDA receptors modulate respiratory drive in fetal sheep. J Physiol 1997;501:415–23.
41. Navarro H, Suguihara C, Soliz A, et al. Effect of L-aspartate on the ventilatory response to hypoxia in sedated newborn piglets. Biol Neonate 1998;73:387–94.
42. Murata Y, Martin CB, Miyake K, et al. Effects of catecholamines on fetal breathing activity in rhesus monkeys. Am J Obstet Gynecol 1981;139:942–7.
43. Bamford OS, Dawes GS, Ward RA. Effects of α_2-adrenergic agonist clonidine and its antagonist idazoxan on the fetal lamb. J Physiol 1986;381:29–37.
44. Bamford OS, Hawkins LH. Central effects of an α_2-adrenergic antagonist on the fetal lamb: a possible mechanism for hypoxic apnea. J Dev Physiol 1990;13:353–8.
45. Giussani DA, Moore PJ, Spencer JAD, et al. α_1 and α_2-adrenoreceptor actions of phentolamine and prazosin on breathing movements in fetal sheep in utero. J Physiol 1995;486:249–55.
46. Joseph SA, Walker DW. Catecholamine neurons in fetal brain; effects on breathing movements and electrocorticogram. J Appl Physiol 1990;69:1903–11.
47. Kitterman JA, Liggins GC, Fewell JE, et al. Inhibition of breathing movements in fetal sheep of sodium meclofenamate. J Physiol 1983;54:687–92.
48. Kitterman JA, Liggins GC, Clements JA, et al. Stimulation of breathing movements in fetal sheep by inhibitors of prostaglandin synthesis. J Dev Physiol 1979;1:453–66.
49. Wallen LD, Murai DT, Clyman RI, et al. Regulation of breathing movements in fetal sheep by prostaglandin E_2. J Appl Physiol 1986;60:526–31.
50. Patrick J, Challis JRG, Cross J. Effects of maternal indomethacin administration on fetal breathing movements in sheep. J Dev Physiol 1987;9:295–300.
51. Murai DT, Wallen LD, Lee CC, et al. Effects of prostaglandins in fetal breathing do not involve peripheral chemoreceptors. J Appl Physiol 1987;62:271–7.
52. Koos BJ. Central effects on breathing in fetal sheep of sodium meclofenamate. J Physiol 1982;330:50–1P.
53. Koos BJ. Central stimulation of breathing movements in fetal lambs by prostaglandin synthetase inhibitors. J Physiol 1985;362:455–66.
54. Guerra FA, Savich RD, Clyman RI, et al. Meclofenamate increases ventilation in lambs. J Dev Physiol 1988;11:1–6.
55. Long WA. Prostaglandins and control of breathing in newborn piglets. J Appl Physiol 1988;64;409–18.
56. Wallen LD, Murai DT, Clyman RI, et al. Effects of meclofenamate on breathing movements in fetal sheep before delivery. J Appl Physiol 1988;64:759–66.
57. Lee DS, Choy P, Davi M, et al. Decrease in plasma prostaglandin E_2 is not essential for the establishment of continuous breathing at birth in sheep. J Dev Physiol 1989;12:145–51.
58. Smith GN, Brien JF, Homan J, et al. Effect of ethanol on ovine fetal and maternal plasma prostaglandin E_2 concentrations and fetal breathing movements. J Dev Physiol 1990;14:23–8.
59. Smith GN, Brien JF, Homan J, et al. Indomethacin reversal of ethanol-induced suppression of ovine fetal breathing movements and relationship to prostaglandin E_2. J Dev Physiol;1990:14:29–35.
60. Watson CS, White SE, Homan JH, et al. Increase cerebral extracellular adenosine and decreased PGE_2 during ethanol-induced inhibition of FBM. J Appl Physiol 1999;86:1410–20.
61. Bennet L, Johnston BM, Vale WW, et al. The central effects of thyrotropin-releasing factor and two antagonists on breathing movements in fetal sheep. J Physiol 1990; 421:1–11.
62. Hanson MA, Moore PJ, Nijhuis JG, et al. Effects of pilocarpine on breathing movements in normal, chemodenervated and brain stem-transected fetal sheep. J Physiol 1988;400:415–24.
63. Fletcher DJ, Hanson MA, Moore PJ, et al. Stimulation of breathing movements by L-5-hydroxytryptophan in fetal sheep during normoxia and hypoxia. J Physiol 1988;404:7575–89.
64. Hasan SU, Lee DS, Gibson DA, et al. Effect of morphine on breathing and behavior in fetal sheep. J Appl Physiol 1988;64:2058–65.
65. Crossley KJ, Nicol MB, Hirst JJ, et al. Suppression of arousal by progesterone in fetal sheep. Reprod Fertil Dev 1997;9:767–73.
66. Nicol MB, Hirst JJ, Walker D, et al. Effect of alteration of maternal plasma progesterone concentrations on fetal behavioural state during late gestation. J Endocrinol 1997;152:379–86.
67. Parkes MJ, Moore PJ, Hanson MA. The effects of inhibition of 3-B hydroxysteroid dehydrogenase activity in sheep fetuses in utero. Cairn: Proceedings of The Society for the Study of Fetal Physiology, 1988:58.
68. Harding R. Fetal pulmonary development: the role of respiratory movements. Equine Vet J Suppl 1997;24:32–9.
69. Sanchez-Esteban J, Tsai SW, Sang J, et al. Effects of mechanical forces on lung-specific gene expression. Am J Med Sci 1998;316:200–4.
70. Blanco CE, Dawes GS, Walker DW. Effects of hypoxia on polysynaptic hind-limb reflexes in new-born lambs before and after carotid denervation. J Physiol 1983;339:467–74.
71. Molteni RA, Melmed MH, Sheldon RE, et al. Induction of fetal breathing by metabolic acidemia and its effects on blood flow to the respiratory muscles. Am J Obstet Gynecol 1980;136:609–20.
72. Hohimer AR, Bissonnette JM. Effects of metabolic acidosis on fetal breathing movements in utero. Respir Physiol 1981;43:99–106.
73. Quilligan EJ, Clewlow F, Johnston BM, et al. Effects of 5-hydroxytryptophan on electrocortical activity and breathing movements of fetal sheep. Am J Obstet Gynecol 1994;141:271–5.
74. Jansen AH, Ioffe S, Chernick V. Stimulation of fetal breathing activity by beta-adrenergic mechanisms. J Appl Physiol 1986;60:1938–45.
75. Bennet L, Gluckman PD, Johnston BM. The effects of corticotrophin-releasing hormone on breathing movements and electrocortical activity of the fetal sheep. J Physiol 1988;23:72–5.

76. Gluckman PD, Gunn TR, Johnston BM. The effect of cooling on breathing and shivering in unanaesthetized fetal lambs in utero. J Physiol 1983;343:495–506.
77. Kuipers IM, Maertzdorf EJ, De Jong DS, et al. Initiation and maintenance of continuous breathing at birth. Pediatr Res 1997;42:163–8.
78. Lagercrantz H, Pequignot JM, Hertzberg T, et al. Birth-related changes of expression and turnover of some neuroactive agents and respiratory control. Biol Neonate 1994;65:145–8.
79. Adamson SL, Richardson BS, Homan J. Initiation of pulmonary gas exchange by fetal sheep in utero. J Appl Physiol 1987;62:989–98.
80. Boddy K, Dawes GS, Fisher R, et al. Foetal respiratory movements, electrocortical activity and cardiovascular responses to hypoxaemia and hypercapnia in sheep. J Physiol 1974;243:599–618.
81. Adamson SL, Kuipers IM, Olson DM. Umbilical cord occlusion stimulates breathing independent of blood gases and pH. J Appl Physiol 1991;70:1796–809.
82. Sawa R, Asakura H, Power G. Changes in plasma adenosine during simulated birth of fetal sheep. J Appl Physiol 1991;70:1524–8.
83. Alvaro RE, Rehan V de Almeida Z, Robertson M, et al. Specificity of a placental factor inhibiting breathing in fetal sheep. Reprod Fertil Dev 1996;8:423–9.
84. Kozuma S, Nishina H, Unno N, et al. Goat fetuses disconnected from the placenta, but reconnected to an artificial placenta, display intermittent breathing movements. Biol Neonate 1999;75:388–97.
85. Martin-Body RL. Brain transections demonstrate the central origin of hypoxic ventilatory depression in carotid body-denervated rats. J Physiol 1988;407:41–52.
86. Martin-Body RL, Johnston BM. Central origin of the hypoxic depression of breathing in the young rabbit. Respir Physiol 1988;71:25–32.
87. Ackland GL, Noble R, Hanson MA. Red nucleus inhibits breathing during hypoxia in neonates. Respir Physiol 1997;110:251–60.
88. Moore PJ, Ackland GL, Hanson MA. Unilateral cooling in the region of locus coeruleus blocks the fall in respiratory output during hypoxia in anaesthetized neonatal sheep. Exp Physiol 1996;81:983–94.
89 Lagercrantz H. Stress, arousal and gene activation at birth. Pediatr Res 1996;11:214–8.
90. Chau AF, Matsurura M, Koos B. Glutamate receptors in the thalamus stimulate breathing and modulate sleep state in fetal sheep. J Soc Gynecol Invest 1996;3:252A,388.
91. Bocking AD, Harding R. Effects of reduced uterine blood flow on electrocortical activity, breathing and skeletal muscle activity in fetal sheep. Am J Obstet Gynecol 1986;154:655–62.
92. Stein P, White SE, Homan J, et al. Altered fetal cardiovascular responses to prolonged hypoxia after sinoaortic denervation. Am J Physiol 1999;276:R340–6.

CHAPTER 29

Postnatal Development of Respiratory Control

Jay P. Farber, PhD

In humans, there are substantial changes in resting breathing pattern during the postnatal period. Most obvious are an increase in duration of inspiration and slowing of respiratory rate. There is also considerable instability of breathing pattern in normal term infants at birth that decreases over a relatively short period of time, but in premature infants instability of breathing pattern remains prominent. Recent investigations offer important insight into basic origins of breathing rhythm (see also Chapter 28) as well as its maturation. Particularly provocative findings have come from in vitro studies using the neonatal rodent nervous system, in which the respiratory rhythm generator is examined in a reduced state.

The role of blood levels of O_2 and CO_2 in modifying breathing pattern during the postnatal period continues to receive considerable attention in human studies and those using animal models. The interest is twofold: (1) the potential role of chemoreception in the development and maintenance of normal respiratory output, and (2) how chemoreception in infants is used to respond to asphyxiant stresses during the postnatal period. There have been several efforts to examine the contribution of chemoreceptors and chemoreceptor pathways to postnatal pathologies, most notably, sudden death in infants (sudden infant death syndrome [SIDS]). These efforts include studies in which possible risk factors for SIDS, such as prenatal exposure to certain drugs of abuse, have been considered. Other investigations have sought to improve our basic understanding of chemoreception and its effects on ventilation. In humans and other species, the ventilatory response to hypoxia matures with respect to both augmentation and suppression of respiratory output. Premature infants, and also some newborn animals, have less of a ventilatory response to increased CO_2 than do infants of a later postnatal period. A variety of in vivo and in vitro animal models have been used effectively to help advance our understanding of these issues. Another exciting and powerful approach is the use of genetic knockout animals or other types of genetic manipulation to gain insight into processes underlying respiratory organization and integration.

This chapter primarily examines the contribution of relatively recent literature to our understanding of postnatal maturation of respiratory control. Such an effort requires the usual caveats with respect to the use of different species and now includes potential limitations of extrapolating from results using in vitro systems. For the former, it is clear that nervous system maturation differs at birth among species, and this can skew the interpretation of postnatal effects. In vitro systems have reduced amounts of nervous system tissue and, in some cases, part of that tissue is not well oxygenated. In addition, patterns of respiratory output generally differ from those typically found in intact animals.

Maturation of Breathing Pattern

Some Developmental Characteristics in Human Infants

Studies in normal term sleeping infants have shown that breathing pattern initially exhibits great variability, which decreases dramatically over the first few days of life.[1] Over the first several months of life, major changes in respiratory timing include an increase in inspiratory duration and slowing of breathing rate during rapid eye movement (REM) and non-REM sleep.[2] Further, periodic breathing, paradoxical movement of the chest wall, and breathing pauses (> 2 s) during sleep all have been shown to decrease over several postnatal months.[3] Siblings of infants who died of SIDS could not be differentiated from control infants with these same variables.[3] Maturation also has been associated with small reductions in periodic breathing intervals in sleeping infants born at normal term, but these changes were larger when infants were born prematurely.[4,5] To more closely examine overall respiratory variability as a potential predictor of SIDS, an index of dispersion of breaths among sequential epochs was used to show that variability around low breathing frequencies was less for infants that subsequently died of SIDS than for age-matched (2 days to 2 months) controls.[6] Also pauses in breathing of between 4 and 30 s during both REM and non-REM sleep were fewer for SIDS infants at about 2 months of age in comparison with controls, but were not different from controls during the early postnatal period.[7] Spontaneous deep breaths or sighs generally are associated with lung mechanoreceptor as well as chemoreceptor activity. Schäfer et al[3] noted that such breaths often preceded an apneic event, but Alvarez et al[8] found that the incidence of spontaneous deep breaths could not be used to predict the occurrence of spontaneous apnea. Nevertheless, the incidence of spontaneous deep breaths was greater in premature infants compared with term infants and also was greater during REM sleep than non-REM sleep.[8] Power law distributions have been used recently to help characterize breathing patterns of premature and older infants.[9] This analysis showed that a single exponent of a power function could characterize the incidence of inadequate breathing or hypopnea. The exponent changed with age to show that the incidence of hypopnea decreased. This effect was modeled in terms of age-dependent increases in tonic input to the respiratory rhythm generator,[9] but considerable caution is required when invoking a specific neural mechanism.[10]

PreBötzinger Complex: A Putative Site for Respiratory Rhythm Generation

Basic characteristics

In vitro preparations from rodent brain stem have produced a crucial basic observation that strongly influences current hypotheses to explain respiratory rhythm generation. Specifically, there is a restricted region of the ventrolateral medulla, called the preBötzinger complex, that is required for respiratory bursting in rodent brain stem or brain slice preparations.[11] Some respiratory neurons in this region have pacemaker properties, that is, they burst spontaneously, and the rate of bursting depends upon membrane potential.[11] These neurons are hypothesized to be critical for generating such respiratory output.[11,12] Pacemaker neurons of preBötzinger complex have been characterized further with optical recordings using calcium-sensitive dye along with neuronal recordings. When burst-generating circuitry was interrupted, pacemaker neurons became desynchronized. This suggested that synaptic coupling was necessary to achieve a bursting output.[13] Currents underlying these pacemaker properties are not identified, but a recent model proposes that a persistent sodium current undergoes rapid activation and then is slowly inactivated.[14] Alternatively (or possibly additionally), it has been proposed that this same general region of the medulla could generate respiratory bursting without invoking pacemaker properties. This model is based on observed neurons that are depolarized by phasic input and then show relatively well-sustained hyperpolarization. When these neurons are organized into a network, a bursting output is produced.[15] This appears to be similar to the concept of excitation followed by activity-dependent suppression of neural network activity proposed by O'Donovan and Chub[16] to explain bursting properties of immature spinal cord. Recently preBötzinger inspiratory neurons, with characteristics necessary for network bursting, were shown to have receptors for substance P and opioids. These receptors may be significant in peptidergic modulation of respiratory frequency.[17] About half of the neurons in this category also had pacemaker properties.

The transmission of rhythmic respiratory drive in the in vitro rodent preparation requires glutamatergic neurotransmission within the preBötzinger region and, further, depends on activation of non-NMDA (*N*-methyl-D-aspartate), as opposed to NMDA, glutamate receptors.[18,19] In fact, mice lacking the gene to produce the critical R1 subunit of the NMDA receptor expressed a respiratory rhythm in vitro that did not differ from controls.[20] Blockade of inhibitory neurotransmission did not stop respiratory bursting in the rodent in vitro system.[21] Although preBötzinger region clearly has received the most recent attention, there is a more rostrally located group of spontaneously bursting respiratory neurons.[22] These cells have been categorized as being preinspiratory. Similar to activity in the preBötzinger complex, blockade of inhibitory neurotransmission could not stop the bursting output of these rostrally located cells.[23] In the mature mouse, some ventrolateral medullary neurons with preinspiratory discharge maintained a bursting discharge during blockade of synaptic transmission.[24] This suggests that pacemaker neurons are part of a normal respiratory rhythm generating circuit, but it does not prove that these neurons are required to produce the respiratory rhythm.

Comparison of results from in vitro and in vivo studies

While glutamatergic non-NMDA receptors are crucial for transmitting respiratory drive in in vitro preparations, results using receptor blockers in intact animals can be much less dramatic. Borday et al[25] studied unanesthetized neonatal (0 to 2 days old) mice and cats after systemic blockade of NMDA and/or non-NMDA receptors. Blockade of non-NMDA receptors in neonatal mice strongly decreased frequency of breathing, but lethal suppression of breathing did not occur until NMDA receptors were blocked as well. Much smaller effects of non-NMDA-receptor blockade were observed in adult mice as well as neonatal and adult cats. Apneustic breathing patterns were observed after combined receptor blockade in adult mice and neonatal and adult cats; this response was attributed to blockade of rostral pontine mechanisms.[25] In this study, the cat, but not the mouse, showed developmental changes in respiratory timing that resembled those found in human maturation. In contrast to results in conscious animals, systemic non-NMDA-receptor blockade either weakened or abolished respiratory (phrenic) motor output in adult decerebrate or pentobarbital-anesthetized cats.[26] Subsequently, it was possible to re-establish respiratory rhythm by elevation of CO_2 levels. It was argued by Borday et al[25] that synaptic mechanisms, probably involving central chemosensitivity, helped to maintain the respiratory network with glutamatergic receptor blockade in conscious intact animals.

Respiratory burst generation: the preBötzinger basis for eupneic breathing?

The most persistent controversy with respect to results from in vitro systems is the relationship of the in vitro respiratory output in rodents to eupnea in intact animals. In vitro preparations tend to have much lower rates of ventilatory bursting with a relatively long burst duration. At least in the early postnatal period, the hypoglossal or cervical motor root burst has a decrementing pattern. Further, maintenence of bursting pattern requires the use of elevated potassium levels in the perfusate in many, but not all, studies. Explanation for the patterns obtained have included the relatively low temperature of the perfusate (~ 28 to 29° C), lack of volume and flow-dependent feedback from lungs, and the reduced amount of neural tissue involved in rhythm generation. None of the preceding issues disqualify the in vitro rodent system as representing basic processes relevant to eupneic breathing. However, it also has been proposed that the burst pattern seen in in vitro systems better corresponds to the gasping breathing pattern observed during severe hypoxic insults. Gasps occurred in hypoxia-insulted intact animals after a period of hyperventilation followed by apnea.[27] The burst pattern of inspiratory motor outflow during gasping lacked the ramp increase observed during eupnea and typically was seen as a brief abrupt effort.

Both eupnea and gasping can be expressed in decerebrate or anesthetized newborn rats.[28] Further, young (8 to 15 days old) decerebrate rats receiving unilateral microinjection of the excitotoxin kainic acid into the preBötzinger region showed suppression of anoxia-induced gasping in most instances, without eupnea being affected consistently.[29] Contrary to this result, blockade of presynaptic N-calcium channels in preBötzinger region of anesthetized adult cats could induce transient apnea that was made permanent using the sodium-channel blocker tetrodotoxin. Under these conditions, hypoxia could still induce gasping.[30] Similarly, when kainic acid was placed in preBötzinger region of anethetized adult cats, apnea could occur.[31] There have been other strenuous objections to the idea that in vitro respiratory rhythm represents gasping. This includes the possible confusion between preBötzinger region and gasping centers in some cited studies as well as the fact that hypoxia does not occur in the preBötzinger region with several in vitro preparations.[15] Notwithstanding the preceding, a recent study by St Jacques and St John[32] extended the type of experiment performed by Pierrefiche et al[26] and is particularly thought provoking. These authors verified that muscimol or kainic acid could induce apnea in some instances when injected unilaterally or bilaterally into preBötzinger region of adult decerebrate rats. However, peripheral chemoreceptor stimulation could temporarily induce eupneic breathing from an apneic animal, and eupneic breathing would resume spontaneously in these animals, typically in less than an hour. This is generally considered to be within the interval that local neural circuits remain suppressed by the drugs used. The authors postulated that preBötzinger region provides excitatory (tonic) input to pontomedullary respiratory circuitry, the loss of which may be easier to overcome in a decerebrate rather than anesthetized animal. Further, since respiration can be driven by chemoreceptor input during apnea, it appears that the preBötzinger region is not required for generating a eupneic respiratory rhythm in adult rats. Note, however, that gasping was still present in several preparations exhibiting apnea.[32] This suggests that there is still uncertainty in our understanding of relationships between anatomic location and functional respiratory output.

Developmental Role of Inhibitory Neurotransmission

In vitro results

In vitro studies in the mouse have produced results of particular interest with respect to development, since medullary slice preparations can be successfully implemented to weaning age. This contrasts with the 0- to 4-day postnatal period most commonly used for in vitro studies in the rat. Intact anesthetized and unanesthetized mice generally had a similar developmental pattern to that observed in humans, that is, prolongation of inspiration and respiratory cycle length[33] (but see[25,34]). Using a tilted sagittal slice (in vitro) preparation from mice of different ages, recordings from hypoglossal neurons (as an index of inspiratory output) showed similar qualitative changes in inspiration and cycle length as for intact animals.[33] With the tilted sagittal slice, large portions of dorsal and ventral respiratory group remain intact. Major developmental changes were observed with respect to inhibitory neurotransmission. Blockade of inhibitory glycinergic input using strychnine in the tilted sagittal slice during the first several postnatal days had no effect on respiratory output. However, after the second postnatal week, bursting rhythm was disrupted severely.[35] Blockade of the γ-aminobutyric acid $(GABA)_A$ receptor using bicuculline also modified neonatal and mature preparations differently. For younger animals there was an increase in inspiratory burst discharge duration and an increase in cycle length;[35] this was comparable to effects obtained from in vitro preparations using newborn rats.[21] Preparations from mature animals on the other hand showed decreased burst duration and respiratory cycle length.[35] At all ages bicuculline caused irregularities in rhythm. Application of the same antagonists to the surface of ventrolateral medulla of anesthetized mice produced similar developmental changes.[35] These results using both in vivo and in vitro preparations are of particular interest because of the comparable behavior of a relatively isolated medullary network to intact preparations. Nonetheless, caution with respect to interpretation of the above in vitro results is required, because individual hypoglossal neurons were tested rather than the mixed output of the hypoglossal nerve. This introduces the possibility that the recorded neurons do not represent the overall output of respiratory neurons.

Alternatively, transverse sections through the medulla can be obtained that contain the preBötzinger region. Use of these sections allows retention of the respiratory output to the upper airway via the hypoglossal nerve, but it excludes other regions of relevance to breathing located in rostral medulla and pons. In contrast to results with the tilted sagittal slice, strychnine caused decreases in respiratory cycle length in animals in the immediate postnatal period as well as in older animals; hypoglossal burst amplitude also increased. There was no suppression of respiratory rhythm.[34] Other evidence of maturation was that the inspiratory output from the hypoglossal nerve changed its character with age from a sharply decrementing discharge to a discharge showing a slower rise and fall of activity.[34] This could reflect an inhibitory modulation of the hypoglossal output, but it also might be due to age-dependent changes in electrophysiologic properties of hypoglossal motor neurons.[36] Another age-dependent difference was that in the immediate postnatal period each preBötzinger neuronal burst caused one burst of activity in the hypoglossal nerve. However, in older mice a coupling occurred between preBötzinger and hypoglossal bursts at a ratio of about 3:1.[34]

The role of inhibitory neurotransmission in respiratory rhythm generation presumably is linked to reciprocal inhibition between inspiratory and expiratory components of the network. In medullary slices from newborn rats, expiration-phased neurons received glycinergic but not GABAergic inhibitory input during inspiration.[37] Nevertheless, as with previous examples, glycinergic input was not required for respiratory rhythm to occur. Using blockade of glycine and $GABA_A$ receptors, effects similar to the burst pattern for the transverse medullary slices from mice were reported.[34,37] Although immaturity of intracellular-extracellular chloride gradient has been implicated in converting effects of inhibitory neurotransmission to an excitatory response,[38] reversal potentials for chloride were at typical adult values in the expiration-phased neurons studied.[37] The $GABA_B$ metabotropic receptor also can modulate respiratory output of in vitro rodent preparations through G protein–coupled change in K^+ conductance.[39] Developmentally, low-voltage-activated Ca^{++} currents in rhythmic neurons of the preBötzinger region were increased by a $GABA_B$-agonist during the early postnatal period, but the same drug decreased these currents during the second postnatal week. In contrast, high-voltage-activated Ca^{++} currents were always decreased by a $GABA_B$-agonist.[40]

In vivo studies

In the arterially perfused adult decerebrate rat, blockade of $GABA_A$ receptors using bicuculline or picrotoxin caused respiratory frequency and amplitude of phrenic nerve discharge to increase. Hypoglossal nerve discharge usually was increased as well. Likewise, glycine-receptor blockade did not eliminate respiratory output, but a low-chloride concentration in the perfusate suppressed respiratory activity.[41] Effects were more dramatic in the adult anesthetized cat, in which bilateral blockade of preBötzinger glycinergic or $GABA_A$ergic plus glycinergic neurotransmission suppressed rhythmic respiration.[42] Taken together, these results suggest that inhibitory neurotransmission is important for expression of breathing rhythm in mature animals.

Role of the Pons

The functional role of the pons in respiratory rhythmogenesis during maturation has been considered in both in vivo and in vitro systems. In decerebrate vagotomized neonatal rats, ablation or lesion of the pontine tegmentum increased inspiratory burst duration between birth and 22 days of age. This effect usually was combined with a decrease in breathing rate. Effective lesioning sites included the rostrolateral pons (parabrachial and Kölliker-Fuse nuclei).[43] Thus, in the rat, the pons appears functional at birth. In opossums, activation of pontine structures using glutamate also produced effects on breathing pattern. The youngest animals tested (~2 to 3 postnatal weeks old) often responded with apnea, but other patterns could be elicited. Older animals generally responded with augmented breathing, usually as an increase in amplitude of diaphragm electromyogram (EMG), with variable effects on breathing rate. It was suggested that rostral pontine input at younger ages may, under some circumstances, disrupt respiratory rhythm.[44] Another insight into pontine respiratory function has been provided using Krox 20 knockout mice. This knockout produces defective hindbrain segmentation such that rhombomeres 3 and 5 are eliminated. Neurons associated with rhombomere 3 (including trigeminal motor and reticular pontine tegmental nuclei) are lost. Intact homozygous Krox 20 knockouts breathed slowly at birth and had many apneic episodes. The hypoventilation disappeared in surviving Krox 20 knockouts over several days, although breathing rate was slower than normal.[45] Similarly, the newborn in vitro Krox 20 preparations, with pons and medulla intact, also had relatively slow respiratory burst rates; however, transection between pons and medulla produced an increase in respiratory burst rate to levels consistent with the normal mouse. The authors argued that caudal pons showed rhythm-promoting effects that were not present in the knockout mice.[45] Of potential interest with respect to pontine modulation of breathing pattern in humans is the case report in which a

TABLE 29–1. Minimal Neurotransmission Requirements for Respiratory Burst Generation

Type of Study	Subject: Newborn	Subject: Adult
In vitro	Non-NMDA glutamatergic	–Non-NMDA glutamatergic –Inhibitory glycinergic?
In vivo	–Non-NMDA glutamatergic –NMDA glutamatergic –Inhibitory amino acids???	–Non-NMDA glutamatergic –NMDA glutamatergic –Inhibitory amino acids

NMDA = *N*-methyl-D-aspartate.

serotonin (5-HT1A) antagonist reversed severe apneusis in a 2-year-old child who had a tumor removed from the pontomedullary region.[46] Apneusis is well known to occur in anesthetized vagotomized animals after lesion of specific rostral pontine nuclei. On the other hand, 5-HT agonists and antagonists also can have prominent respiratory effects at the medullary level.[47]

Summary

While there remain important unresolved questions, studies using in vitro rodent respiratory-rhythm generator and related studies in intact animals have provided new insights with respect to development of brain circuits in respiratory control. These insights are summarized in Figure 29–1 and Table 29–1 and include the following ideas:

1. The reduced respiratory-rhythm generator of neonatal rodents uses preBötzinger neurons with pacemaker and/or other specific electrophysiologic properties in a network dominated by non-NMDA glutamatergic neurotransmission.
2. Tonic and/or phasic synaptic inputs from several possible sources may contribute to expression of the respiratory rhythm.
3. Non-NMDA glutamatergic neurotransmission also has a major influence on the respiratory output of intact rodent neonates, but NMDA-related mechanisms may have more importance in newborns of other species.
4. In more mature mammalian systems, there is increased tolerance for loss of non-NMDA mechanisms.
5. Inhibitory amino acids help to maintain respiratory output in adult animals, and some evidence suggests that glycinergic mechanisms are especially crucial in this regard. Further, the preBötzinger region may be a critical site for inhibitory interactions. It has not been determined whether inhibitory amino acids could play an important role in maintaining respiratory output in some neonates born at a more developed stage than rodents.

Chemoreceptor Modulation of Breathing and Breathing Pattern

Responses to Challenges during Postnatal Development of Humans

Much of the long-term interest in this issue has revolved around the possibility that defects in chemical regulation of breathing could lead to clinical conditions such as apnea of prematurity or major pathologic events such as SIDS. Developmental studies in infants and children have included infants believed to be at risk for SIDS based on

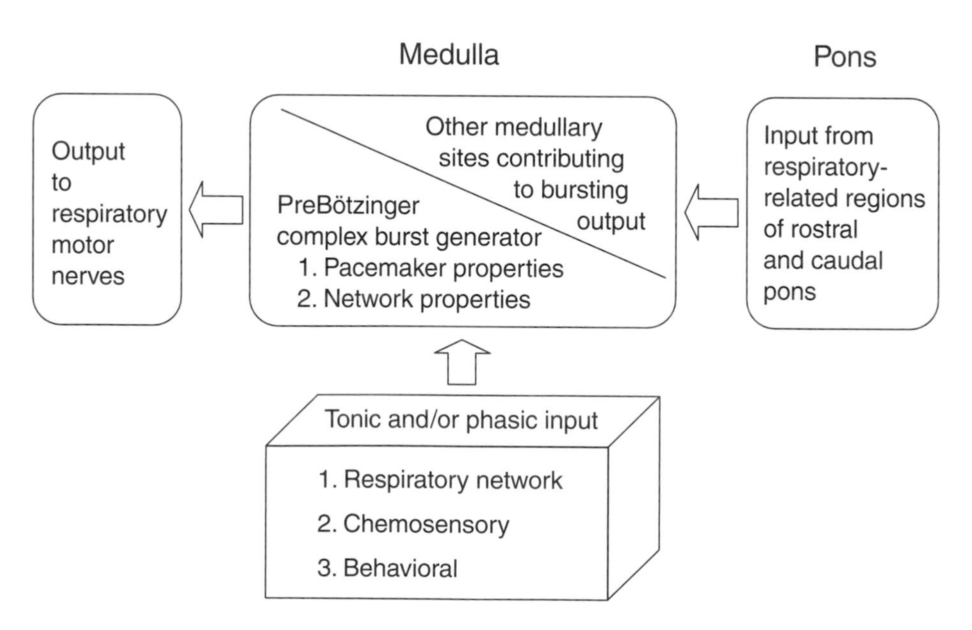

FIGURE 29–1. Components of respiratory-rhythm generation in the central nervous system. Block diagrams relate rhythm-generating properties of the medulla to their basic inputs and outputs.

criteria such as spontaneous respiratory events, belonging to populations at increased risk for SIDS, or being siblings of SIDS infants.

Responses to hypercapnia

Relative ventilatory increases with hypercapnia seem little changed over the first few months of postnatal development;[48] these responses also appear to differ little between newborns and adults.[49] Recent studies have filled in the time ranges of observation. For example, one investigation using a relatively large population could show no age-related changes in percent increase in ventilation per millimeter of mercury increase in CO_2 from the first month to first year of life during non-REM sleep.[3] A similar result was observed in a study carried out in infants between 3 weeks and 3 months of age.[50] End-tidal or transcutaneous P_{CO_2} values when breathing air were age independent and were close to 40 mm Hg in the preceding studies. Children of about 10 years of age were tested in the awake state with CO_2 rebreathing[51] and had responses that generally were comparable to the younger population. Studies using infants with apparent life-threatening events (ALTEs) or siblings of SIDS infants typically have shown no difference in hypercapnic ventilatory responses from "normal" as infants or as older children.[3,51–53] Similarly, infants of mothers who abused narcotics and/or cocaine "during pregnancy" showed relatively subtle effects on hypercapnic ventilatory response when studied between 3 weeks and 5 months of age. However, shifts to the left of the hypercapnic response curve were seen at 3 weeks and 2 months, with a decreased slope of response being present at 2 months.[50] Despite the preceding results, support for the idea that defective chemoreception could be a factor in SIDS has been obtained from postmortem studies of brain tissue from SIDS and non-SIDS infants. In humans, medullary arcuate nucleus may be the equivalent of the ventral medullary surface that participates in chemoreception. Projections exist from the arcuate nucleus to the medullary raphe system,[54] which, likewise, may have chemoreception and/or other circuitry influencing responses to hypercapnia.[55,56] In infants who died and were diagnosed with SIDS, the arcuate nucleus showed decreases in binding of both kainate (glutamatergic) and muscarinic (cholinergic) receptors.[57,58]

In contrast to the preceding, responses of premature infants to hypercapnia are clearly less than those of older infants.[59] Several factors may contribute to ventilatory limitations during CO_2 inhalation in the premature infant, the most obvious being immaturity of chemoreflex mechanisms. A study by Frantz et al[60] showed that occlusion pressure, a generally recognized index of central output, was greatly reduced during CO_2 rebreathing. This occurred in parallel with reduced ventilatory output in premature infants of approximately 30 weeks' gestational age. Although this suggests a deficient chemoreflex response, it is not possible to infer whether the sensory mechanism or integrative processes are immature. Further, the effect also could involve reflex or mechanical properties of the immature thorax. Other factors could play a role in the deficient response of premature infants. For example, an inhibitory airway reflex, resulting in a breathing pause, occurred with a large hypercapnic challenge in premature (31 week old) but not normal term infants.[61] Also, expiratory braking during hypercapnia in premature infants is associated with a decreased breathing rate.[62] Another study of hypercapnic responses in premature infants (35 weeks post conception) showed a smaller rib cage contribution to ventilation responses when infants were tested in the supine position, but overall effect of body position on the hypercapnic response was less clear.[63]

Responses to hypoxia

CHEMOREFLEX. Ventilatory responses related to blood oxygenation can be relatively complex, but the rapidity of peripheral chemoreceptor response to blood oxygenation allows assessment of the initial stimulatory effect. Inhalation of a single breath of O_2 during non-REM sleep did not produce different weight-normalized ventilatory responses at 1, 2, and 3 postnatal months.[64] Similarly, there were no apparent changes in ventilatory response to alternation in O_2 concentration between ~2-day-old and 47-day-old infants.[65] Nonetheless, increases of chemoreflex response could be observed between birth and postnatal day 8 during non-REM sleep, suggesting that there are changes in chemoreflex activity during the early postnatal period.[66] Chemoreflex activity is also present in premature infants,[67,68] but premature infants with bronchopulmonary dysplasia did not respond to alternating breaths of low O_2 at ~38 weeks post conception.[67] However, a group of premature infants with chronic lung disease and lacking an apparent oxygen chemoreflex at birth developed a rapid ventilatory response to hyperoxic challenge by about the 15th postnatal week on average.[69] Animal studies (to be presented later) suggest that early hypoxemia could have impaired the development of carotid body chemoreception of affected infants.

RESPONSES TO SUSTAINED HYPOXIA. With sustained hypoxia in infants, there is a well-characterized increase in breathing followed by a reduction in ventilation. A recent study of premature infants showed that this biphasic response would persist into the second month of postnatal life, but this only represented a postconceptional age of about 35 weeks.[70] There is also evidence that very small preterm infants show only a decrease in ventilation with hypoxia.[71] Even term infants may retain the biphasic response characteristic for at least 2 months when tested with normal bedding at a room temperature of

24°C during non-REM sleep.[72] Since hypoxia can reduce O_2 consumption in newborn mammals,[73] part of the reduction in alveolar (~arterial) P_{CO_2} that accompanies hypoxia could be due to a parallel reduction in CO_2 output. If that is true, the secondary fall in ventilation could be due to the resulting fall in P_{CO_2}. However, similar reductions in ventilation during hypoxia occurred when the fall in arterial P_{CO_2} was partially occluded by inhalation of up to 2% CO_2.[74] A study using a relatively small group of infants (ages 2 to 12 months) born to mothers who smoke showed that no increase in mouth occlusion pressure occurred during hypoxia, whereas it increased in control subjects.[75] This would be an important deficit if it was repeatable in a larger population with better control for age.

Arousal and chemoreceptor stimulation

Besides effects on ventilation, whether an infant arouses with hypoxic and/or hypercapnic stimuli may have relevance to clinical syndromes such as SIDS in certain at-risk groups. The ability to arouse also may play a role in the accidental asphyxiation of infants. This issue has been considered periodically. One relatively recent investigation compared infants born to mothers who are smokers and mothers who are nonsmokers. These infants were tested at between 2 and 3 months of age with progressive lowering of inspired O_2 (5-min intervals at 17%, 15%, and 13% inspired O_2); 85% of 34 infants from mothers who are nonsmokers showed arousal. In the same study, only about 50% of the infants of mothers who smoke aroused during the hypoxic challenge. Infants aroused with hypercapnia at about the same end-tidal P_{CO_2} regardless of whether the mothers were smokers.[76] Similarly, during the first postnatal week, the majority of infants born to substance-abusing mothers showed a lack of arousal to 80 mm Hg inspired O_2 for 3 min; but, using this protocol, normal infants behaved similarly.[77] In the same study, time to arousal with hypercapnia was prolonged in the population with substance-abusing mothers when compared with normal infants.[77] The difference in arousal response to hypoxia in the above studies could have been related to the mode and rapidity of the stimulus. With the issue of accidental asphyxiation by bedding as an impetus, Lijowska et al[78] more fully characterized arousal responses to hypercapnia in infants during the first half-year of life. Results showed stereotypical behaviors of increasing complexity consisting of sighs, startles, thrashing, and full arousal. These activities always occurred in the same sequence and most often did not reach full arousal. Nonetheless, full arousal became more common as CO_2 levels increased. These same behaviors also could take place spontaneously when infants breathed air during sleep.

Responses to Challenges in Animal Models

Responses to hypercapnia

Responses in vivo. Evidence of increasing responsiveness to CO_2 as a ventilatory stimulus has been noted in developing rats. A recent study using both unrestrained animals and decerebrate vagotomized ventilated animals showed increases in tidal volume or inspiratory output at all ages. However, frequency of breathing decreased in rats less than 1 week of age, whereas it increased in older animals. The decrease in breathing frequency occurred largely through an increase in duration of expiration, and could be blocked in the artificially ventilated animals by systemic bicuculline, a $GABA_A$-receptor antagonist. This suggests a possible GABAergic pathway in the immature response.[79] Another study using decerebrate vagotomized rats showed similar effects of CO_2 on inspiratory output, but timing was unaffected over the first 10 postnatal days.[80] Maturation of interaction between chemical and lung mechanoreceptor stimulation was tested by inflating the lungs of rats to cause a prolongation of expiration while varying CO_2 (and O_2) levels. Increased chemical drive reduced the duration of the response, but in conscious rats prolongation of expiration with lung inflation was not reduced with hypercapnia (or hypoxia) at 2 and 5 days of age; however, it was reduced at 8 days of age.[81] Analysis of *c-fos* messenger ribonucleic acid (mRNA) expression 1 day after birth in rats showed that the ventral medullary surface (usually considered to be an important site of medullary chemosensitivity), but not other medullary sites, was activated by high levels of CO_2 for 1 hour. This effect still occurred at day 6, but to a lesser degree. The activation of transcription pathways could reflect early events in maturation of chemoreceptor mechanisms.[82] Genetic tools now are being used to help define parameters of normal and abnormal respiratory chemosensitivity. Brain-stem muscarinic cholinergic pathways are among those implicated in ventilatory responses to CO_2. Knockout of the *ret* proto-oncogene, which is important for neural crest development of muscarinic pathways in mice, results in only about one-third of the normal ventilatory response to hypercapnia.[83] This is an interesting result with respect to the finding of decreased muscarinic-receptor binding in medullary arcuate nucleus of SIDS infants (discussed above). Other evidence of genetic factors in the development of hypercapnic ventilatory response comes from obese Zucker rats (autosomal recessive), in which ventilatory response to hypoxia was similar to that of controls, but response to hypercapnia was blunted.[84] The question of whether the blunted hypercapnic response was due to obesity or to the genotype has been considered by Tankersley and coworkers.[85] They used genetically obese mice (C57BL/6J), homozygous or heterozygous at the OB gene locus. An attenuation of normal ventilatory response to hypercapnia was present before obesity was apparent in these animals, but, as in Zucker rats, ventilatory responses to hypoxia generally were similar to controls.

Responses in vitro. The neonatal brain stem/spinal cords of rats showed an increased rate of bursting with either elevation of bath CO_2[86,87] or reduction of HCO_3^-.[87] This type of response differs notably from that of intact rats of similar ages (see above), even accounting for lack of vagal feedback. The potential complexity of chemoreception by neurons in the brain stem makes it difficult to compare directly in vivo and in vitro studies. Identified sites of medullary chemoreception currently include the ventrolateral medulla, the ventral respiratory group, the nucleus of the solitary tract, and the caudal medullary raphe system. In addition, pontine locus coeruleus and cerebellar fastigial nuclei possess neurons that respond to changes in CO_2 and/or pH.[88] How these different regions are influenced by hypercapnia could notably influence the final response, as would the contribution from arterial chemoreceptors. One potentially important region of chemoreception, the medullary raphe system, shows evidence of developmental changes in sensitivity. Using rat medullary slices, the percentage of raphe neurons stimulated by hypercapnia increased greatly in animals over 11 days of age.[56] A similar phenomenon was observed in raphe neurons grown in culture. In that system, the percentage of neurons suppressed by hypercapnia also decreased with age.[56] Carbon dioxide–excited and –inhibited medullary raphe neurons in culture expressed different phenotypes and often different baseline firing patterns, thereby supporting the possibility of distinct neurophysiologic functions for the two types of responses.[89]

Role of medullary chemoreception in maintenance of eupneic breathing. A critical consideration is whether any sites of central chemoreception are crucial for maintenance of respiratory output. A region that has received particular attention is the putative chemosensory area of the ventrolateral medullary surface. While it is well known that this region has a major impact on the ability of anesthetized animals to breathe adequately, recent investigations have considered the more physiologic states of sleep and wakefulness. Acutely cooling this region has resulted in minimal hypoventilation in adult goats during wakefulness and non-REM sleep.[90] Using an excitatory amino acid agonist to create a more prolonged dysfunction of this region in goats, arterial P_{CO_2} increased by 2 mm Hg, and responsiveness to CO_2 was reduced by over 50%.[91] Cooling specific regions of the ventral medullary surface often produced apnea in neonatal goats under anesthesia but not in the awake state, in which hypopnea was observed instead. After several seconds of cooling, reductions in breathing were greatest during hypercapnic challenges and hyperoxia.[92]

Responses to hypoxia

Besides humans, immature animals of several species exhibit biphasic ventilatory responses to hypoxia. Important studies with respect to the mechanism of biphasic effects have been performed on species as diverse as pig, sheep, cat, rabbit, and rat. To interpret the biphasic response to hypoxia, regions of the brain stem including midbrain, pons, and medulla as well as peripheral chemoreceptors have been considered.

Role of the pons and midbrain. A study by Gluckman and Johnston[93] in fetal sheep has shown convincingly that brain structures higher than the medulla can produce ventilatory depression during hypoxia. Since their finding that lesions of rostrolateral pons abolished hypoxic depression of ventilation in fetal sheep, other investigators have extended the result to neonates and have sought to refine our understanding of the specific locations and neuronal substrates. With respect to midbrain structures, mesencephalic piglets showed depressed ventilation when challenged with hypoxia, and this effect was lessened after transection through caudal mesencephalon.[94] In mesencephalic young rabbits, vagotomized and artificially ventilated to prevent feedback onto respiratory controllers, bilateral ablation of the red nuclei prevented hypoxia-induced depression of ventilation. These same lesions did not block an accompanying biphasic change in arterial pressure. Further, stimulation of the red nucleus profoundly depressed respiratory output.[95] Effects from the pons, as originally suggested by Gluckman and Johnston,[93] appeared to be notable as well, since unilateral cooling of the locus coeruleus region blocked the hypoxia induced fall in ventilatory output in lambs.[96] These authors further suggested that adenosine at this site was a putative neurotransmitter for hypoxic depression based on results of adenosine infusion in animals that did or did not spontaneously express a biphasic ventilatory response. The newborn decerebrate rat also showed a biphasic response of respiratory motor output to hypoxia when tested using constant artificial ventilation and removal of peripheral mechanoreceptor feedback. Further, with elimination of input from carotid bodies, only depression of respiratory output remained, again suggesting that brain-stem mechanisms were important.[97] In a study of the isolated brain stem and spinal cord from neonatal rats, transections at different levels of the brain stem were performed. When the pons was intact and the midbrain removed, reduced O_2 in the superfusate depressed the respiratory output of the preparation. When the dorsal pons and the entire pons was removed, there was progressively less suppression of respiratory output by hypoxia.[98] Depression of ventilation during hypoxia also could be demonstrated in adult animals, and the effect also appeared to depend, in part, on higher brain-stem structures. For example, in a study of carotid-body denervated adult rats, depression of respiratory frequency by hypoxia was reversed by intercollicular decerebration, but higher decerebration failed to reverse this effect.[99]

Role of the medulla and central integration of peripheral input. Despite the preceding discussion, higher brain-stem structures may not account entirely for the depression of breathing during hypoxia in newborns. In piglets, brain-stem blood flow has been shown to be increased during exposure to hypoxia. It was calculated that the increase in blood flow could reduce stimulation of central chemoreceptors and depress the respiratory output.[100] A biphasic respiratory output during hypoxia also has been noted in vitro, using medullary slices from mice containing the preBötzinger complex. Frequency of bursting increased and then decreased when measured from a hypoglossal motor root. Preparations obtained from weanlings showed the preceding effect and augmentation and depression of burst amplitude as well.[101] In either case, the suggestion is that neural circuitry of the medulla can respond directly to hypoxic (anoxic) insult in a biphasic manner. Nitric oxide mechanisms in the medulla also may play a role. It was found that blockade of nitric oxide synthase (NOS) in 15-day-old (but not 5-day-old) rat pups would worsen secondary hypoxic depression of ventilation. The early increase in ventilation with hypoxia was augmented after NOS blockade in the younger rats and blunted in the older rats.[102] The nucleus of the solitary tract (NTS) expressed progressively more NOS with age, and nicotinamide-adenine dinucleotide phosphate (NADPH) diaphorase showed increased staining in NTS subnuclei.[102] The authors suggested that the effects of NOS blockade may involve NTS integration of arterial chemoreceptor input, but other NO effects cannot be excluded. Another potential example of central integration of chemoreceptor input or quite possibly an effect on the arterial chemoreceptor itself (see below also) was observed in a study of anesthetized piglets, in which aminophylline, an adenosine antagonist, prevented hypoxic depression of breathing when carotid bodies were intact but not after denervation.[103]

The vagus nerve influences response to hypoxia in awake newborn lambs. After vagotomy, a biphasic response was still present, but the early ventilatory increase was reduced. This blunting of the early increase in ventilation was eliminated when the upper airway was bypassed, indicating a role for the vagus nerve in promoting airway patency during the response to hypoxia.[104]

Role of arterial chemoreceptors. The actual method of transduction of hypoxic (or hypercapnic) response by carotid body is still a subject of contention among investigators and may differ among species; the present discussion is confined largely to effects on chemoreceptor output. The neural response (ie, increase in discharge) of carotid bodies to hypoxia in intact kittens matured over a period of about 1 month. Interestingly, during the first 2 to 3 weeks, the response was often biphasic. Responses to CO_2 also increased with age, and positive interaction began to occur between hypoxia and hypercapnia.[105,106] Developmental studies, largely in vitro, also have been performed in the rat. Neural discharge of superfused carotid body increased at birth with anoxia or hypoxia and was sensitized further during or after the first postnatal week.[107,108] In the rat carotid body, positive interaction between hypoxia and hypercapnia occurred after the second postnatal week[108] and was present in adults.[109] Membrane properties of petrosal ganglion neurons in rat, representing, in part, the cell bodies for chemoafferent fibers, did not change notably with age and were unlikely to account for age-dependent changes in chemosensitivity.[110] Chronic hypoxia starting in the neonatal period in rats greatly attenuated interaction between the stimuli of hypoxia and carbon dioxide in adult animals.[111] Other evidence suggesting possible impairment of the carotid-body response during chronic hypoxia (in the first 18 postnatal days) was the lack of age-related increase in Ca^{++} flux into carotid-body glomus cells during a hypoxic challenge.[112]

Genetic manipulations. Results using knockout mice indicated that growth factors, including neurotrophin-4/5[113] and brain-derived neurotrophic factor (BDNF), were important for development of visceral afferents, including chemosensory afferents from carotid bodies. Transgenic mice that could not express BDNF had defects in control of breathing during the neonatal period. One of these defects was that breathing did not decrease during hyperoxia, but these same animals were able to increase breathing in response to a hypercapnic challenge. These results are consistent with a loss of peripheral chemoafferents and retention of brain circuitry used for chemoresponses.[113] Other evidence of genetically determined effects on carotid-body chemoresponsiveness was obtained from two inbred rat strains, namely spontaneously hypertensive (SHR) and Fischer 344 (F-344) animals. Using in vitro responses of the carotid body to hypoxia, the carotid sinus nerve discharge and Ca^{++} entry measured using fura 2 dye were dramatically higher in the SHR rats.[114] An earlier study demonstrated greater ventilatory response to hypoxia in SHR rats compared with their genetic normotensive controls,[115] but those results could not be definitively tied to the carotid body.

Chemoreflex response. Assessments of arterial chemoreceptor reflex pathways with brief exposure to hypoxia and/or hyperoxia have been performed in neonatal animals and basically showed species-related differences in onset and development. In kittens, exposure to alternating breaths of hypoxic gas caused responses after the first postnatal week. In the same study responses to CO_2 were present in the youngest animals.[116] When kittens were raised in a hypoxic environment, there were no ventilatory responses to alternations of O_2 concentration to day 14.[117] Two-day-old lambs showed less of a response to changes in O_2 level than animals 10 days of age and older.[118] Additionally, use of sodium cyanide as an intracarotid stimulus increased ventilation observed in piglets tested during the first postnatal week.[119]

Role of Arterial Chemoreceptors in Maturation of Eupneic Breathing. The BDNF knockout mice, besides lacking a response to hyperoxia, also had slow and irregular breathing patterns during the neonatal period.[113] Such effects were even apparent in in vitro assessment of respiratory bursting.[120] These results support the idea that arterial chemoreception may be necessary for expression of normal postnatal respiratory control. Previously, Donnelly and Haddad[121] denervated carotid bodies or carotid plus aortic bodies in the neonatal piglet and found increased incidence of apneas along with increased mortality. Subsequent investigation of carotid-body denervation suggested that increased vulnerability to apnea was age dependent in piglets and occurred when denervations were carried out at about 2 weeks of age.[122] Using a different surgical approach to expose and denervate carotid bodies in piglets, a recent investigation was unable to find either fatalities or notable ventilatory irregularities with carotid-body denervation performed at three postnatal ages. The main effect was transient hypoventilation, which was most marked after carotid-body denervation performed at 20 to 25 postnatal days. Hypoventilation was insignificant for denervations performed at less than 5 postnatal days. Using sodium cyanide injections, evidence of substantial aortic-body chemoreflex activity was obtained from intact animals during the early postnatal period as well as from older animals after chemodenervation. The authors suggested that reorganization of peripheral chemoreceptor responses could occur during the postnatal period and that presence of carotid chemoreceptor input was not required for maturation of respiratory control.[119] A generally similar conclusion was reached by the same group using carotid-body denervation in newborn goats.[123] These conflicting results may be explained partly by species difference, central nervous system versus peripheral effects of BDNF, and the likelihood that the BDNF knockout influenced other chemoreceptor input in addition to that of the carotid body. Nevertheless, the different responses obtained in the three studies using the piglet are difficult to resolve.

Summary

A basic picture of chemical regulation of breathing, at least with respect to hypoxic and hypercapnic challenges, is well established. Yet there have been a number of recent studies in infants and animal models that continue to modify our understanding of the relevant sensory and integrative mechanisms that are applicable during maturation. The immunohistochemical changes observed in the region of the medullary ventral surface of SIDS infants supports the idea that defects in chemoreception could be important. Other results, in general, have not been compelling with respect to specific defects in chemoreception and/or behavioral or ventilatory responses to chemoreception being implicated in SIDS events. However, this statement must be tempered by the fact that some small differences do emerge between normal and at-risk populations of infants. The complexity of the chemoreflex pathways that is emerging currently may indicate that use of external challenges to the system is inadequate to detect nervous system defects that might manifest themselves under some specific set of conditions. Evidence of this possibility is suggested from the studies by Forster and colleagues.[90–92,119,123] In those investigations disruption of either medullary or peripheral chemoreceptor pathways could result in relatively minor or no impairment of resting ventilatory pattern or ventilatory responses to activities like exercise, but defects did occur with specific challenges and during particular behavioral states. None of the defects induced by Forster and co-workers would likely have been missed in the studies in human infants presented in this review, but other deficits may be more difficult to observe. Considering the immunohistochemical defects near the ventral medullary surface of SIDS infants, along with the emerging idea of distributed chemoreceptor function, we need to examine more critically when the loss of one part of the pathway would become apparent.

Failure of chemoreflex responses in chronically hypoxic infants appears most likely due to lack of carotid-body maturation. This is suggested by the lack of changes in ventilation with brief changes in oxygen level in affected infants as well as in chronically hypoxic neonatal animals. Studies of the carotid body itself appear to indicate that chronic hypoxia during the neonatal period impairs carotid-body maturation.

References

1. Fisher JT, Mortola JP, Smith JB, et al. Respiration in newborns: development of the control of breathing. Am Rev Respir Dis 1982;125:650–7.
2. Haddad GG, Epstein RA, Epstein MAF, et al. Maturation of ventilation and ventilatory pattern in normal sleeping infants. J Appl Physiol 1979;46:998–1002.
3. Schäfer T, Schäfer D, Schläfke ME. Breathing, transcutaneous blood gases, and CO_2 response in SIDS siblings and control infants during sleep. J Appl Physiol 1993; 74:88–102.
4. Barrington KJ, Finer NN, Wilkinson MH. Progressive shortening of the periodic breathing cycle duration in normal infants. Pediatr Res 1987;21:247–51.
5. Wilkinson MH, Cranage S, Berger PJ, et al. Changes in the temporal structure of periodic breathing with postnatal development in preterm infants. Pediatr Res 1995; 38:533–8.
6. Schechtman VL, Lee MY, Wilson AJ, Harper RM. Dynamics of respiratory patterning in normal infants and infants

who subsequently died of the sudden infant death syndrome. Pediatr Res 1996;40:571–7.
7. Schechtman VL, Harper RM, Wilson AJ, Southall DP. Sleep apnea in infants who succumb to the sudden infant death syndrome. Pediatrics 1991;87:841–6.
8. Alvarez JE, Bodani J, Fajardo CA, et al. Sighs and their relationship to apnea in the newborn infant. Biol Neonate 1993;63:139–46.
9. Frey U, Silverman M, Barbarasi AL, Suki B. Irregularities and power law distributions in the breathing pattern in preterm and term infants. J Appl Physiol 1998;86:789–97.
10. Bruce EN. Invited editorial on "Irregularities and power law distributions in the breathing pattern in preterm and term infants. J Appl Physiol 1998;86:787–8.
11. Smith JC, Ellengberger H, Ballanyi K, et al. Pre-Bötzinger complex: a brainstem region that may generate respiratory rhythm in mammals. Science 1991;254:726–9.
12. Johnson SM, Smith JC, Funk GD, Feldman JL. Pacemaker behavior of respiratory neurons in medullary slices from neonatal rat. J Neurophysiol 1994;72:2598–608.
13. Koshiya N, Smith JC. Neuronal pacemaker for breathing visualized in vitro. Nature 1999;400:360–3.
14. Butera RJ, Rinzel J, Smith JC. Models of respiratory rhythm generation in the preBötzinger complex. I. Bursting pacemaker neurons. J Neurophysiol 1999;82:382–97.
15. Rekling JC, Feldman JL. PreBötzinger complex and pacemaker neurons: hypothesized site and kernel for respiratory rhythm generation. Ann Rev Physiol 1998; 60:385–405.
16. O'Donovan MJ, Chub N. Population behavior and self organization in the genesis of spontaneous rhythmic activity by developing spinal networks. Semin Cell Dev Biol 1997;8:21–8.
17. Gray PA, Rekling JC, Bocchiaro CM, Feldman JL. Modulation of respiratory frequency by peptidergic input to rhythmogenic neurons in the preBötzinger complex. Science 1999;286:1566–8.
18. Funk GD, Smith JC, Feldman JL. Generation and transmission of respiratory oscillations in medullary slices: role of excitatory amino acids. J Neurophysiol 1993; 70:1497–515.
19. Liu G, Feldman JL, Smith JC. Excitatory amino acid-mediated transmission of inspiratory drive to phrenic motoneurons. J Neurophysiol 1990;64:423–36.
20. Funk GD, Johnson SM, Smith JC, et al. Functional respiratory rhythm generating networks in neonatal mice lacking NMDAR1 gene. J Neurophysiol 1997;78:1414–20.
21. Feldman JL, Smith JC. Cellular mechanisms underlying modulation of breathing pattern in mammals. Annals N Y Acad Sci 1989;563:114–30.
22. Onimaru H, Arata A, Homma I. Intrinsic burst generation of preinspiratory neurons in the medulla of brainstem-spinal cord preparations isolated from newborn rats. Exp Brain Res 1995;106:57–68.
23. Onimaru H, Arata A, Homma I. Inhibitory synaptic inputs to the respiratory rhythm generator in the medulla isolated from newborn rats. Pflugers Arch 1990;417:425–32.
24. Paton JF. Rhythmic bursting of pre- and post-inspiratory neurones during central apnoea in mature mice. J Physiol (Lond) 1997;502:623–39.
25. Borday V, Foutz AS, Nordholm L, Denavit-Saubie M. Respiratory effects of glutamate receptor antagonists in neonate and adult animals. Eur J Pharmacol 1998; 348:235–46.
26. Pierrefiche O, Foutz AS, Champagnat J, Denavit-Saubie M. NMDA and non-NMDA receptors may play distinct roles in timing mechanisms and transmission in the feline respiratory network. J Physiol (Lond) 1994; 474:509–23.
27. Lawson EE, Thach BT. Respiratory patterns during progressive asphyxia in newborn rabbits. J Appl Physiol 1977;43:468–74.
28. Wang W, Fung ML, Darnall RA, St John WM. Characterizations and comparisons of eupnoea and gasping in neonatal rats. J Physiol (Lond) 1996;490:277–92.
29. Huang Q, Zhou D, St John WM. Lesions of regions for in vitro ventilatory genesis eliminate gasping but not eupnea. Respir Physiol 1997;107:111–23.
30. Ramirez JM, Schwarzacher SW, Pierrefiche O, et al. Selective lesioning of the cat preBötzinger complex in vivo eliminates breathing but not gasping. J Physiol (Lond) 1998;507:895–907.
31. Hsieh JH, Chang YC, Su CK, et al. A single minute lesion around the ventral respiratory group in medulla produces fatal apnea in cats. J Auton Nerv Syst 1998; 73:7–18.
32. St Jacques R, St John WM. Transient, reversible apnoea following ablation of the preBötzinger complex in rats. J Physiol (Lond) 1999;520:303–14.
33. Paton JF, Richter DW. Maturational changes in the respiratory rhythm generator of the mouse. Pflugers Arch 1995; 430:115–24.
34. Ramirez JM, Quellmalz UJ, Richter DW. Postnatal changes in the mammalian respiratory network as revealed by the transverse brainstem slice of mice. J Physiol (Lond) 1996;491:799–812.
35. Paton JF, Richter DW. Role of fast inhibitory synaptic mechanisms in respiratory rhythm generation in the maturing mouse. J Physiol (Lond) 1995;484:505–21.
36. Viana F, Bayliss DA, Berger AJ. Repetitive firing properties of developing rat brainstem motoneurones. J Physiol (Lond) 1995;486:745–61.
37. Shao XM, Feldman JL. Respiratory rhythm generation and synaptic inhibition of expiratory neurons in preBötzinger complex: differential roles of glycinergic and GABAergic neural transmission. J Neurophysiol 1997;77:1853–60.
38. Cherubini E, Gaiarsa JL, Ben-Ari Y. GABA: an excitatory transmitter in early postnatal life. Trends Neurosci 1991;14:515–9.
39. Johnson SM, Smith JC, Feldman JL. Modulation of respiratory rhythm in vitro: role of Gi/o protein-mediated mechanisms. J Appl Physiol 1996;80:2120–33.
40. Zhang W, Elsen F, Barnbrock A, Richter DW. Postnatal development of $GABA_B$ receptor–mediated modulation of voltage-activated Ca^{2+} currents in mouse brain-stem neurons. Eur J Neurosci 1999;11:2332–42.
41. Hayashi F, Lipski J. The role of inhibitory amino acids in control of respiratory motor output in an arterially perfused rat. Respir Physiol 1992;89:47–63.

42. Pierrefiche O, Schwarzacher SW, Bischoff AM, Richter DW. Blockade of synaptic inhibition within the preBötzinger complex in the cat suppresses respiratory rhythm generation in vivo. J Physiol (Lond) 1998;509:245–54.
43. Fung ML, St John WM. The functional expression of a pontine pneumotaxic centre in neonatal rats. J Physiol (Lond) 1995;489:579–91.
44. Farber JP. Effects on breathing of rostral pons glutamate injection during opossum development. J Appl Physiol 1990;69:189–95.
45. Jacquin TD, Borday V, Schneider-Maunoury S, et al. Reorganization of pontine rhythmogenic neural networks in Krox-20 knockout mice. Neuron 1996; 17:747–58.
46. Wilken B, Lalley P, Bischoff AM, et al. Treatment of apneustic respiratory disturbance with a serotonin receptor agonist. J Pediatr 1997;130:89–94.
47. Al-Zubaidy ZA, Erickson RL, Greer JJ. Serotonergic and noradrenergic effects on respiratory neural discharge in the medullary slice preparation of neonatal rats. Pflugers Arch 1996;431:942–9.
48. Haddad GG, Leistner HL, Epstein RA, et al. CO_2-induced changes in ventilation and ventilatory pattern in normal sleeping infants. J Appl Physiol 1980;48:684–8.
49. Avery ME, Chernick V, Dutton RE, Permutt S. Ventilatory response to inspired carbon dioxide in infants and adults. J Appl Physiol 1963;18:895–903.
50. McCann EM, Lewis K. Control of breathing in babies of narcotic and cocaine abusing mothers. Early Hum Dev 1991;27:175–86.
51. Glomb WB, Marcus CL, Keens TG, Ward SL. Hypercapnic and hypoxic ventilatory responses in school-aged siblings of sudden infant death syndrome victims. J Pediatr 1992;121:391–7.
52. Coleman JM, Mammel MC, Reardon C, Boros SJ. Hypercarbic ventilatory responses of infants at risk for SIDS. Pediatr Pulmonol 1987;3:226–30.
53. Parks YA, Paton JY, Beardsmore CS, et al. Respiratory control in infants at increased risk for sudden infant death syndrome. Arch Dis Child 1989;64:791–7.
54. Zec N, Filiano JJ, Kinney HC. Anatomic relationships of the human arcuate nucleus of the medulla: a DiI-labeling study. J Neuropathol Exp Neurol 1997;56:509–22.
55. Dreshaj IA, Haxhiu MA, Martin RJ. Role of the medullary raphe nuclei in the respiratory response to CO_2. Respir Physiol 1998;111:15–23.
56. Wang W, Richerson GB. Development of chemosensitivity of rat medullary raphe neurons. Neuroscience 1999; 90:1001–11.
57. Kinney HC, Filiano JJ, Sleeper LA, et al. Decreased muscarinic receptor binding in the arcuate nucleus in sudden infant death syndrome. Science 1995;269:1446–50.
58. Panigraphy A, Filiano JJ, Sleeper LA, et al. Decreased kainate receptor binding in arcuate nucleus of the sudden infant death syndrome. J Neuropathol Exp Neurol 1997;56:1253–61.
59. Rigatto H, Brady JP, de la Torre Verduzco R. Chemoreceptor reflexes in preterm infants: II. The effect of gestational and postgestational age on the ventilatory response to inhaled carbon dioxide. Pediatrics 1975;55:614–20.
60. Frantz ID III, Adler SM, Thach BT, Taeusch HW. Maturational effects on respiratory responses to carbon dioxide in premature infants. J Appl Physiol 1976; 41:41–5.
61. Alvaro RE, de Almeida V, Kwiatkowski K, et al. A developmental study of the dose-response curve of the respiratory sensory reflex. Am Rev Respir Dis 1993;148:1013–7.
62. Eichenwald EC, Ungarelli RA, Stark AR. Hypercapnia increases expiratory braking in preterm infants. J Appl Physiol 1993;75:2665–70.
63. Martin RJ, diFiore JM, Korenke CB, et al. Vulnerability of respiratory control in healthy preterm infants placed supine. J Pediatr 1995;127:609–14.
64. Parks YA, Beardsmore CS, MacFayden UM, et al. The effect of a single breath of 100% oxygen on breathing in infants at 1, 2, and 3 months of age. Am Rev Respir Dis 1991;144:141–5.
65. Calder NA, Williams BA, Kumar P, Hanson MA. The respiratory response of healthy term infants to breath-by-breath alternations in inspired oxygen at two postnatal ages. Pediatr Res 1994;35:321–4.
66. Williams BA, Smyth J, Boon AW, et al. Development of respiratory chemoreflexes in response to alternations of fractional inspired oxygen content in the newborn infant. J Physiol (Lond) 1991;442:81–90.
67. Calder NA, Williams BA, Smyth J, et al. Absence of ventilatory responses to alternating breaths of mild hypoxia and air in infants who have had bronchopulmonary dysplasia: implications for the risk of sudden infant death. Pediatr Res 1994;35:677–81.
68. Rigatto H, Brady JP, de la Torre Verduzco R. Chemoreceptor reflexes in preterm infants: I. The effect of gestational and postgestational age on the ventilatory response to inhalation of 100% and 15% oxygen. Pediatrics 1975;55:604–13.
69. Katz-Salamon M, Eriksson M, Jonsson B. Development of peripheral chemoreceptor function in infants with chronic lung disease and initially lacking hyperoxic response. Arch Dis Child Fetal Neonatal Ed 1996; 75:F4–9.
70. Martin RJ, Difiore JM, Jana L, et al. Persistance of the biphasic ventilatory response to hypoxia in preterm infants. J Pediatr 1998;132:960–4.
71. Alvaro R, Alvarez J, Kwiatkowski K, et al. Small preterm infants (less than or equal to 1500 g) have only a sustained decrease in ventilation in response to hypoxia. Pediatr Res 1992;32:403–6.
72. Cohen G, Malcolm G, Henderson-Smart D. Ventilatory response of the newborn infant to mild hypoxia. Pediatr Pulmonol 1997;24:163–72.
73. Mortola JP, Rezzonico R, Lanthier C. Ventilation and oxygen consumption during acute hypoxia in newborn mammals: a comparative analysis. Respir Physiol 1989; 78:31–43.
74. Rehan V, Haider AZ, Alvaro RE, et al. The biphasic ventilatory response to hypoxia in preterm infants is not due to a decrease in metabolism. Pediatr Pulmonol 1996; 22:287–94.
75. Ueda Y, Stick SM, Sly PD. Control of breathing in infants born to smoking mothers. J Pediatr 1999;135:226–32.

76. Lewis KW, Bosque EM. Deficient hypoxia awakening response in infants of smoking mothers: possible relationship to sudden infant death syndrome. J Pediatr 1995;127:691–9.
77. Ward SL, Bautista DB, Woo MS, et al. Responses to hypoxia and hypercapnia in infants of substance-abusing mothers. J Pediatr 1992;121:704–9.
78. Lijowska AS, Reed NW, Chiodi BA, Thach BT. Sequential arousal and airway-defensive behavior in asphyxial sleep environments. J Appl Physiol 1997;83:219–28.
79. Abu-Shaweesh JM, Dreshaj IA, Thomas AJ, et al. Changes in respiratory timing induced by hypercapnia in maturing rats. J Appl Physiol 1999;87:484–90.
80. Zhou D, Huang Q, Fung ML, et al. Phrenic response to hypercapnia in the unanesthetized, decerebrate, newborn rat. Respir Physiol 1996;104:11–22.
81. Matsuoka T, Mortola JP. Effects of hypoxia and hypercapnia on the Hering-Breuer reflex of the conscious newborn rat. J Appl Physiol 1995;78:5–11.
82. Wickström HR, Holgert H, Hökfelt T, Lagercrantz H. Birth-related expression of c-fos, c-jun and substance P mRNAs in the rat brainstem and pia mater: possible relationship to changes in central chemosensitivity. Dev Brain Res 1999;112:255–66.
83. Burton MD, Kawashima A, Brayer JA, et al. RET proto-oncogene is important for the development of respiratory CO_2 sensitivity. J Auton Nerv Syst 1997;14:137–43.
84. Farkas GA, Schlenker EH. Pulmonary ventilation and mechanics in morbidly obese Zucker rats. Am J Respir Crit Care Med 1994;150:356–62.
85. Tankersley C, Kleeberger S, Russ B, et al. Modified control of breathing in genetically obese (ob/ob) mice. J Appl Physiol 1996;81:716–23.
86. McLean HA, Remmers JE. Respiratory motor output of the sectioned medulla of the neonatal rat. Respir Physiol 1994;96:49–60.
87. Voipio J, Ballanyi K. Interstitial P_{CO_2} and pH, and their role as chemostimulants in the isolated respiratory network of neonatal rats. J Physiol (Lond) 1997;499:527–42.
88. Nattie E. CO_2, brainstem chemoreceptors, and breathing. Prog Neurobiol 1999;59:299–331.
89. Wang W, Pizzonia JH, Richerson GB. Chemosensitivity of rat medullary raphe neurones in primary tissue culture. J Physiol (Lond) 1998;511:433–50.
90. Forster HV, Ohtake PJ, Pan LG, Lowry TF. Effect on breathing of surface ventrolateral medullary cooling in awake, anesthetized and asleep goats. Respir Physiol 1997; 110:187–97.
91. Forster HV, Pan LG, Lowry TF, et al. Breathing of awake goats during prolonged dysfunction of caudal M ventrolateral medullary neurons. J Appl Physiol 1998;84:129–40.
92. Lowry TF, Forster HV, Pan LG, et al. Effect on breathing of ventral medullary surface cooling in neonatal goats. J Appl Physiol 1996;80:1949–57.
93. Gluckman PD, Johnston BM. Lesions in the upper lateral pons abolish the hypoxic depression of breathing in unanesthetized fetal lambs in utero. J Physiol (Lond) 1987;382:373–83.
94. St John WM, St Jacques R, Li A, Darnall RA. Modulation of hypoxic depressions of ventilatory activity in the newborn piglet by mesencephalic mechanisms. Brain Res 1999;819:147–9.
95. Waites BA, Ackland GL, Noble R, Hanson MA. Red nucleus lesions abolish the biphasic respiratory response to isocapnic hypoxia in decerebrate young rabbits. J Physiol (Lond) 1996;495:217–25.
96. Moore PJ, Ackland GL, Hanson MA. Unilateral cooling in the region of locus coeruleus blocks the fall in respiratory output during hypoxia in anaesthetized neonatal sheep. Exp Physiol 1996;81:983–94.
97. Fung ML, Wang W, Darnall RA, St John WM. Characterization of ventilatory response to hypoxia in neonatal rats. Respir Physiol 1996;103:57–66.
98. Okada Y, Kawai A, Muckenhoff K, Scheid P. Role of the pons in hypoxic respiratory depression in the neonatal rat. Respir Physiol 1998;111:55–63.
99. Martin-Body RL. Brain transections demonstrate the central origin of hypoxic ventilatory depression in carotid body–denervated rats. J Physiol (Lond) 1988;407:41–52.
100. Darnall RA, Green G, Pinto L, Hart N. Effect of acute hypoxia on respiration and brain stem blood flow in the piglet. J Appl Physiol 1991;70:251–9.
101. Ramirez JM, Quellmalz UJ, Wilken B. Developmental changes in the hypoxic response of the hypoglossus respiratory motor output in vitro. J Neurophysiol 1997;78:383–92.
102. Gozal D, Gozal E, Torres JE, et al. Nitric oxide modulates ventilatory response to hypoxia in the developing rat. Am J Respir Crit Care Med 1997;155:1755–62.
103. Cattarossi L, Haxhiu-Poskurica B, Haxhiu MA, et al. Carotid bodies and ventilatory response to hypoxia in aminophylline-treated piglets. Pediatr Pulmonol 1995; 20:94–100.
104. Delacourt C, Canet E, Praud JP, Bureau MA. Influence of vagal afferents on diphasic ventilatory response to hypoxia in newborn lambs. Respir Physiol 1995;99:29–39.
105. Carroll JL, Bamford OS, Fitzgerald RS. Postnatal maturation responses to O_2 and CO_2 in the cat. J Appl Physiol 1993;75:2283–91.
106. Marchal F, Bairam A, Haouzi P, et al. Carotid chemoreceptor response to natural stimuli in the newborn kitten. Respir Physiol 1992;87:183–93.
107. Kholwadwala D, Donnelly DF. Maturation of carotid chemoreceptor sensitivity to hypoxia: in vitro studies in the newborn rat. J Physiol (Lond) 1992;453:461–73.
108. Bamford OS, Sterni LM, Wasicko MJ, et al. Postnatal maturation of carotid body and type I cell chemoreception in the rat. Am J Physiol 1999;276:L875–84.
109. Pepper DR, Landauer RC, Kumar P. Postnatal development of CO_2-O_2 interaction in the rat carotid body in vitro. J Physiol (Lond) 1995;485:531–41.
110. Donnelly DF. Developmental changes in membrane properties of chemoreceptor afferent neurons of the rat petrosal ganglia. J Neurophysiol 1999;82:209–15.
111. Landauer RC, Pepper DR, Kumar P. Effects of chronic hypoxaemia from birth upon chemosensitivity in the adult rat carotid body in vitro. J Physiol (Lond) 1995; 485:543–50.
112. Sterni LM, Bamford OS, Wasicko MJ, Carroll JL. Chronic hypoxia abolished the postnatal increase in carotid

body type I cell sensitivity to hypoxia. Am J Physiol 1999;277:L645–52.
113. Erickson JT, Conover JC, Borday V, et al. Mice lacking brain-derived neurotrophic factor exhibit visceral sensory neuron losses distinct from mice lacking NT4 and display a severe developmental deficit in control of breathing. J Neurosci 1996;16:5361–71.
114. Weil JV, Stevens T, Pickett CK, et al. Strain associated differences in hypoxic chemosensitivity of the carotid body in rats. Am J Physiol 1998;274:L767–74.
115. Bee D, Barer G, Wach R, et al. Structure and function of the carotid body in New Zealand genetically hypertensive rats. Q J Exp Physiol 1989;74:691–701.
116. Watanabe T, Kumar P, Hanson MA. Development of respiratory chemoreflexes to hypoxia and CO_2 in unanaesthetized kittens. Respir Physiol 1996; 106:247–54.
117. Hanson MA, Kumar P, Williams BA. The effect of chronic hypoxia upon the development of respiratory chemoreflexes in the newborn kitten. J Physiol (Lond) 1989; 411:563–74.
118. Bureau MA, Begin R. Postnatal maturation of the respiratory response to O_2 in newborn lambs. J Appl Physiol 1982;52:428–33.
119. Lowry TF, Forster HV, Pan LG, et al. Effects on breathing of carotid body denervation in neonatal piglets. J Appl Physiol 1999;87:2128–35.
120. Balkowiec A, Katz DM. Brain-derived neurotrophic factor is required for normal development of the central respiratory rhythm in mice. J Physiol (Lond) 1998; 510:527–33.
121. Donnelly DF, Haddad GG. Prolonged apnea and impaired survival in piglets after sinus and aortic nerve section. J Appl Physiol 1990;68:1048–52.
122. Cote A, Porras H, Meehan B. Age-dependent vulnerability to carotid chemodenervation in piglets. J Appl Physiol 1996;80:323–31.
123. Lowry TF, Forster HV, Pan LG, et al. Effect of carotid body denervation on breathing in neonatal goats. J Appl Physiol 1999;87:1026–34.

CHAPTER 30

Sleep and Respiratory Control

Ronald M. Harper, PhD, David Gozal, MD

The effects of sleep states on breathing of developing infants and children are profound. Alterations in respiratory patterning far exceed immediate metabolic demands, with breathing rates approaching a two-fold increase in waking over quiet sleep (QS), and respiratory rate variability doubling or quadrupling in rapid eye movement (REM) sleep and waking, respectively.[1] In addition to substantial frequency and tidal volume differences between states, normal breathing during sleep is characterized by frequent relatively short pauses in breathing that are associated with transitions in state, body movements, or transient elevations in blood pressure. Disordered breathing, as expressed by hypoxia, hypoventilation, or total cessation of airflow, can emerge during sleep and be associated with marked declines in oxygen saturation sufficiently severe to compromise survival. Certain disorders of state can interfere with ventilation to the extent that neural development is compromised or neural structural elements are damaged such that cognitive function may be severely affected, with the potential to exert deleterious effects years later.[2] Sleep state effects on breathing interact with a number of other structural developmental disorders and respiratory syndromes, often accentuating the primary disorder to intolerable levels for survival. On the other hand, sleep states can assist breathing in other disease conditions and can provide relief in certain circumstances that interfere with ventilation during waking. The objectives of this chapter are to describe developmental characteristics of sleep states, to note some of the brain mechanisms underlying state-related physiologic characteristics, to illustrate normal and abnormal breathing during sleep, and to demonstrate the consequences of sleep-disordered breathing during sleep and the interactions of disease processes or developmental disorders on respiration.

Sleep State Characteristics

States in infants and very young children can be differentiated grossly into two sleep states, as well as waking. Quiet sleep, or non–rapid eye movement (NREM) sleep, is characterized by a pronounced regularity of breathing and a prolongation of inspiratory and expiratory times, leading to a rate decrease of nearly half compared with waking values, with enhanced tidal volume to accommodate appropriate metabolic rate for that state. The QS state typically maintains a degree of postural muscle tone, although often at a reduced level, and diminished variation of heart rate at low frequencies, that is, slow primarily sympathetically mediated changes but enhanced coupling of heart rate with breathing efforts. There is a paucity of eye and body movements; large-amplitude low-frequency (delta) waves are recorded by electroencephalography during QS. Bursts of 12- to 14-Hz electroencephalogram (EEG) sleep "spindles" are characteristic of QS in both *adults and children*; however, maximal development of this phasic spindle activity requires 16 postnatal weeks to emerge.[3] Periods of QS are interspaced with epochs of REM sleep; the latter are normally terminated by a waking period that can be of very short duration. The REM state is characterized by desynchronized EEG activity, comparable to patterns found in waking. In addition, a paralysis of virtually all of the body musculature ensues, except for certain components of the respiratory musculature. The muscle atonia of REM is intermixed with phasic periods of twitches of the periphery, together with rapid eye movements. Respiratory rates typically are enhanced, and heart rate variability at lower frequencies becomes more pronounced; blood pressure also becomes extremely variable, with transient hypotensive periods interspersed with epochs of increased blood pressure. The development of EEG characteristics during sleep and waking states in infants has been described extensively.[3–7] During QS, in particular, maturation of EEG patterns in the first few months of life exhibits unique patterns that reflect thalamocortical development, and helps indicate normal and abnormal neurologic growth that can modify breathing patterns.

Neural Mechanisms Underlying Quiet and REM Sleep

The neural sites underlying the onset and maintenance of quiet and REM sleep continue to be an object of research; however, sufficient insights are available to link certain breathing patterns with properties of state regulatory structures. Areas within the basal forebrain, including regions within the preoptic area, have long been implicated in initiating QS,[8] with stimulation eliciting sleep,

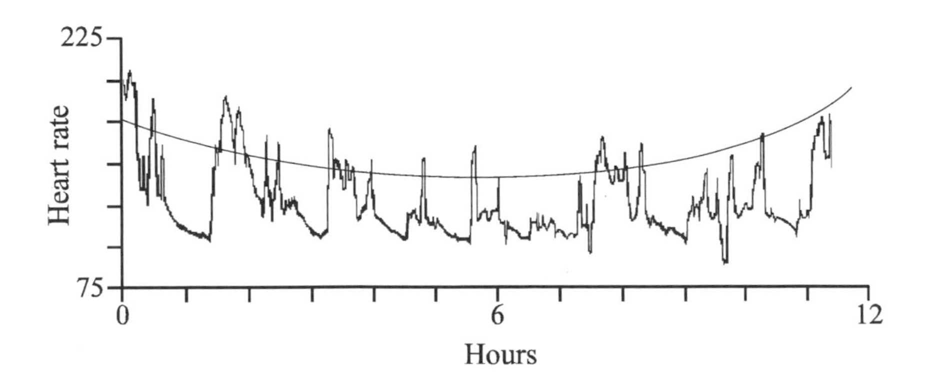

FIGURE 30–1. Plot of minute-by-minute averaged heart rate across a 12-hour night-time recording from a 6-month infant. The near-hourly increases and decreases correspond with periods of rapid eye movement (REM) and quiet sleep (QS), with peaks in the record representing waking (AW) epochs. Note that a gradual decline of heart rate occurs throughout the night (*tracking curve*), with a nadir near 6 hours into the record, followed by a gradual increase over the remainder of the recording—likely a manifestation of circadian influence.

and lesions resulting in pronounced loss of sleep. Single cell discharges suggestive of neurons that selectively fire with the onset of QS have been found in this area.[9,10] Certain features of QS, such as the large synchronous slow waves and bursts of 12- to 14-Hz sleep spindles, depend on the integrity of thalamocortical circuitry and are considered a concomitant characteristic of QS, although these characteristics can be generated during waking states under certain pharmacologic conditions, such as following atropine administration. In addition, adenosine mechanisms may play an important role in metabolic and recovery aspects of QS.[11] Thermoregulatory areas of the anterior hypothalamus interact with sleep mechanisms, with close associations between warming, discharge of thermoregulatory neurons, and induction of sleep.[12]

The principal physiologic characteristics of REM sleep persist after separation of the forebrain from the pons, suggesting that mechanisms underlying this sleep state lie caudal to the diencephalon; of note, areas within the dorsal lateral pons have been particularly implicated in eliciting characteristics of REM sleep state. The atonia of REM, for example, can be abolished by lesions in the dorsal pons, ventral to the locus caeruleus, and phasic somatic events can be terminated by lesions in the pedunculopontine tegmentum.[13] Certain phasic elements, such as the variation of sympathetic and parasympathetic outflow, depend on the integrity of vestibular nuclei,[14] although phasic eye movements remain even when there are lesions in the vestibular sites.[15] A number of brain areas, including the dorsal and caudal raphe,[16,17] locus coeruleus,[17] and ventral medullary surface,[18,19] show a decline of activity during REM sleep; however, most brain sites substantially increase cell discharge during the REM state. Those areas that decrease discharge during REM sleep play significant roles in blood pressure regulation; it is unclear whether the state-related cell patterns in these regions bear a relationship to blood pressure control (and, indirectly, to breathing patterns) during the REM state.

Sleep State Organization

The organization of sleep states undergoes rapid development over the first 6 months of life. Neonates and young infants spend a disproportionate amount of time in REM sleep over waking or QS. The relative amount of QS increases, particularly over the first 3 months of life, and a near-hourly cycle of waking and sleeping appears early in this sequence (Figure 30–1). A 3-hour feeding rhythm is superimposed on the succession of quiet and active sleep periods, and a 24-hour circadian cycle modulates the amplitude of physiologic measures associated with both QS and REM rhythms, as well as waking; the circadian rhythm develops over the first 3 months of life for breathing rate (Figure 30–2), with influences on state appearing as early as during the first month.[20–22] Feeding entrains sleep states, with food intake increasing the probability of REM onset;[23] since the feeding cycle occurs at approximate 3-hourly intervals, the net effect is induction of a REM episode concurrently with termination of those feeding periods; this is followed by near-hourly sequences of quiet and REM sleep periods, which occur until the next feed.

The hourly sleep rhythm lengthens over the course of early life to approach the adult 90-minute sleep period. Sleep states normally are defined by electroencephalographic, eye movement, and neck tonus measures. The pattern of respiratory and heart rate variability can be used as a valuable asset in classification of state, particularly when automatic classification must be performed;[24] the state effects on heart and respiratory rate and variation can be visualized on minute-by-minute plots as seen in Figures 30–1 and 30–2.

A principal signature of QS in adults is the presence of large-amplitude low-frequency (0.5- to 2.0-Hz delta) waves on the EEG. However, QS requires a period of

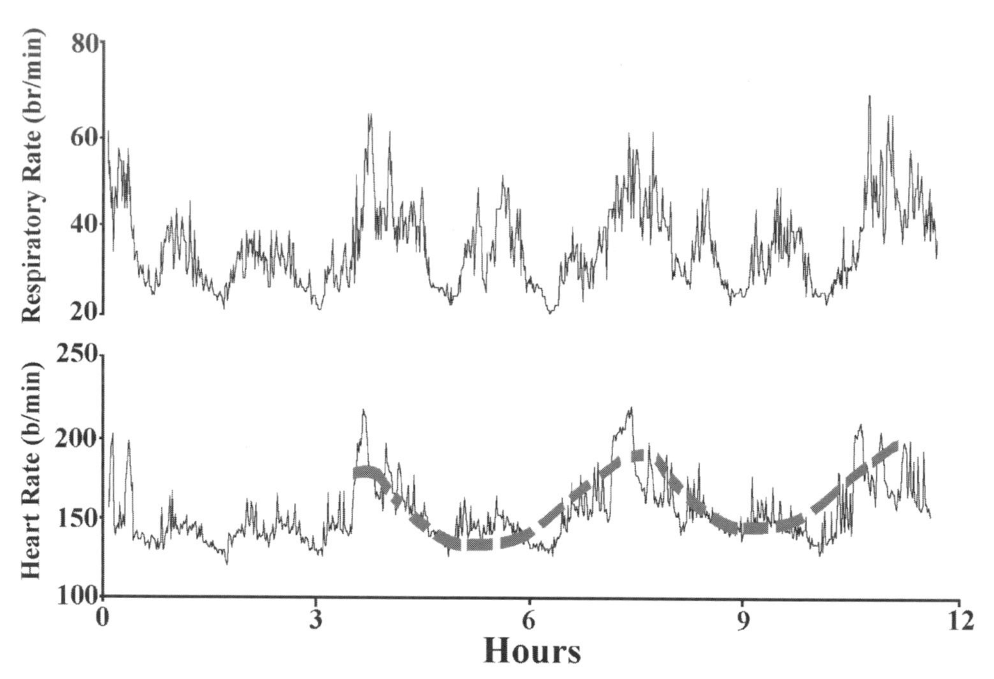

FIGURE 30–2. Minute-by-minute plot of mean respiratory rate and heart rate in a 3-month-old infant demonstrating the presence of near-hourly modulation of breathing and heart rate, together with a 3-hour rhythm, for example, between 4 and 12 hours (see superimposed cartoon of periodic wave [*dashed line*]).

development in the infant, and the principal state of sleep in the newborn is REM sleep. The relative proportion of REM sleep declines and the proportion of QS increases as the infant matures, with relatively equal proportions occurring by 3 months. In addition, the distribution of sleep within a night begins to change from a relatively even distribution in the newborn period to a higher proportion of QS earlier in the night by 1 month of life. Development of the trend of higher proportions of QS early in the night and higher proportions of REM sleep as the night proceeds, characteristic of the adult pattern, does not follow a linear path over 2 to 4 months but is apparent after that time.[21] In addition to the decline in proportion of QS across the night in adults, the amplitude of low frequency waves declines across successive sleep states;[25] a comparable decline occurs in delta amplitude after 2 months of age in infants.[7] Infants 3 months and older show increases in delta amplitude from start to finish of any one QS period. The implication for breathing control in infancy is that QS (either an epoch of QS or across an entire night's recording), despite the seeming constancy in regulation, is not a uniform state after 2 months of age.

In addition to the remarkable decline in REM sleep over the first few months of life is a notable relative increase in the amount of QS between the first 6 months and approximately the ninth year of life. Even more remarkable is the "depth" of QS, as measured by the difficulty to arouse, particularly in children; thresholds for auditory arousal often reach levels 90 dB above waking auditory threshold values.[26]

Development of Respiratory Patterning as a Function of Sleep State

Respiratory rhythm generation depends on bulbopontine respiratory regions; the cyclic activity is modulated further by suprapontine sites that include important efferent projections to areas mediating the sleep-wake cycle, thermoregulation, and circadian rhythmicity. Respiratory control areas also receive afferent inputs from central and peripheral chemoreceptors and from other receptors within the respiratory pump (upper airways, chest wall, and lungs). During fetal life, breathing is discontinuous and coincides with REM-like sleep. After birth, respiratory rhythm is established as a continuous activity to maintain cellular oxygen and carbon dioxide homeostasis.

Respiratory pattern instability during sleep typically is present during early life, such that apneic episodes lasting less than 5 seconds are extremely common in preterm infants, and their frequency is reduced in full-term infants.[27] These apneic episodes are usually of a central nature in the full-term infant and primarily occur during REM sleep. This greater respiratory instability during REM sleep, as compared with NREM sleep, is likely a consequence of phasic inhibitory-excitatory phenomena that characterize REM sleep.

Studies in recently developed transgenic animal models may provide additional and important insights into the respiratory phenotype and its interaction with sleep-wake states. For example, newborn mice with a null mutation in a gene involved in brain-stem development,

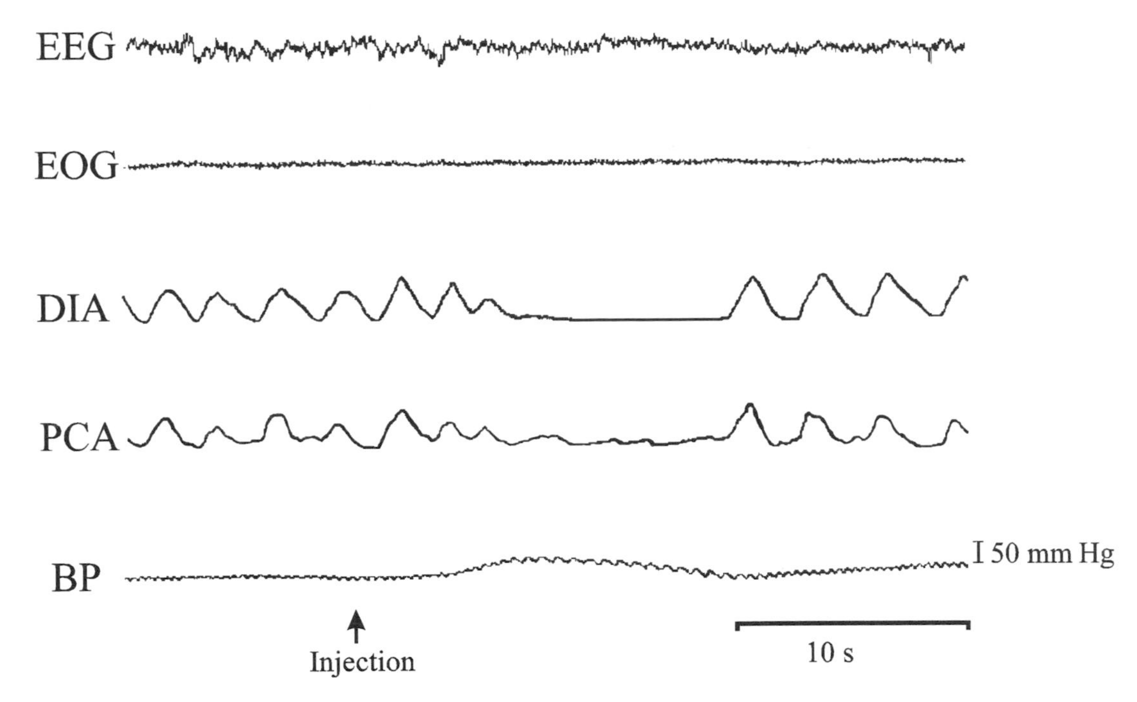

FIGURE 30–3. Loss of diaphragmatic (DIA) and posterior cricoarytenoid (PCA; a laryngeal dilator) muscle activity following a transient elevation of blood pressure (BP) by phenylephrine (INJ) in the cat. EEG = electroencephalogram; EOG = electro-olfactogram. (Reproduced with permission from Marks JD and Harper RM.[34])

Krox, display a high postnatal mortality rate, as well as severe apneic events similar to those observed in extremely premature human infants.[28] In addition, mice that do not express glutamate receptors of the *N*-methyl-D-aspartate (NMDA) type are more susceptible to respiratory depression;[29] while animals with null mutations for a neurotrophic factor, such as brain-derived neurotrophic factor, display excessive respiratory instability after birth as compared with wild-type newborn mice.[30,31] With the evolving understanding of molecular pathways mediating sleep states, it may soon be possible to assess interactions between such state-related genes during development and genes controlling cardiorespiratory regulation.

Consequences of REM Sleep Atonia

An important aspect of REM sleep is the muscular paralysis, or atonia, that is a principal characteristic of the state, in addition to bursts of phasic eye movements. The atonia is widespread and includes virtually all of the musculature, except some of the respiratory musculature; even muscles of the diaphragm are alternately activated during this state.[32] This paralysis is of significant importance in infants, since they have more compliant thoracic walls from not-yet-calcified rib cages and relatively weak intercostal muscles. When intercostal and abdominal wall muscles lose their tone during REM sleep in infants, the increased chest wall compliance leads to significant inward motion of the thoracic wall during inspiratory efforts as a result of negative intrathoracic pressure. The thoracic wall collapse results in greatly diminished thoracic volume and a significant reduction of the actively maintained functional residual capacity.[33] These phenomena are easily recognized by the accompanying paradoxic rib cage/abdominal movements seen during respiratory efforts in REM sleep. Thus, the implications of the effect of REM sleep on breathing are substantial, since the state induces circumstances in which the infant has little reserve oxygen capacity to cope with any additional challenge.

Brain Mechanisms Mediating Drive to Upper Airway and Other Respiratory Musculature

The cranial motor pools innervating muscles of the upper airway include the hypoglossal (XII), XI via X, IX, VII, and V motor pools, and they supply the muscles of the tongue, larynx, styloglossus, dilator nares, tensor veli palatini, and masseter muscles, respectively, all of which can modify airway resistance and lose tone during REM sleep. At least some of these motorneuron pools, including nucleus ambiguus pools supplying XI via X fibers to the laryngeal dilators, are preferentially depressed over diaphragmatic musculature when blood pressure is elevated transiently (Figure 30–3).[34] The loss of tone during such transient elevation of blood pressure has the potential to set the stage for airway collapse.

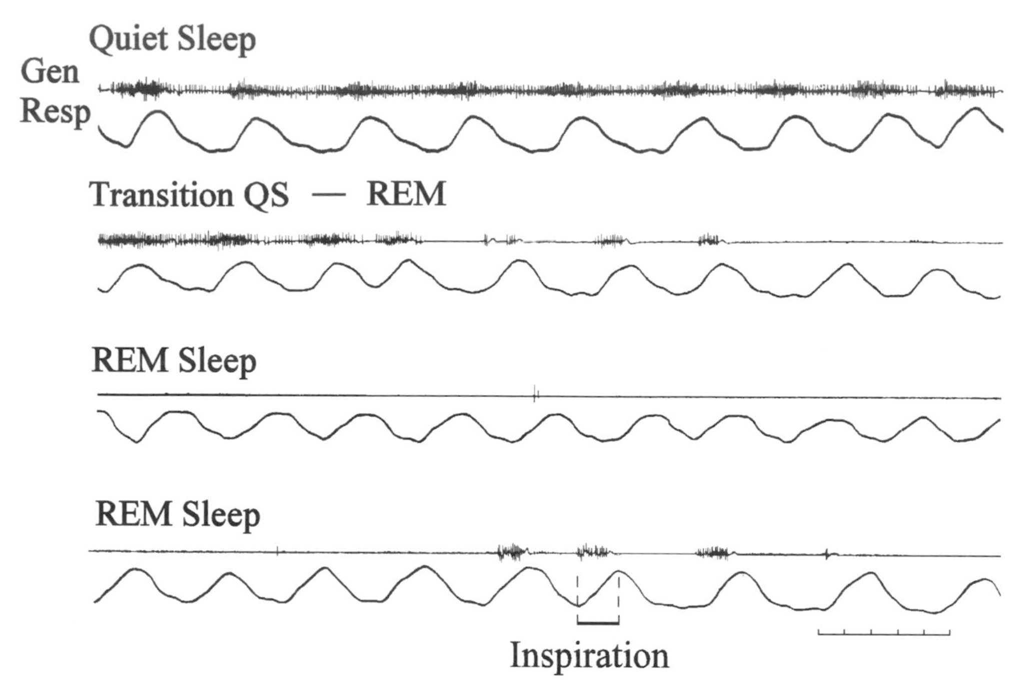

FIGURE 30–4. Genioglossal muscle activity (Gen) during the transition from quiet sleep (QS) to rapid eye movement (REM) sleep in an adult male. Activity is abolished during REM sleep, except for occasional phasic bursts. (Adapted from Sauerland EK and Harper RM.[35])

Loss of Upper Airway Muscle Tone

The loss of muscle tone during REM sleep is of particular importance to upper airway muscles. The consequences of REM sleep atonia on protruder muscles of the tongue, the genioglossi, can be seen for the adult in Figure 30–4.[35] The genioglossi discharge with each breath; that discharge greatly diminishes in REM sleep, except for phasic bursts of activity, which are characteristic of the state. In the adult, the loss of tone in the tongue can lead to relapse of the tongue toward the pharyngeal wall, diminishing the airway caliber; the epiglottis is higher in the infant, effectively reducing the impact of such a tongue relapse. However, other muscles of the upper airway, particularly those responsible for jaw closing (eg, temporalis and masseter), have the potential to modify airway resistance, as may other pharyngeal musculature.

Obstructive Sleep Apnea Syndrome

Obstructive sleep apnea syndrome (OSAS), is a condition during which diaphragmatic, thoracic, and abdominal muscles attempt breathing efforts while the upper airway diameter is severely constricted or collapsed from atonia or inaction of upper airway muscles; this results in cessation or greatly diminished airflow and air exchange. The condition is resolved typically by arousal sufficient to restore upper airway muscle tone. The syndrome is one of the more common disorders of breathing during sleep in children, affecting perhaps as many as 2% of the population during the first decade of life. Repetitive apneic events usually are characterized by loud snoring (although such snoring is not an absolute predictor of sleep apnea) and often are associated with struggling as the child attempts to breathe. The apneic events are associated with oxyhemoglobin desaturation and elevation of partial pressure of arterial CO_2 (Pa_{CO_2}).

The ability to maintain upper airway patency across sleep-wake states and throughout the normal respiratory cycle results from a delicate equilibrium between forces that promote airway closure and dilation. This "balance-of-pressures" concept reflects the current thinking about pathophysiologic mechanisms that underlie the clinical spectrum of obstructive apnea.[36,37]

A smaller cross-sectional area of the upper airway at any point in life is associated with decreased ability to maintain upper airway patency. In adults, the upper airway behaves as predicted by the Starling resistor model. According to this model, under conditions of flow limitation, maximal inspiratory flow is determined by the pressure changes upstream (nasal) to a collapsible site of the upper airway, and flow is independent of downstream (tracheal) pressure generated by the diaphragm. The pressures at which collapse of airway occurs has been termed "critical closing pressure" or P_{crit}.[38] The collapsible segment of the upper airway in children appears to follow a similar model, such that less negative (higher) pressures are present in children with OSAS.[39] Components that affect the upstream segment pressures or increase P_{crit} exert major consequences on the ability to maintain airway patency. The contribution of the various anatomic

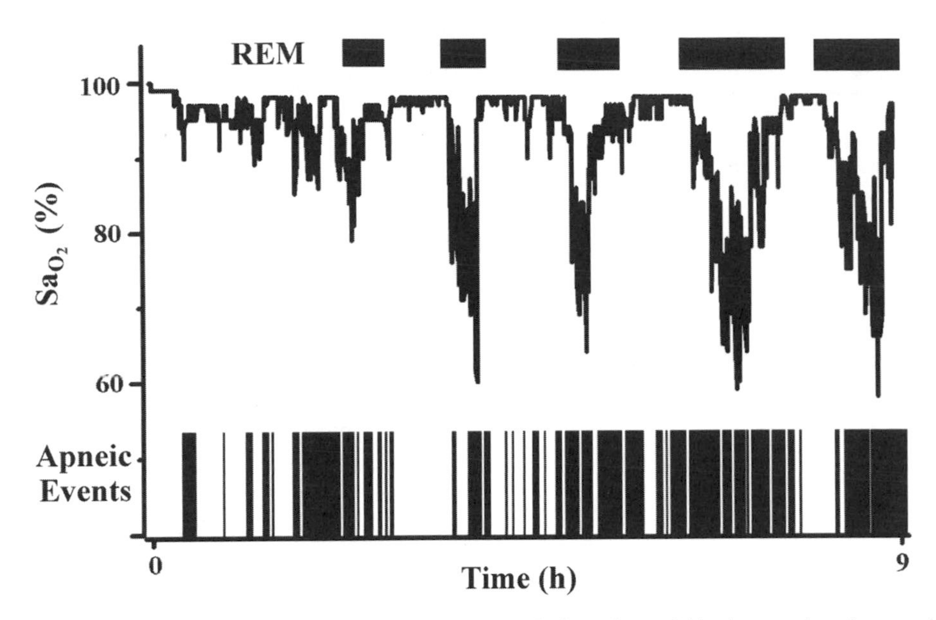

FIGURE 30–5. Overnight recording of pulse oximetry (Sa$_{O_2}$) showing periodic oxyhemoglobin desaturations in a snoring 6-year-old boy with enlarged tonsils and adenoids. Note that the occurrence of obstructive apneic events (*lower panel bars*) and the resulting desaturations coincide with epochs of rapid eye movement (REM) sleep.

nasopharyngeal structures to P_{crit} and the interactions between these structures that lead to upper airway patency or obstruction during sleep are the object of considerable research effort.

Malposition or malinsertion of specific dilating muscles likely exerts major consequences upon the mechanical dilating efficiency. Even if no major weakness is present, the mechanical disadvantage imposed by muscle shortening or by displacements of muscle insertion upon the pharyngeal wall undoubtedly results in diminished ability to stiffen the airway, thus leading to increased collapsibility or elevation of P_{crit}.

Control of upper airway size and stiffness depends on the relative and rhythmic contraction of a host of paired muscles which include palatal, pterygoid, tensor palatini, genioglossus, geniohyoid, and sternohyoid. These muscles promote a patent pharyngeal lumen and contract phasically in close timing relation to phrenic nerve activation. With contraction, these muscles promote motion of soft palate, mandible, tongue, and hyoid bone. Although the coordinated action of these muscles during the respiratory cycle has yet to be deciphered, their output stiffens the pharynx and related structures and enlarges the lumen.

It is important to stress that the optimal activity of these muscles depends on their anatomic arrangement. For example, airway patency is compromised during increased neck flexion by changing the points of attachment of muscles acting on the hyoid bone, such that the resulting vector of their forces may be nullified.

The activity of pharyngeal muscles depends on a variety of state and other factors within the central nervous system, and especially on neural mechanisms that affect brain stem respiratory motorneurons. Wakefulness conveys a supervisory function that assists airway patency, and sedative agents that compromise genioglossal muscle activity may result in significant upper airway compromise.[40] Similarly, and as discussed above, REM sleep atonia may facilitate the occurrence of upper airway collapse in the susceptible child, such that it comes as no surprise that most obstructive sleep apneic events occur in children during REM sleep (Figure 30–5). In addition, mechanoreceptor- and chemoreceptor-mediated genioglossal activity appear to be critical for maintenance of upper airway patency in micrognathic infants,[41] as is demonstrated by changes in genioglossal activity during transitions from oral to nasal breathing, relative to P_{crit}.

There is little evidence to suggest that intrinsic muscle weakness is a major contributor to upper airway dysfunction in conditions other than those associated with neuromuscular disorders. However in the latter, upper airway obstruction is observed frequently during sleep,[42] reinforcing the validity of the balance-of-pressures concept.[36,37]

These considerations demonstrate that several neurally mediated factors may affect overall responses to an added inspiratory load, and that state imposes yet another set of conditional influences on upper airway and overall respiratory behaviors.

Although central and peripheral chemoreceptor drives have not specifically been examined in children with a variety of clinical syndromes leading to OSAS, there is little evidence to suggest that major abnormalities of chemoreceptor control play a significant role in upper airway obstruction during sleep in children with OSAS. Indeed, ventilatory responses to rebreathing hyperoxic hypercapnia in some children and adolescents with OSAS

TABLE 30–1. Medical Conditions Associated with OSAS in Children

Tonsillar and adenoid lymphoid tissue hypertrophy
Achondroplasia, Crouzon's disease, and Apert's syndrome
Neuromuscular disorders (Duchenne muscular dystrophy, spinal muscular atrophy)
Myelomeningocele
Obesity
Pierre Robin syndrome
Cerebral palsy
Down syndrome
Sickle cell disease
Choanal stenosis
Hypothyroidism
Klippel-Feil and Hallermann-Streiff syndromes
Mucopolysaccharidosis
Osteopetrosis
Oropharyngeal papillomatosis
Beckwith-Wiedemann syndrome
Pfeiffer, Prader-Willi, Treacher Collins syndromes

and the mean slopes of the hypercapnic response were similar to those measured in age- and sex-matched control children.[43] Furthermore, no differences were found in the slopes calculated from plotting minute ventilation against oxygen saturation during isocapnic hypoxia.[44] Healthy children adjust ventilatory strategy to short repetitive hypercapnic challenges, while children with OSAS respond to comparable challenges as if neural adjustments to high CO_2 had already been adopted.[45] The blunting of temporal trends in ventilatory responses to CO_2 may derive from long-term changes in neural areas mediating chemosensitivity, including ventral medullary surface areas, following CO_2 exposure; such areas in the cat show long-term neural modification, as indicated by optical imaging techniques.[46]

Diminished laryngeal reflexes to mechanoreceptor and chemoreceptor stimulation with reduced afferent inputs into central neural regions underlying inspiratory inputs may be present. For example, chemoreceptor stimuli, such as increased Pa_{CO_2} or decreased Pa_{O_2}, stimulate the airway dilating muscles in a preferential mode, that is, upper airway musculature are more stimulated than is the diaphragm.[47] This preferential recruitment tends to correct an imbalance of forces acting on the airway and therefore maintains airway patency. Similarly, stimuli resulting from negative pressure in the nose, pharynx, or larynx rapidly stimulates the activity of upper airway dilators, and this effect is also preferential to the upper airway, causing some degree of diaphragmatic inhibition and thus compensating for increases in upstream resistance.[48] The function of these upper airway receptors in children with OSAS is unknown.

Several potential mechanisms contribute to maintenance of upper airway patency during sleep and wakefulness.[49] Each of these mechanisms, or a combination thereof, plays a role in the causation of respiratory compromise in the normal child or in children with clinical problems that predispose to OSAS (Table 30–1). A systematic approach to identification and modification of these mechanisms could lead to improved therapeutic approaches in these patients.

Determination of OSAS usually requires a polysomnograph recording to differentiate central versus obstructive events, precipitation by particular sleep states, cardiovascular sequelae, and associated motoric elements. The consequences of untreated obstructive sleep apnea in young children can be severe. Systemic diastolic hypertension may develop in OSAS patients,[50] and pulmonary hypertension may ensue or complicate underlying cardiac disease such as is seen frequently in Down syndrome.[51] Although the long-term physiologic effects on the cardiovascular system have yet to be described in children, the adult literature suggests the potential for development of a number of cardiovascular morbidities resulting from repetitive hypoxic events associated with recurrent upper airway obstruction and the concurrent transient elevations in arterial pressure accompanying cessation of airflow with sustained inspiratory efforts. Recent evidence of substantial cognitive defects following untreated obstruction is of concern.[2,52] The deficits possibly result from hypoxic damage to neural structures involved in learning and memory.

The most common condition associated with OSAS, adenotonsillar hypertrophy,[53] usually can be resolved by surgery. In more complex cases, however, continuous positive airway pressure administration can be employed and is safe, effective, and usually well-tolerated by children and adolescents with OSAS.[54] Administration of supplemental O_2 usually will improve oxygenation without impairing the drive to breathing or worsening sleep-disordered breathing;[55,56] however, end-tidal CO_2 can rise unexpectedly during supplemental oxygenation, and it should be monitored.

Obstructive Sleep Apnea and Sudden Infant Death Syndrome

A number of pathologic signs that frequently appear at autopsy in victims of sudden infant death syndrome (SIDS) are suggestive of a terminal event associated with airway obstruction, including supradiaphragmatic petechiae, indicative of enhanced negative intrathoracic pressure.[57] However, the extent of petechiae in SIDS is subject to dispute, and it is possible that extreme hypotension may result in petechiae with normal thoracic pressure swings from breathing. Although obstructed breathing is rare in normal infants,[58] infants who later succumb to SIDS show enhanced numbers of obstructed events.[59] Some investigators have reported a relatively fixed respiratory rate (without much variability) in infants who later succumb to SIDS, rather than a

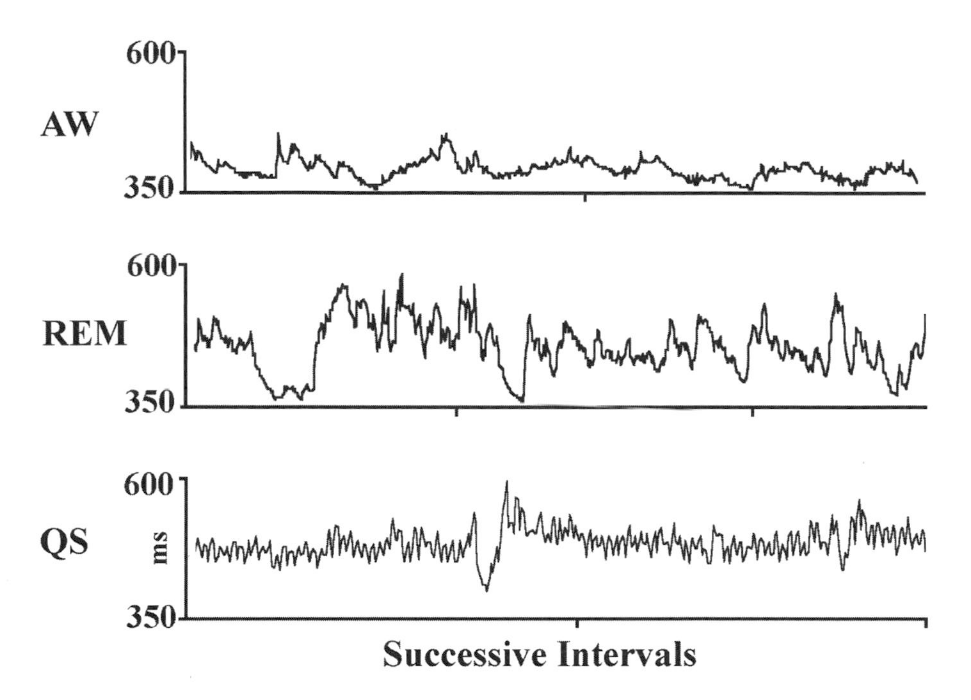

FIGURE 30–6. Successive cardiac R-R intervals during waking (AW), rapid eye movement (REM) sleep, and quiet sleep (QS) from a 40-day-old infant. Note the near-sinusoidal modulation by respiration during QS, and the large slow variation in REM sleep. The x-axis ticks indicate the intervals that sum to 1 minute.

high incidence of apnea.[60] The relative loss of variation in breathing rates derives from a reduction in short apnea, of the type normally encountered from minor variation in blood pressure or small movements, for example. Such determination of short apnea reduction requires careful partitioning of state for adequate determination.

Respiratory Influences on Cardiovascular Action and Blood Pressure Influences on Breathing

One of the more significant aspects of breathing control is the close interdependence of breathing and blood pressure regulation. The respiratory system, using primarily somatic musculature, exerts substantial influence on moment-to-moment blood pressure; conversely, transient elevation of blood pressure can cease breathing efforts, while lowering of blood pressure can greatly increase breathing efforts. The interactions between the systems can be observed readily in breathing influences on heart rate. Inspiratory efforts normally are associated with accelerated heart rate and expiration with deceleration, the result of reflex activity from pulmonary afferents and vagal outflow; the resulting coupling between breathing and heart rate is particularly prominent during QS (Figure 30–6), and measures of that interaction can provide a useful indication of state.[61] In addition, phasic activity during REM sleep induces substantial parasympathetic and sympathetic outflow, resulting in larger but typically slower variation in heart rate. Plots of cardiac beat-to-beat intervals demonstrate the substantial influences exerted normally during each state, with QS exerting a highly cyclic effect on heart variation, and REM sleep showing a lesser extent of modulation by breathing but large slower sources of variation. Waking shows a large variation in heart rate changes; typically, very active periods are accompanied by high heart rates with little variation. The cyclic nature of some of the cardiac rate variation has led to a variety of procedures to measure that variation and to partition sympathetic and parasympathetic influences on the heart. Other procedures focus on momentary effects on breathing that result in transient changes in heart rate, such as responses to gastroesophageal reflux. Particular syndromes exert unique patterns of respiratory-related variation; for example, children with congenital central hypoventilation syndrome show a relative absence of variation of respiratory modulation of heart rate, and infants who later succumb to SIDS also show reduced variation to breathing.

The reciprocal influence of blood pressure on breathing rate is dramatic and of great clinical importance during sleep. Momentary apnea during sleep often occurs as a result of transient elevations in blood pressure, the normal association of blood pressure with arousals or changes in body position. The presence of such short apnea (4 to 5 seconds) should be viewed as a normal occurrence, while their absence is an issue of substantial concern; that is, fixed respiratory rates with few apnea may be a sign of disease or immaturity, since this characteristic indicates that normal regulatory influences are probably inoperative. Such fixed respiratory rates have been detected in infants who later succumb to SIDS,[60] and are found in animals undergoing the initial stages of shock.[62] Of equal importance is the reciprocal aspect of the breathing-blood pressure relationship; loss of blood pressure normally is accompanied by enhanced respiratory efforts, together with recruitment of other somatic musculature with reflex efforts to restore blood pressure.[62,63] Thus, a fall in blood pressure recruits breathing to assist in restoration of perfusion; this process is essential for survival, considering that profound drops in blood pressure occur spontaneously during REM sleep. The REM state is of particular importance in this discussion, since the forebrain influences that assist in maintaining blood pressure from hypothalamic and limbic sites are abolished during REM sleep, leaving management of compensatory blood pressure-breathing interactions principally to local brain stem organization. As discussed below, the cerebellum participates in that compensation, and damage to cerebellar structures may compromise survival under challenges of prolonged apnea or substantial loss of blood pressure.

Cerebellar Influences on Respiration

Regions within the cerebellum have been recognized only recently as playing a role in breathing control, although cerebellar structures have long been implicated in blood pressure regulation. Cerebellar structures have been associated classically with control of movement, particularly in coordination of sequences of motor action so that intentional motor efforts are smoothly executed; a clinical test for cerebellar functioning typically includes a voluntary motor act by the patient (such as touching the nose); the smoothness of the resulting motion is noted. However, certain cognitive abilities, cardiovascular control, and recovery from extreme breathing challenges have been recognized recently as incorporating cerebellar functions. Cardiovascular and breathing control appear to be moderated by cerebellar structures, not for "routine" patterns, but rather for extreme challenges (ie, profound losses of blood pressure or prolonged apnea). For example, damage to the fastigial nucleus of the cerebellum has little effect on normal control of blood pressure, but an animal with bilateral fastigial nuclei lesions succumbs if subjected to significant hypotension by high doses of sodium nitroprusside.[64] A significant issue in this role is that Purkinje cells of the cerebellum are exceptionally sensitive to damage from ischemia;[65] a portion of this damage appears to be mediated via fibers from the inferior olive, a major afferent input to Purkinje cells within the fastigial nucleus. Thus, a pronounced apneic event may establish a circumstance for failure (eliciting damage via hypoxic effects on climbing fibers to Purkinje cells), so that a later blood pressure challenge during REM sleep, a time when protective forebrain mechanisms are unavailable, results in an unrecoverable condition. Cerebellar contributions to breathing in infancy are of particular concern because of the prevalence of cerebellar damage resulting from insults secondary to vascularization issues;[66] the occurrence of developmental abnormalities, such as Chiari Type II (herniated vermis) and Dandy-Walker malformations (absence or hypoplasia of vermis); and the reported incidences of reduced neurotransmitter receptors in structures projecting to the cerebellum of victims of SIDS, including the arcuate nucleus of the ventral medullary surface, and the inferior olive.[67,68] Damage to the cerebellum and immediate projecting structures also has been associated with obstructive sleep apnea and with sudden death in infancy.

Body Position and Breathing Aspects

The incidence of SIDS has been reduced by half in recent years, primarily as a result of avoidance of certain body positions during sleep, especially the prone position.[69] That such a simple intervention results in such an astonishing risk reduction is remarkable. Although several aspects of the prone position may contribute to high risk, including the possibility of suffocation in loose bed clothes,[70] rebreathing of CO_2,[68] or failure to dissipate sufficient heat from the face,[71] the contributions from cerebellar/vestibular influences should not be overlooked, since body position exerts marked effects on cardiovascular control, partially through vestibular/body position sensors.[72–74] These particular issues require further study.

Age and State Effects on Chemosensitivity

One or More Chemosensitive Field?

Almost 40 years ago, areas of the ventrolateral medulla oblongata (VLM) were identified and rapidly accepted as the sites of central chemoreception for CO_2 and/or H^+. Indeed, Mitchell, Loeschcke, and colleagues reported that localized application of acid or CO_2-saturated solutions to the VLM elicited significant cardioventilatory enhancements.[75–77] However, since then, other investigators have postulated that the location of central chemoreceptors is not restricted to the originally described VLM regions, and they have demonstrated the existence of neurons exhibiting intrinsic CO_2 chemosensitivity in many other brain regions,[78–80] suggesting that more than one neural region is capable of fulfilling the requirements for chemosensitivity in response to a stimulus such as hypercapnia.

Neurochemistry of Central Chemosensitivity

The neurotransmitters involved in the intrinsic sensory pathways associated with central chemoreception are unknown. The presence of cholinergic muscarinic receptors in those brain stem areas traditionally associated with CO_2 chemosensitivity appears to play a major role in the neuronal excitation associated with the enhanced ventilatory response to hypercapnia.[81] Additional neurotransmitters also may be involved; opioid receptors have been shown to modulate both hypercapnic and hypoxic chemosensitivities,[82] and γ-aminobutyric acid (GABA) receptors expressed within fast synaptic inhibitory GABAergic pathways reduce the excitation of inspiratory-related neurons and delay initiation of their activity, thereby accounting for the potential prolongation of expiratory duration during hypercapnia.[83] It remains unclear, however, whether all widely distributed chemosensitive neurons participate in a functionally meaningful fashion for the generation of the ventilatory response to hypercapnia, or whether they serve as backup mechanisms that are recruited during particular states (eg, sleep, exercise, or infection). Furthermore, developmental changes occurring in muscarinic receptor expression and in the functional implications of such chemosensitive sites remain undefined thus far.

Maturation of Central Chemosensitivity

Animal data

Central CO_2-chemosensory mechanisms may not be fully functional or mature at birth.[84] When topical application of H^+ to the ventral brain stem is performed, smaller increases in neuronal activity emerge in neonatal cats compared with that in adult animals.[85] Separate studies performed in both newborn and adult rats have demonstrated that hypercapnic ventilatory responses increase with age.[86–89] These findings also have been confirmed in the neonatal primate.[90] However, other studies show that when corrected for body weight, ventilatory responses to hypercapnia in term neonates appear to be similar to those found in adults.[91] Differences in functional chemosensitivity found between various studies may result from the developmental status of any given mammal in relation to its postnatal age. Indeed, premature, but not term, lambs or piglets exhibit an attenuated hypercapnic response.[92,93] Similarly, newborn rats, being immature at birth, also express a lower ventilatory response to hypercapnia at 2 days of life compared with that at 8 days of life.[94] Thus, prematurity and/or factors delaying normal maturation emerge as important contributors to the attenuated hypercapnic response in newborns of various species.

Human data

Hypercapnia elicits a relatively sustained ventilatory increase in human infants at term that is almost entirely due to an increase in tidal volume without consistent change in respiratory frequency.[95,96] In contrast, the ventilatory response to hypercapnia in premature infants is lower, with CO_2 responses increasing with postconceptional age.[97] In preterm infants, the impaired ventilatory increase to hypercapnia is accompanied by a progressive increase in expiratory duration and a consequent frequency reduction over time, both of which appear to be associated with diaphragmatic recruitment during expiration (braking). Braking appears to preserve a high end-expiratory lung volume to optimize gas exchange.[98]

Another important issue involves separation of central and peripheral contributions to the ventilatory response to hypercapnia, an arduous task when testing human subjects. However, when interpreting results of ventilatory challenges with a hypercapnic gas, great care needs to be taken in standardizing the presentation of the stimulus. Although the ventilatory response to hypercapnia generally is believed to indicate the activity of central chemoreceptors, abrupt elevation of inspired CO_2 concentrations also elicits a significant contribution from peripheral chemoreceptors.[99] Such peripheral chemoreceptor–mediated contributions to the hypercapnic response clearly are present in young children, as is demonstrated by larger ventilatory slopes in the response to either endogenous or bolus CO_2 when compared with response to rebreathing or steady state methods.[100] Thus, stimulus presentation, developmental stage, and state (sleep versus awake) need to be incorporated into the interpretation of a test that, a priori, may appear simple to perform.

Beyond infancy, little is known about the development of central chemoreceptor function. In awake prepubertal children, Marcus and colleagues found enhanced ventilatory responses to hypercapnia compared with that in adults using rebreathing techniques, provided that correction of the slopes for body size was performed.[101] Similarly, significant developmental differences in CO_2 responses emerge when the CO_2 stimulus is presented in a step or a ramp fashion.[102] These findings in older children suggest that at some time during the transition from infancy through childhood to adulthood, major changes occur in the relative contributions and integration of peripheral and central chemoreceptor activity. Which mechanisms mediate these developmental changes, and whether they are operative at the carotid body, neural transmission, or central nervous system level, remain unclear.

Effect of Sleep on Carbon Dioxide Responses

When hypercapnic ventilatory responses are conducted in sleeping adults, CO_2 sensitivity is reduced, especially during REM sleep.[103] Although studies in infants are not always in close agreement with those performed in adults,[104,105] a decrease in central chemosensitivity emerges during REM sleep in the young infant when the stimulus is applied using the rebreathing technique.[106] Thus, transition from the wakeful state to the sleep state elicits major decreases in hypercapnic drive, and such changes are accentuated further during REM sleep.

State Effects on Laryngeal Stimulation Reflex Actions on Breathing

Laryngeal chemoreceptors in early life are particularly sensitive to stimulation by agents other than fluids normally encountered during feeding; water stimulation to laryngeal areas of the anesthetized piglet results in prolonged apnea.[107] Thresholds for arousal or coughing responses to clear foreign agents are higher in REM sleep compared with those in QS in adult dogs, resulting in more frequent prolonged apnea in REM rather than waking, as is common in QS.[108]

State Effects on Temperature Control Loss: Consequences for Breathing

The normal influence of descending thermoregulatory mechanisms from hypothalamic regions is abolished by REM sleep.[109,110] Since temperature exerts a major influence on breathing, loss of temperature regulation during REM sleep by these descending mechanisms has the potential to place an infant at risk during elevated or lowered temperatures. The clinical significance for breathing is of some importance; just as infants cannot thermoregulate while under most forms of anesthesia, neither can they regulate temperature in REM sleep. When core temperatures are significantly elevated, as with infections or following immunization, particular attention must be paid to temperature control during sleep. The frequency of central apnea has the potential to increase significantly with increasing temperatures.

The temperature issue is particularly a concern in SIDS, since elevated core temperatures have been reported in victims of the syndrome,[111] perhaps as a result of too-heavy wrapping[112,113] or activated heating systems at night.[71,114] The prone body position, which doubles the risk of SIDS,[69] also enhances the potential for hyperthermia.[113] In the supine position, head covering exerts a significant risk of dangerously elevated core temperature; in both prone and supine positions, excessive body covering should be considered a particular risk, with head covering adding to that risk. The means by which hyperthermia can result in a fatal outcome remain obscure; the inability of respiratory mechanisms to respond to thermal stimulation during REM sleep may be a major factor, as may be unresponsiveness of sympathetic sweating mechanisms for cooling during that state. Recent animal evidence suggests that higher core temperatures diminish "rescue" time for resuscitation from ischemia by gasping.[115] Hyperthermia occurring together with ischemic events results in brain pathology that is comparable to conditions involving much longer ischemic periods without such temperature elevation.[116] A variety of mechanisms may operate to enhance risk from elevated core temperature.

Gasping, Autoresuscitation, and Sleep

The neural sites regulating eupnea may differ from those mediating gasping efforts involved in autoresuscitation.[117–119] Gasping is evoked when tissue hypoxia is sufficiently severe, and it aims to restore perfusion to vital functions.[120] Gasping is used commonly by infants to recover from prolonged apnea as well as loss of blood pressure, and animal evidence suggests that the capability to successfully autoresusitate by gasping is age dependent, with restoration of vital function being more difficult with increasing age.[121,122] As previously noted, gasping mechanisms in animals are affected significantly by core temperature,[115] prenatal nicotine exposure, and maturation.[123,124] In addition, particular components of gasp generation exhibit developmentally regulated dependency on glutamate receptor subtypes and other neurotransmitters.[125,126] Despite the obvious importance of these mechanisms on survival, clarification of issues such as the effect of sleep state on time to effective resuscitation by gasping and proportion of effective survivals, for example, remains to be determined.

Congenital Central Hypoventilation Syndrome

Infants with congenital central hypoventilation syndrome (CCHS; Ondine's curse) exhibit deficient central chemoreception even during wakefulness[127] and a relative loss of breathing drive during sleep.[128,129] This condition can be recognized immediately after birth, particularly with the emergence of QS; ventilation is somewhat improved in REM sleep compared with that in QS. Afflicted infants show chronic respiratory insufficiency in the absence of primary pulmonary, cardiac, neuromuscular, or chest wall disease. Hirschsprung's disease, a condition associated with absence of ganglia in the distal intestinal tract, accompanies a significant proportion of CCHS cases.[129,130] While central chemoreception is diminished even during waking, peripheral chemoreceptor responses are partially preserved,[131] providing a ventilatory stimulus while the patients are alert; however, these patients require ventilatory support during sleep. Maintenance of appropriate CO_2 levels requires vigilant monitoring during periods of rest or sleep. Afflicted patients increase ventilation to exercise,[132] and the increase in ventilation occurs even during passive movement of the periphery during wakefulness[133] and during sleep.[134] Patients frequently show a relative intolerance to high temperatures, and they occasionally show inappropriate responses to transient elevation of blood pressure (eg, syncope to micturation or defecation). A principal physiologic characteristic in CCHS is a near-absence of respiratory-related variation in heart rate;[129,135] this characteristic is especially apparent in QS but is also apparent in waking, as is shown in Figure 30–7; a variety of other

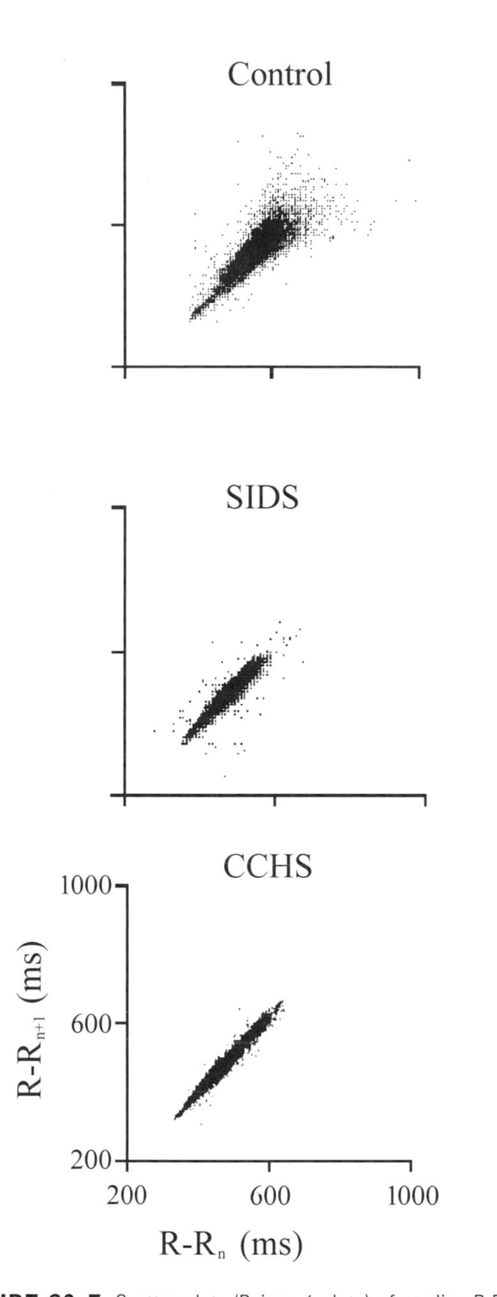

FIGURE 30–7. Scatter plots (Poincaré plots) of cardiac R-R intervals against preceding intervals during quiet sleep (QS) in a patient with congenital central hypoventilation syndrome (CCHS), a control patient, and a subsequent victim of sudden infant death syndrome (SIDS). At slower rates (longer intervals), dispersion is reduced in CCHS and SIDS scatter plots. The largest proportion of variation at these rates derives from respiratory sources, that is diminished in CCHS and future SIDS victims.

cardiac rhythm disturbances including bradycardia and asystole also are apparent.[135,136]

Neuromuscular Disorders and Sleep

Duchenne's Muscular Dystrophy

The ability to ventilate efficiently during sleep depends on the integrity of muscle structure and neural control to those muscles. Maintenance of sustained diaphragmatic, intercostal, and abdominal muscle tone is required to support the prolonged inspiratory efforts of QS, while sustained tone prevents collapse of the upper airway during enhanced negative pressure associated with inspiration. In addition, rapid restoration of muscle tone must occur to overcome minor obstructions and to maintain airway patency, such as the short-term tone restoration that occurs during the phasic activation of upper airway musculature during the REM state.[35] It might be expected that muscle structure and control disorders that afflict children, such as those found in children with neuromuscular disorders, might be associated with disordered breathing during sleep. Duchenne's muscular dystrophy (DMD), a disorder affecting striated muscle structure rather than neural control of the musculature, is the second-most common lethal genetic disorder in males, with an incidence of 1 in 3,300 male births.[137] The disorder results in weakness in striated musculature, including diaphragmatic and accessory respiratory muscles, and affects breathing in waking and sleep; sleep worsens the effects of these defects.

High levels of sleep-disordered breathing,[138] and deaths associated with respiratory failure, are associated with DMD.[139] Since cardiac muscle is also a target of the disorder, cardiomyopathic changes can develop, with involvement of left ventricular contractility as well as right ventricular function. In addition to direct effects of DMD on cardiac muscle that may modify circulation during sleep, the dependency of the cardiovascular system on ventilatory action to assist blood movement may be affected; for example, modified return of venous flow on inspiration, and the resulting failure of interaction between cardiac and respiratory systems, may compromise perfusion.

The symptoms of sleep-disordered breathing in DMD patients, such as daytime sleepiness, fatigue, morning headache, and frequent night-time body repositioning, often are mistaken as components of the primary syndrome, rather than a sleep-related disturbance. Sleep-disordered breathing may occur with normal waking arterial blood gases; thus, night-time polysomnography is required for adequate assessment. Those assessments frequently indicate significant apnea/hypopnea densities with oxygen desaturations, especially during REM sleep.[140–145] Noninvasive ventilatory support with continuous positive or bilevel airway pressure, with or without oxygen supplementation, is the mainstay of therapy once sleep-disordered breathing is diagnosed.

Spinal Muscular Atrophies

Genetic disorders that involve degeneration of the motorneuron pool to the musculature are relatively common; childhood spinal muscular atrophies (SMAs) are a frequent cause of mortality. The lower motorneuron lesions result in initial muscle fasciculations and weakness, followed by atrophy. Signs of the most prevalent form of the disease often can be detected prenatally as a reduction in fetal movements; postnatally, deficiencies in respiratory muscles can be noted by weak cries and respiratory difficulties in addition to the floppiness of other somatic musculature. Survival beyond teenage years is rare. Other less common forms of the disorder appear from 6 months to 2 to 3 years (type II SMA) or from 2 to 3 years (type III SMA) and show better survival rates (eg, into the third decade for type III SMA). The primary characteristic of breathing during sleep results from inadequate neural drive to the musculature (both upper airway and chest); obstructive sleep apnea and hypoventilation should be expected. Since treatment for these syndromes is primarily supportive to prevent complications, determination of sleep-related breathing disorders is a significant concern in maintenance, and intervention to ease specific breathing disorders during sleep (eg, ventilatory support to accommodate sleep-disordered breathing) is of great importance.[146]

Prader-Willi Syndrome

Prader-Willi syndrome (PWS) is a unique genetic condition that results from the loss of paternal contributions for a 2-Mb imprinted region on the proximal long arm of human chromosome 15, in the form of either chromosomal deletions or uniparental disomy.[147] The clinical manifestations of PWS encompass characteristic phenotypic features such as small hands and feet, hypotonia, short stature, obsessive compulsive behaviors, and hypogonadism.[148] The failure to thrive that is characteristically present during early life is later replaced by hyperphagia and development of severe obesity.[149]

Among a number of other unique physiologic characteristics, PWS patients present a unique combination of sleep- and breathing-related manifestations. Indeed, excessive daytime sleepiness with increased frequency of REM sleep periods occurs in a subset of PWS patients, while in others disturbances in circadian rhythmicity with a tendency for multiple microsleep periods is detected.[150,151] In addition, the combination of hypotonia and obesity favor the appearance of obstructive sleep apnea in these patients.

Patients with PWS also display significant alterations in central and peripheral elements of respiratory control that, although not immediately related to their obesity, can be severely impacted by the mechanical consequences of increased adiposity, and that ultimately lead to ventilatory failure.[152,153] An unique and almost universal feature of patients with PWS is the absence of ventilatory responses to peripheral chemoreceptor stimuli;[154–156] this deficiency, leads to abnormal arousal patterns during sleep.[157–159] When untreated, obesity progressively reduces central chemosensitivity as well, with the latter being ameliorated by growth hormone therapy and increased muscle mass.[160]

Achondroplasia

Certain syndromes that are manifested with major craniofacial abnormalities, such as achondroplasia, pose significant concerns for breathing in infancy during sleep. Affected infants frequently exhibit hypoxia during sleep, resulting typically from severe obstructive sleep apnea.[161] On occasion, some remediation is achieved with surgery to enlarge the airway, such as by tonsillectomy and adenoidectomy, but the primary condition of diminished airway diameter is frequently so severe from the structural malformation that continuous positive airway pressure or tracheostomy are required.[162]

Down Syndrome

Children with Down syndrome frequently exhibit a variety of craniofacial and neuromuscular features that predispose to OSAS. Polysomnography reveals that these cases show a disproportionate degree of OSAS with hypoxia and hypoventilation;[163] sleep-disordered breathing improves with tonsillectomy and adenoidectomy, but this intervention often is insufficient to resolve the condition. This latter finding reinforces a suspicion that central neural mechanisms contribute to the impaired breathing during sleep, in addition to the anatomic features.

Myelomeningocele and Chiari II Malformations

Patients afflicted with myelomeningocele or Chiari II malformations frequently exhibit sleep-disordered breathing,[164] and state-related breathing disorders are suspected as causative mechanisms in the sudden unexpected deaths that occur frequently in this population.[165] Moderate or severe breathing disturbances are found in 20% of cases.[164] The largest proportion of affected cases exhibit central apnea, while others show obstructive breathing; obstructed cases are seldom resolved with surgical intervention for tonsillectomy, suggesting that the primary dysfunction is of neural origin.[166] The possible damage to vermis cerebelli structures from foramen magnum herniation in Chiari type II malformation has the potential to interfere with both blood pressure and breathing regulation, particularly under extreme challenges of hypotension or prolonged apnea (see above). Compression of ventral neural surfaces is also a concern. The presence of thoracic or thoracolumbar myelomeningocele, or the addition of severe brain stem malformations, has been shown to enhance the potential for manifesting sleep-disordered breathing.[164] Support for affected patients with Chiari II syndrome must consider the needs for recovery from pronounced hypotension during sleep.

Rett Syndrome

Rett syndrome is a progressive neurodevelopmental disorder of remarkable characteristics; instead of disordered breathing during sleep with recovery of ventilation during waking, breathing in this syndrome is disturbed during waking and normalizes during sleep. The disorder is one of the most common causes of mental retardation; infants develop normally until 6 to 18 months of age, after which they typically regress, losing acquired motor and verbal skills; seizures, autism, ataxia, and stereotypic hand movements frequently develop. Patients typically survive into adulthood. The disorder appears to result from a defect in the *MECP2* gene on the X chromosome;[167] the *MECP2* gene controls gene expression through deoxyribonucleic acid methylation. During waking, patients, who are almost exclusively female (1 in 10,000 to 15,000 females is affected), show periods of hyperventilation followed by central apnea and desaturation. During both REM and QS, however, ventilatory patterns and saturation remain within normal values (although, during REM sleep, saturation may be at slightly lower levels). The disorder in breathing appears to arise from neural mechanisms underlying arousal functions, or possibly from cortical control mechanisms.[168]

Summary

The cardiovascular and respiratory adjustments occurring during state transitions and state changes aim to maintain oxygenation and acid-base homeostasis. Nevertheless, the mechanisms underlying such adjustments may generate transient state-dependent vulnerabilities that, in turn, may develop into life-threatening conditions. Alternatively, the presence of a disease condition affecting the normal functioning of any of the homeostatic mechanisms implicated during the various states may contribute to the particular manifestations and morbidity of such disorders.

Acknowledgment

Aspects of some of these studies were supported by HD-22695.

References

1. Hoppenbrouwers T, Harper RM, Hodgman JE, et al. Polygraphic studies of normal infants during the first six months of life. II. Respiratory rate and variability as a function of state. Pediatr Res 1978;12:120–5.
2. Gozal D, Pope DW. Snoring during early childhood and academic performance at ages 13–14. Pediatrics 2001; 107:1394–99.
3. Sterman MB, Harper RM, Havens B, et al. Quantitative analysis of infant EEG development during QS. Electroencephalogr Clin Neurophysiol 1977;43:371–85.
4. Parmelee AH Jr, Akiyama Y, Schulz MA, et al. Analysis of the electroencephalogram of sleeping infants. Act Nerv Super (Praha) 1969;11:111–5.
5. Parmelee AH Jr, Akiyama Y, Schulz MA., et al. Maturation of EEG activity during sleep in premature infants. Electroencephalogr Clin Neurophysiol 1968;24:319–29.
6. Scher M. Normal electrographic-polysomnographic patterns in preterm and fullterm infants. Semin Pediatr Neurol 1996;3:2–12.
7. Schechtman VL, Harper RK, Harper RM. Distribution of slow-wave EEG activity across the night in developing infants. Sleep 1994;17:316–22.
8. Clemente CD, Sterman MB. Cortical synchronization and sleep patterns in acute restrained and chronic behaving cats induced by basal forebrain stimulation. Electroencephalogr Clin Neurophysiol 1963;24:172–87.
9. Sterman MB, Clemente CD. Forebrain mechanisms for the onset of sleep. In: Petre-Quadrens O, Schlag JD, eds. Basic sleep mechanisms. New York: Academic Press, 1974: 83–97.
10. Szymusiak R. Magnocellular nuclei of the basal forebrain: substrates of sleep and arousal regulation. Sleep 1995; 18:478–500.
11. Benington JH, Heller HC. Restoration of brain energy metabolism as the function of sleep. Prog Neurobiol 1995;45:347–60.
12. Alam MN, McGinty D, Szymusiak R. Neuronal discharge of preoptic/anterior hypothalamic thermosensitive neurons: relation to NREM sleep. Am J Physiol 1995; 269:R1240–9.
13. Shouse MN, Siegel JM. Pontine regulation of REM sleep components in cats: integrity of the pedunculopontine tegmentum (PPT) is important for phasic events but unnecessary for atonia during REM sleep. Brain Res 1992;571:50–63.
14. Morrison AR, Pompeiano O. Vestibular influences during sleep. VI. Vestibular control of autonomic functions during the rapid eye movements of desynchronized sleep. Arch Ital Biol 1970;108:154–80.
15. Perenin MT, Maeda T, Jeannerod M. Are vestibular nuclei responsible for rapid eye movements of paradoxical sleep? Brain Res 1972;43:617–21.
16. McGinty DJ, Harper RM. Dorsal raphe neurons: depression of firing during sleep in cats. Brain Res 1976;101:569–75.
17. Sakai K. Executive mechanisms of paradoxical sleep. Arch Ital Biol 1988;126:239–57.
18. Rector DM, Gozal D, Forster HV, et al. Ventral medullary surface activity during sleep, waking and anesthetic states in the goat. Am J Physiol 1994;267:R1154–60.
19. Richard CA, Rector DM, Harper RK, Harper RM. Optical imaging of the ventral medullary surface across sleep-wake states. Am J Physiol 1999;277:R1239–45.
20. Hoppenbrouwers T, Jensen, DK, Hodgman JE, et al. The emergence of a circadian pattern in respiratory rates: comparison between control infants and subsequent siblings of SIDS. Pediatr Res 1980;14:345–51.
21. Hoppenbrouwers T, Hodgman JE, Sterman MB, Harper RM. Temporal distribution of sleep states, somatic and autonomic activity during the first half year of life. Sleep 1982;5:131–44.
22. Hao H, Rivkees SA. The biological clock of very premature primate infants is responsive to light. Proc Natl Acad Sci U S A 1999;96:2426–9.
23. Harper RM, Hoppenbrouwers T, Bannett D, et al. Effects of feeding on state and cardiac regulation in the infant. Dev Psychobiol 1977;10:507–17.

24. Harper RM, Schechtman VL, Kluge KA. Machine classification of infant sleep state using cardiorespiratory measures. Electroencephalogr Clin Neurophysiol 1987; 67:379–87.
25. Feinberg I, Floyd TC. Systematic trends across the night in human sleep cycles. Psychophysiology 1979;16:283–91.
26. Busby K, Pivik RT. Failure of high intensity auditory stimuli to affect behavioral arousal in children during the first sleep cycle. Pediatr Res 1983;17:802–5.
27. Gaultier CL. Cardiorespiratory adaptation during sleep in infants and children. Pediatr Pulmonol 1995;19:105–17.
28. Jacquin TD, Borday V, Schneider-Maunoury S, et al. Reorganization of pontine rhythmogenic neural networks in Krox-20 knock-out mice. Neuron 1996;17:747–58.
29. Poon CS, Zhou, Z, Champagnat J. NMDA receptor activity in utero averts respiratory depression and anomalous long-term depression in newborn mice. J Neurosci Online 2000;20:RC73. This journal put online on 8/1/96. http://jneurosci.org
30. Erickson JT, Conover JC, Borday V, et al. Mice lacking brain-derived neurotrophic factor exhibit visceral sensory neuron losses distinct from mice lacking NT4 and display a severe developmental deficit in control of breathing. J Neurosci 1996;16:5361–71.
31. Balkowiec A, Katz DM. Brain-derived neurotrophic factor is required for normal development of the central respiratory rhythm in mice. J Physiol 1998;510:527–33.
32. Sieck GC, Trelease RB, Harper RM. Sleep influences on diaphragmatic motor unit discharge. Exp Neurol 1984; 85:316–35.
33. Henderson-Smart DJ, Read DJ. Reduced lung volume during behavioral active sleep in the newborn. J Appl Physiol 1979;46:1081–5.
34. Marks JD, Harper RM. Differential inhibition of the diaphragm and posterior cricoarytenoid muscles induced by transient hypertension across sleep states in intact cats. Exp Neurol 1987;95:730–42.
35. Sauerland EK, Harper RM. The human tongue during sleep: electromyographic activity of the genioglossus muscle. Exp Neurol 1976;51:160–70.
36. Remmers JE, de Groot WJ, Sauerland EK, Anch AM. Pathogenesis of upper airway occlusion during sleep. J Appl Physiol 1978;44:931–8.
37. Brouillette RT, Thach BT. A neuromuscular mechanism maintaining extrathoracic airway patency. J Appl Physiol 1979;46:772–9.
38. Smith PL, Wise RA, Gold AR, et al. Upper airway pressure-flow relationships in obstructive sleep apnea. J Appl Physiol 1988;64:789–95.
39. Marcus CL, McColley SA, Carroll JL, et al. Upper airway collapsibility in children with obstructive sleep apnea syndrome. J Appl Physiol 1994;77:918–24.
40. Hershenson M, Brouillette RT, Olsen E, Hunt CE. The effect of chloral hydrate on genioglossus and diaphragmatic activity. Pediatr Res 1984;18:516–9.
41. Roberts JL, Reed WR, Mathew OP, Thach BT. Control of respiratory activity of the genioglossus muscle in micrognathic infants. J Appl Physiol 1986;61:1523–33.
42. Gozal D. Pulmonary manifestations of neuromuscular disease: Focus on Duchenne muscular dystrophy and spinal muscular atrophy. Pediatr Pulmonol 2000;29:141–50.
43. Marcus CL, Glomb, WB, Basinski DJ, et al. Ventilatory and cardiac responses to hypercapnea and hypoxia during wakefulness in children with the obstructive sleep apnea syndrome. J Appl Physiol 1994;76:314–20.
44. Marcus CL, Gozal D, Arens R, et al. Ventilatory responses during wakefulness in children with obstructive sleep apnea. Am J Respir Crit Care Med 1994;149:715–21.
45. Gozal D, Arens R, Omlin J, et al. Ventilatory response to consecutive short hypercapnic challenges in children with obstructive sleep apnea syndrome. J App Physiol 1995;79:1608–14.
46. Dong X-W, Gozal D, Rector DM, Harper RM. Ventilatory CO_2-induced optical activity changes of the cat ventral medullary surface. Am J Physiol 1993;265:R494–503.
47. Onal E, Lopata M, O'Connor TD. Diaphragmatic and genioglossal electromyogram responses to CO_2 rebreathing in humans. J Appl Physiol 1982;52:438–44.
48. Mathew OP, Abu-Osba YK, Thach BT. Genioglossus muscle responses to upper airway pressure changes: afferent pathways. J Appl Physiol 1982;52:445–50.
49. Kahn A, Groswasser J, Sottiaux M, et al. Mechanisms of obstructive sleep apneas in infants. Biol Neonate 1994; 65:235–9.
50. Marcus CL, Greene MG, Carroll JL. Blood pressure in children with obstructive sleep apnea. Am J Respir Crit Care Med 1998;157:1098–103.
51. Marcus CL, Keens TG, Bautista DB, et al. Obstructive sleep apnea in children with Down syndrome. Pediatrics 1991; 88:132–9.
52. Gozal D. Sleep-disordered breathing and school performance in children. Pediatrics 1996;102:616–20.
53. Marcus CL, Loughlin GM. Obstructive sleep apnea in children. Semin Pediatr Neurol 1996;3:23–8.
54. Marcus CL, Ward SL, Mallory GB, et al. Use of nasal continuous positive airway pressure as treatment of childhood obstructive sleep apnea. J Pediatr 1998; 127:88–94.
55. Aljadeff G, Gozal, D, Bailey-Wahl SL, et al. Effects of overnight supplemental oxygen in obstructive sleep apnea in children. Am J Respir Crit Care Med 1996;153:51–5.
56. Marcus CL, Carroll JL, Bamford O, et al. Supplemental oxygen during sleep in children with sleep-disordered breathing. Am J Respir Crit Care Med 1995;152:1297–301.
57. Krous HF, Jordan J. A comparison of the distribution of petechiae and their significance in sudden infant death syndrome (SIDS), lethal upper airway obstruction, and non-SIDS. In: Harper RM, Hoffman HJ, eds. Sudden infant death syndrome: risk factors and basic mechanisms. New York: PMA Publishing, 1988:91–100.
58. Hoppenbrouwers T, Hodgman JE, Harper RM, et al. Polygraphic studies of normal infants during the first six months of life: III. Incidence of apnea and periodic breathing. Pediatrics 1977;60:418–25.
59. Kahn A, Groswasser J, Rebuffat E, et al. Sleep and cardiorespiratory characteristics of infant victims of sudden

death: a prospective case-control study. Sleep 1992;15: 287–92.
60. Schechtman VL, Harper RM, Wilson AJ, Southall DP. Sleep apnea in infants who succumb to the sudden infant death syndrome. Pediatrics 1991;87:841–6.
61. Harper RM, Schechtman VL, Kluge KA. Machine classification of infant sleep state using cardiorespiratory measures. Electroencephalogr Clin Neurophysiol 1987; 67:379–87.
62. Harper RM, Richard CA, Rector DM. Physiological and ventral medullary surface activity during hypovolemia. Neuroscience 1999;94:579–86.
63. Ohtake PJ, Jennings DB. Ventilation is stimulated by small reductions in arterial pressure in the awake dog. J Appl Physiol 1992;73:1549–57.
64. Lutherer LO, Lutherer BC, Dormer KJ, et al. Bilateral lesions of the fastigial nucleus prevent the recovery of blood pressure following hypotension induced by hemorrhage or administration of endotoxin. Brain Res 1983;269:251–7.
65. Schadé JP, McMenemey WH. Selective vulnerability of the brain in hypoxaemia. Philadelphia (PA): A.A. Davis, 1963.
66. Martin R, Roessmann U, Fanaroff A. Massive intracerebellar hemorrhage in low-birth-weight infants. J Pediatr 1976;89:290–3.
67. Panigrahy A, Filiano JJ, Sleeper LA, et al. Decreased serotonergic receptor binding in rhombic lip-derived regions of the medulla oblongata in the sudden infant death syndrome. J Neuropathol Exp Neurol 2000;59:377–84.
68. Kinney HC, Filiano JJ, Sleeper L, et al. Decreased muscarinic receptor binding in the arcuate nucleus in sudden infant death syndrome. Science 1995;269:1446–50.
69. Willinger M, Hoffman HJ, Wu KT, et al. Factors associated with the transition to nonprone sleep positions of infants in the United States: the National Infant Sleep Position Study. JAMA 1998;280:329–35.
70. Kemp JS, Thach BT. Sudden death in infants sleeping on polystyrene-filled cushions. N Engl J Med 1991; 324:1858–64.
71. Fleming PJ, Blair P, Bacon C, et al. The environment of infants during sleep and the risk of sudden infant death syndrome: results of 1993–5 case-control study for confidential enquiry into stillbirths and deaths in infancy. Br Med J 1996;313:191–5.
72. Harper RM, Kinney HC, Fleming PJ, Thach BT. Sleep influences on homeostatic functions: implications for sudden infant death syndrome. Respir Physiol 2000;119:123–32.
73. Sahni R, Schulze KF, Kashyap S, et al. Body position, sleep states, and cardiorespiratory activity in developing low birth weight infants. Early Hum Dev 1999;54:197–20b.
74. Yates BJ. Vestibular influences on the autonomic nervous system. In: Highstein SM, Cohen B, Buttner-Ennever JA, eds. New directions in vestibular research. New York, NY: New York Academy of Sciences 1996:458–70.
75. Loeschcke HH, Koepchen HP. Versuch fur Lokatisation des Angriffsortes de, Atmungs-und Kreislaufwirkung von Novocain im Liquor cerebrospinalis. Pflugers Arch 1958; 266:623–41.
76. Mitchell RA, Loeschcke HH, Massion WH, Severinghaus JW. Respiratory responses mediated through superficial chemosensitive areas on the medulla. J Appl Physiol 1963;18:523–33.
77. Schlaefke ME. Central chemosensitivity: a respiratory drive. Rev Physiol Biochem Pharmacol 1981;90:171–244.
78. Bruce EN, Cherniack NS. Central chemoreceptors. J Appl Physiol 1987;62:389–402.
79. Sato M, Severinghaus JW, Basbaum A. Medullary CO_2 chemoreceptor identification by c-fos immunocytochemistry. J Appl Physiol 1992;73:96–100.
80. Nattie E. CO_2, brainstem chemoreceptors and breathing. Prog Neurobiol 1999;59:299–331.
81. Nattie EE, Wood J, Mega A, Goritski W. Rostral ventrolateral medulla muscarinic receptor involvement in central ventilatory chemosensitivity. J Appl Physiol 1989; 66:1462–70.
82. Berkenbosch A, Teppema LJ, Olievier CN, Dahan A. Influences of morphine on the ventilatory response to isocapnic hypoxia. Anesthesiology 1997;86:1342–9.
83. Hedner J, Hedner T, Wessberg P, Jonason J. An analysis of the mechanisms by which aminobutyric acid depresses ventilation in the rat. J Appl Physiol 1984;56:849–56.
84. Moss IR, Scarpelli EM. Generation and regulation of breathing in utero: fetal CO_2 response test. J Appl Physiol 1979;47:527–31.
85. Whittaker JAC, Trouth CO, Pan Y, et al. Age differences in responsiveness of brainstem chemosensitive neurons to extracellular pH changes. Life Sci 1990; 46:1699–705.
86. Saetta M, Mortola JP. Interaction of hypoxic and hypercapnic stimuli on breathing pattern in the newborn rat. J Appl Physiol 1987;62:506–12.
87. Ling L, Olson EB Jr, Vidruk EH, Mitchell GS. Attenuation of the hypoxic ventilatory response in adult rats following one month of perinatal hyperoxia. J Physiol (Lond) 1996;495:561–71.
88. Bamford OS, Schuen JN, Carroll JL. Effect of nicotine exposure on postnatal ventilatory responses to hypoxia and hypercapnia. Respir Physiol 1996;106:1–11.
89. Zhou D, Huang Q, Fung ML, et al. Phrenic response to hypercapnia in the unanesthetized, decerebrate newborn rat. Respir Physiol 1996;104:11–22.
90. Guthrie RD, Standaert TA, Hodson WA, Woodrum DE. Sleep and maturation of eucapnic ventilation and CO_2 sensitivity in the premature primate. J Appl Physiol 1980;48:347–54.
91. Rigatto H. Control of ventilation in the newborn. Annu Rev Physiol 1984;46:661–74.
92. Davey MG, Moss TJ, McCrabb GJ, Harding R. Prematurity alters hypoxic and hypercapnic ventilatory responses in developing lambs. Respir Physiol 1996;105:57–67.
93. Segal BS, Inman JDG, Moss IR. Respiratory responses of piglets to hypercapnia during postnatal development. Pediatr Pulmonol 1991;11:113–9.
94. Matsuoka T, Mortola JP. Effects of hypoxia and hypercapnia on the Hering-Breuer reflex of the conscious newborn rat. J Appl Physiol 1995;78:5–11.

95. Krauss AN, Klain DB, Waldman S, Auld PAM. Ventilatory response to carbon dioxide in newborn infants. Pediatr Res 1975;9:46–50.
96. Frantz ID III, Alder SM, Thach BT, Taeusch WH Jr. Maturational effects on respiratory response to carbon dioxide in premature infants. J Appl Physiol 1976; 41:41–5.
97. Rigatto H, Brady JP, de la Torre Verduzco R. Chemoreceptor reflexes in preterm infants. II. The effect of gestational and postnatal age on the ventilatory response to inhaled carbon dioxide. Pediatrics 1975;55:614–21.
98. Noble LM, Carlo WA, Miller MJ, et al. Transient changes in expiratory time during hypercapnia in premature infants. J Appl Physiol 1987;62:1010–3.
99. Gabel RA, Kronenborg RS, Severinghaus JW. Vital capacity breaths of 5% or 15% CO_2 in N_2 or O_2 to test carotid chemosensitivity. Respir Physiol 1973;17:195–208.
100. Rigatto H, Kwiatowski KA, Hasan SU, Cates DB. The ventilatory response to endogenous CO_2 in preterm infants. Am Rev Respir Dis 1991;143:101–4.
101. Marcus CL, Glomb WB, Basinski DJ, et al. Developmental pattern of hypercapnic and hypoxic ventilatory responses from childhood to adulthood. J Appl Physiol 1994;76:314–20.
102. Gozal D, Arens R, Omlin KJ, et al. Maturational differences in step *vs.* ramp hypoxic and hypercapnic ventilatory responses. J Appl Physiol 1994;76:1968–75.
103. Berthon Jones M, Sullivan CE. Ventilation and arousal responses to hypercapnia in normal sleeping humans. J Appl Physiol 1984;57:59–67.
104. Davi M, Sankaran K, McCallum M, et al. Effect of sleep state on chest distortion and on the ventilatory response to CO_2 in neonates. Pediatr Res 1979;13:982–6.
105. Haddad GG, Leistner HL, Epstein RA, et al. CO_2-induced changes in ventilation and ventilatory pattern in normal sleeping infants. J Appl Physiol 1980;48:684–8.
106. Cohen G, Xu C, Henderson-Smart D. Ventilatory response of the sleeping newborn to CO_2 during normoxic rebreathing. J Appl Physiol 1991;71:168–74.
107. Downing SE, Lee JC. Laryngeal chemosensitivity: a possible mechanism for sudden infant death. Pediatrics 1975;55:640–9.
108. Sullivan CE, Murphy E, Kozar LF, Phillipson EA. Waking and ventilatory responses to laryngeal stimulation in sleeping dogs. J Appl Physiol 1978;45:681–9.
109. Parmeggiani PL, Franzini C, Lenzi P. Respiratory frequency as a function of preoptic temperature during sleep. Brain Res 1976;111:253–60.
110. Ni H, Zhang J, Glotzbach S, et al. Dynamic respiratory responses to preoptic/anterior hypothalamic warming in the sleeping cat. Sleep 1994;17:657–64.
111. Stanton AN. Sudden infant death, overheating and cot death. Lancet 1984;ii:1199–201.
112. Gozal D, Colin AA, Daskalovic JY, Jaffe M. Environmental overheating as a cause of transient respiratory chemoreceptor dysfunction in an infant. Pediatrics 1988;82:738–41.
113. Fleming PJ, Levine MR, Azaz Y, Wigfield R. The development of thermoregulation and interactions with the control of respiration in infants: possible relationship to sudden infant death. Acta Paediatr Scand Suppl 1993;389:57–9.
114. Fleming PJ, Gilbert RE, Azaz Y, et al. The interaction between bedding and sleeping position in sudden infant death syndrome: a population-based case-control study. Br Med J 1990;301:85–9.
115. Serdarevich C, Fewell JE. Influence of core temperature on autoresuscitation during repeated exposure to hypoxia in normal rat pups. J Appl Physiol 1999;87:1346–53.
116. Dietrich W, Busto R, Valdes I, Loor Y. Effects of normothermic versus mild hyperthermic forebrain ischaemia in rats. Stroke 1990;21:1318–25.
117. Fung ML, Wang W, St. John WM. Medullary loci critical for expression of gasping in adult rats. J Physiol (Lond) 1994;480:597–611.
118. St. John W. Medullary regions for neurogenesis of gasping: noeud vital or noeuds vitals? J Appl Physiol 1996; 81:1865–77.
119. Ramirez JM, Schwarzacher SW, Pierrefiche O, et al. Selective lesioning of the cat pre-Bötzinger complex in vivo eliminates breathing but not gasping. J Physiol (Lond) 1998;507:895–907.
120. Thach BT, Jacobi MS, Gershan WM. Control of breathing during asphyxia and autoresuscitation. In: Haddad G, Farber JP, eds. Developmental neurobiology of breathing. New York: Marcel Dekker, 1991:681–99.
121. Deshpande P, Khurana A, Hensen P, et al. Failure of the autoresuscitation mechanism in weaning mice: significance of cardiac glycogen and heart rate regulation. J Appl Physiol 1999;87:203–10.
122. Gershan WM, Jacobi MS, Thach BT. Maturation of cardiorespiratory interactions in spontaneous recovery from hypoxic apnea (autoresuscitation). J Pediatr Res 1990;28:87–93.
123. Fewell JE, Smith FG. Perinatal nicotine exposure impairs ability of newborn rats to autoresusitate from apnea during hypoxia. J Appl Physiol 1998;85:2066–74.
124. Gozal D, Torres JE, Gozal YM, Nuckton TJ. Characterization and developmental aspects of anoxia-induced gasping. Biol Neonate 1996;70:280–8.
125. Gozal D, Torres JE. Maturation of anoxia-induced gasping in the rat: potential role for *N*-methyl-D-aspartate glutamate receptors. Pediatr Res 1997;42:872–7.
126. Gozal D, Torres JE, Gozal E, et al. Nitric oxide modulates anoxia-induced gasping in the developing rat. Biol Neonate 1998;73:264–74.
127. Paton JY, Swaminathan S, Sargent CW, Keens TG. Hypoxic and hypercapneic ventilatory responses in awake children with congenital central hypoventilation syndrome. Am Rev Respir Dis 1989;140:368–72.
128. Haddad GG, Mazza NM, Defendini R, et al. Congenital failure of automatic control of ventilation, gastrointestinal motility and heart rate. Medicine (Baltimore) 1978;57:517–26.
129. Verloes A, Elmer C, Lacombe D, et al. Ondine-Hirschsprung syndrome (Haddad syndrome). Further delineation in two cases and review of the literature. Eur J Pediatr 1993;152:75–7.
130. Idiopathic congenital central hypoventilation syndrome diagnosis and management. Official statement,

American Thoracic Society. Am J Respir Crit Care Med 1999;160:368–73.
131. Gozal D, Marcus CL, Shoseyov D, Keens TG. Peripheral chemoreceptor function in children with congenital central hypoventilation syndrome. J Appl Physiol 1993; 74:379–87.
132. Paton JY, Swaminathan S, Sargent CW, et al. Ventilatory response to exercise in children with congenital central hypoventilation syndrome. Am Rev Respir Dis 1993; 147:1185–91.
133. Gozal D, Marcus CL, Ward SL, Keens TG. Ventilatory responses to passive leg motion in children with congenital central hypoventilation syndrome. Am J Respir Crit Care Med 1996;153:761–8.
134. Gozal D, Simakajornboon N. Passive motion of the extremities modifies alveolar ventilation during sleep in patients with CCHS. Am J Respir Crit Care Med 2000; 162:1747–51.
135. Woo MS, Woo MA, Gozal D, et al. Heart rate variability in congenital central hypoventilation syndrome. Pediatr Res 1992;31:291–6.
136. Silvestri JM, Hanna BD, Volgman AS, et al. Cardiac rhythm disturbances among children with idiopathic congenital central hypoventilation syndrome. Pediatr Pulmonol 2000;29:351–8.
137. Emery AH. Population frequencies of inherited neuromuscular diseases—a world survey. Neuromuscul Disord 1991;1:19–29.
138. Labanowski M, Schmidt-Nowara W, Guilleminault C. Sleep and neuromuscular disease: frequency of sleep-disordered breathing in a neuromuscular disease clinic population. Neurology 1996;47:1173–80.
139. Inkley SR, Oldenburg F, Vignos P. Pulmonary function in Duchenne muscular dystrophy related to stage of disease. Am J Med 1974;56:297–306.
140. Smith PEM, Calverley PMA, Edwards RHT. Hypoxemia during sleep in Duchenne muscular dystrophy. Am Rev Respir Dis 1988;137:884–8.
141. Manni R, Ottolini A, Cerveri I, et al. Breathing patterns and $HbSaO_2$ changes during nocturnal sleep in patients with Duchenne's muscular dystrophy. J Neurol 1989; 236:391–4.
142. Barbe F, Quera-Salva A, McCann C, et al. Sleep-related respiratory disturbances in patients with Duchenne muscular dystrophy. Eur Respir J 1994;7:1403–8.
143. Cerveri I, Fanfulla F, Zoia MC, et al. Sleep disorders in neuromuscular diseases. Monaldi Arch Chest Dis 1993; 48:318–21.
144. Redding GJ, Okamoto GA, Guthrie RD, et al. Sleep patterns in nonambulatory boys with Duchenne muscular dystrophy. Arch Phys Med Rehabil 1985;66:818–21.
145. Heckmatt JZ, Loh L, Dubowitz V. Nocturnal hypoventilation in children with nonprogressive neuromuscular disease. Pediatrics 1989;83:250–5.
146. Gozal D. Pulmonary manifestations of neuromuscular disease: focus on Duchenne muscular dystrophy and spinal muscular atrophy. Pediatr Pulmonol 2000; 29:141–50.
147. Lee S, Wevrick R. Identification of novel imprinted transcripts in the Prader-Willi syndrome and Angelman syndrome deletion region: further evidence for regional imprinting control. Am J Hum Genet 2000;66:848–58.
148. Couper R. Prader-Willi syndrome. J Paediatr Child Health 1999;35:331–4.
149. Eiholzer U, Blum WF, Molinari L. Body fat determined by skinfold measurements is elevated despite underweight in infants with Prader-Labhart-Willi syndrome. J Pediatr 1999;134:222–5.
150. Richdale AL, Cotton S, Hibbit K. Sleep and behaviour disturbance in Prader-Willi syndrome: a questionnaire study. J Intellect Disabil Res 1999;43(Pt 5):380–92.
151. Harris JC, Allen RP. Is excessive daytime sleepiness characteristic of Prader-Willi syndrome? The effects of weight change. Arch Pediatr Adolesc Med 1996;150:1288–93.
152. Gozal D, Torres JE, Menendez AA. Longitudinal assessment of hypercapnic ventilatory drive after tracheotomy in a patient with the Prader-Willi syndrome. Eur Respir J 1996;9:1565–8.
153. Smith IE, King MA, Siklos PW, Shneerson JM. Treatment of ventilatory failure in the Prader-Willi syndrome. Eur Respir J 1998;11:1150–2.
154. Arens R, Gozal D, Omlin KJ, et al. Hypoxic and hypercapnic ventilatory responses in Prader-Willi syndrome. J Appl Physiol 1994;77:2224–30.
155. Gozal D, Arens R, Omlin KJ, et al. Absent peripheral chemoreceptor function in Prader-Willi syndrome. J Appl Physiol 1994;77:2231–6.
156. Schluter B, Buschatz D, Trowitzsch E, et al. Respiratory control in children with Prader-Willi syndrome. Eur J Pediatr 1997;156:65–8.
157. Livingston FR, Arens R, Bailey SL, et al. Hypercapnic arousal responses in Prader-Willi syndrome. Chest 1995;108:1627–31.
158. Arens R, Gozal D, Burrell BC, et al. Arousal and cardiorespiratory responses to hypoxia in Prader-Willi syndrome. Am J Respir Crit Care Med 1996;153:283–7.
159. Vgontzas AN, Bixler EO, Kales A, et al. Daytime sleepiness and REM abnormalities in Prader-Willi syndrome: evidence of generalized hypoarousal. Int J Neurosci 1996;87:127–39.
160. Lindgren AC, Hellstrom LG, Ritzen EM, Milerad J. Growth hormone treatment increases CO_2 response, ventilation and central inspiratory drive in children with Prader-Willi syndrome. Eur J Pediatr 1999;158:936–40.
161. Sisk EA, Heatley DG, Borowski BJ, et al. Obstructive sleep apnea in children with achondroplasia: surgical and anesthetic considerations. Otolaryngol Head Neck Surg 1999;120:248–54.
162. Mogayzel PJ Jr, Carroll JL, Loughlin GM, et al. Sleep-disordered breathing in children with achondroplasia. J Pediatr 1998;132:667–71.
163. Marcus CL, Keens TG, Bautista DB, et al. Obstructive sleep apnea in children with Down syndrome. Pediatrics 1991;88:132–9.
164. Waters KA, Forbes P, Morielli A, et al. Sleep-disordered breathing in children with myelomeningocele. J Pediatr 1998;132:672–81.
165. Kirk VG, Morielli A, Brouillette RT. Sleep-disordered breathing in patients with myelomeningocele: the missed diagnosis. Dev Med Child Neurol 1999;41:40–3.

166. Kirk VG, Morielli A, Gozal D, et al. Treatment of sleep-disordered breathing in children with myelomeningocele. Pediatr Pulmonol 2000;30(6):445–62.
167. Amir RE, Van den Veyver IB, Wan M, et al. Rett syndrome is caused by mutations in X-linked MECP2, encoding methyl-CpG-binding protein 2. Nat Genet 1999;23:185–8.
168. Marcus CL, Carroll JL, McColley SA, et al. Polysomnographic characteristics of patients with Rett syndrome. J Pediatr 1994;125:218–24.

CHAPTER 31

Interacting Mechanisms of Physical Activity and Growth in Children

Dan Michael Cooper, MD

Exercise and Growth in Health and Disease

Although adults and children are becoming increasingly sedentary throughout the world, it is ironic that the evolutionary success of modern humans may have resulted, at least in part, from their ability to achieve remarkably high levels of energy expenditure compared with other primates and hominids. As outlined in a novel review by Leonard and Robertson,[1] somewhere between 1.5 to 2.5 million years ago, African savannas expanded at the expense of forest. As a result, food resources became much more widely dispersed. *Homo erectus* (thought to be the direct ancestor of *Homo sapiens*) was able to cope because of an ability to increase physical activity and energy expenditure to that demanded by the need to forage over wider areas.

In modern Western societies, machines and other technologic "advances" have supplanted virtually every physical activity that had been required by early humans for simple survival. The tendency to minimize human energy expenditure is pervasive: for example, even pushing a cart down supermarket aisles, a feeble remnant of foraging for food, is being replaced by internet shopping and home food delivery. But even under these conditions, children continue to spontaneously engage in and enjoy vigorous physical activity (ie, play). This likely represents some innate (genetic) behavior that ultimately leads to a positive physiologic adaptation to the environment.

We now believe that exercise in children is not merely play, but rather, an important aspect of healthy growth and development. Moreover, there appear to be significant long-term health consequences for the child who is unable to engage optimally in physical activity because of environmental, social and psychologic, or physiologic barriers. It is the author's goal here to review recent work showing specific mechanisms that link growth with exercise in children and to highlight the ways in which this information might contribute to a better understanding of how exercise can be optimized in healthy children and in those with chronic disease and disability.

In the first edition of this book 10 years ago, the idea was raised that levels of physical activity and exercise during childhood might play a role in the overall process of growth and development. Understanding of the biologic mechanisms that link exercise with growth has gained clinical importance in the intervening years for a number of reasons. First, it is becoming increasingly apparent that patterns of physical activity during childhood can contribute to the development of deleterious conditions that typically occur later in adulthood, such as osteoporosis, obesity, and heart disease. Enhancing levels of physical activity in an increasingly sedentary population is going to be a profoundly difficult task. It will be made more feasible if the biomedical research community can continue to identify (1) a clear basis for exercise testing and therapy, and (2) accessible markers (biochemical, anatomic) that can be used to gauge the effectiveness of interventions, be they in the context of family, school, or community.

Second, exercise testing is used increasingly to give the clinician insight into cardiorespiratory and metabolic disease mechanisms with specialized groups of patients, such as congenital heart, neuromuscular, and chronic lung disease. The idea that the clinician might gain predictive information or insight into basic disease mechanisms from tests that mimic the "real-life" activities of children is indeed compelling. Hopefully, technologic advances in the acquisition of physiologic responses to exercise will continue to improve, so that this type of noninvasive or, at least, minimally invasive testing paradigm can become increasingly useful in the clinical setting.

Growth Hormone–Insulin-Like Growth Factor Axis and Exercise

Exercise is a naturally occurring and physiologic stimulator of growth hormone (GH) (Figure 31–1),[2] and this suggests the possibility that exercise modulates tissue anabolism by actions of GH. In turn, GH stimulates the synthesis and release of insulin-like growth factor I (IGF-I), and it is the latter that likely mediates many effects of GH on tissues. The GH-IGF-I axis is now known to be a system of growth hormones and mediators that modulate growth in many tissues.

What is particularly intriguing to pediatricians and developmental biologists is that the GH-IGF-I axis also plays a key role in the process of growth and develop-

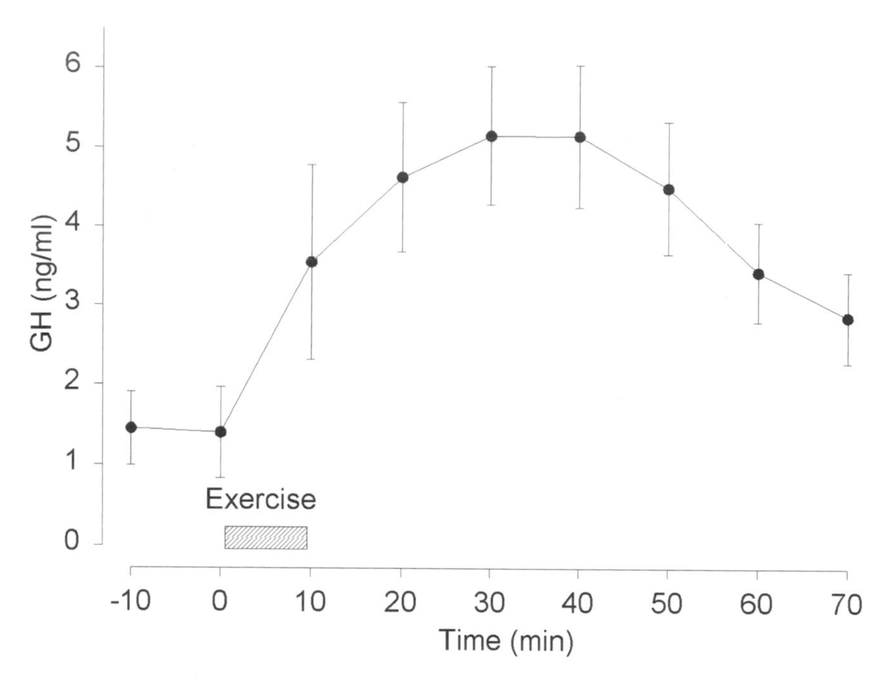

FIGURE 31–1. The effect of a 10-minute high-intensity exercise bout on growth hormone (GH) secretion in female adolescents (N =18). Peak GH was observed at about 32 minutes after the onset of exercise. (Reproduced with permission from Eliakim A et al.[2])

ment. Pulse frequency and amplitude of GH increase throughout childhood and quite substantially during the pubertal growth spurt. Similarly, puberty is characterized by a rapid increase in the upward slope of circulating IGF-I.[3] The regulation of competing demands for energy substrate of these two distinct processes, anabolic responses to exercise and to growth and development, is unknown.

It is not surprising that a number of studies of healthy human beings have demonstrated significant correlations between physical fitness and blood levels of IGF-I.[4–6] In addition, IGF-I is now known to play a key role in exercise-associated muscle hypertrophy at the muscle cellular and molecular levels.[7,8] Presumably, the increased levels of IGF-I are related to the increased anabolism associated with physical fitness.

One mechanism for the association between fitness and IGF-I might be that the increase in GH from individual bouts of exercise eventually leads to increased IGF-I and tissue anabolism. Cuneo et al[9] showed that exogenous GH improved exercise performance and muscle mass in a group of GH-deficient adults. Borer et al,[10] a pioneer in this research, noted that GH pulse frequency and amplitude were reduced and that somatic growth rate fell when exercise was prevented in the hamster. Grindeland et al[11] showed in detrained hypophysectomized rats that GH was required in combination with exercise to effect a retraining of atrophied muscles.

Despite this intriguing evidence, it is clear that the response to training can occur in the absence of GH. For example, work from the author's laboratory has shown that 5 weeks of exercise training in rats rendered GH deficient (by administration of anti-GH releasing hormone antibodies) had the same proportional increase in maximal oxygen uptake as did control animals. Moreover, training seemed to increase the local muscle expression of IGF-I messenger ribonucleic acid (mRNA) and IGF-I protein even in the absence of circulating GH (Figure 31–2).[7,12] Precisely how exercise interacts with the local and systemic expression and modulation of important growth factors remains unknown (Figure 31–3).

Exercise and Growth: The Catabolic Paradox

Recent work from this and other laboratories has demonstrated that physical activity can influence the GH-IGF-I axis in children and adolescents in a number of ways. But a seeming paradox is emerging in which exercise training in children seems to produce significant *catabolic* states as well as the expected *anabolic* adjustments. First, the findings from cross-sectional (ie, steady-state) studies have not been the same as those obtained from prospective exercise training interventions. In a cross-sectional analysis of adolescent females, we found significant correlations between thigh muscle volume (measured by magnetic resonance imaging) and both circulating IGF-I and mean overnight GH concentrations (measured by 20-minute sampling of circulating GH from 8:00 pm to 8:00 am)(Figure 31–4).[13,14] In adolescent males, we also found significant correlations between fitness (assessed as

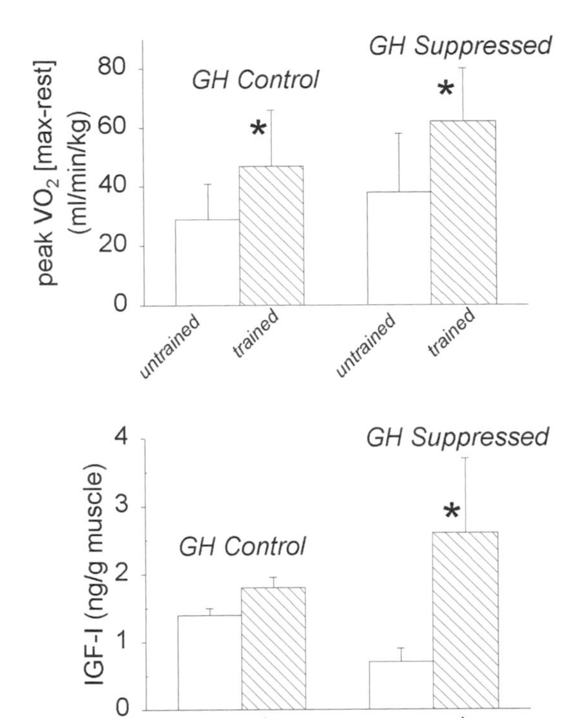

FIGURE 31–2. Evidence for growth hormone (GH)-independent mechanisms of exercise-associated anabolic effects in the rat. In these animals, GH was suppressed using anti-GH releasing hormone antibodies. A program of treadmill exercise training resulted in increased peak oxygen uptake ($\dot{V}_{O_2}$) in both GH-control and GH-suppressed groups (*upper panel*). The increase in fitness was accompanied by significant increases in tissue insulin-like growth factor I (IGF-I) only in the GH-suppressed rats (*lower panel*). $^*p < .05$ for effect of training. These data suggest that training may lead to alterations in local tissue IGF-I that are independent of GH. (Data from Zanconato S et al[7] and Cooper DM et al.[12])

maximal oxygen uptake ($\dot{V}_{O_2}$) per kilogram) and mean overnight GH concentrations.

Fitness was correlated with additional indicators of the bioactivity of IGF-I. It is now known that the IGF-I anabolic effects are modulated by a series of binding proteins.[15] For example, IGFBP-4 inhibits mitogenic effects of IGF-I.[16] In adults IGFBP-4 increases with age,[17,18] suggesting a possible contribution to decreased anabolic function in the elderly. In both male and female adolescents, fitness (assessed either by maximum $\dot{V}_{O_2}$ per kilogram or thigh muscle mass per kilogram) was significantly inversely correlated with IGFBP-4 levels in the circulation. In addition, significant positive correlations were observed between fitness and the ratio of IGF-I/IGFBP-4, the latter being an index of effective IGF-I bioactivity.

Based on these observed correlations between fitness and the GH-IGF-I axis derived from cross-sectional analyses, we hypothesized that a prospective increase in the level of physical activity in children and adolescents would lead to increases in circulating IGF-I. However, this was not what we observed. In a series of prospective exercise training studies we have conducted to date in adolescents, 5 weeks of increased physical activity led to significant decreases in circulating IGF-I (Figure 31–5).[13,14]

While a reduction in circulating IGF-I was most consistently observed in our studies to date, increased physical activity also affected other important components of the GH-IGF-I axis depending on gender and maturational status. For example, training led to significant reductions of circulating growth hormone–binding protein (GHBP) in both adolescent males (–21%) and prepubertal girls (–10%). In humans GHBP is the extracellular component of the GH cell receptor; thus, its circulating levels are felt to reflect the GH-receptor capacity of the tissues. Low levels of GHBP are found in a variety of catabolic states in humans[19] and clearly play a role in the consequent GH-resistant state.

Exercise training in children and adolescents also affected IGF-binding proteins. A significant reduction in IGFBP-3 was seen in all groups studied except for the adolescent females. Over 90% of the IGF-I in the circulating blood is bound by IGFBP-3, and like IGF-I, hepatic production of IGFBP-3 is under the control of GH.[15] The training program affected IGFBP-5 in females only. In the adolescent females, IGFBP-5, which potentiates IGF-I activity,[20] decreased by 10%. In the prepubertal girls, IGFBP-5 substantially increased in the control subjects, but this increase was attenuated by training. The inhibition of IGFBP-5 suggests another potentially "antianabolic" function of exercise in prepubertal children. Finally, there was a dramatic training-associated increase in IGFBP-2 in the male adolescents (+40%). Interestingly, IGFBP-2 is known to inhibit IGF-I anabolic function[15] and is increased by interleukin (IL)-1β in states of increased inflammation.[21]

In summary, exercise training in adolescents led to an unexpectedly consistent reduction in IGF-I levels, despite the observation from cross-sectional studies that fitter people tend to have higher levels of circulating IGF-I. Moreover, the catabolic nature of the adaptation to brief training input was manifest significantly, but differently, in each of the groups by varying effects on GHBP and IGFBPs. Not yet known are the mechanisms of these gender and maturational influences on the GH-IGF-I axis response to increased physical activity.

Evidence That Growth Processes Continue Despite the Catabolic State

Although the brief exercise training protocol led to what appeared to be a catabolic response based on circulating alterations in growth factors, did the data actually show anatomic evidence of catabolism in the research subjects? In our studies of adolescents, there were no differences between training and control groups with regard to

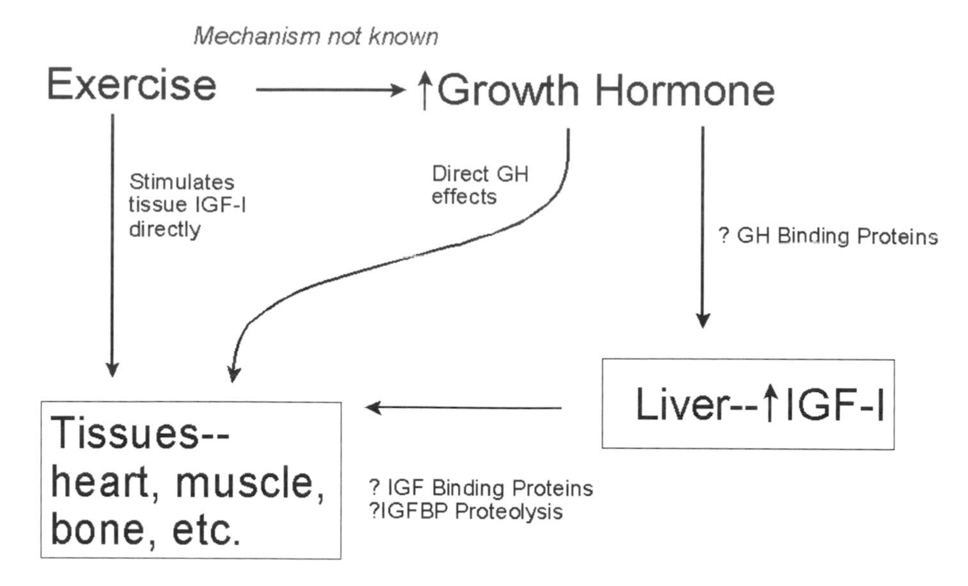

FIGURE 31–3. Possible mechanisms through which exercise interacts with the GH-IGF-I axis. GH = growth hormone; IGF = insulin-like growth factor.

changes in height and weight over the 5-week intervention. In our most recent study of prepubertal girls, however, significant increases in height occurred in both groups, but a significant weight increase was observed only in the control subjects.[22]

Magnetic resonance images of the thigh were obtained to gauge the impact of training on muscle mass, and this led to one of the most consistent findings related to the training intervention. As seen in Figure 31–6, there was a 4 to 5% increase in thigh muscle mass in all three training groups studied to date.[13,14,22] We also found significant increases in more traditional indices of fitness, such as the $\dot{V}_{O_2}$ max—a 12.1% increase in adolescent females, a 3.1% increase in adolescent males, a 6.2% increase in

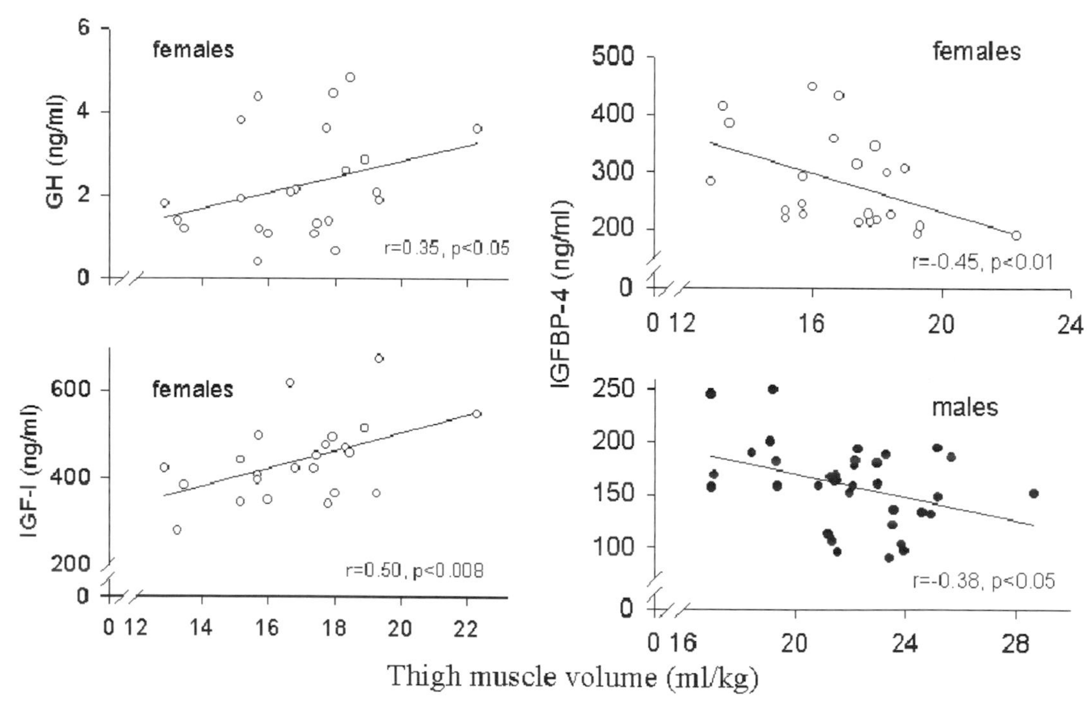

FIGURE 31–4. *Left,* Mean growth hormone (GH) and insulin-like growth factor I (IGF-I) were significantly correlated with muscle mass in adolescent females. Mean GH was significantly correlated with fitness in males as well (not shown). *Right,* Insulin-like growth factor–binding protein 4 (IGFBP-4); known to inhibit anabolic function of IGF-I was *inversely* correlated with muscle mass in both females and males. These data support the observation that the trained state is correlated with increased IGF-I bioactivity. Thigh muscle volume was determined by magnetic resonance imaging. Mean overnight GH was measured by sampling every 20 minutes from 10:00 pm to 8:00 am. (Data from Eliakim et al.[13,14]).

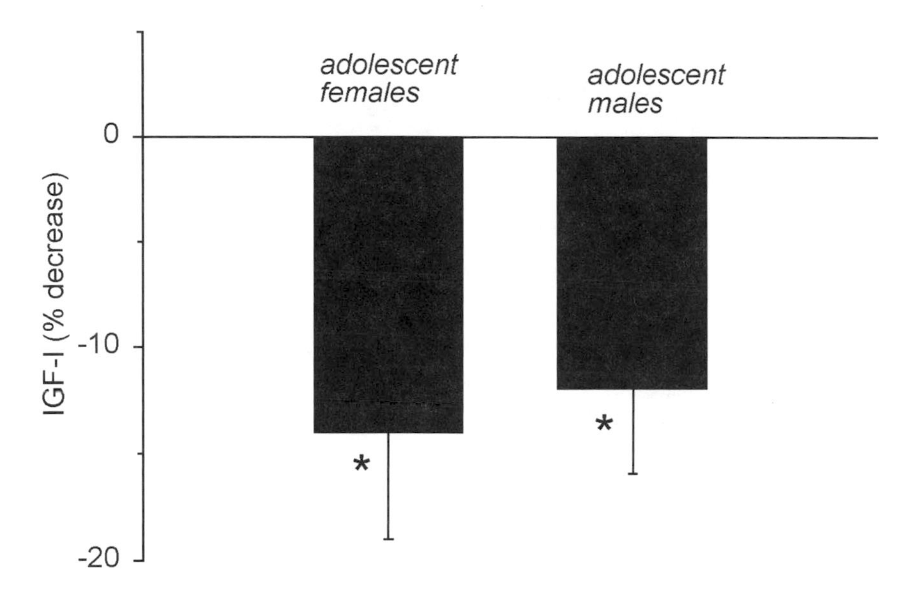

FIGURE 31–5. Effect of 5 weeks of endurance type training on circulating insulin-like growth factor I (IGF-I) in healthy adolescent males and females. Contrary to our expectations, the level of IGF-I actually fell in these two groups. No changes in IGF-I were observed in control* subjects. (Data from Eliakim et al.[13,14] Preliminary data from recent similar studies in prepubertal boys and girls corroborate this finding as well. One such study is Eliakim A, Scheett T, Newcomb R, et al. Fitness, training, and the growth hormone–insulin-like growth factor-I axis in prepubertal girls. J Clin Endo Metab 2001. [In press])

prepubertal females, and a 12.5% increase in prepubertal males. Field tests of exercise capability tended to show even more remarkable positive effects of the exercise training program. For example, in the prepubertal girls tested in 1997, training led to a 20% improvement in the 3-minute run. No statistically significant change was observed in the controls. Finally, almost invariably, the least fit members of the training groups showed the most dramatic improvement.

There remains controversy regarding the response of prepubertal children, particularly girls, to exercise training (see, for example, the review by Pate and Ward[23]). Nonetheless, data from our own recent studies combined with the work of previous investigators do permit some

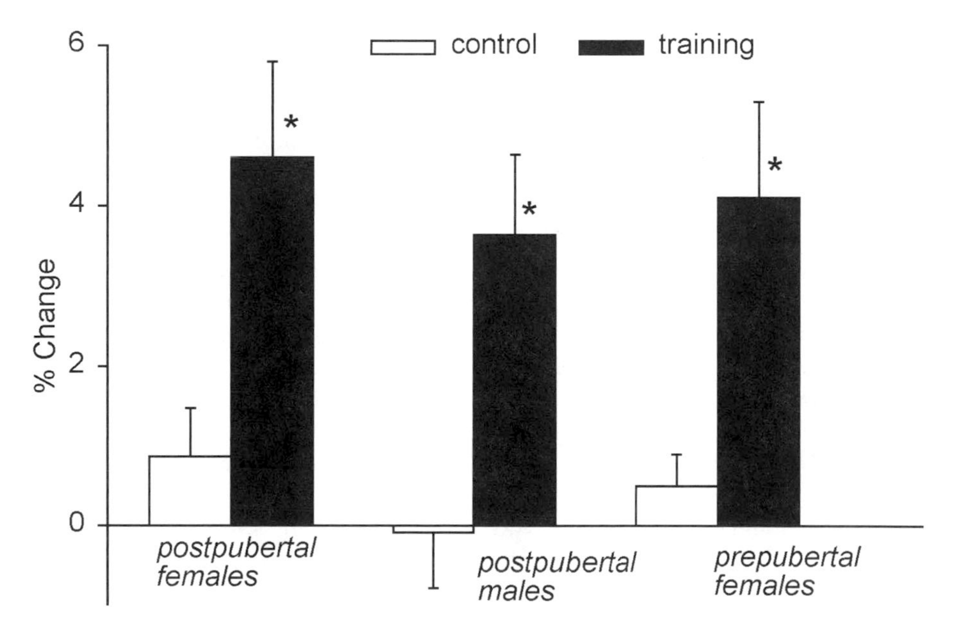

FIGURE 31–6. Effect of 5 weeks of endurance-type training on thigh muscle volume. Muscle volume was estimated using magnetic resonance imaging. There was a consistent finding of significant increases in muscle volume (*$p<.05$) in training compared with control subjects. These increases in muscle mass occurred despite the reduction in circulating levels of insulin-like growth factor I, suggesting that the training had actually led to a catabolic state. (Data from Eliakim et al.[13,14,22])

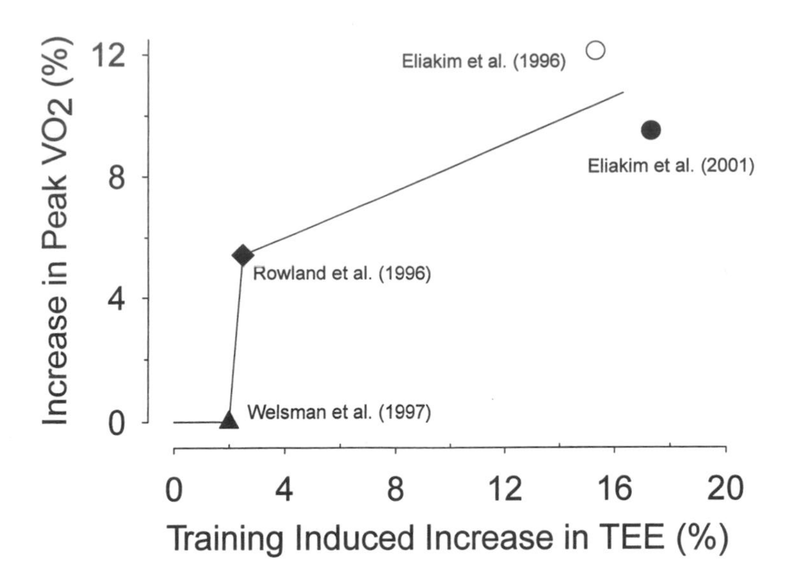

FIGURE 31–7. Relationship between training-associated increase in total energy expenditure (TEE) and increase in peak oxygen uptake ($\dot{V}_{O_2}$). We speculate that a threshold effect exists in which endurance-type training activities must lead to at least a 2 to 3% increase in TEE before any increase in peak $\dot{V}_{O_2}$ can be measured. In addition, once exceeded, it appears that the increase in peak $\dot{V}_{O_2}$ reaches a limit fairly rapidly. Adolescent females seemed to be more responsive to exercise training, perhaps because they were generally less fit than were younger girls. (Data for this graph were estimated from published results of Welsman et al,[24] Rowland and Boyajran,[27] and our previous studies of adolescent and prepubertal girls.[22,28])

reasonable speculation into the dose-response relationship of exercise training in prepubertal girls. We used two recent prospective exercise training studies in this population (one authored by Welsman et al[24] and the other by Rowland et al[25]) with roughly comparable age ranges and an endurance-type (rather than resistive) exercise training protocol. Although neither of these studies used doubly labeled water (DLW) to measure the effect of training on total energy expenditure (TEE), we were able to estimate this effect using the time and duration of the training sessions and the reported increase in heart rate (HR). (Note, we used the relationship between $\dot{V}_{O_2}$ and HR during exercise[26] and the values for TEE found in the present study to estimate the impact of the training on overall energy expenditure.) The results of these estimates are shown in Figure 31–7.[22,24,27,28] This analysis suggests two important features of the exercise dose-response in healthy children. First, there seems to be a minimum of about a 2 to 4% increase in TEE before any change in cardiorespiratory function occurs. Second, the training response appears to reach some maximal level relatively rapidly above this threshold.

These data showed that despite the seeming catabolic state related to the exercise training in children and adolescents, certain growth processes were able to continue. We and others have noted this type of tissue-specific or selective response. For example, a hypoxic environment causes young rats to reduce somatic growth rates and lower circulating levels of IGF-I, while in the lung and right ventricle (obviously, tissues that needs to adapt to the lower fractional concentration of inspired O_2 [FI_{O_2}]) IGF-I mRNA is increased in the right ventricle along with relative lung growth.[29,30]

The Mechanism of Exercise-associated Catabolic States in Children and Adolescents

What is it about exercise that might paradoxically suppress the GH-IGF-I axis? In other pathologic conditions that lead to GH-resistant (ie, high circulating GH) low-IGF-I catabolic states, such as burns, trauma, and sepsis, specific inflammatory cytokines (IL-1β, IL-6, and tumor necrosis factor-α [TNF-α]) often are elevated. Moreover, a wealth of data from in vitro studies now support a causal relationship between these three cytokines and suppression of the GH-IGF-I axis.

The cytokines are a family of low–molecular weight cell-to-cell mediators that regulate many immune and inflammatory responses.[31] While it was recognized in the early 1980s that exercise could induce "acute-phase reactants,"[32] it has been discovered only in the past several years in adults that exercise (primarily involving prolonged and/or exhaustive exercise protocols) leads to increases in circulating levels of inflammatory cytokines.[33] Interleukin-6 is the cytokine most consistently elevated with exercise. Other studies also found exercise-associated elevations in IL-1β and TNF-α.[34–39] In addition, some data suggest that trained adults have sustained increases in circulating TNF-α and IL-1β.[35,38] To our knowledge, these cytokine relationships with exercise have never been studied in children. Moreover, although much work has been done on the role of cytokines in childhood disease, only recently have a few investigators begun to examine the fundamental ways in which cytokine responses mature from early postnatal life to adulthood in healthy subjects.[40]

In the past 2 to 3 years, there has been a substantial number of studies demonstrating specific ways in which cytokines might affect the GH-IGF-I axis and potentially explain the depression in this system that we found after 5 weeks of exercise training in children and adolescents. Interleukins-1β and -6 and TNF-α have a variety of antianabolic effects, including depression of GH-receptor gene expression, inhibition of IGF-I production, and stimulation of IGF-binding proteins that act to inhibit IGF-I function.[41–46]

Moreover, recent studies of the childhood disease juvenile rheumatoid arthritis, an entity characterized by chronic inflammation of joints, high circulating levels of IL-6, and growth retardation, suggest a functionally important role for IL-6 in actual inhibition of growth. De Benedetti et al[47] demonstrated profoundly reduced levels of circulating IGF-I along with growth retardation in transgenic mice that overexpressed IL-6. Remarkably, when the animals were treated with anti-IL-6 antibodies, IGF-I increased and growth rebounded. The preponderance of data strongly suggest that the clinical observation of increased cytokines occurring so frequently with suppression of the GH-IGF-I axis reflects an underlying mechanism rather than an unrelated correlation.

To test the hypothesis that these cytokines might play a role in the adaptation to exercise, we measured the acute effects of exercise on selected cytokines and growth factors in 17 healthy 8- to 11-year-old children (4 females).[48] Designed to mimic patterns and intensity of exercise found in the real lives of American children, the exercise protocol consisted of a 1.5-hour soccer practice (of which about 40 minutes constituted vigorous exercise). Pre- and postexercise urine and saliva samples were obtained in all subjects, and both blood and urine samples were obtained in 9 subjects. The exercise led to significant increases in circulating TNF-α (18 ± 7%, $p < .05$) and IL-6 (125 ± 35%, $p < .01$) as well as a significant increase in the anti-inflammatory cytokine IL-1 receptor antagonist (33 ± 10%, $p < .01$) (Figure 31–8).[48] Urine levels of IL-6 also were substantially increased by exercise (440 ± 137%, $p < .0001$). Circulating levels of IGF-I were reduced to a small but significant degree (−6.4 ± 3.2%, $p < .05$), while IGFBP-1 (known to inhibit IGF-I) was substantially increased (156 ± 40%, $p < .001$). Cytokines are systemically increased following relatively brief exercise in healthy children. This increase may alter critical anabolic agents such as IGF-I and its binding proteins.

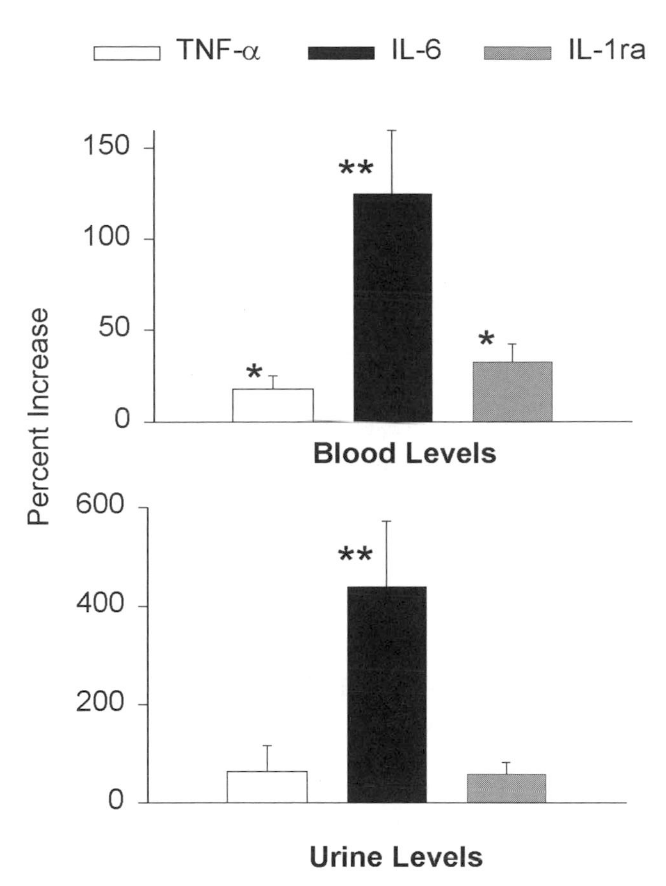

FIGURE 31–8. Effect of a soccer practice–type exercise protocol on serum (n = 9) and urine (n = 17) tumor necrosis factor α (TNF-α), interleukin (IL)-6, and IL-1 receptor antagonist (IL-1ra). Data are expressed as the mean+standard error percent change of each variable. In serum, there were significant elevations in all three of these cytokines with exercise, the most robust response was observed for the inflammatory cytokine IL-6. In urine, a statistically significant and quite substantial response was found for IL-6 alone. *p < .05; **p < .01. (Data from Scheett et al.[48])

Compensatory Mechanisms

The bulk of IGF-I (>99%) circulates in blood by binding to IGF-binding proteins. About 75 to 80% of IGFs circulate in the 150-kD (IGF, IGFBP-3, and an acid labile subunit) form, while the remaining 20 to 25% circulate in the 50-kD form. The half-life of the 150-kD form is about 15 to 20 hours, while that of the smaller 50-kD form is only about 30 minutes. The larger 150-kD complex is not bioavailable to tissues, since it cannot cross the vascular endothelium. For the IGFs from the larger 150-kD form to become bioavailable, this complex needs to be broken down.

One of the mechanisms through which the large 150-kD complex can be disrupted is by the proteolysis of the IGFBP-3. In a recent study of protein turnover in children with cancer, Attard-Montalto et al[49] concluded that "Modification of IGFBP-3 by circulating proteolytic activity may alter IGF bioavailability, allowing protein synthesis to increase during periods of severe catabolic stress." Proteolysis of IGFBP-3 has been observed in a number of other catabolic states, indicating that it may be a more general mechanism of enhancing IGF bioavailability when IGF-I concentrations decrease. These observations, along with our original finding that exercise acutely stimulates IGFBP-3 proteolysis,[50] have led us to hypothesize that IGFBP-3 proteolysis may function during exercise to mitigate the catabolic state. By simultaneously measuring IGFBP-3 proteolysis, the 50- and 150-kD pools of IGF-I, and the mitogenic activity of sera at various stages of exercise training, we propose to develop a powerful new approach to identify mechanisms of "growth versus growth plus exercise" in children and adolescents.

Other potential mechanisms also may explain how growth continues despite neuroendocrine evidence of a catabolic state with exercise training. Training may enhance the number and binding affinity of tissue IGF-I receptors. In a recent publication, we showed that in a naturally occurring low-IGF-I state (ie, the one found in older healthy individuals), there is an increase in IGF-I receptor binding on red blood cells.[18] Moreover, in preliminary data outlined below, exercise training led to increased erythrocyte IGF-I binding. Although the erythrocyte can only reflect tissue binding indirectly, it is a "tissue" that is accessible in studies involving children and adolescents, and it has been used by a number of investigators to gauge the effect of various conditions and interventions (eg, GH-replacement therapy in GH-deficient individuals[51]) on IGF-I tissue binding.

Longer-term Adaptations to Levels of Physical Activity

The idea that physical activity stimulates both anabolic and catabolic mediators may lead to new understanding of how exercise may be useful diagnostically and therapeutically in healthy children and in children with disease and disability. As noted, the inconsistency in studies examining IGF-I and exercise is that cross-sectional data generally show that fitter individuals have higher IGF-I, while prospective (short-term) training studies result in a suppressed GH-IGF-I axis. When the exercise input is not extreme and/or is accompanied by an adequate nutritional response, the overall growth and the local adaptation to exercise training can continue, despite the initial catabolic state (possibly due to one or more of the compensatory mechanisms outlined above). We hypothesize that as the local adaptation to exercise occurs (eg, muscle hypertrophy, angiogenesis, and new mitochondria), the magnitude of the cytokine and/or stress response diminishes. In an ideal adaptation, a rebound or "catch-up" phenomenon then occurs in which a new enhanced anabolic state of the GH-IGF-I axis is eventually achieved.

It is also possible that a longer-term adaptation to increased physical activity may occur in which the GH-IGF-I axis remains depressed even as increased levels of physical activity continue. In this paradigm, local muscle responses can occur, and performance may improve to some degree. However, if the exercise input is of very high intensity and/or if there is not an appropriate nutritional adjustment to the increased metabolic demand, then the GH-IGF-I axis remains depressed and growth is impaired —such as occurs in elite gymnasts[52] or marginally nourished children whose daily living involves heavy physical activities with suboptimal nutrition.[53]

In these otherwise healthy children who train at very high intensities, and in chronically ill children with uncompensated catabolic states (eg, children with cystic fibrosis or juvenile rheumatoid arthritis), bone mineralization often is affected.[54–57] In our own laboratory, we have examined the relationship between fitness, training, and markers of bone formation using available serum and urine markers of bone formation.[58]

Applications to Specific Disease States

Cystic Fibrosis

In 1992 Nixon et al[59] published a pioneering study in the *New England Journal of Medicine* demonstrating a positive relationship between physical fitness and longevity in patients with cystic fibrosis (CF). The research extended a series of previous investigations that had shown the feasibility and possible benefits of exercise as therapy in CF. The idea that a potentially modifiable behavior such as exercise may contribute to patient health and quality of life in CF remains compelling. Despite this, guidelines for the optimal participation of CF patients in exercise training programs are not well developed (see Cooper[60] and Nikolaizik et al[61] and the comprehensive review of Boas[62]). One reason for this lack of guidelines is that the link between physical activity and the regulation of anabolic and catabolic function in CF has not yet been elucidated fully.

There are clearly several mechanisms responsible for the health benefits of exercise in CF. Specific exercise-related effects, such as improved mucociliary clearance, likely play a role.[63] In addition, as noted above, the ability of exercise to stimulate a metabolic state that promotes anabolism contributes to improved health in CF. Recent data demonstrate that anabolic effects of exercise are caused, in large part, by exercise stimulation of the GH-IGF-I axis,[8,64] a system of growth mediators, receptors, and binding proteins that control somatic and tissue growth in many species.[65]

The paradigm that exercise stimulates both anabolic and catabolic mediators is particularly relevant to children and adolescents with CF. Chronic hypoxia, prolonged pulmonary inflammation, increased basal energy expenditure, and malnutrition lead to a catabolic state in many patients with CF, and consistent with this is the recent discovery that circulating levels of IGF-I are low in this population.[66]

Exercise plays an important role in the therapy of children and adolescents with CF, and physiologic indexes of fitness are known to be low in this population.[67,68] The pioneering work of Keens and co-workers[69] and

Orenstein and co-workers[70] demonstrated the feasibility of medically supervised exercise interventions, and their observations have been corroborated more recently by other investigators.[71–73] The compelling conclusion of these investigations is the hope that if exercise programs are implemented in children with CF, then longevity and, perhaps, quality of life may be enhanced.

The paradigms linking exercise with growth, growth factors, and cytokines are particularly relevant to CF. Many children with CF are growth impaired[74,75] and osteopenic.[54,55] Although not well studied to date, it does seem that the mechanism of this growth impairment is associated with abnormal IGF-I regulation. For example, Laursen et al[66,76] and Taylor et al[77] recently noted that IGF-I levels are low in patients with CF. Laursen et al's large study (235 patients) *did not* reveal strong correlations between IGF-I levels and nutritional status, growth, liver disease, or lung function. Moreover, despite the low levels of circulating IGF-I, Dooghe and co-workers[78] recently demonstrated reduced receptor binding of IGF-I on red blood cells of CF patients. This finding was unexpected, since IGF-I receptors are known to be to increased in states of low circulating IGF-I, reflecting compensatory ligand-induced upregulation of tissue receptors (eg, findings from our own laboratory in elderly subjects[18]). Thus, it is apparent that impaired IGF-I function may occur through multiple mechanisms in CF.

In addition to malnutrition (the classic cause of reduced circulating IGF-I[79]) there are a number of possibly interrelated mechanisms for low IGF-I and receptor binding in CF. As noted above, cytokines inhibit the GH-IGF-I axis, and *systemic* increases in proinflammatory cytokines have been observed to accompany excessive local lung inflammation in CF.[80–82] Hypoxia, observed at rest and during exercise in many CF patients,[83] has been shown (by us and others) to inhibit IGF-I levels,[29,84] and children with chronic hypoxia (eg, as occurs in certain congenital heart lesions[85]) have low IGF-I levels. The mechanism of hypoxia-associated reductions in IGF-I is not known, but hypoxia also stimulates proinflammatory cytokines,[86] and these may impair the GH-IGF-I axis.

In summary, it is likely that exercise can promote health in patients with CF by stimulating growth factors. However, because CF patients have a tendency to develop a catabolic state even at rest, care must be taken when recommending exercise programs that will further increase energy expenditure, alter the GH-IGF-I axis, and potentially increase inflammatory cytokines. By researching the specific interactions among exercise, growth factors, and cytokines, we hope to provide a physiologic basis for optimizing the therapeutic use of exercise in patients with CF.

Obesity

The alarming recent increase in type II diabetes in children and adolescents has been triggered by sociocultural and economic factors leading to drastic changes in diet and levels of physical activity in a susceptible population. Alterations in diet and exercise may prove to be useful therapeutic approaches, but they are difficult to implement. Moreover, without clear mechanistic physiologic markers of the metabolic abnormality associated with type II diabetes, diet and exercise regimens will remain imprecise, poorly defined, and ineffective, as has been the case, unfortunately, in other conditions effected by altered energy expenditure.

It is now known that adipose tissue is metabolically active. It appears that the fat mass acts through a hormonal mechanism to maintain itself by limiting lipolysis. For example, levels of GH, one of the major lipolytic hormones, and GH secretion in response to physiologic stimuli such as exercise, are low in adult obese subjects.[87] A vicious cycle then ensues (Figure 31–9) leading to insulin resistance and, in susceptible individuals, frank type II diabetes.

New data indicate that adipocytes produce mediators such as TNF-α that play a pivotal role in insulin sensitivity, possibly by altering insulin-receptor binding in tissues.[88] Growth hormone acts to limit adipocyte TNF-α secretion, as has been demonstrated in GH-deficient individuals in whom TNF-α is high but normalizes when GH is administered. Here, the mechanistic link to physical activity is particularly intriguing: GH pulsatility is enhanced by exercise training in adolescents and adults. Moreover, recent investigations from this and other laboratories demonstrate the acute and chronic inflammatory cytokine response (ie, interleukin-6 and TNF-α) to exercise in both adults and children. The latter information is particularly exciting because it suggests specific mediators that explain the catabolic, as well as the anabolic, potential of physical activity.

Although the potential role of exercise as a therapy for adults with type II diabetes has received substantial attention,[89] far less is known about the specific effects of exercise or training on growth mediators. In children and adolescents with obesity or type II diabetes, there have been few studies focused on cytokine/growth factor responses to exercise. While it seems that the GH-IGF-I and inflammatory cytokine systems are affected by exercise and training in both adults and children, it is only in children that the critical process of growth and development is occurring. Moreover, at no other stage of human development does activity of the GH-IGF-I axis change so rapidly. Thus, a perturbation such as exercise that can modulate the GH-IGF-I axis is unique in children, because of its potential to acutely affect growth as well as to influence health later in life.

Summary

The GH-IGF-I axis regulates growth in many tissues from red blood cells to bones. Thus, efforts to understand

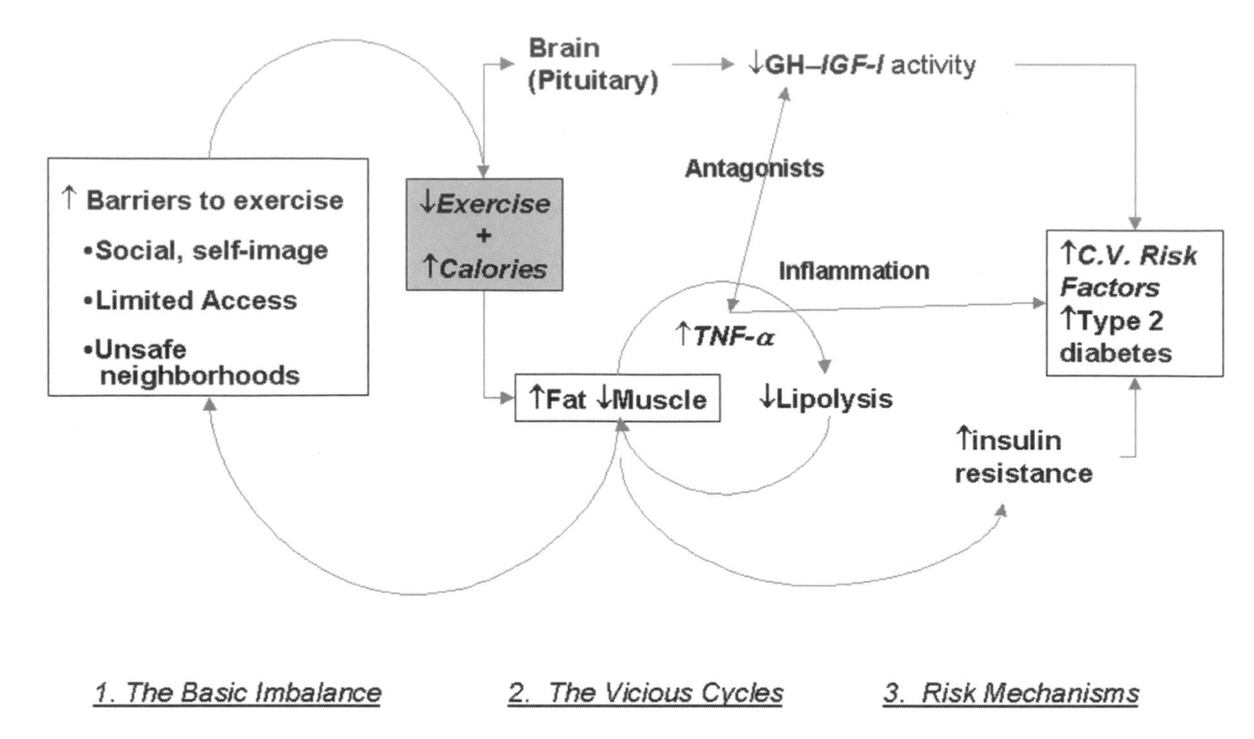

FIGURE 31–9. A model of how social and behavioral factors lead to long-term health problems in children. Physical inactivity reduces anabolic activity of the growth hormone–insulin-like growth factor I (GH-IGF-I) axis, which plays important roles both in attenuating cardiovascular risk factors and in the process of growth and development. Reduced GH exacerbates the problem of increased fat, and fat tissue produces inflammatory mediators, such as tumor necrosis factor α (TNF-α). The inflammatory mediators contribute to insulin resistance, endothelial dysfunction, and, ultimately, increased cardiovascular disease (CV) risk factors. The schemata highlights the vicious cycles in which behavioral and physiologic factors conspire to further reduce exercise frequency in these children.

how physical activity impacts this system will lead to a more fundamental understanding of the mechanisms that control growth and development in children; this will have applications both for healthy children and for those with chronic diseases and disabilities. Specifically, the challenge is to understand how opposing cellular mediators—growth factors on the one hand, inflammatory cytokines and stress hormones on the other—are regulated by exercise and thereby contribute to overall growth and development. This information can be used to better define the boundary between therapeutic effects of exercise (characterized, perhaps, by tissue expression of growth factors) and harmful effects (characterized by excessive tissue cytokine and neuroendocrine stress responses). A scientific basis for determining optimal levels of physical activity in children and adolescents does not yet exist.

Exercise promotes health in children and adolescents and may, under certain circumstances, promote growth.[90] The impact of physical activity during growth and development is of particular importance because of the potential influence on health much later in life. Clearly, the problem of physical inactivity among America's youth is a major health problem of our time, but the benefits of exercise will best be determined by a more thorough understanding of what constitutes both too little as well as too much physical activity. If exercise becomes too strenuous in the healthy child, or if physiologic constraints imposed by a chronic disease or disability render even mild activity painful or injurious, then the adaptive beneficial response may not occur. A substantial increase in injuries in activities such as organized childhood soccer is being observed worldwide[91] and is, perhaps, related to unphysiologically high exercise "inputs" in the developing child. Moreover, in extreme situations of excessive training and self-imposed dietary restriction (eg, as occurs in elite female gymnasts), bone growth is ominously delayed, and this is accompanied by reduced IGF-I. Thus, new research should focus on mechanistic understanding of what constitutes healthy levels of physical activity in children and, consequently, guidelines for children, parents, teachers, and health professionals.

The challenge of understanding how exercise interventions may work to promote health in children and adolescents with obesity or chronic diseases is particularly daunting. It is likely that in children with underlying physiologic constraints, the boundary between therapeutic effects of exercise and harmful effects is less distinct than it is in healthy children. A normally health-promoting exercise input could, in a child with chronic lung or heart disease, become deleterious if, for example, oxygen delivery to tissues were sufficiently impaired. It is a major goal of research in the author's laboratory to better

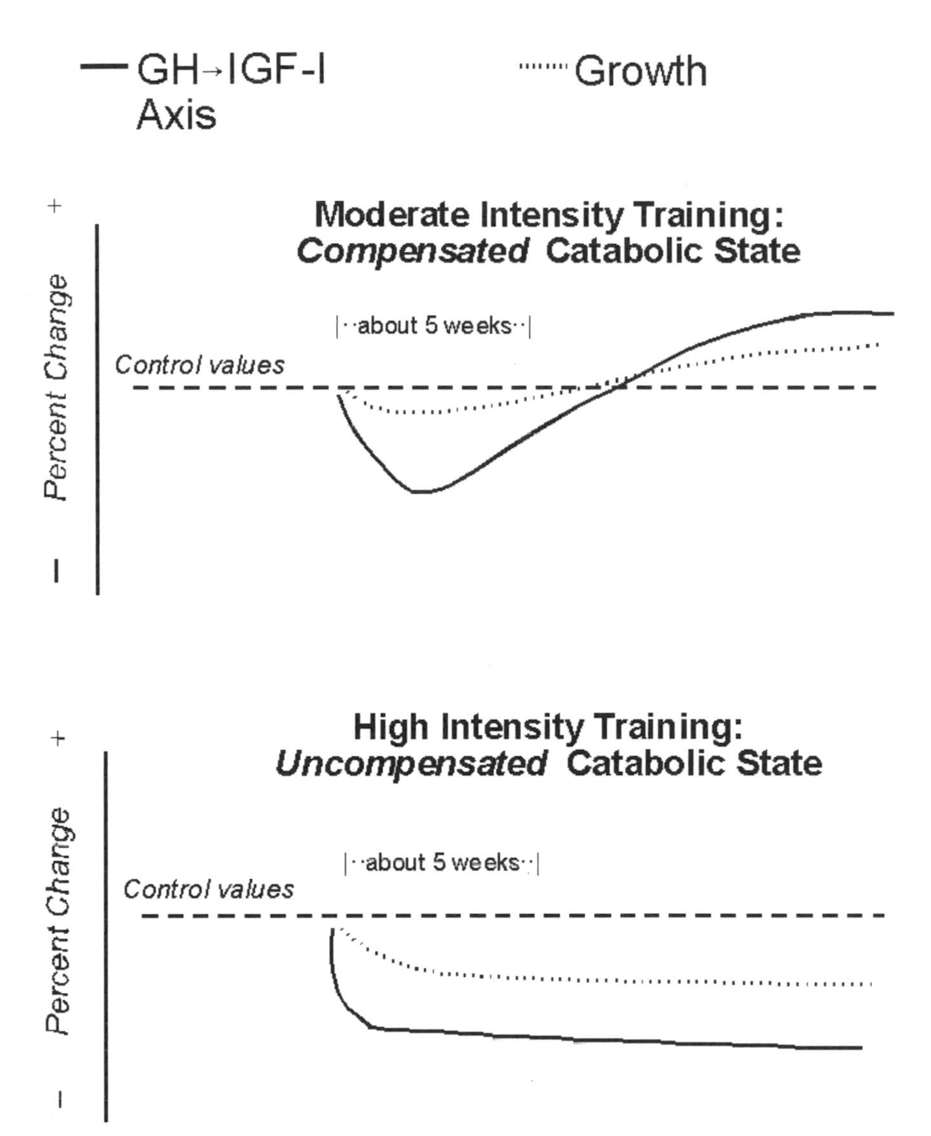

FIGURE 31–10. Interaction of exercise and growth in health and disease. We hypothesize two physiologic states associated with differing levels of physical activity in children and adolescents. *Top*, With moderate-intensity and energy-balanced exercise, a compensated catabolic state is found early in training (about 1 to 5 weeks). Insulin-like growth factor I (IGF-I) may fall, and inflammatory cytokines (not shown) may be elevated. However, as training proceeds, the inflammatory response diminishes and is followed by a rebound in the bioactivity of the growth hormone (GH)-IGF-I axis. Local muscle and somatic growth continue despite the catabolic environment due to compensatory mechanisms (see text) that attenuate the initial suppression of the GH-IGF-I axis. *Bottom*, With high-intensity training, by contrast, the compensatory mechanisms proposed herein are not sufficient. The GH-IGF-I axis remains suppressed throughout the training period, the inflammatory cytokines remain elevated, and somatic growth is impaired. Local muscle adaptation to specific exercises may occur, but with a diminishing response. In children with chronic disease or disability, achieving an optimal exercise response may be more difficult and requires careful monitoring.

understand the "boundary conditions" of the exercise response where adaptation gives way to injury, and, thereby, to provide these children with safe and therapeutic regimens of exercise (Figure 31–10).

Acknowledgments

This work was supported by NICHD RO1 26939, General Clinical Research Center CRC MO1 RR00827-SI, and research support from the Cystic Fibrosis Foundation.

References

1. Leonard WR, Robertson ML. Comparative primate energetics and hominid evolution. Am J Phys Anthropol 1997;102:265–81.
2. Eliakim A, Brasel JA, Cooper DM. GH response to exercise: assessment of the pituitary refractory period, and relationship with circulating components of the GH-IGF-I axis in adolescent females. J Pediatr Endocrinol Metab 2000;12:47–55.

3. Rosenfeld RG. Disorders of growth hormone and insulin-like growth factor secretion and action. In: Sperling MA, ed. Pediatric endocrinology. Philadelphia: W.B. Saunders, 1996:117–70.
4. Poehlman ET, Rosen CJ, Copeland KC. The influence of endurance training on insulin-like growth factor-I in older individuals. Metabolism 1994;43:1401–5.
5. Yeh JK, Aloia JF, Chen M, et al. Effect of growth hormone administration and treadmill exercise on serum and skeletal IGF-I in rats. Am J Physiol 1994;266:E129–35.
6. Koziris LP, Hickson RC, Chatterton RJ, et al. Serum levels of total and free IGF-I and IGFBP-3 are increased and maintained in long-term training. J Appl Physiol 1999; 86:1436–42.
7. Zanconato S, Moromisato DY, Moromisato MY, et al. Effect of training and growth hormone suppression on insulin-like growth factor-I mRNA in young rats. J Appl Physiol 1994;76:2204–9.
8. Adams GR. Role of insulin-like growth factor-I in the regulation of skeletal muscle adaptation to increased loading. In: Holloszy JH, editor. Exercise and sports science reviews. Baltimore: Williams and Wilkins, 1998:31–60.
9. Cuneo RC, Salomon F, Wiles CM, et al. Growth hormone treatment in growth hormone-deficient adults. II. Effects on exercise performance. J Appl Physiol 1991;70:695–700.
10. Borer KT, Nicoski DR, Owens V. Alteration of pulsatile growth hormone secretion by growth-inducing exercise: involvement of endogenous opiates and somatostatin. Endocrinology 1986;118:844–50.
11. Grindeland RE, Roy R, Edgerton VR, et al. Exercise and growth hormone have synergistic effects on skeletal muscle and tibias of suspended rats [abstract]. FASEB J 1991; 5:A1037.
12 Cooper DM, Moromisato DY, Zanconato S, et al. Effect of growth hormone suppression on exercise training and growth responses in young rats. Pediatr Res 1994;35:223–7.
13. Eliakim A, Brasel JA, Mohan S, et al. Physical fitness, endurance training, and the GH-IGF-I system in adolescent females. J Clin Endocrinol Metab 1996;81:3986–92.
14. Eliakim A, Brasel JA, Mohan S, Cooper DM. Increased physical activity and the growth hormone insulin-like growth factor-I axis in adolescent males. Am J Physiol. Regulatory Comparative Integrative Physiol 1998;275: R308–14.
15. Rajaram S, Baylink DJ, Mohan S. Insulin-like growth factor binding proteins in serum and other biological fluids: regulation and functions. Endocr Rev 1997;18:801–831.
16. Mohan S, Bautista C, Wergedal JE, Baylink DJ. Isolation of a novel inhibitory IGF binding protein, a potential local regulator of IGF action in bone cell conditioned medium. Proc Natl Acad Sci U S A 1989;86:8338–42.
17. Honda Y, Landale EC, Strong DD, et al. Recombinant synthesis of insulin-like growth factor binding protein-4 (IGFBP-4): development, validation, and application of a radioimmunoassay for IGFBP-4 in human serum and other biological fluids. J Clin Endocrinol Metab 1996; 81:1389–96.
18. Moromisato D, Roberts CJ, Brasel JA, et al. Erythrocyte insulin-like growth factor-I binding in younger and older males. Clin Endocrinol (Oxf) 1998;48:339–45.
19. Jenkins RC, Ross RJ. Acquired growth hormone resistance in catabolic states. Baillieres Clin Endocrinol Metab 1996; 10:411–9.
20. Mohan S, Libanati C, Dony C, et al. Development, validation, and application of a radioimmunoassay for insulin-like growth factor binding protein-5 in human serum and other biological fluids. J Clin Endocrinol Metab 1995;80:2638–45.
21. Wood TL, O'Donnell SL, Levison SW. Cytokines regulate IGF binding proteins in the CNS. Prog Growth Factor Res 1995;6:181–7.
22. Eliakim A, Scheett TP, Allmendinger N, et al. Training, muscle volume, and energy expenditure in nonobese American girls. J Appl Physiol 2001;90:35–44.
23. Pate RR, Ward DS. Endurance trainability of children and youths. In: Bar-Or O, ed. The child and adolescent athlete. Oxford: Blackwell Science, 1996:130–7.
24. Welsman JR, Armstrong N, Withers S. Responses of young girls to two modes of aerobic training. Br J Sports Med 1997;31:139–42.
25. Rowland TW, Martel L, Vanderburgh P, et al. The influence of short-term aerobic training on blood lipids in healthy 10–12 year old children. Int J Sports Med 1996;17:487–92.
26. Cooper DM, Weiler-Ravell D, Whipp BJ, Wasserman K. Oxygen uptake and heart rate during exercise as a function of growth in children. Pediatr Res 1984;18:845–51.
27. Rowland TW, Boyajian A. Aerobic response to endurance exercise training in children. Pediatrics 1995;96:654–8.
28. Eliakim A, Barstow TJ, Brasel JA, et al. The effect of exercise training on energy expenditure, muscle volume, and maximal oxygen uptake in adolescent females. J Pediatr 1996;129:537–43.
29. Moromisato DY, Moromisato MY, Zanconato S, et al. Effect of hypoxia on lung, heart, and liver insulin-like growth factor-I gene and receptor expression in the newborn rat. Crit Care Med 1996;24:919–24.
30. Russell Jones DL, Leach RM, Ward JP, Thomas CR. Insulin-like growth factor-I gene expression is increased in the right ventricular hypertrophy induced by chronic hypoxia in the rat. J Mol Endocrinol 1993;10:99–102.
31. Aggarwal BB, Puri RK. Human cytokines: their role in disease and therapy. Cambridge: Blackwell Scientific, 1995.
32. Cannon JG, Kluger MJ. Endogenous pyrogen activity in human plasma after exercise. Science 1983;220:617–9.
33. Northoff H, Weinstock C, Berg A. The cytokine response to strenuous exercise. Int J Sports Med 1994;15(Suppl 3: S167–71.
34. Rohde T, MacLean DA, Richter EA, et al. Prolonged submaximal eccentric exercise is associated with increased levels of plasma IL-6. Am J Physiol 1997;273:E85–91.
35. Horne L, Bell G, Fisher B, et al. Interaction between cortisol and tumour necrosis factor with concurrent resistance and endurance training. Clin J Sport Med 1997;7:247–51.
36. Bury TB, Louis R, Radermecker MF, Pirnay F. Blood mononuclear cells mobilization and cytokine secretion during prolonged exercise. Int J Sports Med 1996;17:156–60.
37. Bruunsgaard H, Galbo H, Halkjaer-Kristensen J, et al. Exercise-induced increase in serum interleukin-6 in humans is related to muscle damage. J Physiol (Lond) 1997;499(Pt 3):833–41.

38. Sprenger H, Jacobs C, Nain M, et al. Enhanced release of cytokines, interleukin-2 receptors, and neopterin after long-distance running. Clin Immunol Immunopathol 1992;63:188–95.
39. Ostrowski K, Rohde T, Zacho M, et al. Evidence that interleukin-6 is produced in human skeletal muscle during prolonged running. J Physiol (Lond) 1998;508 (Pt 3):949–53.
40. Lilic D, Cant AJ, Abinun M, et al. Cytokine production differs in children and adults. Pediatr Res 1997;42:237–40.
41. Wolf M, Beohm S, Brand M, Kreymann G. Proinflammatory cytokines interleukin 1 beta and tumor necrosis factor alpha inhibit growth hormone stimulation of insulin-like growth factor I synthesis and growth hormone receptor mRNA levels in cultured rat liver cells. Eur J Endocrinol 1996;135:729–37.
42. Wada Y, Sato M, Niimi M, et al. Inhibitory effects of interleukin-1 on growth hormone secretion in conscious male rats. Endocrinology 1995;136:3936–41.
43. Fan J, Wojnar MM, Theodorakis M, Lang CH. Regulation of insulin-like growth factor IGF-I mRNA and peptide and IGF-binding proteins by interleukin-1. Am J Physiol 1996;270:R621–9.
44. Thissen JP, Verniers J. Inhibition by interleukin-1 beta and tumor necrosis factor-alpha of the insulin-like growth factor I messenger ribonucleic acid response to growth hormone in rat hepatocyte primary culture. Endocrinology 1997;138:1078–84.
45. Frost RA, Lang CH, Gelato MC. Transient exposure of human myoblasts to tumor necrosis factor-alpha inhibits serum and insulin-like growth factor-I stimulated protein synthesis. Endocrinology 1997;138:4153–9.
46. Samstein B, Hoimes ML, Fan J, et al. IL-6 stimulation of insulin-like growth factor binding protein IGFBP-1 production. Biochem Biophys Res Commun 1996; 228:611–5.
47. De Benedetti F, Alonzi T, Moretta A, et al. Interleukin 6 causes growth impairment in transgenic mice through a decrease in insulin-like growth factor-I. A model for stunted growth in children with chronic inflammation. J Clin Invest 1997;99:643–50.
48. Scheett TP, Milles PJ, Ziegler MG, et al. Effect of exercise on cytokines and growth mediators in prepubertal children. Pediatr Res 1999;46:429–34.
49. Attard-Montalto SP, Camacho-Heubner C, Cotterill AM, et al. Changes in protein turnover, IGF-I and IGF binding proteins in children with cancer. Acta Paediatr 1998; 87:54–60.
50. Schwarz AJ, Brasel JA, Hintz RL, et al. Acute effect of brief low- and high intensity exercise on circulating IGF-I, -II, and IGF binding protein-3 and its proteolysis in young healthy men. J Clin Endocrinol Metab 1996;81:3492–7.
51. Mandel S, Moreland E, Nichols V, et al. Changes in insulin-like growth factor-I (IGF-I), IGF binding protein-3, growth hormone binding protein, erythrocyte IGF-I receptor, and growth rate during growth hormone therapy. J Clin Endocrinol Metab 1995;80:190–4.
52. Theintz GE, Howald H, Weiss U, Sizonenko PC. Evidence for a reduction of growth potential in adolescent female gymnasts. J Pediatr 1993;122:306–13.
53. Beaune B, Blonc S, Fellmann N, et al. Serum insulin-like growth factor I and physical performance in prepubertal Bolivian girls of a high and low socioeconomic status. Eur J Appl Physiol 1997;76:98–102.
54. Henderson RC, Madsen CD. Bone density in children and adolescents with cystic fibrosis. J Pediatr 1996;128:28–34.
55. Henderson RC, Specter BB. Kyphosis and fractures in children and young adults with cystic fibrosis. J Pediatr 1994; 125:208–12.
56. Davies UM, Jones J, Reeve J, et al. Juvenile rheumatoid arthritis. Effects of disease activity and recombinant human growth hormone on insulin-like growth factor 1, insulin-like growth factor binding proteins 1 and 3, and osteocalcin. Arthritis Rheum 1997;40:332–40.
57. Cassidy JT, Hillman LS. Abnormalities in skeletal growth in children with juvenile rheumatoid arthritis. Pediatric Rheumatol 1997;23:499–508.
58. Eliakim A, Raisz LG, Brasel JA, Cooper DM. Evidence for increased bone formation following a brief endurance-type training intervention in adolescent males. J Bone Miner Res 1997;12:1708–13.
59. Nixon PA, Orenstein DM, Kelsey SF, Doershuk CF. The prognostic value of exercise testing in patients with cystic fibrosis. N Engl J Med 1992;327:1785–8.
60. Cooper DM. Exercise and cystic fibrosis: the search for a therapeutic optimum. Pediatr Pulmonol 1998;25:143–4.
61. Nikolaizik WH, Knopfli B, Leister E, et al. The anaerobic threshold in patients with cystic fibrosis: comparison of V-slope method, lactate turn points and Conconi test. Pediatr Pulmonol 1998;25:147–53.
62. Boas SR. Exercise recommendations for individuals with cystic fibrosis. Sports Medicine 1997;24:17–37.
63. Lannefors L, Wollmer P. Mucus clearance with three chest physiotherapy regimes in cystic fibrosis: a comparison between postural drainage, PEP and physical exercise. Eur Respir J 1992;5:748–53.
64. Cooper DM. Evidence for and mechanisms of exercise modulation of growth. Med Sci Sports Exerc 1994;26:733–40.
65. LeRoith D. Insulin-like growth factors: molecular and cellular aspects. Boca Raton: CRC Press, 1991.
66. Laursen EM, Juul A, Lanng S, et al. Diminished concentrations of insulin-like growth factor-I in cystic fibrosis. Arch Dis Child 1995;72:494–7.
67. Loutzenhiser JK, Clark R. Physical activity and exercise in children with cystic fibrosis. J Pediatr Nurs 1993;8:112–9.
68. Boas SR, Joswiak ML, Nixon PA, et al. Factors limiting anaerobic performance in adolescent males with cystic fibrosis. Med Sci Sports Exerc 1996;28:291–8.
69. Keens TG, Krastins IR, Wannamaker EM, et al. Ventilatory muscle endurance training in normal subjects and patients with cystic fibrosis. Am Rev Respir Dis 1977; 116:853–60.
70. Orenstein DM, Franklin BA, Doershuk CF, et al. Exercise conditioning and cardiopulmonary fitness in cystic fibrosis. The effects of a three-month supervised running program. Chest 1981;80:392–8.
71. Braggion C, Cornacchia M, Miano A, et al. Exercise tolerance and effects of training in young patients with cystic fibrosis and mild airway obstruction. Pediatr Pulmonol 1989;7:145–52.

72. Stanghelle JK, Hjeltnes N, Bangstad HJ, Michalsen H. Effect of daily short bouts of trampoline exercise during 8 weeks on the pulmonary function and the maximal oxygen uptake of children with cystic fibrosis. Int J Sports Med 1988;9 Suppl 1:32–6.
73. Stanghelle JK, Skyberg D, Haanaes OC. Eight-year follow-up of pulmonary function and oxygen uptake during exercise in 16-year-old males with cystic fibrosis. Acta Paediatr 1992;81:527–31.
74. Thomson MA, Quirk P, Swanson CE, et al. Nutritional growth retardation is associated with defective lung growth in cystic fibrosis: a preventable determinant of progressive pulmonary dysfunction. Nutrition 1995;11:350–4.
75. Byard PJ. The adolescent growth spurt in children with cystic fibrosis. Ann Hum Biol 1994;21:229–40.
76. Laursen T, Jorgensen JO, Christiansen JS. Metabolic effects of growth hormone administered subcutaneously once or twice daily to growth hormone deficient adults. Clin Endocrinol (Oxf) 1994;41:337–43.
77. Taylor AM, Busch A, Thomson A, et al. Relation between insulin-like growth factor-I, body mass index, and clinical status in CF. Arch Dis Child 1997;76:304–9.
78. Dooghe C, Grizard G, Labbe A, et al. Decrease in insulin and insulin-like growth factor I (IGF-I) binding to erythrocytes from patients with cystic fibrosis. Diabetes Metab 1997;23:511–8.
79. Lowe WL Jr, Adamo M, Werner H, et al. Regulation by fasting of rat insulin-like growth factor I and its receptor. Effects on gene expression and binding. J Clin Invest 1989;84:619–26.
80. Elborn JS, Cordon SM, Western P, et al. Tumor necrosis factor, resting energy expenditure and cachexia in cystic fibrosis. Clin Sci 1993;85:563–8.
81. Levy E, Gurbindo C, Lacaille F, et al. Circulating tumor necrosis factor-alpha levels and lipid abnormalities in patients with cystic fibrosis. Pediatr Res 1993;34:162–6.
82. Noah TL, Black HR, Cheng PW, et al. Nasal and bronchoalveolar lavage fluid cytokines in early cystic fibrosis. J Infect Dis 1997;175:638–47.
83. Henke KG, Orenstein DM. Oxygen saturation during exercise in cystic fibrosis. Am Rev Respir Dis 1984;129:708–11.
84. Bernstein D, Jasper JR, Rosenfeld RG, Hintz RL. Decreased serum insulin-like growth factor-I associated with growth failure in newborn lambs with experimental cyanotic heart disease. J Clin Invest 89:1992;1128–32.
85. Barton JS, Hindmarsh PC, Preece MA. Serum insulin-like growth factor 1 in congenital heart disease. Arch Dis Child 1996;75:162–3.
86. Klausen T, Olsen NV, Poulsen TD, et al. Hypoxemia increases serum interleukin-6 in humans. Eur J Appl Physiol 1997;76:480–2.
87. Vettor R, Macor C, Rossi E, et al. Impaired counterregulatory hormonal and metabolic response to exhaustive exercise in obese subjects. Acta Diabetol 2000;34:61–6.
88. Zinman B, Hanley AJ, Harris SB, et al. Circulating tumor necrosis factor-alpha concentrations in a native Canadian population with high rates of type 2 diabetes mellitus. J Clin Endocrinol Metab 1999;84:272–8.
89. Ivy JL, Zderic TW, Fogt DL. Prevention and treatment of non-insulin-dependent diabetes mellitus. Exerc Sport Sci Rev 1999;27:1–35.
90. Torun B, Viteri FE. Influence of exercise on linear growth [review]. Eur J Clin Nutr 1994;48 Suppl 1:S186–9.
91. Backx FJG. Epidemiology of paediatric sports-related injuries. In: Bar-Or O, ed. The child and adolescent athlete. London: Blackwell Scientific, 1996:163–72.

SECTION IV
INFLAMMATION AND PULMONARY DEFENSE MECHANISMS

CHAPTER 32

CILIARY ABNORMALITIES

MICHAEL KASHGARIAN, MD

Siewert first described the triad of bronchiectasis, sinusitis, and situs inversus in 1903.[1] Subsequently, Kartagener reported four patients with similar clinical abnormalities in 1933, and the syndrome has retained his name as an eponym.[2] Although several explanations for the pathogenesis of bronchiectasis in this triad were offered, little was known about the cellular mechanisms involved until 1975. Pedersen and Rebbe described the absence of the dynein arms of the axoneme of immobile human spermatozoa in a patient with Kartagener's syndrome.[3] Pedersen later described similar ciliary defects in nasal mucosa of affected patients, and Afzelius found identical changes in bronchial mucosa of patients with chronic bronchial infections.[4,5] These reports gave birth to the term, "immotile cilia syndrome."[5–11] Additional studies demonstrated that a limited degree of abnormal ciliary movement often was observed in in vitro preparations of the respiratory tract epithelium from such patients, and Sleigh suggested that the term immotile cilia syndrome should be replaced by "primary ciliary dyskinesia" (PCD).[12–16]

Intact mucociliary clearance is essential for pulmonary hygiene.[17–19] Ciliary movement in normal individuals is oriented in one direction. Clearance of the airways is accomplished by the transport of mucus toward the pharynx by the coordinated wavelike movement of the cilia of the epithelium lining the airways. The structure, number, movement, and coordination of the cilia are essential for proper airway function. Impaired or reduced mucociliary function can result from abnormal ciliary function, as seen in PCD changes in the fluidity of mucus, as seen in cystic fibrosis, or a combination of both.[20–25] Although environmental pollution and viral infections are known causes of acquired defects in mucociliary function,[26–28] it is now recognized that a subgroup of patients, predominately in the pediatric age group, suffer from congenital disorders affecting ciliary function.

Clinical Presentation of Primary Ciliary Dyskinesia

Respiratory tract diseases such as sinusitis, otitis media, and bronchitis have been associated with PCD. On the basis of several studies, it is clear that patients with multiple manifestations of chronic upper respiratory disease are likely to have PCD, whereas patients with a single manifestation are not.[16,25,29,30] In addition, ciliary abnormalities similar to those seen in PCD also can be identified in individuals with various respiratory diseases without an intrinsic genetic defect of their ciliary function.[8,12,21,24]

Primary ciliary dyskinesia, which encompasses Kartagener's syndrome, represents a spectrum of ciliary defects, that lead to impaired ciliary motion and result in respiratory dysfunction with chronic and recurrent upper and lower respiratory infections.[9,11,16,31–36] This heterogeneous group of disorders usually is inherited in an autosomal-recessive pattern,[2,10,14,29,37–42] Although a recent report has demonstrated an X chromosome–linked or an autosomal-dominant pattern of inheritance.[43] Studies taking advantage of the evolutionary conservation of the genes encoding for axonemal proteins have identified several candidate genes known to encode components of the ciliary complex. Loss-of-function mutations of these genes have been identified in individual patients, but attempts to conduct linkage studies have been hindered by the heterogeneity of the genetic defects and a lack of consistent linkage between identified mutations and similar ciliary phenotypes in various affected families.[38,44] These autosomal-recessive disorders affect approximately 1 in 16,000 live births. Approximately half of the affected individuals also have situs inversus, which completes the Kartagener triad.

The classic clinical presentation of PCD is chronic respiratory tract disease, which begins in the first year of life and may include rhinitis, sinusitis, otitis media, bronchitis, pneumonia, bronchiectasis, and cough. In addition, males are usually infertile secondary to abnormal sperm

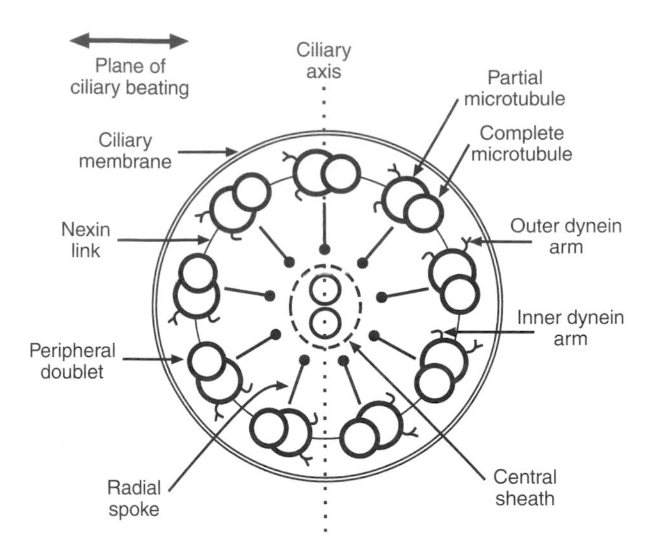

FIGURE 32–1. Ultrastructure of the cilium. This illustration of the structure of the axoneme of a normal cilium demonstrates the central doublet surrounded by nine peripheral microtubule doublets. The central doublet consists of two complete microtubules that are held together by a bridge (which is not visualized in electron micrographs) and surrounded by a central sheath. The outer doublets are each composed of one complete microtubule and one partial microtubule fused together, sharing a common tubule wall. Although outer and inner dynein arms are represented here in the same plane, they actually are separated longitudinally by a distance of approximately 10 nm. Nexin links illustrated here also are not visualized in routine electron microscopy.

motility. More recently, similar defects have been suggested to cause infertility in females when the ciliated epithelium of the fallopian tubes are involved. Sturgess and Turner found that most patients with PCD have cough, rhinitis, sinusitis, and rhinorrhea.[38,45] Greenstone et al reported nasal obstruction, rhinorrhea, and middle ear fluid accumulation as the most common manifestations.[15,16] Mygind et al found the most common manifestations to include nasal polyps as well as sinusitis, bronchiectasis, bronchial pneumonia, and chronic bronchiectasis.[33] Although the clinical spectrum is well characterized, the prevalence of any given ciliary abnormality is less well studied. In addition, published studies have not attempted to correlate specific clinical presentations with specific ultrastructural findings. Some authors have suggested that all children with unexplained chronic respiratory disease, particularly if it starts in the perinatal period, should be investigated for PCD.[25,46] Others have suggested that this approach would yield a relatively low number of abnormalities; in one study, only 6 of 100 cases showed evidence of a ciliary abnormality on the initial electron microscopic study.[25]

Diagnosis of Primary Ciliary Dyskinesia

The diagnosis of PCD is usually made by ultrastructural examination of ciliary epithelial biopsies or brushings of nasal epithelium.[7,16,47–53] Observation of ciliary beat frequency also has been used.[49,54–59] The movement of an individual cilium is produced by the bending of its core axoneme, which is composed of microtubules and associated proteins (Figure 32–1). The microtubules are associated with a number of special function proteins that project at regular positions along the length of the axoneme; these include the dynein arms, nexin links, and radial spokes. Ciliary dynein is a motor protein that hydrolyzes adenosine triphosphate (ATP) to move along a microtubule toward its minus end, the dynein carries with it the adjacent microtubules to generate a sliding force.[57,60–64] The microtubule doublets are held together with nexin links; therefore, during the sliding process, the cilium bends. The spokes connect the outer doublets

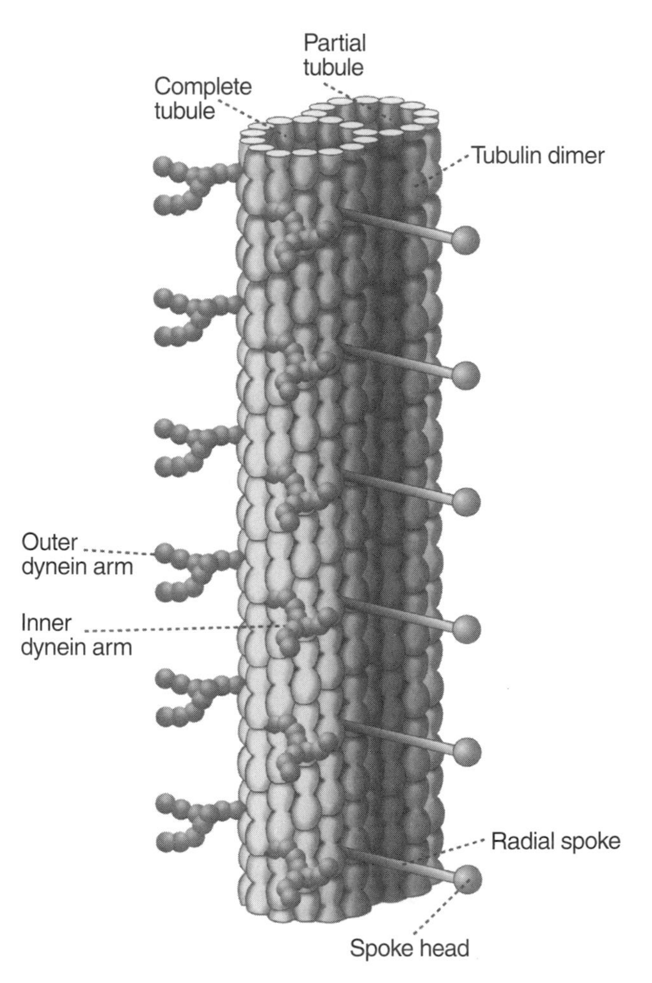

FIGURE 32–2. A computer reconstruction of the outer microtubule doublets as described by Linck.[66] It illustrates that the wall of the microtubule is made up of heterodimers of tubulin. The dynein arms project out from the complete tubule with an axial repeat of approximately 24 nm; inner dynein arms are separated axially from the outer dynein arms by approximately 10 nm. Radial spokes tend to be unevenly spaced along the axial length. This staggering of the outer and inner dynein arms along the axial length makes the routine diagnosis of the absence of either arm difficult, because they are not always visualized in the same plane in an electron micrograph.

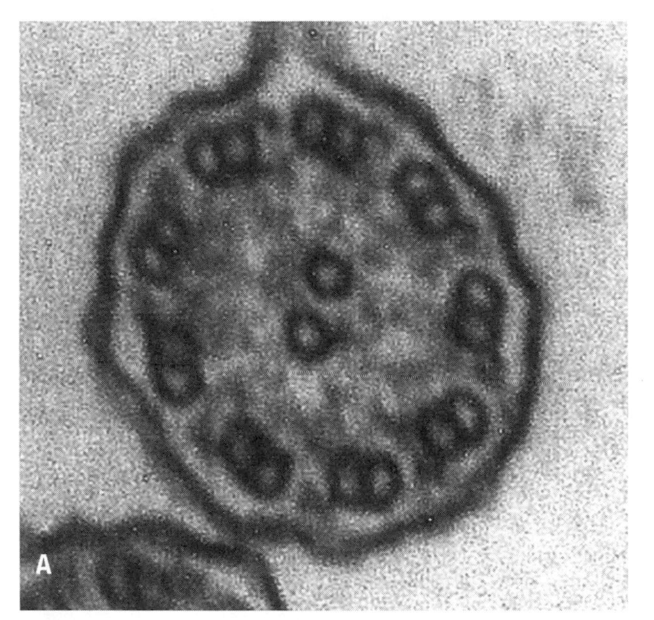

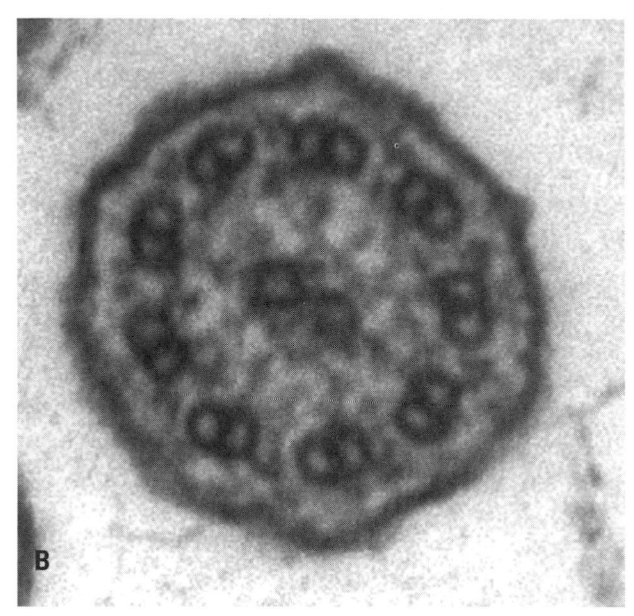

FIGURE 32–3. Electron micrograph of a normal cilium. Electron micrograph demonstrates the normal 9 + 2 configuration of the axoneme. Both inner and outer dynein arms can be identified, but not always on the same microtubule doublet: the outer arms generally are more easily visualized. The spokes are not clearly identified. Clearly, it is necessary to examine more than a single cilium to identify whether there is a specific dyneim arm defect.

to the central doublet and prevent the cilium from buckling. The respiratory epithelium of humans have fields of cilium with microvilli interspersed among the cilia. The movement of cilia is highly coordinated, so that all of the surface cilia move together in a successive wave motion toward the pharynx. This movement is the driving force for cleansing of the airways.

Routine fixation adequately preserves the structure of the cilia for electron microscopy of thin sections, and it is suitable for routine examination of human cilia. Addition of tannic acid to the fixative results in an increase in electron density and contrast and allows clear visualization of the individual components of the ciliary structure.[65] The dynein arms are made more distinct, as are the radial spokes. Linck has proposed a more detailed appraisal of the complex organization of the doublet microtubule and its appendages (Figure 32–2).[66] The illustration demonstrates that the wall of the microtubule is made of

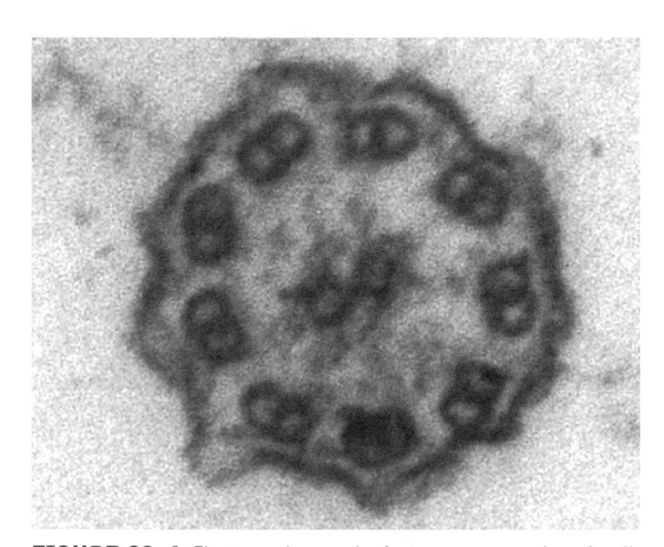

FIGURE 32–4. Electron micrograph of a transverse section of a cilium from a patient with Kartagener's syndrome. Although the axoneme contains the normal component of a 9 + 2 tubule doublets, both inner and outer dynein arms are absent.

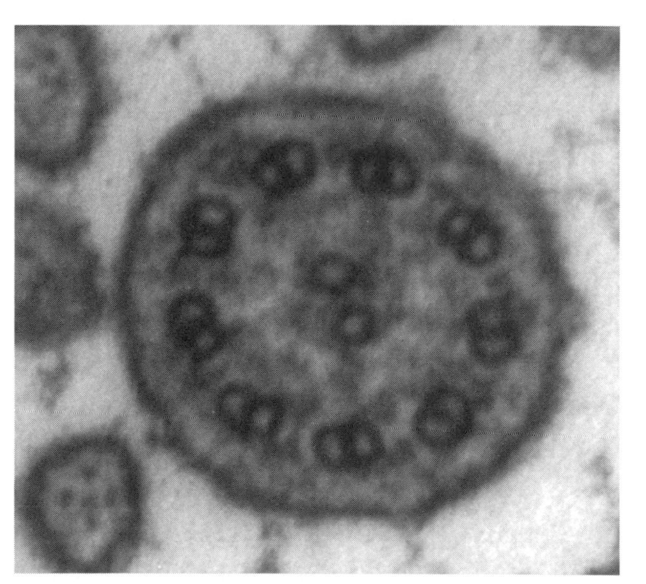

FIGURE 32–5. Electron micrograph illustrating the absence of one of the dynein arms. The normal 9 + 2 orientation is preserved, but only the outer dynein arms can be seen. Notice the inner arms are not seen on any of the doublets even when the outer arm is not visualized.

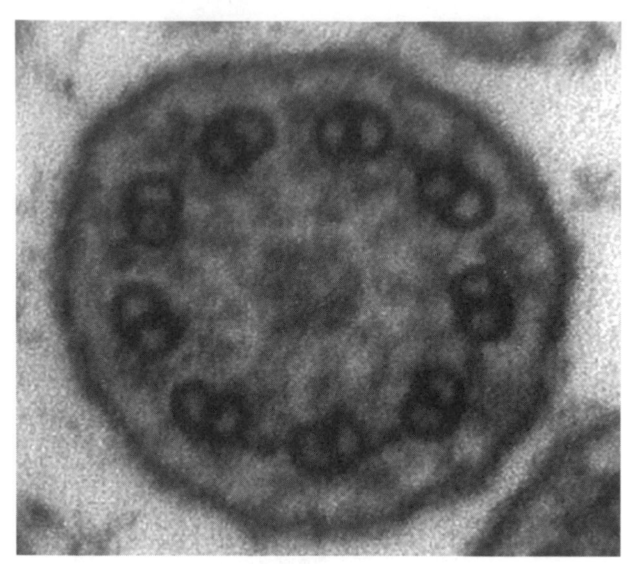

FIGURE 32–6. Electron micrograph illustrating the absence of the central doublet. Absence of the central doublet must be verified by examination of multiple cilia, since axonemal structure is not uniform along the axial length of the cilium.

heterodimers of tubulin arranged in tandem to form protofilaments. Two rows of dynein arms project from the complete tubule. The arms are staggered such that the outer arms are nearer the base than are the corresponding inner arms. The radial spoke triplets are spaced unevenly, with longer spacing nearer the base.

Clinically important defects of ciliary ultrastructure include the lack of dynein arms, microtubular transposition, compound cilia, random ciliary orientation, abnormal length of cilia, radial spoke and nexin link defects, and absence of cilia with brush border metaplasia.[4,7,47,59,67–70] It is important to differentiate conditions, that cause transient ciliary defects that involve only a subset of cilia, such as acute and chronic respiratory

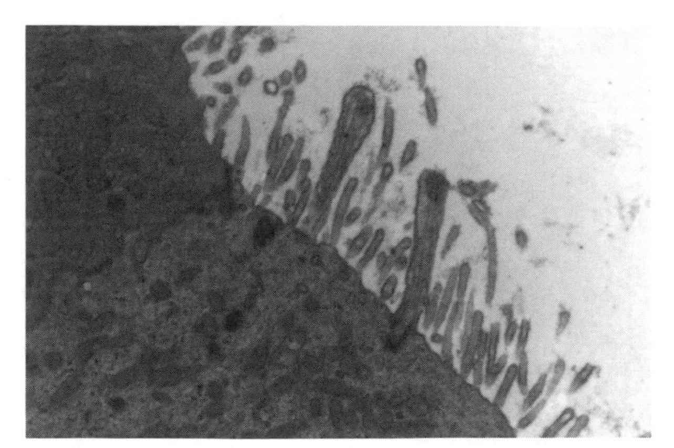

FIGURE 32–7. Electron micrograph illustrating ciliary aplasia. This electron micrograph demonstrates near-complete absence of cilia, with transformation of the apical surface to a brush border pattern. Two cilia are seen arising from the apical surface, but they do not have the normal internal axonemal structure.

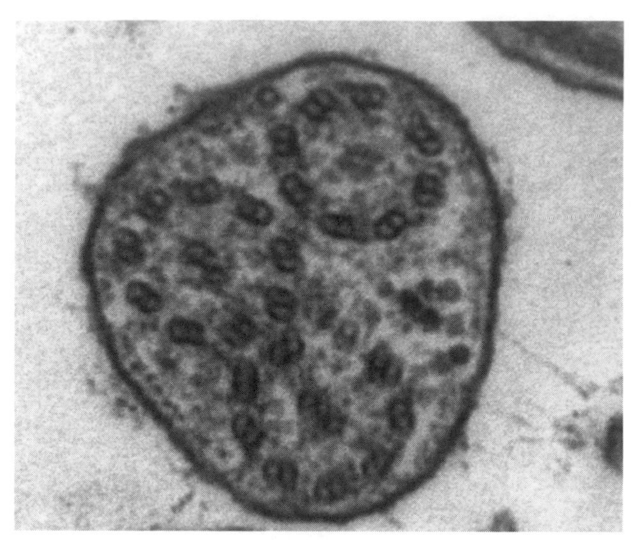

FIGURE 32–8. Electron micrograph illustrating another common abnormality that occurs in chronic inflammation in individuals without an intrinsic defect in ciliary—structure-displacement of the microtubules or reduplication of the axonemal apparatus. This abnormal cilium shows a marked reduplication of the axonemal apparatus with three partially developed axonemes and multiple single tubules without relationship to each other.

inflammation, from true congenital defects (Figure 32–3). In classic Kartagener's syndrome, there is an absence of both inner and outer dynein arms, resulting in a complete dynein arm defect (Figure 32–4). Partial dynein arm defects in which either inner or outer arms are not visualized, and defects in central doublets, generally are not associated with situs inversus and appear to occur as isolated genetic abnormalities (Figures 32–5, and 32–6). Radial spoke defects are more difficult to visualize but generally are considered to be a legitimate entity in this spectrum of genetic ciliary abnormalities. Ciliary aplasia or brush border metaplasia with an absence of cilia in the epithelium may actually be the result of a chronic inflammatory change in an individual with a previous ciliary abnormality (Figures 32–7, and 32–8). Finally, random ciliary orientation, in which the sole ultrastructural defect is that the central doublets are arranged in a random orientation rather than a uniform parallel orientation, can be a cause of PCD (Figure 32–9).

Correlation between the clinical presentation and the ultrastructural pathology in PCD has been reported by several groups.[16,20,21,24,25,29,30,33,49,53,54,71–73] Analysis of our own experience has demonstrated that the number of males and females with PCD roughly equal. No correlation between gender or age and the ultrastructural findings was evident. Random ciliary orientation was the most common defect identified. Structural abnormalities alone, without disordered orientation, was seen in only 21% of biopsies. Many patients with random ciliary orientation also had other structural abnormalities such as reduplication of the ciliary apparatus or misplaced tubular apparatus, but, in general,

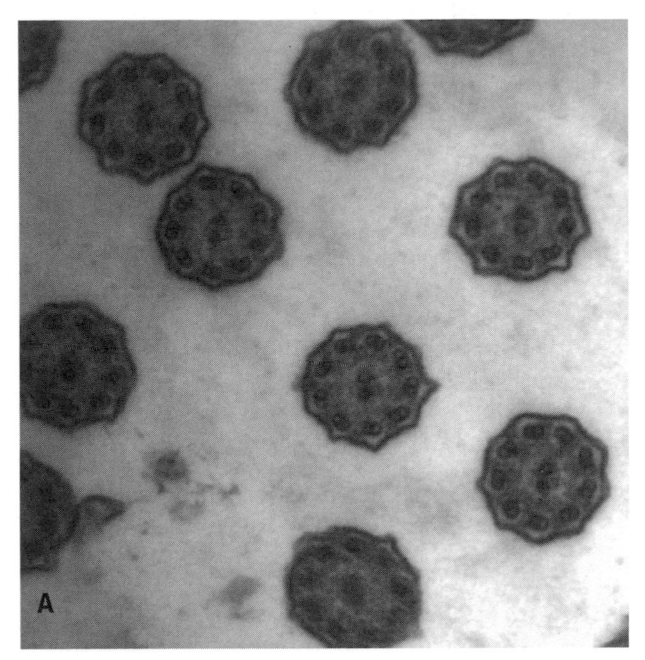

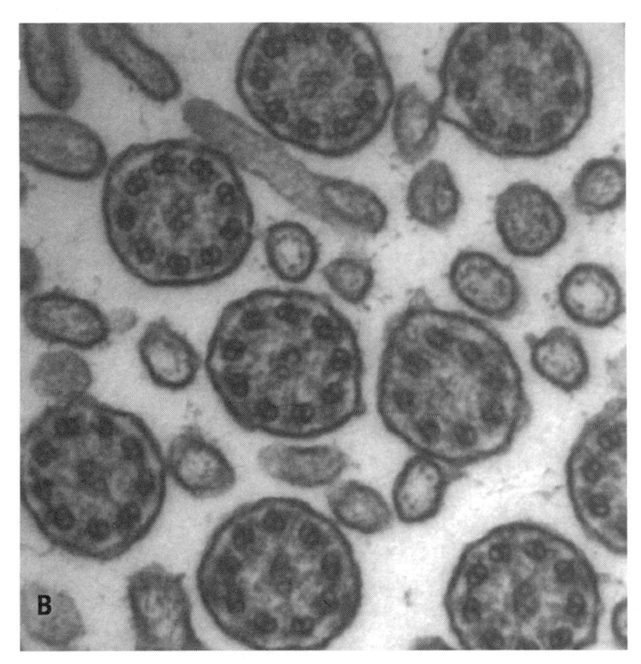

FIGURE 32–9. Electron micrograph illustrating ciliary orientation and disorientation. *A*, Normally, central doublets are aligned in a parallel fashion and oriented in the same direction. This orientation is necessary for the coordinated wave function of the cilia. *B*, The central doublets are oriented in a random fashion; no two ciliary central doublets are in exactly the same plane. Random ciliary orientation is now recognized as a common cause of primary ciliary dyskinesia.

both inner and outer dynein arms were identified in all cases of random ciliary orientation alone. The clinical manifestations in patients with positive biopsies were approximately evenly distributed between sinonasal symptoms, otitis media, and pulmonary manifestations as the presenting clinical picture leading to biopsy. Patients who presented solely with cough were unlikely to have PCD, whereas patients with multiple manifestations had a high likelihood of a ciliary defect.

The diagnosis of PCD should incorporate ultrastructural examination of upper respiratory biopsies. These studies should be correlated with clinical manifestations and, if possible, be confirmed by ciliary function studies. As ciliary ultrastructure can be altered by chronic infection, samples should be obtained when the patients have few respiratory symptoms, and, if positive ciliary defects are identified, repeat sampling should be performed to reduce the possibility of transitory ciliary defects secondary to inflammation. Most clinicians should be able to effectively diagnose PCD using these criteria.

References

1. Siewert AK. Uber einem Fall von bronkiectasie bei einem patientem mit situs inversus vicerum. Berl Klin Wochen 1903;139:139–41.
2. Kartagener M. Pathogenese der Bronchiectasien. Beitr Klin Tuberk 1933;83:489–501.
3. Pedersen H, Rebbe H. Absence of axonemal arms of immotile human spermatozoa. Biol Reprod 1975; 12:541–4.
4. Pedersen H, Mygind N. Absence of axonemal arms in nasal mucosa cilia in Kartagener's syndrome. Nature 1976; 262:494–5.
5. Afzelius BA. A human syndrome caused by immotile cilia. Science 1976;193:317–9.
6. Antonelli M, Modesti A, De Angelis M, et al. Immotile cilia syndrome: radial spokes deficiency in a patient with Kartagener's triad. Acta Paediatr Scand 1981; 70:571–3.
7. Afzelius BA. Ultrastructural basis for ciliary motility. Eur J Respir Dis Suppl 1983;128:280–6.
8. Afzelius BA, Camner P, Mossberg B. Acquired ciliary defects compared to those seen in the immotile-cilia syndrome. Eur J Respir Dis Suppl 1983;127:5–10.
9. Afzelius BA. Immotile-cilia syndrome: ultrastructural features. Eur J Respir Dis Suppl 1982;118:117–22.
10. Afzelius BA. Genetical and ultrastructural aspects of the immotile-cilia syndrome. Am J Hum Genet 1981; 33:852–64.
11. Yarnal JR, Golish JA, Ahmad M, Tomashefski JF. The immotile cilia syndrome: explanation for many a clinical mystery. Postgrad Med 1982;71:195–7.
12. Rossman CM, Forrest JB, Ruffin RE, Newhouse MT. Immotile cilia syndrome in persons with and without Kartagener's syndrome. Am Rev Respir Dis 1980;121: 1011–6.
13. Rossman CM, Forrest JB, Lee RM, Newhouse MT. The dyskinetic cilia syndrome. Ciliary motility in immotile cilia syndrome. Chest 1980;78:580–2.
14. Sleigh MA. Kartagener's syndrome, ciliary defects and ciliary function. Eur J Respir Dis Suppl 1983;127:157–61.
15. Greenstone MA, Dewar A, Cole PJ. Ciliary dyskinesia with normal ultrastructure. Thorax 1983;38:875–6.

16. Greenstone M, Rutman A, Dewar A, et al. Primary ciliary dyskinesia: cytological and clinical features. Q J Med 1988;67:405–23.
17. de Iongh R, Ing A, Rutland J. Mucociliary function, ciliary ultrastructure, and ciliary orientation in Young's syndrome. Thorax 1992;47:184–7.
18. de Iongh R, Rutland J. Orientation of respiratory tract cilia in patients with primary ciliary dyskinesia, bronchiectasis, and in normal subjects. J Clin Pathol 1989;42:613–9.
19. Houtmeyers E, Gosselink R, Gayan-Ramirez G, Decramer M. Regulation of mucociliary clearance in health and disease [comments]. Eur Respir J 1999;13:1177–88.
20. Pedersen M, Mygind N. Rhinitis, sinusitis and otitis media in Kartagener's syndrome (primary ciliary dyskinesia). Clin Otolaryngol 1982;7:373–80.
21. Rayner CF, Rutman A, Dewar A, et al. Ciliary disorientation in patients with chronic upper respiratory tract inflammation. Am J Respir Crit Care Med 1995;151:800–4.
22. Mossberg B, Afzelius BA, Eliasson R, Camner P. On the pathogenesis of obstructive lung disease. A study on the immotile-cilia syndrome. Scand J Respir Dis 1978; 59:55–65.
23. Lurie M, Rennert G, Goldenberg S, et al. Ciliary ultrastructure in primary ciliary dyskinesia and other chronic respiratory conditions: the relevance of microtubular abnormalities. Ultrastruct Pathol 1992;16:547–53.
24. de Iongh RU, Rutland J. Ciliary defects in healthy subjects, bronchiectasis, and primary ciliary dyskinesia. Am J Respir Crit Care Med 1995;151:1559–67.
25. Chapelin C, Coste A, Reinert P, et al. Incidence of primary ciliary dyskinesia in children with recurrent respiratory diseases. Ann Otol Rhinol Laryngol 1997;106:854–8.
26. Harkema JR, Morgan KT, Gross EA, et al. Consequences of prolonged inhalation of ozone on F344/N rats: collaborative studies. Part VII: Effects on the nasal mucociliary apparatus. Res Rep Health Eff Inst 1994;65 (Part 7):3–34.
27. Ohashi Y, Nakai Y, Ikeoka H, et al. Functional and morphological pathology of the nasal mucosa after x-ray irradiation. Clin Otolaryngol 1988;13:435–46.
28. Gabridge MG, Dougherty EP, Gladd MF, Meccoli RA. Effects of heavy metals on structure, function, and metabolism of ciliated respiratory epithelium in vitro. In Vitro Cell Dev Biol 1982;18:1023–32.
29. Afzelius BA. Genetics and pulmonary medicine. 6. Immotile cilia syndrome: past, present, and prospects for the future. Thorax 1998;53:894–7.
30. Barlocco EG, Valletta EA, Canciani M, et al. Ultrastructural ciliary defects in children with recurrent infections of the lower respiratory tract. Pediatr Pulmonol 1991;10:11–7.
31. Zanon P, Calligaro A. The immotile-cilia syndrome. Functional and ultrastructural alterations. Int J Tissue React 1981;3:99–106.
32. Pedersen M. Specific types of abnormal ciliary motility in Kartagener's syndrome and analogous respiratory disorders. A quantified microphoto-oscillographic investigation of 27 patients. Eur J Respir Dis Suppl 1983; 127:78–90.
33. Mygind N, Pedersen M, Nielsen MH. Primary and secondary ciliary dyskinesia. Acta Otolaryngol 1983; 95:688–94.
34. Gonzalez S, von Bassewitz DB, Grundmann E, et al. Atypical cilia in hyperplastic, metaplastic, and dysplastic human bronchial mucosa. Ultrastruct Pathol 1985;8:345–56.
35. Giorgi PL, Oggiano N, Braga PC, et al. Cilia in children with recurrent upper respiratory tract infections: ultrastructural observations. Pediatr Pulmonol 1992;14:201–5.
36. Kaidoglou K, Aivazis V, Alvanou A, et al. Ultrastructural study of bronchial epithelium in chronic respiratory diseases. Histol Histopathol 1991;6:229–33.
37. Janitz K, Wild A, Beck S, et al. Genomic organization of the HSET locus and the possible association of HLA-linked genes with immotile cilia syndrome (ICS). Immunogenetics 1999;49:644–52.
38. Sturgess JM, Thompson MW, Czegledy-Nagy E, Turner JA. Genetic aspects of immotile cilia syndrome. Am J Med Genet 1986;25:149–60.
39. Wilton LJ, Teichtahl H, Temple-Smith PD, De Kretser DM. Kartagener's syndrome with motile cilia and immotile spermatozoa: axonemal ultrastructure and function. Am Rev Respir Dis 1986;134:1233–6.
40. Pedersen M, Morkassel E, Nielsen MH, Mygind N. Kartagener's syndrome. Preliminary report on cilia structure, function, and upper airway symptoms. Chest 1981;80:858–60.
41. Kinney TB, DeLuca SA. Kartagener's syndrome. Am Fam Physician 1991;44:133–4.
42. Losa M, Ghelfi D, Hof E, et al. Kartagener syndrome: an uncommon cause of neonatal respiratory distress? Eur J Pediatr 1995;154:236–8.
43. Narayan D, Krishnan SN, Upender M, et al. Unusual inheritance of primary ciliary dyskinesia (Kartagener's syndrome). J Med Genet 1994;31:493–6.
44. Pennarun G, Escudier E, Chapelin C, et al. Loss-of-function mutations in a human gene related to *Chlamydomonas reinhardtii* dynein IC78 result in primary ciliary dyskinesia. Am J Hum Genet 1999;65:1508–19.
45. Sturgess JM, Chao J, Wong J, et al. Cilia with defective radial spokes: a cause of human respiratory disease. N Engl J Med 1979;300:53–6.
46. Karja J, Nuutinen J. Immotile cilia syndrome in children. Int J Pediatr Otorhinolaryngol 1983;5:275–9.
47. Carlen B, Stenram U. Ultrastructural diagnosis in the immotile cilia syndrome. Ultrastruct Pathol 1987;11: 653–8.
48. Kamada T, Sumimoto R, Shigeto E. Ultrastructural aspect in the immotile cilia syndrome. Hiroshima J Med Sci 1984;33:239–45.
49. Holzmann D, Ott PM, Felix H. Diagnostic approach to primary ciliary dyskinesia: a review. Eur J Pediatr 2000; 159:95–8.
50. Palmblad J, Mossberg B, Afzelius BA. Ultrastructural, cellular, and clinical features of the immotile-cilia syndrome. Annu Rev Med 1984;35:481–92.
51. Panchal A, Koss MN. Role of electron microscopy in interstitial lung disease. Curr Opin Pulm Med 1997;3:341–7.
52. Robson AM, Smallman LA, Gregory J, Drake-Lee AB. Ciliary ultrastructure in nasal brushings. Cytopathology 1993;4:149–59.
53. Smallman LA, Gregory J. Ultrastructural abnormalities of cilia in the human respiratory tract. Hum Pathol 1986; 17:848–55.

54. Bush A, Cole P, Hariri M, et al. Primary ciliary dyskinesia: diagnosis and standards of care. Eur Respir J 1998; 12:982–8.
55. Santamaria F, de Santi MM, Grillo G, et al. Ciliary motility at light microscopy: a screening technique for ciliary defects. Acta Paediatr 1999;88:853–7.
56. Foliguet B, Puchelle E. Apical structure of human respiratory cilia. Bull Eur Physiopathol Respir 1986;22:43–7.
57. Hastie AT, Marchese-Ragona SP, Johnson KA, Wall JS. Structure and mass of mammalian respiratory ciliary outer arm 19S dynein. Cell Motil Cytoskeleton 1988; 11:157–66.
58. Nakano T, Muto H, Yoshioka I. New observations on the fine structure of the normal nasopharyngeal epithelium of the mouse. Auris Nasus Larynx 1986;13:157–68.
59. Toskala E, Rautiainen M, Nuutinen J. Scanning and transmission electron microscopic findings in cilia from human nasal turbinate and sinus mucosa following respiratory infection. Eur Arch Otorhinolaryngol 1994; 251:76–9.
60. Porter ME, Johnson KA. Dynein structure and function. Annu Rev Cell Biol 1989;5:119–51.
61. Satir P. Dynein as a microtubule translocator in ciliary motility: current studies of arm structure and activity pattern. Cell Motil Cytoskeleton 1988;10:263–70.
62. Spungin B, Avolio J, Arden S, Satir P. Dynein arm attachment probed with a non-hydrolyzable ATP analog. Structural evidence for patterns of activity [published erratum appears in J Mol Biol 1988;201:469]. J Mol Biol 1987;197:671–7.
63. Milisav I. Dynein and dynein-related genes. Cell Motil Cytoskeleton 1998;39:261–72.
64. Gibbons IR. Dynein family of motor proteins: present status and future questions. Cell Motil Cytoskeleton 1995; 32:136–44.
65. Valletta EA, Bertini M, Sbarbati A. Tannic acid supplemented fixation improves ultrastructural evaluation of respiratory epithelium in children with recurrent respiratory tract infections. Biotech Histochem 1996;71:245–50.
66. Linck RW. Advances in the ultrastructural analysis of the sperm axoneme. In: Fawcett DW, Bedford JM, eds. The spermatazoon. Baltimore: Urban and Schwarzenberg, 1979.
67. Fox B, Bull TB, Oliver TN. The distribution and assessment of electron-microscopic abnormalities of human cilia. Eur J Respir Dis Suppl 1983;127:11–8.
68. Rautiainen M, Collan Y, Nuutinen J, Afzelius BA. Ciliary orientation in the "immotile cilia" syndrome. Eur Arch Otorhinolaryngol 1990;247:100–3.
69. Phillips JI. Lack of cilia and squamous metaplasia in upper respiratory tract biopsies from children. S Afr Med J 1989;76:355–7.
70. Schneeberger EE, McCormack J, Issenberg HJ, et al. Heterogeneity of ciliary morphology in the immotile-cilia syndrome in man. J Ultrastruct Res 1980;73:34–43.
71. Schidlow DV. Primary ciliary dyskinesia (the immotile cilia syndrome). Ann Allergy 1994;73:457–70.
72. Rossman CM, Lee RM, Forrest JB, Newhouse MT. Nasal ciliary ultrastructure and function in patients with primary ciliary dyskinesia compared with that in normal subjects and in subjects with various respiratory diseases. Am Rev Respir Dis 1984;129:161–7.
73. Torikata C, Kawai T, Nogawa S, et al. Nine Japanese patients with immotile-dyskinetic cilia syndrome: an ultrastructural study using tannic acid–containing fixation. Hum Pathol 1991;22:830–6.

CHAPTER 33

CILIOGENESIS OF AIRWAY EPITHELIUM

LAWRENCE E. OSTROWSKI, PHD

The process of ciliogenesis was carefully recorded by electron microscopists over 30 years ago.[1–4] It is a tribute to the thoroughness of these investigators that their work is still commonly cited as being definitive when describing the morphologic steps of ciliogenesis. However, while the development of cilia indeed occurs by the pattern of morphologic steps described earlier, only in recent years have we begun to develop an understanding of the process of ciliogenesis and its regulation at the molecular and biochemical levels.

This chapter focuses specifically on the development of the hundreds of motile cilia on each ciliated cell that provide the driving force for mucociliary clearance in the airways. Information gained from other systems are included when appropriate to present as complete a summary of our current understanding as possible. The development of a transient, usually single, primary cilium, which has been reported in airway epithelium and occurs in many cell types, has been reviewed elsewhere.[5]

General Features

As mentioned above, the process of ciliogenesis has been the subject of many intensive electron microscopy studies.[1–4,6–12] Whereas the nomenclature and the interpretation of the various structural intermediates observed has varied somewhat between the different investigators, the steps in pathway of ciliogenesis, like the structure of the cilium itself, have been remarkably conserved. Thus ciliogensis in the rat airways[3] appears similar to ciliogenesis in the mouse oviduct.[9] Based on a large series of electron micrographs of the developing rat lung, Sorokin proposed the model illustrated in Figure 33–1.[3] This model is briefly summarized here as a basis for the

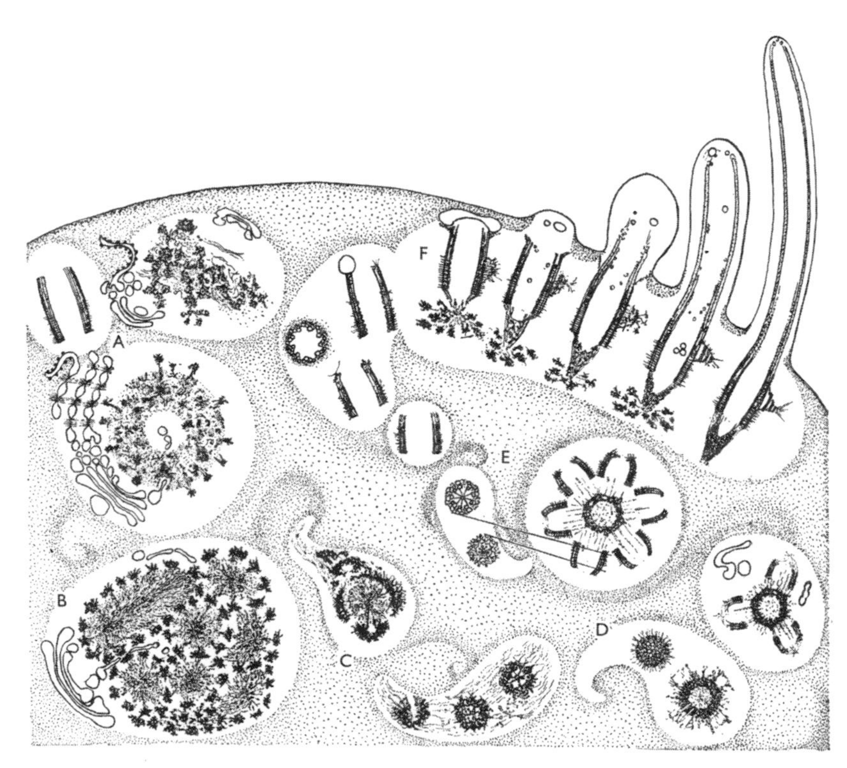

FIGURE 33–1. A schematic representation of ciliogenesis based on a series of electron micrographs of fetal rat lungs. See text for description. (Reproduced with the permission of the Company of Biologists Ltd from Sorokin SP.[3])

remainder of this article; for a more detailed description, please refer to the original work. The first step in ciliogenesis involves the production of the centrioles, which will form the basal bodies of the mature cilia. The mechanisms that control centriole formation are still largely unknown, but studies of centrosomal replication have begun to identify some of the key components.[13,14] γ-Tubulin, which plays a key role in the initiation of microtubule formation,[15] has been localized to the centriole/basal bodies of ciliated epithelial cells.[16] Disruption of the γ-tubulin gene in *Paramecium* prevents the formation of new basal bodies,[17] and it is likely that γ-tubulin is required for the formation of centrioles during ciliogenesis. The first distinct morphologic feature that has been associated with this step is the appearance in the apical cytoplasm of the "fibrogranular aggregates,"[3] which consist of "amorphous clouds of filamentous material"[8] and contain numerous small electron-dense granules referred to as fibrous granules (Figure 33–1, element A). As illustrated, in some sections of cells at this early stage of ciliogenesis, mature centrioles are visible near the fibrogranular aggregates. However, it still is not clear if the original pair of centrioles plays a role in organizing or initiating the formation of this fibrogranular complex. The fibrogranular aggregate has been speculated to be composed largely of precursor material for the assembly of the centrioles. As ciliogenesis proceeds, the granules increase in size and appear to become organized in a row along bundles of fibers (Figure 33–1, elements B and C). The granules are released into the cytoplasm and are believed to mature into deuterosomes, the second distinct precursor in the development of the basal bodies. Deuterosomes are spherical electron-dense bodies, that have an electron-lucent core (Figure 33–1, element D). Recently, it was demonstrated that antibodies against the 230-kD protein pericentriolar material-1 (PCM-1) reacted with fibrous granules but not with deuterosomes in mouse nasal epithelium undergoing ciliogenesis.[18] This suggests that deuterosomes are not formed simply by the fusion of several fibrous granules. It is around the deuterosome that the procentrioles, which will become the basal bodies, are first observed. Depending on the section, one to six procentrioles can be found surrounding a deuterosome (Figure 33–2), and, thus, it appears that the deuterosome is organizing or initiating the formation of the procentrioles, in much the same way that a mature centriole initiates the formation of a daughter centriole during cell mitosis. The procentrioles develop as a cylinder that is orientated with its base near the deuterosome; growth proceeds at the tip in a direction away from the deuterosome (Figure 33–1, elements D and E). At first procentrioles are composed of fine filaments, but, as they mature, singlet, doublet, and finally the nine sets of triplet microtubule fibers appear in the wall. After reaching about half the size of a mature centriole, the immature centrioles

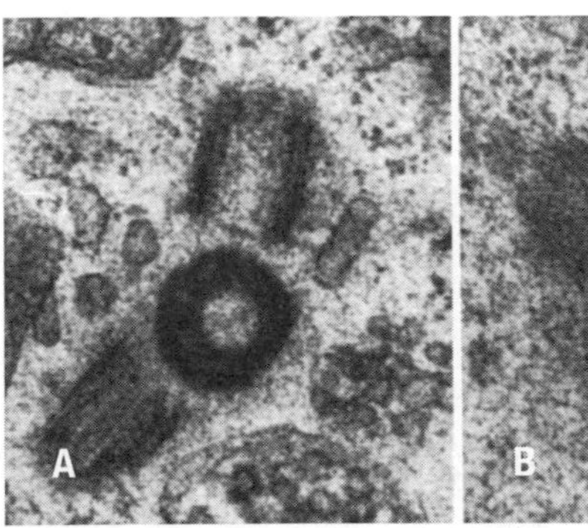

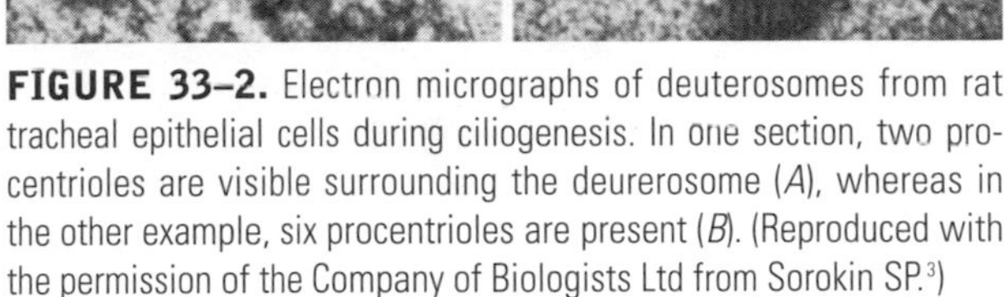

FIGURE 33–2. Electron micrographs of deuterosomes from rat tracheal epithelial cells during ciliogenesis. In one section, two procentrioles are visible surrounding the deurerosome (*A*), whereas in the other example, six procentrioles are present (*B*). (Reproduced with the permission of the Company of Biologists Ltd from Sorokin SP.[3])

move away from the deuterosome and continue to elongate in the cytoplasm. The centrioles migrate to the apical membrane, where they assume their characteristic position as basal bodies for the formation of cilia (Figure 33–1, element F). Here they develop a striated rootlet, a bundle of fibers that extends from the basal body toward the cell interior, and a satellite or basal foot, which projects from the side of the basal body and appears triangular in shape. Recent studies have begun to characterize some of the protein components of the striated rootlet and their expression during ciliogenesis.[19,20] A complex network of actin and intermediate filaments connects the basal bodies to each other and anchors the cilia in the terminal web of the cellular cytoskeleton (Figure 33–3).[21,22] In the mature ciliated cell, basal bodies are arranged such that their basal feet, which point in the direction of the effective stroke, are all orientated in the same direction. However during ciliogenesis, the basal feet appear to be random in their orientation. In addition, the cilia of an individual cell are not formed simultaneously; therefore, different stages of ciliogenesis can be observed in the same cell. Ciliated cells posses numerous long thin microvilli, and many investigators have considered their presence indicative of a "preciliated cell" (Figure 33–4).[9]

The first step in the formation of the actual cilium is the appearance of a small bud in the plasma membrane directly above a basal body. Using freeze-fracture preparations of human nasal epithelium, Carson et al examined the changes in the surface epithelium during ciliogenesis.[7] The first identifiable precursor to the formation of a cilium appears to be a collection of membrane particles, which are destined to become the ciliary necklace. These particles initially appear to be distributed randomly in patches in the membrane and then organized into the strands of the necklace (Figure 33–5). This is followed by the formation of a ciliary bud, with the ciliary necklace in place around the base of the newly forming cilium. The ciliary microtubules then appear as extensions from the

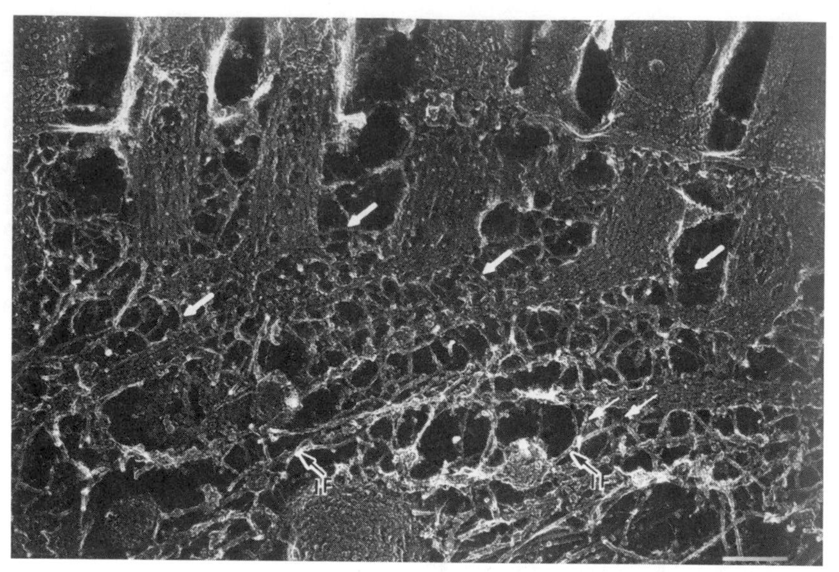

FIGURE 33–3. Quick-freeze deep-etch electron micrograph illustrating the terminal web of a ciliated cell from the chicken trachea. Numerous crossbridges (*thick white arrows*) are evident between the basal bodies and the rootlets. Crossbridges (*thin white arrows*) are also evident between the rootlets and the intermediate filaments (IF, *black arrows*). (Reproduced with the permission of Wiley-Liss Inc. [a subsidiary of John Wiley & Sons Inc.] from Kobayashi N and Hirokawa N.[22])

basal body, and the cilium continues to elongate. Cilia become motile before they are of full length, exhibiting an uncoordinated vibrational pattern. How the basal bodies become orientated in the proper direction and how the beating of the cilia is synchronized is still unknown. In an intriguing study by Boisvieux-Ulrich and Sandoz,[23] microsurgery was used to reverse a segment of the immature oviduct in ovariectomized quail before ciliated cell differentiation had occurred. Following stimulation of oviduct development and differentiation by treatment with estradiol, it was observed that the ciliated cells in the reversed segment of oviduct beat in the opposite direction of cilia in the normal oviduct. Thus, the direction of ciliary beating appears to be determined at an early stage of development, and the authors suggest that this may occur through the inheritance of a cytoskeleton pattern. However, cultures of airway epithelial cells initiated from completely dissociated cell preparations spontaneously become aligned and beat in a synchronous manner,[24] suggesting that, at least in vitro, other factors also may be important. Once the cell has assembled and aligned its full complement of mature cilia, the process of ciliogenesis is complete.

The process of axonemal assembly has been studied most intensively in the unicellular green alga *Chlamydomonas*.[25–28] In this model system, a number of recent studies have identified some of the key steps in the assembly process and some of the proteins involved. One interesting feature of flagellar assembly is that several of the axonemal subunits are assembled in the cytoplasm and transported into the axoneme as large complexes. Thus, there is evidence that radial spokes and dynein arms are assembled in the cytoplasm and transported to the tip of

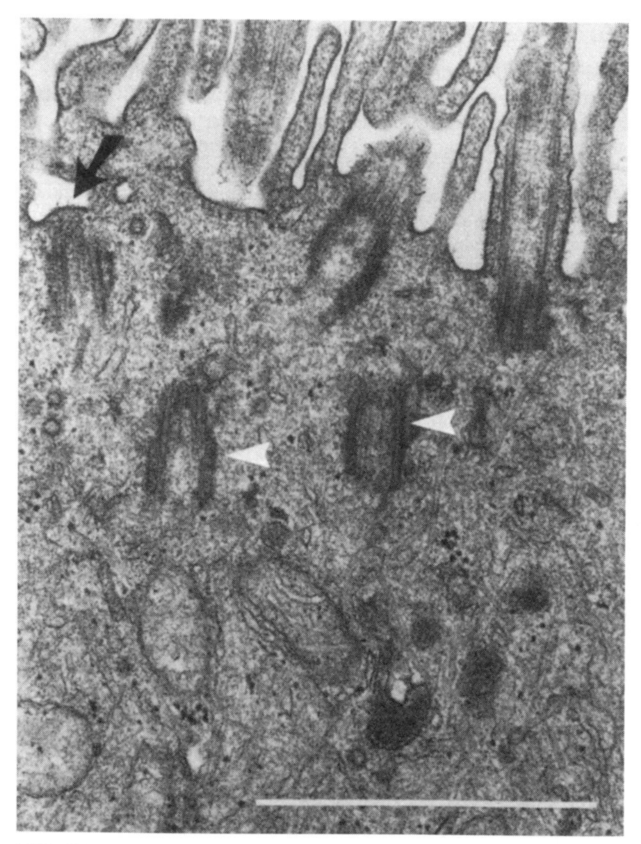

FIGURE 33–4. Electron micrograph illustrating a bud (*black arrow*) of an emergent cilium at a basal body along the luminal border of an epithelial cell heavily populated by microvilli. Also note two subluminal basal bodies (*white arrows*). Bar = 1.0 µm. (Reproduced with permission from Carson JL et al.[7])

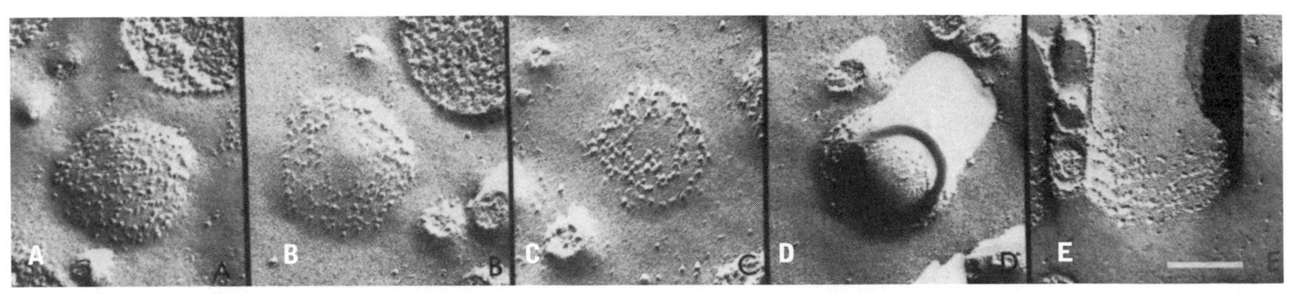

FIGURE 33–5. Freeze-fracture preparations showing the developmental sequence of differentiation of the ciliary necklace during ciliogenesis in normal human nasal epithelium. *A,* Aggregation of membrane-associated particles into patches approximately the diameter of a cilium. Note the random organization of particles in the patch. *B* and *C,* Organization of randomly distributed particles into concentric arrays. *D,* Emergence of a new cilium revealed as a budlike structure with necklace particles at its base. *E,* Mature cilium with basal ciliary necklace. Bar = 0.1 μm. (Reproduced with permission from Carson JL et al.[7])

the growing flagella, where most of the axonemal growth appears to occur. This mode of assembly requires a transport system to move precursors to the ends of the growing microtubules, and, recently, such a system, called intraflagellar transport, has been identified. Intraflagellar transport (IFT) was first described as the bidirectional movement of particles or "rafts" along the axoneme between the outer microtubules and the flagellar membrane.[29] Using a temperature-sensitive mutant of *Chlamydomonas* (*fla*10) that is defective in flagellar assembly, it was demonstrated that at the nonpermissive temperature, IFT did not occur.[30] The *fla*10 mutant contains a temperature-sensitive mutation in one subunit of a heterotrimeric kinesin. Kinesins are plus-end directed microtubule motors, and it now appears that the FLA10 kinesin is responsible for transporting rafts of axonemal proteins or protein complexes along the outer doublets to the tip of the axoneme (Figure 33–6).[31] After the transported proteins have dissociated from the raft, the kinesin and other raft structural proteins are returned to the base of the axoneme through the use of a minus-end directed motor, most likely a cytoplasmic dynein.[32,33] In *Chlamydomonas*, IFT continues after flagellar synthesis is complete, and in *fla*10 mutant cells flagella synthesized at the

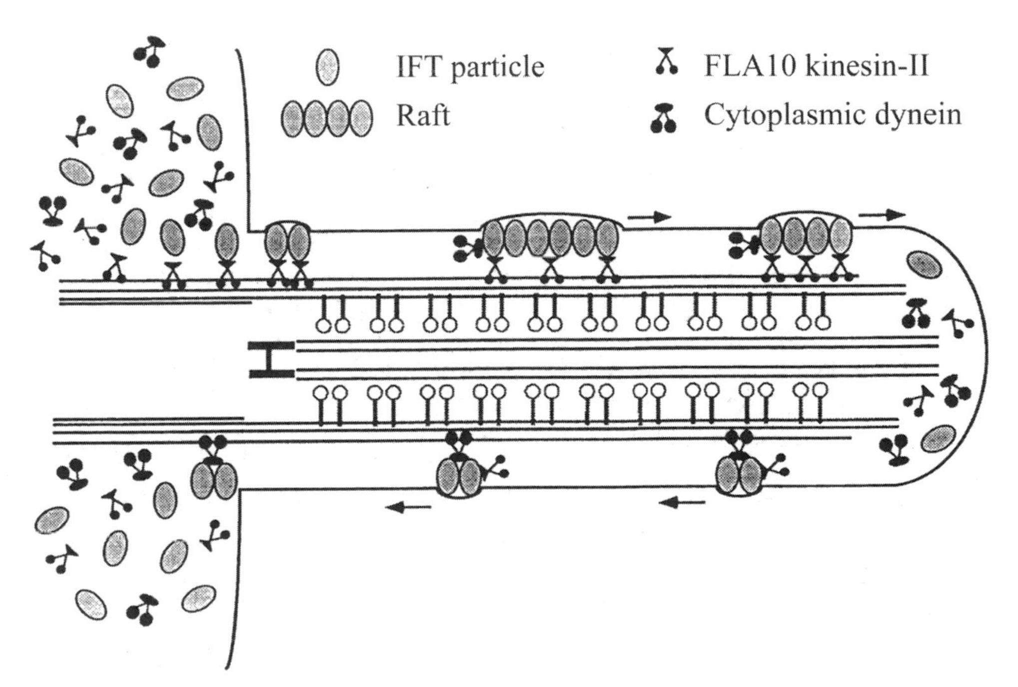

FIGURE 33–6. Model of intraflagellar transport (IFT) in a *Chlamydomonas* flagellum. FLA10 kinesin-II and IFT complexes A and B are highly concentrated around the basal body region of the cell. Multiple copies of complexes A and B associate to form IFT particles. FLA10 kinesin-II binds to the basal bodies, and then IFT particles bind to FLA10 kinesin-II; IFT particles may also bind to the kinesin before docking to the basal bodies. After oligomerization of IFT particles to form rafts, FLA10 kinesin-II transports IFT particles toward the flagellar tip. At the tip, the rafts dissociate into smaller oligomers of IFT particles and are returned to the base of the flagellum by cytoplasmic dynein. (Reproduced with the copyright permission of the Rockefeller University Press from Cole DG et al.[31])

permissive temperature are resorbed after switching to the nonpermissive temperature. Thus IFT is required not only for flagellar assembly but also for maintenance, perhaps being necessary to transport newly synthesized proteins to replace those that undergo turnover. Evidence that this same pathway is operational in mammalian ciliogenesis comes from studies in which targeted gene deletion was used to study the function of the murine homologue of FLA10, KIF3.[34] The targeted deletion of one of the kinesin subunits, KIF3B, resulted in animals that did not survive past midgestation. Among other defects, the null animals exhibited randomized left-right asymmetry and lacked monocilia on the surface of the embryonic node, which is the site of the earliest known left-right asymmetries. About 50% of patients with primary ciliary dyskinesia, an inherited disease characterized by structural defects in the cilia, exhibit situs inversus totalis. The demonstration that animals lacking nodal cilia show defects in left-right asymmetry provides a possible mechanism to explain the association between primary ciliary dyskinesia and situs inversus. It is now recognized that nodal cilia, which are present in the node before the determination of left-right asymmetry, rotate in an anticlockwise direction. It has been proposed that the motion of these nodal cilia acts to create a directional flow of extraembryonic fluid that concentrates an as-yet unidentified signaling molecule to one side of the node; it thereby establishes the development of left-right asymmetry.[34] In the absence of this signal, the determination of left and right is randomized, resulting in the approximately 50% occurrence of situs inversus in primary ciliary dyskinesia patients.[35] Although other studies also have demonstrated a link between the motility of nodal cilia and the development of left-right asymmetry (KIF3A,[36,37] lrd[38,39]) the identification of the putative signaling molecule has not yet been reported. However, the fact that null mutations in subunits of the KIF3 complex do not assemble nodal cilia clearly demonstrates the requirement for kinesin-driven transport in mammalian ciliogenesis. With the increasing availability of in vitro models (see below), studies of the role of KIF3, specifically in ciliogenesis of the airways, should be forthcoming.

Studies of Ciliogenesis During Development and Regeneration

Since the initial descriptions of the ciliogenic process, many investigators have reported on features of ciliogenesis during development or following injury to the airway epithelium.

Ciliogenesis of the airways during development has been examined in many different laboratory animals, including rat,[3,40] hamster,[41] monkey,[42] ferret,[43] rabbit,[4,11] and, more recently, human.[44–46] The major difference between these species appears to be the time during development at which ciliogenesis occurs. Ciliogenesis is initiated at a much earlier stage of development in humans and monkeys and is essentially complete at birth, whereas, in other species, ciliogenesis begins at a later gestational age, and there is a large increase in the number of ciliated cells postnatally.[42] The ferret provides a unique model in that the trachea of this species contains only a few ciliated cells at birth and the number of ciliated cells increases steadily over the first 28 days of life.[47] This allows the study of developmental ciliogenesis postnatally.[43,47] As mentioned above, the process of ciliogenesis appear to be essentially the same in these different models. However, the cell type(s) which undergoes ciliogenesis during development has not been clearly defined. The two most likely pathways for ciliated cells to arise are through the differentiation of a newly formed undifferentiated precursor cell or through the further differentiation of a secretory cell. Evidence exists to support both models of ciliated cell development during differentiation. For example, in a study by Plopper et al, the authors noted that ciliated cells appear before secretory cells in the trachea of the rhesus monkey.[42] However, the authors also reported the presence of cells containing secretory granules undergoing various stages of ciliogenesis. In the newborn ferret, over 65% of the tracheal epithelial cells were identified as secretory, while less than 10% were ciliated. Four weeks after birth the percentage of ciliated cells had increased to greater than 50, while the percentage of secretory cells had decreased to less than 25.[48] Ciliated cells containing secretory granules also have been identified in the human fetal trachea.[46] In all species examined, ciliogenesis is first observed on the membranous portion of the upper trachea. In the human, ciliated cells have been reported in this region as early as the 7th week of gestation, whereas in the cartilaginous region, ciliated cells were not observed until the 12th week of gestation.[45] The process of ciliation proceeds distally from the upper trachea, and, by the 24th week of gestation, the epithelium resembles that of the mature trachea. Cilia present during development are motile and appear to be organized in a coordinate fashion; however, the function of ciliary activity, if any, during development is unknown.[46]

The regeneration of mucociliary epithelium following injury to the airway surface epithelium has been studied by a large number of investigators.[49–52] These studies differ in the animal model used, the type and severity of the injury, and the time required for complete restoration. However, electron micrographs demonstrate the presence of the same intermediate steps described during developmental ciliogenesis, and the process is believed to be the same. For example, Keenan et al studied the regeneration of hamster tracheal epithelium after a denuding mechanical injury.[49] During the first 12 hours after the injury, basal and secretory cells from the adjacent epithelium flatten and migrate into the wound area to rapidly cover the basement membrane with a layer of undifferentiated cells.

Cell proliferation occurred between 24 and 48 hours, and was followed by the appearance of secretory and ciliated cells. By 120 hours after the injury, the epithelium resembled that of the uninjured trachea, although the number of ciliated cells was still reduced. Because the authors first observed "preciliated" cells (defined as large cells with a pale cytoplasm and nucleus) following mitosis of secretory cells and, in addition, identified ciliated and preciliated cells containing periodic acid-Schiff (PAS)-positive droplets, they concluded that the majority of the ciliated cells are derived from secretory cells during the repair process. Similar results have been reported by others.

There is, however, controversy regarding the response of the original ciliated cells to the injury. Although there is only limited evidence that ciliated cells can undergo cell division,[53] there are studies that are not inconsistent with the possibility that ciliated cells, at least under certain conditions, can lose their cilia and then dedifferentiate and participate in the regenerative process. In one study, Van Winkle et al examined the restoration of the normal bronchiolar epithelium following the selective destruction of Clara cells with naphthalene.[54] Following the naphthalene treatment, the differentiated Clara cells became vacuolated and swollen and then exfoliated. The ciliated cells, which were unaffected by naphthalene treatment, became flattened in shape and covered the basal lamina of the terminal bronchioles. A population of squamous cells, with some of the same morphologic features of the flattened ciliated cells, was seen to be actively dividing as determined by 5-bromo-2′-deoxyuridine (BrdU) labeling. This was followed by differentiation of the newly formed progenitor cells into Clara cells. The authors proposed that the squamated (formerly ciliated) cells may be the progenitors responsible for regeneration of the epithelium in the terminal bronchioles under these conditions. In another study, in which weanling ferrets were exposed to sulfur dioxide, ciliated cells in the trachea appeared to shed the apical portion of their cytoplasm, including the cilia and basal bodies.[55] One to 2 days after the injury, ciliogenesis was observed, and after 1 to 2 weeks the epithelium was almost completely reciliated, with no significant change in cell number or mitosis. These studies demonstrate the remarkable plasticity of airway epithelial cells in general and ciliated cells in particular. Further studies, perhaps using newer technologies that follow the fate of individual cells, will need to be performed before firm conclusions can be formed about precursors and progeny of ciliated cells.

Ciliogenesis In Vitro

One of the major advances in the study of ciliogenesis of airway epithelium is the ability to culture undifferentiated epithelial cells in conditions that allow for ciliated cell differentiation and ciliogenesis to take place. With the relative ease of performing carefully controlled experiments in vitro compared to the difficulty of attempting the same studies in vivo, our knowledge of ciliated cell differentiation and ciliogenesis should develop rapidly over the next few years. Many of the early developments in this field used animal models, including dog,[56] guinea pig,[57,58] cow,[59] hamster,[60,61] and rat,[62] but the basic techniques were readily adapted to the study of human tissue. Some of these techniques are described briefly here to highlight a few of the differences between the various models. One important feature of the models described is that they allow for de novo ciliogenesis to occur, as opposed to the maintenance of ciliated cells from the original tissue as is commonly observed in explants of mature ciliated tissues. These explant methods are well suited to study certain features of ciliated cells such as ciliary beat frequency and regulation, but they do not allow the study of the formation of cilia.

As early as 1984, Lee et al reported that tracheal epithelial cells from hamsters undergo ciliogenesis when cultured on collagen gels in media conditioned by mouse 3T3 cells.[61] Both the collagen gel and the use of conditioned media were required for ciliogenesis to take place. Although hamster cells are capable of ciliogenesis when submerged in media, cells from other species show a marked increase in ciliogenesis when cultured on a permeable support at an air-liquid interface. For example, in early studies by Whitcutt et al, tracheal epithelial cells from the guinea pig appeared squamous when grown submerged in media.[57] When cultured in the same media and on the same gelatin membrane but with the apical surface of the culture exposed to air, the guinea pig tracheal epithelial cells produced a mucociliary epithelium similar to that observed in vivo. Similarly, conditions were identified that allowed for the production of a mucociliary epithelium from other species. These early studies not only defined conditions that would permit ciliogenesis in culture, they also identified factors that were of importance to the development of ciliated cells and therefore allowed studies of the regulation of ciliogenesis. Using rat tracheal epithelial cells and the conditions originally described by Kaartinen et al,[62] Davenport and Nettesheim demonstrated that plating cells on a collagen substrate was more important for the development of ciliated cells than for the development of mucous cells.[63] Using this same model system, it also was demonstrated that ciliated cell differentiation was inhibited by $> 90\%$ if the apical surface of the cells were submerged.[64] The requirement of an air-liquid interface for the development of ciliated cells is not absolute and depends both on the species and on the culture conditions. It is clear from studies of development that ciliated cells develop in the fetal state when the lungs and airways are fluid filled. In addition, hamster and human airway cells have been shown to be capable of undergoing ciliogenesis in the submerged state. However, when other factors are kept constant, the degree of mucociliary differentiation is generally improved when airway epithelial cells are cultured at an air-liquid interface. The presence and level of growth factors in the media also has been shown to influence the extent of ciliogenesis. For example, studies by Nettesheim and co-workers, again using rat tracheal epithelial cells, demonstrated that increasing concentrations of epidermal growth factor in the media favored mucous cell differentiation, whereas reducing or eliminating epidermal growth factor from the media increased ciliated cell differentiation.[65,66] It is clear that the balance between secretory and ciliated cell differentiation in the oviduct can be regulated by the levels of estrogen and progesterone.[67–70] Thus ciliated cell differentiation is a regulated process, and identification of the factors controlling the balance of secretory and ciliated cell differentiation in the airways may have clinical applications.

Many laboratories have reported methods that allow ciliogenesis and/or ciliated cell differentiation of human airway epithelial cells in vitro. As in the animal studies, the choice of substrate, the composition of the media, and the presence of an air-liquid interface are important determinants of the amount of ciliated cell differentiation and ciliogenesis that occurs. Several investigators were able to demonstrate ciliogenesis of cultured human nasal cells in submerged cultures by growing the cells unattached to a fixed substrate. Jorissen et al[71] cultured nasal epithelial cells as an undifferentiated monolayer on collagen gels. Collagenase was used to remove sheaths of epithelial cells which were then placed into suspension culture on a rotary shaker, where the cells formed vesicles. Over the next few weeks cells in these vesicles underwent ciliogenesis. Chevillard et al[72] also grew undifferentiated nasal epithelia cells on a collagen gel; however, after these cells reached confluency, the collagen gel detached from the plastic culture dish and formed cord like structures covered with epithelial cells. In these "floating collagen gels," both secretory and ciliated cell differentiation was documented. Hanamure et al reported similar results.[73] These studies demonstrate that the three-dimensional shape of the substrate is important for ciliogenesis to occur in vitro. As with the animal models above, the presence of an air-liquid interface also was shown to increase ciliated cell differentiation in cultures of human epithelium.[74] Extensive ciliogenesis was obtained by de Jong et al[75] in cultures of serially passaged human bronchial epithelial cells through the use of a collagenous substrate, an air-liquid interface, and media conditioned by irradiated mouse fibroblasts (Figure 33–7). Transmission electron microscopy demonstrated all the normal components of ciliogenesis (ie, fibrogranular masses, deuterosomes, procentrioles, basal bodies, and mature cilia) in the air exposed cultures; in contrast, no evidence of ciliogenesis was observed in the submerged cultures. Other investigators have achieved similar results using different media formulations.[76,77] The ability to reproducibly induce human airway epithelial cells to undergo ciliogenesis under carefully controlled conditions in vitro will allow for many interesting and informative experiments to be performed.

Biochemical and Molecular Studies

Analysis of purified axonemes from *Chlamydomonas* flagella by two-dimensional gel electrophoresis indicated that the axoneme itself was composed of over 250 different proteins, many of which are believed to be unique to the axonemal structure.[78] However, perhaps it is not unreasonable to suggest that ciliogenesis may require the coordinate expression of as many as 500 different proteins, if one also includes proteins that are part of the basal apparatus and soluble matrix, membrane proteins that do not purify with the axoneme, and proteins involved in the assembly, maintainence, and regulation of the axoneme. Many of these proteins have been identified recently, mostly in lower organisms, but with the rapid completion of the genome-sequencing project, human homologues of many of these proteins are now becoming available. The identity and functions of many of the structural proteins comprising the axoneme have been described elsewhere (eg, Chapter 32, ref 25–28). In this section, studies of the expression of these proteins during ciliogenesis are discussed.

Tubulin is the most abundant protein in the axoneme; therefore, it is not surprising that its expression and modification has been followed during ciliogenesis. Dirksen and Staprans investigated the incorporation of 3H-leucine into tubulin during ciliogenesis of the newborn mouse oviduct under several experimental conditions.[79] These studies demonstrated the rapid incorporation of labeled tubulin into the axonemal fraction, indicating that the cilia were being assembled from newly synthesized tubulin and not from pre-existing tubulin pools. Since these early studies, several different isoforms of both α- and β-tubulin have been identified. Using monoclonal antibodies against different isoforms of β-tubulin, Renthal et al identified the β-IV isoform as being the major form of β-tubulin in bovine cilia.[80] It would therefore be interesting to study the specific factors regulating the expression of this isoform during ciliogenesis. In addition, axonemal tubulins are known to undergo several post-translational modifications. Studies of human nasal epithelial cells undergoing ciliogenesis in vitro demonstrated that axonemal tubulins were both polyglutamylated and polyglycylated.[81] Polyglutamylation occurred early during ciliogenesis, and tubulin in the centrioles also was polyglutamylated. In contrast, polyglycylation was restricted to axonemal tubulin and was only detected in axonemes already assembled. These post-translational modifications may influence the stability of the axoneme and/or the interactions of microtubule-binding proteins, and determining how these specific

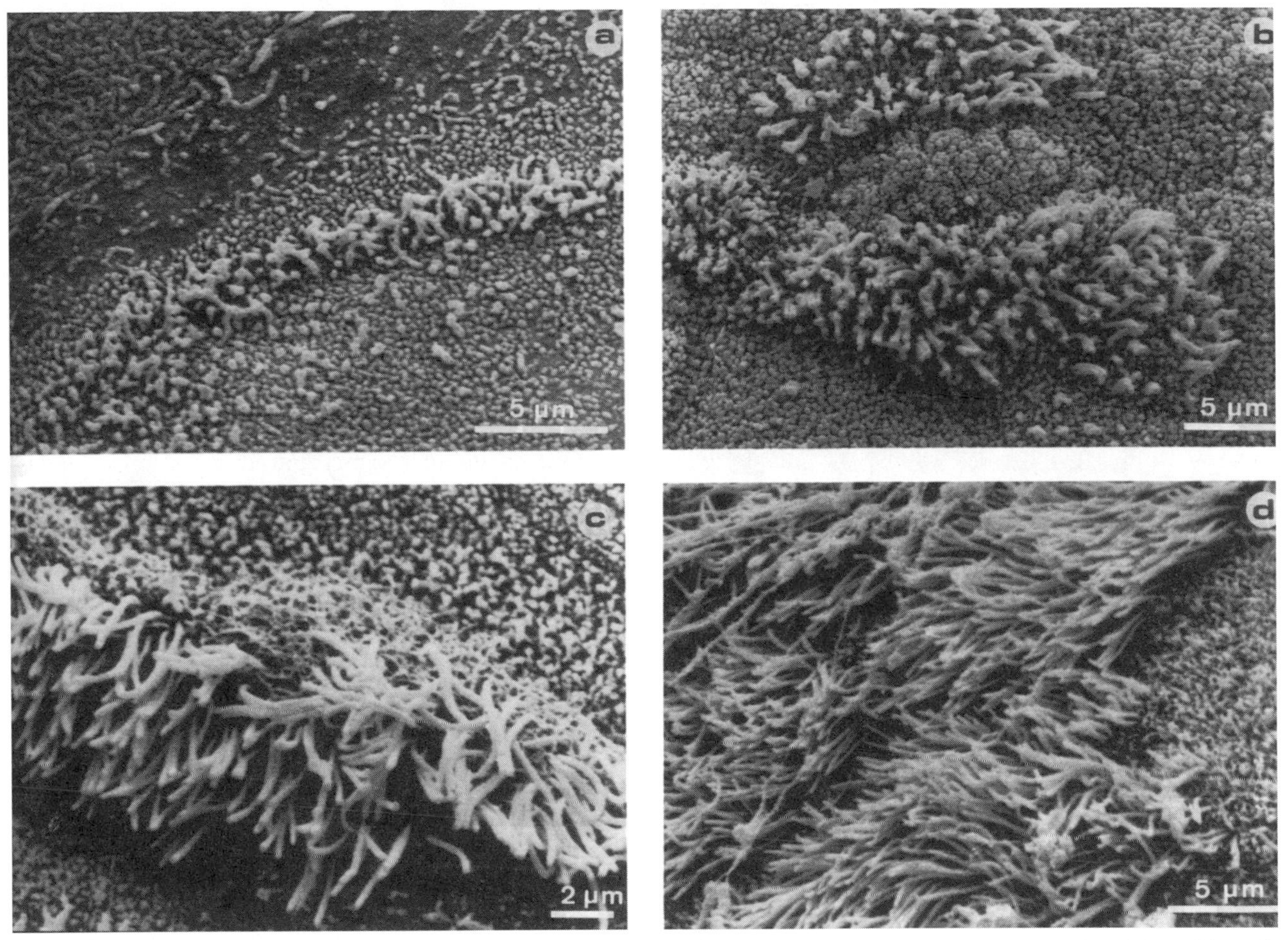

FIGURE 33–7. Ciliogenesis of human bronchial epithelial cells grown on a collagen substrate at an air-liquid interface for 7 (*a*), 14 (*b*), 18 (*c*), and 21 (*d*) days. Bar = 200 nm. (Reproduced with permission from de Jong PM et al,[75] official journal of the American Cancer Thoracic Society; copyright of the American Lung Association.)

modifications occur will be important to a complete understanding of ciliogenesis.

More recently, our laboratory and several others have begun to examine the process of ciliogenesis at the level of transcription. Using primers designed to amplify the conserved catalytic region of axonemal dyneins, Andrews et al[82] cloned partial complementary deoxyribonucleic acids (cDNAs) representing seven different axonemal dynein heavy chains. These cDNA probes were used to analyze the expression of the axonemal dyneins during ciliogenesis of rat tracheal epithelial cells in vitro. It was observed that early in culture, before ciliated cells were present, the expression of axonemal dynein heavy chains was undetectable by Northern blot analysis (Figure 33–8). After the apical surface of the cultures were exposed to air and ciliated cells began to appear, expression of the axonemal dynein heavy chains was dramatically increased. In contrast, the expression of the major cytoplasmic isoform of dynein heavy chain remained relatively constant throughout the culture period. These experiments showed for the first time that the expression of ciliated cell–specific genes is regulated primarily at the transcriptional level and that the expression of these genes appears to be coordinately controlled.

In an extension of these studies, our laboratory used the technique of differential display to identify novel genes that were upregulated during ciliogenesis. By comparing the expression pattern of genes from early undifferentiated cultures of rat tracheal epithelial cells with the expression pattern in later differentiating cultures, we identified several messages that were upregulated specifically in cultures induced to undergo ciliogenesis. Two of these clones, designated KPL1 and KPL2, have been studied in further detail. Full-length cDNAs of both clones were isolated and found to code for previously undescribed genes. KPL1 codes for a small protein that contains a single pleckstrin homology (PH) domain.[83] Pleckstrin homology domains have been demonstrated to bind phosphoinositols and may play an important role in the signal-dependent translocation of proteins to cellular membranes. Whereas the expression of KPL1 clearly is increased in parallel with ciliogenesis of rat tracheal epithelial cells, KPL1 is expressed in a wide variety of tissues. The highest levels of KPL1 are found in brain tissue,

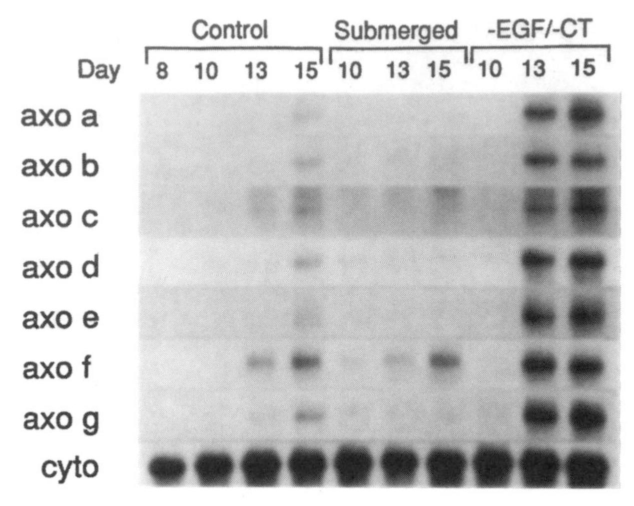

FIGURE 33–8. Analysis of the expression of axonemal dynein heavy chains (axo) during ciliogenesis of rat tracheal epithelial cells in vitro. The cells were cultured under conditions that inhibit (submerged) or increase (removal of epidermal growth factor and cholera toxin, –EGF/–CT) ciliogenesis and harvested on the days indicated. Each of the axonemal dynein heavy chains was strongly induced during ciliogenesis, while the expression of cytoplasmic dynein (cyto) remained constant throughout the culture period. (Reproduced with the permission of the American Society for Cell Biology from Andrews KL et al.[82])

and a recent report by Krappa et al[84] demonstrates that KPL1 associates with post-Golgi membrane vesicles. Thus, the function of increased KPL1 expression during ciliogenesis is still unknown.

In contrast, KPL2 is predicted to code for a much larger protein (> 200 kD) that contains similarities to multiple functional domains.[85] The amino terminus of KPL2 is predicted to form a calponin homology domain, that binds to filamentous actin. A proline-rich region, which may function as a site of interaction with Src homology region 3 (SH3) domains, is present toward the carboxy terminus. In addition, computer analysis demonstrates the presence of three consensus bipartite nuclear localization signals and an adenosine triphosphate–guanosine triphosphate binding site. KPL2 shows a more restricted pattern of expression than KPL1, being most abundant in tissues that contain axonemal structures, such as trachea and testis. The function of this novel protein is still under investigation.

The expression of several centrin isoforms also has been studied during ciliogenesis. Centrins are small calcium-binding proteins that frequently are associated with microtubule organizing centers, including centrioles. In *Chlamydomonas*, centrin is found in the basal body, the striated rootlets, and associated with a subset of inner dynein arms. It also is found near the transition zone, where the axoneme joins the basal body, and it may play a role in flagellar excision. LeDizet et al[86] examined the expression of three human centrin genes during in vitro ciliogenesis of human tracheal epithelial (HTE) cells. Localization studies using an antibody that reacts with multiple centrin isoforms demonstrated the presence of centrin in the basal body and transition zone of human ciliated cells. Analysis of centrin ribonucleic acid (RNA) levels during ciliogenesis of these cultures showed that centrin-1 was not expressed, whereas centrin-3 levels remained relatively constant throughout the culture period. In contrast, centrin-2 RNA levels increased approximately twofold during ciliogenesis. These results suggest that centrin-2 may be the isoform associated with the axoneme and that it may have a specific function in the cilium.

One of the most significant advances in our understanding of ciliogenesis and its regulation has been the identification of the essential role of the transcription factor hepatocyte nuclear factor-3/forkhead homologue 4 (HFH-4) in ciliogenesis. HFH-4 is a member of a family of transcription factors that contain a conserved 100-amino-acid DNA-binding domain known as the winged helix motif. This group of transcription factors has been shown to play a role in the development and differentiation of many different tissues. *HFH-4* has been shown to be expressed both during development and in adult tissues of the lung, brain, testis, and ovary.[87,88] Localization with a specific antibody has demonstrated HFH-4 expression specifically in ciliated cells of the airways, choroid plexus, ependyma, oviduct, and spermatids.[89] Targeted deletion of the *HFH-4* gene in mouse models resulted in animals that are essentially without airway cilia.[90,91] Airway epithelial cells in the mutant mice contained numerous basal bodies and centrioles, indicating that these cells were capable of initiating ciliogenesis. However, the basal bodies were not organized in a single layer just below the apical membrane as in cells from normal mice, but appeared randomly throughout the apical cytoplasm. These results suggest that HFH-4 is required for the expression of a gene responsible for the correct migration and/or positioning of the basal bodies. In addition to the absence of cilia in the airways, HFH-4-null mice lack cilia in the oviduct and brain, and sperm from these animals have been reported to lack flagella, indicating that the pathway of ciliogenesis has been conserved between these tissues, and that HFH-4 plays a key role in the process. Interestingly, approximately 50% of the *HFH-4*-null mice demonstrate situs inversus. As described above, situs inversus is also a feature of primary ciliary dyskinesia, and several recent studies have suggested that the monocilium present on cells of the embryonic node may be crucial for the development of left-right asymmetry. HFH-4 was found to be expressed in the node cells; however, in the *HFH-4*-null animals, the number and appearance of nodal cilia was similar to that found in wild-type mice.[90] Thus, HFH-4 is not required for the assembly of the nodal cilia; however, the absence of HFH-4 results in random left-right asymmetry. Although the exact function of HFH-4 remains to be elucidated, it certainly has a central role in ciliogenesis and provides a definite starting point for future studies of both upstream and downstream events.

Ciliogenesis and Disease

Defects in ciliogenesis may be viewed as a subset of primary ciliary dyskinesia. As discussed in Chapter 32, primary ciliary dyskinesia is a heterogenous disease in which inherited defects in the ciliary apparatus result in impaired mucociliary clearance. Whether certain of these defects are caused by mutations in genes involved in ciliary assembly, such as a kinesin, or genes involved in ciliary function, such as a dynein heavy chain, is unknown at present. Either type of mutation would result in impaired mucociliary clearance and a similar clinical presentation. However, there are reports of rare cases in which individuals have a clear defect in ciliogenesis, as is evidenced by the complete absence of cilia.[92] Because cilia can be lost as a result of secondary causes (eg, infection), reports of ciliary aplasia must be viewed with some skepticism. Recent reports have documented the absence of cilia from multiple biopsies and in patient samples cultured in vitro to allow for ciliogenesis in the absence of secondary effects. Ciliary aplasia may be observed less frequently than other forms of primary ciliary dyskinesia, because a global defect in ciliogenesis may result in embryonic lethality (similar to observations in animal models described above).

Conclusion

Ciliogenesis is the complex process whereby hundreds of different proteins are precisely assembled to form a functioning cilium. The individual cilia are then aligned with hundreds of other cilia, first in the same cell and then with those of adjacent cells, and, finally, the cilia become coordinated in their beat pattern to produce the metachronal wave required for efficient mucociliary clearance. We know surprisingly little about how this process occurs and how it is regulated. Clearly ciliogenesis and mucociliary clearance is important to respiratory health, as is evidenced by the pathology associated with primary ciliary dyskinesia. Although inherited defects of ciliogenesis are rare, cilia are continuously lost due to normal cellular turnover, exposure to pollutants, infections, and, especially, chronic diseases such as asthma and cystic fibrosis. For efficient mucociliary clearance to be restored, the ciliated epithelium must be replaced through active ciliogenesis. With the continuing advances in all areas of scientific research, from the ability to induce differentiation of airway epithelial cells in vitro to the completion of the human genome–sequencing project, it can be expected that a much higher level of understanding of this fundamental developmental process of airway epithelium soon will be achieved. Further studies of ciliogenesis may yield new approaches for intervention in a wide variety of airway diseases.

References

1. Dirksen ER, Crocker TT. Centriole replication in differentiating ciliated cells of mammalian respiratory epithelium. An electron microscopic study. J Microscopie 1965; 5:629–44.
2. Kalnins VI, Porter KR. Centriole replication during ciliogenesis in the chick tracheal epithelium. Z Zellforsch 1969;100(1):1–30.
3. Sorokin SP. Reconstruction of centriole formation and ciliogenesis in mammalian lungs. J Cell Sci 1968;3:207–30.
4. Kanda T, Hilding D. Development of respiratory tract cilia in fetal rabbits. Electron microscopic investigation. Acta Otolaryngol 1968;65:611–24.
5. Wheatley DN, Wang AM, Strugnell GE. Expression of primary cilia in mammalian cells. Cell Biol Int 1996; 20(1):73–81.
6. Anderson RG, Brenner RM. The formation of basal bodies (centrioles) in the rhesus monkey oviduct. J Cell Biol 1971;50(1):10–34.
7. Carson JL, Collier AM, Knowles MR, et al. Morphometric aspects of ciliary distribution and ciliogenesis in human nasal epithelium. Proc Natl Acad Sci U S A 1981;78:6996–9.
8. Dirksen ER. Centriole and basal body formation during ciliogenesis revisited. Biol Cell 1991;72(1–2):31–8.
9. Dirksen ER. Ciliogenesis in the mouse oviduct. A scanning electron microscope study. J Cell Biol 1974;62:899–904.
10. Dirksen ER. Centriole morphogenesis in developing ciliated epithelium of the mouse oviduct. J Cell Biol 1971;51:286–302.
11. Loots GP, Nel PP. Early stages of ciliogenesis in the respiratory epithelium of the nasal cavity of rabbit embryos. Cell Tissue Res 1989;255:589–94.
12. Frisch D, Farbman AI. Development of order during ciliogenesis. Anat Rec 1968;162:221–32.
13. Zimmerman W, Sparks CA, Doxsey SJ. Amorphous no longer: the centrosome comes into focus. Curr Opin Cell Biol 1999;11:122–8.
14. Marshall WF, Rosenbaum JL. How centrioles work: lessons from green yeast. Curr Opin Cell Biol 2000;12:119–25.
15. Schiebel E. Gamma-tubulin complexes: binding to the centrosome, regulation and microtubule nucleation. Curr Opin Cell Biol 2000;12:113–8.
16. Muresan V, Joshi HC, Besharse JC. Gamma-tubulin in differentiated cell types: localization in the vicinity of basal bodies in retinal photoreceptors and ciliated epithelia. J Cell Sci 1993;104(Pt 4):1229–37.
17. Ruiz F, Beisson J, Rossier J, Dupuis-Williams P. Basal body duplication in *Paramecium* requires gamma-tubulin. Curr Biol 1999;9(1):43–6.
18. Kubo A, Sasaki H, Yuba-Kubo A, et al. Centriolar satellites: molecular characterization, ATP-dependent movement toward centrioles and possible involvement in ciliogenesis [published erratum appears in J Cell Biol 1999; 147:1585]. J Cell Biol 1999;147:969–80.

19. Hagiwara H, Aoki T, Ohwada N, Fujimoto T. Identification of a 195 kDa protein in the striated rootlet: its expression in ciliated and ciliogenic cells. Cell Motil Cytoskeleton 2000;45:200–10.
20. Lemullois M, Marty MC. Immunocytochemical study of the formation of striated rootlets during ciliogenesis in quail oviduct. J Cell Sci 1990;95(Pt 3):423–32.
21. Sandoz D, Chailley B, Boisvieux-Ulrich E, et al. Organization and functions of cytoskeleton in metazoan ciliated cells. Biol Cell 1988;63:183–93.
22. Kobayashi N, Hirokawa N. Cytoskeletal architecture and immunocytochemical localization of fodrin in the terminal web of the ciliated epithelial cell. Cell Motil Cytoskeleton 1988;11:167–77.
23. Boisvieux-Ulrich E, Sandoz D. Determination of ciliary polarity precedes differentiation in the epithelial cells of quail oviduct. Biol Cell 1991;72(1–2):3–14.
24. Matsui H, Grubb BR, Tarran R, et al. Evidence for periciliary liquid layer depletion, not abnormal ion composition, in the pathogenesis of cystic fibrosis airways disease. Cell 1998;95:1005–15.
25. Smith EF, Lefebvre PA. The role of central apparatus components in flagellar motility and microtubule assembly. Cell Motil Cytoskeleton 1997;38:1–8.
26. Porter ME. Axonemal dyneins: assembly, organization, and regulation. Curr Opin Cell Biol 1996;8(1):10–7.
27. Curry AM, Rosenbaum JL. Flagellar radial spoke: a model molecular genetic system for studying organelle assembly. Cell Motil Cytoskeleton 1993;24:224–32.
28. Dutcher SK. Flagellar assembly in two hundred and fifty easy-to-follow steps. Trends Genet 1995;11:398–404.
29. Kozminski KG, Johnson KA, Forscher P, Rosenbaum JL. A motility in the eukaryotic flagellum unrelated to flagellar beating. Proc Natl Acad Sci U S A 1993;90:5519–23.
30. Kozminski KG, Beech PL, Rosenbaum JL. The *Chlamydomonas* kinesin-like protein FLA10 is involved in motility associated with the flagellar membrane. J Cell Biol 1995; 131(6 Pt 1):1517–27.
31. Cole DG, Diener DR, Himelblau AL, et al. *Chlamydomonas* kinesin-II-dependent intraflagellar transport (IFT): IFT particles contain proteins required for ciliary assembly in *Caenorhabditis elegans* sensory neurons. J Cell Biol 1998;141:993–1008.
32. Pazour GJ, Dickert BL, Witman GB. The DHC1b (DHC2) isoform of cytoplasmic dynein is required for flagellar assembly. J Cell Biol 1999;144:473–81.
33. Pazour GJ, Wilkerson CG, Witman GB. A dynein light chain is essential for the retrograde particle movement of intraflagellar transport (IFT). J Cell Biol 1998;141: 979–92.
34. Nonaka S, Tanaka Y, Okada Y, et al. Randomization of left-right asymmetry due to loss of nodal cilia generating leftward flow of extraembryonic fluid in mice lacking KIF3B motor protein [published erratum appears in Cell 1999;99:117]. Cell 1998;95:829–37.
35. Noone PG, Bali D, Carson JL, et al. Discordant organ laterality in monozygotic twins with primary ciliary dyskinesia. Am J Med Genet 1999;82:155–60.
36. Marszalek JR, Ruiz-Lozano P, Roberts E, et al. Situs inversus and embryonic ciliary morphogenesis defects in mouse mutants lacking the KIF3A subunit of kinesin-II. Proc Natl Acad Sci U S A 1999;96:5043–8.
37. Takeda S, Yonekawa Y, Tanaka Y, et al. Left-right asymmetry and kinesin superfamily protein KIF3A: new insights in determination of laterality and mesoderm induction by kif3A-/- mice analysis. J Cell Biol 1999; 145:825–36.
38. Supp DM, Witte DP, Potter SS, Brueckner M. Mutation of an axonemal dynein affects left-right asymmetry in inversus viscerum mice. Nature 1997;389:963–6.
39. Supp DM, Brueckner M, Kuehn MR, et al. Targeted deletion of the ATP binding domain of left-right dynein confirms its role in specifying development of left-right asymmetries. Development 1999;126:5495–504.
40. Menco BP, Farbman AI. Genesis of cilia and microvilli of rat nasal epithelia during prenatal development. III. Respiratory epithelium surface, including a comparison with the surface of the olfactory epithelium. J Anat 1987; 152:145–60.
41. McDowell EM, Newkirk C, Coleman B. Development of hamster tracheal epithelium: I. A quantitative morphologic study in the fetus. Anat Rec 1985;213:429–47.
42. Plopper CG, Alley JL, Weir AJ. Differentiation of tracheal epithelium during fetal lung maturation in the rhesus monkey *Macaca mulatta*. Am J Anat 1986;175:59–71.
43. Curtis LN, Carson JL, Collier AM, et al. Features of developing ferret tracheal epithelium: ultrastructural observations of in vivo and in vitro differentiation of ciliated cells. Exp Lung Res 1987;13:223–40.
44. Moscoso G, Nandra K, Driver M. Ciliogenesis and ciliation of the respiratory epithelium in the human fetal cartilaginous trachea. Pathol Res Pract 1989;184:161–7.
45. Moscoso GJ, Driver M, Codd J, Whimster WF. The morphology of ciliogenesis in the developing fetal human respiratory epithelium. Pathol Res Pract 1988;183:403–11.
46. Gaillard DA, Lallement AV, Petit AF, Puchelle ES. In vivo ciliogenesis in human fetal tracheal epithelium. Am J Anat 1989;185:415–28.
47. Leigh MW, Gambling TM, Carson JL, et al. Postnatal development of tracheal surface epithelium and submucosal glands in the ferret. Exp Lung Res 1986;10:153–69.
48. Leigh MW, Cheng PW, Boat TF. Developmental changes of ferret tracheal mucin composition and biosynthesis. Biochemistry 1989;28:9440–6.
49. Keenan KP, Combs JW, McDowell EM. Regeneration of hamster tracheal epithelium after mechanical injury. I. Focal lesions: quantitative morphologic study of cell proliferation. Virchows Arch B Cell Pathol Mol Pathol 1982;41:193–214.
50. Gordon RE, Lane BP. Ciliated cell differentiation in regenerating rat tracheal epithelium. Lung 1984;162:233–43.
51. Barrow RE, Wang CZ, Cox RA, Evans MJ. Cellular sequence of tracheal repair in sheep after smoke inhalation injury. Lung 1992;170:331–8.
52. Erjefalt JS, Erjefalt I, Sundler F, Persson CG. In vivo restitution of airway epithelium. Cell Tissue Res 1995; 281:305–16.
53. Rutten AA, Beems RB, Wilmer JW, Feron VJ. Ciliated cells in vitamin A-deprived cultured hamster tracheal epithelium do divide. In Vitro Cell Dev Biol 1988;24:931–5.

54. Van Winkle LS, Buckpitt AR, Nishio SJ, et al. Cellular response in naphthalene-induced Clara cell injury and bronchiolar epithelial repair in mice. Am J Physiol 1995; 269(6 Pt 1):L800–18.
55. Leigh MW, Carson JL, Gambling TM, Boat TF. Loss of cilia and altered phenotypic expression of ciliated cells after acute sulfur dioxide exposure. Chest 1992;101(3 Suppl): 16S.
56. Kondo M, Finkbeiner WE, Widdicombe JH. Simple technique for culture of highly differentiated cells from dog tracheal epithelium. Am J Physiol 1991;261(2 Pt 1): L106–17.
57. Whitcutt MJ, Adler KB, Wu R. A biphasic chamber system for maintaining polarity of differentiation of cultured respiratory tract epithelial cells. In Vitro Cell Dev Biol 1988;24:420–8.
58. Adler KB, Cheng PW, Kim KC. Characterization of guinea pig tracheal epithelial cells maintained in biphasic organotypic culture: cellular composition and biochemical analysis of released glycoconjugates. Am J Respir Cell Mol Biol 1990;2:145–54.
59. Kondo M, Finkbeiner WE, Widdicombe JH. Cultures of bovine tracheal epithelium with differentiated ultrastructure and ion transport. In Vitro Cell Dev Biol 1993; 29A:19–24.
60. Moller PC, Partridge LR, Cox R, et al. An in vitro system for the study of tracheal epithelial cells. Tissue Cell 1987;19:783–91.
61. Lee TC, Wu R, Brody AR, et al. Growth and differentiation of hamster tracheal epithelial cells in culture. Exp Lung Res 1984;6:27–45.
62. Kaartinen L, Nettesheim P, Adler KB, Randell SH. Rat tracheal epithelial cell differentiation in vitro. In Vitro Cell Dev Biol Anim 1993;29A:481–92.
63. Davenport EA, Nettesheim P. Regulation of mucociliary differentiation of rat tracheal epithelial cells by type I collagen gel substratum. Am J Respir Cell Mol Biol 1996; 14:19–26.
64. Ostrowski LE, Nettesheim P. Inhibition of ciliated cell differentiation by fluid submersion. Exp Lung Res 1995; 21:957–70.
65. Guzman K, Randell SH, Nettesheim P. Epidermal growth factor regulates expression of the mucous phenotype of rat tracheal epithelial cells. Biochem Biophys Res Comm 1995;217:412–8.
66. Clark AB, Randell SH, Nettesheim P, et al. Regulation of ciliated cell differentiation in cultures of rat tracheal epithelial cells. Am J Respir Cell Mol Biol 1995;12: 329–38.
67. Comer MT, Leese HJ, Southgate J. Induction of a differentiated ciliated cell phenotype in primary cultures of Fallopian tube epithelium. Hum Reprod 1998;13: 3114–20.
68. Nayak RK, Zimmerman DR, Albert EN. Electron microscopic studies of estrogen-induced ciliogenesis and secretion in uterine tube of the gilt. Am J Vet Res 1976; 37:189–97.
69. Anderson RG, Hein CE. Estrogen dependent ciliogenesis in the chick oviduct. Cell Tissue Res 1976;171:459–66.
70. Sandoz D, Biosvieux-Ulrich E, Laugier C, Brard E. [Ciliogenesis in the mucous cells of the quail oviduct. II. Hormonal control]. J Cell Biol 1976;71:460–71.
71. Jorissen M, Van der Schueren B, Van den Berghe H, Cassiman JJ. The preservation and regeneration of cilia on human nasal epithelial cells cultured in vitro. Arch Otorhinolaryngol 1989;246:308–14.
72. Chevillard M, Hinnrasky J, Pierrot D, et al. Differentiation of human surface upper airway epithelial cells in primary culture on a floating collagen gel. Epith Cell Biol 1993;2:17–25.
73. Hanamure Y, Deguchi K, Ohyama M. Ciliogenesis and mucus synthesis in cultured human respiratory epithelial cells. Ann Otol Rhinol Laryngol 1994;103: 889–95.
74. Yamaya M, Finkbeiner WE, Chun SY, Widdicombe JH. Differentiated structure and function of cultures from human tracheal epithelium. Am J Physiol 1992;262 (6 Pt 1):L713–24.
75. de Jong PM, van Sterkenburg MA, Hesseling SC, et al. Ciliogenesis in human bronchial epithelial cells cultured at the air-liquid interface. Am J Respir Cell Mol Biol 1994;10:271–7.
76. Gray TE, Guzman K, Davis CW, et al. Mucociliary differentiation of serially passaged normal human tracheobronchial epithelial cells. Am J Respir Cell Mol Biol 1996;14:104–12.
77. Bernacki SH, Nelson AL, Abdullah L, et al. Mucin gene expression during differentiation of human airway epithelia in vitro. Muc4 and muc5b are strongly induced. Am J Respir Cell Mol Biol 1999;20:595–604.
78. Piperno G, Huang B, Luck DJ. Two-dimensional analysis of flagellar proteins from wild-type and paralyzed mutants of *Chlamydomonas reinhardtii*. Proc Natl Acad Sci U S A 1977;74:1600–4.
79. Dirksen ER, Staprans I. Tubulin synthesis during ciliogenesis in the mouse oviduct. Dev Biol 1975;46:1–13.
80. Renthal R, Schneider BG, Miller MM, Luduena RF. Beta IV is the major beta-tubulin isotype in bovine cilia. Cell Motil Cytoskeleton 1993;25:19–29.
81. Million K, Larcher J, Laoukili J, et al. Polyglutamylation and polyglycylation of alpha- and beta-tubulins during in vitro ciliated cell differentiation of human respiratory epithelial cells. J Cell Sci 1999;112(Pt 23):4357–66.
82. Andrews KL, Nettesheim P, Asai DJ, Ostrowski LE. Identification of seven rat axonemal dynein heavy chain genes: expression during ciliated cell differentiation. Mol Biol Cell 1996;7:71–9.
83. Andrews KL, Potdar PD, Nettesheim P, Ostrowski LE. KPL1, which encodes a novel PH domain–containing protein, is induced during ciliated cell differentiation of rat tracheal epithelial cells [in process citation]. Exp Lung Res 2000;26:257–71.
84. Krappa R, Nguyen A, Burrola P, et al. Evectins: vesicular proteins that carry a pleckstrin homology domain and localize to post-Golgi membranes. Proc Natl Acad Sci U S A 1999;96:4633–8.
85. Ostrowski LE, Andrews K, Potdar P, et al. Cloning and characterization of KPL2, a novel gene induced during ciliogenesis of tracheal epithelial cells. Am J Respir Cell Mol Biol 1999;20:675–83.

86. LeDizet M, Beck JC, Finkbeiner WE. Differential regulation of centrin genes during ciliogenesis in human tracheal epithelial cells. Am J Physiol 1998;275(6 Pt 1):L1145–56.
87. Hackett BP, Brody SL, Liang M, et al. Primary structure of hepatocyte nuclear factor/forkhead homologue 4 and characterization of gene expression in the developing respiratory and reproductive epithelium. Proc Natl Acad Sci U S A 1995;92:4249–53.
88. Lim L, Zhou H, Costa RH. The winged helix transcription factor HFH-4 is expressed during choroid plexus epithelial development in the mouse embryo. Proc Natl Acad Sci U S A 1997;94:3094–9.
89. Blatt EN, Yan XH, Wuerffel MK, et al. Forkhead transcription factor HFH-4 expression is temporally related to ciliogenesis. Am J Respir Cell Mol Biol 1999;21:168–76.
90. Brody SL, Yan XH, Wuerffel MK, et al. Ciliogenesis and left-right axis defects in forkhead factor HFH-4-null mice. Am J Respir Cell Mol Biol 2000;23:45–51.
91. Chen J, Knowles HJ, Hebert JL, Hackett BP. Mutation of the mouse hepatocyte nuclear factor/forkhead homologue 4 gene results in an absence of cilia and random left-right asymmetry. J Clin Invest 1998;102:1077–82.
92. DeBoeck K, Jorissen M, Wouters K, et al. Aplasia of respiratory tract cilia. Pediatr Pulmonol 1992;13:259–65.

CHAPTER 34

Immunology and Cellular Defense Mechanisms in the Lung

Zuhair K. Ballas, MD

The lungs and the gastrointestinal (GI) tracts play a unique role in the life of an organism. Both systems provide an interface between the individual and the outside world. For an organism to survive, both systems must have the ability to neutralize threats or dangers from a relatively "hostile" environment. Each system has developed unique approaches to deal with this task. The GI tract evolved specialized cells and specialized lymphoid aggregates. In addition, the GI tract has the added capacity of expunging noxious stimuli, since the GI system is essentially an open one. The pulmonary system has a reduced ability to clear foreign bodies and other stimuli, as it is a closed system. The formidable defensive task of the lungs is readily apparent when one considers that approximately 8,000 to 12,000 L of microorganism-laden air pass through the lungs on a daily basis. Since the lungs face such a prodigious load of microorganisms, one would have expected them to be associated with numerous lymph nodes. However, the lungs do not have afferent lymphatics, and bronchoalveolar-associated lymphoid tissue is rather vestigial in the human lung (unlike the GI-associated lymphoid tissue).[1,2] Instead of organized lymphoid tissue, several filtering, trapping, flushing, and inactivation mechanisms have evolved, in addition to the immune system, for the defense of the bronchopulmonary system. Defenses of the respiratory tract include: (1) barrier defenses, (2) innate immunity, and (3) adaptive immunity (Table 34–1). Such division is arbitrary, however, since interaction between these various systems is the rule rather than the exception. Cytokines and chemokines are soluble mediators that serve as links between various components of the immune system and can exert a negative or positive regulatory effect.

TABLE 34–1. Defenses of the Respiratory Tract

Barrier defenses
Nasal filter
Ciliary activity
Opsonins
Antimicrobial molecules (eg, defensins, collectins, cathelicidins)
Innate immunity
Pattern recognition receptors (eg, Toll-like receptor)
Soluble elements (eg, complement and acute-phase reactants)
Cellular elements (eg, macrophages, neutrophils, natural killer cells, epithelial cells)
Adaptive immunity
Lymphocytes (eg, B cells, Th1, Th2) and their products
Cytokines (eg, interleukins, interferons)
Chemokines (eg, CXCL, XCL, CX3CL, CCL)

Barrier Defenses

The simplest and most immediate defense is a filtering mechanism. This is initiated by the "trapping" of larger particles in the anterior nares; this trapping continues as the air goes through the nasal turbinates, the nasopharynx, and the repeating divisions of bronchi and bronchioles. With every bronchial bifurcation, turbulence creates eddies and allows particle deposition. To help with filtering, a trapping mechanism is provided by the mucous blanket, which is constantly renewed and is moved upward by cilia. Cilia serve as a broom helping to whisk the trapped particles away from the sterile alveoli. For optimal performance, ciliary action must be brisk (which is not the case in cigarette smokers),[3,4] and the mucus has to be of proper viscosity. A thin mucous blanket may not be viscous enough to trap particles; a thick mucous blanket may be too viscous for the cilia to function properly (as is the case in cystic fibrosis).[4,5] In addition to the trapping and flushing mechanisms, cells of the respiratory tree (including serous cells, goblet cells, Clara cells, fibroblasts, epithelial cells, and cells of the immune system) produce a variety of molecules that either exert a direct antimicrobial activity or act as opsonins to facilitate clearance by cells of the immune system. These molecules include lysozyme, lactoferrin, transferrin, fibronectin, and lipopolysaccharide (LPS)-binding proteins. Molecules known as defensins, collectins, and cathelicidins have received considerable attention.[6,7]

Defensins are small (29 to 40 amino acids) cationic peptides that share a motif composed of six cysteines linked by three disulfide bridges. Defensins are divided into α and β subclasses, based on the particular cysteines linked by the disulfide bridges. Defensins are produced by a variety of cells, but the major producers are epithelial cells and neutrophils. Human α defensins and human β defensin 1 (HBD-1) appear to be expressed constitutively, whereas human β defensin 2 (HBD-2) is induced rapidly upon stimulation of the epithelial cells.[8–11]

Defensins have a direct microbicidal activity against gram-negative and gram-positive bacteria, mycobacteria, fungi, and enveloped viruses. The current thinking is that defensins kill their targets by disrupting their membranes and forming ion-permeable membrane channels. Interestingly, the antimicrobial activity of defensins is decreased markedly in the presence of a high salt concentration (as occurs in cystic fibrosis).[8–11]

Another class of antimicrobial molecules that has received attention is that of the collectins.[9–12] Collectins are c-type lectins whose members include surfactant proteins A and D. By virtue of their being lectins, collectins bind to carbohydrate determinants on the surface of bacteria, viruses, and fungi as well as noninfectious particles such as pollen, dust mite allergens, and inorganic particles. Binding to collectins enhances phagocytosis by alveolar macrophages and neutrophils.

Cathelicidins are highly cationic and hydrophobic peptides that have a broad antimicrobial activity. Cathelicidins have been studied most extensively in cows and pigs. However, one cathelicidin (designated hCAP-18 or LL-37) has been well studied in humans. hCAP-18 is found in the specific granules of human neutrophils, in epithelial cells, and in inflamed, but not normal, skin. hCAP-18 also has been found in bronchoalveolar lavage fluid, bronchial epithelial glands, and alveolar macrophages. hCAP-18 has been shown to bind to LPS and, thus, supposedly helps in clearance of bacteria.[9–13]

Innate Immunity

Innate immunity is nonspecific and is phylogenetically older than adaptive immunity. Whereas adaptive immunity can discern and respond to a single amino acid difference on an antigen (eg, human response against pork insulin), innate immunity depends on pattern recognition. The patterns of import are those that are most likely to be present on pathogens and are absent from "self." Examples of such patterns include LPS and peptidoglycans, both of which are absent from cells of mammals. Certain patterns may serve as the "danger signal" of a given class of pathogens. For example, LPS identifies gram-negative bacteria, mannans may identify fungal pathogens, and phosphatidylinositol mannosides and lipoarabinomannans may identify mycobacteria.[9–11,14–16]

There has been a recent explosion in the identification of the various receptors involved in pattern recognition (collectively referred to as pattern recognition receptors or PRR). *Drosophila* is known to have such a receptor, which is called Toll. It appears that humans have Toll-like receptors (TLRs),[11,17–21] which have extracellular, membrane, and cytoplasmic domains. The cytoplasmic domain of a TLR is similar to that of interleukin-1 (IL-1) receptor and is involved in triggering a signaling cascade of events that results, probably through the activation of NFκB, in the transcription of several genes encoding for the synthesis and release of molecules such as antimicrobial peptides and various cytokines.[17–21] While six TLRs have been identified in humans, the ligands of only TLR2 and TLR4 have been identified so far. Toll-like receptor 2 recognizes patterns associated with bacterial lipoproteins on mycobacteria and gram-positive bacteria. Although TLR2 can recognize LPS, TLR4 is the dominant receptor for LPS.[17–21] Arbour et al[22] recently reported that mutations in TLR4 are associated with differences in LPS responsiveness in humans. Missense mutations affecting the extracellular domain of the TLR4 were found to be associated with a blunted response to inhaled LPS in humans. Moreover, Arbour et al[22] found that the wild-type allele of TLR4 rescues the LPS hyporesponsive phenotype in either primary airway epithelial cells or alveolar macrophages obtained from individuals with the TLR4 mutations.

Innate immunity is composed of soluble and cellular elements. The soluble elements include complement and the acute-phase reactants. The cellular elements include macrophages, neutrophils, and natural killer (NK) cells. Unlike the cells of adaptive immunity (T and B lymphocytes), cells of innate immunity do not develop memory and therefore do not exhibit the accelerated and enhanced secondary responses characteristic of adaptive immunity.[14,15]

Although epithelial cells are not traditionally thought of as cellular components of innate immunity, they play an important role in innate lung defenses. Airway epithelium is not just a static barrier but, rather, a dynamic system. A large body of work, much of it done in vitro, indicates that epithelial cells can secrete, and respond to, a number of molecules.[7–14] As mentioned above, epithelial cells can be induced to upregulate HBD-2. Epithelial cells also have been shown to be able to secrete IL-1, IL-5, IL-6, granulocyte-macrophage colony-stimulating factor (GM-CSF), transforming growth factor (TGF)-β, fibronectin, and certain chemokines (see below). Epithelial cells have been shown to express LPS receptors, TLRs, tumor necrosis factor (TNF)-receptors, and adhesion molecules (which can be upregulated with the proper stimulus). In addition to their innate function, epithelial cells serve vital roles in the adaptive immune system,[7–14,17–22] the best example of which is their participation in mucosal immunoglobulin (Ig)A secretion.[23,24] Plasma cells secreting IgA are found just below the basement membrane of epithelial cells and must be transported to the bronchial lumen. Immunoglobulin A is found at the basement membrane in a dimeric form that binds to the so-called poly-Ig receptor (PIR), which is present on the basolateral surface of the overlying epithelial cells. When PIR binds the dimeric IgA, the complex is internalized and carried to the apical surface of the epithelial cell where the PIR is cleaved, leaving a fragment (the secretory component) attached to the dimeric IgA; this complex is then released into the lumen.[23,24]

Dendritic cells (DCs) are believed to be the most potent antigen presenting cells in the body, are abundant in the airways, and are intimately associated with the epithelial cells. It has been estimated that there are up to 700 DC/mm^2 of airway epithelium and that these DCs undergo a rapid turnover with a half-life of around 2 days. In contrast, epidermal Langerhans' cells have a half-life of around 15 days. The DCs are uniquely situated to sample, process, and present incoming antigens to cells of the adaptive immune system. In addition, DCs secrete several cytokines such as interferons and IL-12 that serve to augment and modulate the adaptive immune responses.[15,16,25–29]

Macrophages and neutrophils also are part of innate immunity and play an important role in pulmonary defenses. For example, macrophages, by virtue of their pattern recognition receptors, ingest gram-negative bacteria. Upon doing so, they release a variety of soluble mediators including IL-1, TNF-α, IL-6, IL-12, and IL-8. Each of these mediators triggers a cascade of events. For example, IL-8 acts as a chemotactic factor for neutrophils, whereas IL-12 activates NK cells, which secrete interferon-γ (IFN-γ) and thus skew the differentiation of CD4 cells into Th1 cells (see below). Interleukin-1, IL-6, and TNF-α act as endogenous pyrogens and act on the liver cells to release acute-phase reactants (mannan-binding lectin and C-reactive proteins), which act as opsonins. In addition, C-reactive proteins can help activate the complement cascade.[30–40]

Natural killer cells are large granular lymphocytes which are non-T and non-B cells. They are part of the innate immunity and do not require sensitization for the expression of their function. Natural killer cells can kill tumors of the lymphohematopoietic system, virally infected cells, and certain bacteria (such as salmonellae) and fungi. Moreover, NK cells are a potent source of cytokines and are believed to be a major source of IFN-γ, although they also may secrete IL-5 and IL-13.[41–43]

Of the soluble components of innate immunity, the complement cascade plays a major defensive role against bacteria. Activation of the complement cascade, in addition to opsonization, results in the elaboration of C5a which is a potent neutrophil chemotactic factor.[44] Recent data suggest that complement components may play an important role in regulating adaptive immunity, with a significant part in stimulating the responses of a B cell subset.[45–47]

Adaptive Immunity

Unlike innate immunity, adaptive immunity requires specific sensitization for the expression of its activity. Adaptive immunity is exquisitely specific and has long-lasting memory. Indeed, all people carry in their lymphocytes a record of every antigen to which they have been exposed since birth. Lymphocytes are the cells that mediate adaptive immunity. By virtue of its vast surface area and dual vascularity (bronchial and pulmonary), the pulmonary system is the largest reservoir of lymphocytes in the body.[48–50] It has been estimated that the lung interstitial space contains approximately 10 hr x 10^9 lymphocytes, which is similar to the number of the total circulating lymphocyte pool.[48] Since the lungs have no afferent lymphatics, most of the pulmonary lymphocytes probably are derived from the blood. Lymphocytes are present in several lung compartments: interstitium, epithelium, lamina propria, and bronchoalveolar space (although ~90% of cells in the bronchoalveolar space are macrophages). B cells, albeit only a few, are present in the lamina propria; T cells are present both within and beneath the epithelium. CD8 cells tend to be mostly interepithelial, whereas CD4 cells tend to be subepithelial (in healthy subjects). Smokers and chronic obstructive pulmonary disease (COPD) patients have an increased number of CD8 cells; asthmatics have an increased number of CD4 cells.[48–54] CD8 cells are believed to be killer cells, and CD4 cells are helper cells. However, it is now well established that helper cells are heterogeneous. CD4 cells can be divided into two major subsets: Th1 and Th2. Th1 CD4 lymphocytes secrete several cytokines, prominent among which is IFN-γ. Th2 CD4 lymphocytes also secrete several cytokines, but the prominent ones are IL-4 and IL-5. By virtue of the cytokines they release, Th1 and Th2 CD4 lymphocytes exhibit unique functions. Th1 lymphocytes promote cellular immunity (IFN-γ activates macrophages to kill intracellular microorganisms) and, perhaps, autoimmunity. Th2 lymphocytes, promote IgE synthesis, because IL-4 induces B cells to switch their immunoglobulin isotype from IgM to IgE. It therefore is not surprising that the CD4 lymphocytes found in the airways of allergic asthmatics are mostly Th2 lymphocytes.[48–54] In normal human subjects, most lung lymphocytes have a memory phenotype (CD45RA$^-$, CD45RO$^+$), and most CD4 cells belong to the Th1 subset.[48–55]

Cytokines and Chemokines

As was alluded to above, most of the cells in the lungs secrete one or more soluble mediators. In addition to antimicrobial substances (defensins, cathelicidins, and collectins), cytokines and chemokines play a major role in pulmonary defenses. These soluble mediators act as the link between innate and adaptive defenses. For example, phagocytic cells generate IL-1 and TNF-α that may lead to activation and proliferation of T cells. Dendritic cells secrete several cytokines, and it has been suggested that DCs can be divided into DC1 cells that induce the differentiation of Th1 lymphocytes, and DC2 cells that induce the proliferation of Th2 cells.[56,57] Similarly, human NK cells have been shown to segregate into NK1 cells that secrete IFN-γ and IL-10, and NK2 cells that secrete IL-5 and IL-13.[43]

Of the various cytokines, IL-11 and IL-13 deserve special mention. It has been suggested that IL-13 may induce bronchoconstriction, in an animal model, independent of IgE or eosinophils.[58,59] In an elegant study, Zhu et al[60] reported that mice genetically engineered to constitutively express IL-13 in their lungs developed an inflammatory response in their airways. The inflammatory cells contained eosinophils and macrophages. In addition, these mice developed airway epithelial cell hypertrophy, mucous cell metaplasia, Charcot-Leyden crystal deposition, and subepithelial airway fibrosis. In contrast, mice that constitutively expressed IL-11 in their lungs developed peribronchiolar mononuclear cell infiltrate, subepithelial airway fibrosis, and emphysematous alveoli.[61] Ray et al[62] developed mice whose IL-11 expression was engineered to be under the control of the Clara cell 10-kD protein (CC10) promotor and the reverse tetracycline transactivator to create a lung-specific externally regulable IL-11 expression. Ray et al[62] found that when this IL-11 gene was activated in adulthood (by giving tetracycline to the mice), the mice developed airway remodeling and peribronchiolar nodules, but no emphysematous changes were seen. These data suggest that cytokines may have different effects on the lungs at various stages of development. Age-dependent differences in the effect of various immune mediators currently are receiving more scrutiny.

Occasionally, a knockout mouse model yields some surprising pulmonary results.[63,64] For example, mice whose genes for GM-CSF have been inactivated developed pathologic findings similar to those seen in the human disease pulmonary alveolar proteinosis.[65] These changes were ameliorated upon the administration of aerosolized (but not systemic) GM-CSF.[66] Interestingly, these mice exhibited an increased susceptibility to pulmonary group B streptococcal infection. Granulocyte-macrophage colony-stimulating factor knockout mice displayed a very slow clearance of these bacteria after intratracheal instillation and exhibited increased neutrophilic infiltration (macrophage infiltrates predominated in control mice).[67]

Studies in cytokine knockout mice have revealed important information on the role of various cytokines in particular infections. For example, IL-6 knockout mice have been found to have increased susceptibility to bacterial pneumonias, especially those associated with *Escherichia coli* and *Listeria monocytogenes*.[68–71] Interestingly, pneumonias with these pathogens, but not those with *Streptococcus pneumoniae*, were not associated with peripheral blood neutrophilia in the IL-6 knockout mice.[68–71] Interferon-γ knockout mice were found to have an increased susceptibility to infection with mycobacteria and salmonellae.[72] Indeed, several cases have been reported of humans with mutations in their IFN-γ-receptor genes.[72,73] These patients were able to resist most infections except for those caused by atypical mycobacteria and, in a few cases, salmonellae. An identical picture has been reported in patients with abnormalities in their IL-12 or IL-12-receptor genes.[74,75]

Chemokines are a group of low-molecular weight (8 to 10 kD) compounds that regulate trafficking of various types of leukocytes across cell barriers. At least 40 different chemokines have been identified, and the list is probably far from complete. Chemokines are divided into four groups, each identified by the number of amino acids separating the first two cysteine residues (starting at the N terminus). Traditionally, these groups have been designated CC, CXC, CX3C, and C.[30–32] Each chemokine received a different label; the list became confusing. A new nomenclature has been proposed.[76] The new nomenclature maintains the four categories, but members within each category are numbered sequentially. For example, the CXC family is designated CXCL (L is for ligand; this differentiates them from CXCR, where R stands for receptor), and its members are numbered 1 to 15. The C family is designated XCL (1 and 2, so far); CX3CL has one member, and CCL has 27 members.[76] Cytokines and chemokines are elaborated by several of the cells described above. Airway epithelial cells secrete cytokines (IL-1, IL-5, and IL-6) as well as chemokines (IL-8 or CXCL8 and RANTES [regulated on activation, normal T expressed and secreted] or CCL5). Dendritic cells also secrete cytokines (see above) and chemokines (CCL17, CCL18, CCL22, CCL25, and CCL19). Several chemokines can be secreted by T lymphocytes, and T lymphocytes have receptors for various chemokines; this serves to illustrate the intricate feedback loops that are operant between innate and adaptive immunity.[30–33,35,36,39] Moreover, different chemokine receptors appear to segregate in Th1 vs Th2 lymphocytes. CCR5 and CXCR3 receptors are thought to be on Th1, whereas CCR3, CCR4, and CCR8 are thought to be expressed on Th2.[30,31] This suggests that various chemokines may be involved in attracting either a Th1 or a Th2 lymphocyte. It remains to be seen whether the dominant Th2 expression in asthma is primary or secondary to the elaboration of specific chemokines.

Recent evidence suggests that chemokines may exert different effects in different organs, as seen in a murine model of *Cryptococcus neoformans*. Protective immunity against *C. neoformans*, a common pathogen in human immunodeficiency virus (HIV) infection, is thought to be dependent on a Th1 response, although CD8 T cells also are thought to be important. Huffnagle et al[77] examined the role of CCR5 (a co-receptor for the HIVvirus) in this infection by generating CCR5 knockout mice. They found that after intratracheal instillation of *C. neoformans*, the pulmonary response (local leukocytosis and clearance of the pathogen) was identical to that of the control mice. However, the CCR5 knockout mice were unable to recruit leukocytes to the central nervous system, resulting in lack of clearance of the pathogen and a mortality rate of around 75% (compared to < 10% mortality in controls).

This brief synopsis of various cytokines and chemokines represents just the "tip of the iceberg" in our understanding of the role of these molecules in protecting the organism from various pathogens. A picture is emerging wherein a particular cytokine or chemokine may be the predominant defense against a specific pathogen. Research in the next decade no doubt will bring more exciting and surprising findings in this field.

In summary, the pulmonary system employs several strategies, cells, and molecules to ensure a sterile alveolar space. None of these mechanisms operates on its own. Optimal defense of the lungs relies on carefully choreographed relays, tandems, and cascades of the various components.

References

1. Pabst R. Is BALT a major component of the human lung immune system? Immunol Today 1992;13:119–22.
2. Tschernig T, Pabst R. Bronchus-associated lymphoid tissue (BALT) is not present in the normal adult lung but in different diseases. Pathobiology 2000;68:1–8.
3. Verra F, Escudier E, Lebargy F, et al. Ciliary abnormalities in bronchial epithelium of smokers, ex-smokers, and nonsmokers. Am J Respir Crit Care Med 1995;151: 630–4.
4. Jansen HM, Sachs AP, van Alphen L. Predisposing conditions to bacterial infections in chronic obstructive pulmonary disease. Am J Respir Crit Care Med 1995;151: 2073–80.
5. Trout L, King M, Feng W, et al. Inhibition of airway liquid secretion and its effect on the physical properties of airway mucus. Am J Physiol 1998;274:L258–63.
6. Nicod LP. Pulmonary defense mechanisms. Respiration 1999;66:2–11.
7. Twigg HL III. Pulmonary host defenses. J Thorac Imaging 1998;13:221–33.
8. van Wetering S, Sterk PJ, Rabe KF, Hiemstra PS. Defensins: key players or bystanders in infection, injury, and repair in the lung? J Allergy Clin Immunol 1999;104:1131–8.
9. Nelson S, Summer WR. Innate immunity, cytokines, and pulmonary host defense. Infect Dis Clin North Am 1998; 12:555–67.
10. Ganz T, Lehrer RI. Antimicrobial peptides of vertebrates. Curr Opin Immunol 1998;10:41–4.
11. Diamond G, Legarda D, Ryan LK. The innate immune response of the respiratory epithelium. Immunol Rev 2000;173:27–38.
12. Crouch E, Hartshorn K, Ofek I. Collectins and pulmonary innate immunity. Immunol Rev 2000;173:52–65.
13. Sørensen O, Bratt T, Johnsen AH, et al. The human antibacterial cathelicidin, hCAP-18, is bound to lipoproteins in plasma. J Biol Chem 1999;274:22445–51.
14. Lo D, Feng L, Li L, et al. Integrating innate and adaptive immunity in the whole animal. Immunol Rev 1999; 169:225–39.
15. Medzhitov R, Janeway C Jr. Innate immune recognition: mechanisms and pathways. Immunol Rev 2000;173: 89–97.
16. Zhang P, Summer WR, Bagby GJ, Nelson S. Innate immunity and pulmonary host defense. Immunol Rev 2000; 173:39–51.
17. Modlin RL, Brightbill HD, Godowski PJ. The toll of innate immunity on microbial pathogens. N Engl J Med 1999;340:1834–5.
18. Muzio M, Mantovani A. Toll-like receptors. Microbes Infect 2000;2:251–5.
19. Beutler B. Endotoxin, toll-like receptor 4, and the afferent limb of innate immunity. Curr Opin Microbiol 2000; 3:23–8.
20. Anderson KV. Toll signaling pathways in the innate immune response. Curr Opin Immunol 2000;12:13–9.
21. Bowie A, O'Neill LA. The interleukin-1 receptor/Toll-like receptor superfamily: signal generators for pro-inflammatory interleukins and microbial products. J Leukoc Biol 2000;67:508–14.
22. Arbour NC, Lorenz E, Schutte BC, et al. TLR4 mutations are associated with endotoxin hyporesponsiveness in humans. Nat Genet 2000;25:187–91.
23. Salvi S, Holgate ST. Could the airway epithelium play an important role in mucosal immunoglobulin A production? Clin Exp Allergy 1999;29:1597–605.
24. Norderhaug IN, Johansen FE, Schjerven H, Brandtzaeg P. Regulation of the formation and external transport of secretory immunoglobulins. Crit Rev Immunol 1999; 19:481–508.
25. Holt PG, Stumbles PA. Regulation of immunologic homeostasis in peripheral tissues by dendritic cells: the respiratory tract as a paradigm. J Allergy Clin Immunol 2000; 105:421–9.
26. McWilliam AS, Nelson DJ, Holt PG. The biology of airway dendritic cells. Immunol Cell Biol 1995;73:405–13.
27. McWilliam AS, Napoli S, Marsh AM, et al. Dendritic cells are recruited into the airway epithelium during the inflammatory response to a broad spectrum of stimuli. J Exp Med 1996;184:2429–32.
28. Reid SD, Penna G, Adorini L. The control of T cell responses by dendritic cell subsets. Curr Opin Immunol 2000; 12:114–21.
29. Dupuis M, McDonald DM. Dendritic-cell regulation of lung immunity. Am J Respir Cell Mol Biol 1997;17:284–6.
30. Rossi D, Zlotnik A. The biology of chemokines and their receptors. Annu Rev Immunol 2000;18:217–42.
31. Murdoch C, Finn A. Chemokine receptors and their role in inflammation and infectious diseases. Blood 2000;95: 3032–43.
32. Keane MP, Strieter RM. Chemokine signaling in inflammation. Crit Care Med 2000;28 Suppl:N13–26.
33. Teran LM. CCL chemokines and asthma. Immunol Today 2000;21:235–42.
34. Slifka MK, Whitton JL. Antigen-specific regulation of T cell-mediated cytokine production. Immunity 2000;12:451–7.

35. Cyster JG. Chemokines and cell migration in secondary lymphoid organs. Science 1999;286:2098–102.
36. Baggiolini M. Chemokines and leukocyte traffic. Nature 1998;392:565–8.
37. Dynlacht BD. Regulation of transcription by proteins that control the cell cycle. Nature 1997;389:149–52.
38. Callard R, George AJ, Stark J. Cytokines, chaos, and complexity. Immunity 1999;11:507–13.
39. Ward SG, Bacon K, Westwick J. Chemokines and T lymphocytes: more than an attraction. Immunity 1998; 9:1–11.
40. O'Garra A. Cytokines induce the development of functionally heterogeneous T helper cell subsets. Immunity 1998; 8:275–83.
41. Biron CA. Initial and innate responses to viral infections—pattern setting in immunity or disease. Curr Opin Microbiol 1999;2:374–81.
42. Biron CA, Nguyen KB, Pien GC, et al. Natural killer cells in antiviral defense: function and regulation by innate cytokines. Annu Rev Immunol 1999;17:189–220.
43. Peritt D, Robertson S, Gri G, et al. Differentiation of human NK cells into NK1 and NK2 subsets. J Immunol 1998;161:5821–4.
44. Nonaka M. Origin and evolution of the complement system. Curr Top Microbiol Immunol 2000;248:37–50.
45. Hoffmann JA, Kafatos FC, Janeway CA, Ezekowitz RA. Phylogenetic perspectives in innate immunity. Science 1999;284:1313–8.
46. Carroll MC, Prodeus AP. Linkages of innate and adaptive immunity. Curr Opin Immunol 1998;10:36–40.
47. Fearon DT. The complement system and adaptive immunity. Semin Immunol 1998;10:355–61.
48. Krug N, Tschernig T, Holgate S, Pabst R. How do lymphocytes get into the asthmatic airways? Lymphocyte traffic into and within the lung in asthma. Clin Exp Allergy 1998;28:10–8.
49. Pabst R, Schuster M, Tschernig T. Lymphocyte dynamics in the pulmonary microenvironment: implications for the pathophysiology of pulmonary sarcoidosis. Sarcoidosis Vasc Diffuse Lung Dis 1999;16:197–202.
50. Semenzato G, Bortolin M, Facco M, et al. Lung lymphocytes: origin, biological functions, and laboratory techniques for their study in immune-mediated pulmonary disorders. Crit Rev Clin Lab Sci 1996;33:423–55.
51. Romagnani S. The role of lymphocytes in allergic disease. J Allergy Clin Immunol 2000;105;399–408.
52. Holgate ST. Genetic and environmental interaction in allergy and asthma. J Allergy Clin Immunol 1999;104: 1139–46.
53. Kemeny DM, Vyas B, Vukmanovic-Stejic M, et al. CD8(+) T cell subsets and chronic obstructive pulmonary disease. Am J Respir Crit Care Med 1999;160:S33–7.
54. Saetta M. Airway inflammation in chronic obstructive pulmonary disease. Am J Respir Crit Care Med 1999;160: S17–20.
55. Singh VK, Mehrotra S, Agarwal SS. The paradigm of Th1 and Th2 cytokines: its relevance to autoimmunity and allergy. Immunol Res 1999;20:147–61.
56. Stumbles PA, Thomas JA, Pimm CL, et al. Resting respiratory tract dendritic cells preferentially stimulate T helper cell type 2 (Th2) responses and require obligatory cytokine signals for induction of Th1 immunity. J Exp Med 1998;188:2019–31.
57. Rissoan MC, Soumelis V, Kadowaki N, et al. Reciprocal control of T helper cell and dendritic cell differentiation. Science 1999;283:1183–6.
58. Grunig G, Warnock M, Wakil AE, et al. Requirement for IL-13 independently of IL-4 in experimental asthma. Science 1998;282:2261–3.
59. Wills-Karp M, Luyimbazi J, Xu X, et al. Interleukin-13: central medicator of allergic asthma. Science 1998; 282:2258–61.
60. Zhu Z, Homer RJ, Wang Z, et al. Pulmonary expression of interleukin-13 causes inflammation, mucus hypersecretion, subepithelial fibrosis, physiologic abnormalities, and eotaxin production. J Clin Invest 1999;103:779–88.
61. Waxman AB, Einarsson O, Seres T, et al. Targeted lung expression of interleukin-11 enhances murine tolerance of 100% oxygen and diminishes hyperoxia-induced DNA fragmentation. J Clin Invest 1998:101:1970–82.
62. Ray P, Tang W, Wang P, et al. Regulated overexpression of interleukin 11 in the lung. J Clin Invest 1997;100: 2501–11.
63. Moore TA, Standiford TJ. The role of cytokines in bacterial pneumonia: an inflammatory balancing act. Proc Assoc Am Physicians 1998;110:297–305.
64. Eggleton P, Reid KB. Lung surfactant proteins involved in innate immunity. Curr Opin Immunol 1999;11:28–33.
65. Stanley E, Lieschke GJ, Grail D, et al. Granulocyte/macrophage colony-stimulating factor-deficient mice show no major pertubation of hematopoiesis but develop a characteristic pulmonary pathology. Proc Natl Acad Sci U S A 1994;91:5592–6.
66. Reed JA, Ikegami M, Cianciolo ER, et al. Aerosolized GM-CSF ameliorates pulmonary alveolar proteinosis in GM-CSF-deficient mice. Am J Physiol 1999:276:L556–63.
67. LeVine AM, Reed JA, Kurak KE, et al. GM-CSF-deficient mice are susceptible to pulmonary group B streptococcal infection. J Clin Invest 1999:103:563–9.
68. Dalrymple SA, Slattery R, Aud DM, et al. Interleukin-6 is required for a protective immune response to systemic *Escherichia coli* infection. Infect Immun 1996;64: 3231–5.
69. Dalrymple SA, Lucian LA, Slattery R, et al. Interleukin-6-deficient mice are highly susceptible to *Listeria mono cytogenes* infection: correlation with inefficient neutrophilia. Infect Immun 1995;63:2262–8.
70. Kopf M, Baumann H, Freer G, et al. Impaired immune and acute-phase responses in interleukin-6-deficient mice. Nature 1994;368:339–42.
71. van der Poll T, Keogh CV, Guirao X, et al. Interleukin-6 gene-deficient mice show impaired defense against pneumococcal pneumonia. J Infect Dis 1997;176: 439–44.
72. Jouanguy E, Doffinger R, Dupuis S, et al. IL-12 and IFN-gamma in host defense against mycobacteria and salmonella in mice and men. Curr Opin Immunol 1999;11: 346–51.
73. Dorman SE, Holland SM. Mutation in the signal-transducing chain of the interferon-gamma receptor and

susceptibility to mycobacterial infection. J Clin Invest 1998;101:2364–9.
74. Altare F, Durandy A, Lammas D, et al. Impairment of mycobacterial immunity in human interleukin-12 receptor deficiency. Science 1998;280:1432–5.
75. de Jong R, Altare F, Haagen IA, et al. Severe mycobacterial and *Salmonella* infections in interleukin-12 receptor-deficient patients. Science 1998;280:1435–8.
76. Zlotnik A, Yoshie O. Chemokines: a new classification system and their role in immunity. Immunity 2000; 12:121–7.
77. Huffnagle GB, McNeil LK, McDonald RA, et al. Cutting edge: role of C-C chemokine receptor 5 in organ-specific and innate immunity to *Cryptococcus neoformans*. J Immunol 1999;163:4642–6.

CHAPTER 35

Airway Secretions

Margaret W. Leigh, MD

The upper and lower respiratory tracts are covered by a thin layer of liquid secreted, in large part, by secretory cells in the airway surface epithelium and in the submucosal glands. Current evidence supports two phases of airway surface fluid: a superficial mucous gel, which is propelled by the tips of beating cilia, and an underlying aqueous, periciliary fluid. The effectiveness of mucociliary clearance depends on the density of ciliated cells, the depth of the periciliary fluid, and the rheologic (or viscoelastic) properties of the gel layer. Airway mucus contains large interactive macromolecules, such as mucin-type glycoproteins, which are the major determinants of the viscoelastic properties of the mucous gel. Divalent cations, such as calcium ions, can alter gel properties by interacting with the polyionic mucin molecules to alter conformation and by participating in cross-linking of mucin molecules. Other products in airway secretions that may be involved in gel formation are glycosaminoglycans, deoxyribonucleic acid (DNA), fibrillar actin, serum-type glycoproteins, lysozyme, and lactoferrin. Hydration of the mucous gel greatly influences its physical characteristics by changing the concentration of macromolecules and, hence, the extent of molecular networking. The degree of hydration of the mucous layer and the depth of the periciliary layer are regulated by ion transport across the airway epithelium. This chapter focuses on secretions of human airways, with particular emphasis on the mucin-type glycoproteins and changes in their secretion during development and during disease. For an in-depth review of mucociliary clearance and ion transport, see Chapters 32 and 21, respectively.

Sources

Airway mucus contains a mixture of secretory products from multiple sources (Table 35–1). Normal respiratory tract mucus contains secretory products from goblet cells, submucosal glands, Clara cells, other airway epithelial cells, and alveolar cells. In the presence of injury or infection, airway mucus also may contain substantial amounts of serum transudate and inflammatory cell products. Sputum contains expectorated mucus mixed with varying amounts of saliva, a watery fluid secreted by the salivary glands (parotid glands and submaxillary glands). The composition and properties of saliva are different from airway mucus; therefore, analytic studies must minimize contamination of airway mucous samples with saliva.

Histochemical studies suggest that the primary sources of mucin-type glycoproteins are goblet cells in the surface epithelium, as well as submucosal glands. In

TABLE 35–1. Airway Surface Liquid: Secretory Products and Their Sources

Sources	Secretory Products
Secretory Cells	
Goblet cells	Mucin-type glycoproteins, glycosaminoglycans
Submucosal glands	Mucin-type glycoproteins, glycosaminoglycans, lysozyme, lactoferrin SLPI, PRPs
Clara cells	Surfactant-associated proteins, Clara cell 10-kD protein, SLPI
Other Sources	
Airway epithelium (not specifically goblet cells)	Secretory IgA, lysozyme, defensins, proinflammatory cytokines, arachidonic acid metabolites, neutral lipids and phospholipids, factors that inhibit smooth muscle contraction and submucosal gland secretion
Migratory cells (mast cells, neutrophils, lymphocytes)	Inflammatory mediators, hyaluronic acid, proteases
Intracellular components released by degenerating neutrophils in inflamed airways	DNA, fibrillar actin
Transudation of serum, especially in inflamed airways	Albumin, Igs, α_1-proteinase inhibitor, other serum proteins
Alveolar lining fluid	Phospholipids, surfactant-associated proteins

SLPI = secretory leukocyte protein inhibitor; PRP = proline-rich protein; Ig = immunoglobulin; DNA = deoxyribonucleic acid.

human airways, the estimated volume of secretory cells in submucosal glands greatly exceeds that of goblet cells, leading to the potentially misleading conclusion that the glands produce the majority of secretions. Several lines of evidence suggest that submucosal glands are reservoirs that release their products in response to neurohormonal and possibly inflammatory mediators; whereas, goblet cells secrete at a baseline rate that is modulated only under rather adverse circumstances. In humans and animals that have submucosal glands, cholinergic agonists enhance secretion; in animals without submucosal glands, such as rabbits, these agents do not alter baseline secretion. In dog and cat trachea, unstimulated submucosal gland secretion is minimal, but vagal stimulation results in rapid outpouring of gland secretion, as is demonstrated by hillock formation under tantalum powder[1] or by an increase in fluid recovered by direct micropipette cannulation of the gland duct.[2] When cat tracheal surface epithelium is cultured separately from the submucosal portion containing glands, baseline secretion is unchanged by bethanechol, but gland secretion doubles with exposure to this agent.[3] These observations all support the notion that nonstimulated (basal) secretions are primarily a surface epithelial product, but that augmentation of secretion is primarily a submucosal gland function.

Goblet Cells

In mature tracheobronchial epithelium, goblet cells constitute up to 15 percent of the surface cell population.[4] The prevalence of goblet cells varies and may be markedly increased in airway disease.[5] Goblet cells contain well-developed organelles for glycoprotein synthesis, specifically, rough endoplasmic reticulum and the Golgi apparatus. Goblet cells in the airway epithelium, like their counterparts in the intestinal tract, are filled with electron-lucent and, sometimes, biphasic secretory granules. These secretory granules contain predominantly mucin-type glycoproteins. Histochemical staining with Alcian blue–periodic acid–Schiff (AB-PAS) has been used to characterize the granules in airway secretory cells.[6] Periodic acid–Schiff stain reacts with the vicinyl hydroxyls in glycoconjugates, resulting in a magenta color. Mucins are heavily glycosylated with sugars containing these vicinyl hydroxyls and therefore stain intensely with PAS. Alcian blue binds to acidic moieties, specifically sialic acid and sulfate in glycoconjugates. The prevalence of acidic moieties in glycoconjugates varies; consequently, the intensity of Alcian blue staining varies. The combined staining with Alcian blue and PAS can be used to differentiate mucins containing relatively few acidic moieties (which stain magenta with only a slight blue tint) from those containing abundant acidic moieties (which stain a blue-purple color). Goblet cells in mature tracheobronchial epithelium stain purple with AB-PAS, consistent with acidic mucins.

The mechanism(s) and control of airway goblet cell secretion is less well defined than that for intestinal goblet cell secretion. Most goblet cell secretion occurs by exocytosis of secretory granules (Figure 35–1), but some stimulated release may occur by an apocrine process in which the apical portion of the goblet cell including granules and cytoplasm is expelled (Figure 35–2). Regulation of goblet cell secretion is not completely defined. Several studies suggest that adenosine triphosphate (ATP) may be important for physiologic control of goblet cell secretion.[7,8] Other agents known to enhance goblet cell secretion include neutrophil elastase and cathepsin G,[9] bacterial proteases,[10] platelet activating factor (PAF),[11] serum,[12] and tobacco smoke.[13]

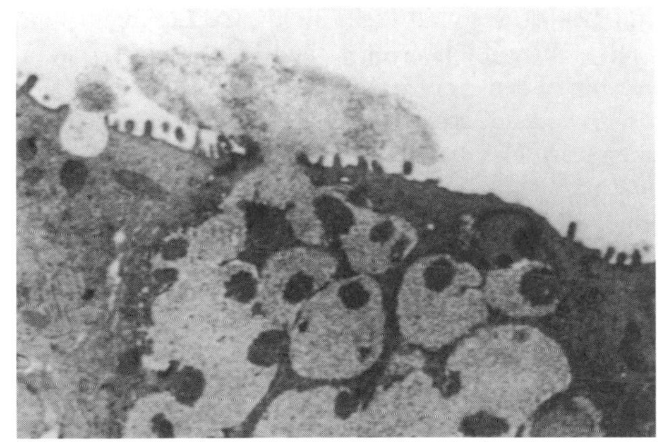

FIGURE 35–1. Photomicrograph (transmission electron microscopy) of secretory cells demonstrating merocrine secretion by simple exocytosis (*left*) and compound exocytosis (*right*), with fusion of secretory granules.

FIGURE 35–2. Photomicrograph (transmission electron microscopy) of airway epithelium demonstrating apocrine secretion after exposure to proteinase. The apical portion of secretory cells, including intact granules and cytoplasm, is cast off.

Most of the developmental changes in airway secretory cells occur during fetal life. The epithelial cell layer of the developing trachea is of endodermal origin and initially resembles that of the developing esophagus.[14] Early secretory cells, present in tracheal epithelium by 12 to 13 weeks, may be separated into two types on the basis of their AB-PAS staining characteristics.[15] The first type contains a few well-defined granules that react only with PAS, and it occasionally contains granules at the apex that also bind Alcian blue. The second type is distended with granules that stain with both PAS and Alcian blue, similar to the goblet cells in adult airways. As the human fetus matures, the first type decreases in prevalence and the second type becomes more prominent, suggesting that the first may be a precursor for the second cell type and that the secretory product changes with maturation. The number of secretory cells in the surface epithelium increases rapidly between 15 and 19 weeks of gestation, reaching a density of 50%; it then decreases to 10 to 15% by 15 weeks of gestation.[16] At birth, the tracheal epithelium resembles that of adults (Figure 35–3).

Submucosal Glands

In humans, submucosal glands are found in the cartilaginous airways, typically located in the submucosal space between the surface epithelium and underlying cartilage. These glands are complex structures containing multiple acini that open into tubules that drain into a collecting duct that opens to the airway surface.[17] The secretory cell types in submucosal glands are mucous cells containing electron-lucent granules, and serous cells containing electron-dense secretory granules.[18] Mucous cells secrete mucin-type glycoproteins; serous cells secrete lysozyme, lactoferrin, secretory leukocyte protein inhibitor (SLPI) proline-rich proteins(PRPs), and glycosaminoglycans.[19] Typically, mucous cells react with both Alcian blue and PAS resulting in a blue-purple staining pattern similar to that of goblet cells in the surface epithelium, but serous cells react only with PAS, resulting in a magenta color. Often, mucous cells and serous cells are segregated into different acini. The submucosal gland duct is ciliated at its opening and appears to be a continuation of the airway surface epithelium. However, the epithelium of the collecting duct consists of tall columnar cells with abundant mitochondria, and it is thought to control the ion and water content of submucosal gland secretions.[17,18] This arrangement allows for hydration of the gel formed by the secreted mucin-type glycoproteins and proteoglycans. Surrounding the glands is a semicontinuous layer of myoepithelial cells that contract and "squeeze" tubules during active gland secretion.[20]

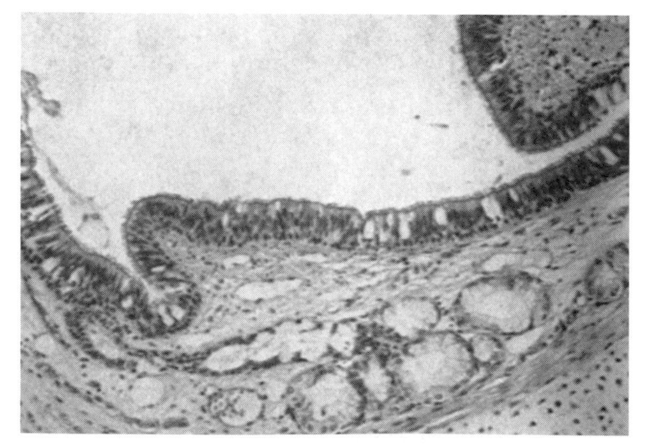

FIGURE 35–3. Cross-section of human trachea in the first day of life. Airway epithelium is mature and submucosal glands are present.

Regulation of submucosal gland secretion primarily involves neural pathways. The most completely studied mechanism for regulation of submucosal gland secretion is the cholinergic neural pathway. Submucosal gland secretion is increased by direct stimulation of the vagus nerve or its branches.[1,2] In addition, parasympathomimetic agents such as acetylcholine, methacholine, and pilocarpine stimulate gland secretion in tracheal explants.[21–23] Cholinergic antagonists such as atropine block gland secretion in response to vagal stimulation or cholinergic agonists. While cholinergic fibers are most prevalent, submucosal glands also contain adrenergic and nonadrenergic noncholinergic (NANC) nerve fibers.[24,25] The role of these neural pathways in regulation of human submucosal gland secretion is undefined. Interestingly, β-adrenergic agents promote gland secretion in some animal species but not in humans.[22,23] Vasoactive intestinal peptide (VIP), one of the neuropeptides associated with NANC fibers, inhibits baseline and methacholine-induced gland secretions in humans, but it has a stimulatory effect in many animal species.[26] Submucosal gland secretion can be stimulated by proteinases, such as cathepsin G and neutrophil elastase,[27,28] although the relative role of these non-neural pathways has not been defined.

Primordial submucosal glands presumably arise from cells in the developing airway epithelium, and first appear at 12 to 14 weeks of gestation as round intraepithelial buds in human trachea.[29] These buds elongate into cylinders that protrude into the submucosal region and then divide to form the two lateral ducts that undergo repeated dichotomous division.[30] These glands first appear near the larynx and they progressively increase in number down the trachea until 17 weeks of gestation, when there is no difference in the gland density in the upper and lower trachea.[31] After 23 weeks of gestation, tracheal glands increase in size but not in number.[31] The timing of development of submucosal glands in bronchi has not been defined as well as for the trachea.

Other Airway Epithelial Cells

Other airway epithelial cells synthesize and release products into the airway lumen. Clara cells, found in the bronchioles of humans, are nonciliated columnar cells that often project into the airway lumen and contain abundant smooth endoplasmic reticulum and apical membrane-bound electron-dense granules.[32] Most of the proteins secreted by Clara cells have a low molecular weight (6,000 to 10,000). The Clara cell 10-kD protein is specific for Clara cells,[33] appears to be a counterpart of rabbit uteroglobin,[34] and is thought to have anti-inflammatory properties.[35] In addition, SLPI has been identified within Clara cells and is thought to protect against protease destruction of the lung.[36] Little is known about regulation of Clara cell secretion.

A number of other secretory products, such as secretory immunoglobulin (Ig) A, arachidonic acid metabolites, cytokines, and lipids are released by airway epithelium, but the specific cell source has not been defined. Some studies suggest that airway epithelium secretes factors that inhibit airway smooth muscle contraction[37] and submucosal gland secretion,[38] because removal of epithelium promotes increased airway tone and gland secretion, respectively. Conceivably, loss of airway surface epithelium from acute or chronic bronchitis could decrease the concentrations of these epithelium-derived relaxing factors resulting in bronchoconstriction and increased gland secretion.

Composition

Airway secretions contain a mixture of respiratory epithelial products (see Table 35–1). Quantification of the volume and components in airway secretions has been difficult. The small volume of the airway lining fluid layer in normal subjects limits our ability to selectively sample and analyze surface fluid composition. The volume of airway mucus production measured by continuous tracheal aspiration in laryngectomized and tracheostomized patients is 0.2 to 0.5 mL/kg of body weight per day;[39] however, this approach most likely overestimates secretion because these airways undoubtedly are irritated by instrumentation. Early compositional studies using expectorated secretions from laryngectomized "normal" subjects or patients with chronic bronchitis demonstrated that the major component of airway secretion is water, accounting for 95% of airway mucus by weight; the solids content includes 2 to 3% proteins and glycoproteins, 1% lipids, and 1% minerals.[40] Another approach to collecting airway surface liquid from normal subjects is the application of preweighed filter paper onto the tracheal or bronchial surface under direct bronchoscopic observation.[41,42] By comparing the wet and dry weights with the preapplication weight of the filter paper, the water content in normal healthy individuals has been estimated at 91 to 93%.[41,42] While mucins are thought to be the major component influencing the viscoelastic properties of normal airway mucus, a number of other components (see Table 35–1) have been identified that may influence mucociliary clearance and other defense mechanisms in the airways.

Mucin-Type Glycoproteins

Mucin-type glycoproteins are heterogeneous high-molecular weight glycoconjugates consisting of a protein core and numerous (typically several hundred) sugar side chains (Figure 35–4). Repulsion of negative charges in adjacent sugar chains is thought to influence molecular structure, resulting in a rigid "bottle-brush" conformation of mucin molecules.[43,44] Characteristically, the sugar side chains of mucin-type glycoproteins are attached by *O*-glycosidic linkages between *N*-acetylgalactosamine (GalNAc) in the sugar side chain and serine or threonine in the peptide core. The sugar side chains are composed of 5 sugars: L-fucose (Fuc), D-galactose (Gal), D-*N*-acetylgalactosamine, D-*N*-acetylglucosamine (GlcNAc), and sialic acid, also known as neuraminic acid (NeuAc). Mucins contain little or no mannose (prevalent in serum and membrane glycoproteins that have *N*-glycosidic linkages) or uronic acid (prevalent in proteoglycans). The overall composition of respiratory mucins is 70 to 80% carbohydrate, 20% protein, and 2 to 7% sulfate.[45,46] The size and structure of mucins are variable: (1) relative molecular mass (M_r) estimates range from 1.8×10^6 to 44×10^6 kD; (2) estimates of peptide core length range from 100 to 600 kD; (3) sugar side chains vary in number, length (typically 1 to 20 sugars/side chain), sugar content, sulfate content, and branching pattern.[47] The central portion of the peptide core is composed of tandem repeats of amino acid sequences that are rich in potential glycosylation

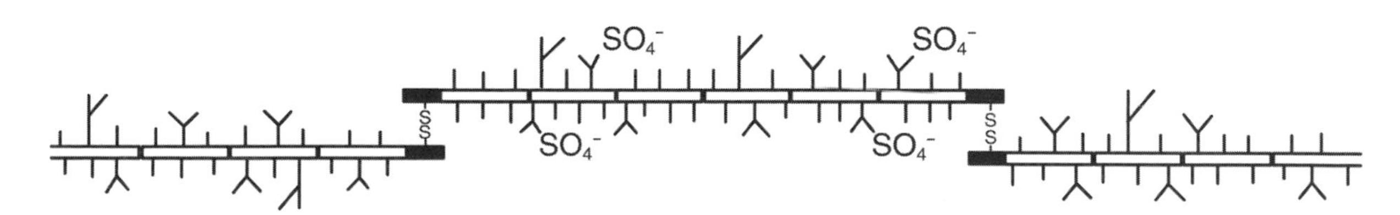

FIGURE 35–4. Structure of a mucin-type glycoprotein. This schematic diagram shows a mucin molecule in the center that is linked to two adjacent mucin molecules by disulfide bonds. Attached to the peptide core of each molecule are multiple sugar side chains of various sizes and branching patterns. The central portion of the peptide core containing tandem repeats of amino acid sequences (*open blocks*) is heavily glycosylated, but the flanking regions (*closed blocks*) are not glycosylated. The nonglycosylated regions contain cysteine residues that allow for disulfide bonds between the ends of adjacent molecules resulting in long cords of mucin molecules.

sites, serine, and threonine.[48,49] A sugar side chain is linked to every third or fourth amino acid in the central portion of the peptide core. The unique sequences for the non-glycosylated terminal regions contain cysteine residues that are thought to link the large mucin molecules through disulfide bonds.[49] These intermolecular disulfide bonds influence the rigidity of the mucous gel.

Synthesis of mucins occurs in stages: first the peptide core is synthesized in the rough endoplasmic reticulum and then sugars are added in a stepwise fashion in the Golgi apparatus. A number of mucin genes that encode the protein core have been identified. At present, nine human mucin genes have been identified and cloned to some degree (Table 35–2).[49–51] For all of these mucin genes, a major portion consists of tandem repeats of variable lengths, encoding peptide sequences of 8 to 169 amino acids. For the presently cloned mucin genes, there is no apparent pattern to the sequence or length of the tandem repeats, except that all are enriched with sequences encoding serine and/or threonine. Human mucin genes expressed in airways include *MUC1*, *MUC2*, *MUC3*, *MUC4*, and *MUC5*; the distribution and extent of expression vary. *MUC1* is a membrane-associated mucin, whereas, the others are secreted. *MUC5* is highly expressed in airways.[52] A number of clones and sequences have been reported for *MUC5*, including *MUC5AC* and *MUC5B*. *MUC4* is expressed fairly equally in the lung, small intestine, colon, stomach, and cervix. *MUC3* is expressed more strongly in the intestine than in the lung. *MUC2* is expressed predominantly in the small intestine and colon, but it may be expressed in diseased airways.[53] One area of active investigation is regulation of mucin gene expression, with particular emphasis on mechanisms by which inflammatory mediators and bacterial products may modulate mucin gene expression.

The first step in glycosylation of the peptide core involves the addition of the first sugar, *N*-acetylgalactosamine, catalyzed by the enzyme mucin peptide αGalNAc transferase that is associated with *cis*-Golgi membranes.[54,55] Each additional sugar is added one-by-one to the growing oligosaccharide chains by a stepwise transfer that is catalyzed by a specific glycosyltransferase.[56] The final structure and length of each oligosaccharide chain is variable, depending on the sequence of additions and specific linkages of the sugars. Some sugar chains are sulfated, specifically the relatively long oligosaccharide chains containing seven or more sugars.[57] Addition of sulfate is catalyzed by sulfotransferase and occurs at the *trans*-Golgi membranes when glycosylation is almost complete.[58] Most of the post-translational modification of mucin molecules occurs in the *trans*-Golgi, where most of the glycosyltransferases and sulfotransferase are located.

Glycosaminoglycans

Glycosaminoglycans (GAGs) are a specific class of glycoconjugates that consist of polyionic polysaccharide chains of variable length. This class of glycoconjugates includes hyaluronic acid, heparan sulfate, keratan sulfate, and chondroitin sulfates A, B, and C.[59] With the exception of keratan sulfate, the polysaccharide chains consist of repeating disaccharide units containing either uronic acid or iduronic acid linked to a hexosamine sugar (GalNAc or GlcNAc). The sugars are sulfated in all GAGs except hyaluronic acid. The negatively charged uronic acids and sulfates are present in high density; consequently, the these large glycoconjugates may interact with mucins and alter the viscoelastic properties of mucus. Early studies of airway secretions did not evaluate glycosaminoglycan or proteoglycan content; however, more recent studies suggest that substantial amounts of these glycoconjugates may be present in airway mucus, particularly in inflamed airways. Hyaluronic acid has been found in asthmatic sputum accounting for 2 to 3% of the dry weight.[60] Hyaluronic acid, chondroitin sulfate, and dermatan sulfate have been identified but not quantitated in airway aspirates from smokers,[61] and chondroitin sulfate has been recovered from sputum samples from patients with chronic bronchitis and cystic fibrosis.[62] The source of GAGs in inflamed airways has not been clearly defined;

TABLE 35–2. Sequences of Tandem Repeats of Cloned Human Mucin Genes

Gene	Sequence of Amino Acids
MUC1	GSTAPPAHGVTSAPDTRPAP (20 aa)
MUC2	PTTTPITTTTTVTPTPTPTGTQT (23 aa)
MUC3	HSTPSFTSSITTTETTS (17 aa)
MUC4	TSSASTGHATPLPVTD (16 aa)
MUC5AC	TTSTTSAP (8 aa)
MUC5B	SSTPGTAHTLTVLTTTATTPTATGSTATP (29 aa)
MUC6	SPFSSTGPMTATSFQTTTTYPTPSHPQTTLPTHVPPFSTSLVTPSTG-TVITPTHAQMATSASIHSTPTGTIPPPTTLKATGSTHTAPPMTPTTS-GTSQAHSSFSTAKTSTSHSHTSSTHHPEVTPTSTTTITPNPTSTGTS-TPVAHTTSATSSRLPTPFTTHSPPTGS (169 aa)
MUC7	TTAAPPTPSATTPAPPSSSAPPE (23 aa)
MUC8	TSCPRPLQEGTPGSRAAHALSRRGHRVHELPTSSPGGDTGF (41 aa)

aa = amino acid; G = glycine; S = serine; T = threonine; A = alanine; P = proline; H = histidine; V = valine; D = aspartic acid; R = arginine; I = isoleucine; Q = glutamine; F = phenylalanine; E = glutamic acid; L = leucine; M = methionine; Y = tyrosine; K = lysine; N = asparagine; C = cysteine.

GAGs may arise from inflammatory cells or from goblet cells and/or submucosal glands. In vitro studies have shown that human and airway mucosa,[63] bovine tracheal serous cells,[64] and canine tracheal epithelial cells[65] release glycoconjugates with proteoglycan characteristics. It is not clear whether these glycoconjugates are released from secretory granules. At least some of the proteoglycans are incorporated into the glycocalyx, coating the surface of epithelial cells, and may be "released" from the surface glycocalyx by protease exposure.[65]

Lipids

Variable amounts of lipids have been identified in airway secretions, particularly in inflamed airways;[40] however, the source has not been defined. In lavaged secretions neutral lipids are most prevalent.[61] These lipids may be bound covalently to mucins.[66] Possible sources of lipids include alveolar surfactant, lipids released or secreted by airway epithelial cells, and lipid components of cell membranes that are shed from disrupted cells.

Lysozyme, Lactoferrin, and Other Factors that Influence Microbe Killing

Several components in airway surface fluid have antimicrobial properties. Lysozyme (muramidase) is a bacteriolytic enzyme that catalyzes the hydrolysis of muramic acid to *N*-acetylglucosamine bonds in bacterial cell walls. Sources of human lung lysozyme include serous cells of submucosal glands, alveolar macrophages, neutrophils, and, to a lesser extent, airway surface epithelial cells.[67–69] In the presence of chronic airway infection and inflammation, concentrations of lysozyme in bronchoalveolar fluid may be seven- to eightfold greater than in normal airways.[70] Lactoferrin, originally isolated from milk, is present in a variety of secretions, including airway secretions. The sources for lung lactoferrin include serous cells of the submucosal glands and activated neutrophils.[71,72] The antimicrobial properties of lactoferrin are attributable to its ability to bind and sequester iron available to iron-dependent bacteria. In addition, lactoferrin has antiviral activity.[73] The concentration of lactoferrin is increased in bronchoalveolar lavage from patients with chronic bronchitis.[70] Defensins are a family of small antimicrobial peptides that have been recovered from a variety of sites within different animal species.[74] One of the defensins, human β defensin 1 (HβD-1), is expressed in airway epithelium from trachea to alveoli;[75] HβD-1 has a broad range of antimicrobial activity against gram-negative organisms, including *Escherichia coli* and *Pseudomonas aeruginosa*.[75]

Airway secretions contain immunoglobulins that play an important role in controlling airway infection. Secretory IgA (sIgA), a complex of secretory component with dimeric IgA, is formed in the airway epithelial cells and secreted into the airway lumen. Immunoglobulin A, synthesized in plasma cells, interacts with an IgA receptor on the basolateral membrane of the airway epithelial cell. This complex is endocytosed, transported to the apical surface in small vesicles, and then discharged as sIgA after proteolytic cleavage of the secretory component. The secretory component protects sIgA from proteinases in airway surface fluid. Approximately 50% of IgA in airway secretions is sIgA.[76] Serum immunoglobulins (IgG and IgA) move across the vascular-airway barrier as transudates. In patients with chronic airway inflammation, the concentration of serum proteins, including immunoglobulins, in airway secretions is increased.[77–79]

Other Proteins

Airway secretions contain a number of other proteins in small concentrations that may influence inflammation or mucus viscosity. Secretory leukocyte proteinase inhibitor is a 12-kD protein that is present in sputum, saliva, and nasal secretions[80] and is thought to arise from serous cells of submucosal glands and Clara cells.[19,68] This small antiproteinase inhibits activity of neutrophil elastase and cathepsin G. The other major antiproteinase in airway secretions is α_1-proteinase inhibitor, a serum protein that moves across the vascular-airway barrier as a transudate. Proline-rich proteins are a family of peptides that are present in airway secretions and are thought to arise from serous cells in submucosal glands.[81] The function of PRPs has not been defined; basic PRPs may interact with acidic mucins and thereby influence mucus viscosity.[82] Clara cell 10-kD protein is found in bronchoalveolar lavage, as well as Clara cells, and is thought to have anti-inflammatory properties based on its ability to inhibit phospholipase A_2.[83,84] Bronchoalveolar lavage fluid also contains surfactant-associated proteins that are thought to interact with surfactant to enhance the low surface tension properties of the alveolar lining fluid. Four surfactant-associated proteins (SP-A, SP-B, SP-C, and SP-D) have been described. While all are synthesized in alveolar type II cells, three (SP-A, SP-B, and SP-C) have been identified in epithelial cells of the nonciliated terminal bronchioles, and one (SP-B) has been identified in gland cells.[85–87] Conceivably, the SPs may interact with the mucus in distal airways and influence adhesiveness of mucus. A number of serum proteins can be detected in airway secretions that filter across the vascular-airway barrier, especially in inflamed airways.[77–79]

Mucus Rheology

Mucus is cleared from the airways by mucociliary clearance and cough. The efficiency of both of these clearance mechanisms depends on the physical properties of the mucous gel, which possesses some of the characteristics of a viscous liquid (eg, molasses) and some of the characteristics of an elastic solid (eg, a rubber band). These viscoelastic or rheologic properties of mucus are determined by the interactions between the large molecules, particularly mucins, in airway secretions. Mucin molecules have polyionic properties attributable to the sulfate and sialic acid moieties in the sugar side chains. Repulsion of negative charges in the adjacent sugar chains is thought to result in the rigid linear structure of mucin molecules.[43,44] Disulfide binding between the nonglycosylated ends of the mucin molecules can result in long chains of rigid mucin molecules. These long chains of highly charged mucin molecules form a tangled network that is thought to be the primary structure of the mucous gel. The polyionic properties of mucin suggest that hydration of this gel should be determined by a Donnan principle in which pH, ionic, and polyionic composition of airway surface fluid are major determinants of mucous gel swelling.[88] Other mucous components may interact with mucins to influence the rigidity and elasticity of mucus. Many of these interactions are nonpermanent and can be rearranged when pressure or force is applied to the mucous gel. When a low-shear force (such as ciliary beat) is applied, these molecular interactions are preserved, and the mucous gel behaves more like an elastic solid. However, when a high shear force (such as a cough) is applied, molecular interactions are disrupted, and the mucous gel behaves more like a viscous liquid.

Measurement of the viscoelastic properties of mucus is complicated, because the mucous gel may be altered or deformed during collection, transport, or analysis resulting in inaccurate measurements. The dynamic nature of mucus viscoelasticity can be measured in a rheometer, in which an oscillatory force is applied to the mucus while monitoring the resultant strain.[89,90] The viscoelastic properties of mucus determine the lag of strain behind stress oscillations. For purely elastic substances there is no lag, but for purely viscous substances the phase lag is 90°. For mucus, the lag phase is between 0° and 90°, and the tangent of the phase lag (tangent δ) is the ratio of viscosity to elasticity. While elasticity remains relatively stable at varying frequencies, viscosity decreases as the frequency of oscillation increases because of the shear forces on the mucous network. Therefore, tangent δ also decreases as the frequency of oscillations increases.

During mucociliary clearance, the mucous gel is subjected to lower shear forces than during cough. King proposes that low shear-rate viscoelastic measurements are more predictive of effects on mucociliary clearance, and high-shear-rate viscoelasity measurements are more predictive of effects on cough clearance.[90] While viscosity and elasticity of the mucous gel influence both mucociliary clearance and cough clearance, the relative importance of these properties for the two clearance mechanisms varies. A low viscosity-to-elasticity ratio (tangent δ) measured at low shear force reflects an elastic gel that is optimal for mucociliary clearance; however, a high viscosity-to-elasticity ratio (tangent δ) at high shear force is optimal for cough clearance. The effects of these physical properties on mucociliary clearance and cough clearance have been assessed in vitro using different models. The mucus-depleted frog palate[91] and the mucus-depleted bovine trachea[92] have been used to assess mucocilary clearance, and a simulated cough machine[93] has been used to assess cough clearance of mucus from different sources and conditions.

Two additional properties of a mucous gel that may influence clearance are adhesiveness and spinability. Mucus adhesiveness is its ability to adhere to the underlying epithelium. Adhesiveness is measured by the force required to separate mucus from a solid surface.[94] These studies demonstrate that mucus adhesiveness is dependent on surface tension, wetability, and hydration.[94–96] Decreased phospholipid content in airway secretions appears to increase surface tension and adhesiveness and thereby impair clearance.[95,96] Mucus spinability is its ability to form a thread when stretched. Measurement of spinability is performed by stretching mucus at a defined rate in a filancemeter until the mucous thread breaks, and then measuring the distance at which the thread breaks.[97] This property is thought to reflect the length of mucin chains; disruption of disulfide bonds in mucin chains with *N*-acetylcysteine decreases spinability.[98] Even though spinability does not correlate with viscoelasticity measures, it does correlate directly with mucociliary clearance[99] and inversely with cough clearance.[100]

Developmental Changes

The secretory function of human airways has not been evaluated during the early stages of development. Mucin gene expression (*MUC4*, *-5AC*, *-5B*, and *-7*) is first detected in human fetal airway tissue in the second trimester.[101] The presence of PAS staining material in the human goblet cells as early as 13 weeks[15] and in the ducts of developing tracheal submucosal glands as early as 16 weeks of gestation[31] further supports the potential for mucin secretion by the second trimester of gestation. At 26 weeks of gestation, the earliest stage studied, explanted human tracheas secrete mucin-type glycoproteins and lysozyme.[102] The rates of baseline and cholinergic-stimulated secretion of mucin-type glycoproteins at 26 to 32 weeks of gestation are similar to those in newborns and children 2 to 6 years old; however, the trend suggests an age-related decrease in the baseline secretory rate (Figure 35–5). The composition of the mucin-type glycoproteins changes little over this time; however, sialic acid and fucose contents increase, and sulfation decreases with age.[103] These changes may alter the charge density and hence the histochemical staining properties as well as the viscoelastic properties of mucus secretions. Unstimulated lysozyme secretion is apparent at 26 to 32 weeks and increases with gestational age (Figure 35–6), but cholin-

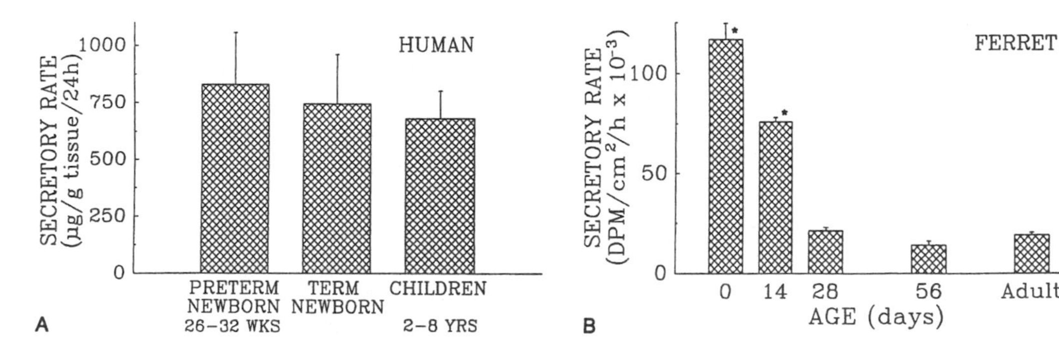

FIGURE 35–5. Age-related changes in tracheal mucin secretion. *A*, Mucin secretory rates (mean + standard error of mean) for human tracheal explants tend to decrease with age, but differences are not significant. (Adapted from Boat TF, Kleinerman JI, Fanaroff AA, Stern RC. Human tracheobronchial secretions: development of mucous glycoprotein and lysozyme secreting systems. Pediatr Res 1977;11:977–80.) *B*, Mucin secretion by ferret tracheal explants decreases with age over the first 28 days of life. *Significant difference compared with adult. (Adapted from Leigh MW et al.[104])

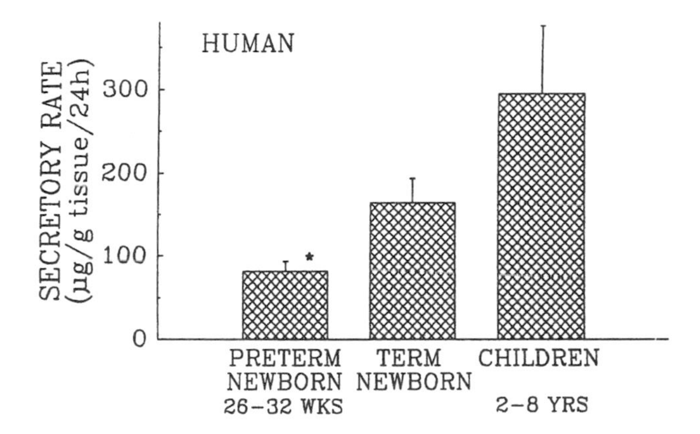

FIGURE 35–6. Age-related changes in tracheal lysozme secretion. Lysozyme secretory rates (mean + standard error of mean) for human tracheal explants increase with age. *Significant difference compared with term newborn. (Adapted from Boat TF et al.[101])

ergic stimulation of lysozyme is not demonstrable until 40 weeks of gestation.[102] The lower output of lysozyme, a bacteriolytic enzyme, may increase the susceptibility of preterm and young infants to bacterial infections of the airways.

Study of the development of airway epithelium and submucosal glands in humans is limited by the scarcity of specimens at many stages of development and the current restrictions on experimental work with fetal tissue. Some reports have shown that the ferret is a useful model for studying developmental changes in secretory structures and their products. Developmental changes in the tracheas of ferrets between birth and 28 days of age are similar to those known to occur in the human between 13 and 20 weeks of gestation.[103] In the first 4 weeks the density of ciliated cells increases from 9 to 54%, the density of secretory cells decreases from 66 to 22%, histochemical staining of the surface epithelial cells changes from predominantly nonacidic to acidic, and submucosal glands develop from intraepithelial buds into complex tubuloacinar structures.[103] The secretory cells in the newborn ferret tracheal epithelium are similar to those in the human fetus at 13 weeks of gestation, and the primordial submucosal glands are similar to those in the human fetus at 12 to 14 weeks of gestation. Newborn ferrets secrete mucin-type glycoproteins at a rate six times greater than that for 28-day-old and adult ferrets (see Figure 35–5). The rate of unstimulated mucin release decreases progressively as the density of secretory cells in the surface epithelium decreases between 0 and 28 days.[104] Stimulation of secretion with cholinergic agonists is not demonstrable until 28 days of age,[104] which suggests that surface epithelial cells are not modulated by these agonists, and that submucosal glands must mature into tubuloacinar structures before their secretion can be regulated. Typical mucin-type glycoproteins (based on their biochemical and physicochemical characteristics) are secreted by ferret tracheal explants at all ages.[105] Mucin amino acid and total carbohydrate contents do not vary with age, but sialic acid[105] content and sulfation[104] increase with age, consistent with the observed changes in histochemical staining. An age-related increase in the activity of sialyltransferase relative to other glycosyltransferases in airway epithelium is consistent with the increased incorporation of sialic acid into mucin.[105]

Pathologic Conditions That Alter Airway Secretions

Airway diseases may involve a number of processes that alter mucus secretions. First, mucus secretions accumulate in disorders that interfere with normal ciliary activity, such as primary ciliary dykinesia, and in acquired conditions such as infection with pertussis or influenza virus.

Second, secretory cells and submucosal glands may secrete increased quantities of mucus in inflammatory conditions, such as acute bacterial or viral infections, exposure to irritants, and asthma. Third, chronic inflammation may lead to goblet cell hyperplasia and submucosal gland hypertrophy, which further increase baseline and stimulated mucus secretion. Fourth, the composition of airway mucus, particularly the content of DNA, glycosaminoglycans, and serum proteins, may be altered in inflammatory condition. Several of these processes are involved in most airway diseases.

Acute Conditions

Infection

Acute tracheobronchitis, generally manifested by increased cough and excessive secretions, is often viral in origin but occasionally results from bacterial infection. The cough and sputum production reflect an outpouring of mucus in response to airway infection and inflammation, as well as ineffective clearance by injured ciliated epithelium.

Hypersecretion in acute tracheobronchitis undoubtedly involves increased release both from secretory cells in the surface epithelium and from glands. In addition, increased amounts of interstitial fluid may move across inflamed mucosa, adding to the volume of surface liquids. Animal studies, such as the early studies of influenza virus infection of ferrets, have demonstrated that respiratory viral infection is associated with depletion of mucous stores in goblet cells of the surface epithelium within several days of inoculation.[106] Neutrophil proteinases and other inflammatory mediators that are increased in infected airways are thought to stimulate secretion by goblet cells and submucosal glands during infection.

Other injurious agents

Human tracheal explants exposed to high concentrations of oxygen release increased amounts of radiolabeled glycoconjugates and lysozyme over the initial 24 to 72 hours.[107] This provides evidence that oxidative stress can act directly and independently of neurohumoral influences on epithelium, to induce a secretory response. Acute exposure of animals to ozone, another oxidant, also increases mucus release.[108] In intact animals, inflammation also plays a role. Specifically, proinflammatory mediators, released by ozone-exposed airway epithelial cells, recruit neutrophils that release elastase, which induces mucus secretion from goblet cells.[109] Hypersecretion has been documented after exposure of animals to noxious agents such as cigarette smoke and SO_2.[110,111] Inflammatory cells and chemokines are thought to mediate mucin secretion following exposure to these agents as well.

Chronic Airway Disease

As a result of a single severe insult, repeated acute insults, or persistent disease, airway remodeling may occur that increases the secretory capability. Three types of changes may occur: goblet cell hyperplasia, goblet cell metaplasia, and submucosal gland hypertrophy. Goblet cell hyperplasia, an increase in the number of goblet cells in the tracheobronchial epithelium (Figure 35–7), is observed in chronic diseases of the airways such as chronic bronchitis, cystic fibrosis, and asthma, as well as after acute insults such as viral infections. One extensively studied animal model of goblet cell hyperplasia is the rat exposed to tobacco smoke.[112] Steroidal and nonsteroidal anti-inflammatory agents can inhibit or totally block cigarette smoke–induced goblet cell hyperplasia.[113,114] In addition, neutrophil-derived proteinases such as cathepsin G and elastase promote goblet cell hyperplasia.[115] Even a single exposure to a large dose of human neutrophil-derived elastase can lead to goblet cell hyperplasia that persists for the life of the animal.[115] These studies suggest that the generation of uninhibited protease activity in the airways in the course of an inflammatory process is a sufficient trigger for goblet cell hyperplasia. It is likely that repeated exposures to proteinases, as in repeated infections or chronic exposure to tobacco smoke, may more effectively induce goblet cell hyperplasia. These same mechanisms are most likely involved in goblet cell metaplasia, the occurrence of goblet cells in areas where they are not typically found, such as in bronchioles.

Submucosal gland hypertrophy also is seen in diseases characterized by chronic inflammation. Submucosal

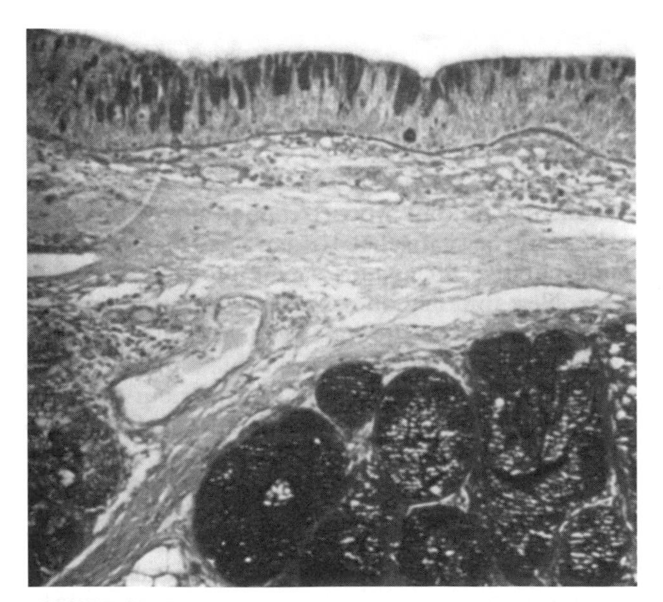

FIGURE 35–7. Goblet cell hyperplasia in airway from an autopsy of a patient who had cystic fibrosis. Note the numerous cells in the surface epithelium that stain dark with Alcian blue–periodic acid–Schiff. The darkly stained structures below the epithelial layer are hypertrophied submucosal glands.

gland size has been assessed semiquantitatively by the Reid index, a ratio of gland thickness to bronchial wall thickness.[116] Enlarged airway submucosal glands (Reid index >0.6) are apparent in chronic diseases such as chronic bronchitis[116] and cystic fibrosis (CF).[117,118] One of the earliest pathologic findings in the lungs of CF patients is gland hypertrophy.[118] However, the size of submucosal glands in newborn infants with CF does not differ from that of matched controls,[119] suggesting that the stimuli that promote gland growth are not present during the fetal period but become activated early in the disease process. Submucosal gland hypertrophy involves not only gland growth but also invasion into the submucosal matrix. Recent studies suggest that metalloproteinases and plasminogen activators degrade extracellular matrix, enabling enlarging glands to invade the submucosal region.[120–122] Gland growth also involves cell proliferation. In hypertrophied CF submucosal glands, the prevalence of proliferating cells is increased compared with that in nonhypertrophied glands from non-CF subjects.[123] Presumably, inflammatory mediators and cytokines influence cell proliferation and expression of the matrix-degrading enzymes to promote gland hypertrophy. These hypertrophied glands contain a larger volume of stored secretory product than do normal glands and therefore secrete more than do normal airways when stimulated.

Asthma

Mucus hypersecretion is a well-recognized pathogenic component of asthma. Widespread mucus plugging of large and small airways is a common pathologic finding in patients dying from status asthmaticus. The chronic inflammation in asthma leads to airway remodeling, including submucosal gland hypertrophy and goblet cell hyperplasia, that increases the secretory potential of asthmatic airways. Numerous inflammatory mediators in asthmatic airways are secretagogues, including histamine, leukotrienes (LC_4, LD_4), PAF, certain prostaglandins ($PGF_{2\alpha}$), and 12- or 15-hydroxyeicosatetraenoic acid (HETE).[23,123–127] More recent studies have shown that interleukin (IL)-9, a T-helper 2 (Th2) lymphocyte cytokine, is increased in allergic asthmatic airway secretions and stimulates *MUC2* and *MUC5AC* transcription and mucin synthesis.[128,129] These studies suggest that IL-9 is a key mediator of the asthmatic response and may be the predominant secretagogue in allergic asthma.[128,129] Analyses of mucus from patients dying from status asthmaticus have shown varying results. While one study identified large amounts of hyaluronic acid but relatively little mucins,[60] another study identified large amounts of mucins and relatively little to no glycosaminoglycans or DNA.[130] Conceivably, these differences may reflect different processes provoking status asthmaticus. For example, status asthmaticus precipitated by exposure to allergens may yield different secretory products than does status asthmaticus precipitated by a respiratory viral infection. Studies to date have not systematically correlated the composition of mucus with clinical data.

Cystic fibrosis

Cystic fibrosis causes a chronic obstructive airway disease characterized by hypertrophy and hyperplasia of the secretory elements, mucus plugging of the airways, and chronic inflammation. These features are similar to the pathologic features seen in asthma and chronic bronchitis. Presumably, similar inflammatory mechanisms mediate these changes. However, in cystic fibrosis there is an enhanced inflammatory response to infection[131,132] that most likely stimulates even greater mucus secretion. In addition, *P. aeruginosa*, the organism that most frequently infects CF airways, releases products that stimulate mucin secretion. *Pseudomonas* elastase stimulates mucin secretion from airway explants,[10] and *P. aeruginosa* lipopolysacchararide upregulates transcription of the mucin gene *MUC 2* in airway epithelial cells.[133] Therefore, multiple mechanisms are stimulating mucin secretion in CF airways chronically infected with *P. aeruginosa.*

Two other characteristic features of cystic fibrosis are the exceptionally viscous sputum and the tendency for chronic infection with *P. aeruginosa* and *Burkholderia cepacia*. These unique characteristics have been the focus for investigation for decades.

ALTERATIONS IN CYSTIC FIBROSIS MUCUS. The exceptionally viscous airway secretions in CF have directed investigators to explore potential CF-related differences in the composition of mucins, hydration of the mucous gel, and presence of other factors in mucus that may increase its rigidity. Early studies suggested a number of compositional differences in CF mucins, including increased fucose content and decreased sialic acid content;[134,135] however, subsequent studies identified no alterations in the fucose and sialic acid content.[136–138] One alteration that has been demonstrated by a variety of approaches is increased sulfation of CF respiratory mucins.[138–142] Studies of expectorated sputum from CF patients demonstrated that the level of mucin sulfation increased with severity of disease,[143] suggesting that chronic infection and inflammation influence sulfation. However, when isolated from inflammatory influences, primary cultures of CF nasal epithelial cells continue to secrete mucins that are more highly sulfated than are those from non-CF nasal cells,[141] suggesting that altered sulfation may result from the basic defect in CF. Further studies are needed to define the mechanism(s) promoting sulfation of mucins in patients with CF. Analysis of sulfated oligosaccharides purified from sputum of a CF patient have identified long branched chains containing an average of 160 to 200 sugar residues; many of these side chains contain varying amounts of a repeating oligosaccharide sequence with sulfate linked to the 6 position of galactose and possibly

N-acetylglucosamine residues.[142–144] Presumably, these long sugar side chains increase the rigidity of the mucin molecule and the gel that incorporates these rigid and highly charged molecules.

Studies of mucus hydration demonstrate that expectorated secretions and bronchoscopic aspirates from CF patients have lower water contents than do those from normal subjects or patients with bronchiectasis (87 to 89% water in CF patients versus 91 to 95% water in bronchiectasis patients and normal subjects).[40,42,143] This relative dehydration could reflect the effects of the basic defect in ion transport (see Chapters 21 and 22).

A third focus has been the influence of chronic infection and inflammation in CF airways on the composition of airway mucus. A number of components, including glycosaminoglycans, proteinases, DNA, and actin have been recovered in higher concentrations from inflamed airways than from uninflamed airways. Each of these components may influence the physical properties of the mucous gel. Several glycosaminoglycans, including hyaluronic acid, chondroitin sulfate, and dermatan sulfate, are more abundant in sputum from patients with chronic bronchitis and CF.[60–62] These highly charged macromolecules can form gels and, therefore, most likely influence the physical properties of the mucous gel. Actin and DNA are thought to have a substantial influence on the physical properties of CF mucus. Purulent airway secretions from CF patients contain high concentrations of DNA thought to arise from degenerating polymorphonuclear neutrophils.[145,146] Large polymerized polyanionic DNA molecules interact with polyionic mucin molecules and increase the viscosity of the mucous gel (Figure 35–8). Enzymatic depolymerization of DNA by deoxyribonuclease (DNase) I reduces the viscosity of purulent CF sputum.[147] A specific interaction between CF mucins and DNA has been suggested by studies showing a marked increase in viscosity and elasticity following addition of DNA to purified CF mucins, but no change in rheologic properties following addition of DNA to purified mucins from patients with bronchitis.[148] In addition to DNA, purulent CF sputum contains a large amount of actin that is thought to arise from degenerating neutrophils.[149] Filamentous actin forms long protease-resistant filaments that become entangled in the mucous gel (see Figure 35–8), adding rigidity to the gel; severing actin filaments by addition of gelsolin reduces viscosity of CF sputum.[149]

Predisposition to Infection with Pseudomonas aeruginosa and Burkholderia cepacia. In CF, chronic colonization of airways with *P. aeruginosa* led to speculation that this bacteria may bind more avidly to CF epithelial cells and/or CF mucus than to normal cells or mucus. Several studies have demonstrated that *Pseudomonas* organisms bind more avidly to CF airway cells than to normal airway cells and that this binding is more apparent with certain genotypes such as ΔF508.[150,151] The *Pseudomonas* component important for binding to epithelial cells is pilin.[152] Recent studies have shown that the specific pilin receptor for *Pseudomonas* binding on epithelial cells, asialoGM1 (a ganglioside component of the cell membrane containing the sugar sequence GalNAcβ1-4Gal), is more prevalent on CF cells than on normal airway cells.[153] Despite this evidence of enhanced *Pseudomonas* binding to epithelial cells, most pathologic sections of CF airways demonstrate *Pseudomonas* organisms within the mucus in the airway lumen instead of attached to the epithelial

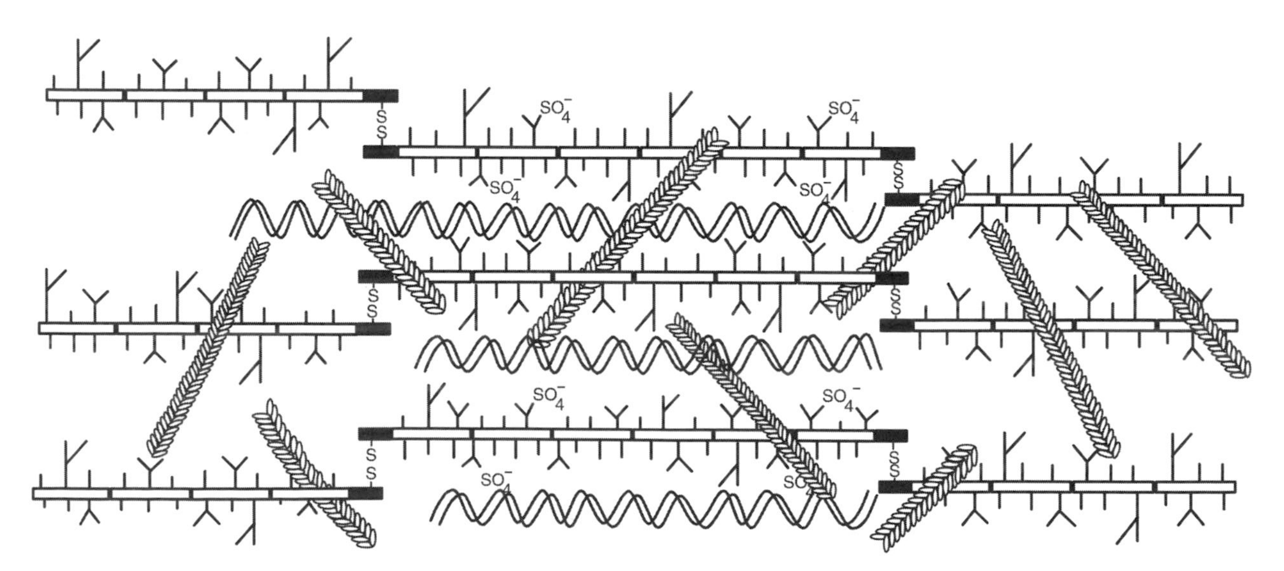

FIGURE 35–8. Postulated structure of purulent airway mucus containing mucin, DNA, and actin. Mucin molecules are shown in the same configuration as in Figure 35–4. Actin (*long strands of leaflets*) and DNA (*double helix*) are present in purulent airway secretions. Both DNA and mucin are large rigid polyionic molecules; presumably, ionic forces influence orientation of DNA molecules within the mucin gel. Filamentous actin can form large rigid filaments; presumably, these filaments become entangled in the mucous gel in a random orientation.

surface.[154] This localization suggests that binding of these bacteria to mucins or other components within the mucous gel limits their access to the epithelial surface. Using different approaches, a number of studies have suggested that *P. aeruginosa* organisms bind more avidly to CF mucins than to normal mucins.[155–158] However, the link between increased binding and alteration in carbohydrate structure of CF mucins has not been identified. Studies of *Pseudomonas* binding to mucins suggest that pilin is not involved.[159,160] Several strains of *P. aeruginosa* bind to respiratory and intestinal mucins by a process that is nonspecific (ie, lacking a specific ligand-receptor interaction).[161,162] A related organism, *B. cepacia* (previously known as *P. cepacia*) binds specifically to mucins[163] by *B. cepacia* mucin–binding adhesin.[164]

Chronic infection of CF airways with *P. aeruginosa* has led to investigation of antimicrobial pathways that may be altered in CF. Airway secretions contain a number of antimicrobial factors, including lysozyme, lactoferrin, and defensins. Levels of lysozyme and lactoferrin are increased in lower airway secretions from patients with chronic obstructive lung diseases including CF.[165–167] Lysozyme, bactericidal for a number of bacterial pathogens in the lung, does not appear to be bactericidal for mucoid and nonmucoid strains of *P. aeruginosa* or *Staphylococcus aureus*.[168] Lactoferrin appears to be hydrolyzed by *Pseudomonas* elastase and/or neutrophil elastase and may therefore have limited activity in chronically infected CF airways.[169] Recent studies suggest that normal and CF epithelial cells secrete other antimicrobial peptides (defensins) that are capable of killing *P. aeruginosa* at low salt concentrations.[170] The recently identified HβD-1 is salt sensitive and is inactivated in CF.[75] These observations provide a potential link between the CF basic defect in ion transport and colonization of airways with *P. aeruginosa*.

Summary and Therapeutic Implications

Airway mucus forms a protective barrier lining for the respiratory tract. The major component of mucus is mucin that is secreted by goblet cells and submucosal glands. At birth goblet cells and submucosal glands are present. Infectious and inflammatory stimuli promote goblet cell hyperplasia, submucosal gland hypertrophy, and hypersecretion of mucus. This hypersecretion is especially prominent in CF, a disease characterized by exaggerated inflammatory response to infection and by chronic infection with *P. aeruginosa*, an organism that releases secretagogues. Excess mucus can cause airway obstruction and predispose patients to respiratory tract infections. The viscoelastic properties of mucus influence its clearability by mucociliary apparatus and cough. Increased concentrations of DNA and fibrillar actin in inflamed airways increase the rigidity of the mucous gel and thereby limit its clearance.

Therapeutic strategies employed to treat disorders characterized by excessive and/or thickened airway secretions include agents to control hypersecretion and agents to disrupt the mucous gel, as well as physical approaches to clear secretions. Agents used to control hypersecretion include anti-inflammatory agents, antibiotics, and anticholinergic agents. Anti-inflammatory agents are used in asthma, CF and other disorders in which excessive inflammation provokes mucus hypersecretion. Use of agents such as corticosteroids and high-dose ibuprofen requires careful attention to the balance of benefits and side effects. Antimicrobial agents are used in CF, bronchiectasis, bronchitis, and other disorders in which chronic infection provokes inflammation and mucus hypersecretion. Use of antimicrobials requires careful attention to the balance of benefits and the potential for selecting organisms that are resistant to usual antibiotics. Atropine and ipratropium may be used to inhibit vagal stimulation of submucosal gland secretion. Other agents presently under investigation in CF are proteinase inhibitors that may block proteinase-stimulated secretion. Mucolytic agents are used to "thin" mucus. The reducing substance, *N*-acetylcysteine, disrupts disulfide bonds that tether mucin molecules in a network and has been used to help clear mucous plugs. However, *N*-acetylcysteine can be irritating to the airways because of the marked hyperosmolarity of formulated preparations. Human recombinant DNase has been used to break down large DNA macromolecules that add rigidity to the mucous gel. Another agent under investigation is gelsolin that severs noncovalent bonds between monomers within actin filaments. Physical approaches to clear secretions include percussion and postural drainage, as well as devices to transmit vibratory forces to airways where these forces can alter the viscoelastic properties of the mucous gel.

References

1. Davis B, Phipps RJ, Nadel JA. A new method for studying tracheal secretion in vitro effect of adrenergic agonists in cats. Chest 1979;75 Suppl:224–5.
2. Ueki I, German VF, Nadel JA. Micropipette measurement of airway submucosal gland secretion. Autonomic effects. Am Rev Respir Dis 1980;121:351–7.
3. Sherman JM, Cheng PW, Tandler B, Boat TF. Mucous glycoproteins from cat tracheal goblet cells and mucous glands separated by EDTA. Am Rev Respir Dis 1981; 124:476–9.
4. Rhodin JA. The ciliated cell. Ultrastructure and function in human tracheal mucosa. Am Rev Respir Dis 1966;93 Suppl:1–15.
5. Ellefsen P, Tos M. Goblet cells in human trachea: quantitative studies of a pathological biopsy material. Arch Otolarygol 1972;95:547–55.
6. Spicer SS, Schulte BA, Chakrin LW. Ultrastructural and histochemical observations of respiratory epithelium and glands. Exp Lung Res 1983;4:137–56.

7. Kim KC, Lee BC. P2 purinoceptor regulation of mucin release by airway goblet cells in primary culture. Br J Pharmacol 1991;103:1053–6.
8. Davis CW, Dowell ML, Lethem M, et al. Goblet cell degranulation in isolated canine tracheal epithelium: response to exogenous ATP, ADP and adenosine. Am J Physiol 1992;262:C1313–23.
9. Kim KC, Nassiri J, Brody JS. Mechanisms of airway goblet cell mucin release; studies with cultured tracheal surface epithelial cells. Am J Respir Cell Mol Biol 1989;1:137–43.
10. Klinger JD, Tandler B, Liedke CM, et al. Proteinases of *Pseudomonas aeruginosa* evoke mucin release by tracheal epithelium. J Clin Invest 1984;74:1669–78.
11. Rieves RD, Goff J, Wu T, et al. Airway epithelial cell mucin release: immunologic quantitation and response to platelet-activating factor. Am J Respir Cell Mol Biol 1992;6:158–67.
12. Boat TF, Polony I, Cheng PW. Mucin release from rabbit tracheal epithelium in response to sera from normal and cystic fibrosis subjects. Pediatr Res 1982;16:792–7.
13. Kuo HP, Rohde JA, Barnes PJ, et al. Cigarette smoke-induced airway goblet cell secretion: dose dependent differential nerve activation. Am J Physiol 1992;263: L161–7.
14. Jeffery PK, Reid L. Ultrastructure of airway epithelium and submucosal gland during development. In: Hodson WA, ed. Development of the lung. New York: Marcel Dekker, 1977; 87–134.
15. DeHaller R. Development of the mucus-secreting elements in the human lung. In: Emery J, ed. The anatomy of the developing lung. London: Heinemann Medical Books, 1969:94–115.
16. Gaillard DA, Lallement AV, Petit AF, Puchelle ES. In vivo ciliogenesis in human fetal tracheal epithelium. Am J Anat 1989;185:415–28.
17. Meyrick B, Sturgess JM, Reid L. A reconstruction of the duct system and secretory tubules of the human bronchial submucosal gland. Thorax 1969;24:729–36.
18. Meyrick B, Reid L. Ultrastructure of cells in human bronchial submucosal glands. J Anat 1970;107:281–99.
19. Basbaum CB, Jany B, Finkbeiner WE. The serous cell. Annu Rev Physiol 1990;52:97–113.
20. Shimura S, Sasaki T, Sasaki H, et al. Contractility of isolated single submucosal gland from trachea. J Appl Physiol 1986;60:1237–47.
21. Chakrin LW, Baker AP, Christian P, et al. Effect of cholinergic stimulation on the release of macromolecules by canine trachea, in vitro. Am Rev Respir Dis 1973;108:69–76.
22. Boat TF, Kleinerman JI. Human respiratory tract secretions. 2. Effect of cholinergic and adrenergic agents on in vitro release of protein and mucous glycoprotein. Chest 1975;67:32–4S.
23. Shelhamer JH, Marom Z, Kaliner M. Immunologic and neuropharmacologic stimulation of mucous glycoprotein release from human airways in vitro. J Clin Invest 1980;66:1400–8.
24. Laitinen A, Partanen M, Hervonen A, et al. Electron microscopic study on the innervation of the human lower respiratory tract. Evidence of adrenergic nerves. Eur J Respir Dis 1985;67:209–15.
25. Laitinen A, Partanen M, Hervonen A, et al. VIP-like immunoreactive nerves in human respiratory tract. Light and electron microscopic study. Histochemistry 1985;82:313–9.
26. Coles SJ, Bhaskar KR, O'Sullivan DD, et al. Airway mucus: composition and regulation of its secretion by neuropeptides in vitro. In: Ciba Foundation Symposium 109. Mucus and mucosa. London: Pitman, 1984:40–60.
27. Sommerhoff CP, Nadel JA, Basbaum CB, Caughey GH. Neutrophil elastase and cathepsin G stimulate secretion from cultured bovine airway gland serous cells. Exp Lung Res 1990;13:25–43.
28. Schuster A, Ueki I, Nadel JA. Neutrophil elastase stimulates tracheal submucosal gland secretion that is inhibited by ICI 200,355. Am J Physiol 1992;262:L86–91.
29. Bucher U, Reid L. Development of the intrasegmental bronchial tree: the pattern of branching and development of cartilage at the various stages of intrauterine life. Thorax 1961;16:207–18.
30. Tos M. Development of the tracheal glands in man. Acta Pathol Microbiol Scand 1966;68 Suppl 185:1–130.
31. Thurlbeck WM, Benjamin B, Reid L. Development and distribution of mucous glands in the foetal human trachea. Br J Dis Chest 1961;55:54–64.
32. Plopper CG, Hill LH, Mariassy AT, et al. Ultrastructure of the non-ciliated bronchiolar epithelial (Clara) cell of mammalian lung. A study of man with comparison of 15 mammalian species. Exp Lung Res 1980;1:171–80.
33. Singh G, Katyal SL, Wong-Chong ML. A quantitative assay for a Clara cell-specific protein and its application in the study of development of pulmonary airways in the rat. Pediatr Res 1986;20:802–5.
34. Mantile G, Miele L, Cordella-Miele E, et al. Human Clara cell 10-kDa protein is the counterpart of rabbit uteroglobin. J Biol Chem 1993;268:20343–51.
35. Miele L, Cordella-Miele E, Mukherjee AB. Uteroglobin: structure, molecular biology, and new perspectives on its function as a phospholipase A2 inhibitor. Endocr Rev 1987;8:474–90.
36. De Water R, Willems LNA, VanMuijen GN, et al. Ultrastructural localization of bronchial antileukoprotease in central and peripheral human airways by a gold-labeling technique using monoclonal antibodies. Am Rev Respir Dis 1986;33:882–90.
37. Farmer SG, Hay DWP. Airway epithelial modulation of smooth-muscle function. The evidence for epithelium-derived inhibitory factor. In: Farmer SG, Hay DWP, eds. The airway epithelium. New York: Marcel Dekker, 1991: 437–83.
38. Sasaki T, Shimura S, Sasaki H, et al. Effect of epithelium on mucus secretion from feline tracheal submucosal glands. J Appl Physiol1989;66:764–70.
39. Toremaln NG. The daily amount of tracheobronchial secretions in man, a method for continuous tracheal aspiration in laryngectomized and tracheostomized patients. Acta Otolaryngol (Stockh) 1960;158 Suppl:43–53.
40. Matthews LM, Spector S, Lemm J, et al. Studies on pulmonary secretion. Am Rev Respir Dis 1963;88:199–204.
41. Boucher RC. Human airway ion transport: part one. Am J Respir Crit Care Med 1994;150:271–81.

42. Boucher RC. Human airway ion transport: part two. Am J Respir Crit Care Med 1994;150:581–93.
43. Lamblin G, Lhermitle M, Degand P, et al. Chemical and physical properties of human bronchial mucous glycoproteins. Biochimie 1979;61:23–43.
44. Rose MC, Voter WA, Brown CF, et al. Structural features of human tracheobronchial mucus glycoprotein. Biochem J 1984;222:371–7.
45. Boat TF, Cheng P-W. Biochemistry of airway mucus secretions. Fed Proc 1980;39:3067–74.
46. Lamblin G, Aubert J-P, Perini JM, et al. Human respiratory mucins. Eur Respir J 1992;5:247–56.
47. Roussel P, Lamblin G, Lhermitte M, et al. The complexity of mucins. Biochimie 1988;70:1471–82.
48. Aubert JP, Porchet N, Crepin M, et al. Evidence for different human tracheobronchial mucin peptides deduced from nucleotide cDNA sequences. Am J Respir Cell Mol Biol 1991;5:178–85.
49. Gum JR. Mucin genes and the proteins they encode: structure, diversity, and regulation. Am J Respir Cell Mol Biol 1992;7:557–64.
50. Gendler SJ, Spicer AP. Epithelial mucin genes. Annu Rev Physiol 1995;57:607–34.
51. Shankar V, Gilmore MS, Elkins RC, Sachdev GP. A novel human mucin cDNA encodes a protein with unique tandem repeat organization. Biochem J 1994;300:295–8.
52. Voynow JA, Rose MC. Quantitation of mucin mRNA in respiratory and intestinal epithelial cells. Am J Respir Cell Mol Biol 1994;11:742–50.
53. Jany BH, Gallup MW, Yan P-S, et al. Human bronchus and intestine express the same mucin gene. J Clin Invest 1991;87:77–82.
54. Roth J. Cytochemical localization of terminal *N*-acetyl-D-galactosamine residues in cellular compartments of intestinal goblet cells: implications for the topology of *O*-glycosylation. J Cell Biol 1984;98:399–406.
55. Abeijon C, Hirschberg CB. Subcellular site of synthesis of the *N*-acetylgalactosamine (a1-0) serine (or threonine) linkage in rat liver. J Biol Chem 1987;262:4153–9.
56. Schachter H. In: Horowitz MI, Pigman W, eds. The glycoconjugates. Vol. III. New York: Academic Press, 1978:87–181.
57. Roussel P, Lamblin G, Degand P, et al. Heterogeneity of the carbohydrate chains of sulfated bronchial glycoproteins isolated from a patient suffering from cystic fibrosis. J Biol Chem 1975;250:2114–22.
58. Hirschberg CB, Snider MD. Topography of glycosylation in the rough endoplasmic reticulum and Golgi apparatus. Ann Rev Biochem 1987;56:63–87.
59. Hascall VC. Proteoglycans: structure and function. In: Ginsburg V, Robbin P, eds. Biology of carbohydrates. Vol. 1. New York: Wiley, 1981:1–49.
60. Sahu S, Lynn WS. Hyaluronic acid in the pulmonary secretions of patients with asthma. Biochem J 1978;173:565–8.
61. Bhaskar KR, O'Sullivan DD, Seltzer J, et al. Density gradient study of bronchial mucus aspirates from healthy volunteers (smokers and nonsmokers) and from patients with tracheostomy. Exp Lung Res 1985;9:289–308.
62. Rahmoune H, Lamblin G, Lafitte J, et al. Chondroitin sulfate in sputum from patients with cystic fibrosis and chronic bronchitis. Am J Respir Cell Mol Biol 1991;5:315–20.
63. Bhaskar KR, O'Sullivan DD, Opaskar-Hincman H, et al. Density gradient analysis of secretions produced in vitro by human and canine airway mucosa: identification of lipids and proteoglycans in such secretions. Exp Lung Res 1986;10:401–22.
64. Paul A, Picard J, Mergey D, et al. Glycoconjugates secreted by bovine tracheal serous cells in culture. Arch Biochem Biophys 1988;260:75–84.
65. Varsano S, Basbaum CB, Forsberg LS, et al. Dog tracheal epithelial cells in culture synthesize sulfated macromolecular glycoconjugates and release them from the cell surface upon exposure to extracellular proteases. Exp Lung Res 1987;13:157–84.
66. Slomiany A, Slomiany BL, Witas H, et al. Isolation of fatty acids covalently bound to the gastric mucus glycoprotein of normal and cystic fibrosis patients. Biochem Biophys Res Commun 1983;113:286–93.
67. Spicer SS, Frayser R, Virella G, Hall BJ. Immunocytochemical localization of lysozymes in respiratory and other tissues. Lab Invest 1977;36:282–95.
68. Konstan MW, Cheng PW, Sherman JM, et al. Human lung lysozyme: sources and properties. Am Rev Respir Dis 1981;123:120–4.
69. Franken C, Meijer CJLM, Dijkman JH. Tissue distribution of antileukoprotease and lysozyme in humans. J Histochem Cytochem 1989;37:493–8.
70. Thompson AB, Bohling T, Payvandi F, Rennard SI. Lower respiratory tract lactoferrin and lysozyme arise primarily in airways and are elevated in association with chronic bronchitis. J Lab Clin Med 1990;115:148–58.
71. Bowes D, Clark AE, Corrin B. Ultrastructural localization of lactoferrin and glycoprotein in human bronchial glands. Thorax 1981;36:108–11.
72. Briggs RC, Glass WF, Montiel MM, Hnilica LS. Lactoferrin: nuclear localization in the human neutrophilic granulocyte. J Histochem Cytochem 1981;29:1128–36.
73. Harmsen MC, Swart PJ, de Bethune MP, et al. Antiviral effects of plasma and milk proteins: lactoferrin shows potent activity against both human immunodeficiency virus and human cytomegalovirus replication in vitro. J Infect Dis 1995;172:380–8.
74. Ganz T, Lehrer RI. Defensins. Pharmacol Ther 1995; 66:191–205.
75. Goldman MJ, Anderson GM, Stolzenberg ED, et al. Human β-defensin-1 is a salt-sensitive antibiotic in lung that is inactivated in cystic fibrosis. Cell 1997;88:553–60.
76. Stockley RA, Afford SC, Burnette D. Assessment of 7S and 11S immunoglobulin A in sputum. Am Rev Respir Dis 1980;22:959–64.
77. Brogan TD, Ryley HC, Neale L, Yassa J. Soluble proteins of bronchopulmonary secretions from patients with cystic fibrosis, asthma and bronchitis. Thorax 1975;36:72–9.
78. Stockley RA, Mistry M, Bradwell AR, Burnette D. A study of plasma proteins in the sol phase of sputum from patients with chronic bronchitis. Thorax 1979;34: 777–82.
79. Stockley RA. Measurement of soluble proteins in lung secretions. Thorax 1984;39:241–7.
80. Kramps JA, Franken C, Dijkman JH. ELISA for quantitative measurement of low molecular weight bronchial

protease inhibitor in human sputum. Am Rev Respir Dis 1984;129:959–63.
81. Warner TF, Azen EA. Proline-rich proteins are present in serous cells of submucosal glands in the respiratory tract. Am Rev Respir Dis 1984;130:115–8.
82. Bailleul V, Richet C, Hayem A, Degand P. Properties rheologiques des secretions bronchiques: mise en evidence et role de polypeptides riches en proline (PRP). Clin Chim Acta 1977;74:115–23.
83. Singh G, Katyal SL. Pulmonary proteins as cell-specific markers. Exp Lung Res 1991;17:245–53.
84. Bedetti CD, Singh J, Singh G, et al. Ultrastructural localization of rat Clara cell 10 kD secretory protein by immuno-gold technique using polyclonal and monoclonal antibodies. J Histochem Cytochem 1987;35:789–94.
85. Phelps DS, Floros J. Localization of surfactant synthesis in human lung by in situ hybridization. Am Rev Respir Dis 1988;137:939–42.
86. Khoor A, Gray ME, Hull WM, et al. Developmental expression of SP-A and SP-A mRNA in the proximal and distal respiratory epithelium in the human fetus and newborn. J Histochem Cytochem 1993;41:1311–9.
87. Khoor A, Stahlman MT, Gray ME, Whitsett JA. Temporal-spatial distribution of SP-B and SP-C proteins and mRNAs in developing respiratory epithelium of human lung. J Histochem Cytochem 1994;42:1187–99.
88. Tam PY, Verdugo P. Control of mucus hydration as a Donnan equilibrium process. Nature 1981;292:340–2.
89. King M. Magnetic microrheometer. In: Braga PC, Allegra L, eds. Methods in bronchial mucology. New York: Raven Press, 1988:73–83.
90. King M. Role of mucus viscoelasticity in cough clearance. Biorheology 1987;24:589–97.
91. Rubin BK, Ramirez O, King M. The mucus depleted frog palate as a model for the study of mucociliary clearance. J Appl Physiol 1990;69:424–9.
92. Wills PJ, Garcia Suarez MJ, Rutman A, et al. The ciliary transportability of sputum is slow on the mucus-depleted bovine trachea. Am J Respir Crit Care Med 1995;151:1255–8.
93. Agarwal M, King M, Rubin BK, Shulka JB. Mucus transport in a miniaturized simulated cough machine: effect of constriction and serous layer simulant. Biorheology 1989;26:977–88.
94. Rubin BK, Ramirez O, King M. The role of mucus rheology and transport in neonatal respiratory distress syndrome and the effect of surfactant therapy. Chest 1992;101: 1080–5.
95. Girod S, Galabert C, Pierrot D, et al. Role of phospholipid lining on respiratory mucus clearance by cough. J Appl Physiol 1991;71:2262–6.
96. Girod S, Galabert C, Lecuirre A, et al. Phospholipid composition and surface-active properties of tracheobronchial secretions from patients with cystic fibrosis and chronic obstructive pulmonary diseases. Pediatr Pulmonol 1992;13:22–7.
97. Zahm JM, Puchelle E, Duvivier C, Didelon J. Spinability of respiratory mucus. Validation of a new apparatus: the Filancemeter. Bull Eur Physiopathol Respir 1986;22: 609–13.
98. Dasgupta B, King M. Reduction in viscoelasticity in cystic fibrosis sputum in vitro using combined treatment with nacystelyn and rhDNase. Pediatr Pulmonol 1996; 22:161–6.
99. Puchelle E, Zahm JM, Duvivier C. Spinability of bronchial mucus: relationship with viscoelasticity and mucus transport properties. Biorheology 1987;20:239–49.
100. King M, Zahm JM, Pierrot D, et al. The role of mucus gel viscosity, spinability, and adhesive properties in clearance by simulated cough. Biorheology 1989;26:737–45.
101. Boat TF, Kleinerman JI, Fanaroff AA, Stern RC. Human tracheobronchial secretions: development of mucous glycoprotein and lysozyme secreting systems. Pediatr Res 1977;11:977–80.
102. Reid CJ, Gould S, Harris A. Developmental expression of mucin genes in the human respiratory tract. Am J Respir Cell Mol Biol 1997;17:592–8.
103. Leigh MW, Gambling TM, Carson JL, et al. Postnatal development of tracheal surface epithelium and submucosal glands in the ferret. Exp Lung Res 1986;10:153–69.
104. Leigh MW, Cheng PW, Carson JL, Boat TF. Developmental changes in glycoconjugate secretion by ferret tracheas. Am Rev Respir Dis 1986;134:784–90.
105. Leigh MW, Cheng PW, Boat TF. Developmental changes of ferret tracheal mucin composition and biosynthesis. Biochemistry 1989;28:9440–6.
106. Francis T, Stuart-Harris CH. Studies on nasal histology of epidemic influenza virus infection in the ferret: the development and repair of the nasal lesion. J Exp Med 1938;68:789–802.
107. Boat TF, Kleinerman JI, Fanaroff AA, Matthews LW. Toxic effects of oxygen on cultured human neonatal respiratory epithelium. Pediatr Res 1973;7:607–15.
108. Phipps RJ, Denas SM, Sielczak MW, Wanner A. Effects of 0.5 ppm ozone on glycoprotein secretion, ion and water fluxes in sheep trachea. J Appl Physiol 1986;60:918–27.
109. Leikauf GD, Simpson LG, Santrock J, et al. Airway epithelial responses to ozone injury. Environ Health Perspect 1995;103(Suppl 2):91–5.
110. King M, Wight A, DeSanctis GT, et al. Mucus hypersecretion and viscoelasticity changes in cigarette-smoking dogs. Exp Lung Res 1989;15:375–89.
111. Miller ML, Andringa A, Rafales L, Vinegar A. Effect of exposure to 500 ppm sulfur dioxide on the lungs of the ferret. Respiration 1985;48:346–54.
112. Lamb D, Reid L. Goblet cell increase in rat bronchial epithelium after exposure to cigarette and cigar smoke. Br Med J 1969;1:33–5.
113. Greig N, Ayers M, Jeffrey PK. The effect of indomethacin on the response of the bronchial epithelium to tobacco smoke. J Pathol 1980;132:1–9.
114. Rogers DF, Jeffrey PK. Inhibition of cigarette smoke-induced airway secretory cell hyperplasia by indomethacin, dexamethasone, prednisolone, or hydrocortisone in the rat. Exp Lung Res 1986;10:285–98.
115. Lucey EC, Stone PJ, Breuer R, et al. Effect of combined human neutrophil cathepsin G and elastase on induction of secretory cell metaplasia and emphysema in hamsters with in vitro observations on elastolysis by these enzymes. Am Rev Respir Dis 1985;132:362–6.

116. Reid L. Measurement of the bronchial mucous gland layer: a diagnostic yardstick in chronic bronchitis. Thorax 1960;15:132–41.
117. Bedrossian CW, Greenberg SD, Singer DB, et al. The lung in cystic fibrosis. A quantitative study including prevalence of pathologic findings among different age groups. Hum Pathol 1976;7:195–204.
118. Lamb L, Reid L. The tracheobronchial submucosal glands in cystic fibrosis: a qualitative and quantitative histochemical study. Br J Dis Chest 1972;66:239–43.
119. Chow CW, Landau LI, Taussig LM. Bronchial mucous glands in the newborn with cystic fibrosis. Eur J Pediatr 1982;139:240–3.
120. Infeld MD, Brennan JA, Davis PB. Human fetal lung fibroblasts promote invasion of the extracellular matrix by normal human tracheobronchial epithelial cells in vitro: a model of early airway gland development. Am J Respir Cell Mol Biol 1993;8:69–78.
121. Tournier JM, Polette M, Hinnrasky J, et al. Expression of gelatinase A, a mediator of extracellular matrix remodeling, by tracheal gland serous cells in culture and in vivo. J Biol Chem 1994;269:25454–64.
122. Lim M, Elfman F, Dohrman A, et al. Upregulation of the 72-kDa type IV collagenase in epithelial and stromal cells during rat tracheal gland morphogenesis. Dev Biol 1995;171:521–30.
123. Leigh MW, Kylander J, Yankaskas JR, Boucher RC. Cell proliferation in bronchial epithelium and submucosal glands of cystic fibrosis patients. Am J Respir Cell Mol Biol 1995;12:605–12.
124. Marom Z, Shelhamer JH, Kaliner M. Effects of arachidonic acid, monohydroxyeicosatetraenoic acid and prostaglandins on release of mucous glycoproteins from human airways in vitro. J Clin Invest 1981; 67:1695–702.
125. Marom Z, Shelhamer JH, Bach MK, et al. Slow-reacting substances, leukotrienes C_4 and D_4 increase release of mucus from airways in vitro. Am Rev Respir Dis 1982; 126:449–51.
126. Marom Z, Shelhamer JH, Sun F, et al. Human airway monohydroxyeicosatetraenoic acid generation and mucus release. J Clin Invest 1983;72:122–7.
127. Steiger J, Bray MA, Subramanian N. Platelet activating factor (PAF) is a potent stimulator of porcine tracheal fluid secretion in vitro. Eur J Pharmacol 1987;142:367–72.
128. Longphre M, Li D, Gallup M, et al. Allergen-induced IL-9 directly stimulates mucin transcription in respiratory epithelial cells. J Clin Invest 1999;104:1375–82.
129. Louahed J, Toda M, Jen J, et al. Interleukin-9 upregulates mucus expression in the airways. Am J Respir Cell Mol Biol 2000;22:649–56.
130. Sheehan JK, Richardson PS, Fung DC, et al. Analysis of respiratory mucus glycoproteins in asthma: a detailed study from a patient who died in status asthmaticus. Am J Respir Cell Mol Biol 1995;13:748–56.
131. Cantin A. Cystic fibrosis lung inflammation: early, sustained and severe. Am J Respir Crit Care Med 1995; 151:939–41.
132. Muhlebach MS, Stewart PW, Leigh MW, Noah TL. Quantitation of inflammatory responses to bacteria in young cystic fibrosis and control patients. Am J Respir Crit Care Med 1999;160:186–91.
133. Li JD, Dohrman AF, Gallup M, et al. Transcriptional activation of mucin by *Pseudomonas aeruginosa* lipopolysaccharide in the pathogenesis of cystic fibrosis lung disease. Proc Natl Acad Sci U S A 1997;94:967–72.
134. Dische Z, di Sant'Agnese P, Pallavicini C, et al. Composition of mucoprotein fractions from duodenal fluid of patients with cystic fibrosis of the pancreas and from controls. Pediatrics 1959;24:74–91.
135. Chernick WS, Barbero GJ. Studies on human tracheobronchial and submaxillary secretions in normal and pathophysiological conditions. Ann NY Acad Sci 1963;106:755–6.
136. Menguy R, Masters VF, Desbaillets L. Salivary mucins of patients with cystic fibrosis: composition and susceptibility to degradation by salivary glycosidases. Gastroenterology 1970;59:257–64.
137. Boat TF, Cheng PW, Wood RE, et al. Tracheobronchial mucus secretion in vivo and in vitro by epithelial tissues from cycstic fibrosis and control subjects. Mod Probl Paediatr 1977;19:141–52.
138. Boat TF, Cheng PW, Iyer R, et al. Human respiratory tract secretions: mucous glycoproteins of nonpurulent tracheobronchial secretions and sputum of patients with bronchitis and cystic fibrosis. Arch Biochem Biophys 1976;177:95–104.
139. Boat TF, Kleinerman JI, Carlson DM, et al. Human respiratory tract secretions: mucous glycoproteins secreted by cultured nasal polyp epithelium from subjects with allergic rhinitis and with cystic fibrosis. Am Rev Respir Dis 1974;110:428–41.
140. Frates RC, Kaizu T, Last JA. Mucus glycoproteins secreted by respiratory epithelial tissue from cystic fibrosis patients. Pediatr Res 1983;17:30–4.
141. Cheng P-W, Boat TF, Cranfill K, et al. Increased sulfation of glycoconjugates by cultured nasal epithelial cells from patients with cystic fibrosis. J Clin Invest 1989;84:68–72.
142. Mendicino J, Sangadala S. Synthesis of sulfated oligosaccharides by cystic fibrosis tracheal epithelial cells. Mol Cell Biochem 1999;201:141–9.
143. Chace KV, Leahy DS, Martin R, et al. Respiratory mucous secretions in patients with cystic fibrosis: relationship between levels of highly sulfated mucin component and severity of the disease. Clin Chim Acta 1983;132:143–55.
144. Sangadala S, Bhat UR, Mendicino J. Structures of high molecular weight sulfated oligosaccharides in human tracheal mucin glycoproteins. Mol Cell Biochem 1993; 126:37–47.
145. Chernick WS, Barbero GJ. Composition of tracheobronchial secretions in cystic fibrosis of the pancreas and bronchiectasis. Pediatrics 1959;24:739–45.
146. Potter JL, Spector S, Matthews LW, et al. Studies on pulmonary secretions: III. The nucleic acids in whole pulmonary secretions from patients with cystic fibrosis, bronchiectasis and laryngectomy. Am Rev Respir Dis 1969;99:909–16.
147. Shak S, Capon DJ, Hellniss R, et al. Recombinant human DNase I reduces viscosity of cystic fibrosis sputum. Proc Natl Acad Sci U S A 1990;87:9188–92.

148. Lethem MI, James SL, Marriott C. The role of mucous glycoproteins in the rheologic properties of cystic fibrosis sputum. Am Rev Respir Dis 1990;142:1053–8.
149. Vasconcellos CA, Allen PG, Wohl ME, et al. Reduction in viscosity of cystic fibrosis sputum by gelsolin. Science 1994;263:969–71.
150. Saiman L, Cacalano G, Grunert D, Prince A. Comparison of adherence of *Pseudomonas aeruginosa* binding to respiratory epithelial cells from cystic fibrosis patients and healthy subjects. Infect Immun 1992;60:2808–14.
151. Zar H, Saiman L, Quittell L, et al. Binding of *Pseudomonas aeruginosa* to respiratory epithelial cells from patients with various mutations in the cystic fibrosis transmembrane regulator. J Pediatr 1995;126:230–3.
152. Irvin RT, Doig P, Lee KK, et al. Characterization of the *Pseudomonas aeruginosa* pilus adhesin: confirmation that the pilin structural protein subunit contains a human epithelial cell-binding domain. Infect Immun 1989;57:3720–6.
153. Imundo L, Barasch J, Prince A, et al. Cystic fibrosis cells have a receptor for pathogenic bacteria on their apical surface. Proc Natl Acad Sci U S A 1995;92:3019–23.
154. Baltimore RS, Christie CDC, Smith GJW. Immunohistopathologic localization of *Pseudomonas aeruginosa* in lungs from patients with cystic fibrosis. Am Rev Respir Dis 1989;140:1650–61.
155. Devaraj N, Sheykhanazari M, Warren WS, Bhavanandan VP. Differential binding of *Pseudomonas aeruginosa* to normal and cystic fibrosis tracheobronchial mucins. Glycobiology 1994;4:307–16.
156. Carnoy C, Ramphal R, Scharfman A, et al. Altered carbohydrate composition of salivary mucins from patients with cystic fibrosis and the adhesion of *Pseudomonas aeruginosa*. Am J Respir Cell Mol Biol 1993;9:323–34.
157. Komiyama K, Habbick BF, Tumber SK. Role of sialic acid in saliva-mediated aggregation of *Pseudomonas aeruginosa* isolated from cystic fibrosis. Infect Immun 1987;55:2364–9.
158. Nelson JW, Tredgett MW, Sheehan JK, et al. Mucinophilic and chemotactic properties of *Pseudomonas aeruginosa* in relation to pulmonary colonization in cystic fibrosis. Infect Immun 1990;58:1489–95.
159. Paranchych W, Sastry PA, Drake D, et al. Pseudomonas pili. Studies on antigenic determinants and mammalian cell receptors. Antibiot Chemother 1985;36:49–57.
160. Ramphal R, Koo L, Ishimoto KS, et al. Adhesion of *Pseudomonas aeruginosa* pilin-deficient mutants to mucin. Infect Immun 1991;59:1307–11.
161. Sajjan U, Reisman J, Doig P, et al. Binding of non-mucoid *Pseudomonas aeruginosa* to normal human intestinal mucin and respiratory mucin from patients with cystic fibrosis. J Clin Invest 1992;89:657–65.
162. Reddy MS. Human tracheobronchial mucin: purification and binding to *Pseudomonas aeruginosa*. Infect Immun 1992;60:1530–5.
163. Sajjan U, Corey M, Karmali M, Forstner J. Binding of *Pseudomonas cepacia* to normal human intestinal mucin and respiratory mucin from patients with cystic fibrosis. J Clin Invest 1992;89:648–56.
164. Sajjan SU, Forstner JF. Identification of the mucin-binding adhesin of *P. cepacia* isolated from patients with cystic fibrosis. Infect Immun 1992;60:1434–40.
165. Gawel J, Rudnik J, Pryjma J, et al. Protein in bronchial secretion of children with chronic obstructive pulmonary diseases. I. Relation to clinical diagnosis. Scand J Respir Dis 1979;60:63–8.
166. Kotlar HK, Harbitz O, Jenssen AO, Smidsrod O. Quantitation of proteins in sputum from patients with chronic obstructive lung disease. II. Determination of albumin, transferrin, alpha-1 acid glycoprotein, IgG, IgM, lysozyme and C3-complement factor. Eur J Respir Dis 1980;61:233–9.
167. Harbitz O, Jennsen AO, Smidsrod O. Lysozyme and lactoferrin in sputum from patients with chronic obstructive pulmonary disease. Eur J Respir Dis 1984;65:512–20.
168. Hughes WT, Koblin BA, Rosenstein BJ. Lysozyme activity in cystic fibrosis. Pediatr Res 1982;16:874–6.
169. Britigan BE, Hayek MB, Doebbeling BN, Fick RB. Transferrin and lactoferrin undergo proteolytic cleavage in pseudomonas-infected lungs of patients with cystic fibrosis. Infect Immun 1993;61:5049–55.
170. Smith JJ, Travis SM, Greenberg EP, Welsh MJ. Cystic fibrosis airway epithelia fail to kill bacteria because of abnormal airway surface fluid. Cell 1996;85:229–36.

CHAPTER 36

PULMONARY MACROPHAGES: ORIGINS, FUNCTIONS, AND CLEARANCE

DAVID W.H. RICHES, PHD, PETER M. HENSON, DVM, PHD

Cells of the mononuclear phagocyte system are present in the lung from the early stages of lung development, wherein they maintain a fluctuating presence throughout the life span of humans, rodents, and other mammals. As illustrated in Figure 36–1, the mononuclear phagocytes of the lung can be subdivided into four populations: (1) sentinel or resident macrophages of the alveoli and airways; (2) interstitial macrophages of the lung parenchyma; (3) circulating blood monocytes that both reside within a marginating pool in the lung microcirculation and also can be induced to migrate from the blood into the air spaces in response to specific needs of both the innate and adaptive immune systems; and (4) pulmonary dendritic cells, a more distantly related member of the mononuclear system whose primary function is the presentation of inhaled antigens to the adaptive immune system. The lungs of cloven-hoofed animals also contain a fifth class of lung mononuclear phagocyte, the pulmonary intravascular macrophage. However, these latter cells are not present in humans, and the reader is referred elsewhere for information about them.[1] The relative proportions of each of these groups of lung macrophages changes throughout life as the specific needs of the lung change. Based on the results of in vitro and in vivo studies, the concept has emerged that the composition of lung mononuclear phagocytes is shaped to a significant extent by the environment and stimuli to which they are exposed.[2–5]

Mononuclear phagocytes are involved in many aspects of host defense against inhaled bacteria, viruses, and particulates as well as in the regulation of acute and chronic inflammatory responses. In addition, lung macrophages play a key role in the resolution of the acute inflammatory response through their ability to recognize and phagocytose apoptotic cells, especially neutrophils.[6,7] However, these cells also significantly contribute to

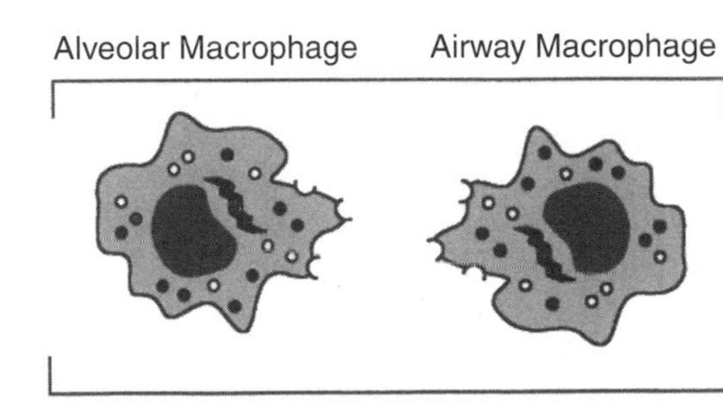

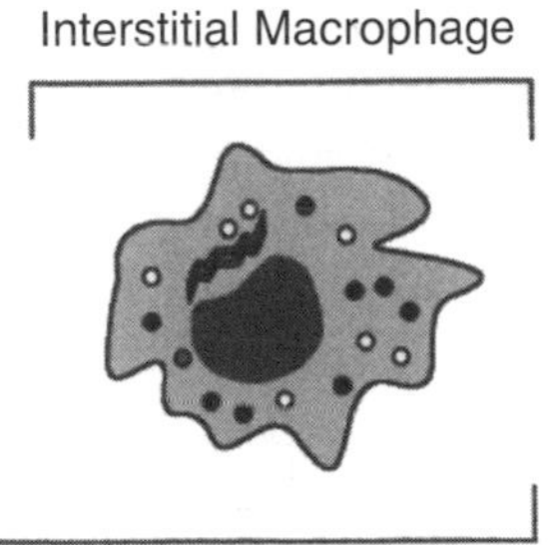

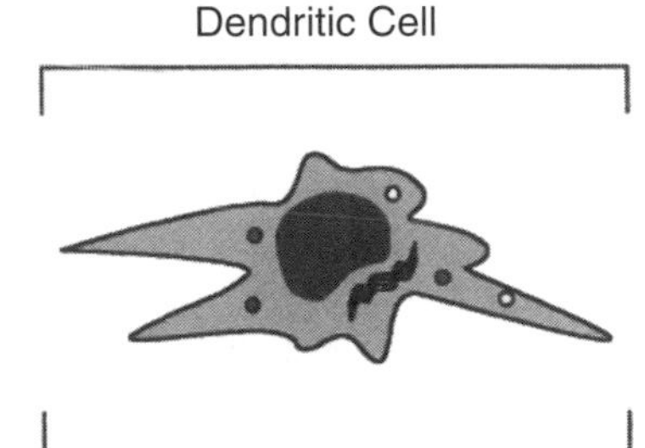

FIGURE 36–1. Macrophage populations and functions in the mature adult lung. Current data suggest that airway and alveolar macrophages are essentially indistinguishable from one another, although definitive studies in which these populations have been separated are currently lacking. Pulmonary dendritic cells, a more distantly related member of the mononuclear phagocyte family, exhibit distinct functions from pulmonary macrophages.

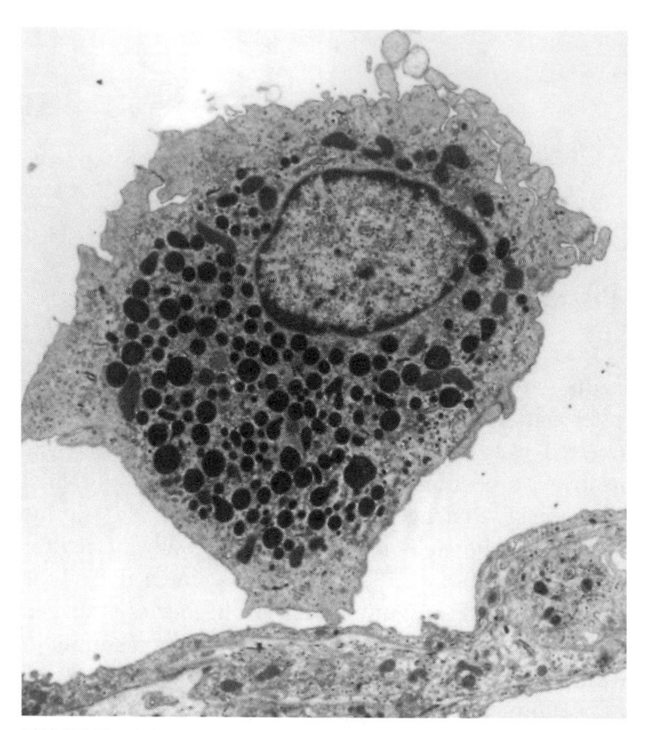

FIGURE 36–2. Electron micrograph of a human alveolar macrophage. Note the high content of vesicles. These cells often contain phagocytosed proteinaceous material as well as pulmonary surfactant—the latter sometimes having the appearance of lamellar bodies (post-stained with uranyl acetate and Reynold's lead stain, original magnification × 4900). (Courtesy of Jan Henson.)

chronic inflammation, remodeling, and fibrosis as a consequence of the production of growth and survival factors that collectively support the proliferation of mesenchymal and epithelial cells in addition to preventing their death (as reviewed by Riches[8]). Last, recent studies have shown that primitive macrophages appear in the developing lung before the establishment of the early blood-forming elements in the liver and bone marrow, raising the possibility of their involvement in early lung development and embryonic remodeling.[9,10] In this chapter, we review the cells of the mononuclear phagocyte system that are represented in the lung, and discuss their origins, functions, and ultimately, their fate. Due to space constraints, we focus principally on alveolar and airway macrophages. These cells are morphologically similar to other macrophages, although they often exhibit some distinct traits, such as abundant mitochondria and well-developed endoplasmic reticulum and granules (Figure 36–2). In addition, alveolar macrophages often contain lamellar bodies containing ingested pulmonary surfactant. For areas not directly related to these cells, we refer the reader to recent reviews or primary articles.

Origins

The results from research conducted during the past 30 years have greatly improved our understanding of the origin and kinetics of lung mononuclear phagocytes, both under steady state conditions and during lung inflammation. Much of this work has been possible through the use of radioisotopically labeled cells,[11,12] as well as through the development of monoclonal antibodies and other phenotypic markers that have been used to identify mononuclear phagocytes in general, and to classify different developmental stages and phenotypic variants of these cells.[13–15]

Local Proliferation of Fetal and Adult Lung Macrophages

Macrophages first appear in the developing lung prior to the establishment of the primitive blood-forming elements of the fetal liver. The fetal lung develops from the laryngotracheal groove and, in rats, can first be discerned at day 10.5 of gestation. By day 14, the bronchial tree has begun to develop and is surrounded by loosely organized mesenchyme; it is at this stage that macrophages, often referred to as "angle" cells, can first be identified within the developing lung structures.[10,16] Studies by Sorokin and colleagues have shown these cells to be actively proliferating in response to the myeloid growth factors, granulocyte-macrophage colony-stimulating factor (GM-CSF) and macrophage CSF (M-CSF), that are produced by the cells of the developing lung stroma.[17,18] The importance of these mononuclear phagocyte growth factors in the proliferation, differentiation, and survival of alveolar macrophages has been clarified somewhat in mice, in which the genes encoding GM-CSF and M-CSF have been deleted by gene targeting (as in the GM-CSF-null mice) or inactivated through a natural mutation of the M-CSF gene (as in op/op mice). Mice deficient in GM-CSF exhibit a phenotype in which the number of alveolar macrophages is diminished, and the mice display a lung pathology similar to that seen in patients with pulmonary alveolar proteinosis.[19,20] These observations suggest that the turnover and/or removal of alveolar surfactant and other proteinaceous material is regulated by alveolar macrophages, and that the development and functions of these cells is dependent on GM-CSF. Similarly, the lungs of op/op mice also have markedly reduced numbers of alveolar macrophages;[21,22] while mice deficient in both GM-CSF and M-CSF (obtained by crossing GM-CSF-null mice with op/op mice) develop severe progressive pulmonary inflammation associated with frequent bacterial pneumonia and the accumulation of proteinaceous material within the alveoli.[23]

While these studies have provided important insights into the development and functions of macrophages in the lung, there are still fundamental gaps in our knowledge about the functions of primitive macrophages in the developing lung. It is also unclear where these primitive macrophages come from and which growth factors regulate their development. Perhaps these cells are required in the formations of the gas exchange units. Alternatively, perhaps primitive macrophages phagocytose cells that are destined to die during development in a similar fashion to the proposed role of macrophages in cell clearance in developmental systems in *Caenorhabditis elegans* and *Drosophila melanogaster*.[24] Consistent with this possibility are the results of studies conducted by Hume and colleagues[9] in which macrophages are initially found to be distributed throughout the embryo by day 9.5 and have been shown to be localized between the digits of development forelimbs of mice at later developmental stages.

There also remains a dearth of information, especially in humans, regarding the origins of alveolar and airway macrophages in the lungs of adults under steady state (ie, noninflamed) conditions. Early studies in mice suggested that resident alveolar macrophages originate almost exclusively from circulating blood monocytes.[12] However, other studies challenge this notion. For example, studies conducted in mice have provided compelling data to suggest that the alveolar macrophage can be derived from locally proliferating cells.[25–29] Nakata et al[30] confirmed this important point in a recent study of bone marrow allografts in human recipients by showing that proliferating alveolar macrophages of both donor and recipient origins were present in the lung, and that cells of donor origin gradually replaced cells of recipient origin approximately 60 days' post-transplantation. However, it is not clear whether the proliferating pool of alveolar macrophages is derived from circulating monoblasts or promonocytes, and severe monocytopenia induced by corticosteroids or chemotherapy has little effect on the number of alveolar macrophages.[26,31] In addition, in the study by Nakata et al[30] the monocyte population of the blood was exclusively of donor origin as early as day 41 post-transplantation, yet the alveolar macrophage population still contained recipient genotypes even after day 83. Similarly, using microsatellite analysis Kjellstrom and colleagues[32] have shown that recipient genotypes are still detected in populations of alveolar macrophages up to 6 months after allogeneic bone marrow transplantation. Many questions still remain to be addressed. For example, if the replicating pool is derived from blood-borne (and bone marrow-derived) progenitor cells, where do their progenitors reside in the lung, and at what stage in myeloid development do these cells migrate from the blood into the lung? Answers to these questions currently are lacking in the lung. However, studies on the origin of resident peritoneal macrophages have suggested that the proliferation and differentiation of these cells takes place in the milky spots of the omentum.[33,34] Furthermore, the milky spots appear to be a source within the peritoneal cavity of both GM-CSF and M-CSF, and macrophages are absent from the milky spots in op/op mice.[35] In addition, experimental omentectomy in rats has been found to result in a marked decline in both peritoneal macrophage number and in peritoneal defense mechanisms.[36] Thus, if the site of peritoneal macrophage proliferation and differentiation is also the major source of M-CSF and GM-CSF, perhaps the same is true in the lung. If so, this would point to a potentially important role of the airway and alveolar epithelium in the proliferation, differentiation, and survival of resident alveolar and airway macrophages.

Monocyte Influx during Pulmonary Inflammation

While many questions exist about the origin and kinetics of resident lung macrophages, there is general agreement that in response to the specific need to defend the airways and gas exchange surfaces of the lung, monocytes can be induced rapidly to migrate from the blood into the air spaces when the capacity of the resident cells becomes overwhelmed. Following transmigration, monocytes rapidly differentiate into macrophages and carry out many responses and functions that are critical to the recognition and elimination of bacteria, particulates, and other inhaled materials. In general, the process of monocyte migration occurs subsequent to an initial rapid accumulation of neutrophils that peaks approximately 1 to 2 days after the initiation of an inflammatory response. In a similar fashion to neutrophils, the migration of monocytes into the air spaces is initiated by the expression of several key chemotactic factors. These include the complement activation fragments, C5a and $C5a_{desArg}$,[37] and fragments of the connective tissue matrix (including fibronectin) that are released following proteolytic cleavage by metalloproteinases and other enzymes that are secreted or released by recently recruited neutrophils.[38] In addition, abundant evidence now supports the key role of chemokines, especially CC-chemokines that include MCP-1, MIP-1α, and MIP-1β and which, as discussed later, are secreted by resident alveolar macrophages and airway (and probably alveolar) epithelial cells. It also has been recognized recently that neutrophils secrete granule-associated chemokines such as interleukin (IL)-8 and MIP-1α[39] in addition to retaining a limited capacity to synthesize chemokines and other proinflammatory cytokines.[40]

In response to chemotactic factors, monocytes become localized to the vascular endothelium through the engagement of the selectins, integrins, and other tethering and adhesive molecules prior to their transmigration across the endothelium, basement membrane, and epithelium to gain access to the air spaces. Intratracheal instillation of inflammatory stimuli, such as lipopolysaccharide (LPS), stimulates the accumulation of large numbers of monocytes in the air spaces, which peak in number roughly 3 to 5 days after the initiation of the inflammatory response.[41] Upon arrival in the air spaces, monocytes rapidly differentiate into macrophages and often are referred to as "responsive" or "inflammatory" macrophages. In vitro and in vivo studies have revealed much information about the stimuli that are capable of inducing this differentiation response, as well as details of the underlying mechanisms. Several serum components, cytokines that include IL-10, and a variety of other well-defined monocyte stimuli such as 1α,25-dihydroxyvitamin D_3 have been shown to induce monocyte-macrophage differentiation.[42–44] In addition, M-CSF and GM-CSF have been shown to support the survival of these cells during the inflammatory response, and, as might be expected, the levels of M-CSF and GM-CSF wax and wane with the genesis and resolution of the inflammatory response.[45] Important insights into the role of M-CSF as a monocyte-macrophage survival factor have come from an elegant study by Lagasse and Weissman.[46] They showed that the requirement for M-CSF in promoting the survival of monocytes at the critical stage of monocyte-macrophage differentiation could be overcome by expressing the prosurvival protein, Bcl-2, under the influence of a monocyte-specific promoter in transgenic mice. Monocytes isolated from the Bcl-2-transgenic mice were able to undergo monocyte-macrophage differentiation in the absence of M-CSF, whereas monocytes isolated from wild-type mice became apoptotic in the absence of M-CSF and were unable to differentiate into macrophages. Importantly, these investigators also reported that enforced expression of Bcl-2 in monocytes resulted in rescue of the monocyte and macrophages deficiences observed in op/op mice.[46] Thus, the survival response to M-CSF is critical to the development of both resident tissue macrophages as well as for promoting monocyte-macrophage differentiation.

In summary, macrophages exist in the lung as resident sentinel cells of both the alveolar surfaces and the airways. However, in response to specific threats to the epithelial surfaces, whether these be in the form of bacterial infections, particulate overloads, or other inflammatory stimuli, the sentinel macrophages can be supplemented rapidly by circulating blood monocytes, which then differentiate into so-called inflammatory macrophages. In addition, during prolonged pulmonary inflammation, macrophages also accumulate in the interstitium of the thickened alveolar septa. These cells also can contribute to the pathogenesis of chronic pulmonary inflammation and ultimately fibrosis, through their capacity to secrete chemokines, cytokines, and growth factors that can influence the proliferation and survival of both mesenchymal and epithelial cells.[47,48] In the next section, we discuss aspects of macrophage function in the defense of the lung, and how these functions can become dysregulated during acute and chronic lung inflammation.

Functions

The functions of lung macrophages are many and varied and relate to a number of issues including (1) the dynamics and proportions of different macrophage types that

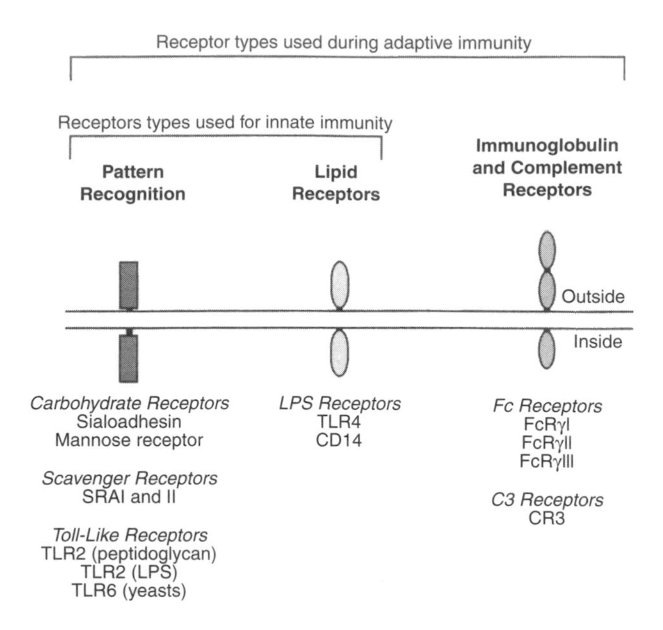

FIGURE 36–3. Pattern recognition and other receptors involved in the uptake of particulates, bacteria, and apoptotic cells. LPS = lipopolysaccharide.

are present, (2) their location, and (3) the stimuli or conditions that they encounter. Thus, in considering the functions of lung macrophages, these issues also must be considered. Broadly speaking, this discussion focuses on the functions of macrophages in the steady state and during lung inflammation.

Macrophage Functions in the Normal Lung

Macrophages fulfil several key functions in the normal lung that are important in maintaining the fine balance that prevents the lung from responding to inappropriate immune and inflammatory stimuli, yet renders it "primed" to respond when its limited capacity to remove, digest, or sequester commonly encountered microorganisms, particulates, or other antigens becomes overwhelmed.

Phagocytosis of microorganisms and particulates

Principal among the functions of sentinel alveolar and airway macrophages is the ability to kill, phagocytose, digest and/or sequester bacteria, yeasts, and other particulates that enter the air spaces (or are generated therein) at varying rates throughout the lives of both urban and rural man. Alveolar and airway macrophages phagocytose particulate material via a plethora of cell surface receptors (Figure 36–3). Surfactant proteins A and D are recognized by specific receptors and play a key role in the removal of pulmonary surfactant.[49–52] In addition, recent data support the contention that the surfactant proteins A and D, which belong to the collectin family, play important roles both in the innate protection of the gas exchange surfaces via their ability to act as bacterial opsonins, and in suppressing inappropriate inflammatory responses, respectively.[53–55] Lung macrophages also express a variety of receptors often referred to as "pattern recognition" receptors, which are important in the innate recognition of inhaled material. These include scavenger receptors and carbohydrate recognition receptors that recognize repetitive patterns of lipids and carbohydrates that are often specific to particular groups of microorganisms. In addition, macrophages express toll-like receptors, which bind LPS, peptidoglycan, unmethylated CpG repeats found primarily in bacterial DNA, and yeast cell walls,[56,57] as well as CD14, which recognizes LPS bound to lipopolysaccharide binding protein a serum protein that promotes the dissociation of large complexes of LPS (LBP).[58] Last, lung macrophages also express receptors for immunoglobulin G (IgG) and complement component C3, which promote the phagocytosis of bacteria[57,59–61] in the context of both the innate immune system (alternative pathway of complement activation) and the adaptive immune system (leading to specific antibody formation).

Immune system suppression

Given their continuous exposure to ambient air, the airways and gas exchange surfaces of the lung are constantly exposed to inhaled antigens and particulates that have the potential to activate both the innate and adaptive immune systems. However, the lung has evolved a mechanism of tolerance to commonly encountered antigens that appears to be functionally equivalent to the well-recognized phenomenon of oral tolerance. Tolerance is mediated at the level of both the airway dendritic cells and the T cell, and the resident alveolar and airway macrophages are the primary cells that cause immune system suppression.[62] The ability of resident alveolar and airway macrophages to suppress T cell activation in response to both polyclonal and specific antigens is not shared by macrophages from other organs and tissues, or by circulating blood monocytes.[63] Data reported by Thepen and colleagues[64,65] have shown convincingly that depletion of alveolar and airway macrophages in rodents with liposome-encapsulated chlodronate potentiates the response to pulmonary immunization with intratracheally instilled TNP-KLH an experimental hapten-antigen. As illustrated in Figure 36–4, several soluble factors released by lung macrophages contribute to the immune suppression mediated by these cells. These include NO·, prostaglandin E_2, and immunosuppressive cytokines, especially IL-10 and transforming growth factor β (TGF-β).[44,66–68]

Clearly, since the lung is constantly exposed to potentially infectious or inflammatory stimuli, maintaining its epithelial surfaces in a state of immune suppression represents an Achilles' heel. This raises the question of how the lung is able to promote the activation of the adaptive immune system in response to appropriate needs. The answer appears to lie, at least in part, in the ability of proinflammatory cytokines to overcome macrophage-mediated immune system suppression. Insights into how the immune suppressive activity of lung macrophages can be overcome have emerged recently from studies reported by Bilyk and Holt. As summarized in Figure 36–4, exposure of lung macrophages to proinflammatory cytokines, especially tumor necrosis factor α (TNF-α) and GM-CSF results in a downregulation of suppressive activity.[69] In addition, during the evolution of an inflammatory response in the lung, the proportion of lung mononuclear phagocytes becomes skewed from one dominated by resident alveolar and airway macrophages, to one in which blood monocytes and monocyte-derived

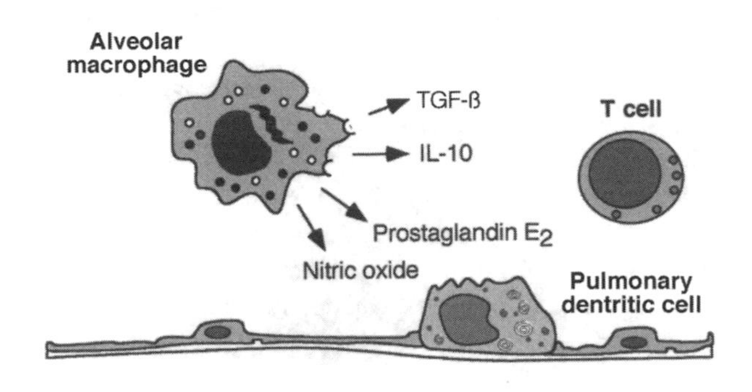

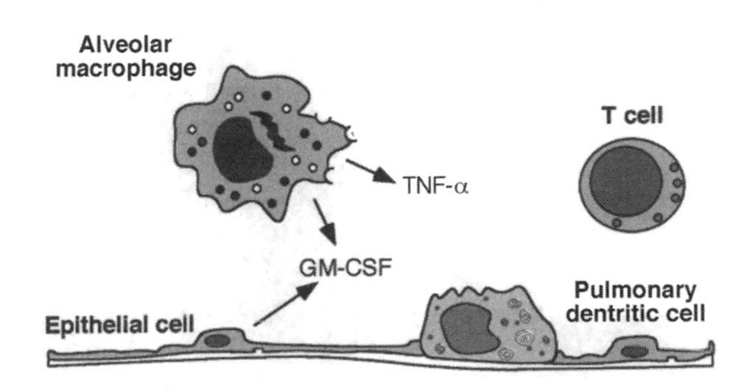

FIGURE 36–4. Mechanisms of immune suppression of T cell and dendritic cell function in the lung by resident alveolar macrophages. *A*, Key regulators of immune suppression of antigen-presenting activity and T cell activation. *B*, The mechanism by which proinflammatory cytokines overcome immune suppression to allow the activation of the adaptive immune system; antigen presentation and T cell activation are enabled in the absence of suppression. TGF = transforming growth factor; IL = interleukin; TNF = tumor necrosis factor; GM-CSF = granulocyte-macrophage colony-stimulating factor. (Reproduced with permission from Riches DWH. Monocytes, macrophages and dendritic cells of the lung. In: Murray J, Nadal J, Mason RS, Bouchay N, eds. Textbook of respiratory medicine, 2nd ed. Philadelphia, PA: W.B. Saunders, 2000:385–412.)

inflammatory macrophages predominate. As discussed earlier, immunosuppressive activity is not expressed by blood monocytes, hence shifting the balance toward immune stimulation.[63] Furthermore, in the presence of GM-CSF and TNF-α, monocytes preferentially differentiate toward a dendritic cell phenotype,[70] further skewing the environment toward antigen-presenting activity. Thus, while in the normal (ie, noninflamed) lung environment, lung macrophages tend to damp down the immune system, pulmonary inflammation changes this environment to one in which the adaptive immune system can be activated.

Oxidant production

The generation of reactive oxygen and reactive nitrogen free radicals is critical to host defense against commonly encountered bacteria. The role of reactive oxygen species, especially $O_2^{\cdot-}$, H_2O_2 and $OH^{\cdot}$, in host defense of the lung is well illustrated in diseases associated with deficiencies in their production such as chronic granulomatous disease (CGD), as well as in mice in which key components of the NADPH (the reduced form of nicotinamide-adenine dinucleotide phosphate) oxidase have been disrupted following homologous recombination in embryonic stem cells.[71,72] In both CGD and p47*phox* (-/-) mice, there is a uniform deficiency in the ability to control pulmonary and other infections.[73] However, while reactive oxygen species are critical to normal host defense, inappropriate production by alveolar and airway macrophages results in severe injury to airway and alveolar epithelia, often contributing to fibroproliferation and further damage to the alveolar-capillary units. Such a situation exists, for example, in survivors of the adult respiratory distress syndrome (ARDS) or in individuals who have been exposed to bioactive particulates such as quartz or silica.[74] Inappropriate oxidant production also has been detected in patients with bronchietasis, and H_2O_2 levels in breath condensates of these patients have been linked to disease severity.[75]

In addition to reactive oxygen species, airway and alveolar macrophages also are capable of producing the reactive nitrogen free radical, NO·, by the oxidation of L-arginine under the influence of inducible nitric oxide synthase (*iNOS*).[76] Studies of the role of NO· in the defense of the lung in humans have been difficult. However, deletion of the *iNOS* gene in mice has shown that macrophages derived from these animals are incapable of producing NO· in response to stimulation,[77] and, importantly, these animals are considerably more sensitive to airway infections with *Listeria monocytogenes* and *Mycobacterium tuberculosis* than are wild-type mice.[77] Also, NO· has been shown to react with H_2O_2 to produce the longer-living and more toxic peroxynitrite free radical, which also can contribute to epithelial injury.[78] Thus, while both reactive oxygen and reactive nitrogen free radicals play an important role in the defense of the lung against potentially pathogenic bacteria, they also can cause inappropriate injury to the epithelial surfaces.

Lipid mediator, cytokine, and chemokine production

Resident alveolar and airway macrophages are the first phagocytes to encounter inhaled microorganisms and particulates. Positioned as they are, they represent an important cell type involved in the activation of the innate and adaptive immune systems, through there ability to produce proinflammatory cytokines, chemokines, and lipid mediators. Collectively, these early responses promote the recruitment and activation of other inflammatory cells, initially neutrophils, and then later, monocytes and lymphocytes. Thus, while resident alveolar and airway macrophages respond by producing protein and lipid mediators, they also promote the transition between the normal lung and the inflamed lung.

Studies conducted over 20 years ago initially suggested that macrophages in general, and alveolar macrophages in particular, are capable of hydrolyzing phospholipids containing arachidonic acid at the sn-2 position in response to exposure to a variety of proinflammatory stimuli including zymosan particles and LPS.[79] Hydrolysis of arachidonyl-containing phosphatidylcholine species by phospholipase A_2 enyzmes[80] results in the formation of two key substrates for the production of the lipid mediators: (1) lysophosphatidylcholine, which upon acetylation at the sn-2 production by acetyltransferases, leads to the production of platelet activating factor (PAF) species;[81] and (2) arachidonic acid, which serves as a substrate for the production of prostaglandins and leukotrienes (as reviewed by Riches and colleagues).[82]

Platelet activating factor is produced within minutes of exposure of alveolar macrophages to inflammatory stimuli and exhibits broad proinflammatory activities that include (1) chemotactic activity toward neutrophils and monocytes, (2) potentiation of adhesive interactions between neutrophils and vascular endothelial cells, and (3) potent bronchoconstrictive and vasodilative properties. In addition, PAF primes neutrophils, monocytes, and macrophages for enhanced responses to other proinflammatory stimuli, such as LPS and chemotactic formyl peptides, as well as enhancing the production of cytokines such as TNF-α.[83,84]Arachidonic acid is oxidized to prostaglandins (PGs) and leukotrienes (LTs) by cyclooxygenase and lipoxygenase enzyme pathways, respectively. Among the PGs produced by alveolar macrophages, PGE_2, PGD_2, PGI_2, and thromboxane A_2 play important roles in the control of vascular tone and in the inhibition of macrophage functions.[85] Basal PG production is catalyzed by the constitutively expressed enzyme COX-1. However, proinflammatory stimuli including LPS, PAF, and phagocytic particles upregulate the expression of the inducible COX-2 enzyme, thereby resulting in an amplification in the production of PGs.[86,87] The main LT produced by alveolar macrophages is LTB_4; LTB_4 is synthesized rapidly in response to stimulation with LPS and phagocytic particles, and it exhibits potent chemotactic activity toward neutrophils.[88] Studies conducted by Rankin and colleagues[88] and Martin and colleagues[89] have indicated that LTB_4 is the principal neutrophil chemotactic substance produced in the lung prior to the synthesis of IL-8 at later time points during the induction of the early inflammatory response.

In addition to the basic studies that have led to the elucidation of the nature and functions of lipid mediators, recently developed receptor antagonists that prevent lipid mediator binding or pharmacologic agents that interfere with lipid mediator synthesis and/or metabolism have begun to be tested in clincial trails. For example, zileuton, a 5′-lipoxygenase pathway inhibitor, has been shown to reduce TNF-α levels in the airways of patients with asthma,[90] while at the same time improving lung function and physiology.[91] On the other hand, PAF receptor antagonists have proven ineffective so far in altering airway function in asthmatic patients.[92] These latter findings are consistent with the notion that PAF is involved in the initiation of the inflammatory response, and that once established, its involvement is more limited and, hence, is not inhibitable by specific receptor antagonists.

While the early production of lipid mediators represents an important mechanism through which the inflammatory response in the lung can be intitiated and regulated, the production of cytokines and chemotactic chemokines by macrophages and airway and alveolar epithelial cells is of great significance to the development of both acute and chronic inflammatory responses. Cytokines that contribute to the development of the inflammatory response include TNF-α and IL-1β. Inhibition of TNF-α function with either humanized monoclonal antibodies or so-called TNF "receptorglobulins" has proven effective in controlling inflammation in rheumatoid arthritis and inflammatory bowel disease. However, while they held great promise in the treatment of ARDS and sepsis, the results from clinical trails have been disappointing.[93,94] Similarly, treatment regimens directed at inhibiting IL-1β responses in patients with sepsis also have failed to influence survival.[95] The explanation for the failure of cytokine-directed therapies is likely similar to that for the inability of PAF receptor antagonists to prevent ongoing inflammation in asthma (ie, the production of, and response to, TNF-α and IL-1β has already occurred by the time the patient is treated).[96]

In addition to early response cytokines, exposure of alveolar macrophages to LPS, particulates, and TNF-α induces the de novo synthesis of a variety of chemotactic chemokines that stimulate the recruitment of neutrophils, eosinophils, monocytes, and lymphocytes into the lung. The human chemokine family comprises four closely related subfamilies that have been classified on the basis of the presence and pattern of conserved cysteine residues, namely the C, CC, CXC, and CXXXC families (as reviewed by Kunkel, Keane, and colleagues[97,98]). The CC and CXC families appear to be of principal importance to the development of the inflammatory response. Members of the CC family generally are involved in the chemotaxis of mononuclear cells, while the CXC family chemokines are involved mainly in neutrophil chemotaxis, although some members (eg, non-ELR-motif-containing CXC chemokines such as IP-10) are produced in response to interferon (IFN)-γ and help regulate the angiogenic response.[99,100] In vitro and in vivo studies have revealed that both alveolar and airway macrophages are capable of producing CXC chemokines, especially IL-8, in the settings of acute and chronic lung inflammation in patients with ARDS, idiopathic pulmonary fibrosis (IPF), bronchiolitis obliterans with organizing pneumonia (BOOP), and cystic fibrosis.[101–104] Likewise, CC chemokines, such as MIP-1α, are produced by macrophages in interstitial lung diseases.[105,106] In summary, resident macrophages of the airways and alveoli play a key role in the initiation of the inflammatory response in the lung through their ability to respond to inhaled bacteria, viruses, particulates, and other pathogenic aerosols and gases (eg, ozone) with the production of a panoply of lipid mediators, cytokines, and chemokines. Collectively, these substances initiate, amplify, and perpetuate the inflammatory response by stimulating the transmigration of other inflammatory cells from the blood to the air spaces and by their effects on the airway and alveolar epithelium. For example, epithelial cells respond poorly to LPS, yet they express IL-8 and ENA-78 in response to TNF-α, which is initially produced by alveolar macrophages in response to LPS.[107]

Functions during Pulmonary Inflammation

While some macrophage functions are similar in both the normal and the inflamed lung, pulmonary inflammation with its recruitment and differentiation of monocytes into macrophages results in the expression of a number of functions not associated with the normal lung. In this section, we highlight some of the changes in macrophage functions that are of significance to the maintenance of the inflammatory response, the dysregulated transition to aberrant wound repair and fibrosis, and the resolution of inflammation and restoration of normal tissue structure and function.

Lung remodeling

The architecture of the lung is largely maintained by the extracellular connective tissue matrix (ECM), which provides the framework of support for the epithelial and mesenchymal cells, the airways, and the pulmonary circulation. Lung macrophages, particularly inflammatory macrophages, contribute both to matrix degradation

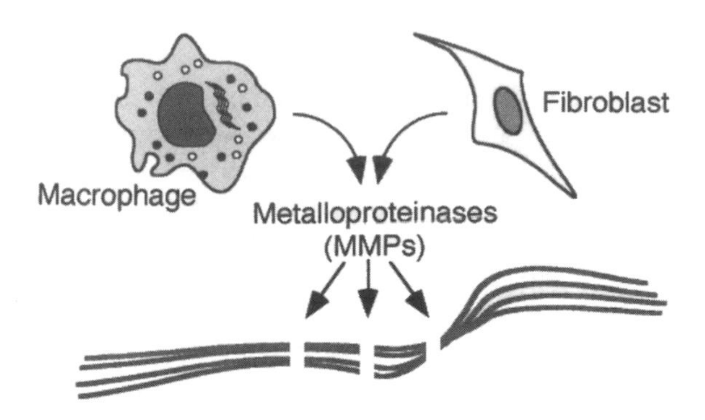

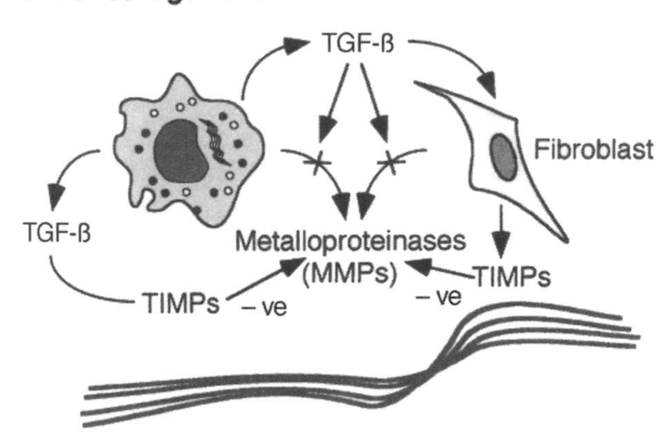

FIGURE 36–5. *A*, Regulation of collagen matrix deposition and removal and *B*, proposed mechanisms of dysregulation of interstitial lung diseases, particularly idiopathic pulmonary fibrosis (IPF). TGF = transforming growth factor; TIMP = tissue inhibitor of metalloproteinase. (Reproduced with permission from Chan ED et al.[108])

during the early stages of lung repair and to matrix synthesis. These functions are mediated respectively by (1) metalloproteinases and other matrix-degrading enzymes, and (2) growth and survival factors. Dysregulation of both matrix degradation and matrix synthesis can have severe consequences for the lung and have been implicated in disorders as diverse as emphysema and pulmonary fibrosis (as reviewed by Riches[8] and Chan et al[108]).

The ability of macrophages to degrade collagen, elastin and other components of the ECM has been recognized for many years. Consisting mainly of metalloproteinases, cysteine and serine proteases, and acid hydrolases, many of these enzymes can act both intracellularly and extracellularly. As illustrated in Figure 36–5, collagen degradation by macrophages is mediated mainly by matrix metalloproteinase-1 (MMP-1), which is activated by MMP-3,[109–111] a metalloproteinase that also is secreted by LPS-stimulated human alveolar macrophages. In addition, monocytes and macrophages secrete MMP-9, an enzyme that cleaves degraded collagen.[109] Thus, macrophages secrete a repertoire of proteinases that collectively promote collagen breakdown. It seems likely that following extracellular cleavage, macrophages ingest portions of the partially degraded ECM and complete the process of full matrix degradation in the endosomal and lysosomal system. Macrophages also contribute to matrix degradation by their ability to regulate metalloproteinase production by fibroblasts. Several macrophage-derived cytokines have been implicated in this process including TNF-α, IL-1β, and platelet-derived growth factor (PDGF). Thus, matrix degradation and débridement is mediated by subtle interactions between both macrophages and fibroblasts, and by cross-talk between these cells by proinflammatory cytokine growth factors.

Macrophages also play a key role in repair following lung injury. The initial studies by Leibovitch and Ross in 1975 first highlighted the importance of macrophages in wound repair in the skin.[112] Since then, there has developed a broadening appreciation of the role of macrophages as a source of fibroblast and epithelial cell growth and survival factors in the repair process. In addition, through their ability to secrete CC chemokines and both non-ELR- and ELR-motif-containing CXC chemokines, macrophages actively contribute to the regulation of tissue angiogenesis.[99] It should be noted, however, that dysregulation of macrophage growth factor production likely contributes to inappropriate lung repair responses and fibrosis. For example, macrophages are a rich source of TGF-β, a critically important growth factor in the genesis of pulmonary fibrosis, especially in the early stages.[113] Transforming growth factor β potentiates tissue fibrosis through its pleiotropic activities. In addition to its well-established ability to stimulate the synthesis of collagen I and III by fibroblasts,[114,115] TGF-β stimulates the production of tissue inhibitor of metalloproteinases (TIMPs),[116] while inhibiting the expression of MMP-1 and MMP-2. Thus, inappropriate and/or continued production of TGF-β markedly shifts the balance of the lung ECM from débridement to fibrosis. Macrophages are also a source of insulin-like growth factor I (IGF-I), whose activities have been shown to include (1) those of a fibroblast progression-type growth factor, and (2) potent stimulation of collagen gene expression by fibroblasts.[117] Studies by Uh and colleagues[48] have shown that IGF-I is expressed at greatly increased levels by alveolar macrophages and alveolar epithelial cells in IPF. Also, IGF-I was shown to be expressed by interstitial macrophages, and the level of expression by these cells was found to be associated with disease severity in IPF patients.[48] Recent studies also have highlighted the importance of IGF-I as a survival factor that acts to inhibit apoptosis in cells bearing the IGF-I receptor.[118,119] In addition, macrophages secrete PDGF, and blocking studies of bronchoalveolar lavage fluid from patients with IPF have shown that PDGF contributes to fibroblast proliferation.[120] Thus, collectively macrophages may directly and indirectly play a role in the regulation of fibrosis through

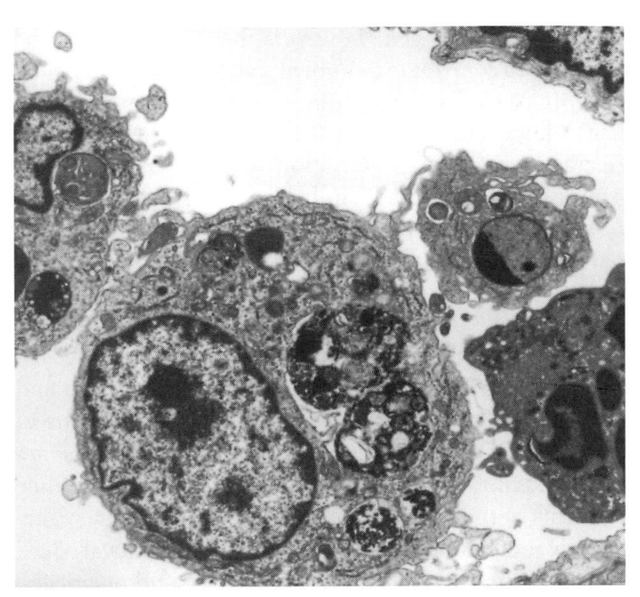

FIGURE 36–6. Electron micrograph of an alveolar macrophage that has phagocytosed two apoptotic neutrophils. The neutrophils are already in the process of being digested by the macrophage. Phagocytosis of apoptotic cells by macrophages occurs rapidly and "silently" (post-stained with uranyl acetate and Reynold's lead stain, original magnification × 5400). (Courtesy of Jan Henson and Galeen Smith.)

their ability to express a wide repertoire of growth factors, chemokines, and cytokines that influence mesenchymal cell proliferation and survival, collagen matrix synthesis, and angiogenesis of the evolving fibrotic lesions.

Removal of senescent cells

Macrophages have long been recognized as key elements in the removal of dead and damaged cells from tissues, a process essential for normal tissue homeostasis and the return of injured structures to their characteristic structure and function. This is perhaps more relevant in the lungs than elsewhere, because of the potential in the respiratory tract for cell damage from external inhaled particulates and other factors. In recent years, development of the concept of programmed cell death or apoptosis has focused more specific attention on these clearance roles and their mechanisms. Apoptosis must be seen as a two-step phenomenon, in which an unwanted or potentially damaged cell first undergoes a variety of changes that ensure its inability to replicate (deoxyribonucleic acid [DNA] fragmentation and nuclear condensation) as well as alterations to its surface that allow it to be recognized and removed from the tissue. This removal is the critical second phase of the overall process, and, not surprisingly, macrophages are especially efficient in performing the removal. Figure 36–6 is an electron micrographic illustration of an alveolar macrophage containing two phagocytosed apoptotic neutrophils.

Some of the earliest studies of apoptotic cell uptake into macrophages were in fact carried out in the lung in attempts to understand resolution of pulmonary inflammation. The extremely efficient removal of neutrophils that had accumulated in the early stages of the inflammation led to the demonstration of uptake into macrophages within the air spaces.[7,121] On the other hand, observation of the engulfment phenomenon, in this case ingestion of "microphages" by "macrophages" as described by Metchnikoff[122], predated these studies by almost a century, even though the concept of apoptosis was not introduced until the 1970s. However, the phenomenon extends way beyond the process of inflammation. Removal of unwanted cells is essential to development, tissue remodeling, establishment and maintenance of the immune system, control of neoplastic alterations, and general responses to injury. In development of the *C. elegans* larva, exactly 131 of approximately 960 total cells are destined to undergo apoptosis and removal. As outlined above, during development of the lung, cells that have performed their early essential functions also become apoptotic and are removed.

Most tissue cells have the ability to recognize and remove such cells, including epithelial cells, fibroblasts, and endothelial cells.[123–125] However, in vitro macrophages appear to express a greater array of relevant receptors and to ingest apoptotic cells at a greater rate and to a greater extent.[126] Over the last few years a host of potential receptors for recognition and removal of apoptotic cells have been identified, for the most part by use of antibodies or ligands that block the uptake of apoptotic cells directly incubated with the macrophages in vitro. Many of receptors involved in the uptake of apoptotic cells are the same pattern recognition receptors that are involved in the uptake of bacteria and other particulates, such as scavenger receptors; others include integrins, complement receptors, receptors of the innate immune system, and some unique candidates arising from specific studies of apoptotic cell removal in nematodes, insects, or mammals.[123–125,127,128] The evolutionary breadth again emphasizes its primitive nature and importance.

Surprisingly, much less is known about the surface changes on the apoptotic cells that are recognized. The only well-characterized alteration is a redistribution of membrane phospholipids that results in expression of phosphatidylserine (PS) in the outer membrane leaflet. Normally phospholipids are distributed asymmetrically, and PS is maintained on the inner leaflet. During cell activation, PS may be moved to the outside by a phospholipid "scramblase," but is rapidly re-internalized as a consequence of aminophospholipid translocases. In apoptosis the scramblase is stimulated, and the rectifying translocase is inactivated, resulting in persistent PS expression. This is the basis of one assay for apoptosis, the ability to bind PS-recognizing annexin V. Other surface changes probably involve alteration of membrane carbohydrates and perhaps altered expression of some proteins (eg, those on lymphocytes or intercellular adhesion molecule 3 (ICAM-3).[129] One of the reasons for this lack of information could be that some of the ligands are not new or unique in nature, but rather are redistributed on the cell surface so that low-affinity "receptors" on the macrophage bind with a high enough avidity to stimulate ingestion.

A particularly important candidate receptor that has been identified and cloned recently[127] specifically recognizes the polar head group of PS. This PS receptor appears to be critical for the actual uptake of apoptotic cells,[130] even if some of the other receptors play a more important role in initial tethering of the apoptotic cell to the macrophage surface.[130] Another potentially important recognition mechanism appears to involve members of the collectin family of molecules (including the related C1q). Here, the globular head groups bind the apoptotic cells (to ligands, which at this point are unknown), and their collagenous tails interact with macrophage receptors, of which surface calreticulin may be one of the most important.[131,132] However, what is clearly lacking at this stage in our general understanding of these important processes, is which of these multiply redundant mechanisms really drives recognition and uptake in vivo. In this regard it is relevant that C1q-deficient mice show abnormal clearance of apoptotic cells in the kidney and peritoneum,[133] and in early experiments, surface protein A–and surface protein D–knockout animals show defective clearance from the lungs (unpublished observations). Although PS-receptor knockouts are not yet available, there are reports that annexin can block uptake in vivo,[134] and, in our own studies, an apoptotic cell line that does not express PS on its membrane was not cleared normally from the lungs unless PS was deliberately introduced into the outer membrane (unpublished observations).

In what might be considered the normal process, apoptotic cells are removed in situ, one at a time, before they disintegrate and release potentially toxic materials into the tissue. Characteristically, removal is quiet and efficient and, because of this, difficult to observe. Most importantly it does not result in local inflammation. This is in contrast to the presumed effect of cell disruption and necrosis, which initiates a local inflammatory response as a protective measure. Uptake of apoptotic cells into macrophages in vitro does not initiate synthesis and secretion[135,136] of proinflammatory mediators and, in fact, actively suppresses such production.[136] This suppression also appears to be initiated by ligation of the PS receptor[127,130] and is due in part to the synthesis, release, and activation of TGF-β.[136] Direct instillation of apoptotic cells into an inflamed lung rapidly and markedly initiates the production and release of TGF-β from macrophages in the lesion; at the same time, it promotes a more rapid resolution (unpublished observations). The current model suggests that apoptotic cell stimulation of such anti-inflammatory molecules explains the quiet removal and participates in resolution of inflammation. If prolonged, however, the TGF-β would be expected to contribute in its own way to tissue remodeling and, in particular, to fibrotic changes. For example, in CD44-knockout mice, an apparent defect in apoptotic cell clearance and TGF-β activation resulted in accelerated, prolonged, and lethal pulmonary inflammation in response to bleomycin (unpublished observations) with reduction in the normal fibrosis seen in this system. In more general terms, the current paradigm suggests that macrophages (and immature dendritic cells) have the ability to distinguish between apoptotic and necrotic cells—one of which leads to suppression of inflammation and activation of the adaptive immune response, and one of which leads to their activation. These concepts are expressed most clearly in the "Danger" hypothesis.[137] While elements of these ideas are extremely attractive, the reality is likely much more complex. For example, removal of cell debris, particularly membranous material and organelles, seems to be mediated by the same groups of receptors as is removal of intact apoptotic cells. Therefore, we feel a more likely scenario may be a balance between anti-inflammatory and proinflammatory macrophage stimuli that can lead to complex and time-dependent responses in the lung.

One of the early studies of apoptotic cell removal showed that resident alveolar macrophages were inefficient in recognition and uptake of senescent neutrophils.[121] We now know that they express only low levels of the PS receptor. The efficacy of resident interstitial macrophages has not been addressed. During inflammatory reactions the influx of new macrophages from blood and local replication results in a population with increased PS-receptor expression and increased ability to remove apoptotic cells and to release TGF-β. Whether the inflammatory environment also increases these properties in the resident cells is not clear, nor is there full characterization of these receptors, their modulation, and the appropriate cell functions in the different lung macrophage populations. One such function in mature macrophages appears to be not only uptake of the apoptotic cells but also their rapid digestion within the phagosomes, again emphasizing the overall efficiency of the system. Intriguingly, however, not all apoptotic cell contents are destroyed at the same rate. Thus, during removal of neutrophils, some of the neutrophil elastase may remain for a while within the macrophage phagosome, conceivably available for subsequent release and action. On a larger scale, organisms originally ingested by soon-to-become apoptotic cells may escape exposure to extracellular antibody or complement and survive within the phagosomes of the macrophage after ingestion of the apoptotic cells containing them.

Clearance

The above discussion of cell clearance in pulmonary inflammation naturally leads one to question the mechanisms by which the accumulating macrophages are removed. During the resolving phase, the alveoli may be full of macrophages that, in only a few days, are completely gone. Potential routes and mechanisms of removal include, clearance by the mucociliary escalator with ultimate destruction in the gut, migration back into the bloodstream, emigration to the lymphatics and local lymph nodes, or local death (apoptotic or otherwise) with clearance by other macrophages or by the epithelium. Despite the potential importance of this process, it has received remarkably little investigation. At one point the lung was even cited as a potential route of clearance for macrophages from other sites in the body that entered the bloodstream (directly or from lymphatics), lodged in the pulmonary circulation, migrated into the alveolus, and were cleared through the airways. However, studies of peritoneal macrophages by Bellingan et al[138] and at our own institution (unpublished observations) show this not to be the case. Macrophages appear for the most part to be cleared locally. However, the lung is a special case, and it must be supposed that a significant proportion of these cells that reach the air spaces are cleared through the mucociliary escalator.

There is no evidence for movement back to the bloodstream. However, elegant studies in the 1980s by Bice and associates[139] suggested a route of clearance to the local lymph nodes. Two interesting caveats must be applied to this investigation. The actual markers detected were fluorescent particles, and, although shown originally in macrophages within the alveoli, they could have been passed to the lymph nodes by some other mechanism than within macrophages. The recent recognition that immature dendritic cells are avidly phagocytic and, in the process of subsequent maturation, migrate to the local lymph nodes to initiate adaptive immune responses raises other possibilities. How many of the phagocytic macrophage-like cells in a pulmonary inflammation are, in fact, dendritic cells? Do true macrophages migrate to the lymph nodes? Are apoptotic macrophages ingested by immature dendritic cells, with the resulting potential processing of contained antigens for presentation to the immune system?

A reasonable additional suggestion for clearance is that some, or many, of the macrophages themselves become apoptotic and are cleared locally by other macrophages or even by tissue cells. On the other hand, a study in inflamed peritoneum suggested that local death and removal was not of significant importance, and emphasized the lymph node route as critical.[138] The potential rapidity of uptake and digestion means that mere examination for the presence of apoptotic macrophages in lesions is not likely to answer this question, although Bellingan et al[138] did address this issue. While blood monocytes have been examined extensively for induction of apoptosis and the pathways involved, less attention has been paid to macrophages, and even less to macrophage subsets. As discussed earlier, in many tissues, including the lung, resident macrophages are known to live for a long time. Something, then, must distinguish the resident cell from an inflammatory macrophage that either migrates away or dies in situ. A current prevailing concept in apoptosis is that cells are maintained actively in a living state by stimuli that induce antiapoptotic signals. These include appropriate growth factors (including M-CSF for macrophages) or ligation of adhesion molecules. Little is known about this type of regulation in macrophages within the lung and whether resident cells and inflammatory macrophages show differential susceptibility to such signals.

Concluding Comments

Our understanding of how macrophages contribute to the growth, defense, inflammation, repair, and function of the lung has improved greatly in recent years. In this chapter, we have attempted to illustrate some of the current dogmas and concepts that have been established, as well as highlight areas that require further research. Clearly, there are more questions than answers, but the application of current and emerging technologies can be expected to provide great insights into the role(s) and functions of macrophages in coming years. For example, while GM-CSF-deficient op/op mice, and chemically induced macrophage-deficient mice have helped in our understanding of the fundamental roles of macrophages in the lung, we have little knowledge about the role of primitive macrophages in lung development and function. Unfortunately, *c-fms*-null mice die during embryonic development most likely due to the need for the M-CSF receptor in the function of the placenta. However, the development of conditional knockout animals may allow this question to be addressed, and may provide clear answers about general macrophage functions in the adult. There are also emerging data[140] to suggest that defective uptake of apoptotic neutrophils may contribute to chronic inflammatory diseases of the lung, such as in cystic fibrosis or recurrent infections. Thus, an understanding of how macrophages handle these cells, and the mechanisms that result in impaired cell uptake, is clearly indicated. Last, the role of the macrophage in innate protection of the lung currently is undergoing a revival in interest, and this surely will provide a better understanding of the fundamental mechanisms of macrophage involvement in lung immunity.

Acknowledgments

The authors wish to acknowledge the members of our laboratories who, over the years, have contributed to some of the work discussed in this review. In addition, we wish to thank Jan Henson for preparing the electron micrographs. This work was supported by PHS grants HL65326, HL 56556, and HL55549 (to D.W.H.R.) and GM48211 and HL60980 (to P.M.H.) from the National Institutes of Health.

References

1. Brain JD, Molina RM, Warner AE. Pulmonary intravascular macrophages. In: Lipscomb MF, Russell SW, eds. Lung macrophages and dendritic cells in health and disease. Vol. 102. New York: Marcel Dekker, 1997:131–49.
2. Laszlo DJ, Henson PM, Remigio LK, et al. Development of functional diversity in mouse macrophages. Mutual exclusion of two phenotypic states. Am J Pathol 1993; 143:587–97.
3. Lake FR, Noble PW, Henson PM, Riches DW. Functional switching of macrophage responses to tumor necrosis factor-alpha (TNF alpha) by interferons. Implications for the pleiotropic activities of TNF alpha. J Clin Invest 1994;93:1661–9.
4. Henson PM, Riches DW. Modulation of macrophage maturation by cytokines and lipid mediators: a potential role in resolution of pulmonary inflammation. Ann N Y Acad Sci 1994;725: 298–308.
5. Riches DW. Signalling heterogeneity as a contributing factor in macrophage functional diversity. Semin Cell Biol 1995;6:377–84.
6. Savill J, Haslett C. Granulocyte clearance by apoptosis in the resolution of inflammation. Semin Cell Biol 1995; 6:385–93.
7. Haslett C. Granulocyte apoptosis and its role in the resolution and control of lung inflammation. Am J Respir Crit Care Med 1999;160:S5–11.
8. Riches DWH. Macrophage involvement in wound repair, remodeling and fibrosis. In: Clark RAF, ed. The molecular and cellular biology of wound repair. New York: Plenum Press, 1996:95–141.
9. Hume DA, Monkley SJ, Wainwright BJ. Detection of c-fms protooncogene in early mouse embryos by whole mount in situ hybridization indicates roles for macrophages in tissue remodelling. Br J Haematol 1995;90:939–42.
10. Sorokin SP, Hoyt RF Jr, Blunt DG, McNelly NA. Macrophage development: II. Early ontogeny of macrophage populations in brain, liver, and lungs of rat embryos as revealed by a lectin marker. Anat Rec 1992;232:527–50.
11. van Furth R, Diesselhoff-den Dulk MMC, Mattie H. Quantitative study on the production and kinetics of mononuclear phagocytes during an acute inflammatory reaction. J Exp Med 1973;138:1314–30.
12. Blusse van Oud Alblas A, van der Linden-Schrever B, van Furth R. Origin and kinetics of pulmonary macrophages during an inflammatory reaction induced by intravenous administration of heat-killed bacillus Calmette-Guérin. J Exp Med 1981;154:235–52.
13. Rabinowitz SS, Gordon S. Macrosialin, a macrophage-restricted membrane sialoprotein differentially glycosylated in response to inflammatory stimuli [published erratum appears in J Exp Med 1992;175:309]. J Exp Med 1991;174:827–36.
14. de Bruijn MF, Slieker WA, van der Loo JC, et al. Distinct mouse bone marrow macrophage precursors identified by differential expression of ER-MP12 and ER-MP20 antigens. Eur J Immunol 1994;24:2279–84.
15. Clarke S, Gordon S. Myeloid-specific gene expression. J Leukoc Biol 1998;63:153–68.
16. Sorokin SP, Hoyt RF Jr. Macrophage development: I. Rationale for using *Griffonia simplicifolia* isolectin B_4 as a marker for the line. Anat Rec 1992;232:520–6.
17. Sorokin SP, McNelly NA, Blunt DG, Hoyt RF Jr. Macrophage development: III. Transformation of pulmonary macrophages from precursors in fetal lungs and their later maturation in organ culture. Anat Rec 1992; 232:551–71.
18. Sorokin SP, McNelly NA, Hoyt RF Jr. CFU-rAM, the origin of lung macrophages, and the macrophage lineage. Am J Physiol 1992;263:L299–307.
19. Dranoff G, Crawford AD, Sadelain M, et al. Involvement of granulocyte-macrophage colony-stimulating factor in pulmonary homeostasis. Science 1994;264:713–6.
20. Huffman JA, Hull WM, Dranoff G, et al. Pulmonary epithelial cell expression of GM-CSF corrects the alveolar proteinosis in GM-CSF-deficient mice. Am Soc Clin Invest 1996;97:649–55.
21. Wiktor-Jedrzejczak W, Bartocci A, Ferrante AW Jr, et al. Total absence of colony-stimulating factor 1 in the macrophage-deficient osteopetrotic (op/op) mouse. Proc Natl Acad Sci U S A 1990;87:4828–32.
22. Wiktor-Jedrzejczak W, Ratajczak MZ, Ptasznik A, et al. CSF-1 deficiency in the *op/op* mouse has differential effects on macrophage populations and differentiation stages. Exp Hematol 1992;20:1004–10.
23. Lieschke GJ, Stanley ER, Grail D, et al. Mice lacking both macrophage- and granulocyte-macrophage colony-stimulating factor have macrophages and coexistent osteopetrosis and severe lung disease. Blood 1994;84:27–35.
24. Franc NC, White K, Ezekowitz RA. Phagocytosis and development: back to the future. Curr Opin Immunol 1999;11:47–52.
25. Tarling JD, Coggle JE. Evidence for the pulmonary origin of alveolar macrophages. Cell Tissue Kinet 1982;15:577–84.
26. Tarling JD, Coggle JE. The absence of effect on pulmonary alveolar macrophage numbers during prolonged periods of monocytopenia. J Reticuloendothel Soc 1982; 31:221–4.
27. Coggle JE, Tarling JD. Cell kinetics of pulmonary alveolar macrophages in the mouse. Cell Tissue Kinet 1982; 15:139–43.
28. Sawyer RT, Strausbauch PH, Volkman A. Resident macrophage proliferation in mice depleted of blood monocytes by strontium-90. Lab Invest 1982;46:165–70.
29. Sawyer RT. The ontogeny of pulmonary alveolar macrophages in parabiotic mice. J Leukocyte Biol 1986; 40:347–54.
30. Nakata K, Gotoh H, Watanabe J, et al. Augmented proliferation of human alveolar macrophages after allogeneic bone marrow transplantation. Blood 1999;93:667–73.
31. Lin H, Kuhn C, Chen D. Effects of hydrocortisone acetate on pulmonary alveolar macrophage colony-forming cells. Am Rev Respir Dis 1982;125:712–5.
32. Kjellstrom C, Ichimura K, Chen XJ, et al. The origin of alveolar macrophages in the transplanted lung: a longitudinal microsatellite-based study of donor and recipient DNA. Transplantation 2000;69:1984–6.
33. Wijffels JF, Hendrickx RJ, Steenbergen JJ, et al. Milky spots in the mouse omentum may play an important role in

the origin of peritoneal macrophages. Res Immunol 1992;143:401–9.
34. Cranshaw ML, Leak LV. Milky spots of the omentum: a source of peritoneal cells in the normal and stimulated animal. Arch Histol Cytol 1990;53:165–77.
35. Zhu H, Naito M, Umezu H, et al. Macrophage differentiation and expression of macrophage colony-stimulating factor in murine milky spots and omentum after macrophage elimination. J Leukoc Biol 1997;61:436–44.
36. Agalar F, Sayek I, Cakmakci M, et al. Effect of omentectomy on peritoneal defence mechanisms in rats. Eur J Surg 1997;163:605–9.
37. Marder SR, Chenoweth DE, Goldstein IM, Perez HD. Chemotactic responses of human peripheral blood monocytes to the complement-derived peptides C5a and C5a desArg. J Immunol 1985;134:3325–31.
38. Doherty DE, Henson PM, Clark RA. Fibronectin fragments containing the RGDS cell-binding domain mediate monocyte migration into the rabbit lung. A potential mechanism for C5 fragment-induced monocyte lung accumulation. J Clin Invest 1990;86:1065–75.
39. Jaovisidha P, Peeples ME, Brees AA. et al. Respiratory syncytial virus stimulates neutrophil degranulation and chemokine release. J Immunol 1999;163:2816–20.
40. Siddiqui RA, Akard LP, Garcia JG, et al. Chemotactic migration triggers IL-8 generation in neutrophilic leukocytes. J Immunol 1999;162:1077–83.
41. Doherty DE, Downey GP, Schwab B III, et al. Lipolysaccharide-induced monocyte retention in the lung. Role of monocyte stiffness, actin assembly, and CD18-dependent adherence. J Immunol 1994;153:241–55.
42. Musson RA. Human serum induces maturation of human monocytes in vitro. Am J Pathol 1983;111:331–40.
43. Proveddini DM, Deftos LJ, Manolagas SC. 1,25-dihydroxyvitamin D_3 promotes in vitro morphologic and enzymatic changes in normal human monocytes consistent with their differentiation into macrophages. Bone 1986;7:23–8.
44. Allavena P, Piemonti L, Longoni D, et al. IL-10 prevents the differentiation of monocytes to dendritic cells but promotes their maturation to macrophages. Eur J Immunol 1998;28:359–69.
45. Metcalf D. The molecular control of blood cells. Cambridge: Harvard University Press, 1988.
46. Lagasse E, Weissman IL. Enforced expression of Bcl-2 in monocytes rescues macrophages and partially reverses osteopetrosis in *op/op* mice. Cell 1997;89:1021–31.
47. Adamson IY, Letourneau HL, Bowden DH. Comparison of alveolar and interstitial macrophages in fibroblast stimulation after silica and long or short asbestos. Lab Invest 1991;64:339–44.
48. Uh S-T, Inoue Y, King TE Jr, et al. Morphometric analysis of insulin-like growth factor-I localization in lung tissues of patients with idiopathic pulmonary fibrosis. Am J Respir Crit Care Med 1998;158:1626–35.
49. Holmskov U, Mollenhauer J, Madsen J, et al. Cloning of gp-340, a putative opsonin receptor for lung surfactant protein D. Proc Natl Acad Sci U S A 1999;96:10794–9.
50. Holmskov U, Lawson P, Teisner B, et al. Isolation and characterization of a new member of the scavenger receptor superfamily, glycoprotein-340 (gp-340), as a lung surfactant protein-D binding molecule. J Biol Chem 1997;272:13743–9.
51. Chroneos ZC, Abdolrasulnia R, Whitsett JA, et al. Purification of a cell-surface receptor for surfactant protein A. J Biol Chem 1996;271:16375–83.
52. Pison U, Wright JR, Hawgood S. Specific binding of surfactant apoprotein SP-A to rat alveolar macrophages. Am J Physiol 1992;262:L412–7.
53. Korfhagen TR, Sheftelyevich V, Burhans MS, et al. Surfactant protein-D regulates surfactant phospholipid homeostasis in vivo. J Biol Chem 1998;273:28438–43.
54. LeVine AM, Bruno MD, Huelsman KM, et al. Surfactant protein A–deficient mice are susceptible to group B streptococcal infection. J Immunol 1997;158:4336–40.
55. LeVine AM, Whitsett JA, Gwozdz JA, et al. Distinct effects of surfactant protein A or D deficiency during bacterial infection on the lung [in process citation]. J Immunol 2000;165:3934–40.
56. Aderem A, Ulevitch RJ. Toll-like receptors in the induction of the innate immune response. Nature 2000; 406:782–7.
57. Ozinsky A, Underhill DM, Fontenot JD, et al. The repertoire for pattern recognition of pathogens by the innate immune system is defined by cooperation between toll-like receptors [in process citation]. Proc Natl Acad Sci U S A 2000;97:13766–71.
58. Wright SD, Ramos RA, Tobias PS, et al. CD14, a receptor for complexes of lipopolysaccharide (LPS) and LPS binding protein [comments]. Science 1990;249:1431–3.
59. Krieg AM. Mechanisms and applications of immune stimulatory CpG oligodeoxynucleotides. Biochim Biophys Acta 1999;1489:107–16.
60. Linehan SA, Martinez-Pomares L, Gordon S. Mannose receptor and scavenger receptor: two macrophage pattern recognition receptors with diverse functions in tissue homeostasis and host defense. Adv Exp Med Biol 2000;479:1–14.
61. Lien E, Sellati TJ, Yoshimura A, et al. Toll-like receptor 2 functions as a pattern recognition receptor for diverse bacterial products. J Biol Chem 1999;274:33419–25.
62. Holt PG. Regulation of antigen-presenting cell function(s) in lung and airway tissues. Eur Respir J 1993;6:120–9.
63. Holt PG. Inhibitor activity of unstimulated alveolar macrophages on T-lymphocyte blastogenic response. Am Rev Respir Dis 1978;118:791–3.
64. Thepen T, Hoeben K, Breve J, Kraal G. Alveolar macrophage elimination in vivo is associated with an increase in pulmonary immune responses in mice. J Exp Med 1989;170: 499–509.
65. Thepen T, McMenamin C, Oliver J, et al. Regulation of immune response to inhaled antigen by alveolar macrophages: differential effects of in vivo alveolar macrophage elimination on the induction of tolerance vs. immunity. Eur J Immunol 1991;21:2845–50.
66. Lipscomb MF, Pollard AM, Yates JL. A role for TGF-beta in the suppression by murine bronchoalveolar cells of lung dendritic cell initiated immune responses. Reg Immunol 1993;5:151–7.
67. Roth MD, Golub SH. Human pulmonary macrophages utilize prostaglandins and transforming growth factor β1

to suppress lymphocyte activation. J Leukoc Biol 1993; 53:366–71.
68. Kawabe T, Isobe K-I, Hassegawa Y, et al. Immunosuppressive activity induced by nitric oxide in culture supernatant of activated rat alveolar macrophages. Immunology 1992;76:72–8.
69. Bilyk N, Holt PG. Inhibition of the immunosuppressive activity of resident pulmonary alveolar macrophages by granulocyte/macrophage colony-stimulating factor. J Exp Med 1993;177:1773–7.
70. Caux C, Dezutter-Dambuyant C, Schmitt D, Banchereau J. GM-CSF and TNF-alpha cooperate in the generation of dendritic Langerhan's cells. Nature 1992;360:258–61.
71. Jackson SH, Gallin JI, Holland SM. The p47phox mouse knock-out model of chronic granulomatous disease. J Exp Med 1995;182:751–8.
72. Tauber AI, Borregaard N, Simons E, Wright J. Chronic granulomatous disease: a syndrome of phagocyte oxidase deficiencies. Medicine 1983;62:286–309.
73. Chang YC, Segal BH, Holland SM, et al. Virulence of catalase-deficient *Aspergillus nidulans* in p47phos -/- mice. Implications for fungal pathogenicity and host defense in chronic granulomatous disease. J Clin Invest 1998;101:1843–50.
74. Castranova V, Vallyathan V, Ramsey DM, et al. Augmentation of pulmonary reactions to quartz inhalation by trace amounts of iron-containing particles. Environ Health Perspect 1997;105:1319–24.
75. Loukides S, Horvath I, Wodehouse T, et al. Airway inflammation is important in the development and progression of many lung diseases, including bronchiectasis. Am J Respir Crit Care Med 1998;158:991–4.
76. Xie Q-W, Cho HJ, Calaycay J, et al. Cloning and characterization of inducible nitric oxide synthase from mouse macrophages. Science 1992;256:225–8.
77. MacMicking JD, Nathan C, Hom G, et al. Altered responses to bacterial infection and endotoxic shock in mice lacking inducible nitric oxide synthase. Cell 1995; 81:641–50.
78. Gow AJ, Thom SR, Ischiropoulos H. Nitric oxide and peroxynitrite-mediated pulmonary cell death. Am J Physiol 1998;274:L112–8.
79. Humes JL, Bonney RJ, Pelus L, et al. Macrophages synthesis and release prostaglandins in response to inflammatory stimuli. Nature 1977;269:149–51.
80. Leslie CC. Properties and regulation of cytosolic phospholipase A2. J Biol Chem 1997;272:16709–12.
81. Albert DH, Snyder F. Biosynthesis of 1-alkyl-2-acetyl-sn-glycero-3-phosphocholine (platelet-activating factor) from 1-alkyl-2-acyl-sn-glycero-3-phosphocholine by rat alveolar macrophages. Phospholipase A2 and acetyltransferase activities during phagocytosis and ionophore stimulation. J Biol Chem 1983;258:97–102.
82. Riches DW, Channon JY, Leslie CC, Henson PM. Receptor-mediated signal transduction in mononuclear phagocytes. Prog Allergy 1988;42:65–122.
83. Lo CJ, Cryer HG, Fu M, Kim B. Endotoxin-induced macrophage gene expression depends on platelet-activating factor. Arch Surg 1997;132:1342–7.
84. Maier RV, Hahnel GB, Fletcher JR. Platelet-activating factor augments tumor necrosis factor and procoagulant activity. J Surg Res 1992;52:258–64.
85. Hsueh W. Prostaglandin biosynthesis in pulmonary macrophages. Am J Pathol 1979;97:137–48.
86. Hempel SL, Monick MM, Hunninghake GW. Lipopolysaccharide induces prostaglandin H synthase-2 protein and mRNA in human alveolar macrophages and blood monocytes. J Clin Invest 1994;93:391–6.
87. Thivierge M, Rola-Pleszczynski M. Up-regulation of inducible cyclooxygenase gene expression by platelet-activating factor in activated rat alveolar macrophages. J Immunol 1995;154:6593–9.
88. Rankin JA, Sylvester I, Smith S, et al. Macrophages cultured in vitro release leukotriene B4 and neutrophil attractant/activation protein (interleukin 8) sequentially in response to stimulation with lipopolysaccharide and zymosan. J Clin Invest 1990;86:1556–64.
89. Martin TR, Raugi G, Merritt TL, Henderson WR Jr. Relative contribution of leukotriene B4 to the neutrophil chemotactic activity produced by the resident human alveolar macrophage. J Clin Invest 1987;80:1114–24.
90. Wenzel SE. Antileukotriene drugs in the management of asthma [comments]. JAMA 1998;280:2068–9.
91. Busse WW, McGill KA, Horwitz RJ. Leukotriene pathway inhibitors in asthma and chronic obstructive pulmonary disease. Clin Exp Allergy 1999;29(Suppl 2):110–5.
92. Evans DJ, Barnes PJ, Cluzel M, O'Connor BJ. Effects of a potent platelet-activating factor antagonist, SR27417A, on allergen-induced asthmatic responses. Am J Respir Crit Care Med 1997;156:11–6.
93. Abraham E, Glauser MP, Butler T, et al. p55 Tumor necrosis factor receptor fusion protein in the treatment of patients with severe sepsis and septic shock. A randomized controlled multicenter trial. Ro 45-2081 Study Group. JAMA 1997;277:1531–8.
94. Abraham E, Anzueto A, Gutierrez G, et al. Double-blind randomised controlled trial of monoclonal antibody to human tumour necrosis factor in treatment of septic shock. NORASEPT II Study Group [comments]. Lancet 1998;351:929–33.
95. Opal SM, Fisher CJ Jr, Dhainaut JF, et al. Confirmatory interleukin-1 receptor antagonist trial in severe sepsis: a phase III, randomized, double-blind, placebo-controlled, multicenter trial. The Interleukin-1 Receptor Antagonist Sepsis Investigator Group [comments]. Crit Care Med 1997;25:1115–24.
96. Abraham E. Why immunomodulatory therapies have not worked in sepsis. Intensive Care Med 1999;25:556–66.
97. Kunkel SL, Lukacs NW, Strieter RM, Chensue SW. The role of chemokines in the immunopathology of pulmonary disease. Forum (Genova) 1999;9:339–55.
98. Keane MP, Strieter RM. Chemokine signaling in inflammation. Crit Care Med 2000;28:N13–26.
99. Strieter RM, Polverini PJ, Kunkel SL, et al. The functional role of the ELR motif in CXC chemokine-mediated angiogenesis. J Biol Chem 1995;270:27348–57.
100. Moore BB, Keane MP, Addison CL, et al. CXC chemokine modulation of angiogenesis: the importance of balance

between angiogenic and angiostatic members of the family. J Invest Med 1998;46:113–20.
101. Carre PC, Mortenson RL, King TEJ, et al. Increased expression of the interleukin-8 gene by alveolar macrophages in idiopathic pulmonary fibrosis. A potential mechanism for the recruitment and activation of neutrophils in lung fibrosis. J Clin Invest 1991;88:1802–10.
102. Donnelly SC, Strieter RM, Kunkel SL, et al. Interleukin-8 and development of adult respiratory distress syndrome in at risk patient groups. Lancet 1993;341:643–7.
103. Carre PC, King TE Jr, Mortensen R, Riches DWH. Cryptogenic organizing pneumonia: increased expression of interleukin-8 and fibronectin genes by alveolar macrophages. Am J Respir Cell Mol Biol 1994;10:100–5.
104. Khan TZ, Wagener JS, Bost T, et al. Early pulmonary inflammation in infants with cystic fibrosis. Am J Respir Crit Care Med 1995;151:1075–82.
105. Standiford TJ, Rolfe MW, Kunkel SL, et al. Macrophage inflammatory protein-1 alpha expression in interstitial lung disease. J Immunol 1993;151:2852–63.
106. Smith RE, Strieter RM, Zhang K, et al. A role for C-C chemokines in fibrotic lung disease. J Leukoc Biol 1995;57:782–7.
107. Standiford TJ, Kunkel SL, Basha MA, et al. Interleukin-8 gene expression by a pulmonary epithelial cell line. A model for cytokine networks in the lung. J Clin Invest 1990;86:1945–53.
108. Chan ED, Worthen GS, Augustin A, et al. Inflammation in the pathogenesis of interstitial lung diseases. In: Schwarz MI, Kim TE Jr, eds. Interstitial lung disease. Hamilton (ON): B.C. Decker, 1997;135–64.
109. Welgus HG, Campbell EJ, Cury JD, et al. Neutral metalloproteinases produced by human mononuclear phagocytes. Enzyme profile, regulation, and expression during cellular development. J Clin Invest 1990;86:1496–502.
110. Campbell EJ, Cury JD, Lazarus CJ, Wegus HG. Monocyte procollagenase and tissue inhibitor of metalloproteinases. Identification, chacterization, and regulation of secretion. J Biol Chem 1987;262:15862–8.
111. Campbell EJ, Cury JD, Shapiro SD, et al. Neutral proteinases of human mononuclear phagocytes. Cellular differentiation markedly alters cell phenotype for serine proteinases, metalloproteinases, and tissue inhibitor of metalloproteinases. J Immunol 1991;146:1286–93.
112. Leibovitch SJ, Ross R. The role of macrophage in wound repair. A study with hydrocortisone and antimacrophage serum. Am J Pathol 1975;78:71–100.
113. Khalil N, Bereznay O, Sporn M, Greenberg AH. Macrophage production of transforming growth factor beta and fibroblast collagen synthesis in chronic pulmonary inflammation. J Exp Med 1989;170:727–37.
114. Heine UI, Munoz EF, Flanders KC, et al. Colocalization of TGF-beta 1 and collagen I and III, fibronectin and glycosaminoglycans during lung branching morphogenesis. Development 1990;109:29–36.
115. Roberts AB, Sporn MB, Assoian RK, et al. Transforming growth factor type beta: rapid induction of fibrosis and angiogenesis in vivo and stimulation of collagen formation in vitro. Proc Natl Acad Sci U S A 1986;83:4167–71.
116. Wright JK, Cawston TE, Hazleman BL. Transforming growth factor beta stimulates the production of the tissue inhibitor of metalloproteinases (TIMP) by human synovial and skin fibroblasts. Biochim Biophys Acta 1991;1094:207–10.
117. Goldstein RH, Poliks CF, Pilch PF, et al. Stimulation of collagen formation by insulin and insulin-like growth factor I in cultures of human lung fibroblasts. Endocrinology 1989;124:964–70.
118. Wang L, Ma W, Markovich R, et al. Insulin-like growth factor I modulates induction of apoptotic signaling in H9C2 cardiac muscle cells. Endocrinology 1998;139:1354–60.
119. Singleton JR, Randolph AE, Feldman EL. Insulin-like growth factor I receptor prevents apoptosis and enhances neuroblastoma tumorigenesis. Cancer Res 1996;56:4522–9.
120. Thornton SC, Robbins JM, Penny R, Breit SN. Fibroblast growth factors in connective tissue disease associated interstitial lung disease. Clin Exp Immunol 1992;90:447–52.
121. Newman S, Henson J, Henson P. Phagocytosis of senescent neutrophils by human monocyte-derived macrophages and rabbit inflammatory macrophages. J Exp Med 1982;156:430–42.
122. Metchnikoff E. Lectures on the comparative pathology of inflammation. Delivered at the Pasteur Institute 1891. New York: Dover Publications, 1968:xx–224.
123. Fadok VA, Henson PM. Apoptosis: getting rid of the bodies. Curr Biol 1998;8:R693–5.
124. Fadok VA. Clearance: the last and often forgotten stage of apoptosis. J Mammary Gland Biol Neoplasia 1999;4:203–11.
125. Savill,J. Apoptosis. Phagocytic docking without shocking [news; comments]. Nature 1998;392:442–3.
126. Parnaik R, Raff MC, Scholes J. Differences between the clearance of apoptotic cells by professional and non-professional phagocytes. Curr Biol 2000;10:857–60.
127. Fadok VA, Bratton DL, Rose DM, et al. A receptor for phosphatidylserine-specific clearance of apoptotic cells [comments]. Nature 2000;405:85–90.
128. Savill J, Fadok V. Corpse clearance defines the meaning of cell death [in process citation]. Nature 2000;407:784–8.
129. Moffatt OD, Devitt A, Bell ED, et al. Macrophage recognition of ICAM-3 on apoptotic leukocytes. J Immunol 1999;162:6800–10.
130. Fadok VA, de Cathelineau A, Daleke DL, et al. Loss of phospholipid asymmetry and surface exposure of phosphatidylserine is required for phagocytosis of apoptotic cells by macrophages and fibroblasts. J Biol Chem 2001;276:1071–7.
131. Sim RB, Moestrup SK, Stuart GR, et al. Interaction of C1q and the collectins with the potential receptors calreticulin (cC1qR/collectin receptor) and megalin. Immunobiology 1998;199:208–24.
132. Ogden CA, deCathelineau AM, Hoffmann, P, et al. C1q and collectin engagement of cell surface calreticulin stimulates macropinocytosis and uptake of apototic cells. J Exp Med. [In Press]

133. Taylor PR, Carugati A, Fadok VA, et al. A hierarchical role for classical pathway complement proteins in the clearance of apoptotic cells in vivo. J Exp Med 2000;192:359–66.
134. van den Eijnde SM, Lips J, Boshart L, et al. Spatiotemporal distribution of dying neurons during early mouse development. Eur J Neurosci 1999;11:712–24.
135. Stern M, Savill J, Haslett C. Human monocyte-derived macrophage phagocytosis of senescent eosinophils undergoing apoptosis. Mediation by alpha v beta 3/CD36/thrombospondin recognition mechanism and lack of phlogistic response. Am J Pathol 1996;149:911–21.
136. Fadok VA, McDonald PP, Bratton DL, Henson PM. Regulation of macrophage cytokine production by phagocytosis of apoptotic and post-apoptotic cells. Biochem Soc Trans 1998;26:653–6.
137. Matzinger P. An innate sense of danger. Semin Immunol 1998;10:399–415.
138. Bellingan GJ, Caldwell H, Howie SE, et al. In vivo fate of the inflammatory macrophage during the resolution of inflammation: inflammatory macrophages do not die locally, but emigrate to the draining lymph nodes. J Immunol 1996;157:2577–85.
139. Harmsen AG, Muggenburg BA, Snipes MB, Bice DE. The role of macrophages in particle translocation from lungs to lymph nodes. Science 1985;230:1277–80.
140. Pryjma J, Kaszuba-Zwoinska J, Pawlik J, et al. Alveolar macrophages of children suffering from recurrent infections of respiratory tract are less efficient in eliminating apoptotic neutrophils. Pediatr Pulmonol 1999;27:167–73.

CHAPTER 37

The Role of Oxidant Injury in the Pathogenesis of Bronchopulmonary Dysplasia

Jonathan M. Davis, MD, Richard Parad, MD, MPH

Bronchopulmonary dysplasia (BPD) is a chronic lung disease that develops in newborn infants treated with oxygen and positive-pressure mechanical ventilation for a primary lung disorder. Bronchopulmonary dysplasia generally occurs in premature infants, although it can be seen in critically ill full-term infants. The use of new treatment modalities has significantly improved the outcome for many critically ill infants. As a result, more infants are surviving the newborn period, but developing BPD. This is important, since the development of BPD is associated with significant long-term pulmonary and neurologic sequelae.[1] Bronchopulmonary dysplasia has become an extremely important complication of neonatal intensive care and the most common form of chronic lung disease in infants.

Bronchopulmonary dysplasia was first described in 1967 by Northway, who documented the clinical course, radiographic findings, and histopathologic lung changes in a group of infants who had received oxygen and ventilatory support for treatment of respiratory distress syndrome (RDS).[2] Northway originally postulated that oxygen toxicity was the primary cause of BPD, and there is increasing evidence implicating reactive oxygen species in the pathogenesis of BPD. However, positive-pressure ventilation, prematurity, genetic predisposition, inflammation, infection (prenatal and postnatal), and excessive fluid administration also may play important roles. The detailed cellular and molecular mechanisms causing BPD and possible prevention strategies still have not been well established.

This chapter reviews the definition and incidence of BPD, pathophysiologic changes, detailed mechanisms associated with the pathogenesis, long-term outcome, and new therapeutic intervention strategies for the prevention of BPD in high-risk infants.

Definition and Incidence of Bronchopulmonary Dysplasia

As the care of neonates has improved, the criteria defining BPD have changed. Many infants developing chronic lung disease do not require prolonged mechanical ventilation. Several studies have defined BPD as simply the requirement for oxygen supplementation at 28 days of life with or without an abnormal chest radiograph.[3,4] Shennan and colleagues suggested that the need for oxygen supplementation at 36 weeks' postconceptual gestational age may be a more accurate predictor of ultimate pulmonary outcome.[5] Other investigators have found that the only method to definitively establish the diagnosis of BPD is the presence of chronic respiratory symptoms (ie, asthma, repeated pulmonary infections) requiring treatment with bronchodilators or corticosteroids in the first year or two of life.[6] The definition of BPD may need to be more flexible and not restricted to a single point in time to properly define patients who develop long-term pulmonary sequelae. Recently, the term "chronic lung disease" (CLD) has been used to describe both preterm and full-term infants developing chronic respiratory dysfunction. For simplicity, we will use the term BPD to encompass the more general term, CLD.

The incidence of BPD depends on the definition used and the patient population studied. Several recent studies have indicated that surfactant replacement therapy has significantly improved survival in very low-birth-weight infants, while simultaneously decreasing the incidence and severity of BPD.[7,8] Although it appears from these studies that the incidence of BPD (20 to 60% of infants < 1,500 g) has decreased slightly after the introduction of surfactant therapy, the prevalence, or total number of infants with BPD, has increased secondary to improved survival. A better understanding of the pathophysiologic abnormalities in BPD as well as basic mechanisms involved in the lung injury process are needed urgently.

Pathophysiologic Changes

Infants with BPD demonstrate abnormalities in clinical status, chest radiograph, cardiopulmonary function, and morphologic examination of the lung. The severity of BPD is directly proportional to the degree of the pathophysiologic insult. In the early stages, an increase in pulmonary resistance and airway reactivity can be demonstrated.[9] As the disease progresses in severity, airway obstruction can become more significant and expiratory flow limitation can develop.[10] The increased resistance may cause increased work of breathing and abnormalities in ventilation-perfusion matching, resulting in increased oxygen requirements. Functional residual capacity can be reduced initially because of atelectasis, but it can be elevated in later stages of BPD because of excessive air trapping and hyperinflation. A marked decrease in lung compliance can occur and appears to correlate well with morphologic and radiographic changes in the lung.

The pulmonary circulation in infants with BPD can be abnormal, with endothelial cell degeneration and proliferation, medial muscle hypertrophy, peripheral extension of smooth muscle, and vascular obliteration.[11] The vascular alterations can lead to increased pulmonary vascular pressures and the development of cor pulmonale.[12] Pulmonary hypertension unresponsive to O_2 supplementation has been associated with a poor prognosis and has generated trials examining the use of inhaled nitric oxide (iNO) in infants with significant BPD.[13,14]

Pathologic Changes

Detailed morphologic analyses on lungs of infants with BPD recently have been completed.[15] Bronchopulmonary dysplasia appears to proceed as a continuous process through distinct pathologic stages from acute lung injury, which is characterized by an exudative phase, to proliferative and reparative phases. If normal reparative processes and new lung growth occur, then BPD may resolve spontaneously. However, if lung growth and repair do not proceed normally, then BPD can become more severe.

Airways

The upper airways (ie, trachea, main bronchi) of infants with BPD may reveal significant abnormalities, depending on the duration of intubation. Grossly, mucosal edema or necrosis may be focal or more diffuse. The earliest histologic changes include patchy loss of cilia from columnar epithelial cells, which can then become dysplastic or necrotic, resulting in breakdown of the epithelial lining. Necrotic areas may involve the mucosa or extend into the submucosa. Infiltration of inflammatory cells (neutrophils, lymphocytes) into these areas may be prominent. Goblet cells may become hyperplastic, resulting in increased mucus production, which can mix with cellular debris. Granulation tissue may develop in areas that have been damaged from the endotracheal tube or from repeated suctioning procedures. Mucosal cells may regenerate or ultimately be replaced by stratified squamous epithelium or metaplastic epithelium, if the injury process continues.

The most significant pathologic changes occurring in infants with BPD are seen in the terminal bronchioles and alveolar ducts. Hyaline membranes that appear during the acute phase of RDS become covered with a thin dysplastic epithelial lining made up primarily of type II alveolar cells. These membranes may then become incorporated into the underlying airway. Edema, inflammation, exudate, and necrosis of epithelial cells can occur as the process continues. Necrotizing bronchiolitis may occur if the damage is particularly severe. Cellular debris, inflammatory cells, and proteinaceous exudate can accumulate and obstruct many of the terminal airways and the distal lung. This process may actually be beneficial, because it protects the distal alveoli from further damage from oxygen and mechanical ventilation. Fibroblast proliferation and activation in response to this insult may lead to peribronchial fibrosis and obliterative fibroproliferative bronchiolitis. Smooth muscle hypertrophy and associated bronchospasm can cause narrowing in small airways leading to small airway obstruction.

Alveoli

The earliest findings seen in the alveoli involve interstitial or alveolar edema. Focal areas of atelectasis, inflammation, exudate, and fibroblast proliferation develop later. As the disease progresses, normal alveolar architecture is disrupted with areas of atelectasis becoming more widespread and alternating with areas of marked hyperinflation. These hyperinflated areas can become emphysematous blebs. Destruction of alveoli can occur resulting in alveolar hypoplasia and a decrease in surface area available for gas exchange. Interstitial and alveolar fibrosis can develop leading to impaired fluid clearance and decreased lung compliance. Capillary beds can be severely damaged, and medial muscle hypertrophy of pulmonary arterioles can develop, resulting in marked pulmonary hypertension.

Several investigators have suggested recently that a new form of BPD has emerged in the postsurfactant era, primarily involving an arrest of lung development.[16] Infants dying with BPD may have fewer alveoli that are larger in size, with less inflammation and secondary fibrotic changes compared to that seen in the past, suggesting that an arrest in alveolarization (especially secondary alveolar crest formation) is occurring. This condition is commonly referred to as alveolar simplification. Chronically ventilated preterm baboons appear to be an excellent model in which to study BPD. Animals treated with appropriate concentrations of oxygen and ventilatory strategies to prevent volutrauma have been shown to develop pulmonary pathologic lesions similar to those seen in < hr 1,000 g infants, such as alveolar hypoplasia, variable saccular wall fibrosis, and minimal airway disease.[16] The baboon lungs demonstrated significantly decreased alveolization and capillary vasculature compared with term controls. This model demonstrates that impaired alveolization and capillary development

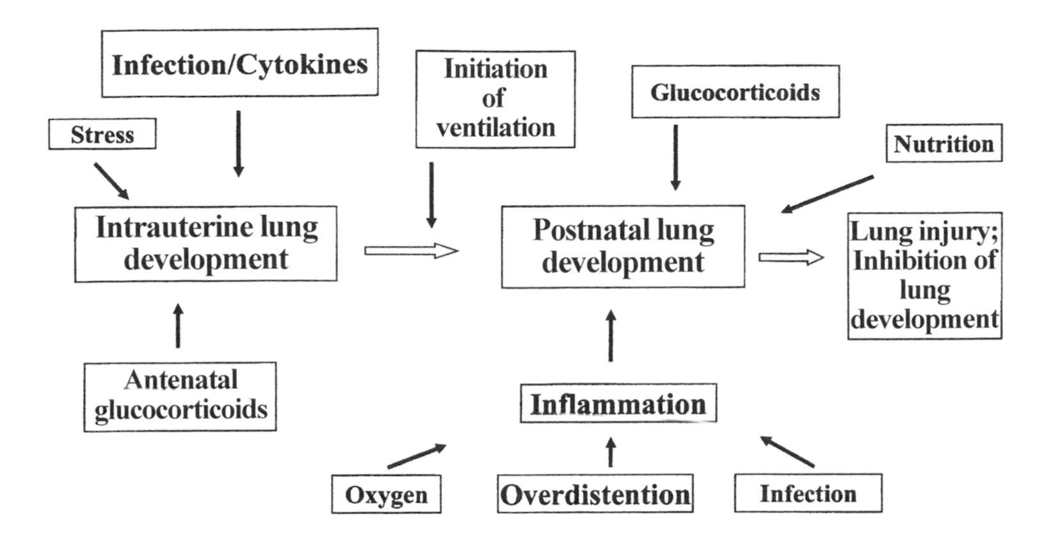

FIGURE 37–1. Pathogenesis of bronchopulmonary dysplasia (BPD) involving both prenatal and postnatal factors. (Adapted from Jobe AH.[16])

occur in immature lungs, even in the absence of marked hyperoxia (although even room air is supraphysiologic) and high ventilation settings. A better understanding of the pathogenesis of BPD may lead to the development of new therapeutic interventions.

Pathogenesis

The pathogenesis of BPD is complex, involving both prenatal and postnatal insults to the lung (Figure 37–1). A variety of factors can cause epithelial, interstitial, and endothelial injuries resulting in the release of multiple inflammatory mediators that increase vascular and epithelial permeability and induce a potent inflammatory response.[17,18] Water and protein leak into the alveoli and can interfere with surfactant function, further diminishing lung compliance.[19] Chemotactic mediators recruit and activate several inflammatory cell types in the alveolar and interstitial spaces, resulting in the release of reactive oxygen species and proteases. Alterations in oxidant-antioxidant and protease-antiprotease balance result in further inflammatory changes and lung damage (amplification phenomenon), potentially interfering with the structural development of the lung.

Prenatal Events

Subclinical intrauterine infection and the ensuing inflammatory response have now been shown to be important in the etiology of preterm labor and premature rupture of membranes.[20,21] There is also growing evidence that prenatal infection and inflammation are major risk factors for the subsequent development of BPD. Although several investigators have found a lower incidence of RDS in preterm infants born to mothers with chorioamnionitis and funisitis (possibly due to increased in utero stress) as compared to preterm infants born to mothers without chorioamnionitis, they also observed a significantly higher incidence of BPD in these same infants.[22] This suggests that although intrauterine infection may accelerate lung maturation, it may also "prime the lung," causing significant inflammation and subsequent lung injury. Antenatal exposure of the lung to proinflammatory cytokines appears to be a major risk factor for the development of BPD. Ghezzi and associates found a higher amniotic fluid interleukin (IL)-8 level (> 11.5 ng/mL) in mothers whose fetuses developed BPD compared to those whose fetuses did not (91% versus 15%, $p = .01$).[23] Infants exposed to elevated amniotic fluid tumor necrosis factor (TNF)-α levels and amniotic fluid infection have been found to have an increased incidence of RDS, prolonged requirements for supplemental oxygen and mechanical ventilation, and longer hospital stays compared with nonexposed infants.[21] Injection of endotoxin into the amniotic fluid of pregnant sheep 6 days before delivery was found to significantly increase lung compliance (59%), gas volume (twofold), and concentrations of surfactant lipids and proteins.[24] These effects were qualitatively larger than those achieved with betamethasone. White blood cell counts and messenger ribonucleic acid (mRNA) for various cytokines were increased in fetal membranes and lungs after endotoxin exposure, suggesting an early inflammatory response in the fetal lung. Similarity in the pattern of expression of cytokines suggests a common pathway for the initiation of preterm labor and also injury to the lung and the central nervous system of the fetus.

The use of antenatal corticosteroids has been shown to enhance fetal lung maturation and lower the risk for developing RDS; the effects on the incidence of BPD are more controversial.[25] Antenatal treatment with beta-

TABLE 37–1. Reactive Oxygen Species

Radical	Symbol	Antioxidant
Superoxide anion	O_2^-	Superoxide dismutase, uric acid, vitamin E
Singlet oxygen	$^1O_2$	ß-Carotene, uric acid, vitamin E
Hydrogen peroxide	H_2O_2	Catalase, glutathione peroxidase, glutathione
Hydroxyl radical	OH^-	Vitamins C and E
Peroxide radical	LOO^-	Vitamins C and E
Hydroperoxyl radical	LOOH	Glutathione transferase, glutathione peroxidase

L = lipid.

methasone has been shown repeatedly to have multiple direct beneficial effects on the fetal lung, including improved lung compliance, lung volumes, surfactant production, and antioxidant enzyme activity.[26] Betamethasone also may prevent lung damage in the fetus indirectly by reducing maternal cytokine production and exposure in the fetus. Repetitive courses of prenatal corticosteroids also have been used routinely and are associated with further improvements in lung mechanics and reduced oxidative stress in the lung.[27] However, multiple courses of antenatal steroids do appear to significantly reduce both somatic and lung growth in the fetus, which may be detrimental to long-term pulmonary function.[28]

Postnatal Events

Imbalance of Oxidants and Antioxidants

Under normal conditions, a delicate balance exists between the production of reactive oxygen species (ROS) and the antioxidant defenses that protect cells in vivo. Reactive oxygen species are molecules with extra electrons in their outer ring, and they are toxic to living tissues (Table 37–1). Oxygen has a unique molecular structure and is abundant within cells. It readily accepts free electrons generated by oxidative metabolism within the cell, producing free radicals. The balance may be disturbed by increased ROS production under a variety of conditions (Table 37–2). Alternatively, ROS can increase due to an inability to quench production, because of inadequate antioxidant defenses. Damage caused by ROS includes cell membrane destruction, mitochondrial injury, protein nitration, inactivation of growth factors, and modification of nucleic acids.[1]

The premature infant appears to be especially susceptible to ROS-induced damage, because adequate concentrations of antioxidants may be absent at birth. Frank and Groseclose have studied the development of the antioxidant enzymes superoxide dismutase (SOD), catalase, and glutathione peroxidase in the lungs of rabbits during late gestation.[29] The marked increase in these enzymes during the latter part of gestation parallels the maturation pattern of pulmonary surfactant (Figure 37–2). These developmental changes in the fetal lung allow proper ventilation by reducing surface tension, and provide for

TABLE 37–2. Sources of Reactive Oxygen Species

Normal cellular metabolism
Hyperoxia
Ischemia/reperfusion
Respiratory burst of neutrophils/mononuclear cells
Arachadonic acid metabolism

the transition from the relative hypoxia of intrauterine development to the oxygen-rich extrauterine environment. Premature birth before the upregulation of sufficient quantities of these antioxidant enzymes as well as other ROS scavengers (eg, vitamin E, ascorbic acid, glutathione, ceruloplasmin) may result in an imbalance between oxidants and antioxidants and an increased risk for the development of BPD.[30]

Oxygen radicals have been shown to be involved in the pathogenesis of BPD. Expired pentane and ethane have been measured as indirect evidence of free radical–induced lipid peroxidation in the first week of life and have been found to be elevated significantly in neonates subsequently developing BPD.[31] Similarly, plasma concentrations of allantoin, an oxidation byproduct of uric acid, has been shown to be elevated significantly in the first 48 hours of life in infants developing BPD, compared to controls.[32] Varsila and colleagues analyzed proteins in tracheal aspirates in the first week of life and found evidence of protein oxidation (carbonyl formation) in infants developing chronic lung disease.[33] Banks and associates found a fourfold increase in plasma 3-nitrotyrosine concentration in infants developing BPD compared to controls, indicating increased evidence of reactive nitrogen species (endogenous nitric

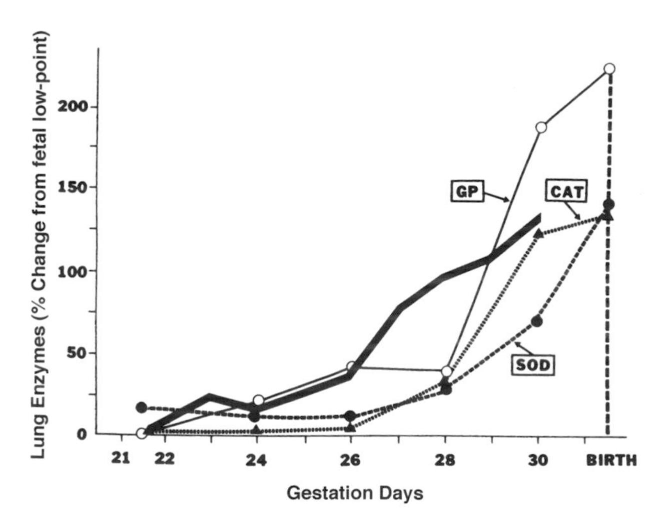

FIGURE 37–2. Developmental changes in antioxidant levels and activity during gestation. The increases in superoxide dismutase (SOD), catalase (CAT), and glutathione peroxidase (GP) late in gestation are similar to those seen for pulmonary surfactant (*dark, thick line*). (Adapted from Frank L and Groseclose EE.[29])

oxide reacting with superoxide) modifying serum proteins.[34] Most important, the multicenter STOP-ROP (supplemental therapeutic oxygen for prethreshold retinopathy of prematurity) trial examined whether exposing premature infants to higher inspired oxygen concentrations would prevent the development of severe ROP. Although the effects of the increased oxygen were minimal on the eyes, exposed infants had dramatic increases (55%) in the incidence of BPD and pulmonary infections.[35] These studies all demonstrate that ROS are intimately involved in the development of acute lung and chronic lung disease in newborn infants.

Further evidence for the role of ROS in lung injury comes from several studies that have shown that antioxidant supplementation with SOD and catalase reduces cell damage, increases survival, and prevents lung injury from prolonged hyperoxia and mechanical ventilation.[36–38] In addition, genetically engineered mice overexpressing either CuZnSOD or MnSOD survive longer, whereas mice with disrupted CuZnSOD genes die more rapidly in a hyperoxic environment compared to normal diploid controls.[39–41] All of these studies confirm the critical role of the intricate balance between the production of ROS and antioxidant defenses in the development of lung injury.

Effects of mechanical ventilation

Treatment of RDS with positive-pressure ventilation exposes the lungs to inspiratory pressures capable of causing pathologic changes. Although the initial phases of lung injury in BPD are the result of the primary disease process (eg, RDS), superimposed positive-pressure mechanical ventilation appears to add to the lung injury and to provoke a complex inflammatory cascade that ultimately leads to chronic lung disease. Barotrauma is the term generally used to describe the lung injury that occurs secondary to positive-pressure mechanical ventilation; however, volutrauma from excessive tidal volume ventilation may be a more appropriate term to describe this lung injury process.[42]

The role of barotrauma in BPD depends on several factors, including the structure of the tracheobronchial tree and the physiologic effects of surfactant deficiency. With surfactant deficiency, surface tension forces are elevated, aeration is unequal, and most terminal alveoli are collapsed. The pressure needed to distend these poorly compliant saccules is high and is transmitted to the terminal bronchioles and alveolar ducts. Nilsson and colleagues showed that even brief periods of positive-pressure ventilation cause bronchiolar epithelial damage in the lung, with the severity of the injury correlating with the amount of peak pressure used.[43] Tremblay and associates observed that mechanical ventilation with excessive tidal volumes and low positive end-expiratory pressures (PEEP) causes marked elevations in cytokine production in the lung.[44] This suggests that the damaging effects of oxygen and mechanical ventilation in the lung occur via similar pathways, primarily involving activation of the inflammatory cascade that ultimately leads to the development of acute lung injury and BPD.

Strategies to prevent lung injury have resulted in frequent and continuous changes in methods of ventilation. With the increased use of nasal continuous positive airway pressure (NCPAP), many preterm infants can be managed without the need for mechanical ventilation, which minimizes injury to the lung. Synchronized intermittent mandatory ventilators (SIMVs) and high-frequency devices also have been studied. Bernstein and associates reported that infants of < hr 1000 g receiving SIMV developed significantly less BPD compared to those receiving conventional ventilation.[45] Several multicenter trials have demonstrated that high-frequency oscillatory ventilation (HFOV) or high-frequency jet ventilation (HFJV) using high volume alveolar recruitment strategies in conjunction with surfactant replacement therapy reduced complications of mechanical ventilation (eg, pulmonary interstitial emphysema [PIE], pneumothorax) and lowered the incidence of BPD compared to conventional ventilation.[46,47] Regardless of the type of ventilation strategy used, it is imperative to avoid even brief periods of overventilation, because higher tidal volumes and hypocarbia are associated with a higher risk for the development of lung injury in critically ill neonates with RDS as well as adults with ARDS (adult RDS).[44,48]

The use of surfactant replacement therapy has resulted in dramatic decreases in complications of mechanical ventilation. Surfactant permits more equal distribution of pressures and ventilation to all alveoli, prevents overdistention of air spaces and bronchioles, and stabilizes airways. A major benefit of surfactant therapy has been the reduction of ventilator pressures and pulmonary air leak. However, BPD continues to be an important problem, despite the widespread use of exogenous surfactant and strategies to minimize lung injury using mechanical ventilation (ie, permissive hypercapnia).[49] Van Marter and associates recently studied 452 premature infants weighing from 500 to 1,500 g at birth, born at specific neonatal centers in either Boston or New York, and found the incidence of BPD to be significantly higher in Boston (22%) compared to New York (4%), even after adjusting for baseline risk.[50] Using multivariate analyses to examine differences in specific respiratory care practices during the first week of life, most of the increased risk of BPD was explained simply by the incidence of early initiation of mechanical ventilation, although the use of both exogenous surfactant and indomethacin further increased the risk. This suggests that attempts to minimize the use of mechanical ventilation using NCPAP (with or without exogenous surfactant) should lower the incidence and severity of BPD in high-risk infants.

Inflammation

Marked inflammation in the lung and inhibition of alveolarization appear to begin a cascade of destruction and abnormal repair that develops into BPD. The initial stimulus activating the inflammatory process in the lung may be ROS, mechanical ventilation, infectious agents, or other stimuli that result in the attraction and activation of leukocytes. Activated leukocytes are predominantly neutrophils and macrophages, both of which have the potential for further release of ROS and a variety of other inflammatory mediators.[51–53] There is also evidence suggesting that eosinophils may play a role in this inflammatory process and contribute to the development of BPD.[54]

Among the toxic products released from injured cells are the lipid products from plasma membranes that are metabolized arachidonic acid and lysoplatelet activating factor (Figure 37–2). Arachidonic acid may be catalyzed by lipoxygenase, giving rise to various cytokines and leukotrienes. Alternatively, it may be altered by cyclooxygenase to produce thromboxane, prostaglandin, or prostacyclin. Cytokines are low–molecular weight peptides that are released by immune cells in the lung; they modulate gene expression in response to injury and participate in acute-phase reactions and tissue remodeling, and are thus important in regulating the inflammation and healing processes involved in BPD (Table 37–3).[55] Release of early response cytokines such as TNF-α, IL-1β, IL-8, and TGF-β by macrophages and the presence of soluble adhesion molecules (ie, selectins) may impact other cells to release chemoattractants and to recruit neutrophils; this further amplifies the inflammatory response.[56–58] Elevated concentrations of proinflammatory cytokines in conjunction with reduced anti-inflammatory products (ie, IL-10) usually appear in tracheal aspirates within a few hours of life in infants subsequently developing BPD.[59–61] Sunday and colleagues studied the lungs of preterm baboons who developed BPD and found increased numbers of neuroendocrine cells, which release bombesin-like peptides.[62] Administration of specific antibodies that blocked the action of these peptides was associated with a decrease in the severity of lung injury in this animal model of BPD. All these agents and the activated leukocytes that accompany them cause significant pulmonary

TABLE 37–3. Inflammatory Mediators and Bronchopulmonary Dysplasia

Mediators	Specific Examples
Proinflammatory	
Cytokines	IL-1β, IL-1, IL-6, IL-11, TNF-α
Chemokines	IL-8, MIP-1α
Chemoattractants	LTB_4, LTE_4, C3a, C5a
Anti-inflammatory	
Cytokines	IL-4, IL-10, ?IL-6

IL = interleukin; TNF = tumor necrosis factor; MIP = macrophage inflammatory protein; LT = leukotriene; C = complement.

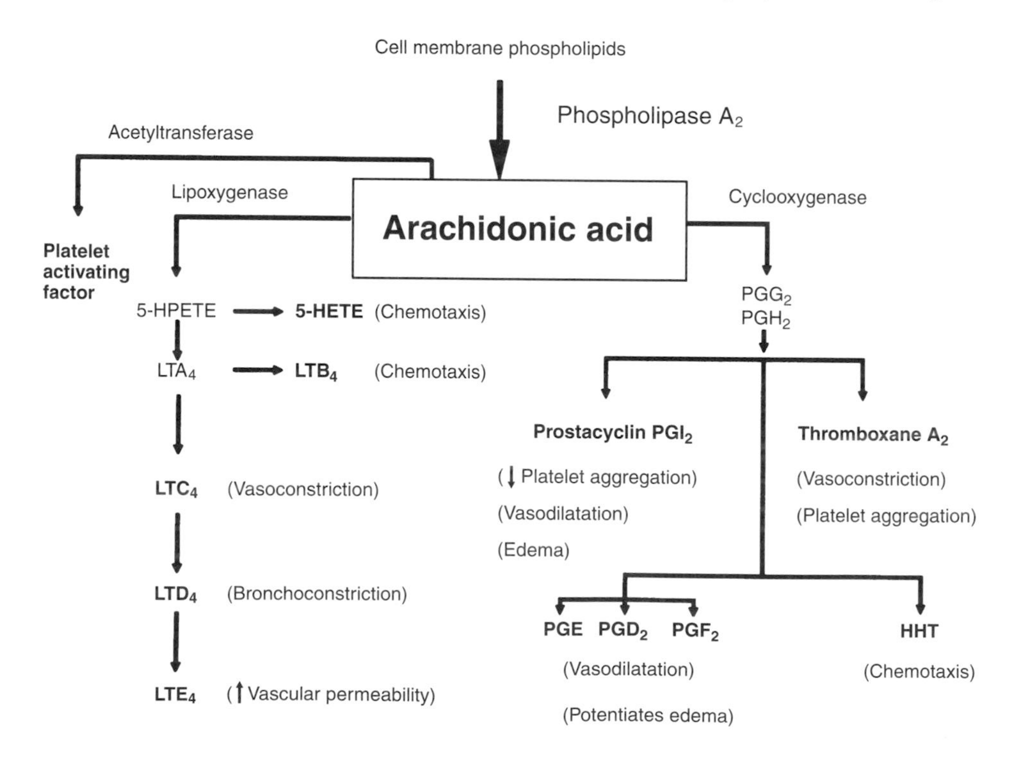

FIGURE 37–3. Schematic representation of the metabolism of cell membrane lipids to arachidonic acid, which initiates the inflammatory cascade. The various metabolic pathways are shown with the agents that are produced and their function in the inflammatory process. HETE = hydroxyeicosatetraenoic acid; HHT = hydroxyheptadecatrienoic acid; HPETE = hydroxyperoxyeicosatetraenoic acid; LT = leukotriene; PG = prostaglandin.

damage, including breakdown of capillary endothelial integrity and leakage of larger molecules (eg, albumin) into alveolar spaces. Albumin leakage and associated pulmonary edema are known to inhibit surfactant function and have been postulated to be important factors in the development of BPD.[63]

The release of elastase and collagenase from activated neutrophils directly destroys the elastin and collagen framework of the lung. The breakdown products of collagen (ie, hydroxyproline), elastin (ie, desmosine), and basement membranes (ie, laminin) have been recovered in the urine of infants with BPD.[64,65] The major defense against the action of elastase activity is α_1-proteinase inhibitor, which may be inactivated by ROS.[66] Increased elastase activity accompanied by compromised antiproteinase function may result in an imbalance that has been demonstrated in tracheal aspirates and serum of infants developing BPD.[67,68] Therapy with exogenous antiproteases could potentially restore this delicate balance and prevent the development of BPD. This hypothesis has been tested in a pilot study in which premature neonates requiring assisted ventilation were treated with intravenous doses of α_1-proteinase inhibitor over the first 2 weeks of life.[69] A trend toward reductions in both the incidence of BPD and the need for continued ventilatory support was noted with α_1-proteinase inhibitor treatment. Further studies examining the safety and efficacy of various doses are underway currently.

As the acute cycle of injury continues with further production and accumulation of inflammatory mediators, significant injury to the lung can occur during a particularly critical period of rapid growth (ie, six divisions from 24 to 40 weeks' gestation). Watterberg and associates have demonstrated that extremely premature infants have evidence of adrenal insufficiency at birth with the lowest serum cortisol concentrations during the first week of life, correlating with increased lung inflammation and adverse respiratory outcome.[70] Pilot studies examining early treatment with low-dose hydrocortisone in extremely low-birth-weight infants increased the likelihood of survival without BPD, a benefit that was particularly apparent in infants born to mothers with chorioamnionitis.[71] Larger multicenter trials are being planned, but these studies all clearly support the notion that this abnormal inflammatory process is intimately involved in the acute and the chronic changes that occur in the lungs of infants with BPD.

Infection

Ureaplasma urealyticum has been recovered from cervical cultures of pregnant women and implicated as a possible cause of chorioamnionitis, prematurity, and BPD.[72,73] Several investigators have cultured the upper genital tract of mothers prior to delivery and tracheal aspirates from preterm infants after delivery and found that BPD developed significantly more often in infants colonized with *Ureaplasma* compared to those with negative cultures.[74] In contrast, other studies have found that although *Ureaplasma* was detected frequently (by culture or polymerase chain reaction) in many low-birth-weight infants, its presence was not associated with the development of BPD.[75,76] Other investigators have suggested that both prenatal and postnatal infections act as a potent stimulus for the inflammatory response, with recruitment of leukocytes, release of ROS, and activation of the arachidonic cascade, ultimately leading to BPD. Since preterm infants are relatively immunodeficient at birth (both cellular and humoral arms), they are much more susceptible to colonization and subsequent infection with a variety of infectious agents (eg, virus, bacteria, fungi) that may affect the severity of BPD.[77,78]

Effect of nutritional status

The nutritional status of the premature infant is important in the development of BPD. Adequate calories and essential nutrients for growth may be lacking during a period of stress and growth; vital components for immunologic and antioxidant defenses may be inadequate; and the nutritional supplements provided may actually contribute to ongoing damage.

Premature infants have increased nutritional requirements because of increased metabolic needs and rapid growth requirements. Superimposed lung disease may further increase energy expenditures (due to increased work of breathing) in infants with limited nutritional reserves. If these increased energy needs are not met by exogenous sources, the infant develops a catabolic state, which is probably a major contributing factor in the pathogenesis of BPD. Inadequate nutrition, which could interfere with normal growth and maturation of the lung, may potentiate the deleterious effects of oxygen and barotrauma. Newborn rats with inadequate caloric intake have decreased lung weights, protein levels, and deoxyribonucleic acid (DNA) content.[78] These abnormalities were even greater in pups that were nutritionally deprived at birth and then exposed to hyperoxia.

Antioxidant enzymes play a vital role in the protection of the lung, and many of these enzymes have trace elements (eg, copper, zinc, selenium) that are an integral part of their structure. Deficiencies in these elements may predispose the lung to further injury, whereas supplementation may provide protection to the lung and prevent hyperoxic lung damage.[79,80] The repair of elastin and collagen is limited in animals that are undernourished, and copper and zinc may be necessary for this repair.[81] Vitamin deficiency also has been postulated to be important in the development of BPD. Increasing serum levels of vitamin E, a natural antioxidant that prevents peroxidation of lipid membranes, initially was thought to prevent BPD.[82] However, subsequent clinical trials have been unable to demonstrate any positive effects in the prevention of BPD.[83] Current nursery feeding and hyperalimentation regimens appear to provide adequate amounts of vitamin E for preterm infants. Concentrations of vitamin A (ie, retinol) may be deficient in premature neonates, and this vitamin appears to be important in maintaining cell integrity and in tissue repair.[84] Several investigators have found lower serum retinol levels in cord blood and in the first month of life in infants who subsequently developed BPD.[85,86] Despite adequate supplementation, some infants remain vitamin A deficient, presumably from increased absorption of parenteral vitamin A into the tubing of the intravenous administration set or due to higher nutritional requirements. A multicenter trial of vitamin A supplementation in premature infants at risk for developing BPD recently demonstrated that large doses of intramuscular vitamin A given three times per week was associated with a small (7%) but significant reduction in the incidence of BPD, suggesting that vitamin A deficiency is an important contributor to lung injury.[87]

Large volumes of intravenous fluids often are administered to premature infants to provide adequate fluid requirements (due to increased insensible water losses) and sufficient calories. Excessive fluid administration can be associated with the development of a patent ductus arteriosus and pulmonary edema, which can lead to increased oxygen and ventilator requirements and the development of BPD.[88] Early closure of the ductus using indomethacin or surgical ligation has been associated with improvements in pulmonary function, but these approaches have not affected the incidence of chronic lung disease.

Influence of genetic factors

Numerous investigators have observed that neonates were more likely to develop BPD if there was a strong family history of atopy and asthma. Nickerson and Taussig found a positive family history of asthma in 77% of infants with RDS who subsequently developed BPD, compared with only 33% of infants who did not.[89] Bertrand and colleagues evaluated the relationship between prematurity, RDS, and the need for mechanical ventilation to a family history of airway hyper-reactivity.[90] The severity of lung disease was directly related to the degree of prematurity and the duration of oxygen exposure. However, siblings and mothers of infants with the most significant lung disease had evidence of airway reactivity, suggesting that all three factors are involved in determining long-term outcome. When histocompatibility loci (ie, human leukocyte antigens [HLAs]) were examined, Clark and associates found that only infants with HLA-A2 developed BPD, again suggesting that other underlying factors that are poorly understood may be important in the pathogenesis of BPD.[91] More recently, Hagan et al reported that a family history of asthma is associated with an increase in the overall severity of BPD in premature infants but does not appear to be a causative factor.[92]

Outcome

Most neonates who develop BPD ultimately achieve normal lung function and thrive, although significant complications may occur that increase the risk of dying in the first year of life. During infancy, continued normal lung growth should result in slow improvement of pulmonary function and weaning from oxygen therapy. However, other respiratory problems (eg, reactive airway disease and repeated pulmonary infections) and abnormal neurologic development are additional abnormalities that may occur and require careful follow-up.

Although pulmonary function in most survivors with BPD improves over time with continued lung growth and permits normal activity, abnormalities detected by pulmonary function testing may remain through adolescence. Follow-up studies of children who had BPD have shown an increased incidence of wheezing and other clinical respiratory symptoms that may continue into later years.[93] In addition, pulmonary function studies have demonstrated increased airway resistance and reactivity, decreased lung compliance, ventilation-perfusion mismatch, abnormal exercise tolerance, and blood gas abnormalities (eg, increased Pa_{CO_2}) in older children with a history of BPD.[94] The most significant abnormalities were found in children who had clinical respiratory symptoms such as wheezing and repeated pulmonary infections, especially early in their childhood (< hr 2 years of age).[95] Baraldi and colleagues demonstrated progressive improvements in pulmonary function tests over the first 2 years of life in infants with BPD, although evidence of airway dysfunction continued to persist.[96] It appears that abnormal pulmonary function and distress are greatest in the first 2 years of life in infants with BPD. Significant improvement in pulmonary function appears to occur from years 7 through 10, indicating that pulmonary abnormalities from BPD persist well into childhood and continue to improve slowly over time. This confirms the observation that BPD is generally less severe than that seen in the era before use of surfactant replacement therapy and is associated with a better outcome if it does develop.

Prevention Strategies

A multidisciplinary approach to the prevention of BPD in infants is needed. The use of prenatal steroids in mothers at high risk of delivering significantly premature infants appears to reduce the severity and incidence of BPD.[25] The early use of NCPAP in infants with respiratory distress may eliminate the need for mechanical ventilation in some infants and facilitate successful extubation in other low-birth-weight infants.[97] The use of exogenous surfactant replacement therapy in premature infants with significant RDS can reduce mortality and the severity and incidence of BPD, although the total number of survivors with BPD increases. Exogenous surfactant may also prevent lung injury in full-term infants with pneumonia or meconium aspiration syndrome.[98] Aggressive treatment of symptomatic patent ductus arteriosus may reduce the severity of BPD and should include fluid restriction, diuretics, indomethacin, or surgical closure. Ventilator pressures and inspired oxygen concentrations should be reduced as low and as soon as possible to reduce hypocarbia, volutrauma, air leak, and oxygen toxicity.

Aggressive nutritional support is critical in helping to promote normal lung growth, maturation, and repair. It also protects the lung from the damaging effects of hyperoxia, infection, and barotrauma. Systemic supplementation with vitamin A in sufficient quantities to establish normal serum retinol concentrations has been reported to reduce the incidence of BPD, although the need to administer repeated doses through the intramuscular route has limited the widespread use of this therapy.

The early use of synchronized mechanical ventilation or high-frequency ventilation (HFV) in newborn infants with significant RDS may reduce the severity and incidence of BPD.[46,47] The combined use of HFV and surfactant replacement may prevent significant lung damage in premature and term infants with significant lung disease unresponsive to surfactant replacement and conventional mechanical ventilation.[99] Further conclusive evidence of the beneficial effects of both synchronized ventilation and HFV in premature infants is needed.

Inhaled nitric oxide also is being used clinically to treat both term and preterm infants with pulmonary hypertension secondary to severe pulmonary parenchymal disease.[100] In term infants, iNO has been shown to lower pulmonary vascular resistance, improve oxygenation, and reduce the need for extracorporeal membrane oxygenation (ECMO) in many critically ill newborns. Inhaled NO also has been used in premature infants with significant RDS and has been shown to improve oxygenation, although the incidence of BPD does not appear to be reduced.[101] Low-dose iNO appears to possess anti-inflammatory properties that might be advantageous in premature infants. However, caution should be used with administration of iNO and high concentrations of oxygen. Synergistic pulmonary cytotoxicity and surfactant dysfunction have been reported to occur in several in vitro and in vivo studies secondary to the formation of peroxynitrite ($ONOO^-$), a potent reactive nitrogen species.[102,103]

Some studies have suggested that the early use of corticosteroids may reduce the incidence and severity of BPD, but significant concerns exist regarding increased mortality, side effects (ie, ileal perforation), and long-term sequelae (eg, cerebral palsy).[104] The most promising method for preventing the development of BPD appears to be prophylactic supplementation of human recombinant antioxidant enzymes. This seems to be a logical strategy in preventing BPD, because ROS appear to play a major role in the pathogenesis of lung injury, and premature infants are known to be relatively deficient in antioxidant enzymes at birth. Several animal studies have shown that prolonged exposure to high oxygen concentrations can cause severe lung damage and death, and administration of antioxidants can prevent many of these complications.[1,31–33,105–107] Recombinant human CuZnSOD (rhSOD) has been administered prophylactically to the lungs of premature infants at high risk for developing BPD. In preliminary studies in premature infants, the prophylactic use of both single and multiple intratracheal doses of rhSOD appeared to mitigate inflammatory changes and severe lung injury from oxygen and mechanical ventilation, with no apparent associated toxicity.[108,109] In animal studies, the rhSOD appeared to localize both in intracellular and extracellular compartments following intratracheal instillation with significant quantities of active protein present 48 hours after the dose is given.[110] National collaborative trials using prophylactic intratracheal rhSOD in premature infants at high risk for developing BPD recently have been completed. Premature infants with a birth weight of 600 to 1,200 g receiving intratracheal instillation of rhSOD at birth appeared to have no significant pulmonary improvement at 28 days of life or at 36 weeks' postconceptual age. However, at 1 year corrected age, rhSOD-treated infants had significantly (44%) fewer episodes of respiratory illness (eg, wheezing, asthma, and pulmonary infections) severe enough to require treatment with bronchodilators or corticosteroids compared to placebo controls.[111] This suggests that rhSOD did prevent long-term pulmonary injury from ROS in high-risk premature infants. Further therapeutic intervention trials are needed to ultimately develop a therapy that can prevent or significantly ameliorate this important chronic lung disease.

References

1. Davis JM, Rosenfeld WN. Bronchopulmonary dysplasia. In: Avery GB, Fletcher MA, MacDonald MG, eds. Neonatology, 5th ed. Philadelphia: Lippincott Williams & Wilkins, 1999;509–32.
2. Northway WH Jr, Rosan RC, Porter DY. Pulmonary disease following respirator therapy of hyaline-membrane disease. N Engl J Med 1967;276:357–68.
3. Bancalari E, Abdenour GE, Feller R, Gannon J. Bronchopulmonary dysplasia: clinical presentation. J Pediatr 1979;95:819–23.
4. Avery ME, Tooley WH, Keller JB, et al. Is chronic lung disease in low birth weight infants preventable? A survey of eight centers. Pediatrics 1987;79:26–30.
5. Shennan AT, Dunn MS, Ohlsson A, et al. Abnormal pulmonary outcomes in premature infants: prediction from oxygen requirement in the neonatal period. Pediatrics 1988;82:527–32.

6. Palta M, Sadek M, Barnet JH, et al. Evaluation of criteria for chronic lung disease in surviving very low birth weight infants. Newborn Lung Project. J Pediatr 1998;132: 57–63.
7. Kresch MJ, Clive JM. Meta-analyses of surfactant replacement therapy of infants with birth weights less than 2000 grams. J Perinatol 1998;18:276–83.
8. Battin M, Ling EW, Whitfield MF, et al. Has the outcome for extremely low gestational age (ELGA) infants improved following recent advances in neonatal intensive care? Am J Perinatol 1998;15:469–77.
9. Goldman SL, Gerhardt T, Sonni R, et al. Early prediction of chronic lung disease by pulmonary function testing. J Pediatr 1983;102:613–7.
10. Tepper RS, Morgan WJ, Cota K, Taussig LM. Expiratory flow limitation in infants with bronchopulmonary dysplasia. J Pediatr 1986;109:1040–6.
11. Abman SH. Pulmonary hypertension in infants with bronchopulmonary dysplasia: clinical aspects. In: Bancalari E, Stocker JT, eds. Bronchopulmonary dysplasia. Washington (DC): Hemisphere Publishing, 1988:221.
12. Subhedar NV, Shaw NJ. Changes in pulmonary arterial pressure in preterm infants with chronic lung disease. Arch Dis Child Fetal Neonatal Ed 2000;82:F243–7.
13. Berman W Jr, Yabek SM, Dillon T, et al. Evaluation of infants with bronchopulmonary dysplasia using cardiac catheterization. Pediatrics 1982;70:708–12.
14. Banks BA, Seri I, Ischiropoulos H, et al. Changes in oxygenation with inhaled nitric oxide in severe bronchopulmonary dysplasia. Pediatrics 1999;103:610–8.
15. Cherukupalli K, Larson JE, Rotschild A, Thurlbeck WM. Biochemical, clinical, and morphologic studies on lungs of infants with bronchopulmonary dysplasia. Pediatr Pulmonol 1996;22:215–29.
16. Jobe AH. The new BPD: an arrest of lung development. Pediatr Res 1999;46:641–3.
17. Groneck P, Gotz-Speer B, Opperman M, et al. Association of pulmonary inflammation and increased microvascular permeability during the development of bronchopulmonary dysplasia: a sequential analysis of inflammatory mediators in respiratory fluids of high-risk neonates. Pediatrics 1994;93:712–8.
18. Pierce MR, Bancalari E. The role of inflammation in the pathogenesis of bronchopulmonary dysplasia. Pediatr Pulmonol 1995;19:371–8.
19. Jobe AH. Pulmonary surfactant therapy. N Engl J Med 1993;328:712–8.
20. Yoon BH, Romero R, Jun JK, et al. Amniotic fluid cytokines (interleukin-6, tumor necrosis factor-alpha, interleukin-1 beta, and interleukin-8) and the risk for the development of bronchopulmonary dysplasia. Am J Obstet Gynecol 1997;177:825–30.
21. Hitti J, Krohn MA, Patton DL, et al. Amniotic fluid tumor necrosis factor-alpha and the risk of respiratory distress syndrome among preterm infants. Am J Obstet Gynecol 1997;177:50–6.
22. Watterberg KL, Demers LM, Scott SM, Murphy S. Chorioamnionitis and early lung inflammation in infants in whom bronchopulmonary dysplasia develops. Pediatrics 1996;97:210–5.
23. Ghezzi F, Gomez R, Romero R, et al. Elevated interleukin-8 concentrations in amniotic fluid of mothers whose neonates subsequently develop bronchopulmonary dysplasia. Eur J Obstet Gynecol Reprod Biol 1998;78:5–10.
24. Jobe AH, Newnham JP, Willet KE, et al. Effects of antenatal endotoxin and glucocorticoids on the lungs of preterm lambs. Am J Obstet Gynecol 2000;18:401–8.
25. Crowley PA. Antenatal corticosteroid therapy: a meta-analysis of the randomized trials, 1972 to 1994. Am J Obstet Gynecol 1995;173:322–35.
26. Polk DH, Ikegami M, Jobe AH, et al. Preterm lung function after retreatment with antenatal betamethasone in preterm lambs. Am J Obstet Gynecol 1997;176:308–15.
27. Walther FJ, Jobe AH, Ikegami M. Repetitive prenatal glucocorticoid therapy reduces oxidative stress in the lungs of preterm lambs. J Appl Physiol 1998;85:273–8.
28. Banks BA, Cnaan A, Morgan MA, et al. Multiple courses of antenatal corticosteroids and outcome of premature neonates. North American Thyrotropin-Releasing Hormone Study Group. Am J Obstet Gynecol 1999; 181:709–17.
29. Frank L, Groseclose EE. Preparation for birth into an O_2-rich environment: the antioxidant enzymes in the developing rabbit lung. Pediatr Res 1984;18:240–4.
30. Jain A, Mehta T, Auld PA, et al. Glutathione metabolism in newborns: evidence for glutathione deficiency in plasma, bronchoalveolar lavage fluid, and lymphocytes in prematures. Pediatr Pulmonol 1995;20:160–6.
31. Ogihara T, Okamoto R, Kim HS, et al. New evidence for the involvement of oxygen radicals in triggering neonatal chronic lung disease. Pediatr Res 1996;39:117–9.
32. Pitkanen OM, Hallman M, Andersson SM. Correlation of free oxygen radical-induced lipid peroxidation with outcome in very low birth weight infants. J Pediatr 1990; 116:760–4.
33. Varsila E, Pesonen E, Andersson S. Early protein oxidation in the neonatal lung is related to the development of chronic lung disease. Acta Paediatr 1995;84:1296–9.
34. Banks BA, Ischiropoulos H, McClelland M, et al. Plasma 3-nitrotyrosine is elevated in premature infants who develop bronchopulmonary dysplasia. Pediatrics 1998;101:870–4.
35. The STOP-ROP Multicenter Study Group. Supplemental therapeutic oxygen for prethreshold retinopathy of prematurity—a randomized, controlled trial. Pediatrics 2000;105:295–310.
36. Davis JM, Rosenfeld WN, Sanders RJ, Gonenne A. Prophylactic effects of recombinant human superoxide dismutase in neonatal lung injury. J Appl Physiol 1993; 74:2234–41.
37. Padmanabhan RV, Gudapaty R, Liener IE, et al. Protection against pulmonary oxygen toxicity in rats by the intratracheal administration of liposome-encapsulated superoxide dismutase or catalase. Am Rev Respir Dis 1985;132:164–7.
38. Turrens JF, Crapo JD, Freeman BA. Protection against oxygen toxicity by intravenous injection of liposome-entrapped catalase and superoxide dismutase. J Clin Invest 1984;73:87–95.
39. White CW, Avraham KB, Shanley PF, Groner Y. Transgenic mice with expression of elevated levels of copper-zinc

superoxide dismutase in the lungs are resistant to pulmonary oxygen toxicity. J Clin Invest 1991;87:2162–8.
40. Wispe JR, Warner BB, Clark JC, et al. Human Mn-superoxide dismutase in pulmonary epithelial cells of transgenic mice confers protection from oxygen injury. J Biol Chem 1992;267:23937–41.
41. Carlsson LM, Jonsson J, Edlun T, Marklund SL. Mice lacking extracellular superoxide dismutase are more sensitive to hyperoxia. Proc Natl Acad Sci U S A 1995;92:6264–8.
42. Dreyfuss D, Saumon G. Should the lung be rested or recruited? Am J Respir Crit Care Med 1994;149:1066–7.
43. Nilsson R, Grossman G, Robertson B. Lung surfactant and the pathogenesis of neonatal bronchiolar lesions induced by artificial ventilation. Pediatr Res 1978;12:249–55.
44. Tremblay L, Valenza F, Ribeiro SP, et al. Injurious ventilatory strategies increase cytokines and c-fos m-RNA expression in an isolated rat lung model. J Clin Invest 1997;99:944–52.
45. Bernstein G, Mannino FL, Heldt GP, et al. Randomized multicenter trial comparing synchronized and conventional intermittent mandatory ventilation in neonates. J Pediatr 1996;128:453–63.
46. Clark RH, Gerstmann DR, Null DM, deLemos RA. Prospective, randomized comparison of high-frequency oscillatory and conventional ventilation in respiratory distress syndrome. Pediatrics 1992;89:5–12.
47. Keszler M, Modanlou HD, Brudno DS, et al. Multicenter controlled clinical trial of high-frequency jet ventilation in preterm infants with uncomplicated respiratory distress syndrome. Pediatrics 1997;100:593–9.
48. Garland JS, Buck RK, Allred EN, Leviton A. Hypocarbia before surfactant therapy appears to increase bronchopulmonary dysplasia risk in infants with respiratory distress syndrome. Arch Pediatr Adolesc Med 1995;149:617–22.
49. Mariani G, Cifuentes J, Carlo WA. Randomized trial of permissive hypercapnia in preterm infants. Pediatrics 1999;104:1082–8.
50. Van Marter LJ, Allred EN, Pagano M, et al. Do clinical markers of barotrauma and oxygen toxicity explain interhospital variation in rates of chronic lung disease? The Neonatology Committee for the Developmental Network. Pediatrics 2000;105:1194–201.
51. Jones CA, Cayabyab RG, Kwong KY, et al. Undetectable interleukin (IL)-10 and persistent IL-8 expression early in hyaline membrane disease: a possible developmental basis for the predisposition to chronic lung inflammation in preterm newborns. Pediatr Res 1996;39:966–75.
52. Brus F, van Oeveren W, Okken A, Bambang SO. Activation of circulating polymorphonuclear leukocytes in preterm infants with severe idiopathic respiratory distress syndrome. Pediatr Res 1996;39:456–63.
53. Groneck P, Speer CP. Inflammatory mediators and bronchopulmonary dysplasia. Arch Dis Child Fetal Neonatal Ed 1995;73:F1–3.
54. Raghavender B, Smith JB. Eosinophil cationic protein in tracheal aspirates of preterm infants with bronchopulmonary dysplasia. J Pediatr 1997;130:944–7.
55. Ozdemir A, Brown MA, Morgan WJ. Markers and mediators of inflammation in neonatal lung disease. Pediatr Pulmonol 1997;23:292–306.
56. Blobe GC, Schiemann WP, Lodish HF. Role of transforming growth factor beta in human disease. N Engl J Med 2000;342:1350–8.
57. Jonsson B, Tullus K, Brauner A, et al. Early increase of TNF alpha and IL-6 in tracheobronchial aspirate fluid indicator of subsequent chronic lung disease in preterm infants. Arch Dis Child Fetal Neonatal Ed 1997;77:F198–201.
58. Ramsay PL, O'Brian SE, Hegemier S, Welty SE. Early clinical markers for the development of bronchopulmonary dysplasia: soluble E-selectin and ICAM-1. Pediatrics 1998;102:927–32.
59. Munshi UK, Niu JO, Siddiq MM, Parton LA. Elevation of interleukin-8 and interleukin-6 precedes the influx of neutrophils in tracheal aspirates from preterm infants who develop bronchopulmonary dysplasia. Pediatr Pulmonol 1997;24:331–6.
60. Kotecha S, Chan B, Azam N, et al. Increase in interleukin-8 and soluble intercellular adhesion molecule-1 in bronchoalveolar lavage fluid from premature infants who develop chronic lung disease. Arch Dis Child Fetal Neonatal Ed 1995;72:F90–6.
61. Jonsson B, Li YH, Noack G, et al. Downregulatory cytokines in tracheobronchial aspirate fluid from infants with chronic lung disease of prematurity. Acta Paediatr 2000;89:1375–80.
62. Sunday ME, Yoder BA, Cuttitta F, et al. Bombesin-like peptide mediates lung injury in a baboon model of bronchopulmonary dysplasia. J Clin Invest 1998;102:584–94.
63. Bland RD, Albertine KH, Carlton DP, et al. Chronic lung injury in preterm lambs: abnormalities of the pulmonary circulation and lung fluid balance. Pediatr Res 2000;48:64–74.
64. Bruce MC, Wedig KE, Jentoft N, et al. Altered urinary excretion of elastin cross-links in premature infants who developed bronchopulmonary dysplasia. Am Rev Respir Dis 1985;131:568–72.
65. Alnahhas MH, Karathanasis P, Kriss VM, et al. Elevated laminin concentrations in lung secretions of preterm infants supported by mechanical ventilation are correlated with radiographic abnormalities. J Pediatr 1997;131:555–60.
66. Ossanna PJ, Test ST, Matheson NR, et al. Oxidative regulation of neutrophil elastase-α-1-proteinase inhibitor interactions. J Clin Invest 1986;77:1939–51.
67. Sluis KB, Darlow BA, Vissers MC, Winterbourn CC. Proteinase-antiproteinase balance in tracheal aspirates from neonates. Eur Respir J 1994;7:251–9.
68. Merritt TA, Cochrane CG, Holcomb K, et al. Elastase and α_1-proteinase inhibitor activity in tracheal aspirates during respiratory distress syndrome. Role of inflammation in the pathogenesis of bronchopulmonary dysplasia. J Clin Invest 1983;72:656–66.
69. Stiskal JA, Dunn MS, Shennan AT, et al. Alpha1-proteinase inhibitor therapy for the prevention of chronic lung disease of prematurity: a randomized, controlled trial. Pediatrics 1998;101:89–94.
70. Watterberg KL, Scott SM, Backstrom C, et al. Links between early adrenal function and respiratory outcome in preterm infants: airway inflammation and patent ductus arteriosus. Pediatrics 2000;105:320–4.

71. Watterberg KL, Gerdes JS, Gifford KL, Lin HM. Prophylaxis against early adrenal insufficiency to prevent chronic lung disease in premature infants. Pediatrics 1999; 104:1258–63.
72. Wang EE, Ohlsson A, Kellner JD. Association of *Ureaplasma urealyticum* colonization with chronic lung disease of prematurity: results of a meta-analysis. J Pediatr 1995;127:640–4.
73. Alfa MJ, Embree JE, Degagne P, et al. Transmission of *Ureaplasma urealyticum* from mothers to full- and preterm infants. Pediatr Infect Dis J 1995;14:341–5.
74. Li YH, Brauner A, Jonsson B, et al. *Ureaplasma urealyticum*-induced production of proinflammatory cytokines by macrophages. Pediatr Res 2000;48:114–9.
75. Da Silva O, Gregson D, Hammerberg O. Role of *Ureaplasma urealyticum* and *Chlamydia trachomatis* in development of bronchopulmonary dysplasia in very low birth weight infants. Pediatr Infect Dis J 1997;16:364–9.
76. Heggie AD, Jacobs MR, Butler VT, et al. Frequency and significance of isolation of *Ureaplasma urealyticum* and *Mycoplasma hominis* from cerebrospinal fluid and tracheal aspirate specimens from low birth weight infants. J Pediatr 1994;124:956–61.
77. Gonzalez A, Sosenko IR, Chandar J, et al. Influence of infection on patent ductus arteriosus and chronic lung disease in premature infants weighing 1000 grams or less. J Pediatr 1996;128:470–8.
78. Frank L, Groseclose E. Oxygen toxicity in newborn rats: the adverse effects of undernutrition. J Appl Physiol 1982; 53:1248–55.
79. Darlow BA, Inder TE, Graham PJ, et al. The relationship of selenium status to respiratory outcome in the very low birth weight infant. Pediatrics 1995;96:314–9.
80. Forman HJ, Rotman EI, Fisher AB. Roles of selenium and sulfur-containing amino acids in protection against oxygen toxicity. Lab Invest 1983;49:148–53.
81. O'Dell BL, Kilburn KH, McKenzie WN, Thurston RJ. The lung of the copper-deficient rat: a model for developmental pulmonary emphysema. Am J Pathol 1978; 91:413–32.
82. Ehrenkranz RA, Bonta BW, Ablow RC, Warshaw JB. Amelioration of bronchopulmonary dysplasia after vitamin E administration: a preliminary report. N Engl J Med 1978;299:564–9.
83. Saldanha RL, Cepeda EE, Poland RL. The effect of vitamin E prophylaxis on the incidence and severity of bronchopulmonary dysplasia. J Pediatr 1982;101:89–93.
84. Brandt RB, Mueller DG, Schroeder JR, et al. Serum vitamin A in premature and term neonates. J Pediatr 1978; 92:101–4.
85. Shenai JP. Vitamin A supplementation in very low birth weight neonates: rationale and evidence. Pediatrics 1999; 104:1369–74.
86. Hustead VA, Gutcher GR, Anderson SA, Zachman RD. Relationship of vitamin A (retinol) status to lung disease in the preterm infants. J Pediatr 1984;105:610–5.
87. Tyson JE, Wright LL, Oh W, et al. Vitamin A supplementation for extremely-low-birth-weight infants. National Institute of Child Health and Human Development Neonatal Research Network. N Engl J Med 1999;340:1962–8.
88. Van Marter LJ, Leviton A, Allred EN, et al. Hydration during the first days of life and the risk of bronchopulmonary dysplasia in low birth weight infants. J Pediatr 1990;116:942–9.
89. Nickerson BG, Taussig LM. Family history of asthma in infants with bronchopulmonary dysplasia. Pediatrics 1980;65:1140–4.
90. Bertrand JM, Riley SP, Popkin J, Coates AL. The long-term pulmonary sequelae of prematurity: the role of familial airway hyperreactivity and the respiratory distress syndrome. N Engl J Med 1985;312:742–5.
91. Clark DA, Pincus LG, Oliphant M, et al. HLA-A2 and chronic lung disease in neonates. JAMA 1982;248: 1868–9.
92. Hagan R, Minutillo C, French N, et al. Neonatal chronic lung disease, oxygen dependency, and a family history of asthma. Pediatr Pulmonol 1995;20:277–83.
93. Jacob SV, Coates AL, Lands LC, et al. Long-term pulmonary sequelae of severe bronchopulmonary dysplasia. J Pediatr 1998;133:193–200.
94. Gross SJ, Iannuzzi DM, Kveselis DA, Anbar RD. Effect of preterm birth on pulmonary function at school age: a prospective controlled study. J Pediatr 1998;133:188–92.
95. Hakulinen AL, Heinonen K, Lansimies E, Kiekara O. Pulmonary function and respiratory morbidity in school-age children born prematurely and ventilated for neonatal respiratory insufficiency. Pediatr Pulmonol 1990;8:226–32.
96. Baraldi E, Filippone M, Trevisanuto D, et al. Pulmonary function until two years of life in infants with bronchopulmonary dysplasia. Am J Respir Crit Care Med 1997;155:149–55.
97. Higgins RD, Richter SE, Davis JM. Nasal continuous positive airway pressure facilitates extubation of very low birth weight neonates. Pediatrics 1991;88:999–1003.
98. Lotze A, Mitchell BR, Bulas DI, et al. Multicenter study of surfactant (beractant) use in the treatment of term infants with severe respiratory failure. Survanta in Term Infants Study Group. J Pediatr 1998;132:40–7.
99. Davis JM, Richter SE, Kendig JW, Notter RH. High frequency jet ventilation and surfactant treatment of newborns with severe respiratory failure. Pediatr Pulmonol 1992;13:108–12.
100. Kinsella JP, Abman SH. Clinical approach to inhaled nitric oxide therapy in the newborn with hypoxemia. J Pediatr 2000;136:717–26.
101. Kinsella JP, Walsh WF, Bose CL, et al. Inhaled nitric oxide in premature neonates with severe hypoxaemic respiratory failure: a randomized controlled trial. Lancet 1999; 354:1061–5.
102. Robbins CG, Davis JM, Merritt TA, et al. Combined effects of nitric oxide and hyperoxia on surfactant function and pulmonary inflammation. Am J Physiol Lung Cell Mol Physiol 1995;269:L545–50.
103. Narula P, Xu J, Kazzaz JA, et al. Synergistic cytotoxicity from nitric oxide and hyperoxia in cultured lung cells. Am J Physiol 1998;274:L411–6.
104. Yeh TF, Lin YJ, Huang CC, et al. Early dexamethasone therapy in preterm infants: a follow-up study. Pediatrics 1998;101:E7.

105. Jacobson JM, Michael JR, Jafri MH Jr, Gurtner GH. Antioxidants and antioxidant enzymes protect against pulmonary oxygen toxicity in the rabbit. J Appl Physiol 1990;68:1252–9.
106. Tanswell AK, Freeman BA. Liposome-entrapped antioxidant enzymes prevent lethal O_2 toxicity in the newborn rat. J Appl Physiol 1987;63:347–52.
107. Davis JM. Superoxide dismutase: a role in the prevention of chronic lung disease. Biol Neonate 1998;74:29–34.
108. Rosenfeld WN, Davis JM, Parton L, et al. Safety and pharmacokinetics of recombinant human superoxide dismutase administered intratracheally to premature neonates with respiratory distress syndrome. Pediatrics 1996;97:811–7.
109. Davis JM, Rosenfeld WN, Richter SE, et al. Safety and pharmacokinetics of multiple doses of recombinant human CuZn superoxide dismutase administered intratracheally to premature neonates with respiratory distress syndrome. Pediatrics 1997;100:24–30.
110. Sahgal N, Davis JM, Robbins C, et al. Localization and activity of recombinant human CuZn superoxide dismutase after intratracheal administration. Am J Physiol Lung Cell Mol Physiol 1996;271:L230–5.
111. Davis JM, Rosenfeld WN, Parad R, et al. Improved pulmonary outcome at one year corrected age in premature neonates treated with recombinant human superoxide dismutase. Pediatr Res 2000;47:395A.

CHAPTER 38

VIRUS-INDUCED INFLAMMATION IN AIRWAYS

JAMES E. GERN, MD

The natural history of asthma can be influenced strongly by viral infections that promote airway inflammation. Infections with respiratory viruses such as respiratory syncytial virus (RSV) and parainfluenza virus (PIV) are the principal cause of wheezing illnesses in infants and, in some children, herald the onset of asthma. In fact, it has been proposed that certain childhood infections provide a sufficient immune response to influence the eventual development of the immune system and modify the risk of subsequent allergy and asthma. In older children and adults, viral infections continue to influence asthma disease activity by being frequent triggers of acute symptoms. In this regard, common cold viruses such as rhinovirus (RV) are isolated most commonly during exacerbations of asthma in the spring and fall, while influenza and RSV are isolated in a significant number of wheezing children and asthmatics during the winter season.

Viruses can affect airway function and symptoms by directly damaging tissues in the airway or by inducing an antiviral inflammatory response. For viruses such as RV that do not cause appreciable damage to the airway lining, even during severe colds, virus-induced inflammation may be responsible for the majority of clinical effects of the cold; this is especially true during the latter stages of the illness, when viral replication is low or has ceased. This review discusses the unique features of virus-induced inflammation and their relationship to reduced airway function; it also explores potential interactions with the pathogenic processes of allergy and asthma. Finally, prospects for the development of specific therapies for virus-induced wheezing illnesses are explored.

Viral Inoculation Studies

Experimental infection with respiratory viruses has provided a convenient means to study the pathogenesis of wheezing with viral respiratory infections, while controlling for confounding factors such as the time and dose of inoculation and the type of virus producing the illness. There are, however, important differences between natural and experimental infections with RV. For example, natural infections produce a broader range of illness severity, and it is likely that some or all of the viruses used to inoculate volunteers are attenuated and produce relatively mild clinical illnesses. Perhaps as a result, it is unusual for subjects with asthma to experience clinically significant exacerbations of asthma or changes in FEV_1 (forced expiratory volume in 1 second),[1] although aerosol inoculation with RV has been shown to increase peak-flow variability.[2]

Despite these limitations, studies using experimental inoculation with viruses such as RV, RSV, and influenza have enabled the analysis of viral effects on upper and lower airway physiology and have provided a system to evaluate potential interactions between allergen exposure and viral infection.

Rhinovirus and Infection of the Lower Airway

There is little doubt that some respiratory viruses (ie, influenza virus, RSV, and PIV) infect lower airway tissues and cause tissue inflammation and lower airway obstruction. Several lines of evidence suggest that RV infections also can extend into the lower airway, and that effects on asthma are initiated by ensuing lower airway inflammation. For example, case reports and epidemiologic studies have linked RV to lower airway syndromes such as bronchitis, bronchiolitis, and pneumonia.[3-8] In addition, experimental RV inoculation increases lower airway inflammation, as indicated by increased submucosal lymphocytes and epithelial eosinophils in bronchial biopsies,[9] and increases in the number of neutrophils in bronchial lavage fluid.[10] Furthermore, RV can replicate in cultured bronchial epithelial cells and at temperatures approximating those found in the lower airway.[11] Finally, although RV is difficult to culture from lower airway secretions obtained via bronchoalveolar lavage (BAL),[12] RV ribonucleic acid (RNA) was detected in BAL cells and biopsy specimens from volunteers after experimental inoculation with RV16.[13,14] These data suggest that, at least under some conditions, RV infections extend into the lower airway and induce bronchial inflammation that could contribute to virus-induced exacerbations of asthma.

Viral Effects on Airway Responsiveness

One of the cardinal features of asthma is airway hyperresponsiveness, which is defined as the increased sensitivity of the airways to irritants or allergen, causing

TABLE 38–1. Potential Effects of Viral Infections on Neural Regulation of the Airway

Enhanced parasympathetic efferent signal
↓ M_2-receptor function
Interference with nonadrenergic noncholinergic neurons
↓ Nitric oxide production
Sensory C fiber activation
↑ Neuropeptide release
↑ Response to neuropeptides
Epithelial cell damage
Sensory nerve irritation
↓ Endopeptidase activity

bronchoconstriction. Therefore, it is of interest that several types of viral infections, including experimental infection with certain strains of RV (RV16, but not RV39 or RV Hanks), influenza virus, and RSV can cause changes in airway responsiveness to histamine, methacholine, or allergen.[15] For example, Cheung and colleagues[16] inoculated 14 subjects with mild asthma with either RV16 (type 16 rhinovirus) or placebo and found that airway responsiveness transiently increased during the acute infection and returned to baseline levels by 1 week after the inoculation. In addition to increasing the sensitivity of the airway, RV16 infection also increased the *maximal* response to inhaled methacholine for up to 15 days after the acute infection. Furthermore, there is evidence that experimental infection with RV16 induces greater changes in airway responsiveness in volunteers with respiratory allergy[17,18] or mild allergic asthma,[9] suggesting a potential mechanism for the greater severity of lower airway effects with naturally acquired RV infections in patients with asthma.

Effects of Viral Infections on Neural Regulation of the Airway

Viral infections could potentially cause bronchoconstriction and increased airway responsiveness through several mechanisms (Table 38–1). Although neural mechanisms of virus-induced bronchoconstriction and airway obstruction are of great interest, they are particularly difficult to study in humans, because definitive experiments often require the disruption of neural tissue. Consequently, much of our understanding has been gained through the use of animal models of respiratory viral infections.

Parasympathetic nerves are the major autonomic innervation of the airway, and effects of viral infection on this system have been well documented. Parasympathetic nerves release acetylcholine, which binds to M_3-muscarinic receptors on airway smooth muscle, producing bronchoconstriction. An important regulatory mechanism in this system is the M_2-autoreceptor on the neuron.[19] When acetylcholine is released, M_2-receptors are activated and inhibit subsequent release of acetylcholine, providing a negative-feedback loop. Studies in animals infected with PIVs indicate that acute viral infections are associated with dysfunction of the M_2-receptors.[20] This effect may be caused directly by the virus or may be a result of virus-induced cellular inflammation. Interestingly, eosinophils do not contribute to virus-induced M_2-receptor dysfunction unless animals have been sensitized with allergen before viral inoculation.[19] In addition to the findings in animal models, there are preliminary studies to indicate that naturally acquired viral infections in humans also may be associated with M_2-receptor dysfunction, and that this may contribute to virus-induced increases in airway responsiveness.[21]

In addition to promoting parasympathetic activity, viral infections also may inhibit mechanisms that normally serve to oppose airway smooth muscle contraction. The nonadrenergic inhibitory neural response is defective in tracheal smooth muscle from RSV-infected cotton rats,[22] and the release of the putative mediator, nitric oxide, is decreased in hyper-responsive tracheas from infected guinea pigs.[23]

Respiratory viral illness may provoke asthma by stimulating airway sensory nerve fibers that can initiate bronchoconstrictor reflexes via the brain stem, and/or cause airway edema and smooth muscle contraction via the release of neuropeptides such as substance P and neurokinin A.[24,25] There is evidence that viral infections can potentiate the release of neuropeptides and/or sensitivity to these potent inflammatory mediators. For example, the hyper-responsiveness to histamine and cholinergic challenge of tracheas from bovine PIV-3 infected guinea pigs is blocked by depleting neuropeptides from sensory C fibers with capsaicin prior to viral inoculation.[26] Furthermore, an increased airway contractile response to neuropeptides has been observed in influenza virus A-infected ferret tracheas and in guinea pigs infected with PIVs.[26–29] Finally, rats with current or recent viral illnesses have markedly enhanced plasma extravasation from airway postcapillary venules after stimulation of neuropeptide release from airway C fibers.[30–33]

Virus-mediated epithelial damage may promote activation of sensory nerves and the effects of neuropeptides in the airway. For example, if the epithelial barrier is compromised, exposed sensory nerves may be stimulated more easily by inhaled particles and inflammatory mediators. Damaged epithelium also may have reduced activity of neutral endopeptidase, an enzyme that inactivates substance P and neurokinin A.[27,29,30,34]

In summary, information gained from animal models has been key to defining potential neural pathways for virus-induced airway dysfunction. Although interpretation of this information can be limited by the potential of interspecies differences in airway physiology, there has been noteworthy progress in defining interfaces between cellular inflammation and neural activation and/or dysfunction.

Virus-Induced Inflammation

There is evidence to suggest that the immune response to a virus plays a major role in the pathogenesis of upper and lower respiratory symptoms. For example, RV infections do not cause extensive epithelial cell destruction even when severe cold symptoms are present.[35] Second, the severity of respiratory symptoms correlates closely with the influx of inflammatory cells and increases in cytokines and mediators in nasal secretions.[10,36–39] Whether these factors are participating in symptom pathogenesis or are markers of severe disease has not yet been established. Third, studies in rodents have demonstrated that morbidity of viral infections can be amplified by the passive transfer of certain T cell subsets or clones.[40–43]

Although the immune responses to viruses are complex and involve multiple airway cells, cytokines, and mediators, there are a few cells and mediators that are likely to play key roles in this process. For example, the airway epithelial cell is the principal host cell for most respiratory viruses, although limited replication of influenza virus and RSV has also been observed in mononuclear cells. In addition, RV can infect airway smooth muscle cells and submucosal gland cells in tissue culture.[44,45] If these findings are confirmed in vivo, it would raise the possibility that viral replication in these cells could directly affect muscle cell responsiveness and airway mucus secretion, respectively.

Viral replication within epithelial cells is a central event in the initiation of airway immune responses and inflammatory processes (Figure 38–1). Viral replication in the epithelial cell triggers intracellular signaling pathways, including activation of NFκB,[46–49] GATA,[49] and AP-1.[50] These intracellular messengers bind to a number of gene promotors, leading to increased activity of a number of proinflammatory genes including cytokines and chemokines, and increased expression of adhesion and major histocompatibility complex (MHC) molecules.[51,52] In addition to activation of gene transcription, infection with RSV has been shown to increase steady state levels of RANTES messenger RNA by increasing mRNA stability.[53]

Activation of epithelial cells may be an important pathway to adversely affect respiratory physiology, especially in the context of allergy and asthma. For example, virus-induced cytokines (ie, tumor necrosis factor α [TNF-α], granulocyte colony-stimulating factor [G-CSF], and interferon [IFN]-γ) and chemokines (ie, interleukin [IL]-8, macrophage inflammatory protein [MIP]-1α, and RANTES)[10,39,54–56] can recruit and activate inflammatory cells (ie, neutrophils, eosinophils, and activated T cells)[57,58] that have been linked to asthma. In addition, viral replication and cytokines that are induced by viral infections can upregulate adhesion molecule expression on epithelial cells[59] and recruited inflammatory cells.

Unlike RSV and influenza virus, which can destroy large numbers of epithelial cells in vivo or in vitro, only a small subset of epithelial cells becomes infected with RV.[60,61] Using in situ hybridization and RV-specific probes, it has been demonstrated that specialized nonciliated cells that overlie lymphoid follicles in adenoidal tissue express large amounts of intercellular adhesion molecule 1 [ICAM-1] (the receptor used by over 90% of RV serotypes) and are especially susceptible to RV infection.[62] Determining whether the level of ICAM-1 expression, or some other factor, conveys susceptibility to these cells has yet to be determined.

There is evidence that endothelial cells are also activated early during the course of upper respiratory infections and may contribute to airway dysfunction during respiratory illnesses through several pathways. First, upregulation of adhesion molecules by cytokines such as TNF-α is an important factor in the recruitment of inflammatory cells. Perhaps of equal or greater importance is the transudation of plasma proteins from the vascular tissue of the nasal mucosa, leading to increased nasal secretions and congestion.[63] Peak levels of plasma proteins such as albumin and immunoglobulin G (IgG) coincide with the time of maximal cold symptoms[63] and increases in bronchial responsiveness,[16] suggesting that similar processes occur in the lower airway. Activation of kinins has been advanced as a possible mechanism for cold-induced increased endothelial permeability;[36,64] however, a bradykinin antagonist, NPC 567, did not improve cold symptoms in a clinical trial.[65] Finally, vasodilation is likely to contribute to edema of the nasal mucosa and possibly the lower airway during viral respiratory infections. Leukotrienes are increased in nasal secretions during viral infections,[56] and studies are underway to determine whether leukotriene receptor blockers can relieve cold-related nasal congestion.

Immediately following the transudation of fluids into the airway, products of goblet cells and mucin glands are increased.[63,66] Mechanisms of mucin gene upregulation and goblet cell degranulation now are being elucidated, and potent stimuli include cytokines (ie, TNF-α, IL-9) and bacterial cell wall components.[67,68] Activation of the epithelial growth factor (EGF) receptor has been identified as a key mechanism for the differentiation and degranulation of goblet cells; EGF may be activated by a number of different stimuli.[69] Since secreted mucus is a major contributor to upper and lower airway obstruction during viral respiratory infections, development of specific inhibitors of this process could be an important advance in the therapy of exacerbations of asthma and other disorders characterized by overproduction of mucus.

As a result of epithelial-derived chemokines and increased expression of endothelial adhesion molecules,

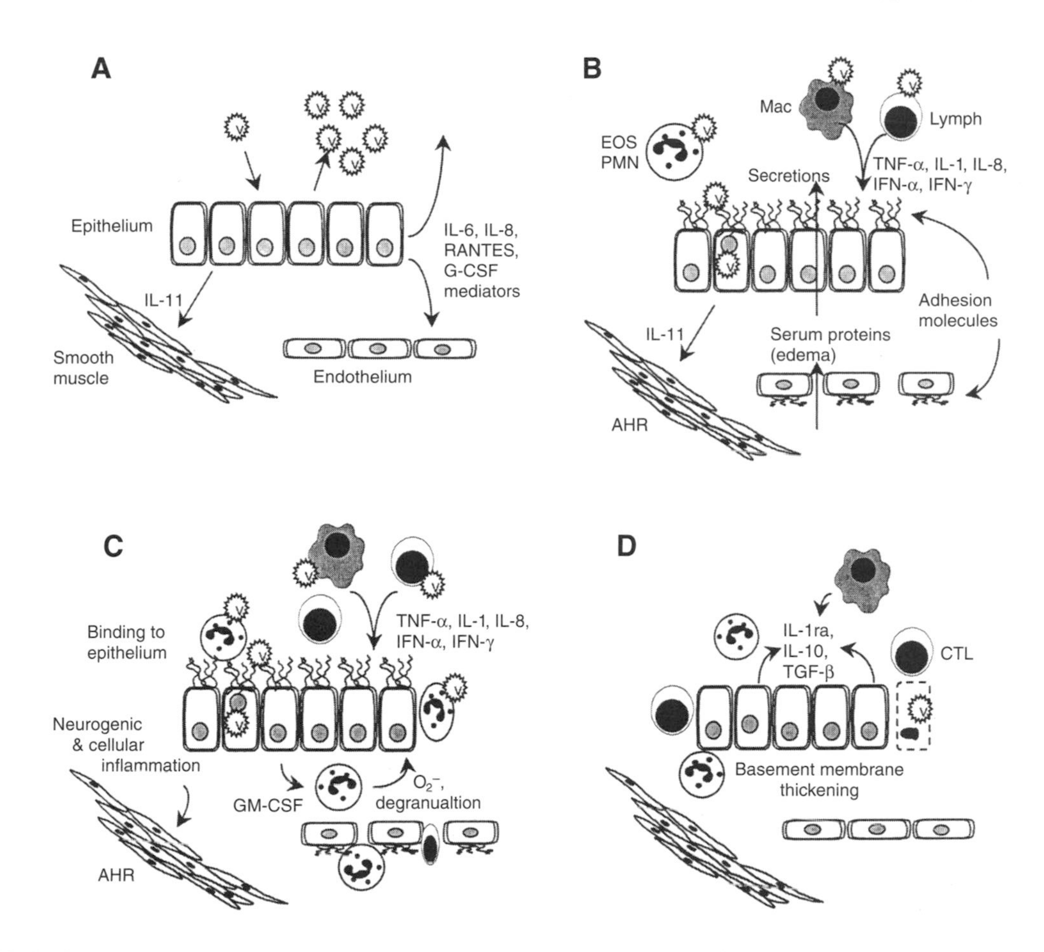

FIGURE 38–1. Cellular inflammatory responses to respiratory viral infection. *A*, Viral replication and epithelial activation. Respiratory viral infections are initiated when a virus enters a host epithelial cell; viral replication causes the release of new infectious particles and activates secretion of cytokines, chemokines, and mediators by the epithelial cells. *B*, Activation of resident airway cells. Viral particles released into the airway cause activation of resident cells in the airway, including macrophages, lymphocytes, and granulocytes. Cytokines from epithelial cells and other resident airway cells increase adhesion molecule expression and airway responsiveness. *C*, Cell recruitment and activation. The combination of chemokine secretion and increased adhesion molecule expression causes recruitment and activation of additional leukocytes, which further adds to airway inflammation and increased responsiveness. *D*, Resolution. Cytotoxic T cells kill virus-infected cells, and cytokines such as interleukin (IL)-10, IL-1 receptor agonist (IL-1ra), and transforming growth factor (TGF)-ß are likely to play a role in the downregulation of airway inflammation after viral infection. Increased numbers of airway lymphocytes and eosinophils may persist for weeks after the viral infection. The steps illustrated in this diagram can occur sequentially or in parallel, and the timing depends on factors related to both the host and virus. RANTES = regulated on activation, normal T expressed and secreted; G-CSF = granulocyte colony-stimulating factor; TNF = tumor necrosis factor; IFN = interferon; EOS = eosinophil; PMN = polymorphonuclear leukocyte; mac = macrophage; lymph = lymphocyte; GM-CSF = granulocyte-macrophage colony-stimulating factor; CTL = cytotoxic lymphocyte; O_2^- = superoxide; AHR = airway hyper-responsiveness. (Adapted from Folkerts G et al.[15])

leukocytes are recruited into airway secretions during the acute stages of viral infections. Neutrophils are the main cells found in nasal and lower airway secretions during acute viral infections,[35,70] and increases in blood and nasal neutrophils correlate with cold and asthma symptom scores and cold-induced changes in airway hyper-responsiveness.[39] Once recruited to the airway, respiratory viruses can activate neutrophil inflammatory functions, as indicated by enhancement of superoxide responses, chemotaxis, and adhesion.[71] In addition, proteases released by activated neutrophils are potent secretagogues for airway submucosal glands.[72]

Although the neutrophil is the predominant cell in nasal secretions during acute viral infections, eosinophil granular proteins also have been detected in the nasal secretions of children with wheezing illnesses caused by RV or RSV.[54,73,74] In addition, increases in sputum eosinophilic cationic protein (ECP) during the acute phase of experimentally-induced RV infection has been shown to correlate with increased airway responsiveness in a group of adult asthmatics after experimental inoculation with RV16.[75] Experiments conducted in vitro indicate that RV does not activate eosinophils directly;[76] it is likely that eosinophil activation is secondary to the activity of virus-

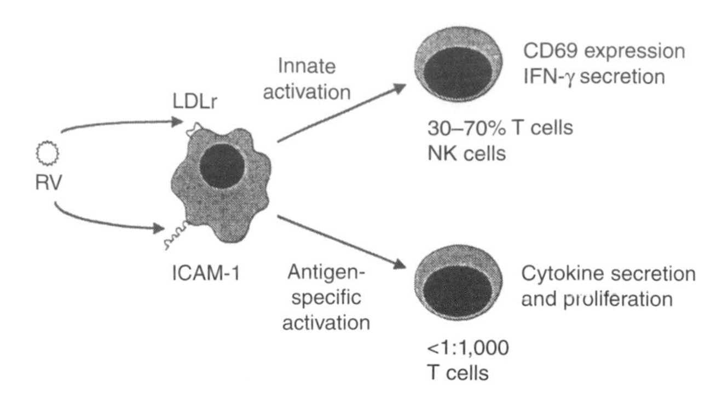

FIGURE 38–2. Two mechanisms for virus-induced lymphocyte activation. Respiratory viruses such as rhinovirus (RV) can bind to antigen-presenting cells such as macrophages, B cells, or dendritic cells via specific receptors (eg, intercellular adhesion molecule 1 [ICAM-1] and the low-density lipoprotein receptor [LDLr]). Innate responses can be activated through the secretion of soluble factors such as interferon (IFN)-α, interleukin (IL)-12, and/or IL-18, leading to increased CD69 expression and IFN-γ secretion by T cells and natural killer (NK) cells. In addition, antigen presentation can activate a smaller subset of antigen-specific T cells. (Adapted from Gern GE et al.[77])

induced mediators or cytokines secreted by T cells, epithelial cells, or other airway cells.[77]

Mononuclear cells also are recruited to the upper and lower airway during acute viral infections.[9,78] Macrophages, which predominate in lower airway secretions, can bind RV in vitro, and secrete cytokines that have antiviral (ie, IFN-α) and/or proinflammatory (ie, IL-1, TNF-α) effects.[79,80] Virus-activated macrophages and lymphocytes likely help to clear viruses and virus-infected cells from the airway.

Lymphocyte responses may be of particular importance because of their central role in orchestrating antiviral responses. Viruses can activate T cells via either innate or antigen-specific pathways (Figure 38–2). Innate immune responses to a virus can occur rapidly (within 24 to 48 hours) after exposure to the virus and may be caused by soluble mediators such as IFN-α secreted by antigen-presenting cells.[77,81,82] Virus-specific T cell responses generally are not detectable in the airway or blood until 7 to 10 days after inoculation with the virus; however, T cell responses to either influenza or RV can be cross-reactive to different viral serotypes.[83–85] Since different serotypes of either RV or influenza virus can cause many infections in the same host over a lifetime, T cell reactivity to a particular strain of virus can be detected in some seronegative individuals.[86] These mechanisms to rapidly activate T cells and NK cells may serve to enhance antiviral responses and limit viral replication.

Perhaps of equal importance to proinflammatory mechanisms are the pathways to downregulate virus-induced immune response to promote healing of the airway and lung tissue. Nitric oxide (NO), which is increased both in asthma and during upper respiratory infections, may have complex effects on airway physiology. On the one hand, NO is a potent vasodilator and may increase airway wall edema and thereby increase airway obstruction in asthma. On the other hand, NO may have beneficial effects including inhibition of viral (including RV) replication[87] and bronchodilation through relaxation of airway smooth muscle. The overall effect of NO may be beneficial, since greater NO production during experimentally induced RV infections correlated with a smaller increase in airway responsiveness.[88]

In addition, virus-induced secretion of cytokines with antiviral properties has been investigated. Respiratory viruses can stimulate IL-10 secretion, which, in turn, can downregulate antigen presentation by monocytes.[89] In addition, IL-10 secretion from peripheral blood mononuclear cells (PBMCs) was impaired in allergic individuals following experimentally induced infection with influenza.[90] This suggests that allergic individuals may have a reduced capacity to suppress virus-induced inflammation following the acute phase of infection.

Finally, IL-1 receptor antagonist (IL-1ra) has been detected in the nasal secretions of volunteers infected with RV.[91] Interleukin-1ra binds to IL-1 receptors without causing activation and thereby blocks the proinflammatory effects of active forms of IL-1. Interestingly, RV infection induces secretion of a brief and modest peak of IL-1β 2 days after inoculation, whereas IL-1ra is secreted in much greater amounts for up to 3 days after inoculation. These findings suggest that IL-1ra may be an important regulator of inflammatory effects mediated by the IL-1 receptor during common cold infections.

Interactions between Viral Infections and Allergic Inflammation

Several studies have been designed to test the hypothesis that there are specific interactions between allergen- and virus-induced inflammation. In one set of studies, lower airway responses to allergen in subjects with allergic rhinitis were evaluated before, during, and after experimental inoculation with RV.[17,92–95] Rhinovirus infections increased airway responsiveness to histamine, methacholine, and allergen and increased the probability of developing a late-phase allergic response after whole lung antigen inhalation.[95] Effects of RV on airway responsiveness were most pronounced in subjects that developed a late allergic response after allergen inhalation.[92] Furthermore, those subjects that developed a late allergic response to allergen after RV infection also had a greater increase in plasma histamine levels after the inhaled allergen challenge.[92]

In studies using bronchoscopy, RV infection caused an increased release of histamine into the lower airways after segmental allergen challenge, and augmented the

TABLE 38–2. Distinct Immune Responses to Viral Infections in Infants With Recurrent Wheezing

Observation	Outcome	References
↑ RSV-specific IgE	↑ Risk of recurrent wheezing in infancy	Welliver et al[99]
↑ ECP (serum or nasal secretions)		Koller et al[100] and Reijonen et al[101]
↓ (IFN-γ secretion (PBMC, ex vivo)		Renzi et al[102]
Eosinophilia or lack of eosinopenia	Persistant wheezing—age 6 yr	Martinez et al[103]
Transient ↑IgE		Martinez et al[103]

RSV = respiratory syncytial virus; IgE = immunoglobulin E; ECP = eosinophilic cationic protein; IFN = interferon; PBMC = peripheral blood mononuclear cell.

recruitment of both total leukocytes and eosinophils into the airway 48 hours after allergen challenge.[93] These effects were noted only in allergic individuals, indicating that RV infection specifically enhanced allergen-induced responses in the airway.

The possibility that exposure to allergen might enhance the severity of viral illness also has been evaluated in two separate studies.[96,97] Neither nasal challenge with allergen nor natural exposure to ragweed during the peak of the season accentuated the severity of experimentally induced infections with RV16 and influenza virus, respectively. In fact, nasal allergen challenge delayed the onset and shortened the duration of RV16 colds. One possible explanation for this effect is that a component of the allergen-induced immune response has antiviral activity, and, in support of this theory, it has been demonstrated that eosinophil-derived neurotoxin, which is a potent RNase, can inhibit replication of RSV.[98] Second, it is possible that the preceding allergen-induced inflammation leads, in turn, to the activation of anti-inflammatory mechanisms (eg, secretion of IL-10), and that these factors attenuate the viral illness. Whatever the mechanism, the findings of this study do not suggest that allergic inflammation leads to more severe respiratory viral infections, or that this mechanism contributes to the pathogenesis of virus-induced exacerbations of asthma.

Effect of Host Immune Factors on Respiratory Viral Infections

Studies to evaluate the relationship between the immune response to viruses and the outcome or sequelae of respiratory viral infections have been performed. In infants with bronchiolitis, several immune responses measured at the time of the acute infection have been associated with either recurrent wheezing or the eventual development of asthma (Table 38–2).[99–103] These findings support the hypothesis that infants at risk for recurrent wheezing may have either an ineffective antiviral immune response or an enhanced inflammatory responses to viral infections that may augment virus-induced airway obstruction. Prospective studies to evaluate immune responses to viruses before the onset of severe respiratory infections in infants are needed to test this hypothesis.

There is also evidence that immune responses to common cold viruses affects the course of respiratory infections in experimentally infected volunteers. Despite the use of standardized lots of viral inoculum, standardized inoculation techniques, and the enrollment of seronegative subjects, there has been considerable individual variability in the severity of respiratory symptoms[104–106] and in the amount of virus detected in nasal secretions following experimental inoculation.[17,92,95] This variability suggests that there are host factors other than the quantity of virus-specific antibody that limit viral replication and the severity of clinical symptoms.

To test for relationships between virus-induced lymphocyte responses and the outcomes of viral infections, PBMCs from seronegative volunteers were tested for virus-specific proliferation and IFN-γ secretion in tissue culture.[86] Following the blood test, the volunteers were inoculated with RV16, and quantitative viral cultures were performed on samples of nasal lavage obtained during the acute cold. The results of this study showed that vigorous RV-specific lymphocyte responses before the cold (either proliferation or IFN-γ secretion) were associated with reduced viral shedding after inoculation. These findings suggest that variations in virus-induced T cell responses contribute to the individual variability in viral shedding during experimentally induced, and perhaps naturally acquired, RV infections in subjects with respiratory allergy or asthma. Additional studies are underway to determine whether T cell responses and IFN-γ secretion to viral infection are different in patients with asthma, and whether this may help to explain the increased lower airway sequella of RV infections in asthma.

Summary and Implications for Therapy

Viral respiratory infections can adversely affect airway function in all age groups. In infancy, respiratory viruses such as RSV cause transient episodes of wheezing that may be recurrent. In addition, there are indications that the immune response to respiratory viruses may be different, and perhaps ineffective, in some infants that are predisposed to recurrent wheezing or asthma. Finally, in older children and adults with established asthma, common cold viruses such as RV frequently trigger acute symptoms of asthma.

These findings suggest that antiviral therapies may be able to reduce the morbidity of wheezing illnesses in all age groups. Furthermore, preventing severe RSV infections in infancy either through vaccination or antiviral medications may potentially reduce the incidence of asthma in childhood. Administration of a monoclonal neutralizing antibody to RSV (palivizumab) has proved to be an effective strategy to prevent RSV infection in premature and high-risk infants, but this therapy is too expensive for general use.[107] Vaccines for RSV are being developed and may provide a more practical strategy for disease prevention. A greater understanding of the role of RSV infection in the initiation of asthma and the risk factors for severe RSV infection is needed to design more comprehensive and cost-effective programs to prevent RSV-related morbidity.

Exacerbations of asthma in older children and adults frequently are triggered by common cold viruses, notably RV, and influenza infections. Although vaccination is recommended for people with asthma, standard vaccination is not an option for prophylaxis of RV-induced exacerbations of asthma due to the large number (> 100) of RV serotypes. In the absence of an RV vaccine, antiviral agents have the potential to either treat or prevent virus-induced exacerbations of asthma, although there are still a few barriers to overcome. Experience with antiviral medications such as the influenza neuraminidase inhibitors has demonstrated that treatment needs to be started early in the disease course to produce clinical benefit; similar restraints apply to new medications such as soluble ICAM-1 that prevent RV binding or uncoating.[108]

Another potential barrier to treatment is cost. Although prophylactic treatment with anti-RV medications during the fall and spring cold seasons may not be practical for normal individuals because of the anticipated high cost of the new medications, this approach may be cost effective for children and adults at increased risk for RV-related morbidity because of asthma or chronic obstructive pulmonary disease. Whether the new antiviral agents that interfere with viral attachment or enzymes (3C protease inhibitors)[109] can prevent exacerbations of asthma if used regularly or, better yet, if started at the first sign of a cold, remains to be determined.

Another critical challenge is to determine why individuals with allergy and lower airway inflammation are so susceptible to the effects of respiratory viruses, such as RV, that cause mild disease in normal individuals. Data in infants infected with RSV suggest that immune responses to this virus are distinct in children who subsequently develop recurrent wheezing and asthma, and host factors that are associated with greater viral replication in adults are beginning to be identified. Remaining challenges include establishing whether antiviral immune responses are determined solely by genetics or whether environment factors play a significant role in their development. In addition, it will be important to ascertain which elements of the antiviral, or perhaps anti-inflammatory, immune responses are impaired in patients with recurrent wheezing. Are immune abnormalities associated with asthma only in response to allergens, or is there also a fundamental defect in the immune response to respiratory viruses? The answers to these questions may provide new therapeutic targets for asthma and respiratory viral illnesses.

Acknowledgment

This work was supported by grants AI40685 and AI34891 from the National Institutes of Health.

References

1. Fleming HE, Little FF, Schnurr D, et al. Rhinovirus-16 colds in healthy and in asthmatic subjects: similar changes in upper and lower airways. Am J Respir Crit Care Med 1999;160:100–8.
2. Grünberg K, Timmers MC, De Klerk EPA, et al. Experimental rhinovirus 16 infections causes variable airway obstruction in subjects with atopic asthma. Am J Respir Crit Care Med 1999;160:1375–80.
3. Kellner G, Popow-Kraupp T, Kundi M, et al. Clinical manifestations of respiratory tract infections due to respiratory syncytial virus and rhinoviruses in hospitalized children. Acta Paediatr Scand 1989;78:390–4.
4. Horn MEC, Brain E, Gregg I, et al. Respiratory viral infection in childhood. A survey in general practice, Roehampton 1967–1972. J Hyg (Camb) 1975;74:157–68.
5. Monto AS, Cavallaro JJ. The Tecumseh study of respiratory illness II. Patterns of occurrence of infection with respiratory pathogens. Am J Epidemiol 1971;94:280–9.
6. Nicholson KG, Kent J, Hammersley V, Cancio E. Risk factors for lower respiratory complications of rhinovirus infections in elderly people living in the community: prospective cohort study. BMJ 1996;313:1119–23.
7. Henderson FW, Clyde WA Jr, Collier AM, et al. The etiologic and epidemiologic spectrum of bronchiolitis in pediatric practice. J Pediatr 1979;95:183–90.
8. Las Heras J, Swanson VL. Sudden death of an infant with rhinovirus infection complicating bronchial asthma: case report. Pediatr Pathol 1983;1:319–23.
9. Fraenkel DJ, Bardin PG, Sanderson G, et al. Lower airway inflammation during rhinovirus colds in normal and in asthmatic subjects. Am J Respir Crit Care Med 1995; 151:879–86.
10. Jarjour NN, Gern JE, Kelly EAB, et al. The effect of an experimental rhinovirus 16 infection on bronchial lavage neutrophils. J Allergy Clin Immunol 2000;105:1169–77.
11. Schroth MK, Grimm E, Frindt P, et al. Rhinovirus replication causes RANTES production in primary bronchial epithelial cells. Am J Respir Cell Mol Biol 1999;20:1220–8.
12. Halperin SA, Eggleston PA, Hendley JO, et al. Pathogenesis of lower respiratory tract symptoms in experimental rhinovirus infection. Am Rev Respir Dis 1983;128:806–10.
13. Gern JE, Galagan DM, Jarjour NN, et al. Detection of rhinovirus RNA in lower airway cells during experimentally-

induced infection. Am J Respir Crit Care Med 1997; 155:1159–61.

14. Papadapoulos NG, Bates PJ, Bardin PG, et al. Rhinoviruses infect the lower airways. J Infect Dis 2000;181:1875–84.
15. Folkerts G, Busse WW, Nijkamp FP, et al. State of the art: virus-induced airway hyperresponsiveness and asthma. Am J Respir Crit Care Med 1998;157:1708–20.
16. Cheung D, Dick EC, Timmers MC, et al. Rhinovirus inhalation causes long-lasting excessive airway narrowing in response to methacholine in asthmatic subjects in vivo. Am J Respir Crit Care Med 1995;152:1490–6.
17. Gern JE, Calhoun WJ, Swenson C, et al. Rhinovirus infection preferentially increases lower airway responsiveness in allergic subjects. Am J Respir Crit Care Med 1997; 155:1872–6.
18. Bardin PG, Sanderson G, Robinson BS, et al. Experimental rhinovirus infection in volunteers. Eur Respir J 1996; 9:2250–5.
19. Fryer AD, Costello RW, Jacoby DB. Muscarinic receptor dysfunction in asthma. Allergy Clin Immunol Int 2000; 12:63–7.
20. Fryer AD, Jacoby DB. Parainfluenza virus infection damages inhibitory M_2 muscarinic receptors on pulmonary parasympathetic nerves in the guinea pig. Br J Pharmacol 1991;102:267–71.
21. Keen H, Hurst V, Jack S, et al. Loss of function of pulmonary M_2 receptors in subjects with mild bronchial hyperreactivity during a respiratory viral infection. Eur Respir J 1998;12:149S.
22. Colasurdo GN, Hemming VG, Prince GA, et al. Human respiratory syncytial virus affects nonadrenergic noncholinergic inhibition in cotton rat airways. Am J Physiol Lung Cell Mol Physiol 1995;12:L1006–11.
23. Folkerts G, Linde van der HJ, Nijkamp FP. Virus-induced airway hyperresponsiveness in guinea pigs is related to a deficiency in nitric oxide. J Clin Invest 1995;95:26–30.
24. Kowalski ML, Didier A, Kaliner MA. Neurogenic inflammation in the airways. I. Neurogenic stimulation induces plasma protein extravasation into the rat airway lumen. Am Rev Respir Dis 1989;140:101–9.
25. Piedimonte G, Hoffman JIE, Husseini WK, et al. NK1 receptors mediate neurogenic inflammatory increase in blood flow in rat airways. J Appl Physiol 1993;74:2462–8.
26. Ladenius ARC, Folkerts G, Linde van der HJ, Nijkamp FP. Potentiation by viral respiratory infection of ovalbumin-induced guinea pig tracheal hyperresponsiveness: role for tachykinins. Br J Pharmacol 1995;115:1048–52.
27. Dusser DJ, Jacoby DB, Djokic TD, et al. Virus induces airway hyperresponsiveness to tachykinins: role of neutral endopeptidase. J Appl Physiol 1989;67:1504–11.
28. Saban R, Dick EC, Fishleder RI, Buckner CK. Enhancement by parainfluenza 3 infection of contractile responses to substance P and capsaicin in airway smooth muscle from the guinea pig. Am Rev Respir Dis 1987;136:586–91.
29. Jacoby DB, Tamaoki J, Borson DB, Nadel JA. Influenza infection causes airway hyperresponsiveness by decreasing enkephalinase. J Appl Physiol 1988;64:2653–8.
30. Borson DB, Brokaw JJ, Sekizawa K, et al. Neutral endopeptidase and neurogenic inflammation in rats with respiratory infections. J Appl Physiol 1989;66:2653–8.
31. Piedimonte G, Nadel JA, Umeno E, McDonald DM. Sendai virus infection potentiates neurogenic inflammation in the rat trachea. J Appl Physiol 1990;68:754–60.
32. McDonald DM. Respiratory tract infections increase susceptibility to neurogenic inflammation in the rat trachea. Am Rev Respir Dis 1988;137:1432–40.
33. Yoshihara S, Chan B, Yamawaki I, et al. Plasma extravasation in the rat trachea induced by cold air is mediated by tachykinin release from sensory nerves. Am J Respir Crit Care Med 1995;151:1011–7.
34. Maggi CA, Patacchini R, Perretti F, et al. The effect of thiorphan and epithelium removal on contractions and tachykinin release produced by activation of capsaicin-sensitive afferents in the guinea-pig isolated bronchus. Naunyn Schmiedebergs Arch Pharmacol 1990;341:74–9.
35. Winther B, Farr B, Thoner RB, et al. Histopathologic examination and enumeration of polymorphonuclear leukocytes in the nasal mucosa during experimental rhinovirus colds. Acta Otolaryngol (Stockh) 1984;413 Suppl:19–24.
36. Naclerio RM, Proud D, Lichtenstein LM, et al. Kinins are generated during experimental rhinovirus colds. J Infect Dis 1988;157:133–42.
37. Einarsson O, Geba GP, Zhu Z, et al. Interleukin-11: stimulation in vivo and in vitro by respiratory viruses and induction of airways hyperresponsiveness. J Clin Invest 1996;97:915–24.
38. Proud D, Gwaltney JM Jr, Hendley JO, et al. Increased levels of interleukin-1 are detected in nasal secretions of volunteers during experimental rhinovirus colds. J Infect Dis 1994;169:1007–13.
39. Grünberg K, Timmers MC, Smits HH, et al. Effect of experimental rhinovirus 16 colds on airway hyperresponsiveness to histamine and interleukin-8 in nasal lavage in asthmatic subjects *in vivo*. Clin Exp Allergy 1997; 27:36–45.
40. Folkerts G, Verheyen A, Janssen M, Nijkamp FP. Virus-induced airway hyperresponsiveness in the guinea pig can be transferred by bronchoalveolar cells. J Allergy Clin Immunol 1992;90:364–72.
41. Cannon MJ, Openshaw PJM, Askonas BA. Cytotoxic T cells clear virus but augment lung pathology in mice infected with respiratory syncytial virus. J Exp Med 1988; 168:1163–8.
42. Alwan WH, Record FM, Openshaw PJM. CD4+ T-cells clear virus but augment disease in mice infected with respiratory syncytial virus—comparison with the effects of CD8+ T-cells. Clin Exp Immunol 1992;88:527–36.
43. Alwan WH, Kozlowska WJ, Openshaw PJ. Distinct types of lung disease caused by functional subsets of antiviral T cells. J Exp Med 1994;179:81–9.
44. Hakonarson H, Maskeri N, Carter C, et al. Mechanism of rhinovirus-induced changes in airway smooth muscle responsiveness. J Clin Invest 1998;102:1732–41.
45. Yamaya M, Sekizawa K, Suzuki T, et al. Infection of human respiratory submucosal glands with rhinovirus: effects on cytokine and ICAM-1 production. Am J Physiol 1999;277(2 Pt 1):L362–71.
46. Zhu Z, Tang W, Wu Y, et al. Rhinovirus stimulation of interleukin-6 in vivo and in vitro. Evidence for nuclear

factor kappa B–dependent transcriptional activation. J Clin Invest 1996;97:421–30.

47. Zhu Z, Tang W, Gwaltney JMJ, et al. Rhinovirus stimulation of interleukin-8 in vivo and in vitro: role of NF-kappaB. Am J Physiol 1997;273(4 Pt 1):L814–24.
48. Jamaluddin M, Casola A, Garofalo RP, et al. The major component of IkappaBalpha proteolysis occurs independently of the proteasome pathway in respiratory syncytial virus–infected pulmonary epithelial cells. J Virol 1998;72:4849–57.
49. Papi A, Johnston SL. Respiratory epithelial cell expression of vascular cell adhesion molecule-1 and its up-regulation by rhinovirus infection via NF-kappaB and GATA transcription factors. J Biol Chem 1999;274:30041–51.
50. Mastronarde JG, Monick MM, Mukaida N, et al. Activator protein-1 is the preferred transcription factor for cooperative interaction with nuclear factor-kappaB in respiratory syncytial virus–induced interleukin-8 gene expression in airway epithelium. J Infect Dis 1998;177:1275–81.
51. Garofalo R, Mei F, Espejo R, et al. Respiratory syncytial virus infection of human respiratory epithelial cells up-regulates class I MHC expression through the induction of IFN-beta and IL-1 alpha. J Immunol 1996; 157:2506–13.
52. Olszewska-Pazdrak B, Casola A, Saito T, et al. Cell-specific expression of RANTES, MCP-1, and MIP-1alpha by lower airway epithelial cells and eosinophils infected with respiratory syncytial virus. J Virol 1998;72:4756–64.
53. Koga T, Sardina E, Tidwell RM, et al. Virus-inducible expression of a host chemokine gene relies on replication-linked mRNA stabilization. Proc Nat Acad Sci U S A 1999;96:5680–5.
54. Teran LM, Seminario MC, Shute JK, et al. RANTES, macrophage-inhibitory protein 1α, and the eosinophil product major basic protein are released into upper respiratory secretions during virus-induced asthma exacerbations in children. J Infect Dis 1999;179:677–81.
55. Noah TL, Henderson FW, Wortman IA, et al. Nasal cytokine production in viral acute upper respiratory infection of childhood. J Infect Dis 1995;171:584–92.
56. van Schaik SM, Tristram DA, Nagpal IS, et al. Increased production of IFN-gamma and cysteinyl leukotrienes in virus-induced wheezing. J Allergy Clin Immunol 1999;103:630–6.
57. Kameyoshi Y, Dorschner A, Mallet AI, et al. Cytokine RANTES released by thrombin-stimulated platelets is a potent attractant for human eosinophils. J Exp Med 1992;176:587–92.
58. Zhang L, Redington AE, Holgate ST. RANTES: a novel mediator of allergic inflammation? Clin Exp Allergy 1994;24:899–904.
59. Papi A, Johnston SL. Rhinovirus infection induces expression of its own receptor intercellular adhesion molecule 1 (ICAM-1) via increased NF-kappaB-mediated transcription. J Biol Chem 1999;274:9707–20.
60. Arruda E, Mifflia TE, Gwaltney JM Jr, et al. Localization of rhinovirus replication in vitro with in situ hybridization. J Med Virol 1991;54:634–8.
61. Bardin PG, Johnston SL, Sanderson G, et al. Detection of rhinovirus infection of the nasal mucosa by oligonucleotide *in situ* hybridization. Am J Respir Cell Mol Biol 1994; 10:207–13.
62. Arruda E, Boyle TR, Winther B, et al. Localization of human rhinovirus replication in the upper respiratory tract by in situ hybridization. J Infect Dis 1995;171:1329–33.
63. Igarashi Y, Skoner DP, Doyle WJ, et al. Analysis of nasal secretions during experimental rhinovirus upper respiratory infections. J Allergy Clin Immunol 1993;92:722–31.
64. Proud D, Naclerio RM, Gwaltney JM, Hendley JO. Kinins are generated in nasal secretions during natural rhinovirus colds. J Infect Dis 1990;161:120–3.
65. Higgins PG, Barrow GI, Tyrrell DA. A study of the efficacy of the bradykinin antagonist, NPC 567, in rhinovirus infections in human volunteers. Antiviral Res 1990; 14:339–44.
66. Yuta A, Doyle WJ, Gaumond E, et al. Rhinovirus infection induces mucus hypersecretion. Am J Physiol Lung Cell Mol Physiol 1998;274:L1017–23.
67. Longphre M, Li D, Gallup M, et al. Allergen-induced IL-9 directly stimulates mucin transcription in respiratory epithelial cells. J Clin Invest 1999;104:1375–82.
68. Basbaum C, Lemjabbar H, Longphre M, et al. Control of mucin transcription by diverse injury-induced signaling pathways. Am J Respir Crit Care Med 1999;160(5 Pt 2): S44–8.
69. Takeyama K, Dabbagh K, Lee HM, et al. Epidermal growth factor system regulates mucin production in airways. Proc Nat Acad Sci U S A 1999;96:3081–6.
70. Everard ML, Swarbrick A, Wrightham M, et al. Analysis of cells obtained by bronchial lavage of infants with respiratory syncytial virus infection. Arch Dis Child 1994; 71:428–32.
71. Busse WW, Vrtis RF, Steiner R, Dick EC. *In vitro* incubation with influenza virus primes human polymorphonuclear leukocyte generation of superoxide. Am J Respir Cell Mol Biol 1991;4:347–54.
72. Schuster A, Fahy JV, Ueki I, Nadel JA. Cystic fibrosis sputum induces a secretory response from airway gland serous cells that can be prevented by neutrophil protease inhibitors. Eur Respir J 1995;8:10–4.
73. Heymann PW, Rakes GP, Hogan AD, et al. Assessment of eosinophils, viruses and IgE antibody in wheezing infants and children. Int Arch Allergy Immunol 1995; 107:380–2.
74. Garofalo R, Kimpen JLL, Welliver RC, Ogra PL. Eosinophil degranulation in the respiratory tract during naturally acquired respiratory syncytial virus infection. J Pediatr 1992;120:28–32.
75. Grünberg K, Smits HH, Timmers MC, et al. Experimental rhinovirus 16 infection. Effects on cell differentials and soluble markers in sputum in asthmatic subjects. Am J Respir Crit Care Med 1997;156(2 Pt 1):609–16.
76. Handzel ZT, Busse WW, Sedgwick JB, et al. Eosinophils bind rhinovirus and activate virus-specific T cells. J Immunol 1998;160:1279–84.
77. Gern JE, Vrtis R, Kelly EAB, et al. Rhinovirus produces non-specific activation of lymphocytes through a monocyte-dependent mechanism. J Immunol 1996;157:1605–12.
78. Levandowski RA, Weaver CW, Jackson GG. Nasal secretion leukocyte populations determined by flow cytometry

during acute rhinovirus infection. J Med Virol 1988; 25:423–32.

79. Gern JE, Dick EC, Lee WM, et al. Rhinovirus enters but does not replicate inside monocytes and airway macrophages. J Immunol 1996;156:621–7.
80. Hayden FG, Albrecht JK, Kaiser DL, Gwaltney JM Jr. Prevention of natural colds by contact prophylaxis with intranasal alpha$_2$-interferon. N Engl J Med 1986;314:71–5.
81. Tough DF, Borrow P, Sprent J. Induction of bystander T cell proliferation by viruses and type I interferon *in vivo*. Science 1996;272:1947–50.
82. Sareneva T, Matikainen S, Kurimoto M, Julkunen I. Influenza A virus–induced IFN-alpha/beta and IL-18 synergistically enhance IFN-gamma gene expression in human T cells. J Immunol 1998;160:6032–8.
83. Rimmelzwaan GF, Osterhaus ADME. Cytotoxic T lymphocyte memory: role in cross-protective immunity against influenza? Vaccine 1995;13:703–5.
84. Gern JE, Dick EC, Kelly EAB, et al. Rhinovirus-specific T cells recognize both shared and serotype-restricted viral epitopes. J Infect Dis 1997;175:1108–14.
85. Wimalasundera SS, Katz DR, Chain BM. Characterization of the T cell response to human rhinovirus in children: implications for understanding the immunopathology of the common cold. J Infect Dis 1997;176:755–9.
86. Parry DE, Busse WW, Sukow KA, et al. Rhinovirus-induced peripheral blood mononuclear cell responses and outcome of experimental infection in allergic subjects. J Allergy Clin Immunol 2000;105:692–8.
87. Sanders SP, Siekierski ES, Porter JD, et al. Nitric oxide inhibits rhinovirus-induced cytokine production and viral replication in a human respiratory epithelial cell line. J Virol 1998;72:934–42.
88. de Gouw HWFM, Grünberg K, Schot R, et al. Relationship between exhaled nitric oxide and airway hyperresponsiveness following experimental rhinovirus infection in asthmatic subjects. Eur Respir J 1998;11:126–32.
89. Stockl J, Vetr H, Majdic O, et al. Human major group rhinoviruses downmodulate the accessory function of monocytes by inducing IL-10. J Clin Invest 1999; 104:957–65.
90. Gentile DA, Patel A, Ollila C, et al. Diminished IL-10 production in subjects with allergy after infection with influenza A virus. J Allergy Clin Immunol 1999; 103:1045–8.
91. Yoon HJ, Zhu Z, Gwaltney JM Jr, Elias JA. Rhinovirus regulation of IL-1 receptor antagonist in vivo and in vitro: a potential mechanism of symptom resolution. J Immunol 1999;162:7461–9.
92. Calhoun WJ, Swenson CA, Dick EC, et al. Experimental rhinovirus 16 infection potentiates histamine release after antigen bronchoprovocation in allergic subjects. Am Rev Respir Dis 1991;144:1267–73.
93. Calhoun WJ, Dick EC, Schwartz LB, Busse WW. A common cold virus, rhinovirus 16, potentiates airway inflammation after segmental antigen bronchoprovocation in allergic subjects. J Clin Invest 1994;94:2200–8.
94. Gern JE, Busse WW. The effects of rhinovirus infections on allergic airway responses. Am J Respir Crit Care Med 1995;152:S40–5.
95. Lemanske RF Jr, Dick EC, Swenson CA, et al. Rhinovirus upper respiratory infection increases airway hyperreactivity and late asthmatic reactions. J Clin Invest 1989; 83:1–10.
96. Avila PC, Abisheganaden JA, Wong H, et al. Effects of allergic inflammation of the nasal mucosa on the severity of rhinovirus 16 cold. J Allergy Clin Immunol 2000; 105:923–32.
97. Exelbert RL, Skoner DP, Gentile DA, et al. Upper airway response in ragweed-primed and unprimed adult subjects during experimental infection with influenza A (FLU) virus. J Allergy Clin Immunol 2000;105:S198.
98. Domachowske JB, Dyer KD, Bonville CA, Rosenberg HF. Recombinant human eosinophil-derived neurotoxin/RNase 2 functions as an effective antiviral agent against respiratory syncytial virus. J Infect Dis 1998;177:1458–64.
99. Welliver RC, Wong DT, Rijnaldo D, Ogra PL. Predictive value of respiratory syncytial virus–specific IgE responses for recurrent wheezing following bronchiolitis. J Pediatr 1986;109:776–80.
100. Koller DY, Wojnarowski C, Herkner KR, et al. High levels of eosinophilic cationic protein in wheezing infants predict the development of asthma. J Allergy Clin Immunol 1997;99:752–6.
101. Reijonen TM, Korppi M, Kleemola M, et al. Nasopharyngeal eosinophil cationic protein in bronchiolitis—relation to viral findings and subsequent wheezing. Pediatr Pulmonol 1997;24:35–41.
102. Renzi PM, Turgeon JP, Yang JP, et al. Cellular immunity is activated and a TH-2 response is associated with early wheezing in infants after bronchiolitis. J Pediatr 1997; 130:584–93.
103. Martinez FD, Stern DA, Wright AL, et al. Differential immune responses to acute lower respiratory illnesses in early life and subsequent development of persistent wheezing and asthma. J Allergy Clin Immunol 1998; 102:915–20.
104. Doyle WJ, Skoner DP, Fireman P, et al. Rhinovirus 39 infection in allergic and nonallergic subjects. J Allergy Clin Immunol 1992;89:968–78.
105. Eggleston PA, Hendley JO, Gwaltney JM Jr. Mediators of immediate hypersensitivity in nasal secretions during natural colds and rhinovirus infection. Acta Otolaryngol (Stockh) 1984;413:25–35.
106. Turner RB, Weingand KW, Yeh CH, Leedy DW. Association between interleukin-8 concentration in nasal secretions and severity of symptoms of experimental rhinovirus colds [comments]. Clin Infect Dis 1998;26:840–6.
107. Storch GA. Humanized monoclonal antibody for prevention of respiratory syncytial virus infection. Pediatrics 1998;102:648–51.
108. Turner RB, Wecker MT, Pohl G, et al. Efficacy of tremacamra, a soluble intercellular adhesion molecule 1, for experimental rhinovirus infection—a randomized clinical trial. J Am Med Assoc 1999;281:1797–804.
109. Patick AK, Binford SL, Brothers MA, et al. In vitro antiviral activity of AG7088, a potent inhibitor of human rhinovirus 3C protease. Antimicrob Agents Chemother 1999;43:2444–50.

CHAPTER 39

Fibroproliferative Response: Molecular Mediators and Pathophysiologic Relevance

Oliver Eickelberg, MD, Alfin G. Vicencio, MD

The human body is composed of two major compartments, a cellular and an extracellular compartment, of which the interstitium is an important part. Both compartments are damaged with tissue injury, and the ensuing healing process involves regeneration of both the cellular mass and the extracellular matrix (ECM). This healing process is based on one of the most conserved cascades of events in physiology, the response to injury. In the case of normal wound healing, this response leads to a complete functional *restitutio ad integrum*, which ensures tissue homeostasis. Independent of the type of tissue affected, this cascade follows a well-defined sequence that includes initiation and execution of (1) the coagulation cascade, (2) an inflammatory response (associated with angiogenesis, formation of granulation tissue, reepithelialization of denuded areas), and (3) a fibroproliferative response (including proliferation of mesenchymal cells and increased synthesis of the ECM) (Figure 39–1).[1–3] It was the discovery and delineation of these distinct phases in the course of cutaneous wound healing that led to the designation of the expression fibroproliferative response (FPR) as a single entity.

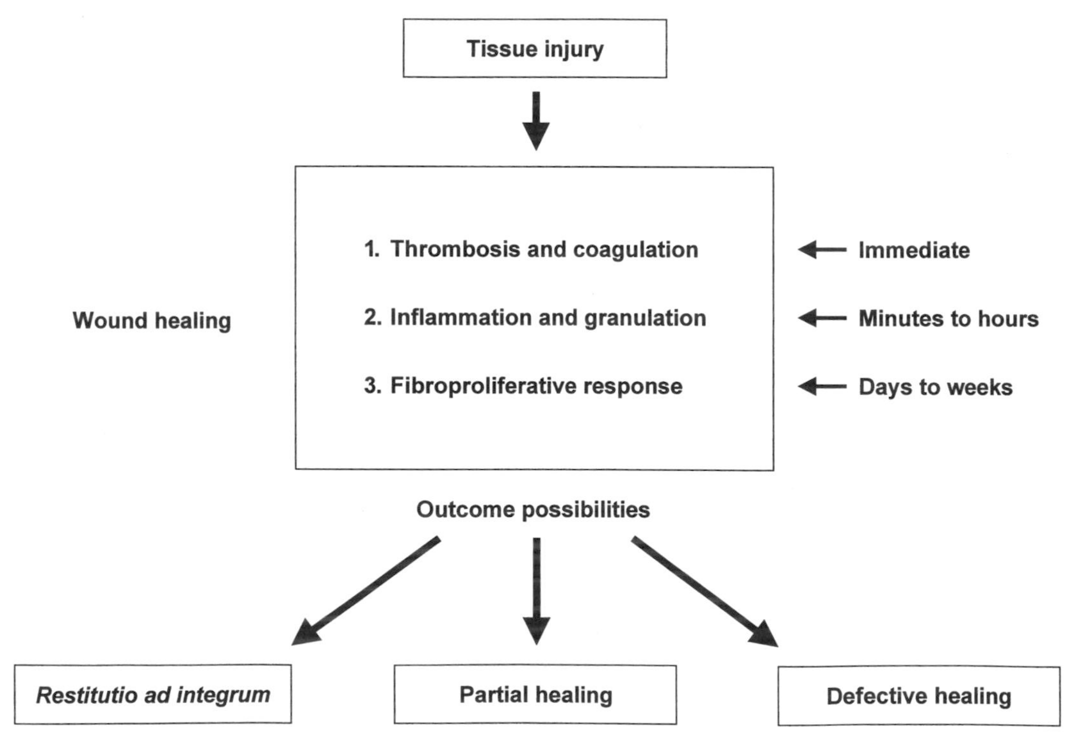

FIGURE 39–1. Response to injury. Injury triggers a well-defined sequence of events in an attempt to restore tissue integrity. Immediately following injury, thrombosis and coagulation initiate the cascade of events responsible for wound healing, preventing blood loss and further damage. Subsequent migration of inflammatory cells to the site of injury promotes the healing process, along with increased blood flow and formation of granulation tissue. Finally, the fibroproliferative response, which encompasses proliferation of mesenchymal cells and increased synthesis of the ECM, completes the cascade. If all three phases function properly, damaged tissue is partially, if not completely restored. If, on the other hand, these processes are perturbed or continue unregulated, healing may be defective, ultimately compromising tissue function.

The FPR comprises two distinct phenomenologic mechanisms that are closely intercalated (Figure 39–2). The initial phase is triggered by a variety of growth factors and encompasses the proliferation of local mesenchymal cells to regenerate the mesenchymal cell population (eg, fibroblasts in the skin, stellate cells in the liver, or myofibroblasts in the lung or arteries). This proliferative phase, which varies in intensity and duration, is closely followed by a phase of increased synthesis of ECM molecules, most notably the collagens. Under physiologic conditions, the FPR ensures sufficient restoration of tissue architecture and is, therefore, essential for restoring tissue integrity after injury.[4] However, the FPR can also threaten tissue homeostasis under circumstances of dysregulated feedback control. Under physiologic conditions, a network of regulatory processes terminates the FPR after restoration of tissue architecture. However, if these negative feedback mechanisms malfunction, deposition of ECM continues unregulated and eventually leads to fibrotic restructuring of affected tissues, ultimately compromising their functions. This can be attributable to two major causes: the initial insult was too severe to allow for sufficient repair or the initial insult was followed by repeated injuries, continuously driving the FPR.[5] Accordingly, the fine balance between timed onset and offset of the FPR is at the center of current research of fibrotic diseases. Identifying its molecular mediators will prove instrumental in targeting future therapies of such diseases.

Fibrotic Diseases

Fibrotic diseases, such as those seen in the lung, kidney, or liver, represent major medical problems associated with progressive loss of organ function and even death. Whereas the incidence of the more classic disorders, such as idiopathic pulmonary fibrosis (IPF) and hepatic fibrosis, is on the rise, an estimated 45% of the deaths in the United States can be attributed to diseases that exhibit some features of fibroproliferative disorders, including arteriosclerosis, diabetes, stroke, and myocardial infarction. Fibrotic diseases have long been associated with irreversible accumulation of inert extracellular material, preventing the affected tissue or organ from exercising its physiologic functions. Therapeutic options have been limited, and the disease is generally regarded as irreversible.[6,7] However, recent advances in the understanding of both the pathogenesis of fibrosis and the molecular mediators driving fibrogenesis have led to a redefinition of fibrotic diseases. It is now widely accepted that the ECM, even in pathologic situations, is subjected to constant remodeling, with a continuous turnover of more than 5% per day.[8] It is this balance between synthesis and degradation that, when severely biased toward synthesis, results in unregulated accumulation of ECM in fibrotic disease states (Figure 39–3). However, these mechanisms also suggest that the state of fibrosis can be modified, perhaps even reversed, by modulating this balance, either through increased degradation or decreased synthesis.

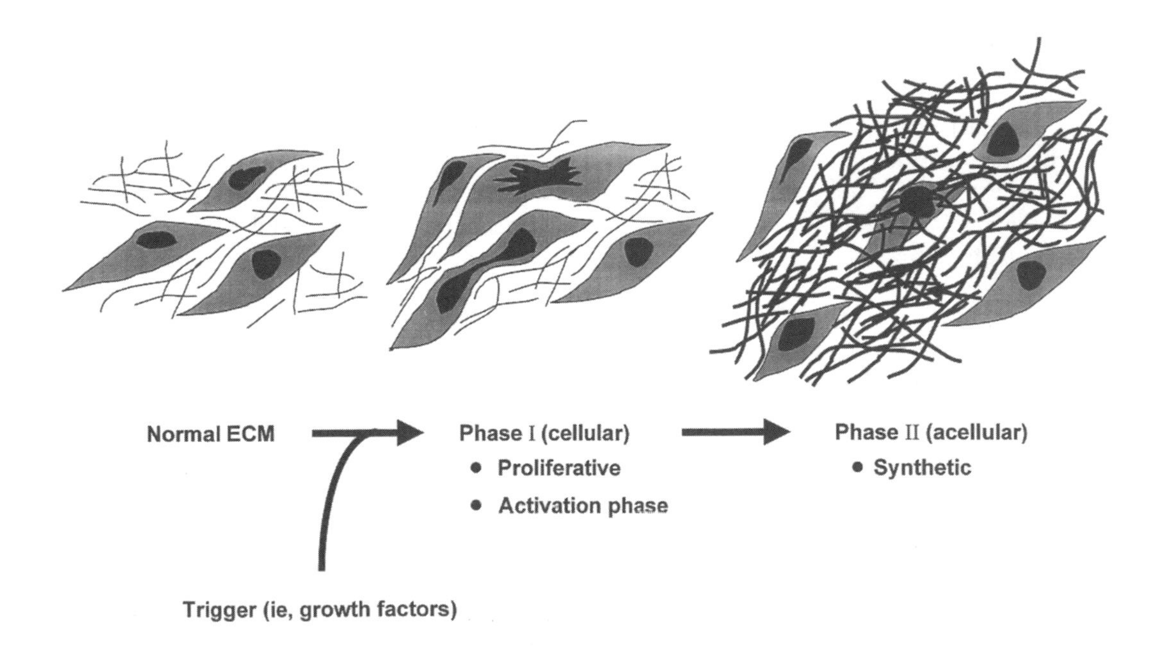

FIGURE 39–2. The fibroproliferative response (FPR). The final phase in the wound healing process, the FPR, is triggered by a variety of growth factors released as a result of injury. Initially, local mesenchymal cells are activated and proliferate to regenerate the cell population. Following the proliferative phase, the repopulated mesenchymal cells increase their synthesis rate of collagens and other ECM molecules, thus restoring tissue integrity.

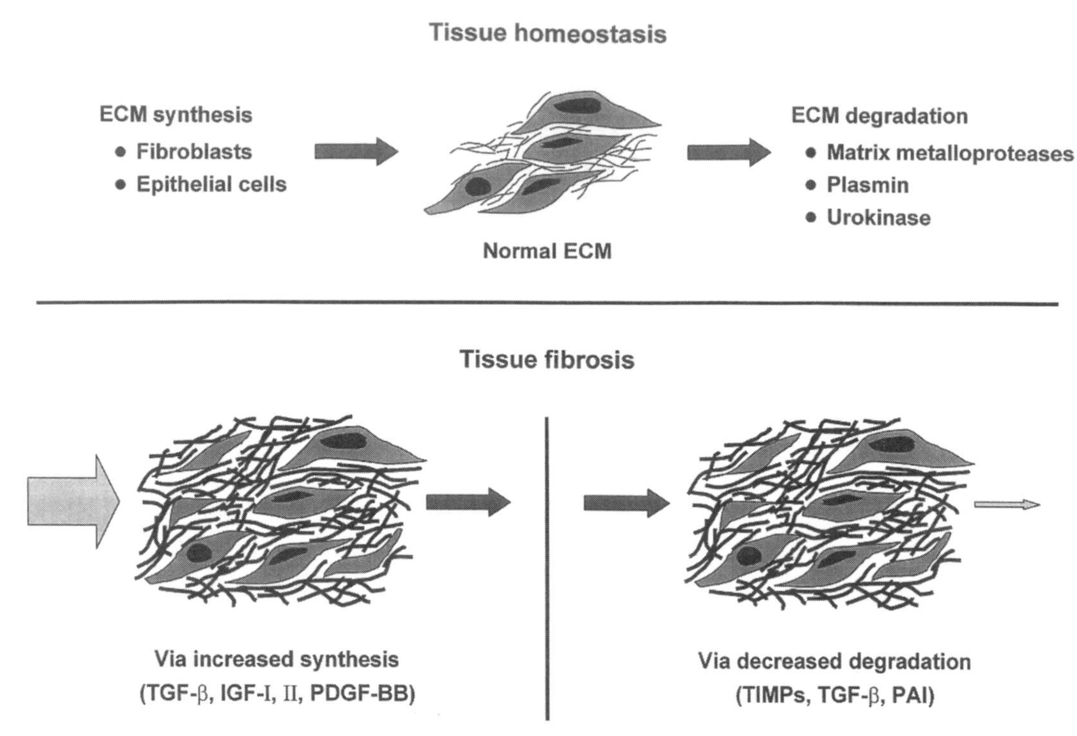

FIGURE 39–3. Extracellular matrix (ECM) balance. Under normal conditions, each tissue is aiming for homeostasis. Thus, the functional and static integrity of the ECM is provided through a dynamic and continuous turnover rate that is balanced between synthesis and degradation. Numerous factors contribute to this fine balance. Fibrosis can be the result of dysregulation of this balance, secondary to an ongoing and unregulated increase in ECM synthesis (ie, via increased TGF-β expression) or a decrease in the rate of ECM degradation (ie, via increased expression of tissue inhibitor of matrix metalloprotease [TIMP]; decreased expression of protease). IGF = insulin-like growth factor; PAI = plasminogen activator inhibitor-BB; PDGF-BB = platelet-derived growth factor.

In this respect, new therapeutic options have recently emerged that target these mechanisms, either by inhibition of ECM synthesis (interferon-γ, transforming growth factor-β [TGF-β] antagonism), or by stimulation of ECM degradation (matrix metalloproteases or urokinase).[9–14]

As an organ becomes fibrotic, both quantitative and qualitative changes in the composition of the ECM occur. Quantitatively, the overall content of collagenous and noncollagenous ECM components increases 3 to 5 fold. Qualitatively, this increased overall deposition is accompanied by a shift from low-density basement membrane-like ECM (eg, type IV collagen) to high-density, fibril-forming ECM (eg, type I and III collagen).[15] This phase of increased ECM deposition is preceded by increased proliferation of mesenchymal cells, which is predominant in early phases of the disease. Closely following injury of any etiology, this proliferative response is also known as "activation," which comprises the transition of resident quiescent cells into proliferative, fibrogenic, and contractile myofibroblasts.[16,17] These cells often exhibit characteristic markers of activation, such as α-smooth muscle actin.[18] Therefore, most of the disease states associated with fibrosis exhibit the two characteristic features of the FPR: proliferation of mesenchymal cells accompanied by increased deposition of ECM molecules.

Hamman and Rich reported a key observation in 1944 in their original description of three patients with idiopathic lung fibrosis.[19] Following pathologic examination in these cases, which were seen at Johns Hopkins University between 1931 and 1933, it was revealed that "the alveolar walls were tremendously thickened; in the early stages of the process crowded with fibroblasts which, at later stages, were replaced by mature scar tissue." By these simple but accurate pathologic observations, Hamman and Rich defined the FPR in one sentence. Although the etiology and pathophysiology of idiopathic lung fibrosis remain enigmatic, it is believed that during the course of the disease, a predominantly proliferative and cellular response of mesenchymal cells slowly progresses to a more fibrotic and acellular response.[20] The close resemblance between normal wound healing and fibrotic lung disease may be interpreted in a way that "fibrosis is a wound that doesn't stop healing."

To more clearly elucidate the operating mechanisms of this group of diseases, researchers have long relied on bleomycin instillation into the trachea of animals as a model for lung fibrosis. Bleomycin instillation leads to rapid development of fibrosis, as assessed by increased deposition of collagens within the interstitial space of the lung, and thus reproduces many of the pathologic findings of lung fibrosis, although recently this has been questioned.[21] Whereas the expression of many growth factors and cytokines in the lung is affected by bleomycin instillation, research soon focused on members of the TGF-β family. Transforming growth factor-β is known to be a major mediator of fibrosis in vitro, and subsequent analysis of the time course of collagen deposition in bleomycin models has demonstrated that this accumulation is immediately preceded by a peak in TGF-β transcription and activity.[22–24] These observations, in agreement with findings that anti-TGF-β therapy leads to a reduction of lung fibrosis,[25] have led to the hypothesis that TGF-β is the main soluble mediator initiating the fibrotic response in the lung. In 1997, this was further substantiated by Gauldie's group, who used an adenovirus system to deliver active TGF-β into the lungs of adult rats.[26] These studies showed that local administration of bioactive TGF-β into rodent lungs reproduces many of the characteristics of lung fibrosis. Whereas multiple studies have confirmed this idea over the past years, current research has now focused on TGF-β signal transduction mechanisms and on how a TGF-β-dominated response can result in tissue fibrosis.

The Transforming Growth Factor-β System

In the late 1970s and early 1980s, it was discovered that polypeptides secreted by Moloney sarcoma virus-infected mouse 3T3 cells had the ability to confer a "transformed" phenotype (anchorage-independent growth) to non-neoplastic cells such as normal rat kidney (NRK) fibroblasts.[27,28] When these peptides were also found in tumor extracts other than sarcomas, the name was changed from "sarcoma growth factor" to "transforming growth factor."[29] In 1983, it was found that this transforming activity was, in fact, the result of a combined action of two entirely different peptides, subsequently designated TGF-α and TGF-β.[30] Transforming growth factor-α was found to be an analogue of epidermal growth factor (EGF), whereas TGF-β was totally unrelated to any known polypeptide. Although the name transforming growth factor was thus designated in the context of this observation, this nomenclature is somewhat misleading, as TGF-β is one of the most powerful tumor suppressors and antiproliferative growth factors known.

Transforming growth factor-β is the prototypic member of a large, and still growing, family of polypeptide growth factors that exert a multiplicity of effects on most cell types. Members within the TGF-β superfamily (including bone morphogenetic proteins, activins, inhibins) are uniquely characterized by the invariant positioning of seven cysteine residues leading to a structural core motif known as the "cysteine knot." Transforming growth factor-β plays an important and nonredundant role in embryonic development and cellular differentiation, regulates cellular proliferation, induces synthesis of ECM proteins, and modulates the immune response.[31–33] Transforming growth factor-β is secreted as a biologically inactive precursor molecule containing a pre-prodomain, the latency-associated peptide (LAP). Complex proteolytic processing by the endoprotease furin then releases the pre-prodomain and generates a homodimer of mature TGF-β. This homodimer is still held inactive through noncovalent association of the released LAP with TGF-β. All forms of secreted TGF-β either appear in the form of the small latent complex (100 kD, containing TGF-β associated with LAP), or the large latent complex (220 kD, containing TGF-β associated with LAP and the secretory glycoprotein latent TGF-β binding protein [LTBP]). Proteolytic processing of these complexes by proteases, such as plasmin or matrix metalloproteases, therefore represents one major step in the regulation of TGF-β bioactivity.[31–33]

Signal transduction mechanisms of TGF-β began to be unraveled after the cloning of three membrane-bound TGF-β receptors in 1991–92, designated TβRI, TβRII, and TβRIII (or betaglycan).[34–37] The cloning and characterization of the TGF-β receptors was a milestone in the field of signal transduction, as TβRI and TβRII were the first membrane-bound receptors exhibiting serine-threonine kinase activity and hence represented the introduction of a novel signaling mechanism, in addition to the well-known tyrosine kinase receptor system. The cloning of Smad molecules beginning in 1995 then led to the discovery of pathway-specific transcription factors that directly interacted with the signal transducing TGF-β receptor, TβRI. The founding member of the Smad family was isolated from *Drosophila* using a genetic screen to find mutants that exacerbated the effect of weak decapentaplegic (dpp) alleles, members of the TGF-β superfamily in *Drosophila*.[38,39] This gene was subsequently named *mad*, for *mothers against decapentaplegic*. The discovery of *mad* led to the identification of three related genes in *Caenorhabditis elegans*, termed *sma-2*, *sma-3*, and *sma-4*, because a mutation in these genes causes small body size.[40] In 1996, the first human Smad was identified, originally because pancreatic cancer was associated with frequent mutations in this locus.[41,42] It was therefore named DPC4 (for "deleted in pancreatic carcinoma locus 4"). Because of its homology with the *sma* and *mad* genes, it was then also termed Smad4, as were all subsequently isolated members of this family. To date, eight Smad isoforms have been cloned and characterized, which are classified into three subgroups according to their function: (1) receptor-regulated Smads, which directly function as substrate molecules for phosphorylated type I receptors (Smad1, 2,

3, 58); (2) the common Smad4, which is the binding partner for all receptor-regulated Smads and facilitates their translocation into the nucleus; and (3) inhibitory Smads (Smad6 and 7), which inhibit the association of receptor-regulated Smads with the type I receptors. The entire Smad family shares similar structural features, including an amino-terminal DNA-binding domain (termed MH1 domain) and a carboxy-terminal transactivating domain (termed MH2 domain).[31,33,43]

In the current model of TGF-β signal transduction (Figure 39–4), biologic effects of TGF-β are achieved after binding of TGF-β to the ligand-binding receptor isotype, TβRII. This leads to the formation or stabilization of a heterotetrameric complex of TβRI and TβRII, followed by transphosphorylation of TβRI in a region known as the GS domain by the constitutively phosphorylated TβRII. Finally, the subsequent phosphorylation of the receptor-associated cytoplasmic effector molecules Smad2 and Smad3 by TβRI then leads to heterooligomerization of phosphorylated Smad2 or 3 with the common Smad4, and the modulation of gene transcription in the nucleus. The type III TGF-β receptor (betaglycan) is a widely expressed heparan sulfate and chondroitin sulfate proteoglycan that binds TGF-β with high affinity through its protein core but has no apparent intrinsic signaling activity. Betaglycan is said to facilitate ligand binding to TβRII, but recent reports have indicated that its role may be far more complex than that, exhibiting positive or negative effects on TGF-β signaling, depending on the cell-type analyzed.[31–33]

Transforming Growth Factor-β and Fibrosis: Mechanisms and Hypotheses

How can such a potent growth factor elicit completely divergent responses dependent on the cellular context? In some instances, TGF-β leads to massive accumulation of ECM; in others, it only affects cellular differentiation. Although most mammalian tissues express three TGF-β isoforms (TGF-β1, -β2, and -β3), these isoforms generally lead to qualitatively identical biologic responses in vitro, with the exception that TGF-β2 exhibits a lower affinity to the TβR complex than TGF-β1 and -β3. Knockout experiments of these isoforms, however, have generated different phenotypes, indicating that specific temporal or spatial expression patterns of these isoforms determine the knockout phenotypes, rather than different cellular effects elicited by each isoform.[44]

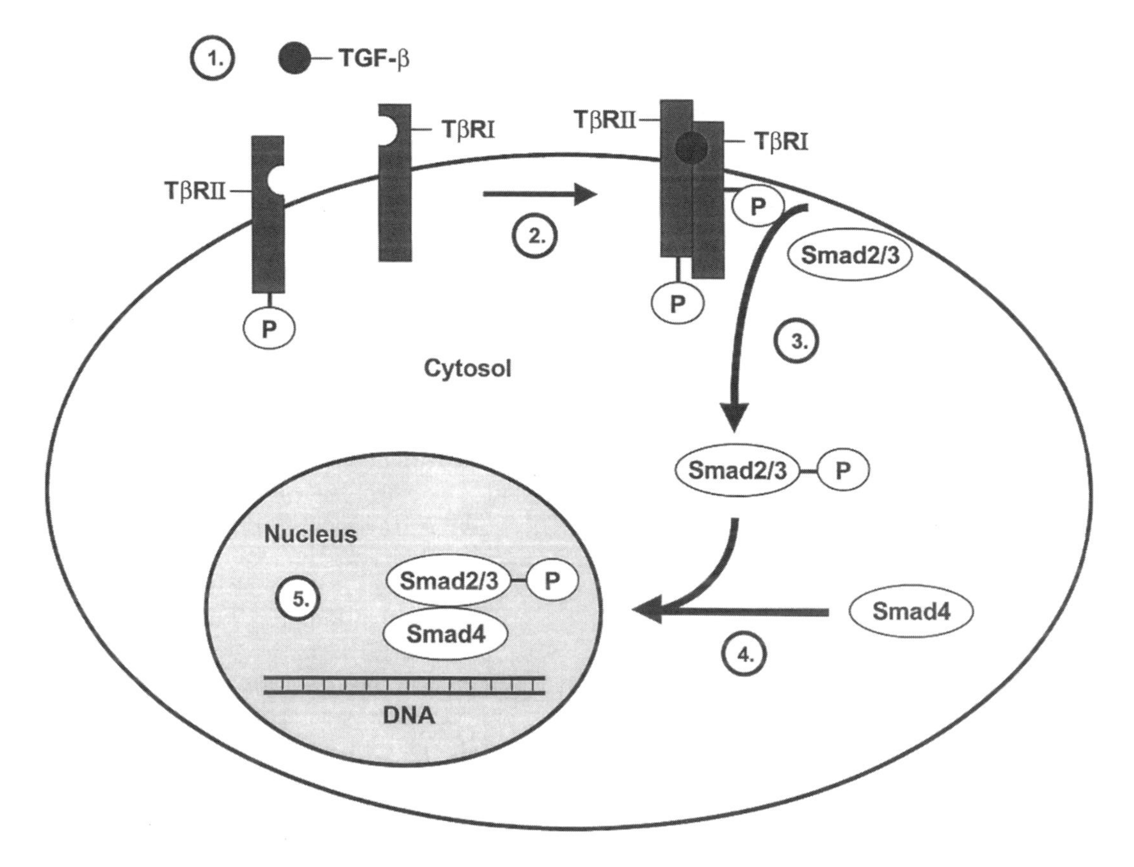

FIGURE 39–4. TGF-β signal transduction. 1. TGF-β signaling is initiated when TGF-β ligand binds to TβRII. 2. This induces the formation of a TβRI-TβRII complex and subsequent phosphorylation of TβRI by TβRII. 3. TβRI then phosphorylates the downstream effector molecules Smad2 or Smad3. 4. Once phosphorylated, Smad2/3 can dimerize with Smad4, and 5. Enter the nucleus, where the complex acts as a transcription factor.

Similarly, Smad2, Smad3, and Smad4 knockout mice exhibit significantly different phenotypes, an observation, which has led to attempts to characterize their non-redundant and non-complementary roles in TGF-β signaling.[45] These findings are especially intriguing comparing Smad2 and Smad3, as the peptide sequence of Smad2 differs from that of Smad3 only by an insert of 30 amino acids within the MH1 domain. This insert prevents binding of Smad3 to DNA. In addition to this structural difference, the availability of cell populations derived from mouse embryos deficient in either Smad2 or Smad3 has recently shed light on the relative importance of each factor on TGF-β-induced signaling. In contrast to the TGF-β isoforms, Smad2 and Smad3 not only seem to be temporally and spatially differentially expressed in vivo, but they also seem to have different functions on a cellular level. Interestingly, c-fos, Smad7, and TGF-β1 induction by TGF-β is Smad3-dependent, whereas MMP-2 expression is Smad2-dependent.[46] Moreover, fibronectin induction, which, to a large extent, is also seen in the FPR, is independent of either Smad, whereas growth inhibition in a variety of cell types seems to be Smad2 or 3 dependent.[47–50]

In addition to the specific contributions of Smad isoforms, the outcome of a TGF-β response furthermore is dependent on the activation of simultaneously activated signaling pathways, such as the mitogen-activated protein kinase (MAPK) or activator protein-1 (AP-1) pathway (Figure 39–5).[33] The specific contribution of each of these pathways likely determines the outcome of the response of a given cell to TGF-β stimulation. This entails that the specific availability and activation of distinct signal transduction pathways determine whether a TGF-β-driven signal results in complete healing, or persistence of the FPR, as seen in tissue fibrosis. Specifically in the case of lung fibrosis, TGF-β is known as the major profibrotic cytokine, as previously discussed. Many of these effects seem to be mediated by the protein JunD, a member of the AP-1 family of transcription factors.[10,51] Therefore, it remains to be analyzed whether lung fibrosis is the result of a preferentially activated signal transduction pathway, such as the AP-1 pathway. Overall, Smad expression is significantly downregulated in the lung with age (Eickelberg O, Vicencio A, unpublished observations). The prevalence of one pathway (AP-1) versus another (eg, Smads), or the prevalence of one Smad isoform (eg, Smad3) versus another (eg, Smad2) may shift a TGF-β response to fibrosis, whereas this response in an environment of relatively abundant Smad molecules would lead to a predominantly antiproliferative response. The future elucidation of such mechanisms will more than likely clarify the tissue-specific effects of TGF-β, and hopefully lead to the discovery of novel therapeutic options for the treatment of fibrotic diseases.

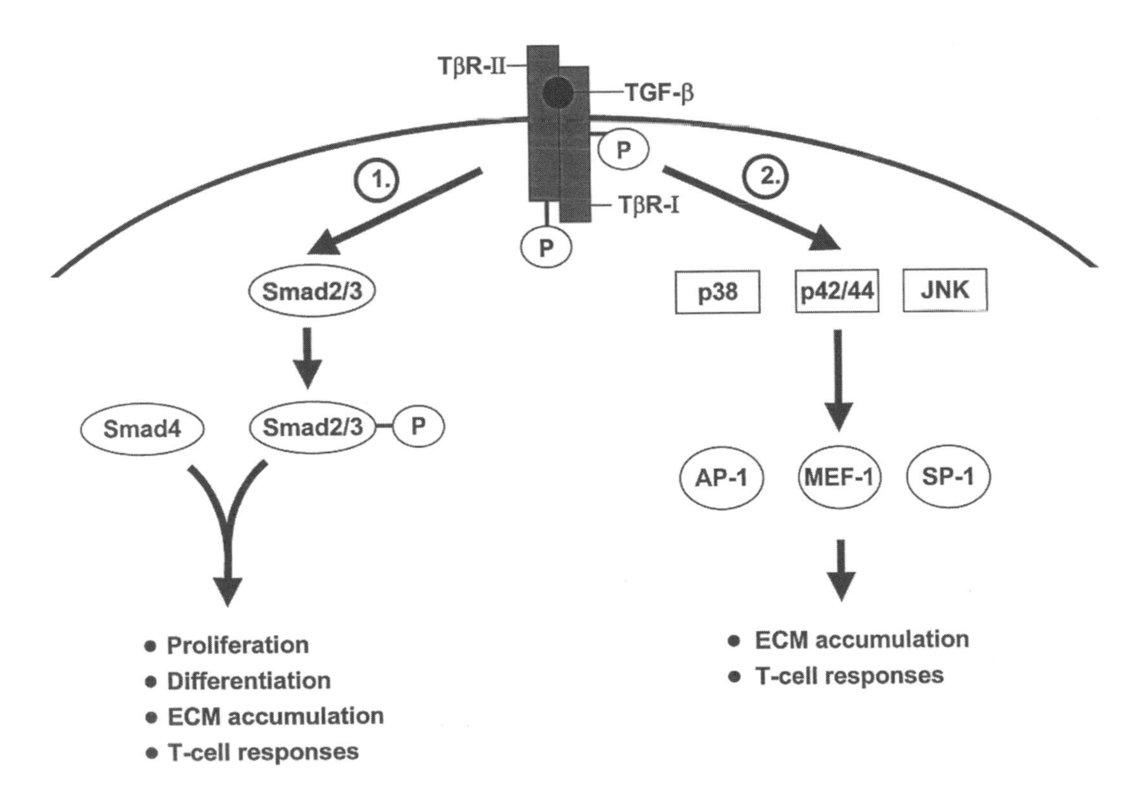

FIGURE 39–5. Alternate pathways in TGF-β signaling. 1. TGF-β leads to well-described activation of Smads. 2. It also activates an array of Smad-independent signaling pathways, including the AP-1 and MAPK pathway. Interaction occurs between these pathways at multiple levels, and the cellular response to TGF-β is dependent on the coactivation of all pathways. JNK = cJun N-terminal kinase.

Relevance of Transforming Growth Factor-β to Pediatric Lung Disease

Although the more classic fibrotic diseases, such as IPF, are rare in the pediatric age group, other diseases exhibit similar features that place the FPR and its regulatory mechanisms at the center of pediatric respiratory research. For example, bronchopulmonary dysplasia (BPD), a clinical entity seen in premature infants who are often exposed to high oxygen concentrations and mechanical ventilation, exhibits features characteristic of an early FPR response.[52] Prior to the widespread use of surfactant, alveolar fibrosis was a major pathologic stigma of the disease. As ventilation strategies have improved, classic fibrotic changes have become less apparent, and an arrest of lung development represents the major pathologic finding in BPD.[52] Nevertheless, the lungs of these patients show increases in myofibroblast proliferation, with persistence of these cells in terminal airways.[53] Furthermore, Zhou and colleagues demonstrated the importance of TGF-β during early lung development by selectively overexpressing active TGF-β1 in the mouse lung using a surfactant protein C (SP-C) promoter.[54] In these studies, the lungs of transgenic mice revealed striking alterations in the distribution of α-smooth muscle actin (a marker for myofibroblasts) and collagen III, as well as a dramatic arrest in branching morphogenesis which led to premature death during the perinatal period. Consistent with these observations, a more recent study showed that attenuation of TGF-β signaling can restore branching morphogenesis in a similar in vitro scenario.[55] Thus, in BPD, damage incurred by high oxygen concentrations or mechanical ventilation could be a trigger for disease onset through TGF-β-dependent mechanisms.

Whereas the TGF-β system offers new theories regarding poorly characterized entities such as BPD, it also has led to novel approaches to more established diseases such as asthma. Traditionally, asthma has been characterized by airway inflammation and destruction; however, ideas about the pathophysiology of asthma have undergone several modifications over recent years.[56,57] Currently, deposition of collagen in the subepithelial basement membranes of asthmatic airways is regarded as a key factor in the development of this disease, and investigators have linked such changes to increased expression of TGF-β.[57,58] Importantly, the expression and release of epithelial TGF-β seems to be resistant to traditional asthma therapies such as corticosteroids.[59] Thus, understanding the TGF-β system and its relation to chronic asthma may lead to more effective therapies for steroid-resistant disease. A better understanding of organ fibrosis, BPD, asthma, and even diseases not yet associated with excess ECM accumulation will follow the elucidation of specific signal transduction pathways activated by TGF-β. Modification of such pathways will likely lead to new classes of specific and individualized therapies for the treatment of these diseases.

References

1. O'Kane S, Ferguson MW. Transforming growth factor beta s and wound healing. Int J Biochem Cell Biol 1997; 29:63–78.
2. Eckes B, Zigrino P, Kessler D, et al. Fibroblast-matrix interactions in wound healing and fibrosis. Matrix Biol 2000; 19:325–32.
3. Clark RA. Fibrin and wound healing. Ann N Y Acad Sci 2001;936:355–67.
4. Mutsaers SE, Bishop JE, McGrouther G, Laurent GJ. Mechanisms of tissue repair: from wound healing to fibrosis. Int J Biochem Cell Biol 1997;29:5–17.
5. Franklin TJ. Therapeutic approaches to organ fibrosis. Int J Biochem Cell Biol 1997;29:79–89.
6. Egan JJ. New treatments for pulmonary fibrosis? [in process citation]. Lancet 1999;354:1839–40.
7. Mason RJ, Schwarz MI, Hunninghake GW, Musson RA. NHLBI Workshop Summary. Pharmacological therapy for idiopathic pulmonary fibrosis: past, present, and future. Am J Respir Crit Care Med 1999;160:1771–7.
8. Laurent GJ. Biochemical pathways leading to collagen deposition in pulmonary fibrosis. Ciba Found Symp 1985;114:222–33.
9. Ziesche R, Hofbauer E, Wittmann K, et al. A preliminary study of long-term treatment with interferon gamma-1b and low-dose prednisolone in patients with idiopathic pulmonary fibrosis [see comments]. N Engl J Med 1999; 341:1264–9.
10. Eickelberg O, Pansky A, Koehler E, et al. Molecular mechanisms of TGF-(beta) antagonism by interferon (gamma) and cyclosporine A in lung fibroblasts. FASEB J 2001; 15:797–806.
11. Schermuly RT, Gunther A, Ermert M, et al. Conebulization of surfactant and urokinase restores gas exchange in perfused lungs with alveolar fibrin formation. Am J Physiol Lung Cell Mol Physiol 2001;280:L792–800.
12. Corbel M, Caulet-Maugendre S, Germain N, et al. Inhibition of bleomycin-induced pulmonary fibrosis in mice by the matrix metalloproteinase inhibitor batimastat. J Pathol 2001;193:538–45.
13. Taniyama Y, Morishita R, Nakagami H, et al. Potential contribution of a novel antifibrotic factor, hepatocyte growth factor, to prevention of myocardial fibrosis by angiotensin II blockade in cardiomyopathic hamsters. Circulation 2000;102:246–52.
14. Hironaka K, Sakaida I, Matsumura Y, et al. Enhanced interstitial collagenase (matrix metalloproteinase-13) production of Kupffer cell by gadolinium chloride prevents pig serum-induced rat liver fibrosis. Biochem Biophys Res Commun 2000;267:290–5.
15. Katzenstein AL, Myers JL. Idiopathic pulmonary fibrosis: clinical relevance of pathologic classification. Am J Respir Crit Care Med 1998;157:1301–15.
16. Halayko AJ, Camoretti-Mercado B, Forsythe SM, et al. Divergent differentiation paths in airway smooth muscle

culture: induction of functionally contractile myocytes. Am J Physiol 1999;276:L197–206.
17. Halayko AJ, Solway J. Molecular mechanisms of phenotypic plasticity in smooth muscle cells. J Appl Physiol 2001; 90:358–68.
18. Berk BC. Vascular smooth muscle growth: autocrine growth mechanisms. Physiol Rev 2001;81:999–1030.
19. Hamman BL, Cue JI, Miller FB, et al. Helicopter transport of trauma victims: Does a physician make a difference? J Trauma 1991;31:490–4.
20. Ward PA, Hunninghake GW. Lung inflammation and fibrosis. Am J Respir Crit Care Med 1998;157:S123–9.
21. Borzone G, Moreno R, Urrea R, et al. Bleomycin-induced chronic lung damage does not resemble human idiopathic pulmonary fibrosis. Am J Respir Crit Care Med 2001;163:1648–53.
22. Hoyt DG, Lazo JS. Alterations in pulmonary mRNA encoding procollagens, fibronectin and transforming growth factor-beta precede bleomycin-induced pulmonary fibrosis in mice. J Pharmacol Exp Ther 1988; 246:765–71.
23. Raghow B, Irish P, Kang AH. Coordinate regulation of transforming growth factor beta gene expression and cell proliferation in hamster lungs undergoing bleomycin-induced pulmonary fibrosis. J Clin Invest 1989;84:1836–42.
24. Breen E, Shull S, Burne S, et al. Bleomycin regulation of transforming growth factor-beta mRNA in rat lung fibroblasts. Am J Respir Cell Mol Biol 1992;6:146–52.
25. Wang Q, Wang Y, Hyde DM, et al. Reduction of bleomycin induced lung fibrosis by transforming growth factor beta soluble receptor in hamsters. Thorax 1999;54:805–12.
26. Sime PJ, Xing Z, Graham FL, et al. Adenovector-mediated gene transfer of active transforming growth factor-beta1 induces prolonged severe fibrosis in rat lung. J Clin Invest 1997;100:768–76.
27. de Larco JE, Todaro GJ. Growth factors from murine sarcoma virus-transformed cells. Proc Natl Acad Sci U S A 1978;75:4001–5.
28. Todaro GJ, De Larco JE. Growth factors produced by sarcoma virus-transformed cells. Cancer Res 1978;38:4147–54.
29. Roberts AB, Lamb LC, Newton DL, et al. Transforming growth factors: isolation of polypeptides from virally and chemically transformed cells by acid/ethanol extraction. Proc Natl Acad Sci U S A 1980;77:3494–8.
30. Anzano MA, Roberts AB, Smith JM, et al. Sarcoma growth factor from conditioned medium of virally transformed cells is composed of both type alpha and type beta transforming growth factors. Proc Natl Acad Sci U S A 1983;80:6264–8.
31. Massague J. TGF-beta signal transduction. Annu Rev Biochem 1998;67:753–91.
32. Piek E, Heldin CH, ten Dijke P. Specificity, diversity, and regulation in TGF-beta superfamily signaling. FASEB J 1999;13:2105–24.
33. Massague J. How cells read TGF-beta signals. Nat Rev Mol Cell Biol 2000;1:169–78.
34. Wang XF, Lin HY, Ng-Eaton E, et al. Expression cloning and characterization of the TGF-beta type III receptor. Cell 1991;67:797–805.
35. Lopez-Casillas F, Cheifetz S, Doody J, et al. Structure and expression of the membrane proteoglycan betaglycan, a component of the TGF-beta receptor system. Cell 1991; 67:785–95.
36. Lin HY, Wang XF, Ng-Eaton E, et al. Expression cloning of the TGF-beta type II receptor, a functional transmembrane serine/threonine kinase. Cell 1992;68:775–85.
37. Franzen P, ten Dijke P, Ichijo H, et al. Cloning of a TGF beta type I receptor that forms a heteromeric complex with the TGF beta type II receptor. Cell 1993;75:681–92.
38. Sekelsky JJ, Newfeld SJ, Raftery LA, et al. Genetic characterization and cloning of mothers against dpp, a gene required for decapentaplegic function in *Drosophila melanogaster*. Genetics 1995;139:1347–58.
39. Raftery LA, Twombly V, Wharton K, Gelbart WM. Genetic screens to identify elements of the decapentaplegic signaling pathway in *Drosophila*. Genetics 1995;139: 241–54.
40. Savage C, Das P, Finelli AL, et al. *Caenorhabditis elegans* genes sma-2, sma-3, and sma-4 define a conserved family of transforming growth factor beta pathway components. Proc Natl Acad Sci U S A 1996;93:790–4.
41. Hahn SA, Schutte M, Hoque AT, et al. DPC4, a candidate tumor suppressor gene at human chromosome 18q21.1. Science 1996;271:350–3.
42. Thiagalingam S, Lengauer C, Leach FS, et al. Evaluation of candidate tumour suppressor genes on chromosome 18 in colorectal cancers. Nat Genet 1996;13:343–6.
43. Miyazono K, ten Dijke P, Heldin CH. TGF-beta signaling by Smad proteins. Adv Immunol 2000;75:115–57.
44. Bottinger EP, Letterio JJ, Roberts AB. Biology of TGF-beta in knockout and transgenic mouse models. Kidney Int 1997;51:1355–60.
45. Weinstein M, Yang X, Deng C. Functions of mammalian Smad genes as revealed by targeted gene disruption in mice. Cytokine Growth Factor Rev 2000;11:49–58.
46. Piek E, Ju WJ, Heyer J, et al. Functional characterization of transforming growth factor-beta signaling in Smad2- and Smad3-deficient fibroblasts. J Biol Chem 2001;276: 19945–53.
47. Ashcroft GS, Yang X, Glick AB, et al. Mice lacking Smad3 show accelerated wound healing and an impaired local inflammatory response. Nat Cell Biol 1999;1:260–6.
48. von Gersdorff G, Susztak K, Rezvani F, et al. Smad3 and Smad4 mediate transcriptional activation of the human Smad7 promoter by transforming growth factor-beta. J Biol Chem 2000;275:11320–6.
49. Nagarajan RP, Chen Y. Structural basis for the functional difference between Smad2 and Smad3 in FAST-2 (forkhead activin signal transducer-2)-mediated transcription. Biochem J 2000;350(Pt 1):253–9.
50. Nagarajan RP, Zhang J, Li W, Chen Y. Regulation of Smad7 promoter by direct association with Smad3 and Smad4. J Biol Chem 1999;274:33412–8.
51. Verrecchia F, Tacheau C, Schorpp-Kistner M, et al. Induction of the AP-1 members c-Jun and JunB by TGF-beta/Smad suppresses early Smad-driven gene activation. Oncogene 2001;20:2205–11.
52. Jobe AJ. The new BPD: an arrest of lung development. Pediatr Res 1999;46:641–3.

53. Toti P, Buonocore G, Tanganelli P, et al. Bronchopulmonary dysplasia of the premature baby: an immunohistochemical study. Pediatr Pulmonol 1997;24:22–8.
54. Zhou L, Dey CR, Wert SE, Whitsett JA. Arrested lung morphogenesis in transgenic mice bearing an SP-C-TGF-beta 1 chimeric gene. Dev Biol 1996;175:227–38.
55. Zhao J, Shi W, Chen H, Warburton D. Smad7 and Smad6 differentially modulate transforming growth factor beta-induced inhibition of embryonic lung morphogenesis. J Biol Chem 2000;275:23992–7.
56. Holgate ST. Epithelial damage and response. Clin Exp Allergy 2000;30(Suppl 1):37–41.
57. Busse WW, Banks-Schlegel S, Wenzel SE. Pathophysiology of severe asthma. J Allergy Clin Immunol 2000;106:1033–42.
58. Holgate ST, Davies DE, Lackie PM, et al. Epithelial-mesenchymal interactions in the pathogenesis of asthma. J Allergy Clin Immunol 2000;105:193–204.
59. Puddicombe SM, Polosa R, Richter A, et al. Involvement of the epidermal growth factor receptor in epithelial repair in asthma. FASEB J 2000;14:1362–74.

INDEX